Cooking Light.

ANNUAL
RECIPES 2007

Oxmoor
House.

Our Year at Cooking Light.

This morning, I spent a couple of hours working in the Test Kitchens. I love being in the TK; as the place where we prepare and review all the recipes that appear in the magazine, it's the heart of *Cooking Light.*

The setup is impressive: There are eight cooking stations, each outfitted with the residential-caliber appliances, amenities and hardware required for duplicating the way you, our readers, will cook our recipes. And the chefs and home economists who are the magazine's TK professionals work at those stations just as they would at their own home kitchens. Well, that statement needs some qualification—their days usually start before 7 a.m., and they cook until Taste Testing, which is usually sometime around noon. That testing involves representatives from the whole staff, who rate each dish based on a variety of factors, including nutrition, appearance, and, certainly, taste. If a dish passes on all criteria, it will run in the magazine. If not, the dish either gets revised and re-tested, or it fails altogether.

On any given workday, not all the TK professionals are cooking for the tasting; some of the chefs might be making a dish we'll photograph for the next issue. Or maybe a couple of them will be out filling a market order, or at their desks editing tested recipes.

That's why our TK is a busy, energetic, and highly creative laboratory. And without it, this 2007 edition of *Cooking Light Annual Recipes*—indeed, the magazine itself—could scarcely exist. To get a feel for the TK's prodigious output, consider that this cookbook contains all 1,000 recipes we published last year. And Vanessa Taylor Johnson, the Test Kitchens Director who manages the work, the people, and the physical space, estimates the staff probably prepared 5,000 recipes in total to get to that figure. (That number accounts for the multiple re-tests some recipes require, for the real dishes we photograph, and for the recipes that for one reason or another simply don't pass.)

Step into our Test Kitchens on any morning, and the first thing you might hear is the whirring of a mixer or the sizzling of meat in a skillet. You might also hear what Test Kitchens Director Vanessa Johnson calls "counter conversation"—staffers gathering around the kitchen counter to discuss recipes.

As you can imagine, producing every story represented in this book is a point of pride for the *Cooking Light* staff. But some features stand out among our favorites:

- Our "Cooking Class" series this year highlighted One Great Dish, and the secrets you need to move from novice to master of cakes, pizza, pot roasts, and more.
- As America's top healthy food and lifestyle magazine, *Cooking Light* takes seriously its commitment in examining what the latest nutrition news means for you. Over the last year, we discussed the merits of the hypertension-easing DASH eating plan in August, foods that enhance brain function in September, and dishes with the antioxidant lycopene in October. Each story was accompanied by terrific recipes.
- The popularity of *Cooking Light* Supper Clubs™ across the United States inspired a fresh crop of stories in our September issue, which was fully stocked with brand-new, easy-to-do party ideas.
- The enthusiastic reception to our signature Holiday Cookbook in November encouraged us to devote even more pages to it this year, with recipes for everything from appetizers to desserts. This year's rendition also has lots of great menus, as well as new approaches for the season's best entertaining and gift giving.
- From the year's first issue to the last, our perennially top-rated stories—Reader Recipes, Lighten Up, and SuperFast—have rendered some of the year's very best recipes.

These stories are why the magazine's staff—the TK professionals as well as the rest of the people who produce every issue—believes that this edition of *Cooking Light Annual Recipes* may just be the best ever. My colleagues and I hope you enjoy cooking from it in your own TK—that is, the one in your home.

Very truly yours,

Editor in Chief

Forget delivery! Learn how to make pizza—hot and tasty—at home in our cooking class (page 330).

Gather friends for a casual meal featuring Frogmore Stew (page 302).

Our Summer Cookbook (page 169) capitalizes on sensational seasonal produce including fresh, vibrant berries.

Our Favorite Recipes

Not all recipes are created equal. At *Cooking Light*®, only those that have passed muster with our Test Kitchens staff and food editors—not an easy crowd to please—make it onto the pages of our magazine. We rigorously test each recipe, often two or three times, to ensure not only that they're healthy and reliable, but also that they taste as good as they possibly can. So which of our recipes are our favorites? They're the ones readers keep calling and writing about, the ones our staff whip up for their own families and friends. They're not always the ones that rated the highest, but they're the dishes that are definitely the most memorable.

◀ **Buttermilk Sorbet with Strawberries** *(page 184):* Refreshing, tart, and nutritious, this fruity dessert will have you begging for seconds.

Dijon Chicken Stew with Potatoes and Kale *(page 48):* This soothing and nutritious stew combines Dijon mustard, potatoes, and kale to lighten your wintertime blues.

Tenderloin Sandwich (*page 289*):
Fire up the grill to create a delicious classic sandwich topped with Dijon mustard, romaine lettuce, red onions, and tomato slices.

Green Pumpkinseed and Cranberry Crispy Bars (*page 165*):
Here's a creative take on the classic Rice Krispies bars. Savor the taste of cranberry, marshmallows, and pumpkin seeds as a crunchy—and healthy—snack.

Asian Chicken Lettuce Wraps (*page 24*):
For a surefire way to introduce Asian fare to your kids, prepare this fun dish at your next family get-together.

Oven-Roasted Tomatoes with Goat Cheese (*page 64*):
The concentrated flavor of the tomatoes blends beautifully with aged balsamic vinegar and crumbled goat cheese.

Our Favorite Recipes

▶ **Swiss Enchiladas**
(page 164):
Share this cheesy, satisfying casserole with friends at tailgates and potluck dinners. We promise this lightened version is just as tasty and enjoyable as the original.

▼ **Pulled Chicken Sandwiches**
(page 172):
The spices and bright flavors add zest to this summertime favorite. Serve with corn on the cob when entertaining friends and neighbors.

◀ **Summer Berry Medley with Limoncello and Mint** *(page 215):* Italian lemon-flavored liqueur brightens the fresh flavors of raspberries, blackberries, strawberries, and blueberries in this sweet and tangy dessert.

▼ **Chinese-Style Stove-Top Pot Roast with Noodles** *(page 363):* The fusion of ginger, soy sauce, star anise, and Chinese five-spice powder creates a pungent and attractive Asian dish.

Lemon Angel Food Cupcakes *(page 137)*: Decorate these cupcakes with flirty—and edible—flowers such as pansies or rosebuds. Your party guests will love the refined beauty and style.

Our Favorite Recipes

◀ **Chocolate Fudge Brownie Ice Cream**
(*page 261*):
A chocolate lover's delight, this homemade dessert pleases your taste buds without teasing your thighs.

▼ **Spicy Chicken Cakes with Horseradish Aïoli**
(*page 269*):
Garnished with aïoli, a garlic mayonnaise from France, these delectable cakes are great served with sweet potatoes and steamed asparagus.

Our Favorite Recipes

▶ **Tres Leche Cake** *(page 311)*: Three types of milk come together brilliantly with rum to create a moist, tender cake topped with meringue.

▼ **Spinach Fettuccine** *(page 274)*: This lightened version combines bacon, spinach, and pecorino Romano cheese for a beautiful dish that's not only healthy, but delicious.

▲ Oven-Fried Chicken (*page 382*): The secret for an extra crispy crust is cornmeal. Enjoy the great taste and superior texture of this classic fried dish without experiencing the fat.

◄ Ice Cream Treasures (*page 191*): Savor this crunchy delight. Cereal, coconut, almonds, and toffee bars mix beautifully with reduced-fact vanilla ice cream for the perfect summer dessert.

11

Our Favorite Recipes

▶ **Irish Cream Brownies** *(page 379):* The creamy, chocolaty appeal of Bailey's Irish Cream enhances the rich, fudgy flavor of these brownies.

▼ **Spaghetti and Meatballs** *(page 338):* Enjoy this lightened version of the American classic with ground sirloin and turkey Italian sausage. Fresh herbs and Parmigiano-Reggiano cheese complete this satisfying and comforting dish.

Vanilla Bean Pudding
(page 293):
Simple ingredients and easy-to-follow instructions help you make this homemade dessert with superior results.

▲ **Shrimp and White Bean Salad with Creamy Lemon-Dill Dressing** *(page 279):* This easy, toss-together, no-cook dish can be prepared in just over thirty minutes.

▶ **Cinnamon-Sugar Cookies** *(page 166):* A hint of spice adds flair to the traditional buttery and sweet flavors of these delicate treats.

Our Favorite Recipes

◀ **Spicy Shrimp Cakes with Corn and Avocado Salsa** (*page 383*): Experiment with nontraditional party fare by serving these delightful starters. We promise your guests will love the rich, spicy flavors and a change from the norm.

▼ **Pide with Yogurt Dip** (*page 42*): Create this homemade Turkish appetizer with simple ingredients straight from your kitchen.

Our Favorite Recipes

Fajita Turkey Burgers *(page 219):*
Prepare this lean protein dish after a late-afternoon workout. The fresh cilantro, salsa, and avocado add flair to this quick supper.

Harvest Pie *(page 398):*
Taste the season with this gorgeous autumn dessert, which features butternut squash in place of pumpkin.

▼ **Fresh Lime Chiffon Cake** *(page 199):*
Moist, light, and refreshing, this three-layer dessert tastes just as wonderful as it looks. Garnish with mint, blueberries, and lime wedges for a splashing and classic treat.

Sweet Potato Casserole *(page 426):*
A pecan-laced streusel topping perfects the subtle, satisfyingly sweet flavor of this classic Thanksgiving side dish.

Blueberry Cheesecake Ice Cream *(page 263):*
Homemade ice cream allows you to find a balance between flavor, texture, and nutrition. The fruity mix of blueberries makes this dessert a definite family favorite.

contents

©2006 by Oxmoor House, Inc.
Book Division of Southern Progress Corporation
P.O. Box 2463, Birmingham, Alabama 35201

ISBN-10: 0-8487-3071-2
ISBN-13: 978-0-8487-3071-0
ISSN:1091-3645

Printed in the United States of America
First printing 2006

Be sure to check with your health-care provider before making any changes in your diet.

Oxmoor House, Inc.
Editor in Chief: Nancy Fitzpatrick Wyatt
Executive Editor: Katherine M. Eakin
Copy Chief: Allison Long Lowery

Cooking Light ® Annual Recipes 2007
Editor: Heather Averett
Copy Editor: Jacqueline Giovanelli
Editorial Assistant: Rachel Quinlivan, R.D.
Photography Director: Jim Bathie
Director of Production: Laura Lockhart
Senior Production Manager: Greg A. Amason
Production Assistant: Faye Porter Bonner

Contributors:
Designer: Carol Damsky
Indexer: Mary Ann Laurens
Interns: Jill Baughman, Ashley Leath, Mary Katherine Pappas, Lucas Whittington, Laura K. Womble

To order additional publications, call 1-800-765-6400.
For more books to enrich your life, visit **oxmoorhouse.com**

Cover: *Mexican Black Bean Sausage Chili* (*page 45*)
Page 1: *Shortcakes with Fresh Berries* (*page 303*)

Cooking Light ®
Editor in Chief: Mary Kay Culpepper
Executive Editor: Billy R. Sims
Art Director: Susan Waldrip Dendy
Managing Editor: Maelynn Cheung
Senior Food Editor: Alison Mann Ashton
Features Editor: Phillip Rhodes
Projects Editor: Mary Simpson Creel, M.S., R.D.
Food Editor: Ann Taylor Pittman
Associate Food Editors: Julianna Grimes Bottcher, Timothy Q. Cebula
Assistant Food Editor: Kathy C. Kitchens, R.D.
Assistant Editors: Cindy Hatcher, Brandy Rushing
Test Kitchens Director: Vanessa Taylor Johnson
Senior Food Stylist: Kellie Gerber Kelley
Food Stylist: M. Kathleen Kanen
Test Kitchens Professionals: Sam Brannock, Kathryn Conrad, Mary H. Drennen, Jan Jacks Moon, Tiffany Vickers, Mike Wilson
Assistant Art Director: Maya Metz Logue
Senior Designers: Fernande Bondarenko, J.Shay McNamee
Designer: Brigette Mayer
Senior Photographer: Randy Mayor
Senior Photo Stylist: Cindy Barr
Photo Stylists: Jan Gautro, Leigh Ann Ross
Studio Assistant: Melissa Hoover
Copy Chief: Maria Parker Hopkins
Senior Copy Editor: Susan Roberts
Copy Editor: Johannah Paiva
Production Manager: Liz Rhoades
Production Editors: Joanne McCrary Brasseal, Hazel R. Eddins
Administrative Coordinator: Carol D. Johnson
Office Manager: Rita K. Jackson
Editorial Assistant: Abigail Banks
Correspondence Editor: Michelle Gibson Daniels
Interns: SaBrina Bone, Melissa Marek, Lauri Short, Megan Voelkel

CookingLight.com
Editor: Jennifer Middleton Richards
Online Producer: Abigail Masters

5 Surprisingly Healthful Foods

The latest research shows they deserve a prominent place in a smart diet.

Scientists are currently looking beneath the surface at mushrooms, avocados, and peanuts—as well as once-maligned eggs and coffee. Redeeming qualities for each of these five foods are coming to light. They have nutritional respect and deserve a place at your table. All five are easy to enjoy on their own, or try them in our delicious recipes.

QUICK & EASY
Caramelized Onion, Canadian Bacon, and Egg Sandwiches

Great for breakfast, lunch, or dinner, this sandwich would be well paired with a simple fruit salad. Use yellow onions if you prefer intensely sweet caramelized onions. The sandwich also is tasty on toasted whole wheat English muffins.

- 2 teaspoons canola oil
- 2½ cups thinly vertically sliced onion
- ½ teaspoon sugar
- ½ teaspoon tarragon vinegar
- ¼ teaspoon salt
- ¼ teaspoon freshly ground black pepper
- 4 Canadian bacon slices
- Cooking spray
- 4 large eggs
- 8 (1½-ounce) slices hearty white bread, toasted (such as Pepperidge Farm)

1. Heat oil in a large nonstick skillet over medium-high heat. Add onion and next 4 ingredients; sauté 8 minutes or until golden. Remove onion mixture from pan. Add bacon to pan; cook 1 minute on each side or until lightly browned. Remove bacon from pan.
2. Wipe pan clean with paper towels.

Coat pan with cooking spray. Reduce heat to medium. Add eggs to pan; cook 2 minutes on each side or until desired degree of doneness. Layer 1 bacon slice, ¼ cup onion mixture, and 1 egg on each of 4 toast slices. Top with remaining toast slices. Yield: 4 servings (serving size: 1 sandwich).

CALORIES 363 (27% from fat); FAT 11g (sat 2.3g, mono 4.6g, poly 2.5g); PROTEIN 18.5g; CARB 51.3g; FIBER 5.5g; CHOL 225mg; IRON 3mg; SODIUM 934mg; CALC 89mg

Poached Eggs with White Corn Polenta

Either a breakfast or a light dinner, this dish uses white cornmeal for a creamy polenta. If you can find it, use imported Italian white polenta since the grain is very fine, resulting in a soft texture. Make an extra batch of salsa as a topping for bruschetta.

SALSA:
- ⅓ cup chopped bottled roasted red bell peppers
- 1 tablespoon chopped fresh basil
- ½ teaspoon extravirgin olive oil
- ⅛ teaspoon salt
- 1 large plum tomato, seeded and diced (about ⅓ cup)

POLENTA:
- 4 cups water
- 1½ cups frozen white corn kernels, thawed
- 1 cup white cornmeal or dry polenta
- ½ teaspoon salt, divided
- 3 tablespoons grated fresh Parmesan cheese
- 1 teaspoon butter
- ¼ teaspoon freshly ground black pepper

EGGS:
- 4 large eggs
- Cooking spray

REMAINING INGREDIENT:
- 2 bacon slices, cooked and crumbled

1. To prepare salsa, combine first 5 ingredients; set aside.
2. To prepare polenta, bring water to a boil in a medium saucepan. Add corn, cornmeal, and ¼ teaspoon salt. Cook 2 minutes or until cornmeal mixture returns to a boil, stirring constantly. Reduce heat to low; cook 20 minutes or until thick, stirring frequently. Stir in remaining ¼ teaspoon salt, Parmesan cheese, butter, and black pepper. Cover and keep warm.
3. To prepare eggs, while polenta cooks, add water to a large skillet, filling two-thirds full; bring to a boil. Reduce heat; simmer. Break an egg into each of 4 (6-ounce) custard cups coated with cooking spray. Place custard cups in simmering water in pan. Cover pan; cook 6 minutes or until set. Remove custard cups from water; carefully remove eggs from custard cups.
4. Spoon about 1 cup polenta onto each of 4 plates; top each serving with about 3 tablespoons salsa and 1 poached egg. Sprinkle evenly with bacon. Yield: 4 servings.

CALORIES 307 (30% from fat); FAT 10.3g (sat 3.4g, mono 4g, poly 1.6g); PROTEIN 14.2g; CARB 40.5g; FIBER 4.6g; CHOL 221mg; IRON 1.9mg; SODIUM 664mg; CALC 78mg

Peanut Butter

Misconception: This creamy spread is an indulgence best enjoyed only occasionally because it's high in fat and calories.

Why It's Good For You: At least five major studies confirm that eating peanuts can lower risk for coronary heart disease. "Suffice it to say that eating peanut butter or peanuts has been associated with lower total cholesterol, lower LDL or 'bad' cholesterol, and lower triglycerides," says Richard Mattes, Ph.D., R.D., a professor of nutrition at Purdue University.

Even better, these health benefits seem to occur without promoting weight gain. One reason could be that peanut butter is a stick-to-the-ribs kind of food. Peanut butter is high in fat and calories, but a small amount can quell hunger. A tablespoon or two of peanut butter is all it takes to net a world of benefits for both the heart and waistline.

Eggs

Misconception: Eggs are high in dietary cholesterol, so they don't have a place in my heart-healthy diet.

Why They're Good for You: Eggs contain a variety of substances that appear to promote good health. Choline, a nutrient that is critical to brain function, is one example. Scientists at the University of North Carolina find adding choline to the diets of pregnant animals improves memory performance in their offspring.

Eggs are also being studied because they contain lutein and zeaxanthin, antioxidants that may keep eyes healthy and ward off the leading cause of blindness, macular degeneration. A recent report in the *Journal of Nutrition* suggests that we look at the egg as a whole package: Eggs are inexpensive, contain the highest-quality protein on the planet, and are loaded with small amounts of vital nutrients, including folate, riboflavin, selenium, B12, and choline.

Coffee

Misconception: The only thing you get from drinking coffee is a caffeine buzz.

Why It's Good for You: The average cup of coffee has hundreds of different chemical compounds. Maybe that's why news reports about coffee vacillate between lauding its health benefits and labeling it harmful. Still, the benefits of coffee seem to outweigh the negatives.

Some Arizona researchers recently discovered that caffeinated coffee helps improve memory in older adults. A new study from the United Kingdom suggests that small amounts of coffee consumed throughout the day can increase alertness and improve performance on all kinds of tasks. Preliminary studies suggest regular coffee drinking may lower the risk of type 2 diabetes. A new report in the *Journal of the American Medical Association* finds that people who drink a daily four to six cups have a 28 percent lower risk of developing this illness than folks who drink less than two cups each day. Speculation is that caffeine deserves the credit, though it could be an antioxidant phenolic compound called chlorogenic acid.

Avocados

Misconception: I shouldn't eat avocados because they're high in fat.

Why They're Good for You: A lot of attention centers on the fact that avocados are rich in monounsaturated fat, the heart-healthy kind. Yet scientists are now more interested in the active compounds in avocados that might help prevent cancer. One recent study found that those compounds can inhibit the growth of prostate cancer cells. While conducting the study, these researchers found avocados are loaded with a variety of antioxidants, including familiar disease-fighting compounds such as lutein, beta-carotene, and vitamin E.

Another recently discovered benefit is that avocados help the body absorb phytochemicals from other foods. Researchers from Ohio State University recently reported that pairing avocados with salsa or salad allows for better absorption of antioxidants in those foods. The lycopene in tomatoes or the beta-carotene in carrots may be better absorbed if there's a slice or two of avocado in the bowl. Scientists suspect that the fat content of avocados helps the body absorb these antioxidants.

Mushrooms

Misconception: Mushrooms are a low-calorie food with little nutritional benefit.

Why They're Good for You: They may be 90 percent water and have only 18 calories per cup, but mushrooms are getting serious scientific attention. Laboratory reports and animal studies show that compounds in mushrooms may do everything from bolster immune function to suppress breast and prostate cancers to decrease tumor size. Penn State researchers find that mushrooms harbor large amounts of an antioxidant called L-ergothioneine. The scientific buzz is that fungi, for the moment, are the only foods that contain this compound.

While scientists work to figure out how these findings will translate to dietary advice, there are plenty of reasons to enjoy mushrooms. Clare Hasler, Ph.D., a well-known expert in functional foods and executive director of the Robert Mondavi Institute for Wine and Food Science at the University of California, Davis, points out that mushrooms offer a healthy helping of the blood pressure–lowering mineral potassium. "Most people might be surprised to learn that while orange juice is touted as one of the highest potassium foods, one medium portobello mushroom actually has more potassium," she says. "And five white button mushrooms have more potassium than an orange."

Café au Lait Chiffon Pie

(pictured on page 226)

Since the filling is not cooked, be sure to use pasteurized egg whites.

CRUST:
1½ cups chocolate graham cracker crumbs (about 10 cookie sheets)
2 tablespoons sugar
2 tablespoons butter, melted
1 large pasteurized egg white
Cooking spray

FILLING:
1½ cups water
½ cup freshly ground dark roast coffee
3 cups miniature marshmallows
⅓ cup 1% low-fat milk
2 large pasteurized egg whites
2 tablespoons sugar
1 (8-ounce) container frozen reduced-calorie whipped topping, thawed and divided

REMAINING INGREDIENT:
3 tablespoons grated semisweet chocolate

1. Preheat oven to 350°.
2. To prepare crust, combine cracker crumbs and 2 tablespoons sugar, stirring well with a whisk. Add butter and 1 egg white; toss with a fork until moist. Press mixture into bottom and up sides of a 9-inch pie plate coated with cooking spray. Bake at 350° for 8 minutes; cool completely on a wire rack.
3. To prepare filling, brew water and coffee in a coffee maker according to manufacturer's directions. Place brewed coffee in a small saucepan; bring to a boil. Cook until reduced to ⅓ cup (about 15 minutes). Add marshmallows and milk. Cook over medium heat until marshmallows melt, stirring constantly. Pour mixture into a large bowl; cover and let stand until mixture thickens, stirring occasionally (about 30 minutes).
4. Place 2 egg whites in a medium bowl; beat with a mixer at high speed until foamy. Gradually add 2 tablespoons sugar, beating at high speed until stiff peaks form. Gently fold half of egg

white mixture into marshmallow mixture; gently fold in remaining egg white mixture. Fold in 1⅔ cups whipped topping. Spoon filling into prepared crust. Cover with plastic wrap; chill until firm (about 5 hours to overnight).
5. Cut pie into 8 wedges. Top each serving with 1 tablespoon whipped topping (reserve remaining whipped topping for another use); sprinkle each serving with about 1 teaspoon grated semisweet chocolate. Yield: 8 servings.

CALORIES 262 (28% from fat); FAT 8.2g (sat 5.1g, mono 1.8g, poly 0.2g); PROTEIN 3.5g; CARB 43.5g; FIBER 0.9g; CHOL 8mg; IRON 0.2mg; SODIUM 62mg; CALC 17mg

Mocha-Almond Latte Freeze

Any coffee will work here, but a darker French roast coffee has a rich, strong flavor that pairs nicely with chocolate. The recipe makes more double-strength coffee than you need; freeze leftover coffee in ice cube trays for iced coffee drinks (or use leftover coffee in Café au Lait Chiffon Pie [recipe at left]). Once frozen, coffee cubes can be stored in zip-top plastic bags for up to three months.

3 cups water
1 cup freshly ground French roast coffee
¼ cup fat-free milk
¼ cup ice cubes
1 teaspoon unsweetened cocoa
½ cup vanilla low-fat frozen yogurt
½ teaspoon grated semisweet chocolate
1 tablespoon canned refrigerated light whipped cream (such as Reddi-wip)
½ teaspoon chocolate syrup
1 teaspoon sliced almonds, toasted

1. Brew water and coffee in a coffee maker according to manufacturer's directions. Cover and chill. Reserve ¼ cup chilled coffee (reserve remaining coffee for another use).
2. Place ¼ cup chilled coffee, milk, ice cubes, and cocoa in a blender; process until smooth. Add yogurt and grated chocolate; process until smooth. Pour mixture into a tall glass; top with

whipped cream. Drizzle with chocolate syrup, and sprinkle with almonds. Serve immediately. Yield: 1 serving (serving size: about 1¼ cups).

CALORIES 168 (23% from fat); FAT 4.2g (sat 2g, mono 1.6g, poly 0.4g); PROTEIN 7.6g; CARB 26.8g; FIBER 1g; CHOL 9mg; IRON 0.9mg; SODIUM 94mg; CALC 222mg

Avocado-Tomatillo Dip with Cumin Pita Chips

CHIPS:
3 (6-inch) pitas, split in half horizontally
Cooking spray
1 teaspoon cumin seeds, crushed
1 teaspoon dried oregano
½ teaspoon kosher salt

DIP:
½ pound tomatillos (about 5 large)
½ cup chopped onion
2 tablespoons chopped fresh cilantro
1 teaspoon finely chopped seeded jalapeño pepper
½ teaspoon salt
⅓ cup fat-free sour cream
2 ripe peeled avocados, seeded and coarsely chopped

1. Preheat oven to 375°.
2. To prepare chips, coat rough side of each pita half with cooking spray; sprinkle evenly with cumin seeds, oregano, and kosher salt. Cut each pita half into 8 wedges; arrange wedges in a single layer on baking sheets. Bake at 375° for 15 minutes or until golden brown.
3. To prepare dip, discard husks and stems from tomatillos. Place tomatillos in a small saucepan; cover with water. Bring to a boil; cook 5 minutes or until tender. Drain and cool to room temperature. Place tomatillos, onion, cilantro, jalapeño, and ½ teaspoon salt in a blender or food processor, and process until smooth. Add sour cream and avocado; process until smooth. Serve with chips. Yield: 12 servings (serving size: about 2½ tablespoons dip and 4 chips).

CALORIES 106 (42% from fat); FAT 5g (sat 0.7g, mono 2.9g, poly 0.8g); PROTEIN 2.6g; CARB 13.9g; FIBER 2.8g; CHOL 1mg; IRON 0.9mg; SODIUM 266mg; CALC 33mg

Getting It All In

Certainly, the best way to consume these five healthful foods is to just eat them. Our recipes suggest ways to introduce or incorporate them into your diet. And you can also enjoy them in the following ways:

Avocados

• Add a few slices to a smoked turkey sandwich.

• Top chili or other thick soups with chunks of avocado.

• Place several slices atop garlic-rubbed bruschetta.

• Enjoy an avocado "bowl"—cut an avocado in half, remove the seed, and fill the cavity with balsamic vinegar. Sprinkle with coarse sea salt, and scoop out the flesh from the skin with a spoon.

Coffee

• If you're not a big fan of black coffee, try a milder-tasting latte instead (just be sure to use low-fat or fat-free milk).

• Mix coffee and hot chocolate for a hot, sweet mocha drink.

• Reduce brewed coffee, and combine it with a little ancho chile powder, sugar, salt, and pepper to make a glaze for pork tenderloin.

Eggs

• Slice a hard-cooked egg, and add to a salad.

• Keep hard-cooked eggs on hand for a quick snack or breakfast on the go.

• Top corn tortillas with scrambled eggs, shredded reduced-fat Cheddar cheese, and bottled salsa for a quick brunch burrito.

Mushrooms

• Toss a handful of sliced mushrooms into the eggs you scramble for breakfast.

• Add finely chopped mushrooms to the ground beef mixture for hamburgers.

• Stir a little ⅓-less-fat cream cheese into sautéed finely chopped mushrooms for an appetizer spread for crostini.

• Top mashed potatoes with a dollop of commercial pesto and a generous scoop of sautéed mushrooms.

Peanut butter

• Instead of cream cheese or jelly, spread a couple tablespoons of peanut butter onto your bagel or toast.

• Add two tablespoons peanut butter to vanilla low-fat milk shake, and blend until smooth.

• Make peanut butter s'mores: Spread a graham cracker with peanut butter, and sprinkle with mini marshmallows. Microwave a few seconds until the marshmallows melt, and top with another cracker.

Classic for Company Menu

serves 4

Searing the pork tenderloin before roasting seals in the juices.

Herb-crusted pork tenderloin*

Wild Mushroom and Rice Timbales

Steamed green beans with minced shallots

* Heat 2 teaspoons olive oil in a large non-stick skillet over medium-high heat. Add 1 (1-pound) trimmed pork tenderloin; brown all sides, and remove from heat. Combine 2 tablespoons Dijon mustard, 2 teaspoons chopped fresh thyme, 2 teaspoons chopped fresh parsley, and 1 teaspoon chopped fresh rosemary in a small bowl. Rub mustard mixture on pork. Bake at 375° for 15 minutes or until a thermometer registers 160°. Cut into ¼-inch-thick slices.

Wild Mushroom and Rice Timbales

Timbales are metal molds used to shape rice and custard mixtures. Ramekins, glass custard cups, or dry measuring cups make a fine substitute. Serve with roasted chicken, beef, or pork, or with salmon.

½ cup dried porcini mushrooms, chopped (about ½ ounce)
1 cup boiling water
1½ cups water
¾ cup brown rice blend (such as Lundberg)
½ teaspoon salt, divided
4 teaspoons olive oil, divided
½ cup diced red onion
1½ cups coarsely chopped portobello mushroom cap (about 1 cap)
1 (8-ounce) package presliced button mushrooms
1 tablespoon chopped fresh or 1 teaspoon dried thyme
¼ cup (1 ounce) grated fresh Parmesan cheese
¼ teaspoon freshly ground black pepper
Cooking spray
Thyme leaves (optional)

1. Place porcini mushrooms in a small bowl; cover with 1 cup boiling water. Let stand 20 minutes or until soft. Drain in a sieve over a bowl, reserving liquid.

2. Place reserved mushroom liquid, 1½ cups water, rice, and ¼ teaspoon salt in a large saucepan; bring to a boil. Cover, reduce heat, and simmer 50 minutes or until rice is tender.

3. While rice cooks, heat 2 teaspoons oil in a large nonstick skillet over medium-high heat. Add onion; sauté 2 minutes. Add remaining 2 teaspoons oil, ⅛ teaspoon salt, portobello mushrooms, and button mushrooms; cook 5 minutes or until mushrooms are tender and liquid almost evaporates, stirring frequently. Stir in remaining ⅛ teaspoon salt, porcini mushrooms, and chopped thyme.

4. Remove rice from heat; stir in mushroom mixture, cheese, and pepper.

5. Coat 4 timbales or 4 (6-ounce) ramekins with cooking spray. Pack about 1 cup rice mixture into each timbale; invert onto plates. Garnish with thyme, if desired. Yield: 4 servings (serving size: 1 timbale).

CALORIES 239 (30% from fat); FAT 7.9g (sat 1.8g, mono 3.9g, poly 0.6g); PROTEIN 9.3g; CARB 36.8g; FIBER 4.3g; CHOL 5mg; IRON 2mg; SODIUM 415mg; CALC 96mg

How to Make Sushi

1. *Place 1 nori sheet, shiny side down, on a sushi mat covered with plastic wrap, with long edge toward you. Pat ¾ cup rice mixture evenly over nori with moist hands, leaving a 1-inch border on one long end of nori.*

2. *Spread 1 tablespoon avocado mixture over rice. Arrange 8 shrimp pieces, 2 chives, and 2 cucumber strips along bottom third of rice-covered nori.*

3. *Lift edge of nori closest to you; fold over filling. Lift bottom edge of sushi mat; roll toward top edge, pressing firmly on sushi roll. Continue rolling to top edge; press mat to seal sushi roll.*

Avocado and Shrimp Sushi

Serve sushi with the typical accompaniments of wasabi, low-sodium soy sauce, and pickled ginger.

- 2 cups uncooked short-grain white rice
- ¼ cup seasoned rice vinegar
- 1 tablespoon wasabi (Japanese horseradish)
- 1 avocado, peeled and mashed
- 1½ tablespoons finely chopped fresh cilantro
- 24 large shrimp, cooked, peeled, and halved crosswise (about 8 ounces)
- 6 nori (seaweed) sheets
- 12 chives
- 12 (7-inch-long) julienne-cut seeded peeled cucumber strips

1. Prepare rice according to package directions. Stir in vinegar; cover and cool to room temperature.
2. Combine wasabi and avocado in a small bowl; set aside. Combine cilantro and shrimp in another small bowl; toss well.
3. Cut off one-quarter of nori sheets along a short edge, and discard. Place 1 nori sheet, shiny side down, on a sushi mat covered with plastic wrap, with long edge toward you. Pat ¾ cup rice mixture evenly over nori with moist hands, leaving a 1-inch border on one long end of nori. Spread 1 tablespoon avocado mixture over rice. Arrange 8 shrimp pieces, 2 chives, and 2 cucumber strips along bottom third of rice-covered nori.
4. Lift edge of nori closest to you; fold over filling. Lift bottom edge of sushi mat; roll toward top edge, pressing firmly on sushi roll. Continue rolling to top edge; press mat to seal sushi roll. Let rest, seam side down, 5 minutes. Slice crosswise into 8 pieces. Repeat procedure with remaining nori, rice mixture, avocado mixture, shrimp mixture, chives, and cucumber. Yield: 6 servings (serving size: 8 pieces).

CALORIES 365 (16% from fat); FAT 6.5g (sat 1g, mono 3.4g, poly 1g); PROTEIN 13.2g; CARB 60.3g; FIBER 3.9g; CHOL 57mg; IRON 4.3mg; SODIUM 311mg; CALC 35mg

Citrus-Marinated Mushrooms

- ¼ cup rice vinegar
- 2 tablespoons sugar
- 2 tablespoons fresh lime juice
- 1 tablespoon low-sodium soy sauce
- ¾ teaspoon crushed red pepper
- ¼ teaspoon salt
- 4 garlic cloves, thinly sliced
- 1 teaspoon grated orange rind
- 2 teaspoons extravirgin olive oil
- 1 teaspoon dark sesame oil
- ½ teaspoon grated lime rind
- 1 pound mushrooms, halved
- 2 tablespoons chopped fresh parsley

1. Combine first 7 ingredients in a small saucepan. Bring to a boil; cook 1 minute or until sugar dissolves. Remove from heat; stir in orange rind, oils, and lime rind. Combine vinegar mixture and mushrooms in a large bowl; toss well. Cover; refrigerate overnight. Add parsley; toss to combine. Yield: 6 servings (serving size: about ⅔ cup).

CALORIES 63 (34% from fat); FAT 2.4g (sat 0.3g, mono 1.4g, poly 0.5g); PROTEIN 3.1g; CARB 8.6g; FIBER 1.2g; CHOL 0mg; IRON 0.5mg; SODIUM 188mg; CALC 7mg

Grilled Peanut Butter and Banana Split Sandwich

- 2 (1-ounce) slices firm white sandwich bread
- 1 teaspoon butter, softened
- 1 tablespoon creamy peanut butter
- 2 teaspoons honey
- ½ teaspoon semisweet chocolate minichips
- 1 large strawberry, thinly sliced
- ½ small banana, cut lengthwise into 3 slices (about 2 ounces)
- 1 tablespoon pineapple jam

1. Spread one side of each bread slice with ½ teaspoon butter. Combine peanut butter and honey; spread over plain side of 1 bread slice. Sprinkle with chocolate chips; top evenly with strawberry slices and banana slices.

Continued

2. Spread pineapple jam over plain side of remaining bread slice. Carefully assemble sandwich, buttered sides out.
3. Heat a small nonstick skillet over medium-high heat. Add sandwich; cook 2 minutes on each side or until lightly browned. Yield: 1 serving (serving size: 1 sandwich).

CALORIES 436 (30% from fat); FAT 14.5g (sat 4.2g, mono 6g, poly 3.2g); PROTEIN 9.4g; CARB 72g; FIBER 4.6g; CHOL 10mg; IRON 3mg; SODIUM 497mg; CALC 100mg

Curried Peanut-Squash Soup

Cooking spray
2 cups thinly vertically sliced onion
1 tablespoon curry powder
1½ teaspoons ground cumin
¾ teaspoon salt, divided
¼ teaspoon ground red pepper
2 garlic cloves, minced
4 cups fat-free, less-sodium chicken broth
2 cups chopped peeled butternut squash
1 cup shredded carrot
1 cup frozen green peas, thawed
1½ cups cooked brown basmati rice
¾ cup sliced green onions
6 tablespoons creamy peanut butter
¼ cup chopped fresh cilantro
6 lime wedges
Green onion strips (optional)

1. Heat a large Dutch oven over medium heat. Coat pan with cooking spray. Add 2 cups onion; cook 6 minutes or until tender, stirring occasionally. Stir in curry powder, cumin, ½ teaspoon salt, pepper, and garlic. Cook 1 minute, stirring constantly. Add broth, squash, and carrot; bring to a boil. Cover, reduce heat, and simmer 20 minutes or until squash is tender. Stir in peas; cook, uncovered, 1 minute. Stir in ¼ teaspoon salt, rice, and next 3 ingredients. Cook 1 minute or until thoroughly heated. Serve with lime wedges; garnish with green onion strips, if desired. Yield: 6 servings (serving size: 1⅓ cups soup and 1 lime wedge).

CALORIES 252 (33% from fat); FAT 9.3g (sat 1.9g, mono 4.2g, poly 2.5g); PROTEIN 9.7g; CARB 35.7g; FIBER 7.3g; CHOL 0mg; IRON 2.5mg; SODIUM 677mg; CALC 91mg

Indoor Grilling

Just because it's cold outside doesn't mean you have to give up grilling. Here are the best tools—and recipes—for the job.

Thanks to a variety of new grill pans, contact grills, and electric grills, you can achieve great grilled flavor indoors. Burgers are a natural choice, but fish, steaks, and even fruit fare well on an indoor grill.

Rum-Spiked Grilled Pineapple with Toasted Coconut

Grilling caramelizes the sugars in the fruit for a light dessert that is delicious on its own or served with low-fat vanilla ice cream. Any firm fruit, such as peaches and apricots, lends itself to grilling.

¼ cup packed light brown sugar
¼ cup dark spiced rum (such as Captain Morgan's)
1 pineapple, peeled, cored, halved lengthwise, and sliced lengthwise into 12 wedges (about 1½ pounds)
1 tablespoon butter
2 tablespoons sweetened coconut, toasted
Low-fat vanilla ice cream (optional)

1. Combine sugar and rum in a microwave-safe bowl. Microwave at HIGH 1½ minutes or until sugar dissolves. Brush rum mixture evenly over pineapple wedges.
2. Heat butter in a grill pan over medium-high heat. Add pineapple; grill 3 minutes on each side or until grill marks form and pineapple is thoroughly heated. Sprinkle with coconut. Serve with ice cream, if desired. Yield: 6 servings (serving size: 2 pineapple wedges and 1 teaspoon coconut).

CALORIES 136 (17% from fat); FAT 2.5g (sat 1.4g, mono 0.8g, poly 0.1g); PROTEIN 0.7g; CARB 24g; FIBER 1.7g; CHOL 5mg; IRON 0.5mg; SODIUM 22mg; CALC 23mg

Asian Chicken Lettuce Wraps

Kids love these. For picky eaters, just prepare all the ingredients, and let everyone garnish their wraps.

1 tablespoon canola oil
1 tablespoon dark sesame oil
1 tablespoon rice vinegar
1 tablespoon low-sodium soy sauce
1½ teaspoons chili garlic sauce (such as Sriracha)
1 teaspoon grated peeled fresh ginger
½ teaspoon grated orange rind
2 garlic cloves, minced
Dash of sea salt
4 (6-ounce) skinless, boneless chicken breast halves
Cooking spray
8 Boston lettuce leaves (about 1 head)
1 cup fresh mint leaves (about 10 ounces)
½ cup bean sprouts (about 2 ounces)
1 lime, cut into 8 wedges
Chopped peanuts (optional)

1. Combine first 9 ingredients in a small bowl; stir with a whisk. Reserve 2 tablespoons oil mixture. Place remaining oil mixture in a large zip-top plastic bag. Add chicken breast halves to bag; seal and marinate in refrigerator 1 hour, turning occasionally. Remove chicken from bag, and discard marinade.
2. Heat a large nonstick grill pan over medium-high heat. Coat pan with cooking spray. Add chicken to pan; grill 12 minutes or until chicken is done, turning once. Let stand 5 minutes before cutting into thin slices. Divide chicken evenly among lettuce leaves; top each lettuce leaf with 2 tablespoons mint, 1 tablespoon sprouts, and about 1 teaspoon reserved oil mixture. Serve with lime wedges. Garnish with peanuts, if desired. Yield: 4 servings (serving size: 2 wraps and 2 lime wedges).

CALORIES 265 (32% from fat); FAT 9.3g (sat 1.3g, mono 4g, poly 3.1g); PROTEIN 40.7g; CARB 3.3g; FIBER 1g; CHOL 99mg; IRON 2.2mg; SODIUM 363mg; CALC 47mg

Classic Beef Shish Kebabs

The trick with these kebabs is to cook the meat separately from the vegetables so nothing overcooks. You can prepare this recipe on a grill pan, but you'll need to cook the kebabs in batches. An electric indoor grill is ideal for this recipe. It has a larger surface area so you can cook everything at once, starting with the onion and pepper kebabs, and later adding other kebabs with shorter cooking times so everything is finished cooking in about 10 minutes.

  1 tablespoon olive oil, divided
  1 teaspoon chopped fresh
     rosemary
  3 large garlic cloves, minced
  1 pound beef tenderloin, trimmed
     and cut into 1-inch cubes
  ½ teaspoon kosher salt, divided
  ½ teaspoon freshly ground black
     pepper, divided
  2 teaspoons fresh lemon juice
  2 cups cherry tomatoes
  1 large red onion, cut into 1-inch
     pieces
  1 yellow bell pepper, seeded and
     cut into 1-inch pieces
  ½ pound cremini mushrooms,
     stemmed and halved
    Cooking spray

1. Combine 2 teaspoons oil, rosemary, and garlic in a large zip-top bag. Add beef; seal and marinate in refrigerator 1 hour, turning occasionally. Remove beef from bag, and discard marinade. Thread beef evenly onto 6 (12-inch) wooden skewers; sprinkle with ¼ teaspoon salt and ¼ teaspoon black pepper.
2. Combine remaining 1 teaspoon oil and juice in a large bowl. Add tomatoes, onion, bell pepper, and mushrooms, tossing to coat. Thread vegetables separately onto 12 (12-inch) skewers; sprinkle with remaining ¼ teaspoon salt and ¼ teaspoon black pepper. Place beef and vegetable kebabs on an electric grill coated with cooking spray. Grill tomato and mushroom kebabs 7 minutes. Grill beef kebabs 9 minutes or until desired degree of doneness. Grill onion and pepper kebabs 10 minutes. Remove vegetables from skewers. Yield: 6 servings (serving size: 1 beef kebab and about 1 cup vegetables).

CALORIES 156 (36% from fat); FAT 6.2g (sat 1.7g, mono 3.1g, poly 0.5g); PROTEIN 17.1g; CARB 8.9g; FIBER 1.8g; CHOL 35mg; IRON 1.6mg; SODIUM 196mg; CALC 29mg

---

QUICK & EASY
Grilled Salmon with Garlic, Lemon, and Basil

We found that fish cooks best on a nonstick grill pan with a dome-shaped lid (see "Our Improvised Indoor Grilling System," page 26), so the fish steams while it gets great grill marks. Serve with a tossed green salad and couscous.

SAUCE:
  2 tablespoons chopped fresh basil
  ½ teaspoon grated lemon rind
  2 tablespoons fresh lemon juice
  1 tablespoon extravirgin olive oil
  2 garlic cloves, minced

FISH:
    Cooking spray
  4 (6-ounce) salmon fillets
  ½ teaspoon kosher salt
  ¼ teaspoon freshly ground black
     pepper

1. To prepare sauce, combine first 5 ingredients in a small bowl; set aside.
2. To prepare fish, heat a nonstick grill pan over medium-high heat. Coat pan with cooking spray. Sprinkle fish evenly with salt and pepper; add fish to pan. Cover and grill 4 minutes on each side or until fish flakes easily when tested with a fork or until desired degree of doneness. Serve with sauce. Yield: 4 servings (serving size: 1 fillet and about 1 tablespoon sauce).

CALORIES 309 (48% from fat); FAT 16.6g (sat 3.6g, mono 8.4g, poly 3.5g); PROTEIN 36.4g; CARB 1.3g; FIBER 0.2g; CHOL 87mg; IRON 0.7mg; SODIUM 316mg; CALC 27mg

---

QUICK & EASY
Grilled Halibut with Lemon-Caper Vinaigrette

Halibut is a light-textured white fish, but this simple vinaigrette could be used on any grilled fish. You can prepare extra vinaigrette to toss with salad greens.

VINAIGRETTE:
  1½ tablespoons fresh lemon juice
  1 tablespoon extravirgin olive oil
  1½ teaspoons finely chopped shallot
  1 teaspoon chopped capers
  ¼ teaspoon kosher salt
  ¼ teaspoon freshly ground black
     pepper

FISH:
    Cooking spray
  4 (6-ounce) halibut fillets
  ½ teaspoon kosher salt
  2 tablespoons chopped fresh chives

1. To prepare vinaigrette, combine first 6 ingredients in a small bowl; stir with a whisk.
2. To prepare fish, heat a nonstick grill pan over medium-high heat. Coat pan with cooking spray. Sprinkle fish with ½ teaspoon salt. Add fish to pan; grill 4 minutes on each side or until fish flakes easily when tested with a fork or until desired degree of doneness. Spoon vinaigrette over fish. Sprinkle with chives. Yield: 4 servings (serving size: 1 fillet, about 2 teaspoons vinaigrette, and 1½ teaspoons chives).

CALORIES 221 (30% from fat); FAT 7.4g (sat 1.1g, mono 4g, poly 1.6g); PROTEIN 35.6g; CARB 0.5g; FIBER 0.1g; CHOL 54mg; IRON 1.5mg; SODIUM 531mg; CALC 83mg

Indoor Grilling Tools

Electric Open Grill

Although this type of equipment can hog space in a small kitchen, we like electric grills because the heat coils are built into the unit (under the cooking grates) for consistent heat. Most have a large cooking surface, which makes it handy to prepare a lot of food, as in the Classic Beef Shish Kebabs (recipe on page 25). They're also nice for tableside grilling.

Our Favorite: The Bonjour Power 1800 Grill & Griddle ($80) has a generous 11 x 16–inch cooking surface, but stores upright to take up as little space as possible in the kitchen. Of the electric models we tested, this one did the best job of getting hot, maintaining heat, and creating nice grill marks (it's become a popular piece of equipment in our Test Kitchens). And there's a bonus: Just flip the unit over for a griddle to make pancakes for a crowd or use as a warming tray. Cleanup is easy, as well, because of the nonstick surface, and the electrical cord simply detaches so you can immerse the grill in water.

Stovetop Grill Pan

These have become standard equipment in many kitchens because you can pull one out to grill fish, vegetables, even bread and fruit at a moment's notice. The best models are nonstick (for easy cleanup), though many cooks also like cast-iron grills like those made by Lodge. Some cast-iron pans require seasoning or the food will stick (coat the pan with vegetable oil and heat it in a 350° oven for one hour).

Our Favorite: All-Clad's Stainless Nonstick 12-inch Round Grill Pan ($100) has a high-quality large surface to stand up to everyday use. Our runner-up was the cast-iron Lodge Logic Square Grill Pan ($25), which comes preseasoned.

Stovetop Grill Pan with Panini Press

This relatively new category of grill pan is a stovetop (nonelectric) panini maker—basically, a grill pan with a separate heavy cast-iron press to weigh down a sandwich. The pans were created to capitalize on the popularity of panini sandwiches.

Our Favorite: none. Using a cast-iron skillet (which you likely already have) or any heavy skillet to weigh down a sandwich in a grill pan works just as well as a panini press. In addition, most models come with instructions to preheat the press—an awkward and potentially hazardous process that isn't necessary.

Electric Contact Grill/Panini Maker

Contact grills, (panini makers), have a hinged grill surface to cook food from top and bottom simultaneously, so there's no need to turn during cooking. The downsides of contact grills are that delicate foods can be crushed if the plates aren't adjustable, and vegetables often steam before they caramelize.

Our Favorite: none. We found these grills were cumbersome to use and store. In addition, they didn't get hot enough to create decent grill marks, which enhance the appearance of the food.

Our Improvised Indoor Grilling System

When you use a grill pan, the heat comes only from the bottom of the pan, cooking the food slowly from the bottom up. So we set about looking for a high-domed lid that would retain the heat and allow hot air to circulate around the food. We found what we wanted by using All-Clad's 12½-inch Dome Cover ($51), which fits the manufacturer's 12-inch Round Grille Pan ($100). Together, the two pieces create an excellent indoor cooking system: The interior of the food is done when the exterior is golden brown and caramelized—and it takes far less time than an open grill.

Pressed Cuban Sandwich with Garlic Dijon Butter

Use a cast-iron skillet or a brick covered with foil to weigh down the sandwiches.

BUTTER:

- 1 garlic head
- 1 teaspoon olive oil
- 1 tablespoon Dijon mustard
- 1½ teaspoons butter, softened

SANDWICHES:

- 4 (3-ounce) hoagie rolls, cut in half lengthwise
- 8 sandwich-length pickle slices
- ¼ pound thinly sliced smoked turkey
- ¼ pound thinly sliced turkey ham
- 8 (¾-ounce) slices low-fat Swiss cheese (such as Jarlsberg)

Cooking spray

1. Preheat oven to 350°.

2. To prepare butter, remove white papery skin from garlic head (do not peel or separate cloves); drizzle with oil. Wrap head in foil. Bake at 350° for 1 hour; cool 10 minutes. Separate cloves; squeeze to extract garlic pulp. Discard skins. Combine garlic pulp, mustard, and butter in a small bowl; set aside.

3. To prepare sandwiches, scoop out inside of roll halves, leaving ½-inch shells. Discard bread pieces. Spread about 2 teaspoons garlic butter over cut sides of top and bottom halves of each roll. Arrange pickles, turkey, ham, and cheese evenly on bottom halves of rolls; top with top halves.

4. Heat a nonstick grill pan over medium-high heat. Coat pan with cooking spray. Add 2 sandwiches to pan. Place a cast-iron or heavy skillet on top of sandwiches, and press gently to flatten. Grill 4 minutes on each side or until cheese melts and bread is toasted. Repeat procedure with remaining sandwiches. Cut sandwiches in half diagonally, and serve immediately. Yield: 8 servings (serving size: ½ sandwich).

CALORIES 166 (24% from fat); FAT 4.4g (sat 1.4g, mono 1.5g, poly 1g); PROTEIN 13g; CARB 19.6g; FIBER 2.3g; CHOL 20mg; IRON 1.2mg; SODIUM 776mg; CALC 194mg

Steakhouse Steak

We call for flank steak in this recipe, but the dry rub seasoning would work well on any cut of meat. For a special occasion, try it on filet mignon.

RUB:

- 1 tablespoon whole black peppercorns
- 1 teaspoon kosher salt
- 1 teaspoon dry mustard
- ½ teaspoon garlic powder
- ¼ teaspoon dried thyme

REMAINING INGREDIENTS:

- 1 (1-pound) flank steak, trimmed
- Cooking spray
- Chopped fresh parsley (optional)

1. To prepare rub, heat a small skillet over medium heat. Add peppercorns; cook 1 minute or until fragrant. Transfer toasted peppercorns to a spice grinder; grind until fine. Combine ground peppercorns, salt, mustard, garlic powder, and thyme in a small bowl. Rub peppercorn mixture evenly over steak. Let stand 10 minutes.

2. Heat a nonstick grill pan over medium-high heat. Coat steak with cooking spray; grill 7 minutes on each side or until desired degree of doneness. Let stand 5 minutes before slicing. Garnish with parsley, if desired. Yield: 4 servings (serving size: 3 ounces meat).

CALORIES 171 (34% from fat); FAT 6.5g (sat 2.4g, mono 2.4g, poly 0.3g); PROTEIN 25g; CARB 1.6g; FIBER 0.5g; CHOL 37mg; IRON 2mg; SODIUM 533mg; CALC 36mg

> You can **achieve** the appearance of food cooked **outdoors** with indoor grilling.

dinner tonight

Eggs for Supper

Eggs are the key to these quick and comforting suppers.

Eggs Menu 1
serves 4

Cajun Quiche in a Rice Crust

Bibb-strawberry salad*

Low-fat butter pecan ice cream with low-fat caramel sauce

* Combine 4 cups torn Bibb lettuce leaves, 1 cup sliced strawberries, ½ cup sliced carrot, and 2 tablespoons chopped fresh mint in a large bowl. Drizzle with 1 tablespoon bottled poppy seed dressing; toss well to coat.

Game Plan

1. Prepare quiche crust.

2. Sauté onion, celery, bell pepper, garlic, and sausage.

3. While quiche bakes:
- Slice and chop ingredients for salad
- Assemble and dress salad

Cajun Quiche in a Rice Crust

If you don't have cooked rice, use boil-in-a-bag rice and follow the microwave directions. Cool the rice slightly before adding the egg.

TASTE TIP: Adjust the amount of hot pepper sauce in the filling to suit your taste.

TOTAL TIME: 45 MINUTES

CRUST:

- 2 cups cooked long-grain white rice, cooled
- 1 teaspoon garlic powder
- 1 teaspoon onion powder
- ½ teaspoon salt
- 1 large egg, lightly beaten
- Cooking spray
- ¼ cup (1 ounce) reduced-fat shredded Cheddar cheese

FILLING:

- ½ cup prechopped onion
- ½ cup prechopped celery
- ½ cup prechopped red bell pepper
- 1 teaspoon bottled minced garlic
- 3 ounces andouille sausage or kielbasa, chopped (about ⅔ cup)
- ¾ cup egg substitute
- 2 large egg whites, lightly beaten
- ¼ cup plain fat-free yogurt
- ¼ teaspoon salt
- ¼ teaspoon hot pepper sauce (such as Tabasco)
- ¼ cup (1 ounce) reduced-fat shredded Cheddar cheese

1. Preheat oven to 375°.

2. To prepare crust, combine first 5 ingredients. Spread into bottom and up sides of a 9-inch pie plate coated with cooking spray. Sprinkle bottom of crust evenly with ¼ cup cheese.

3. To prepare filling, heat a medium nonstick skillet over medium-high heat. Coat pan with cooking spray. Add onion and next 4 ingredients; sauté 5 minutes. Spoon into prepared crust. Combine egg substitute and next 4 ingredients; stir with a whisk until well blended. Pour egg substitute mixture over sausage mixture. Sprinkle with ¼ cup cheese. Bake at 375° for 30 minutes or until center is set. Let stand 5 minutes before serving. Yield: 4 servings (serving size: 1 wedge).

CALORIES 291 (32% from fat); FAT 10.3g (sat 4.5g, mono 3.7g, poly 1.6g); PROTEIN 19.5g; CARB 29.4g; FIBER 0.9g; CHOL 79mg; IRON 2.8mg; SODIUM 623mg; CALC 181mg

Eggs Menu 2

serves 4

Quick Avgolemono, Orzo, and Chicken Soup

Ricotta-garlic pita wedges*

Tossed salad with bottled Greek dressing

*Preheat broiler. Combine ⅓ cup part-skim ricotta cheese, 1 teaspoon chopped fresh oregano, ⅛ teaspoon salt, ⅛ teaspoon freshly ground black pepper, and 1 minced garlic clove in a small bowl. Place 8 pita wedges on a baking sheet; broil 2 minutes or until toasted. Top each wedge with 4 teaspoons ricotta mixture. Broil 1 minute or until cheese is lightly browned.

Game Plan

1. While broiler preheats:
- Prepare ricotta mixture for pitas
- Boil broth for soup

2. While soup simmers:
- Prepare salad
- Broil pita wedges

QUICK & EASY
Quick Avgolemono, Orzo, and Chicken Soup

Avgolemono (ahv-goh-LEH-moh-noh) is a tangy Greek soup that combines chicken broth, eggs, and lemon juice. Traditional versions include rice; our interpretation uses orzo.

MAKE-AHEAD TIP: Prepare the soup up to three days ahead and refrigerate (do not freeze). Reheat over gentle heat.

TOTAL TIME: 35 MINUTES

- 6 cups fat-free, less-sodium chicken broth
- 1 teaspoon finely chopped fresh dill
- ½ cup uncooked orzo
- 4 large eggs
- ⅓ cup fresh lemon juice
- 1 cup shredded carrot
- ¼ teaspoon salt
- ¼ teaspoon pepper
- 8 ounces skinless, boneless chicken breast, cut into bite-sized pieces

1. Bring broth and dill to a boil in a large saucepan. Add orzo. Reduce heat, and simmer 5 minutes or until orzo is slightly tender. Remove from heat.

2. Place eggs and juice in a blender; process until smooth. Remove 1 cup broth from pan with a ladle, making sure to leave out orzo. With blender on, slowly add broth; process until smooth.

3. Add carrot, salt, pepper, and chicken to pan. Bring to a simmer over medium-low heat, and cook 5 minutes or until chicken and orzo are done. Reduce heat to low. Slowly stir in egg mixture; cook 30 seconds, stirring constantly (do not boil). Yield: 4 servings (serving size: 2 cups).

CALORIES 228 (25% from fat); FAT 6.3g (sat 1.9g, mono 2.2g, poly 1g); PROTEIN 25.3g; CARB 16.6g; FIBER 2.9g; CHOL 244mg; IRON 2.6mg; SODIUM 855mg; CALC 68mg

Eggs Menu 3

serves 4

Shrimp and Egg Flower Soup

Snow pea and water chestnut salad*

Store-bought almond cookies

* Combine 4 cups fresh snow peas, 2 tablespoons chopped green onions, and 1 (5-ounce) can drained, sliced water chestnuts in a large bowl. Combine 2 tablespoons rice wine vinegar, 1 tablespoon low-sodium soy sauce, 2 teaspoons toasted sesame seeds, 1 teaspoon sugar, and 2 teaspoons dark sesame oil. Drizzle vinaigrette over snow pea mixture; toss well to coat.

Game Plan

1. While broth mixture comes to a boil:
- Prepare salad
- Shred carrot, slice green onions, and beat eggs

QUICK & EASY
Shrimp and Egg Flower Soup

Better than takeout, this fast Cantonese-style menu works both for weeknight dining and impromptu entertaining. Drizzle the egg into the soup while stirring to create "flowers."

QUICK TIP: To save time, purchase frozen, peeled, and deveined shrimp.

TOTAL TIME: 45 MINUTES

- 2 tablespoons cornstarch
- 2 tablespoons water
- 5 cups fat-free, less-sodium chicken broth
- 1 tablespoon dry sherry
- 1 tablespoon low-sodium soy sauce
- 1½ teaspoons grated peeled fresh ginger
- 1 teaspoon dark sesame oil
- 2 cups (4 ounces) presliced mushrooms
- 1 cup shredded carrot
- 1 cup frozen petite peas, thawed
- ¾ pound medium shrimp, peeled and deveined, cut lengthwise
- 2 large eggs, lightly beaten
- ¼ cup thinly sliced green onions

1. Combine cornstarch and water in a small bowl, stirring with a whisk.

2. Combine cornstarch mixture, broth, and next 4 ingredients in a large saucepan. Bring to a boil. Add mushrooms and carrot; cook 2 minutes. Add peas and shrimp; cook 3 minutes or until shrimp are done. Remove from heat. Slowly drizzle egg into broth mixture, stirring constantly. Stir in onions. Yield: 4 servings (serving size: 2 cups).

CALORIES 226 (23% from fat); FAT 5.7g (sat 1.4g, mono 1.3g, poly 1.1g); PROTEIN 26.7g; CARB 15.6g; FIBER 4g; CHOL 235mg; IRON 4.1mg; SODIUM 841mg; CALC 104mg

Eggs Menu 4
serves 4

Sunny Frittata

Pineapple salad*

Mango sorbet

*Combine 4 cups cubed fresh pineapple and 1 cup halved red grapes in a medium bowl. Combine 2 tablespoons orange juice, 1 tablespoon honey, ⅛ teaspoon ground red pepper, and a dash of salt in a small bowl. Drizzle juice mixture over pineapple mixture; sprinkle evenly with 2 tablespoons toasted sweetened coconut and 2 tablespoons chopped macadamia nuts.

Game Plan

1. While oven preheats:
- Dice ham, slice green onions, and shred cheese
- Mix egg substitute and seasonings
- Sauté frittata filling

2. While frittata bakes:
- Prepare pineapple salad

QUICK & EASY
Sunny Frittata

A combination of egg substitute, Cheddar cheese, and orange bell pepper lends the frittata a cheerful hue. Substitute red or green bell pepper, if you prefer. Stir the egg mixture while it cooks for the first two minutes to keep it from browning too much.

TOTAL TIME: 45 MINUTES

2 cups egg substitute
½ cup fat-free milk
¼ teaspoon salt
¼ teaspoon black pepper
Cooking spray
⅔ cup (4 ounces) diced ham
½ cup diced orange bell pepper
½ cup thinly sliced green onions
¼ cup (1 ounce) reduced-fat shredded Cheddar cheese

1. Preheat oven to 375°.
2. Combine first 4 ingredients in a small bowl, stirring well with a whisk.

3. Heat a medium nonstick skillet over medium-high heat. Coat pan with cooking spray. Add ham, bell pepper, and onions; sauté 2 minutes. Stir in egg mixture. Reduce heat to medium, and cook 5 minutes, stirring occasionally during first 2 minutes. Top with cheese. Wrap handle of pan with foil; bake at 375° for 12 minutes or until center is set. Cut frittata into 4 wedges. Yield: 4 servings (serving size: 1 wedge).

CALORIES 194 (37% from fat); FAT 8g (sat 2.7g, mono 2.1g, poly 2.2g); PROTEIN 24.8g; CARB 4.6g; FIBER 0.9g; CHOL 28mg; IRON 3.1mg; SODIUM 401mg; CALC 153mg

---

menu of the month

Valentine's Dinner

Set the table and light the candles for this romantic menu for two.

Valentine's Day Menu
serves 2

Wild Mushroom Soup

Toasted baguette slices

Rosemary Shrimp Scampi Skewers

Carrot Couscous with Fresh Chives

Steamed haricots verts

Bittersweet Chocolate Pudding with Raspberries

Chardonnay

Espresso

MAKE AHEAD
Wild Mushroom Soup

Any combination of mushrooms will work well in this savory starter that can be made up to a day in advance. Reheat over medium heat. Serve with thin toasted baguette slices lightly brushed with olive oil and sprinkled with salt as a nice dipper for the soup.

½ teaspoon butter
½ teaspoon olive oil
2 tablespoons finely chopped celery
2 tablespoons finely chopped shallots
2 tablespoons finely chopped carrot
Cooking spray
1 cup thinly sliced button mushrooms
2 cups thinly sliced shiitake mushroom caps
1 (14-ounce) can fat-free, less-sodium chicken broth
1 teaspoon dry sherry
½ teaspoon chopped fresh parsley
¼ teaspoon chopped fresh tarragon
¼ teaspoon freshly ground black pepper
⅛ teaspoon salt

1. Heat butter and oil in a large nonstick skillet over medium-high heat. Add celery, shallots, and carrot; sauté 3 minutes or until lightly browned. Spoon vegetable mixture into a medium bowl.
2. Coat pan with cooking spray. Add button mushrooms; sauté 3 minutes or until lightly browned. Add button mushrooms to vegetable mixture. Coat pan with cooking spray. Add shiitake mushrooms; sauté 3 minutes or until lightly browned. Add shiitake mushrooms to vegetable mixture.
3. Combine vegetable mixture and broth in a medium saucepan; bring to a boil over medium heat. Cover, reduce heat, and simmer 30 minutes. Stir in sherry and remaining ingredients. Simmer, uncovered, 5 minutes. Yield: 2 servings (serving size: about 1¼ cups).

CALORIES 69 (35% from fat); FAT 2.7g (sat 0.7g, mono 1.3g, poly 0.4g); PROTEIN 5.7g; CARB 7.1g; FIBER 2.4g; CHOL 3mg; IRON 1.2mg; SODIUM 485mg; CALC 27mg

1. *Working with 1 rosemary sprig at a time, hold leafy end of sprig in 1 hand. Strip leaves off sprig with other hand, leaving ½ inch of leaves attached to leafy end. Thread 3 shrimp onto each rosemary skewer.*

Rosemary Shrimp Scampi Skewers

Threading shrimp on rosemary-branch skewers imparts flavor to the dish and scent to your table. Bamboo skewers also work quite well. Serve with steamed haricots verts.

    1   tablespoon dry white wine
    1   teaspoon fresh lemon juice
    1   teaspoon olive oil
    ⅛   teaspoon salt
    ⅛   teaspoon freshly ground black pepper
    1   garlic clove, minced
   18   large shrimp, peeled and deveined
        (about ¾ pound)
    6   (6-inch) rosemary sprigs
  Cooking spray
  Lemon wedges (optional)

1. Combine first 6 ingredients in a zip-top plastic bag. Add shrimp to bag; seal and shake to coat. Marinate in refrigerator 30 minutes, turning bag occasionally.
2. Remove shrimp from marinade; discard marinade. Working with 1 rosemary sprig at a time, hold leafy end of sprig in 1 hand. Strip leaves off sprig with other hand, leaving ½ inch of leaves attached to leafy end. Thread 3 shrimp onto each rosemary skewer.

3. Heat a grill pan over medium-high heat. Coat both sides of skewers with cooking spray. Arrange 3 skewers on pan; cook 2 minutes on each side or until shrimp are done. Remove from pan; keep warm. Repeat procedure with remaining skewers. Serve with lemon wedges, if desired. Yield: 2 servings (serving size: 3 skewers).

CALORIES 208 (23% from fat); FAT 5.2g (sat 0.9g, mono 2.1g, poly 1.4g); PROTEIN 34.7g; CARB 2.4g; FIBER 0.1g; CHOL 259mg; IRON 4.2mg; SODIUM 400mg; CALC 93mg

QUICK & EASY • MAKE AHEAD
Carrot Couscous with Fresh Chives

    ⅔   cup carrot juice
   1½   teaspoons fresh lemon juice
    ¼   teaspoon salt
    ⅛   teaspoon freshly ground black pepper
    ½   cup uncooked couscous
    2   teaspoons olive oil
    2   tablespoons chopped fresh chives

1. Bring first 4 ingredients to a simmer over medium-high heat; gradually stir in couscous. Remove from heat; cover and let stand 5 minutes. Drizzle with oil; fluff with a fork. Sprinkle with chives; toss to combine. Yield: 2 servings (serving size: about ¾ cup).

CALORIES 236 (19% from fat); FAT 4.9g (sat 0.7g, mono 3.4g, poly 0.6g); PROTEIN 6.4g; CARB 41.4g; FIBER 3g; CHOL 0mg; IRON 1mg; SODIUM 323mg; CALC 33mg

Bittersweet Chocolate Pudding with Raspberries

    ½   cup sugar
    2   teaspoons cornstarch
    1   teaspoon vanilla extract
  Dash of salt
    1   large egg, lightly beaten
    1   large egg white, lightly beaten
    1   cup 1% low-fat milk
    ½   cup evaporated fat-free milk
    2   ounces bittersweet chocolate, chopped
    ½   cup raspberries
    4   teaspoons shaved white chocolate

1. Combine first 6 ingredients in a medium bowl, stirring well with a whisk.
2. Combine milks in a medium saucepan; bring to a simmer. Remove from heat; add bittersweet chocolate to pan, stirring until chocolate melts. Gradually stir about one-fourth of hot chocolate mixture into egg mixture; add egg mixture to remaining chocolate mixture in pan, stirring constantly. Cook over medium heat 5 minutes or until mixture is thick and creamy, stirring constantly. Pour into a bowl; cover surface of pudding with plastic wrap. Chill. Top with raspberries and white chocolate. Yield: 4 servings (serving size: about ½ cup pudding, 2 tablespoons raspberries, and 1 teaspoon white chocolate).

CALORIES 276 (30% from fat); FAT 9.2g (sat 4.5g, mono 1.8g, poly 0.8g); PROTEIN 7.9g; CARB 44.5g; FIBER 2g; CHOL 55mg; IRON 0.8mg; SODIUM 143mg; CALC 174mg

inspired vegetarian

Beans, Italian Style

Dried beans and legumes are as fundamental as pasta in the Italian kitchen.

MAKE AHEAD
Lentil and Herb Salad

Lentils are popular across Italy. Technically not a "bean," lentils are legumes. Unlike beans, lentils require no soaking. Serve as a side salad, or add a cup of diced mozzarella, and it makes a light main dish.

    1   cup dried lentils
    ½   cup finely chopped red onion
    2   tablespoons finely chopped fresh flat-leaf parsley
    1   tablespoon finely chopped fresh basil
    ½   teaspoon salt
    ⅛   teaspoon freshly ground black pepper
    3   tablespoons red wine vinegar
    2   tablespoons olive oil

1. Place lentils in a large saucepan. Cover with water to 2 inches above lentils; bring to a boil. Reduce heat, and simmer 45 minutes or until tender. Drain well.

2. Place lentils in a large bowl. Stir in onion and next 4 ingredients. Add vinegar and oil; toss well. Serve at room temperature. Yield: 7 servings (serving size: about ½ cup).

CALORIES 127 (28% from fat); FAT 3.9g (sat 0.5g, mono 2.9g, poly 0.4g); PROTEIN 6.4g; CARB 17.6g; FIBER 4.2g; CHOL 0mg; IRON 1.7mg; SODIUM 178mg; CALC 28mg

---

Bean Basics

Dried beans should always be soaked, preferably for 8 hours or overnight. Soaking softens the exterior wall of the beans and enables them to cook evenly and considerably more quickly than if you didn't soak them at all. It's easy: Sort and wash the beans; place them in a large bowl. Add water to cover to 2 inches above the beans. Cover the bowl, and let the beans stand 8 hours or overnight. Drain and rinse the beans.

If you're in a hurry, you can use the quick-soak method, though it may not soften the beans uniformly and may result in uneven cooking. However, it's a convenient alternative. Simply cook the beans briefly in boiling water for 2 minutes, and let them stand for at least 1 hour.

Simmer beans slowly, with barely a bubble apparent in the pot, in plenty of water to allow room for expansion. This gentle process ensures the beans cook evenly, and when done, are tender yet firm to the bite. Don't salt the beans before cooking. Salt the beans when they're fully cooked and still hot.

Store any leftover cooked beans in tightly closed containers in the refrigerator for three to four days. You can also freeze them for several months. To do so, spread them in a single layer on a baking sheet, and freeze; then place them in an airtight container.

Cannellini Minestrone

This is a marvelously flavorful soup from the northwestern region of Liguria, also known as the Italian Riviera. Dried mushrooms and Swiss chard are both commonly used ingredients there.

  2 cups dried cannellini beans
  8 cups water
  1 cup dried porcini mushrooms
     (about 1 ounce)
  1 teaspoon salt
  ⅛ teaspoon freshly ground black
     pepper
  1 tablespoon olive oil
  1 cup finely chopped onion
  ½ cup finely chopped celery
  1 garlic clove, minced
  2 tablespoons finely chopped fresh
     flat-leaf parsley
  1 tablespoon finely chopped fresh
     basil
  ½ teaspoon crushed red pepper
  1 (14.5-ounce) can diced tomatoes,
     drained
  1 (4.5-ounce) can chopped green
     chiles
  3 cups torn Swiss chard (about 1
     pound)
  4 teaspoons olive oil

1. Sort and wash beans; place in a large bowl. Cover with water to 2 inches above beans; cover and let stand 8 hours or overnight. Drain and rinse beans.

2. Combine beans and 8 cups water in a large Dutch oven; bring to a boil. Cover, reduce heat, and simmer 1½ hours or until beans are tender.

3. Combine mushrooms and boiling water to cover in a small bowl. Cover and let stand 30 minutes or until tender. Drain and chop.

4. Place 2 cups cooked beans in a blender or food processor. Process until smooth; return pureed beans to pan. Stir in salt and pepper.

5. Heat 1 tablespoon oil in a large nonstick skillet over medium heat. Add onion, celery, and garlic; cook 10 minutes or until vegetables are tender. Stir in mushrooms, parsley, and next 4 ingredients; cook 3 minutes, stirring frequently. Add onion mixture and chard to beans in

---

pan; bring to a boil. Reduce heat, and simmer 10 minutes or until chard is tender. Ladle soup into individual bowls; drizzle with 4 teaspoons oil. Yield: 8 servings (serving size: about 1⅓ cups soup and ½ teaspoon oil).

CALORIES 250 (17% from fat); FAT 4.7g (sat 0.7g, mono 3.1g, poly 0.7g); PROTEIN 15.1g; CARB 39.7g; FIBER 10.7g; CHOL 0mg; IRON 7.3mg; SODIUM 492mg; CALC 171mg

---

Tomato and Bean Bruschetta

Bruschetta is one of Tuscany's premier appetizers—you'll find it served with all manner of toppings, including beans. The right bread is essential; a country-style loaf is a sturdy base for the thick bean spread. To cook dried cannellini, follow steps 1 and 2 in Cannellini Minestrone (recipe at left).

     Cooking spray
  1 cup chopped seeded peeled plum
     tomato
  1 garlic clove, minced
  1 cup cooked cannellini beans
  ½ teaspoon salt
     Dash of crushed red pepper
  4 ounces country white bread,
     diagonally sliced into 8 (¼-inch)
     pieces and toasted
  4 teaspoons extravirgin
     olive oil
  ¼ cup thinly sliced fresh
     basil

1. Heat a large nonstick skillet over medium heat. Coat pan with cooking spray. Add tomato and garlic; cook 2 minutes, stirring constantly.

2. Add beans, salt, and pepper to pan, mashing beans with a fork. Cook 1 minute or until thoroughly heated. Remove from heat. Spread bean mixture evenly over bread slices; drizzle each slice with ½ teaspoon olive oil, and top each with 1½ teaspoons basil. Yield: 4 servings (serving size: 2 bruschetta).

CALORIES 180 (30% from fat); FAT 5.9g (sat 0.7g, mono 3.8g, poly 0.8g); PROTEIN 6.6g; CARB 27.3g; FIBER 5.6g; CHOL 0mg; IRON 1.7mg; SODIUM 446mg; CALC 38mg

Bean and Barley Soup

This is an especially nutritious soup; barley adds another source of soluble fiber. This recipe quick-soaks the beans, but you can soak the beans overnight, if you wish. Pureeing some of the beans adds extra body to the soup.

   1   cup dried borlotti or pinto beans
   1   tablespoon olive oil
   2   cups finely chopped red onion
   1   cup finely chopped fresh flat-leaf parsley
   ½   cup finely chopped celery
   ½   cup finely chopped carrot
   ½   cup chopped fresh basil
   9   cups water
   2   cups organic vegetable broth (such as Swanson Certified Organic)
   2   bay leaves
   ⅓   cup uncooked pearl barley
   ½   teaspoon salt
   ½   teaspoon freshly ground black pepper
   ½   teaspoon hot sauce
   2   tablespoons grated fresh Parmesan cheese

1. Sort and wash beans; place in a large saucepan. Cover with water to 2 inches above beans; bring to a boil. Cook 2 minutes; remove from heat. Cover and let stand 1 hour. Drain beans. Wipe pan dry with a paper towel.
2. Heat oil in pan over medium-high heat. Add onion, parsley, celery, carrot, and basil; cook 3 minutes, stirring frequently. Add beans, 9 cups water, broth, and bay leaves; bring to a boil. Reduce heat, and simmer 1 hour and 15 minutes or until beans are tender. Discard bay leaves.
3. Place ¾ cup beans and ¾ cup cooking liquid in a blender; process until smooth. Return pureed bean mixture to pan. Stir in barley, salt, pepper, and hot sauce; bring to a boil. Reduce heat, and simmer 30 minutes or until barley is done. Ladle soup into individual bowls; sprinkle with cheese. Yield: 4 servings (serving size: 1¼ cups soup and 1½ teaspoons cheese).

CALORIES 308 (16% from fat); FAT 5.4g (sat 1.1g, mono 2.9g, poly 0.8g); PROTEIN 14.6g; CARB 52.6; FIBER 12.5g; CHOL 2mg; IRON 4.4mg; SODIUM 676mg; CALC 154mg

Soak, Then Cook
Cooking times for dried beans vary. Use this chart as a guide.

Bean variety	Soaking time	Cooking time
Borlotti, pinto, and cranberry	8 hours or overnight	1½ hours
Black-eyed peas	8 hours or overnight	30 to 45 minutes
Cannellini or Great Northern	8 hours or overnight	1½ hours
Chickpeas	8 hours or overnight	1 to 1½ hours
Fava beans	8 hours or overnight	1 to 1½ hours (whole beans) 30 to 45 minutes (skinned and split beans)
Lentils	None	30 to 45 minutes

Tuscan Vegetable and Bean Soup with Cheese Croutons

In the summer, this soup is delicious when served at room temperature with a little drizzle of extravirgin olive oil on top in place of the cheese-topped crouton.

   1   cup dried borlotti or pinto beans
   8   cups water
   2   tablespoons olive oil
   1½ cups finely chopped onion (about 1 large)
   ½   cup chopped celery
   1   tablespoon chopped fresh parsley
   1   garlic clove, minced
   5   cups cold water
   2   cups (½-inch) slices zucchini (about 2 medium)
   1½ cups (½-inch) cubed Yukon gold or red potato (about 8 ounces)
   1   cup (1-inch) cut green beans (about ¼ pound)
   ¾   cup (½-inch) slices carrot
   1   cup canned tomato puree (about ½ [16-ounce] can)
   1   teaspoon salt
   ½   teaspoon freshly ground black pepper
   2   cups chopped Swiss chard or fresh spinach
   6   (½-inch-thick) slices country white bread (about 4 ounces)
   6   tablespoons (about 1½ ounces) grated fresh Parmesan cheese

1. Sort and wash beans; place in a large bowl. Cover with water to 2 inches above beans; cover and let stand 8 hours or overnight. Drain and rinse beans.
2. Combine beans and 8 cups water in a large Dutch oven; bring to a boil. Cover, reduce heat, and simmer 1½ hours or until beans are tender. Drain and set aside.
3. Heat oil in a large saucepan over medium-high heat. Add onion, celery, parsley, and garlic to pan; sauté 2 minutes. Add beans, 5 cups water, and next 7 ingredients. Bring to a boil; reduce heat, and simmer 35 minutes. Add chard; simmer 5 minutes or until chard is tender.
4. Preheat broiler.
5. Place bread slices on a baking sheet; top each with 1 tablespoon cheese. Broil 2 minutes or until cheese melts and bread is lightly toasted. Ladle soup into individual bowls; top with cheese croutons. Yield: 6 servings (serving size: 1⅓ cups soup and 1 crouton).

CALORIES 237 (27% from fat); FAT 7g (sat 1.6g, mono 3.8g, poly 0.7g); PROTEIN 9.3g; CARB 37.3g; FIBER 7.3g; CHOL 4mg; IRON 2.8mg; SODIUM 831mg; CALC 138mg

Canned Beans Substitution

To substitute canned beans for dry (though they'll have a softer texture), use two cups rinsed, drained canned beans for every cup of dried beans in a recipe.

Menu Makeovers

We stepped up to the plate when two families asked for our help with their dining dilemmas.

Our readers face a range of kitchen challenges, from figuring out what to cook for dinner on busy weeknights (and how to avoid preparing the same dishes over and over) to cooking just one meal for the family instead of catering to each picky eater. When we posted a query on CookingLight.com to find two families that would be interested in a menu makeover, the number of responses was amazing. And after carefully sifting through them all, we selected The Dickinson's and the Wall's—two families that encompass common dilemmas: a newlywed couple and a family with two young children. We're sure you'll recognize some of their challenges—and appreciate our strategies.

MAKE AHEAD
Two-Potato Mash

This sweet-and-salty blend is a delicious way to obtain vitamin A. It also fulfills Russ Wall's desire for simple dishes he can prepare and the Dickinsons' request for ways to work different vegetables into their diet.

     2   pounds sweet potatoes
     1   cup fat-free sour cream,
         divided
    ¼   cup packed brown sugar
    ¼   cup butter, divided
     1   teaspoon kosher salt, divided
    ¼   teaspoon ground cinnamon
     1   (22-ounce) bag frozen mashed
         potatoes (such as Ore-Ida)
    2¼ cups fat-free milk
    ½   teaspoon black pepper

1. Pierce sweet potatoes with a fork; arrange in a circle on paper towels in microwave. Microwave at HIGH 12 minutes or until tender, rearranging potatoes after 6 minutes. Let stand 5 minutes. Peel potatoes; mash. Add ½ cup sour cream, sugar, 2 tablespoons butter, ½ teaspoon salt, and cinnamon, stirring until blended. Keep warm.
2. Heat frozen mashed potatoes in a large microwave-safe bowl according to package directions, omitting salt and fat. Add milk, remaining ½ cup sour cream, remaining 2 tablespoons butter, remaining

½ teaspoon salt, and pepper, stirring to combine. Spoon sweet potato mixture over mashed potatoes, swirling with a spoon. (Do not blend in completely.) Yield: 12 servings (serving size: about ⅔ cup).

CALORIES 234 (22% from fat); FAT 5.8g (sat 3g, mono 1.6g, poly 0.1g); PROTEIN 5.1g; CARB 41.3g; FIBER 3.2g; CHOL 13mg; IRON 0.3mg; SODIUM 378mg; CALC 119mg

MAKE AHEAD
Beef, Cheese, and Noodle Bake

This family-friendly casserole is a great way to incorporate more vegetables into your children's food.

     1   (8-ounce) package small elbow
         macaroni
         Cooking spray
     1   cup prechopped onion
     1   cup preshredded carrot
     2   teaspoons bottled minced garlic
     1   pound lean ground sirloin
     1   cup tomato sauce
     1   teaspoon kosher salt, divided
    ½   teaspoon freshly ground black pepper
     1   cup fat-free milk
     2   tablespoons all-purpose flour
    ⅛   teaspoon ground nutmeg
    1½ cups (6 ounces) 2% reduced-fat
         shredded sharp Cheddar cheese
         (such as Cracker Barrel), divided

1. Preheat oven to 350°.
2. Cook pasta according to package directions, omitting salt and fat; drain. Lightly coat pasta with cooking spray.
3. Heat a Dutch oven over medium-high heat. Coat pan with cooking spray. Add onion and carrot, and sauté 4 minutes. Add garlic; sauté 1 minute. Add ground beef; cook 5 minutes or until browned, stirring to crumble. Add tomato sauce, ½ teaspoon salt, and pepper. Cook 2 minutes or until most of liquid evaporates.
4. Add pasta to beef mixture in pan, stirring to combine. Spoon pasta mixture into an 11 x 7–inch baking dish coated with cooking spray.
5. Place milk, flour, nutmeg, and remaining ½ teaspoon salt in a medium saucepan; stir with a whisk until blended. Cook over medium heat 2 minutes or until thickened, stirring constantly with a whisk. Add 1 cup cheese, stirring until smooth. Pour cheese mixture over pasta mixture; stir. Top evenly with remaining ½ cup cheese. Bake at 350° for 20 minutes or until lightly browned. Let stand 5 minutes before serving. Yield: 8 servings (serving size: about 1 cup).

CALORIES 283 (24% from fat); FAT 7.7g (sat 4.2g, mono 2.4g, poly 0.7g); PROTEIN 22.3g; CARB 30.1g; FIBER 2.1g; CHOL 46mg; IRON 3.1mg; SODIUM 622mg; CALC 209mg

---

Get Organized

Organize the pantry by storing common foods together—canned foods with canned foods; rice and other starchy sides together; oils, vinegars, and condiments grouped together, etc. Discard any spices that are more than two years old. Then organize the spices in alphabetical order, using a permanent marker on the outside of the spice jar. (It's also a good idea to mark the date of purchase on the bottom of spice jars so you know when to discard them.)

Sasha Wall, of Sterling, Virginia, is an evaluation and research manager in the education field. She's also the primary meal planner, shopper, and cook for her husband, Russ, a police officer who works nights, and daughters Sophie, seven, and Maddy, five.

Challenge: Russ needs quick, easy recipes he can prepare on his days off. "He would make us dinner if he knew what and how to cook," says Sasha.

Solution: Choose recipes with short ingredient lists and few steps. Citrus–Glazed Chicken Thighs (recipe on page 35), for example, deliver wonderful flavor, thanks to an easy marinade (Russ can even recruit the girls to help measure ingredients). We also suggested that Sasha provide Russ with a short list of recipes to concentrate on. That way, he can develop a solid repertoire, rather than being distracted by too many choices.

Challenge: Cook one meal for everyone instead of preparing one dish for the parents and another for the kids. "We always have to make two, or sometimes three, meals a night," says Sasha. "What can we make that everyone will eat?"

Solution: Teach kids that Mom and Dad are not short-order cooks. Even as toddlers, children can and should eat what their parents eat. Encourage kids to sample new foods (offer one new food at a time), but don't force the issue. Hungry kids will eat what's available, especially if they have a choice (see "Clean the Fridge, Feed the Family," page 35).

Challenge: Stop wasting food. "We buy food and often throw it out if we don't have time to cook it," says Sasha.

Solution: The best way to avoid waste is to buy only what you need. People tend to purchase big packages of food because they think it saves money, but the strategy doesn't work if they end up throwing away half the package. If you buy a large package of meat or poultry, divide it into single-recipe portions in heavy-duty zip-top plastic bags, label, and freeze at once. You can also add marinades or rubs to the meat or poultry before freezing, so it's ready for grilling, baking, or broiling when thawed.

Challenge: Improve meal planning and kitchen organization. "I can't seem to plan a week of menus so that I only have to shop once a week," says Sasha.

Solution: Before shopping, sit down and select the recipes you plan to make for the week (keep in mind that some will yield enough for leftovers for lunch or dinner another day). Check your pantry, refrigerator, and freezer to see which ingredients you already have, and make a list of those you need. Also take an inventory of the fridge and pantry to toss old or duplicate ingredients (see "Get Organized," page 33). To reduce last-minute trips to the store, keep a running list of items you need—as soon as you run out of something, add it to the list. Sites such as CookingLight.com allow you to print a shopping list at no charge. Keep a copy on the fridge, and as you run out of an ingredient, check it off.

The Feedback: After devoting a weekend to rearranging the kitchen, purging expired items, organizing the pantry, and relocating cooking tools for more convenience, "It's amazing how much space I have now, and how I can see everything at once," Sasha says. "Tomorrow, we'll grill the chicken we marinated and froze. I plan to make sautéed spinach and precut refrigerated potatoes by experimenting and putting together flavors that we like, and tasting as we go."

Wall's Shopping List

Produce department:
1 lime*
1 pound asparagus
2 pounds sweet potatoes
Bagged baby spinach
Bottled minced garlic*
Bottled ground fresh ginger*

Meat department:
1½ pounds skinless, boneless chicken thighs

Baking and condiment aisles:
Low-sodium soy sauce*
Honey*
Cooking spray*
Olive oil*
Balsamic vinegar*
All-purpose flour*
Brown sugar*
Ground cinnamon*
Ground red pepper*
Kosher salt*
Black pepper (preferably whole peppercorns to grind as needed)*

Frozen food department:
1 (22-ounce) bag refrigerated potato wedges (such as Ore-Ida)

Dairy department:
100% pure orange juice*
Fat-free milk*
1 (8-ounce) carton fat-free sour cream

* You may have these items on hand.

Wall Family Supper Menu

Citrus–Glazed Chicken Thighs
Sautéed spinach
Roasted potato wedges

Citrus-Glazed Chicken Thighs

Chicken thighs cook quickly and come with built-in portion control: Two two-ounce chicken thighs are the appropriate serving of meat. The sweet-tangy sauce is easy to make and drizzles nicely over rice or couscous.

    1   cup orange juice
    2   tablespoons low-sodium soy sauce
    2   tablespoons honey
    2   teaspoons bottled minced garlic
    2   teaspoons bottled ground fresh
        ginger (such as Spice World)
    ½   teaspoon grated lime rind
    ¼   to ½ teaspoon ground red pepper
    12 (2-ounce) skinless, boneless
        chicken thighs
        Cooking spray
    1   tablespoon all-purpose flour
    ½   teaspoon salt

1. Place first 7 ingredients in a large zip-top plastic bag. Add chicken; seal bag, and marinate in refrigerator 1 hour, turning occasionally. Remove chicken from bag, reserving marinade.
2. Preheat broiler.
3. Place chicken on a foil-lined jelly-roll pan coated with cooking spray; broil 8 minutes on each side or until done.
4. While chicken cooks, place reserved marinade, flour, and salt in a small saucepan, stirring with a whisk until blended. Bring to a boil over medium-high heat. Reduce heat, and cook 1 minute or until thickened. Serve sauce with chicken. Yield: 6 servings (serving size: 2 thighs and 2½ tablespoons sauce).

CALORIES 189 (23% from fat); FAT 4.7g (sat 1.2g, mono 1.4g, poly 1.1g); PROTEIN 23g; CARB 12.1g; FIBER 0.2g; CHOL 94mg; IRON 1.5mg; SODIUM 470mg; CALC 18mg

Thai-Style Ground Beef

This dish appeals to adults and kids alike, which answers Sasha Wall's challenge to prepare one dinner that satisfies the whole family. Serve with lime wedges. Enjoy leftovers with warm tortillas.

        Cooking spray
    1   cup thinly sliced leek
    1   teaspoon bottled minced garlic
    1   pound lean ground sirloin
    1   teaspoon red curry paste (such as
        Thai Kitchen)
    1   cup tomato sauce
    ½   cup light coconut milk
    ¼   teaspoon grated lime rind
    1½ tablespoons fresh lime juice
    1   tablespoon brown sugar
    1   tablespoon Asian fish sauce
    3   cups hot cooked short-grain rice
        Iceberg lettuce wedges (optional)
        Chopped cilantro (optional)
        Chopped green onions (optional)

1. Heat a large skillet over medium-high heat. Coat pan with cooking spray. Add leek; sauté 5 minutes. Add garlic; sauté 1 minute. Add beef; cook 7 minutes or until lightly browned, stirring to crumble. Stir in curry paste and tomato sauce; cook until half of liquid evaporates (about 2 minutes). Add milk and next 4 ingredients; cook 2 minutes or until slightly thickened. Serve with rice and lettuce wedges, if desired. Garnish with cilantro and green onions, if desired. Yield: 4 servings (serving size: about ½ cup beef mixture and ¾ cup rice).

CALORIES 353 (16% from fat); FAT 6.4g (sat 3.2g, mono 1.7g, poly 0.6g); PROTEIN 23.1g; CARB 51.5g; FIBER 2.8g; CHOL 49mg; IRON 6.3mg; SODIUM 723mg; CALC 29mg

Balsamic Roasted Asparagus

This is a supereasy side dish that Russ Wall can prepare for dinner on his nights off, and the Dickinsons can enjoy, too.

    1   pound asparagus
    1   tablespoon olive oil
    1   tablespoon balsamic vinegar
    ½   teaspoon kosher salt
    ½   teaspoon bottled minced garlic
    ¼   teaspoon freshly ground black
        pepper

1. Preheat oven to 425°.
2. Snap off tough ends of asparagus. Place in a jelly-roll pan. Drizzle with olive oil and vinegar; sprinkle with salt, garlic, and pepper, tossing to coat. Bake at 425° for 10 minutes, turning once. Yield: 4 servings.

CALORIES 67 (48% from fat); FAT 3.6g (sat 0.5g, mono 2.7g, poly 0.3g); PROTEIN 2.5g; CARB 5.7g; FIBER 2.5g; CHOL 0mg; IRON 0.5mg; SODIUM 236mg; CALC 26mg

Mediterranean Couscous

Quick-cooking couscous is now even better since it's available in a whole wheat version. Fresh sage gives this side dish an earthy taste and aroma.

    1¾ cups fat-free, less-sodium chicken
        broth
    ¾   cup whole wheat couscous
    1   cup grape tomatoes, halved
    ½   cup chopped seeded peeled
        cucumber
    ½   cup chopped red bell pepper
    ¼   cup sliced green onions
    ¼   teaspoon grated lemon rind
    2   tablespoons fresh lemon juice
    4   teaspoons extravirgin olive oil
    1   tablespoon chopped fresh sage
    ½   teaspoon salt
    ½   teaspoon freshly ground black
        pepper

1. Bring broth to a boil in a medium saucepan; gradually stir in couscous. Remove from heat; cover and let stand 5 minutes. Fluff with a fork. Combine couscous, tomatoes, and remaining ingredients in a large bowl. Yield: 4 servings (serving size: about 1 cup).

CALORIES 150 (32% from fat); FAT 5.4g (sat 0.7g, mono 3.7g, poly 0.5g); PROTEIN 4.8g; CARB 22.1g; FIBER 4.4g; CHOL 0mg; IRON 1.2mg; SODIUM 467mg; CALC 25mg

---

Clean the Fridge, Feed the Family

Don't wait until produce has gone bad to clean out the fridge. Instead, plan a salad bar night and use what's left over from other recipes. It's a good way to encourage children to be more adventurous eaters.

Shannon Olsen Dickinson and Brian Dickinson are newlyweds in Las Vegas, and they're learning to mesh two styles of eating. Shannon lost 75 pounds after graduating from college and has kept it off for 10 years by eating wisely and exercising every morning before heading to work.

Challenge: Eat more fruits and vegetables. "I love produce, but Brian could live without it," says Shannon. "I'd like to find a way to make it appealing to both of us."

Solution: A great way to incorporate vegetables is to roast a mélange of seasonal favorites to serve with meat, poultry, or fish. Combine precut potato wedges (such as Simply Potatoes), baby carrots, sliced fennel bulb, and asparagus in a baking pan. Drizzle with a little extravirgin olive oil; sprinkle with salt, pepper, and dried or fresh rosemary. Toss and bake at 425° for 25 minutes or until golden and tender. Also, use fruits as toppings for savory dishes, as in the Jerk Pork Tenderloin with Fresh Pineapple Chutney (recipe on page 37).

Challenge: Rely less on prepackaged foods for breakfast and lunch.

Solution: Eating packaged breakfast bars and frozen entrées for lunch five days a week becomes boring, so we encouraged Shannon and Brian to add pizzazz to breakfast with a thick, rich Blackberry-Mango Breakfast Shake (recipe on page 38). Frozen blackberries, silken tofu, sliced mango, orange juice, and a touch of honey create a satisfying, high-protein beverage that's ready in minutes and keeps them full for hours. Homemade muffins such as Whole-Grain Blackberry Spice Muffins (recipe on page 37) also call for frozen blackberries, so they can enjoy a high-fiber, antioxidant-rich fruit in two delicious recipes.

Leftovers can help at lunchtime. Many *Cooking Light* recipes yield four or six servings. After dinner, pack what's left to enjoy for lunch the next day. Other lunch-friendly choices are salads such as Mediterranean Couscous (recipe on page 35), which travels well and can be served chilled or at room temperature.

Challenge: Find recipes that they can prepare together. "My husband is eager to help but doesn't have much of a repertoire beyond grilling meat," says Shannon.

Solution: Cooking together is a great way for couples to bond and learn to cook. Our advice: Select recipes that appeal to both of you, and try at least one new dish each week (keep track of those you enjoy to prepare again). Divide the work: If one of you is an expert chopper and dicer, let the other rinse vegetables and mix spice rubs.

Challenge: Find whole-grain foods they both enjoy. "I would love to try some of the grains I read about in the magazine," says Shannon, "but I have no idea how to prepare them."

Solution: If a recipe looks good and contains a whole grain like bulgur, quinoa, or brown rice, try it. Most cookbooks and magazines give explicit directions on how to prepare a particular grain. Once you've sampled different varieties, you'll feel more confident substituting them in other recipes, such as using quinoa in place of rice in a pilaf.

The Feedback: "The main things we have changed are the types of foods we eat," says Shannon. "I am more adventurous when I look at recipes, and I am now more willing to prepare a recipe with a vegetable we've never tried because you showed me how easy it is to add them to a rice or couscous recipe or just roast them for a side dish."

Dickinson's Shopping List

Produce department:

2 onions*
1 red bell pepper
1 yellow bell pepper
1 garlic bulb or bottled minced garlic*
1 bunch green onions*
1 package fresh mint*
1 bunch fresh cilantro*
1 fresh pineapple (available peeled and cored)

Meat department:

1¼ pounds pork tenderloin

Baking/condiment/canned foods/ grains aisles:

Dark brown sugar*
Extravirgin olive oil*
Cooking spray*
Kosher salt*
Black pepper (preferably whole peppercorns to grind as needed)*
Garlic powder*
Dried thyme*
Ground red pepper (cayenne)*
Apple-pie spice
Dried rosemary*
Cider vinegar*
Basmati rice*
1 (14-ounce) can fat-free, less-sodium chicken broth*
1 (14-ounce) can light coconut milk*

* You may have these items on hand.

Dinner at the Dickinson's Menu

Skillet Onions, Peppers, and Garlic

Mint-Cilantro and Coconut Rice

Jerk Pork Tenderloin with Fresh Pineapple Chutney

Skillet Onions, Peppers, and Garlic

This simple veggie side has plenty of flavor and color and takes just 15 minutes to prepare. For a touch of heat, add a few dashes of your favorite hot sauce or a pinch of ground red pepper. If you love the taste of rosemary, use up to one teaspoon dried or fresh.

- 2 teaspoons olive oil
- 1 cup thinly sliced red bell pepper
- 1 cup thinly sliced yellow bell pepper
- 1 cup vertically sliced sweet onion
- 1 teaspoon minced garlic
- ½ teaspoon dried rosemary
- ¼ teaspoon salt
- ¼ teaspoon freshly ground black pepper

1. Heat oil in a large nonstick skillet over medium-high heat. Add bell peppers and onion; cook 13 minutes or until onion is tender, stirring frequently. Add garlic, rosemary, salt, and black pepper; cook 2 minutes, stirring frequently. Yield: 3 cups (serving size: about ¾ cup).

CALORIES 55 (40% from fat); FAT 2.4g (sat 0.3g, mono 1.7g, poly 0.2g); PROTEIN 1g; CARB 7.5g; FIBER 1.9g; CHOL 0mg; IRON 0.4mg; SODIUM 119mg; CALC 24mg

Mint-Cilantro and Coconut Rice

Basmati rice has a naturally nutty flavor that is delicious with the herbs. This recipe can easily be doubled.

- 2 teaspoons olive oil
- 1 cup uncooked basmati rice
- ¼ cup sliced green onions
- ¾ cup fat-free, less-sodium chicken broth
- ¼ cup light coconut milk
- ½ teaspoon kosher salt
- ¼ teaspoon freshly ground black pepper
- 2 tablespoons chopped fresh mint
- 2 tablespoons chopped fresh cilantro

1. Heat oil in a medium saucepan over medium-high heat. Add rice; sauté 3 minutes. Add onion; sauté 1 minute. Stir in broth, milk, salt, and pepper. Bring to a boil; cover, reduce heat, and simmer 17 minutes or until liquid is absorbed and rice is tender, stirring once after 10 minutes. Stir in mint and cilantro; cover and let stand 5 minutes. Yield: 4 cups (serving size: about ¾ cup).

CALORIES 218 (15% from fat); FAT 3.8g (sat 1.3g, mono 2g, poly 0.4g); PROTEIN 4.6g; CARB 42.1g; FIBER 0.7g; CHOL 0mg; IRON 0.4mg; SODIUM 326mg; CALC 10mg

Jerk Pork Tenderloin with Fresh Pineapple Chutney

For more heat and spicy flavor, use up to one tablespoon Easy Jerk Seasoning. Sprinkle the versatile seasoning over meat, chicken, or seafood, and grill, bake, or broil. It's even tasty over popcorn. Store in a jar or plastic container with a tight-fitting lid. The chutney is also delicious over chicken and fish.

PORK:
- 1 teaspoon olive oil
- 1 (1¼-pound) pork tenderloin, trimmed
- 2 teaspoons Easy Jerk Seasoning

CHUTNEY:
- Cooking spray
- ½ cup finely chopped onion
- 2 cups finely chopped fresh pineapple (about ½ cored pineapple)
- 1 tablespoon dark brown sugar
- 1 tablespoon cider vinegar
- ⅛ teaspoon salt
- Dash of freshly ground black pepper

1. Preheat oven to 425°.
2. To prepare pork, heat oil in a large ovenproof skillet over medium-high heat. Rub pork with 2 teaspoons Easy Jerk Seasoning. Add pork to pan; cook 3 minutes, turning to brown all sides. Place pan in oven; bake at 425° for 25 minutes or until a thermometer registers 160° (slightly pink). Let stand 10 minutes before slicing.

3. To prepare chutney, heat a medium saucepan over medium-high heat. Coat pan with cooking spray. Add onion; cook 5 minutes or until lightly browned. Add pineapple and remaining 4 ingredients. Cover, reduce heat, and simmer 15 minutes or until thickened, stirring occasionally. Serve over pork. Yield: 4 servings (serving size: 3 ounces pork and about ½ cup chutney).

CALORIES 276 (32% from fat); FAT 9.8g (sat 3.2g, mono 4.3g, poly 0.9g); PROTEIN 31.5g; CARB 14.8g; FIBER 1.6g; CHOL 97mg; IRON 1.9mg; SODIUM 377mg; CALC 25mg

EASY JERK SEASONING:
- 1 tablespoon garlic powder
- 2½ teaspoons kosher salt
- 2 teaspoons dried thyme
- 1½ teaspoons apple-pie spice
- 1 teaspoon ground red pepper

1. Combine all ingredients in a small bowl. Yield: 10 servings (serving size: about ½ teaspoon).

CALORIES 5 (0% from fat); FAT 0.1g (sat 0g, mono 0g, poly 0g); PROTEIN 0.2g; CARB 1.1g; FIBER 0.4g; CHOL 0mg; IRON 0.3mg; SODIUM 471mg; CALC 6mg

Whole-Grain Blackberry Spice Muffins

Coarsely chop the blackberries, and freeze them until ready to stir into the batter. To freeze the muffins, let cool, and place in zip-top plastic bags. Reheat in microwave 20 seconds.

- 2 cups all-purpose flour (about 9 ounces)
- 1 cup rolled oats
- 1 cup packed dark brown sugar
- 1½ teaspoons baking powder
- ½ teaspoon baking soda
- ½ teaspoon salt
- ½ teaspoon apple-pie spice
- 1 cup fat-free milk
- 3 tablespoons butter, melted
- 1 teaspoon vanilla extract
- 1 large egg, lightly beaten
- 1½ cups frozen blackberries, coarsely chopped
- Cooking spray
- ¼ cup granulated sugar

Continued

1. Preheat oven to 400°.

2. Lightly spoon flour into dry measuring cups; level with a knife. Combine flour and next 6 ingredients in a large bowl. Make a well in center of mixture. Combine milk, butter, vanilla, and egg in a small bowl; add to flour mixture, stirring just until moist. Gently stir in blackberries.

3. Spoon ¼ cup batter into each of 17 paper-lined muffin cups coated with cooking spray. Bake at 400° for 16 minutes. Sprinkle muffins evenly with granulated sugar; bake 3 minutes or until muffins spring back when touched lightly in center. Cool in pans 10 minutes on wire racks. Yield: 17 muffins (serving size: 1 muffin).

CALORIES 177 (15% from fat); FAT 3g (sat 1.2g, mono 1.1g, poly 0.4g); PROTEIN 3.5g; CARB 34.3g; FIBER 1.8g; CHOL 18mg; IRON 1.4mg; SODIUM 181mg; CALC 68mg

Blackberry-Mango Breakfast Shake

Use silken tofu to achieve a smooth consistency. If you don't like the seeds in blackberries, substitute frozen blueberries. This delicious, creamy drink is loaded with protein, fiber, and heart-protective vitamin C. Store leftovers in the refrigerator up to one day, but stir before serving.

1½ cups frozen blackberries
 1 cup refrigerated mango slices (such as Del Monte)
 1 cup (about 6½ ounces) low-fat tofu (such as Silken soft)
 1 cup orange juice
 3 tablespoons honey

1. Place all ingredients in a blender; process until smooth. Yield: 4 servings (serving size: 1 cup).

CALORIES 155 (4% from fat); FAT 0.8g (sat 0.1g, mono 0.2g, poly 0.4g); PROTEIN 4g; CARB 35.9g; FIBER 3.7g; CHOL 0mg; IRON 1mg; SODIUM 39mg; CALC 44mg

Guilt-Free Lasagna

A trim yet tasty chicken-and-ham casserole is easier on the waistline—and conscience—of a Maine reader.

Courtney Sparks of Casco, Maine, first tried the Chicken-Ham Lasagna at work, when a coworker brought in leftovers. The rich and creamy dish was a hit, but Sparks knew it could be lighter.

Of concern to us was the heavy cream sauce, the use of full-fat dairy products, and two tablespoons of butter per serving. Since the original recipe made more sauce than needed, we cut back on those ingredients. The casserole's sodium was also a problem. We were able to trim an impressive 546 milligrams sodium per portion by omitting the butter and salt. Substituting fat-free, less-sodium chicken broth for regular chicken broth and reducing the amount of cheese saved another 360 milligrams sodium per serving.

Chicken-Ham Lasagna

To shorten prep time, skin, bone, and shred rotisserie chicken; add to sauce.

 2 cups fat-free, less-sodium chicken broth
 ½ teaspoon freshly ground black pepper, divided
 1 pound skinless, boneless chicken breast, cut into bite-sized pieces, divided
 3 cups 1% low-fat milk
 ⅓ cup all-purpose flour (about 1½ ounces)
1½ cups (6 ounces) freshly grated Parmesan cheese, divided
 ¼ cup chopped fresh parsley
 Cooking spray
 12 no-cook lasagna noodles (8 ounces)
 8 ounces thinly sliced 96% fat-free deli ham, chopped
 Chopped fresh parsley (optional)

1. Preheat oven to 350°.

2. Place broth and ¼ teaspoon pepper in a large skillet over medium-high heat, and bring to a boil. Add chicken; cover, reduce heat, and simmer 10 minutes or until chicken is done. Remove chicken from pan with a slotted spoon; set aside.

3. Combine milk, flour, and remaining ¼ teaspoon pepper; stir with a whisk until smooth. Add milk mixture to broth in pan. Bring to a boil over medium-high heat, stirring constantly. Cook 1 minute or until mixture thickens, stirring constantly. Remove from heat. Add 1 cup cheese and parsley, stirring until cheese melts.

4. Spread 1 cup sauce over bottom of a 13 x 9–inch baking dish coated with cooking spray. Arrange 3 lasagna noodles over sauce. Spoon ¾ cup sauce evenly over noodles. Top evenly with one-third of ham and one-third of chicken. Repeat layers twice, ending with noodles. Top with remaining sauce. Sprinkle evenly with remaining ½ cup cheese.

5. Cover with foil very lightly coated with cooking spray; bake at 350° for 30 minutes. Remove and discard foil; bake an additional 10 minutes or until cheese is lightly browned. Sprinkle with parsley, if desired. Yield: 8 servings.

CALORIES 260 (24% from fat); FAT 7g (sat 3.7g, mono 2g, poly 0.8g); PROTEIN 28.9g; CARB 18g; FIBER 0.8g; CHOL 57mg; IRON 1.9mg; SODIUM 740mg; CALC 295mg

WINE NOTE: You need a comfort wine to go with an unfussy dish like this. The ideal wine needs to be inexpensive and uncomplicated. Australian shiraz is a good choice. Annie's Lane Shiraz 2002 from Australia's Clare Valley ($15) is a simple blast of berriness with a soft texture.

	BEFORE	AFTER
SERVING SIZE		
	1 piece	
CALORIES PER SERVING		
	735	260
FAT		
	47.1g	7g
PERCENT OF TOTAL CALORIES		
	58%	24%

Breakfast Breads

Begin your day on a wholesome note with one of these tasty, satisfying treats.

Whole Wheat, Oatmeal, and Raisin Muffins

1 cup whole wheat flour (about 4¾ ounces)
¼ cup granulated sugar
¼ cup packed brown sugar
2 tablespoons untoasted wheat germ
2 tablespoons wheat bran
1½ teaspoons baking soda
1 teaspoon ground cinnamon
½ teaspoon salt
1½ cups quick-cooking oats
⅓ cup chopped pitted dates
⅓ cup raisins
⅓ cup dried cranberries
1 cup low-fat buttermilk
¼ cup canola oil
1 teaspoon vanilla extract
1 large egg, lightly beaten
½ cup boiling water
Cooking spray

1. Lightly spoon flour into a dry measuring cup; level with a knife. Combine flour and next 7 ingredients in a large bowl, stirring with a whisk. Stir in oats, dates, raisins, and cranberries. Make a well in center of mixture. Combine buttermilk, oil, vanilla, and egg; add to flour mixture, stirring just until moist. Stir in boiling water. Let batter stand 15 minutes.
2. Preheat oven to 375°.
3. Spoon batter into 12 muffin cups coated with cooking spray. Bake at 375° for 20 minutes or until muffins spring back when touched lightly in center. Remove muffins from pans immediately; place on a wire rack. Yield: 12 servings (serving size: 1 muffin).

CALORIES 204 (28% from fat); FAT 6.4g (sat 0.8g, mono 3.2g, poly 1.8g); PROTEIN 4.6g; CARB 34.7g; FIBER 3.4g; CHOL 19mg; IRON 1.4mg; SODIUM 288mg; CALC 43mg

---

QUICK & EASY
Lemon-Scented Olive Oil Muffins

MUFFINS:

1 cup all-purpose flour (about 4½ ounces)
½ cup granulated sugar
1 teaspoon baking powder
¼ teaspoon salt
½ cup fat-free sour cream
2 tablespoons extravirgin olive oil
1½ tablespoons fat-free milk
1½ tablespoons grated lemon rind
2 teaspoons fresh lemon juice
1 large egg, lightly beaten
1 large egg white, lightly beaten
Cooking spray

GLAZE:

1 cup sifted powdered sugar
½ teaspoon grated lemon rind
3 tablespoons fresh lemon juice

REMAINING INGREDIENT:

Grated lemon rind (optional)

1. Preheat oven to 350°.
2. To prepare muffins, lightly spoon flour into a dry measuring cup; level with a knife. Combine flour, sugar, baking powder, and salt in a large bowl; stir well with a whisk. Make a well in center of mixture.
3. Combine sour cream and next 6 ingredients in a small bowl; stir well with a whisk. Add to flour mixture, stirring just until moist.
4. Spoon batter evenly into 10 muffin cups coated with cooking spray. Bake at 350° for 25 minutes or until muffins spring back when touched lightly in center. Remove from pans immediately. Cool completely on a wire rack.
5. To prepare glaze, combine powdered sugar, ½ teaspoon rind, and 3 tablespoons juice in a small bowl; stir with a whisk until smooth. Spread about 1 teaspoon glaze over each muffin; let stand 5 minutes or until set. Garnish with lemon rind, if desired. Yield: 10 servings (serving size: 1 muffin).

CALORIES 166 (19% from fat); FAT 3.5g (sat 0.7g, mono 2.4g, poly 0.3g); PROTEIN 2.9g; CARB 31.2g; FIBER 0.4g; CHOL 22mg; IRON 0.7mg; SODIUM 131mg; CALC 53mg

---

Sweet Potato and Pecan Flapjacks

1¼ cups all-purpose flour (about 5½ ounces)
¼ cup chopped pecans, toasted
3 tablespoons yellow cornmeal
2 teaspoons baking powder
½ teaspoon salt
½ teaspoon ground cinnamon
1 cup fat-free milk
1 cup mashed cooked sweet potato
3 tablespoons brown sugar
1 tablespoon canola oil
½ teaspoon vanilla extract
2 large egg yolks
2 large egg whites
Cooking spray

1. Lightly spoon flour into dry measuring cups; level with a knife. Combine flour and next 5 ingredients in a large bowl, stirring with a whisk.
2. Combine milk and next 5 ingredients, stirring until smooth; add to flour mixture, stirring just until combined. Beat egg whites with a mixer at high speed until soft peaks form; fold egg whites into batter. Let batter stand 10 minutes.
3. Heat a nonstick griddle or nonstick skillet over medium-high heat. Coat griddle or pan with cooking spray. Spoon about ¼ cup batter per pancake onto griddle or pan. Cook 2 minutes or until tops are covered with bubbles and edges look cooked. Carefully turn pancakes over, and cook 2 minutes or until bottoms are lightly browned. Yield: 6 servings (serving size: 2 pancakes).

CALORIES 276 (26% from fat); FAT 7.9g (sat 1.1g, mono 4.1g, poly 2.1g); PROTEIN 7.7g; CARB 43.7g; FIBER 2.8g; CHOL 71mg; IRON 2.7mg; SODIUM 419mg; CALC 166mg

Steps to Tender Quick Bread

These breakfast breads fall into the category of quick breads and rely on a three-step process:

- Stir together dry ingredients.
- Mix wet ingredients.
- Combine wet and dry ingredients with a few strokes to moisten the dry ingredients. The mixture will be slightly lumpy.

Pancakes and waffles also fall into the category of quick breads because they are leavened with baking powder or baking soda, as compared to yeast breads that require long rising times before baking. They're mixed together much like muffins, but have a higher liquid–to–dry ingredient ratio and are usually beaten with a whisk to make the batter more pourable.

QUICK & EASY • MAKE AHEAD
FREEZABLE

Pear and Walnut Muffins

Fragrant pears and walnuts make an unbeatable combination.

½ cup chopped walnuts
1 cup all-purpose flour (about 4½ ounces)
⅓ cup whole wheat flour (about 1½ ounces)
1½ teaspoons baking powder
½ teaspoon baking soda
½ teaspoon salt
⅔ cup packed brown sugar
2 tablespoons canola oil
2 teaspoons vanilla extract
1 (8-ounce) carton plain fat-free yogurt
1 large egg, lightly beaten
1½ cups finely diced peeled pear
Cooking spray
3 tablespoons turbinado sugar

1. Preheat oven to 400°.
2. Place walnuts in a food processor; process until finely ground.
3. Lightly spoon flours into dry measuring cups; level with a knife. Combine flours and next 3 ingredients in a

medium bowl; stir well with a whisk. Stir in ground walnuts. Make a well in center of mixture.
4. Combine brown sugar and next 4 ingredients in a small bowl; add to flour mixture, stirring just until moist. Fold in pear.
5. Spoon batter into 15 muffin cups coated with cooking spray; sprinkle with turbinado sugar. Bake at 400° for 20 minutes or until muffins spring back when touched lightly in center. Remove from pans immediately. Place on a wire rack. Serve warm or at room temperature. Yield: 15 servings (serving size: 1 muffin).

CALORIES 149 (30% from fat); FAT 4.9g (sat 0.5g, mono 1.6g, poly 2.5g); PROTEIN 3.1g; CARB 23.9g; FIBER 1.3g; CHOL 14mg; IRON 1mg; SODIUM 191mg; CALC 76mg

QUICK & EASY • MAKE AHEAD
FREEZABLE

Blueberry Oatmeal Muffins

This family favorite gets a twist with the addition of whole wheat flour and oatmeal.

1⅔ cups quick-cooking oats
⅔ cup all-purpose flour (about 3 ounces)
½ cup whole wheat flour (about 2⅓ ounces)
¾ cup packed light brown sugar
2 teaspoons ground cinnamon
1 teaspoon baking powder
1 teaspoon baking soda
¾ teaspoon salt
1½ cups fat-free buttermilk
¼ cup canola oil
2 teaspoons grated lemon rind
2 large eggs, lightly beaten
2 cups frozen blueberries
2 tablespoons all-purpose flour
2 tablespoons granulated sugar

1. Preheat oven to 400°.
2. Place oats in a food processor; pulse 5 or 6 times until oats resemble coarse meal. Place in a large bowl.
3. Lightly spoon ⅔ cup all-purpose flour and wheat flour into dry measuring cups; level with a knife. Add flours and next 5 ingredients to oats in bowl; stir well with a whisk. Make a well in center of mixture.

4. Combine buttermilk, oil, rind, and eggs in small bowl; stir well with a whisk. Add to flour mixture, stirring just until moist.
5. Toss berries with 2 tablespoons flour, and gently fold into batter.
6. Spoon batter into 16 muffin cups lined with paper liners; sprinkle with 2 tablespoons granulated sugar. Bake at 400° for 18 minutes or until muffins spring back when touched lightly in center. Remove from pans immediately. Place on a wire rack. Serve warm or at room temperature. Yield: 16 servings (serving size: 1 muffin).

CALORIES 170 (26% from fat); FAT 5g (sat 0.6g, mono 2.5g, poly 1.4g); PROTEIN 4g; CARB 28.6g; FIBER 2g; CHOL 27mg; IRON 1.2mg; SODIUM 256mg; CALC 65mg

QUICK & EASY • FREEZABLE

Apricot-Bran Honey Cakes

1½ cups diced dried apricots (about 7 ounces)
6 tablespoons butter
⅓ cup apricot nectar
2 tablespoons honey
¾ cup all-purpose flour (about 3⅓ ounces)
¾ cup oat bran
1 teaspoon baking soda
½ teaspoon salt
¼ cup packed brown sugar
1 teaspoon vanilla extract
1 (8-ounce) carton plain fat-free yogurt
1 large egg, lightly beaten
1 large egg white, lightly beaten
Cooking spray

1. Preheat oven to 400°.
2. Combine first 4 ingredients in a small saucepan; place over high heat. Bring to a boil. Reduce heat; simmer 3 minutes or until apricots are plump. Remove from heat; cool.
3. Lightly spoon flour into dry measuring cups; level with a knife. Combine flour, bran, baking soda, and salt in a medium bowl; stir well with a whisk. Make a well in center of mixture.
4. Combine sugar and next 4 ingredients in a small bowl; stir well with a whisk.

Add sugar mixture to flour mixture, stirring just until combined. Gently fold in apricot mixture.

5. Spoon ½ cup batter into each of 7 (6-ounce) ramekins coated with cooking spray. Place ramekins on a jelly-roll pan. Bake at 400° for 15 minutes or until golden brown. Place on a wire rack. Serve warm or at room temperature. Yield: 7 servings (serving size: 1 cake).

CALORIES 313 (33% from fat); FAT 11.5g (sat 5.3g, mono 4.6g, poly 0.8g); PROTEIN 7.6g; CARB 49.1g; FIBER 3.5g; CHOL 57mg; IRON 2.6mg; SODIUM 465mg; CALC 99mg

---

Quick Tips for Revamping Your Quick Bread Recipes

Use these tips to create your own quick breads.

• Low-fat buttermilk, sour cream, and yogurt add rich flavor and can be substituted for some of the fat in a recipe. You may need to experiment with the quantities. Replacing too much of the fat with these ingredients can result in tough, rubbery baked goods.

• Replace up to half of the amount of all-purpose flour in a recipe with whole wheat flour, a good source of fiber. You might notice subtle differences, such as a slightly denser texture, because wheat flour doesn't rise as high. Experiment with other flours, such as oat, barley, spelt, *kamut*, and amaranth. All are relatively easy to work with and lend distinctive flavors and an even more diverse nutritional profile to baked goods. For instance, barley flour produces baked goods with a moist, tender texture and a sweet, nutty flavor, while oat flour adds many heart-healthy benefits.

• Add ground flaxseed. Whether it's a few tablespoons or ½ cup, flaxseed lends nuttiness.

• Chopped nuts, nut meal, or nut oils add healthful fats.

• Dried, fresh, or frozen fruits contribute sweetness, flavor, and nutrition with few calories and little fat.

Winners' Circle

Cooking Light Ultimate Reader Recipe Contest finalists bring fresh flavors from around the country.

More than 2,500 creative cooks from across the country sent us recipes for the first annual *Cooking Light* Ultimate Reader Recipe Contest. Entrants developed recipes for one of four categories: starters and drinks, entrées, sides and salads, and desserts. Recipes included one of four Golden spoon sponsor products: Ronzoni Healthy Harvest Whole Wheat Blend Pasta; Swanson Broth; 3-A-Day Milk, Cheese, or Yogurt; and Hellmann's/Best Foods Mayonnaise.

The top recipes were prepared in the magazine's Test Kitchens to determine the finalists, who traveled to Birmingham, Alabama, to make their recipes for a panel of outside judges. Following a long day of tasting and intense discussion, the judges chose category winners, who each received $5,000. And one of those winners took home the grand prize of $10,000 and an active family vacation valued at $5,000. The big winner was Karen Tedesco, whose recipe for Crunchy Shrimp with Toasted Couscous and Ginger-Orange Sauce won the entrées category and the top contest prize. Her standout creation fulfilled the requirements for a winning recipe: It was unique, flavorful, and easily reproducible for a home cook.

Crunchy Shrimp with Toasted Couscous and Ginger-Orange Sauce

(pictured on page 227)

GRAND PRIZE WINNER
CATEGORY WINNER—ENTRÉES

"The sauce that accompanies the shrimp is one of my favorites. I've used it as a dipping sauce for vegetables, and to top grilled chicken and salmon."

—Karen Tedesco,
Webster Groves, Missouri

SAUCE:
- 1 cup orange juice
- 2 tablespoons reduced-fat mayonnaise
- 1½ tablespoons fat-free, less-sodium chicken broth
- 1 tablespoon chopped fresh cilantro
- 1 teaspoon grated peeled fresh ginger
- 1 teaspoon fresh lime juice
- ½ teaspoon ground cumin
- ¼ teaspoon salt
- ¼ teaspoon ground red pepper

COUSCOUS:
- 1 cup uncooked couscous
- 1½ cups fat-free, less-sodium chicken broth
- ½ cup orange juice
- ½ teaspoon salt
- ⅓ cup chopped green onions
- 2 tablespoons sliced almonds, toasted
- 1 tablespoon unsalted butter

SHRIMP:
- 20 jumbo shrimp, peeled and deveined (about 1 pound)
- 1 large egg white, lightly beaten
- ½ cup panko (Japanese breadcrumbs)
- 1 teaspoon chopped fresh cilantro
- ½ teaspoon grated peeled fresh ginger
- ⅛ teaspoon freshly ground black pepper
- 1 tablespoon canola oil

REMAINING INGREDIENT:
- 2 cups trimmed watercress

Continued

1. To prepare sauce, bring 1 cup orange juice to a boil in a small saucepan over medium-high heat; cook until reduced to ¼ cup (about 10 minutes). Remove from heat; cool completely. Stir in mayonnaise and next 7 ingredients; set aside.

2. To prepare couscous, place couscous in a large nonstick skillet over medium-high heat; cook 3 minutes or until toasted, stirring constantly. Add 1½ cups broth, ½ cup orange juice, and ½ teaspoon salt; bring to a boil. Remove from heat; cover and let stand 5 minutes. Fluff with a fork; add onions, almonds, and butter, stirring until butter melts. Keep mixture warm.

3. To prepare shrimp, combine shrimp and egg white in a large bowl, tossing to coat. Combine panko, 1 teaspoon cilantro, ½ teaspoon ginger, and black pepper in a large zip-top plastic bag. Add shrimp to bag; seal bag, and shake to coat.

4. Heat oil in a large nonstick skillet over medium-high heat; arrange shrimp in a single layer in pan. Cook 2 minutes on each side or until done.

5. Place ¾ cup couscous on each of 4 plates; top each with ½ cup watercress and 5 shrimp. Drizzle each with 1½ tablespoons sauce. Yield: 4 servings.

CALORIES 376 (25% from fat); FAT 10.6g (sat 2.7g, mono 4.1g, poly 2g); PROTEIN 17.6g; CARB 51.9g; FIBER 3.9g; CHOL 61mg; IRON 2.1mg; SODIUM 763mg; CALC 84mg

WINE NOTE: The one-two punch of ginger and orange in this shrimp dish is a main consideration in pairing it with wine, as is the texture. Crunchy textures like this are best balanced by wines that have a good amount of tingling crisp acidity. As it happens, riesling satisfies both needs here. It's got the exotic fruitiness to stand up to the ginger and orange, a pureness that complements the shrimp, and a bolt of acidity that cuts through the crunch. The most fruity, crisp, and light rieslings come from Germany. Try Selbach-Oster "Zeltinger Sonnenuhr" Riesling Spätlese 2004 from the Mosel-Saar-Ruwer region of Germany ($33).

STAFF FAVORITE • MAKE AHEAD
Pide with Yogurt Dip

CATEGORY WINNER—STARTERS AND DRINKS

"I used to buy this bread at a Turkish market in Germany. I couldn't find it in the United States and started to make it myself. Knead the dough until it feels like the soft underside of a woman's arm (the instruction from a Turkish cookbook)."

—Sabine Zempleni, Lincoln, Nebraska

DIP:

- 1 cup fat-free plain yogurt
- ½ cup minced green onions
- 1 tablespoon fresh lemon juice
- 2 teaspoons chopped fresh dill
- ½ teaspoon salt
- ¼ teaspoon freshly ground black pepper
- 2 garlic cloves, minced
- 1 (8-ounce) block ⅓-less-fat cream cheese, softened

PIDE:

- 8 cups all-purpose flour (about 36 ounces)
- 2 teaspoons salt
- 1 package dry yeast (about 2¼ teaspoons)
- 2⅓ cups warm water (100° to 110°)
- Cooking spray
- 1 large egg yolk, lightly beaten
- 1 teaspoon nigella seeds

1. To prepare dip, combine first 8 ingredients, stirring with a whisk until blended and smooth. Cover and chill.

2. To prepare pide (PEE-dah), lightly spoon flour into dry measuring cups; level with a knife. Combine flour, salt, and yeast in a large bowl. Add water; stir until a soft dough forms. Turn dough out onto a lightly floured surface. Knead until smooth and elastic (about 10 minutes). Place dough in a large bowl coated with cooking spray, turning to coat top. Cover and let rise in a warm place (85°), free from drafts, 1 hour.

3. Preheat oven to 500°.

4. Place a 13 x 15–inch baking sheet in oven; heat 10 minutes.

5. Place egg yolk in a small bowl; set aside. Remove baking sheet from oven;

lightly coat with cooking spray. Quickly turn dough out onto preheated baking sheet. Pat or roll dough to edges of pan, being careful not to touch hot pan. Brush dough with egg yolk; sprinkle with nigella seeds.

6. Bake at 500° for 18 minutes or until golden brown. Remove from oven; release pide from baking sheet with a thin spatula. Place on a wire rack. Using a serrated knife, divide bread by making 4 lengthwise cuts and 3 crosswise cuts to form 20 equal portions. Serve warm or at room temperature with dip. Yield: 20 servings (serving size: 1 piece pide and about 1½ tablespoons dip).

NOTE: Nigella seeds are black onion seeds that have a nutty, peppery flavor. They're used in India and the Middle East as a seasoning for breads, vegetables, and legumes.

CALORIES 224 (14% from fat); FAT 3.4g (sat 1.9g, mono 0.9g, poly 0.3g); PROTEIN 7.3g; CARB 40.1g; FIBER 1.6g; CHOL 19mg; IRON 2.5mg; SODIUM 353mg; CALC 44mg

MAKE AHEAD
Roasted Vegetable-Rosemary Chicken Soup

CATEGORY WINNER—SALADS AND SIDES

"This hearty soup has a wonderful flavor because the vegetables are roasted first, which caramelizes and intensifies the taste."

—Bev Jones, Brunswick, Missouri

- 1 cup (1-inch) cubed carrot
- 1 cup (1-inch) cubed onion
- 1 cup coarsely chopped mushrooms
- 1 cup (1-inch) pieces celery
- 1 cup (1-inch) pieces red bell pepper
- 2 tablespoons extravirgin olive oil
- 1 cup water
- 2 tablespoons chopped fresh rosemary
- ¼ teaspoon salt
- 4 (14-ounce) cans fat-free, less-sodium chicken broth
- 2 garlic cloves, minced
- 1 pound skinless, boneless chicken breast, cut into ½-inch pieces
- 2 cups uncooked whole wheat rotini pasta

1. Preheat oven to 375°.

2. Combine first 5 ingredients in a large bowl; drizzle with oil, and toss well to coat. Arrange vegetable mixture in a single layer on a jelly-roll pan lined with foil. Bake at 375° for 50 minutes or until browned, stirring occasionally.

3. Combine water and next 5 ingredients in a large Dutch oven; bring to a boil. Reduce heat, and simmer 30 minutes. Add roasted vegetables; simmer 30 minutes. Bring soup to a boil. Add pasta; simmer 10 minutes, stirring occasionally. Yield: 8 servings (serving size: about 1 cup).

CALORIES 176 (25% from fat); FAT 4.8g (sat 0.8g, mono 3g, poly 0.7g); PROTEIN 17.9g; CARB 15.5g; FIBER 2.3g; CHOL 33mg; IRON 1.5mg; SODIUM 450mg; CALC 45mg

---

MAKE AHEAD

One-Bowl Chocolate Mocha Cream Cake

CATEGORY WINNER—DESSERTS

"Cake is my favorite dessert—especially frosted cake."

—Anna Ginsberg, Austin, Texas

CAKE:

    2 cups all-purpose flour (about 9 ounces)
    1 cup granulated sugar
    1 cup packed dark brown sugar
    ¾ cup unsweetened cocoa
    1½ teaspoons baking soda
    1½ teaspoons baking powder
    ½ teaspoon salt
    1 cup reduced-fat mayonnaise
    3 tablespoons canola oil
    1 cup hot strong brewed coffee
    2 teaspoons vanilla extract
    ⅓ cup semisweet chocolate morsels
Cooking spray

MOCHA CREAM:

    ¼ cup boiling water
    1 tablespoon instant coffee granules
    1 (7-ounce) jar marshmallow creme
    1 (8-ounce) container frozen light whipped topping, thawed
    ⅓ cup light chocolate syrup (such as Hershey's Lite Syrup)

1. Preheat oven to 350°.

---

2. To prepare cake, lightly spoon flour into dry measuring cups; level with a knife. Combine flour and next 6 ingredients in a large bowl. Add mayonnaise and oil; beat with a mixer at low speed until well blended. Slowly add brewed coffee and vanilla; beat at low speed 1 minute or until well blended. Stir in chocolate; pour batter into a 13 x 9–inch baking pan coated with cooking spray. Bake at 350° for 30 minutes or until a wooden pick inserted in center comes out clean. Cool completely in pan on a wire rack.

3. To prepare mocha cream, combine water and coffee granules in a large bowl; stir until granules dissolve. Add marshmallow creme; beat with a mixer at low speed until smooth. Fold in whipped topping. Spread mocha cream over top of cake; drizzle with chocolate syrup. Chill until ready to serve. Yield: 16 servings.

CALORIES 315 (23% from fat); FAT 8.1g (sat 3.2g, mono 2.6g, poly 1.9g); PROTEIN 2.6g; CARB 60g; FIBER 1.8g; CHOL 0mg; IRON 1.8mg; SODIUM 390mg; CALC 46mg

---

QUICK & EASY

Pumpkin Pie Shake

FINALIST—STARTERS AND DRINKS

"Seeking an all-American taste in a beverage, I came up with this idea."

—Vivian Levine, Summerfield, Florida

    2 cups vanilla reduced-fat ice cream (such as Healthy Choice), softened
    1 cup fat-free milk
    ⅔ cup canned pumpkin
    ¼ cup packed brown sugar
    ¾ teaspoon pumpkin-pie spice
    3 tablespoons frozen fat-free whipped topping, thawed
Pumpkin-pie spice (optional)

1. Place first 5 ingredients in a blender; process until smooth. Pour ¾ cup ice cream mixture into each of 4 glasses. Top each with about 2 teaspoons whipped topping; sprinkle with the additional pumpkin-pie spice, if desired. Yield: 4 servings.

CALORIES 198 (13% from fat); FAT 2.8g (sat 1.8g, mono 0.6g, poly 0.1g); PROTEIN 6.1g; CARB 38g; FIBER 1.4g; CHOL 18mg; IRON 1.3mg; SODIUM 180mg; CALC 157mg

---

China Pattern Menu

serves 4

Five-spice chicken*

Asian Coleslaw

Steamed sugar snap peas

* Heat 2 teaspoons canola oil in a large nonstick skillet over medium-high heat. Sprinkle 1 pound chopped chicken breast tenders with ½ teaspoon salt, ½ teaspoon five-spice powder, and ¼ teaspoon freshly ground black pepper. Add chicken to pan; cook 4 minutes. Stir in ½ cup julienne-cut red bell pepper; sauté 3 minutes or until soft. Add 4 cups baby spinach to pan; cook 2 minutes or until chicken is done. Spread 1 teaspoon lime mayonnaise on each of 4 flour tortillas. Divide chicken mixture evenly among tortillas. Roll up tortillas.

MAKE AHEAD

Asian Coleslaw

(pictured on page 226)

FINALIST—SALADS AND SIDES

—Christina Keyes, Española, New Mexico

    7 cups shredded napa (Chinese) cabbage
    1 cup shredded red cabbage
    1 cup chopped daikon radish
    1 cup chopped green onions
    1 cup loosely packed fresh cilantro leaves
    1 cup frozen green peas, thawed
    3 tablespoons sesame seeds
    ¾ cup reduced-fat mayonnaise
    3 tablespoons white wine vinegar
    1 tablespoon soy sauce
    ½ teaspoon dark sesame oil
    ¼ teaspoon ground red pepper
    ¼ cup sliced almonds

1. Combine first 7 ingredients in a large bowl. Combine mayonnaise and next 4 ingredients, stirring with a whisk. Add mayonnaise mixture to cabbage mixture; toss well. Sprinkle with almonds. Cover and chill at least 1 hour before serving. Yield: 12 servings (serving size: about ⅔ cup coleslaw and 1 teaspoon almonds).

CALORIES 79 (50% from fat); FAT 4.4g (sat 0.8g, mono 1.6g, poly 1.8g); PROTEIN 2.4g; CARB 7.6g; FIBER 2.2g; CHOL 0mg; IRON 0.6mg; SODIUM 224mg; CALC 58mg

Snowy Weekend Getaway

A little advance preparation can go a long way to make your short escape delightful and delicious.

The most memorable vacations aren't necessarily the most extravagant. Sometimes a casual weekend with close friends means much more than a stay at a posh resort. This winter, find a cozy cottage or cabin to share, build a fire, and toast to the simple pleasures in life.

Winter Breakfast Menu
serves 6

Baked Pears with Streusel Filling

Smoked Salmon and Onion Frittata

Bagels

Fruit salad

Coffee

Lunch on the Snowshoe Trail Menu
serves 6

Lentil Soup with Balsamic-Roasted Winter Vegetables
or
Mexican Black Bean Sausage Chili

Onion and Fontina Beer Batter Bread

Orange-Infused Cherry-Almond Biscotti

Hot chocolate

Dinner by the Fire Menu
serves 6

Cheese Crostini with Prosciutto

Winter Orange Salad
or
Belgian Endive and Apple Salad with Cranberry Vinaigrette

Roasted Shallot and Butternut Squash Pasta

Chocolate-Cappuccino Parfaits

Pinot noir

QUICK & EASY • MAKE AHEAD
Baked Pears with Streusel Filling

This breakfast or brunch dish requires surprisingly little effort. Prepare the streusel up to two days in advance, stirring in the pecans just before baking to preserve their texture.

STREUSEL:
- ¼ cup all-purpose flour (about 1 ounce)
- ¼ cup packed brown sugar
- 1½ tablespoons butter, melted
- 1 tablespoon honey
- ½ teaspoon ground cinnamon
- ¼ teaspoon salt
- ¼ teaspoon ground allspice
- ¼ cup chopped pecans, toasted

PEARS:
- 3 Anjou pears, peeled and cut in half lengthwise
- ⅓ cup apple juice
- 1½ tablespoons apple brandy

1. Preheat oven to 375°.
2. To prepare streusel, lightly spoon flour into a dry measuring cup; level with a knife. Combine flour and next 6 ingredients in a bowl. Stir with a fork until mixture resembles coarse meal. Stir in pecans.
3. To prepare pears, using a melon baller or spoon, scoop out core from each pear half. Spoon streusel evenly into pear halves. Place pear halves, cut sides up, in an 8-inch square baking dish. Pour apple juice and apple brandy into dish. Cover dish with foil. Bake at 375° for 30 minutes. Uncover and bake an additional 5 minutes. Serve pears warm. Drizzle evenly with cooking liquid. Yield: 6 servings (serving size: 1 pear half and about 1 tablespoon cooking liquid).

CALORIES 200 (27% from fat); FAT 6.6g (sat 1.8g, mono 3.2g, poly 1.2g); PROTEIN 1.5g; CARB 34.4g; FIBER 4g; CHOL 8mg; IRON 0.8mg; SODIUM 124mg; CALC 26mg

Smoked Salmon and Onion Frittata

- 1 tablespoon olive oil, divided
- 1 cup vertically sliced onion
- ¼ cup thinly sliced green onions
- 1 tablespoon minced fresh thyme
- ½ teaspoon freshly ground black pepper, divided
- Cooking spray
- 2 cups preshredded potatoes (such as Simply Potatoes)
- 3 ounces smoked salmon, chopped
- 2½ ounces ⅓-less-fat cream cheese, cut into small pieces
- ⅛ teaspoon salt
- 2 cups egg substitute

1. Heat 1½ teaspoons oil in an 8-inch cast-iron skillet over medium heat. Add 1 cup onion; sauté 5 minutes or until tender. Remove from heat. Stir in green onions, thyme, and ¼ teaspoon pepper. Remove onion mixture from skillet; set aside.
2. Preheat broiler.
3. Coat skillet with cooking spray. Combine potatoes, remaining 1½ teaspoons oil, and remaining ¼ teaspoon pepper. Press potato mixture into bottom of skillet. Broil 15 minutes or until potatoes are crisp and golden.
4. Reduce oven temperature to 375°.
5. Spread onion mixture over potato mixture; sprinkle with salmon, cheese, and salt. Pour egg substitute over the top. Bake at 375° for 38 minutes or until puffy and lightly browned. Yield: 6 servings (serving size: 1 wedge).

CALORIES 163 (30% from fat); FAT 5.4g (sat 2.1g, mono 2.7g, poly 0.5g); PROTEIN 13.5g; CARB 14.9g; FIBER 1.2g; CHOL 12mg; IRON 2mg; SODIUM 572mg; CALC 46mg

The roasted root vegetables in the soup balance the sharp flavors of endive and radicchio in the salad.

Lentil Soup with Balsamic-Roasted Winter Vegetables

Radicchio-endive winter salad*

Coffee and almond biscotti

*Combine 3 cups chopped radicchio and 3 cups chopped endive in a large bowl. Combine 2 tablespoons orange juice, 2 teaspoons extravirgin olive oil, ¼ teaspoon salt, and ⅛ teaspoon freshly ground black pepper in a small bowl, stirring well. Add dressing to salad greens, tossing to coat.

MAKE AHEAD

Lentil Soup with Balsamic-Roasted Winter Vegetables

The flavor of this dish improves on the second day, so it's ideal to make in advance. Add the chard just before serving to preserve its color. Stir in a little water when you reheat the soup if it's too thick.

1⅔   cups cubed peeled sweet potato, (about 8 ounces)
1⅔   cups cubed peeled parsnip (about 8 ounces)
1⅔   cups cubed peeled carrot (about 8 ounces)
  2   tablespoons balsamic vinegar
  2   tablespoons olive oil
  ⅛   teaspoon kosher salt
  1   cup (4 ounces) chopped pancetta
  1   cup chopped shallots (about 6 large)
  1   cup chopped red onion (about 1 medium)
  1   tablespoon fresh thyme leaves
  1   tablespoon minced garlic
  1   tablespoon balsamic vinegar
  ½   teaspoon black pepper
  ¼   cup dry white wine
1¼   cups dried lentils
  6   cups fat-free, less-sodium chicken broth, divided
  8   cups Swiss chard, trimmed and chopped (about 9 ounces)

1. Preheat oven to 375°.

2. Combine first 6 ingredients in a large bowl; toss well. Arrange vegetable mixture in a single layer on a large foil-lined jelly-roll pan; bake at 375° for 30 minutes or until lightly browned, stirring occasionally. Set aside.

3. Cook pancetta in a Dutch oven over medium-high heat 8 minutes or until crisp. Remove from pan with a slotted spoon; set aside. Add shallots and onion to drippings in pan; cook 15 minutes or until golden brown. Add thyme, garlic, 1 tablespoon vinegar, and pepper, and cook 1 minute. Add wine, scraping pan to loosen browned bits. Add pancetta, lentils, and 4 cups broth to pan. Bring to a boil. Cover, reduce heat, and simmer 30 minutes. Add remaining 2 cups broth and roasted vegetables to pan, and simmer, uncovered, 15 minutes. Add chard, and cook 2 minutes or until wilted. Yield: 6 servings (serving size: about 1½ cups).

CALORIES 373 (28% from fat); FAT 11.7g (sat 3.5g, mono 6.4g, poly 1.6g); PROTEIN 18.8g; CARB 51g; FIBER 15.3g; CHOL 14mg; IRON 6.4mg; SODIUM 875mg; CALC 118mg

MAKE AHEAD

Mexican Black Bean Sausage Chili

(pictured on page 225)

You may need to thin the chili with water if you've made it ahead.

SAUSAGE:

  3   tablespoons dry red wine
  2   tablespoons sherry vinegar
  2   tablespoons minced garlic
1½   tablespoons Hungarian sweet paprika
  2   teaspoons ancho chili powder
  1   teaspoon ground cumin
  ½   teaspoon dried oregano
  ½   teaspoon ground coriander
  ½   teaspoon black pepper
Dash of kosher salt
  ¾   pound lean ground pork
  ¾   pound ground turkey breast

CHILI:

  2   tablespoons olive oil
  2   cups diced onion (about 2 medium)
  1   tablespoon ground cumin
  1   tablespoon finely minced garlic
  2   teaspoons dried oregano
  3   chipotle chiles, canned in adobo sauce, minced
  4   (15-ounce) cans black beans, rinsed and drained, divided
  3   cups fat-free, less-sodium chicken broth, divided
  3   cups water
  2   (14.5-ounce) cans no salt–added diced tomatoes, drained
  ¼   cup freshly squeezed lime juice
  ¼   cup very finely chopped cilantro, divided
Low-fat sour cream (optional)
Sliced green onions (optional)

1. To prepare sausage, combine first 12 ingredients in a large bowl. Cover and refrigerate overnight.

2. To prepare chili, heat oil in a large saucepan over medium-high heat. Add sausage mixture; cook 7 minutes or until browned, stirring to crumble. Add onion and next 4 ingredients; cook 4 minutes or until onion is tender. Place 1½ cups black beans and 1 cup broth in a food processor; process until smooth. Add pureed beans, remaining beans, remaining 2 cups broth, water, and tomatoes to pan; bring to a boil. Reduce heat, and simmer, partially covered, 45 minutes or until slightly thick. Stir in juice and cilantro. Ladle about 1¾ cups chili into each of 6 bowls. Garnish each serving with sour cream and green onions, if desired. Yield: 6 servings.

CALORIES 395 (27% from fat); FAT 11g (sat 2.9g, mono 6g, poly 2.1g); PROTEIN 35.3g; CARB 40.4g; FIBER 13.7g; CHOL 78mg; IRON 6mg; SODIUM 989mg; CALC 128mg

Onion and Fontina Beer Batter Bread

Bake this quick bread before you leave town, or mix the dry ingredients, sauté the onions, and grate the cheese in advance, then bake the loaf on-site.

- 1 tablespoon olive oil
- 1 cup diced onion
- 3 cups all-purpose flour (about 13½ ounces)
- 3 tablespoons sugar
- 2 teaspoons baking powder
- 1 teaspoon salt
- 1 cup (4 ounces) grated fontina cheese
- 1 (12-ounce) bottle beer (such as amber ale)
- Cooking spray
- ¼ cup butter, melted and divided

1. Preheat oven to 375°.
2. Heat oil in a large nonstick skillet over medium heat. Add onion, and sauté 6 minutes or until tender. Cool to room temperature.
3. Lightly spoon flour into dry measuring cups, and level with a knife. Combine flour, sugar, baking powder, and salt in a bowl; make a well in center of mixture. Add onion, cheese, and beer; stir just until moist.
4. Spoon batter into a 9 x 5–inch loaf pan coated with cooking spray; drizzle evenly with 2 tablespoons butter. Bake at 375° for 35 minutes; brush with remaining 2 tablespoons butter. Bake an additional 23 minutes or until a wooden pick inserted in center comes out clean. Cool 5 minutes in pan on a wire rack; remove from pan. Cool completely on wire rack. Yield: 16 servings (serving size: 1 slice).

CALORIES 149 (30% from fat); FAT 5g (sat 2.3g, mono 2.1g, poly 0.3g); PROTEIN 3.5g; CARB 22.2g; FIBER 0.8g; CHOL 12mg; IRON 1.2mg; SODIUM 259mg; CALC 61mg

Orange-Infused Cherry-Almond Biscotti

When buying dried cherries, look for those without added sugar. Serve with coffee or tea.

- 1¾ cups all-purpose flour (about 7½ ounces)
- 1 cup whole wheat pastry flour (about 5⅛ ounces)
- 1 cup sugar
- 2 teaspoons baking powder
- ¾ teaspoon salt
- 2 tablespoons melted butter
- 1 tablespoon grated orange rind
- 1 tablespoon fresh orange juice
- ½ teaspoon almond extract
- 3 large eggs, lightly beaten
- ¾ cup dried sweet cherries, chopped
- ¾ cup slivered almonds, toasted and chopped
- Cooking spray (optional)

1. Preheat oven to 350°.
2. Lightly spoon flours into dry measuring cups; level with a knife. Combine flours, sugar, baking powder, and salt in a large bowl; stir with a whisk. Combine butter, rind, juice, almond extract, and eggs in a bowl; stir with a whisk. Add egg mixture to flour mixture; stir until a soft dough forms. Stir in cherries and almonds. Turn dough out onto a lightly floured surface; knead lightly 8 times. Divide dough in half. Shape each portion into an 11-inch-long roll. Place rolls 4 inches apart on a baking sheet coated with cooking spray or lined with parchment paper.
3. Bake at 350° for 25 minutes or until golden. Remove rolls from pan, and cool 10 minutes on a wire rack. Cut each roll diagonally into 20 (½-inch) slices. Carefully stand slices upright on baking sheet.
4. Reduce oven temperature to 325°.
5. Bake biscotti 20 minutes or until almost firm (biscotti will be slightly soft in center but will continue to harden as they cool). Remove from baking sheet; cool completely on a wire rack. Yield: 40 biscotti (serving size: 1 biscotto).

CALORIES 83 (23% from fat); FAT 2.1g (sat 0.5g, mono 1g, poly 0.4g); PROTEIN 2g; CARB 14.3g; FIBER 1.1g; CHOL 17mg; IRON 0.6mg; SODIUM 79mg; CALC 26mg

Cheese Crostini with Prosciutto

This fast, simple appetizer complements pastas, soups, and salads. You can grate the cheese in advance.

- 6 (1-ounce) slices ciabatta bread
- 2 garlic cloves, halved
- ¼ cup (1 ounce) grated fresh Parmesan cheese
- 2 ounces thinly sliced prosciutto
- ½ teaspoon freshly ground black pepper

1. Preheat broiler.
2. Place bread on a baking sheet. Broil 1 minute or until lightly browned. Rub 1 side of each bread slice with cut half of garlic. Discard garlic. Sprinkle cheese evenly over bread. Broil 1 minute or until cheese melts. Arrange prosciutto evenly over bread. Sprinkle evenly with pepper. Yield: 6 servings (serving size: 1 piece).

CALORIES 127 (25% from fat); FAT 3.5g (sat 1.4g, mono 1.2g, poly 0.4g); PROTEIN 7.2g; CARB 16.6g; FIBER 1g; CHOL 13mg; IRON 1mg; SODIUM 442mg; CALC 78mg

Winter Orange Salad

You'll find the best oranges this time of year. Mix the vinaigrette and prepare the greens up to two days in advance, storing each component separately until it's time to toss the salad. Keep the greens chilled and covered with a damp towel.

VINAIGRETTE:

- 3 tablespoons sherry vinegar
- 2 tablespoons fresh orange juice
- 2 tablespoons minced shallots
- 2 tablespoons sugar
- 2 teaspoons extravirgin olive oil
- 1 teaspoon dry mustard
- ½ teaspoon salt

SALAD:

- 3 cups orange sections (about 3 large oranges)
- 3 cups torn romaine lettuce
- 3 cups torn red leaf lettuce
- 3 cups baby spinach leaves
- 1 cup thinly sliced red onion
- ½ cup (2 ounces) crumbled feta cheese

1. To prepare vinaigrette, combine first 7 ingredients in a small bowl; stir with a whisk. Set aside.

2. To prepare salad, combine orange sections, romaine, red leaf lettuce, and spinach in a large bowl. Add onion and cheese. Pour vinaigrette over salad mixture; toss gently to coat. Yield: 6 servings (serving size: about 2 cups).

CALORIES 119 (29% from fat); FAT 3.9g (sat 1.6g, mono 1.6g, poly 0.3g); PROTEIN 3.1g; CARB 21.5g; FIBER 5.1g; CHOL 8mg; IRON 1.3mg; SODIUM 329mg; CALC 107mg

---

Choice Ingredient: Belgian Endive

"Versatile" best describes the Belgian endive, a member of the chicory family. Belgian endive has a slightly bitter flavor and crunchy texture that's great for dips and salads, or grilled or braised as a side dish. For the best flavor, buy small, firm heads with white leaves and yellow tips. Refrigerate them wrapped in a dry paper towel for three to five days. Be sure to separate the leaves and rinse well before using. Our Belgian Endive and Apple Salad with Cranberry Vinaigrette (recipe at right) features this unique green.

MAKE AHEAD

Belgian Endive and Apple Salad with Cranberry Vinaigrette

Make the vinaigrette, toast the nuts, and prepare the greens up to two days in advance. Substitute walnut or olive oil if hazelnut oil isn't available. To reduce prep time, use bagged Italian blend greens.

VINAIGRETTE:

- 1 cup cranberry juice cocktail
- ¾ cup sweetened dried cranberries
- ¼ cup red wine vinegar
- 3 tablespoons finely chopped shallots
- 1 garlic clove, minced
- 1 tablespoon hazelnut oil
- ¼ teaspoon kosher salt
- ¼ teaspoon freshly ground black pepper

SALAD:

- 3 tablespoons chopped walnuts
- 2 teaspoons brown sugar
- 1 teaspoon butter, melted
- ¼ teaspoon ground cinnamon
- ⅛ teaspoon ground allspice
- ⅛ teaspoon freshly ground black pepper
- 3 cups torn radicchio
- 3 cups baby spinach
- ¼ cup (1 ounce) Stilton cheese, crumbled
- 2 Fuji apples, thinly sliced (about 1 pound)
- 2 heads Belgian endive, cut lengthwise into strips

1. To prepare vinaigrette, combine juice and cranberries in a small saucepan; bring to a boil. Reduce heat; simmer 10 minutes or until most of liquid evaporates. Remove from heat; stir in vinegar, shallots, and garlic. Drizzle oil into pan, stirring with a whisk until blended. Stir in salt and ¼ teaspoon pepper. Cool to room temperature.

2. Preheat oven to 350°.

3. To prepare salad, combine walnuts and next 5 ingredients; toss well. Spread on a foil-lined baking sheet. Bake at 350° for 5 minutes or until toasted.

4. Combine radicchio and remaining 4 ingredients in a large bowl. Add vinaigrette and walnuts; toss well. Yield: 6 servings (serving size: 2⅓ cups).

CALORIES 205 (31% from fat); FAT 7.1g (sat 1.6g, mono 2.4g, poly 2.2g); PROTEIN 2.9g; CARB 36.8g; FIBER 6.4g; CHOL 7mg; IRON 1.2mg; SODIUM 158mg; CALC 64mg

---

MAKE AHEAD

Roasted Shallot and Butternut Squash Pasta

SQUASH:

- 3 tablespoons olive oil, divided
- 3 butternut squash, halved lengthwise and seeded (about 3½ pounds)
- 8 shallots, peeled (about ½ pound)
- ⅓ cup fat-free, less-sodium chicken broth
- 2 tablespoons chopped fresh sage
- 2 tablespoons crème fraîche
- 2 tablespoons dry white wine
- 1 teaspoon kosher salt
- ¾ teaspoon freshly ground black pepper
- 2 garlic cloves, chopped

PASTA:

- 12 ounces uncooked penne (tube-shaped pasta)
- ⅔ cup (about 2½ ounces) shredded Asiago cheese, divided
- Cooking spray

1. Preheat oven to 375°.

2. To prepare squash, drizzle 1 tablespoon oil in bottom of a roasting pan. Place squash, cut sides down, and shallots in pan. Bake, uncovered, at 375° for 45 minutes or until tender. Cool. Scoop pulp from squash; discard peels. Reserve 1½ cups pulp. Place remaining 2 tablespoons oil, remaining pulp, shallots, broth, and next 6 ingredients in a food processor; process until smooth.

3. Reduce oven temperature to 350°.

4. To prepare pasta, cook pasta in boiling water 7 minutes or until almost tender. Drain. Combine reserved 1½ cups pulp, pureed mixture, pasta, and ⅓ cup cheese in a large bowl; stir gently. Spoon mixture into a 13 x 9–inch baking dish coated with cooking spray; cover with foil.

Continued

5. Bake at 350° for 30 minutes. Uncover; sprinkle with remaining ⅓ cup cheese. Bake 5 minutes or until cheese melts. Yield: 6 servings (serving size: 1⅓ cups).

CALORIES 475 (24% from fat); FAT 12.7g (sat 4.3g, mono 6.3g, poly 1g); PROTEIN 15g; CARB 80.8g; FIBER 7.5g; CHOL 16mg; IRON 4.3mg; SODIUM 386mg; CALC 276mg

WINE NOTE: For the dinner menu, a single red wine that can carry you through from the crostini to the pasta makes sense. Pinot noir has a kind of sweet-meaty earthiness that mirrors prosciutto and is a foil to the saltiness of the cheese. And the deep savory sweetness of roasted squash in the pasta is echoed by pinot noir more than by just about any other red variety. Try Laetitia Pinot Noir 2004 from the Arroyo Grande Valley of California ($20). (This dry red wine isn't a good match for the parfait, so plan to serve coffee or tea with dessert.)

cooking class

Simply Wonderful Stew

Hearty and nourishing, stew is the antidote to winter's chill.

This year, we devote the Cooking Class column to mastering classic dishes. For January/February, the spotlight is on a winter favorite: stew. Once you learn the eight steps to prepare stew (see page 50), you'll achieve winning results every time.

MAKE AHEAD

Chocolate-Cappuccino Parfaits

Assemble and freeze the parfaits up to a day ahead. You can place the parfait glasses in the freezer about 30 minutes before assembling to help the layers firm up quickly.

- 4½ cups chocolate low-fat ice cream, softened
- 2 tablespoons instant coffee granules
- ¼ cup cold brewed coffee
- 6 tablespoons frozen reduced-calorie whipped topping, thawed
- ¾ teaspoon ground cinnamon

1. Combine ice cream and coffee granules, stirring until coffee granules dissolve. Spoon ¼ cup ice cream mixture into each of 6 (8-ounce) parfait glasses. Drizzle each serving with 1 teaspoon brewed coffee. Repeat layers, ending with ice cream mixture. Cover and freeze until firm. Just before serving, top each parfait with 1 tablespoon whipped topping and ⅛ teaspoon cinnamon. Yield: 6 servings (servings size: 1 parfait).

CALORIES 163 (20% from fat); FAT 3.6g (sat 2g, mono 0.8g, poly 0.1g); PROTEIN 3.1g; CARB 30.1g; FIBER 0.2g; CHOL 8mg; IRON 0.7mg; SODIUM 83mg; CALC 125mg

STAFF FAVORITE • MAKE AHEAD
FREEZABLE

Dijon Chicken Stew with Potatoes and Kale

- 4 teaspoons olive oil, divided
- 2 cups sliced leek
- 4 garlic cloves, minced
- ⅓ cup all-purpose flour (about 1½ ounces)
- 1 pound skinless, boneless chicken thighs, cut into bite-sized pieces
- ½ pound skinless, boneless chicken breast, cut into bite-sized pieces
- ½ teaspoon salt, divided
- ½ teaspoon freshly ground black pepper, divided
- 1 cup dry white wine
- 3 cups fat-free, less-sodium chicken broth, divided
- 1 tablespoon all-purpose flour
- 1½ cups water
- 2 tablespoons Dijon mustard
- 2 cups (½-inch) cubed peeled white potato (about 1 pound)
- 8 cups loosely packed torn kale (about 5 ounces)
- Crushed red pepper (optional)

1. Heat 1 teaspoon oil in a Dutch oven over medium-high heat. Add leek; sauté 6 minutes or until tender and golden brown. Add garlic; sauté 1 minute. Spoon leek mixture into a large bowl.

2. Place ⅓ cup flour in a shallow bowl or pie plate. Dredge chicken in flour, shaking off excess. Heat remaining 1 tablespoon oil in pan over medium-high heat. Add half of chicken mixture; sprinkle with ⅛ teaspoon salt and ⅛ teaspoon black pepper. Cook 6 minutes, browning on all sides. Add browned chicken to leek mixture. Repeat procedure with remaining chicken mixture, ⅛ teaspoon salt, and ⅛ teaspoon black pepper.

3. Add wine to pan, scraping pan to loosen browned bits. Combine 1 cup broth and 1 tablespoon flour, stirring with a whisk until smooth. Add broth mixture, remaining 2 cups broth, water, and mustard to pan; bring to a boil. Stir in chicken mixture, remaining ¼ teaspoon salt, and remaining ¼ teaspoon black pepper. Cover, reduce heat, and simmer 30 minutes.

4. Stir in potato. Cover and simmer 30 minutes or until potato is tender. Stir in kale; cover and simmer 10 minutes. Garnish with crushed red pepper, if desired. Yield: 6 servings (serving size: 1½ cups).

CALORIES 324 (22% from fat); FAT 7.9g (sat 1.5g, mono 3.5g, poly 1.7g); PROTEIN 30.9g; CARB 33.7g; FIBER 5g; CHOL 85mg; IRON 4.6mg; SODIUM 659mg; CALC 180mg

Use the Right Equipment

Although no fancy equipment is needed to make a good stew, it's great if you have a Dutch oven. These are heavy cast-iron or stainless steel pots with tight-fitting lids. Some of the best are cast-iron with an enameled coating. The enamel prevents any reaction that might occur between ingredients and metal that could give your stew an off flavor, and it keeps the cast iron from retaining the scent or flavor of stews past. Two other good-to-have tools: tongs for flipping the meat, and a flat-edged wooden spatula for deglazing.

Choose the Right Cuts of Meat

For **beef** stew, purchase readily available beef stew meat. These chunks of beef come from tougher parts of the steer or animal—the shoulder, leg, and butt—which are sometimes collectively referred to as "chuck." As they simmer over low heat, they become tender and offer great flavor to the stew.

For **lamb** stews, purchase a boned leg of lamb, trim it well, and cut into cubes. A friendly butcher might even do this for you. Or look for lamb stew meat, which is usually cut-up scraps from leg of lamb. Meat from the leg adds great flavor to any stew.

When searching for **pork** for stews, seek out pork shoulder, often called Boston butt pork roast, which is a fattier cut with a lot of flavor that needs to cook for a long time. Or choose lean pork tenderloin, which becomes tender in a shorter amount of time.

Use a combination of boneless, skinless **chicken** breasts and thighs for chicken stews. The breast meat has a pleasantly firm texture, while the thighs offer meaty richness similar to that of pork.

Sauté the Aromatics

Begin cooking by sautéing onions, garlic, leeks, or shallots until golden brown. The caramelized surface on these aromatics infuses the stew with flavor and fragrance. Remove from the pan once browned.

Dredge in Flour

Dredging the meat—placing the pieces in a bowl of flour, tossing to coat, then shaking off the excess—results in a tasty crust. When the meat is seared, the flour coating cooks quickly, sealing juices inside the meat. It also makes an instant mini roux that sticks to the bottom of the pan—a roux being a flour-and-fat combo that thickens stews.

Brown the Meat

Make sure there is a thin layer of oil in the bottom of the pan. Cook the meat over medium-high heat, so the edges of the meat quickly sear and brown, but the meat remains uncooked. Brown the meat in batches so as not to overcrowd the pan; if the pan is too crowded, the meat will steam and not brown. Don't worry if the bottom of the pan develops a thick dark brown coating—as long as it does not burn. You actually want this to occur; the browned bits will add a deep richness to the gravy. Remove the browned meat from the pan so you can deglaze.

Deglaze the Pan

Deglazing refers to the process of adding liquid, usually wine, to the pan, and boiling while scraping up the browned bits on the bottom of the pan. The browned bits dissolve and add flavor to the gravy.

Keep the Heat Low

After you return the meat and aromatics to the pan and cover them with the desired liquid, it is very important to simmer. As mentioned, stews are best made with tougher cuts of meat. Slowly cooking stew over low heat so the liquid barely simmers breaks tissues down into tender morsels. If cooked too fast, the meat will become overly firm and tough.

Add Vegetables Later

It's best to add vegetables such as potatoes and carrots to stews after the meat has had a chance to cook for a while. This ensures that the meat will be fork tender, while the vegetables retain their shape and character without becoming overcooked.

Stew vs. Braise

Most of us think of a stew as a mixture of meat and vegetables in a rich, meaty sauce. Technically, a stew consists of small pieces of meat that are seared and then cooked while immersed in liquid. A braise involves one or a few larger pieces of meat that are seared and cooked in liquid that comes less than halfway up the sides of the meat. Both a stew and a braise result in a rich gravy and tender meat.

Great Today, Even Better Later

Stews taste great as soon as the meat becomes tender, and it's hard to resist diving into the pot when the whole house is fragrant with simmering wine, onions, and herbs. But if you have leftovers, cool and keep them in the refrigerator overnight—you'll be rewarded with even better taste the next day, after flavors have had more time to marry.

Or freeze leftovers for up to three months. Freeze individual or double servings in heavy-duty zip-top plastic bags, which will take up minimal space in your freezer. Thaw overnight in the refrigerator, and reheat gently over medium heat.

Make-Ahead Meal for Entertaining and Busy Lives

Because they can be prepared ahead and reheated, stews are ideal for entertaining. Make the stew in the morning, or a day or two ahead, and place in the refrigerator. You'll be free to enjoy a glass of wine and a relaxing visit with guests as the stew reheats. Working parents may want to make a stew, or two, over the weekend and then enjoy the reheated leftovers during the week.

1. *Gather the right equipment. Use a Dutch oven, a large pan with a tight-fitting lid, for the best results. A flat wooden spatula works well to deglaze the pan (step 6).*

2. *Use the right cuts of meat for the recipe. If cuts are too lean, the meat might end up tough in the stew.*

3. *Sauté aromatics (onions, garlic, etc.) until golden brown to deepen their flavor, then remove from the pan.*

4. *Dredge the meat in flour, and shake off the excess.*

5. *Brown the meat to create a delicious crust that locks in juices and establishes flavorful browned bits that stick to the bottom of the pan.*

6. *Deglaze the pan, scraping the bottom of the pan as you add the liquid. The browned bits that are scraped up give the stew lots of flavor.*

7. *Simmer over low heat to ensure the meat gets tender.*

8. *Add vegetables after the meat has cooked a while so they won't become overdone and so they will retain their shape and texture.*

Two-Potato Lamb Stew with Roasted Garlic

Roast another head of garlic for pasta sauces, pizzas, or spread onto bread or stirred into mashed potatoes. Wrap separately in foil, and refrigerate for up to five days.

- 1 garlic head
- Cooking spray
- 4 cups coarsely chopped onion
- 4 garlic cloves, minced
- 1/3 cup all-purpose flour (about 1½ ounces)
- 2 pounds boneless leg of lamb, trimmed and cut into bite-sized pieces
- 2 teaspoons olive oil
- 1 teaspoon salt, divided
- ½ teaspoon freshly ground black pepper, divided
- 1 cup dry red wine
- 3 cups less-sodium beef broth
- 2½ cups (1-inch) cubed peeled sweet potato (about 10 ounces)
- 2½ cups (1-inch) cubed peeled Yukon gold potato (about 10 ounces)
- 2½ cups (½-inch) slices peeled parsnip (about 10 ounces)
- 1 tablespoon chopped fresh rosemary

1. Preheat oven to 350°.
2. Remove white papery skin from garlic head (do not peel or separate cloves). Wrap garlic head in foil. Bake at 350° for 45 minutes or until tender; cool 10 minutes. Separate cloves; squeeze to extract pulp. Discard skins.
3. Heat a Dutch oven over medium-high heat. Coat pan with cooking spray. Add onion; sauté 10 minutes or until tender and golden brown. Add 4 garlic cloves; sauté 1 minute. Spoon onion mixture into a bowl.
4. Place flour in a shallow bowl or pie plate. Dredge lamb in flour, shaking off excess. Heat oil in pan over medium-high heat. Add half of lamb mixture; sprinkle with ¼ teaspoon salt and ⅛ teaspoon pepper. Cook 6 minutes, browning on all sides. Add browned lamb to onion mixture. Repeat procedure with remaining lamb mixture, ¼ teaspoon salt, and ⅛ teaspoon pepper.

5. Add wine to pan, scraping pan to loosen browned bits. Stir in lamb mixture and broth; bring to a boil. Cover, reduce heat, and simmer 1 hour or until lamb is just tender.
6. Stir in potatoes and parsnip. Cover and simmer 30 minutes. Stir in roasted garlic, remaining ½ teaspoon salt, remaining ¼ teaspoon pepper, and rosemary; simmer 10 minutes. Yield: 8 servings (serving size: 1⅓ cups).

CALORIES 316 (30% from fat); FAT 10.5g (sat 3.9g, mono 4.8g, poly 0.9g); PROTEIN 20.6g; CARB 35.4g; FIBER 4.9g; CHOL 58mg; IRON 2.5mg; SODIUM 526mg; CALC 60mg

Provençal Pork Stew with Olives and Fennel

Niçoise olives hail from Provence and add a mellow nuttiness to this French stew; be sure to warn diners, though, that these olives are unpitted.

- 1 tablespoon olive oil, divided
- 4 cups sliced fennel bulb (about 2 bulbs)
- 3½ cups thinly sliced onion (about 2 large)
- 8 garlic cloves, minced
- 1/3 cup all-purpose flour (about 1½ ounces)
- 2 pounds pork tenderloin, trimmed and cut into bite-sized pieces
- ½ teaspoon salt, divided
- ½ teaspoon freshly ground black pepper, divided
- 1 cup dry white wine
- 1 cup fat-free, less-sodium chicken broth
- 1 tablespoon herbes de Provence
- 3 (14.5-ounce) cans diced tomatoes, undrained
- ½ cup niçoise olives
- Chopped fresh parsley (optional)

1. Heat 1 teaspoon oil in a large Dutch oven over medium-high heat. Add fennel and onion; sauté 8 minutes or until tender. Add garlic; sauté 2 minutes. Spoon fennel mixture into a large bowl.
2. Place flour in a shallow bowl or pie plate. Dredge pork in flour, shaking off excess. Heat remaining 2 teaspoons oil in

pan over medium-high heat. Add half of pork mixture; sprinkle with ⅛ teaspoon salt and ⅛ teaspoon pepper. Cook 6 minutes, browning on all sides. Add browned pork to fennel mixture. Repeat procedure with remaining pork mixture, ⅛ teaspoon salt, and ⅛ teaspoon pepper.
3. Add wine to pan, scraping pan to loosen browned bits. Stir in pork mixture, broth, herbes de Provence, and tomatoes; bring to a boil. Cover, reduce heat, and simmer 45 minutes or until pork is just tender.
4. Stir in remaining ¼ teaspoon salt, remaining ¼ teaspoon pepper, and olives. Simmer 10 minutes or until pork is tender and sauce is thick. Sprinkle with parsley, if desired. Yield: 8 servings (serving size: 1½ cups).

CALORIES 275 (28% from fat); FAT 8.7g (sat 2g, mono 5.2g, poly 1g); PROTEIN 27.3g; CARB 22.5g; FIBER 5.2g; CHOL 74mg; IRON 3mg; SODIUM 649mg; CALC 84mg

Lamb Stew with Chickpeas and Pomegranate Molasses

Pomegranate molasses is thick, tangy, sweet, and slightly bitter. Look for it in Middle Eastern markets.

- Cooking spray
- 2 cups chopped red onion
- 6 garlic cloves, minced
- 1/3 cup all-purpose flour (about 1½ ounces)
- 2 pounds boneless leg of lamb, trimmed and cut into bite-sized pieces
- 1 tablespoon olive oil
- 1 teaspoon salt, divided
- 2 tablespoons pomegranate molasses
- 2 (14-ounce) cans less-sodium beef broth
- 2 cups (¼-inch) slices carrot
- 1 (15-ounce) can chickpeas (garbanzo beans), rinsed and drained
- 2 tablespoons chopped fresh mint
- ½ teaspoon freshly ground black pepper
- 4 cups hot cooked couscous

Continued

1. Heat a large Dutch oven over medium-high heat. Coat pan with cooking spray. Add onion; sauté 10 minutes or until tender and golden brown. Add garlic; sauté 1 minute. Spoon onion mixture into a large bowl.

2. Place flour in a shallow bowl or pie plate. Dredge lamb in flour, shaking off excess. Heat oil in pan over medium-high heat. Add half of lamb mixture; sprinkle with ¼ teaspoon salt. Cook 6 minutes, browning on all sides. Add browned lamb to onion mixture. Repeat procedure with remaining lamb mixture and ¼ teaspoon salt.

3. Add molasses and broth to pan, scraping pan to loosen browned bits; bring to a boil. Stir in lamb mixture. Cover, reduce heat, and simmer 1 hour or until lamb is just tender.

4. Stir in carrot and chickpeas. Simmer, uncovered, 45 minutes or until lamb is very tender. Remove from heat; stir in remaining ½ teaspoon salt, mint, and pepper. Serve over couscous. Yield: 8 servings (serving size: ¾ cup stew and ½ cup couscous).

CALORIES 384 (27% from fat); FAT 11.5g (sat 4.1g, mono 5.2g, poly 1.1g); PROTEIN 23.4g; CARB 44.9g; FIBER 4.5g; CHOL 58mg; IRON 3.3mg; SODIUM 652mg; CALC 66mg

Pork Stew with Cipollini, Mushrooms, and Chestnuts

    4   cups fat-free, less-sodium chicken
        broth
 1½   ounces dried mushroom
        medley
        Cooking spray
    1   pound cipollini onions, peeled
    5   garlic cloves, minced
   ⅓   cup all-purpose flour
    2   pounds boneless Boston butt pork
        roast, trimmed and cut into
        bite-sized pieces
    2   teaspoons olive oil
   ¾   teaspoon salt, divided
   ½   teaspoon black pepper, divided
    1   cup dry white wine
    2   teaspoons dried rubbed sage
 1½   cups (1-inch) slices carrot
    1   cup coarsely chopped bottled
        chestnuts

1. Bring broth and mushrooms to a boil in a medium saucepan. Remove from heat; cover and let stand 20 minutes or until tender. Drain mushrooms in a colander over a bowl, reserving broth.

2. Heat a large Dutch oven over medium-high heat. Coat pan with cooking spray. Add onions; sauté 6 minutes or until lightly browned. Add garlic; sauté 1 minute. Spoon onion mixture into a large bowl.

3. Place flour in a shallow bowl or pie plate. Dredge pork in flour, shaking off excess. Heat oil in pan over medium-high heat. Add half of pork mixture; sprinkle with ⅛ teaspoon salt and ⅛ teaspoon pepper. Cook 6 minutes, browning on all sides. Add browned pork to onion mixture. Repeat procedure with remaining pork mixture, ⅛ teaspoon salt, and ⅛ teaspoon pepper.

4. Add wine to pan, scraping pan to loosen browned bits. Stir in reserved broth, pork mixture, and sage; bring to a boil. Cover, reduce heat, and simmer 40 minutes or until pork is almost tender.

5. Stir in carrot. Simmer, uncovered, 20 minutes. Stir in mushrooms, ½ teaspoon salt, ¼ teaspoon pepper, and chestnuts; simmer 10 minutes. Yield: 8 servings (serving size: about 1 cup).

CALORIES 276 (26% from fat); FAT 8.1g (sat 2.4g, mono 3.9g, poly 1g); PROTEIN 23.9g; CARB 26.2g; FIBER 4g; CHOL 63mg; IRON 3.3mg; SODIUM 520mg; CALC 54mg

> Stew is the quintessential comfort food. It's easy to make, and its success just depends on following a few simple steps.

Basic Beef Stew with Carrots and Mushrooms

A crowd-pleaser, this recipe is justifiably a classic. Purchase precut lean stew beef, or cut lean beef sirloin or chuck into bite-sized pieces. White potatoes, not to be confused with baking potatoes, are waxy in texture and hold up well in soups and stews; you can substitute red potatoes. Halve any mushrooms that are larger than 1½ inches.

    1   tablespoon olive oil, divided
    1   pound small cremini
        mushrooms
        Cooking spray
    2   cups chopped onion
    3   garlic cloves, minced
   ⅓   cup all-purpose flour (about
        1½ ounces)
    2   pounds lean beef stew meat, cut
        into bite-sized pieces
   ¾   teaspoon salt, divided
    1   cup dry red wine
    1   tablespoon chopped fresh
        thyme
    2   (14-ounce) cans less-sodium beef
        broth
    1   bay leaf
    2   cups (¾-inch) cubed peeled white
        potato (about 1 pound)
 1½   cups (1-inch) slices carrot (about
        12 ounces)
   ½   teaspoon freshly ground black
        pepper
        Thyme sprigs (optional)

1. Heat 1 teaspoon oil in a large Dutch oven over medium-high heat. Add mushrooms; sauté 5 minutes or until mushrooms begin to brown. Spoon into a large bowl. Lightly coat pan with cooking spray. Add onion; sauté 10 minutes or until tender and golden brown. Add garlic; sauté 1 minute. Add onion mixture to mushroom mixture.

2. Place flour in a shallow bowl or pie plate. Dredge beef in flour, shaking off excess. Heat remaining 2 teaspoons oil in pan over medium-high heat. Add half of beef mixture; sprinkle with ⅛ teaspoon salt. Cook 6 minutes, browning on all

sides. Add browned beef to mushroom mixture. Repeat procedure with remaining beef mixture and ⅛ teaspoon salt.

3. Add wine to pan, scraping pan to loosen browned bits. Add chopped thyme, broth, and bay leaf; bring to a boil. Stir in beef mixture. Cover, reduce heat to medium-low, and simmer 1 hour or until beef is just tender.

4. Stir in potato and carrot. Simmer, uncovered, 1 hour and 15 minutes or until beef and vegetables are very tender and sauce is thick, stirring occasionally. Stir in remaining ½ teaspoon salt and pepper. Discard bay leaf. Garnish with thyme sprigs, if desired. Yield: 8 servings (serving size: about 1 cup).

CALORIES 303 (29% from fat); FAT 9.8g (sat 3.2g, mono 4.7g, poly 0.6g); PROTEIN 26.4g; CARB 26.8g; FIBER 2.3g; CHOL 71mg; IRON 3.9mg; SODIUM 494mg; CALC 54mg

---

MAKE AHEAD • FREEZABLE
Beef Stew with Red Wine, Dried Plums, and Celery Root

1	tablespoon olive oil, divided
2	cups chopped onion
3	garlic cloves, minced
⅓	cup all-purpose flour
2	pounds lean beef stew meat, cut into bite-sized pieces
1	teaspoon salt, divided
2	cups dry red wine
2	(14-ounce) cans less-sodium beef broth
2	thyme sprigs
½	vanilla bean (optional)
½	teaspoon black pepper
4	cups (¾-inch) cubed peeled celeriac (celery root; about 1 pound)
16	pitted dried plums

1. Heat 1 teaspoon oil in a large Dutch oven over medium-high heat. Add onion; sauté 10 minutes or until tender and golden brown. Add garlic; sauté 1 minute. Spoon onion mixture into a large bowl.

2. Place flour in a shallow bowl or pie plate. Dredge beef in flour, shaking off excess. Heat remaining 2 teaspoons oil in pan over medium-high heat. Add half of beef mixture; sprinkle with ¼ teaspoon

salt. Cook 6 minutes, browning on all sides. Add browned beef to onion mixture. Repeat procedure with remaining beef mixture and ¼ teaspoon salt.

3. Add wine to pan, scraping pan to loosen browned bits. Bring to a boil; reduce heat, and simmer 10 minutes or until liquid is reduced to about 1 cup. Add beef mixture, broth, thyme, and vanilla bean half, if desired. Bring mixture to a simmer. Stir in remaining ½ teaspoon salt and pepper. Cover, reduce heat to medium-low, and simmer 1 hour or until beef is just tender.

4. Discard thyme sprigs and vanilla bean half. Stir in celeriac and dried plums. Simmer, uncovered, 1 hour or until beef and vegetables are very tender and sauce is thick, stirring occasionally. Yield: 8 servings (serving size: 1 cup).

CALORIES 297 (30% from fat); FAT 9.9g (sat 3.3g, mono 4.7g, poly 0.6g); PROTEIN 25.1g; CARB 27.2g; FIBER 3.4g; CHOL 71mg; IRON 3.8mg; SODIUM 608mg; CALC 65mg

---

MAKE AHEAD • FREEZABLE
Chicken Stew with Shallots, Cider, and Butternut Squash

4	teaspoons olive oil, divided
1	cup sliced shallots (about 6 medium)
1	teaspoon curry powder
⅓	cup all-purpose flour (about 1½ ounces)
1¼	pounds skinless, boneless chicken thighs, cut into bite-sized pieces
¾	pound skinless, boneless chicken breast, cut into bite-sized pieces
1	teaspoon salt, divided
½	teaspoon black pepper, divided
2	cups fermented dry cider
1	(14-ounce) can fat-free, less-sodium chicken broth, divided
1	tablespoon all-purpose flour
1	cup water
2	cups (½-inch) cubed peeled butternut squash (about 1 pound)
¼	cup sliced almonds, toasted

Chopped fresh parsley (optional)

1. Heat 1 teaspoon oil in a Dutch oven over medium-high heat. Add shallots; sauté 5 minutes or until tender and golden brown. Add curry powder; sauté 1 minute. Spoon shallot mixture into a large bowl.

2. Place ⅓ cup flour in a shallow bowl or pie plate. Dredge chicken in flour, shaking off excess. Heat remaining 1 tablespoon oil in pan over medium-high heat. Add half of chicken mixture; sprinkle with ¼ teaspoon salt and ⅛ teaspoon pepper. Cook 6 minutes, browning on all sides. Add browned chicken to shallot mixture. Repeat procedure with remaining chicken mixture, ¼ teaspoon salt, and ⅛ teaspoon pepper.

3. Add cider to pan, scraping pan to loosen browned bits. Combine 1 cup broth and 1 tablespoon flour, stirring with a whisk until smooth. Add broth mixture, remaining broth, and water to pan; bring to a boil. Stir in chicken mixture, remaining ½ teaspoon salt, and remaining ¼ teaspoon pepper. Cover, reduce heat, and simmer 40 minutes, stirring occasionally.

4. Stir in squash. Simmer, uncovered, 55 minutes or until chicken and squash are very tender and sauce thickens. Spoon about 1 cup stew into each of 6 bowls; sprinkle each serving with 2 teaspoons almonds and parsley, if desired. Yield: 6 servings.

CALORIES 328 (27% from fat); FAT 9.7g (sat 1.8g, mono 4.9g, poly 2g); PROTEIN 35.8g; CARB 24.4g; FIBER 2.9g; CHOL 111mg; IRON 3.1mg; SODIUM 628mg; CALC 85mg

. . . And Ready in Just About 20 Minutes

Here's more than a week's worth of quick entrées to get dinner on the table in a flash.

QUICK & EASY
Indian-Style Shrimp with Yogurt Sauce

Garam masala is a blend of Indian spices that may include cardamom, coriander, cumin, fennel, black pepper, and a variety of Northern Indian spices. The rich yogurt sauce counters the peppery shrimp. Serve over quick-cooking brown rice.

- 1 (6-ounce) carton plain low-fat yogurt
- 2 tablespoons chopped fresh cilantro
- 2 teaspoons canola oil
- 1½ teaspoons bottled minced garlic
- 1½ pounds large shrimp, peeled and deveined
- 1½ teaspoons garam masala
- ⅛ teaspoon salt
- ⅛ teaspoon ground red pepper

1. Spoon yogurt onto several layers of heavy-duty paper towels; spread to ½-inch thickness. Cover with additional paper towels; let stand 5 minutes. Scrape into a bowl using a rubber spatula. Stir in cilantro. Cover and refrigerate.
2. Heat oil in a large nonstick skillet over medium-high heat. Add garlic; sauté 1 minute. Add shrimp; sprinkle shrimp with garam masala, salt, and pepper. Cook 6 minutes or until shrimp are done. Serve with yogurt sauce. Yield: 4 servings (serving size: 1 cup shrimp and 1 tablespoon yogurt sauce).

CALORIES 180 (22% from fat); FAT 4.4g (sat 1g, mono 1.8g, poly 1.3g); PROTEIN 29.4g; CARB 4g; FIBER 0.3g; CHOL 255mg; IRON 4.3mg; SODIUM 393mg; CALC 132mg

QUICK & EASY • MAKE AHEAD
Corn and Potato Chowder

If you prefer a hotter bite, add extra ground red pepper or some minced seeded jalapeño pepper to this thick and hearty, corn-studded soup.

- Cooking spray
- 1½ cups prechopped green bell pepper
- 1 cup chopped green onions, divided (about 1 bunch)
- 2 cups frozen corn kernels
- 1¼ cups water
- 1 teaspoon seafood seasoning (such as Old Bay)
- ¾ teaspoon dried thyme leaves
- ⅛ teaspoon ground red pepper
- 1 pound baking potatoes, cut into ½-inch pieces
- 1 cup half-and-half
- ¼ cup chopped parsley
- ¾ teaspoon salt
- ½ cup (2 ounces) shredded reduced-fat sharp Cheddar cheese

1. Heat a Dutch oven over medium-high heat. Coat pan with cooking spray. Add bell pepper and ¾ cup green onions, and sauté 4 minutes or until lightly browned.
2. Increase heat to high; add corn and next 5 ingredients; bring to a boil. Cover, reduce heat, and simmer 10 minutes or until potatoes are tender. Remove from heat, and stir in half-and-half, parsley, and salt. Place about 1½ cups soup in each of 4 bowls; sprinkle each with 2 tablespoons cheese and 1 tablespoon green onions. Yield: 4 servings.

CALORIES 343 (27% from fat); FAT 10.2g (sat 6.4g, mono 3.1g, poly 0.5g); PROTEIN 11.5g; CARB 53.3g; FIBER 7g; CHOL 41mg; IRON 2.5mg; SODIUM 654mg; CALC 219mg

QUICK & EASY
Skillet Fillets with Cilantro Butter

Substitute any mild white fish such as cod, flounder, or orange roughy for the tilapia. Serve with sautéed spinach and additional lemon wedges. Grate the rind before squeezing the lemon for easier preparation.

- ¼ teaspoon salt
- ¼ teaspoon ground cumin
- ⅛ teaspoon ground red pepper
- 4 (6-ounce) tilapia fillets
- Cooking spray
- 1 lemon, quartered
- 2 tablespoons butter, softened
- 2 tablespoons finely chopped fresh cilantro
- ½ teaspoon grated lemon rind
- ¼ teaspoon paprika
- ⅛ teaspoon salt

1. Combine first 3 ingredients; sprinkle over both sides of fish. Heat a large nonstick skillet over medium-high heat. Coat pan with cooking spray. Coat both sides of fish with cooking spray; place in pan. Cook 3 minutes on each side or until fish flakes easily when tested with a fork or until desired degree of doneness. Place fish on a serving platter; squeeze lemon quarters over fish.
2. Place butter and remaining 4 ingredients in a small bowl; stir until well blended. Serve with fish. Yield: 4 servings (serving size: 1 fillet and about 2 teaspoons cilantro butter).

CALORIES 194 (32% from fat); FAT 6.9g (sat 3.1g, mono 2.5g, poly 0.6g); PROTEIN 30.5g; CARB 1.2g; FIBER 0.2g; CHOL 88mg; IRON 0.7mg; SODIUM 354mg; CALC 32mg

QUICK & EASY
Dried Cherry–Toasted Almond Turkey Salad Sandwiches

For a quick meal, serve with baked chips.

- ¼ cup slivered almonds (about 1 ounce)
- ¼ cup plain fat-free yogurt
- 3 tablespoons low-fat mayonnaise
- 1 teaspoon bottled ground fresh ginger (such as Spice World)
- ⅛ teaspoon crushed red pepper
- ¾ cup thinly sliced celery
- ¼ cup chopped red onion
- ¼ cup dried cherries
- ¼ cup golden raisins
- 8 ounces roasted turkey breast, chopped
- 4 (6-inch) whole wheat pitas, cut in half

1. Heat a small nonstick skillet over medium-high heat. Add almonds; cook 2 minutes or until toasted, stirring constantly. Remove from heat; set aside.

2. Combine yogurt, mayonnaise, ginger, and pepper in a medium bowl. Add almonds, celery, and next 4 ingredients, stirring well. Spoon ⅓ cup turkey mixture into each pita half. Yield: 4 servings (serving size: 2 stuffed pita halves).

CALORIES 398 (20% from fat); FAT 8.7g (sat 1.4g, mono 4.1g, poly 2.4g); PROTEIN 25.9g; CARB 56.1g; FIBER 6.9g; CHOL 51mg; IRON 3.5mg; SODIUM 501mg; CALC 93mg

---

QUICK & EASY • MAKE AHEAD
Creole Chicken and Vegetables

Enjoy the taste of summer anytime by using frozen bell peppers and frozen okra in this speedy Creole dish. Serve over rice.

  Cooking spray
  1 pound chicken breast tenders
  2 cups frozen pepper stir-fry (such as Bird's Eye brand), thawed
  1 cup frozen cut okra, thawed
  ¾ cup thinly sliced celery
  ¾ teaspoon sugar
  ½ teaspoon salt
  ½ teaspoon dried thyme
  ¼ teaspoon ground red pepper
  1 (14.5-ounce) can diced tomatoes, undrained
  ¼ cup chopped fresh parsley
  1 tablespoon butter

1. Heat a large nonstick skillet over medium-high heat. Coat pan with cooking spray. Add chicken; cook 3 minutes on each side or until browned. Add pepper stir-fry and next 6 ingredients, stirring to combine. Pour tomatoes over chicken mixture; bring to a boil. Cover, reduce heat, and simmer 5 minutes. Uncover; cook 3 minutes. Add parsley and butter, stirring until butter melts. Yield: 4 servings (serving size: 1 cup).

CALORIES 199 (20% from fat); FAT 4.4g (sat 1.8g, mono 1.5g, poly 0.5g); PROTEIN 28.3g; CARB 11g; FIBER 3.2g; CHOL 73mg; IRON 1.9mg; SODIUM 550mg; CALC 71mg

---

QUICK & EASY
Pork and Stir-Fried Vegetables with Spicy Asian Sauce

Use your favorite sliced vegetables in place of the zucchini and bell pepper; mushrooms and water chestnuts would also be good. To round out the meal, serve with quick-cooking rice stick noodles.

  1 teaspoon canola oil
  ¼ cup hoisin sauce
  ¼ cup ketchup
  1 teaspoon low-sodium soy sauce
  ½ teaspoon bottled minced garlic
  ⅛ to ¼ teaspoon ground red pepper
  1 (1-pound) pork tenderloin, trimmed, cut into ½-inch pieces
  1 teaspoon black pepper
  ¼ teaspoon salt
  2 teaspoons dark sesame oil
  1 cup presliced zucchini
  1 cup presliced red bell pepper
  1 teaspoon bottled ground fresh ginger (such as Spice World)
  ½ cup chopped green onions
  1 teaspoon toasted sesame seeds

1. Heat canola oil in a large nonstick skillet over medium-high heat. Combine hoisin sauce and next 4 ingredients, stirring until blended; set side. Add pork to pan; sprinkle with black pepper and salt. Cook 3 minutes on each side or until done. Remove from pan. Add sesame oil to pan. Add zucchini, bell pepper, and ginger; stir-fry 4 minutes or until bell pepper is tender. Stir in onions and pork. Add hoisin mixture to pan; toss to coat. Sprinkle with sesame seeds. Yield: 4 servings (serving size: about 1 cup).

CALORIES 244 (31% from fat); FAT 8.5g (sat 1.9g, mono 3.6g, poly 2.3g); PROTEIN 25.6g; CARB 15.6g; FIBER 1.7g; CHOL 74mg; IRON 2mg; SODIUM 678mg; CALC 24mg

---

QUICK & EASY
Broiled Flank Steak with Salsa Verde

This piquant green sauce makes a great accompaniment to broiled or grilled pork, or steamed white fish. A little goes a long way, so use it sparingly. Serve with roasted potato wedges.

SALSA:
  1 cup cilantro leaves
  1 cup flat-leaf parsley leaves
  3 tablespoons water
  2 tablespoons extravirgin olive oil
  1 tablespoon fresh lime juice
  2 teaspoons capers, rinsed and drained
  1 teaspoon Dijon mustard
  3 cornichons
  1 garlic clove, peeled

STEAK:
  1 (1½-pound) flank steak, trimmed
  ½ teaspoon salt
  ½ teaspoon freshly ground black pepper
  Cooking spray

1. Preheat broiler.

2. To prepare salsa, place first 9 ingredients in a food processor; process until smooth, scraping sides of bowl occasionally. Place salsa in a bowl; cover and set aside.

3. To prepare steak, sprinkle both sides evenly with salt and pepper. Place on a broiler pan coated with cooking spray; broil 6 minutes on each side or until desired degree of doneness. Cut steak diagonally across grain into thin slices; serve with salsa. Yield: 6 servings (serving size: 3 ounces steak and about 1 tablespoon salsa).

CALORIES 279 (46% from fat); FAT 14.3g (sat 4.6g, mono 7.4g, poly 0.8g); PROTEIN 32g; CARB 3.9g; FIBER 0.3g; CHOL 62mg; IRON 2.9mg; SODIUM 364mg; CALC 37mg

Quinoa Salad with Toasted Pistachios and Dried Pineapple

Fluffy quinoa offers a crunchy texture to this filling salad. Closely related to Swiss chard and spinach, quinoa is a good source of protein, fiber, and iron. Toast the quinoa before cooking if you prefer a nuttier flavor.

1½ cups water
¾ cup uncooked quinoa
¼ cup shelled, chopped pistachios (about 1 ounce)
2 cups rotisserie chicken breast, chopped
⅓ cup chopped green onions
⅓ cup chopped dried pineapple
1 tablespoon toasted sesame oil
1½ teaspoons bottled ground fresh ginger (such as Spice World)
½ teaspoon ground cumin
½ teaspoon salt
¼ teaspoon crushed red pepper

1. Bring water to a boil in a small saucepan. Add quinoa. Cover, reduce heat, and simmer 12 minutes.
2. Heat a small skillet over medium-high heat. Add pistachios, and cook 2 minutes or until lightly toasted, stirring frequently. Transfer pistachios to a large bowl; add cooked quinoa, chicken, and remaining ingredients. Toss gently. Yield: 4 servings (serving size: 1 cup).

CALORIES 344 (28% from fat); FAT 10.7g (sat 1.6g, mono 4.7g, poly 3.7g); PROTEIN 27g; CARB 32.5g; FIBER 3.7g; CHOL 60mg; IRON 3.2mg; SODIUM 362mg; CALC 42mg

Soft Black Bean Tostadas

Turn this dish into a quick vegetarian-friendly one by omitting the chicken.

SALSA:
½ cup chopped peeled avocado
½ cup chopped seeded tomato
¼ cup thinly sliced green onions
2 teaspoons fresh lime juice
¼ teaspoon salt

REMAINING INGREDIENTS:
2 tablespoons water
2 tablespoons fresh lime juice
½ teaspoon ground cumin
⅛ teaspoon salt
⅛ teaspoon ground red pepper
1 (15-ounce) can black beans, rinsed and drained
4 (8-inch) flour tortillas
1 cup shredded roasted skinless, boneless chicken breast
¾ cup (3 ounces) preshredded Monterey Jack cheese
1 cup shredded iceberg lettuce
½ cup fat-free sour cream

1. Preheat broiler.
2. To prepare salsa, combine first 5 ingredients in a small bowl. Toss gently, and set aside.
3. Place 2 tablespoons water and next 5 ingredients in a blender; process until smooth.
4. Place tortillas on a baking sheet, and spread about ¼ cup black bean mixture over each tortilla. Top each with ¼ cup chicken and 3 tablespoons cheese. Broil 2 minutes or until cheese melts and tortilla edges are just beginning to brown.
5. Top each tortilla with ¼ cup lettuce, ¼ cup salsa, and 2 tablespoons sour cream. Cut each tortilla into 4 wedges. Yield: 4 servings (serving size: 1 tostada).

CALORIES 410 (32% from fat); FAT 14.4g (sat 5.9g, mono 5.9g, poly 1.4g); PROTEIN 25.3g; CARB 47.7g; FIBER 7.2g; CHOL 49mg; IRON 3.7mg; SODIUM 858mg; CALC 264mg

new american classics

Ham and Two-Cheese Spoon Bread

Neither a bread pudding nor a soufflé, spoon bread is beloved throughout the South as both a main course and side dish for breakfast, lunch, and dinner. We've given it new life with the addition of ham and Parmesan cheese.

Ham and Two-Cheese Spoon Bread

2¾ cups fat-free milk
2 teaspoons sugar
1 teaspoon dried thyme
⅛ teaspoon ground red pepper
¾ cup yellow cornmeal
2 large egg yolks, lightly beaten
Cooking spray
1 cup chopped onion
8 ounces 33%-less-sodium ham, diced
1 cup (4 ounces) shredded reduced-fat sharp Cheddar cheese
¼ cup (1 ounce) grated fresh Parmesan cheese
4 large egg whites

1. Preheat oven to 375°.
2. Combine first 4 ingredients in a medium saucepan over medium-high heat. When mixture begins to simmer, gradually add cornmeal in a slow, steady stream, stirring well with a whisk. Cook 3 minutes or until thickened and smooth, stirring constantly. Transfer cornmeal mixture to a large bowl. Add yolks, stirring with a whisk. Let mixture stand 10 minutes.
3. Heat a large nonstick skillet over medium-high heat. Coat pan with cooking spray. Add onion; sauté 6 minutes or until tender. Add to cornmeal mixture. Recoat pan with cooking spray. Add ham; sauté 5 minutes or until ham begins to brown. Add to cornmeal mixture. Stir cheeses into cornmeal mixture.
4. Beat egg whites with a mixer at high speed until stiff peaks form (do not overbeat). Gently stir one-third of egg whites into cornmeal mixture; gently fold in remaining egg whites. Using a rubber spatula, scrape cornmeal mixture into a 1½-quart soufflé or deep baking dish coated with cooking spray. Bake at 375° for 50 minutes or until puffed, golden brown, and just set in center. Serve immediately. Yield: 8 servings (serving size: about 1 cup).

CALORIES 201 (29% from fat); FAT 6.4g (sat 3.3g, mono 1.3g, poly 0.4g); PROTEIN 16.6g; CARB 18.3g; FIBER 1.3g; CHOL 78mg; IRON 1.1mg; SODIUM 586mg; CALC 219mg

Launching A Lunch Club

Take brown-bagging to a new level.

Hop on the bandwagon with the latest in lunchtime plans—lunch clubs. The following recipes are based on guidelines for nutritional balance from the Healthy Lunch Club at the Minneapolis-based furniture retailer Room and Board. The club offers quick, economical meals—with healthful food. Here's how it works: Every day three members each prepare enough lunch to feed 10 people. They follow a few guidelines. Each member's contribution should have no more than 500 calories and 15 grams of fat per serving, and should contain whole grains and at least one serving of fruits and vegetables. Once members have cooked, they take two weeks off from kitchen duty while the others take over. Most people spend about $40 to $50 to create the meals. Each of these recipes can serve at least 10 people. They might just inspire you and your coworkers to form your own lunch club, and make your workplace both healthier and tastier.

QUICK & EASY • MAKE AHEAD
Greek Bulgur Salad with Chicken

This dish plays off the traditional Greek salad. Bulgur and chicken make it substantial enough for lunch. The flavors meld slowly, so it's ideal to serve the following day.

4½   cups water
  3   cups uncooked medium bulgur
  ¾   cup fresh lemon juice (about 3 lemons), divided
  2   teaspoons salt, divided
2½   cups chopped skinless, boneless rotisserie chicken breast
2½   cups chopped peeled cucumber
  2   cups halved grape tomatoes
  1   cup chopped fresh parsley
  ½   cup thinly sliced fresh basil
  ½   cup finely chopped red onion
  ½   cup (2 ounces) crumbled feta cheese
  ¼   cup extravirgin olive oil
  ½   teaspoon black pepper
 10   kalamata olives, pitted and chopped

1. Combine water, bulgur, ½ cup juice, and 1 teaspoon salt in a large saucepan; bring to a boil over medium-high heat. Cover, reduce heat, and simmer 5 minutes. Remove from heat; let stand 15 minutes or until liquid is absorbed. Uncover and cool to room temperature.
2. Combine ¼ cup juice, 1 teaspoon salt, chicken, and remaining 9 ingredients in a large bowl; toss to combine. Add cooled bulgur mixture; toss well to combine. Cover and chill. Yield: 10 servings (serving size: about 1⅔ cups).

CALORIES 305 (33% from fat); FAT 11.1g (sat 2.7g, mono 6g, poly 1.5g); PROTEIN 16.7g; CARB 37.6g; FIBER 8.8g; CHOL 36mg; IRON 2.3mg; SODIUM 651mg; CALC 82mg

MAKE AHEAD
Rosemary Chicken Noodle Soup

Add the noodles to the soup just before serving. You can bring the noodles to work in a zip-top plastic bag. Make the soup the night before, cool to room temperature, and refrigerate; reheat in the microwave or in a slow cooker set on high.

  4   cups hot cooked whole wheat blend wide egg noodles (about 3½ cups uncooked)
  1   tablespoon olive oil
  2   teaspoons salt, divided
  8   cups water
  4   cups fat-free, less-sodium chicken broth
  2   cups chopped onion
  1   cup chopped celery
  2   tablespoons dried rosemary
1½   pounds skinless, boneless chicken thighs
1½   pounds skinless, boneless chicken breast
  1   (10-ounce) package preshredded carrot
  1   (8-ounce) package presliced mushrooms
  ⅓   cup finely chopped fresh parsley
  1   (6-ounce) package fresh baby spinach
  ¼   cup fresh lemon juice
  ½   teaspoon black pepper

1. Combine noodles, oil, and ½ teaspoon salt; toss well to coat.
2. Combine water and next 6 ingredients in a large Dutch oven; add ½ teaspoon salt. Bring to a boil. Cover, reduce heat, and simmer 30 minutes. Remove chicken from pan, and cool slightly. Shred chicken with 2 forks.
3. Add carrot and mushrooms to pan; bring to a boil. Reduce heat, and simmer 6 minutes or until carrot is tender. Add shredded chicken, parsley, spinach, and 1 teaspoon salt; cook 3 minutes or until spinach wilts. Stir in noodle mixture, lemon juice, and pepper. Cook 1 minute. Yield: 10 servings (serving size: 2 cups).

CALORIES 291 (17% from fat); FAT 5.6g (sat 1.2g, mono 2.2g, poly 1.4g); PROTEIN 34.5g; CARB 27.1g; FIBER 5.4g; CHOL 96mg; IRON 3.3mg; SODIUM 791mg; CALC 71mg

MAKE AHEAD • FREEZABLE

Garden-Style Lasagna

You can use onions, broccoli, and pre-chopped matchstick-cut carrots in addition to precooked noodles to speed up preparation. If you make the lasagna ahead, let it cool completely, then cover and chill. The next day, heat single servings in the microwave. Freeze leftovers for dinner.

Cooking spray
2 cups chopped onion
4 garlic cloves, minced
2 teaspoons olive oil, divided
2 cups chopped zucchini (about 8 ounces)
2 cups chopped yellow squash (about 8 ounces)
2 cups thinly sliced carrot (about 8 ounces)
2 cups chopped broccoli (about 6 ounces)
1 teaspoon salt, divided
½ cup all-purpose flour (about 2¼ ounces)
3½ cups 1% low-fat milk
1 cup (4 ounces) grated fresh Parmesan cheese, divided
¼ teaspoon freshly ground black pepper
Dash of nutmeg
1 (10-ounce) package frozen chopped spinach, thawed and drained
1½ cups 1% low-fat cottage cheese
2 cups (8 ounces) preshredded part-skim mozzarella cheese, divided
12 precooked lasagna noodles

1. Preheat oven to 375°.

2. Heat a large Dutch oven over medium-high heat. Coat pan with cooking spray. Add onion to pan; sauté 4 minutes or until lightly browned. Add garlic; sauté 1 minute. Spoon onion mixture into a large bowl.

3. Heat 1 teaspoon oil in pan over medium-high heat. Add zucchini and yellow squash; sauté 4 minutes or until tender and just beginning to brown. Add to onion mixture.

4. Heat 1 teaspoon oil in pan over medium-high heat. Add carrot; sauté

4 minutes or until tender. Add broccoli; sauté 4 minutes or until crisp-tender. Add to onion mixture. Sprinkle with ½ teaspoon salt; toss well.

5. Lightly spoon flour into a dry measuring cup; level with a knife. Place flour in a medium saucepan. Gradually add milk, stirring with a whisk until blended. Bring to a boil over medium heat; cook 2 minutes or until thick, stirring constantly. Remove from heat. Add ½ teaspoon salt, ½ cup Parmesan, pepper, and nutmeg; stir until smooth. Stir in spinach.

6. Combine cottage cheese and 1½ cups mozzarella; stir well. Spread ½ cup spinach mixture in bottom of a 13 x 9–inch baking dish coated with cooking spray. Arrange 4 noodles over spinach mixture in dish, and top with half of cottage cheese mixture (about 1½ cups), half of onion mixture (about 2½ cups), and about 1 cup spinach mixture. Repeat layers, ending with noodles. Spread remaining spinach mixture over noodles; sprinkle with ½ cup Parmesan and ½ cup mozzarella.

7. Cover and bake at 375° for 20 minutes. Uncover and bake an additional 20 minutes or until cheese is bubbly and beginning to brown. Let stand 10 minutes before serving. Yield: 12 servings.

CALORIES 272 (27% from fat); FAT 8.3g (sat 4.4g, mono 2.5g, poly 0.5g); PROTEIN 18.5g; CARB 31.2g; FIBER 3.6g; CHOL 20mg; IRON 1.4mg; SODIUM 589mg; CALC 456mg

MAKE AHEAD
Breadsticks Two Ways

Serve these alongside soups or salads. You can make the entire batch with just one of the toppings, if you prefer.

  1 (11-ounce) can refrigerated soft breadstick dough
  2 tablespoons reduced-fat shredded Cheddar cheese
  1 tablespoon diced pickled jalapeño peppers
  2 tablespoons grated fresh Parmesan cheese
  1 tablespoon minced pitted kalamata olives

1. Preheat oven to 375°.

2. Unroll dough; cut in half crosswise. Sprinkle one dough half with Cheddar cheese and peppers; press lightly into dough. Cut dough half in half crosswise. Separate dough into 12 strips. Twist each piece into a 6-inch-long strip; place on a baking sheet.

3. Sprinkle Parmesan and olives over second half of dough; press lightly into dough. Cut dough half in half crosswise. Separate dough into 12 strips. Twist each piece into a 6-inch-long strip; place on a second baking sheet. Bake breadsticks at 375° for 12 minutes or until golden brown. Cool on wire racks. Yield: 24 breadsticks (serving size: 2 breadsticks).

CALORIES 83 (23% from fat); FAT 2.1g (sat 0.7g, mono 0.6g, poly 0.5g); PROTEIN 2.6g; CARB 12.8g; FIBER 0.4g; CHOL 1mg; IRON 0.8mg; SODIUM 247mg; CALC 20mg

MAKE AHEAD
Black Pepper Corn Bread

To keep the bread moist, seal the cooled bread in plastic wrap, and don't slice it until you're ready to serve.

  ⅓ cup all-purpose flour (about 1½ ounces)
1⅓ cups cornmeal
  2 teaspoons baking powder
  ¾ teaspoon salt, divided
  ½ teaspoon coarsely ground black pepper
  1 cup frozen corn kernels, thawed
  1 cup fat-free milk
  3 tablespoons butter, melted and divided
  2 tablespoons honey
  3 large eggs
    Cooking spray

1. Preheat oven to 400°.

2. Lightly spoon flour into a dry measuring cup; level with a knife. Combine flour, cornmeal, baking powder, ½ teaspoon salt, and pepper in a large bowl; stir well with a whisk.

3. Place corn and milk in a blender or food processor; process until smooth. Add 2 tablespoons butter, honey, and eggs; process until combined. Add milk mixture to cornmeal mixture; stir just until combined.

4. Spoon batter into a 13 x 9–inch baking dish coated with cooking spray. Bake at 400° for 15 minutes or until a wooden pick inserted in center comes out clean. Cool in pan 5 minutes on a wire rack. Lightly brush corn bread with 1 tablespoon butter; sprinkle evenly with ¼ teaspoon salt. Serve warm, or cool completely in pan on a wire rack. Yield: 12 servings (serving size: 1 piece).

CALORIES 144 (28% from fat); FAT 4.5g (sat 1.9g, mono 1.8g, poly 0.5g); PROTEIN 4.4g; CARB 22g; FIBER 1.6g; CHOL 61mg; IRON 1.2mg; SODIUM 278mg; CALC 80mg

MAKE AHEAD
Hearty Beef and Potato Stew

    Cooking spray
16 garlic cloves, crushed
  2 cups chopped onion
  3 pounds boneless chuck roast, trimmed and cut into 2-inch cubes, divided
  1 cup dry red wine
1½ cups chopped carrot
  2 teaspoons chopped fresh rosemary
1¾ teaspoons salt
  ½ teaspoon black pepper
  2 bay leaves
1¼ cups water, divided
  1 cup less-sodium beef broth
  2 (14.5-ounce) cans diced tomatoes, undrained
2½ pounds peeled baking potatoes, cut into 1-inch pieces
  1 tablespoon flour
    Chopped parsley (optional)
  2 (8-ounce) baguettes, each cut into 6 equal portions

1. Preheat oven to 300°.

2. Heat a large Dutch oven over medium-high heat. Coat pan with cooking spray. Add garlic; sauté 1 minute or until garlic just begins to brown. Remove garlic from pan with a slotted spoon; place in a large bowl. Coat pan with cooking spray. Add onion; sauté 3 minutes or until tender. Add onion to garlic. Coat pan with cooking spray. Add half of beef to pan; sauté 5 minutes or until browned on all sides. Add browned beef and any accumulated

Continued

juices to onion mixture. Coat pan with cooking spray. Add remaining beef to pan; sauté 5 minutes or until browned on all sides. Add beef and any accumulated juices to onion mixture.

3. Add wine to pan; bring to a boil, scraping pan to loosen browned bits. Add beef mixture. Stir in carrot, rosemary, salt, pepper, and bay leaves. Stir in 1 cup water, broth, and tomatoes. Bring to a boil; cook 1 minute. Remove from heat; cover and bake at 300° for 1½ hours. Remove from oven; uncover and stir in potatoes. Combine ¼ cup water and flour; stir with a whisk until smooth. Stir flour mixture into stew. Cover and bake an additional 1½ hours or until beef is tender. Discard bay leaves. Sprinkle with parsley, if desired. Serve with bread. Yield: 12 servings (serving size: about 1 cup stew and 1 portion bread).

CALORIES 440 (29% from fat); FAT 14.3g (sat 5.4g, mono 6.1g, poly 0.9g); PROTEIN 28.4g; CARB 45.9g; FIBER 4g; CHOL 64mg; IRON 4.5mg; SODIUM 753mg; CALC 97mg

Pesto Chicken Salad Sandwiches

(pictured on page 228)

Substitute baguettes for focaccia, if you want. Prepare the chicken salad at home the night before, then assemble the sandwiches at work the next day.

½ cup low-fat mayonnaise
⅓ cup plain fat-free yogurt
⅓ cup commercial pesto (such as Buitoni)
1½ tablespoons fresh lemon juice
½ teaspoon salt
½ teaspoon black pepper
4 cups cubed skinless, boneless rotisserie chicken breast
1 cup diced celery
⅓ cup chopped walnuts, toasted
1 (1-pound) focaccia bread, cut in half horizontally, toasted, and cut into 20 slices
1 (12-ounce) bottle roasted red bell peppers, drained and chopped
10 romaine lettuce leaves

1. Combine first 6 ingredients in a large

bowl, stirring with a whisk. Stir in chicken, celery, and walnuts.

2. Spread ½ cup salad onto each of 10 bread slices. Top each serving with about 2 tablespoons bell pepper, 1 lettuce leaf, and one bread slice. Yield: 10 servings (serving size: 1 sandwich).

CALORIES 324 (28% from fat); FAT 10g (sat 1.2g, mono 0.6g, poly 2.2g); PROTEIN 26.4g; CARB 31.6g; FIBER 1.6g; CHOL 55mg; IRON 2.3mg; SODIUM 725mg; CALC 39mg

MAKE AHEAD

Chicken Enchilada Casserole

Make ahead; microwave servings to reheat.

1 tablespoon canola oil
1 cup prechopped fresh onion
1½ teaspoons ground cumin
1 teaspoon chili powder
¼ teaspoon garlic salt
Dash of ground red pepper
2 (15.5-ounce) cans Great Northern beans, rinsed and drained
2 cups shredded skinless, boneless rotisserie chicken
1 cup thinly sliced green onions, divided
½ cup sliced ripe olives, divided
18 (6-inch) corn tortillas
Cooking spray
2 cups (8 ounces) preshredded reduced-fat 4-cheese Mexican blend cheese, divided
1 cup 1% low-fat milk
½ cup chopped fresh cilantro
1 (16-ounce) jar green salsa
10 tablespoons reduced-fat sour cream
Cilantro sprigs (optional)

1. Heat oil in a large nonstick skillet over medium heat. Add prechopped onion; cook 3 minutes or until tender, stirring frequently. Stir in cumin, chili powder, garlic salt, and pepper; cook 1 minute. Stir in beans; cook 2 minutes. Remove from heat. Add shredded chicken, ½ cup green onions, and 7 tablespoons ripe olives; stir well.

2. Preheat oven to 350°.

3. Layer 6 tortillas on bottom of a 13 x 9–inch baking dish coated with cooking spray. Spread 2 cups chicken mixture over

tortillas; sprinkle with ¾ cup cheese. Repeat layers once. Top with remaining 6 tortillas.

4. Place milk, chopped cilantro, and salsa in a blender, and process until smooth. Pour over top of tortillas. Cover and bake at 350° for 35 minutes. Uncover, sprinkle with ½ cup cheese, ½ cup green onions, and 1 tablespoon olives. Bake 5 minutes or until cheese melts. Serve with sour cream. Garnish with cilantro sprigs, if desired. Yield: 10 servings (serving size: 1 casserole slice and 1 tablespoon sour cream).

CALORIES 353 (30% from fat); FAT 11.8g (sat 4.2g, mono 4.2g, poly 1.8g); PROTEIN 23.5g; CARB 45.8g; FIBER 7.9g; CHOL 45mg; IRON 2.5mg; SODIUM 734mg; CALC 396mg

MAKE AHEAD

Mac and Cheese with Roasted Tomatoes

Cooking spray
8 plum tomatoes, cut into ¼-inch-thick slices (about 2 pounds)
1 tablespoon olive oil
1 tablespoon minced fresh thyme
¾ teaspoon salt, divided
4 garlic cloves, thinly sliced
1 pound uncooked multigrain whole wheat elbow macaroni (such as Barilla Plus)
½ cup all-purpose flour (about 2¼ ounces)
5 cups 1% low-fat milk
1½ cups (6 ounces) shredded extrasharp white Cheddar cheese
1 cup (4 ounces) shredded fontina cheese
½ teaspoon black pepper
½ cup (2 ounces) grated fresh Parmesan cheese
⅓ cup dry breadcrumbs
½ teaspoon paprika

1. Preheat oven to 400°.

2. Cover a baking sheet with aluminum foil, and coat foil with cooking spray. Arrange tomato slices in a single layer on baking sheet. Drizzle oil over tomatoes. Sprinkle with thyme, ¼ teaspoon salt, and garlic. Bake at 400° for 35 minutes or until tomatoes start to dry out.

3. Cook pasta according to package directions, omitting salt and fat. Drain well.

4. Lightly spoon flour into a dry measuring cup; level with a knife. Place flour in a large Dutch oven; gradually add milk, stirring with a whisk until blended. Cook over medium heat 8 minutes or until thick and bubbly, stirring constantly with a whisk. Add ½ teaspoon salt, Cheddar, fontina, and pepper, stirring until cheese melts. Remove from heat. Stir in tomatoes and pasta. Spoon into a 13 x 9–inch baking dish coated with cooking spray. Combine Parmesan cheese, breadcrumbs, and paprika; sprinkle over pasta mixture. Bake at 400° for 25 minutes or until bubbly. Yield: 10 servings (serving size: about 1 cup).

CALORIES 411 (31% from fat); FAT 14g (sat 6.9g, mono 2.9g, poly 0.9g); PROTEIN 22.8g; CARB 49.9g; FIBER 4.7g; CHOL 39mg; IRON 2.5mg; SODIUM 638mg; CALC 414mg

Cuban-Style Red Beans and Rice

A classic Latin *sofrito*—pork fat, tomato paste, onion, garlic, bell pepper, herbs, and spices—gives this dish complexity. Prepare it the night before, cool to room temperature, and refrigerate; reheat single servings in the microwave the next day. Serve with Black Pepper Corn Bread (recipe on page 59).

    8 bacon slices
    1 teaspoon olive oil
 1½ cups chopped onion
 1½ cups chopped green bell pepper
        (about 1 medium)
    4 garlic cloves, minced
    2 tablespoons tomato paste
    2 cups uncooked long-grain rice
 1½ teaspoons dried oregano
 1½ teaspoons ground cumin
    1 teaspoon salt
   ½ teaspoon black pepper
    1 bay leaf
    2 cups water
    3 (14-ounce) cans fat-free, less-
        sodium chicken broth, divided
    3 (16-ounce) cans red beans, rinsed
        and drained
  Sliced green onions (optional)

1. Cook bacon in a Dutch oven over medium heat until crisp. Remove bacon from pan, reserving 1 tablespoon drippings in pan; crumble bacon, and set aside. Add oil to pan. Add onion and bell pepper; sauté over medium-high heat 4 minutes or until onion is tender. Add garlic; sauté 1 minute or just until garlic begins to brown. Add tomato paste; cook 1 minute, stirring constantly. Add rice and next 4 ingredients; cook 2 minutes, stirring constantly.

2. Add reserved bacon and bay leaf to pan; stir in water and 2 cans broth. Bring to a boil; cover, reduce heat, and simmer 20 minutes or until rice is tender. Remove from heat; discard bay leaf. Stir in third can of broth and beans. Cook 5 minutes over low heat or until thoroughly heated, stirring frequently. Garnish with green onions, if desired. Yield: 10 servings (serving size: about 1⅓ cups).

CALORIES 287 (11% from fat); FAT 4.5g (sat 1.3g, mono 1.9g, poly 0.5g); PROTEIN 11.8g; CARB 49.3g; FIBER 7.5g; CHOL 7mg; IRON 2.1mg; SODIUM 883mg; CALC 25mg

Chicken Muffuletta

This make-ahead sandwich is a lighter take on an old New Orleans favorite. Use a fork to scrape the bread and hollow the loaves.

    3 cups chopped seeded tomato
        (about 2 medium)
  Cooking spray
    8 cups diced peeled eggplant (about
        1 pound)
 1½ cups chopped onion
    2 teaspoons chopped fresh thyme
   ¼ teaspoon black pepper
 1⅓ cups chopped pimiento-stuffed
        olives (about 7 ounces)
   ⅔ cup (2 ounces) chopped reduced-
        fat hard salami
   ¼ cup chopped pepperoncini (about
        5 medium)
    1 tablespoon olive oil
    1 tablespoon balsamic vinegar
    4 ounces sharp provolone cheese,
        finely diced (about 1 cup)
    4 (8-ounce) loaves French bread
    1 pound skinless, boneless rotisserie
        chicken breast, thinly sliced

1. Spread tomato evenly onto several layers of heavy-duty paper towels. Cover with additional paper towels; let stand 10 minutes.

2. Heat a large nonstick skillet over medium-high heat. Coat pan with cooking spray. Add eggplant and onion, and sauté 10 minutes or until eggplant is tender and beginning to brown. Stir in thyme and pepper; cook 1 minute, stirring occasionally. Spoon eggplant mixture into a large bowl.

3. Coat pan with cooking spray. Add tomato; cook 2 minutes, stirring frequently. Stir tomato into eggplant mixture. Cool to room temperature.

4. Stir olives and next 5 ingredients into eggplant mixture.

5. Cut bread loaves in half horizontally. Hollow out top and bottom halves of bread, leaving ½-inch-thick shells; reserve torn bread for another use. Spread about 3 tablespoons olive mixture over bottom half of each loaf. Arrange sliced chicken evenly on bottom halves. Top chicken evenly with remaining olive mixture; cover with top halves of loaves. Wrap loaves with plastic wrap; refrigerate up to 24 hours. Cut each loaf into 3 pieces just before serving. Yield: 12 servings (serving size: 1 piece).

CALORIES 329 (22% from fat); FAT 8.2g (sat 2.8g, mono 2.7g, poly 0.7g); PROTEIN 21.7g; CARB 44.9g; FIBER 3.1g; CHOL 45mg; IRON 3.1mg; SODIUM 1,004mg; CALC 96mg

Make your workplace more healthful and happy by launching a lunch club today!

Black Bean-Quinoa Salad with Basil-Lemon Dressing

Edamame makes a tasty substitute for lima beans in this recipe. For an attractive presentation, serve the salad on a bed of baby greens or spinach.

1½ cups uncooked quinoa
  3 cups organic vegetable broth (such as Swanson Certified Organic)
  1 (14-ounce) package reduced-fat firm tofu, cut into ¼-inch cubes
  3 tablespoons olive oil, divided
1¼ teaspoons salt, divided
  1 cup chopped fresh basil
  2 teaspoons grated lemon rind
  3 tablespoons fresh lemon juice
  2 tablespoons Dijon mustard
  1 teaspoon sugar
  ½ teaspoon freshly ground black pepper
  3 garlic cloves, minced
  1 (10-ounce) package frozen baby lima beans
  4 cups chopped tomato (about 3 medium)
  ½ cup sliced green onions
  ½ cup chopped carrot
  1 (15-ounce) can black beans, rinsed and drained

1. Combine quinoa and broth in a saucepan; bring to a boil over medium-high heat. Cover, reduce heat, and simmer 15 minutes or until broth is absorbed and quinoa is tender. Remove from heat.
2. Place tofu on several layers of paper towels; cover with additional paper towels. Let stand 5 minutes. Heat 1 tablespoon oil in a large nonstick skillet over medium-high heat. Add tofu; sprinkle with ¼ teaspoon salt. Sauté 9 minutes or until lightly browned. Remove from heat; cool completely.
3. Combine 2 tablespoons oil, 1 teaspoon salt, basil, and next 6 ingredients in a large bowl; stir with a whisk until blended. Stir in quinoa.
4. Cook lima beans according to package directions, omitting salt and fat. Cool completely. Add lima beans, tofu, tomato, onions, carrot, and beans to quinoa mixture; stir gently to combine. Store, covered, in refrigerator until ready to serve. Yield: 10 servings (serving size: 1 cup).

CALORIES 232 (24% from fat); FAT 6.2g (sat 0.6g, mono 3.7g, poly 1.2g); PROTEIN 9.8g; CARB 35.1g; FIBER 6.7g; CHOL 0mg; IRON 3.8mg; SODIUM 722mg; CALC 68mg

Oat-Topped Fig Muffins

1½ cups all-purpose flour (about 6¾ ounces)
  1 cup whole wheat pastry flour (about 5⅛ ounces)
  ½ cup sugar
  1 teaspoon baking powder
  1 teaspoon baking soda
  ½ teaspoon salt
1½ cups low-fat buttermilk
1¼ cups chopped dried figs
  2 tablespoons canola oil
  1 teaspoon vanilla extract
  1 large egg
Cooking spray
  ⅓ cup packed brown sugar
  ¼ cup quick-cooking oats
  1 tablespoon butter

1. Preheat oven to 400°.
2. Lightly spoon flours into measuring cups; level with a knife. Combine flours, sugar, and next 3 ingredients in a large bowl; stir with a whisk. Make a well in center of mixture.
3. Place buttermilk, figs, oil, vanilla, and egg in a food processor; process until well blended. Add fig mixture to flour mixture, stirring just until combined. Spoon batter into 12 muffin cups coated with cooking spray.
4. Combine brown sugar, oats, and butter in a small bowl; toss with a fork until combined. Sprinkle oat mixture evenly over muffins. Bake at 400° for 18 minutes or until a wooden pick inserted in center of a muffin comes out clean. Cool in pans on a wire rack 5 minutes; remove muffins from pans, and cool completely on rack. Yield: 12 muffins (serving size: 1 muffin).

CALORIES 83 (23% from fat); FAT 2.1g (sat 0.7g, mono 0.6g, poly 0.5g); PROTEIN 2.6g; CARB 12.8g; FIBER 0.4g; CHOL 1mg; IRON 0.8mg; SODIUM 247mg; CALC 20mg

Smoked Mozzarella, Bacon, and Tomato Strata

This savory bread pudding needs to stand overnight. Bake it while you get ready for work in the morning. For less smoky flavor, use regular mozzarella cheese or Cheddar.

3½ cups 1% low-fat milk
1¼ cups part-skim ricotta cheese (such as Sargento)
  ⅓ cup chopped fresh cilantro
  1 teaspoon salt
  ½ teaspoon freshly ground black pepper
  ½ teaspoon ground cumin
  5 large eggs, lightly beaten
1½ cups diced plum tomato
1½ cups fresh or frozen corn kernels
1¼ cups thinly sliced green onions, divided
  ½ teaspoon ground coriander
  1 (16-ounce) loaf multigrain bread, cubed
Cooking spray
  1 cup (4 ounces) shredded smoked mozzarella cheese
  4 slices bacon, cooked and chopped

1. Combine first 7 ingredients; stir with a whisk until well blended.
2. Combine tomato, corn, 1 cup green onions, and coriander.
3. Arrange half of bread cubes in bottom of a 13 x 9–inch baking dish coated with cooking spray. Sprinkle evenly with half of tomato mixture, ½ cup cheese, and half of bacon. Pour half of milk mixture over top. Repeat procedure with remaining bread, tomato mixture, and milk mixture. Sprinkle with ½ cup cheese, remaining bacon, and ¼ cup green onions. Cover and refrigerate 8 hours or overnight.
4. Preheat oven to 350°.
5. Uncover strata. Bake at 350° for 50 minutes or until set. Yield: 10 servings.

CALORIES 309 (26% from fat); FAT 9g (sat 4.5g, mono 2.7g, poly 0.7g); PROTEIN 17.5g; CARB 41.5g; FIBER 2.3g; CHOL 130mg; IRON 2.4mg; SODIUM 778mg; CALC 254mg

Shrimp and Tofu Pad Thai

Pad thai is perhaps the best-known Thai dish to Americans. Slightly under-cooking the noodles will preserve their texture when reheating them the next day. Cook this dish the night before, cool to room temperature, and refrigerate; reheat single servings in the microwave the next day.

  2 tablespoons peanut oil, divided
  1 pound extrafirm tofu, drained and cut into ½-inch cubes
  2 cups finely shredded napa (Chinese) cabbage
  6 tablespoons rice vinegar
 ¼ cup Thai fish sauce (such as Three Crabs)
  3 tablespoons brown sugar
  2 tablespoons ketchup
  2 tablespoons creamy peanut butter
  1 tablespoon lime juice
  1 teaspoon chili garlic sauce (such as Lee Kum Kee)
 ¼ cup water
  1 teaspoon cornstarch
  1 pound medium shrimp, cooked and peeled
  2 cups thinly sliced green onions
 ½ cup chopped fresh cilantro
  1 pound uncooked wide rice noodles (*bánh pho*)

1. Heat 1 tablespoon oil in a large non-stick skillet over medium-high heat. Add tofu; sauté 4 minutes or until lightly browned on all sides. Spoon tofu into a large bowl. Add cabbage to pan; sauté 30 seconds or until just beginning to wilt. Add cabbage to tofu. Remove pan from heat.
2. Combine vinegar and next 6 ingredients. Combine water and cornstarch, stirring with a whisk; stir into vinegar mixture.
3. Heat 1 tablespoon oil in pan over medium-high heat. Add shrimp; sauté 1 minute. Add vinegar mixture; bring to a boil, and cook 1 minute, stirring frequently. Add shrimp mixture, green onions, and cilantro to cabbage mixture; toss to combine.
4. Cook noodles according to package directions, omitting salt and fat. Drain well. Add noodles to cabbage mixture; toss well. Yield: 10 servings (serving size: about 1½ cups).

CALORIES 339 (21% from fat); FAT 7.8g (sat 1.5g, mono 2.7g, poly 3.2g); PROTEIN 16.8g; CARB 48.8g; FIBER 2g; CHOL 88mg; IRON 2.7mg; SODIUM 819mg; CALC 80mg

enlightened cook

Pure and Simple Cuisine

Chef and author Michel Nischan's family garden inspires his cooking and his readers.

All gardens are special. But some, like the backyard garden of chef and cookbook author Michel Nischan, are more special than most. It's the inspiration for his new cookbook, *Homegrown Pure and Simple: Great Healthy Food from Garden to Table*, the follow-up to his first book, the James Beard Award–winning *Taste Pure and Simple: Irresistible Recipes for Good Food and Good Health.* Here are some of Nischan's recipes.

Shiitake Mushroom Rice Cakes

Use a pair of kitchen shears to cut up the dried mushrooms; it's easier than using a knife. You can substitute olive or canola oil for grapeseed oil.

1½ cups boiling water
  1 ounce dried shiitake mushrooms, chopped
  3 tablespoons grapeseed oil, divided
 ¼ cup minced shallots
  2 cups diced fresh shiitake mushroom caps (about 4 ounces)
  1 cup uncooked sushi rice
 ¾ cup sake
 ¼ cup low-sodium soy sauce
  1 cup water
 ¼ cup thinly sliced green onions
Cooking spray
 ½ cup panko (Japanese breadcrumbs)
  2 tablespoons black sesame seeds

1. Place boiling water and dried mushrooms in a small bowl. Cover and let stand 30 minutes. Drain mushrooms, reserving liquid.
2. Heat 1 tablespoon oil in a large saucepan over medium heat. Add shallots to pan; sauté 2 minutes or until tender. Add fresh and rehydrated mushrooms to pan; cook 5 minutes or until tender. Add rice to pan; cook 2 minutes, stirring constantly. Stir in sake; cook 3 minutes or until liquid is nearly absorbed, stirring constantly. Stir in ½ cup reserved mushroom liquid and soy sauce; cook 3 minutes or until liquid is nearly absorbed, stirring constantly. Add remaining mushroom liquid, ½ cup at a time, stirring constantly until each portion of liquid is absorbed before adding the next. Add 1 cup water, ¼ cup at a time, stirring constantly until each portion of water is absorbed before adding the next (about 16 minutes total). Stir in green onions.
3. Form 9 cakes using a ⅓ cup dry measuring cup coated with cooking spray. Place cakes on a platter. Cover and chill 3 hours.
4. Remove from refrigerator. Place panko in a shallow bowl. Place sesame seeds in a shallow bowl. Dredge each cake in panko on one side and sesame seeds on other side.
5. Heat 1 tablespoon oil in a large non-stick skillet over medium-high heat. Add 5 cakes to pan; cook 3 minutes on each side or until lightly browned. Transfer to a platter. Repeat procedure with 1 tablespoon oil and remaining cakes. Yield: 9 servings (serving size: 1 cake).

CALORIES 185 (28% from fat); FAT 5.7g (sat 0.5g, mono 0.8g, poly 3.2g); PROTEIN 3.1g; CARB 23.7g; FIBER 1.1g; CHOL 0mg; IRON 4.2mg; SODIUM 252mg; CALC 8mg

Strawberry Mint Sauce

This luscious strawberry sauce is delicious drizzled over vanilla ice cream, pound cake, or biscuits. If you can find lemon verbena in local markets, it's a great substitute for mint. Use any type of good-quality local honey that's available.

    2   cups chopped strawberries (about
        1 pint)
    ½   cup honey
    ¼   cup fresh mint leaves
    2   tablespoons fresh lemon juice

1. Place strawberries, honey, and mint in a small saucepan. Bring to a simmer over medium heat; cook 1 minute or until honey dissolves. Place strawberry mixture in a blender or food processor; process until smooth. Strain through a fine sieve into a bowl; discard solids. Stir in lemon juice. Yield: 1¾ cups (serving size: about ¼ cup).

CALORIES 80 (2% from fat); FAT 0.2g (sat 0g, mono 0g, poly 0.1g); PROTEIN 0.5g; CARB 21.2g; FIBER 0.6g; CHOL 0mg; IRON 0.6mg; SODIUM 2mg; CALC 14mg

Grilled Herbed Pork Tenderloin

    ¼   cup fresh oregano leaves
    ¼   cup fresh sage leaves
    ¼   cup fresh orange juice
    ¼   cup honey
    2   tablespoons grated lemon rind
    2   tablespoons grapeseed oil
    1   tablespoon coarsely ground black
        pepper
    ¼   teaspoon salt
    6   garlic cloves, peeled
    2   (1-pound) pork tenderloins, trimmed
    ¼   teaspoon salt
    Cooking spray

1. Place first 9 ingredients in a blender or food processor; process until almost smooth. Pour mixture into a large heavy-duty, zip-top plastic bag. Add pork to bag; seal. Marinate in refrigerator 2 hours, turning bag occasionally.
2. Prepare grill.

3. Remove pork from marinade. Discard marinade. Sprinkle pork with ¼ teaspoon salt. Place pork on grill rack coated with cooking spray; cover and grill 25 minutes or until a thermometer registers 155° (slightly pink), turning pork after 15 minutes. Let stand 10 minutes before cutting into slices. Yield: 8 servings (serving size: 3 ounces pork).

CALORIES 214 (24% from fat); FAT 5.8g (sat 1.5g, mono 2g, poly 1.6g); PROTEIN 24.4g; CARB 15.7g; FIBER 0.3g; CHOL 74mg; IRON 1.6mg; SODIUM 168mg; CALC 29mg

Seared Tuna and Radish Salad with Wasabi Dressing

SALAD:
    ½   cup fresh snow peas
    1   cup torn Bibb lettuce
    1   cup thinly sliced radishes (about 4
        ounces)
    2   tablespoons chopped fresh mint
    2   tablespoons chopped fresh cilantro
    2   tablespoons radish sprouts
    1½ tablespoons fresh lemon juice
    1½ tablespoons mirin (sweet rice wine)
    1   teaspoon canola oil
    4   (6-ounce) sushi-grade tuna steaks
    ½   teaspoon kosher salt

DRESSING:
    3   tablespoons silken tofu
    1½ tablespoons wasabi powder
    1   tablespoon rice vinegar
    1   tablespoon fresh lemon juice
    1   tablespoon mirin (sweet rice wine)
    5   tablespoons water

1. To prepare salad, cook snow peas in boiling water 3 minutes or until crisp-tender. Drain and rinse with cold water; drain. Cut peas crosswise into thin slices. Combine peas, lettuce, and next 6 ingredients in a medium bowl; set aside.
2. Heat oil in a large nonstick skillet over medium-high heat. Sprinkle fish with salt. Add fish to pan; cook 2 minutes on each side or until desired degree of doneness. Let stand 2 minutes. Cut into ¼-inch-thick slices.
3. To prepare dressing, place tofu and next 4 ingredients in a food processor,

and process until smooth. With processor on, slowly pour water through food chute; process until well blended. Serve fish over salad; drizzle with dressing just before serving. Yield: 4 servings (serving size: 5 ounces fish, ¾ cup salad, and 2 tablespoons dressing).

CALORIES 280 (12% from fat); FAT 3.6g (sat 0.5g, mono 1g, poly 1g); PROTEIN 41.8g; CARB 10.7g; FIBER 1.1g; CHOL 77mg; IRON 2.2mg; SODIUM 428mg; CALC 64mg

Oven-Roasted Tomatoes with Goat Cheese

"I like to dry my own tomatoes," says Michel Nischan. "That way, I can control the moisture content and have tomatoes that are moist, meaty, and syrupy with the concentrated flavor of sun-dried tomatoes. Ripe peaches, figs, cherries, apricots, and nectarines can also be dried using this method." Use good-quality aged balsamic vinegar to bring out the sweetness of the fruit.

    6   tomatoes, halved (about 1¼ pounds)
    2   tablespoons extravirgin olive oil,
        divided
    1   tablespoon balsamic vinegar
    ½   teaspoon kosher salt
    ¼   teaspoon freshly ground black
        pepper
    2   tablespoons crumbled goat cheese
    12 rosemary sprigs

1. Preheat oven to 200°.
2. Place a wire rack over a baking sheet; set aside.
3. Combine tomatoes, 1 tablespoon oil, and vinegar; toss gently. Place tomatoes, cut sides up, on rack. Sprinkle with salt and pepper.
4. Bake at 200° for 6 hours or until tender and slightly syrupy (do not overbake or tomatoes will be tough and chewy). Remove from oven; cool completely. Place ½ teaspoon cheese on each tomato half. Fold slightly; secure each tomato half with 1 rosemary sprig. Place on a serving platter; drizzle with 1 tablespoon oil. Yield: 6 servings (serving size: 2 tomato halves).

CALORIES 88 (65% from fat); FAT 6.4g (sat 1.7g, mono 4g, poly 0.6g); PROTEIN 2.4g; CARB 6.5g; FIBER 1.9g; CHOL 4mg; IRON 0.5mg; SODIUM 189mg; CALC 31mg

Come to Your Senses

Smart cooks use all five senses in the kitchen. These examples show you how to let taste, touch, sight, smell, and sound guide your cooking.

Skillet Chicken Breast Aglio e Olio

Chicken benefits from the strong flavors of garlic, capers, and cherry peppers in the sauce for this dish. **TASTE** the sauce before serving to be sure the flavors are balanced. You can adjust the amount capers to suit your taste. Breadcrumbs serve as a thickener, lending the sauce body and texture. Serve with green beans and rice.

MAKE AHEAD
Curried Sunflower Brittle

If you use color changes as cooking cues for the sunflower seed kernels, curry powder, or sugar mixture, they might become overcooked and bitter. For this brittle you need to go with **SMELL**. Sugar has no scent until it begins to caramelize; the key to this recipe is adding sunflower seeds right at that point. Store in an airtight container up to one week.

Cooking spray
- 1 cup unsalted, untoasted sunflower seed kernels
- ½ teaspoon curry powder
- ⅛ teaspoon salt
- 1¼ cups sugar
- ¼ cup water
- 2 tablespoons light-colored corn syrup

1. Line a baking sheet with foil; coat foil with cooking spray. Coat flat surface of a metal spatula with cooking spray; set aside.
2. Heat a large nonstick skillet over medium-high heat. Add kernels; cook until they release a toasted aroma (about 3 minutes), stirring frequently. Place in a bowl; wipe pan with a paper towel.
3. Heat pan over medium-high heat. Add curry powder; cook until fragrant (about 30 seconds), stirring constantly. Add curry to kernels. Sprinkle with salt; stir to combine.
4. Combine sugar, water, and corn syrup in a saucepan. Bring mixture to a boil over medium-high heat, stirring occasionally until sugar dissolves. Continue to cook, without stirring, until first sign of caramel fragrance (about 3 minutes).
5. Remove from heat; stir in kernel mixture. Rapidly spread mixture to about ⅛-inch thickness onto prepared baking sheet using prepared spatula. Cool

completely; break into small pieces. Yield: 16 servings (serving size: 1 ounce).

CALORIES 111 (31% from fat); FAT 3.8g (sat 0.4g, mono 0.7g, poly 2.5g); PROTEIN 1.8g; CARB 19.2g; FIBER 0.8g; CHOL 0mg; IRON 0.5mg; SODIUM 24mg; CALC 11mg

Spanish-Style Shrimp with Garlic

(pictured on page 231)

To determine when the shrimp are done, **LOOK** for the characteristic pink or orange marks and check to see that the shrimp flesh has changed from translucent to opaque white. Serve this tapas-style dish with grilled bread, if desired.

- 1 tablespoon extravirgin olive oil
- ⅛ teaspoon ground red pepper
- 6 garlic cloves, thinly sliced
- 1 bay leaf
- 1 pound large shrimp, peeled and deveined
- ¼ teaspoon salt
- 2 tablespoons chopped fresh parsley
- 4 lemon wedges

1. Heat oil in a large nonstick skillet over medium heat. Add pepper, garlic, and bay leaf; cook 2 minutes, stirring constantly. Increase heat to medium-high. Add shrimp; sauté until shrimp have pink or orange markings and white, opaque flesh (about 4 minutes). Remove from heat. Sprinkle with salt. Discard bay leaf. Sprinkle with parsley, and serve with lemon wedges. Yield: 4 servings (serving size: ½ cup shrimp and 1 lemon wedge).

CALORIES 161 (31% from fat); FAT 5.5g (sat 0.9g, mono 3g, poly 1.1g); PROTEIN 23.4g; CARB 3.2g; FIBER 0.2g; CHOL 172mg; IRON 2.9mg; SODIUM 317mg; CALC 70mg

- 6 (6-ounce) skinless, boneless chicken breast halves
- ½ teaspoon salt, divided
- ⅓ cup all-purpose flour (about 1½ ounces)
- 2 tablespoons butter
- 1 tablespoon olive oil
- 8 garlic cloves, thinly sliced
- 2 to 3 tablespoons capers, drained
- 4 pickled hot cherry peppers, halved and seeded
- 1 cup organic vegetable broth (such as Swanson Certified Organic)
- 1 tablespoon dry breadcrumbs
- 3 tablespoons chopped fresh flat-leaf parsley

1. Sprinkle chicken with ¼ teaspoon salt. Dredge chicken in flour.
2. Heat butter and oil in a large nonstick skillet over medium heat. Add chicken; cook 4 minutes on each side or until browned. Add garlic; cook 30 seconds. Add capers and peppers; cook 30 seconds. Add broth; bring to a boil. Reduce heat, and simmer 5 minutes or until chicken is done. Stir in breadcrumbs; cook until liquid thickens (about 1 minute). Taste sauce, and add ¼ teaspoon salt, if needed. Remove from heat; sprinkle with parsley. Yield: 6 servings (serving size: 1 chicken breast half and about 2½ tablespoons sauce).

CALORIES 286 (27% from fat); FAT 8.5g (sat 3.3g, mono 3.3g, poly 0.9g); PROTEIN 40.9g; CARB 9.1g; FIBER 0.6g; CHOL 109mg; IRON 2mg; SODIUM 831mg; CALC 42mg

Beef Tenderloin Bruschetta with Brown Butter

Use **SOUND** to judge when the mustard seeds are ready. As with microwave popcorn, when a second of time passes between pops, the seeds are done.

½ cup diced mango
2 tablespoons chopped fresh cilantro
2 tablespoons lime juice
2 teaspoons finely chopped serrano chile
½ teaspoon sugar
¼ teaspoon salt
⅛ teaspoon ground turmeric
1½ teaspoons canola oil
½ teaspoon yellow mustard seeds, divided
1½ teaspoons butter, melted
Cooking spray
1 (4-ounce) beef tenderloin steak, trimmed (1 inch thick)
⅛ teaspoon salt
⅛ teaspoon pepper
16 (¼-ounce) diagonal slices French bread baguette, toasted (½ inch thick)

1. Combine first 7 ingredients in a small bowl; cover and let stand at room temperature 15 minutes.
2. Heat oil in a small nonstick skillet over medium-high heat. Add 1 mustard seed to pan; cook until seed pops (about 90 seconds). Add remaining seeds; stir to coat with oil. Cover and cook seeds 30 seconds or until they begin to pop, gently shaking the pan. Stir in butter and cover. Cook until 1 second passes between pops, shaking pan constantly (about 30 seconds). Remove from heat. Scrape mustard seed mixture into mango mixture; stir gently. Let stand 5 minutes.
3. Heat pan over medium-high heat. Coat pan with cooking spray. Sprinkle beef with ⅛ teaspoon salt and pepper. Add beef to pan; cook 3 minutes on each side or until desired degree of doneness. Let rest 5 minutes. Cut across grain into very thin slices.
4. Divide beef slices evenly among baguette slices. Top each bruschetta with 1½ teaspoons mango mixture. Serve immediately. Yield: 8 servings (serving size: 2 bruschetta).

CALORIES 88 (29% from fat); FAT 2.8g (sat 1g, mono 1.2g, poly 0.4g); PROTEIN 4.4g; CARB 12.1g; FIBER 0.6g; CHOL 11mg; IRON 0.9mg; SODIUM 216mg; CALC 5mg

QUICK & EASY
Pan-Grilled Flank Steak with Chermoula

While you can use **TOUCH** to determine steak doneness, **SIGHT** is also a useful tool. As steak passes from rare into medium rare, red juice beads begin to form on its surface. The juice flows more and turns pink as the steak heads toward medium. Steak cooked beyond medium releases brown juice. *Chermoula* is a versatile North African herb-and-spice sauce. Use a cast-iron grill pan for this dish, as a nonstick grill pan can't handle high heat.

CHERMOULA:
1 cup fresh parsley leaves
1 cup fresh cilantro leaves
3 tablespoons less-sodium beef broth
2 tablespoons fresh lime juice
1 tablespoon extravirgin olive oil
1 tablespoon paprika
1 teaspoon ground cumin
½ teaspoon ground coriander
¼ teaspoon salt
¼ teaspoon ground red pepper
2 garlic cloves, peeled

STEAK:
1 (1½-pound) flank steak, trimmed
¼ teaspoon salt
¼ teaspoon freshly ground black pepper
Cooking spray

1. To prepare chermoula, place first 11 ingredients in a food processor; process until finely chopped, scraping sides of bowl occasionally.
2. To prepare steak, sprinkle steak with ¼ teaspoon salt and black pepper. Heat a cast-iron grill pan over high heat. Coat pan with cooking spray. Cook steak 4 minutes; turn and look for red beads forming on surface to indicate steak is approaching medium rare. Cook 4 minutes or until desired degree of doneness. Let rest 5 minutes. Cut steak diagonally across grain into thin slices. Serve with sauce. Yield: 6 servings (servings size: 3 ounces steak and 1½ tablespoons sauce).

CALORIES 195 (41% from fat); FAT 8.9g (sat 2.7g, mono 4.1g, poly 0.5g); PROTEIN 25.3g; CARB 2.6g; FIBER 1.2g; CHOL 37mg; IRON 2.9mg; SODIUM 284mg; CALC 55mg

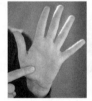  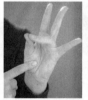

| Rare | Medium-Rare | Medium | Medium-well | Well-done |

Keep in Touch

When checking steaks for doneness, nothing is as accurate as a meat thermometer, says Kathryn Conrad, a member or the *Cooking Light* Test Kitchens staff. However, this touch test is easy and effective.

Shake one hand so it's completely relaxed. Conrad suggests that if you're a righty, shake your left hand; lefty, shake your right hand. Then, with the index finger of your other hand, gently press the soft part of your "test" hand just below the thumb. This is the feel of a rare steak.

Touch the thumb and forefinger together on your test hand, then press lightly below the thumb. This is how a medium-rare steak feels. Touch your thumb and middle finger of your test hand together: medium steak. Touch your thumb to the ring finger: medium-well steak. Touch your thumb to your pinky finger; the texture of your flesh just below your thumb is similar to that of a well-done steak.

WINE NOTE: As far as wine is concerned, flank steak is a pretty easygoing partner—many red wines would work well—but the chermoula is a different story. Garlic, lime, paprika, cumin, cilantro, and coriander are all dominant seasonings that make this dish sizzle. But they can also make wine fizzle. Best bet: a soft, thick, fruit-driven red that will act to "cushion" all the spice. Try Geyser Peak's 2001 Shiraz from Sonoma County, California ($18).

MAKE AHEAD • FREEZABLE
Vanilla Bean Angel Food Cake

Your sense of **TOUCH** will tell you when the vanilla seeds are thoroughly mixed into the sugar. Also, you'll know the cake has finished baking when you press the surface and it springs back. Serve with fresh berries or fat-free whipped topping, if desired.

- 1½ cups sugar, divided
- 1 (2-inch) piece vanilla bean, split lengthwise
- 1 cup sifted cake flour (about 4 ounces)
- 12 large egg whites
- ½ teaspoon cream of tartar
- ¼ teaspoon salt
- 1 teaspoon lemon juice

1. Preheat oven to 325°.
2. Place ¾ cup sugar in a small bowl. Scrape seeds from vanilla bean, and add seeds to sugar; discard bean. Work vanilla seeds into sugar with fingers until well combined.
3. Combine flour and sugar mixture, stirring with a whisk to combine.
4. Beat egg whites with a mixer at high speed until foamy. Add cream of tartar and salt; beat until soft peaks form. Add ¾ cup sugar, 2 tablespoons at a time, beating until stiff peaks form. Beat in juice. Sift flour mixture over egg white mixture, ¼ cup at a time; fold in after each addition.
5. Spoon batter into an ungreased 10-inch tube pan, spreading evenly. Break air pockets by cutting through batter with a knife. Bake at 325° for 50 minutes or until cake springs back when lightly touched. Invert pan; cool completely. Loosen cake from sides of pan using a narrow metal spatula. Invert cake onto plate. Yield: 12 servings (serving size: 1 slice).

CALORIES 144 (0% from fat); FAT 0.1g (sat 0g, mono 0g, poly 0g); PROTEIN 4.3g; CARB 31.7g; FIBER 0.1g; CHOL 0mg; IRON 0.6mg; SODIUM 105mg; CALC 4mg

MAKE AHEAD • FREEZABLE
Butter Crust Sandwich Bread

TOUCH guides you in three ways as you make this bread: Knead the dough until it feels smooth and elastic; press it to see if it has risen enough; and then tap the baked loaf to determine if it has finished baking. Serve toasted with preserves, or use for sandwiches.

- 1 tablespoon sugar
- 1 package dry yeast (about 2¼ teaspoons)
- 1 cup warm fat-free milk (100° to 110°)
- 2 tablespoons butter, melted and cooled, divided
- 3¼ cups all-purpose flour, divided (about 14½ ounces)
- 1 teaspoon salt
- Cooking spray

1. Dissolve sugar and yeast in warm milk in a large bowl; let stand 5 minutes. Stir in 1 tablespoon butter. Lightly spoon flour into dry measuring cups; level with a knife. Add 3 cups flour and salt to yeast mixture; stir until a soft dough forms. Turn dough out onto a floured surface. Knead until smooth and elastic (about 8 minutes); add enough of remaining ¼ cup flour, 1 tablespoon at a time, to prevent dough from sticking to hands (dough will feel tacky).
2. Place dough in a large bowl coated with cooking spray, turning to coat top. Cover and let rise in a warm place (85°), free from drafts, 1 hour or until doubled in size. (Gently press two fingers into dough. If indentation remains, dough has risen enough.) Punch dough down; cover and let rest 5 minutes.
3. Roll dough into a 14 x 7–inch rectangle on a lightly floured surface. Roll up rectangle tightly, starting with a short edge, pressing firmly to eliminate air pockets; pinch seam and ends to seal. Place roll, seam side down, in an 8 x 4½–inch loaf pan coated with cooking spray. Lightly coat surface of dough with cooking spray, and cover; let rise in a warm place (85°), free from drafts, 30 minutes or until doubled in size.
4. Preheat oven to 400°.
5. Uncover loaf; drizzle surface of loaf with 1 tablespoon butter, gently spreading with a pastry brush. Cut a ¼-inch-deep slit lengthwise down center of loaf using a sharp knife.
6. Bake at 400° for 30 minutes or until bread is browned on bottom and sounds hollow when tapped. Cool on wire rack. Yield: 1 loaf; 10 servings (serving size: 1 slice).

CALORIES 187 (16% from fat); FAT 3.3g (sat 1.5g, mono 0.9g, poly 0.5g); PROTEIN 5.3g; CARB 33.7g; FIBER 1.2g; CHOL 7mg; IRON 2mg; SODIUM 264mg; CALC 38mg

Oil Drill

According to Lidia Bastianich, restaurateur, TV host, and cookbook author, an informal olive oil tasting lets the home cook exercise all five senses in the kitchen. Take four oils, each from a different region. **See** the color, **inhale** the aroma, **feel** the viscosity with your fingers, **hear** it run quickly or dribble slowly from the bottle, and, finally, **taste** its fruitiness or peppery bite. "Sample each one by itself with just a bit of bread. Use a slice of green apple to clear and reassess your palate. Go back and forth and come up with adjectives for each," she suggests.

Toasted Coconut Rice

Your sense of **SMELL** comes into play when toasting the cardamom and coconut, and sautéing the garlic, as each ingredient releases its unique fragrance to indicate that it has cooked enough.

¼ teaspoon ground cardamom
1 cup flaked sweetened coconut
1 tablespoon extravirgin olive oil
1 garlic clove, minced
2 cups long-grain rice
3½ cups water
1½ teaspoons salt
1 teaspoon butter
2 tablespoons chopped fresh cilantro

1. Heat a saucepan over medium-high heat. Add cardamom; cook, stirring constantly, until fragrant (about 15 seconds). Transfer to a small bowl.
2. Add coconut to pan; cook, stirring constantly, until fragrant and just beginning to brown (about 2 minutes). Add to cardamom.
3. Add oil and garlic to pan. Sauté, stirring frequently, just until garlic is fragrant but not browned (about 20 seconds). Stir in rice; sauté 3 minutes. Stir in coconut mixture, water, and salt; bring to a simmer. Cover, reduce heat to medium-low, and cook 20 minutes or until liquid is absorbed. Fluff with a fork. Add butter, stirring gently until melted. Stir in cilantro. Yield: 10 servings (serving size: about ¾ cup).

CALORIES 198 (24% from fat); FAT 5.3g (sat 3.4g, mono 1.3g, poly 0.3g); PROTEIN 2.9g; CARB 34.2g; FIBER 0.9g; CHOL 1mg; IRON 1.8mg; SODIUM 385mg; CALC 14mg

> # With practice, a cook can use smell more as a guide than an alarm.

Creole Cookin' Menu
serves 6
Chicken and Andouille Jambalaya
Spinach-orange salad*
Mango sorbet

*Combine 1 (6-ounce) bag baby spinach leaves, ⅓ cup thinly sliced red onion, and 1½ cups orange sections in a large bowl, tossing gently. Whisk together 2 tablespoons olive oil, 4 teaspoons Dijon mustard, 1 tablespoon fresh lemon juice, 1 tablespoon water, ¼ teaspoon salt, ⅛ teaspoon crushed red pepper, and 1 teaspoon minced garlic. Toss dressing with spinach mixture.

STAFF FAVORITE
Chicken and Andouille Jambalaya

Consider **SOUND** when cooking this dish. The andouille sizzles loudly at first, then quiets as it renders fat, indicating that it's nearly done. The vegetables cook softly as they release liquid. But the noise increases as they start to caramelize. Don't worry if the bottom of the pan becomes dark brown in parts before you add the broth; it deepens the flavor of the dish.

2 tablespoons canola oil
1½ cups andouille sausage (about 7½ ounces), cut into ¼-inch-thick slices
3 cups finely chopped red bell pepper
3 cups finely chopped yellow onion
2 cups finely chopped celery
2 bay leaves
2½ cups chopped skinless, boneless chicken breast
1½ teaspoons finely chopped jalapeño pepper
1 teaspoon salt
1 teaspoon dried basil
1 teaspoon dried oregano
½ teaspoon dried thyme
¼ teaspoon freshly ground black pepper
⅛ teaspoon ground red pepper
3 garlic cloves, minced
½ cup tomato puree
2¾ cups fat-free, less-sodium chicken broth
1½ cups basmati rice
1 cup thinly sliced green onions

---

1. Heat oil in a large Dutch oven over medium-high heat. Add sausage; cook until sizzling quiets (about 8 minutes), stirring occasionally.
2. Add bell pepper, onion, celery, and bay leaves; cook until vegetables are golden brown, sizzle loudly, and begin to squeak (about 14 minutes), stirring occasionally. Add chicken and next 8 ingredients; cook 4 minutes, stirring occasionally.
3. Add tomato puree; cook 2 minutes, stirring occasionally. Add broth, and bring to a boil. Stir in rice. Cover, reduce heat, and simmer 20 minutes. Discard bay leaves. Stir in green onions. Yield: 6 servings (serving size: 1⅓ cups).

CALORIES 484 (25% from fat); FAT 13.7g (sat 3.8g, mono 6.3g, poly 2.7g); PROTEIN 30.5g; CARB 63.3g; FIBER 5.7g; CHOL 78mg; IRON 3.9mg; SODIUM 835mg; CALC 79mg

---

QUICK & EASY
Celery and Mushroom Salad with Parmigiano-Reggiano

In a simple dish like this, flavor balance is essential. Sample the dressing before coating the vegetables, and adjust the lemon juice to suit your **TASTE**. The flavor of the extravirgin olive oil will greatly influence how this dish tastes. Add salt a little at a time until the dressing tastes properly seasoned. Add freshly ground black pepper to the mix, if desired.

4 cups sliced cremini mushrooms
2 cups thinly sliced celery
2 tablespoons extravirgin olive oil
2 tablespoons fresh lemon juice, divided
½ teaspoon salt, divided
½ cup (2 ounces) shaved Parmigiano-Reggiano cheese

1. Combine mushrooms and celery in a large bowl. Combine oil, 1 tablespoon juice, and ¼ teaspoon salt in a small bowl, stirring well with a whisk. Taste oil mixture; add remaining 1 tablespoon juice and ¼ teaspoon salt, if needed.
2. Add oil mixture to mushroom mixture; toss gently. Taste again; if any

remaining juice and salt have not yet been added, stir in, if needed. Top with cheese. Yield: 5 servings (serving size: 1 cup).

CALORIES 117 (67% from fat); FAT 8.7g (sat 2.7g, mono 5.2g, poly 0.6g); PROTEIN 5.9g; CARB 4.9g; FIBER 1.2g; CHOL 8mg; IRON 0.4mg; SODIUM 466mg; CALC 168mg

inspired vegetarian

Spring for a Party

Lead the season with this simple, tasty assortment of finger foods and drink.

Sometimes it seems that spring will never arrive. The calendar reads "March," but there's still a chilly wind blowing and the daffodils are struggling to make an appearance. To rush the season, throw a party. These delectable meat-free goodies will appeal to all partygoers, vegetarian or not.

QUICK & EASY • MAKE AHEAD
Roasted Tomatillo-Mango Salsa with Spiced Tortilla Chips

Keep a close watch when pulsing the salsa in the food processor; it should have a chunky consistency.

CHIPS:
10 (6-inch) flour tortillas
Cooking spray
1 tablespoon chili powder
1 teaspoon ground cumin
¼ teaspoon salt

SALSA:
1½ pounds fresh tomatillos
1 large jalapeño pepper
1 large onion, peeled and quartered
4 unpeeled garlic cloves
½ cup fresh cilantro leaves
1 tablespoon fresh lime juice
1 teaspoon salt
3 cups finely diced peeled mango (about 2 large)

1. Preheat oven to 450°.
2. To prepare chips, lightly coat tortillas with cooking spray. Combine chili powder, cumin, and ¼ teaspoon salt in a small bowl; sprinkle evenly over tortillas. Cut each tortilla into 4 wedges. Arrange wedges in a single layer on a baking sheet. Bake at 450° for 7 minutes or until crisp and golden.
3. Preheat broiler.
4. To prepare salsa, discard husks and stems from tomatillos. Remove stem from jalapeño. Place tomatillos, jalapeño, onion, and garlic on a broiler pan coated with cooking spray. Broil 8 minutes or until tomatillos and onion are lightly charred (about 8 minutes), turning once; cool.
5. Peel garlic. Place garlic, tomatillos, jalapeño, onion, cilantro, lime juice, and 1 teaspoon salt in a food processor; pulse 10 times or until ingredients are coarsely chopped. Place tomatillo mixture in a large bowl; stir in mango. Serve with chips. Yield: 20 servings (serving size: ⅓ cup salsa and 2 chips).

CALORIES 81 (19% from fat); FAT 1.7g (sat 0.4g, mono 0.7g, poly 0.4g); PROTEIN 2g; CARB 15.1g; FIBER 1.7g; CHOL 0mg; IRON 0.9mg; SODIUM 259mg; CALC 30mg

MAKE AHEAD
Provençal Deviled Eggs

An assortment of dried herbs, herbes de Provence commonly contains basil, lavender, rosemary, thyme, fennel seed, and marjoram. Look for it where other dried spices are sold.

1 tablespoon chopped sun-dried tomatoes, packed without oil
12 hard-cooked large eggs, shelled
⅓ cup low-fat mayonnaise
1 tablespoon chopped pitted kalamata olives
2 teaspoons chopped fresh parsley
2 teaspoons chopped capers
½ teaspoon dried herbes de Provence
½ teaspoon Dijon mustard
¼ teaspoon salt
¼ teaspoon freshly ground black pepper
Chopped fresh parsley (optional)

1. Combine boiling water and tomatoes in a bowl. Cover; let stand 30 minutes or until tender. Drain and set aside.
2. Cut eggs in half lengthwise; remove yolks. Place 8 yolks in a medium bowl; reserve 4 yolks for another use. Add tomatoes, mayonnaise, and next 7 ingredients to bowl; stir well. Spoon 1½ teaspoons egg mixture into each egg white half. Sprinkle with additional chopped parsley, if desired. Yield: 2 dozen (serving size: ½ egg).

CALORIES 41 (66% from fat); FAT 3g (sat 0.7g, mono 1g, poly 0.9g); PROTEIN 2.8g; CARB 0.7g; FIBER 0.1g; CHOL 71mg; IRON 0.3mg; SODIUM 103mg; CALC 11mg

MAKE AHEAD • FREEZABLE
Yellow Pepper Pesto Terrine

Substitute red bell peppers, if desired.

PESTO:
2 large yellow bell peppers
1 cup basil leaves, chopped
¼ cup dry breadcrumbs
1 tablespoon pine nuts, toasted
1 tablespoon olive oil
½ teaspoon salt
¼ teaspoon ground black pepper
4 garlic cloves, peeled

CHEESE FILLING:
2 (8-ounce) blocks fat-free cream cheese, softened
1 (8-ounce) block ⅓-less-fat cream cheese, softened
2 tablespoons grated Parmesan cheese
¼ teaspoon salt
¼ teaspoon ground red pepper

ADDITIONAL INGREDIENTS:
Fresh basil leaves (optional)
48 table wafer crackers

1. Preheat broiler.
2. To prepare pesto, cut bell peppers in half lengthwise; discard seeds and membranes. Place pepper halves, skin sides up, on a foil-lined baking sheet; flatten with hand. Broil 10 minutes or until *Continued*

blackened. Place in a zip-top plastic bag; seal. Let stand 15 minutes. Peel and discard skin.

3. Place peppers, chopped basil, and next 6 ingredients in a blender or food processor; process until smooth.

4. To prepare cheese filling, combine cheeses, ¼ teaspoon salt, and red pepper in a medium bowl; stir well.

5. Line an 8 x 4–inch loaf pan with plastic wrap, allowing plastic wrap to extend over edges of pan. Spread about 1 cup cheese filling in bottom of pan. Spread ½ cup pesto over cheese mixture. Repeat procedure with remaining cheese filling and pesto, ending with cheese filling. Cover and refrigerate 6 hours or overnight.

6. To serve, invert terrine onto a platter; remove plastic wrap. Garnish with additional basil leaves, if desired. Serve with crackers. Yield: 24 servings (serving size: about 2 tablespoons terrine and 2 crackers).

CALORIES 89 (40% from fat); FAT 4g (sat 1.7g, mono 0.6g, poly 0.2g); PROTEIN 5.1g; CARB 8.7g; FIBER 0.4g; CHOL 9mg; IRON 0.2mg; SODIUM 229mg; CALC 52mg

QUICK & EASY • MAKE AHEAD
FREEZABLE
Peanuts with Indian Spices

This easy appetizer can keep up to a week in an airtight container. If you have leftovers after the party, enjoy them as a snack or salad topping.

  2 tablespoons ground coriander
  2 tablespoons brown sugar
  1 tablespoon ground cumin
1½ teaspoons salt
  ½ teaspoon freshly ground black pepper
  ½ teaspoon ground red pepper
  3 large egg whites
  6 cups unsalted, dry-roasted peanuts
  3 tablespoons black sesame seeds
Cooking spray

1. Preheat oven to 300°.
2. Combine first 6 ingredients in a bowl.
3. Place egg whites in a medium bowl; beat with a mixer at medium speed

1 minute or until frothy. Add spice mixture, peanuts, and sesame seeds; stir well. Spread mixture in a single layer on 2 jelly-roll pans coated with cooking spray. Bake at 300° for 30 minutes or until nuts are dry and roasted, stirring occasionally. Cool completely. Yield: 6 cups (serving size: ¼ cup).

CALORIES 228 (74% from fat); FAT 18.8g (sat 2.6g, mono 9.2g, poly 5.9g); PROTEIN 9.4g; CARB 9.3g; FIBER 3.5g; CHOL 0mg; IRON 1mg; SODIUM 158mg; CALC 28mg

MAKE AHEAD
Tunisian Sweet and Hot Pepper-Tomato Relish

Here's a zesty condiment to spark up a crudité platter. It can be made up to three days in advance. Look for harissa, a North African paste made of chiles, garlic, and spices, in international markets. This relish can easily be doubled; however, you will probably have to roast the peppers in two batches.

  3 large red bell peppers
1¾ cups chopped seeded peeled tomato
  ¼ cup chopped fresh flat-leaf parsley
  1 teaspoon grated lemon rind
  2 tablespoons fresh lemon juice
  1 tablespoon extravirgin olive oil
  1 tablespoon commercial harissa or hot pepper sauce (such as Tabasco)
  1 teaspoon sugar
  1 teaspoon ground cumin
  ¼ teaspoon salt
  ⅛ teaspoon freshly ground black pepper
  2 garlic cloves, minced
  3 (6-inch) pitas, each split and cut into 4 wedges

1. Preheat broiler.
2. Cut bell peppers in half lengthwise; discard seeds and membranes. Place pepper halves, skin sides up, on a foil-lined baking sheet; flatten with hand. Broil 15 minutes or until blackened. Place in a zip-top plastic bag; seal. Let stand 15 minutes. Peel and cut into ½-inch pieces; place in a large bowl.
3. Heat a medium, heavy skillet over high heat. Add tomato; cook 8 minutes or until thick, stirring constantly. Add tomato to bell pepper in bowl. Stir in parsley and next 9 ingredients. Serve with pita wedges. Yield: 12 servings (serving size: about 3 tablespoons relish and 2 pita wedges).

CALORIES 73 (20% from fat); FAT 1.6g (sat 0.2g, mono 0.9g, poly 0.3g); PROTEIN 2.2g; CARB 13.3g; FIBER 1.8g; CHOL 0mg; IRON 0.8mg; SODIUM 133mg; CALC 24mg

QUICK & EASY
Sparkling Pomegranate Cocktail

This simple, delicious cocktail can easily be doubled to serve more guests. For an equally delightful nonalcoholic version, simply mix one part pomegranate juice to two parts sparkling water.

  2 cups pomegranate juice (such as POM Wonderful)
1½ cups lemon-flavored sparkling water
  ½ cup berry-flavored vodka or plain vodka
Lemon rind strips (optional)

1. Combine first 3 ingredients in a pitcher. Pour ½ cup into each of 8 ice-filled glasses. Garnish with lemon rind strips, if desired. Yield: 8 servings.

CALORIES 195 (0% from fat); FAT 0g; PROTEIN 0g; CARB 44g; FIBER 0g; CHOL 0mg; IRON 0.7mg; SODIUM 1mg; CALC 1mg

> These make-ahead dishes are easy on the host and just as easy on the guests— no forks required.

Goat Cheese Tarts with Lemon-Fig Compote

These dainty little bites are surprisingly simple to prepare. The phyllo pastry shells are sold in the frozen food section in the supermarket; thaw before filling. Prepare the compote up to two days in advance, and store it in the refrigerator.

COMPOTE:

    2   cups finely chopped dried black
        Mission figs
    1   cup water
    ½   cup Marsala wine
    1   tablespoon brown sugar
    1   tablespoon grated lemon rind
    1   tablespoon fresh lemon juice
    ⅛   teaspoon salt

TARTS:

    2   (2.1-ounce) packages mini
        phyllo shells (such as Athens)
    ½   cup (4 ounces) fat-free cream
        cheese, softened
    1   (4-ounce) package goat cheese
    1   large egg white
    1   tablespoon 1% low-fat
        milk
    2   tablespoons powdered sugar
    1   tablespoon all-purpose flour
    ⅛   teaspoon salt

1. To prepare compote, combine first 7 ingredients in a medium saucepan. Bring to a boil. Cover, reduce heat, and simmer 20 minutes, stirring occasionally. Simmer, uncovered, until mixture reduces to about 1 cup (about 30 minutes). Remove from heat; cool.

2. Place fig mixture in a food processor; pulse 5 times or until finely chopped. Place in a small bowl; cover and chill.

3. To prepare tarts, preheat oven to 350°.

4. Arrange phyllo shells in a single layer on a jelly-roll pan. Combine cheeses in a medium bowl; beat with a mixer at medium speed until smooth. Add egg white; beat well. Add milk; beat well. Combine powdered sugar, flour, and salt; add to cheese mixture, beating well.

5. Spoon about 1½ teaspoons cheese mixture into each phyllo shell. Bake at 350° for 15 minutes or until lightly browned. Cool on a wire rack. Top each tart with about 1½ teaspoons compote. Yield: 15 servings (serving size: 2 tarts).

CALORIES 120 (29% from fat); FAT 3.8g (sat 1.2g, mono 1.6g, poly 0.4g); PROTEIN 3.4g; CARB 17.8g; FIBER 1.6g; CHOL 4mg; IRON 1mg; SODIUM 132mg; CALC 54mg

How to Make Phyllo Triangles and Shells

If you want to make your own phyllo shells, begin by thawing frozen phyllo dough in the refrigerator overnight. Wrap unused dough in plastic wrap, and store in the refrigerator up to one week. While you work, cover extra dough with a slightly dampened towel to prevent the dough from drying out. We also give instructions below for making phyllo triangles.

1. *Carefully remove one sheet at a time. Layer four sheets, one atop the other, for a sturdy pastry. Coat all but the top layer with cooking spray to prevent tearing.*

2. *Use a pizza cutter to cut dough in half vertically, creating two long sections. Use cooking spray to bond any tearing that occurs while working.*

3. *To make shells: Cut the two long sections (from Step 2) into thirds to create six squares. Line a muffin tin and bake for 20 minutes, then fill and serve.*

4. *To make triangles: Working with one section at a time, drop a tablespoon of filling onto the bottom. Leave a one-inch border around filling to allow for folding.*

5. *Gently fold into a triangle. Start at the filling end and fold forward in a flag pattern. Avoid wrapping too tightly; the filling will spill out during baking.*

Slow Cooking for Fast Times

If your schedule's crowded, use a slow cooker this morning for a memorable make-ahead meal tonight.

Slow Cooker Chicken Paprikash

Serve this dish with egg noodles, orzo, rice, or mashed potatoes. Use preshredded carrots to speed up preparation.

- 3 tablespoons all-purpose flour
- 2 pounds skinless, boneless chicken breast, cut into ½-inch strips
- 2 cups chopped onion (about 1 large)
- 1¼ cups fat-free, less-sodium chicken broth
- 1 cup chopped red bell pepper
- ½ cup shredded carrot
- 2 tablespoons Hungarian sweet paprika
- 2 teaspoons bottled minced garlic
- 1 teaspoon salt
- 1 teaspoon freshly ground black pepper
- 1 (8-ounce) package presliced mushrooms
- 1¼ cups reduced-fat sour cream

1. Combine flour and chicken in a medium bowl; toss well. Add chicken mixture, onion, and next 8 ingredients to an electric slow cooker. Cover and cook on LOW for 8 hours.

2. Stir in sour cream. Yield: 6 servings (serving size: 1 cup).

CALORIES 316 (25% from fat); FAT 8.8g (sat 4.5g, mono 2.2g, poly 1.1g); PROTEIN 40.6g; CARB 17.3g; FIBER 3g; CHOL 114mg; IRON 2.3mg; SODIUM 627mg; CALC 123mg

Slow Cooker Char Siu Pork Roast

Char siu is a Chinese version of barbecue. Serve with sticky or long-grain white rice and a steamed or stir-fried medley of bell peppers, carrots, snow peas, sliced baby corn, and water chestnuts.

- ¼ cup low-sodium soy sauce
- ¼ cup hoisin sauce
- 3 tablespoons ketchup
- 3 tablespoons honey
- 2 teaspoons bottled minced garlic
- 2 teaspoons grated peeled fresh ginger
- 1 teaspoon dark sesame oil
- ½ teaspoon five-spice powder
- 2 pounds boneless Boston butt pork roast, trimmed
- ½ cup fat-free, less-sodium chicken broth

1. Combine first 8 ingredients in a small bowl, stirring well with a whisk. Place in a large zip-top plastic bag. Add pork to bag; seal. Marinate in refrigerator at least 2 hours, turning occasionally.

2. Place pork and marinade in an electric slow cooker. Cover and cook on LOW for 8 hours.

3. Remove pork from slow cooker using a slotted spoon; place on a cutting board or work surface. Cover with aluminum foil; keep warm.

4. Add broth to sauce in slow cooker. Cover and cook on LOW 30 minutes or until sauce thickens. Shred pork with 2 forks; serve with sauce. Yield: 8 servings (serving size: 3 ounces pork and ¼ cup sauce).

CALORIES 227 (38% from fat); FAT 9.5g (sat 3.1g, mono 3.9g, poly 1.1g); PROTEIN 21.6g; CARB 12.7g; FIBER 0.4g; CHOL 73mg; IRON 1.7mg; SODIUM 561mg; CALC 30mg

Apricot and Lamb Tagine

Serve over hot couscous with a side of steamed green beans.

TAGINE:

- 2 cups diced onion (about 1 large)
- ½ cup orange juice
- ½ cup less-sodium beef broth
- 2 tablespoons honey
- 1 tablespoon grated lemon rind
- 1 tablespoon fresh lemon juice
- 2 teaspoons bottled minced garlic
- 2 teaspoons grated peeled fresh ginger
- 1½ teaspoons salt
- 1 teaspoon ground coriander
- ½ teaspoon ground cumin
- ¼ teaspoon freshly ground black pepper
- 2 pounds boneless leg of lamb, trimmed and cut into bite-sized pieces
- 2 (3-inch) cinnamon sticks
- 1 (6-ounce) package dried apricots, halved

REMAINING INGREDIENTS:

- 4 cups cooked couscous
- ¼ cup slivered almonds, toasted
- ¼ cup chopped fresh parsley

1. To prepare tagine, combine first 15 ingredients in an electric slow cooker. Cover and cook on LOW for 8 hours. Discard cinnamon sticks.

2. Place ½ cup couscous on each of 8 plates. Top each serving with ½ cup lamb mixture, 1½ teaspoons almonds, and 1½ teaspoons parsley. Yield: 8 servings.

CALORIES 451 (37% from fat); FAT 18.7g (sat 7.1g, mono 8.1g, poly 1.7g); PROTEIN 26.2g; CARB 43.2g; FIBER 3.6g; CHOL 81mg; IRON 3.3mg; SODIUM 515mg; CALC 52mg

A **pot** you don't have to watch and that's easy to **clean** afterward—slow cooking is a **recipe** for dinner on **busy days.**

Mediterranean Roast Turkey

Serve this slow cooker roast with mashed potatoes and garnish with fresh thyme sprigs, if desired.

- 2 cups chopped onion (about 1 large)
- ½ cup pitted kalamata olives
- ½ cup julienne-cut drained oil-packed sun-dried tomato halves
- 2 tablespoons fresh lemon juice
- 1½ teaspoons bottled minced garlic
- 1 teaspoon Greek seasoning mix (such as McCormick's)
- ½ teaspoon salt
- ¼ teaspoon freshly ground black pepper
- 1 (4-pound) boneless turkey breast, trimmed
- ½ cup fat-free, less-sodium chicken broth, divided
- 3 tablespoons all-purpose flour

1. Place first 9 ingredients in an electric slow cooker. Stir in ¼ cup chicken broth. Cover and cook on LOW for 7 hours.
2. Combine ¼ cup broth and flour in a small bowl; stir with a whisk until smooth. Add broth mixture to slow cooker. Cover and cook on LOW 30 minutes. Cut turkey into slices. Yield: 8 servings (serving size: about 4 ounces turkey and about ⅓ cup onion mixture).

CALORIES 368 (26% from fat); FAT 10.7g (sat 2.2g, mono 5.6g, poly 2g); PROTEIN 55.3g; CARB 9.8g; FIBER 1.2g; CHOL 159mg; IRON 3.2mg; SODIUM 527mg; CALC 44mg

Curried Squash and Apple Soup

This make-ahead recipe keeps in the refrigerator up to four days and up to two months in the freezer. For a main dish option, add cooked, diced chicken or turkey breast to the pot in the last 20 minutes of cooking. Serve garnished with a dollop of sour cream and chopped cilantro.

- 3 cups fat-free, less-sodium chicken broth
- 2 cups chopped onion (about 1 large)
- 2 teaspoons bottled minced garlic
- 1½ teaspoons grated peeled fresh ginger
- 1 teaspoon salt
- 1 teaspoon red curry powder
- ½ teaspoon ground coriander
- ½ teaspoon freshly ground black pepper
- 2 pounds cubed peeled butternut squash (3 cups)
- 2 apples, cored, peeled, and diced (1 pound, 2 cups)

1. Place all ingredients in an electric slow cooker. Cover and cook on LOW for 8 hours or until squash is tender.
2. Place half of squash mixture in a blender, and process until smooth. Pour pureed mixture into a large bowl. Repeat procedure with remaining squash mixture. Yield: 8 servings (serving size: 1 cup).

CALORIES 95 (4% from fat); FAT 0.5g (sat 0.1g, mono 0.1g, poly 0.1g); PROTEIN 2.6g; CARB 22.4g; FIBER 3.8g; CHOL 0mg; IRON 1.2mg; SODIUM 446mg; CALC 73mg

Beef Goulash

Garnish bowls of this dish with reduced-fat sour cream and chopped fresh parsley.

- ⅓ cup all-purpose flour (about 1½ ounces)
- 2 pounds lean beef stew meat, cut into bite-sized pieces
- 4 cups diced peeled baking potato (about 1½ pounds)
- 2 cups chopped onion (about 1 large)
- 1 cup (¼-inch-thick) slices carrot
- 1 cup chopped red bell pepper (about 1 medium)
- ⅓ cup ketchup
- 1 tablespoon Worcestershire sauce
- 2 teaspoons Hungarian sweet paprika
- 2 teaspoons minced garlic
- 1 teaspoon salt
- 1 (10-ounce) can double-strength beef broth

1. Combine flour and beef in a medium bowl; toss well. Place beef mixture, potato, and remaining ingredients in an electric slow cooker. Cover and cook on LOW for 8 hours. Yield: 8 servings (serving size: 1 cup).

CALORIES 304 (25% from fat); FAT 8.3g (sat 3g, mono 3.4g, poly 0.4g); PROTEIN 25.4g; CARB 31.3g; FIBER 3.2g; CHOL 72mg; IRON 3.5mg; SODIUM 744mg; CALC 33mg

---

Not Your Mother's Slow Cooker

Remember Mom's original three-quart cylindrical pot that didn't come out of its avocado-colored electric base? Slow cookers have changed. Here are our favorites.

Hamilton Beach 5-Quart Double Dish Slow Cooker ($40): This model offers two ways to cook—prepare one dish in the five-quart stoneware bowl, or use the divided nonstick Double Dish to cook two separate recipes at the same time.

Rival 6-Quart Versaware Slow Cooker ($60): The Eurostyle stoneware pot functions as a slow cooker in a removable electric base. The pot can also be used on the stovetop for cooking or reheating, or in the oven to roast, bake, or broil. Afterward, use it to store leftovers in the refrigerator or freezer.

Rival 5.5-Quart Recipe Smart Pot ($100): Offers programmable settings for temperature and cooking time and stays warm for up to four hours after the cooking cycle is completed. Use your own recipe, or choose from more than 200 preprogrammed recipes digitally stored in the electronic display.

Cuisinart 6.5-Quart Slow Cooker ($150): A sleek, stainless steel exterior houses a generously sized removable pot. Nice features include automatic "warm" setting after cooking is complete, retractable electrical cord storage, and a cooking rack that accommodates ramekins or other bakeware.

Indonesian Dinners

Spice up suppertime with these Indonesian-inspired dishes.

Indonesian Dinner Menu 1
serves 4

Chicken Saté with Peanut Sauce

Assorted vegetable sauté*

White rice with green onions

*Heat 1 tablespoon canola oil over medium-high heat in a large skillet. Add 2 cups snow peas, 2 cups julienne-cut shiitake mushrooms, and 1 cup julienne-cut red bell pepper to pan. Stir in 1 tablespoon low-sodium soy sauce, 1 teaspoon lime juice, ½ teaspoon crushed red pepper, ¼ teaspoon salt, and a dash of sugar; sauté 5 minutes or until vegetables just begin to soften.

Game Plan

1. While broiler preheats:
   • Soak skewers in water
   • Prepare spice paste
   • Cook rice
2. While chicken marinates:
   • Prepare peanut sauce
3. While chicken cooks:
   • Cook vegetables

Chicken Saté with Peanut Sauce

Classic Indonesian satés feature skewered meat, fish, or poultry that is grilled or broiled.

TOTAL TIME: 45 MINUTES

SATÉ:
- ½ cup chopped shallots (about 4)
- 2 tablespoons dark brown sugar
- 1 tablespoon minced fresh ginger
- 1 tablespoon sambal oelek (chile paste with garlic)
- 1 tablespoon low-sodium soy sauce
- 2 teaspoons coriander seeds
- 2 teaspoons canola oil
- 1 teaspoon fish sauce
- ½ teaspoon turmeric
- ½ teaspoon black peppercorns
- Dash of freshly ground nutmeg
- 4 garlic cloves
- 2 whole cloves
- 1½ pounds chicken breast tenders

PEANUT SAUCE:
- ½ cup reduced-fat creamy peanut butter
- ⅓ cup water
- 3 tablespoons lime juice
- 1 tablespoon low-sodium soy sauce
- 2 teaspoons dark brown sugar
- 1 teaspoon hot paprika
- 1 teaspoon Sriracha (hot chile sauce, such as Huy Fong)

REMAINING INGREDIENT:
Cooking spray

1. Preheat broiler.
2. To prepare saté, place first 13 ingredients in a food processor, and process until smooth. Place shallot mixture and chicken in a large zip-top plastic bag; seal and marinate in refrigerator 10 minutes.
3. To prepare peanut sauce, combine peanut butter and next 6 ingredients in a medium bowl; stir well with a whisk.
4. Remove chicken from bag; discard marinade. Thread chicken onto 8 (12-inch) wooden skewers. Place skewers on rack of a broiler or roasting pan coated with cooking spray. Broil 12 minutes or until done. Serve with peanut sauce. Yield: 4 servings (serving size: 2 skewers and about ¼ cup sauce).

CALORIES 424 (33% from fat); FAT 15.5g (sat 3.2g, mono 1.3g, poly 0.9g); PROTEIN 47.2g; CARB 23.7g; FIBER 2.7g; CHOL 99mg; IRON 2.6mg; SODIUM 745mg; CALC 37mg

Indonesian Dinner Menu 2
serves 4

Fried Rice (Nasi Goreng)

Spinach soup*

Fresh pineapple cubes

*Heat a Dutch oven over medium-high heat. Coat pan with cooking spray. Add ½ cup chopped onion, ½ cup chopped green bell pepper, ½ teaspoon salt, ¼ teaspoon freshly ground black pepper, and 1 minced garlic clove to pan; sauté 2 minutes. Add 4 cups fat-free, less-sodium chicken broth and 2 cups frozen whole kernel corn, thawed. Bring to a boil; cook 10 minutes. Add 1 (6-ounce) package fresh baby spinach; cook until wilted.

Game Plan

1. Assemble ingredients for fried rice.
2. Cook soup.
3. While soup cooks:
   • Prepare fried rice

Fried Rice
Nasi Goreng

We recommend topping this fried rice with diced cucumbers and tomatoes, but for a more traditional Indonesian accompaniment, top it with a fried egg. Sambal oelek is a spicy table condiment from Southeast Asia; look for it in gourmet grocery stores and Asian markets.

TOTAL TIME: 35 MINUTES

TASTE TIP: Use two tablespoons serrano chile if you prefer spicier rice.

2 teaspoons canola oil
⅓ cup minced shallots (about 3)
1 to 2 tablespoons minced serrano chile
1 tablespoon sambal oelek (chile paste with garlic)
2 teaspoons fish sauce
2 teaspoons low-sodium soy sauce
¼ teaspoon salt
4 garlic cloves, minced
2 cups diced cooked chicken breast
2 cups diced cooked shrimp (about 12 ounces)
3 cups cooked rice
½ cup diced cucumber
½ cup diced tomato

1. Heat oil in a large nonstick skillet over medium-high heat. Add shallots and chile to pan; sauté 2 minutes or until shallots are lightly browned. Add chile paste, fish sauce, soy sauce, salt, and garlic to pan; cook 1 minute or until sauce becomes fragrant. Add chicken, shrimp, and rice to pan, stirring to coat with sauce. Cook 2 minutes or until thoroughly heated, stirring occasionally. Place about 1½ cups rice mixture on each of 4 plates, and sprinkle each serving with 2 tablespoons cucumber and 2 tablespoons tomato. Yield: 4 servings.

CALORIES 430 (13% from fat); FAT 6.2g (sat 1.2g, mono 2.5g, poly 1.7g); PROTEIN 44.1g; CARB 46.1g; FIBER 2.3g; CHOL 225mg; IRON 5.8mg; SODIUM 717mg; CALC 62mg

Indonesian Dinner Menu 3
serves 4

Steamed Clams with Thai Basil and Chiles

Rice noodles with cilantro

Cardamom-spiced iced coffee*

*Combine 4 cups strong brewed coffee, ¼ cup sweetened condensed milk, and ⅛ teaspoon cardamom in a medium bowl, stirring until blended. Chill. Serve over ice.

Game Plan

1. Prepare iced coffee.
2. Prepare ingredients for clams.
3. While noodles cook:
   • Cook clams

Steamed Clams with Thai Basil and Chiles

Look for oyster sauce—a concentrated sauce made of oysters, brine, and soy sauce—in the Asian foods section of the supermarket. Substitute sweet basil if Thai basil isn't available.

TOTAL TIME: 40 MINUTES

TASTE TIP: For even spicier and more traditional flavor, use two teaspoons Thai bird chile instead of serrano. Look for bird chiles at an Asian market.

1 tablespoon canola oil
4 garlic cloves, chopped
2 teaspoons minced serrano chile
⅓ cup dry white wine
1 tablespoon fish sauce
2 teaspoons oyster sauce
1 teaspoon sugar
½ teaspoon freshly ground black pepper
3 pounds littleneck clams in shells, scrubbed
1 cup chopped fresh Thai basil

1. Heat oil in a large nonstick skillet over medium-high heat. Add garlic; sauté 1 minute or until golden. Add chile; sauté 10 seconds. Stir in wine and next 4 ingredients. Bring to a boil. Add clams; cover and cook 7 minutes or until shells open. Add basil; cover and cook 1 minute. Discard any unopened shells. Remove clams from pan with a slotted spoon. Serve with sauce. Yield: 4 servings (serving size: about 13 clams and about ⅓ cup sauce).

CALORIES 298 (21% from fat); FAT 6.9g (sat 0.6g, mono 2.3g, poly 2.1g); PROTEIN 44.2g; CARB 12g; FIBER 0.6g; CHOL 116mg; IRON 48.1mg; SODIUM 559mg; CALC 183mg

Indonesian Dinner Menu 4
serves 4

Shrimp in Yellow Sauce

Coconut rice*

Shrimp crackers

*Combine 1 cup long-grain rice; 1¼ cups fat-free, less-sodium chicken broth; 1 teaspoon salt; and 2 teaspoons canola oil in a medium saucepan over high heat; bring to a boil. Reduce heat, and add ½ cup light coconut milk and ½ stalk fresh lemongrass, crushed. Cover and simmer 15 minutes or until liquid is absorbed. Let stand 10 minutes; fluff with a fork.

Game Plan

1. While rice cooks:
   • Process and cook spice paste
2. While rice stands:
   • Cook shrimp

Shrimp in Yellow Sauce

TOTAL TIME: 35 MINUTES

TASTE TIP: For authentic flavor, use shrimp paste (such as Lee Kum Kee) in place of fish sauce.

SPICE PASTE:
½ teaspoon grated lime rind
2 tablespoons lime juice
1 to 2 teaspoons sambal oelek (chile paste with garlic)
1 teaspoon fish sauce
½ teaspoon coriander seeds
½ teaspoon turmeric
3 garlic cloves
2 shallots, chopped
1 (1-inch) piece fresh ginger, peeled

REMAINING INGREDIENTS:
Cooking spray
1 cup light coconut milk
1 pound large shrimp, peeled and deveined
Chopped cilantro (optional)

Continued

1. To prepare spice paste, place first 9 ingredients in a food processor; process until smooth.

2. Heat a large nonstick skillet over medium-high heat. Coat pan with cooking spray. Add spice paste to pan; sauté 1 minute or until fragrant. Add coconut milk and shrimp; simmer 4 minutes or until shrimp are done. Garnish with cilantro, if desired. Yield: 4 servings (serving size: about ¾ cup).

CALORIES 175 (26% from fat); FAT 5.1g (sat 3.2g, mono 0.3g, poly 0.8g); PROTEIN 24.4g; CARB 8.1g; FIBER 0.4g; CHOL 172mg; IRON 3.4mg; SODIUM 302mg; CALC 72mg

in season

Think Green

Spring's delicate vegetables enliven speedy starters, entrées, and sides.

Asparagus stalks and pea shoots working up through the cool ground are true harbingers of spring. After a winter of slow-simmering stews and braises, early spring is the time to reach for delicate baby greens and lettuces, crisp young peas, and assorted herbs to create tasty dishes that require minimal cooking. Venture to your favorite grocer, farm stand, or your own garden to find vegetables at their peak.

Chicken Scaloppine with Spring Herb Salad

Haricots verts are delicate green beans, sometimes called French green beans.

CHICKEN:
- 4 (6-ounce) skinless, boneless chicken breast halves
- 1 cup whole buttermilk
- ½ teaspoon salt
- ½ cup all-purpose flour (about 2¼ ounces)
- 2 teaspoons dried tarragon
- ½ teaspoon freshly ground black pepper
- 1 tablespoon canola oil

SALAD:
- 2½ cups haricots verts (about 8 ounces)
- 4 cups baby spinach leaves (about 2 ounces)
- 2 cups trimmed arugula (about 1 ounce)
- 2 cups trimmed watercress (about 1 ounce)
- ⅓ cup fresh flat-leaf parsley leaves
- 1 tablespoon chopped fresh chives
- 2 tablespoons finely chopped shallots
- 2 tablespoons fresh lemon juice
- 2 tablespoons olive oil
- 1 tablespoon champagne vinegar
- 1 teaspoon Dijon mustard
- ¼ teaspoon salt
- ⅛ teaspoon freshly ground black pepper

1. To prepare chicken, place each chicken breast half between 2 sheets of heavy-duty plastic wrap; pound each piece to ½-inch thickness using a meat mallet or rolling pin. Combine chicken and buttermilk in a large zip-top plastic bag; seal. Marinate in refrigerator 2 hours, turning bag occasionally. Remove chicken from bag; discard marinade.

2. Pat chicken dry with paper towels; sprinkle with ½ teaspoon salt. Combine flour, tarragon, and ½ teaspoon black pepper in a shallow bowl. Dredge chicken in flour mixture; shake off excess. Heat canola oil in a large nonstick skillet over medium-high heat. Add chicken; cook 3 minutes on each side or until done.

3. To prepare salad, place haricots verts in a large saucepan of boiling water; cook 3 minutes. Drain and plunge haricots verts into ice water; drain. Place haricots verts, spinach, and next 4 ingredients in a large bowl. Combine shallots and remaining 6 ingredients in a small bowl, stirring with a whisk. Spoon 3 tablespoons shallot mixture over spinach mixture; toss gently to coat. Place 2 cups salad mixture onto each of 4 plates; top each serving with 1 chicken breast half. Drizzle chicken evenly with remaining shallot mixture. Yield: 4 servings.

CALORIES 314 (31% from fat); FAT 10.7g (sat 1.7g, mono 6.3g, poly 1.7g); PROTEIN 41.9g; CARB 11.5g; FIBER 3g; CHOL 100mg; IRON 3mg; SODIUM 610mg; CALC 99mg

QUICK & EASY
Three-Cheese Chicken Penne Florentine
(pictured on page 229)

Fresh spinach, chicken, and a combination of cheeses make this dish comforting enough for the last days of winter yet fresh enough for the first days of spring. You also can cook the pasta mixture in individual eight-ounce ramekins; bake for 15 minutes.

- 1 teaspoon olive oil
- Cooking spray
- 3 cups thinly sliced mushrooms
- 1 cup chopped onion
- 1 cup chopped red bell pepper
- 3 cups chopped fresh spinach
- 1 tablespoon chopped fresh oregano
- ¼ teaspoon freshly ground black pepper
- 1 (16-ounce) carton 2% low-fat cottage cheese
- 4 cups hot cooked penne (about 8 ounces uncooked tube-shaped pasta)
- 2 cups shredded roasted skinless, boneless chicken breast
- 1 cup (4 ounces) shredded reduced-fat sharp Cheddar cheese, divided
- ½ cup (2 ounces) grated fresh Parmesan cheese, divided
- ½ cup 2% reduced-fat milk
- 1 (10¾-ounce) can condensed reduced-fat, reduced-sodium cream of chicken soup, undiluted

1. Preheat oven to 425°.

2. Heat oil in a large nonstick skillet coated with cooking spray over medium-high heat. Add mushrooms, onion, and bell pepper; sauté 4 minutes or until tender. Add spinach, oregano, and black pepper; sauté 3 minutes or just until spinach wilts.

3. Place cottage cheese in a food processor; process until very smooth. Combine spinach mixture, cottage cheese, pasta, chicken, ¾ cup Cheddar cheese, ¼ cup Parmesan cheese, milk, and soup in a large bowl. Spoon mixture into a 2-quart baking dish coated with cooking spray. Sprinkle with ¼ cup Cheddar cheese and ¼ cup Parmesan cheese. Bake at 425° for 25 minutes or until lightly browned and bubbly. Yield: 8 servings (serving size: about 1 cup).

CALORIES 345 (25% from fat); FAT 9.7g (sat 5.1g, mono 3.1g, poly 1g); PROTEIN 31.7g; CARB 32.9g; FIBER 2.1g; CHOL 56mg; IRON 2mg; SODIUM 532mg; CALC 275mg

---

QUICK & EASY
Pizza Primavera

Use pencil-thin asparagus stalks, which will be done when the pizza has finished cooking.

1 (12-ounce) prebaked pizza crust (such as Mama Mary's)
1 teaspoon olive oil
1 garlic clove, minced
⅓ cup (about 1½ ounces) shredded part-skim mozzarella cheese, divided
1 cup arugula leaves
2 ounces thinly sliced prosciutto
6 basil leaves, torn
½ cup (1-inch) diagonally cut asparagus
1 cup sliced fresh mushrooms
¼ cup (1 ounce) grated Parmigiano-Reggiano

1. Preheat oven to 400°. Place a baking sheet in oven.
2. Brush pizza crust with oil. Sprinkle crust with garlic and 3 tablespoons mozzarella. Top with arugula and next 4 ingredients. Sprinkle with 7 teaspoons mozzarella and Parmigiano-Reggiano. Place pizza on preheated baking sheet; bake at 400° for 20 minutes or until golden brown. Let stand 5 minutes before cutting into 4 wedges. Yield: 4 servings (serving size: 1 wedge).

CALORIES 360 (35% from fat); FAT 14.1g (sat 3.9g, mono 4.4g, poly 5.6g); PROTEIN 15.9g; CARB 43.3g; FIBER 2.1g; CHOL 18mg; IRON 3.7mg; SODIUM 613mg; CALC 210mg

---

Roasted Baby Spring Vegetables

Use white balsamic vinegar to maintain the vegetables' vibrant hue. Look for baby carrots with tops, which have tender texture and subtly sweet flavor. Small carrots packed and sold as "baby" carrots are actually whittled-down mature vegetables.

3 tablespoons white balsamic vinegar
1 tablespoon chopped shallots
1 pound baby carrots with tops
1 tablespoon olive oil
½ teaspoon salt
¼ teaspoon freshly ground black pepper
12 fingerling potatoes, halved lengthwise (about 1¼ pounds)
1 (6-ounce) bag radishes, halved (about 1¾ cups)
2 cups (2-inch) slices asparagus (about 1 pound)
1 tablespoon chopped fresh flat-leaf parsley
1 tablespoon chopped fresh chives

1. Preheat oven to 500°.
2. Combine vinegar and shallots in a small bowl; set aside.
3. Trim green tops from carrots; discard tops. Combine carrots and next 5 ingredients in bottom of a roasting pan, tossing gently to combine. Bake at 500° for 20 minutes or until vegetables begin to brown, stirring occasionally. Remove pan from oven; add shallot mixture and asparagus, tossing to combine. Return pan to oven; bake 5 minutes. Stir in parsley and chives. Yield: 7 servings (serving size: 1 cup).

CALORIES 127 (16% from fat); FAT 2.2g (sat 0.3g, mono 1.4g, poly 0.3g); PROTEIN 3.9g; CARB 24.6g; FIBER 3.9g; CHOL 0mg; IRON 2.7mg; SODIUM 232mg; CALC 52mg

---

Greens Guide

Artichoke
Flavor: mild, faintly nutty
Select: specimens that are heavy for their size, with tight, olive-green leaves
Use: sautéed, stuffed, roasted, boiled, or steamed with other vegetables or on its own

Asparagus
Flavor: grassy
Select: young, tender, bright green stalks; the more mature the plant, the thicker the stalk
Use: as a side dish or added to salads, soups, and pasta

Belgian Endive
Flavor: mildly bitter
Select: firm heads with white yellow- or red-tinged leaves (Belgian endive is cultivated in a dark environment to preserve its delicate color)
Use: in salads or stuffed with a mild filling as an appetizer

Chervil
Flavor: like parsley (its cousin), with a hint of anise
Select: curly, dark green leaves
Use: in salads, as a garnish, or anywhere you'd use parsley

Sorrel
Flavor: tart, lemony, and a little sour
Select: bright green, crisp leaves (sorrel looks similar to spinach); the more mature the plant, the more bitter the flavor
Use: in salads and soups; anywhere you want an acidic top note

Watercress
Flavor: peppery, with a touch of mustard (it's a member of the mustard family)
Select: brightly colored leaves
Use: in salads, as a garnish, and as a substitute for arugula

Greens Storage Tip
Spring's fragile herbs and vegetables don't have a long shelf life. Store in the refrigerator, and use them as soon as possible, within two to three days of purchase.

Artichoke, Chanterelle, and Cipollini Sauté

March marks the beginning of peak season for artichokes. The smaller the artichoke, the more tender its texture.

  3 cups water
2½ tablespoons fresh lemon juice, divided
  2 pounds baby artichokes
  1 tablespoon butter, divided
  1 (10-ounce) bag cipollini onions, peeled and halved (about 2 cups)
  1 tablespoon olive oil
2½ tablespoons finely chopped shallots
2½ ounces fresh chanterelle mushrooms, halved
  2 garlic cloves, minced
 ½ cup dry white wine
  1 cup sugar snap peas
  1 tablespoon chopped fresh parsley
 ½ teaspoon salt
 ⅛ teaspoon freshly ground black pepper
  6 tablespoons (1½ ounces) shredded Parmesan cheese

1. Combine water and 2 tablespoons juice. Working with one artichoke at a time, bend back outer green leaves of artichoke, snapping at base, until reaching light green leaves. Trim about ¼ inch from top of artichoke. Cut off stem of artichoke to within ¼ inch of base; peel stem. Cut artichoke in half vertically. Place artichoke halves in lemon water. Set aside.
2. Melt 1½ teaspoons butter in a large nonstick skillet over medium-high heat. Add onions; cook 3 minutes or until onions begin to brown, stirring occasionally. Remove onions from pan, and set aside.
3. Add 1½ teaspoons butter and oil to pan, stirring until butter melts. Add shallots, mushrooms, and garlic; sauté 1½ minutes or until shallots are tender. Add onions and wine; cook 3 minutes or until wine almost evaporates. Drain artichokes. Stir artichokes and peas into onion mixture; cook 3 minutes or until artichokes are tender. Remove from heat;

stir in 1½ teaspoons juice, parsley, salt, and pepper. Sprinkle with cheese. Yield: 6 servings (serving size: about 1 cup artichoke mixture and 1 tablespoon cheese).

CALORIES 190 (30% from fat); FAT 6.4g (sat 2.8g, mono 2.8g, poly 0.5g); PROTEIN 9.5g; CARB 24.8g; FIBER 8.7g; CHOL 10mg; IRON 2.6mg; SODIUM 481mg; CALC 184mg

QUICK & EASY

Poached Salmon with Creamy Herb Sauce

Poach the salmon for 10 minutes, then let it stand for another 10 minutes to finish cooking. It will be translucent in the center when it's completely cooked.

SALMON:
  2 cups dry white wine
  2 cups water
  3 tablespoons sliced shallots
  6 black peppercorns
  4 lemon slices
  2 parsley sprigs
  4 (6-ounce) skinless salmon fillets (about 1 inch thick)

SAUCE:
 ½ cup low-fat mayonnaise
 ¼ cup chopped fresh sorrel
 ¼ cup fat-free sour cream
  2 tablespoons chopped fresh chervil
  1 tablespoon chopped fresh parsley
  2 teaspoons chopped fresh dill
  2 teaspoons Dijon mustard
  1 teaspoon fresh lemon juice
 ¼ teaspoon salt
 ¼ teaspoon freshly ground black pepper

REMAINING INGREDIENTS:
  3 cups sugar snap peas, trimmed
  8 cups torn Bibb lettuce (about 5 ounces)

1. To prepare salmon, combine first 6 ingredients in a large skillet; bring to a boil. Add fish to pan. Cover, reduce heat, and simmer 10 minutes (fish may not be

completely cooked). Remove from heat. Let stand, covered, 10 minutes. Remove fish from pan with a slotted spoon; place on a dish. Cover and chill. Discard cooking liquid.
2. To prepare sauce, combine mayonnaise and next 9 ingredients in a small bowl; cover and chill.
3. Cook peas in boiling water 1 minute or until crisp-tender. Drain and rinse with cold water; drain. Arrange 2 cups lettuce and ¾ cup peas on each of 4 plates. Top each serving with 1 salmon fillet and about 3 tablespoons sauce. Yield: 4 servings.

CALORIES 411 (38% from fat); FAT 17.4g (sat 4.1g, mono 6.7g, poly 5.6g); PROTEIN 41.1g; CARB 19.2g; FIBER 4.2g; CHOL 87mg; IRON 2.3mg; SODIUM 684mg; CALC 132mg

QUICK & EASY

Ginger-Garlic Broccolini

Broccolini is a cross between broccoli and Chinese kale; sometimes it's labeled "baby broccoli." It has a subtle peppery bite and crunchy texture.

  1 tablespoon canola oil
  2 teaspoons minced peeled fresh ginger
 ¼ teaspoon crushed red pepper
  2 garlic cloves, minced
  1 pound Broccolini, trimmed
 ¾ teaspoon salt
 ¼ cup mirin (sweet rice wine)
 ¼ cup water

1. Heat oil in a large nonstick skillet over medium-high heat. Add ginger, pepper, and garlic; sauté 30 seconds. Add Broccolini and salt, and sauté 2 minutes. Add mirin and water; cover and cook over low heat 10 minutes or until tender. Yield: 4 servings.

CALORIES 109 (29% from fat); FAT 3.5g (sat 0.3g, mono 2.1g, poly 1.1g); PROTEIN 3.7g; CARB 12.4g; FIBER 1.3g; CHOL 0mg; IRON 0.9mg; SODIUM 472mg; CALC 75mg

Creative Contest Recipes

Here are more winning recipes from the 2006 *Cooking Light* Ultimate Reader Recipe Contest finalists.

QUICK & EASY
Chipotle-Lime Crab Crisps

FINALIST—STARTERS AND DRINKS

"These appetizers combine sweet crab, Parmesan cheese, jícama, bell pepper, cilantro, and mayonnaise highlighted with fiery chipotles. A little crab goes a long way in these appetizers."

—Bob Gadsby, Great Falls, Montana

48 baked tortilla chips
½ cup reduced-fat mayonnaise
1 teaspoon chopped canned chipotle chile in adobo sauce
1 tablespoon fresh lime juice
¾ pound lump crabmeat, shell pieces removed
¼ cup (1 ounce) grated fresh Parmesan cheese
2 tablespoons finely chopped peeled jícama
2 tablespoons thinly sliced green onions
2 tablespoons finely chopped red bell pepper
2 tablespoons finely chopped fresh cilantro
1 tablespoon finely chopped celery
1 avocado, peeled and diced

1. Preheat oven to 350°.
2. Arrange tortilla chips in a single layer on 2 baking sheets.
3. Combine mayonnaise, chile, and juice, stirring with a whisk.
4. Combine crab and next 6 ingredients in a medium bowl. Add mayonnaise mixture, stirring until well combined. Spoon about 1 tablespoon crab mixture onto each chip. Bake at 350° for 5 minutes or until thoroughly heated; top chips evenly with avocado. Yield: 16 servings (serving size: 3 crisps).

CALORIES 85 (35% from fat); FAT 3.3g (sat 0.6g, mono 1.5g, poly 0.8g); PROTEIN 5.1g; CARB 9.1g; FIBER 1.2g; CHOL 18mg; IRON 0.4mg; SODIUM 211mg; CALC 44mg

MAKE AHEAD
Sour Cream Panna Cotta with Blackberry-Zinfandel Compote

FINALIST—DESSERTS

"I developed this light but rich-tasting dessert for a get-together dinner for fitness instructors. I've made this for other entertaining events because I can prepare it ahead of time, which I love."

—Camilla Saulsbury, Nacogdoches, Texas

PANNA COTTA:

2½ teaspoons unflavored gelatin
¼ cup water
1¼ cups evaporated fat-free milk
½ cup powdered sugar
1 vanilla bean, split lengthwise
2 cups reduced-fat sour cream
¼ teaspoon ground cardamom

COMPOTE:

3 cups frozen blackberries, thawed and divided
¼ cup zinfandel or other fruity dry red wine
3 tablespoons granulated sugar

REMAINING INGREDIENT:

8 mint sprigs

1. To prepare panna cotta, sprinkle gelatin over water in a small bowl; let stand 10 minutes. Bring milk, powdered sugar, and vanilla bean to a boil in a medium saucepan over medium-high heat. Remove pan from heat; remove vanilla bean with a slotted spoon. Scrape seeds from vanilla bean. Stir seeds into milk mixture; discard bean.
2. Add gelatin mixture to milk mixture, stirring with a whisk until gelatin dissolves. Add sour cream and cardamom; stir until well combined. Divide mixture evenly among 8 (6-ounce) custard cups. Cover and refrigerate for 8 hours or overnight.
3. To prepare compote, place 1 cup blackberries, wine, and granulated sugar in a food processor, and process until smooth. Strain blackberry mixture through a fine sieve into a medium saucepan, and discard solids. Bring mixture to a boil over medium-high heat, and cook 1 minute. Remove from heat; add 2 cups blackberries. Cool completely.
4. Loosen edges of custards with a knife or rubber spatula. Place a dessert plate, upside down, on top of each cup; invert onto plates. Serve with compote; top with mint sprigs. Yield: 8 servings (serving size: 1 panna cotta, about ¼ cup compote, and 1 mint sprig).

CALORIES 219 (32% from fat); FAT 7.7g (sat 4.7g, mono 2.2g, poly 0.4g); PROTEIN 6.6g; CARB 30.3g; FIBER 2.9g; CHOL 34mg; IRON 0.6mg; SODIUM 89mg; CALC 218mg

For *Cooking Light* readers, being healthy means eating healthy, being active, and living well.

Whole Wheat Blend Rotini with Spicy Turkey Sausage and Mustard Greens

FINALIST—ENTRÉES
—Jeff Violette, Oakland, Maine

1 (14-ounce) can fat-free, less-sodium chicken broth, divided
4 quarts water
1 (13.5-ounce) package uncooked whole wheat blend rotini (corkscrew pasta)
 Cooking spray
1½ cups chopped yellow onion (about 1 large)
2 garlic cloves, minced
1 pound hot turkey Italian sausage
8 ounces bagged prewashed cut mustard greens
½ cup half-and-half
½ cup (2 ounces) grated fresh pecorino Romano cheese
½ teaspoon kosher salt
¼ teaspoon freshly ground black pepper

1. Place ½ cup broth in a small saucepan over medium heat; simmer until reduced to 3 tablespoons (about 6 minutes). Remove from heat.
2. Combine water and remaining broth in a large Dutch oven. Bring to a boil over high heat; stir in pasta. Cook, uncovered, 10 minutes or until al dente. Drain well; place pasta in a large bowl. Keep warm.
3. Heat a Dutch oven over medium heat. Coat pan with cooking spray. Add onion; cook 4 minutes or until tender, stirring occasionally. Add garlic; cook 1 minute, stirring constantly. Remove casings from sausage. Add sausage to pan; cook 6 minutes or until browned, stirring to crumble. Stir in greens; cook 2 minutes or until greens wilt. Add reduced broth, half-and-half, and cheese. Cook 4 minutes or until cheese melts and mixture thickens, stirring frequently.
4. Add sausage mixture to pasta, and sprinkle with salt and pepper. Toss well. Serve immediately. Yield: 8 servings (serving size: 1¼ cups).

CALORIES 328 (29% from fat); FAT 10.4g (sat 4.3g, mono 3.4g, poly 2.3g); PROTEIN 20.6g; CARB 40.7g; FIBER 5.4g; CHOL 61mg; IRON 3.3mg; SODIUM 635mg; CALC 164mg

Super Soups

These nurturing one-dish meals make it easy to enjoy a variety of nutrient-rich foods.

Mushroom, Barley, and Beef Soup

Try to use hulled barley for this soup—it's a less refined form of the grain that provides more fiber and iron than pearled barley, which will also work nicely. Beef stew meat also contributes iron and selenium.

½ cup dried porcini mushrooms (about ¼ ounce)
1 cup boiling water
 Cooking spray
3½ cups sliced cremini mushrooms (about 8 ounces)
1½ cups chopped onion (about 1 medium)
½ cup finely chopped carrot (about 1 medium)
½ cup finely chopped celery
½ cup finely chopped parsnip (about 1 small)
2 garlic cloves, minced
1 tablespoon olive oil
12 ounces lean beef stew meat, cut into bite-sized pieces
6 cups less-sodium beef broth, divided
2 cups water
½ teaspoon salt
¼ teaspoon freshly ground black pepper
2 thyme sprigs
1 cup uncooked barley
2 tablespoons chopped fresh parsley

1. Place porcini mushrooms in a medium bowl; cover with boiling water. Cover and let stand 30 minutes or until tender. Drain mushrooms in a colander over a bowl, reserving liquid. Chop mushrooms; set aside.
2. Heat a Dutch oven over medium-high heat. Coat pan with cooking spray. Add cremini mushrooms and onion; sauté 10 minutes or until lightly browned. Spoon onion mixture into a medium bowl. Recoat pan with cooking spray. Add carrot, celery, parsnip, and garlic; sauté 4 minutes or until lightly browned. Add carrot mixture to onion mixture.
3. Heat oil in pan over medium-high heat. Add beef; cook 3 minutes, browning on all sides. Add 1 cup broth to pan, scraping pan to loosen browned bits. Add 5 cups broth, chopped porcini, porcini liquid, onion mixture, 2 cups water, salt, pepper, and thyme. Bring to a boil; cover, reduce heat to medium-low, and simmer 1 hour or until beef is just tender.
4. Discard thyme sprigs. Stir in barley; cover and cook 30 minutes or until barley is al dente. Uncover and cook 15 minutes. Remove from heat; sprinkle with parsley. Yield: 6 servings (serving size: about 1½ cups soup and 1 teaspoon parsley).

CALORIES 318 (27% from fat); FAT 9.6g (sat 2.9g, mono 4.6g, poly 0.9g); PROTEIN 25.7g; CARB 32.5g; FIBER 7.4g; CHOL 58mg; IRON 3.8mg; SODIUM 700mg; CALC 47mg

Ribollita with Herb Pesto

The intensely aromatic pesto is also good tossed with hot pasta.

SOUP:
1½ teaspoons extravirgin olive oil
2½ cups chopped red onion (1 large)
½ cup chopped carrot (about 1 large)
½ cup chopped celery
2 garlic cloves, chopped
1¾ cups (¼-inch) cubed Yukon gold potato (about 1 medium)
2 teaspoons chopped fresh sage
6 cups fat-free, less-sodium chicken broth
6 cups stemmed sliced Swiss chard (about 1 bunch)
½ teaspoon salt
¼ teaspoon freshly ground black pepper
1 (15-ounce) can pinto beans, rinsed and drained

HERB PESTO:

½ cup chopped basil leaves

¼ cup walnuts, toasted

2 tablespoons chopped fresh flat-leaf parsley

1 tablespoon extravirgin olive oil

1 tablespoon hot water

1 teaspoon chopped rosemary leaves

½ teaspoon thyme leaves (optional)

½ teaspoon fresh lemon juice

¼ teaspoon salt

⅛ teaspoon freshly ground black pepper

2 garlic cloves, minced

REMAINING INGREDIENT:

8 (1-ounce) slices Italian bread, toasted

1. To prepare soup, heat 1½ teaspoons oil in a large Dutch oven over medium-high heat. Add onion, carrot, and celery; sauté 6 minutes or until onion is tender. Add chopped garlic; cook 1 minute. Stir in potato and sage. Stir in broth; bring to a boil. Cover, reduce heat, and simmer 10 minutes. Stir in chard; simmer 10 minutes or until potato is tender. Add ½ teaspoon salt, ¼ teaspoon pepper, and beans. Simmer 5 minutes or until hot. Remove from heat; keep warm.

2. To prepare herb pesto, place basil and next 10 ingredients in a food processor. Process until smooth, scraping sides with a spatula. Spread 1½ teaspoons pesto over each bread slice. Ladle 1 cup soup into each of 8 bowls. Tuck 1 pesto-topped bread slice into each serving. Yield: 8 servings.

CALORIES 232 (26% from fat); FAT 6.7g (sat 1g, mono 2.9g, poly 2.5g); PROTEIN 9g; CARB 35.7g; FIBER 7g; CHOL 0mg; IRON 3mg; SODIUM 866mg; CALC 100mg

Soup is a delicious way to fit in a variety of colorful produce.

Red Lentil Mulligatawny with Apple-Celery Salsa

This rich, creamy soup will thicken as it cools. Thin it with hot water, a tablespoon at a time, to the desired consistency. Lentils provide fiber, folate, and protein, as well as iron. The fresh topping adds vitamin C, plus a dose of quercetin.

SALSA:

⅔ cup finely chopped Granny Smith apple

¼ cup finely chopped celery

1 tablespoon chopped fresh cilantro

1 tablespoon fresh lime juice

SOUP:

3½ cups fat-free, less-sodium chicken broth

1 cup dried small red lentils

1 cup chopped onion

1½ cups light coconut milk

3 tablespoons tomato paste

1 teaspoon grated peeled fresh ginger

½ teaspoon ground cumin

⅛ teaspoon ground turmeric

1 teaspoon fresh lime juice

½ teaspoon salt

¼ teaspoon freshly ground black pepper

1. To prepare salsa, combine first 4 ingredients; cover and chill.

2. To prepare soup, place broth, lentils, and onion in a Dutch oven over medium-high heat; bring to a boil. Cover, reduce heat, and simmer 15 minutes or until lentils are tender. Pour half of lentil mixture into a blender; let stand 5 minutes. Process until smooth. Pour pureed lentil mixture into a bowl. Pour remaining lentil mixture into blender; process until smooth. Add coconut milk and next 4 ingredients; process until smooth. Return pureed lentil mixture and coconut milk mixture to pan. Cover and simmer over medium heat 10 minutes. Remove from heat; stir in 1 teaspoon juice, salt, and pepper. Ladle about 1 cup soup into each of 4 bowls; top each serving with ¼ cup salsa. Yield: 4 servings.

CALORIES 280 (19% from fat); FAT 5.9g (sat 4.4g, mono 0.1g, poly 0.1g); PROTEIN 17.6g; CARB 42.4g; FIBER 9.6g; CHOL 0mg; IRON 4.1mg; SODIUM 677mg; CALC 50mg

Farro Minestrone with Brussels Sprouts, Butternut Squash, and Chestnuts

Spelt (called farro in Italy) is an ancient, unhybridized form of wheat that adds fiber to this soup.

1 cup uncooked spelt (farro, about 6 ounces)

1 tablespoon extravirgin olive oil

1 cup coarsely chopped onion

½ cup finely chopped carrot (about 1 small)

⅓ cup finely chopped celery

3 ounces pancetta, chopped

2 garlic cloves, minced

5 cups fat-free, less-sodium chicken broth

⅓ cup dry white wine

1½ cups bottled chestnuts, halved

1 cup diced peeled butternut squash

1 cup quartered Brussels sprouts (about 5 ounces)

¼ teaspoon freshly ground black pepper

1 cup grape tomatoes, halved

1 ounce shaved pecorino Romano cheese

1. Place spelt in a large saucepan. Cover with water to 2 inches above spelt; bring to a boil. Reduce heat, and simmer 20 minutes or until tender. Drain; set aside.

2. Heat oil in a Dutch oven over medium-high heat. Add onion, carrot, celery, pancetta, and garlic; sauté 8 minutes or until mixture is very fragrant and beginning to brown. Stir in broth and wine, scraping pan to loosen browned bits. Add chestnuts, squash, Brussels sprouts, and pepper; bring to a boil. Reduce heat, and simmer, uncovered, 10 minutes. Stir in spelt and tomatoes; cover and cook 10 minutes. Ladle about 1 cup soup into each of 6 bowls; sprinkle evenly with cheese. Yield: 6 servings.

CALORIES 333 (27% from fat); FAT 10.1g (sat 3.4g, mono 2.5g, poly 0.7g); PROTEIN 11.7g; CARB 52.8g; FIBER 5.4g; CHOL 15mg; IRON 2.9mg; SODIUM 638mg; CALC 125mg

Substitute Gruyère or Jack cheese for the Cheddar in the grilled cheese sandwich, if desired.

Winter Potage
Grilled cheese sandwich*
Light pound cake

*Heat a medium nonstick skillet over medium-high heat; coat pan with cooking spray. Sauté ½ cup thinly sliced onion 6 minutes or until golden. Remove from pan; set aside. Spread each of 4 slices of rustic sourdough bread with 1 teaspoon Dijon mustard; top each with 1 tablespoon onion and 3 tablespoons reduced-fat sharp Cheddar cheese. Top each with 1 bread slice. Reduce heat to medium. Coat pan with cooking spray; cook sandwiches 2 minutes on each side or until cheese melts.

Winter Potage

A hearty combination of six vegetables gives layers of flavor to this soup. A squeeze of fresh lemon and a little cracked black pepper at the table brighten each bowl.

    1 teaspoon olive oil
    1 teaspoon butter
    1 cup thinly sliced leek (about 1 large)
    ½ cup sliced celery
    2 garlic cloves, minced
    2 cups chopped broccoli florets
    2 cups baby spinach leaves
    1 cup frozen shelled edamame
    1 cup frozen petite green peas
    1 tablespoon rice
    ⅛ teaspoon ground red pepper
    3 cups fat-free, less-sodium chicken broth
 1½ cups water
 1½ teaspoons fresh lemon juice
    ¼ teaspoon salt
    ¼ teaspoon black pepper
       Lemon wedges (optional)
       Cracked black pepper (optional)

1. Heat oil and butter in a Dutch oven over medium-high heat. Add leek and celery; sauté 4 minutes or until tender.

Stir in garlic; cook 1 minute. Add broccoli and next 5 ingredients. Stir in broth and water; bring to a boil. Reduce heat, cover, and simmer 20 minutes or until vegetables are soft.

2. Place one-third of vegetable mixture in a food processor or blender; process until smooth. Pour pureed mixture into a large bowl; repeat procedure with remaining vegetable mixture. Stir in juice, salt, and ¼ teaspoon black pepper. Garnish with lemon wedges and cracked black pepper, if desired. Yield: 4 servings (serving size: 1½ cups).

CALORIES 152 (25% from fat); FAT 4.2g (sat 0.9g, mono 1.5g, poly 1.2g); PROTEIN 10g; CARB 19.3g; FIBER 6.4g; CHOL 3mg; IRON 3.2mg; SODIUM 540mg; CALC 101mg

Black-Eyed Pea Posole with Pork and Collard Greens

Black-eyed peas stand in for the traditional hominy in this version of the Mexican dish posole. Peas are an excellent source of folate, while greens infuse the soup with vitamin A.

    1 poblano pepper
       Cooking spray
    ¾ pound boneless pork shoulder, trimmed and cut into ½-inch cubes
    3 cups fat-free, less-sodium chicken broth, divided
    4 cups loosely packed bagged, prewashed, chopped collard greens (about 8 ounces)
    1 cup chopped red onion
    1 cup chopped tomatillos
    ½ cup chopped fresh cilantro
    2 teaspoons finely chopped jalapeño pepper
    ½ teaspoon dried Mexican oregano (such as McCormick's)
    2 garlic cloves, chopped
    1 (15-ounce) can black-eyed peas, rinsed and drained
    ¼ teaspoon salt
    ¼ teaspoon black pepper
    6 lime wedges

1. Preheat broiler.
2. Place 1 poblano pepper on a foil-lined

baking sheet; broil 3 inches from heat 8 minutes or until blackened and charred, turning after 6 minutes. Place in a heavy-duty zip-top plastic bag; seal. Let stand 15 minutes. Peel and discard skin; discard seeds, membrane, and stem. Coarsely chop pepper; set aside.

3. Heat a Dutch oven over medium-high heat. Coat pan with cooking spray. Add pork; cook 4 minutes, browning on all sides. Add 1 cup broth, scraping pan to loosen browned bits. Stir in 2 cups broth, chopped roasted poblano, greens, and next 6 ingredients. Bring to a boil; cover, reduce heat, and simmer 40 minutes or until pork is tender. Stir in peas, salt, and black pepper; simmer, uncovered 5 minutes or until thoroughly heated. Serve with lime wedges. Yield: 6 servings (serving size: about 1 cup soup and 1 lime wedge).

CALORIES 153 (28% from fat); FAT 4.7g (sat 1.5g, mono 1.9g, poly 0.7g); PROTEIN 15.4g; CARB 12.5g; FIBER 3.7g; CHOL 38mg; IRON 1.7mg; SODIUM 422mg; CALC 73mg

Lentil and Spinach Soup with Roasted Red Pepper and Pomegranate Molasses
(pictured on page 228)

Spinach, plus garnishes of roasted red pepper and pomegranate molasses, enrich this satisfying soup with antioxidants.

    6 cups water
 1½ cups dried lentils
    2 garlic cloves, chopped
    1 bay leaf
    1 (3-inch) cinnamon stick
    4 cups diced Japanese eggplant (about 2)
    1 cup chopped onion
    1 thyme sprig
    1 tablespoon extravirgin olive oil
    4 cups less-sodium beef broth, divided
    ½ cup chopped fresh flat-leaf parsley
    1 (6-ounce) package baby spinach
    1 teaspoon salt
    ½ teaspoon freshly ground black pepper
    8 teaspoons pomegranate molasses
    ½ cup thinly sliced bottled roasted red bell pepper

1. Place first 5 ingredients in a Dutch oven over medium-high heat; bring to a boil. Reduce heat, and simmer 20 minutes. Discard bay leaf and cinnamon stick. Set lentil mixture aside.

2. Preheat oven to 450°.

3. Place eggplant, onion, and thyme in a 13 x 9–inch baking dish. Drizzle with oil; toss to coat. Bake at 450° for 30 minutes, stirring after 15 minutes. Stir in 1 cup broth; bake 10 minutes. Discard thyme; add eggplant mixture to lentil mixture.

4. Stir 3 cups broth and parsley into lentil mixture; bring to a boil over medium-high heat. Cover, reduce heat, and simmer 10 minutes. Remove from heat. Add spinach; stir gently until spinach wilts. Stir in salt and pepper. Ladle about 1 cup soup into each of 8 bowls; drizzle each serving with 1 teaspoon pomegranate molasses, and top with about 1 tablespoon roasted red bell pepper. Yield: 8 servings.

CALORIES 224 (8% from fat); FAT 2g (sat 0.3g, mono 1.3g, poly 0.3g); PROTEIN 13.3g; CARB 40g; FIBER 7g; CHOL 0mg; IRON 5.1mg; SODIUM 563mg; CALC 57mg

WINE NOTE: One wine works well with the earthy, bitter, and sweet flavors in this soup: pinot noir. Good pinot noir demonstrates an earthiness of its own, plus an attractive bitterness and a "sweet spot" of cherry-pomegranate fruitiness. Try Pedroncelli "F. Johnson Vineyard" 2003 from Sonoma County, California ($15).

Get your USDA daily recommended servings of fruits and vegetables with a nutrient-rich bowl of soup.

lighten up

Ramen Noodle Salad, Revamped

An Asian side dish is transformed from a rarity to a regular feature in a Massachusetts reader's line-up.

Stacy Legrand of Westborough, Massachusetts, strives for a healthy lifestyle, which includes cooking meals at home most weeknights and exercising regularly. But her recipe for Asian Pasta Salad didn't seem to fit into her health-conscious repertoire. So we've helped revamp it.

The dressing contained the bulk of the fat, calories, and sodium, so it took some tweaking. First, the amount of canola oil was reduced from ¾ cup to 2 tablespoons, shaving 100 calories and 12 grams of fat per serving. To add depth and volume to the dressing, we added less-sodium beef broth, which contributes negligible calories and sodium per portion. A bit of freshly ground black pepper adds a spicy note, while a discreet ¼ teaspoon salt bumped up the flavor.

We substituted Chinese plain noodles for the ramen noodles. Swapping noodles and adding beef broth, a smidgen of salt, and a little pepper for the noodle flavor packets lowered the sodium by more than 317 milligrams per serving.

Even though the seeds and nuts provide mostly heart-healthy unsaturated fats, we reduced the amounts of both to keep calories in check, and we toasted them to heighten their flavors.

BEFORE	AFTER
SERVING SIZE	
¾ cup	
CALORIES PER SERVING	
388	130
FAT	
28.3g	4g
PERCENT OF TOTAL CALORIES	
66%	28%

Asian Pasta Salad

Use any combination of nuts and seeds. This salad would also be good with sliced bell pepper or shiitake mushrooms. Serve as an accompaniment to pepper steak or pork chops glazed with hoisin sauce. Look for the wheat noodles labeled as *plain* for this salad.

2 tablespoons sliced almonds
2 tablespoons unsalted sunflower seed kernels
1 (8-ounce) package Chinese noodles, crumbled (such as KA-ME)
⅓ cup white wine vinegar
⅓ cup less-sodium beef broth
¼ cup sugar
2 tablespoons canola oil
¼ teaspoon salt
¼ teaspoon freshly ground black pepper
1 cup chopped green onions
1 (10-ounce) package angel hair slaw

1. Heat a medium nonstick skillet over medium heat. Add first 3 ingredients to pan; cook 3 minutes or until lightly toasted, stirring frequently.

2. Combine vinegar and next 5 ingredients in a small bowl, stirring with a whisk.

3. Combine toasted noodle mixture, green onions, and slaw in a large bowl. Add vinegar mixture, tossing well. Let stand 5 minutes. Yield: 12 servings (serving size: about ¾ cup).

CALORIES 130 (28% from fat); FAT 4g (sat 0.3g, mono 1.9g, poly 1.3g); PROTEIN 3g; CARB 20.9g; FIBER 1.5g; CHOL 0mg; IRON 0.5mg; SODIUM 165mg; CALC 12mg

Whole-Grain Pastas

Reap the nutritional benefits of whole grains with these flavorful dishes.

Soba (SOH-buh) is a Japanese pasta made with buckwheat and wheat flour. For more heat, add ½ teaspoon crushed red pepper instead of ¼ teaspoon.

QUICK & EASY

Kamut Spirals with Chicken-Artichoke Wine Sauce

Kamut (kuh-MOOT) gets its name from the ancient Egyptian word for "wheat." Its grains are up to three times larger and boast up to 40 percent more protein than standard wheat grains. Kamut is also high in lipids, amino acids, vitamins, and minerals.

- 1 (12-ounce) package kamut spirals
- 2 tablespoons olive oil
- 1½ pounds chicken breast tenders, cut into bite-sized pieces
- 4 garlic cloves, minced
- ½ cup white wine
- ½ teaspoon salt
- ¼ teaspoon freshly ground black pepper
- 2 (15-ounce) cans artichoke quarters, rinsed, drained, and finely chopped
- ½ cup (2 ounces) grated Parmigiano-Reggiano cheese
- ⅓ cup finely chopped fresh basil
- Chopped fresh basil (optional)

1. Cook pasta according to package directions, omitting salt and fat.
2. Heat oil in a large skillet over medium-high heat. Add chicken to pan; sauté 2 minutes or until browned. Add garlic; sauté 1 minute. Add wine, salt, pepper, and artichokes; simmer 5 minutes or until sauce is thickened and chicken is done. Remove from heat; stir in cheese and ⅓ cup basil. Place sauce and pasta in a large bowl; stir gently to combine. Garnish with chopped basil, if desired. Yield: 6 servings (serving size: 1⅓ cups).

CALORIES 434 (19% from fat); FAT 9.2g (sat 2.7g, mono 4.5g, poly 1.2g); PROTEIN 40.1g; CARB 49g; FIBER 4.7g; CHOL 72mg; IRON 4.3mg; SODIUM 629mg; CALC 156mg

---

QUICK & EASY

Sausage and Bean Ragù on Quinoa Macaroni

Quinoa (KEEN-wah) is a South American grain prized for its high protein content. Use whole wheat macaroni, which includes eight essential amino acids, if you can't find it.

- 1 (16-ounce) package quinoa macaroni
- 1 tablespoon olive oil
- 1 cup finely chopped onion (about 1 medium)
- 2 garlic cloves, minced
- 1 pound bulk turkey Italian sausage
- ½ cup dry white wine
- ½ cup fat-free, less-sodium chicken broth
- ½ teaspoon fennel seeds
- ¼ teaspoon freshly ground black pepper
- 2 (16-ounce) cans cannellini beans or other white beans, rinsed and drained
- 2 (14.5-ounce) cans diced tomatoes, undrained
- ½ cup (2 ounces) shaved Romano cheese

1. Cook pasta according to package directions, omitting salt and fat.
2. Heat oil in a large nonstick skillet over medium-high heat. Add onion and garlic; sauté 3 minutes. Add sausage; cook until browned, stirring to crumble. Stir in wine, scraping pan to loosen browned bits. Add broth and next 4 ingredients; bring to a boil. Reduce heat, and simmer 15 minutes.
3. Add pasta, stirring well. Top evenly with cheese. Serve immediately. Yield: 8 servings (serving size: 1½ cups pasta mixture and 1 tablespoon cheese).

CALORIES 410 (24% from fat); FAT 10.7g (sat 3.6g, mono 3.2g, poly 2.4g); PROTEIN 23.4g; CARB 58.9g; FIBER 8.9g; CHOL 41mg; IRON 4.4mg; SODIUM 729mg; CALC 141mg

---

- 8 ounces shiitake mushrooms
- 9 cups fat-free, less-sodium chicken broth
- 1 (5-inch) piece peeled fresh ginger, sliced
- 1 whole garlic head, peeled and crushed
- 3 tablespoons yellow miso (soybean paste)
- 1 (14-ounce) package extrafirm tofu, drained and diced
- 1 tablespoon dark sesame oil
- ¼ teaspoon crushed red pepper
- 12 ounces buckwheat soba noodles
- 1½ cups shredded napa (Chinese) cabbage
- ½ cup shredded carrots
- ½ cup finely sliced green onions
- 2 tablespoons toasted sesame seeds

1. Remove stems from mushrooms. Reserve stems. Slice mushroom caps into ¼-inch julienne strips; set aside.
2. Combine stems, broth, ginger, and garlic in a large saucepan; bring to a boil. Reduce heat, and simmer 15 minutes. Strain broth through a sieve into a bowl; discard solids. Add miso to broth, stirring well with a whisk. Add tofu. Cover and keep warm.
3. Heat oil in a large nonstick skillet over medium-high heat. Add mushrooms caps and pepper to pan; sauté 3 minutes or until browned. Add to broth mixture.
4. Cook noodles according to package directions, omitting salt and fat. Drain and rinse with cold water; drain.
5. Place ⅔ cup noodles into each of 6 shallow bowls; pour 1½ cups hot broth mixture over each serving. Garnish each serving with ¼ cup cabbage, about 1½ tablespoons carrots, about 1½ tablespoons onions, and 1 teaspoon sesame seeds. Yield: 6 servings.

CALORIES 423 (21% from fat); FAT 10g (sat 1.8g, mono 3g, poly 4.3g); PROTEIN 22.9g; CARB 63.1g; FIBER 7.7g; CHOL 0mg; IRON 9.9mg; SODIUM 905mg; CALC 142mg

Fiber Count

The Whole Grains Council offers the following fiber content information for various whole-grain pastas, based on a two-ounce serving size. By contrast, two ounces of store brand refined durum semolina—or "white"—pasta has two grams of fiber.

All Whole Grains (made from only 100% whole grains)

Manufacturer	Grain	Fiber Content
Lundberg Farm	Brown rice	3 grams
Mrs. Leeper's (AIPC)	Corn	4 grams
American Italian Pasta Co.	Wheat	5 grams
American Italian Pasta Co.	Multigrain	5 grams
Bionaturae	Wheat	5 grams
Eden	Kamut and buckwheat	5 grams
Eden	Kamut and quinoa	5 grams
Gia Russa	Wheat	5 grams
Purity Foods Vita-Spelt	Spelt	5 grams
Eden	Kamut	6 grams
Hodgson Mill	Wheat	6 grams
Racconto/Bella Terra	Wheat	6 grams
Racconto/Bella Terra	8 whole grains	7 grams
Eden	Rye	8 grams

Whole Grains Plus Other Ingredients

Hodgson Mill	Wheat/egg/vegetable	5 grams
Hodgson Mill	Wheat/flax	6 grams
Food for Life	Multigrain	7 grams
Lifestream (Nature's Path)	Whole grain and flax	8 grams

Whole and Refined Grain Blends

Healthy Harvest	Wheat	3 grams
Barilla PLUS	Wheat, oats, spelt, and barley	4 grams

Tips from the Test Kitchens

Whole-grain foods contain all three parts of a grain's seed or kernel—bran, germ, and endosperm—while refined grains contain only the endosperm. Consequently, whole-grain pastas cook differently from their refined counterparts. Our Test Kitchens professionals offer these pointers:

• **Do not overcook** whole-grain pastas. We found that the package instructions for the pastas are an accurate gauge of cooking time. Overcooked, they tend to become even mushier than overcooked regular pasta.

• **Serve immediately.** Cooked whole-grain pastas dry out more quickly than refined-flour pastas.

• **Coat immediately.** Toss these pastas in sauce as soon after cooking as possible to keep them moist and supple.

• **Consider creamier sauces,** which tend to adhere to the whole-grain pastas better than tomato-based sauces.

• **For skeptics, start mild** with a whole-grain pasta blend. These mix the flavor and texture of regular pasta with whole grains and cook in a way you are more likely to be familiar with.

Creamy Spinach Lasagna

A less-sweet marinara sauce helps balance the flavor of this dish, with its smooth spinach sauce and rich mozzarella topping.

> 12 cooked whole wheat lasagna noodles
> 1 tablespoon olive oil
> 2¼ cups chopped onion (about 2 medium)
> 2 garlic cloves, minced
> 1 (16-ounce) package frozen chopped spinach, thawed, drained, and squeezed dry
> ⅓ cup all-purpose flour (about 1½ ounces)
> 3 cups 2% reduced-fat milk
> ½ teaspoon salt
> ¼ teaspoon freshly ground black pepper
> ¼ teaspoon ground red pepper
> 1 (26-ounce) jar marinara sauce
> Cooking spray
> 1½ cups (6 ounces) shredded part-skim mozzarella cheese
> Parsley sprigs (optional)

1. Cook pasta according to package directions, omitting salt and fat.

2. Preheat oven to 375°.

3. Heat oil in a large skillet over medium heat. Add onion; cook 10 minutes or until onion is browned, stirring occasionally. Stir in garlic and spinach. Reduce heat, cover, and cook 3 minutes or until spinach is tender. Set aside.

4. Lightly spoon flour into a dry measuring cup; level with a knife. Combine flour, milk, salt, black pepper, and red pepper in a small saucepan, stirring with a whisk. Bring to a boil over medium-high heat, stirring frequently. Reduce heat, and simmer 1 minute, stirring frequently. Add 2 cups milk mixture to spinach mixture. Cover remaining milk mixture, and set aside.

5. Spread ½ cup marinara sauce in bottom of a 13 x 9–inch baking dish coated with cooking spray. Arrange 3 lasagna noodles over sauce; top with half of spinach mixture. Top with 3 lasagna noodles, 1 cup marinara sauce, and
Continued

¾ cup cheese. Layer 3 lasagna noodles, remaining spinach mixture, and 3 lasagna noodles. Top with remaining marinara sauce. Pour reserved milk mixture over top, and sprinkle with ¾ cup cheese. Bake at 375° for 50 minutes or until lasagna is browned on top. Garnish with parsley sprigs, if desired. Yield: 8 servings (serving size: 1 piece).

CALORIES 328 (25% from fat); FAT 9.3g (sat 3.8g, mono 3.6g, poly 1.2g); PROTEIN 17.3g; CARB 45.6g; FIBER 6.9g; CHOL 19mg; IRON 3.1mg; SODIUM 726mg; CALC 371mg

QUICK & EASY
Macaroni Salad with Gorgonzola

Serve this over a bed of fresh arugula or gourmet greens for an attractive presentation. If you prefer, substitute crumbled goat cheese for Gorgonzola.

  8 ounces whole wheat macaroni
  1 cup diced red bell pepper (about 1 medium)
  1 cup diced Granny Smith apple (about 1 medium)
  3 tablespoons chopped pecans, toasted
  ⅓ cup reduced-fat sour cream
  2 tablespoons champagne vinegar
  1 tablespoon low-fat mayonnaise
  ¾ teaspoon salt
  2 cups arugula, chopped
  ¼ cup (2 ounces) crumbled Gorgonzola cheese

1. Cook pasta according to package directions, omitting salt and fat. Drain. Add bell pepper, apple, and pecans.
2. Combine sour cream and next 3 ingredients. Stir until blended. Pour over macaroni mixture, tossing to coat. Stir in arugula, and sprinkle with cheese. Yield: 8 servings (serving size: ¾ cup).

CALORIES 173 (31% from fat); FAT 5.9g (sat 2.5g, mono 1.5g, poly 0.9g); PROTEIN 6.6g; CARB 26g; FIBER 3.7g; CHOL 10mg; IRON 1.3mg; SODIUM 344mg; CALC 72mg

You'll find whole-grain pasta in most major supermarkets. Look for specialty varieties in health-food stores.

Brown Rice Penne with Eggplant

Brown rice pasta has a firm texture that partners well with hearty toppings. It's also good in baked pasta dishes. Top with freshly ground black pepper for even more spicy heat.

  1 (16-ounce) package brown rice penne (or ziti)
  1 tablespoon olive oil
  3 cups cubed eggplant (about 1 small)
  1 cup finely chopped onion (about 1 medium)
  3 garlic cloves, minced
  1 teaspoon salt
  ¼ teaspoon crushed red pepper
  1 (26-ounce) jar fat-free pasta sauce (such as Muir Glen Organic)
  ⅓ cup finely chopped fresh basil
  1½ cups (6 ounces) preshredded Italian-blend or Parmesan cheese, divided

1. Cook pasta according to package directions, omitting salt and fat. Drain.
2. Heat oil in a large skillet over medium-high heat. Add eggplant and onion; sauté 8 minutes or until onion is browned. Stir in garlic; sauté 3 minutes. Add salt, pepper, and pasta sauce; bring to a simmer. Reduce heat, and cook 5 minutes. Remove from heat; stir in basil.
3. Toss eggplant mixture with pasta. Sprinkle with 1 cup cheese; toss gently. Top with ½ cup cheese. Serve immediately. Yield: 8 servings (serving size: 1¼ cups pasta).

CALORIES 353 (18% from fat); FAT 7.1g (sat 3.1g, mono 2.7g, poly 0.4g); PROTEIN 11.5g; CARB 56.3g; FIBER 5g; CHOL 17mg; IRON 4.2mg; SODIUM 430mg; CALC 202mg

Spelt Spaghetti with Shiitakes and Pecan Cream

The use of nuts to thicken sauces has been recorded in recipes dating back to medieval Rome. This luscious, creamy sauce features toasted pecans. If you can't find spelt pasta, use whole wheat instead.

  1 (12-ounce) package spelt spaghetti (such as Vita-Spelt)
  1½ cups 1% low-fat milk
  ½ cup chopped pecans, toasted
  2 teaspoons olive oil
  3 cups chopped shiitake mushroom caps (about 8 ounces)
  ½ cup diced shallots
  4 garlic cloves, minced
  1¼ teaspoons salt
  2 tablespoons chopped fresh parsley

1. Cook pasta according to package directions, omitting salt and fat.
2. Place milk and pecans in a blender or food processor; process until smooth. Set aside.
3. Heat oil in a large nonstick skillet over medium-high heat. Add mushrooms, shallots, and garlic; sauté 3 minutes or until golden. Stir in pecan mixture and salt; bring to a boil. Reduce heat, and simmer 5 minutes or until slightly thickened.
4. Remove from heat. Add pasta; toss gently to combine. Sprinkle with parsley, and serve immediately. Yield: 6 servings (serving size: 1⅓ cups pasta and 1 teaspoon parsley).

CALORIES 321 (28% from fat); FAT 10.1g (sat 1.2g, mono 5.1g, poly 2.2g); PROTEIN 12.2g; CARB 49.3g; FIBER 6.1g; CHOL 2.4mg; IRON 3mg; SODIUM 534mg; CALC 87mg

Straw and Hay Alfredo with Roasted Asparagus

This dish derives its name from the color contrast of the two types of pasta. Because it mixes the earthiness of whole wheat with the familiarity of regular pasta, it's a delicious introduction to whole-grain pastas. Truffle oil adds a pleasant, earthy undertone; you can substitute extravirgin olive oil. As with all alfredo dishes, serve immediately.

    2 cups 1% low-fat milk
    ⅓ cup (3 ounces) ⅓-less-fat cream
       cheese
    2 tablespoons all-purpose flour
    1 teaspoon salt
    1 teaspoon butter
    3 garlic cloves, minced
    1 cup (4 ounces) grated Parmigiano-
       Reggiano cheese
    1 pound asparagus, trimmed and cut
       into 2-inch pieces (about 2 cups)
       Cooking spray
    8 ounces uncooked whole wheat
       spaghetti
    8 ounces uncooked spaghetti
    2 tablespoons truffle oil
    ¼ teaspoon freshly ground black
       pepper

1. Preheat oven to 425°.
2. Place first four ingredients in a blender; process until smooth.
3. Melt butter in a saucepan over medium-high heat. Add garlic; sauté 30 seconds. Add milk mixture to pan; cook 3 minutes or until mixture simmers, stirring constantly. Cook 2 minutes or until thickened, stirring constantly. Remove from heat; stir in cheese. Cover.
4. Place asparagus on a jelly-roll pan coated with cooking spray. Bake at 425° for 10 minutes or until browned, stirring once.
5. Cook pastas according to package directions, omitting salt and fat; drain.
6. Place pastas and asparagus in a large bowl. Add cheese mixture, tossing well. Add truffle oil and pepper; toss gently. Serve immediately. Yield: 8 servings (serving size: 1 cup).

CALORIES 296 (35% from fat); FAT 11.4g (sat 5.2g, mono 4.7g, poly 0.8g); PROTEIN 14.5g; CARB 34.9g; FIBER 3.7g; CHOL 21mg; IRON 2.8mg; SODIUM 602mg; CALC 276mg

Frozen Assets

It's smart to have a variety of ingredients in your freezer.

Even if you prefer fresh, seasonal ingredients, having a selection of frozen fruits, vegetables, and other staples in the freezer empowers you to make fabulous dinners on the spur of the moment.

QUICK & EASY
Sesame Chicken Edamame Bowl

Frozen stir-fry mixes and frozen shelled edamame save prep time and don't require thawing. The slightly sweet and nutty stir-fried vegetables complement the delicately flavored chicken. You can serve this over udon noodles or rice stick noodles instead of rice.

    2 teaspoons canola oil
    1 tablespoon minced peeled fresh
       ginger
    2 teaspoons minced peeled fresh
       lemongrass
    2 garlic cloves, minced
    1 pound skinless, boneless chicken
       breast, cut into bite-sized pieces
    2 cups frozen shelled edamame
       (green soybeans)
    2 cups frozen bell pepper stir-fry
       mix
    2 tablespoons low-sodium soy
       sauce
    1 tablespoon mirin (sweet rice
       wine)
    1 teaspoon dark sesame oil
    ¼ teaspoon cornstarch
    ½ cup (¼-inch) diagonally cut green
       onions
    2 teaspoons dark sesame seeds
    ½ teaspoon salt
    2 cups hot cooked brown rice

1. Heat canola oil in a large nonstick skillet over medium-high heat. Add ginger, lemongrass, and garlic; sauté 1 minute or just until mixture begins to brown. Add chicken; sauté 2 minutes.

Add edamame and stir-fry mix; sauté 3 minutes. Combine soy sauce, mirin, sesame oil, and cornstarch, stirring with a whisk. Add to pan; cook 1 minute. Remove from heat. Stir in onions, sesame seeds, and salt. Serve over rice. Yield: 6 servings (serving size: ⅔ cup chicken mixture and ⅓ cup rice).

CALORIES 277 (21% from fat); FAT 6.5g (sat 0.7g, mono 2.3g, poly 2.6g); PROTEIN 25.5g; CARB 27.1g; FIBER 5.4g; CHOL 44mg; IRON 2.4mg; SODIUM 452mg; CALC 72mg

QUICK & EASY • MAKE AHEAD
Spice-Berry Balsamic Sauce

The warm spices complement the flavor punch from the black pepper and balsamic vinegar in this all-purpose sauce. Use one type of berry or a frozen-berry mixture. Serve warm over low-fat frozen yogurt, pancakes, or French toast.

    ½ cup cranberry juice cocktail
    ⅓ cup packed brown sugar
    1 tablespoon balsamic vinegar
    ⅛ teaspoon ground cardamom
    ⅛ teaspoon ground cinnamon
    ⅛ teaspoon freshly ground black
       pepper
    1 (12-ounce) package frozen berries
       (blueberries, strawberries, and
       raspberries)
    1 (3-inch) cinnamon stick
    2 tablespoons cornstarch
    2 tablespoons water

1. Combine first 8 ingredients in a medium saucepan; bring to a boil. Combine cornstarch and water, stirring with a whisk; add to fruit mixture. Boil 1 minute, stirring constantly. Discard cinnamon stick. Yield: 2 cups (serving size: 2 tablespoons).

CALORIES 33 (1% from fat); FAT 0g; PROTEIN 0.1g; CARB 8.5g; FIBER 0.5g; CHOL 0mg; IRON 0.3mg; SODIUM 3mg; CALC 9mg

QUICK & EASY
Skillet Paella

This one-dish meal makes the most of saffron-enhanced rice, shrimp, and chicken with summer vegetables from the freezer. Substitute a dash of turmeric if you don't have saffron.

  2 teaspoons olive oil
  1 cup chopped red onion
  ½ cup chopped celery
  1 teaspoon dried oregano
  1½ cups uncooked basmati rice
  ¼ teaspoon saffron threads, crushed
  1 pound skinless, boneless chicken breast, cut into bite-sized pieces
  3 cups fat-free, less-sodium chicken broth
  1 cup frozen whole-kernel corn
  ½ cup chopped bottled roasted red bell peppers
  1 teaspoon salt
  1 (10-ounce) package frozen chopped spinach, thawed
  ¼ pound medium shrimp, peeled and deveined
  ½ cup frozen green peas, thawed

1. Heat oil in a large nonstick skillet over medium-high heat. Add onion, celery, and oregano; sauté 4 minutes. Add rice, saffron, and chicken; sauté 3 minutes. Add broth and next 5 ingredients; bring to a boil. Cover, reduce heat, and simmer 15 minutes or until rice is done. Stir in peas. Yield: 6 servings (serving size: about 1½ cups).

CALORIES 256 (12% from fat); FAT 3.5g (sat 0.7g, mono 1.5g, poly 0.7g); PROTEIN 27.2g; CARB 29g; FIBER 3.5g; CHOL 73mg; IRON 2.8mg; SODIUM 748mg; CALC 111mg

QUICK & EASY • MAKE AHEAD
Cheddar Corn Bread with Pepitas

The green pumpkinseeds, or *pepitas*, lend crunch, while the green chiles add spicy heat. Pepitas are sold at large grocery stores or Mexican markets. Serve this bread with chili, spice-rubbed pork tenderloin, or as a savory snack with salsa.

  ½ cup (2 ounces) reduced-fat shredded Cheddar cheese
  ¼ cup nonfat buttermilk
  1 (10-ounce) package frozen cream-style corn, thawed
  1 (8½-ounce) package corn muffin mix (such as Jiffy)
  1 (4.5-ounce) can chopped green chiles, drained
     Cooking spray
  ¼ cup unsalted pumpkinseed kernels

1. Preheat oven to 400°.
2. Combine first 5 ingredients in a large bowl, stirring until dry ingredients are moistened. Spoon into an 8-inch square baking dish coated with cooking spray. Sprinkle top of batter with pumpkinseeds. Bake at 400° for 20 minutes or until a wooden pick inserted in center comes out clean. Yield: 8 servings.

CALORIES 204 (30% from fat); FAT 6.9g (sat 2.3g, mono 2.4g, poly 1.2g); PROTEIN 6g; CARB 30.5g; FIBER 1.3g; CHOL 12mg; IRON 1.6mg; SODIUM 436mg; CALC 107mg

QUICK & EASY
Sweet Corn and Hominy Quesadillas

This quesadilla has plenty of cheese and vegetables, so eat it with a knife and fork. Serve as a side dish with chipotle-spiced chicken, black beans, and chunky salsa.

  1 (10-ounce) package frozen cream-style corn, thawed
  12 (6-inch) corn tortillas
  ¾ cup (3 ounces) shredded reduced-fat Cheddar cheese
  1 (15.5-ounce) can white hominy, rinsed and drained
  6 tablespoons chopped green onions
  ¼ cup chopped fresh cilantro
  2 tablespoons canned chopped green chiles
     Cooking spray

1. Spread about 2½ tablespoons corn over each of 6 tortillas. Sprinkle 2 tablespoons cheese over each; top each with ¼ cup hominy, 1 tablespoon onions, 2 teaspoons cilantro, 1 teaspoon chiles, and 1 tortilla. Heat a large nonstick skillet over medium-high heat. Coat pan

with cooking spray. Place 2 quesadillas in pan; cook 3 minutes on each side or until tortillas are lightly browned. Set aside, and keep warm. Repeat procedure with remaining quesadillas. Cut each quesadilla into 4 wedges. Yield: 6 servings (serving size: 4 wedges).

CALORIES 200 (23% from fat); FAT 5g (sat 2.2g, mono 1.1g, poly 0.8g); PROTEIN 7.3g; CARB 34.3g; FIBER 4.2g; CHOL 11mg; IRON 0.4mg; SODIUM 335mg; CALC 143mg

STAFF FAVORITE
Shrimp Florentine with Caramelized Garlic

Make sure to buy frozen loose-leaf spinach for this recipe since you can measure just what you need. Purchase fresh, peeled garlic to save on prep time.

GARLIC:
  ½ teaspoon kosher salt
  20 garlic cloves, peeled
     Cooking spray

SHRIMP:
  2 teaspoons olive oil
  1 pound medium shrimp, peeled and deveined
  1 teaspoon butter
  ¾ cup half-and-half
  ½ cup fat-free, less-sodium chicken broth
  ⅓ cup (about 1½ ounces) grated Parmesan cheese
  ¼ teaspoon salt
  ¼ teaspoon crushed red pepper
  ⅛ teaspoon black pepper
  2 cups frozen loose-leaf spinach, thawed, drained, and squeezed dry
  4 cups hot cooked linguine (about 8 ounces uncooked pasta)

1. Preheat oven to 350°.
2. To prepare garlic, combine ½ teaspoon kosher salt and garlic in a bowl. Place garlic mixture on a jelly-roll pan coated with cooking spray. Bake at 350° for 25 minutes or until browned, stirring occasionally.
3. To prepare shrimp, heat oil in a large nonstick skillet over medium-high heat. Add shrimp; sauté 3 minutes or until done. Remove shrimp from pan.

4. Melt butter in pan over medium heat. Stir in half-and-half and next 5 ingredients. Cook 1 minute or until cheese melts, stirring constantly. Stir in shrimp and spinach; cook 1 minute. Combine shrimp mixture, garlic mixture, and pasta in a large bowl; toss well. Serve immediately. Yield: 4 servings (serving size: 1½ cups).

CALORIES 484 (24% from fat); FAT 13.1g (sat 5.8g, mono 4.4g, poly 1.6g); PROTEIN 38.2g; CARB 51.1g; FIBER 5.2g; CHOL 202mg; IRON 6.6mg; SODIUM 811mg; CALC 362mg

---

Five Frozen Fare Advantages

- Some frozen ingredients retain more nutritional attributes than fresh, which can spoil or lose nutrients as they sit on the shelf. Frozen fruits and vegetables are picked at the peak of nutritional value, when fully ripe and loaded with flavor, and are typically processed shortly after harvest.
- You can generally count on the quality and consistency of frozen foods, such as berries, corn, peas, and shrimp.
- Since March is not a time of year when fresh, locally grown berries, peas, or corn are in the produce aisle, frozen options are a ready and affordable alternative.
- Using frozen ingredients means nothing is wasted because you can measure what's needed in a recipe and put the rest back in the freezer.
- You can save time by cooking with frozen ingredients. Some foods, like stir-fry mixes or frozen shelled edamame, can be added to recipes straight from the freezer without defrosting. Since frozen produce has already been washed and trimmed, you save prep time, as well.

To supplement frozen ingredients, add fresh herbs, toasted nuts, freshly grated cheeses, or prepare a simple sauce for a satisfying home-cooked meal.

Sweet Spreads

Fruit curds add a delightful, tangy note to a variety of sweet treats.

Curd is a common teatime treat, usually slathered on toast or scones. And it is versatile: British cooks also use it as a filling in trifles, tarts, and cakes. Even the all-American lemon meringue pie is, essentially, lemon curd wearing a crown of meringue.

Traditional versions are made with egg yolks and plenty of butter. We use whole eggs and cornstarch, then stir in a couple of tablespoons of butter at the end to achieve the velvety texture expected from curd, but with less fat and fewer calories. Homemade curd will keep in the refrigerator for up to one week; you also can freeze it in a heavy-duty zip-top bag (thaw frozen curd in the refrigerator and use it within one week of thawing).

MAKE AHEAD
Lemon Curd

Fresh lemons are a must in this recipe and give it unbeatable flavor. For a lime-curd variation, substitute lime rind and juice.

- 1 cup plus 2 tablespoons sugar
- 1 tablespoon cornstarch
- ⅛ teaspoon salt
- 1 cup fresh lemon juice (about 5 medium lemons)
- 3 large eggs, lightly beaten
- 2 tablespoons butter
- 1 teaspoon grated lemon rind

1. Combine first 3 ingredients in a medium, heavy saucepan, stirring with a whisk. Stir in juice and eggs; bring to a boil over medium heat, stirring constantly with a whisk. Reduce heat, and simmer 1 minute or until thick, stirring constantly. Remove from heat; add butter and lemon rind, stirring gently until butter melts.

2. Spoon mixture into a medium bowl; cool. Cover and chill at least 6 hours or overnight (mixture will thicken as it cools). Yield: 2½ cups (serving size: 1 tablespoon).

CALORIES 35 (26% from fat); FAT 1g (sat 0.5g, mono 0.3g, poly 0.1g); PROTEIN 0.5g; CARB 6.4g; FIBER 0g; CHOL 18mg; IRON 0mg; SODIUM 17mg; CALC 2mg

---

STAFF FAVORITE • MAKE AHEAD
Triple Berry Curd

The combination of berries gives this curd a vibrant color, and frozen berries make it easy to enjoy year-round.

- 1 cup frozen blackberries, thawed
- 1 cup frozen blueberries, thawed
- 1 cup frozen raspberries, thawed
- ⅔ cup sugar
- 1 tablespoon cornstarch
- ⅛ teaspoon salt
- 2 tablespoons fresh lemon juice
- 3 large eggs, lightly beaten
- 2 tablespoons butter

1. Place all berries in a blender, and process until smooth. Press berry mixture through a sieve over a medium bowl using back of a spoon, reserving 1 cup puree; discard seeds. Reserve any remaining puree for another use; store in refrigerator.

2. Combine sugar, cornstarch, and salt in a medium, heavy saucepan, stirring with a whisk. Stir in 1 cup puree, juice, and eggs. Bring to a boil over medium heat, stirring constantly with a whisk. Reduce heat, and simmer 1 minute or until thick, stirring constantly. Remove from heat; add butter, stirring gently until butter melts. Cool.

3. Spoon mixture into a medium bowl; cover and chill at least 6 hours or overnight (mixture will thicken as it cools). Yield: 2½ cups (serving size: 1 tablespoon).

CALORIES 29 (31% from fat); FAT 1g (sat 0.5g, mono 0.3g, poly 0.1g); PROTEIN 0.6g; CARB 4.8g; FIBER 0.4g; CHOL 17mg; IRON 0.3mg; SODIUM 18mg; CALC 4mg

Pineapple Curd

Serve this tangy tropical curd over pound cake and top it with toasted coconut and chopped macadamia nuts.

½ cup sugar
1 tablespoon cornstarch
⅛ teaspoon salt
1 cup pineapple juice
2 tablespoons fresh lemon juice
3 large eggs, lightly beaten
2 tablespoons butter

1. Combine first 3 ingredients in a medium, heavy saucepan, stirring with a whisk. Stir in juices and eggs; bring to a boil over medium heat, stirring constantly with a whisk. Reduce heat, and simmer 1 minute or until thick, stirring constantly. Remove from heat; add butter, stirring gently until butter melts.
2. Spoon mixture into a medium bowl; cool. Cover and chill at least 6 hours or overnight (mixture will thicken as it cools). Yield: 2½ cups (serving size: 1 tablespoon).

CALORIES 25 (32% from fat); FAT 0.9g (sat 0.5g, mono 0.3g, poly 0.1g); PROTEIN 0.5g; CARB 3.6g; FIBER 0g; CHOL 17mg; IRON 0.1mg; SODIUM 17mg; CALC 3mg

Very Berry Tarts

This is a great make-ahead dessert for a cocktail buffet, weekend brunch, or spring luncheon. You can prepare the curd and whipped topping mixture in advance; refrigerate separately until you're ready to serve. If you have prepared the other curd varieties, use all three on the dessert tray.

1 cup vanilla low-fat yogurt
½ teaspoon grated lemon rind
½ cup frozen fat-free whipped topping, thawed
½ cup plus 2 tablespoons Triple Berry Curd (recipe on page 89)
2 (2.1-ounce) packages mini phyllo shells (such as Athens)
Grated lemon rind (optional)

1. Spoon yogurt onto several layers of heavy-duty paper towels; spread to ½-inch thickness. Cover with additional paper towels; let stand 5 minutes. Scrape yogurt into a bowl using a rubber spatula.
2. Combine yogurt and ½ teaspoon rind. Gently fold in whipped topping.
3. Spoon 1 teaspoon Triple Berry Curd into each phyllo shell; top each with 2 teaspoons yogurt mixture. Garnish with additional lemon rind, if desired. Serve immediately. Yield: 15 servings (serving size: 2 tarts).

CALORIES 63 (36% from fat); FAT 2.5g (sat 0.3g, mono 1.2g, poly 0.4g); PROTEIN 1g; CARB 8.4g; FIBER 0.1g; CHOL 7mg; IRON 0.4mg; SODIUM 43mg; CALC 30mg

Sour Cream Scones

Whole wheat flour adds nutty flavor to a basic scone recipe. Split one in half, and fill with your choice of curd.

1½ cups all-purpose flour (about 6¾ ounces)
⅔ cup whole wheat flour (about 3 ounces)
⅓ cup packed brown sugar
2 tablespoons granulated sugar
2 teaspoons baking powder
½ teaspoon baking soda
¼ teaspoon salt
⅔ cup reduced-fat sour cream
3 tablespoons butter, melted and cooled
1 large egg white, lightly beaten
⅓ cup dried currants or raisins
Cooking spray
1 tablespoon granulated sugar
¼ teaspoon ground cinnamon

1. Preheat oven to 400°.
2. Lightly spoon flours into dry measuring cups; level with a knife. Combine flours and next 5 ingredients in a large bowl; stir well with a whisk.
3. Combine sour cream, butter, and egg white in a small bowl. Add sour cream mixture to flour mixture, stirring just until moist. Stir in currants.
4. Turn dough out onto a lightly floured surface; knead lightly 6 to 12 times with floured hands. (Dough will be crumbly.)

Divide dough in half. Pat each half into a 6-inch circle on a baking sheet coated with cooking spray. Cut each circle into 6 wedges; do not separate.
5. Combine 1 tablespoon granulated sugar and cinnamon. Lightly coat top of dough with cooking spray. Sprinkle with cinnamon mixture. Bake at 400° for 15 minutes or until lightly browned. Yield: 1 dozen (serving size: 1 scone).

CALORIES 175 (25% from fat); FAT 4.8g (sat 2.9g, mono 1.3g, poly 0.3g); PROTEIN 3.6g; CARB 30.2g; FIBER 1.4g; CHOL 14mg; IRON 1.3mg; SODIUM 219mg; CALC 81mg

Strawberry-Kiwifruit Pizza in a Cookie Crust

We used the Pineapple Curd (recipe at left) in this family-style dessert, but Lemon Curd (recipe on page 89) would be just as tasty. Fresh blueberries, halved grapes, sliced banana, and plum wedges are other topping ideas. Serve the pizza immediately or the crust will become soggy.

1 (18-ounce) package refrigerated sugar cookie dough
½ cup flaked sweetened coconut, toasted
Cooking spray
1 (8-ounce) block fat-free cream cheese, softened
1 tablespoon lemon juice
¾ cup Pineapple Curd (recipe at left)
6 large strawberries, sliced
3 kiwifruit, peeled and sliced

1. Preheat oven to 350°.
2. Place cookie dough in a large bowl; knead in coconut until well combined. Pat dough into a 12 x 8–inch rectangle on a baking sheet coated with cooking spray. Bake at 350° for 18 minutes or until lightly browned. Cool completely on a wire rack.
3. Combine cream cheese and juice in a medium bowl; beat with a mixer at medium speed until well blended. Spread evenly over prepared crust, leaving a ½-inch border. Spread Pineapple Curd over cream cheese mixture. Arrange sliced strawberries and kiwifruit on top of curd.

Serve immediately. Yield: 12 servings (serving size: 1 piece).

CALORIES 279 (39% from fat); FAT 12.2g (sat 4g, mono 5.9g, poly 1.3g); PROTEIN 5.6g; CARB 37.9g; FIBER 1.2g; CHOL 32mg; IRON 1.1mg; SODIUM 327mg; CALC 86mg

MAKE AHEAD
Chocolate-Berry Cream Pie

This dessert can be prepared a day in advance, but wait to spread the topping until you're ready to serve.

CRUST:

1 cup chocolate wafer crumbs (about 20 cookies; such as Nabisco's Famous Chocolate Wafers)
2 tablespoons brown sugar
1 tablespoon butter, melted
1 egg white, lightly beaten
Cooking spray

FILLING:

1 cup fat-free cottage cheese
½ cup (4 ounces) fat-free cream cheese, softened
6 tablespoons granulated sugar
2 tablespoons all-purpose flour
1 teaspoon vanilla extract
⅛ teaspoon salt
2 large eggs
1 large egg yolk

REMAINING INGREDIENT:

¾ cup Triple Berry Curd (recipe on page 89)

1. Preheat oven to 350°.
2. To prepare crust, combine first 4 ingredients in a small bowl; stir with a fork until moist. Press into bottom and 1 inch up sides of a 9-inch pie plate coated with cooking spray. Bake at 350° for 8 minutes; cool on a wire rack.
3. To prepare filling, place cottage cheese and next 5 ingredients in a food processor; process 1 minute or until smooth. Add eggs and egg yolk; process until smooth. Spoon filling into prepared crust. Bake at 350° for 35 minutes or until set. Cool completely on a wire rack. Cover and chill at least 4 hours or overnight.

4. To serve, spread Triple Berry Curd evenly over top. Yield: 8 servings (serving size: 1 wedge).

CALORIES 218 (26% from fat); FAT 6.3g (sat 2.6g, mono 2.1g, poly 1g); PROTEIN 10.9g; CARB 29.6g; FIBER 0.8g; CHOL 99mg; IRON 1.2mg; SODIUM 249mg; CALC 56mg

MAKE AHEAD
Gingerbread Cake with Cream Cheese Frosting

CAKE:

⅓ cup granulated sugar
¼ cup butter, softened
¼ cup molasses
1 large egg
1½ cups all-purpose flour (about 6¾ ounces)
2 teaspoons ground ginger
½ teaspoon baking soda
¼ teaspoon ground nutmeg
⅛ teaspoon salt
⅛ teaspoon ground cloves
⅔ cup fat-free milk
1 teaspoon vanilla extract
Cooking spray

FROSTING:

¼ cup (2 ounces) fat-free cream cheese, softened
¼ cup (2 ounces) ⅓-less-fat cream cheese, softened
1 teaspoon vanilla extract
⅛ teaspoon salt
1¾ cups powdered sugar

REMAINING INGREDIENT:

⅓ cup Lemon Curd (recipe on page 89)

1. Preheat oven to 350°.
2. To prepare cake, place granulated sugar and butter in a medium bowl; beat with a mixer at high speed 2 minutes or until well combined. Add molasses and egg; beat well.
3. Lightly spoon flour into dry measuring cups; level with a knife. Combine flour and next 5 ingredients in a medium bowl. Add flour mixture and milk alternately to sugar mixture, beginning and ending with flour mixture. Stir in 1 teaspoon vanilla. Spoon batter into an 8-inch square pan coated with cooking spray. Bake at 350° for 30 minutes or until a wooden pick

inserted in center comes out clean. Cool completely on a wire rack.
4. To prepare frosting, place cheeses, 1 teaspoon vanilla, and ⅛ teaspoon salt in a large bowl; beat with a mixer at medium speed until light and fluffy. Gradually add powdered sugar; beat at low speed just until blended (do not overbeat). Spread frosting evenly over top of cake. Top each serving with Lemon Curd. Yield: 12 servings (serving size: 1 cake piece and about 1½ teaspoons curd).

CALORIES 246 (22% from fat); FAT 5.9g (sat 3.5g, mono 1.3g, poly 0.3g); PROTEIN 4.1g; CARB 44.3g; FIBER 0.5g; CHOL 39mg; IRON 1.2mg; SODIUM 198mg; CALC 51mg

Caribbean Bananas Flambé with Pineapple Curd over Frozen Yogurt

Make the curd and freeze scoops of frozen yogurt in advance.

¼ cup packed brown sugar
1 tablespoon granulated sugar
¼ teaspoon ground cinnamon
2 ripe unpeeled bananas
3 tablespoons fresh lime juice (about 2 limes)
1 tablespoon butter
¼ cup dark rum
2 cups vanilla fat-free frozen yogurt
½ cup Pineapple Curd (recipe on page 90)

1. Combine first 3 ingredients in a medium bowl.
2. Peel bananas; cut each in half lengthwise. Cut each half into 4 pieces. Brush bananas with juice; dredge in sugar mixture.
3. Melt butter in a large nonstick skillet over medium-high heat; add bananas. Cook 2 minutes, turning bananas after 1 minute. Remove from heat; pour rum into one side of pan. Ignite rum with a long match; let flames die down.
4. Spoon ½ cup frozen yogurt into each of 4 dessert dishes; top each with 4 banana pieces and 2 tablespoons Pineapple Curd. Serve immediately. Yield: 4 servings.

CALORIES 312 (14% from fat); FAT 4.7g (sat 2.8g, mono 1.3g, poly 0.3g); PROTEIN 4.6g; CARB 57.4g; FIBER 2.2g; CHOL 43mg; IRON 0.6mg; SODIUM 99mg; CALC 122mg

Meat Loaf

Learn all you need to master—and trim down—this treasured American classic.

Meat loaf holds an honored spot in the pantheon of all-American foods, and all you need to prepare a meat loaf is ground meat (be it beef, pork, turkey, or lamb), a few seasonings, perhaps a vegetable or two, and some kind of binder (usually breadcrumbs and/or eggs) to hold it all together. That equation leaves lots of room for invention, including lower-fat versions. Slimming down this suppertime standby is just a matter of technique. Doing so not only improves flavor but also does a lot to boost meat loaf's nutritional profile.

MAKE AHEAD • FREEZABLE
Diner Meat Loaf "Muffins"

Sit down to a meat loaf in a half hour with this recipe. Serve with steamed green beans and roasted potato wedges for an at-home version of a blue-plate special.

 1 teaspoon olive oil
 1 cup finely chopped onion
 ½ cup finely chopped carrot
 1 teaspoon dried oregano
 2 garlic cloves, minced
 1 cup ketchup, divided
 1½ pounds ground beef, extralean
 1 cup finely crushed fat-free saltine crackers (about 20)
 2 tablespoons prepared mustard
 1 teaspoon Worcestershire sauce
 ¼ teaspoon freshly ground black pepper
 2 large eggs, lightly beaten
 Cooking spray

1. Preheat oven to 350°.
2. Heat oil in a large nonstick skillet over medium-high heat. Add onion, carrot, oregano, and garlic, and sauté 2 minutes. Cool onion mixture.
3. Combine onion mixture, ½ cup ketchup, beef, and next 5 ingredients in a large bowl.
4. Spoon meat mixture into 12 muffin cups coated with cooking spray. Top each with 2 teaspoons ketchup. Bake at 350° for 25 minutes or until a thermometer registers 160°. Let stand 5 minutes. Yield: 6 servings (serving size: 2 "muffins").

CALORIES 276 (28% from fat); FAT 8.6g (sat 3g, mono 4g, poly 0.8g); PROTEIN 28.7g; CARB 21.7g; FIBER 1.8g; CHOL 131mg; IRON 3.9mg; SODIUM 759mg; CALC 48mg

STAFF FAVORITE • MAKE AHEAD
FREEZABLE
Classic Meat Loaf
(pictured on page 230)

Three types of ground meat lends depth. Serve with roasted carrots and onions.

 1 (1½-ounce) slice white bread
 2 tablespoons fat-free milk
 ½ cup ketchup, divided
 ⅔ pound ground beef, extralean
 ½ pound lean ground veal
 6 ounces lean ground pork
 ½ cup chopped onion
 ⅓ cup chopped fresh parsley
 1 tablespoon Dijon mustard
 1 teaspoon dried basil
 ¾ teaspoon salt
 ¼ teaspoon black pepper
 2 large egg whites, lightly beaten
 Cooking spray

1. Preheat oven to 350°.
2. Place bread in a food processor; pulse 10 times or until coarse breadcrumbs measure 1½ cups.
3. Combine breadcrumbs and milk in a large bowl; let stand 5 minutes. Add 2 tablespoons ketchup, beef, and next 9 ingredients.
4. Shape meat mixture into a 9 x 5–inch loaf on a broiler pan coated with cooking spray. Spread 6 tablespoons ketchup over top of meat loaf. Bake at 350° for 1 hour or until a thermometer registers 160°. Let stand 10 minutes. Cut loaf into 12 slices. Yield: 6 servings (serving size: 2 slices).

CALORIES 231 (31% from fat); FAT 7.9g (sat 3.1g, mono 3.2g, poly 0.8g); PROTEIN 26.7g; CARB 13.2g; FIBER 0.9g; CHOL 79mg; IRON 2.3mg; SODIUM 764mg; CALC 49mg

New Blue Plate Special Menu
serves 6

Barbecue Meat Loaf
Creamy coleslaw*
Dinner rolls

*Combine ⅓ cup reduced-fat mayonnaise, 2 tablespoons cider vinegar, ¼ teaspoon salt, and ¼ teaspoon ground red pepper in a small bowl, stirring with a whisk to blend. Combine 1 (12-ounce) bag coleslaw, ½ cup diced red bell pepper, and ½ cup diced yellow bell pepper in a large bowl. Add dressing, stirring well to combine.

MAKE AHEAD • FREEZABLE
Barbecue Meat Loaf

Use your family's favorite barbecue sauce to prepare this simple meat loaf.

 1½ pounds ground beef, extralean
 ½ cup dry breadcrumbs
 ½ cup chopped onion
 1 tablespoon barbecue sauce
 1 tablespoon prepared mustard
 1½ teaspoons chili powder
 1 teaspoon garlic powder
 ½ teaspoon salt
 ½ teaspoon freshly ground black pepper
 2 large egg whites, lightly beaten
 Cooking spray
 ¼ cup plus 1 teaspoon barbecue sauce

1. Preheat oven to 350°.
2. Combine first 10 ingredients in a large bowl.
3. Shape meat mixture into a 9 x 5–inch loaf on a broiler pan coated with cooking spray. Spread ¼ cup plus 1 teaspoon barbecue sauce over top of meat loaf. Bake at 350° for 1 hour or until a thermometer registers 160°. Let stand 10 minutes. Cut loaf into 12 slices. Yield: 6 servings (serving size: 2 slices).

CALORIES 203 (24% from fat); FAT 5.4g (sat 2.2g, mono 2.2g, poly 0.5g); PROTEIN 27.3g; CARB 10.5g; FIBER 1.1g; CHOL 61mg; IRON 3.2mg; SODIUM 517mg; CALC 26mg

MAKE AHEAD • FREEZABLE
Iberian Meat Loaf

Olives and paprika are common throughout the Iberian Peninsula, which is dominated by Spain. Use Spanish smoked paprika for more authentic flavor.

1½ pounds ground turkey breast
1 (8-ounce) can tomato sauce, divided
1 cup chopped onion
½ cup dry breadcrumbs
½ cup chopped fresh parsley
⅓ cup sliced pitted manzanilla (or green) olives
1½ teaspoons paprika
1½ teaspoons chopped fresh oregano
½ teaspoon ground coriander
¼ teaspoon black pepper
2 large egg whites, lightly beaten
1 garlic clove, minced
Cooking spray

1. Preheat oven to 350°.
2. Combine turkey, ½ cup tomato sauce, and next 10 ingredients in a large bowl.
3. Shape mixture into a 9 x 5–inch loaf on a broiler pan coated with cooking spray. Spread ½ cup tomato sauce evenly over top of meat loaf. Bake at 350° for 1 hour or until a thermometer registers 165°. Let stand 10 minutes. Cut meat loaf into 12 slices. Yield: 6 servings (serving size: 2 slices).

CALORIES 203 (22% from fat); FAT 4.9g (sat 1.3g, mono 0.9g, poly 1.2g); PROTEIN 25.9g; CARB 13.4g; FIBER 2.1g; CHOL 56mg; IRON 2.4mg; SODIUM 888mg; CALC 49mg

How to Make Great Meat Loaf

1. *Sauté the aromatics (onions, garlic, carrot, and the like); this intensifies their flavor in the final product.*

2. *Use your hands to combine the ingredients in a large bowl.*

3. *Shape a free form meat loaf on a broiler pan coated with cooking spray.*

4. *Brush ketchup or other liquid across the top of the loaf.*

5. *Use a meat thermometer to test the loaf's internal temperature for doneness (160° for ground beef, pork, or veal; 165° for ground poultry).*

6. *Let the loaf stand 10 minutes before slicing. Slice and serve.*

Choose the Meat

Meat is the main ingredient, and the one that most influences texture and flavor. Fatty cuts like regular ground chuck or ground beef (may be called "85 percent lean," but it's a hefty 15 percent fat by weight) are out because nearly all that fat will end up in the final product. Breadcrumbs, crackers, or whatever is used to bind the loaf will absorb the extra fat cooked out of the meat. While that makes for a moist texture, it isn't nutritionally sound. We found that 92 percent lean and 96 percent extra lean ground beef work fine, especially when combined with a smaller amount of ground pork, which adds a bit of moisture.

Ultralean ground turkey breast can also be used for a leaner meat loaf, but it makes for a dry final product. So we combined ground turkey breast with ground turkey or ground pork and added a little extra liquid to the mix.

Bind It

We also experimented with various binding agents, including traditional breadcrumbs and eggs or egg whites. We learned to let the overall flavor of the meat loaf determine the binder. Our Diner Meat Loaf "Muffins" (recipe on page 92) use crushed saltines, whereas our Asian-Style Meat Loaves (recipe on page 95) use chopped rice crackers.

You also can use fresh or dry breadcrumbs: It takes about twice as many fresh breadcrumbs to equal the binding capacity of dried. A good rule of thumb is to use 1 cup fresh breadcrumbs (or ½ cup dried breadcrumbs) for every 1½ pounds of meat.

Add a Little Extra Liquid

Because lower-fat meat loaf relies on leaner cuts of meat and poultry, it helps to add slightly higher amounts of liquid flavorings like ketchup, salsa, and milk to keep the loaf moist and compensate for the lower amounts of fat.

Don't Forget the Eggs

Whole eggs and egg whites are interchangeable in most of these recipes, as both are adept at holding the multiple ingredients in a meat loaf together. We used egg whites most often in these recipes to keep fat down, and also because other higher-fat ingredients were already adding flavor.

Choose a Form

Meat loaf recipes can be made in a loaf pan, with a free-form shape, or in a muffin tin. Free-form loaves cook more quickly than those in a loaf pan, and muffin tin loaves cook in about half the time of a full-size loaf.

Let It Stand

Meat loaf firms as it stands: 10 minutes is usually sufficient. But you'll find that loaves become even firmer, and much easier to slice for sandwiches when allowed to stand in the refrigerator overnight. Slice what you need for dinner tonight, then refrigerate the leftovers in a chunk to cut, slice, or crumble as needed.

Versatile Leftovers

For many of us, the real appeal of meat loaf is enjoying the leftovers. These are some of our favorite ways to enjoy it the next day.

- Sliced on a sandwich
- Crumbled as taco or enchilada filling
- Crumbled and mixed with bottled marinara over pasta
- Thinly sliced on gourmet crackers
- Reheated and topped with refrigerated mashed potatoes (such as Simply Potatoes) for a speedy shepherd's pie

Handle with Care

Meat loaf is one of the easiest dinners to prepare and uses ingredients found in any supermarket. But you should use care when handling any raw meat.

- When shopping, pick up ground meat just before checking out.
- Refrigerate or freeze meat right away.
- Cook or freeze ground meat within two days. Use frozen meat within four months.
- Wash your hands before and after handling raw ground meat. Wash utensils, countertops, cutting boards, the sink, and anything else that comes into contact with raw meat with hot, soapy water.
- Use a meat thermometer to gauge the internal temperature of meat loaf. Cook ground beef, pork, and veal to 160° and ground poultry to 165°.
- Reheat any type of meat loaf to an internal temperature of 165°. Note: We found that very lean ground beef may still be pink when fully cooked, so be sure to use a meat thermometer to test its doneness.
- Cooked meat loaf will keep in the refrigerator up to four days and in the freezer up to three months (ground poultry) or four months (beef, pork, or veal).

Santa Fe Meat Loaf

Slicing the loaf reveals a hidden layer of cheese. Leftovers are especially good on a sandwich. Serve with a tossed green salad and corn bread.

Cooking spray
½ cup chopped onion
⅓ cup finely chopped red bell
     pepper
1 teaspoon chili powder
½ teaspoon ground cumin
4 garlic cloves, minced
1 tablespoon minced canned
     chipotle chile in adobo
     sauce
½ pound 7%-fat ground turkey
1 pound ground turkey breast
¾ cup dry breadcrumbs
⅔ cup mild chunky salsa,
     divided
1 teaspoon dried oregano
6 slices 30%-less-fat center-cut
     bacon (such as Oscar Mayer),
     cooked and crumbled
2 large egg whites, lightly
     beaten
¾ cup (3 ounces) reduced-fat finely
     shredded Mexican-style four
     cheese blend (such as Kraft 2%
     milk)

1. Preheat oven to 350°.
2. Heat a large nonstick skillet over medium-high heat. Coat pan with cooking spray. Add onion and next 4 ingredients to pan; sauté 1½ minutes or until onion is tender. Stir in chipotle chile; sauté 30 seconds. Remove from pan; cool. Combine onion mixture, turkey, turkey breast, breadcrumbs, ⅓ cup salsa, oregano, bacon, and egg whites in a large bowl.
3. Place half of turkey mixture in an 8 x 4–inch loaf pan coated with cooking spray. Arrange cheese over top, leaving a ½-inch border around edges. Arrange remaining turkey mixture over cheese, pressing edges to pack. Spread ⅓ cup salsa over top of meat loaf. Bake at 350° for 1 hour and 25 minutes or until a thermometer registers 165°. Let stand 10 minutes. Remove meat loaf from pan; cut into 12 slices. Yield: 6 servings (serving size: 2 slices).

CALORIES 288 (33% from fat); FAT 10.5g (sat 4g, mono 3.3g, poly 1.6g); PROTEIN 31.5g; CARB 14.8g; FIBER 1.4g; CHOL 88mg; IRON 2.2mg; SODIUM 876mg; CALC 256mg

Italian-Style Meat Loaf

Line the bottom part of the broiler pan with aluminum foil for easy cleanup.

1½ pounds 92%-lean ground beef
1 cup fat-free tomato-basil pasta
     sauce, divided
½ cup Italian-seasoned breadcrumbs
½ cup (2 ounces) preshredded fresh
     Parmesan cheese
½ cup finely chopped onion
⅓ cup chopped fresh flat-leaf
     parsley
1 teaspoon garlic powder
½ teaspoon dried basil
½ teaspoon dried oregano
½ teaspoon salt
¼ teaspoon black pepper
2 large egg whites, lightly beaten
Cooking spray

1. Preheat oven to 350°.
2. Combine beef, ½ cup pasta sauce, and next 10 ingredients in a large bowl. Shape mixture into an 8 x 4–inch loaf on a broiler pan coated with cooking spray. Brush ½ cup pasta sauce over top of meat loaf. Bake at 350° for 1 hour and 10 minutes or until a thermometer registers 160°. Let stand 10 minutes. Cut meat loaf into 12 slices. Yield: 6 servings (serving size: 2 slices).

CALORIES 263 (42% from fat); FAT 12.1g (sat 5.7g, mono 4.7g, poly 0.6g); PROTEIN 27.8g; CARB 11.9g; FIBER 1.4g; CHOL 67mg; IRON 3.3mg; SODIUM 859mg; CALC 175mg

WINE NOTE: Anything Italian-style seems like a candidate for Chianti, but with a humble meat loaf like this, something more full-bodied is best. A California syrah has enough concentration to mirror the density of the ground beef, and it makes the meat loaf seem just a bit grander. Try Arrowood's Grand Archer 2001 Syrah from Sonoma County, California (about $20).

Asian-Style Meat Loaves

Serve with stir-fried broccoli rabe and steamed rice.

1 (3½-ounce) package plain rice
     crackers (such as KA-ME)
1 pound ground turkey breast
½ pound lean ground pork
1 cup chopped green onions
½ cup hoisin sauce, divided
½ cup chopped red bell pepper
½ cup drained chopped canned
     water chestnuts
1 tablespoon low-sodium soy
     sauce
1 tablespoon grated peeled fresh
     ginger
¼ teaspoon salt
3 garlic cloves, minced
2 large egg whites, lightly beaten
Cooking spray

1. Preheat oven to 350°.
2. Place crackers in a food processor; process until finely chopped.
3. Combine cracker crumbs, turkey, pork, green onions, ¼ cup hoisin, and next 7 ingredients in a large bowl.
4. Shape mixture into 6 (5 x 2½–inch) loaves on a broiler pan coated with cooking spray; spread 2 teaspoons hoisin over top of each meat loaf. Bake at 350° for 45 minutes or until a thermometer registers 165°. Let stand 5 minutes. Yield: 6 servings (serving size: 1 loaf).

CALORIES 288 (16% from fat); FAT 5g (sat 1.8g, mono 1.9g, poly 0.9g); PROTEIN 29.5g; CARB 28.2g; FIBER 1.9g; CHOL 76mg; IRON 1.7mg; SODIUM 651mg; CALC 33mg

Mini loaves cook
in about half
the time of a
full-size loaf.

. . . And Ready in Just about 20 Minutes

More than a week's worth of quick entrées get dinner on the table in a flash

Turkey and Bean Chili

Balance the heat from the poblano pepper and fiery chili powder with a garnish of light sour cream.

    1   cup prechopped red onion
   ⅓   cup chopped seeded poblano
        chile (about 1)
    1   teaspoon bottled minced garlic
  1¼   pounds ground turkey
    2   tablespoons tomato paste
    1   tablespoon chili powder
    2   teaspoons dried oregano
    1   teaspoon ground cumin
   ¼   teaspoon salt
   ¼   teaspoon black pepper
    1   (19-ounce) can cannellini beans,
        rinsed and drained
    1   (14.5-ounce) can diced tomatoes,
        undrained
    1   (14-ounce) can fat-free,
        less-sodium chicken broth
   ½   cup chopped fresh cilantro
    6   lime wedges

1. Heat a large saucepan over medium heat. Add first 4 ingredients; cook 6 minutes or until turkey is done, stirring frequently to crumble. Stir in tomato paste and next 8 ingredients; bring to a boil. Reduce heat, and simmer 10 minutes. Stir in cilantro. Serve with lime wedges. Yield: 6 servings (serving size: about 1 cup chili and 1 lime wedge).

CALORIES 211 (28% from fat); FAT 6.5g (sat 1.7g, mono 1.9g, poly 1.6g); PROTEIN 22.5g; CARB 16.4g; FIBER 4.7g; CHOL 54mg; IRON 3.4mg; SODIUM 474mg; CALC 52mg

Filet Mignon with Sweet Bourbon-Coffee Sauce

Roast refrigerated potato wedges for a quick side.

   ½   cup water
    3   tablespoons bourbon
  1½   teaspoons sugar
   ½   teaspoon beef-flavored bouillon
        granules
   ½   teaspoon instant coffee granules
   ½   teaspoon black pepper
   ¼   teaspoon salt
    4   (4-ounce) beef tenderloin steaks,
        trimmed (about 1 inch thick)
        Cooking spray
    2   tablespoons chopped fresh parsley

1. Combine first 5 ingredients in a small bowl; set aside.
2. Sprinkle pepper and salt over both sides of steaks. Heat a medium nonstick skillet over medium-high heat. Coat pan with cooking spray. Add steaks; cook 2 minutes on each side. Reduce heat to medium; cook steaks 2 minutes or until desired degree of doneness. Transfer steaks to a platter; cover and keep warm.
3. Add bourbon mixture to pan; cook over medium-high heat until mixture is reduced to ¼ cup (about 3 minutes). Serve sauce over beef; sprinkle with parsley. Yield: 4 servings (serving size: 1 steak, 1 tablespoon sauce, and 1½ teaspoons parsley).

CALORIES 178 (27% from fat); FAT 5.3g (sat 2g, mono 2.1g, poly 0.2g); PROTEIN 22.4g; CARB 2.1g; FIBER 0.1g; CHOL 52mg; IRON 1.5mg; SODIUM 371mg; CALC 21mg

Wasabi and Panko-Crusted Pork with Gingered Soy Sauce

Panko are coarse white breadcrumbs used in this quick and easy interpretation of the Japanese dish *tonkatsu*. Look for panko and wasabi paste in the ethnic-foods section of the supermarket. Substitute chicken broth if you don't have sake or sherry on hand. Serve with rice and steamed snow peas and carrots for a complete meal.

   ⅔   cup panko (Japanese breadcrumbs)
    1   large egg white, lightly beaten
    4   (4-ounce) boneless center-cut loin
        pork chops (about ½ inch thick)
    1   teaspoon peanut oil
        Cooking spray
   ⅛   teaspoon salt
    1   tablespoon bottled ground fresh
        ginger (such as Spice World)
   ⅓   cup fat-free, less-sodium chicken
        broth
    2   tablespoons sake or dry sherry
    2   tablespoons low-sodium soy sauce
    2   teaspoons sugar
    1   teaspoon wasabi paste
   ⅓   cup thinly sliced green onions

1. Place panko in a shallow dish. Place egg white in another shallow dish. Dip pork in egg white; dredge in panko.
2. Heat oil in a large nonstick skillet coated with cooking spray over medium-high heat; add pork. Cook 4 minutes on each side or until done. Remove pork from pan; sprinkle with salt.
3. Reduce heat to medium. Add ginger to pan; cook 30 seconds, stirring constantly. Combine broth and next 4 ingredients in a small bowl, stirring well with a whisk. Add broth mixture to pan, scraping pan to loosen browned bits. Stir in green onions. Spoon sauce over pork. Yield: 4 servings (serving size: 1 pork chop and about 1 tablespoon sauce).

CALORIES 215 (28% from fat); FAT 6.8g (sat 2.1g, mono 2.9g, poly 0.8g); PROTEIN 24.5g; CARB 10.8g; FIBER 0.9g; CHOL 65mg; IRON 1.1mg; SODIUM 454mg; CALC 15mg

Shrimp Arrabbiata

    6   ounces fresh linguine
    2   tablespoons olive oil, divided
    1   pound large shrimp, peeled and
        deveined
   ¼   teaspoon salt
   ½   cup prechopped onion
    2   teaspoons bottled minced garlic
   ½   teaspoon dried basil
   ½   teaspoon crushed red pepper
    2   tablespoons tomato paste
    1   (14.5-ounce) can diced tomatoes,
        undrained
    2   tablespoons chopped fresh parsley

1. Cook pasta according to package directions, omitting salt and fat. Drain and keep warm.

2. Heat 1 tablespoon oil in a large nonstick skillet over medium-high heat. Sprinkle shrimp with salt; add shrimp to pan. Cook 2 minutes on each side or until shrimp are done. Transfer shrimp to a bowl. Heat 1 tablespoon oil in pan. Add onion, garlic, basil, and red pepper to pan; sauté 1 minute. Add tomato paste and tomatoes; bring to a boil. Cook 3 minutes or just until sauce begins to thicken. Return shrimp to pan; cook 1 minute or until thoroughly heated. Add parsley to pan, stirring well. Serve over pasta. Yield: 4 servings (serving size: about 1 cup shrimp mixture and 1 cup pasta).

CALORIES 343 (26% from fat); FAT 10g (sat 1.4g, mono 6g, poly 1.7g); PROTEIN 29.4g; CARB 33.1g; FIBER 3.7g; CHOL 172mg; IRON 4.6mg; SODIUM 594mg; CALC 91mg

QUICK & EASY
Andouille and Red Beans with Rice

Prepare and bake a corn bread mix while the red beans and rice are cooking.

1 (3½-ounce) bag boil-in-bag long-grain rice
Cooking spray
4 ounces andouille sausage, diced
1 cup chopped red bell pepper
1 cup prechopped onion
1½ to 2 teaspoons salt-free Cajun seasoning
1 teaspoon dried thyme leaves
½ teaspoon hot pepper sauce (such as Tabasco)
1 (16-ounce) can dark kidney beans, rinsed and drained
1 (14-ounce) can fat-free, less-sodium chicken broth
¼ cup chopped fresh parsley
½ teaspoon salt

1. Cook rice according to package directions, omitting salt and fat.

2. Heat a large nonstick skillet over medium-high heat. Coat pan with cooking spray. Add sausage; cook 3 minutes or until lightly browned. Using a slotted spoon, transfer sausage to a bowl, and keep warm.

3. Add bell pepper and next 4 ingredients to pan; sauté 3 minutes or until onion is tender. Add beans and broth to pan; cook 8 minutes or until thick, mashing half of beans. Add sausage, parsley, and salt to pan; cook 1 minute or until thoroughly heated, stirring occasionally. Serve bean mixture over rice. Yield: 4 servings (serving size: about ¾ cup bean mixture and about ½ cup rice).

CALORIES 245 (21% from fat); FAT 5.6g (sat 2.1g, mono 2.4g, poly 0.8g); PROTEIN 11.7g; CARB 37g; FIBER 4.2g; CHOL 20mg; IRON 2.7mg; SODIUM 900mg; CALC 41mg

QUICK & EASY
Clams Parmesan

Serve this speedy entrée over angel hair pasta to soak up the flavorful broth.

4 pounds littleneck clams
¼ cup fresh lemon juice
½ teaspoon black pepper
½ cup (2 ounces) preshredded fresh Parmesan cheese
2 tablespoons dry breadcrumbs
2 tablespoons chopped fresh basil
2 tablespoons chopped fresh oregano
2 tablespoons chopped fresh parsley
2 teaspoons olive oil

1. Combine first 3 ingredients in a large nonstick skillet. Cover and cook over medium heat 8 minutes or until shells open. Discard any unopened shells.

2. While clams cook, combine cheese and next 4 ingredients in a small bowl; set aside.

3. Transfer clam mixture to a large bowl. Sprinkle with cheese mixture, and drizzle with oil. Yield: 3 servings (serving size: 20 clams, ½ cup broth, and about ½ teaspoon oil).

CALORIES 414 (20% from fat); FAT 9.4g (sat 3.8g, mono 4g, poly 0.8g); PROTEIN 19.5g; CARB 8.8g; FIBER 0.5g; CHOL 44mg; IRON 13.3mg; SODIUM 406mg; CALC 308mg

QUICK & EASY
Quick Choucroute

This choucroute version is inspired by the classic Alsatian braise of pork, sausage, apples, and sauerkraut. Serve with rye or pumpernickel bread to soak up the sauce.

2 teaspoons canola oil
1 pound boneless center-cut loin pork chops, cut into ½-inch slices
¼ teaspoon freshly ground black pepper
⅛ teaspoon kosher salt
1 cup chopped Golden Delicious apple (about 1)
¾ cup thinly sliced onion (about 1 medium)
1 bay leaf
1 (12-ounce) bottle light beer
2 cups sauerkraut, rinsed and drained
½ pound low-fat smoked sausage, cut diagonally into ½-inch slices
⅓ cup chopped fresh parsley
2 tablespoons prepared horseradish
1 tablespoon whole-grain mustard

1. Heat oil in a large nonstick skillet over medium-high heat. Sprinkle pork with pepper and salt. Add pork to pan; sauté 2 minutes. Remove pork from pan, and keep warm.

2. Add apple, onion, and bay leaf to pan; cook 2 minutes or until onion is lightly browned. Add beer, scraping pan to loosen browned bits. Add sauerkraut and sausage; bring to a simmer, and cook 5 minutes. Return pork to pan; cover and cook 2 minutes or until pork is thoroughly heated. Discard bay leaf. Stir in parsley. Serve with horseradish and mustard. Yield: 4 servings (serving size: 2 cups pork mixture, 1½ teaspoons horseradish, and ¾ teaspoon mustard).

CALORIES 307 (32% from fat); FAT 11g (sat 3.3g, mono 5.1g, poly 1.5g); PROTEIN 31g; CARB 19.9g; FIBER 3.3g; CHOL 84mg; IRON 3.2mg; SODIUM 837mg; CALC 53mg

Spicy Chicken Quesadillas

Serve these quesadillas with a tossed green salad.

- ¼ cup thinly sliced green onions (about 2)
- 2 tablespoons chopped cilantro
- 1 tablespoon chopped pickled jalapeño peppers
- 1 cup chopped cooked chicken (about 8 ounces)
- 4 (8-inch) flour tortillas
- ¾ cup (3 ounces) reduced-fat shredded Cheddar cheese
- Cooking spray
- ¾ cup salsa

1. Combine first 3 ingredients in a small bowl; stir until blended.

2. Place ¼ cup chopped chicken over half of each tortilla. Sprinkle each with 3 tablespoons cheese and 1 tablespoon onion mixture; fold tortillas in half.

3. Heat a large nonstick skillet over medium-high heat. Coat pan with cooking spray. Place 2 quesadillas in pan. Cook 2 minutes on each side or until lightly browned. Repeat procedure with remaining quesadillas. Cut each quesadilla in half. Serve with salsa. Yield: 4 servings (serving size: 1 quesadilla and 3 tablespoons salsa).

CALORIES 328 (30% from fat); FAT 10.9g (sat 4.8g, mono 4.1g, poly 1.5g); PROTEIN 27.9g; CARB 29.4g; FIBER 2.1g; CHOL 65mg; IRON 2.5mg; SODIUM 786mg; CALC 248mg

Spiced Chicken and Greens with Pomegranate Dressing

Round out this early spring dish with a hearty multigrain baguette.

CHICKEN:
- Cooking spray
- 1 teaspoon chili powder
- ¼ teaspoon salt
- 4 (6-ounce) skinless, boneless chicken breast halves

DRESSING:
- ⅓ cup pomegranate juice
- 3 tablespoons red wine vinegar
- 2 teaspoons sugar
- 2 teaspoons canola oil
- ¼ teaspoon salt
- ¼ teaspoon crushed red pepper

SALAD:
- 1 (5-ounce) package gourmet salad greens
- ½ cup thinly sliced red onion
- ¾ cup orange sections (about 2 medium oranges)
- ⅓ cup dried cranberries
- ¼ cup (1 ounce) crumbled Gorgonzola cheese

1. To prepare chicken, heat a large non-stick skillet over medium heat. Coat pan with cooking spray. Sprinkle chili powder and salt over chicken. Add chicken to pan; cook 5 minutes on each side or until done. Remove chicken from pan; let stand 3 minutes. Cut chicken across grain into thin slices; set aside.

2. To prepare dressing, combine juice and next 5 ingredients in a small bowl; stir well with whisk.

3. To prepare salad, place greens on a serving platter; top with onion, orange, cranberries, and chicken slices. Sprinkle evenly with cheese; pour dressing over salad. Yield: 4 servings (serving size: 2 cups salad, about 4½ ounces chicken, and 2 tablespoons dressing).

CALORIES 333 (18% from fat); FAT 6.7g (sat 2.3g, mono 2.4g, poly 1.2g); PROTEIN 42.2g; CARB 27.1g; FIBER 5.4g; CHOL 105mg; IRON 2mg; SODIUM 527mg; CALC 115mg

new american classics

Lean Philly Cheesesteaks

It doesn't matter that there isn't a steak in a Philly cheesesteak sandwich—it's still the stuff of legend.

This delicious, messy treat consists of thinly sliced beef, melted cheese, and sweet grilled onions, all served on a crusty roll.

Lean Philly Cheesesteaks

- 1 tablespoon olive oil
- 1½ cups thinly sliced onion
- 1 cup sliced red bell pepper
- 1 cup sliced green bell pepper
- 5 garlic cloves, minced
- 2 teaspoons sugar
- 2 teaspoons white wine vinegar
- 1 teaspoon dried oregano
- ¼ teaspoon salt
- 4 ounces light processed cheese, cubed (such as Velveeta Light)
- 3 tablespoons less-sodium beef broth
- 12 ounces thinly sliced, low-sodium deli roast beef, shredded
- 4 hot dog buns, toasted

1. Heat oil in a large nonstick skillet over medium-high heat. Add onion, bell peppers, and garlic; sauté 4 minutes or until golden brown. Reduce heat, and cook 8 minutes or until tender, stirring occasionally. Stir in sugar, vinegar, oregano, and salt. Add cheese; cook 2 minutes or until cheese melts, stirring constantly.

2. Combine broth and beef in a microwave-safe bowl. Microwave at HIGH 1 minute or until hot.

3. Place 3 ounces beef mixture in each bun; top each with ½ cup cheese mixture. Serve immediately. Yield: 4 servings (serving size: 1 sandwich).

CALORIES 379 (29% from fat); FAT 12.3g (sat 4.2g, mono 4.6g, poly 1.4g); PROTEIN 31.8g; CARB 35.2g; FIBER 2.6g; CHOL 56mg; IRON 4.1mg; SODIUM 942mg; CALC 253mg

Global Grocery

Supermarkets and superstores are now the places to find ingredients that once required a trip to a specialty market.

Food magazines, including this one, have often been taken to task for using too many "hard-to-find" ingredients in recipes, such as exotic produce or ethnic seasonings. Until recently. Today, there's a good chance that most of what you need to prepare authentic ethnic or chef-inspired contemporary recipes can be found at local supermarkets or superstores like Wal-Mart and Target. These companies cater to mainstream America, which includes burgeoning Latino and Asian populations, as well as to customers who are more food savvy than ever before.

With that in mind, we feature five ingredients here, once available only in specialty and ethnic groceries—now widely accessible in large supermarkets and superstores, and possibly even in your neighborhood market.

Marinated Vegetable Salad with Queso Fresco

(pictured on page 233)

This vibrant side salad lends itself to improvisation. Start with our basics, including tomatoes, zucchini, jícama, black beans, and **queso fresco** with a salsa vinaigrette. From there, you might add sliced olives, corn, diced avocado, or radishes. It's great with grilled chicken.

- 1 cup diced tomatoes
- 1 cup diced zucchini
- 1 cup diced jícama
- ½ cup thinly sliced green onions
- 2 tablespoons chopped, pickled jalapeños
- 1 (15-ounce) can black beans, drained and rinsed
- ½ cup bottled salsa
- 3 tablespoons fresh lime juice
- 1½ tablespoons canola oil
- ½ cup chopped fresh cilantro
- ¼ teaspoon freshly ground black pepper
- 2 cups torn romaine lettuce
- ¼ cup (1 ounce) shredded queso fresco

1. Combine first 6 ingredients in a large bowl. Combine salsa, juice, and oil, stirring with a whisk. Pour dressing over tomato mixture. Cover and chill 1 hour.
2. Add cilantro and pepper to bowl; toss gently. Serve over lettuce. Sprinkle with cheese. Yield: 4 servings (serving size: 1¼ cups salad and 1 tablespoon cheese).

CALORIES 174 (37% from fat); FAT 7.1g (sat 1.3g, mono 3.5g, poly 1.8g); PROTEIN 7.3g; CARB 21.7g; FIBER 8.1g; CHOL 5mg; IRON 2mg; SODIUM 536mg; CALC 102mg

Crab Cakes with Red Pepper Mayonnaise

Panko lends the crab cakes a nice, crunchy crust. These cakes are large enough to serve as a main dish, but you also can form smaller appetizer cakes.

RED PEPPER MAYONNAISE:
- 1 red bell pepper
- ⅓ cup reduced-fat mayonnaise
- 1 garlic clove
- Dash of hot pepper sauce (such as Tabasco)

CRAB CAKES:
- ⅓ cup reduced-fat mayonnaise
- ¼ cup minced red onion
- ¼ cup minced red bell pepper
- 2 tablespoons minced celery
- 1½ teaspoons fresh lemon juice
- 1 egg white, lightly beaten
- 1 pound lump crabmeat, shell pieces removed
- 1¼ cups panko (Japanese breadcrumbs), divided
- 2 tablespoons butter, divided
- 10 cups trimmed watercress (about 10 ounces)
- 6 lemon wedges (optional)

1. Preheat broiler.
2. To prepare mayonnaise, cut bell pepper in half lengthwise; discard seeds and membranes. Place pepper halves, skin sides up, on a foil-lined baking sheet; flatten with hand. Broil 12 minutes or until blackened. Place in a zip-top plastic bag; seal. Let stand 10 minutes. Peel pepper. Place pepper, ⅓ cup mayonnaise, garlic, and pepper sauce in a food processor. Process until smooth; transfer to a bowl, and chill.
3. To prepare crab cakes, combine ⅓ cup mayonnaise, onion, next 5 ingredients, and ¾ cup panko in a large bowl; stir until well combined. Form into 6 patties; dredge patties in ½ cup panko. Heat 1 tablespoon butter in a large nonstick skillet over medium-high heat. Add 3 patties to pan; cook 10 minutes or until lightly browned and cooked through, turning once. Remove from pan, and keep warm. Repeat procedure with 1 tablespoon butter and remaining patties. Serve with watercress and red pepper mayonnaise. Garnish with lemon wedges, if desired. Yield: 6 servings (serving size: 1 crab cake, about 1½ cups watercress, and about 1½ tablespoons mayonnaise).

CALORIES 234 (34% from fat); FAT 8.8g (sat 3.5g, mono 1.7g, poly 2.7g); PROTEIN 22g; CARB 15.2g; FIBER 1.4g; CHOL 96mg; IRON 0.9mg; SODIUM 625mg; CALC 165mg

WINE NOTE: Albariño from Spain is a good choice. Nora Albariño 2004 from Rias Baxais ($16) is zesty, with a hint of citrus, starfruit, and dried peach.

Queso Fresco

Queso fresco is the most widely used cheese in Mexican cooking. The firm-textured fresh white cheese (its name translates as "fresh cheese") is slightly salty, with a mild, tangy taste similar to farmer's cheese. Like other fresh cheeses, queso fresco is lower in fat and sodium (despite its salty flavor) than aged cheeses. It's easily crumbled to sprinkle on dishes like enchiladas and tamales, as well as soups like black bean and tortilla. It also makes a tasty addition to cold vegetable salads. And although it softens, it doesn't melt when heated; queso fresco is classically used in the filling for chile relleños and quesadillas. For a snack, heat some on corn tortillas and top with a dollop of salsa.

Queso fresco is usually made with cow's milk. It's sold in various shapes and sizes, most commonly in rounds, but it may also be packaged in cottage-cheeselike tubs. Store leftovers tightly wrapped in the refrigerator, and use within two weeks or by the package freshness date, whichever comes first.

Asian Noodles

Looking for an alternative to Italian pasta? Check your market's Asian section. You will likely find Chinese lo mein noodles made with wheat flour in widths similar to those of spaghetti, linguine, or fettuccine, as well as Japanese buckwheat soba noodles as fine as angel hair.

You may also want to try *sai fun* or cellophane noodles made with mung bean paste. When soaked in water, the opaque noodles become a tangle of clear, long, wispy strands to add to soups or stir-fried dishes. There are also both thick and thin noodles made with rice flour.

Asian noodles used in stir-fries are precooked and served as a base for the cooked vegetables, meats, and other ingredients. For soups, the noodles can be stirred into the broth to soften and absorb flavor. Many traditional cold salads and side dishes are made with cooked noodles. Except for different cooking times, Asian noodles are generally interchangeable with one another and Italian pasta. Store leftover dried Asian pasta in an airtight container.

Chipotles in Adobo Sauce

Chipotle chile peppers in adobo sauce are smoked jalapeños canned in a sauce of tomatoes, onions, garlic, spices, and vinegar. Taking a cue from Mexican cooks, we often reach for these to add complex, smoky flavor to a dish. If these fiery chiles are new to you, start easy—a little goes a long way.

Chipotles are a natural in barbecue recipes. Braised and stewed meats and poultry, and chili with and without meat, are also good partners. Add minced chipotles to turkey burgers, or stir a little into mayonnaise to spread on sandwiches. Chipotles are a nice addition to bean dips, soups, salsas, and even scrambled eggs.

No recipe requires an entire can of chipotles. Leftovers can be refrigerated in a clean, tightly covered container for several months. Or, place one chile and some sauce in each compartment of a plastic ice-cube tray, and freeze. (Or puree the peppers and their sauce, and freeze the leftovers in ice-cube trays.) Store the cubes in the freezer in a zip-top plastic bag, and use as needed.

Guava Paste

Dense, sweet guava paste is sold canned or in bricks and is prized in Latin countries, where it's often cut into thin slices and layered with cream cheese. The rosy, fruit-leatherlike paste has several other uses.

Simmered with spices and chiles, guava paste's exotic, slightly acidic taste makes a superb base for barbecue sauces and fruit ketchups to serve with spareribs and other pork dishes. It similarly flatters shellfish.

Traditionally, Latin bakers use guava paste as a tasty filling for little pastries or cookies. Its natural partners include ginger and tropical fruits such as pineapple and mango. It adds a lovely flavor to treats like homemade ice cream or sorbet.

Finely chopping guava paste before adding it to hot liquids helps it melt more quickly. Store leftovers in a covered container in the refrigerator for up to three weeks.

Panko

For fried foods with a satisfying crunch, a growing number of chefs and cooks are using panko, or Japanese breadcrumbs. Panko is usually made from loaves of specially baked white bread with the crusts removed. (Tan panko is made from crusted bread.)

Panko's irregular-shaped crumbs are both larger and lighter than American dried breadcrumbs. It's ideal for breading every kind of fish, from flat catfish fillets to rings of calamari. When making crab cakes, the porous crumbs can be used both as a binder (in place of crackers) and as a coating. When cooked, panko crumbs stay remarkably crisp.

Because panko browns really well and doesn't become soggy, it makes an appealing crunchy topping for broiled oysters, salmon steaks, and virtually any oven-baked casserole. The crumbs are neutral-flavored and pair well with herb and spice seasonings. Remember the trick of oven "frying" skinless chicken with crushed corn flakes? Panko makes the pieces even crunchier, more delicious, and more delicate. The breadcrumbs keep indefinitely stored in an airtight container.

Mongolian Hot Pot

This is a popular soup in northern China. Cooking goes quickly, so you'll want to prep all the ingredients first. Simmering the **soba noodles** in the broth helps thicken the soup.

2½ tablespoons grated peeled fresh ginger
2 tablespoons low-sodium soy sauce
¼ teaspoon crushed red pepper
8 ounces flank steak, thinly sliced and cut into 1½-inch lengths
2 large garlic cloves, minced
Cooking spray
7 cups thinly sliced bok choy (about 1 pound)
1 cup thinly sliced shiitake mushrooms (about 2 ounces)
1 cup (¼-inch-thick) slices carrot
½ cup thinly sliced green onions
2 cups hot water
2 tablespoons hoisin sauce
2 (14-ounce) cans less-sodium beef broth
4 ounces uncooked soba (buckwheat) noodles
1 tablespoon rice vinegar
1½ teaspoons dark sesame oil

1. Combine first 5 ingredients in a large zip-top plastic bag, and seal. Marinate in refrigerator 2½ hours, turning bag occasionally.
2. Heat a small Dutch oven over high heat. Coat pan with cooking spray. Add beef mixture to pan; stir-fry 1 minute or until browned. Remove beef mixture from pan; set aside.
3. Add bok choy, mushrooms, carrot, and onions to pan; stir-fry 2 minutes or until bok choy begins to wilt. Add 2 cups hot water, hoisin, and broth; bring to a boil. Stir in noodles. Reduce heat; simmer 5 minutes or until noodles are done. Stir in beef mixture and vinegar. Ladle 1½ cups soup into each of 6 bowls; drizzle each serving with ¼ teaspoon oil. Yield: 6 servings.

CALORIES 197 (26% from fat); FAT 5.6g (sat 1.9g, mono 2.2g, poly 0.7g); PROTEIN 13.4g; CARB 24.2g; FIBER 2.8g; CHOL 17mg; IRON 2mg; SODIUM 633mg; CALC 102mg

Pumpkin-Black Bean Soup

This Caribbean-inspired soup combines pumpkin, black beans, tomatoes, and sherry. It's topped with a tangy shower of **queso fresco**. Use vegetable broth to make this a meatless meal.

1½ cups drained diced canned tomatoes
2 (15-ounce) cans black beans, drained and rinsed
1 teaspoon olive oil
Cooking spray
1½ cups finely chopped onion
1 teaspoon ground cumin
3 garlic cloves, minced
3 cups fat-free, less-sodium chicken broth
2 tablespoons sherry vinegar
½ teaspoon freshly ground black pepper
1 (15-ounce) can pumpkin
2 tablespoons dry sherry
1 cup (4 ounces) crumbled queso fresco
½ cup sliced green onions
Pumpkinseed kernels (optional)

1. Place tomatoes and beans in a food processor; process until about half the beans are smooth. Set aside.
2. Heat oil in a Dutch oven coated with cooking spray over medium-high heat. Add onion to pan; sauté 5 minutes or until lightly browned. Add cumin and garlic; sauté 1 minute. Add bean mixture, broth, and next 3 ingredients; bring to a boil. Cover, reduce heat, and simmer 20 minutes. Stir in sherry. Ladle about 1 cup soup into each of 6 bowls; sprinkle evenly with queso fresco and green onions. Garnish with pumpkinseed kernels, if desired. Yield: 6 servings.

CALORIES 175 (16% from fat); FAT 3.1g (sat 1.2g, mono 1.1g, poly 0.2g); PROTEIN 10g; CARB 29.2g; FIBER 9.3g; CHOL 6mg; IRON 3mg; SODIUM 785mg; CALC 139mg

Cold Asian Noodle Salad with Ponzu Vinaigrette

You can use any type of **Asian wheat** or **egg noodle**. Keep Italian-style linguine on hand as a substitute.

Cooking spray
½ pound medium shrimp, peeled and deveined
1 (6-ounce) package chow mein stir-fry noodles (chuka soba)
1 cup haricots verts, cut into 2-inch pieces (about 4 ounces)
1 cup thinly sliced shiitake mushroom caps (about 2 ounces)
⅓ cup chopped red onion
¼ cup matchstick-cut carrots
6 tablespoons commercial ponzu sauce (such as Kikkoman)
2 tablespoons toasted sesame oil
2 teaspoons black sesame seeds

1. Heat a medium nonstick skillet over medium-high heat. Coat pan with cooking spray. Add shrimp; sauté 5 minutes or until done. Remove from heat.
2. Cook noodles according to package instructions, omitting salt and fat. Drain; rinse with cold water. Drain well.
3. Combine noodles, shrimp, haricots verts, and next 3 ingredients in a large bowl. Combine ponzu and sesame oil in a small bowl, stirring with a whisk. Add oil mixture to noodle mixture; toss gently to coat. Add sesame seeds, tossing gently. Cover and chill 45 minutes, stirring occasionally. Yield: 4 servings (serving size: 1½ cups).

CALORIES 316 (27% from fat); FAT 9.5g (sat 1.4g, mono 3.2g, poly 4.1g); PROTEIN 18.4g; CARB 40.1g; FIBER 1.7g; CHOL 86mg; IRON 2.4mg; SODIUM 795mg; CALC 60mg

Blazin' Baked Beans

Chipotle chiles in adobo sauce add smoky-depth. Serve with Pork Tenderloin with Guava Bourbon Sauce (recipe on page 103).

¼ pound finely diced bacon slices
1½ cups chopped onion
⅓ cup packed dark brown sugar
3 tablespoons Dijon mustard
2 tablespoons finely chopped chipotle chile, canned in adobo sauce
5 (16-ounce) cans navy beans, rinsed and drained
1 (18-ounce) jar low-sodium barbecue sauce
Cooking spray

1. Preheat oven to 350°.
2. Cook bacon in a large nonstick skillet over medium-high heat until crisp. Remove bacon from pan, reserving 1 tablespoon drippings in pan, and set bacon aside. Add onion to drippings in pan; sauté 3 minutes.
3. Combine bacon, onion, sugar, and next 4 ingredients in a large bowl; toss well. Spoon bean mixture into a 13 x 9–inch or 2½-quart baking dish coated with cooking spray. Bake at 350° for 45 minutes. Yield: 21 servings (serving size: ½ cup).

CALORIES 167 (22% from fat); FAT 4.1g (sat 1.4g, mono 1.7g, poly 0.8g); PROTEIN 8.7g; CARB 24.9g; FIBER 5.1g; CHOL 5mg; IRON 1.9mg; SODIUM 520mg; CALC 49mg

Guava-Candied Ginger Gelato

⅓ cup nonfat dry milk
1 (12-ounce) can evaporated fat-free milk
7 ounces guava paste, cut into ½-inch pieces
1 teaspoon vanilla extract
⅛ teaspoon salt
4 large egg yolks
1 cup 2% reduced-fat milk
¼ cup finely chopped crystallized ginger (about 1 ounce)
Crystallized ginger (optional)
Mint sprigs (optional)

Some of Our Other Favorite Ingredients

These are a few more ingredients that formerly were available only at ethnic or gourmet markets. Lately, we've found them in large supermarkets. You can find recipes that use all of these at CookingLight.com.

Ingredient	What is It?	How to Use It
Sriracha	Moderately hot Thai sauce made with sun-ripened chiles, sugar, vinegar, salt, and garlic	As a condiment in place of ketchup (it's great on eggs, burgers, and French fries), in barbecue sauce; add a dash of Sriracha and a little sautéed pancetta to bottled marinara to make a quick arrabbiata sauce for pasta
Edamame	High-protein fresh green soybeans with a flavor similar to green peas or sweet lima beans; sold in the frozen foods section	As a snack or side dish sprinkled with kosher salt; add to salads and stir-fried dishes; puree as a dip with cut-up raw vegetables or pita bread
Nutella	Italian-made chocolate-hazelnut spread; its makers claim that, worldwide, it outsells all other brands of nut butter combined	Slathered on apples; spread on crepes or waffles with sliced banana; used in place of creamy peanut butter in almost any dessert
Fresh lemongrass	A sour-lemony herb popular in Thai and Vietnamese cooking; looks like an overgrown green onion	Coarsely chopped and added to soups, stews, sauces, etc. (remove pieces before serving)
Fresh bay leaves	An herb native to the Mediterranean; lends woodsy flavor to all manner of dishes	Add to soups, stews, and sauces to deepen their flavor (use 1 fresh leaf for every 2 dried, and remove before serving)

1. Combine first 3 ingredients in a medium saucepan over low heat. Cook 15 minutes or until guava paste dissolves, stirring constantly.

2. Combine vanilla, salt, and yolks in a large bowl, stirring with a whisk. Gradually add milk mixture to bowl, stirring constantly with a whisk. Return mixture to pan. Cook over medium heat 10 minutes or until mixture thinly coats back of a spoon or registers 160° on a thermometer, stirring constantly with a whisk (do not boil). Remove from heat, and stir in reduced-fat milk. Immediately pour mixture into a bowl. Cover and chill 3 hours. Pour mixture into freezer can of an ice-cream freezer; freeze according to manufacturer's instructions. Stir in chopped ginger. Spoon gelato into a freezer-safe container. Cover and freeze 2 hours or until firm. Garnish with additional ginger and mint, if desired. Yield: 8 servings (serving size: about ½ cup).

CALORIES 174 (15% from fat); FAT 2.9g (sat 1.2g, mono 1.2g, poly 0.4g); PROTEIN 7.1g; CARB 29.9g; FIBER 0.3g; CHOL 107mg; IRON 0.6mg; SODIUM 130mg; CALC 234mg

Southwestern Lamb Stew

Chipotle chiles, tomatoes, and beer add vibrant flavors to the sauce. Serve over mashed potatoes.

    2   pounds lamb stew meat,
        trimmed
    ½   teaspoon salt
    ¼   teaspoon freshly ground black
        pepper
        Cooking spray
    5½ cups vertically sliced onion
        (about 1 large)
    ¾   cup less-sodium beef broth
    2   to 3 tablespoons finely chopped
        chipotle chiles, canned in adobo
        sauce
    2   tablespoons tomato paste
    1   teaspoon ground cumin
    1   teaspoon chili powder
    1   (14.5-ounce) can diced tomatoes,
        undrained
    1   (12-ounce) bottle beer
    ¼   cup chopped fresh cilantro

1. Preheat oven to 350°.

2. Sprinkle lamb with salt and pepper. Heat a large Dutch oven over medium-high heat. Coat pan with cooking spray. Add lamb; cook 8 minutes, browning on all sides. Remove lamb from pan; set aside. Add onion to pan; sauté 5 minutes or until golden brown. Add broth; cook until liquid evaporates, scraping pan to loosen browned bits. Stir in chiles and next 5 ingredients. Return lamb to pan; bring to a boil. Cover and bake at 350° for 1 hour and 15 minutes or until lamb is tender. Sprinkle with cilantro. Yield: 4 servings (serving size: about 1¾ cups stew and 1 tablespoon cilantro).

CALORIES 395 (28% from fat); FAT 12.4g (sat 4.3g, mono 4.9g, poly 1.2g); PROTEIN 48.4g; CARB 14.8g; FIBER 3.8g; CHOL 147mg; IRON 5.1mg; SODIUM 795mg; CALC 56mg

QUICK & EASY

Pork Tenderloin with Guava Bourbon Sauce

This dish is easy enough to make for a weeknight supper and special enough to serve to company.

    1   cup fat-free, less-sodium chicken
        broth
    2   ounces finely chopped guava
        paste
    1   (1¼-pound) pork tenderloin,
        trimmed
    1   teaspoon salt
    ½   teaspoon freshly ground black
        pepper
        Cooking spray
    1   teaspoon canola oil
    ½   cup finely chopped shallots
    3   tablespoons bourbon
    1½ tablespoons whole grain mustard

1. Combine broth and guava paste in a small saucepan; bring to a boil. Reduce heat, and simmer 2 minutes or until guava dissolves, stirring constantly. Set mixture aside.

2. Sprinkle pork tenderloin with salt and pepper. Heat a large nonstick skillet over medium-high heat. Coat pan with cooking spray. Add pork to pan; cook 6 minutes, browning on all sides. Remove pork from pan.

3. Add oil and shallots to pan; sauté 1 minute. Add bourbon; cook 30 seconds or until liquid almost evaporates. Stir in broth mixture. Return pork to pan, cover, and simmer 13 minutes or until a thermometer registers 160° (slightly pink). Remove pork from pan; let stand 15 minutes before cutting into slices. Remove pan from heat; gently stir in mustard. Yield: 4 servings (serving size: 3 ounces pork and 3 tablespoons sauce).

CALORIES 284 (30% from fat); FAT 9.4g (sat 2.8g, mono 4.2g, poly 1.2g); PROTEIN 30.6g; CARB 14.7g; FIBER 1g; CHOL 94mg; IRON 2.2mg; SODIUM 887mg; CALC 25mg

QUICK & EASY

Mixed Salad with Hoisin Vinaigrette and Crisp Panko Chicken

Omit the chili powder to prepare kid-friendly chicken fingers.

CHICKEN:

    ½   cup panko (Japanese breadcrumbs)
    ½   teaspoon salt
    ¼   teaspoon chili powder
    ¼   teaspoon freshly ground black
        pepper
    1   pound chicken breast tenders, cut
        into 1-inch pieces
        Cooking spray

SALAD:

    2   tablespoons white wine vinegar
    1½ tablespoons hoisin sauce
    1   tablespoon finely chopped peeled
        fresh ginger
    1   tablespoon Dijon mustard
    2   teaspoons canola oil
    1½ teaspoons low-sodium soy
        sauce
    1   teaspoon toasted sesame oil
    1   large garlic clove, minced
    1   cup cherry tomatoes, halved
    ½   cup chopped green onions
    1   (8-ounce) package field greens
        salad mix

1. Preheat oven to 375°.

2. To prepare chicken, combine first 4 ingredients in a medium bowl. Add

Continued

chicken, tossing to coat. Arrange chicken in a single layer on a baking sheet coated with cooking spray. Bake at 375° for 15 minutes or until chicken is done and lightly browned, stirring once.

3. To prepare salad, place vinegar and next 7 ingredients in a food processor; process until well combined.

4. Combine tomatoes, green onions, and salad mix in a large bowl; add vinegar mixture, tossing to coat. Place about 1 cup salad mixture on each of 4 plates; top each serving with about 1 cup chicken. Yield: 4 servings.

CALORIES 242 (27% from fat); FAT 7.2g (sat 1.3g, mono 3g, poly 2g); PROTEIN 28.8g; CARB 14.4g; FIBER 2.8g; CHOL 73mg; IRON 1.7mg; SODIUM 622mg; CALC 29mg

technique

Think Thin

Pound boneless cuts of meat to trim cooking time and boost tenderness.

Seared Duck Breast with Ruby Port Sauce

Use your pounding tool to crush spices to a coarse consistency. Serve with rice and steamed green beans.

DUCK:

- 1 pound boneless duck breast halves, thawed and skinned
- 1 tablespoon pink peppercorns, crushed
- 1 teaspoon coriander seeds, crushed
- ¾ teaspoon salt
- 3 garlic cloves, minced
- 2 teaspoons olive oil, divided

SAUCE:

- 2 cups ruby port
- ¼ cup packed brown sugar
- ¼ cup sherry vinegar
- 1 tablespoon half-and-half
- 2 teaspoons butter
- Chopped fresh flat-leaf parsley (optional)

1. To prepare duck, place breast halves between 2 sheets of heavy-duty plastic wrap; pound each piece to ¼-inch thickness with a meat mallet or small heavy skillet.

2. Combine crushed peppercorns, crushed coriander seeds, salt, and garlic. Rub peppercorn mixture evenly over both sides of duck; let stand 15 minutes.

3. Heat 1 teaspoon oil in a large nonstick skillet over medium-high heat. Add half of duck; cook 1 minute on each side or until desired degree of doneness. Remove duck from pan; keep warm. Repeat procedure with 1 teaspoon oil and remaining duck.

4. To prepare sauce, combine port, sugar, and vinegar in a saucepan. Bring to a boil over medium-high heat; cook until reduced to ½ cup (about 10 minutes). Remove from heat. Add half-and-half and butter; stir until butter melts. Cut duck breasts crosswise into thin slices. Drizzle with sauce, and sprinkle with parsley, if desired. Yield: 4 servings (serving size: 3 ounces duck and 2 tablespoons sauce).

CALORIES 453 (15% from fat); FAT 7.5g (sat 2.4g, mono 3.3g, poly 0.8g); PROTEIN 31.9g; CARB 32.5g; FIBER 0.4g; CHOL 169mg; IRON 6mg; SODIUM 594mg; CALC 46mg

QUICK & EASY
Peppered Steak with Horseradish-Chive Cream

- ½ cup fat-free sour cream
- 2 tablespoons chopped fresh chives
- 1 tablespoon prepared horseradish
- 1 teaspoon Worcestershire sauce
- 1 (1-pound) boneless sirloin steak
- 1 tablespoon freshly ground black pepper
- 2 tablespoons balsamic vinegar
- ½ teaspoon salt
- 2 garlic cloves, minced
- Cooking spray

1. Prepare grill.

2. Combine first 4 ingredients in a small bowl, stirring until well blended. Cover and chill.

3. Place steak between 2 sheets of heavy-duty plastic wrap, and pound to ¼-inch thickness using a meat mallet or small heavy skillet. Combine pepper, vinegar, salt, and garlic in a small bowl. Rub steak with vinegar mixture.

4. Place steak on grill rack coated with cooking spray; grill 2 minutes on each side or until desired degree of doneness. Cut steak diagonally across grain into thin slices. Yield: 4 servings (serving size: 3 ounces steak and 2 tablespoons cream).

CALORIES 198 (25% from fat); FAT 5.5g (sat 2.2g, mono 2g, poly 0.3g); PROTEIN 26g; CARB 9.8g; FIBER 0.6g; CHOL 73mg; IRON 3.4mg; SODIUM 411mg; CALC 68mg

QUICK & EASY
Lemon-Arugula Chicken Paillard

A *paillard* (PI-yahrd) is a piece of meat pounded thin and grilled quickly or sautéed. To make this colorful dish even more striking, use a combination of red and yellow tomatoes.

- 2 teaspoons grated lemon rind
- 3 tablespoons fresh lemon juice
- 2 teaspoons extravirgin olive oil
- 1 garlic clove, crushed
- ½ teaspoon salt, divided
- ½ teaspoon freshly ground black pepper, divided
- 4 cups trimmed arugula
- 4 (6-ounce) skinless, boneless chicken breast halves
- Cooking spray
- 1 cup grape or cherry tomatoes, halved (about 6 ounces)
- ⅓ cup dry white wine

1. Combine first 4 ingredients in a large bowl. Sprinkle with ¼ teaspoon salt and ¼ teaspoon pepper. Add arugula; toss well.

2. Place each chicken breast half between 2 sheets of heavy-duty plastic wrap; pound each piece to ¼-inch thickness using a meat mallet or small heavy skillet. Sprinkle both sides of chicken with ¼ teaspoon salt and ¼ teaspoon pepper.

3. Heat a grill pan or a large nonstick skillet over medium-high heat. Coat pan with cooking spray. Add chicken, and cook 4 minutes on each side or until done. Remove chicken from pan, and keep warm.

4. Add tomatoes and wine to pan. Cook 2 minutes or until liquid almost evaporates. Yield: 4 servings (serving size:

1 chicken paillard, ¾ cup arugula mixture, and ¼ cup tomato mixture).

CALORIES 239 (17% from fat); FAT 4.6g (sat 0.9g, mono 2.2g, poly 0.8g); PROTEIN 40.3g; CARB 4.2g; FIBER 1g; CHOL 99mg; IRON 1.8mg; SODIUM 416mg; CALC 59mg

How to Make a Chicken Paillard

1. *Trim off excess fat, and place the meat between two sheets of heavy-duty plastic wrap.*

2. *With a meat pounder, mallet, or small heavy skillet, firmly pound the entire surface until the meat is ¼ to ½ inches thick, depending on the recipe. If you pound the meat too hard or thin, it will tear.*

3. *Remove plastic wrap when the meat is evenly pounded.*

QUICK & EASY
Chicken Roulade with Herbed Cheese and Prosciutto

"Roulade" is a French term for a thin cut of meat that is stuffed, rolled, then browned before being roasted or braised. Substitute chives for parsley, if desired.

4 (6-ounce) skinless, boneless chicken breast halves
½ teaspoon salt
½ teaspoon freshly ground black pepper
2 tablespoons light garlic and herb spreadable cheese (such as Alouette Light)
2 ounces prosciutto, chopped
16 large spinach leaves, stemmed
8 ounces uncooked fettuccine
2 tablespoons chopped fresh flat-leaf parsley
¼ teaspoon salt
4 teaspoons extravirgin olive oil, divided
2 tablespoons white wine
2 tablespoons water

1. Place each chicken breast half between 2 sheets of heavy-duty plastic wrap; pound each piece to ¼-inch thickness using a meat mallet or small heavy skillet. Sprinkle both sides of chicken with ½ teaspoon salt and pepper.
2. Combine cheese and prosciutto in a small bowl. Spread 1½ teaspoons cheese mixture over each breast half. Place 4 spinach leaves on each breast half; flatten with hand. Roll up chicken, jelly-roll fashion, starting with narrow end. Secure chicken rolls at 1-inch intervals with twine. Set aside.
3. Cook pasta according to package directions, omitting salt and fat. Drain well. Place pasta in a large bowl. Sprinkle with parsley and ¼ teaspoon salt. Drizzle with 2 teaspoons oil; toss gently to coat. Cover and keep warm.
4. Heat 2 teaspoons oil in a large nonstick skillet over medium-high heat. Place chicken in pan, and cook 6 minutes, browning on all sides. Add wine and water. Cover, reduce heat to medium-low, and cook 6 minutes or until

chicken is done. Remove chicken from pan, and let stand 2 minutes. Remove twine, and cut each roulade crosswise into 5 equal pieces.
5. Place about 1 cup pasta mixture on each of 4 plates; top each with 5 pieces roulade. Serve immediately. Yield: 4 servings.

CALORIES 495 (21% from fat); FAT 11.5g (sat 3.2g, mono 5.2g, poly 2g); PROTEIN 51.8g; CARB 43.6g; FIBER 2.9g; CHOL 113mg; IRON 4.3mg; SODIUM 850mg; CALC 81mg

QUICK & EASY
Chipotle-Orange Chicken Cutlets

4 (6-ounce) skinless, boneless chicken breast halves
1 tablespoon butter
1 tablespoon canola oil
⅓ cup all-purpose flour (about 1½ ounces)
2 teaspoons ground cumin
½ teaspoon salt
½ cup thawed orange juice concentrate, undiluted
½ cup water
2 teaspoons finely chopped chipotle chile, canned in adobo sauce (about 1 chile)
2 tablespoons water (optional)
2 cups hot cooked brown rice
⅓ cup chopped fresh cilantro
Cilantro sprigs (optional)

1. Place each chicken breast half between 2 sheets of heavy-duty plastic wrap; pound each piece to ¼-inch thickness using a meat mallet or small heavy skillet.
2. Melt butter and oil in a large nonstick skillet over low heat.
3. Combine flour, cumin, and salt in a shallow dish. Dip chicken in orange juice concentrate; dredge in flour mixture. Reserve concentrate.
4. Increase heat to medium-high. Heat pan 2 minutes or until butter starts to brown. Add chicken; cook 3 minutes on each side or until done. Remove from pan; keep warm.
5. Stir in reserved concentrate, ½ cup water, and chile. Bring to a boil; cook

Continued

2 minutes. (Thin sauce with 2 table-spoons water, if needed.)

6. Combine rice and chopped cilantro. Serve with chicken. Garnish with cilantro sprigs, if desired. Yield: 4 servings (serving size: 1 chicken breast half, 2 tablespoons sauce, and ½ cup rice mixture).

CALORIES 419 (20% from fat); FAT 9.5g (sat 2.8g, mono 3.7g, poly 2g); PROTEIN 43g; CARB 38g; FIBER 2.4g; CHOL 106mg; IRON 2mg; SODIUM 239mg; CALC 45mg

QUICK & EASY
Orange Duck Breast Salad

If the duck breasts you select are thicker than an inch, butterfly them first to make it easier to pound them thin and even.

- ½ cup fresh orange juice (about 2 oranges)
- 3 tablespoons white wine vinegar
- 4 teaspoons brown sugar
- 2 teaspoons Dijon mustard
- 2 teaspoons canola oil
- ⅛ teaspoon salt
- ⅛ teaspoon freshly ground black pepper
- 1 garlic clove, minced
- ¾ pound boneless duck breast halves, thawed and skinned
- 4 cups cubed sourdough bread (about 7 ounces)
- 2 teaspoons olive oil
- Cooking spray
- 10 cups mixed salad greens
- ⅓ cup pitted prunes, quartered
- 3 teaspoons chopped walnuts, toasted

1. Preheat oven to 350°.

2. Combine first 8 ingredients; stir well.

3. Place each duck breast half between 2 sheets of heavy-duty plastic wrap; pound each piece to ¼-inch thickness using a meat mallet or small heavy skillet. Place duck in a large zip-top plastic bag. Add half of juice mixture; seal and marinate in refrigerator 30 minutes.

4. Combine cubed bread and oil; toss well. Arrange bread on a jelly-roll pan. Bake at 350° for 20 minutes, stirring once. Set aside.

5. Remove duck from bag; discard marinade. Heat a large nonstick skillet over medium heat. Coat pan with cooking spray. Add duck; cook 3 minutes on each side or until desired degree of doneness. Remove from pan. Cut duck into ¼-inch slices.

6. Combine toasted bread cubes, greens, prunes, and walnuts in a large bowl. Drizzle with remaining half of juice mixture; toss well. Place greens mixture on each of 4 plates. Top with duck slices. Yield: 4 servings (serving size: 2 ounces duck and 2 cups greens mixture).

CALORIES 402 (26% from fat); FAT 11.6g (sat 2.2g, mono 5.2g, poly 3.1g); PROTEIN 26.2g; CARB 51.6g; FIBER 6.3g; CHOL 65mg; IRON 9mg; SODIUM 593mg; CALC 158mg

How to Butterfly a Breast

1. *With larger poultry breasts and thick steaks, it's best to butterfly the meat before pounding it thin. To butterfly a breast, slice it lengthwise, cutting to—but not through—the other side.*

2. *Open halves, laying the breast flat.*

inspired vegetarian

Vegetable Pancakes

Hot off the griddle: Croquettes and patties sizzle with fresh flavors and spring produce.

You can make these flavorful pancakes for a meal or side dish. Using pantry or refrigerator staples, each is packed with vegetables, enhanced with grated cheeses, fresh herbs, onion or garlic, and touched up with simple seasonings to flaunt spring flavors. Then, more vegetables are heaped on top or served alongside, making these vegetable pancakes wholesome, filling, and perfect for springtime meals.

Herbed Chicken Dinner Menu
serves 4

While these pancakes can stand alone as a meatless main dish, they make a delightful side for simple sautéed chicken.

Lemon and rosemary chicken*

Potato-Zucchini Skillet Pancakes with Cherry Tomato Salad

Fresh green beans

*Combine 1 tablespoon fresh lemon juice, 2 teaspoons chopped fresh rosemary, 1 teaspoon salt, and ½ teaspoon freshly ground black pepper. Rub herb mixture over 4 (6-ounce) skinless, boneless chicken breast halves. Heat 2 teaspoons olive oil in a large nonstick skillet over medium-high heat. Add chicken to pan; sauté 6 minutes on each side or until done.

Potato-Zucchini Skillet Pancakes with Cherry Tomato Salad

These potato pancakes make an ideal base for the tangy olive and tomato salad.

PANCAKES:

- 3 cups shredded peeled Yukon gold potato (about 1 pound)
- 2 cups shredded zucchini (about 8 ounces)
- 1 cup shredded onion (about 1 small)
- ½ cup egg substitute
- ¼ cup matzo meal
- ¼ teaspoon salt
- Dash of freshly ground black pepper
- 4 teaspoons canola oil, divided

SALAD:

- 3 cups quartered cherry tomatoes
- 2 tablespoons chopped pitted kalamata olives
- 2 tablespoons chopped fresh parsley
- 1 teaspoon extravirgin olive oil
- ¼ teaspoon salt
- ¼ teaspoon freshly ground black pepper

1. To prepare pancakes, place first 3 ingredients in a clean kitchen towel, and squeeze out excess liquid. Combine potato mixture, egg substitute, and next 3 ingredients in a large bowl, and stir gently to blend.

2. Heat 1 teaspoon canola oil in a nonstick griddle or large nonstick skillet over medium heat. Spoon about 1 cup potato mixture into hot pan, spreading to a 6-inch diameter. Cook 3 minutes on each side or until lightly browned and cooked through. Transfer to a plate; keep warm. Repeat procedure with 3 teaspoons oil and remaining potato mixture.

3. To prepare salad, combine tomatoes and remaining 5 ingredients in a medium bowl; toss gently. Serve salad on top of pancakes. Yield: 4 servings (serving size: 1 pancake and about ¾ cup salad).

CALORIES 242 (31% from fat); FAT 8.4g (sat 0.8g, mono 5.2g, poly 1.9g); PROTEIN 8.3g; CARB 34.6g; FIBER 3.8g; CHOL 0mg; IRON 2.7mg; SODIUM 504mg; CALC 35mg

Shredded Carrot-Ginger Pancakes with Asian Dipping Sauce

Serve these easy pancakes as an accompaniment to stir-fried rice with tofu and steamed sugar snap or snow peas. If you have a griddle, you can cook all the pancakes in one batch.

PANCAKES:

- 2½ cups coarsely shredded carrot (about 1 pound)
- ½ cup chopped green onions
- 1 teaspoon minced garlic
- 1 teaspoon grated peeled fresh ginger
- ½ cup egg substitute
- 3 tablespoons cracker meal
- ¼ teaspoon salt
- 1 tablespoon canola oil, divided
- Cooking spray
- Green onion strips (optional)

SAUCE:

- 2 tablespoons low-sodium soy sauce
- 1½ tablespoons water
- ½ teaspoon minced garlic
- ½ teaspoon grated peeled fresh ginger
- ½ teaspoon rice wine vinegar

1. To prepare pancakes, combine first 4 ingredients in a large bowl. Combine egg substitute, cracker meal, and salt in a small bowl. Add egg mixture to carrot mixture; stir to blend.

2. Heat 1½ teaspoons oil in a nonstick griddle or large nonstick skillet coated with cooking spray over medium-low heat. Using about ¼ cup batter per pancake, spoon 4 pancakes onto hot pan, spreading each to a 4-inch diameter. Cook 4 minutes on each side or until bottoms are lightly browned and cooked through. Transfer to a plate; keep warm. Repeat procedure with 1½ teaspoons oil and remaining batter. Garnish with green onion strips, if desired.

3. To prepare dipping sauce, combine soy sauce and remaining 4 ingredients in a small bowl, and stir with a whisk. Serve with pancakes. Yield: 4 servings (serving size: 2 pancakes and 1 tablespoon sauce).

CALORIES 129 (28% from fat); FAT 4g (sat 0.3g, mono 2.1g, poly 1.2g); PROTEIN 5g; CARB 18.1g; FIBER 3.9g; CHOL 0mg; IRON 1.3mg; SODIUM 562mg; CALC 60mg

Bulgur, Spinach, and Toasted Walnut Pancakes

A tomato salad tossed with olive oil, fresh lemon juice, parsley, and mint is a tasty side for these hearty pancakes.

- 2 cups boiling water
- 1 cup uncooked bulgur
- ⅓ cup finely chopped walnuts
- 2 tablespoons low-sodium soy sauce
- Cooking spray
- ¾ cup finely chopped onion
- 1 garlic clove, minced
- 2 cups chopped fresh, tightly packed spinach
- ¼ teaspoon salt
- ½ cup orange juice
- 2 large egg yolks
- ¼ cup whole wheat flour (about 1⅕ ounces)
- 2 large egg whites
- 1 tablespoon canola oil
- 2 cups loosely packed spinach leaves
- Orange rind strips (optional)

1. Combine 2 cups boiling water and bulgur in a bowl; cover and let stand 20 minutes. Drain well, and press out excess liquid.

2. Heat walnuts in a large skillet over medium heat until walnuts are hot. Add soy sauce; cook 20 seconds or until liquid evaporates, stirring constantly. Remove from pan. Wipe pan with a paper towel.

3. Heat pan over medium-high heat. Coat pan with cooking spray. Add onion; sauté 5 minutes or until golden. Add garlic; sauté 30 seconds. Add chopped spinach; cook 30 seconds. Add bulgur, walnuts, and salt; stir well.

4. Combine juice and egg yolks in a large bowl. Add bulgur mixture. Lightly spoon flour into a dry measuring cup; level with a knife. Add flour to bulgur mixture; stir well. Beat egg whites with a mixer at high speed until soft peaks form. Fold whites into bulgur mixture.

5. Heat oil in a nonstick griddle or large nonstick skillet over medium heat. Pour ½ cup batter per pancake onto hot pan, spreading each to a 5-inch diameter.

Continued

Cook 5 minutes or until bottoms are browned. Carefully turn pancakes over; cook 4 minutes or until bottoms are golden. Transfer to a plate; keep warm.

6. Heat pan over medium-high heat. Add spinach leaves; cook 2 minutes or until spinach wilts, stirring constantly. Serve with pancakes. Garnish with rind strips, if desired. Yield: 4 servings (serving size: 2 pancakes and about ¼ cup wilted spinach).

CALORIES 338 (36% from fat); FAT 13.7g (sat 1.8g, mono 4.1g, poly 6.5g); PROTEIN 14.6g; CARB 45.2g; FIBER 9.7g; CHOL 106mg; IRON 5.7mg; SODIUM 560mg; CALC 179mg

Seven Steps to Perfect Pancakes

1. Use a nonstick griddle or a skillet with low sloping sides that will make it easier to use a spatula to flip or check pancakes.

2. Preheat the griddle or skillet until it is hot enough to sizzle a drop of water.

3. For several recipes, cooking spray is used in addition to coating the skillet very lightly with canola oil. Tilt the skillet to spread the oil evenly over the surface or use a silicone brush, if you have one.

4. Never crowd the pancakes. Leave enough space to be able to turn them without a collision.

5. Don't rush the cooking. Use medium heat, and allow enough time for the pancake to turn golden brown on the underside. Cooking over higher heat will brown the exterior before the interior is done.

6. If the batter is soft, the top layer will be evenly covered with tiny bubbles. For substantial batters, like rice, you need to lift an edge and peek at the underside. A well-browned underside will guarantee that the pancake won't break or crumble when it's flipped.

7. Keep cooked pancakes warm on a heatproof platter in a 200° oven.

Arborio Rice, Parmesan, and Green Pea Pancakes

On the side, serve roasted red peppers with olive oil and chopped fresh thyme.

Cooking spray
½ cup finely chopped onion
1 cup uncooked Arborio rice or other short-grain rice
2¾ cups water
¾ teaspoon salt
1 cup fresh or frozen green peas
½ cup (2 ounces) freshly grated Parmigiano-Reggiano cheese
2 large egg whites, lightly beaten
1 large egg, lightly beaten
2 teaspoons canola oil
Thinly shaved Parmigiano-Reggiano cheese (optional)

1. Heat a large saucepan over medium heat. Coat pan with cooking spray. Add onion; cook 5 minutes or until tender, stirring occasionally. Add rice; cook 1 minute, stirring constantly. Add 2¾ cups water and salt; bring to a boil. Cover, reduce heat to low, and cook 15 minutes. Stir in peas and grated cheese; cook 2 minutes, stirring constantly. Cover, remove from heat, and let stand 15 minutes.

2. Combine egg whites and egg in a large bowl. Add rice mixture, stirring until blended.

3. Heat oil in a nonstick griddle or large nonstick skillet over medium heat. Spoon ½ cup rice mixture per pancake onto hot pan, spreading each to a 4-inch diameter. Cook 6 minutes on each side or until bottoms are browned. Garnish with shaved cheese, if desired. Yield: 4 servings (serving size: 2 pancakes).

CALORIES 224 (31% from fat); FAT 7.8g (sat 2.7g, mono 3.2g, poly 1.2g); PROTEIN 11.7g; CARB 26.4g; FIBER 2.7g; CHOL 115mg; IRON 1.4mg; SODIUM 677mg; CALC 142mg

Brown Rice and Mushroom Pancakes

Unlike our other recipes, these crunchy pancakes are cooked over medium-high heat. Extra mushrooms, onions, and bell peppers sautéed for the pancake base are reserved for a simple sauce that complements the pancakes.

5 teaspoons olive oil, divided
5 cups thinly sliced mushrooms (12 ounces)
½ cup finely chopped onion
½ cup finely chopped red bell pepper
1 garlic clove, minced
1 tablespoon chopped fresh thyme
¾ teaspoon salt
¼ teaspoon black pepper
1 cup organic vegetable broth (such as Swanson Certified Organic)
1 teaspoon cornstarch
3 cups cooked brown rice
2 tablespoons dry breadcrumbs
2 large eggs, lightly beaten

1. Heat 2 teaspoons oil in a large nonstick skillet over medium heat. Add mushrooms, onion, and bell pepper; cook 10 minutes or until liquid evaporates, stirring occasionally. Add garlic; cook 1 minute. Stir in thyme, salt, and black pepper. Remove 1 cup mushroom mixture, and set aside. Increase heat to medium-high. Add broth and cornstarch to pan; bring to a boil. Cook 1 minute, stirring constantly. Keep warm.

2. Combine reserved 1 cup mushroom mixture, brown rice, breadcrumbs, and eggs; mix well.

3. Heat 1 tablespoon oil in a nonstick griddle or large nonstick skillet over medium-high heat. Spoon about ½ cup rice batter per pancake onto hot pan, spreading each to a 4-inch diameter. Cook 5 minutes on each side or until bottoms are golden brown. Serve with mushroom sauce. Yield: 4 servings (serving size: 2 pancakes and ⅓ cup sauce).

CALORIES 315 (29% from fat); FAT 10.2g (sat 2g, mono 6g, poly 1.6g); PROTEIN 10.4g; CARB 46.6g; FIBER 3.6g; CHOL 106mg; IRON 2.2mg; SODIUM 651mg; CALC 48mg

Double Corn Pancakes with Jalapeño and Chunky Tex-Mex Tomato Sauce

Serve these corn-studded pancakes with a black bean salad to round out the meal. They also make a great savory breakfast treat if you serve them with a little butter rather than the tomato sauce.

SAUCE:

    1 tablespoon canola oil
 ¼ cup finely chopped onion
1½ teaspoons chili powder
    1 teaspoon ground cumin
    2 (14.5-ounce) cans no salt–added diced tomatoes, undrained
 ¼ teaspoon salt
 ¼ cup chopped fresh cilantro

PANCAKES:

 ½ cup all-purpose flour (about 2¼ ounces)
    1 cup yellow cornmeal
    2 teaspoons baking powder
 ¼ teaspoon salt
    1 cup canned whole-kernel corn, rinsed and drained
 ¼ cup sliced green onions
    2 teaspoons minced seeded jalapeño pepper
    1 cup 1% low-fat milk
    2 tablespoons canola oil, divided
    2 large eggs, lightly beaten

1. To prepare sauce, heat 1 tablespoon oil in a medium saucepan over low heat. Add chopped onion; cover and cook 5 minutes or until golden brown, stirring occasionally. Stir in chili powder and cumin; cook 20 seconds, stirring constantly.
2. Add tomatoes; bring to a boil. Cover, reduce heat, and simmer 15 minutes. Uncover and cook 5 minutes or until slightly thickened. Stir in ¼ teaspoon salt and cilantro.
3. To prepare pancakes, lightly spoon flour into a dry measuring cup; level with a knife. Combine flour, cornmeal, baking powder, and ¼ teaspoon salt in a large bowl; stir with a whisk. Fold in corn, green onions, and jalapeño.

4. Combine milk, 1 tablespoon oil, and eggs in a small bowl; stir well with a whisk. Add to cornmeal mixture, stirring just until combined. Let batter stand 10 minutes.
5. Heat 1 tablespoon oil in a nonstick griddle or large nonstick skillet over medium heat. Spoon about ⅓ cup batter per pancake onto hot pan. Cook 4 minutes or until tops are covered with bubbles and edges looked cooked. Carefully turn pancakes; cook 2 minutes or until bottoms are lightly browned. Serve immediately with sauce. Yield: 4 servings (serving size: 2 pancakes and ½ cup sauce).

CALORIES 458 (29% from fat); FAT 14.6g (sat 2.1g, mono 7.6g, poly 3.9g); PROTEIN 12.4g; CARB 66.8g; FIBER 6.7g; CHOL 108mg; IRON 3.6mg; SODIUM 814mg; CALC 273mg

dinner tonight

Chicken Suppers

A bird in the hand makes for speedy, satisfying chicken suppers.

Chicken Supper Menu 1
serves 4

Chicken with Lime Sauce

Cumin roasted potatoes*

Green beans

*Preheat oven to 500°. Cut 2 large unpeeled baking potatoes into ½-inch slices. Arrange slices on a baking sheet coated with cooking spray. Combine 1 tablespoon extravirgin olive oil, 1 teaspoon ground cumin, 1 teaspoon bottled minced garlic, ½ teaspoon salt, and ¼ teaspoon ground red pepper in a small bowl. Spoon mixture over potato slices, tossing well to coat. Bake at 500° for 20 minutes or until done.

Game Plan

1. While oven preheats:
• Cut potatoes, and coat with oil mixture
2. While potatoes cook:
• Cook chicken
• Cook green beans

Chicken with Lime Sauce

A silky sauce coats the chicken with rich, tangy flavor. Substitute lemon if you don't have a lime on hand. For a splash of color, garnish with chopped parsley or chives.

TOTAL TIME: 40 MINUTES

    4 (6-ounce) skinless, boneless chicken breast halves
 ¼ teaspoon salt
 ¼ teaspoon freshly ground black pepper
    2 teaspoons olive oil
Cooking spray
 ¾ cup fat-free, less-sodium chicken broth
    1 tablespoon brown sugar
    3 tablespoons lime juice, divided
    2 teaspoons Dijon mustard
    2 tablespoons water
    1 teaspoon cornstarch
    1 tablespoon butter

1. Place each chicken breast half between 2 sheets of heavy-duty plastic wrap; pound to ¼-inch thickness using a meat mallet or small heavy skillet. Sprinkle chicken with salt and pepper.
2. Heat oil in a large nonstick skillet coated with cooking spray over medium-high heat. Add chicken; cook 4 minutes on each side or until browned. Remove from pan; keep warm.
3. Add broth, sugar, 2 tablespoons juice, and mustard to pan, and cook over medium heat, scraping pan to loosen browned bits.
4. Combine 2 tablespoons water and cornstarch in a small bowl. Add cornstarch mixture to pan; stir well with a whisk. Bring to a boil over medium-high heat; cook 1 minute or until slightly thick. Whisk in 1 tablespoon lime juice and butter, stirring until butter melts. Return chicken to pan; simmer 2 minutes or until chicken is thoroughly heated. Yield: 4 servings (serving size: 1 chicken breast half and 2 tablespoons sauce).

CALORIES 260 (26% from fat); FAT 7.5g (sat 2.7g, mono 3.1g, poly 0.8g); PROTEIN 40.7g; CARB 5.4g; FIBER 0.1g; CHOL 106mg; IRON 1.8mg; SODIUM 382mg; CALC 32mg

Chicken Supper Menu 2

serves 4

Chicken Enchiladas with Salsa Verde

Spanish rice*

Black beans

*Cook 2 slices bacon in a large nonstick skillet over medium heat until crisp. Remove bacon from pan; crumble. Add ½ cup chopped onion and 2 minced garlic cloves to drippings in pan; cook 4 minutes, stirring occasionally. Add 1 cup rice; 2 cups fat-free, less-sodium chicken broth; and 1 (14.5-ounce) can drained diced tomatoes. Stir to combine. Bring to a boil. Cover, reduce heat, and simmer 20 minutes or until rice is tender. Stir in crumbled bacon and ⅓ cup sliced green onions just before serving.

Game Plan

1. Cook bacon, and chop onion and garlic for enchiladas and rice.
2. While rice cooks:
• Preheat oven
• Prepare enchiladas
3. While enchiladas bake:
• Cook beans

QUICK & EASY

Chicken Enchiladas with Salsa Verde

A squeeze of lime juice brightens the flavor of this hearty Mexican dish. The enchiladas are mild, so serve with hot sauce, if desired. If you can't find queso fresco, use ¼ cup shredded Monterey Jack cheese or Monterey Jack with jalapeño peppers.

TOTAL TIME: 45 MINUTES

QUICK TIP: Buy a rotisserie chicken at the supermarket, and use the breast meat for this recipe. Use the leftover meat for sandwiches.

    1 cup chopped onion
    ¼ cup chopped fresh cilantro
    2 garlic cloves, minced
    1 (7-ounce) bottle salsa verde (such as Herdez)
    2 cups shredded cooked chicken breast
    ⅓ cup (3 ounces) ⅓-less-fat cream cheese, softened
    1 cup fat-free, less-sodium chicken broth
    8 (6-inch) corn tortillas
  Cooking spray
    ¼ cup (1 ounce) crumbled queso fresco
    ½ teaspoon chili powder
    4 lime wedges
  Cilantro sprigs (optional)

1. Preheat oven to 425°.
2. Place first 4 ingredients in a blender; process until smooth. Combine chicken and cream cheese in a large bowl. Stir in ½ cup salsa mixture. Reserve remaining salsa mixture.
3. Bring broth to a simmer in a medium skillet. Working with one tortilla at a time, add tortilla to pan; cook 20 seconds or until moist, turning once. Remove tortilla; drain on paper towels. Spoon about ¼ cup chicken mixture down center of tortilla; roll up. Place tortilla, seam-side down, in an 11 x 7–inch baking dish coated with cooking spray. Repeat procedure with remaining tortillas, broth, and chicken mixture.
4. Pour reserved salsa mixture over enchiladas; sprinkle evenly with queso fresco and chili powder. Bake at 425° for 18 minutes or until thoroughly heated. Serve with lime wedges. Garnish with cilantro sprigs, if desired. Yield: 4 servings (serving size: 2 enchiladas and 1 lime wedge).

CALORIES 327 (26% from fat); FAT 9.5g (sat 4.4g, mono 2.9g, poly 1.3g); PROTEIN 28.5g; CARB 31g; FIBER 3.3g; CHOL 78mg; IRON 1.8mg; SODIUM 493mg; CALC 149mg

---

Chicken Supper Menu 3

serves 4

Penne and Chicken Tenderloins with Spiced Tomato Sauce

Romaine salad with anchovy and fresh basil vinaigrette*

Warm sourdough bread

*Combine 1½ teaspoons anchovy paste, 1½ teaspoons Dijon mustard, and 1 tablespoon red wine vinegar. Add 2 tablespoons canola oil, stirring constantly with a whisk. Stir in 1 tablespoon chopped fresh basil. Place 8 cups torn romaine lettuce leaves in a large bowl. Add dressing, tossing to coat. Sprinkle salad with ¼ cup shredded Parmesan cheese.

Game Plan

1. Boil water for pasta.
2. While pasta sauce cooks:
• Make salad dressing
• Cook pasta
• Heat bread

QUICK & EASY

Penne and Chicken Tenderloins with Spiced Tomato Sauce

Any small pasta will work in this entrée.

TOTAL TIME: 36 MINUTES

    1 teaspoon ground fennel seed
    1 teaspoon dried basil
    ½ teaspoon salt
    ½ teaspoon ground coriander
    ¼ teaspoon freshly ground black pepper
    1 pound chicken breast tenders, cut into 1-inch pieces
    1 tablespoon olive oil
    4 garlic cloves, minced
    4 cups canned diced tomatoes, undrained
    1 cup white wine
    8 ounces uncooked penne
    ¼ cup (1 ounce) freshly grated Parmigiano-Reggiano cheese
    ¼ cup chopped fresh basil

1. Combine first 5 ingredients in a small bowl; rub over chicken.

2. Heat oil in a large nonstick skillet over medium-high heat. Add chicken; cook 4 minutes, turning once. Remove from pan; set aside.

3. Reduce heat to medium. Add garlic to pan; sauté 30 seconds or until soft. Add tomatoes and wine, scraping pan to loosen browned bits. Bring to a boil. Reduce heat, and simmer 15 minutes. Add chicken, and simmer 5 minutes.

4. Cook pasta according to package directions, omitting salt and fat. Drain. Toss pasta with chicken mixture in a large bowl. Sprinkle with cheese and basil. Yield: 4 servings (serving size: about 1½ cups).

CALORIES 356 (19% from fat); FAT 7.4g (sat 2g, mono 3.2g, poly 1.1g); PROTEIN 33.5g; CARB 38.4g; FIBER 4.3g; CHOL 72mg; IRON 3.1mg; SODIUM 527mg; CALC 106mg

reader recipes

Three Tasty Winners

More finalists from the 2005 Cooking Light Ultimate Reader Recipe Contest.

Banana Rum Coconut Cookies

FINALIST—DESSERTS
—Christine Dohlmar, Valrico, Florida

⅔ cup packed dark brown sugar
½ cup ripe mashed banana (about 1 medium)
½ cup reduced-fat mayonnaise
1 teaspoon rum
¾ cup all-purpose flour (about 3⅓ ounces)
1 cup quick-cooking oats
½ cup flaked sweetened coconut
½ cup golden raisins
½ cup chopped walnuts
1 teaspoon baking powder
¼ teaspoon ground cinnamon
⅛ teaspoon ground nutmeg
Dash of ground ginger

1. Preheat oven to 350°.

2. Place first 4 ingredients in a large bowl; beat with a mixer at medium speed until blended. Lightly spoon flour into dry measuring cups; level with a knife. Combine flour, oats, and remaining 7 ingredients, stirring with a whisk. Stir flour mixture into banana mixture. Drop dough by 2 tablespoonfuls onto parchment paper–lined baking sheets. Bake at 350° for 19 minutes or until lightly browned. Remove from pan; cool completely on a wire rack. Yield: 20 cookies (serving size: 1 cookie).

CALORIES 118 (28% from fat); FAT 3.7g (sat 1.1g, mono 0.3g, poly 1.5g); PROTEIN 1.7g; CARB 19.9g; FIBER 1.1g; CHOL 0mg; IRON 0.6mg; SODIUM 86mg; CALC 26mg

QUICK & EASY
Colorful Quick Quinoa Grecian Salad
(pictured on page 231)

FINALIST—SALADS AND SIDES
"I worked at a natural foods market and discovered all kinds of new grains. Since then, I have been experimenting in the kitchen and came up with this recipe during the peak of summer's harvest."
—Margee Berry, White Salmon, Washington

2 cups uncooked quinoa
3 cups fat-free, less-sodium chicken broth
2 tablespoons extravirgin olive oil
1 teaspoon grated lemon rind
2 teaspoons fresh lemon juice
1 teaspoon sherry vinegar
1 teaspoon minced fresh mint
½ teaspoon sea salt
1 cup cherry tomatoes, quartered
1 cup thinly sliced radicchio
½ cup chopped yellow bell pepper
½ cup chopped English cucumber
⅓ cup (about 1½ ounces) crumbled reduced-fat feta cheese
3 tablespoons chopped pitted kalamata olives
1 tablespoon minced shallots

1. Place quinoa in a large bowl; cover with water. Let stand 5 minutes; rinse well, and drain.

2. Bring broth to a boil in a large saucepan; stir in quinoa. Cover, reduce heat, and simmer 15 minutes or until liquid is absorbed. Uncover; fluff with a fork. Cool to room temperature.

3. Combine oil and next 5 ingredients in a large bowl. Add quinoa, tomatoes, and remaining ingredients; toss well. Yield: 10 servings (serving size: 1 cup).

CALORIES 186 (30% from fat); FAT 6.3g (sat 0.9g, mono 3.9g, poly 1.2g); PROTEIN 5.9g; CARB 25.1g; FIBER 3.1g; CHOL 1mg; IRON 2.5mg; SODIUM 367mg; CALC 37mg

Chicken Piccata with Summer Vegetable Pasta

FINALIST—ENTRÉES
"This recipe reflects how my family tries to eat. We keep vegetables and whole grains as the bulk of the meal, and use lean proteins and other ingredients to add flavor."
—Erin Mylroie, St. George, Utah

Olive oil–flavored cooking spray
1 cup (¼-inch) strips red bell pepper (about 1 medium)
¾ cup thinly sliced onion (about ½ large onion)
1½ cups matchstick-cut zucchini (about 1 medium)
1¼ cups matchstick-cut yellow squash (about 1 medium)
1 cup cherry tomatoes, halved
2 garlic cloves, minced
8 ounces uncooked whole wheat blend spaghetti
¾ cup (3 ounces) grated fresh Parmesan cheese, divided
½ cup thinly sliced fresh basil
4 (6-ounce) skinless, boneless chicken breast halves, trimmed
¼ teaspoon salt
½ teaspoon freshly ground black pepper, divided
½ cup all-purpose flour (about 2¼ ounces)
2 teaspoons olive oil
1½ cups fat-free, less-sodium chicken broth
6 tablespoons fresh lemon juice
2 tablespoons capers
½ cup sliced green onions
1 tablespoon butter

Continued

1. Heat a large nonstick skillet over medium-high heat. Coat pan with cooking spray. Add bell pepper and onion; sauté 8 minutes or until tender and beginning to brown. Place onion mixture in a large bowl; keep warm. Return pan to medium-high heat. Recoat pan with cooking spray. Add zucchini and yellow squash; sauté 4 minutes or until crisp-tender. Add tomatoes and garlic; sauté 2 minutes. Add squash mixture to onion mixture. Keep warm.

2. Cook pasta according to package directions, omitting salt and fat. Drain pasta in a colander over a bowl, reserving ½ cup cooking liquid. Add pasta and reserved cooking liquid to vegetable mixture, stirring to combine. Add ½ cup Parmesan cheese and basil; toss to combine. Keep warm.

3. Sprinkle both sides of chicken breasts with salt and ¼ teaspoon black pepper. Place flour in a shallow bowl. Dredge chicken in flour, turning to coat; shake off excess flour.

4. Heat a large nonstick skillet over medium-high heat. Coat pan with cooking spray. Add oil to pan, swirling to coat. Add chicken, and cook 4 minutes on each side or until done. Remove from pan; keep warm.

5. Add broth, juice, and capers to pan, scraping pan to loosen browned bits. Bring to a boil; cook 3 minutes. Remove from heat. Add green onions, butter, and ¼ teaspoon black pepper; stir until butter melts.

6. Arrange about 1 cup pasta mixture on each of 4 plates; top each serving with 1 chicken breast half, ¼ cup sauce, and 1 tablespoon cheese. Serve immediately. Yield: 4 servings.

CALORIES 588 (20% from fat); FAT 13.2g (sat 5.2g, mono 4.8g, poly 1.6g); PROTEIN 57.8g; CARB 62.3g; FIBER 10.5g; CHOL 119mg; IRON 5.3mg; SODIUM 798mg; CALC 267mg

new american classic

Cheesecake with Fresh Strawberry Sauce

Cheesecake has been an American favorite since Colonial days. We can't think of a sweeter way to welcome spring.

STAFF FAVORITE • MAKE AHEAD
Cheesecake with Fresh Strawberry Sauce

(pictured on page 232)

If you make this cake in a nine-inch springform pan, cut the baking time by about 15 minutes. The center of the cake may appear looser than expected, but it will become firmer as it chills overnight.

CHEESECAKE:

½ cup sugar
20 reduced-calorie vanilla wafers
⅛ teaspoon salt, divided
3 large egg whites, divided
Cooking spray
1½ cups sugar
3 tablespoons cornstarch
2 (8-ounce) blocks ⅓-less-fat cream cheese, softened
½ cup (4 ounces) block-style fat-free cream cheese, softened
1 teaspoon vanilla extract
1 teaspoon fresh lemon juice
4 large eggs
Strawberries (optional)

SAUCE:

4 cups sliced strawberries (about 1½ pounds)
½ cup water
2 tablespoons sugar
1 tablespoon water
2 teaspoons cornstarch
2 teaspoons fresh lemon juice

1. Preheat oven to 350°.

2. To prepare cheesecake, place ½ cup sugar, wafers, and dash salt in a food processor; process until mixture resembles sand. Place 1 egg white in a small bowl; stir with a whisk until frothy. With processor on, add 2 tablespoons egg white through food chute, processing until blended (discard remaining frothy egg white). Firmly press mixture into bottom and slightly up sides of an 8-inch springform pan coated with cooking spray. Bake at 350° for 10 minutes; cool completely on a wire rack.

3. Reduce oven to 300°.

4. Combine 1½ cups sugar, 3 tablespoons cornstarch, and dash salt in a large bowl. Add cheeses; beat with a mixer at medium-high speed until smooth. Reduce mixer speed to low. Add vanilla and 1 teaspoon juice; beat just until combined. Add eggs, 1 at a time, beating after each addition just until incorporated. Add 2 egg whites; beat just until incorporated.

5. Pour cheese mixture into prepared pan. Bake at 300° for 1 hour and 15 minutes or until a 3-inch circle in center of cheesecake barely jiggles when side of pan is tapped. Turn oven off. Leave cheesecake in oven with door open 30 minutes. Remove cheesecake from oven; run a knife around outside edge. Cool to room temperature on a wire rack. Cover and chill at least 8 hours. Garnish cake with strawberries, if desired.

6. To prepare sauce, combine sliced strawberries, ½ cup water, and 2 tablespoons sugar in a small saucepan over medium-high heat; bring to a boil. Reduce heat, and simmer 5 minutes. Strain mixture through a sieve into a bowl, pressing lightly with a spatula; discard solids. Return mixture to pan. Combine 1 tablespoon water and 2 teaspoons cornstarch in a small bowl, stirring with a whisk. Add cornstarch mixture to pan. Bring to a boil; cook 1 minute, stirring constantly. Transfer mixture to a bowl; cool to room temperature. Stir in 2 teaspoons juice. Yield: 16 servings (serving size: 1 slice cheesecake and about 2 tablespoons sauce).

CALORIES 245 (31% from fat); FAT 8.4g (sat 4.7g, mono 2.4g, poly 0.4g); PROTEIN 6.6g; CARB 36.8g; FIBER 0.9g; CHOL 75mg; IRON 0.6mg; SODIUM 216mg; CALC 49mg

Everyday Chinese

Enjoy better-than-takeout dishes with these fast weeknight recipes.

QUICK & EASY • MAKE AHEAD
Edamame Dumplings

Round gyoza wrappers are perfect for the dumplings, but square wonton wrappers may be easier to find. Look for them in the refrigerated produce section of the supermarket. Wonton wrappers are lightly coated with cornstarch, which makes them easier to work with.

SAUCE:
- 2 tablespoons chopped green onions
- 2 tablespoons low-sodium soy sauce
- 1 teaspoon honey

DUMPLINGS:
- 1 cup frozen shelled edamame (green soybeans)
- 1 teaspoon fresh lemon juice
- 1 teaspoon dark sesame oil
- ½ teaspoon ground cumin
- ¼ teaspoon salt
- 20 wonton wrappers
- 2 teaspoons cornstarch
- Cooking spray
- ½ cup water, divided

1. To prepare sauce, combine first 3 ingredients in a small bowl, stirring with a whisk.
2. To prepare dumplings, cook edamame according to package directions; drain. Rinse with cold water; drain well. Place edamame, juice, oil, cumin, and salt in a food processor; process until smooth.
3. Working with 1 wonton wrapper at a time (cover remaining wrappers with a damp towel to prevent drying), spoon about 1 teaspoon edamame mixture in center of wrapper. Moisten edges of dough with water; fold opposite corners to form a triangle, pinching points to seal. Place dumplings on a large baking sheet sprinkled with cornstarch.

4. Heat a large nonstick skillet over medium-high heat. Coat pan with cooking spray. Arrange half of dumplings in a single layer in pan; reduce heat to medium. Cook 1 minute or until bottoms begin to brown; turn. Add ¼ cup water to pan; cover. Cook 30 seconds; uncover. Cook 1 minute or until liquid evaporates. Remove from pan; keep warm. Repeat procedure with remaining dumplings and water. Serve immediately with sauce. Yield: 4 servings (serving size: 5 dumplings and 1 tablespoon sauce).

CALORIES 191 (16% from fat); FAT 3.3g (sat 0.5g, mono 1g, poly 1.8g); PROTEIN 8.2g; CARB 31.2g; FIBER 2.9g; CHOL 4mg; IRON 2.4mg; SODIUM 657mg; CALC 47mg

QUICK & EASY
Stir-Fried Beef with Ginger-Carrot Sauce

For added heat, serve with extra chile pepper sauce on the side. Our Test Kitchens staff regularly uses Sriracha, a thick sauce made from ground sun-dried hot chiles and garlic. See page 102 for more information about Sriracha.

- 12 ounces flank steak, trimmed
- 1 tablespoon cornstarch
- ½ teaspoon salt
- ⅛ teaspoon freshly ground white pepper
- 1 tablespoon peanut oil, divided
- 1 large green bell pepper, chopped (about 1½ cups)
- 1 cup thinly sliced carrot
- 2 teaspoons minced fresh ginger
- 1 cup fat-free, less-sodium chicken broth
- 1 teaspoon chile paste with garlic (such as sambal oelek)
- 2 cups hot cooked rice

1. Cut steak diagonally across grain into thin slices. Combine steak, cornstarch, salt, and white pepper in a bowl, tossing to coat; set aside.
2. Heat 2 teaspoons oil in a large nonstick skillet over medium heat. Add steak; stir-fry 4 minutes or until browned. Remove steak from pan. Add 1 teaspoon oil to pan. Add bell pepper, carrot, and ginger; stir-fry 2 minutes or until carrot is tender. Add broth and chile paste; cook 3 minutes. Return steak to pan; cook 1 minute or until thoroughly heated. Serve over rice. Yield: 4 servings (serving size: 1¼ cups steak mixture and ½ cup rice).

CALORIES 290 (28% from fat); FAT 9g (sat 2.8g, mono 3.8g, poly 1.4g); PROTEIN 21.5g; CARB 29.6g; FIBER 2.3g; CHOL 26mg; IRON 2.7mg; SODIUM 462mg; CALC 47mg

QUICK & EASY
Shrimp Cilantro Fried Rice

Put leftover cooked white rice to good use in this fragrant, colorful dish.

- 2 teaspoons peanut oil
- 1 teaspoon dark sesame oil
- ¼ cup finely chopped carrot
- 1 teaspoon minced peeled fresh ginger
- ¼ teaspoon crushed red pepper
- 3 garlic cloves, minced
- 4 cups cooked long-grain rice
- 1 cup chopped cooked shrimp
- 2 tablespoons low-sodium soy sauce
- ½ cup chopped fresh cilantro

1. Heat oils in a large nonstick skillet over medium-high heat. Add carrot, ginger, pepper, and garlic; sauté 1 minute. Add rice; sauté 2 minutes. Stir in shrimp and soy sauce; sauté 1 minute. Remove from heat; stir in cilantro. Yield: 4 servings (serving size: about 1 cup).

CALORIES 276 (14% from fat); FAT 4.4g (sat 0.5g, mono 2.1g, poly 1.4g); PROTEIN 11.1g; CARB 47.1g; FIBER 1.2g; CHOL 56mg; IRON 3.1mg; SODIUM 341mg; CALC 35mg

Wild Mushroom and Chicken Stir-Fry

Wild mushrooms add meaty texture and earthy taste. You can substitute sliced button or baby portobello mushrooms. Serve with lo mein noodles.

- 1 pound skinless, boneless chicken breast, sliced crosswise
- 1 tablespoon cornstarch, divided
- ½ teaspoon salt, divided
- ⅛ teaspoon freshly ground white pepper
- 3 tablespoons oyster sauce
- 1 tablespoon water
- ½ teaspoon sugar
- 1 tablespoon peanut oil
- 1 garlic clove, minced
- 1 cup snow peas, trimmed
- 1 cup sliced shiitake mushrooms
- 1 cup sliced oyster mushroom caps
- ¾ cup fat-free, less-sodium chicken broth
- ½ cup chopped green onions

1. Combine chicken, 1 teaspoon cornstarch, ¼ teaspoon salt, and pepper in a medium bowl; set aside.
2. Combine oyster sauce, water, sugar, 2 teaspoons cornstarch, and ¼ teaspoon salt in a small bowl; set aside.
3. Heat oil in a large nonstick skillet over medium-high heat. Add chicken mixture and garlic; sauté 3 minutes. Add snow peas and mushrooms; sauté 2 minutes. Stir in broth; bring to a boil. Stir in oyster sauce mixture; cook 30 seconds or until thickened. Remove from heat; stir in onions. Yield: 4 servings (serving size: 1¼ cups).

CALORIES 203 (22% from fat); FAT 5g (sat 0.6g, mono 2.4g, poly 1.4g); PROTEIN 28.4g; CARB 7.4g; FIBER 1.7g; CHOL 66mg; IRON 1.6mg; SODIUM 537mg; CALC 31mg

Cooking simple, authentic-tasting Chinese food is easy. Recipes can be prepared with everyday ingredients and a nonstick skillet.

Hot and Sour Pork with Cabbage

Use packaged preshredded green cabbage to lessen chopping time. Ketchup adds sweet, tangy flavor.

- 1 (1-pound) pork tenderloin, trimmed and cut into strips
- 1 tablespoon cornstarch, divided
- ½ teaspoon white pepper
- ¼ teaspoon salt
- 1 tablespoon water
- ½ cup ketchup
- 1 tablespoon sugar
- 1 tablespoon Sriracha (hot chile sauce, such as Huy Fong)
- 2 teaspoons low-sodium soy sauce
- 1 tablespoon peanut oil
- 3 garlic cloves, minced
- 12 cups coarsely chopped green cabbage (about 2 pounds)
- ⅓ cup chopped green onions

1. Combine pork, 1 teaspoon cornstarch, white pepper, and salt in a medium bowl; set aside.
2. Combine 2 teaspoons cornstarch and 1 tablespoon water in a small bowl; set aside.
3. Combine ketchup and next 3 ingredients in a small bowl; set aside.
4. Heat oil in a large nonstick skillet over medium-high heat. Add pork mixture and garlic; sauté 2 minutes. Remove pork from pan; set aside. Add cabbage to pan; sauté 2 minutes. Add ketchup mixture; sauté 2 minutes. Stir in pork; sauté 1 minute. Stir in cornstarch mixture; cook 30 seconds or until thick. Remove from heat; stir in onions. Yield: 4 servings (serving size: 1½ cups).

CALORIES 282 (24% from fat); FAT 7.6g (sat 1.6g, mono 3.7g, poly 1.7g); PROTEIN 26.6g; CARB 30.1g; FIBER 0.9g; CHOL 68mg; IRON 3.2mg; SODIUM 791mg; CALC 142mg

Garlic Pork with Tomato and Basil
(pictured on page 233)

Serve with fiery chile sauce on the side.

- 12 ounces pork tenderloin, thinly sliced
- 2 teaspoons cornstarch, divided
- ¼ teaspoon salt
- ⅛ teaspoon freshly ground white pepper
- 3 tablespoons cold water
- 2 tablespoons oyster sauce
- 1 teaspoon sugar
- 1 teaspoon Sriracha (hot chile sauce, such as Huy Fong)
- 2 teaspoons peanut oil
- 2 teaspoons minced fresh garlic
- 2 cups chopped seeded plum tomatoes (about 3 tomatoes)
- ¾ cup chopped fresh basil
- ¼ cup chopped green onions (about 2 onions)
- 2 cups hot cooked brown rice

1. Combine pork, 1 teaspoon cornstarch, salt, and pepper in a small bowl, tossing to coat.
2. Combine water, oyster sauce, sugar, Sriracha, and 1 teaspoon cornstarch in a small bowl.
3. Heat oil in a large nonstick skillet over medium-high heat. Add garlic and pork mixture, and sauté 3 minutes or until pork is done. Add tomatoes; sauté 1 minute. Add cornstarch mixture, and cook 1 minute or until thickened. Stir in basil. Remove from heat, and sprinkle with onions. Serve with rice. Yield: 4 servings (serving size: 1 cup pork mixture and ½ cup rice).

CALORIES 257 (22% from fat); FAT 6.2g (sat 1.6g, mono 2.7g, poly 1.4g); PROTEIN 21.2g; CARB 28.5g; FIBER 2.9g; CHOL 55mg; IRON 2mg; SODIUM 294mg; CALC 39mg

Noodle Salad with Shrimp and Mint

Purchase precooked peeled and deveined shrimp from the seafood department at your grocery store.

- 1 (7-ounce) package uncooked vermicelli
- 2 tablespoons lime juice
- 2 tablespoons low-sodium soy sauce
- 1 tablespoon honey
- 2 teaspoons chopped fresh mint
- 2 teaspoons dark sesame oil
- ¼ teaspoon salt
- 2 garlic cloves, minced
- 1 pound cooked shrimp, chopped
- 1 tablespoon chopped green onions
- Lime wedges (optional)

1. Cook pasta according to package directions, omitting salt and fat; drain.
2. Combine lime juice and next 6 ingredients in a small bowl, stirring well.
3. Combine pasta and shrimp in a large bowl. Drizzle with dressing; toss to coat. Sprinkle with onions. Serve immediately with lime wedges, if desired. Yield: 4 servings (serving size: 1¼ cups).

CALORIES 334 (12% from fat); FAT 4.3g (sat 0.5g, mono 0.9g, poly 1g); PROTEIN 31.6g; CARB 43.4g; FIBER 1.8g; CHOL 223mg; IRON 5.6mg; SODIUM 672mg; CALC 43mg

Citrus Soy Chicken Drumsticks

For an irresistible appetizer, prepare this recipe with two pounds of chicken drummettes instead of drumsticks. Serve the rest of the bottle of sake with the meal.

- 8 chicken drumsticks (about 2 pounds), skinned
- 1 teaspoon finely chopped fresh ginger
- ¼ teaspoon salt
- Cooking spray
- ½ cup sake (rice wine)
- ¼ cup fresh orange juice
- 2 tablespoons sugar
- 2 tablespoons low-sodium soy sauce
- 1 tablespoon fresh lemon juice
- ¼ cup chopped green onions

1. Combine chicken, ginger, and salt in a large bowl, tossing to coat. Heat a large nonstick skillet over medium-high heat. Coat pan with cooking spray. Add chicken, and cook 6 minutes or until browned on all sides. Add sake and next 4 ingredients; cook 1 minute. Cover, reduce heat, and simmer 10 minutes or until chicken is done. Remove chicken from pan; keep warm. Bring sauce to a boil. Cook until sauce is reduced to ½ cup (about 5 minutes). Return chicken to pan, turning to coat. Sprinkle green onions over chicken. Yield: 4 servings (serving size: 2 drumsticks).

CALORIES 196 (23% from fat); FAT 5g (sat 1.3g, mono 1.5g, poly 1.2g); PROTEIN 26.7g; CARB 9.8g; FIBER 0.3g; CHOL 103mg; IRON 1.7mg; SODIUM 529mg; CALC 24mg

Curry Shrimp with Noodles

Cut prep time by purchasing frozen peeled and deveined shrimp. Thaw in cold water before adding to the recipe.

- ⅓ cup ketchup
- 1 tablespoon fresh lime juice
- 2 teaspoons soy sauce
- 2 teaspoons sugar
- 1 teaspoon red curry powder
- 1 (8-ounce) package rice noodles
- 2 teaspoons peanut oil
- ½ cup vertically sliced white onion
- 2 garlic cloves, minced
- 1 pound large shrimp, peeled and deveined
- 4 lime wedges

1. Combine first 5 ingredients in a bowl.
2. Cook noodles according to package directions, omitting salt and fat; drain.
3. Heat oil in a large nonstick skillet over medium-high heat. Add onion and garlic; cook 1 minute, stirring constantly. Add shrimp; cook 5 minutes or until shrimp are done, stirring frequently. Add noodles and ketchup mixture, tossing to combine; cook 3 minutes or until thoroughly heated. Serve immediately with lime wedges. Yield: 4 servings (serving size: about 1½ cups noodles and 1 lime wedge).

CALORIES 379 (9% from fat); FAT 3.9g (sat 0.7g, mono 1.3g, poly 1.3g); PROTEIN 29.5g; CARB 54.8g; FIBER 0.9g; CHOL 221mg; IRON 5.2mg; SODIUM 570mg; CALC 68mg

Szechuan Green Beans with Ground Pork

Szechuan cuisine refers to the hot, spicy dishes characteristic of the vast Szechuan province in southwestern China. You can substitute lean ground chicken or turkey for pork and asparagus for green beans.

- ½ pound lean ground pork
- 1 teaspoon cornstarch
- ⅛ teaspoon salt
- ⅛ teaspoon freshly ground white pepper
- 1 teaspoon peanut oil
- 2½ cups (1-inch) cut green beans
- 1 teaspoon minced fresh garlic
- 2 tablespoons hoisin sauce
- 2 teaspoons low-sodium soy sauce
- 1 teaspoon sugar
- 1 teaspoon crushed red pepper
- 2 cups hot cooked white rice

1. Combine first 4 ingredients in a medium bowl. Heat oil in a large nonstick skillet over medium-high heat. Add pork mixture, beans, and garlic; cook 3 minutes or until pork loses its pink color, stirring to crumble.
2. Combine hoisin and next 3 ingredients in a small bowl, stirring with a whisk. Add hoisin mixture to pan. Cook 2 minutes or until thoroughly heated, stirring frequently. Serve over rice. Yield: 4 servings (serving size: 1 cup pork mixture and ½ cup rice).

CALORIES 254 (24% from fat); FAT 6.8g (sat 2.2g, mono 3.5g, poly 1.1g); PROTEIN 14.6g; CARB 32.5g; FIBER 3.3g; CHOL 43mg; IRON 1.5mg; SODIUM 323mg; CALC 47mg

Chinese Cooking Essentials

One trick to cooking Chinese dishes anytime is to keep a few basic ingredients on hand. These items can be found at any well-stocked supermarket.

- **Chicken broth** is often thickened with cornstarch to create glossy, smooth sauces for various meat and vegetable combinations.
- **Cornstarch** is used to thicken sauces or as a light coating for pan-fried recipes.
- Used in small amounts, **dark sesame oil** lends toasted, nutty flavor.
- Fresh **garlic** cloves offer a pungent, bold flavor.
- Fresh **ginger** lends a peppery bite with subtle sweetness. Store a zip-top plastic bag of pureed fresh ginger in the freezer—just break off pieces as needed.
- Chinese chefs favor **green onions** for their mild flavor and vibrant color. Green onions are often added to dishes just before serving to maintain their fresh, delicate flavor.
- Sweet-spicy, thick **hoisin sauce** is made with soybeans, garlic, chile peppers, and spices. It's used to season meat, poultry, and seafood dishes, and is also served as a condiment.
- **Honey** imparts subtle sweetness and smooth texture to sauces.
- Keep fresh **lemons** on hand. The juice adds tangy, fresh flavor; the rind imparts a fragrant, citrusy aroma and bright taste.
- **Low-sodium soy sauce** adds saltiness and a characteristic earthy flavor to almost all Chinese dishes.
- Dark-brown, rich-tasting **oyster sauce** is often added to stir-fries and used as a table condiment.
- Mild-tasting, all-purpose **peanut oil** has a high smoke point, making it ideal for stir-frying. If you're allergic to peanuts, substitute canola or corn oil.
- Season with **white pepper,** which has milder flavor than black pepper and is often used in light-colored sauces.

Ground Turkey and Tofu

You can use chicken breast or lean pork instead of turkey. Cut chicken or pork into cubes, then grind it in a food processor.

  1 (14-ounce) package water-packed firm reduced-fat tofu, drained and cut into 1-inch cubes
  ⅛ teaspoon salt
  ⅛ teaspoon freshly ground white pepper
  1 pound ground turkey breast
  ¼ cup hoisin sauce
  1 tablespoon rice vinegar
  1 tablespoon low-sodium soy sauce
  2 teaspoons sugar
  1 teaspoon cornstarch
  ¼ teaspoon crushed red pepper
  3 garlic cloves, minced
Cooking spray
  ½ cup frozen green peas, thawed
  ¼ cup chopped green onions

1. Place tofu in a single layer on several layers of paper towels; cover with additional paper towels. Let stand 30 minutes, pressing down occasionally.
2. Combine salt, white pepper, and turkey in a large bowl. Combine hoisin and next 6 ingredients in a medium bowl, stirring with a whisk.
3. Heat a large nonstick skillet over medium-high heat. Coat pan with cooking spray. Add tofu; cook 6 minutes or until browned on all sides, stirring occasionally. Remove tofu from pan; keep warm. Recoat pan with cooking spray; add turkey mixture to pan. Cook 3 minutes or until turkey loses its pink color, stirring to crumble. Stir in hoisin mixture, tofu, and peas; cook 2 minutes or until thoroughly heated. Sprinkle with green onions. Yield: 4 servings (serving size: 1¼ cups).

CALORIES 275 (27% from fat); FAT 8.4g (sat 2.1g, mono 1.1g, poly 3.1g); PROTEIN 31.5g; CARB 17.4g; FIBER 1.7g; CHOL 56mg; IRON 2.4mg; SODIUM 881mg; CALC 70mg

---

Braided Salmon

For a shorter prep time, omit the braiding step. Cut salmon fillet into four (six-ounce) pieces, and cook as directed in braided method.

  2 teaspoons finely chopped fresh ginger
  ½ teaspoon salt
  ½ teaspoon peanut oil
  1 (1½-pound) skinless salmon fillet
  ½ cup chopped green onions
  2 teaspoons low-sodium soy sauce
  1 teaspoon dark sesame oil

1. Combine ginger, salt, and peanut oil in a small bowl. Brush over fillet; set aside.
2. Combine onions, soy sauce, and sesame oil in a small bowl.
3. Cut salmon lengthwise into 3 (15 x 1–inch) ropes; reserve remaining salmon for another use. Braid ropes; secure with wooden picks. Place braid in an 11 x 7–inch baking dish. Cover dish with plastic wrap. Microwave at HIGH 2 minutes or until desired degree of doneness. Let stand 2 minutes. Microwave at HIGH 2 minutes.
4. Remove dish from microwave. Drizzle onion mixture over fish. Yield: 4 servings (serving size: 4 ounces fish and 1 tablespoon sauce).

CALORIES 258 (44% from fat); FAT 12.7g (sat 2.9g, mono 5.5g, poly 3.3g); PROTEIN 32.6g; CARB 1.3g; FIBER 0.4g; CHOL 84mg; IRON 0.8mg; SODIUM 455mg; CALC 26mg

WINE NOTE: As simply prepared as this salmon is, the final touch of soy sauce, sesame oil, and green onions gives the dish lots of punch. For any prospective wine partner, the challenge is to stand up to each of these dramatic flavors. A superfruity, nonoaky white such as Theo Minges "Gleisweiler Hölle" Riesling Spatlese 2004 from Pfalz, Germany, $20, is a fine counterpoint.

Blended Holiday

Easter and Passover have some food traditions in common. Here's a menu created to bring them all to the table.

H ere's a holiday riddle: What spring celebration features lamb, eggs, and children hunting for edible treats?

If you guessed Easter or Passover, you're right. If you said both, you get extra points, because at this time of year Christian and Jewish traditions have much in common. That's good news for the estimated one million interfaith couples in the United States, who can find common ground to celebrate both holidays at one table.

Smoked Trout Mousse

Kosher dietary law prohibits mixing meat and dairy, hence the use of sour cream substitute in this recipe and Asparagus Spears with Smoked Salmon Spirals (recipe at right). Use kosher gelatin, available in supermarket ethnic foods aisles this time of year. Serve with matzo.

 4 hard-cooked large eggs
  Cooking spray
 ½ cup chicken broth
 ½ cup water
 1 tablespoon unflavored kosher gelatin
 10 ounces skinless, boneless smoked trout
 2 tablespoons fresh lemon juice
 ½ teaspoon freshly ground black pepper
 ½ cup sour cream substitute (such as Tofutti Sour Supreme)
 ¼ cup chopped fresh chives
 4 teaspoons chopped fresh dill
  Fresh chives (optional)

1. Peel eggs. Slice each egg in half lengthwise; remove yolk. Reserve yolks for another use. Finely chop egg white. Set aside.

2. Coat a 7½ x 3–inch loaf pan with cooking spray; line pan with plastic wrap. Set aside.

3. Combine chicken broth and water. Place broth mixture in a 2-cup glass measure; sprinkle gelatin over mixture. Let stand 5 minutes. Microwave mixture at HIGH 30 seconds; stir until gelatin dissolves. Chill 15 minutes or until mixture begins to thicken.

4. Place trout in a food processor; pulse 10 times or until finely chopped. Add gelatin mixture, lemon juice, and pepper; process until well combined. Place trout mixture in a large bowl; fold in sour cream substitute, ¼ cup chives, and dill. Spoon trout mixture into prepared pan; cover and chill overnight. Sprinkle with egg white. Garnish with chives, if desired. Yield: 12 servings.

CALORIES 69 (44% from fat); FAT 3.4g (sat 1.2g, mono 0.5g, poly 0.6g); PROTEIN 8.8g; CARB 0.8g; FIBER 0g; CHOL 19mg; IRON 0.2mg; SODIUM 102mg; CALC 5mg

Asparagus Spears with Smoked Salmon Spirals

Use hearty asparagus spears for this easy appetizer. You can blanch the asparagus and combine the sour cream substitute, dill, and tarragon up to a day ahead, and refrigerate separately.

 24 asparagus spears
 3 tablespoons sour cream substitute (such as Tofutti Sour Supreme)
 1 teaspoon chopped fresh dill
 1 teaspoon chopped fresh tarragon
 4 ounces sliced smoked salmon, cut into 24 (¼-inch-wide) strips
  Dill sprigs (optional)

1. Snap off tough ends of asparagus. Cook asparagus in boiling water 3 minutes or until crisp-tender; drain. Rinse with cold water; drain. Pat dry.

2. Combine sour cream substitute, chopped dill, and tarragon in a small bowl. Spread about ½ teaspoon dill mixture over one side of each salmon strip. Wrap 1 salmon strip around each asparagus spear with dill mixture touching asparagus. Garnish with dill sprigs, if desired. Yield: 8 servings (serving size: 3 spears).

CALORIES 38 (47% from fat); FAT 2g (sat 1.1g, mono 0.3g, poly 0.2g); PROTEIN 3.4g; CARB 2.8g; FIBER 0.6g; CHOL 3.3mg; IRON 0.7mg; SODIUM 142mg; CALC 9mg

Potato and Double-Horseradish Salmon

Horseradish is used in two forms—prepared and wasabi powder (Japanese horseradish). Prepare the salmon, through Step 3, up to one day ahead. Bake just before serving.

- ¼ cup Dijon mustard
- 3 tablespoons prepared horseradish
- 1½ teaspoons chopped fresh thyme
- 1 teaspoon wasabi powder (dried Japanese horseradish)
- 8 (6-ounce) skinless salmon fillets
- 1 teaspoon salt
- ½ teaspoon freshly ground black pepper
- 1 cup instant potato flakes
- Cooking spray

1. Preheat oven to 400°.

2. Combine first 4 ingredients in a small bowl. Sprinkle salmon evenly with salt and pepper; brush both sides of salmon with mustard mixture.

3. Place potato flakes in a shallow dish; dredge salmon in potato flakes.

4. Heat a large nonstick skillet over medium-high heat. Coat pan with cooking spray. Lightly spray salmon with cooking spray. Add salmon to pan; cook 2 minutes on each side or until golden. Wrap handle of skillet with foil. Bake at 400° for 6 minutes or until fish flakes easily when tested with a fork or until desired degree of doneness. Serve immediately. Yield: 8 servings (serving size: 1 fillet).

CALORIES 378 (33% from fat); FAT 13.9g (sat 3.2g, mono 5.9g, poly 3.4g); PROTEIN 38.8g; CARB 22.6g; FIBER 1.9g; CHOL 87mg; IRON 1.1mg; SODIUM 589mg; CALC 43mg

Marinated Lamb with Orange Chimichurri

Chimichurri is an Argentinean condiment commonly served with roasted and grilled meats. Here, it's a delicious match for lamb. Chimichurri also makes a nice tapas-style appetizer with toast points. For the freshest results, prepare the chimichurri while the roast stands.

LAMB:

- 3 tablespoons Dijon mustard
- 2 teaspoons grated orange rind
- 1 teaspoon ground cumin
- 1 teaspoon paprika
- ¼ teaspoon ground cinnamon
- ¼ teaspoon crushed red pepper
- 6 garlic cloves, minced
- 1 (4-pound) boneless leg of lamb, trimmed
- 1 teaspoon salt
- ¼ teaspoon freshly ground black pepper
- Cooking spray

ORANGE CHIMICHURRI:

- 1 cup packed fresh cilantro leaves
- ⅔ cup packed fresh basil leaves
- ½ cup packed fresh parsley leaves
- ⅓ cup fresh orange juice
- 2 tablespoons fresh lemon juice
- 1 tablespoon extravirgin olive oil
- ½ teaspoon salt
- ¼ teaspoon ground cumin
- ¼ teaspoon freshly ground black pepper
- 2 garlic cloves, peeled

1. To prepare lamb, combine first 7 ingredients in a small bowl; rub over lamb. Place lamb in a large zip-top plastic bag; seal. Marinate in refrigerator 2 hours, turning occasionally.

2. Preheat oven to 400°.

3. Remove lamb from bag; discard marinade. Sprinkle lamb evenly with 1 teaspoon salt and ¼ teaspoon pepper. Roll lamb; secure lamb at 2-inch intervals with twine. Place lamb on a rack of a broiler pan or roasting pan coated with cooking spray; place rack in pan. Bake at 400° for 55 minutes or until a thermometer registers 145° (medium-rare) or desired degree of doneness. Let roast stand 20 minutes before slicing.

4. To prepare orange chimichurri, place cilantro and remaining 9 ingredients in a food processor; process until smooth. Serve with lamb. Yield: 8 servings (serving size: 3 ounces lamb and 1½ tablespoons orange chimichurri).

CALORIES 343 (37% from fat); FAT 14g (sat 4.4g, mono 6.2g, poly 1.4g); PROTEIN 47.6g; CARB 4.1g; FIBER 0.9g; CHOL 150mg; IRON 5mg; SODIUM 734mg; CALC 49mg

How to Roll Lamb

1. *Sprinkle lamb evenly with 1 teaspoon salt and ¼ teaspoon pepper. Roll lamb.*

2. *Secure lamb at 2-inch intervals with twine.*

Vanilla Balsamic Chicken

After scraping out the seeds from the vanilla bean for the sauce, add the pod to a canister of sugar. The scent of the bean will permeate the sugar. Serve the chicken with a tossed green salad.

½ cup fat-free, less-sodium chicken broth
½ cup balsamic vinegar
¼ cup finely chopped shallots
¼ cup packed brown sugar
¼ teaspoon grated orange rind
¼ cup fresh orange juice
1 (2-inch) piece vanilla bean, split lengthwise
¾ teaspoon salt, divided
16 skinless, boneless chicken thighs (about 2 pounds)
Cooking spray
½ teaspoon freshly ground black pepper
Orange rind strips (optional)

1. Preheat oven to 450°.
2. Combine first 6 ingredients in a small saucepan. Scrape seeds from vanilla bean; stir seeds into broth mixture, reserving bean for another use. Bring to a boil. Reduce heat, and simmer until reduced to ½ cup (about 20 minutes). Stir in ¼ teaspoon salt.
3. Arrange chicken in a single layer in bottom of a roasting pan coated with cooking spray. Sprinkle chicken evenly with ½ teaspoon salt and pepper. Bake at 450° for 10 minutes.
4. Brush half of broth mixture over chicken; bake 5 minutes. Brush remaining broth mixture over chicken; bake 15 minutes or until a thermometer registers 180°. Garnish with orange rind, if desired. Yield: 8 servings (serving size: 2 chicken thighs).

CALORIES 209 (24% from fat); FAT 5.5g (sat 1.4g, mono 1.7g, poly 1.4g); PROTEIN 27.5g; CARB 10.9g; FIBER 0.2g; CHOL 115mg; IRON 1.8mg; SODIUM 371mg; CALC 29mg

Roast Vegetable Medley

Use true baby carrots, which are sweet and tender, instead of shaved-down regular carrots.

1 cup baby carrots with tops (about 5 ounces)
1½ tablespoons extravirgin olive oil
2½ teaspoons chopped fresh oregano
2½ teaspoons chopped fresh mint
¾ teaspoon salt
½ teaspoon dried marjoram
½ teaspoon freshly ground black pepper
24 garlic cloves, peeled
8 large shallots, peeled and halved lengthwise
3 red bell peppers, cut into 1-inch pieces (about 1¼ pounds)
1 large yellow squash, halved lengthwise and cut into 1-inch pieces (about 6 ounces)
1 fennel bulb, cut into ½-inch thick wedges (about 15 ounces)
1 large zucchini, halved lengthwise and cut into 1-inch pieces (about 7 ounces)
Cooking spray

1. Preheat oven to 450°.
2. Place 1 oven rack in upper third of oven, and place second rack in lower third of oven.
3. Cut tops off carrots; discard tops. Combine carrots and remaining ingredients except cooking spray in a large bowl; toss to combine. Divide vegetable mixture evenly between 2 jelly-roll pans coated with cooking spray. Bake at 450° for 12 minutes, stirring once; exchange positions of pans on oven racks. Bake 12 additional minutes or until vegetables begin to brown, stirring once. Yield: 8 servings (serving size: about ¾ cup).

CALORIES 89 (31% from fat); FAT 3.1g (sat 0.4g, mono 2g, poly 0.4g); PROTEIN 3g; CARB 14.3g; FIBER 3.6g; CHOL 0mg; IRON 1.1mg; SODIUM 253mg; CALC 59mg

MAKE AHEAD
Date-Nut Haroset

A part of every seder, *haroset* is a thick condiment that symbolizes the mortar the Jews prepared when they were slaves in Egypt. Recipes vary but typically include fruit, nuts, and honey.

1¼ cups whole pitted dates
⅔ cup dried figs
⅔ cup dried apricots
2 tablespoons raisins
¼ cup kosher sweet red wine
1 tablespoon fresh lemon juice
2 teaspoons honey
¼ teaspoon ground cinnamon
⅛ teaspoon ground nutmeg
1 Granny Smith apple, peeled, cored, and shredded
½ cup kosher miniature marshmallows
⅓ cup finely chopped walnuts

1. Place first 4 ingredients in a food processor. Pulse 4 times or until coarsely chopped, scraping sides of bowl occasionally. Add wine and next 5 ingredients. Pulse 2 times to combine (mixture should be slightly chunky but spreadable). Place fruit mixture in a large bowl; stir in marshmallows and walnuts. Cover and refrigerate at least 2 hours or overnight. Yield: 4 cups (serving size: 2 tablespoons).

CALORIES 51 (15% from fat); FAT 0.9g (sat 0.1g, mono 0.1g, poly 0.6g); PROTEIN 0.6g; CARB 11.1g; FIBER 1.2g; CHOL 0mg; IRON 0.3mg; SODIUM 2mg; CALC 13mg

Fallen Chocolate Cake with Cherry Red Wine Sauce

SAUCE:
- ⅔ cup sugar
- ½ cup kosher red wine
- 1 pound frozen pitted unsweetened cherries

CAKE:
- ½ cup shelled pistachios
- Cooking spray
- 1¼ cups sugar, divided
- ¼ cup water
- 4 ounces bittersweet chocolate, coarsely chopped
- Dash of salt
- ½ cup unsweetened cocoa
- 3 large eggs, lightly beaten
- ½ teaspoon vanilla extract
- ⅛ teaspoon almond extract
- 4 large egg whites

1. Combine first 3 ingredients in a saucepan; bring to a boil. Reduce heat; simmer until reduced to 2 cups (about 30 minutes). Chill.
2. Preheat oven to 350°.
3. Place pistachios in a food processor; process until finely ground. Sprinkle pistachios over bottom of a 9-inch springform pan coated with cooking spray.
4. Combine 1 cup sugar and water in a medium saucepan; bring to a boil. Remove from heat; stir in chocolate and salt, stirring until chocolate melts. Add cocoa, stirring with a whisk until well blended. Add 3 eggs, 1 at a time, stirring well after each addition. Stir in extracts.
5. Beat egg whites with a mixer at high speed until foamy. Gradually add ¼ cup sugar, 1 tablespoon at a time, beating until stiff peaks form. Gently stir one-fourth of egg white mixture into chocolate mixture; gently fold in remaining egg white mixture. Spoon into pan. Bake at 350° for 25 minutes or until a wooden pick inserted in center comes out nearly clean. Cool to room temperature; run a knife around outside edge. Serve with sauce. Yield: 12 servings (serving size: 1 slice cake and 2½ tablespoons sauce).

CALORIES 262 (23% from fat); FAT 6.6g (sat 2.3g, mono 1.7g, poly 0.9g); PROTEIN 5.5g; CARB 46.2g; FIBER 2.4g; CHOL 53mg; IRON 1mg; SODIUM 49mg; CALC 18mg

Splendid Soufflés

All you need to know to master the preparation of savory or sweet soufflés

Mastering a soufflé is a culinary accomplishment, though it needn't be difficult. Success depends on two simple techniques: First, whip egg whites properly, and second, fold the egg whites gently into a flavored base. With a little practice, you'll be turning out tasty soufflés like a pro.

Bacon, Potato, and Gruyère Soufflés

White potatoes work best for this recipe. Although they're similar in appearance to the russet (or baking potato), white potatoes, sometimes labeled "boiling" potatoes, have lighter skin and less-starchy flesh.

- Cooking spray
- 2 tablespoons dry breadcrumbs
- 1¾ pounds peeled white potatoes, cut into 1-inch pieces (about 3 medium)
- ¾ cup low-fat buttermilk
- ⅓ cup fat-free, less-sodium chicken broth
- ½ teaspoon salt
- ½ teaspoon freshly ground black pepper
- 1 large egg
- 1½ teaspoons butter
- 1 cup thinly sliced leek (about 1 large)
- ¾ cup (3 ounces) finely grated Gruyère cheese
- 2 bacon slices, cooked and crumbled
- 6 large egg whites

1. Lightly coat 6 (8-ounce) soufflé dishes with cooking spray. Sprinkle evenly with breadcrumbs. Set aside.
2. Place potatoes in a medium saucepan; cover with water. Bring to a boil. Reduce heat, and simmer 20 minutes or until very tender; drain. Cool. Place potatoes, buttermilk, and next 4 ingredients in a food processor; process until smooth. Transfer potato mixture to a large bowl.
3. Position oven rack to lowest level, and remove middle rack. Preheat oven to 425°.
4. Melt butter in a nonstick skillet over medium-high heat. Add leek to pan; sauté 6 minutes or until tender. Add leek, cheese, and bacon to potato mixture; stir well to combine.
5. Place egg whites in a large mixing bowl; beat with a mixer at high speed until stiff peaks form (do not overbeat). Gently fold one-fourth of egg whites into potato mixture; gently fold in remaining egg whites. Gently spoon mixture into prepared dishes. Sharply tap dishes on counter 2 or 3 times to level. Place dishes on a baking sheet; place baking sheet on bottom rack of a 425° oven. Immediately reduce oven temperature to 350° (do not remove soufflés from oven). Bake 40 minutes or until a wooden pick inserted in side of soufflé comes out clean. Serve immediately. Yield: 6 servings (serving size: 1 soufflé).

CALORIES 253 (28% from fat); FAT 7.9g (sat 4.1g, mono 2.5g, poly 0.6g); PROTEIN 13.7g; CARB 32.2g; FIBER 2.9g; CHOL 57mg; IRON 1.2mg; SODIUM 447mg; CALC 211mg

Begin with the Right Equipment

Soufflé dishes have tall, straight sides and are available in various sizes and volumes. The sides support the batter as it ascends, and the capacity determines the soufflé's height. So, if you select an appropriate-sized dish, your soufflé should rise two to three inches above the dish with no additional support required. Our recipes each specify sizes for baking dishes: 8-ounce dishes for individual soufflés and a 1½-quart dish for the Sweet Potato Soufflé (recipe on page 123). If you don't have these sizes, it's safe to go up to the next size, but don't use smaller dishes.

In our recipes, all of the soufflé bases are made on the stovetop, so they simply require a heavy saucepan, a whisk, and a wooden spoon. An electric mixer with a whisk attachment is the only equipment required to whip the egg whites. (We tested with a stand mixer, but a powerful handheld mixer works as well.) If you happen to have a copper bowl, bring it out. While most large metal or glass bowls will suffice, whipping egg whites in a copper bowl helps prevent overbeating and results in a more stable mixture.

The broad, flat surface of a rubber spatula makes it the best tool for folding.

Prepare the Dish

The first step to making a soufflé is to prepare the baking dish by lightly greasing the sides. Butter is traditional, but we call for a light coating of cooking spray to keep fat and calories to a minimum.

Once the dish has been lightly greased, sprinkle it with something that will give the soufflé traction as it rises during cooking. Sugar is the best for sweet soufflés; use breadcrumbs or finely grated cheese for savory.

Make the Base

The two basic components of a soufflé are the base and the beaten egg whites. The base is a starchy sauce, custard, or fruit puree that gives the dish its charac-teristic flavor. It's thickened on the stovetop, and then enriched with egg yolk and flavorings in a method known as *bouillie* (bool-YEE).

The recipes employ the bouillie method because it yields soufflés that are tender, light, and sturdy all at the same time. Generally speaking, dessert soufflés are lighter than savory ones. The air (from the whipped egg whites and heat expansion) won't sustain the weight of a dense savory soufflé after cooking, but dessert soufflés hold their dramatic puffed appearance just a bit longer.

Whip the Egg Whites

Egg whites incorporate more air if they're not completely cold, so separate the eggs first. Leave the whites out on the counter for about 20 minutes before whipping—just long enough to take off the chill.

Carefully separate eggs, so the whites contain no trace of yolk. (If a bit of yolk strays into the whites, remove it with a clean spoon.) Take care also to place egg whites in a clean bowl with no residual fat, and use a clean whisk attachment to whip them. This ensures that the whites remain untainted by even the smallest amount of fat, which prevents them from reaching optimal volume.

Keep a watchful eye on the egg whites once they reach the soft peak stage because they will progress quickly to firm peak. You will recognize soft peaks when you lift the beaters and the egg whites droop or slope gently. Stiff peaks stand at attention. If they visibly lose their luster, they're overbeaten, and you'll need to begin anew with fresh egg whites.

Lighten the Base

Once the base is prepared and cooled to room temperature, and the egg whites are whipped, the next step is to lighten the base by folding about a quarter of the egg whites into the base. With this step complete, it's easier to incorporate the remaining egg whites and maintain their volume.

Bake the Soufflé

Before preheating the oven, position the rack to the lowest setting, and remove the middle rack, allowing at least six inches above the soufflé dish. Baking the soufflé near the bottom heat source ensures it will rise to its maximum height, and keeping it as far away as possible from a potential top heat source prevents overbrowning before the center cooks. (Make sure the oven is preheated and ready before you whip the egg whites so that you can put the soufflé batter directly into the oven.)

Gently spoon the batter into the prepared dish, and tap the dish sharply on the counter a few times. This allows the batter to settle and make full contact with the sides of the dish so it rises high.

Once you place the soufflé in the oven, immediately reduce the oven temperature. The initial higher temperature gives the egg whites a blast of heat to encourage inflation of the batter. If you don't reduce the temperature, the top will become too brown.

Resist the urge to open the oven door as the soufflé bakes. Doing so allows cooler air into the oven and will cause the soufflé to deflate.

Test for Doneness

Test for doneness by inserting a wooden pick into the side of the soufflé. If it comes out clean, the soufflé is done. However, there are degrees of doneness, and determining the difference is a matter of personal preference. Some cooks prefer soufflés with a moist center, while others prefer more firm soufflés. To understand the difference, think of soft versus hard scrambled eggs. (Moist soufflés collapse more quickly.)

Serve It

Soufflés begin deflating as soon as they're removed from the oven, so time the meal to serve them immediately (although they're still delicious even after they've fallen). Ensure stress-free timing with the recipes by preparing the base and separating the egg whites in advance. Using this strategy and a bit of last-minute assembly, you can serve soufflés with confidence.

1. *Use soufflé dishes with tall, straight sides. A powerful stand mixer with a whisk attachment will incorporate the most air into egg whites; use a rubber or silicone spatula to fold the egg whites into the base.*

2. *Lightly coat the entire soufflé dish with cooking spray. Add breadcrumbs or sugar, and roll the dish around until it's completely covered.*

3. *The base gives the soufflé its characteristic flavor. After the base is cooked and cooled, egg yolks and flavorings, such as vanilla or lemon juice, are added to enrich the dish.*

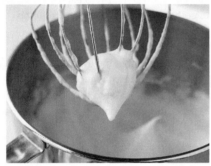

4. *Whip the egg whites to stiff satiny peaks, but do not overbeat them. Egg whites have reached the stiff peak stage when they stand up. Overbeaten egg whites look dry and grainy.*

5. *Gently fold the egg whites into the base, incorporating as much air as possible. "Cut" down the center and up the sides of the bowl, making an S motion with a spatula, rotating the bowl as you go.*

6. *The soufflé is done when it's puffed and set. To make sure it's completely cooked, insert a wooden pick or skewer horizontally into the side. If it comes out clean, the soufflé is ready.*

Mango-Macadamia Soufflés

SOUFFLÉS:

Cooking spray
- 2 tablespoons sugar
- 2 cups chopped peeled ripe mango (about 2 medium)
- ¾ cup mango nectar
- ½ cup sugar
- 3 tablespoons cornstarch
- ⅛ teaspoon salt
- ¼ cup butter
- 2 large egg yolks
- 6 large egg whites
- 3 tablespoons chopped macadamia nuts

SAUCE:
- ¾ cup fat-free sweetened condensed milk
- ½ cup fresh lime juice (about 4 limes)
- 2 tablespoons water

1. Position oven rack to lowest level, and remove middle rack. Preheat oven to 425°.

2. To prepare soufflés, lightly coat 8 (8-ounce) soufflé dishes with cooking spray. Sprinkle evenly with 2 tablespoons sugar. Set aside.

3. Place mango and nectar in a blender; process until smooth. Combine ½ cup sugar, cornstarch, and salt in a medium saucepan over medium-high heat, stirring with a whisk. Add mango mixture to pan; stir until blended. Bring to a boil. Cook 1 minute or until mixture is thick and bubbly, stirring constantly; remove from heat. Stir in butter. Transfer mixture to a large bowl; cool to room temperature. Stir in egg yolks.

4. Place egg whites in a large mixing bowl; beat with a mixer at high speed until stiff peaks form (do not overbeat). Gently fold one-fourth of egg whites into mango mixture; gently fold in remaining egg whites. Gently spoon mixture into prepared dishes; sprinkle evenly with macadamia nuts. Sharply tap dishes 2 or 3 times on counter to level. Place dishes on a baking sheet; place baking sheet on bottom rack of a 425°

oven. Immediately reduce temperature to 350° (do not remove soufflés from oven). Bake 30 minutes or until a wooden pick inserted in side of soufflé comes out clean.

5. To prepare sauce, combine condensed milk, juice, and water, stirring well with a whisk. Serve with soufflés. Yield: 8 servings (serving size: 1 soufflé and about 2½ tablespoons sauce).

CALORIES 304 (28% from fat); FAT 9.5g (sat 3.7g, mono 4.8g, poly 0.5g); PROTEIN 6.7g; CARB 50.5g; FIBER 1.4g; CHOL 68mg; IRON 0.3mg; SODIUM 162mg; CALC 101mg

Sweet Potato Soufflé

Savory and sweet, this soufflé can be served as a side dish or dessert.

Cooking spray
¼ cup granulated sugar, divided
2 sweet potatoes (about 1 pound, 12 ounces)
2 tablespoons butter, softened
¼ cup all-purpose flour (about 1 ounce)
½ cup half-and-half
1 tablespoon grated orange rind
⅓ cup fresh orange juice
¼ cup packed dark brown sugar
1 teaspoon ground cinnamon
¾ teaspoon salt
2 large egg yolks
5 large egg whites

1. Position oven rack to lowest level, and remove middle rack. Preheat oven to 425°.

2. Coat a 1½-quart soufflé dish with cooking spray. Sprinkle evenly with 2 tablespoons granulated sugar. Set aside.

3. Pierce potatoes with a fork; arrange on paper towels in microwave oven. Microwave at HIGH 10 minutes or until tender, rearranging potatoes after 5 minutes. Let stand 5 minutes. Peel potatoes. Combine potatoes and butter, and mash with a potato masher until smooth.

4. Lightly spoon flour into a dry measuring cup; level with a knife. Place flour, potato mixture, half-and-half, and next 6 ingredients in a food processor; process until smooth. Transfer potato mixture to a large bowl.

5. Place egg whites in a large mixing bowl; beat with a mixer at high speed until soft peaks form. Add 2 tablespoons granulated sugar, 1 tablespoon at a time, beating until stiff peaks form (do not overbeat). Gently fold one-fourth of egg white mixture into potato mixture; gently fold in remaining egg white mixture. Gently spoon mixture into prepared dish. Sharply tap dish 2 or 3 times on counter to level. Place dish on a baking sheet; place baking sheet in a 425° oven. Immediately reduce oven temperature to 375° (do not remove soufflé from oven). Bake 1 hour or until soufflé is puffy, golden, and set. Serve immediately. Yield: 6 servings.

CALORIES 259 (26% from fat); FAT 7.5g (sat 4.3g, mono 2.3g, poly 0.5g); PROTEIN 6.9g; CARB 41g; FIBER 3.1g; CHOL 88mg; IRON 1.3mg; SODIUM 414mg; CALC 84mg

Beet Soufflés with Lemony Horseradish Crème Fraîche

Serve this spectacular jewel-toned soufflé with roast beef and steamed asparagus for a special spring dinner.

3 small beets (about 12 ounces)
3 tablespoons fresh lemon juice, divided
1 (½-ounce) slice French bread
Cooking spray
½ cup all-purpose flour (about 2¼ ounces)
¾ teaspoon salt, divided
1½ cups fat-free milk
2 large egg yolks
5 large egg whites
2 tablespoons sugar
¼ cup crème fraîche
2 teaspoons prepared horseradish

1. Leave root and 1-inch stem on beets; scrub with a brush. Place in a medium saucepan; cover with water. Bring to a boil. Cover, reduce heat, and simmer 35 minutes or until tender. Drain and rinse with cold water. Drain; cool. Trim off beet roots; rub off skins. Place beets and

2 tablespoons juice in a food processor; process until smooth. Set aside.

2. Position oven rack to lowest level, and remove middle rack. Preheat oven to 425°.

3. Place bread in a food processor, and process until finely ground. Lightly coat 8 (8-ounce) soufflé dishes with cooking spray. Sprinkle evenly with crumbs. Set dishes aside.

4. Lightly spoon flour into a dry measuring cup; level with a knife. Combine flour and ½ teaspoon salt in a medium saucepan over medium-high heat. Gradually add milk, stirring constantly with a whisk; bring to a boil. Cook 2 minutes, stirring constantly. Remove from heat. Transfer mixture to a large bowl; cool to room temperature. Stir in beet mixture and egg yolks.

5. Place egg whites in a large mixing bowl; beat with a mixer at high speed until soft peaks form. Add sugar, 1 tablespoon at a time, beating until stiff peaks form (do not overbeat). Gently fold one-fourth of egg white mixture into beet mixture; gently fold in remaining egg white mixture. Gently spoon mixture into prepared dishes. Sharply tap dishes on counter 2 or 3 times to level. Place dishes on a baking sheet; place baking sheet on bottom rack of a 425° oven. Immediately reduce oven temperature to 350° (do not remove soufflés from oven). Bake 40 minutes or until a wooden pick inserted in side of soufflé comes out clean.

6. Combine 1 tablespoon juice, ¼ teaspoon salt, crème fraîche, and horseradish, stirring well with a whisk. Serve with soufflés. Yield: 8 servings (serving size: 1 soufflé and about 1 tablespoon sauce).

CALORIES 126 (29% from fat); FAT 4g (sat 2.1g, mono 0.5g, poly 0.2g); PROTEIN 6.2g; CARB 16.2g; FIBER 1.2g; CHOL 59mg; IRON 0.8mg; SODIUM 318mg; CALC 73mg

Double Chocolate Soufflés with Warm Fudge Sauce

You can prepare the ingredients ahead, spoon the batter into soufflé dishes, cover, and freeze until you're ready to cook them. They can go straight from the freezer to the oven. Make the sauce ahead, too, and simply warm it before serving. This recipe received our Test Kitchens' highest rating.

SOUFFLÉS:

Cooking spray
2   tablespoons sugar
½   cup sugar
3   tablespoons all-purpose flour
3   tablespoons unsweetened cocoa
⅛   teaspoon salt
1¼ cups fat-free milk
3   ounces bittersweet chocolate, chopped
1   teaspoon vanilla extract
1   large egg yolk
6   large egg whites

SAUCE:

1   tablespoon butter
⅓   cup sugar
2   tablespoons unsweetened cocoa
1   tablespoon all-purpose flour
½   cup fat-free milk
½   ounce bittersweet chocolate, chopped

1. Position oven rack to lowest level, and remove middle rack. Preheat oven to 425°.
2. To prepare soufflés, lightly coat 6 (8-ounce) soufflé dishes with cooking spray. Sprinkle evenly with 2 tablespoons sugar. Set aside.
3. Combine ½ cup sugar and next 3 ingredients in a medium saucepan over medium-high heat, stirring with a whisk. Gradually add 1¼ cups milk, stirring constantly with a whisk; bring to a boil. Cook 2 minutes or until slightly thick, stirring constantly with a whisk; remove from heat. Add 3 ounces chocolate; stir until smooth. Transfer mixture to a large bowl; cool to room temperature. Stir in vanilla and egg yolk.
4. Place egg whites in a large mixing bowl; beat with a mixer at high speed until stiff peaks form (do not overbeat). Gently fold one-fourth of egg whites into chocolate mixture; gently fold in remaining egg white mixture. Gently spoon mixture into prepared dishes. Sharply tap dishes 2 or 3 times on counter to level. Place dishes on a baking sheet; place baking sheet on bottom rack of 425° oven. Immediately reduce oven temperature to 350° (do not remove soufflés from oven). Bake 40 minutes or until a wooden pick inserted in side of soufflé comes out clean.
5. To prepare sauce, melt butter in a small saucepan over medium-high heat. Add ⅓ cup sugar, 2 tablespoons cocoa, and 1 tablespoon flour; stir well with a whisk. Gradually add ½ cup milk, stirring well with a whisk; bring to a boil. Cook 1 minute or until slightly thick, stirring constantly with a whisk. Remove from heat; add ½ ounce chocolate, stirring until smooth. Serve warm with soufflés. Yield: 6 servings (serving size: 1 soufflé and about 2 tablespoons sauce).

CALORIES 315 (26% from fat); FAT 9g (sat 5.1g, mono 1.8g, poly 0.3g); PROTEIN 9.1g; CARB 51.8g; FIBER 2.9g; CHOL 41mg; IRON 1.4mg; SODIUM 153mg; CALC 79mg

Lemon Soufflés with Buttermilk Sauce

Buttermilk sauce complements this tart lemon soufflé.

SOUFFLÉS:

Cooking spray
2   tablespoons sugar
¾   cup sugar, divided
2   tablespoons all-purpose flour
⅛   teaspoon salt
⅔   cup 2% reduced-fat milk
3   tablespoons butter
1   tablespoon grated lemon rind
⅓   cup fresh lemon juice
2   large egg yolks
5   large egg whites

SAUCE:

¼   cup sugar
2   tablespoons all-purpose flour
⅛   teaspoon salt
¾   cup low-fat buttermilk
1   large egg, lightly beaten

1. Position oven rack to lowest level, and remove middle rack. Preheat oven to 425°.
2. To prepare soufflés, lightly coat 8 (8-ounce) soufflé dishes with cooking spray. Sprinkle evenly with 2 tablespoons sugar. Set aside.
3. Combine ½ cup sugar, 2 tablespoons flour, and ⅛ teaspoon salt in a heavy saucepan over medium heat, stirring with a whisk. Gradually add reduced-fat milk, stirring well with a whisk; bring to a boil. Cook 1 minute or until thick and bubbly, stirring constantly. Remove from heat. Add butter; stir well. Transfer mixture to a large bowl; cool to room temperature. Add rind, juice, and egg yolks; stir until blended.
4. Place egg whites in a large mixing bowl; beat with a mixer at high speed until soft peaks form. Add ¼ cup sugar, 1 tablespoon at a time, beating until stiff peaks form (do not overbeat). Gently fold one-fourth of egg white mixture into lemon mixture, and gently fold in remaining egg white mixture. Gently spoon mixture into prepared dishes. Sharply tap dishes 2 or 3 times on counter to level. Place dishes on a baking sheet; place baking sheet on bottom rack of 425° oven. Immediately reduce oven temperature to 350° (do not remove soufflés from oven). Bake 40 minutes or until a wooden pick inserted in side of soufflé comes out clean.
5. To prepare sauce, combine ¼ cup sugar, 2 tablespoons flour, and ⅛ teaspoon salt in a small saucepan over medium-low heat. Combine buttermilk and egg, stirring well with a whisk. Gradually add buttermilk mixture to pan, stirring constantly with a whisk. Cook 10 minutes or until a thermometer registers 160°, stirring constantly with a whisk. Serve sauce with soufflés. Yield: 8 servings (serving size: 1 soufflé and about 1½ tablespoons sauce).

CALORIES 216 (28% from fat); FAT 6.7g (sat 3.7g, mono 2g, poly 0.5g); PROTEIN 5.7g; CARB 34.5g; FIBER 0.2g; CHOL 91mg; IRON 0.5mg; SODIUM 184mg; CALC 65mg

Chesapeake Treasures

Maryland's famed estuary yields some of the country's most delectable shellfish.

The Chesapeake Bay is home to what many consider the most delicious crabs and oysters in the world. Centuries ago, the Algonquin Indians dubbed the waters *Chesepioc*, or "great shellfish bay." While blue crabs exist all along the East Coast, they thrive in the Chesapeake's waters, which form North America's largest estuary, stretching almost 200 miles from its freshwater origin in Havre de Grace, Maryland, to its salty union with the Atlantic in Norfolk, Virginia.

Oysters Chesapeake

This dish combines two of the Chesapeake's most beloved foods: oysters and crabs. Cook on the bottom broiler rack, or the breadcrumbs will burn before the oysters are cooked through.

    2 tablespoons reduced-fat
       mayonnaise
    2 tablespoons reduced-fat sour
       cream
    1 tablespoon minced chives
    ⅛ teaspoon salt
    ⅛ teaspoon freshly ground black
       pepper
    2 bacon slices, cooked and
       crumbled (drained)
    1 (6½-ounce) can lump crabmeat,
       undrained
    1 (1-ounce) slice white bread
    1 teaspoon butter, melted
    12 shucked oysters
    Lemon wedges (optional)
    Fresh minced chives (optional)

1. Preheat broiler.
2. Combine first 7 ingredients in a medium bowl; stir gently.
3. Place bread in a food processor; process until coarse crumbs measure ½ cup. Combine breadcrumbs and butter in a small bowl.
4. Arrange oysters on a broiler pan. Spoon about 1 tablespoon crab mixture over each oyster; sprinkle each with about 1 teaspoon breadcrumb mixture. Broil 7 minutes or until tops are browned and oysters are done. Serve with lemon wedges and garnish with chives, if desired. Yield: 6 servings (serving size: 2 oysters).

CALORIES 124 (47% from fat); FAT 6.5g (sat 2.4g, mono 2.2g, poly 1.3g); PROTEIN 11.2g; CARB 4.4g; FIBER 0.1g; CHOL 52mg; IRON 2.4mg; SODIUM 469mg; CALC 56mg

Soft-Shell Crab Sandwiches

    4 jumbo soft-shell crabs,
       cleaned
    3 tablespoons all-purpose flour
    1 teaspoon Old Bay seasoning
    1 tablespoon butter
    ¼ cup Lemon Tartar Sauce (recipe at
       right)
    8 (1-ounce) slices French bread
    12 (¼-inch-thick) slices plum
       tomato
    4 Bibb lettuce leaves

1. Rinse crabs; pat dry with paper towels.
2. Combine flour and Old Bay seasoning in a shallow dish. Dredge crabs in flour mixture.
3. Melt butter in a large skillet over medium-high heat until butter begins to brown. Add crabs; cook 3 minutes, gently pressing body and legs against pan. Turn crabs; cook 3 minutes or until brown and cooked through. Drain on paper towels.
4. Spread 1 tablespoon Lemon Tartar Sauce over each of 4 bread slices. Top each with 1 crab, 3 tomato slices, 1 lettuce leaf, and 1 bread slice. Yield: 4 servings.

CALORIES 324 (22% from fat); FAT 7.9g (sat 3.5g, mono 1.4g, poly 1.2g); PROTEIN 29.2g; CARB 33g; FIBER 1.5g; CHOL 112mg; IRON 2.9mg; SODIUM 981mg; CALC 211mg

Lemon Tartar Sauce

    ⅓ cup reduced-fat sour cream
    ⅓ cup finely chopped sweet pickles
    ¼ cup light mayonnaise
    1 tablespoon grated lemon rind
    ¼ teaspoon salt

1. Combine all ingredients in a small bowl, stirring well. Yield: 6 servings (serving size: 2 tablespoons).

CALORIES 65 (69% from fat); FAT 5g (sat 1.7g, mono 1.2g, poly 2g); PROTEIN 0.7g; CARB 4.6g; FIBER 0.2g; CHOL 10mg; IRON 0.1mg; SODIUM 270mg; CALC 24mg

Crab Cakes

    3 (1-ounce) slices white bread
    ¼ cup finely chopped green onions
    2 tablespoons chopped fresh dill
    2 tablespoons reduced-fat mayonnaise
    ¼ teaspoon black pepper
    2 large egg whites
    1 pound lump crabmeat, shell pieces
       removed
    1 tablespoon canola oil, divided
    Cooking spray

1. Preheat oven to 400°.
2. Place bread in a food processor; process until coarse crumbs measure 1½ cups. Combine breadcrumbs, green onions, and next 5 ingredients. Divide crab mixture into 6 equal portions, shaping each into a 1-inch-thick patty.
3. Heat 1½ teaspoons oil in a large non-stick skillet over medium-high heat. Add 3 patties; cook 1 minute on each side. Remove from pan; place on a jelly-roll pan coated with cooking spray. Repeat procedure with 1½ teaspoons oil and remaining patties. Bake at 400° for 20 minutes or until thoroughly heated and golden. Yield: 6 servings (serving size: 1 crab cake).

CALORIES 140 (28% from fat); FAT 4.3g (sat 0.6g, mono 1.8g, poly 1.6g); PROTEIN 16g; CARB 8.4g; FIBER 0.5g; CHOL 59mg; IRON 1.1mg; SODIUM 382mg; CALC 94mg

A D-I-Y Crab Feast

Chesapeake locals regularly throw impromptu crab feasts. Fortunately, you don't have to live along the Chesapeake Bay to savor the sweet meat of a fresh blue crab. Linton's Seafood (www.lintonsseafood.com) in Crisfield, Maryland, will ship steamed or live blue crabs. These Chesapeake delicacies don't come cheap—prices vary seasonally and can run more than $50 for a dozen—although crab lovers will argue they're worth the cost.

All you need for an old-fashioned crab feast are crabs, beer, wooden mallets, sharp knives, plenty of napkins, newspapers to spread across the table, and a large stockpot.

Popular side dishes include corn on the cob, sliced tomatoes, potato salad, and coleslaw. The Chesapeake Bay Program, a watershed advocacy group, offers these crab cooking tips:

• A bushel has 60 to 70 crabs, enough to feed 10 to 12 people. If you're serving crabs with many other side dishes, a bushel could feed as many as 15 people.

• Cook only live crabs. Once a crab dies, bacteria grow quickly.

• Keep the crabs cool until you get them in the pot. Put them in a cooler on a tray with ice beneath it to keep the crabs out of the melted ice. (If the crabs get in the water, they'll use up the water's oxygen and suffocate.)

• Steam crabs until they're bright orange, 25 to 30 minutes.

Steamed Blue Crabs

Rinse 24 live blue crabs with cold water. Combine 24 ounces beer, 1 cup white vinegar, and 1 sliced lemon in a 19-quart stockpot fitted with a vegetable steamer; bring to a simmer. Using tongs, place half of crabs on top of steamer and sprinkle with ¼ cup Old Bay seasoning. Repeat process with remaining crabs and ¼ cup Old Bay seasoning. Cover tightly and simmer for 25 minutes or until crabs are bright orange and done. Yield: 4 to 6 servings.

Spring Fingerling Potato Salad with Crab, Asparagus, and Watercress

This easy-to-prepare salad is an excellent choice for a special spring luncheon.

    1 pound fingerling potatoes
    1 pound asparagus spears, steamed
       and chilled
    ¼ teaspoon salt, divided
    ¼ cup light mayonnaise
    ¼ cup bottled low-sodium chili
       sauce
    3 tablespoons finely chopped
       chives
    2 tablespoons finely chopped fresh
       flat-leaf parsley
    2 tablespoons capers, drained
    2 teaspoons sugar
    8 cups trimmed watercress (about
       2 bunches)
    1 pound lump crabmeat, shell pieces
       removed

1. Place potatoes in a medium saucepan; cover with water. Bring to a boil. Reduce heat; simmer 10 minutes or until tender. Drain. Chill. Cut potatoes into ½-inch-thick slices. Sprinkle potatoes and asparagus with ⅛ teaspoon salt.
2. Combine ⅛ teaspoon salt, mayonnaise, and next 5 ingredients in a small bowl, stirring well with a whisk.
3. Arrange watercress on a large platter. Arrange potatoes, asparagus, and crabmeat over watercress. Serve immediately with dressing on the side. Yield: 4 servings (serving size: one-fourth of salad and 2 tablespoons dressing).

CALORIES 343 (18% from fat); FAT 6.8g (sat 1.4g, mono 1.5g, poly 3.6g); PROTEIN 30.3g; CARB 42.1g; FIBER 5.7g; CHOL 106mg; IRON 5.4mg; SODIUM 812mg; CALC 231mg

Oysters with Two Sauces

If you don't have rock salt, set the oysters on a bed of crushed ice.

      Rock salt
    24 shucked oysters
     4 lemon wedges
     ½ cup Mignonette Sauce
        (recipe below)
     6 tablespoons Cucumber-
        Horseradish Relish (recipe on
        page 127)

1. Cover a platter 1 inch deep with rock salt. Nestle oysters in rock salt, and garnish with lemon wedges. Serve with Mignonette Sauce and Cucumber-Horseradish Relish. Yield: 4 servings (serving size: 6 oysters, 2 tablespoons Mignonette Sauce, and 1½ tablespoons Cucumber-Horseradish Relish).

CALORIES 97 (21% from fat); FAT 2.2g (sat 0.7g, mono 0.3g, poly 0.8g); PROTEIN 6.7g; CARB 14.7g; FIBER 0.7g; CHOL 45mg; IRON 6.2mg; SODIUM 332mg; CALC 57mg

MAKE AHEAD
Mignonette Sauce

    1   cup dry white wine
    ½   cup red wine vinegar
    ¼   cup minced shallots
    1½ teaspoons black peppercorns,
        crushed
    ⅛   teaspoon salt

1. Place wine and vinegar in a small saucepan; bring to a boil. Cook until reduced to ¾ cup (about 5 minutes). Stir in shallots, peppercorns, and salt. Chill 2 hours. Yield: ¾ cup (serving size: 2 tablespoons).

CALORIES 15 (0% from fat); FAT 0g; PROTEIN 0.3g; CARB 4.5g; FIBER 0.1g; CHOL 0mg; IRON 0.3mg; SODIUM 53mg; CALC 6mg

MAKE AHEAD
Cucumber-Horseradish Relish

¾ cup finely chopped cucumber
2 tablespoons fresh lemon juice
2 teaspoons sugar
2 teaspoons chopped fresh dill
2 teaspoons prepared horseradish
⅛ teaspoon salt

1. Combine all ingredients in a small bowl. Cover and chill 2 hours. Yield: ⅔ cup (serving size: about 5 teaspoons).

CALORIES 10 (0% from fat); FAT 0g; PROTEIN 0.2g; CARB 2.4g; FIBER 0.1g; CHOL 0mg; IRON 0.1mg; SODIUM 50mg; CALC 5mg

---

Oyster Safety

Before buying oysters, make sure the shells are tightly closed, indicating they're still alive. Keep them on ice for the trip home. Then keep the oysters refrigerated, and consume them within a day or two. They need some oxygen to survive, so never store them in an airtight container.

Concerns about the dangers of eating oysters in months that don't contain an "r"—a caveat that predates reliable refrigeration—have largely been laid to rest. Still, oysters aren't at their peak quality from May through August when they spawn, which inhibits their size and flavor.

Vibrio vulnificus, a type of bacteria commonly found in warm seawater, can contaminate raw shellfish. Though the risk of illness from the bacteria is rare in healthy people, anyone with a compromised immune system should eat thoroughly cooked shellfish. And because of that bacteria, you may want to avoid warm-water oysters—such as those from the Gulf of Mexico—in summer months.

Fava Beans

Discover the legume that's been a Mediterranean mainstay for centuries.

Fava beans have been a staple of Mediterranean and Middle Eastern cuisines for centuries, and more American cooks are becoming familiar with them. In fact, you may already know them, as favas go by many names: broad beans, horse beans, English beans, faba beans, and Windsor beans. They can star in appetizers, omelets, salads, soups, dips, pasta dishes, and casseroles. Many home cooks like to add favas to minestrone soup, and favas can sometimes substitute for garbanzos in falafel patties.

They're a sublime delicacy: emerald green with a firm texture and subtle nutty flavor. In season from late March to early May, they can be found in specialty and ethnic markets and in supermarkets. It's worth a little extra effort to enjoy them in the following recipes.

QUICK & EASY
Fava Bean, Asparagus, and Pasta Soup

This soup uses two spring vegetables: favas and asparagus. Acini di pepe is a small round pasta often used in soups; you can substitute orzo, if you prefer.

4½ pounds unshelled fava beans (about 2¼ cups shelled)
1 tablespoon olive oil
⅓ cup finely chopped shallots
⅓ cup finely chopped carrot
½ cup uncooked acini di pepe (about 3 ounces)
2 tablespoons dry sherry
4 cups fat-free, less-sodium chicken broth
1 cup water
1⅓ cups (1-inch) sliced asparagus
1 tablespoon fresh lemon juice
¼ teaspoon salt
6 tablespoons grated fresh Parmesan cheese
2 tablespoons chopped fresh chives

1. Remove beans from pods; discard pods. Cook beans in boiling water 1 minute. Remove beans with a slotted spoon. Plunge beans into ice water; drain. Remove tough outer skins from beans; discard skins.

2. Heat oil in a medium saucepan over medium-high heat. Add shallots and carrot; sauté 2 minutes (do not brown). Stir in pasta; sauté 2 minutes. Add sherry; cook 10 seconds or until liquid evaporates. Add broth and water; bring to a boil. Reduce heat, and simmer 6 minutes. Add beans and asparagus; cook 4 minutes or until asparagus is crisp-tender. Remove from heat; stir in juice and salt. Top with cheese and chives. Yield: 6 servings (serving size: about 1⅓ cups soup, 1 tablespoon cheese, and 1 teaspoon chives).

CALORIES 200 (21% from fat); FAT 4.8g (sat 1.6g, mono 2.3g, poly 0.4g); PROTEIN 11.9g; CARB 27.6g; FIBER 5.5g; CHOL 5mg; IRON 2.6mg; SODIUM 481mg; CALC 133mg

QUICK & EASY
Bigilla

This Maltese dip is traditionally made with dried favas, but using fresh beans means they don't need to be soaked overnight first and slashes the cooking time. Serve with crackers or crusty bread.

4 pounds unshelled fava beans (2 cups shelled)
2 tablespoons capers
1½ tablespoons extravirgin olive oil
1 tablespoon minced fresh parsley
1 tablespoon chopped jalapeño pepper
1 tablespoon fresh lemon juice
1 teaspoon salt
¼ teaspoon freshly ground black peppercorns
2 garlic cloves, chopped

1. Remove beans from pods; discard pods. Cook beans in boiling water 1 minute. Remove beans with a slotted spoon. Plunge beans into ice water;

Continued

drain. Remove tough outer skins from beans; discard skins.

2. Place beans in a medium saucepan; cover with water, and bring to a boil. Cover, reduce heat, and simmer 20 minutes or until tender. Drain and rinse with cold water; drain. Place beans and remaining ingredients in a food processor; process until smooth. Yield: 8 servings (serving size: ¼ cup).

CALORIES 61 (43% from fat); FAT 2.9g (sat 0.5g, mono 2g, poly 0.4g); PROTEIN 2.9g; CARB 6.4g; FIBER 2.2g; CHOL 0mg; IRON 1mg; SODIUM 382mg; CALC 14mg

When You Can't Find Fresh

Fresh fava beans have a fleeting season, but they're available in other forms to enjoy all year long.

Peeled frozen beans can be used in place of fresh, with slightly increased cooking times (follow the directions on the label).

Many people are familiar with **dried** favas, often found at supermarkets. Check out ethnic markets for shelled and sliced dried favas imported from Italy.

Canned or **bottled** favas are available in most supermarkets, but these tend to be the least favorable way to enjoy these beans. Often, the tough outer skin hasn't been removed, and the beans can be high in sodium. If you use canned or bottled beans, be sure to rinse and drain (and peel, if necessary) them first.

Fava Bean Risotto with Fresh Mozzarella and Prosciutto

This entrée is a delicious springtime one-dish meal. You can use 2¼ cups fresh shelled green peas in place of the favas, or a combination of both.

> 4½ pounds unshelled fava beans (about 2¼ cups shelled)
> 2 ounces thinly sliced prosciutto (about ½ cup)
> Cooking spray
> 2½ cups fat-free, less-sodium chicken broth
> 2 cups water
> 1 tablespoon butter
> 1½ cups chopped leek (about 2 medium)
> 2 garlic cloves, minced
> 1½ cups uncooked Arborio rice
> 1 teaspoon chopped fresh thyme
> ⅓ cup dry white wine
> ¾ teaspoon salt
> ¼ teaspoon freshly ground black pepper
> 2 cups trimmed arugula
> 4 ounces fresh mozzarella cheese, cut into ¼-inch cubes

1. Preheat oven to 400°.

2. Remove beans from pods; discard pods. Cook beans in boiling water 1 minute. Remove beans with a slotted spoon. Plunge beans into ice water; drain. Remove tough outer skins from beans; discard skins. Set beans aside.

3. Arrange prosciutto in a single layer on a baking sheet coated with cooking spray; bake at 400° for 7 minutes or until crisp. Set aside.

4. Bring broth and 2 cups water to a simmer in a medium saucepan (do not boil); keep warm over low heat.

5. Melt butter in a medium sauté pan over medium-high heat. Add leek and garlic; sauté 3 minutes or until tender. Add rice and thyme; cook 2 minutes, stirring constantly. Reduce heat to medium. Add wine; cook 1 minute or until liquid is nearly absorbed, stirring constantly. Add broth mixture, ½ cup at a time, stirring frequently until each portion of broth is absorbed before adding

the next (about 20 minutes total). Stir in beans, salt, and pepper; cook 2 minutes, stirring frequently.

6. Remove from heat; stir in arugula and cheese. Top with prosciutto. Yield: 6 servings (serving size: about 1 cup risotto and about 2 teaspoons prosciutto).

CALORIES 266 (26% from fat); FAT 7.6g (sat 4.4g, mono 2.4g, poly 0.5g); PROTEIN 13.9g; CARB 35.4g; FIBER 4.7g; CHOL 28mg; IRON 2.3mg; SODIUM 691mg; CALC 167mg

Fresh Spring Fare Menu
serves 4

Based on seasonal ingredients, this menu is as refreshing as it is tasty.

Orecchiette with Fresh Fava Beans, Ricotta, and Shredded Mint

Roasted asparagus with lemon and Parmesan*

Garlic bread

*Toss 1 pound trimmed asparagus with 2 teaspoons extravirgin olive oil; sprinkle with ¼ teaspoon salt and ¼ teaspoon crushed red pepper. Bake at 425° for 5 minutes or until crisp-tender. Toss asparagus with 1½ teaspoons grated lemon rind, and top with 2 tablespoons shredded Parmesan cheese.

QUICK & EASY
Orecchiette with Fresh Fava Beans, Ricotta, and Mint

While fava beans are best, frozen lima beans or green peas can be used in a pinch.

> 2 pounds unshelled fava beans (about 1 cup shelled)
> 1 pound uncooked orecchiette pasta ("little ears" pasta)
> 1 teaspoon extravirgin olive oil
> ¾ teaspoon salt
> 1 cup part-skim ricotta cheese
> ½ cup (2 ounces) grated fresh Parmesan cheese
> ½ cup coarsely chopped fresh mint
> ½ teaspoon freshly ground black pepper
> Mint sprigs (optional)

1. Remove beans from pods; discard pods. Cook beans in boiling water 1 minute. Remove beans with a slotted spoon. Plunge beans into ice water; drain. Remove tough outer skins from beans; discard skins. Set beans aside.

2. Cook pasta according to package directions, omitting salt and fat. Drain pasta, reserving 1 cup pasta water. Place pasta in a large bowl; add oil and salt. Toss well.

3. Combine 1 cup reserved pasta water, ricotta cheese, Parmesan cheese, chopped mint, and pepper. Add beans and cheese mixture to pasta mixture; toss to combine. Garnish with mint sprigs, if desired. Yield: 6 servings (serving size: about 1 cup).

CALORIES 507 (16% from fat); FAT 8.8g (sat 4.1g, mono 2.5g, poly 1.3g); PROTEIN 29.2g; CARB 85.5g; FIBER 4.7g; CHOL 25mg; IRON 6.2mg; SODIUM 540mg; CALC 255mg

Fava, Sweet Pea, and Sugar Snap Salad

Mint and green peas are a classic spring combination. If you're a fan of edamame, use it in place of either the green peas or fava beans.

    4   pounds unshelled fava beans
        (about 2 cups shelled)
    2   cups sugar snap peas, trimmed
    1   cup shelled green peas (about
        1 pound unshelled)
    ¼   cup thinly sliced fresh mint
    2   ounces prosciutto, thinly sliced
        (about ½ cup)
    3   tablespoons red wine vinegar
    1   tablespoon extravirgin olive oil
    2   teaspoons Dijon mustard
    ¼   teaspoon salt
    ¼   teaspoon freshly ground black
        pepper

1. Remove beans from pods; discard pods. Cook beans and snap peas in boiling water 1 minute or until snap peas are crisp-tender. Remove beans and snap peas with a slotted spoon. Plunge beans and snap peas into ice water; drain. Remove tough outer skins from beans; discard skins.

2. Combine beans, snap peas, green peas, mint, and prosciutto in a large bowl. Combine vinegar and remaining 4 ingredients in a small bowl; stir with a whisk. Pour over bean mixture, and toss well. Yield: 8 servings (serving size: ½ cup).

CALORIES 99 (29% from fat); FAT 3.2g (sat 0.7g, mono 1.4g, poly 0.4g); PROTEIN 6.6g; CARB 11.7g; FIBER 4g; CHOL 6mg; IRON 1.9mg; SODIUM 267mg; CALC 44mg

Fava Beans with Tomato and Onion

Serve this colorful side dish with salmon.

    4½ pounds unshelled fava beans
        (about 2¼ cups shelled)
    2   cups sliced, halved plum tomatoes
        (about 4)
    1   cup vertically sliced sweet
        onion
    1   tablespoon red wine vinegar
    2   teaspoons extravirgin
        olive oil
    1   teaspoon minced fresh garlic
    ¼   teaspoon salt
    ¼   teaspoon freshly ground black
        pepper
        Cooking spray
    ½   teaspoon sugar
    ½   teaspoon red wine vinegar
    ⅛   teaspoon salt

1. Preheat oven to 425°.

2. Remove beans from pods; discard pods. Cook beans in boiling water 1 minute. Remove beans with a slotted spoon. Plunge beans into ice water; drain. Remove tough outer skins from beans; discard skins.

3. Combine beans, tomatoes, and next 6 ingredients in a 13 x 9–inch baking dish coated with cooking spray, tossing well. Bake bean mixture at 425° for 20 minutes, stirring once.

4. Combine sugar, ½ teaspoon vinegar, and ⅛ teaspoon salt in a small bowl, stirring until sugar dissolves. Drizzle over bean mixture, tossing gently to coat. Yield: 5 servings (serving size: ½ cup).

CALORIES 123 (16% from fat); FAT 2.2g (sat 0.3g, mono 1.4g, poly 0.4g); PROTEIN 6.5g; CARB 20.3g; FIBER 5.1g; CHOL 0mg; IRON 1.4mg; SODIUM 182mg; CALC 39mg

Shelling Fresh Favas

When shopping for favas, select small pods; those that bulge with beans are past their prime. Two pounds unshelled beans yield about 1 cup shelled.

Preparing and cooking fava beans involves three simple steps.

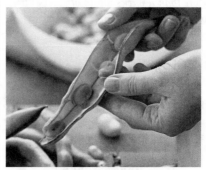

1. *Remove beans from their pods.*

2. *Cook shelled beans in boiling water for 1 minute. Remove beans with a slotted spoon. Plunge beans into ice water; drain.*

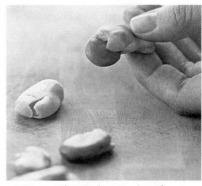

3. *Remove the tough outer skins from beans by pinching the outer skin between your thumb and forefinger; discard skins.*

After this, the beans are ready to use in any recipe.

. . . And Ready in Just About 20 Minutes

More than a week's worth of quick entrées to get dinner on the table in a flash

QUICK & EASY

Lamb Chops in Fennel-Tomato-Caper Sauce

Serve this dish with rice to soak up the flavorful sauce.

```
 8  (4-ounce) lamb loin chops,
      trimmed
¼  teaspoon salt, divided
¼  teaspoon black pepper,
      divided
Cooking spray
½  cup prechopped onion
 1  teaspoon bottled minced
      garlic
½  teaspoon fennel seeds
 1  tablespoon capers
 1  (14.5-ounce) can diced tomatoes,
      undrained
```

1. Sprinkle lamb chops with ⅛ teaspoon salt and ⅛ teaspoon pepper. Heat a large nonstick skillet over medium-high heat. Coat pan with cooking spray. Add lamb to pan; cook 2 minutes on each side or until lightly browned. Remove lamb from pan. Add ⅛ teaspoon salt, ⅛ teaspoon pepper, onion, and garlic to pan; sauté 2 minutes.

2. Place fennel seeds in a heavy-duty zip-top plastic bag; seal. Crush seeds with a rolling pin. Add seeds, capers, and tomatoes to pan; bring to a boil. Return lamb to pan. Cover, reduce heat, and cook 6 minutes or until desired degree of doneness. Yield: 4 servings (serving size: 2 lamb chops and ½ cup sauce).

CALORIES 228 (31% from fat); FAT 7.8g (sat 2.8g, mono 3.1g, poly 0.7g); PROTEIN 28.3g; CARB 9.6g; FIBER 1.1g; CHOL 86mg; IRON 3.3mg; SODIUM 551mg; CALC 75mg

QUICK & EASY

Broiled Salmon with Marmalade-Dijon Glaze

Although quick enough for a hectic weeknight, this dish will impress guests. Serve with salad and roasted potatoes.

```
½  cup orange marmalade
 1  tablespoon Dijon mustard
½  teaspoon garlic powder
½  teaspoon salt
¼  teaspoon black pepper
⅛  teaspoon ground ginger
 4  (6-ounce) salmon fillets
Cooking spray
```

1. Preheat broiler.

2. Combine first 6 ingredients in a small bowl, stirring well. Place fish on a jelly-roll pan coated with cooking spray. Brush half of marmalade mixture over fish; broil 6 minutes. Brush fish with remaining marmalade mixture; broil 2 minutes or until fish flakes easily when tested with a fork or until desired degree of doneness. Yield: 4 servings (serving size: 1 fillet).

CALORIES 377 (32% from fat); FAT 13.4g (sat 3.1g, mono 5.8g, poly 3.3g); PROTEIN 36.6g; CARB 27.3g; FIBER 0.4g; CHOL 87mg; IRON 0.8mg; SODIUM 488mg; CALC 42mg

QUICK & EASY

Orange-Scented Couscous Salad with Almonds, Cilantro, and Cucumber

Cut wonton wrappers into wedges, coat with cooking spray, and sprinkle with sesame seeds. Bake until crisp, and serve with the salad.

```
 1  cup orange juice, divided
½  cup water
 1  teaspoon salt, divided
 1  teaspoon ground coriander
¼  teaspoon ground cinnamon
¼  teaspoon black pepper,
      divided
 1  cup uncooked couscous
¼  cup sweetened dried cranberries
¼  cup sliced almonds
1½  cups chopped, cooked chicken
      breast
 1  cup chopped cucumber
⅓  cup prechopped red onion
 3  tablespoons chopped fresh
      cilantro
 1  tablespoon fresh lime juice
 2  teaspoons Dijon mustard
1½  tablespoons extravirgin
      olive oil
```

1. Combine ¾ cup orange juice, water, ½ teaspoon salt, coriander, cinnamon, and ⅛ teaspoon pepper in a saucepan; bring to a boil. Remove from heat; add couscous and cranberries. Cover and let stand 5 minutes; fluff with a fork. Transfer couscous mixture to a large bowl.

2. Heat a small skillet over medium heat. Add nuts to pan; cook 3 minutes or until toasted, stirring frequently. Add nuts, chicken, and next 3 ingredients to couscous mixture; toss.

3. Combine ¼ cup orange juice, ½ teaspoon salt, ⅛ teaspoon pepper, lime juice, and mustard, stirring with a whisk. Gradually add oil to juice mixture, stirring constantly with a whisk. Drizzle juice mixture over couscous mixture, tossing to coat. Yield: 4 servings (serving size: 1½ cups).

CALORIES 396 (24% from fat); FAT 10.7g (sat 1.5g, mono 6.4g, poly 1.8g); PROTEIN 24.1g; CARB 49.7g; FIBER 4.1g; CHOL 45mg; IRON 1.4mg; SODIUM 690mg; CALC 58mg

Chicken-Peanut Chow Mein

Chow mein noodles are often labeled *chuka soba*. If you can't find them in the Asian section of the supermarket, substitute spaghetti or linguine. Chop and measure the ingredients while you wait for the water to boil.

- 1 cup precut matchstick-cut carrots
- 1 cup snow peas, trimmed
- 2 (6-ounce) packages chow mein noodles
- 1 tablespoon dark sesame oil, divided
- ½ pound skinless, boneless chicken breast
- 3 tablespoons low-sodium soy sauce, divided
- ¾ cup fat-free, less-sodium chicken broth
- 2 tablespoons oyster sauce
- 1 teaspoon sugar
- ¼ teaspoon crushed red pepper
- 1 cup presliced mushrooms
- 2 teaspoons bottled fresh ground ginger (such as Spice World)
- 1 cup (1-inch) sliced green onions
- 2 tablespoons dry-roasted peanuts, coarsely chopped

1. Cook carrots, snow peas, and noodles in boiling water 3 minutes; drain.
2. Heat 2 teaspoons oil in a large nonstick skillet over medium-high heat. Cut chicken crosswise into thin strips. Add chicken and 1 tablespoon soy sauce to pan; stir-fry 3 minutes. Remove chicken from pan; keep warm.
3. Combine 2 tablespoons soy sauce, broth, oyster sauce, sugar, and pepper, stirring well. Heat 1 teaspoon oil over medium-high heat. Add mushrooms and ginger to pan; stir-fry 3 minutes. Add broth mixture, and cook 1 minute. Add noodle mixture and chicken to pan; cook 1 minute, tossing to combine. Sprinkle with onions and peanuts. Yield: 4 servings (serving size: 1½ cups noodle mixture, ¼ cup onions, and 1½ teaspoons peanuts).

CALORIES 471 (17% from fat); FAT 8.7g (sat 1.4g, mono 3g, poly 2.6g); PROTEIN 27.8g; CARB 72.6g; FIBER 2.7g; CHOL 33mg; IRON 2.2mg; SODIUM 807mg; CALC 43mg

Beef with Sugar Snap Peas

Flank steak slices cook quickly, so remove the steak from the pan as soon as it's no longer pink, and it will be cooked perfectly.

- 1 (3½-ounce) bag boil-in-bag brown rice
- 1 (12-ounce) flank steak, trimmed
- 2 tablespoons low-sodium soy sauce, divided
- ¾ cup fat-free, less-sodium chicken broth
- ¼ cup hoisin sauce
- 2 teaspoons cornstarch
- 2 teaspoons dark sesame oil
- 1 cup sliced onion
- 1 tablespoon bottled fresh ground ginger (such as Spice World)
- 3 cups frozen sugar snap peas
- 1 cup preshredded carrot

1. Cook rice according to package directions, omitting salt and fat.
2. Cut steak diagonally across grain into thin slices. Combine steak and 1 tablespoon soy sauce; toss to coat. Combine 1 tablespoon soy sauce, broth, hoisin, and cornstarch; stir well with a whisk.
3. Heat oil in a large nonstick skillet over medium-high heat. Add steak mixture; sauté 1½ minutes or until lightly browned. Remove steak from pan. Add onion and ginger to pan; sauté 2 minutes. Add peas and carrot, and sauté 2 minutes. Stir in steak mixture; sauté 30 seconds. Add broth mixture; bring to a boil. Cook 1 minute or until slightly thick, stirring constantly. Serve immediately over rice. Yield: 4 servings (serving size: 1 cup beef mixture and ½ cup rice).

CALORIES 361 (24% from fat); FAT 9.7g (sat 3g, mono 2.7g, poly 0.6g); PROTEIN 24.3g; CARB 40g; FIBER 5.1g; CHOL 30mg; IRON 3mg; SODIUM 677mg; CALC 98mg

Shrimp and Calamari Salad

Double the shrimp if you can't find squid.

- 6 cups water
- ¾ pound large shrimp, peeled and deveined
- ¾ pound cleaned, skinless squid
- 1½ cups thinly sliced fennel (about ½ bulb)
- 1 cup thinly sliced celery
- ½ cup precut matchstick-cut carrots
- ¼ cup prechopped red onion
- 3 tablespoons chopped fresh parsley
- 3 tablespoons fresh lemon juice
- 1 tablespoon extravirgin olive oil
- ¾ teaspoon salt
- ¼ teaspoon freshly ground black pepper
- 4 cups mixed salad greens

1. Bring 6 cups water to a boil in a large saucepan. Add shrimp to pan; cook 3 minutes. Add squid to pan; cook 1 minute or until done. Drain and rinse with cold water; drain and cool.
2. Combine fennel and next 8 ingredients in a large bowl. Add shrimp mixture to bowl; toss well. Arrange 1 cup greens on each of 4 plates; top each serving with about 1½ cups shrimp mixture. Yield: 4 servings.

CALORIES 238 (25% from fat); FAT 6.5g (sat 1.1g, mono 3g, poly 1.4g); PROTEIN 32.4g; CARB 12g; FIBER 3g; CHOL 327mg; IRON 3.9mg; SODIUM 667mg; CALC 142mg

Spiced Pork with Bourbon Reduction Sauce

Substitute chicken broth for bourbon, if you prefer. Serve with couscous or rice.

SAUCE:

½ cup bourbon
¼ cup packed dark brown sugar
¼ cup low-sodium soy sauce
3 tablespoons cider vinegar
1½ teaspoons bottled minced garlic
½ teaspoon black pepper

PORK:

½ teaspoon chili powder
¼ teaspoon ground cinnamon
⅛ teaspoon ground allspice
⅛ teaspoon salt
1 (1-pound) pork tenderloin, trimmed
Cooking spray

1. To prepare sauce, combine first 6 ingredients in a medium saucepan; bring mixture to a boil. Reduce heat to medium; cook until reduced to ½ cup (about 11 minutes), stirring frequently. Remove from heat.
2. To prepare pork, combine chili powder, cinnamon, allspice, and salt, stirring well; rub evenly over pork. Cut pork crosswise into 12 slices.
3. Heat a large nonstick skillet over medium-high heat. Coat pan with cooking spray. Add pork to pan; cook 4 minutes on each side or until desired degree of doneness. Serve with sauce. Yield: 4 servings (serving size: 3 pork slices and 2 tablespoons sauce).

CALORIES 277 (13% from fat); FAT 4g (sat 1.4g, mono 1.8g, poly 0.5g); PROTEIN 24.9g; CARB 16.7g; FIBER 0.5g; CHOL 74mg; IRON 2.2mg; SODIUM 673mg; CALC 29mg

---

lighten up

Coffee Cake for a New Generation

A lighter and tastier version becomes a family favorite.

Elisabeth Ferraiuolo of Connecticut loves baking and cooking. Part of her kitchen savvy came from her grandmother, Elisabeth Masucci, who emigrated from Italy as a teenager and baked from scratch. Elizabeth remembers Walnut Coffee Cake as a staple at her grandmother's house, where it was often served to guests or for dessert. Here's how we lightened it.

Using butter instead of shortening, and less of it, trimmed 102 calories and 11 grams of fat per serving. The original recipe also contained 43 milligrams of cholesterol per slice, so we swapped fat-free egg substitute for whole eggs and fat-free buttermilk for the full-fat version to lower the cholesterol to a negligible 19 milligrams per serving. A touch of salt balances the flavors in the cake. Even the nut swirl mixture had a few modifications: We reduced the amount of walnuts slightly to cut calories and fat, and used dark brown sugar for a more full-bodied flavor than that of plain brown sugar.

BEFORE	AFTER
SERVING SIZE	
1 slice	
CALORIES PER SERVING	
421	298
FAT	
22.8g	9g
PERCENT OF TOTAL CALORIES	
49%	27%

Walnut Coffee Cake

Chop the walnuts to the size of small peas to ensure they're evenly distributed in the cake. Substitute pecans for walnuts, if desired.

¾ cup packed dark brown sugar
⅓ cup chopped walnuts
1 teaspoon ground cinnamon
3¼ cups all-purpose flour (about 14½ ounces)
2 teaspoons baking soda
1 teaspoon baking powder
¼ teaspoon salt
1½ cups granulated sugar
10 tablespoons butter, softened
¾ cup egg substitute
1 teaspoon vanilla extract
1½ cups fat-free buttermilk
Cooking spray

1. Preheat oven to 350°.
2. Combine first 3 ingredients in a small bowl. Set aside.
3. Lightly spoon flour into dry measuring cups; level with a knife. Combine flour, baking soda, baking powder, and salt in a medium bowl, stirring well with a whisk.
4. Combine sugar and butter in a large bowl; beat with a mixer at medium-high speed until well combined (about 3 minutes). Add egg substitute; beat 3 minutes or until combined. Beat in vanilla.
5. Add flour mixture and buttermilk alternately to butter mixture, beginning and ending with flour mixture, beating well after each addition and scraping sides of bowl. Spoon half of batter into a 10-inch Bundt pan coated with cooking spray. Sprinkle half of brown sugar mixture evenly over batter; spoon remaining batter into pan. Top with remaining brown sugar mixture.
6. Bake at 350° for 55 minutes or until a wooden pick inserted in center comes out clean. Cool in pan 10 minutes on a wire rack; remove from pan. Cool completely on wire rack. Yield: 16 servings (serving size: 1 slice).

CALORIES 298 (27% from fat); FAT 9g (sat 4.7g, mono 2.1g, poly 1.6g); PROTEIN 5.1g; CARB 50.3g; FIBER 0.9g; CHOL 19mg; IRON 1.7mg; SODIUM 326mg; CALC 68mg

Simple Sauces From the Pantry

Armed with a well-stocked kitchen, you can use on-hand staples to deliciously dress up meat, poultry, fish, and pasta in a hurry.

Having a well-stocked pantry can spare time and frustration when you're throwing a meal together at the last minute, or searching for ways to perk up a weeknight dinner. Armed with your favorite pantry staples, the possibilities for great sauce combinations are enticing.

Broiled Salmon Fillets with Curried Chutney Sauce

This quick, sweet-and-sour sauce puts chutney to good use, while cider vinegar and curry powder add tang and deepen the flavor. The sauce also pairs well with grilled chicken breasts. Serve the fillets and sauce with rice and haricot verts, if desired.

- ¾ cup fat-free, low-sodium chicken broth
- ⅓ cup prepared mango chutney
- 2 tablespoons cider vinegar
- 1 teaspoon curry powder
- ½ teaspoon salt, divided
- 4 (6-ounce) salmon fillets (about 1 inch thick)
- ¼ teaspoon freshly ground black pepper
- Cooking spray

1. Preheat broiler.
2. Combine first 4 ingredients and ¼ teaspoon salt in a small saucepan; bring to a boil over medium heat. Reduce heat, and cook until reduced to ½ cup (about 8 minutes).
3. Sprinkle fillets with ¼ teaspoon salt and pepper. Place fish, skin side down, on a broiler pan coated with cooking spray. Broil 10 minutes or until fish flakes easily when tested with a fork or until desired degree of doneness. Serve with sauce. Yield: 4 servings (serving size: 1 fillet and 2 tablespoons sauce).

CALORIES 338 (35% from fat); FAT 13.2g (sat 3.1g, mono 5.7g, poly 3.2g); PROTEIN 36.7g; CARB 15.7g; FIBER 0.4g; CHOL 87mg; IRON 1.1mg; SODIUM 785mg; CALC 27mg

Rigatoni with Green Olive–Almond Pesto and Asiago Cheese

This made-in-the-processor pasta sauce combines olives and almonds for a twist on traditional pesto. It's also nice as a base on pizza. Green Spanish manzanilla olives are packed in brine.

- 1 pound uncooked rigatoni
- 1¼ cups (6 ounces) pitted manzanilla (or green) olives
- ½ cup sliced almonds, toasted
- ½ cup fresh flat-leaf parsley leaves
- ¼ teaspoon freshly ground black pepper
- 1 large garlic clove
- 2 tablespoons water
- 1 teaspoon white wine vinegar
- ½ cup (2 ounces) grated Asiago cheese

1. Cook pasta according to package directions, omitting salt and fat. Drain pasta, reserving 6 tablespoons cooking liquid.
2. Place olives and next 4 ingredients in a food processor; pulse 3 times or until coarsely chopped. With processor on, add 2 tablespoons water and vinegar through food chute, processing until mixture is finely chopped. Combine pasta, ¼ cup reserved cooking liquid, and olive mixture in a large bowl; toss well. Add enough of remaining cooking liquid to make pasta mixture moist, tossing well to coat. Sprinkle with cheese. Serve immediately. Yield: 6 servings (serving size: 1⅔ cups).

CALORIES 424 (29% from fat); FAT 13.6g (sat 2.3g, mono 7.6g, poly 2.4g); PROTEIN 15.3g; CARB 61.6g; FIBER 3.5g; CHOL 8mg; IRON 3.2mg; SODIUM 510mg; CALC 136mg

Pork Medallions with Porcini Mushroom Sauce

Dried mushrooms will keep for up to six months in an airtight container.

- 1½ cups (1½ ounces) dried porcini mushrooms
- 1½ cups boiling water
- 1 (1-pound) pork tenderloin, trimmed and cut crosswise into 8 pieces
- 1 teaspoon freshly ground black pepper
- 1 teaspoon minced fresh rosemary
- ¾ teaspoon salt
- 1 garlic clove, crushed
- 2 teaspoons olive oil
- 1 teaspoon butter
- ¾ cup diced red onion
- ½ cup dry Marsala or Madeira
- 1 cup fat-free, less-sodium chicken broth
- Rosemary sprigs (optional)

1. Combine mushrooms and 1½ cups boiling water in a bowl. Cover and let stand 30 minutes or until tender. Drain in a colander over a bowl, reserving 1 cup liquid. Finely chop mushrooms.

Continued

2. Place each piece of pork between 2 sheets of heavy-duty plastic wrap, and pound to ½-inch thickness using a meat mallet or small heavy skillet. Sprinkle both sides of pork with pepper.

3. Combine minced rosemary, salt, and garlic in a small bowl; mash with a fork into a paste. Heat oil and butter in a large nonstick skillet over medium-high heat. Add garlic paste; sauté 30 seconds. Add pork; cook 2 minutes on each side. Remove from pan. Add onion to pan; sauté 5 minutes or until tender. Add mushrooms and Marsala, and cook 1 minute. Add reserved mushroom liquid and broth; bring to a boil. Cook until reduced to 1½ cups (about 10 minutes). Reduce heat to medium-low. Return pork to pan; cook 3 minutes or until thoroughly heated. Garnish with rosemary sprigs, if desired. Yield: 4 servings (serving size: 2 pieces pork and ⅓ cup sauce).

CALORIES 269 (25% from fat); FAT 7.6g (sat 2.2g, mono 4g, poly 0.9g); PROTEIN 28.2g; CARB 13.2g; FIBER 2.5g; CHOL 76mg; IRON 4mg; SODIUM 612mg; CALC 28mg

Bow Tie Pasta with Roasted Red Pepper and Cream Sauce

Bottled roasted red peppers at the base of this rich sauce deliver ample flavor and save the effort of roasting your own. Balsamic vinegar helps balance the natural sweetness of the peppers.

  1 pound uncooked farfalle (bow tie pasta)
  2 teaspoons extravirgin olive oil
  ½ cup finely chopped onion
  1 (12-ounce) bottle roasted red bell peppers, drained and coarsely chopped
  2 teaspoons balsamic vinegar
  1 cup half-and-half
  1 tablespoon tomato paste
  ⅛ teaspoon ground red pepper
  1 cup (4 ounces) freshly grated Parmigiano-Reggiano cheese, divided
Thinly sliced fresh basil (optional)

1. Cook pasta according to package directions, omitting salt and fat.

2. Heat oil in a large skillet over medium heat. Add onion, and cook 8 minutes or until tender, stirring frequently. Add bell peppers; cook 2 minutes or until thoroughly heated. Increase heat to medium-high. Stir in vinegar; cook 1 minute or until liquid evaporates. Remove from heat; cool 5 minutes.

3. Place bell pepper mixture in a blender; process until smooth. Return bell pepper mixture to pan; cook over low heat until warm. Combine half-and-half and tomato paste in a small bowl, stirring with a whisk. Add tomato mixture to bell pepper mixture, stirring with a whisk until well combined. Stir in ground red pepper.

4. Combine pasta and bell pepper mixture in a large bowl. Add ½ cup cheese, tossing to coat. Spoon 1⅓ cups pasta into each of 6 bowls; top each with about 1½ tablespoons cheese. Garnish with basil, if desired. Yield: 6 servings.

CALORIES 424 (23% from fat); FAT 10.7g (sat 5.6g, mono 3.7g, poly 0.5g); PROTEIN 17.6g; CARB 62.9g; FIBER 3g; CHOL 32mg; IRON 2.9mg; SODIUM 383mg; CALC 222mg

Classic Combination Menu
serves 6

Crisp purchased breadsticks and a salad dressed with a freshly made Dijon vinaigrette round out this family-friendly pasta dinner.

Penne with Triple-Tomato Sauce

Tossed salad*

Breadsticks

*Combine 6 cups mixed salad greens, ½ cup thinly sliced radish, ½ cup presliced mushrooms, and 1 seeded and thinly sliced yellow bell pepper in a large bowl. Combine 2 tablespoons extravirgin olive oil, 1 tablespoon water, 1 tablespoon red wine vinegar, 1 teaspoon Dijon mustard, and ¼ teaspoon freshly ground black pepper in a small bowl; stir well with a whisk. Toss dressing with salad. Sprinkle with ⅓ cup shaved fresh Parmesan cheese.

Penne with Triple-Tomato Sauce

Sun-dried, fresh, and canned tomatoes carry this sauce. You can use reserved oil from the sun-dried tomatoes instead of olive oil to sauté the onion.

  1 teaspoon olive oil
  ½ cup finely chopped onion
  2 garlic cloves, minced
  ¼ cup chopped drained oil-packed sun-dried tomato halves
  1 teaspoon sugar
  ¼ teaspoon salt
  ¼ teaspoon freshly ground black pepper
  4 plum tomatoes, chopped (about ½ pound)
  1 (14.5-ounce) can diced tomatoes, undrained
  12 ounces uncooked penne
  ½ cup (4 ounces) goat cheese
  ¼ cup finely chopped fresh flat-leaf parsley
Freshly ground black pepper (optional)
Basil sprigs (optional)

1. Heat oil in a large nonstick skillet over medium-high heat. Add onion, and sauté 4 minutes or until tender. Add garlic, and sauté 1 minute. Add sun-dried tomatoes and next 5 ingredients. Reduce heat to medium, and cook 20 minutes or until liquid almost evaporates, stirring frequently.

2. While tomato mixture cooks, prepare pasta according to package directions, omitting salt and fat. Drain; return pasta to pan. Stir in tomato mixture, cheese, and parsley. Garnish with black pepper and basil sprigs, if desired. Yield: 6 servings (serving size: 1⅓ cups).

CALORIES 325 (22% from fat); FAT 8g (sat 4.4g, mono 2.3g, poly 0.4g); PROTEIN 13.2g; CARB 51.6g; FIBER 3.9g; CHOL 15mg; IRON 2.8mg; SODIUM 302mg; CALC 90mg

Sautéed Chicken Breasts with Creamy Walnut Sauce

This recipe turns walnuts into a rich, bread-thickened sauce that, in the Liguria region (on Italy's northwest coast), is traditionally used to dress pasta.

    2   (1½-ounce) slices day-old white
        bread
    1   cup fat-free, low-sodium chicken
        broth
    ⅓   cup walnuts, toasted
    ¼   cup fresh flat-leaf parsley leaves
    2   teaspoons fresh lemon juice
    ½   teaspoon salt
    ¼   teaspoon freshly ground black
        pepper
    ⅛   teaspoon ground red pepper
    2   garlic cloves, chopped
    6   (6-ounce) skinless, boneless
        chicken breast halves
    ¼   teaspoon salt
    ¼   teaspoon freshly ground black
        pepper
    1   teaspoon olive oil
    1   teaspoon butter
    6   cups fresh baby spinach
    2   tablespoons chopped fresh
        flat-leaf parsley

1. Trim crusts from bread. Chop bread; combine bread and broth in a small bowl. Let stand 10 minutes. Place bread mixture, walnuts, and next 6 ingredients in a food processor; process until smooth.
2. Sprinkle chicken with ¼ teaspoon salt and ¼ teaspoon black pepper.
3. Heat oil and butter in a large nonstick skillet over medium-high heat. Add chicken; cook 7 minutes on each side or until done. Remove chicken from pan; keep warm. Add broth mixture to pan; cook until hot and slightly thick, scraping pan to loosen browned bits.
4. To serve, place 1 cup spinach on each of 6 plates. Place 1 chicken breast half on each serving; top each with about 2½ tablespoons sauce. Sprinkle 1 teaspoon chopped parsley over each serving. Yield: 6 servings.

CALORIES 286 (24% from fat); FAT 7.6g (sat 1.4g, mono 1.8g, poly 3.2g); PROTEIN 42.4g; CARB 11.5g; FIBER 2.6g; CHOL 100mg; IRON 2.8mg; SODIUM 586mg; CALC 59mg

Shelf Lives

Pantry item	Will keep, unopened
Low-acid canned goods, such as beans, carrots, corn, peas, soups, and stews	2 to 5 years
Vinegar; dry pasta	2 years
Chopped or minced garlic	18 months
Olives; high-acid canned goods, such as juices, fruit, pickles, tomatoes, and foods in vinegar-based sauce	12 to 18 months
Maple syrup; salsa; chutney; sun-dried tomatoes packed in oil; jarred or canned nuts	12 months
Olive or vegetable oils; dried mushrooms	6 months

QUICK & EASY
Pork Chops with Maple Mustard Glaze

Maple syrup makes a fine stand-in for honey or sugar in sauces. Here, it adds a rich, sweet note to herbed mustard sauce. This sauce goes nicely with sautéed chicken breasts as well.

    1   teaspoon butter
    4   (4-ounce) boneless pork loin
        chops, trimmed
    ½   teaspoon salt
    ¼   teaspoon freshly ground black pepper
    ½   cup fat-free, less-sodium chicken
        broth
    ¼   cup pure maple syrup
    2   tablespoons Dijon mustard
    1   teaspoon chopped fresh sage
    1   teaspoon chopped fresh thyme
    2   teaspoons heavy cream

1. Melt butter in a large nonstick skillet over medium heat. Sprinkle pork chops evenly with salt and pepper; add pork to pan. Cook 4 minutes on each side or until lightly browned. Remove from pan; keep warm.
2. Add broth and next 4 ingredients to pan. Bring to a boil, and cook 3 minutes or until slightly thick. Stir in cream, and reduce heat to medium. Return pork to pan; simmer 3 minutes or until pork is done, turning once. Yield: 4 servings (serving size: 1 pork chop and about 1 tablespoon sauce).

CALORIES 214 (22% from fat); FAT 5.2g (sat 1.9g, mono 1.9g, poly 0.6g); PROTEIN 26.3g; CARB 14.6g; FIBER 0.3g; CHOL 68mg; IRON 1.2mg; SODIUM 751mg; CALC 38mg

QUICK & EASY
Lemon Sole with Lemon-Caper Sauce

    1   tablespoon extravirgin olive oil
    4   (6-ounce) lemon sole fillets
    ½   teaspoon salt
    ¼   teaspoon freshly ground black
        pepper
    1   teaspoon butter
    1   garlic clove, minced
    ¾   cup fat-free, less-sodium chicken
        broth
    2   tablespoons capers, rinsed,
        drained, and minced
    1   tablespoon fresh lemon
        juice
    1   tablespoon minced fresh flat-leaf
        parsley

1. Heat oil in a large nonstick skillet over medium heat. Sprinkle fish with salt and pepper. Add fish to pan; cook 3 minutes on each side or until fish flakes easily when tested with a fork or until desired degree of doneness. Remove fish from pan; keep warm.
2. Melt butter in pan. Add garlic; cook 1 minute or until lightly browned. Add broth, scraping pan to loosen browned bits. Bring to a boil; cook until reduced to ¼ cup (about 6 minutes). Stir in capers and juice; cook 3 minutes or until sauce is slightly thick. Remove from heat; stir in parsley. Serve immediately. Yield: 4 servings (serving size: 1 fillet and 1 tablespoon sauce).

CALORIES 202 (29% from fat); FAT 6.6g (sat 1.5g, mono 3.5g, poly 0.9g); PROTEIN 32.7g; CARB 1.3g; FIBER 0.4g; CHOL 84mg; IRON 0.9mg; SODIUM 640mg; CALC 39mg

Garden Party

Celebrate Mother's Day, a graduation, or a bridal shower with an inviting outdoor luncheon.

Garden Party Menu
serves 6

Blackberry-Chambord Royale

Truffled Asparagus Crostini

Melon, Serrano Ham, and Arugula Salad

Curried Chicken Salad Sandwiches

Lemon Angel Food Cupcakes

Blackberry-Chambord Royale

This simple yet elegant aperitif is garnished with icy blackberries. Purchase fresh berries, and freeze them in a single layer on a baking sheet so they will hold their shape.

2 tablespoons Chambord (raspberry-flavored liqueur)
2 cups fresh blackberries, frozen
1 (750-milliliter) bottle Champagne or sparkling wine, chilled

1. Pour 1 teaspoon Chambord into each of 6 Champagne flutes. Place 3 berries in each glass. Pour about ⅔ cup Champagne into each glass. Serve immediately. Yield: 6 servings.

CALORIES 121 (0% from fat); FAT 0.2g (sat 0g, mono 0g, poly 0.1g); PROTEIN 0.5g; CARB 8.5g; FIBER 2.5g; CHOL 0mg; IRON 0.7mg; SODIUM 6mg; CALC 26mg

---

QUICK & EASY
Truffled Asparagus Crostini

Aromatic truffle oil and sharp-nutty Manchego cheese add lots of flavor with minimal effort. If you can't find Manchego, use Parmigiano-Reggiano cheese instead. Chopping the cooked asparagus into small but not fine pieces makes the crostini easy to eat while retaining the crisp-tender texture of the vegetables.

24 (1-inch) slices French bread baguette
1 pound asparagus spears, trimmed
2½ teaspoons truffle oil or extravirgin olive oil
¼ teaspoon salt
⅛ teaspoon freshly ground black pepper
½ cup (2 ounces) grated Manchego cheese

1. Preheat broiler.
2. Arrange baguette slices in a single layer on a large baking sheet; broil 1 minute or until lightly browned. Remove from oven; turn over, and broil 1 minute or until lightly browned. Remove from oven; cool on pan.
3. Fill a large skillet with water to a depth of 1 inch; bring to a boil over medium-high heat. Add asparagus; cook 2 minutes or until crisp-tender. Drain and plunge asparagus into ice water; drain. Chop asparagus to measure 2 cups. Place in a bowl. Add oil, salt, and pepper; toss well to coat.
4. Top each bread slice with 1 rounded tablespoon asparagus mixture; place on a baking sheet. Sprinkle cheese evenly over crostini. Broil 1 minute or until cheese begins to melt. Serve warm. Yield: 6 servings (serving size: 4 crostini).

CALORIES 164 (24% from fat); FAT 4.3g (sat 1.7g, mono 1.5g, poly 0.2g); PROTEIN 6.8g; CARB 26g; FIBER 2.2g; CHOL 7mg; IRON 2.8mg; SODIUM 474mg; CALC 63mg

---

QUICK & EASY
Melon, Serrano Ham, and Arugula Salad

Serrano ham is the air-cured ham common in Spanish tapas. Many supermarkets carry it in the deli section.

3 tablespoons sherry vinegar
1 teaspoon canola oil
1 teaspoon molasses
¼ teaspoon salt
¼ teaspoon ground cumin
¼ teaspoon freshly ground black pepper
1 garlic clove, minced
6 cups cubed peeled cantaloupe (about 1 [3-pound] melon)
3 ounces serrano ham, trimmed and cut into ¼-inch pieces
8 cups loosely packed trimmed arugula
¼ cup (1 ounce) shaved Manchego cheese

1. Combine first 7 ingredients in a large bowl, stirring well with a whisk. Add cantaloupe and ham; toss gently to coat.
2. Arrange arugula in an even layer on a serving platter. Top with cantaloupe mixture; sprinkle evenly with cheese. Serve immediately. Yield: 6 servings (serving size: about 2 cups).

CALORIES 122 (31% from fat); FAT 4.3g (sat 1.6g, mono 1.7g, poly 0.7g); PROTEIN 7.6g; CARB 15.7g; FIBER 0.5g; CHOL 16mg; IRON 1.1mg; SODIUM 432mg; CALC 118mg

---

QUICK & EASY • MAKE AHEAD
Curried Chicken Salad Sandwiches

You can prepare the chicken salad up to a day ahead and refrigerate.

24 (1-ounce) slices pumpernickel bread
Cooking spray
2½ tablespoons finely chopped onion
1½ tablespoons dark brown sugar
1½ tablespoons cider vinegar, divided
2 cups chopped roasted skinless, boneless chicken breast
3 tablespoons reduced-fat mayonnaise
½ teaspoon curry powder
⅛ teaspoon salt

1. Trim crusts from bread slices; cut slices into triangles.

2. Heat a small nonstick skillet over medium-high heat. Coat pan with cooking spray. Add onion to pan; sauté 5 minutes. Combine sugar and 1½ teaspoons vinegar, stirring with a whisk until sugar dissolves. Add sugar mixture to pan, scraping pan to loosen browned bits. Remove from heat; cool to room temperature.

3. Combine onion mixture, 1 tablespoon vinegar, chicken, and remaining 3 ingredients. Place about 2 tablespoons chicken mixture on each of 12 bread slices. Top with remaining bread slices. Yield: 6 servings (serving size: 2 sandwiches).

CALORIES 271 (16% from fat); FAT 4.8g (sat 1g, mono 1.2g, poly 1.2g); PROTEIN 20.5g; CARB 36.3g; FIBER 4.5g; CHOL 40mg; IRON 2.6mg; SODIUM 606mg; CALC 57mg

---

STAFF FAVORITE • MAKE AHEAD

Lemon Angel Food Cupcakes

Sifting the flour mixture thoroughly three times incorporates the powdered sugar for a light, tender cupcake. Top with tiny edible pansy blossoms or rosebuds for decoration. Store extra cupcakes in an airtight container, or send them home with guests as party favors.

CUPCAKES:
- ½ cup cake flour (about 2 ounces)
- ¾ cup powdered sugar
- ¾ cup egg whites (about 5 large eggs)
- ⅛ teaspoon salt
- ¾ teaspoon cream of tartar
- ½ cup granulated sugar
- ½ teaspoon vanilla extract
- 2 teaspoons grated lemon rind

LEMON FROSTING:
- ¼ cup butter, softened
- 2 cups powdered sugar
- 1 tablespoon 1% low-fat milk
- 1 to 2 tablespoons freshly squeezed lemon juice
- Edible flowers such as pansies or rosebuds (optional)

1. Preheat oven to 350°.

2. Place 16 paper muffin cup liners in muffin cups. Set aside.

3. To prepare cupcakes, lightly spoon cake flour into dry measuring cups; level with a knife. Sift together flour and ¾ cup powdered sugar into a medium bowl; repeat procedure 2 times.

4. Beat egg whites and salt with a mixer at high speed until frothy (about 1 minute). Add cream of tartar, and beat until soft peaks form. Add granulated sugar, 1 tablespoon at a time, beating until stiff peaks form. Sprinkle flour mixture over egg white mixture, ¼ cup at a time; fold in after each addition. Stir in vanilla and rind.

5. Divide batter evenly among prepared muffin cups. Bake at 350° for 18 minutes or until lightly browned. Remove from pan; let cool completely on a wire rack.

6. To prepare frosting, beat butter with a mixer at high speed until fluffy. Gradually add 2 cups powdered sugar; beat at low speed just until blended. Add milk and lemon juice; beat until fluffy. Add more lemon juice as needed to adjust consistency. Spread 2 tablespoons lemon frosting over each cupcake. Garnish with edible pansies and rosebuds, if desired. Yield: 16 cupcakes (serving size: 1 cupcake).

CALORIES 144 (18% from fat); FAT 2.9g (sat 1.8g, mono 0.8g, poly 0.1g); PROTEIN 1.6g; CARB 28.9g; FIBER 0.1g; CHOL 8mg; IRON 0.3mg; SODIUM 58mg; CALC 4mg

---

inspired vegetarian

Terrific Greens

Whether raw or cooked, these leafy greens add nutrition and pizzazz to any meal.

Dark green, leafy vegetables are among the first to come up in the garden and make an appearance at farmers' markets. In addition to offering good nutritional value, their presence will brighten your dinner plate. When you discover the wonderful versatility and captivating flavors of greens, these vegetables are bound to become a staple in your weeknight repertoire.

QUICK & EASY

Mushroom and Spinach Frittata with Goat Cheese

Arugula is a good substitute for spinach if you prefer to use it instead.

- 2½ cups refrigerated shredded hash brown potatoes (such as Simply Potatoes)
- 1 tablespoon olive oil, divided
- 1 teaspoon freshly ground black pepper, divided
- ½ teaspoon kosher salt, divided
- Cooking spray
- 4 cups thinly sliced cremini or button mushrooms (about 8 ounces)
- 1 cup chopped onion
- 4 cups coarsely chopped spinach (about 4 ounces)
- 1 tablespoon chopped fresh or 1 teaspoon dried thyme
- 1 garlic clove, minced
- 1¾ cups egg substitute
- ½ cup (2 ounces) crumbled goat cheese

1. Preheat oven to 375°.

2. Combine potatoes, 2 teaspoons oil, ½ teaspoon pepper, and ¼ teaspoon salt in a medium bowl. Press potatoes into bottom and up sides of a 10-inch deep-dish pie plate coated with cooking spray. Bake at 375° for 10 minutes.

3. Heat 1 teaspoon oil in a large nonstick skillet coated with cooking spray over medium-high heat. Add mushrooms and onion to pan; sauté 6 minutes or until tender. Add ½ teaspoon pepper, ¼ teaspoon salt, spinach, thyme, and garlic; cook 3 minutes or until spinach wilts. Cool slightly; stir in egg substitute and cheese.

4. Pour mushroom mixture over potato mixture. Bake at 375° for 30 minutes or until set. Cool 5 minutes; cut into 6 wedges. Yield: 6 servings.

CALORIES 168 (24% from fat); FAT 4.4g (sat 1.7g, mono 2.1g, poly 0.3g); PROTEIN 12.4g; CARB 21g; FIBER 2.7g; CHOL 4mg; IRON 2.5mg; SODIUM 412mg; CALC 61mg

Five More Great Greens

The selection and wide variety of dark green, leafy vegetables go beyond what we feature here, and they're often interchangeable in recipes.

Broccoli rabe

Despite the name, broccoli rabe, also called rapini, is closely related to the turnip. It's a pleasantly pungent-tasting vegetable that is often substituted for broccoli; cooks frequently place more emphasis on its spicy, slender stalks and jagged leafy greens than its small florets. When selecting rabe, look for deep green, tight, compact bud clusters (yellow flower buds are a sign of age).

Collard greens

This cousin of cabbage and kale tastes like a cross between the two and is a good substitute for the latter. Collards are an excellent source of vitamins A and C, calcium, and iron. Look for crisp green leaves with no evidence of yellowing or wilting.

Dandelion greens

This distinctive weed grows both wild and cultivated. The pale green, saw-toothed leaves have a tangy flavor. They can be eaten raw or cooked like spinach, and are an excellent source of vitamin A.

Mustard greens

There are different varieties of this peppery leafy green, ranging in shape, size, and pungent flavor. Look for crisp young leaves with a rich green color. Mustard greens are an excellent source of thiamine and riboflavin.

Swiss chard

A member of the beet family, Swiss chard has large curled leaves on ribbed stems. There are several varieties, including rainbow, ruby, and white, which all are good sources of vitamin A and vitamin C.

Roasted Beet and Citrus Salad

The sweet flavors of roasted beets and tangerines balance the earthy flavor of the beet greens. If small golden beets are unavailable, substitute red ones.

1½ pounds small golden beets
Cooking spray
 ¼ cup orange juice
  1 tablespoon cider vinegar
  1 tablespoon olive oil
  1 teaspoon honey
 ¼ teaspoon salt
 ¼ teaspoon freshly ground black pepper
  1 garlic clove, minced
  4 cups mixed salad greens
  3 cups chopped beet greens (about 3 ounces)
1½ cups tangerine or orange sections, halved crosswise (about 8 tangerines)
  2 tablespoons shaved fresh Parmesan cheese
  1 tablespoon coarsely chopped walnuts, toasted

1. Preheat oven to 400°.
2. Leave root and 1-inch stem on beets; scrub with a brush. Place beets on a jelly-roll pan coated with cooking spray. Lightly coat beets with cooking spray. Bake at 400° for 45 minutes or until tender. Cool beets slightly. Trim off roots; rub off skins. Cut beets in half.
3. Combine orange juice and next 6 ingredients in a medium bowl, stirring with a whisk. Add beets, tossing gently to coat. Remove beets with a slotted spoon, and set aside, reserving juice mixture in bowl. Add salad greens and beet greens to bowl; toss well. Place about 1 cup greens mixture on each of 6 salad plates; top each with about 1½ cups beets, ¼ cup tangerine sections, 1 teaspoon cheese, and ½ teaspoon nuts. Serve immediately. Yield: 6 servings.

CALORIES 143 (38% from fat); FAT 4.2g (sat 0.8g, mono 2.2g, poly 1g); PROTEIN 4.6g; CARB 24.8g; FIBER 6.1g; CHOL 2mg; IRON 2.1mg; SODIUM 263mg; CALC 119mg

Spring Greens Pie

Even though we call for specific greens here, your options include a variety of dark green, leafy vegetables. You will need to purchase several bunches of beets. After trimming the greens for this recipe, roast the beets for later or serve them as a side dish with the meal (see Roasted Beet and Citrus Salad, recipe at left, for instructions).

Cooking spray
  1 cup thinly sliced green onions
 ½ cup sliced shallots (about 5)
10 cups bagged prewashed baby spinach (about 3 [6-ounce] packages)
  5 cups trimmed arugula (about 9 ounces)
  4 cups chopped beet greens (about 4 ounces)
 ½ cup part-skim ricotta cheese
 ½ cup (2 ounces) shredded part-skim mozzarella cheese
 ½ cup coarsely chopped fresh parsley
 ¼ cup chopped fresh dill
 ½ teaspoon salt
 ½ teaspoon fennel seeds
 ½ teaspoon black pepper
  8 sheets frozen phyllo dough, thawed

1. Preheat oven to 375°.
2. Heat a large nonstick skillet over medium-high heat. Coat pan with cooking spray. Add onions and shallots; cook 4 minutes or until golden. Remove onion mixture from pan; set aside. Add spinach to pan; cook 6 minutes or until wilted, stirring occasionally. Place spinach in a colander. Add arugula and beet greens to pan; cook 3 minutes or until wilted. Place arugula mixture on top of spinach in colander, and drain, pressing until barely moist.
3. Combine onion mixture, spinach mixture, and cheeses in a large bowl. Stir in parsley and next 4 ingredients.
4. Place one sheet of phyllo dough on a large cutting board or work surface (cover remaining dough to keep from drying); lightly coat with cooking spray. Place sheet in a 10-inch deep-dish pie

plate coated with cooking spray, gently pressing into bottom and up sides of pan, letting ends of phyllo overlap top of pan. Repeat procedure with remaining phyllo sheets, placing in a crisscross pattern. Spoon spinach mixture evenly over phyllo. Fold overlapping ends of phyllo toward center of pan. Coat ends of phyllo with cooking spray, and gently press to hold shape.

5. Bake at 375° for 40 minutes or until golden. Cool 15 minutes on a wire rack; cut into wedges. Yield: 4 servings (serving size: 1 wedge).

CALORIES 250 (26% from fat); FAT 7.3g (sat 3.6g, mono 2.6g, poly 0.6g); PROTEIN 13.4g; CARB 32.9g; FIBER 5.5g; CHOL 18mg; IRON 5.5mg; SODIUM 739mg; CALC 365mg

Sicilian-Style Greens over Polenta

You can use any combination of dark green, leafy vegetables to equal 12 cups.

Cooking spray
4 cups chopped Belgian endive (about 4 ounces)
4 cups chopped kale (about 4 ounces)
4 cups chopped turnip greens (about 4 ounces)
1/3 cup golden raisins
1/4 teaspoon salt
1 cup yellow cornmeal
1/4 teaspoon crushed red pepper
2 cups organic vegetable broth (such as Swanson Certified Organic)
1 cup fat-free milk
1/2 cup (2 ounces) grated fresh Parmesan cheese, divided
2 teaspoons olive oil
1 garlic clove, thinly sliced
1/4 cup dry breadcrumbs
4 teaspoons pine nuts, toasted

1. Heat a large nonstick skillet over medium heat. Coat pan with cooking spray. Add endive; cook 1 minute or until endive begins to wilt, stirring constantly. Add kale; cook 1 minute or until

kale begins to wilt, stirring constantly. Add turnip greens; cook 1 minute or until greens begin to wilt. Stir in raisins and salt. Cover, reduce heat, and simmer 6 minutes or until greens are tender; set mixture aside.

2. Combine cornmeal and pepper in a saucepan over medium-high heat. Gradually add broth and milk, stirring with whisk; bring to boil. Cover, reduce heat, and simmer 10 minutes; stir occasionally. Add 1/4 cup cheese.

3. Heat oil in a small skillet over medium heat. Add garlic; cook 1 minute or until lightly browned, stirring constantly. Stir in breadcrumbs; cook 1 minute or until golden brown, stirring frequently. Remove from heat; stir in 1/4 cup cheese.

4. Spoon 1 cup polenta onto each of 4 plates; top each serving with 1 cup greens mixture. Sprinkle each with 2 tablespoons breadcrumb mixture and 1 teaspoon pine nuts. Yield: 4 servings.

CALORIES 336 (20% from fat); FAT 7.3g (sat 2.4g, mono 2.6g, poly 1.6g); PROTEIN 12.3g; CARB 55.8g; FIBER 5.4g; CHOL 10mg; IRON 3.7mg; SODIUM 662mg; CALC 340mg

Clean Greens

Store greens unwashed in plastic bags in the refrigerator crisper; any added moisture will cause them to spoil more rapidly. Use within five days of purchasing. When you're ready to prepare them, remove unwanted stems and tear the leaves into small pieces.

Simply running the greens under cold water in the sink in a colander isn't enough to remove grit. Instead, dunk them in a large bowl or sink filled with cold water. The dirt will sink to the bottom while the greens rise to the top. Remove the greens by hand, and repeat the procedure. Dunking and soaking is the only method that removes all the dirt. Next, spin the greens in a large salad spinner unless the recipe calls for cooking the greens. In that case, cook them with the water that clings to them.

Cucumber and Arugula-Stuffed Pitas with Mimosa Vinaigrette

The term "mimosa" is most often associated with the drink made from orange juice and Champagne. But a garnish including a hard-cooked egg yolk, such as in the dressing for this sandwich, is also referred to as mimosa.

2 tablespoons finely chopped pepperoncini peppers
2 tablespoons goat cheese, softened
1 tablespoon water
1 tablespoon fresh lemon juice
1 1/2 teaspoons olive oil
1/4 teaspoon salt
1/4 teaspoon freshly ground black pepper
1 hard-cooked large egg, grated
1 garlic clove, minced
2 cups chopped arugula
1 cup chopped romaine lettuce
8 (1/4-inch-thick) slices tomato
4 (6-inch) whole wheat pitas, cut in half
1 cup (1/4-inch-thick) slices peeled cucumber

1. Combine first 9 ingredients in a large bowl; add arugula and romaine lettuce, tossing gently to coat.

2. Place 1 tomato slice in each pita half; divide cucumber slices evenly among pita halves. Place about 1/4 cup arugula mixture in each pita half. Yield: 4 servings (serving size: 2 pita halves).

CALORIES 251 (22% from fat); FAT 6.1g (sat 1.7g, mono 2.3g, poly 1.2g); PROTEIN 10.1g; CARB 42.8g; FIBER 6.4g; CHOL 56mg; IRON 3.1mg; SODIUM 736mg; CALC 61mg

Pasta with Beans and Greens

This recipe comes together quickly; prepare the cheese sauce while the pasta and green beans are cooking. Combine both mixtures right before serving to retain the dish's creamy consistency.

    8   ounces uncooked cavatappi
    2   cups (1-inch) cut green beans
        (about 12 ounces)
    1   tablespoon butter
    2   tablespoons all-purpose flour
    3   cups 1% low-fat milk
    ¾   cup (3 ounces) grated fresh
        Parmesan cheese
    ½   teaspoon salt
    ⅛   teaspoon black pepper
    ⅛   teaspoon crushed red pepper
    2   garlic cloves, crushed
    3   cups coarsely chopped spinach
        (about 3 ounces)
    3   cups coarsely chopped kale (about
        4 ounces)
    ⅓   cup chopped fresh mint
    ¼   cup (1 ounce) shaved fresh
        Parmesan cheese

1. Cook pasta according to package directions, omitting salt and fat. Add beans to pan halfway through cooking time. Drain well.
2. Melt butter in a medium saucepan over medium heat. Add flour, stirring with a whisk. Gradually add milk; cook until slightly thick and bubbly (about 8 minutes), stirring constantly with a whisk. Add grated Parmesan cheese and next 4 ingredients, stirring until cheese melts. Keep warm.
3. Combine pasta mixture, spinach, kale, and mint in a large bowl. Stir in milk mixture, tossing gently to coat. Spoon 1½ cups pasta mixture onto each of 6 plates; top each serving with 2 teaspoons shaved Parmesan cheese. Serve immediately. Yield: 6 servings.

CALORIES 328 (25% from fat); FAT 9g (sat 5.3g, mono 2.4g, poly 0.6g); PROTEIN 18.4g; CARB 44.4g; FIBER 3.9g; CHOL 23mg; IRON 3.4mg; SODIUM 607mg; CALC 462mg

in season

Green, Gold, and Glorious

Delicate and velvety, the avocado needs little coaxing to shine.

It's hard to think of the avocado as a fruit—a berry, in fact, marked by a single large seed—partly because it's so often used in salads, sandwiches, and other savory dishes. Yet between its nutty, subtle taste and buttery, sensuous texture, the avocado distinguishes itself as one of nature's most sublime fruits.

Roasted Garlic, Poblano, and Red Pepper Guacamole

When storing this guacamole, press plastic wrap against its surface to help keep it from oxidizing and turning brown. You can use it to liven up a turkey sandwich or as a condiment in a vegetable wrap. If time is tight, serve with baked tortilla chips.

GUACAMOLE:

    6   garlic cloves, unpeeled
    1   red bell pepper
    1   poblano pepper
    ¼   cup finely chopped green onions
    2   tablespoons chopped fresh cilantro
    2   teaspoons fresh lime juice
    ¼   teaspoon kosher salt
    1   ripe peeled avocado, seeded and
        coarsely mashed

CHIPS:

    6   (6-inch) corn tortillas, each cut
        into 8 wedges
    2   teaspoons fresh lime juice
    ¼   teaspoon kosher salt
        Cooking spray

1. Preheat oven to 450°.
2. To prepare guacamole, wrap garlic cloves in foil; bake at 450° for 15 minutes or until soft. Let cool slightly; remove skins. Place garlic in a medium bowl; mash with a fork.

3. Preheat broiler.
4. Cut peppers in half lengthwise; discard seeds and membranes. Place pepper halves, skin sides up, on a foil-lined baking sheet; flatten with hand. Broil 15 minutes or until blackened, turning frequently. Place in a zip-top plastic bag; seal. Let stand 10 minutes. Peel and finely chop. Add peppers, onions, and next 4 ingredients to garlic; stir well.
5. Reduce heat to 425°.
6. To prepare chips, combine tortilla wedges, 2 teaspoons juice, and ¼ teaspoon salt in a large bowl, tossing to coat. Arrange tortillas in a single layer on a baking sheet coated with cooking spray. Bake at 425° for 10 minutes or until crisp and lightly browned, turning once. Cool 5 minutes. Serve with guacamole. Yield: 8 servings (serving size: 2½ tablespoons guacamole and 6 chips).

CALORIES 87 (38% from fat); FAT 3.7g (sat 1g, mono 1.9g, poly 0.8g); PROTEIN 2.1g; CARB 13.2g; FIBER 3.1g; CHOL 0mg; IRON 0.4mg; SODIUM 151mg; CALC 40mg

Mango-Avocado Margarita

Rub the rim of each glass with a lime wedge, then coat rims with salt and chili powder.

    2   cups ice cubes
    1   cup chopped peeled mango
        (about 1 large)
    6   tablespoons chopped ripe peeled
        avocado
    6   tablespoons fresh lime juice
    ¼   cup tequila
    ¼   cup orange juice
    2   tablespoons sugar
    2   tablespoons Triple Sec (orange-
        flavored liqueur)
    4   lime wedges (optional)

1. Place first 8 ingredients in a blender; process until smooth.
2. Pour mixture into 4 glasses. Serve drinks with lime wedges, if desired. Serve immediately. Yield: 4 servings (serving size: 1 cup).

CALORIES 162 (22% from fat); FAT 4g (sat 1.1g, mono 2.1g, poly 0.7g); PROTEIN 1.1g; CARB 23g; FIBER 1.7g; CHOL 0mg; IRON 0.1mg; SODIUM 2mg; CALC 10mg

Assorted Avocados

The hundreds of avocado varieties break down into three distinct species: Mexican (smallest, highest oil content), Guatemalan (medium), and West Indian (largest, leanest).

Hass avocados are by far Mexico's most popular variety. A hybrid of Mexican and Guatemalan species, Hass avocados typically weigh between four and eight ounces, and have pebbly skin that turns from dark green to nearly black as they ripen.

Fuerte avocados, also a Mexican-Guatemalan hybrid, feature a more classic pear shape than Hass fruits and smooth, shiny skins that grow dull and spotted as they ripen.

Reed avocados are larger and rounder than other California avocados. Reeds maintain their firmness even when they're ripe.

Florida avocados are mostly West Indian in origin. These varieties have smooth skin and grow to be much larger than their California counterparts. Booth, Lula, Simmonds, and Taylor are among the more popular Florida varieties.

Selecting and Storing Avocados

To choose ripe avocados, look for avocados that yield slightly to the touch. They should feel heavy for their size, and solid; the skin shouldn't be pulling away from the flesh, and the pit shouldn't rattle when the fruit is shaken. The skin on Hass avocados will have a dark brownish-black color when ripe.

To ripen avocados at home, choose unblemished fruits that feel firm to the touch. Accelerate the ripening process by storing them in a closed paper bag.

Once ripe, you can keep whole avocados in the refrigerator for up to a week. Sliced avocados will keep for up to three days. Squeeze lemon or lime juice on a cut avocado to prevent discoloration, and cover tightly with plastic wrap.

Red Snapper Cakes with Avocado-Tomatillo Sauce

Serve with roasted new potatoes and asparagus.

SAUCE:

    4 garlic cloves, peeled
    1 tomatillo, husked and quartered
       (about 3 ounces)
    ½ Vidalia or other sweet onion,
       quartered
    ½ jalapeño pepper, seeded
       Cooking spray
    9 tablespoons chopped ripe peeled
       avocado
    ¼ cup fresh cilantro leaves
    1 tablespoon fresh lime juice
    ½ teaspoon salt

CAKES:

    3 (1-ounce) slices bread
    ½ cup finely chopped Vidalia or
       other sweet onion
    ½ cup finely chopped red bell pepper
    2 tablespoons chopped fresh
       cilantro
    2 tablespoons capers, drained
    2 tablespoons fat-free mayonnaise
    ½ teaspoon salt
    ½ teaspoon ground coriander
    ¼ teaspoon freshly ground black
       pepper
   14 ounces finely chopped skinless
       red snapper
    2 large egg whites, lightly beaten
    1 teaspoon butter

1. Preheat broiler.
2. To prepare sauce, combine first 4 ingredients on a jelly-roll pan coated with cooking spray. Broil 12 minutes or until blackened, stirring once. Cool slightly. Place tomatillo mixture in a blender; add avocado, ¼ cup cilantro, juice, and ½ teaspoon salt. Process until smooth. Cover and chill.
3. Preheat oven to 400°.
4. To prepare cakes, place bread in a food processor; pulse 10 times or until coarse crumbs measure 2 cups. Combine 1 cup breadcrumbs, ½ cup onion, and next 9 ingredients in a large bowl; stir until well blended. Divide snapper mixture into 12 equal portions (about ¼ cup each), shaping

each into a ½-inch-thick patty. Dredge patties in 1 cup breadcrumbs.
5. Melt butter in a large nonstick skillet coated with cooking spray over medium heat. Add cakes; cook 2 minutes on each side or until browned. Wrap handle of pan with foil; place in oven. Bake cakes at 400° for 8 minutes or until cooked through. Spoon about 2½ tablespoons sauce on each of 6 plates; top sauce with 2 cakes. Yield: 6 servings.

CALORIES 261 (34% from fat); FAT 9.9g (sat 2g, mono 4.4g, poly 2g); PROTEIN 17.3g; CARB 27.7g; FIBER 3g; CHOL 27mg; IRON 0.8mg; SODIUM 588mg; CALC 55mg

Chilled Avocado Soup with Tortilla Chips

    1 cup canned cannellini beans,
       rinsed and drained
    1 cup chopped peeled cucumber
    ½ cup fat-free buttermilk
    1 tablespoon fresh lime juice
    ⅛ teaspoon chipotle chile powder
    1 (14-ounce) can fat-free,
       less-sodium chicken broth
    1 ripe peeled avocado
    ½ teaspoon salt, divided
    1 tablespoon chopped fresh cilantro
    2 (6-inch) corn tortillas, halved and
       cut into ⅛-inch-thick strips
       Cooking spray
    ⅛ teaspoon ground cumin
    ⅛ teaspoon chipotle chile powder

1. Place first 7 ingredients in a blender; add ¼ teaspoon salt. Process until smooth; stir in ⅛ teaspoon salt and cilantro. Cover and chill 2 hours.
2. Preheat oven to 400°.
3. Lightly coat tortilla strips with cooking spray. Combine ⅛ teaspoon salt, cumin, and ⅛ teaspoon chile powder in a small bowl; sprinkle cumin mixture over strips, tossing gently to coat. Arrange strips in a single layer on a baking sheet. Bake at 400° for 5 minutes or until crisp. Cool in pan. Place 1 cup soup in each of 4 bowls; top evenly with tortilla strips. Yield: 4 servings.

CALORIES 152 (49% from fat); FAT 8.2g (sat 2.2g, mono 4.3g, poly 1.6g); PROTEIN 6.2g; CARB 18.4g; FIBER 4.5g; CHOL 0mg; IRON 1.2mg; SODIUM 576mg; CALC 89mg

Seafood Avocado Salad with Ginger

If serving this salad chilled, add the avocado just before tossing it with the lime juice mixture. If bay scallops aren't available, substitute coarsely chopped sea scallops.

       2 quarts water
      ¾ pound large shrimp, peeled and
          deveined
      ¾ pound bay scallops
       1 cup chopped celery
       1 cup chopped cucumber
      ½ cup chopped carrot
      ½ cup chopped green onions
      ½ pound coarsely chopped cooked
          lobster meat
       1 finely chopped peeled ripe
          avocado
       3 tablespoons fresh lime juice
       2 tablespoons chopped fresh
          cilantro
       1 tablespoon sugar
       1 tablespoon seasoned rice vinegar
       1 tablespoon fish sauce
       2 teaspoons grated peeled fresh
          ginger
       1 teaspoon Thai roasted chile paste
       6 cups trimmed arugula

1. Bring 2 quarts water to a boil in a large saucepan; reduce heat to medium, and simmer. Add shrimp; cook 3 minutes or until done. Remove shrimp with a slotted spoon. Add scallops to pan; cook 3 minutes or until done. Drain; cool 10 minutes. Combine shrimp, scallops, celery, and next 5 ingredients in a large bowl; toss well.
2. Combine lime juice and next 6 ingredients in a medium bowl, stirring with a whisk. Add cilantro mixture to shrimp mixture, tossing to coat.
3. Place 1 cup arugula on each of 6 plates; top each with about 1 cup seafood mixture. Yield: 6 servings.

CALORIES 232 (27% from fat); FAT 7g (sat 2.1g, mono 2.8g, poly 1.4g); PROTEIN 30.5g; CARB 12g; FIBER 3.7g; CHOL 134mg; IRON 2.1mg; SODIUM 658mg; CALC 115mg

Seared Shrimp Cocktail with Tropical Chipotle-Avocado Salsa

This dish makes an impressive first course for a dinner party. Shrimp picks up flavor quickly and doesn't need to marinate for more than half an hour.

    1½ cups finely chopped fresh
          pineapple
       9 tablespoons chopped peeled ripe
          avocado
      ½ cup finely chopped tomato
      ⅓ cup chopped green onions
       2 tablespoons chopped fresh basil
       2 teaspoons fresh lemon juice
       1 teaspoon minced chipotle chile,
          canned in adobo sauce
      ½ teaspoon sugar
      ½ teaspoon salt, divided
      30 large unpeeled shrimp (about
          1½ pounds)
       1 tablespoon dry sherry
       1 tablespoon low-sodium soy sauce
      ½ teaspoon ground cumin
       3 garlic cloves, minced
       2 teaspoons olive oil
       6 lime wedges (optional)

1. Combine first 8 ingredients in a medium bowl; stir in ¼ teaspoon salt. Cover and chill.
2. Peel and devein shrimp, leaving tails intact. Combine shrimp, sherry, and next 3 ingredients in a large zip-top plastic bag; seal and shake to coat shrimp. Marinate in refrigerator 30 minutes.
3. Heat oil in a large nonstick skillet over medium-high heat. Remove shrimp from bag; discard marinade. Add shrimp to pan; sprinkle with ¼ teaspoon salt. Cook 2 minutes on each side or until shrimp are done. Spoon ⅓ cup salsa into each of 6 martini glasses; place 5 shrimp on rim of each glass. Garnish each glass with a lime wedge, if desired. Yield: 6 servings.

CALORIES 197 (34% from fat); FAT 7.4g (sat 1.6g, mono 3.5g, poly 1.6g); PROTEIN 24.3g; CARB 9.7g; FIBER 1.8g; CHOL 172mg; IRON 3.1mg; SODIUM 467mg; CALC 76mg

Blackened Chicken and Grilled Avocado Tacos

The avocado will dry slightly in the pan, intensifying its flavor. Choose a ripe but firm avocado so it will hold its shape as it cooks.

       4 (6-ounce) skinless, boneless
          chicken breast halves
       1 tablespoon paprika
       1 teaspoon ground cumin
       1 teaspoon dried oregano
      ¾ teaspoon sugar
      ¾ teaspoon garlic powder
      ½ teaspoon salt
      ½ teaspoon dried thyme
      ¼ teaspoon ground red pepper
       1 tablespoon fresh lime juice
       1 ripe peeled avocado, cut into
          16 slices
          Cooking spray
       8 (6-inch) corn tortillas
       2 cups shredded romaine lettuce
       1 cup bottled low-sodium salsa
          (such as Green Mountain Gringo)
      ¼ cup fat-free sour cream
      ¼ cup finely chopped red onion

1. Place chicken between 2 sheets of plastic wrap; pound to ½-inch thickness using a meat mallet or small heavy skillet. Combine paprika and next 7 ingredients in a small bowl. Sprinkle evenly over chicken; let stand 10 minutes.
2. Combine juice and avocado in a medium bowl, tossing to coat. Heat a grill pan over medium-high heat. Coat pan with cooking spray. Grill avocado 2 minutes on each side or until well marked; remove from pan.
3. Place chicken in pan. Cook 4 minutes on each side or until done. Let chicken stand 5 minutes; cut chicken crosswise into ¼-inch-thick slices.
4. Warm tortillas according to package directions. Divide chicken evenly among tortillas; top each with 2 avocado slices, ¼ cup lettuce, 2 tablespoons salsa, 1½ teaspoons sour cream, and 1½ teaspoons onion. Yield: 4 servings (serving size: 2 tacos).

CALORIES 423 (25% from fat); FAT 11.6g (sat 3g, mono 5.1g, poly 2.6g); PROTEIN 45.2g; CARB 38g; FIBER 5.7g; CHOL 100mg; IRON 3mg; SODIUM 675mg; CALC 158mg

Spice Rubs

Easy spice rubs punch up the flavor on the grill.

Spice Rub Menu 1

serves 4

Pork Chops with Carolina Rub

Stove-top barbecue beans*

Coleslaw

*Melt 1 tablespoon butter in a saucepan over medium-high heat. Add ½ cup chopped onion and 1 minced garlic clove; sauté 3 minutes. Stir in ⅓ cup ketchup, 2 tablespoons brown sugar, 2 tablespoons prepared mustard, 2 tablespoons fresh lemon juice, 2 tablespoons low-sodium soy sauce, 1 teaspoon chili powder, and 2 (15.5-ounce) cans drained and rinsed Great Northern beans. Cook 10 minutes, stirring occasionally.

Game Plan

1. While grill heats:
- Prepare seasoning mixture
- Season pork
- Let pork stand
- Chop and measure ingredients for beans

2. While pork stands:
- Prepare beans
- Toss slaw

QUICK & EASY
Pork Chops with Carolina Rub

Season the pork chops and let them stand about 10 minutes before they're grilled. This allows the meat time to absorb the flavorful spice rub. For a nice side dish to accompany these pork chops, consider purchasing preshredded coleslaw mix and low-fat bottled dressing from the supermarket.

TOTAL TIME: 42 MINUTES

1 teaspoon garlic powder
1 teaspoon onion powder
1 teaspoon sugar
1 teaspoon paprika
1 teaspoon chili powder
1 teaspoon freshly ground black pepper
½ teaspoon salt
4 (4-ounce) center-cut pork loin chops
Cooking spray
¼ cup barbecue sauce

1. Prepare grill.
2. Combine first 7 ingredients in a small bowl. Rub pork with spice mixture; let stand 10 minutes.
3. Place pork on grill rack coated with cooking spray. Grill 4 minutes. Turn pork; grill 2 minutes. Brush each chop with 1 tablespoon sauce, and grill 2 minutes or until desired degree of doneness. Yield: 4 servings (serving size: 1 pork chop).

CALORIES 185 (34% from fat); FAT 6.9g (sat 2.4g, mono 3g, poly 0.7g); PROTEIN 24.6g; CARB 5g; FIBER 0.8g; CHOL 65mg; IRON 1.1mg; SODIUM 477mg; CALC 35mg

Spice Rub Menu 2

serves 4

Grilled Beef and Pepper Sandwich

Vegetable chips

Pineapple shake*

*Place 4 scoops vanilla low-fat ice cream, 3 cups 2% reduced-fat milk, 2 cups chopped fresh pineapple, 3 tablespoons brown sugar, and ½ teaspoon vanilla extract in a blender; process until smooth.

Game Plan

1. While grill heats:
- Prepare seasoning mixture for steak
- Season steak
- Let steak stand
- Halve and seed peppers

2. While steak and peppers cook:
- Prepare mayonnaise mixture

3. While steak and peppers stand:
- Prepare shake

4. Assemble sandwiches.

QUICK & EASY
Grilled Beef and Pepper Sandwich

TOTAL TIME: 45 MINUTES

2 teaspoons grated lemon rind
1 teaspoon dried rosemary
1 teaspoon olive oil
1 teaspoon Dijon mustard
½ teaspoon freshly ground black pepper
¼ teaspoon salt
2 garlic cloves, minced
1 (1-pound) flank steak, trimmed
Cooking spray
2 red bell peppers
⅓ cup reduced-fat mayonnaise
3 tablespoons finely grated Parmesan cheese
1 tablespoon fresh lemon juice
1 garlic clove, minced
1 (10-ounce) round focaccia bread, cut in half horizontally

1. Prepare grill.
2. Combine first 7 ingredients in a small bowl. Rub spice mixture over one side of steak; let stand 10 minutes.
3. Place steak on grill rack coated with cooking spray, and grill 8 minutes on each side or until desired degree of doneness. Let steak stand 10 minutes. Cut steak diagonally across grain into thin slices.
4. Cut bell peppers in half lengthwise; discard seeds and membranes. Flatten peppers with hand. Place peppers, skin-side down, on grill rack; grill 12 minutes or until blackened. Place peppers in a zip-top plastic bag; seal. Let stand 10 minutes. Peel and cut each half into quarters.
5. Combine mayonnaise, cheese, juice, and 1 garlic clove in a small bowl, stirring well. Spread about ¼ cup mayonnaise mixture onto cut side of each bread half. Arrange beef evenly over bottom half; top with peppers. Cover with top bread half, pressing gently. Cut sandwich into 4 wedges. Yield: 4 servings (serving size: 1 wedge).

CALORIES 427 (29% from fat); FAT 13.9g (sat 4.6g, mono 5.9g, poly 2.4g); PROTEIN 31g; CARB 45.3g; FIBER 2.8g; CHOL 47.9mg; IRON 4.2mg; SODIUM 719mg; CALC 69mg

Spice Rub Menu 3

serves 4

Roadhouse Steaks with Ancho Chile Rub

Mashed potatoes

Iceberg wedges with creamy blue cheese dressing*

*Cut a small head of iceberg lettuce into 8 wedges. Rinse under cold water; drain. Arrange 2 lettuce wedges on each of 4 plates; top each serving with 6 quartered cherry tomatoes. Combine ⅓ cup low-fat buttermilk, 3 tablespoons reduced-fat mayonnaise, 2 tablespoons white wine vinegar, and ¼ teaspoon salt, stirring well with a whisk. Stir in 2 tablespoons crumbled blue cheese. Drizzle dressing evenly over salads.

Game Plan

1. While grill heats:
- Prepare seasoning mixture
- Season steaks
- Let steaks stand
- Chop and measure ingredients for salad

2. While steaks stand:
- Prepare salad
- Prepare potatoes

QUICK & EASY

Roadhouse Steaks with Ancho Chile Rub

Ancho chile powder is made from ground, smoked, dried poblano peppers; it gives this rub a subtle smoky heat. For a milder flavor, cut back on the ground black pepper or ancho chile powder, and omit the ground red pepper.

TOTAL TIME: 32 MINUTES

- 4 teaspoons Worcestershire sauce
- 1 tablespoon freshly ground black pepper
- 2 teaspoons ancho chile powder
- 1 teaspoon Dijon mustard
- ½ teaspoon salt
- ½ teaspoon ground cumin
- ⅛ teaspoon ground red pepper
- 2 garlic cloves, minced
- 4 (4-ounce) beef tenderloin steaks, trimmed
- Cooking spray

1. Prepare grill.

2. Combine first 8 ingredients in a small bowl. Rub spice mixture evenly over steaks; let stand 10 minutes.

3. Place steaks on a grill rack coated with cooking spray. Grill 5 minutes on each side or until desired degree of doneness. Yield: 4 servings (serving size: 1 steak).

CALORIES 177 (36% from fat); FAT 7.1g (sat 2.4g, mono 2.6g, poly 0.4g); PROTEIN 22.3g; CARB 3.9g; FIBER 1g; CHOL 59mg; IRON 2.1mg; SODIUM 441mg; CALC 34mg

Spice Rub Menu 4

serves 4

Spice-Rubbed Pork Skewers with Tomatoes

Peanutty couscous*

Limeade

*Place 1½ cups fat-free, less-sodium chicken broth in a 1½-quart casserole dish. Cover and microwave at HIGH 3 minutes. Stir in 1 (5.7-ounce) box couscous. Cover and let stand 5 minutes. In a small bowl, combine 3 tablespoons low-sodium soy sauce, 1 tablespoon peanut oil, ½ teaspoon crushed red pepper, and ¼ teaspoon garlic powder. Fluff couscous with a fork; stir in soy mixture, 2 tablespoons chopped roasted peanuts, and 2 sliced green onions.

Game Plan

1. While grill heats:
- Prepare seasoning mixture
- Slice pork
- Season pork
- Let pork stand

2. While pork stands:
- Prepare couscous

3. While couscous stands:
- Grill pork skewers

QUICK & EASY

Spice-Rubbed Pork Skewers with Tomatoes

If using wooden skewers, soak them in about two inches of water for approximately 15 minutes while the grill heats, and pat them dry before adding the meat and tomatoes. This prevents the skewers from burning on the grill.

TOTAL TIME: 40 MINUTES

- 1 tablespoon brown sugar
- 1 teaspoon ground coriander
- ½ teaspoon garlic powder
- ½ teaspoon freshly ground black pepper
- ¼ teaspoon salt
- ¼ teaspoon ground cumin
- ⅛ teaspoon ground ginger
- 1 (1-pound) pork tenderloin, trimmed
- 1 teaspoon chile paste
- 16 cherry tomatoes
- Cooking spray
- 2 tablespoons low-sodium soy sauce
- 1 teaspoon dark sesame oil

1. Prepare grill.

2. Combine first 7 ingredients. Cut pork in half crosswise; cut each half into 8 lengthwise strips. Combine pork strips and chile paste in a shallow dish; toss to coat. Sprinkle brown sugar mixture evenly over pork; toss to coat. Let pork stand 10 minutes.

3. Thread 1 pork strip and 1 tomato onto each of 16 (10-inch) wooden skewers. Place skewers on a grill rack coated with cooking spray. Grill 3 minutes on each side or until desired degree of doneness. Combine soy sauce and oil; drizzle over pork. Yield: 4 servings (serving size: 4 skewers).

CALORIES 196 (30% from fat); FAT 6.6g (sat 2g, mono 2.6g, poly 1g); PROTEIN 25.5g; CARB 8.2g; FIBER 1.2g; CHOL 75mg; IRON 1.8mg; SODIUM 507mg; CALC 18mg

Tasty Tagines

These aromatic Moroccan stews are one-pot meals good for casual get-togethers or supper any weeknight.

Just as the cook in many American kitchens has her own potato salad or apple pie recipe, in Morocco, the tagine is the dish defined household by household, and each family's recipe is a closely guarded secret. Preparing a tagine—basically a covered, braised stew—is an easy introduction to the flavors of Morocco. You can use any meat, poultry, or fish, flavored with a blend of aromatics such as paprika, ginger, or coriander and dressed up with fresh herbs.

The word "tagine" also refers to the glazed earthenware platter topped with a distinctive conical lid in which the food is cooked and served. But you don't need one; our recipes call for a Dutch oven to do the job. Nor do you have to trek to North Africa to fill your spice rack, since the warm and pungent seasonings used in a tagine—cinnamon, cumin, ground ginger, or turmeric—are available in any supermarket.

Zucchini Ribbons with Saffron Couscous

This easy side combines common flavors of Morocco: saffron-enhanced couscous balanced with zucchini and carrots.

    4   zucchini (about 2 pounds)
    2   tablespoons olive oil, divided
    ½   cup finely diced onion (about
        1 small)
    ½   cup finely diced carrot (about
        1 small)
    1   (14-ounce) can fat-free,
        less-sodium chicken broth
    1   teaspoon salt, divided
    ¼   teaspoon saffron threads, crushed
    ¼   teaspoon freshly ground black
        pepper, divided
    1¼ cups uncooked couscous
    ½   cup frozen green peas
    2   tablespoons chopped fresh
        cilantro

1. Using a vegetable peeler, shave zucchini into ribbons; set aside.
2. Heat 2 teaspoons oil over medium-high heat in a medium saucepan. Add onion and carrot; sauté 3 minutes. Add broth, ½ teaspoon salt, saffron, and ⅛ teaspoon pepper; bring to a boil. Stir in

couscous and peas. Remove from heat; cover and let stand 5 minutes. Fluff with a fork. Keep warm.
3. Heat 4 teaspoons oil in a large nonstick skillet over medium-high heat. Add zucchini ribbons, and sauté 1 minute or until tender. Stir in ½ teaspoon salt and ⅛ teaspoon pepper. Serve over couscous mixture. Sprinkle evenly with cilantro. Yield: 8 servings (serving size: ½ cup couscous, ¼ cup zucchini, and ¾ teaspoon cilantro).

CALORIES 169 (20% from fat); FAT 3.8g (sat 0.6g, mono 2.6g, poly 0.5g); PROTEIN 5.9g; CARB 28.3g; FIBER 3.6g; CHOL 0mg; IRON 1mg; SODIUM 414mg; CALC 34mg

QUICK & EASY • MAKE AHEAD
Ras el Hanout

Some versions of this complex Moroccan spice blend may contain up to 50 spices.

    2   teaspoons ground ginger
    2   teaspoons ground coriander
    1½ teaspoons ground cinnamon
    1½ teaspoons freshly ground black
        pepper
    1½ teaspoons ground turmeric
    1¼ teaspoons ground nutmeg
    1   teaspoon ground allspice
    ½   teaspoon ground cloves

1. Combine all ingredients; store in an airtight container. Yield: about 3½ tablespoons (serving size: 1 teaspoon).

CALORIES 9 (26% from fat); FAT 0.3g (sat 0.1g, mono 0.1g, poly 0.1g); PROTEIN 0.2g; CARB 1.6g; FIBER 0.8g; CHOL 0mg; IRON 0.4mg; SODIUM 1mg; CALC 12mg

Tagine of Chicken and Chickpeas

Use all chicken thighs or all chicken breasts, if you prefer. This savory tagine blends paprika, ginger, and turmeric to season the chicken and sauce.

    1   teaspoon Hungarian sweet
        paprika
    ½   teaspoon ground ginger
    ½   teaspoon ground turmeric
    ¼   teaspoon freshly ground black
        pepper
    1   pound skinless, boneless chicken
        breast halves
    1   pound skinless, boneless chicken
        thighs (about 4)
    1   tablespoon olive oil
    2   cups diced onion (about
        2 medium)
    2   cups chopped seeded plum
        tomato (about 3)
    ¼   teaspoon salt
    1   (15½-ounce) can chickpeas
        (garbanzo beans), rinsed and
        drained
    2   tablespoons chopped fresh
        cilantro

1. Combine first 4 ingredients in a small bowl; rub spice mixture evenly over chicken. Heat oil in a large nonstick skillet over medium-high heat. Add chicken to pan; cook 3 minutes on each side or until lightly browned. Transfer chicken to a cutting board; cool slightly. Cut into slices, and return to pan. Add onion; sauté 3 minutes. Add tomato and salt; cover and cook 15 minutes. Add chickpeas; cover and cook 15 minutes, stirring occasionally. Stir in cilantro. Yield: 4 servings (serving size: 1½ cups).

CALORIES 363 (24% from fat); FAT 9.7g (sat 1.6g, mono 4.5g, poly 2.6g); PROTEIN 44.9g; CARB 23g; FIBER 5.9g; CHOL 123mg; IRON 3.6mg; SODIUM 646mg; CALC 70mg

Familiar Technique

A tagine acquires its characteristic flavor from slow cooking and a blend of herbs and spices appropriate to the meat or fish. We've adapted our recipes to work in your kitchen by searing the meat to shorten the cooking time. After searing, the meat braises in the oven to absorb the flavors of the aromatics and broth. Even though a traditional sauce is mainly made up of water and oil or butter, we used low-fat broths to enhance the flavor of our tagines and to produce satisfying, healthful stews.

Authentic Yet Accessible Flavors

Certain ingredients are quintessentially Moroccan and give our dishes authentic flavor. We include a simple, versatile recipe for Ras el Hanout (recipe on page 145), a traditional blend of Moroccan spices that flavors our version of Turkey Kefta (recipe on page 148)—spicy-sweet meatballs simmered on a bed of caramelized onions—as well as a beef tagine. Another signature Moroccan flavoring, preserved lemon, imparts a unique pickled zest. You can purchase preserved lemon in larger grocery stores and ethnic markets, but we improvise by cooking chopped whole lemon, olive oil, water, and sugar for a fish tagine recipe. Saffron adds a typical Moroccan essence. We call for crushing and soaking saffron threads in liquid to release their unique and pungent flavors during cooking.

Besides the spices and seasonings that accent a tagine, various fruits and vegetables contribute to nuances on the theme. Depending upon the season, vine-ripened tomatoes, tender zucchini, sweet peas, fresh fava beans, or delicate fennel bulbs accompany morsels of beef, lamb, or chicken cooked in sauces redolent of saffron, ginger powder, cinnamon, or cumin. Many tagines also incorporate a delicate, sweet touch of honey, dates, figs, or apricots.

Preserved Lemon

If you purchase preserved or salted lemon for Moroccan cooking, make sure salt is the only added ingredient. You don't want other spices, herbs, or pickling spices to interfere with the flavor of a dish. Rinse the salted lemon to reduce the sodium content. You also can use the liquid in salad dressings (especially grated carrot or cucumber salads), add it to a tapenade with olives, chiles, and parsley, or use it to jazz up hummus.

Traditional Tools

You don't need special equipment to prepare tagines, but these items add authenticity:

- Look for a **tagine dish** at most cookware stores, Moroccan import stores, or via the Internet (at www.tagines.com, www.lecreuset.com, and www.surlatable.com). Cast iron, copper, and aluminum allow the best heat conduction. If you buy a traditional glazed earthenware tagine, you will need to season it before use. To do so, use a pastry brush to paint the glazed base with vegetable oil, and place it in a 200° oven until the oil is absorbed, which may take two to eight hours. Repeat the process at least once. Make sure to follow the manufacturer's instructions for cooking in and cleaning your tagine, and be aware that some tagines are for decorative purposes only. Since most tagine dishes generally hold a limited amount of food, consider following our lead and preparing the recipe in a Dutch oven. You can then serve it in a tagine dish.
- If you develop a taste for Moroccan cooking, you will want a vessel called a **couscoussière,** which is used to create the perfectly fluffy, lump-free pasta consumed across North Africa. This steamer can be purchased at www.berbertrading.com and www.surlatable.com. Two-tiered couscoussières allow you to cook a stew or meat in the lower tier, which then steams the couscous in the upper tier.

Simple Preparation

In addition to the subtle balance of flavors, the appeal of serving a tagine lies in its easy preparation. Our Test Kitchens provide these pointers to make tagines fail-safe.

- For tagines using stew meats with cinnamon, rub the meat with a blend of peppery-sweet spices and sear it before covering the Dutch oven and baking the dish. We used this method with the Tagine of Lamb and Apricots in Honey Sauce (recipe on page 147) because when cinnamon is sautéed with other aromatics, it tends to become ropelike and results in an undesirable grainy sauce.
- For some tagines—like the Beef Tagine with Dried Plums and Toasted Almonds (recipe on page 148)—we sautéed the aromatics first to release the spices' oils, which rendered a more robust flavor and a smooth-textured sauce.
- Because leaner cuts of stew meat tend to dry out, watch the tagine closely near the end of the cooking time. Check the sauce every 20 to 30 minutes to make sure it's not sticky or dry. Add water or broth by one-quarter cupfuls if the sauce seems overly thick; if too runny, remove the lid, increase the heat slightly, and allow the sauce to reduce.

Servicing the Meal

Round out your meal with a basket of warm flatbread and simple sides. We include recipes for several basic side dishes that can be prepared while the tagine bakes. Couscous is also an ideal accompaniment because the fluffy grains soak up the tagine sauce, and it's quite easy to prepare. Once the different components are ready, bring the Dutch oven to the table, and serve the tagine and the side dishes family style. After all, the tagine is a casual dish that is meant to be relished with friends and family.

Tagine of Lamb and Apricots in Honey Sauce

Prepare this tagine a day ahead, and you will be rewarded with more complex flavors. Wildflower honey provides an aromatic essence to this dish in lieu of the traditional orange-flower water. You can add one-quarter cupfuls of water or broth to the sauce during cooking if it's too thick. Serve with flatbread.

  1 teaspoon salt
  1 teaspoon ground turmeric
  ¾ teaspoon ground cinnamon
  ¼ teaspoon freshly ground black
     pepper
  2 pounds lamb stew meat
  2 teaspoons olive oil
  2 cups chopped onion (about
     2 medium)
  1 cup less-sodium beef broth
  ¼ cup honey
  1 (3-inch) cinnamon stick
  1 cup chopped dried apricots
  ¼ cup slivered almonds, toasted

1. Preheat oven to 425°.
2. Combine first 5 ingredients in a large bowl. Toss gently to coat. Heat oil in a Dutch oven over medium-high heat. Add lamb mixture; cook 5 minutes, browning on all sides and stirring frequently. Add onion, and cook 2 minutes, stirring once. Stir in broth, honey, and cinnamon stick. Cover and bake at 425° for 45 minutes. Stir in apricots, and bake 15 minutes. Discard cinnamon stick, and sprinkle evenly with almonds. Yield: 5 servings (serving size: 1 cup lamb mixture and about 2½ teaspoons almonds).

CALORIES 403 (33% from fat); FAT 15g (sat 5.1g, mono 7.3g, poly 1.5g); PROTEIN 40.5g; CARB 26.9g; FIBER 2.8g; CHOL 120mg; IRON 4.3mg; SODIUM 681mg; CALC 54mg

WINE NOTE: From cabernet sauvignon to syrah and Bordeaux to Rioja, there's hardly a red wine that doesn't work with lamb. In this dish, the savoriness of the lamb is underscored by the fruity sweetness of the apricots and honey. This goes well with zinfandel, a thick, rich wine that has a dense fruitiness of its own. Try Folie à Deux's 2002 zinfandel from Amador County, California ($18).

Fish Tagine with Preserved Lemon and Tomatoes

Firm white fish such as mahimahi, halibut, or sea bass are particularly good in this recipe. Use more or less saffron according to your taste. We suggest serving with basmati rice.

  Cooking spray
  2 tablespoons finely chopped whole
     lemon
  1 tablespoon water
  1 tablespoon olive oil, divided
  1 teaspoon sugar
  ⅛ teaspoon saffron threads, crushed
  3 tablespoons chopped fresh
     flat-leaf parsley
  3 tablespoons chopped fresh cilantro
  ¾ teaspoon salt
  ½ teaspoon Hungarian sweet paprika
  ½ teaspoon ground cumin
  ¼ teaspoon freshly ground black
     pepper
 12 pitted green olives, thinly sliced
  2 garlic cloves, minced
 1½ pounds mahimahi
  2 cups thinly sliced onion (about 1)
  4 cups coarsely chopped seeded
     tomato (about 2 pounds)
  Cilantro leaves (optional)

1. Heat a small nonstick skillet over medium-high heat. Coat pan with cooking spray. Add lemon, 1 tablespoon water, ½ teaspoon oil, and sugar; cook 3 minutes or until water evaporates and mixture just begins to brown, stirring frequently. Set aside.
2. Place 2½ teaspoons oil in a small microwave-safe bowl, and microwave at HIGH 10 seconds at a time just until oil is heated. Stir in saffron; let stand 10 minutes.
3. Combine lemon mixture, saffron mixture, parsley, and next 7 ingredients in a large zip-top plastic bag. Add fish to bag, and seal. Marinate in refrigerator 30 minutes, turning occasionally.
4. Preheat oven to 400°.
5. Layer 1 cup onion and 2 cups tomato on bottom of a 13 x 9–inch baking dish coated with cooking spray. Remove fish from bag, reserving marinade. Top tomato with fish; pour marinade over fish.

Cover with 2 cups tomato and 1 cup onion. Cover with foil. Bake at 400° for 40 minutes or until fish flakes easily when tested with a fork or until desired degree of doneness.
6. Transfer fish and vegetables to a serving platter. Drizzle remaining liquid over fish. Garnish with cilantro leaves, if desired. Serve immediately. Yield: 4 servings (serving size: 6 ounces fish, ¾ cup vegetable mixture, and about 1 tablespoon sauce).

CALORIES 290 (28% from fat); FAT 9g (sat 1.3g, mono 4.8g, poly 1.9g); PROTEIN 37.7g; CARB 14g; FIBER 3.1g; CHOL 54mg; IRON 2.5mg; SODIUM 794mg; CALC 124mg

Eggplant and Tomato Tagine

You can turn this flavorful topping for rice or couscous into a main dish by adding canned chickpeas.

 11 cups (¾-inch) cubed peeled
     eggplant (about 2 pounds)
  ¾ teaspoon salt, divided
  Cooking spray
  1 tablespoon olive oil
  1 cup finely diced red bell pepper
     (about 1 large)
  2 tablespoons tomato paste
  1 teaspoon Hungarian sweet
     paprika
  1 teaspoon ground cumin
  2 garlic cloves, minced
  1 (28-ounce) can diced tomatoes,
     undrained
  ¼ teaspoon freshly ground black
     pepper
  1 tablespoon fresh lemon juice

1. Sprinkle eggplant with ¼ teaspoon salt; let stand 20 minutes. Rinse; pat dry.
2. Preheat oven to 425°.
3. Place eggplant on a jelly-roll pan coated with cooking spray. Coat eggplant with cooking spray. Bake at 425° for 30 minutes or until eggplant is tender, stirring once.
4. Heat oil in a large nonstick skillet over medium-high heat. Add bell pepper to pan, and sauté 5 minutes or until soft. Set aside.

Continued

5. Combine tomato paste and next 4 ingredients in a small Dutch oven over medium-high heat. Bring to a boil; simmer 3 minutes. Add eggplant to pan; cook 5 minutes. Add ½ teaspoon salt and black pepper. Stir in juice; garnish with bell pepper. Yield: 6 servings (serving size: 1 cup tomato mixture and about 2 tablespoons bell pepper).

CALORIES 98 (25% from fat); FAT 2.7g (sat 0.4g, mono 1.7g, poly 0.4g); PROTEIN 3.3g; CARB 18.3g; FIBER 8.1g; CHOL 0mg; IRON 1.1mg; SODIUM 373mg; CALC 42mg

Fennel with Sweet Onion in Tomato Vinaigrette

Fennel is a pale green bulb with long stalks that is often mistaken for celery, but its feathery fronds and flavor are distinctive. Avoid fennel with flowering buds, which indicate that it's too mature. Store it wrapped in plastic in the crisper drawer of your refrigerator for up to four days. To cut down on prep time, use a mandoline or food processor to slice the fennel.

1 cup chopped peeled plum tomato (about 2)
2 tablespoons white wine vinegar
2 teaspoons extravirgin olive oil
1 teaspoon ground cumin
½ teaspoon salt
¼ teaspoon freshly ground black pepper
1 garlic clove, minced
3 cups thinly sliced fennel bulb (about 1 medium)
2 cups thinly sliced Vidalia or other sweet onion (about 2 medium)
2 tablespoons chopped fresh parsley
1 tablespoon fresh lemon juice
8 kalamata olives, pitted and quartered

1. Place tomato in a medium bowl; mash lightly with back of a spoon. Add vinegar and next 5 ingredients to bowl; toss to combine. Add fennel and remaining ingredients; cover and chill. Yield: 6 servings (serving size: about 1 cup).

CALORIES 63 (44% from fat); FAT 3.1g (sat 0.4g, mono 2.1g, poly 0.4g); PROTEIN 1.5g; CARB 8.4g; FIBER 2.8g; CHOL 0mg; IRON 0.9mg; SODIUM 313mg; CALC 43mg

Beef Tagine with Dried Plums and Toasted Almonds

Dried plums and honey sweeten this tagine's sauce.

1 tablespoon olive oil
2 teaspoons Ras el Hanout (recipe on page 145)
1½ pounds boneless sirloin steak, cut into 1-inch cubes
2 cups chopped onion (about 2 medium)
1 cup water
1½ teaspoons salt
1 (14-ounce) can less-sodium beef broth
1½ cups pitted dried plums
3 tablespoons honey
⅓ cup slivered almonds, toasted

1. Preheat oven to 425°.
2. Heat oil in a Dutch oven over medium-high heat. Add Ras el Hanout; cook 30 seconds, stirring constantly. Add beef; cook 3 minutes. Add onion, water, salt, and broth. Cover and bake at 425° for 1 hour. Stir in plums and honey; cook 15 minutes. Sprinkle with almonds. Yield: 6 servings (serving size: ¾ cup beef mixture and about 2½ teaspoons almonds).

CALORIES 352 (29% from fat); FAT 11.3g (sat 2.5g, mono 6.2g, poly 1.4g); PROTEIN 29.6g; CARB 34.3g; FIBER 4.4g; CHOL 49mg; IRON 2.5mg; SODIUM 772mg; CALC 69mg

QUICK & EASY • MAKE AHEAD
Grated Carrots with Cumin-Orange Dressing

½ teaspoon ground cumin
3 cups grated carrot
¼ cup golden raisins
3 tablespoons fresh orange juice
1 tablespoon fresh lemon juice
1 tablespoon chopped fresh parsley
1 tablespoon chopped fresh cilantro
2 teaspoons olive oil
¼ teaspoon salt

1. Place cumin in a small skillet. Cook over medium heat 2 minutes or until toasted and fragrant, stirring frequently.

2. Combine cumin, carrot, and remaining ingredients in a bowl. Cover and chill. Yield: 6 servings (serving size: ½ cup).

CALORIES 62 (25% from fat); FAT 1.7g (sat 0.2g, mono 1.1g, poly 0.2g); PROTEIN 0.9g; CARB 11.9g; FIBER 1.9g; CHOL 0mg; IRON 0.4mg; SODIUM 138mg; CALC 25mg

Turkey Kefta with Sweet Onion and Raisin Sauce

In Morocco, the word *kefta* refers to ground meat—usually turkey, beef, or lamb. Serve with rice or couscous.

4 cups thinly vertically sliced Vidalia or other sweet onion
½ cup raisins
¾ teaspoon salt
½ teaspoon black pepper
½ teaspoon Ras el Hanout (recipe on page 145)
1 (14-ounce) can fat-free, less-sodium chicken broth
½ cup finely chopped fresh parsley
¼ cup dry breadcrumbs
1 teaspoon salt
½ teaspoon Ras el Hanout
½ teaspoon freshly ground black pepper
1 egg, lightly beaten
1¼ pounds ground turkey breast
¼ cup slivered almonds, toasted

1. Combine first 6 ingredients in a Dutch oven; bring to a boil. Reduce heat, and simmer 10 minutes or until sauce thickens, stirring occasionally.

2. Combine parsley and next 6 ingredients in a large bowl; shape mixture into 20 meatballs. Place meatballs on top of onion mixture; cover and cook 20 minutes or until done. Sprinkle evenly with almonds. Yield: 4 servings (serving size: 5 meatballs, ½ cup onion mixture, and 1 tablespoon almonds).

CALORIES 246 (19% from fat); FAT 5.2g (sat 0.8g, mono 2.7g, poly 1.1g); PROTEIN 27.6g; CARB 22g; FIBER 3.1g; CHOL 94mg; IRON 2.4mg; SODIUM 857mg; CALC 68mg

Choosing Foods That Are Right For You

To learn what—and how much—you should eat, using the USDA's free interactive Web site can help.

It was good news when the U.S. Departments of Agriculture and Health and Human Services released the updated Dietary Guidelines for Americans last year. First, the guidelines acknowledged that everyone has different dietary needs, depending on gender, age, weight, and physical activity. Second, they urged everyone to watch overall calorie consumption and eat more heart-healthy fats, whole grains, fruits, vegetables, and fat-free or low-fat dairy products.

That's great—what could be better than dietary recommendations tailored to your personal needs? And to help you determine exactly what those needs are, the USDA introduced MyPyramid.gov, a free online food guide complete with interactive tools to help you learn what nutrition experts say you should eat and how your diet stacks up to their recommendations. Check it out today! We've also included recipes here that can help you with your personal plan—whatever it may be.

Mozzarella Chicken Sandwich

This sandwich provides two grain servings from the ciabatta, a little more than two servings of meat from the chicken, and half a dairy serving from the cheese. Serve this chicken sandwich with orange wedges and baked chips.

- ¼ cup (about 2 ounces) sun-dried tomato pesto (such as Classico)
- 2 tablespoons fat-free mayonnaise
- ¾ pound skinless, boneless chicken breasts
- ¼ teaspoon pepper
- ⅛ teaspoon salt
- 1 teaspoon olive oil
- 1 (8-ounce) loaf ciabatta
- 12 large basil leaves
- ¾ cup (3 ounces) shredded part-skim mozzarella cheese
- ½ cup sliced bottled roasted red bell peppers
- 1 large tomato, thinly sliced

1. Combine pesto and mayonnaise in a small bowl, stirring to blend.
2. Sprinkle chicken with pepper and salt. Heat oil in a large nonstick skillet over medium-high heat. Add chicken, and cook 3 minutes on each side or until done. Remove chicken to a cutting board, and cool slightly. Cut chicken lengthwise into thin slices.
3. Preheat broiler.
4. Cut ciabatta in half horizontally. Place bread, cut sides up, on a baking sheet. Broil 3 minutes or until lightly browned. Remove bread from pan. Spread pesto mixture evenly over cut sides of bread. Arrange chicken slices evenly over bottom half of bread. Top chicken evenly with basil leaves, and sprinkle cheese over top. Place bottom half on baking sheet, and broil 2 minutes or until cheese melts. Arrange bell pepper and tomato over cheese, and cover with top half of bread. Cut into 4 equal pieces. Yield: 4 servings (serving size: 1 sandwich).

CALORIES 394 (31% from fat); FAT 13.4g (sat 3.9g, mono 7.4g, poly 1.1g); PROTEIN 31.3g; CARB 37.3g; FIBER 2g; CHOL 63mg; IRON 2.8mg; SODIUM 796mg; CALC 187mg

Eggplant Parmesan

Japanese eggplants are thinner and longer than the globe eggplants found in most grocery stores. Look for this variety at an Asian market if your supermarket doesn't carry it; substitute two (one-pound) globe eggplants if the Asian variety isn't available. One serving of this Italian classic constitutes about two cups of a vegetable allotment.

- 1½ tablespoons olive oil, divided
- 1 garlic clove, minced
- 1 teaspoon dried oregano
- ¼ teaspoon crushed red pepper
- 2 (14.5-ounce) cans no salt–added whole tomatoes, undrained and coarsely chopped
- ¼ teaspoon salt
- ¼ teaspoon freshly ground black pepper
- 4 Japanese eggplants, cut in half lengthwise (about 2 pounds)
- Cooking spray
- ½ cup grated Parmesan cheese
- ⅓ cup dry breadcrumbs

1. Preheat broiler.
2. Heat 1½ teaspoons oil in a medium saucepan over medium heat. Add garlic; cook 2 minutes or until fragrant, stirring occasionally. Add oregano, red pepper, and tomatoes; simmer 5 minutes or until thick. Add salt and black pepper, and keep warm.
3. Place eggplant halves, cut sides up, in bottom of a broiler pan coated with cooking spray. Brush evenly with 1 tablespoon oil. Broil 5 minutes or until slightly browned and tender. Spoon ½ cup tomato mixture over each eggplant half; top each half with 1 tablespoon cheese and about 2 teaspoons breadcrumbs. Broil 5 minutes or until cheese is browned. Yield: 4 servings (serving size: 2 eggplant halves).

CALORIES 278 (31% from fat); FAT 9.7g (sat 2.7g, mono 4.8g, poly 1.3g); PROTEIN 11.6g; CARB 42.6g; FIBER 18.1g; CHOL 9mg; IRON 3mg; SODIUM 396mg; CALC 237mg

Citrus Waffles with Marmalade Compote

(pictured on page 236)

One serving of this simple breakfast contributes about ½ cup serving of fruit and about two ounces of grains.

COMPOTE:
- ¼ cup reduced-sugar orange marmalade (such as Smucker's)
- 1 tablespoon fresh orange juice
- 1 teaspoon fresh lemon juice
- 1 teaspoon honey
- 2 cups fresh orange sections (about 2 oranges)

WAFFLES:
- ¾ cup all-purpose flour (about 3¾ ounces)
- ¾ cup whole wheat flour (about 3½ ounces)
- ½ cup packed brown sugar
- ¼ cup toasted wheat germ
- 1¼ teaspoons baking powder
- 1 teaspoon baking soda
- ¼ teaspoon salt
- ¼ teaspoon nutmeg
- 1⅓ cups buttermilk
- ⅓ cup water
- 2 tablespoons canola oil
- 1 teaspoon grated orange rind
- 1 large egg, lightly beaten
- Cooking spray
- Powdered sugar

1. To prepare compote, place first 4 ingredients in a small saucepan over medium-low heat; cook 2 minutes or until marmalade melts. Reduce heat, and gently stir in orange sections; keep warm.
2. To prepare waffles, lightly spoon flours into dry measuring cups, and level with a knife. Combine flours, brown sugar, and next 5 ingredients in a large bowl, stirring with a whisk. Combine buttermilk and next 4 ingredients in a small bowl. Add milk mixture to flour mixture, stirring just until moist. Coat a waffle iron with cooking spray; preheat. Spoon about ⅓ cup batter per 4-inch waffle onto hot waffle iron, spreading batter to edges. Cook 5 minutes or until steaming stops, and repeat procedure with remaining batter. Sift powdered sugar over tops of waffles. Serve with orange compote. Yield: 6 servings (serving size: 2 waffles and ⅓ cup compote).

CALORIES 309 (24% from fat); FAT 8.3g (sat 1.9g, mono 3.7g, poly 2.1g); PROTEIN 8.5g; CARB 52.5g; FIBER 4.5g; CHOL 43mg; IRON 2.3mg; SODIUM 492mg; CALC 169mg

QUICK & EASY

Creamy Spinach and Tofu Spaghetti

This pasta dish blends tofu and spinach to create a creamy sauce. The whole wheat spaghetti provides a serving of whole grains.

- 2 cups cherry tomatoes, halved
- Cooking spray
- 4 teaspoons olive oil, divided
- ½ teaspoon freshly ground black pepper, divided
- 2 cups tightly packed fresh baby spinach (about 1¼ ounces)
- 1½ cups cubed reduced-fat silken tofu (about 6 ounces)
- 1 cup fresh basil leaves
- ¼ cup (1 ounce) grated fresh pecorino Romano cheese
- 1 tablespoon red wine vinegar
- ¾ teaspoon salt
- 2 garlic cloves, minced
- 4 cups hot cooked whole wheat spaghetti (about 8 ounces uncooked)
- 2 tablespoons pine nuts, toasted

1. Preheat oven to 450°.
2. Place tomatoes, cut sides up, on a jelly-roll pan coated with cooking spray. Drizzle tomatoes with 2 teaspoons oil, and sprinkle evenly with ¼ teaspoon pepper. Bake at 450° for 7 minutes or until tender.
3. Place 2 teaspoons oil, ¼ teaspoon pepper, spinach, and next 6 ingredients in a food processor; process until smooth.
4. Combine spinach mixture and pasta in a large skillet; cook over low heat 2 minutes or until thoroughly heated, stirring occasionally. Gently stir in tomatoes and pine nuts. Serve immediately. Yield: 4 servings (serving size: about 1¼ cups).

CALORIES 306 (31% from fat); FAT 10.6g (sat 2.1g, mono 4.8g, poly 2.6g); PROTEIN 14g; CARB 43.4g; FIBER 8g; CHOL 7mg; IRON 3.1mg; SODIUM 573mg; CALC 138mg

Edamame Dip
(pictured on page 235)

You won't need encouragement to eat your veggies when you serve this hearty, nutty dip with a variety of crisp vegetables such as jícama, bell pepper strips, steamed sugar snap peas, and carrot sticks.

1½ cups frozen shelled edamame (green soybeans), thawed and cooked
½ cup water
¼ cup chopped red onion
3 tablespoons chopped fresh cilantro
2 tablespoons rice vinegar
1 tablespoon olive oil
1½ teaspoons chili garlic sauce (such as Lee Kum Kee)
½ teaspoon salt
1 (16-ounce) can cannellini beans or other white beans, rinsed and drained

1. Place all ingredients in a food processor, and process until smooth. Serve immediately, or cover and chill. Yield: 2½ cups (serving size: about 3 tablespoons edamame mixture).

CALORIES 61 (37% from fat); FAT 2.5g (sat 0.4g, mono 1.1g, poly 0.7g); PROTEIN 4g; CARB 6.1g; FIBER 1.2g; CHOL 0mg; IRON 0.7mg; SODIUM 120mg; CALC 23mg

Pineapple Teriyaki Salmon
(pictured on page 234)

You can round out the meal with sautéed haricots verts and quick-cooking couscous.

2 tablespoons brown sugar
2 tablespoons low-sodium soy sauce
1 teaspoon finely grated orange zest
1 (6-ounce) can pineapple juice
½ teaspoon salt, divided
2 teaspoons canola oil
4 (6-ounce) salmon fillets (about 1 inch thick)
¼ teaspoon freshly ground black pepper
Grated orange rind (optional)

1. Combine first 4 ingredients and ¼ teaspoon salt in a small saucepan over high heat, and bring to a boil. Reduce heat, and simmer until reduced to ¼ cup (about 15 minutes). Set aside.
2. Preheat oven to 400°.
3. Heat oil in a large nonstick skillet over medium-high heat. Sprinkle both sides of fish with ¼ teaspoon salt and pepper. Add fish to pan; cook 3 minutes. Turn fish over, and place in oven; bake at 400° for 3 minutes. Remove from oven; brush 1 tablespoon sauce over each fillet. Return to oven, and cook 1 minute or until fish flakes easily when tested with a fork or until desired degree of doneness. Sprinkle with orange rind, if desired. Yield: 4 servings (serving size: 1 salmon fillet).

CALORIES 339 (41% from fat); FAT 15.4g (sat 3.3g, mono 7g, poly 3.9g); PROTEIN 36.8g; CARB 11.2g; FIBER 0.2g; CHOL 87mg; IRON 1mg; SODIUM 644mg; CALC 34mg

Roasted Pepper and Goat Cheese Pasta

Pureeing the roasted peppers into a sauce is an easy way to add a generous vegetable serving to a meal. To make this a vegetarian dish, substitute vegetable broth for chicken broth.

3 large red bell peppers (about 1½ pounds)
5 teaspoons olive oil, divided
2 garlic cloves, minced
½ cup fat-free, less-sodium chicken broth
2 tablespoons lemon juice
2 teaspoons sugar
¾ teaspoon salt
¼ teaspoon freshly ground black pepper
⅛ teaspoon crushed red pepper
¼ cup chopped fresh basil
4 cups hot cooked bow tie pasta (8 ounces uncooked)
½ cup (2 ounces) crumbled goat cheese

1. Preheat broiler.
2. Cut bell peppers in half lengthwise; discard seeds and membranes. Place pepper halves, skin sides up, on a foil-lined baking sheet; flatten with hand. Broil 8 minutes or until blackened. Place peppers in a zip-top plastic bag; seal. Let stand 20 minutes. Peel; place peppers in a blender.
3. Heat 2 teaspoons oil in small skillet over medium heat. Add garlic; sauté 1 minute. Remove from heat; let stand 5 minutes. Add garlic mixture, 1 tablespoon oil, broth, and next 5 ingredients to blender with peppers; process until smooth. Combine bell pepper mixture and basil with pasta. Sprinkle with cheese. Yield: 4 servings (serving size: about 1 cup pasta mixture and 2 tablespoons cheese).

CALORIES 342 (26% from fat); FAT 9.8g (sat 3.1g, mono 5.1g, poly 1.2g); PROTEIN 12.1g; CARB 53.4g; FIBER 4.6g; CHOL 7mg; IRON 2.8mg; SODIUM 549mg; CALC 48mg

WINE NOTE: A simple pasta dish doesn't need a superpricey wine. Instead take a tip from Italian trattorias and serve a simple, bracingly fresh white like pinot grigio. It's the ultimate no-frills, no-fuss wine, and its light citrus/almond/hay notes are great with goat cheese. Try Lagaria 2004 pinot grigio from Delle Venezie, Italy ($9).

Ham and Cheese Toasted Sandwiches

This quick and tasty sandwich packs nutrition for breakfast or lunch.

¼ cup (2 ounces) tub-style light cream cheese
1 tablespoon chopped fresh basil
1 teaspoon Dijon mustard
¼ teaspoon freshly ground black pepper
8 (1-ounce) slices whole wheat bread
4 ounces low-fat deli ham
8 (¼-inch-thick) slices tomato (about 1 large)
¼ cup (2 ounces) shredded reduced-fat sharp Cheddar cheese

1. Preheat broiler.

Continued

2. Combine first 4 ingredients in small bowl; stir well.

3. Spread about 1 tablespoon cream cheese mixture over each of 4 bread slices. Top each with 1 ounce ham, 2 tomato slices, and 1 tablespoon Cheddar cheese. Place sandwich halves and remaining 4 slices bread on a baking sheet. Broil 2 minutes or until cheese is melted and bread is lightly browned. Top sandwich halves with remaining bread slices. Serve immediately. Yield: 4 servings (serving size: 1 sandwich).

CALORIES 246 (31% from fat); FAT 8.6g (sat 4.3g, mono 2.8g, poly 1.1g); PROTEIN 16g; CARB 28.6g; FIBER 4.2g; CHOL 25mg; IRON 2.4mg; SODIUM 859mg; CALC 174mg

QUICK & EASY
Pecan White and Brown Rice Pilaf

Using part instant white rice and part instant brown rice can help make the switch to whole grains easier.

 2 teaspoons olive oil
 1 cup finely chopped onion
 1 bay leaf
 2 cups water
 1 cup fat-free, less-sodium chicken broth
 ½ cup instant white rice
 ½ cup instant brown rice
 ½ cup uncooked bulgur
 1 tablespoon dried cranberries or currants
 ½ teaspoon salt
 ¼ teaspoon freshly ground black pepper
 ¼ cup chopped pecans, toasted
 2 tablespoons chopped fresh parsley

1. Heat olive oil in a large saucepan over medium-high heat. Add onion; sauté 4 minutes or until tender. Add bay leaf; cook 1 minute. Add water and next 7 ingredients; bring to a boil. Cover, reduce heat, and simmer 8 minutes or until rice is tender. Remove from heat; discard bay leaf. Stir in pecans and parsley. Yield: 6 servings (serving size: ½ cup).

CALORIES 188 (27% from fat); FAT 5.6g (sat 0.6g, mono 3.3g, poly 1.4g); PROTEIN 4.3g; CARB 31.7g; FIBER 3.9g; CHOL 0mg; IRON 1mg; SODIUM 268mg; CALC 32mg

New Chicken Dinner Menu
serves 4

The simple preparation of the springtime side dishes means that the chicken—and its rich, sweet-tart sauce—is the star of this meal.

Chicken with Balsamic-Fig Sauce
Roasted new potatoes*
Fresh asparagus

*Preheat oven to 450°. Combine 2 cups refrigerated packaged new potato wedges (such as Simply Potatoes), 2 teaspoons chopped fresh rosemary, 2 teaspoons olive oil, ¾ teaspoon salt, and ½ teaspoon freshly ground black pepper in a medium bowl. Spread potato mixture in a single layer on a jelly-roll pan. Bake at 450° for 15 minutes or until golden.

QUICK & EASY
Chicken with Balsamic-Fig Sauce

To help you with your calculations for the MyPyramid, this recipe yields about four ounces cooked meat from one chicken breast.

 4 (6-ounce) skinless, boneless chicken breast halves
1½ tablespoons fresh thyme leaves, divided
 ½ teaspoon salt, divided
 ¼ teaspoon freshly ground black pepper
 1 tablespoon olive oil
 1 tablespoon butter
 ¾ cup chopped onion
 ½ cup fat-free, less-sodium chicken broth
 ¼ cup balsamic vinegar
 2 teaspoons low-sodium soy sauce
 ½ cup finely chopped dried figs (such as Mission)

1. Sprinkle both sides of chicken evenly with 1½ teaspoons thyme, ¼ teaspoon salt, and pepper. Heat oil in a large non-stick skillet over medium-high heat. Add chicken; cook 6 minutes on each side or until done. Remove from pan; keep warm.

2. Reduce heat to medium; add butter to pan. Add onion; sauté 3 minutes. Add broth, vinegar, soy sauce, and figs. Simmer until sauce is reduced to 1 cup (about 3 minutes). Add 1 tablespoon thyme and ¼ teaspoon salt. Cut chicken breast halves lengthwise on diagonal into slices. Serve sauce over chicken. Yield: 4 servings (serving size: 4 ounces chicken and ¼ cup sauce).

CALORIES 355 (28% from fat); FAT 11g (sat 3.6g, mono 4.9g, poly 1.5g); PROTEIN 41.3g; CARB 21.6g; FIBER 3g; CHOL 116mg; IRON 2.1mg; SODIUM 563mg; CALC 71mg

QUICK & EASY
Five-Spice Tilapia with Citrus Ponzu Sauce

One serving of this fish provides almost all five ounces of meat recommended for those on an 1,800-calorie meal plan.

 2 tablespoons thinly sliced green onions
 2 tablespoons orange juice
 1 tablespoon lemon juice
 1 tablespoon low-sodium soy sauce
 2 teaspoons rice wine vinegar
 1 teaspoon brown sugar
 ¼ teaspoon bottled ground fresh ginger (such as Spice World)
 ½ teaspoon five-spice powder
 ¼ teaspoon salt
 ¼ teaspoon ground red pepper
 4 (6-ounce) tilapia fillets
 2 teaspoons canola oil

1. Combine first 7 ingredients in a small bowl.

2. Combine five-spice powder, salt, and pepper. Sprinkle both sides of fish evenly with spice mixture.

3. Heat oil in a large nonstick skillet over medium-high heat. Add fish to pan; cook 2 minutes on each side or until fish flakes easily when tested with a fork or until desired degree of doneness. Remove from pan, and serve with sauce. Yield: 4 servings (serving size: 1 fillet and 1 tablespoon sauce).

CALORIES 217 (27% from fat); FAT 6.6g (sat 1.8g, mono 1.9g, poly 2.3g); PROTEIN 37g; CARB 3.1g; FIBER 0.2g; CHOL 125mg; IRON 1mg; SODIUM 332mg; CALC 8mg

Roast Chicken

Master a basic technique, then explore delicious variations for this comforting classic.

Few entrées are as familiar and welcoming as a succulent roast chicken. It's often the star of homey weeknight suppers and company-worthy dinners. Roast chicken's broad appeal is well deserved because its neutral-tasting meat harmonizes with many flavors, from those of Lemon-Rosemary Roast Chicken with Potatoes (recipe on page 155) to Oven Barbecue Beer-Can Chicken (recipe at right).

Although picking up a rotisserie chicken at the supermarket is a convenient option, there are a number of advantages to roasting your own bird at home. Taste is the best reason—you can use virtually any combination of herbs and spices to suit your preference. Roasting a chicken allows you to control the sodium as well as the quality of the ingredients. Best of all, it's simple, mostly hands-free cooking if you follow a few steps (see "Six Steps to Great Chicken," page 156).

Chipotle-Lime Roast Chicken with Tomatillo Sauce

Tomatillos look like small green tomatoes in papery husks. Combining them with chipotle chile powder gives this chicken Mexican flair.

- 1 (3¾-pound) whole roasting chicken
- 2 teaspoons butter, softened
- 1 teaspoon chipotle chile powder
- 1 teaspoon grated lime rind
- ¾ teaspoon salt, divided
- ½ teaspoon ground cumin
- 4 garlic cloves, minced and divided
- Cooking spray
- 8 ounces tomatillos
- 1 onion, quartered
- ¼ cup chopped fresh cilantro
- 1 tablespoon fresh lime juice
- 1 (4.5-ounce) can chopped green chiles, undrained
- Chopped fresh cilantro (optional)

1. Preheat oven to 375°.
2. Remove and discard giblets and neck from chicken; trim excess fat. Starting at neck cavity, loosen skin from breast and drumsticks by inserting fingers, gently pushing between skin and meat.
3. Combine butter, chile powder, rind, ½ teaspoon salt, cumin, and 1 garlic clove in a small bowl. Rub seasoning mixture under loosened skin and over breast and drumsticks. Tie ends of legs together with twine. Lift wing tips up and over back; tuck under chicken. Place chicken, breast side up, on a rack coated with cooking spray; place rack in roasting pan.
4. Discard husks and stems from tomatillos; cut into quarters. Arrange tomatillos and onion evenly around chicken. Bake at 375° for 40 minutes.
5. Increase oven temperature to 450°, and bake an additional 20 minutes or until a thermometer inserted in meaty part of thigh registers 170°. Remove chicken from pan; let stand 15 minutes.
6. Place tomatillos and onion in a food processor. Add ¼ teaspoon salt, 3 garlic cloves, ¼ cup cilantro, juice, and chiles; process until smooth.
7. Remove skin from chicken; discard. Carve chicken, and serve with sauce. Sprinkle with cilantro, if desired. Yield: 4 servings (serving size: 5 ounces meat and about ½ cup sauce).

CALORIES 299 (36% from fat); FAT 12.1g (sat 3.9g, mono 4.1g, poly 2.5g); PROTEIN 36.9g; CARB 9.6g; FIBER 2.4g; CHOL 111mg; IRON 2.9mg; SODIUM 694mg; CALC 51mg

Oven Barbecue Beer-Can Chicken

- 1 (3¾-pound) whole roasting chicken
- 3 tablespoons ketchup
- 3 tablespoons chili sauce
- 2 teaspoons Worcestershire sauce
- 1 teaspoon chili powder
- 1 teaspoon cider vinegar
- ¼ teaspoon freshly ground black pepper
- ⅛ teaspoon salt
- 1 garlic clove, minced
- 1 (12-ounce) can beer
- 3 tablespoons barbecue smoked seasoning (such as Hickory Liquid Smoke)

1. Preheat oven to 375°.
2. Remove and discard giblets and neck from chicken; trim excess fat. Starting at neck cavity, loosen skin from breast and drumsticks by inserting fingers, gently pushing between skin and meat.
3. Combine ketchup and next 7 ingredients in a bowl. Reserve ¼ cup ketchup mixture; rub remaining ketchup mixture under loosened skin and over breast and drumsticks. Lift wing tips up and over back; tuck under chicken.
4. Discard ½ cup beer. Add barbecue smoked seasoning to can. Holding chicken upright with body cavity facing down, insert beer can into cavity. Place chicken in a roasting pan, and spread legs out to form a tripod to support chicken. Bake at 375° for 40 minutes.
5. Increase oven temperature to 450°, and bake an additional 30 minutes or until a thermometer inserted in meaty part of thigh registers 170°. Lift chicken slightly using tongs; place spatula under can. Carefully lift chicken and can; place on a cutting board. Let stand 15 minutes. Gently lift chicken using tongs or insulated rubber gloves; carefully twist can, and remove from cavity.
6. Remove skin from chicken; discard. Carve chicken, and serve with reserved ¼ cup sauce. Yield: 4 servings (serving size: 5 ounces meat and 1 tablespoon sauce).

CALORIES 269 (32% from fat); FAT 9.6g (sat 2.6g, mono 3.6g, poly 2.2g); PROTEIN 35.8g; CARB 8g; FIBER 0.4g; CHOL 106mg; IRON 2.1mg; SODIUM 700mg; CALC 26mg

Use the Right Equipment

Use a heavy metal roasting pan and a cooking rack. The pan will catch the flavorful juices that drip as the bird roasts. The rack elevates the bird off the pan, allowing the chicken to roast rather than simmer.

You'll also need a kitchen thermometer. Since oven temperatures vary, a thermometer is the truest test of doneness. The USDA recommends that whole chickens be cooked to 180°. Our recipes direct you to pull the bird from the oven at 170°, and let it stand 15 minutes. The internal temperature of the chicken continues to rise as it stands, reaching the desired temperature without overcooking and drying out. Check the accuracy of your thermometer by immersing the stem in at least two inches of boiling water and waiting 30 seconds to check the reading. If it registers 212°, it's accurate.

Select the Best Bird

Our recipes call for meaty "roasting" chickens. Because they're older and larger than broilers-fryers, they have more muscle and fat. When the fat cooks off, the roast chicken is moist and tasty.

Overall, we find roasting a fresh bird offers better results in terms of flavor and texture than frozen chicken. Look for a fresh, never-frozen chicken at larger supermarkets. There are subtle differences among free-range, organic, and traditional farm-raised birds.

Read the label, and look for a bird that contains no added ingredients. Chicken is often injected with water, broth, or saline. This slightly increases the weight of the bird and flavors it.

Store and Handle Properly

Cook a whole fresh chicken within one to two days after purchasing. If you start with a frozen chicken, let it thaw in the refrigerator overnight. Never thaw a chicken at room temperature—that allows bacteria to grow. Always make sure the chicken has thawed completely before cooking because a partially frozen chicken can cook unevenly and overbrown on the outside before the interior reaches the proper temperature.

Many people wash chickens before roasting them to reduce the risk of salmonella. In fact, cooking the bird to the proper temperature is the only safeguard against bacteria, and rinsing can spread bacteria to the sink or other areas where water may splash. We do not call for rinsing chickens before cooking.

Prepare the Bird

Roasting the chicken with the skin intact flavors and moistens the lean breast meat as it cooks. Most of the fat cooks off, but some is absorbed from the skin into the meat.

Herbs and spices rubbed over the outside of the chicken will only flavor the skin, but seasonings rubbed under the skin will permeate the meat. Since our recipes call to remove and discard the skin after roasting, it's important to rub seasonings directly on the flesh.

To loosen the skin, start at the neck cavity. Insert your fingers between the skin and flesh, and work all the way to the drumsticks, pressing gently as you go. Take care not to tear the skin because this will cause it to shrink during roasting, exposing the meat beneath. Without the protection of the skin, the meat dries out easily. Once the skin is loose, it's simple to rub seasonings on the meat.

Seasoning can be as simple as a little salt and pepper, but chicken marries well with a variety of flavors. However, there are other tricks that contribute to a tasty bird. Stuff the cavity, and the meat absorbs flavor from the inside out. Brining (soaking the chicken in a mixture of water, salt, sugar, and spices before roasting) is another technique that delivers a moist and delicious bird.

Classic technique for roast chicken calls to truss or secure the bird with twine. With the exception of Oven Barbecue Beer-Can Chicken, our recipes call for trussing the chicken. We recommend this procedure mostly for aesthetic purposes.

Roast

The key to a beautifully roasted chicken is to keep the lean breast meat moist while allowing time to fully cook the legs. Although we discard the skin, browning is another consideration since crisp skin provides a shield for the delicate meat. High-heat roasting produces a beautifully bronzed bird, but it may also toughen the meat. Chicken cooked at a low temperature comes out moist but yields a lackluster-looking bird. A combination of high and low heat produces the best results. Our recipes direct you to begin at 375° and increase the oven temperature to finish the cooking.

Carve

Once you've roasted the perfect bird, wait at least 15 minutes before carving. This allows the internal temperature of the chicken to reach the proper level (180°), and the juices to redistribute throughout the meat.

To carve the bird, first remove and discard the skin. Use a sharp knife to remove each leg by cutting through the joint where the thigh attaches to the body. You can then separate the drumstick and the thigh by cutting through the joint where they meet. Serve each piece whole, or cut the meat away from the bone. Carve the breast meat by holding the knife parallel to the breast and thinly slicing. Or cut away the whole breast, and slice it on a cutting board.

Take Stock

Thrifty cooks know that making stock yields a high return on your investment because you make use of the chicken carcass. Another advantage is that homemade stock should be virtually sodium-free, whereas commercial broths can be high in sodium.

It's easy to make and there's no substitute for the flavor of homemade chicken stock in soups, stews, sauces, and other dishes.

The Skinny on Chicken

The skin from a whole bird accounts for about half of its fat. However, roasting with the skin adds moisture and protects lean meat from drying out. We routinely call to cook the chicken with the skin on, removing it before serving, which substantially reduces the fat (some of the fat from the skin absorbs into the meat during roasting). Roasting a whole chicken this way yields a bird with about 36 percent of its calories from fat—most of it unsaturated.

Lemon-Rosemary Roast Chicken with Potatoes

A green salad is all you'll need to round out the meal. Garnish with rosemary sprigs.

    1   (3¾-pound) whole roasting chicken
    2   tablespoons olive oil, divided
    2   teaspoons chopped fresh
        rosemary
    1   teaspoon grated lemon rind
    ¾   teaspoon salt, divided
    ½   teaspoon freshly ground black
        pepper, divided
    3   garlic cloves, minced
    Cooking spray
    3   baking potatoes, peeled and cut
        into 1½-inch pieces (about
        2 pounds)
    4   lemon wedges

1. Preheat oven to 375°.
2. Remove and discard giblets and neck from chicken; trim excess fat. Starting at neck cavity, loosen skin from breast and drumsticks by inserting fingers, gently pushing between skin and meat.
3. Combine 1 tablespoon oil, rosemary, rind, ½ teaspoon salt, ¼ teaspoon pepper, and garlic in a small bowl. Rub seasoning mixture under loosened skin and over breast and drumsticks. Tie ends of legs together with twine. Lift wing tips up and over back, and tuck under chicken. Place chicken, breast side up, on a rack coated with cooking spray, and place rack in a roasting pan.
4. Toss potatoes with 1 tablespoon oil. Arrange potato mixture evenly around chicken. Bake at 375° for 40 minutes.
5. Increase oven temperature to 450°, and bake an additional 20 minutes or until a thermometer inserted in meaty part of thigh registers 170°. Remove chicken from pan; let stand 15 minutes. Sprinkle potatoes with ¼ teaspoon salt and ¼ teaspoon pepper.
6. Remove skin from chicken; discard. Carve chicken, and serve with potatoes and lemon wedges. Yield: 4 servings (serving size: 5 ounces meat, about 1½ cups potatoes, and 1 lemon wedge).

CALORIES 522 (28% from fat); FAT 16.5g (sat 3.5g, mono 8.5g, poly 2.9g); PROTEIN 41.6g; CARB 49.8g; FIBER 5.4g; CHOL 106mg; IRON 4.4mg; SODIUM 568mg; CALC 68mg

WINE NOTE: Roast chicken is very versatile with wine, and so are the seasonings used here. In the winter, serve this dish with an earthy red wine like pinot noir. In summer, try Beaujolais, an exuberantly fruity red best served slightly chilled. Try George Dubeouf's "Fleurie" Beaujolais 2004 ($12).

Roast Chicken with Mint-Cilantro Pesto

    1   (3¾-pound) whole roasting
        chicken
    ¼   cup fresh mint leaves
    ¼   cup fresh cilantro leaves
    2   tablespoons water
    1   teaspoon olive oil
    ½   teaspoon salt
    ¼   teaspoon freshly ground black
        pepper
    1   garlic clove
    Cooking spray

1. Preheat oven to 375°.
2. Remove and discard giblets and neck from chicken; trim excess fat. Starting at neck cavity, loosen skin from breast and drumsticks by inserting fingers, gently pushing between skin and meat.
3. Place mint leaves and next 6 ingredients in a food processor, and process until finely ground. Rub herb mixture under loosened skin and over breast and drumsticks. Tie ends of legs together with twine. Lift wing tips up and over back, and tuck under chicken. Place chicken, breast side up, on a rack coated with cooking spray, and place rack in a roasting pan.
4. Bake at 375° for 40 minutes.
5. Increase oven temperature to 450°, and bake chicken an additional 20 minutes or until a thermometer inserted in meaty part of thigh registers 170°. Remove chicken from pan, and let stand 15 minutes. Remove skin from chicken, and discard. Carve chicken, and serve immediately. Yield: 4 servings (serving size: 5 ounces meat).

CALORIES 250 (38% from fat); FAT 10.6g (sat 2.7g, mono 4.4g, poly 2.3g); PROTEIN 35.6g; CARB 0.6g; FIBER 0.2g; CHOL 106mg; IRON 1.9mg; SODIUM 403mg; CALC 24mg

Roast Chicken with Wild Rice Stuffing

    Cooking spray
    ½   cup chopped onion
    ¾   cup long-grain and wild rice blend
    1   garlic clove, minced
    1½ cups water
    ⅓   cup chopped dried figs
    1½ tablespoons pine nuts, toasted
    ¾   teaspoon salt, divided
    1   (3¾-pound) whole roasting chicken
    2   teaspoons butter, softened
    ¾   teaspoon ground cumin
    ½   teaspoon ground coriander
    ½   teaspoon crushed red pepper
    ¼   teaspoon ground cinnamon

1. Preheat oven to 375°.
2. Heat a nonstick saucepan over medium-high heat. Coat pan with cooking spray. Add onion to pan; sauté 4 minutes. Add rice and garlic to pan; sauté 1 minute. Add 1½ cups water to pan; bring to a boil. Cover, reduce heat, and simmer 20 minutes or until rice is almost tender. Stir in figs, nuts, and ¼ teaspoon salt.
3. Remove and discard giblets and neck from chicken; trim excess fat. Starting at neck cavity, loosen skin from breast and drumsticks by inserting fingers, gently pushing between skin and meat.
4. Combine ½ teaspoon salt, butter, and remaining 4 ingredients in a small bowl. Rub seasoning mixture under loosened skin and over breast and drumsticks. Stuff rice mixture into chicken cavity. Tie ends of legs together with twine. Lift wing tips up and over back; tuck under chicken. Place chicken, breast side up, on a rack coated with cooking spray; place rack in a roasting pan.
5. Bake at 375° for 40 minutes.
6. Increase oven temperature to 450°, and bake an additional 20 minutes or until a thermometer inserted in meaty part of thigh registers 170°. Remove chicken from pan; let stand 15 minutes.
7. Remove skin from chicken; discard. Carve chicken, and serve with stuffing. Yield: 4 servings (serving size: 5 ounces meat and about ½ cup rice).

CALORIES 245 (35% from fat); FAT 9.4g (sat 2.7g, mono 3.1g, poly 2.3g); PROTEIN 25.3g; CARB 14.5g; FIBER 1.8g; CHOL 74mg; IRON 1.9mg; SODIUM 471mg; CALC 44mg

1. *Separate the skin from the flesh, and rub the seasoning mixture directly on the meat.*

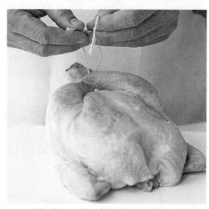

2. *Tie the ends of the legs of the chicken together with twine for a professional presentation.*

3. *The bird cooks more evenly when it's elevated off the pan atop vegetables or a rack.*

4. *Insert the thermometer into the meaty part of the thigh to get an accurate temperature reading. This is the slowest cooking part of the bird.*

5. *Remove and discard the skin before serving for a substantial fat savings.*

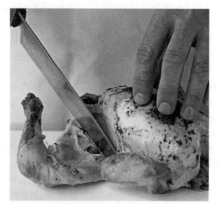

6. *Use a sharp knife to remove the legs first. Hold the knife parallel to the chicken breast, and slice thinly.*

Chicken Roasted in Bay Leaves

Placing bay leaves in the chicken cavity infuses the bird with a subtle herbed aroma as it roasts.

CHICKEN:
- 1 (3¾-pound) whole roasting chicken
- ½ teaspoon salt
- ¼ teaspoon freshly ground black pepper
- 16 bay leaves
- 4 celery stalks, halved lengthwise and crosswise
- 2 carrots, peeled and halved
- 1 onion, quartered

GRAVY:
- ¼ cup brandy
- 1½ cups fat-free, less-sodium chicken broth
- 2 tablespoons whipping cream
- 3 tablespoons water
- 2 tablespoons all-purpose flour
- ¼ teaspoon salt

1. Preheat oven to 375°.

2. To prepare chicken, remove and discard giblets and neck from chicken; trim excess fat. Starting at neck cavity, loosen skin from breast and drumsticks by inserting fingers, gently pushing between skin and meat. Rub ½ teaspoon salt and pepper under loosened skin and over breast and drumsticks. Place 8 bay leaves under loosened skin; place 8 bay leaves in cavity.

3. Tie ends of legs together with twine. Lift wing tips up and over back; tuck under chicken. Place celery, carrot, and onion in a single layer in a roasting pan. Place chicken, breast side up, on top of vegetables.

4. Bake at 375° for 40 minutes.

5. Increase oven temperature to 450°, and bake an additional 20 minutes or until a thermometer inserted in meaty part of thigh registers 170°. Using tongs or insulated rubber gloves, remove chicken from pan, tilting slightly to drain juices. Let stand 15 minutes. Remove vegetables from pan with a slotted spoon; reserve.

6. To prepare gravy, place a zip-top plastic bag in a 2-cup glass measure. Pour brandy into bag; add drippings from pan. Let stand 2 minutes (fat will rise to top). Seal bag; carefully snip off bottom corner of bag. Drain drippings into measuring cup, stopping before fat layer reaches opening; discard fat.

7. Return vegetables to pan. Add brandy mixture, broth, and cream to pan; cook 10 minutes over medium heat, scraping pan to loosen browned bits. Remove vegetables from pan using a slotted spoon; discard. Combine water and flour in a small bowl, stirring with a whisk until well blended to form a slurry; add slurry and ¼ teaspoon salt to pan, stirring constantly. Simmer 1 minute or until slightly thick.

8. Remove skin from chicken, and discard. Discard bay leaves. Carve chicken, and serve with gravy. Yield: 4 servings (serving size: 5 ounces meat and about ¼ cup gravy).

CALORIES 306 (36% from fat); FAT 12.3g (sat 4.3g, mono 4.4g, poly 2.3g); PROTEIN 37.1g; CARB 4.5g; FIBER 0.7g; CHOL 117mg; IRON 2.1mg; SODIUM 704mg; CALC 33mg

Classic Roast Chicken with Gravy

Be sure the butter is softened so it combines thoroughly with the herbs.

CHICKEN:

- 1 (3¾-pound) whole roasting chicken
- 1 tablespoon butter, softened
- ½ teaspoon salt
- ½ teaspoon dried thyme
- ½ teaspoon dried oregano
- ½ teaspoon dried rubbed sage
- ⅛ teaspoon freshly ground black pepper
- 2 carrots, peeled and halved
- 4 stalks celery, halved
- 1 onion, quartered

GRAVY:

- ½ cup dry white wine
- 1½ cups fat-free, less-sodium chicken broth
- 2 tablespoons all-purpose flour
- 3 tablespoons water
- ¼ teaspoon salt

1. Preheat oven to 375°.

2. To prepare chicken, remove and discard giblets and neck from chicken; trim excess fat. Starting at neck cavity, loosen skin from breast and drumsticks by inserting fingers, gently pushing between skin and meat.

3. Combine butter and next 5 ingredients in a small bowl. Rub seasoning mixture under loosened skin and over breast and drumsticks. Tie ends of legs together with twine. Lift wing tips up and over back; tuck under chicken. Place carrots, celery, and onion in a single layer in a roasting pan. Place chicken, breast side up, on top of vegetables.

4. Bake at 375° for 40 minutes.

5. Increase oven temperature to 450°, and bake an additional 20 minutes or until a thermometer inserted in meaty part of thigh registers 170°. Using tongs or insulated rubber gloves, remove chicken from pan, tilting slightly to drain juices. Let stand 15 minutes. Remove vegetables from pan with a slotted spoon; reserve.

6. To prepare gravy, place a zip-top plastic bag in a 2-cup glass measure. Pour wine into bag; add drippings from pan. Let stand 2 minutes (fat will rise to top). Seal bag; carefully snip off bottom corner of bag. Drain drippings into measuring cup, stopping before fat layer reaches opening; discard fat.

7. Return vegetables to pan. Add wine mixture and broth to pan; cook 10 minutes over medium heat, scraping pan to loosen browned bits. Remove vegetables from pan using a slotted spoon; discard. Combine flour and water in a small bowl, stirring with a whisk to form a slurry; add slurry and ¼ teaspoon salt to pan, stirring constantly. Simmer 1 minute or until slightly thick.

8. Remove skin from chicken; discard. Carve chicken, and serve with gravy. Yield: 4 servings (serving size: 5 ounces meat and about ¼ cup gravy).

CALORIES 287 (39% from fat); FAT 12.4g (sat 4.4g, mono 4.3g, poly 2.3g); PROTEIN 37g; CARB 4.4g; FIBER 0.9g; CHOL 114mg; IRON 2.4mg; SODIUM 721mg; CALC 35mg

How to Make Good Gravy

Preparing pan gravy, a delicious way to make use of the browned bits and drippings from the chicken, is one of the best reasons to roast your own bird.

1. *To prepare gravy, place a zip-top plastic bag in a 2-cup glass measure. Pour wine into bag; add drippings from pan. Let stand 2 minutes (fat will rise to top). Seal bag; carefully snip off bottom corner of bag. Drain drippings into measuring cup, stopping before fat layer reaches opening; discard fat.*

2. *Return vegetables to pan. Add wine mixture and broth to pan; cook 10 minutes over medium heat, scraping pan to loosen browned bits.*

. . . And Ready in Just About 20 Minutes

More than a week's worth of quick entrées to get dinner on the table in a flash

Linguine with Asparagus, Parmesan, and Bacon

(pictured on page 235)

Start with hot tap water, and cover the pot with the lid—the water for cooking the pasta will come to a boil faster. Look for prechopped onion in the produce section.

    3   cups (1-inch) sliced asparagus
        (about 1 pound)
    1   (9-ounce) package refrigerated
        linguine
    4   bacon slices (uncooked)
    1   cup chopped onion
    2   teaspoons bottled minced garlic
    1   teaspoon dried oregano
    2   cups grape or cherry tomatoes
    ¾   cup fat-free, less-sodium chicken
        broth
    1   tablespoon butter
    ¼   teaspoon salt
    ¼   teaspoon freshly ground black
        pepper
    2   tablespoons fresh lemon juice
    ½   cup (2 ounces) preshredded
        Parmesan cheese
    Shaved Parmesan cheese (optional)

1. Cook asparagus and pasta according to pasta package directions, omitting salt and fat. Drain; set aside.
2. Cook bacon in a large nonstick skillet over medium-high heat until crisp. Remove bacon from pan, reserving 2 teaspoons drippings in pan. Cool bacon slightly, and crumble. Add onion, garlic, and oregano to drippings in pan; sauté 4 minutes or until onion is lightly browned. Add tomatoes; cook 2 minutes. Add broth; bring to a boil. Stir in

butter, salt, and pepper; remove from heat. Place asparagus mixture in a large bowl; add tomato mixture and juice, tossing well. Top with bacon and shredded cheese. Garnish with shaved Parmesan, if desired. Yield: 4 servings (serving size: 2 cups pasta mixture and 2 tablespoons cheese).

CALORIES 360 (30% from fat); FAT 11.9g (sat 5.3g, mono 3.9g, poly 0.8g); PROTEIN 16.9g; CARB 46.1g; FIBER 5.6g; CHOL 23mg; IRON 1.3mg; SODIUM 683mg; CALC 171mg

Moroccan Swordfish with Caper-Yogurt Sauce

SAUCE:

    ½   cup plain low-fat yogurt
    1   tablespoon chopped fresh mint
    1½ teaspoons capers, drained
    ¼   teaspoon bottled minced garlic
    Dash of salt
    Dash of freshly ground black
        pepper

FISH:

    1   teaspoon paprika
    ½   teaspoon ground coriander
    ¼   teaspoon salt
    ¼   teaspoon ground ginger
    ¼   teaspoon ground cumin
    ¼   teaspoon ground cinnamon
    ⅛   teaspoon ground red pepper
    4   (6-ounce) swordfish steaks (about
        ¾ inch thick)
    Cooking spray
    Mint sprigs (optional)

1. To prepare sauce, combine first 6 ingredients in a small bowl.
2. To prepare fish, heat a nonstick grill pan over medium-high heat. Combine paprika and next 6 ingredients; sprinkle over both sides of fish. Lightly coat both sides of fish with cooking spray; add fish to pan. Cook 4 minutes on each side or until fish flakes easily when tested with a fork or until desired degree of doneness. Serve with sauce. Garnish with mint sprigs, if desired. Yield: 4 servings (serving size: 1 steak and 2 tablespoons sauce).

CALORIES 222 (29% from fat); FAT 7.2g (sat 2.1g, mono 2.7g, poly 1.6g); PROTEIN 34.3g; CARB 3.1g; FIBER 0.6g; CHOL 66mg; IRON 1.8mg; SODIUM 383mg; CALC 73mg

Beef and Vegetable Kebabs

Using the broiler lets you enjoy the taste of kebabs year-round; they're also great cooked on the grill. Serve over rice.

    1   pound boneless sirloin steak,
        trimmed and cut into 1-inch cubes
    8   (1-inch) pieces yellow bell pepper
        (about 1 pepper)
    8   small mushrooms (about 4 ounces)
    8   (1-inch) pieces green onions (about 2)
    8   cherry tomatoes
    1   teaspoon kosher salt
    ½   teaspoon dried thyme
    ¼   teaspoon freshly ground black
        pepper
    Cooking spray
    2   teaspoons canola oil

1. Preheat broiler.
2. Divide first 5 ingredients evenly among 4 (12-inch) skewers, and sprinkle with salt, thyme, and black pepper. Place on a broiler pan coated with cooking spray; drizzle kebabs with oil.
3. Broil 10 minutes or until desired degree of doneness, turning once. Yield: 4 servings (serving size: 1 kebab).

CALORIES 218 (41% from fat); FAT 10g (sat 3.2g, mono 4.1g, poly 1.4g); PROTEIN 26.5g; CARB 4.7g; FIBER 0.7g; CHOL 56mg; IRON 2mg; SODIUM 529mg; CALC 33mg

Pork Chops with Ginger-Cherry Sauce

You may use any variety of fruit preserves. Serve with egg noodles tossed with chopped fresh parsley.

    1   teaspoon dark sesame oil
    4   (4-ounce) center-cut boneless
        pork chops, trimmed
    ½   teaspoon salt
    ¼   teaspoon freshly ground black
        pepper
    ½   cup cherry preserves
    2   teaspoons low-sodium soy sauce
    1   teaspoon bottled ground fresh
        ginger (such as Spice World)
    1   teaspoon seasoned rice vinegar

1. Heat oil in a nonstick skillet over medium-high heat. Sprinkle pork with salt and pepper; add to pan. Cook 4 minutes on each side; remove pork from pan.
2. Combine preserves and remaining 3 ingredients in a small bowl. Add preserves mixture to pan; reduce heat, and cook 2 minutes or until slightly thick, stirring constantly. Return pork to pan; cook 2 minutes or until thoroughly heated. Yield: 4 servings (serving size: 1 pork chop and 2 tablespoons sauce).

CALORIES 275 (26% from fat); FAT 7.8g (sat 2.6g, mono 3.4g, poly 1g); PROTEIN 23.5g; CARB 26.8g; FIBER 0.1g; CHOL 67mg; IRON 1mg; SODIUM 453mg; CALC 19mg

Bistro Dinner Salad

This is a perfect light and quick yet refined meal. The mustard tarragon vinaigrette complements the slightly bitter salad greens, while the pear adds a hint of sweetness.

    3 tablespoons finely chopped
       walnuts
    4 large eggs
    Cooking spray
    2 bacon slices (uncooked)
    8 cups gourmet salad greens
    ¼ cup (1 ounce) crumbled blue
       cheese
    1 Bartlett pear, cored and thinly
       sliced
    1 tablespoon white wine vinegar
    1 tablespoon extravirgin olive oil
    ½ teaspoon dried tarragon
    ½ teaspoon Dijon mustard
    4 (1-inch-thick) slices French bread
       baguette, toasted

1. Place nuts in a small skillet; cook over medium-high heat 3 minutes or until lightly browned, shaking pan frequently. Remove from heat; set aside.
2. Break 1 egg into each of 4 (6-ounce) custard cups coated with cooking spray. Cover with plastic wrap, and microwave at HIGH 40 seconds or until set; let stand 1 minute. Remove eggs from cups; drain on paper towels.
3. Cook bacon in a skillet over medium-high heat until crisp. Remove bacon

from pan, reserving 1 teaspoon drippings. Cool bacon slightly, and crumble. Combine walnuts, bacon, greens, blue cheese, and pear in a large bowl.
4. Combine 1 teaspoon reserved drippings, vinegar, oil, tarragon, and mustard in small bowl; stir with a whisk. Drizzle over greens mixture; toss gently. Arrange 2 cups salad mixture on each of 4 serving plates; top each serving with 1 egg and 1 toast slice. Yield: 4 servings.

CALORIES 393 (39% from fat); FAT 17g (sat 4.7g, mono 6.9g, poly 3.2g); PROTEIN 16.9g; CARB 44.7g; FIBER 8.8g; CHOL 222mg; IRON 3.1mg; SODIUM 605mg; CALC 150mg

Stir-Fried Chicken Salad

The pan sauce here doubles as a piquant vinaigrette for the main-dish salad. Serve with crunchy breadsticks, if you wish.

    ¼ cup fat-free, less-sodium chicken
       broth
    2 tablespoons rice wine vinegar
    1 tablespoon Thai fish sauce
    1 tablespoon low-sodium soy sauce
    1 tablespoon bottled chopped garlic
    2 teaspoons sugar
    1 pound skinless, boneless chicken
       breast tenders
    1 tablespoon peanut oil
    4 cups mixed salad greens
    ¼ cup chopped fresh basil
    ½ cup thinly sliced red onion
    2 tablespoons finely chopped
       unsalted, dry-roasted peanuts
    Lime wedges (optional)

1. Combine first 6 ingredients in a medium bowl. Add chicken to broth mixture, stirring to coat. Let stand 3 minutes.
2. Heat oil in a large nonstick skillet over medium-high heat. Drain chicken, reserving marinade. Add chicken to pan; cook 4 minutes or until done, stirring frequently. Stir in reserved marinade. Reduce heat; cook 1 minute or until slightly thick. Remove pan from heat.
3. Combine greens and basil in a large bowl. Add chicken mixture, tossing well. Place 1¼ cups salad mixture on each of 4 plates. Top each serving with 2 tablespoons onion and 1½ teaspoons

peanuts. Serve immediately. Serve with lime wedges, if desired. Yield: 4 servings.

CALORIES 214 (30% from fat); FAT 7.2g (sat 1.3g, mono 3g, poly 2.2g); PROTEIN 29.1g; CARB 8g; FIBER 2g; CHOL 66mg; IRON 2mg; SODIUM 594mg; CALC 60mg

Fresh Tuna Tacos

This is a great dish for a casual supper; let everyone assemble their own tacos.

    ¾ teaspoon chili powder
    ½ teaspoon ground cumin
    ½ teaspoon sugar
    ¼ teaspoon salt
    ⅛ teaspoon chipotle chile powder or
       chile powder
    1 pound Yellowfin tuna fillet (about
       ¾ inch thick)
    Cooking spray
    8 (6-inch) corn tortillas
    1 cup sliced peeled avocado (about
       1 medium)
    ½ cup vertically sliced onion
    ¼ cup fresh cilantro leaves
    24 pickled jalapeño slices
    8 teaspoons reduced-fat sour
       cream
    4 lime wedges

1. Combine first 5 ingredients in a small bowl; sprinkle spice mixture evenly over both sides of fish.
2. Heat a grill pan over high heat. Coat pan with cooking spray. Add fish; cook 2 minutes on each side or until medium-rare or desired degree of doneness. Cut fish into ¼-inch-thick slices.
3. Warm tortillas according to package directions. Divide fish evenly among tortillas; top each with 2 tablespoons avocado, 1 tablespoon onion, 1½ teaspoons cilantro, 3 jalapeño slices, and 1 teaspoon sour cream. Serve tacos with lime wedges. Yield: 4 servings (serving size: 2 filled tacos and 1 lime wedge).

CALORIES 331 (24% from fat); FAT 9g (sat 2g, mono 4.1g, poly 1.7g); PROTEIN 31.5g; CARB 32.3g; FIBER 5.3g; CHOL 55mg; IRON 2.3mg; SODIUM 408mg; CALC 138mg

Feta and Pepperoncini Barley Salad

Serve cantaloupe wedges and warm pita bread to complete the menu. Barley and navy beans are excellent sources of dietary fiber in this salad.

1½ cups water
⅔ cup uncooked quick-cooking barley
1 cup (4 ounces) crumbled feta cheese with basil and sun-dried tomatoes
1 cup halved grape or cherry tomatoes
½ cup finely chopped pepperoncini peppers
½ cup chopped bottled roasted red bell peppers
2 tablespoons chopped fresh basil
1 tablespoon capers, drained
1 tablespoon cider vinegar
1 tablespoon extravirgin olive oil
½ teaspoon bottled minced garlic
1 (16-ounce) can navy beans, rinsed and drained

1. Bring 1½ cups water to a boil in a medium saucepan; add barley. Cover, reduce heat, and simmer 18 minutes or until liquid is absorbed and barley is tender. Drain and rinse with cold water; drain well.
2. While barley cooks, combine feta cheese and remaining 9 ingredients in a large bowl; toss well. Add barley; toss gently until combined. Serve immediately. Yield: 4 servings (serving size: 1¼ cups).

CALORIES 317 (31% from fat); FAT 10.8g (sat 5g, mono 4g, poly 1.1g); PROTEIN 14.3g; CARB 42.6g; FIBER 10.5g; CHOL 25mg; IRON 4.2mg; SODIUM 973mg; CALC 250mg

Mussels and Clams with Curry Coconut Sauce over Noodles

If you don't have a serrano chile, substitute ¼ teaspoon crushed red pepper.

1 (7-ounce) package rice noodles
1 tablespoon olive oil
1 teaspoon bottled minced garlic
1 serrano chile, seeded and thinly sliced
1 cup fat-free, less-sodium chicken broth
1 tablespoon green curry paste
1 teaspoon bottled ground fresh ginger (such as Spice World)
1 (14-ounce) can light coconut milk
1½ pounds mussels, scrubbed and debearded
1½ pounds littleneck clams, scrubbed
2 cups grape or cherry tomatoes
1 cup chopped fresh cilantro, divided
¼ cup fresh lime juice
4 lime wedges

1. Cook noodles according to package directions, omitting salt and fat. Drain; set aside.
2. While noodles cook, heat oil in a large Dutch oven over medium heat. Add garlic and chile, and sauté 1 minute. Stir in broth, curry paste, ginger, and coconut milk; bring to a boil.
3. Add mussels and clams. Cover, reduce heat, and simmer 5 minutes or until shells open; discard any unopened shells. Remove from heat. Stir in tomatoes, ½ cup cilantro, and juice; toss well. Place 1 cup noodles in each of 4 shallow bowls; top each serving with 4 mussels and 4 clams. Drizzle sauce evenly over shellfish; sprinkle each serving with 2 tablespoons cilantro. Serve with lime wedges. Yield: 4 servings.

CALORIES 405 (25% from fat); FAT 11.3g (sat 5.3g, mono 3.3g, poly 1g); PROTEIN 19.6g; CARB 56.7g; FIBER 2.1g; CHOL 49mg; IRON 6.3mg; SODIUM 548mg; CALC 69mg

reader recipes

Learning From Experience

A young aspiring chef improvises to create a tasty pasta toss.

Eighteen-year-old Christina Provo of Lakeville, Indiana, loves inventing recipes, and she has been honing her skills. Three years ago, she created the Asparagus and Parmesan Pasta Toss one day when she wanted something more exciting than a sandwich for lunch. "I based the dish on things we had on hand in the kitchen," Provo says. "And we had some ingredients we needed to use up."

She says the main reason she loves cooking is for the experience of creating something new. "You never know how it's going to turn out until it's finished, even if you've made it before," Provo says. "I like the surprise."

Asparagus and Parmesan Pasta Toss

1 red bell pepper
1 pound uncooked mostaccioli pasta (tube-shaped pasta)
Cooking spray
3 garlic cloves, minced
2 cups presliced mushrooms
½ to 1 teaspoon crushed red pepper
½ teaspoon salt
¼ teaspoon dried marjoram
⅛ teaspoon dried oregano
⅛ teaspoon freshly ground black pepper
1 (14.5-ounce) can diced tomatoes, undrained
2¾ cups (1-inch) pieces asparagus (about 12 ounces)
½ cup (2 ounces) grated fresh Parmesan, divided

1. Preheat broiler.
2. Cut bell pepper in half lengthwise; discard seeds and membranes. Place pepper halves, skin sides up, on a foil-lined

baking sheet; flatten with hand. Broil 15 minutes or until blackened. Place in a zip-top plastic bag; seal. Let stand 10 minutes. Peel and cut into strips.

3. Cook pasta according to package directions, omitting salt and fat.

4. Heat a large nonstick skillet over medium-high heat. Coat pan with cooking spray. Add garlic, and cook 1 minute. Add mushrooms; cook 4 minutes or until liquid evaporates. Add bell pepper, crushed red pepper, and next 5 ingredients. Bring to a simmer; cook 7 minutes. Stir in asparagus; cook 4 minutes or until crisp-tender. Combine mushroom mixture, pasta, and ¼ cup cheese in a large bowl, tossing well to combine. Sprinkle ¼ cup cheese over pasta. Yield: 8 servings (serving size: 1⅓ cups).

CALORIES 124 (29% from fat); FAT 4g (sat 1.7g, mono 1g, poly 0.4g); PROTEIN 7.1g; CARB 16.5g; FIBER 3.7g; CHOL 10mg; IRON 2.4mg; SODIUM 456mg; CALC 104mg

---

QUICK & EASY
Creamy Herb Summer Pasta

"I rely on pasta as a staple, and this certainly qualifies as an easy side dish. You can serve it warm or chilled."
—Caroline Markunas, Birmingham, Alabama

> 8 ounces uncooked elbow macaroni
> 2 teaspoons minced shallots
> 2 teaspoons olive oil
> ½ teaspoon red wine vinegar
> ¼ teaspoon salt
> ⅛ teaspoon black pepper
> ¼ cup fat-free sour cream
> 1 tablespoon chopped fresh parsley

1. Cook pasta according to package directions, omitting salt and fat. Drain.

2. Combine shallots, oil, vinegar, salt, and pepper, stirring with a whisk. Stir in sour cream and parsley. Combine pasta and shallot mixture; toss well. Yield: 8 servings (serving size: ½ cup).

CALORIES 247 (12% from fat); FAT 3.4g (sat 0.6g, mono 1.8g, poly 0.6g); PROTEIN 8.1g; CARB 45.2g; FIBER 1.4g; CHOL 1mg; IRON 2.3mg; SODIUM 162mg; CALC 35mg

---

Flavorful Fare Menu
serves 4

The Caribbean spices on the fish go surprisingly well with the Indian-accented pilaf.

Aromatic Swordfish Steaks

Basmati rice pilaf*

Sautéed spinach

*Heat 1 tablespoon canola oil in a large saucepan over medium-high heat. Add 1 cup basmati rice to pan; sauté 2 minutes. Add 1 (14-ounce) can light coconut milk and ¾ cup fat-free, less-sodium chicken broth to pan; bring to a boil. Cover, reduce heat, and simmer 20 minutes or until tender. Transfer rice to a bowl. Add 3 tablespoons chopped pistachios, 3 tablespoons golden raisins, 3 tablespoons chopped fresh parsley, ¼ teaspoon garam masala, and ¼ teaspoon salt; toss well.

QUICK & EASY
Aromatic Swordfish Steaks

"I wanted an easy and delicious way to prepare fish with exotic flair. After returning home from a trip to Jamaica with a suitcase full of spices, I went to work, and this is the result."
—Karen Harris, Castle Rock, Colorado

> ¾ cup plain yogurt
> 1 tablespoon Jamaican jerk seasoning (such as Spice Islands)
> 1 tablespoon fresh lemon juice
> 1 teaspoon garlic powder
> 1 teaspoon ground cumin
> 1 teaspoon chili powder
> ½ teaspoon ground cinnamon
> ½ teaspoon ground ginger
> 4 (6-ounce) swordfish steaks (about ¾ inch thick)
> Cooking spray

1. Combine first 8 ingredients in a large zip-top plastic bag. Add fish, turning to coat. Cover and refrigerate 1 hour, turning bag occasionally.

2. Prepare grill.

3. Remove fish from bag. Discard marinade. Place fish on grill rack coated with cooking spray; grill 4 minutes on each side or until fish flakes easily when tested with a fork or until desired degree of doneness. Yield: 4 servings (serving size: 1 steak).

CALORIES 241 (30% from fat); FAT 8.5g (sat 2.8g, mono 3g, poly 1.7g); PROTEIN 35.5g; CARB 3.8g; FIBER 0.7g; CHOL 72mg; IRON 1.8mg; SODIUM 406mg; CALC 69mg

---

Roasted Garlic, Tomato, and Basil Squares

"My sister prepared a delectable but very high-fat tomato-basil tart. I wanted to find a light version and came up with this appetizer."
—Erin Mylroie, St. George, Utah

> 1 package dry yeast (about 2¼ teaspoons)
> ¼ teaspoon sugar
> 1 cup warm water (100° to 110°)
> 3 cups all-purpose flour (about 13½ ounces), divided
> 1 teaspoon salt
> Cooking spray
> 1 whole garlic head
> 2 tablespoons yellow cornmeal
> 2 cups chopped plum tomato (about 9 ounces)
> 1 cup (4 ounces) shredded part-skim mozzarella cheese
> ½ cup chopped fresh basil
> ¼ cup (1 ounce) grated fresh Parmesan cheese
> 2 tablespoons light mayonnaise
> ¼ teaspoon salt
> ¼ teaspoon freshly ground black pepper

1. Dissolve yeast and sugar in 1 cup warm water in a large bowl; let stand 5 minutes. Lightly spoon flour into dry measuring cups; level with a knife. Add 2¾ cups flour and 1 teaspoon salt to yeast mixture, stirring until well blended. Turn dough out onto a floured surface. Knead until smooth and elastic (about 5 minutes); add enough of remaining ¼ cup flour, 1 tablespoon at a time, to prevent dough from sticking to hands.

2. Place dough in a large bowl coated with cooking spray, turning to coat top. Cover and let rise in a warm place (85°),
Continued

free from drafts, 1 hour or until doubled in size.

3. Preheat oven to 400°.

4. While dough rises, remove white papery skin from garlic head (do not peel or separate cloves). Wrap head in foil. Bake at 400° for 40 minutes; cool 10 minutes. Separate cloves; squeeze to extract garlic pulp. Discard skins.

5. Cover a baking sheet with parchment paper, and sprinkle with cornmeal. Place dough on prepared baking sheet. Roll dough into a 15 x 10–inch rectangle. Lightly coat dough with cooking spray. Bake at 400° for 10 minutes or until lightly browned; remove from oven. Combine garlic pulp, tomato, and remaining 6 ingredients in a medium bowl. Spread cheese mixture over crust; bake at 400° for 15 minutes or until lightly browned. Let stand 10 minutes. Cut into 12 squares. Yield: 12 servings (serving size: 1 square).

CALORIES 168 (17% from fat); FAT 3.2g (sat 1.4g, mono 0.6g, poly 0.2g); PROTEIN 6.9g; CARB 27.4g; FIBER 1.4g; CHOL 8mg; IRON 1.8mg; SODIUM 289mg; CALC 93mg

---

QUICK & EASY
Soon Du Bu

"After I got married, my Korean mother-in-law taught me to make some traditional Korean recipes so my husband wouldn't pine away for her delicious cooking. This recipe is one of my favorites because it's easy and quick. Serve it with steamed white rice."

—Elan Perry, Marietta, Georgia

  2 teaspoons dark sesame oil
  ¼ pound medium shrimp, peeled and coarsely chopped
  ¼ teaspoon salt
  ¼ teaspoon crushed red pepper
  ⅛ teaspoon black pepper
  2 garlic cloves, minced
  ¾ cup fat-free, less-sodium chicken broth
  1 (14-ounce) package reduced-fat firm tofu, drained
  ½ cup finely chopped zucchini
  ¼ cup green onions, cut into 2-inch pieces
  1 large egg, lightly beaten

1. Heat oil in a large saucepan over medium heat. Add shrimp; sauté 2 minutes. Add salt, red pepper, black pepper, and garlic; sauté 1 minute. Add chicken broth and tofu, stirring to crumble tofu. Cover, reduce heat, and simmer 10 minutes. Stir in zucchini, onions, and egg; cook 5 minutes. Yield: 4 servings (serving size: about ¾ cup).

CALORIES 117 (37% from fat); FAT 4.8g (sat 0.9g, mono 1.6g, poly 1.7g); PROTEIN 14.1g; CARB 3.8g; FIBER 0.8g; CHOL 96mg; IRON 2mg; SODIUM 511mg; CALC 60mg

---

QUICK & EASY
Greek Shrimp Cocktail with Lemon-Yogurt Cream

"I created this first course when my garden was overflowing with mint and tomatoes, and our gourmet cooking group was preparing a dinner with a Mediterranean theme."

—Jamie Miller, Maple Grove, Minnesota

  3 cups water
  1 cup organic vegetable broth (such as Swanson Certified Organic)
  1 pound medium shrimp, peeled and deveined
  3 tablespoons finely chopped fresh flat-leaf parsley, divided
  1½ tablespoons finely chopped fresh mint
  1 tablespoon red wine vinegar
  2 teaspoons extravirgin olive oil
  ½ teaspoon dried oregano
  2 garlic cloves, minced
  1 cup finely chopped seeded cucumber
  1 cup finely chopped seeded tomato
  ⅓ cup (about 1½ ounces) reduced-fat crumbled feta
  ¼ cup finely chopped red onion
  2 tablespoons chopped pitted kalamata olives
  ¼ teaspoon freshly ground black pepper
  ½ cup plain fat-free yogurt
  1 teaspoon grated lemon rind
  2 teaspoons fresh lemon juice
  1 teaspoon honey
  8 lemon wedges

1. Combine 3 cups water and broth in a medium saucepan; bring to a boil. Add shrimp; cook 3 minutes or until done. Drain and rinse with cold water; drain.

2. Combine 2 tablespoons parsley, mint, and next 4 ingredients, stirring with a whisk. Stir in cucumber and next 4 ingredients. Add shrimp, tossing gently to combine. Sprinkle with pepper.

3. Combine yogurt, rind, juice, and honey in a small bowl, stirring with a whisk. Serve over shrimp mixture. Sprinkle with 1 tablespoon parsley; serve with lemon wedges. Yield: 8 servings (serving size: about ⅔ cup shrimp mixture, 1 tablespoon yogurt cream, and 1 lemon wedge).

CALORIES 118 (30% from fat); FAT 3.9g (sat 0.9g, mono 1.8g, poly 0.6g); PROTEIN 14g; CARB 6.6g; FIBER 0.9g; CHOL 88mg; IRON 1.8mg; SODIUM 298mg; CALC 90mg

---

MAKE AHEAD
Toni's Banana Chocolate Chip Walnut Bread

"I adapted this from a vegan muffin recipe to create a healthful snack my always-hungry teenagers can enjoy on the go."

—Toni Goodman, Lake Oswego, Oregon

  2 cups mashed ripe banana (about 4)
  1 cup vanilla fat-free yogurt
  ½ cup reduced-fat vanilla soy milk
  ¼ cup canola oil
  ½ teaspoon vanilla extract
  4 cups whole wheat pastry flour (about 20½ ounces)
  1 cup sugar
  2 teaspoons baking powder
  2 teaspoons baking soda
  1 teaspoon ground cinnamon
  ½ teaspoon salt
  1 cup semisweet chocolate chips
  ½ cup chopped walnuts
  Cooking spray

1. Preheat oven to 350°.

2. Place first 5 ingredients in a food processor; process until smooth.

3. Lightly spoon flour into dry measuring cups; level with a knife. Combine flour and next 5 ingredients in a large bowl. Add banana mixture to flour mixture, stirring just until moist. Stir in chocolate chips and walnuts until well combined. Divide mixture evenly between 2 (9 x 5–inch) loaf pans coated with cooking spray.

4. Bake at 350° for 50 minutes or until a wooden pick inserted in center comes out clean. Cool in pans on a wire rack 10 minutes. Remove from pans; cool completely. Yield: 2 loaves; 16 servings per loaf (serving size: 1 slice).

CALORIES 150 (29% from fat); FAT 4.9g (sat 1.2g, mono 1.8g, poly 1.6g); PROTEIN 3.2g; CARB 25.8g; FIBER 2.7g; CHOL 0mg; IRON 0.9mg; SODIUM 153mg; CALC 41mg

enlightened cook

Fine Food in Wild Places

Carole Latimer, who leads adventure trips for women, raises camp cuisine to a new level.

Tony's Breakfast Couscous

Latimer received this recipe from the husband of one of her guides, and it quickly became a favorite way to start the day. You can prepare it the night before, and serve warm or cold. The recipe is easy to double to serve more people. Use any combination of dried fruits you like—cherries, apples, blueberries, or raspberries. You can substitute one cup fat-free milk for dry, and decrease the water to ¼ cup.

1¼ cups water
½ cup nonfat dry milk
½ cup uncooked couscous
¼ cup dried cranberries
¼ cup raisins
¼ cup chopped walnuts, toasted
2 tablespoons brown sugar
½ teaspoon ground cinnamon
⅛ teaspoon salt

1. Bring 1¼ cups water to a boil in a small saucepan; stir in milk and remaining ingredients. Remove from heat. Cover; let stand 10 minutes. (Mixture will thicken as it cools.) Yield: 3 servings (serving size: ⅔ cup).

CALORIES 305 (21% from fat); FAT 6.9g (sat 0.7g, mono 1g, poly 4.8g); PROTEIN 9.6g; CARB 53.7g; FIBER 3.3g; CHOL 2mg; IRON 1.1mg; SODIUM 169mg; CALC 174mg

Sri Lankan Beef Curry Dinner

Latimer recommends serving this stew the first night in camp. You can prep the ingredients at home, and then cook the rice at camp.

1 tablespoon ground coriander
2 teaspoons ground cumin
1 teaspoon ground fennel
1 teaspoon ground turmeric
4 teaspoons freshly ground black pepper
2 teaspoons salt
2½ pounds boneless sirloin steak, trimmed and cut into 1½-inch cubes
Cooking spray
3 cups chopped onion (about 2 medium)
2 teaspoons grated fresh ginger
3 garlic cloves, minced
2 red jalapeño peppers, minced
3 cups light coconut milk
2 tablespoons white wine vinegar
2 (1 x 3–inch) lemon rind strips
6 cups hot cooked basmati rice

1. Cook first 4 ingredients in a small saucepan over medium-low heat 7 minutes or until toasted, stirring occasionally.
2. Combine toasted spices, black pepper, salt, and beef in a large bowl. Cover and marinate in refrigerator 1 hour.
3. Heat a large saucepan over medium-high heat. Coat pan with cooking spray. Add onion, ginger, garlic, and jalapeños; sauté 3 minutes or until onion is tender. Remove onion mixture from pan. Recoat pan with cooking spray. Add half of beef; cook 6 minutes, browning on all sides. Remove beef from pan. Repeat procedure with remaining beef. Return onion mixture and beef to pan; stir in milk, vinegar, and rind, scraping pan to loosen browned bits. Bring to a boil. Cover, reduce heat, and simmer 2 hours or until beef is very tender. Discard rind. Serve over rice. Yield: 8 servings (serving size: about ⅔ cup beef mixture and ¾ cup rice).

CALORIES 414 (25% from fat); FAT 11.7g (sat 6.5g, mono 2.6g, poly 0.3g); PROTEIN 33.5g; CARB 42.9g; FIBER 2.1g; CHOL 90mg; IRON 4.9mg; SODIUM 653mg; CALC 33mg

Chile Corncakes

It's difficult to tote fresh milk and eggs into the wilderness, so Latimer reconstitutes dry milk and eggs instead. For this recipe, you can substitute two large eggs and one cup fat-free milk for the dry versions; you'll need to decrease the water to ¾ cup. Serve these savory cakes with sour cream and salsa for breakfast or dinner.

½ cup whole wheat flour (about 2⅜ ounces)
½ cup all-purpose flour (about 2¼ ounces)
1 cup yellow cornmeal
½ cup dried egg mix
⅓ cup nonfat dry milk
2 teaspoons baking powder
1 teaspoon salt
2 cups water
½ cup fresh corn kernels
¼ cup canola oil
1 (4.5-ounce) can chopped green chiles, drained
6 tablespoons reduced-fat sour cream
6 tablespoons fat-free bottled salsa

1. Lightly spoon flours into dry measuring cups; level with a knife. Combine flours, cornmeal, and next 4 ingredients in a large bowl; make a well in center of mixture. Add 2 cups water, corn, oil, and chiles, stirring just until moist.
2. Pour about ⅓ cup batter per pancake onto a hot nonstick griddle or nonstick skillet. Cook 3 minutes or until tops are covered with bubbles and edges look
Continued

cooked. Carefully turn pancakes over; cook 2 minutes or until bottoms are lightly browned. Serve with sour cream and salsa. Yield: 6 servings (serving size: 2 corncakes, 1 tablespoon sour cream, and 1 tablespoon salsa).

CALORIES 335 (30% from fat); FAT 11.3g (sat 1.5g, mono 5.6g, poly 3g); PROTEIN 10.4g; CARB 47.4g; FIBER 3.6g; CHOL 8mg; IRON 2.1mg; SODIUM 850mg; CALC 209mg

lighten up

Enticing Enchiladas

We trim down a 30-year-old casserole recipe for a Nevada couple with heart-healthy goals.

Swiss Enchiladas originated with a recipe clipped from a newspaper in the 1970s, when Diane Webber's husband, Robert, was a graduate student. Diane, of Las Vegas, Nevada, says they took the cheesy dish to her work potlucks and his department functions. In recent years, Webber prepared the casserole for tailgate parties and other get-togethers since it can easily be doubled, and the unexpected nutty flavor from the Swiss cheese in a familiar tortilla-chicken combination made it a hit. However, the two have become more health-conscious and strive to incorporate more vegetables, chicken, and fish into their diets. They asked *Cooking Light* to lighten it.

BEFORE	AFTER
SERVING SIZE	
1 enchilada	
CALORIES PER SERVING	
783	419
FAT	
54.2g	13.2g
PERCENT OF TOTAL CALORIES	
62%	28%

Swiss Enchiladas

Add a dash of cumin or paprika to the onions, if you'd like. You can also use purchased rotisserie chicken to cut down on the prep time.

Cooking spray
1½ cups chopped onion
2 cups chopped roasted skinless, boneless chicken breast (about 2 breast halves)
2 garlic cloves, minced
2 (4.5-ounce) cans diced green chiles, undrained
1 (14.5-ounce) can petite diced tomatoes, undrained
2 cups 2% reduced-fat milk
2 tablespoons all-purpose flour
¼ teaspoon salt
6 (8-inch) fat-free flour tortillas
2 cups (8 ounces) shredded Swiss cheese, divided

1. Preheat oven to 350°.
2. Heat a large nonstick skillet over medium-high heat. Coat pan with cooking spray. Add onion; cook 5 minutes or until tender, stirring occasionally. Stir in chicken, garlic, chiles, and tomatoes. Reduce heat, and simmer 7 minutes or until liquid evaporates. Set aside.
3. Combine milk and flour in a small saucepan over medium-high heat; cook 5 minutes or until mixture thickens, stirring constantly with a whisk. Stir in salt.
4. Warm tortillas according to package directions. Spoon about ½ cup chicken mixture and about 2½ tablespoons cheese down center of each tortilla; roll up. Arrange filled tortillas in bottom of a 13 x 9–inch baking dish coated with cooking spray. Pour milk mixture over tortillas, and top evenly with 1 cup cheese. Bake at 350° for 25 minutes or until cheese is bubbly. Remove from oven.
5. Preheat broiler.
6. Broil casserole 3 minutes or until cheese begins to brown. Yield: 6 servings (serving size: 1 enchilada and about ⅓ cup sauce).

CALORIES 419 (28% from fat); FAT 13.2g (sat 7.9g, mono 3.7g, poly 0.8g); PROTEIN 33.2g; CARB 41.8g; FIBER 4.3g; CHOL 79mg; IRON 2.1mg; SODIUM 726mg; CALC 474mg

Cobb Salad with Green Goddess Dressing

Cobb Salad with Green Goddess Dressing

DRESSING:
½ cup plain fat-free yogurt
¼ cup reduced-fat mayonnaise
3 tablespoons white wine vinegar
3 tablespoons chopped green onions
2 tablespoons chopped fresh flat-leaf parsley
1 tablespoon chopped fresh chives
2 teaspoons anchovy paste
1 teaspoon chopped fresh tarragon
¼ teaspoon freshly ground black pepper
⅛ teaspoon salt
1 garlic clove, minced

SALAD:
8 cups torn romaine lettuce
1 cup trimmed watercress
1½ cups chopped cooked chicken breast
2 tomatoes, each cut into 8 wedges (about 1 pound)
2 hard-cooked large eggs, each cut into 4 wedges
½ cup diced peeled avocado
¼ cup (1½ ounces) crumbled blue cheese

1. To prepare dressing, place first 11 ingredients in a blender or food processor; process until smooth. Chill.
2. To prepare salad, combine lettuce and watercress in a large bowl. Place 2 cups lettuce mixture on each of 4 plates. Arrange 6 tablespoons chicken, 4 tomato wedges, 2 egg wedges, 2 tablespoons avocado, and 1 tablespoon cheese over each serving. Serve each salad with ¼ cup dressing. Yield: 4 servings.

CALORIES 273 (39% from fat); FAT 11.8g (sat 3.6g, mono 4.3g, poly 2.5g); PROTEIN 25.7g; CARB 16.3g; FIBER 3.8g; CHOL 158mg; IRON 3.2mg; SODIUM 637mg; CALC 196mg

Bake Sales Go Big Time

A once-quaint tradition now nets big bucks for important causes. Here are recipes and plans to make your own fund-raiser a sweet success.

Long the province of church ladies and high school football moms, bake sales have hit the big time. Altruists around the country, including many top restaurant chefs, are finding that yesterday's quaint tradition is a foolproof way to raise significant amounts of cash for good causes.

Plan a Profitable Bake Sale

Don't ask too much of any single person. After your group of key planners sets specific monetary and civic goals for the sale, seek other volunteers and partners with modest, clear requests.

Publicize. Include someone with media experience in your planning committee. Post flyers and place notices of the sale in all relevant bulletins and newsletters. Also, bone up on the charity and engage local media with concise notes highlighting what makes your event different and interesting.

Pick a friendly, high-traffic location that, if outdoors, comes with a rain site. Set up where there will be lots of customers who both support your cause and are likely to be interested in your wares. Check with the town or city clerk for information on necessary permits.

Packaging matters. Wrappings should suggest their contents are fresh and appetizing.

Be creative. Pick a theme, such as a summer kick-off Memorial Day sale. Integrate local celebrities into the event, or tie in cooking demos or raffles of especially elaborate desserts. Encourage bakers to print labels bearing creative names for their wares.

STAFF FAVORITE • MAKE AHEAD

Green Pumpkinseed and Cranberry Crispy Bars

We loved this creative take on the traditional Rice Krispies bar. Green pumpkinseeds are also sometimes sold as *pepitas*. In humid weather, cool the bars in the refrigerator to keep them from becoming too sticky.

Cooking spray
½ cup raw green pumpkinseeds
¼ cup butter
1 (8-ounce) package miniature marshmallows (about 5 cups)
1 teaspoon vanilla extract
⅛ teaspoon salt
5 cups oven-toasted rice cereal (such as Rice Krispies)
1 cup dried cranberries

1. Heat a large nonstick skillet over medium-high heat. Coat pan with cooking spray. Add pumpkinseeds; cook 4 minutes or until seeds begin to pop and lightly brown, stirring frequently. Remove from heat; cool.
2. Lightly coat a 13 x 9–inch baking dish with cooking spray; set aside. Melt butter in a large saucepan over medium heat. Stir in marshmallows; cook 2 minutes or until smooth, stirring constantly. Remove from heat; stir in vanilla and salt. Stir in reserved seeds, cereal, and cranberries. Scrape mixture into prepared dish using a rubber spatula.
3. Lightly coat hands with cooking spray; press cereal mixture evenly into dish. Cool completely. Cut into 16 bars. Yield: 16 servings (serving size: 1 bar).

CALORIES 152 (29% from fat); FAT 4.9g (sat 2.2g, mono 1.4g, poly 1g); PROTEIN 1.9g; CARB 26.3g; FIBER 0.7g; CHOL 7.5mg; IRON 0.9mg; SODIUM 115mg; CALC 5mg

MAKE AHEAD • FREEZABLE

Strawberry Jam Crumb Cake

For convenience, you can freeze this breakfast treat for up to two weeks.

CRUMB TOPPING:
¼ cup all-purpose flour (about 1 ounce)
¼ cup packed brown sugar
¼ teaspoon ground cinnamon
2 tablespoons chilled butter, cut into small pieces

CAKE:
Cooking spray
1¼ cups all-purpose flour (about 5½ ounces)
½ teaspoon baking powder
¼ teaspoon baking soda
⅛ teaspoon salt
⅔ cup powdered sugar
¼ cup butter, softened
½ teaspoon vanilla extract
1 large egg
6 tablespoons fat-free milk
2 tablespoons fresh lemon juice
¼ cup reduced-sugar strawberry spread (such as Smucker's)

1. To prepare crumb topping, lightly spoon ¼ cup flour into a dry measuring cup; level with a knife. Combine flour, brown sugar, and cinnamon in a small bowl. Cut in 2 tablespoons butter with a pastry blender or 2 knives until mixture resembles coarse meal; set topping aside.
2. Preheat oven to 350°.
3. To prepare cake, lightly coat an 8-inch springform pan with cooking spray; set aside. Lightly spoon 1¼ cups flour into dry measuring cups; level with a
Continued

knife. Combine flour, baking powder, baking soda, and salt in a small bowl; set aside.

4. Combine powdered sugar and ¼ cup butter in a large bowl; beat with a mixer at medium speed until well blended (about 2 minutes). Add vanilla and egg; beat 2 minutes. Combine milk and juice; add to sugar mixture, and beat 2 minutes.

5. Add half of flour mixture to sugar mixture; stir until smooth. Add remaining flour mixture, and stir just until combined.

6. Spoon half of batter into prepared pan, spreading evenly. Top with strawberry spread. Spoon remaining batter over strawberry layer, spreading evenly. Sprinkle reserved crumb topping evenly over batter. Bake at 350° for 45 minutes or until a wooden pick inserted in center comes out clean. Cool 10 minutes in pan on a wire rack; remove from pan. Cool completely on wire rack. Yield: 12 servings (serving size: 1 wedge).

CALORIES 191 (30% from fat); FAT 6.3g (sat 3.8g, mono 1.7g, poly 0.3g); PROTEIN 2.5g; CARB 31.7g; FIBER 0.5g; CHOL 33mg; IRON 0.9mg; SODIUM 123mg; CALC 32mg

---

STAFF FAVORITE

Cinnamon-Sugar Cookies

Buttery and sweet with a hint of spice, these cookie jar favorites are right for any occasion. If you prefer a slightly chewier cookie, reduce baking time to 10 minutes. A sprinkling of large-grained turbinado sugar makes a pretty presentation to attract buyers.

    1   cup granulated sugar
    6   tablespoons butter, softened
    1   tablespoon light corn
        syrup
    1   teaspoon vanilla extract
    1   large egg
    1   cup cake flour (about 4
        ounces)
    ¾   cup all-purpose flour (about
        3⅓ ounces)
    1   teaspoon baking powder
    1   teaspoon baking soda
    ¼   teaspoon salt
    ¼   teaspoon ground cinnamon
    ¼   cup turbinado sugar
    ½   teaspoon ground cinnamon

1. Place granulated sugar and butter in a bowl; beat with a mixer at medium speed until well blended (about 3 minutes). Add syrup, vanilla, and egg; beat 3 minutes or until well blended.

2. Lightly spoon flours into dry measuring cups; level with a knife. Combine flours, baking powder, baking soda, salt, and ¼ teaspoon cinnamon. Add flour mixture to butter mixture; stir until just combined. Wrap in plastic wrap; chill 1 hour.

3. Preheat oven to 375°.

4. Combine turbinado sugar and ½ teaspoon cinnamon in a small bowl. Shape dough into 48 balls, about 1 teaspoon each. Roll balls in cinnamon-sugar mixture. Place 2 inches apart on ungreased baking sheets. Bake at 375° for 12 minutes or until golden on bottom. Cool on wire racks. Yield: 48 cookies (serving size: 1 cookie).

CALORIES 105 (27% from fat); FAT 3.1g (sat 1.9g, mono 0.8g, poly 0.2g); PROTEIN 1.2g; CARB 18.2g; FIBER 0.3g; CHOL 16mg; IRON 0.5mg; SODIUM 122mg; CALC 15mg

---

STAFF FAVORITE • MAKE AHEAD
FREEZABLE

Sour Cream Coffeecake Muffins

Fold the batter just four times to swirl in the sugar mixture, not fully blend it.

    ½   cup packed dark brown
        sugar
    ¼   cup chopped pecans
    1½ teaspoons ground cinnamon
    1   cup granulated sugar
    ¼   cup butter, softened
    ½   cup egg substitute
    1   cup reduced-fat sour cream
    2   tablespoons water
    1   teaspoon vanilla extract
    1¾ cups all-purpose flour (about
        7¾ ounces)
    1   teaspoon baking powder
    ½   teaspoon baking soda
    ½   teaspoon salt
        Cooking spray
    6   tablespoons powdered
        sugar
    3   teaspoons fresh orange juice
        Dash of salt

1. Preheat oven to 400°.

2. Combine first 3 ingredients; set aside.

3. Place granulated sugar and butter in a large bowl; beat with a mixer at medium speed until well blended (about 3 minutes). Add egg substitute; beat 3 minutes. Beat in sour cream, water, and vanilla.

4. Lightly spoon flour into dry measuring cups; level with a knife. Combine flour, baking powder, baking soda, and salt in a large bowl, stirring well with a whisk. Make a well in center of mixture; add sour cream mixture. Stir just until combined.

5. Place 3 tablespoons brown sugar mixture in a small bowl; set aside. Sprinkle surface of batter with remaining brown sugar mixture. Gently fold batter 4 times.

6. Place 18 paper muffin cup liners in muffin cups; coat liners with cooking spray. Spoon batter into prepared cups. Sprinkle batter evenly with reserved brown sugar mixture. Bake at 400° for 25 minutes or until a wooden pick inserted in center comes out clean. Remove muffins from pan immediately; place on a wire rack. Cool 10 minutes.

7. Combine powdered sugar, juice, and dash of salt in a small bowl, stirring until smooth. Drizzle powdered sugar mixture evenly over muffins. Yield: 18 servings (serving size: 1 muffin).

CALORIES 182 (28% from fat); FAT 5.7g (sat 2.8g, mono 1.4g, poly 0.6g); PROTEIN 2.9g; CARB 30.4g; FIBER 0.6g; CHOL 14mg; IRON 1mg; SODIUM 176mg; CALC 53mg

Bake some yummy cookies, gingerbread, muffins, or snack cakes for a good cause today.

Gingerbread Loaf

This aromatic, spice-filled loaf cake is even more moist the next day, so it's well suited to make ahead for a bake sale. Check your local supermarket for small disposable loaf pans; half-size loaves may be ideal for a bake sale. This recipe also makes 3 (3½ x 5½–inch) loaves; bake them for 50 minutes.

1¾ cups all-purpose flour (about 7¾ ounces)
¾ cup whole wheat flour (about 3⅓ ounces)
2 teaspoons baking powder
1 teaspoon ground ginger
½ teaspoon baking soda
¼ teaspoon salt
¼ teaspoon ground cardamom
¼ teaspoon ground cinnamon
Dash of nutmeg
1 cup warm 1% low-fat milk (100° to 110°)
½ cup molasses
¼ cup canola oil
3 tablespoons prune baby food
2 large eggs, lightly beaten
¾ cup packed dark brown sugar
½ cup golden raisins
Cooking spray
2 tablespoons finely chopped walnuts

1. Preheat oven to 350°.
2. Lightly spoon flours into dry measuring cups; level with a knife. Combine flours, baking powder, and next 6 ingredients in a large bowl.
3. Combine milk and next 4 ingredients in a medium bowl, stirring with a whisk until blended. Add sugar, stirring until well blended. Make a well in center of flour mixture. Add milk mixture to flour mixture; stir just until combined. Stir in raisins. Scrape batter into a 9 x 5–inch loaf pan coated with cooking spray, using a rubber spatula. Sprinkle walnuts in a 2½-inch-wide strip down center of loaf.
4. Bake at 350° for 1 hour or until a wooden pick inserted in center comes out clean. Cool in pan on a wire rack. Yield: 16 servings (serving size: 1 slice).

CALORIES 207 (22% from fat); FAT 5.2g (sat 0.7g, mono 2.5g, poly 1.7g); PROTEIN 3.8g; CARB 37.7g; FIBER 1.4g; CHOL 27mg; IRON 1.9mg; SODIUM 165mg; CALC 94mg

Send a Message Fortune Cookies

These cookies are ideal for bake sales trying to promote a cause; customize the fortune to suit the occasion. Bake three cookies at a time so they'll be soft enough to shape. Tuck your message into the cookie while shaping. If the cookies become too brittle, return them to the oven for a few seconds to soften.

½ cup bread flour (about 2⅓ ounces)
½ cup sugar
1 teaspoon vanilla extract
2 large egg whites

1. Lightly spoon flour into a dry measuring cup; level with a knife. Place flour, sugar, extract, and egg whites in a food processor; process until blended. Scrape batter into a bowl using a rubber spatula; cover and chill 1 hour.
2. Preheat oven to 400°.
3. Cover 2 large baking sheets with parchment paper. Draw 3 (3-inch) circles on paper. Turn paper over; secure with masking tape. Spoon 1 teaspoon batter into center of each of 3 drawn circles; spread evenly to fill circle. Place one sheet in oven, and bake at 400° for 5 minutes or until cookies are brown just around edges. Remove from oven. Working quickly, loosen edges of cookies with a spatula, and turn over.
4. Lay handle of a wooden spoon and a prepared fortune along center of 1 cookie. Fold cookie over so edges meet over spoon handle; press edges together. Remove spoon. Gently pull ends of cookie down over rim of a small bowl (or jar); hold for a few seconds or until set. Repeat with remaining cookies.
5. Repeat baking and shaping procedures until all of batter is used. Cool cookies completely; store in an airtight container. Yield: 18 cookies (serving size: 1 cookie).

CALORIES 37 (0% from fat); FAT 0.1g (sat 0g, mono 0g, poly 0g); PROTEIN 0.9g; CARB 8.4g; FIBER 0.1g; CHOL 0mg; IRON 0.2mg; SODIUM 6mg; CALC 1mg

How to Make Fortune Cookies

1. *Spoon 1 teaspoon batter into center of each of 3 drawn circles; spread evenly to fill circle.*

2. *Lay handle of a wooden spoon and a prepared fortune along center of 1 cookie. Fold cookie over so edges meet over spoon handle; press edges together. Remove spoon.*

3. *Gently pull ends of cookie down over rim of a small bowl (or jar); hold for a few seconds or until set. Repeat with remaining cookies.*

Double Apple Bran Muffins

Oat bran, the outer casing of an oat, is high in fiber. Apples and applesauce make these healthful muffins sweet and moist. If making ahead, individually wrap cooled muffins, and freeze for up to one week.

½ cup packed brown sugar
¼ cup butter, softened
1 large egg
1 large egg white
¾ cup fat-free milk
¼ cup unsweetened applesauce
1 tablespoon molasses
½ teaspoon vanilla extract
1 cup all-purpose flour (about 4½ ounces)
1½ cups oat bran
1½ teaspoons baking powder
¾ teaspoon salt
½ teaspoon ground cinnamon
½ cup coarsely chopped, peeled Granny Smith apple
2 teaspoons turbinado sugar (optional)

1. Preheat oven to 400°.
2. Place 12 paper muffin cup liners in muffin cups; set aside. Combine brown sugar and butter in a medium bowl; beat with a mixer at medium-high speed until light and fluffy (about 5 minutes). Add egg; beat 1 minute or until well blended. Beat in egg white until well blended. Add milk, applesauce, molasses, and vanilla; beat at low speed until well blended.
3. Lightly spoon flour into a dry measuring cup; level with a knife. Combine flour, bran, and next 3 ingredients in a large bowl; make a well in center of mixture. Add milk mixture to flour mixture, stirring just until moist. Gently stir in apple.
4. Spoon batter evenly into prepared muffin cups. Sprinkle evenly with turbinado sugar, if desired. Bake at 400° for 18 minutes or until muffins spring back when touched lightly in center. Yield: 12 servings (serving size: 1 muffin).

CALORIES 174 (29% from fat); FAT 5.6g (sat 2.8g, mono 1.6g, poly 0.8g); PROTEIN 5.2g; CARB 32.5g; FIBER 3g; CHOL 28mg; IRON 1.9mg; SODIUM 258mg; CALC 80mg

Chocolate-Banana Snack Cake

This easy-to-make snack cake has deep chocolate taste. For more banana flavor and a slight crunch, top the cake with crumbled banana chips before baking. You can sell the cake whole or package individual pieces.

½ cup unsweetened applesauce
1 cup granulated sugar
¼ cup butter, softened
½ cup mashed ripe banana
2 large eggs
1 teaspoon instant coffee granules
1 teaspoon vanilla extract
1 cup all-purpose flour (about 4½ ounces)
½ cup unsweetened cocoa
½ teaspoon baking soda
¼ teaspoon salt
Powdered sugar (optional)

1. Preheat oven to 350°.
2. Spoon applesauce onto several layers of heavy-duty paper towels; spread to ½-inch thickness. Cover with additional paper towels; let stand 5 minutes. Scrape applesauce into a bowl using a rubber spatula.
3. Combine sugar and butter in a large bowl; beat with a mixer at medium speed until light and fluffy (about 2 minutes). Add applesauce and banana, beating until blended. Add eggs, 1 at a time, beating well after each addition. Beat in coffee and vanilla.
4. Lightly spoon flour into a dry measuring cup; level with a knife. Combine flour, cocoa, baking soda, and salt, stirring well with a whisk. Add flour mixture to egg mixture; stir just until combined. Scrape batter into an 8-inch baking pan lined with parchment paper, spreading evenly. Bake at 350° for 40 minutes or until a wooden pick inserted in center comes out clean. Cool in pan on a wire rack. Sprinkle with powdered sugar, if desired. Yield: 16 servings (serving size: 1 piece).

CALORIES 128 (28% from fat); FAT 3.9g (sat 2.2g, mono 1.1g, poly 0.2g); PROTEIN 2.3g; CARB 22.5g; FIBER 1.4g; CHOL 34mg; IRON 0.9mg; SODIUM 106mg; CALC 10mg

Triple Fruit Cookies

Make these cookies up to a week in advance, since they freeze well. Dried fruits are available in most supermarkets and health food stores.

⅔ cup packed brown sugar
⅓ cup butter, softened
¼ cup light-colored corn syrup
2 tablespoons fresh orange juice
1 teaspoon vanilla extract
1 large egg
1½ cups all-purpose flour (about 6¾ ounces)
½ teaspoon baking soda
½ teaspoon baking powder
½ teaspoon ground cinnamon
¼ teaspoon salt
¼ teaspoon ground allspice
¼ cup dried blueberries
¼ cup dried cranberries
¼ cup dried cherries
¼ cup flaked sweetened coconut

1. Preheat oven to 350°.
2. Place sugar and butter in a medium bowl; beat with a mixer at medium speed until well blended (about 3 minutes). Add syrup, juice, vanilla, and egg; beat until well combined (about 2 minutes).
3. Lightly spoon flour into dry measuring cups; level with a knife. Combine flour, baking soda, and next 4 ingredients. Add flour mixture to butter mixture; stir just until combined. Add blueberries, cranberries, cherries, and coconut; stir gently.
4. Drop dough by rounded teaspoonfuls 2 inches apart onto ungreased baking sheets. Bake at 350° for 12 minutes or until golden. Cool on pans 1 minute. Remove cookies from pans, and cool on wire racks. Yield: 48 cookies (serving size: 2 cookies).

CALORIES 108 (26% from fat); FAT 3.1g (sat 1.9g, mono 0.8g, poly 0.7g); PROTEIN 1.2g; CARB 19g; FIBER 0.7g; CHOL 16mg; IRON 0.6mg; SODIUM 90mg; CALC 17mg

Summer Cookbook

Here are some creative ways to use the season's best produce and flavors in starters, entrées, sides, and desserts.

Winning Beginnings

From sweet gazpacho to spicy salsas, these appetizers will be a hit at your next get-together.

QUICK & EASY
Prosciutto-Wrapped Figs Stuffed with Blue Cheese

12 large fresh black Mission figs, trimmed
2 ounces blue cheese, cut into 12 cubes
2 ounces thinly sliced prosciutto, cut into 12 strips
¼ cup balsamic vinegar
2 tablespoons honey
⅛ teaspoon freshly ground black pepper
Dash of salt
Cooking spray

1. Cut each fig in half vertically, cutting to, but not through, base of fig. Spread slightly apart. Place 1 cube of cheese inside each fig, and gently close to seal. Wrap one prosciutto strip around each fig.
2. Prepare grill.
3. Combine vinegar and next 3 ingredients in a small saucepan; bring to a boil. Reduce heat, and simmer until thick, about 10 minutes. Cool.
4. Place figs on a grill rack coated with cooking spray; grill 6 minutes, turning occasionally, until prosciutto is crisp. Drizzle each fig with balsamic syrup.

Yield: 6 servings (serving size: 2 stuffed figs and 1½ teaspoons balsamic syrup).

CALORIES 178 (21% from fat); FAT 4.4g (sat 2.3g, mono 0.8g, poly 0.3g); PROTEIN 5.6g; CARB 32.2g; FIBER 3.7g; CHOL 16mg; IRON 0.7mg; SODIUM 342mg; CALC 98mg

MAKE AHEAD
Chunky Tomato-Fruit Gazpacho

2 cups finely chopped tomatoes (about ¾ pound)
2 cups finely diced honeydew melon (about ¾ pound)
2 cups finely diced cantaloupe (about ¾ pound)
1 cup finely diced mango (about 1 medium)
1 cup finely diced seeded peeled cucumber (about 1 medium)
1 cup finely diced nectarines (about 3 medium)
1 cup fresh orange juice (about 4 oranges)
½ cup finely chopped Vidalia or other sweet onion
¼ cup chopped fresh basil
3 tablespoons chopped fresh mint
3 tablespoons fresh lemon juice
1 teaspoon sugar
½ teaspoon salt
1 jalapeño pepper, seeded and finely chopped

1. Combine all ingredients in a large bowl. Cover and chill at least 2 hours. Yield: 7 servings (serving size: 1 cup).

CALORIES 95 (5% from fat); FAT 0.5g (sat 0.1g, mono 0.1g, poly 0.2g); PROTEIN 2.1g; CARB 23g; FIBER 2.8g; CHOL 0mg; IRON 0.9mg; SODIUM 189mg; CALC 33mg

Tomatoes

History: The Europeans initially rejected this plant, prized by the Aztecs as a health food, falsely believing the tomato was poisonous. The reputation of tomatoes improved when the French later dubbed them "love apples."
Varieties: Beefsteak, globe, plum, grape, and cherry are the most familiar types. Summer brings a bumper crop of heirloom tomatoes that come in myriad shapes and hues, including purple, bicolored, striped, orange, and yellow.
Availability: Although fresh tomatoes are available year-round, their peak season is June through September.
To select: Look for "a bright red, crimson color on the exterior and firmness," says Tony DiMare, of the 77-year-old, family-owned DiMare Company. For tomatoes of other hues, "you're still looking for bright color and firmness."
To store: Keep tomatoes at room temperature prior to consumption, says DiMare. "Don't refrigerate tomatoes because cold temperatures, below 55 degrees, destroy the integrity, texture, and taste." To speed up the ripening process, put tomatoes in a brown paper bag at room temperature. Plan to eat more delicate heirloom tomatoes the day you buy them. "Heirloom-type tomatoes don't typically have a long shelf life," DiMare says.
To cook: "I like to use plum tomatoes for fresh tomato sauce or salsa because of their solid content," DiMare says. He also likes to eat sliced tomatoes with buffalo mozzarella, oregano, salt, and pepper, dressed with olive oil and balsamic vinegar.

Jamaica Margaritas

Hibiscus blossoms can be found at Latin grocery stores. Simmering the blossoms in a sugar-water mixture infuses more flavor than just steeping them in warm water. This drink is especially good when made with premium-quality tequila.

    1   cup dried hibiscus blossoms
        (about 2 ounces)
    3   cups water
    ¾   cup sugar
    1¼ cups tequila
    ½   cup fresh lime juice
    ⅓   cup Triple Sec or other orange-
        flavored liqueur
    8   lime slices

1. Place blossoms in a strainer; rinse with cold water. Combine blossoms, 3 cups water, and sugar in a medium saucepan; bring to a boil. Reduce heat, and simmer 10 minutes. Strain into a bowl; discard blossoms. Cover and chill hibiscus mixture.
2. Combine hibiscus mixture, tequila, juice, and Triple Sec. Serve over ice. Garnish with lime slices. Yield: 8 servings (serving size: ½ cup margarita and 1 lime slice).

CALORIES 205 (0% from fat); FAT 0g; PROTEIN 0.1g; CARB 24.7g; FIBER 0.1g; CHOL 0mg; IRON 0mg; SODIUM 3mg; CALC 4mg

Minted Raspberry-Hibiscus Agua Fresca

    8   cups water
    2   cups fresh raspberries
    ¼   cup coarsely chopped fresh mint
        leaves
    6   rose hip and hibiscus tea bags
        (such as Pompadour brand)
    ¾   cup sugar
    1   tablespoon fresh lemon juice
    8   mint sprigs

1. Bring 8 cups water to a boil in a large saucepan. Add raspberries, mint, and tea bags. Remove from heat. Let stand 1 hour at room temperature. Remove tea bags; strain mixture through a sieve,

reserving liquid. Discard solids. Add sugar and juice to tea, stirring until sugar dissolves. Garnish with mint sprigs. Yield: 8 servings (serving size: 1 cup tea and 1 mint sprig).

CALORIES 77 (0% from fat); FAT 0g; PROTEIN 0.1g; CARB 19.8g; FIBER 0.3g; CHOL 0mg; IRON 0.2mg; SODIUM 2mg; CALC 6mg

Pita Chips with Eggplant Caviar

Prepare the pita chips ahead, and store in an airtight container up to four days.

PITA CHIPS:
    4   (6-inch) pitas
        Cooking spray
    ¼   teaspoon salt

CAVIAR:
    1   eggplant, cut in half lengthwise
        (about 1½ pounds)
    2   tablespoons chopped fresh flat-
        leaf parsley
    2   tablespoons minced shallots
    2   tablespoons extravirgin olive oil
    2   tablespoons fresh lemon juice
    1   tablespoon capers, drained and
        chopped
    ¼   teaspoon salt
    ¼   teaspoon black pepper
    2   canned anchovy fillets, patted dry
        and minced
    1   garlic clove, minced
        Parsley sprigs
        Lemon wedges (optional)

1. Preheat oven to 350°.
2. To prepare pita chips, split pitas; cut each half into 8 wedges. Place wedges in a single layer on a baking sheet coated with cooking spray; coat wedges with cooking spray. Sprinkle with ¼ teaspoon salt. Bake at 350° for 15 minutes or until lightly browned.
3. Preheat broiler.
4. To prepare caviar, place eggplant halves, cut sides up, on a baking sheet coated with cooking spray. Lightly coat eggplant with cooking spray, and broil 15 minutes or until tender. Remove from oven. Cool on pan 10 minutes; peel. Coarsely chop pulp; place in a medium

bowl. Add parsley and next 8 ingredients, stirring until blended. Garnish with parsley sprigs; serve with pita chips and lemon wedges, if desired. Yield: 8 servings (serving size: 8 pita chips and ¼ cup eggplant caviar).

CALORIES 137 (27% from fat); FAT 4.1g (sat 0.6g, mono 2.8g, poly 0.6g); PROTEIN 3.9g; CARB 21.7g; FIBER 3.1g; CHOL 1mg; IRON 1.1mg; SODIUM 379mg; CALC 38mg

Okra, Corn, and Jalapeño Skillet Salsa

Blending prime summer produce, this salsa is great over grilled chicken or pork or with baked tortilla chips. This recipe doubles easily for a crowd.

    1   tablespoon canola oil
    1   cup fresh yellow corn kernels
        (about 2 ears)
    1   pound okra, cut into ½-inch
        pieces (about 3½ cups)
    1   cup chopped fresh spinach
    ¼   cup bottled pickled jalapeño
        pepper slices
    ¾   cup chopped tomato (about
        1 medium)
    1   tablespoon fresh lime juice
    ⅛   teaspoon salt
    ⅛   teaspoon black pepper
    1   garlic clove, minced

1. Heat oil in a large nonstick skillet over medium-high heat. Add corn; sauté 3 minutes. Add okra; sauté 3 minutes. Stir in spinach and jalapeño; cook 2 minutes. Remove from heat; stir in tomato and remaining ingredients. Yield: 8 servings (serving size: ½ cup).

CALORIES 64 (35% from fat); FAT 2.5g (sat 0.2g, mono 1.3g, poly 0.9g); PROTEIN 2.6g; CARB 10g; FIBER 2.7g; CHOL 0mg; IRON 0.8mg; SODIUM 110mg; CALC 54mg

Fresh Corn Blinis with Smoked Salmon and Chive Cream

Classic blinis are nutty buckwheat flour pancakes topped with sour cream and caviar. Our version has silver-dollar-sized sweet corn pancakes crowned with cold-smoked salmon. To prevent the blinis from becoming soggy, arrange in a single layer on a platter.

½ cup reduced-fat sour cream
1 tablespoon minced fresh chives
1 ear shucked corn
⅓ cup all-purpose flour (about 1½ ounces)
2 tablespoons fine-ground yellow cornmeal
½ cup 1% low-fat milk
1 large egg yolk
¼ teaspoon salt
¼ teaspoon black pepper
1 large egg white
Cooking spray
4 ounces cold-smoked salmon, cut into 24 (2-inch) strips
Chopped fresh chives (optional)

1. Combine sour cream and minced chives in a small bowl. Cover mixture, and refrigerate.
2. Cut kernels from ear of corn. Scrape remaining pulp from cob using dull side of a knife blade. Discard cob. Set corn aside.
3. Lightly spoon flour into a dry measuring cup; level with a knife. Combine flour and cornmeal in a medium bowl; make a well in center of mixture. Combine milk and egg yolk in a small bowl; stir well with a whisk. Add milk mixture to flour mixture, and stir with a whisk just until moist. Stir in corn, salt, and pepper.
4. Place egg white in a bowl; beat with a mixer at high speed until foamy. Gently fold egg white into corn mixture.
5. Heat a large nonstick skillet over medium heat. Coat pan with cooking spray. Spoon about 1 tablespoon batter per blini onto pan, spreading to about 2-inch diameter. Cook 2 minutes or until tops are covered with bubbles and edges begin to set. Carefully turn blinis over;

cook 1 minute. Transfer blinis to a serving platter, and arrange in a single layer; keep warm. Repeat process with remaining batter. Top each blini with 1 piece salmon and 1 teaspoon sour cream mixture. Garnish with chopped chives, if desired. Yield: 8 servings (serving size: 3 topped blinis).

CALORIES 102 (33% from fat); FAT 3.7g (sat 1.7g, mono 1.2g, poly 0.4g); PROTEIN 6.2g; CARB 11.2g; FIBER 0.7g; CHOL 35mg; IRON 0.7mg; SODIUM 386mg; CALC 45mg

---

QUICK & EASY

Panzanella Salad with Bacon, Tomato, and Basil

Make the tomato mixture a day ahead; toss with bread and lettuce just before serving.

3 tablespoons balsamic vinegar
2 teaspoons extravirgin olive oil
½ teaspoon salt
¼ teaspoon black pepper
2 garlic cloves, minced
4 cups coarsely chopped tomato (about 1⅓ pounds)
½ cup vertically sliced red onion
¼ cup chopped fresh basil
6 bacon slices, cooked and crumbled
1 (8-ounce) loaf day-old French bread, cut into 1-inch cubes
Cooking spray
2 cups torn romaine lettuce

1. Preheat oven to 350°.
2. Combine first 5 ingredients in a bowl; stir with a whisk. Add tomato, onion, basil, and bacon; toss well. Set aside.
3. Arrange bread cubes in a single layer on a baking sheet; lightly coat bread with cooking spray. Bake at 350° for 15 minutes or until toasted; cool. Add bread and lettuce to tomato mixture; toss gently. Serve immediately. Yield: 6 servings (serving size: about 1¾ cups).

CALORIES 190 (29% from fat); FAT 6.2g (sat 1.6g, mono 3.1g, poly 1g); PROTEIN 6.8g; CARB 27.7g; FIBER 3.1g; CHOL 5mg; IRON 2mg; SODIUM 541mg; CALC 50mg

---

Basil

History: A native of India, basil is a member of the mint family.

Varieties: "If I could only have one [variety], it would be Genoa Green (sweet green basil). That's what I use to make pesto," says Susan Belsinger, coauthor of *Basil, An Herb Lover's Guide*. Her other favorites include Mrs. Burns lemon basil, Aussie Sweetie, cinnamon basil, and sweet Thai basil.

Availability: Genoa Green is available year-round in supermarkets, but summer is the herb's best season; Belsinger compares basil to tomatoes in that the herb is far superior grown and picked in season. You can find other varieties like purple opal or anise at farmers' markets. Nurseries and farmers' markets also sell plants you can cultivate yourself.

To select: "Look for basil that isn't wilted and doesn't have dark spots," advises Belsinger. And if you're growing your own, harvest on a sunny day. "An herb cut on a cloudy day doesn't have as strong a flavor because the sun hasn't had a chance to bring out its essential oils," says Belsinger.

To store: "Treat basil like a cut flower," Belsinger says. Place stems in a glass of water for up to a week (change the water every few days).

To cook: Match the variety to the dish. Belsinger likes to use lemon basil in gelatos and tea or lemonade. Try cinnamon basil in baked goods. Thai basil holds up well to the strong flavors of spicy cuisines. And, of course, you can always turn a bumper crop of basil into pesto.

Main Dishes

These entrées will add sizzle to your menu and highlight the brightest flavors of the season.

Pulled Chicken Sandwiches

(pictured on page 238)

The chicken and sauce can be made up to two days ahead and stored in the refrigerator. Reheat in a saucepan before serving.

CHICKEN:

- 2 tablespoons dark brown sugar
- 1 teaspoon paprika
- 1 teaspoon chili powder
- ¾ teaspoon ground cumin
- ½ teaspoon ground chipotle chile pepper
- ½ teaspoon salt
- ¼ teaspoon ground ginger
- 2 pounds skinless, boneless chicken thighs
- Cooking spray

SAUCE:

- 2 teaspoons canola oil
- ½ cup finely chopped onion
- 2 tablespoons dark brown sugar
- 1 teaspoon chili powder
- ½ teaspoon garlic powder
- ½ teaspoon dry mustard
- ¼ teaspoon ground allspice
- ⅛ teaspoon ground red pepper
- 1 cup ketchup
- 2 tablespoons cider vinegar
- 1 tablespoon molasses

REMAINING INGREDIENTS:

- 8 (2-ounce) sandwich rolls, toasted
- 16 hamburger dill chips

1. Prepare grill.

2. To prepare chicken, combine first 7 ingredients in a small bowl. Rub spice mixture evenly over chicken. Place chicken on a grill rack coated with cooking spray; cover and grill 20 minutes or until a thermometer registers 180°. Turn occasionally. Let stand 5 minutes. Shred with 2 forks.

3. To prepare sauce, heat oil in a medium saucepan over medium heat. Add onion; cook 5 minutes or until tender, stirring occasionally. Stir in 2 tablespoons sugar, 1 teaspoon chili powder, garlic powder, and next 3 ingredients; cook 30 seconds. Stir in ketchup, vinegar, and molasses; bring to a boil. Reduce heat, and simmer 10 minutes or until slightly thick, stirring occasionally. Stir in chicken; cook 2 minutes or until thoroughly heated.

4. Place about ⅓ cup chicken mixture on bottom half of each roll; top each serving with 2 pickle chips and top roll half. Yield: 8 servings (serving size: 1 sandwich).

CALORIES 365 (23% from fat); FAT 9.1g (sat 2.8g, mono 2.6g, poly 2.6g); PROTEIN 28.2g; CARB 42.8g; FIBER 2g; CHOL 94mg; IRON 3.4mg; SODIUM 877mg; CALC 78mg

Asian-Style Grilled Cornish Hens

Raspberry vinegar provides a fruity, lightly tart note in the marinade for this dish.

- 3 tablespoons raspberry vinegar
- 2 tablespoons hoisin sauce
- 1 tablespoon dark sesame oil
- 1 tablespoon low-sodium soy sauce
- 1 teaspoon Sriracha (hot chile sauce, such as Huy Fong)
- 4 garlic cloves, minced
- 4 (1½-pound) Cornish hens, skinned and split in half lengthwise
- Cooking spray

1. Combine first 6 ingredients in a large zip-top plastic bag. Add hens to bag; seal and marinate in refrigerator overnight, turning occasionally. Remove hens from bag; discard marinade.

2. Prepare grill.

3. Place hens on a grill rack coated with cooking spray, and grill 10 minutes on each side or until a thermometer registers 180°. Yield: 8 servings (serving size: ½ Cornish hen).

CALORIES 213 (30% from fat); FAT 7.2g (sat 1.7g, mono 2.5g, poly 2.1g); PROTEIN 32.4g; CARB 2.5g; FIBER 0.2g; CHOL 146mg; IRON 1.2mg; SODIUM 235mg; CALC 23mg

Grilled Shrimp Skewers with Summer Fruit Salsa

Fresh fruit and succulent grilled shrimp capture the essence of summer in this flavorful dish.

SALSA:

- ½ cup chopped ripe plum (about 1)
- ½ cup diced apricots (about 2)
- ½ cup diced nectarine (about 1)
- 1 teaspoon grated lime rind
- 3 tablespoons fresh lime juice
- 2 tablespoons thinly sliced fresh mint
- 2 tablespoons diced red onion
- 1 tablespoon minced seeded serrano chile
- 1 tablespoon honey
- ¼ teaspoon salt
- ⅛ teaspoon ground red pepper
- 12 sweet cherries, pitted and halved
- 1 green onion, finely chopped

SHRIMP:

- 2 tablespoons butter, melted
- 2 teaspoons fresh lemon juice
- ¼ teaspoon salt
- 1 garlic clove, minced
- 24 jumbo shrimp, peeled and deveined (about 2 pounds)
- Cooking spray
- 6 lime wedges
- Mint sprigs (optional)

1. To prepare salsa, combine first 13 ingredients in a medium bowl. Cover and chill 1 hour.

2. Prepare grill.

3. To prepare shrimp, place butter and next 4 ingredients in a large bowl; toss to coat. Thread 4 shrimp onto each of 6 (12-inch) skewers. Place kebabs on a grill rack coated with cooking spray; grill 3 minutes on each side or until shrimp are done. Serve with salsa and lime wedges. Garnish with mint sprigs, if desired. Yield: 6 servings (serving size: 1 kebab, ⅓ cup salsa, and 1 lime wedge).

CALORIES 242 (25% from fat); FAT 6.8g (sat 2.9g, mono 1.5g, poly 1.3g); PROTEIN 31.6g; CARB 13.4g; FIBER 1.5g; CHOL 240mg; IRON 4.1mg; SODIUM 449mg; CALC 94mg

Grilled Chicken Mojito Sandwiches

A mojito is a rum, lime juice, and mint cocktail that originated in Cuba. This sandwich features those flavors and makes for a great lunch or casual dinner.

DRESSING:

- ¼ cup reduced-fat mayonnaise
- 3 tablespoons minced fresh mint
- ¼ teaspoon finely grated lime rind
- 1 tablespoon fresh lime juice
- 1 teaspoon sugar
- 1 teaspoon minced serrano chile (with seeds)

SANDWICH:

- 3 tablespoons fresh lime juice
- 2 tablespoons dark rum
- 1 tablespoon minced fresh mint
- 1 teaspoon ground cumin
- 1 garlic clove, crushed
- 1 pound chicken breast tenders
- 4 (¼-inch-thick) slices Vidalia or other sweet onion
- Cooking spray
- ¼ teaspoon salt
- ¼ teaspoon freshly ground black pepper
- 4 (2-ounce) French rolls, halved
- 8 (¼-inch-thick) tomato slices
- 4 red leaf lettuce leaves

1. To prepare dressing, combine first 6 ingredients in a small bowl, stirring with a whisk. Cover and chill.

2. To prepare sandwich, combine 3 tablespoons lime juice and next 4 ingredients in a large zip-top plastic bag. Add chicken; seal and marinate in refrigerator 15 minutes, turning occasionally.

3. Prepare grill.

4. Remove chicken from bag; discard marinade. Place chicken and onion on grill rack coated with cooking spray. Grill 4 minutes on each side or until chicken is done and onion is tender. Remove from grill; sprinkle chicken with salt and pepper.

5. Grill roll halves, cut sides down, until lightly toasted, about 1 minute.

6. Spread about 1 tablespoon dressing over bottom half of each roll. Top each serving with 3 ounces chicken, 1 onion slice, 2 tomato slices, and 1 lettuce leaf; cover with top halves of rolls. Yield: 4 servings (serving size: 1 sandwich).

CALORIES 370 (15% from fat); FAT 6.1g (sat 1.5g, mono 1.9g, poly 2g); PROTEIN 32.5g; CARB 43.3g; FIBER 3.9g; CHOL 66mg; IRON 2.9mg; SODIUM 705mg; CALC 99mg

---

Peaches

History: "An apple is an excellent thing—until you have tried a peach," claimed writer George du Maurier. And many would agree. Ever since this juicy fruit was first grown in China, poets have waxed lyrical over its charms. It's also the state fruit of Georgia.

Varieties: Peaches are in season from May to October. The Crest and Elegant Lady are two popular kinds found at supermarkets. Newer types include the small Saturn (its squat, elliptical shape resembles the planet for which it's named) and white peaches, such as the Babcock, White Lady, and Sugar Giant.

Availability: The fruit is in abundant supply in supermarkets in June. You'll find more unusual varieties at farmers' markets.

To select: "It's all about the senses," says Tim Cooper, owner of Cooper Farms in Fairfield, Texas, which cultivates 20 varieties of peaches. "A peach needs to have a good color, and the touch needs to be slightly soft, but not too soft, which means it's getting ripe. When you walk up to a peach stand, if you smell peaches when you get there, you know they're ripe."

To store: "If they're not quite as ripe as you'd like them, just set them on the kitchen table in a bowl," says Cooper. "If they're ripe, put them in the fridge, and they'll keep for a few days."

To cook: Cooper loves peach cobbler and peach ice cream. Peaches are also good in sauces and chutneys.

Corn Bread Shortcake with Ham and Fresh Peach Salsa

This dish features the down-home flavors of corn bread, smoked ham, and peaches. The dressy presentation lends itself to a memorable summer dinner. You can also try this versatile salsa with grilled pork tenderloin or duck breast.

SALSA:

- 3 cups diced peeled peaches
- ¼ cup dried cranberries, chopped
- ¼ cup fresh orange juice
- 3 tablespoons minced shallots
- 2 tablespoons chopped fresh cilantro
- 1 tablespoon brown sugar
- 1 tablespoon fresh lime juice
- ¼ teaspoon ground cumin
- ⅛ teaspoon ground red pepper

SHORTCAKE:

- ½ cup all-purpose flour (about 2¼ ounces)
- 1¼ cups cornmeal
- 2 tablespoons granulated sugar
- 1½ teaspoons baking powder
- ½ teaspoon salt
- 1¼ cups low-fat buttermilk
- 2 tablespoons canola oil
- 1 large egg, lightly beaten
- Cooking spray

REMAINING INGREDIENTS:

- 9 (1½-ounce) slices 33%-less-sodium smoked ham
- Cilantro sprigs (optional)

1. To prepare salsa, combine first 9 ingredients in a bowl, and toss gently. Cover and chill 1 hour.

2. Preheat oven to 425°.

3. To prepare shortcake, lightly spoon flour into a dry measuring cup; level with a knife. Combine flour, cornmeal, and next 3 ingredients, stirring well with a whisk. Make a well in center of mixture. Combine buttermilk, oil, and egg in a bowl; add to flour mixture. Stir just until moist. Spoon batter into an 8-inch square baking pan coated with cooking spray. Bake at 425° for 20 minutes or

Continued

June 173

until a wooden pick inserted in center comes out clean. Cool in pan 5 minutes on a wire rack. Turn shortcake out onto a cutting board or work surface; cut into 9 equal pieces.

4. Heat a large nonstick skillet over medium-high heat. Coat pan with cooking spray. Add ham to pan, and sauté 1 minute on each side or until lightly browned. Remove from heat; keep warm.

5. Cut shortcake pieces in half horizontally. Place 1 bottom half on each of 9 plates; top each serving with 1 tablespoon salsa, 1 ham slice, and top half of shortcake. Top each serving with 2 tablespoons salsa. Garnish with cilantro sprigs, if desired. Yield: 9 servings.

CALORIES 264 (27% from fat); FAT 7.8g (sat 1.8g, mono 3.8g, poly 1.6g); PROTEIN 12g; CARB 37.3g; FIBER 2.7g; CHOL 51mg; IRON 1.4mg; SODIUM 679mg; CALC 98mg

Cavatappi with Arugula Pesto and Cherry Tomatoes

Peppery arugula complements the sweetness of ripe tomatoes. Use heirloom tomatoes, if available, for even better flavor. Substitute fusilli for cavatappi, if desired. Serve immediately.

PESTO:
- 5 cups trimmed arugula
- ½ cup (2 ounces) grated fresh Parmesan cheese
- ¼ cup pine nuts, toasted
- 1 tablespoon lemon juice
- ¾ teaspoon salt
- ¼ teaspoon freshly ground black pepper
- 1 garlic clove, minced
- ⅓ cup water
- 2 tablespoons extravirgin olive oil

REMAINING INGREDIENTS:
- 1 pound uncooked cavatappi
- 2 cups red and yellow cherry tomatoes, halved (about ¾ pound)
- 2 tablespoons pine nuts, toasted

1. To prepare pesto, place first 7 ingredients in a food processor; process until finely minced. With processor on, slowly pour ⅓ cup water and oil through food chute; process until well blended.

2. Cook pasta according to package directions, omitting salt and fat. Drain. Combine pesto, pasta, and tomatoes in a large bowl; toss well. Sprinkle pine nuts over pasta. Serve immediately. Yield: 6 servings (serving size: 1⅓ cups pasta and 1 teaspoon nuts).

CALORIES 425 (29% from fat); FAT 13.7g (sat 2.8g, mono 6.3g, poly 3.7g); PROTEIN 14.6g; CARB 61.5g; FIBER 3.2g; CHOL 6mg; IRON 2.1mg; SODIUM 412mg; CALC 135mg

WINE NOTE: There's nothing more satisfying than a light pasta dish and a glass of cold, fresh, dry Italian white wine. Pinot grigio fills the bill exactly, and it's a steal, too. For one that's thirst-quenching and loaded with personality, try Alois Lageder Pinot Grigio 2004 from the Trentino Alto Adige region ($12).

Sandwich Night Menu
serves 4

These crab sandwiches are a snap to prepare. Pick up a package of cabbage-and-carrot coleslaw mix, and toss it with light coleslaw dressing for a quick side.

Summer Crab Rolls

Coleslaw

Limeade*

*Combine ¾ cup sugar and ¾ cup water in a microwave-safe dish; microwave at HIGH 3 minutes or until sugar dissolves. Add 2 cups water and ½ cup fresh lime juice. Serve over ice.

QUICK & EASY • MAKE AHEAD
Summer Crab Rolls

Make these crab rolls ahead, and take them on a picnic. You can find a 12-pack of dinner rolls in the bakery section of your local supermarket. Substitute lobster or chopped shrimp for crab, if desired.

- ¼ cup finely chopped Vidalia or other sweet onion
- ¼ cup low-fat mayonnaise
- 2 tablespoons chopped fresh chives
- 1 tablespoon Dijon mustard
- 1 teaspoon fresh lemon juice
- ½ teaspoon hot pepper sauce (such as Tabasco)
- 1 pound lump crabmeat, drained and shell pieces removed
- 1½ tablespoons butter, softened
- 12 (1-ounce) dinner rolls, cut in half horizontally
- 12 Boston lettuce leaves (about 1 small head)
- 6 plum tomatoes, each cut into 4 slices

1. Combine first 7 ingredients in a large bowl; toss well.

2. Spread butter onto cut sides of rolls. Heat a large nonstick skillet over medium heat. Place 6 roll halves, cut sides down, in pan 1 minute or until toasted. Repeat procedure with remaining roll halves. Spoon ¼ cup crab mixture onto each bottom roll half. Top each with 1 lettuce leaf and 2 tomato slices; top with remaining roll halves. Yield: 6 servings (serving size: 2 rolls).

CALORIES 320 (23% from fat); FAT 8.3g (sat 2g, mono 1.2g, poly 3.2g); PROTEIN 22.2g; CARB 40.8g; FIBER 2.9g; CHOL 83mg; IRON 3.4mg; SODIUM 696mg; CALC 132mg

These **main dishes** demonstrate creative ways to use the **season's** best produce and flavors.

Spicy Jerk Chicken Kebabs with Bell Peppers and Pineapple

1 teaspoon whole allspice
1 teaspoon black peppercorns
4 whole cloves
¼ cup packed brown sugar
¼ cup fresh lime juice
¼ cup low-sodium soy sauce
2 tablespoons Worcestershire sauce
2 teaspoons paprika
2 teaspoons dried thyme leaves
8 garlic cloves
3 large shallots, peeled and cut in half
1 (3-inch) piece peeled fresh ginger, thinly sliced
1 jalapeño pepper, halved and seeded
2 pounds skinless, boneless chicken breast, cut into 1-inch pieces
2 cups (1-inch) cubed pineapple (about 1 medium)
1½ cups (1-inch) pieces red bell pepper (about 1 large)
1½ cups (1-inch) pieces green bell pepper (about 1 large)
1 teaspoon salt
½ teaspoon black pepper
Cooking spray

1. Heat a small skillet over medium-high heat. Add first 3 ingredients to pan; cook 1 minute or until lightly toasted and fragrant.
2. Place spices, sugar, and next 9 ingredients in a blender; process until smooth. Combine spice mixture and chicken in a large zip-top plastic bag; seal and marinate in refrigerator 2 hours, turning occasionally.
3. Prepare grill.
4. Remove chicken from bag, reserving marinade. Thread chicken, pineapple, and bell peppers alternately onto each of 8 (12-inch) skewers. Brush reserved marinade onto pineapple and bell peppers. Sprinkle evenly with salt and pepper. Place kebabs on a grill rack coated with cooking spray. Grill 8 minutes or until chicken is done. Yield: 8 servings (serving size: 1 kebab).

CALORIES 170 (9% from fat); FAT 1.6g (sat 0.4g, mono 0.4g, poly 0.4g); PROTEIN 27.2g; CARB 10.9g; FIBER 1.4g; CHOL 66mg; IRON 1.6mg; SODIUM 527mg; CALC 34mg

Chicken with Corn and Cheese Sauce

You can thin the sauce with more milk, if necessary. Also try the sauce with grilled steak or pork chops, in baked potatoes, or poured over boiled new potatoes.

SAUCE:
1 teaspoon butter
2 cups fresh corn kernels (about 3 ears)
1 cup finely chopped red onion
2 teaspoons chili powder
1 cup coarsely chopped peeled tomato
½ cup 2% reduced-fat milk
½ cup (4 ounces) block-style fat-free cream cheese
2 cups (8 ounces) shredded extrasharp Cheddar cheese
½ teaspoon salt
¼ teaspoon black pepper
¼ teaspoon hot pepper sauce (such as Tabasco)

CHICKEN:
8 (6-ounce) skinless, boneless chicken breast halves
½ teaspoon salt
¼ teaspoon black pepper
Cooking spray
¼ cup chopped fresh chives

1. Prepare grill.
2. To prepare sauce, melt butter in a large saucepan over medium heat. Add corn and onion. Cover and cook 10 minutes or until onion is tender, stirring occasionally. Stir in chili powder; cook 1 minute. Stir in tomato; cook 2 minutes. Stir in milk and cream cheese; cook 6 minutes over low heat, stirring frequently. Stir in Cheddar cheese, ½ teaspoon salt, ¼ teaspoon pepper, and pepper sauce; cook 4 minutes or until melted, stirring frequently. Cover sauce, and keep warm.
3. To prepare chicken, sprinkle chicken with ½ teaspoon salt and ¼ teaspoon pepper. Place chicken on grill rack coated with cooking spray; grill 4 minutes on each side or until done. Serve chicken with sauce; sprinkle with chives. Yield: 8 servings (serving size: 1 chicken breast half, ⅓ cup sauce, and 1½ teaspoons chives).

CALORIES 371 (31% from fat); FAT 12.6g (sat 6.3g, mono 3.7g, poly 1g); PROTEIN 50.3g; CARB 13.6g; FIBER 1.6g; CHOL 132mg; IRON 1.7mg; SODIUM 696mg; CALC 275mg

---

Corn

History: A type of grass, corn is a New World food.

Varieties: Sweet white corn (called Country Gentleman) and the larger-kernel yellow (Golden Bantam) are the most popular varieties. Other types include Seneca Tomahawk, Providence Delectable, Ambrosia, and Lancelot.

Availability: May through September is peak season; look for specialty varieties at farmers' markets.

To select: "A fresh husk is the number one thing to look for," says Jane Weber, co-owner of Weber Farm in Bettendorf, Iowa. "And nice deep-brown silk tips or ends mean it's ripe, but the whole silk shouldn't be dried up. If you open just the tip of the husk, you can see if the kernels have filled out all the way to the end of the ear." Kernels should be plump and milky when pinched.

To store: The sugars in corn begin to turn to starch as soon as it's harvested, so plan to eat it as soon as possible. You can store it in its husk in the refrigerator for up to a day.

To cook: Sweet summer corn requires minimal cooking. "Bring the water to a boil, put the corn in, and bring it back to a boil; it'll be done in a few minutes," says Weber. Serve it on the cob, or cut the kernels from the cob to use in soups, salads, succotash, salsas, and other dishes.

Charmoula-Marinated Swordfish Steaks

Charmoula is a Moroccan marinade typically made from cilantro, oil, lemon juice, cumin, and garlic. The blend also complements poultry.

⅓ cup chopped fresh cilantro
3 tablespoons fresh lemon juice
2 teaspoons extravirgin olive oil
1 teaspoon ground coriander
1 teaspoon ground cumin
1 teaspoon paprika
¼ teaspoon ground ginger
2 garlic cloves, minced
6 (6-ounce) swordfish steaks (about 1½ inches thick)
¾ teaspoon salt
¼ teaspoon freshly ground black pepper
Cooking spray
6 lemon wedges

1. Combine first 8 ingredients in a large zip-top plastic bag. Add fish to bag; seal and marinate in refrigerator 1 hour, turning occasionally.
2. Prepare grill.
3. Remove fish from bag; discard marinade. Sprinkle fish with salt and pepper. Place fish on a grill rack coated with cooking spray; grill 5 minutes on each side or until fish flakes easily when tested with a fork or until desired degree of doneness. Serve with lemon wedges. Yield: 6 servings (serving size: 1 steak and 1 lemon wedge).

CALORIES 216 (34% from fat); FAT 8.1g (sat 2g, mono 3.7g, poly 1.6g); PROTEIN 31.8g; CARB 2.2g; FIBER 0.5g; CHOL 62mg; IRON 1.6mg; SODIUM 439mg; CALC 17mg

Spiced Chicken Skewers

(pictured on page 237)

The mild acids in yogurt make it a great base for a tenderizing marinade.

KEBABS:
¾ cup plain low-fat yogurt
1 tablespoon grated peeled fresh ginger
2 teaspoons ground coriander
2 teaspoons paprika
1 teaspoon ground cumin
¼ teaspoon ground cardamom
¼ teaspoon ground turmeric
¼ teaspoon saffron threads, crushed
⅛ teaspoon ground cinnamon
⅛ teaspoon ground cloves
3 garlic cloves, minced
2 pounds skinless, boneless chicken thighs, cut into 1-inch chunks
1 red onion, cut into 1-inch chunks (about 8 ounces)
1 large red bell pepper, cut into 1-inch chunks (about 8 ounces)
1 zucchini, cut into 1-inch chunks (about 8 ounces)
Cooking spray
½ teaspoon salt
½ teaspoon freshly ground black pepper

RAITA:
½ cup plain low-fat yogurt
⅓ cup diced seeded tomato
¼ cup cucumber, peeled, seeded, grated, and squeezed dry
¼ cup reduced-fat sour cream
1 tablespoon minced seeded jalapeño pepper
1½ teaspoons chopped fresh cilantro
¼ teaspoon ground cumin
¼ teaspoon salt

1. To prepare kebabs, combine first 12 ingredients in a large zip-top plastic bag; seal and marinate in refrigerator overnight, turning bag occasionally.
2. Prepare grill.
3. Remove chicken from bag; discard marinade. Thread chicken, onion, bell pepper, and zucchini alternately on each of 8 (12-inch) wooden skewers. Coat kebabs with cooking spray, and sprinkle

with ½ teaspoon salt and black pepper. Place kebabs on grill rack coated with cooking spray. Grill 25 minutes or until chicken is done, turning occasionally. Remove from grill; keep warm.
4. To prepare raita, combine ½ cup yogurt and remaining 7 ingredients in a small bowl. Serve with kebabs. Yield: 8 servings (serving size: 1 kebab and about 2 tablespoons raita).

CALORIES 189 (29% from fat); FAT 6g (sat 2g, mono 1.7g, poly 1.3g); PROTEIN 24.9g; CARB 8.5g; FIBER 1.7g; CHOL 99mg; IRON 1.7mg; SODIUM 344mg; CALC 81mg

Crab and Scallop Seviche Cocktails

If bay scallops aren't available, cut sea scallops into quarters.

¾ cup fresh lime juice (about 6 limes)
½ cup finely diced Vidalia or other sweet onion
½ pound bay scallops
1½ cups Clamato juice
1 cup chopped seeded tomato
2 tablespoons minced jalapeño
2 tablespoons chopped fresh cilantro
1 cup chopped peeled avocado (about 1 medium)
½ pound lump crabmeat, drained and shell pieces removed
6 cilantro sprigs (optional)
6 lime wedges (optional)
6 ounces baked tortilla chips

1. Combine first 3 ingredients in a medium bowl. Cover and chill 2 hours.
2. Place Clamato juice in a small saucepan. Bring to a boil, and cook until reduced to ½ cup (about 12 minutes). Chill reduced juice.
3. Add Clamato juice, tomato, jalapeño, and cilantro to scallop mixture. Fold in avocado and crabmeat. Garnish with cilantro sprigs and lime wedges. Serve with chips. Yield: 6 servings (serving size: 1 cup seviche and 1 ounce chips).

CALORIES 313 (30% from fat); FAT 10.4g (sat 1.8g, mono 5.2g, poly 2.4g); PROTEIN 19.4g; CARB 36.1g; FIBER 4.3g; CHOL 56mg; IRON 1.5mg; SODIUM 719mg; CALC 119mg

Summer Herb Chimichurri with Grilled Steak

Chimichurri is a thick and flavorful herb sauce. Fresh basil and dried marjoram stand in for traditional parsley in this version of the Argentine favorite.

   1 tablespoon olive oil
 ½ cup finely chopped shallots (about 3 ounces)
   8 garlic cloves, minced
   2 tablespoons fresh lemon juice
   1 tablespoon sherry vinegar
 ¼ teaspoon crushed red pepper
   1 cup chopped arugula
 ¼ cup finely chopped fresh basil
   1 teaspoon dried marjoram
 ¾ teaspoon salt, divided
 ½ teaspoon freshly ground black pepper, divided
 ½ teaspoon Spanish smoked paprika
   1 (1-pound) flank steak, trimmed
Cooking spray

1. Heat oil in a small nonstick skillet over medium-high heat. Add shallots and garlic; sauté 3 minutes or until tender. Remove from heat; stir in juice, vinegar, and red pepper. Cool. Combine shallot mixture, arugula, basil, and marjoram in a small bowl. Stir in ¼ teaspoon salt and ¼ teaspoon black pepper. Set aside.
2. Prepare grill.
3. Combine paprika, remaining ½ teaspoon salt, and remaining ¼ teaspoon black pepper. Rub paprika mixture over steak. Place steak on a grill rack coated with cooking spray; grill 6 minutes on each side or until desired degree of doneness. Let stand 5 minutes. Cut steak diagonally across grain into thin slices. Spoon sauce down center of slices, and serve. Yield: 4 servings (serving size: 3 ounces steak and 3 tablespoons sauce).

CALORIES 218 (41% from fat); FAT 9.9g (sat 3.1g, mono 5g, poly 0.7g); PROTEIN 25g; CARB 6.8g; FIBER 0.7g; CHOL 42mg; IRON 2.2mg; SODIUM 496mg; CALC 51mg

On The Side

Summer produce yields inventive accompaniments.

Sweet Corn and Parmesan Flans

(pictured on page 239)

For a pretty presentation, use a combination of red, orange, and yellow tear-drop tomatoes.

Cooking spray
2½ cups fresh corn kernels (about 5 ears)
   1 cup 1% low-fat milk
 ⅓ cup grated Parmesan cheese
   1 teaspoon flour
 ½ teaspoon salt
 ¼ teaspoon freshly ground black pepper
   4 large eggs
 18 small tear-drop cherry tomatoes (pear-shaped), halved
   2 tablespoons thinly sliced basil

1. Preheat oven to 350°.
2. Heat a large nonstick skillet over medium heat. Coat pan with cooking spray. Add corn, and cook 5 minutes or until tender, stirring occasionally. Remove from heat. Set aside 1 cup corn kernels.
3. Place remaining corn in a food processor; pulse 5 times or until coarsely chopped. Add milk and next 5 ingredients to food processor; pulse 4 times or until combined.
4. Pour about ½ cup corn mixture into each of 6 (6-ounce) ramekins coated with cooking spray. Place ramekins in a 13 x 9–inch baking pan; add hot water to pan to a depth of 1 inch. Bake at 350° for 35 minutes or until center barely moves when ramekins are touched. Remove ramekins from pan; cool 5 minutes on a wire rack. Invert flans onto 6 plates. Garnish each serving with about 2½ tablespoons corn kernels, 6 tomato halves, and 1 teaspoon basil. Yield: 6 servings.

CALORIES 152 (35% from fat); FAT 5.9g (sat 2.2g, mono 2g, poly 1g); PROTEIN 9.8g; CARB 17g; FIBER 2.4g; CHOL 147mg; IRON 1.2mg; SODIUM 344mg; CALC 125mg

Spiced Marinated Tomatoes

Serve with a grilled burger or chicken. You can prepare this recipe up to two days in advance. The longer the tomatoes marinate, the more flavor they acquire. Remove the seeds from the pepper if you prefer mild heat.

   4 cups halved red, yellow, or orange cherry tomatoes
 ⅓ cup thinly sliced green onions (about 4)
   4 garlic cloves, minced
   1 jalapeño pepper, thinly sliced
 ⅓ cup white balsamic vinegar
   1 tablespoon light brown sugar
   1 tablespoon extravirgin olive oil
   2 teaspoons minced peeled fresh ginger
   1 teaspoon ground cumin
 ½ teaspoon salt
 ½ teaspoon freshly ground black pepper

1. Combine first 4 ingredients in a large bowl. Combine vinegar and remaining 6 ingredients in a small bowl. Pour vinegar mixture over tomato mixture, tossing to coat. Chill 1 hour. Yield: 8 servings (serving size: ½ cup).

CALORIES 58 (31% from fat); FAT 2g (sat 0.3g, mono 1.3g, poly 0.3g); PROTEIN 1g; CARB 10.1g; FIBER 1.2g; CHOL 0mg; IRON 0.8mg; SODIUM 159mg; CALC 17mg

Oven-Fried Okra

1½ cups yellow cornmeal
 ¾ teaspoon kosher salt, divided
 ½ teaspoon freshly ground black pepper
Dash of ground red pepper
 ½ cup fat-free buttermilk
   1 large egg, lightly beaten
   1 pound fresh okra pods, trimmed and cut into ¾-inch slices (about 3 cups)
Cooking spray

1. Preheat oven to 450°.
2. Combine cornmeal, ½ teaspoon salt,
Continued

black pepper, and red pepper in a shallow dish; set aside.

3. Combine buttermilk and egg in a large bowl, stirring with a whisk. Add okra; toss to coat. Let stand 3 minutes.

4. Dredge okra in cornmeal mixture. Place okra on a jelly-roll pan coated with cooking spray. Lightly coat okra with cooking spray. Bake at 450° for 40 minutes, stirring once. Sprinkle with ¼ teaspoon salt. Yield: 8 servings (serving size: about ½ cup).

CALORIES 144 (4% from fat); FAT 0.7g (sat 0.2g, mono 0.3g, poly 0.1g); PROTEIN 4.5g; CARB 29.3g; FIBER 2.6g; CHOL 27mg; IRON 1.3mg; SODIUM 204mg; CALC 68mg

---

MAKE AHEAD

Citrus Pickled Red Onion and Golden Beet Salad with Green Beans

Grate ½ teaspoon orange rind before squeezing the fruit for juice.

QUICK TIP: Since beets' leafy green tops leach moisture from the root, trim them to about one inch to prevent the loss of nutrients. Use the greens in salads or wilted sides, much like you would collards or other hearty greens. Store trimmed beets wrapped in plastic in the refrigerator for up to three weeks, and gently wash before use.

  1 pound golden beets
  1 teaspoon extravirgin olive oil
  2 cups thinly sliced red onion
      (about 2 large)
  1 cup fresh orange juice (about
      4 oranges)
  ½ cup fresh lemon juice
  1 teaspoon salt
  1 cup water
  1 pound green beans, trimmed
  1 tablespoon fresh lemon juice
  1 tablespoon extravirgin olive oil
  ½ teaspoon grated orange rind
  ¼ teaspoon salt
  ¼ teaspoon freshly ground black
      pepper
  1 garlic clove, minced

1. Preheat oven to 350°.
2. Leave root and 1-inch stem on beets; scrub with a brush. Place beets in center of a baking sheet lined with aluminum foil. Drizzle with 1 teaspoon oil. Bake at 350° for 1 hour or until beets are tender. Cool completely. Peel and cut each beet into 8 wedges. Combine beets, onion, and next 3 ingredients in a large bowl. Cover and chill overnight.
3. Bring 1 cup water to a boil in a medium saucepan; add beans. Cook 3 minutes or until beans are crisp-tender. Drain and rinse with cold water; drain. Place beans in a large bowl.
4. Drain beet mixture, reserving 2 tablespoons marinade. Add beet mixture to green beans, and toss gently. Combine reserved marinade, 1 tablespoon lemon juice, and remaining 5 ingredients in a small bowl; stir with a whisk. Pour marinade mixture over beet mixture; toss gently. Yield: 6 cups (serving size: about 1 cup).

CALORIES 88 (32% from fat); FAT 3.1g (sat 0.4g, mono 2.2g, poly 0.4g); PROTEIN 2.2g; CARB 14.8g; FIBER 4.8g; CHOL 0mg; IRON 0.9mg; SODIUM 336mg; CALC 56mg

---

Green Beans

History: Green beans (also called snap beans) are a legume with an edible pod. Their scientific name, *Phaseolus*, means "small boat." Some varieties of beans have a string along the seam of the pod (hence the old-fashioned name "string bean"); breeding has eliminated the string in some kinds. Ask when you're buying to be sure.

Varieties: Green beans range in size from svelte haricots verts to large wax beans.

Availability: Green beans are a year-round grocery store standby, but May to October is their prime time. Heirloom varieties of the legumes are available at many farmers' markets.

To select: "Snap beans should snap when you bend them," says Brian Axdahl of Axdahl Farms in Stillwater, Minnesota, which cultivates 13 varieties of green beans. "A darker green bean with a more slender appearance is preferable." Try to avoid beans that are spotty.

To store: Tightly wrapped in plastic, "they can last about 10 days in the refrigerator," says Axdahl.

To cook: Green beans are versatile—braise, boil, steam, or stir-fry them.

Grilled Vegetable Focaccia

Grill the vegetables while the dough rises. Try other toppings, such as thinly sliced tomato, on the focaccia.

  1 package active dry yeast (about
      2¼ teaspoons)
  4 teaspoons sugar
  1⅓ cups warm water (100° to 110°)
  ¼ cup extravirgin olive oil, divided
  3 cups all-purpose flour (about
      13½ ounces), divided
  2 teaspoons dried oregano
  1½ teaspoons salt, divided
  ½ teaspoon fennel seeds
      Cooking spray
  2 tablespoons balsamic vinegar
  6 ounces zucchini, cut into
      ¼-inch-thick slices
  1 yellow bell pepper, seeded and
      quartered
  1 red onion, cut into ¼-inch-thick
      slices
  ½ teaspoon freshly ground black
      pepper
  ¼ cup shredded Romano cheese
  ¼ cup thinly sliced fresh basil

1. Dissolve yeast and sugar in 1⅓ cups warm water and 2 tablespoons oil in a large bowl; let stand 5 minutes.
2. Lightly spoon flour into dry measuring cups; level with a knife. Combine 2⅔ cups flour, oregano, 1 teaspoon salt, and fennel seeds; stir well. Stir flour mixture into yeast mixture. Turn dough out onto a floured surface. Knead until smooth and elastic (about 5 minutes); add enough of remaining ⅓ cup flour, 1 tablespoon at a time, to prevent dough from sticking to hands (dough will feel sticky). Place dough in a large bowl coated with cooking spray, turning to coat top. Cover and let rise in a warm place (85°), free from drafts, 1½ hours or until doubled in size. (Gently press two fingers into dough. If indentation remains, dough has risen enough.) Press dough out onto a jelly-roll pan coated with cooking spray. Cover and let rise 30 minutes.
3. Prepare grill.
4. Combine 2 tablespoons oil and vinegar in a small bowl. Brush oil mixture

evenly over zucchini, bell pepper, and onion. Sprinkle with ½ teaspoon salt and black pepper. Place vegetables on a grill rack coated with cooking spray. Grill zucchini 4 minutes on each side or until cooked through. Grill bell peppers and onions 6 minutes on each side or until tender. Remove vegetables from grill. Cool completely. Cut bell peppers into ¼-inch-thick strips.

5. Preheat oven to 425°.

6. Arrange vegetables evenly over surface of dough, and sprinkle with cheese. Bake at 425° for 27 minutes or until golden. Sprinkle with basil. Transfer to a wire rack; cool 10 minutes before serving. Yield: 12 servings.

CALORIES 182 (28% from fat); FAT 5.6g (sat 1g, mono 3.6g, poly 0.6g); PROTEIN 4.8g; CARB 28.3g; FIBER 1.7g; CHOL 2mg; IRON 2mg; SODIUM 323mg; CALC 42mg

---

QUICK & EASY
Chili Powder and Cumin-Rubbed Corn on the Cob

Soak the corn for 20 minutes before grilling to prevent the husks from burning.

 6 ears corn with husks
 1½ tablespoons butter, melted
 1 teaspoon chili powder
 ½ teaspoon salt
 ½ teaspoon ground cumin
 ¼ teaspoon freshly ground black pepper
 ⅛ teaspoon ground red pepper
 6 lime wedges

1. Place corn in cold water, and soak 20 minutes.
2. Prepare grill.
3. Combine butter and next 5 ingredients in a small bowl.
4. Pull husks back from corn; scrub silks from corn. Brush butter mixture evenly over corn. Wrap husks around corn. Place on a grill rack, and grill 16 minutes or until done, turning occasionally. Serve with lime wedges. Yield: 6 servings (serving size: 1 ear of corn and 1 lime wedge).

CALORIES 151 (28% from fat); FAT 4.7g (sat 1.7g, mono 1.7g, poly 0.9g); PROTEIN 4.7g; CARB 27.6g; FIBER 4.1g; CHOL 8mg; IRON 0.9mg; SODIUM 243mg; CALC 7mg

---

Corn Muffins with Jalapeños and Lime Butter

We call for jalapeños in these peppery muffins, but to make them even hotter, try a tablespoon of minced habanero instead.

 6 tablespoons butter, softened and divided
 1 cup chopped sweet onion
 2 garlic cloves, minced
 1 cup fresh corn kernels (about 2 ears)
 2 teaspoons minced jalapeño
 1 teaspoon salt, divided
 1 cup all-purpose flour (about 4½ ounces)
 1 cup yellow cornmeal
 ¼ cup sugar
 1 teaspoon baking powder
 ½ teaspoon baking soda
 ½ teaspoon chili powder
 1¼ cups fat-free buttermilk
 2 large eggs, lightly beaten
 1 large egg white, lightly beaten
 Cooking spray
 1 tablespoon fresh lime juice
 1 tablespoon honey

1. Preheat oven to 400°.
2. Melt 1 tablespoon butter in a large nonstick skillet over medium-high heat. Add onion and garlic to pan; cook 2 minutes, stirring occasionally. Add corn, jalapeño, and ¼ teaspoon salt; cook 2 minutes. Remove from heat; add 2 tablespoons butter, tossing to melt.
3. Lightly spoon flour into a dry measuring cup; level with a knife. Combine flour, ¾ teaspoon salt, cornmeal, and next 4 ingredients in a large bowl. Make a well in center of mixture. Combine buttermilk, eggs, and egg white in a large bowl. Add onion mixture to buttermilk mixture. Add buttermilk mixture to flour mixture, stirring just until moist. Spoon batter into 15 muffin cups coated with cooking spray. Bake at 400° for 20 minutes or until lightly browned. Cool in pan 5 minutes on a wire rack; remove from pan. Cool muffins completely on wire rack.
4. Combine 3 tablespoons butter, juice, and honey in a small bowl. Serve with muffins. Yield: 15 servings (serving size:

1 muffin and about 1 teaspoon lime butter).

CALORIES 160 (30% from fat); FAT 5.4g (sat 3.1g, mono 1.5g, poly 0.4g); PROTEIN 3.9g; CARB 24g; FIBER 1g; CHOL 40mg; IRON 0.9mg; SODIUM 300mg; CALC 53mg

---

Penne with Corn, Roasted Poblanos, Avocado, and Tomato

Serve this hearty side dish with grilled fish. Or you can add a little chopped roasted chicken breast to the pasta toss to make it an entrée.

 2 poblano peppers
 2 red bell peppers
 2 ears shucked corn
 2 tablespoons fresh lime juice
 1 tablespoon extravirgin olive oil
 1 teaspoon salt
 ½ teaspoon freshly ground black pepper
 ½ teaspoon ground cumin
 1 garlic clove, minced
 4 cups hot cooked penne (about 8 ounces uncooked pasta)
 2 cups halved grape tomatoes
 1 cup finely chopped onion
 ¼ cup chopped fresh cilantro
 1 chopped peeled avocado
 ¾ cup (3 ounces) queso fresco

1. Preheat broiler.
2. Cut poblano and bell peppers in half lengthwise; discard seeds and membranes. Place pepper halves, skin sides up, on a foil-lined baking sheet; flatten with hand. Add corn to baking sheet. Broil 18 minutes or until peppers are blackened and corn is lightly browned, turning corn occasionally. Place peppers in a zip-top plastic bag; seal. Let stand 10 minutes. Peel and coarsely chop. Cut kernels from ears of corn.
3. Combine lime juice and next 5 ingredients in a large bowl. Add peppers, corn, pasta, and next 4 ingredients; toss. Top with cheese. Yield: 8 servings (serving size: 1 cup pasta and 1½ tablespoons cheese).

CALORIES 234 (29% from fat); FAT 7.5g (sat 1.6g, mono 4.1g, poly 1g); PROTEIN 7.8g; CARB 37.2g; FIBER 4.7g; CHOL 3mg; IRON 1.9mg; SODIUM 325mg; CALC 52mg

Scalloped Vidalia Onions

Sweet onions in creamy sauce with a hint of sherry are a great side dish for a special dinner and wonderful with any red meat or poultry.

    4   pounds Vidalia or other sweet
        onions, trimmed and quartered
    Cooking spray
    1½ teaspoons olive oil
    ⅔   cup dry sherry
    1   tablespoon butter
    2   tablespoons all-purpose flour
    1   cup 1% low-fat milk
    ¼   cup (1 ounce) shredded Gruyère
        cheese
    ¾   teaspoon salt
    ¼   teaspoon black pepper

1. Preheat oven to 400°.
2. Place onions in a 13 x 9–inch baking dish coated with cooking spray. Drizzle with oil, tossing to coat. Bake at 400° for 40 minutes, stirring halfway through cooking time. Remove from oven. Drizzle sherry over onions; stir to combine. Bake an additional 40 minutes, stirring once.
3. Melt butter in a small saucepan over medium heat. Add flour, stirring with a whisk until smooth. Gradually add milk, stirring with a whisk until blended; bring to a boil. Cook 1 minute, stirring constantly. Remove from heat. Add cheese, salt, and pepper, stirring until smooth.
4. Pour milk mixture over onions, stirring to combine. Bake at 400° for 20 minutes or until mixture is thick and beginning to brown on top. Remove from oven. Let stand 10 minutes before serving. Yield: 8 servings (serving size: about ⅔ cup).

CALORIES 164 (26% from fat); FAT 4.7g (sat 2.1g, mono 2g, poly 0.4g); PROTEIN 6.4g; CARB 23.1g; FIBER 2.3g; CHOL 11mg; IRON 0.6mg; SODIUM 160mg; CALC 196mg

---

MAKE AHEAD
Yukon Gold Potato Salad

    2   pounds Yukon gold potatoes
    ½   cup light mayonnaise
    2   tablespoons white wine vinegar
    1   tablespoon Dijon mustard
    ½   teaspoon salt
    ¼   teaspoon freshly ground black
        pepper
    ¼   teaspoon dried tarragon
    ¼   cup thinly sliced green onions
    2   tablespoons chopped fresh
        flat-leaf parsley

1. Place potatoes in a saucepan. Cover with water to 2 inches above potatoes; bring to a boil. Reduce heat, and simmer 20 minutes or until tender. Drain. Cool. Peel and cut potatoes into 1-inch cubes. Place potatoes in a large bowl.
2. Combine mayonnaise and next 5 ingredients. Add mayonnaise mixture to potatoes; toss gently to coat. Stir in onions and parsley. Cover and chill 1 hour. Yield: 6 servings (serving size: about 1 cup).

CALORIES 204 (31% from fat); FAT 7g (sat 1.1g, mono 1.6g, poly 4g); PROTEIN 3.2g; CARB 32.9g; FIBER 3g; CHOL 7mg; IRON 0.7mg; SODIUM 428mg; CALC 19mg

---

MAKE AHEAD
Grilled Ratatouille

Prepare and refrigerate up to two days ahead.

    1   peeled eggplant, halved lengthwise
        (about 1 pound)
    1   teaspoon kosher salt, divided
    2   zucchini, halved lengthwise
    1   red bell pepper, halved lengthwise
    1   green bell pepper, halved lengthwise
    1   red onion, quartered
    Cooking spray
    1   cup diced plum tomato (about 2)
    1   tablespoon extravirgin olive oil
    2   teaspoons herbes de Provence
    ¼   teaspoon freshly ground black
        pepper
    1   garlic clove, minced

1. Sprinkle cut sides of eggplant with ¾ teaspoon salt. Let drain 1 hour. Rinse well; pat dry with paper towels.
2. Prepare grill.
3. Coat eggplant, zucchini, bell peppers, and onion with cooking spray. Place vegetables on a grill rack coated with cooking spray; grill 5 minutes on each side or until tender. Cool.
4. Coarsely chop vegetables, and place in a large bowl. Stir in ¼ teaspoon salt, tomato, and remaining ingredients. Yield: 8 servings (serving size: ½ cup).

CALORIES 50 (36% from fat); FAT 2g (sat 0.3g, mono 1.3g, poly 0.3g); PROTEIN 1.4g; CARB 8g; FIBER 3.2g; CHOL 0mg; IRON 0.5mg; SODIUM 229mg; CALC 18mg

---

Bell Peppers

History: Along with hot chile peppers, sweet bell peppers are part of the *Capsicum* botanical family. Christopher Columbus brought them back from the New World to Spain, where cooks quickly embraced their use.

Varieties: There are more than 100 sweet pepper varieties, including green, red, orange, yellow, and purple bell peppers.

Availability: Bell peppers are at their best from July through September. Green, red, orange, and yellow bell peppers are available at most supermarkets; you'll find more exotic colors and other varieties at specialty stores and farmers' markets.

To select: "Look for firm, nicely colored [for its respective color] fruit," says Robert Schueller, spokesperson for Melissa's World Variety Produce. Peppers should be fragrant at the stem end. Avoid peppers that are damp because they can mold.

To store: If you plan to use peppers within a day or two, keep them at room temperature for better flavor, Schueller advises. You also can store peppers in a plastic bag in the refrigerator for up to a week. Be sure to wash and cut the fruit just before using it.

To cook: With their firm texture and sweet flavor, bell peppers are a natural on the grill. Schueller also recommends slicing them to dip into hummus, as well as chopping and adding them to pizza and potato salad.

Garden Herb Salad with Roasted Shallot Vinaigrette

The sweetness of the shallot in the vinaigrette dressing plays well off the herbs.

 1 shallot, peeled
 2 tablespoons red wine vinegar
 1 tablespoon extravirgin olive oil
 1 teaspoon sugar
 1 teaspoon Dijon mustard
 ¼ teaspoon salt
 ¼ teaspoon black pepper
 1 (4-ounce) package herb salad mix

1. Preheat oven to 400°.
2. Wrap shallot in foil. Bake at 400° for 35 minutes; cool 10 minutes. Mince. Combine shallot, vinegar, oil, sugar, mustard, salt, and pepper in a large bowl; stir well with a whisk. Add salad mix; toss well to coat. Yield: 6 servings (serving size: 1⅔ cups).

CALORIES 29 (74% from fat); FAT 2.4g (sat 0.3g, mono 1.7g, poly 0.3g); PROTEIN 0.6g; CARB 2.9g; FIBER 0.6g; CHOL 0mg; IRON 0.3mg; SODIUM 136mg; CALC 10mg

---

QUICK & EASY
Lemony Couscous with Mint, Dill, and Feta

You can substitute regular couscous for whole wheat. Add cubed rotisserie chicken to make this a light lunch.

 2 cups water
 1 tablespoon extravirgin olive oil
 1 teaspoon salt
 1 large garlic clove, minced
 1 (10-ounce) box whole wheat couscous
 1⅔ cups grape or cherry tomatoes, halved (about 1 pint)
 1½ cups diced English cucumber
 ⅓ cup chopped green onions
 ⅓ cup fresh lemon juice
 2 tablespoons chopped fresh mint
 1 tablespoon chopped fresh dill
 1 (4-ounce) package crumbled feta cheese

1. Combine first 4 ingredients in a medium saucepan; bring to a boil. Gradually stir in couscous. Remove from heat. Cover and let stand 5 minutes. Fluff with a fork; cool.
2. Combine couscous, tomatoes, and next 5 ingredients in a large bowl; toss well. Add cheese. Yield: 8 servings (serving size: 1 cup couscous mixture and 2 tablespoons cheese).

CALORIES 202 (25% from fat); FAT 5.5g (sat 2.4g, mono 2g, poly 0.6g); PROTEIN 7.7g; CARB 33.1g; FIBER 5.4g; CHOL 13mg; IRON 1.6mg; SODIUM 458mg; CALC 97mg

---

Dinner Made Easy Menu
serves 4

This salad pairs nicely with simple broiled or grilled fish, such as snapper or grouper. Use the middle rack in the oven to cook the fish, so the breading doesn't burn.

Strawberry, Cucumber, and Basil Salad

Broiled snapper*

Sautéed carrot coins

*Sprinkle 4 (6-ounce) snapper fillets with ½ teaspoon salt and ¼ teaspoon freshly ground black pepper. Dredge fish in 1 cup panko (Japanese breadcrumbs). Place fish on a rack coated with cooking spray; place rack in a broiler pan. Broil 12 minutes or until fish flakes easily when tested with a fork. Serve with lemon wedges, if desired.

QUICK & EASY
Strawberry, Cucumber, and Basil Salad

Serve as a side salad, starter, or snack.

 4 cups hulled strawberries, quartered (1 pound)
 2 tablespoons thinly sliced fresh basil
 2 teaspoons balsamic vinegar
 1 teaspoon sugar
 2 cucumbers, peeled, halved lengthwise, seeded, and thinly sliced (about 2 cups)
 1 teaspoon freshly squeezed lemon juice
 ¼ teaspoon salt
 ¼ teaspoon freshly ground black pepper

1. Combine first 4 ingredients in a large bowl, and toss gently to coat. Cover and chill 1 hour.
2. Combine cucumbers and juice; toss to coat. Add cucumber mixture, salt, and pepper to strawberry mixture; toss gently to combine. Serve immediately. Yield: 4 servings (serving size: 1½ cups).

CALORIES 49 (9% from fat); FAT 0.5g (sat 0.1g, mono 0.1g, poly 0.3g); PROTEIN 1.1g; CARB 11.6g; FIBER 3.1g; CHOL 0mg; IRON 0.6mg; SODIUM 150mg; CALC 26mg

---

QUICK & EASY
Japanese-Style Cucumber and Radish Salad

Inspired by *sunomono*, a Japanese salad often made with sliced cucumber and daikon radish, this variation is a refreshing no-cook option to serve alongside grilled salmon or teriyaki-style chicken skewers.

 ½ cup thinly sliced sweet onion
 8 sliced radishes (about 4 ounces)
 1 English cucumber, peeled, halved lengthwise, and sliced (about 10 ounces)
 ¼ cup rice wine vinegar
 2 teaspoons canola oil
 1 teaspoon dark sesame oil
 ¼ teaspoon salt
 ⅛ teaspoon crushed red pepper
 1 teaspoon sesame seeds, toasted

1. Combine first 3 ingredients in a medium bowl.
2. Combine vinegar and next 4 ingredients in a small bowl; stir until blended. Drizzle vinegar mixture over cucumber mixture, tossing to coat. Cover with plastic wrap, and chill 15 minutes. Sprinkle with sesame seeds before serving. Yield: 6 servings (serving size: about ½ cup).

CALORIES 39 (62% from fat); FAT 2.7g (sat 0.3g, mono 1.3g, poly 0.9g); PROTEIN 0.7g; CARB 3.2g; FIBER 0.5g; CHOL 0mg; IRON 0.9mg; SODIUM 14mg; CALC 106mg

Elote

Grilled corn on the cob is a popular street food in Oaxaca, Mexico.

    3 tablespoons fat-free mayonnaise
    2 teaspoons fresh lime juice
    2 tablespoons finely grated
       Parmesan cheese
    ½ teaspoon chili powder
    ¼ teaspoon ground red pepper
    ¼ teaspoon ground cumin
    ⅛ teaspoon salt
    4 ears shucked corn
    Cooking spray

1. Prepare grill.
2. Combine mayonnaise and juice in a small bowl. Combine cheese and next 4 ingredients in another small bowl.
3. Place corn on a grill rack coated with cooking spray. Grill corn 12 minutes or until tender, turning frequently. Remove corn from grill; brush with mayonnaise mixture, and sprinkle with cheese mixture. Serve immediately. Yield: 4 servings (serving size: 1 ear of corn).

CALORIES 145 (17% from fat); FAT 2.8g (sat 0.8g, mono 0.8g, poly 0.9g); PROTEIN 5.7g; CARB 29g; FIBER 4.3g; CHOL 3mg; IRON 0.9mg; SODIUM 227mg; CALC 34mg

Lemon-Orange Fennel Salad

    4 cups thinly sliced fennel bulb
       (about 2 bulbs)
    2 cups orange sections (about
       3 oranges)
    1 cup lemon sections, peeled (about
       2 lemons)
    ½ cup thinly sliced red onion
    2 tablespoons chopped fresh mint
    1 tablespoon chopped fresh parsley
    1 tablespoon chopped fennel fronds
    1 tablespoon extravirgin olive oil
    1 tablespoon fresh lemon juice
    ½ teaspoon salt
    ¼ teaspoon freshly ground black
       pepper

1. Combine all ingredients in a large bowl; toss gently to coat. Chill 1 hour. Yield: 6 servings (serving size: 1 cup).

CALORIES 82 (29% from fat); FAT 2.6g (sat 0.3g, mono 1.7g, poly 0.3g); PROTEIN 1.8g; CARB 16g; FIBER 4.5g; CHOL 0mg; IRON 0.8mg; SODIUM 229mg; CALC 67mg

Fruit Slaw

Prepare and refrigerate the dressing up to a day ahead, and toss it with the other ingredients just before serving.

DRESSING:
    ⅓ cup low-fat mayonnaise
    ⅓ cup reduced-fat sour cream
    2 teaspoons grated lime rind
    2 tablespoons chopped fresh
       cilantro
    2 tablespoons fresh lime juice
       (about 2 limes)
    1 teaspoon sugar
    1 teaspoon curry powder
    ¾ teaspoon salt
    ¼ teaspoon freshly ground black
       pepper

REMAINING INGREDIENTS:
    2 cups diced pineapple
    2 cups sliced peeled peaches (about
       4 peaches)
    1 cup sliced peeled mango (about 1
       mango)
    1 cup seedless red grapes, halved
    1 (16-ounce) package coleslaw

1. To prepare dressing, combine first 9 ingredients in a small bowl.
2. Combine pineapple and remaining 4 ingredients in a large bowl. Add mayonnaise mixture to coleslaw mixture; toss well. Serve immediately. Yield: 10 servings (serving size: 1 cup).

CALORIES 88 (18% from fat); FAT 1.8g (sat 0.6g, mono 0.5g, poly 0.5g); PROTEIN 1.6g; CARB 18.8g; FIBER 1g; CHOL 3mg; IRON 0.6mg; SODIUM 265mg; CALC 41mg

Desserts

Fresh fruit stars in tarts, parfaits, crisps, and sorbets.

Nectarine Tarte Tatin

Using a stainless-steel skillet makes it easier to see when the sugar has caramelized, but you can use a nonstick pan. You'll use the same skillet to prepare the tarte tatin like an upside-down cake, layering pie dough over the fruit and finishing it in the oven.

    7   nectarines
    ½   cup sugar
    2   tablespoons water
    1½ teaspoons fresh lemon juice
    2   teaspoons butter
    ¾   teaspoon vanilla extract
    ½   (15-ounce) package refrigerated
        pie dough (such as Pillsbury)

1. Preheat oven to 425°.
2. Cut 1 nectarine in half, and set aside; cut remaining half in half. Cut remaining 6 nectarines into quarters.
3. Combine sugar, water, and juice in a 12-inch stainless-steel skillet. Cook 2 minutes or until sugar is golden (do not stir). Remove from heat; stir in butter and vanilla. Let stand 3 minutes.
4. Place nectarine half, cut side down, in center of sugar mixture; arrange nectarine quarters, cut side down, around center. Return pan to medium heat. Cook 10 minutes or until sugar mixture is bubbly (do not stir). Remove from heat; let stand 3 minutes.
5. Roll pie dough into a 12-inch circle on a lightly floured surface. Place dough over nectarine mixture, fitting dough between nectarines and skillet.
6. Bake at 425° for 15 minutes or until lightly browned. Remove from oven, and cool 10 minutes. Carefully invert tart onto a serving plate. Cut into wedges. Yield: 10 servings (serving size: 1 wedge).

CALORIES 183 (32% from fat); FAT 6.6g (sat 2.9g, mono 2.7g, poly 0.8g); PROTEIN 1.8g; CARB 30.4g; FIBER 1.6g; CHOL 6mg; IRON 0.3mg; SODIUM 84mg; CALC 6mg

MAKE AHEAD • FREEZABLE

Strawberry Margarita Sorbet

Tequila and fresh, ripe strawberries are a delicious match in this dessert. Prepare it up to a day ahead.

- 2 cups water
- 1 cup sugar
- ½ cup tequila
- 1 teaspoon grated lime rind
- ½ cup fresh lime juice (about 4 limes)
- 1 teaspoon grated orange rind
- ⅓ cup fresh orange juice (about 2 oranges)
- 2 cups hulled strawberries

1. Combine water and sugar in a medium saucepan, stirring until sugar dissolves; bring to a boil. Cook 5 minutes. Pour sugar mixture into a medium bowl; stir in tequila and next 4 ingredients.

2. Place strawberries in a food processor; process until smooth. Add strawberry puree to sugar mixture; stir well. Cover and refrigerate 3 hours or until chilled.

3. Pour strawberry mixture into freezer can of an ice-cream freezer, and freeze according to manufacturer's instructions. Spoon mixture into a freezer-safe container; cover and freeze 8 hours or until almost firm. Yield: 8 servings (serving size: ½ cup).

CALORIES 167 (2% from fat); FAT 0.3g (sat 0g, mono 0g, poly 0.1g); PROTEIN 0.7g; CARB 33.4g; FIBER 1.7g; CHOL 0mg; IRON 0.4mg; SODIUM 1mg; CALC 16mg

---

QUICK & EASY • MAKE AHEAD

Peaches with Cava and Lemon Verbena

You can find lemon verbena plants at your local nursery. Some farmers' markets and specialty stores also sell fresh sprigs of it. If you can't find it, cook strips of lemon rind with the wine, and add ½ teaspoon grated lemon rind before serving. Cava is an affordable Spanish sparkling wine now widely available in this country.

- 10 (3-inch) lemon verbena leaves
- 1 (750-milliliter) bottle Cava or other sparkling wine
- ½ cup sugar
- 6 cups sliced peaches (about 2 pounds)
- ½ teaspoon minced lemon verbena leaves

1. Combine whole verbena leaves and wine in a large saucepan; bring to a boil over medium heat. Cook until reduced to 1 cup (about 15 minutes). Remove and discard leaves. Add sugar, stirring until dissolved. Add peaches; bring to a boil. Remove from heat. Cover and chill. Stir in minced verbena leaves just before serving. Yield: 5 servings (serving size: 1 cup).

CALORIES 157 (3% from fat); FAT 0.5g (sat 0g, mono 0.1g, poly 0.1g); PROTEIN 1.9g; CARB 39.5g; FIBER 2.7g; CHOL 0mg; IRON 1.1mg; SODIUM 11mg; CALC 23mg

---

MAKE AHEAD • FREEZABLE

Blackberry-Mascarpone Ice Cream

Mascarpone cheese lends the ice cream rich texture.

- 2 cups 2% reduced-fat milk
- ½ cup sugar
- ⅓ cup half-and-half
- 2 tablespoons maple syrup
- 1 tablespoon fresh lemon juice
- ⅛ teaspoon salt
- 1 large egg, lightly beaten
- ¼ cup (2 ounces) mascarpone cheese
- 3¼ cups fresh blackberries, divided
- ¼ cup sugar

1. Combine first 7 ingredients in a large, heavy saucepan over medium-low heat, stirring well with a whisk. Heat to 160° or until tiny bubbles form around edge of pan, stirring frequently (do not boil). Remove from heat. Add cheese, stirring until smooth. Cool completely.

2. Place 2 cups blackberries and ¼ cup sugar in a blender or food processor, and process until smooth. Strain blackberry mixture through a sieve into a large bowl; discard solids. Cover and chill.

3. Pour milk mixture into freezer can of an ice-cream freezer, and freeze according to manufacturer's instructions. When ice cream is almost set, with machine still running, pour pureed blackberries into freezer can; process until set. Spoon ice cream into a freezer-safe container; cover and freeze 1 hour or until firm. Serve with 1¼ cups blackberries. Yield: 6 servings (serving size: ¾ cup ice cream and about 3 tablespoons blackberries).

CALORIES 261 (29% from fat); FAT 8.5g (sat 4.5g, mono 2.5g, poly 0.6g); PROTEIN 6g; CARB 41.9g; FIBER 0g; CHOL 60mg; IRON 0.8mg; SODIUM 115mg; CALC 159mg

Brandied Berry Milk Shake

2 cups vanilla low-fat ice cream
½ cup blackberries
½ cup blueberries
½ cup sliced strawberries
½ cup 1% low-fat milk
¼ cup brandy

1. Place all ingredients in a blender; process until smooth. Yield: 4 servings (serving size: 1 cup).

CALORIES 182 (18% from fat); FAT 3.7g (sat 2.1g, mono 1g, poly 0.3g); PROTEIN 4.7g; CARB 24.3g; FIBER 1.9g; CHOL 19mg; IRON 0.4mg; SODIUM 65mg; CALC 153mg

---

Berries

History: Strawberries, blackberries, raspberries, and blueberries were once only harvested in the wild but now are cultivated.

Varieties: Strawberries, blackberries, raspberries, and blueberries are among the perennial favorites. Other types include boysenberries, gooseberries, huckleberries, lingonberries, and loganberries.

Availability: Strawberries lead the pack with an April-to-June peak season. Other berries are available from May until August (black), October (blue), and November (raspberry). All are found at supermarkets. Farmers' markets and gourmet stores also sell more exotic kinds, such as golden or black raspberries.

To select: Look for plump, bright-colored berries. Strawberries should have their green caps still attached; other berries shouldn't (which is a sure sign they were picked too soon).

To store: Keep berries refrigerated in a moisture-proof container for up to three days; wash them just before using them.

To cook: Fresh berries need little embellishment. They're excellent in jam, baked goods, and sauces for sweet or savory dishes.

Raspberry Tart

Prepare this tart to showcase a bumper crop of fresh raspberries. Briefly freezing the dough makes it easier to roll into an even layer, and then press into the pan.

PASTRY:
1 cup all-purpose flour (about 4½ ounces)
2 tablespoons sugar
¼ teaspoon salt
2 tablespoons chilled butter, cut into small pieces
2 tablespoons chilled vegetable shortening
3 tablespoons ice water

PASTRY CREAM:
½ cup sugar
2 tablespoons cornstarch
⅛ teaspoon salt
1 cup 1% low-fat milk
1 large egg yolk, lightly beaten
½ teaspoon vanilla extract

REMAINING INGREDIENTS:
3 (6-ounce) containers fresh raspberries
3 tablespoons red currant jelly

1. Preheat oven to 375°.
2. To prepare pastry, lightly spoon flour into a dry measuring cup; level with a knife. Combine flour, 2 tablespoons sugar, and ¼ teaspoon salt in a bowl. Cut in butter and shortening with a pastry blender or 2 knives until mixture resembles coarse meal. Sprinkle surface with ice water, 1 tablespoon at a time; toss with a fork until moist and crumbly (do not form a ball).
3. Gently press mixture into a 4-inch circle on plastic wrap, and cover. Chill 10 minutes. Slightly overlap 2 sheets of plastic wrap on a slightly damp surface. Unwrap and place chilled dough on plastic wrap. Cover dough with 2 additional sheets of overlapping plastic wrap. Roll dough, still covered, into an 11-inch circle. Place dough in freezer 5 minutes or until plastic wrap can be easily removed. Remove top sheets of plastic wrap; fit dough, plastic wrap side up, into a 9-inch round removable-bottom tart pan. Press dough against bottom and sides of pan. Remove remaining plastic wrap. Pierce bottom and sides of dough with a fork; bake at 375° for 20 minutes. Cool on a wire rack.
4. To prepare pastry cream, combine ½ cup sugar, cornstarch, and ⅛ teaspoon salt in a small saucepan over medium heat. Gradually add milk, stirring with a whisk. Stir in egg yolk; bring to a boil, stirring constantly. Cook 1 minute, stirring constantly. Remove from heat; stir in vanilla. Scrape into a bowl. Press plastic wrap onto surface of pastry cream. Place bowl in a large ice-filled bowl. Cool completely, stirring occasionally.
5. Spoon pastry cream into crust; spread evenly. Top with raspberries, starting from center. Place jelly in a small microwave-safe bowl; microwave at HIGH 10 seconds at a time, stirring well, until jelly is warmed through and thinned. Apply jelly in an even layer over tart using a pastry brush. Chill tart 15 minutes or until jelly sets; cover loosely with plastic wrap, and chill at least 45 minutes before serving. Yield: 8 servings (serving size: 1 slice).

CALORIES 250 (26% from fat); FAT 7.3g (sat 3.4g, mono 2g, poly 1.4g); PROTEIN 3.8g; CARB 43.4g; FIBER 4.6g; CHOL 34mg; IRON 1.3mg; SODIUM 147mg; CALC 60mg

---

Buttermilk Sorbet with Strawberries

Garnish each serving with fresh mint sprigs, if desired.

SORBET:
2 cups low-fat buttermilk
¼ cup sugar
¼ cup light corn syrup

STRAWBERRIES:
3 cups sliced fresh strawberries (about 1 pound)
1 tablespoon sugar

1. To prepare sorbet, combine first 3 ingredients in a medium bowl, stirring until sugar dissolves. Pour mixture into freezer can of an ice-cream freezer;

freeze according to manufacturer's instructions. Spoon sorbet into a freezer-safe container; cover and freeze 1 hour or until firm.

2. To prepare strawberries, combine strawberries and 1 tablespoon sugar; let stand 10 minutes. Spoon berries into serving bowls, and top with sorbet. Yield: 4 servings (serving size: ¾ cup sorbet and about ¾ cup strawberries).

CALORIES 206 (6% from fat); FAT 1.4g (sat 0.7g, mono 0.4g, poly 0.2g); PROTEIN 4.8g; CARB 46.5g; FIBER 2.3g; CHOL 5mg; IRON 0.6mg; SODIUM 155mg; CALC 161mg

Fresh Cherry and Plum Crisp

Serve warm with low-fat ice cream.

½ cup all-purpose flour (about 2¼ ounces)
½ cup packed brown sugar
¼ cup slivered almonds
½ cup regular oats
3 tablespoons cold butter
¼ teaspoon ground cinnamon
¼ teaspoon salt
4 cups chopped ripe plums (about 2 pounds)
4 cups pitted sweet cherries (about 1½ pounds)
2 tablespoons all-purpose flour
⅓ cup granulated sugar
⅛ teaspoon salt
Cooking spray

1. Preheat oven to 400°.
2. Lightly spoon flour into a dry measuring cup; level with a knife. Place flour, brown sugar, and almonds in a food processor; pulse 5 times or until blended. Add oats, butter, cinnamon, and ¼ teaspoon salt; pulse 5 times or until mixture is crumbly. Set aside.
3. Combine plums and next 4 ingredients in a large bowl; toss well. Spoon plum mixture into a 13 x 9–inch baking dish coated with cooking spray. Sprinkle with oat mixture. Bake at 400° for 35 minutes or until bubbly. Yield: 8 servings.

CALORIES 313 (23% from fat); FAT 7.9g (sat 3.1g, mono 3g, poly 1.1g); PROTEIN 4.4g; CARB 60.7g; FIBER 4.6g; CHOL 11mg; IRON 1.5mg; SODIUM 147mg; CALC 43mg

MAKE AHEAD
Vanilla Berry Parfaits with Meringue Cookies

CUSTARD:
2½ cups 2% reduced-fat milk
1 vanilla bean, split lengthwise
⅓ cup sugar
3 tablespoons cornstarch
⅛ teaspoon salt
3 egg yolks
1 tablespoon butter

REMAINING INGREDIENTS:
¼ cup raspberry preserves
1 tablespoon framboise (raspberry brandy)
1⅔ cups fresh blackberries (about 5½ ounces)
1⅓ cups fresh raspberries (about 6 ounces)
1 cup fresh blueberries (about 4½ ounces)
12 large fat-free vanilla meringue cookies (such as Miss Meringue), divided

1. To prepare custard, place milk in a medium saucepan. Scrape seeds from bean; add seeds and bean to milk. Heat milk mixture over medium heat to 180° or until tiny bubbles form around edge (do not boil); discard bean.
2. Combine sugar and next 3 ingredients in a large bowl; stir well with a whisk. Gradually add hot milk mixture to sugar mixture, stirring constantly with a whisk. Return milk mixture to pan; cook over medium heat until thick and bubbly (about 5 minutes), stirring constantly. Remove from heat. Add butter, stirring until melted. Pour into a bowl; cool completely. Cover and chill at least 4 hours.
3. Combine preserves and framboise in a large bowl. Reserve 6 blackberries, 6 raspberries, and 6 blueberries. Fold remaining berries into preserves mixture.
4. Reserve 6 cookies. Place remaining cookies in a large zip-top plastic bag. Crush cookies using a rolling pin.
5. Spoon ¼ cup custard into each of 6 tall glasses; spoon ⅓ cup berry mixture over each serving; top each serving with ⅓ cup crushed meringues, ¼ cup custard, and ⅓ cup berry mixture. Top each

serving with 1 blackberry, 1 raspberry, 1 blueberry, and 1 cookie. Yield: 6 servings (serving size: 1 parfait).

CALORIES 268 (21% from fat); FAT 6.3g (sat 3.2g, mono 2.1g, poly 0.6g); PROTEIN 5.8g; CARB 48.8g; FIBER 3.7g; CHOL 115mg; IRON 0.6mg; SODIUM 125mg; CALC 149mg

QUICK & EASY
Grilled Summer Stone Fruit with Cherry-Port Syrup

Look for firm fruit, which will maintain its shape when grilled. Use any combination of fruit you prefer.

SYRUP:
1¾ cups ruby port
⅔ cup sugar
¼ cup dried tart cherries
2 tablespoons red wine vinegar

FRUIT:
2 apricots, halved and pitted
2 peaches, halved and pitted
2 nectarines, halved and pitted
2 plums, halved and pitted
1½ tablespoons canola oil
1 tablespoon sugar
¼ teaspoon ground cinnamon
Cooking spray
4 cups vanilla low-fat ice cream

1. To prepare syrup, combine first 4 ingredients in a medium saucepan over medium-high heat; bring to a boil. Cook 10 minutes or until slightly syrupy. Cover and set aside.
2. Prepare grill.
3. To prepare fruit, brush outsides of apricots, peaches, nectarines, and plums with oil, and sprinkle cut sides evenly with 1 tablespoon sugar and cinnamon. Place fruit on a grill rack coated with cooking spray. Grill 4 minutes on each side or until tender. Place fruit on a cutting board; cool 5 minutes. Cut each fruit half into 4 slices.
4. Place ½ cup ice cream into each of 8 bowls. Top each serving with 8 pieces of fruit and 3 tablespoons syrup. Serve immediately. Yield: 8 servings.

CALORIES 291 (19% from fat); FAT 6.1g (sat 2.1g, mono 2.5g, poly 1g); PROTEIN 4.2g; CARB 49.8g; FIBER 1.7g; CHOL 18mg; IRON 0.5mg; SODIUM 52mg; CALC 115mg

Creative Crepes

Versatile, convenient crepes can be made ahead or made to order. Pair them with an array of fillings any time of day.

Folded, rolled, or stacked, crepes transition effortlessly from humble to haute cuisine. This superthin pancake can be one of the most versatile building blocks in the kitchen. A simple combination of flour, sugar, eggs, milk, water, and just a touch of butter, crepes are delicious in both savory and sweet recipes. Once you master the basic techniques for making the batter and cooking the crepes, variations abound with the simple addition of spices or herbs, and the possibilities for fillings are almost endless.

MAKE AHEAD
Basic Crepes

Although you'll only need about three tablespoons batter to make each crepe, we found a ¼-cup dry measuring cup is the best tool to scoop and pour the batter into the pan so the crepes cook evenly. The small amount of sugar gives the crepes a golden appearance and crisp edges without adding noticeable sweetness, so this recipe works in both savory and sweet applications.

    1 cup all-purpose flour (about 4½ ounces)
    2 teaspoons sugar
    ¼ teaspoon salt
    1 cup low-fat 1% milk
    ½ cup water
    2 teaspoons butter, melted
    2 large eggs

1. Lightly spoon flour into a dry measuring cup; level with a knife. Combine flour, sugar, and salt in a small bowl. Place milk, water, melted butter, and eggs in a blender. Add flour mixture to milk mixture, and process until smooth. Cover batter; chill 1 hour.

2. Heat an 8-inch nonstick crepe pan or skillet over medium heat. Pour a scant ¼ cup batter into pan; quickly tilt pan in all directions so batter covers pan with a thin film. Cook about 1 minute. Carefully lift edge of crepe with a spatula to test for doneness. Crepe is ready to turn when it can be shaken loose from pan and underside is lightly browned. Turn crepe over, and cook 30 seconds or until center is set.

3. Place crepe on a towel; cool completely. Repeat procedure with remaining batter, stirring batter between crepes. Stack crepes between single layers of wax paper to prevent sticking. Yield: 13 crepes (serving size: 1 crepe).

CALORIES 62 (23% from fat); FAT 1.6g (sat 0.8g, mono 0.5g, poly 0.2g); PROTEIN 2.6g; CARB 8.9g; FIBER 0.3g; CHOL 35mg; IRON 0.6mg; SODIUM 70mg; CALC 29mg

HERBED CREPES VARIATION: Add 1 teaspoon chopped fresh parsley and 1 teaspoon chopped fresh chives to the Basic Crepe batter.

ESPRESSO CREPES VARIATION: Add 2 teaspoons instant espresso powder to the Basic Crepe batter.

BUCKWHEAT CREPES VARIATION: Omit ⅔ cup all-purpose flour and add ⅔ cup buckwheat flour to the Basic Crepe recipe.

CINNAMON CREPES VARIATION: Add 1 teaspoon ground cinnamon to the Basic Crepe batter.

Herbed Wild Mushroom Bundles

    6 green onions
    1½ teaspoons butter
    1¾ cups diced shiitake mushroom caps (about 4 ounces)
    1⅓ cups diced oyster mushrooms (about 4 ounces)
    1 (8-ounce) package cremini mushrooms, coarsely chopped
    ⅓ cup dry white wine
    1 tablespoon ⅓-less-fat cream cheese
    1 tablespoon chopped fresh flat-leaf parsley
    2 teaspoons minced fresh chives
    ½ teaspoon salt
    ½ teaspoon chopped fresh thyme
    ⅛ teaspoon freshly ground black pepper
    8 Herbed Crepes (recipe at left)
    Cooking spray

1. Remove green tops from green onions. Cut onion tops lengthwise into ⅛-inch-wide strips to form 8 ties. Drop green onion strips in boiling water, and cook 10 seconds or until limp. Drain onion strips; set aside. Chop white portion of each onion.

2. Melt butter in a medium nonstick skillet over medium heat. Add chopped onions and mushrooms; cook 5 minutes or until mushrooms release their moisture and darken. Add wine to pan; cook 2 minutes or until liquid almost evaporates. Remove from heat; stir in cheese and next 5 ingredients.

3. Preheat oven to 350°.

4. Spoon ⅓ cup mushroom mixture into center of 1 crepe. Gather edges of crepe, and crimp to seal, forming a purse. Tie 1 green onion strip around crimped top of bundle. Repeat procedure with remaining crepes, mushroom mixture, and green onion strips. Place bundles in a 13 x 9–inch baking dish coated with cooking spray. Bake at 350° for 15 minutes or until crepes are thoroughly heated. Yield: 8 servings (serving size: 1 bundle).

CALORIES 92 (29% from fat); FAT 3g (sat 1.5g, mono 0.8g, poly 0.3g); PROTEIN 4.9g; CARB 12.4g; FIBER 1.5g; CHOL 38mg; IRON 1.3mg; SODIUM 236mg; CALC 48mg

Crepes 101

Prepare the Batter

Making crepe batter is quick and easy. Simply combine all the wet ingredients in a blender, add the dry ingredients, and blend briefly.

Next, cover the batter and let it rest, chilled, for one hour. Harold McGee, author of *On Food and Cooking*, explains that this allows "the proteins and damaged starch to absorb water," ensuring the crepes will be tender. The air incorporated into the batter will also dissipate, so the crepes will be paper-thin. After the crepe batter rests, stir it with a whisk to make sure the flour is evenly dispersed, and stir occasionally throughout the cooking process for the same reason.

It's important for the batter to reach the right consistency—similar to that of heavy whipping cream. This produces a thin, even crepe with enough structure to hold together. Different flours or types of milk, the amount of fat, and other factors have a subtle impact on the final consistency.

The Pan and Process

The classic French crepe pan is heavy with distinctly angled shallow edges, somewhat like the sloping sides of an omelet pan. Though not expensive, crepe pans have limited utility.

We tested all of these recipes with an eight-inch nonstick skillet with great results. The nonstick surface is essential because Basic Crepes (recipe on page 186) doesn't use additional fat in the pan to cook the crepes.

The trickiest part of the process is swirling just the right amount of batter in the pan. It's not difficult, but it takes practice. Even seasoned cooks use the first crepe as practice, so don't be discouraged if it takes a couple of times to get the hang of it. The crepes don't have to be uniform or perfectly round.

Success lies in preheating the pan to the correct temperature and mastering the swirl. You want to distribute a thin layer of batter quickly over the base of the hot pan so the crepe will have uniform thickness and cook evenly. Start by adding the batter to the center of the pan. Gently tilt the pan in a circular motion so the batter runs to, but not up, the sides of the pan.

Our crepe recipes only call for about three tablespoons of batter per crepe. Because timing is critical to producing a smooth, even crepe, we recommend scooping the batter with a ¼-cup dry measuring cup. Fill it just three-quarters full, and then add the batter to the pan all at once.

Cook Quickly

Because it's so thin, a crepe cooks very quickly. Check to see if it's done after about one minute. Simply lift one edge of the crepe with a spatula, and gently shake the pan. If the edges of the crepe appear to be crisp, the underside is brown, and it shakes loose from the pan, it's time to turn. It will need to cook only briefly— about 30 seconds—on the other side, just long enough to set the center of the crepe.

Make Extras

Crepes are a choice make-ahead food. You can cook them up to four or five days in advance, stack them between layers of wax paper, slip them in a large zip-top plastic bag, seal, and refrigerate. They will also keep in the freezer for up to two months. If freezing, make sure to stack the crepes between layers of wax paper and wrap them securely with a double layer of plastic wrap. Be sure to allow the frozen crepes to thaw overnight in the refrigerator before using.

Filling

Crepes pair well with a wide variety of flavors. For breakfast, fill the crepes with sausage and cheese. Try Cherry and Orange Blintzes (recipe on page 189) for brunch. Fill lunch crepes with chicken, pork, or vegetables. Dinner crepes can take center stage, or try our Herbed Wild Mushroom Bundles (recipe on page 186) as a side dish for a special meal.

Sauce

Though it's strictly optional, saucing the crepes introduces another flavor dimension and brings polish to a finished crepe. Make a sauce to complement the desired filling, such as the Asiago sauce we paired with Crepes with Ratatouille (recipe on page 190). For an easy option, use store-bought condiments, such as hoisin sauce with Asian-inspired filling, or bottled barbecue sauce with chicken or pork filling.

Paris Street Crepe Favorites

For the most part, Paris is a city where people sit down to dine, whether it's lingering over lunch or settling into a table at a sidewalk café for afternoon coffee. One notable exception is the many freestanding crepe stands that dot the city's sidewalks, where customers can grab a quick, cheap, and delicious snack to enjoy on the go. Some cafés also have walk-up windows where passersby can order take-out crepes. Fillings range from sweet (fruit, sugar, chocolate) to savory (cheese, ham, and vegetables). Crepes filled with Nutella (the Italian chocolate-hazelnut spread) are perhaps the most popular variety, though purists may argue that *crêpes beurre-sucre*—with butter and sugar—are the best way to enjoy this French specialty.

How to Make Great Crepes

1. An 8-inch nonstick skillet or crepe pan, ¼-cup dry measuring cup, and a rubber spatula are the only things needed to cook beautiful crepes. But a blender and whisk ensure a smooth batter.

2. Simply combine all of the ingredients, and blend to make the batter.

3. The consistency of the batter after it rests should be about that of (unwhipped) heavy whipping cream.

4. Add the batter to the center of the pan, and gently tilt the pan in a circular motion, allowing the batter to reach the sides of the pan.

5. The edges of the crepe should be crisp, the underside brown, and the center will come loose if you gently shake the pan. These visual cues alert you that the crepe is ready to flip.

6. The ultimate convenience food, crepes will keep five days if stacked between layers of wax paper and chilled. Or freeze them up to two months.

7. Spoon filling evenly down the center of the crepes.

8. Stack, roll, or fold crepes for a variety of presentation options.

Smoked Salmon Buckwheat Pinwheels

Look for packaged sliced smoked salmon. Conveniently, each slice should be one ounce.

½ cup (4 ounces) fat-free cream cheese, softened
3 tablespoons fat-free sour cream
1 (3-ounce) package ⅓-less-fat cream cheese, softened
8 Buckwheat Crepes (recipe on page 186)
3 tablespoons minced fresh chives
8 (1-ounce) slices cold-smoked salmon

1. Combine first 3 ingredients; stir until smooth. Spread about 1 tablespoon cheese mixture evenly over each crepe. Sprinkle each with about 1 teaspoon chives; top each with 1 salmon slice. Roll up each crepe, jelly-roll fashion. Cover and chill 1 hour. Cut each roll crosswise into 10 pinwheels. Yield: 20 servings (serving size: 4 pinwheels).

CALORIES 62 (38% from fat); FAT 2.6g (sat 1.2g, mono 0.8g, poly 0.2g); PROTEIN 4.8g; CARB 4.5g; FIBER 0.7g; CHOL 29mg; IRON 0.4mg; SODIUM 316mg; CALC 22mg

Espresso Crepes with Ice Cream and Dark Chocolate Sauce

Since both the crepes and chocolate sauce can be made ahead, this is the simplest of desserts. If you make the sauce ahead, warm it just before serving.

⅓ cup half-and-half
2 tablespoons honey
3 ounces semisweet chocolate, chopped
8 Espresso Crepes (recipe on page 186)
2 cups low-fat coffee ice cream

1. Combine half-and-half and honey in a small saucepan over medium heat; cook 3 minutes or until tiny bubbles

form around edge of pan, stirring frequently (do not boil). Remove from heat. Add chocolate; stir until smooth.
2. Fold each crepe in half; fold in half again. Place 1 crepe on each of 8 plates. Top each serving with ¼ cup coffee ice cream; drizzle with 4 teaspoons sauce. Yield: 8 servings.

CALORIES 229 (28% from fat); FAT 7.1g (sat 4g, mono 0.8g, poly 0.2g); PROTEIN 6.2g; CARB 25.5g; FIBER 0.8g; CHOL 45mg; IRON 0.6mg; SODIUM 105mg; CALC 93mg

Cherry and Orange Blintzes

This crepe doubles as either a delicious dessert or brunch offering.

½ cup (4 ounces) ⅓-less-fat cream cheese, softened
¼ cup packed brown sugar
¼ cup (2 ounces) fat-free cream cheese, softened
2 teaspoons grated orange rind
⅛ teaspoon salt
¼ cup fresh orange juice
⅓ cup dried sweet cherries
8 Basic Crepes (recipe on page 186)
Cooking spray
2 teaspoons powdered sugar

1. Preheat oven to 350°.
2. Combine first 5 ingredients in a bowl, stirring until blended. Combine juice and cherries in a small microwave-safe bowl. Microwave at HIGH 30 seconds; let stand 10 minutes. Drain and coarsely chop cherries. Stir cherries into cheese mixture.
3. Spoon 3 tablespoons cheese mixture in center of each crepe; fold sides and ends over. Place crepes, seam sides down, in a 13 x 9–inch baking dish coated with cooking spray. Cover and bake at 350° for 15 minutes or until blintzes are thoroughly heated. Sprinkle with powdered sugar. Serve immediately. Yield: 4 servings (serving size: 2 blintzes).

CALORIES 317 (29% from fat); FAT 10.1g (sat 5.8g, mono 3g, poly 0.5g); PROTEIN 10.4g; CARB 45.1g; FIBER 2g; CHOL 92mg; IRON 1.8mg; SODIUM 412mg; CALC 132mg

Chicken, Spinach, and Mushroom Crepes

This recipe comes together in a flash for a delicious weeknight supper.

Cooking spray
1 cup thinly sliced onion
1 (8-ounce) package presliced mushrooms
3 cups chopped cooked chicken breast
½ cup sliced green onions
¾ teaspoon salt, divided
1 (10-ounce) package frozen chopped spinach, thawed, drained, and squeezed dry
1 tablespoon butter
2 tablespoons all-purpose flour
1¼ cups 2% reduced-fat milk
¼ teaspoon black pepper
10 Basic Crepes (recipe on page 186)
½ cup (2 ounces) shredded Monterey Jack cheese with jalapeño peppers

1. Heat a large nonstick skillet over medium-high heat. Coat pan with cooking spray. Add 1 cup onion and mushrooms to pan; sauté 5 minutes or until mushrooms release their moisture and darken. Stir in chicken, green onions, ¼ teaspoon salt, and spinach.
2. Melt butter in a small saucepan over medium heat. Add flour to pan; stir with a whisk until blended. Cook 1 minute, stirring constantly. Gradually add milk to pan, stirring constantly with a whisk; cook 5 minutes or until thick. Remove from heat. Stir in ½ teaspoon salt and pepper. Pour milk mixture over chicken mixture; stir to combine.
3. Preheat broiler.
4. Spoon about ½ cup chicken mixture in center of each crepe; fold sides and ends over. Place, seam sides down, in a 13 x 9–inch baking pan coated with cooking spray. Sprinkle crepes evenly with cheese. Broil 2 minutes or until lightly browned. Yield: 5 servings (serving size: 2 crepes).

CALORIES 411 (30% from fat); FAT 13.8g (sat 6.7g, mono 4.1g, poly 1.4g); PROTEIN 40.1g; CARB 30.9g; FIBER 3.7g; CHOL 164mg; IRON 3.6mg; SODIUM 719mg; CALC 308mg

Crepes with Ratatouille

Oven-roasted vegetables make a tasty filling for this meatless main-dish crepe.

FILLING:

    5   cups chopped eggplant (about
        ¾ pound)
  3½   cups chopped zucchini (about
        2 medium)
  1½   cups chopped seeded plum
        tomato (about ¾ pound)
    1   cup chopped red bell pepper
    ½   cup chopped onion
    2   garlic cloves, minced
    1   teaspoon olive oil
    ¾   teaspoon salt
    ¼   teaspoon black pepper
        Cooking spray
    2   tablespoons chopped fresh basil
    2   tablespoons chopped fresh parsley

SAUCE:

    1   cup 1% low-fat milk
    1   tablespoon all-purpose flour
    ½   cup (2 ounces) grated Asiago
        cheese
    2   tablespoons (1 ounce) fat-free
        cream cheese, softened
        Dash of ground nutmeg
    2   tablespoons dry white wine
    ⅛   teaspoon salt
    ⅛   teaspoon freshly ground black
        pepper

REMAINING INGREDIENT:

    8   Basic Crepes (recipe on page 186)

1. Preheat oven to 450°.
2. To prepare filling, combine first 6 ingredients in a large bowl. Drizzle with oil, and sprinkle with ¾ teaspoon salt and ¼ teaspoon pepper; toss to coat. Spread vegetable mixture in an even layer on a jelly-roll pan coated with cooking spray. Bake at 450° for 45 minutes or until vegetables are lightly browned, stirring every 15 minutes. Transfer vegetable mixture to a bowl; cool 2 minutes. Stir in basil and parsley.
3. Increase oven temperature to 500°.
4. To prepare sauce, combine milk and flour in a saucepan over medium-high heat; bring to a boil. Cook 1 minute or until thick, stirring constantly with a

whisk. Remove from heat. Add cheeses and nutmeg; stir with a whisk until smooth. Stir in wine, ⅛ teaspoon salt, and ⅛ teaspoon pepper. Add 2 tablespoons sauce to vegetable mixture; stir until combined.
5. Spoon 3 tablespoons vegetable mixture in center of each crepe; fold sides and ends over. Place, seam sides down, in an 11 x 7–inch baking dish coated with cooking spray. Top crepes with remaining sauce. Bake at 500° for 10 minutes or until crepes are lightly browned. Yield: 4 servings (serving size: 2 crepes).

CALORIES 308 (29% from fat); FAT 9.9g (sat 4.7g, mono 3.1g, poly 1g); PROTEIN 15.6g; CARB 39.9g; FIBER 6.5g; CHOL 85mg; IRON 2.7mg; SODIUM 775mg; CALC 315mg

WINE NOTE: Sauvignon blanc is a good match with dishes made up of mostly vegetables and herbs. Snappy, fresh, and herbal itself, the wine plays up the flavors in these crepes with delicious results. Try the tasty, well-priced Chateau Souverain 2004 sauvignon blanc from California's Alexander Valley ($14).

Cinnamon Crepes with Peaches and Cream Cheese

Make the filling and crepes ahead, and chill until you're ready to use them.

    1   cup powdered sugar
    1   cup fat-free cottage cheese
    ¾   cup (6 ounces) ⅓-less-fat cream
        cheese, softened
    2   teaspoons fresh lemon juice,
        divided
  3½   cups sliced peeled peaches (about
        1 pound)
    1   teaspoon granulated sugar
    1   teaspoon amaretto (almond-
        flavored liqueur)
    6   Cinnamon Crepes (recipe on page
        186)
    2   tablespoons sliced almonds, toasted

1. Place powdered sugar, cheeses, and 1½ teaspoons juice in a food processor; process until smooth. Spoon mixture into a bowl; cover and chill 1 hour.

2. Combine ½ teaspoon juice, peaches, granulated sugar, and amaretto in a bowl; toss gently. Let stand 15 minutes; toss gently.
3. Place one crepe on each of 6 plates. Spoon ½ cup cheese mixture in center of each crepe; roll up. Top each with ½ cup peach mixture; sprinkle with 1 teaspoon almonds. Serve immediately. Yield: 6 servings (serving size: 1 crepe).

CALORIES 301 (29% from fat); FAT 9.6g (sat 5g, mono 3.1g, poly 0.7g); PROTEIN 10.7g; CARB 43.5g; FIBER 2g; CHOL 60mg; IRON 1mg; SODIUM 334mg; CALC 90mg

lighten up

Sweet Success

An ice cream treat is revamped for a Missouri grandmother and her family.

Ice Cream Treasures is a favorite family treat. "I remember making it for the first time with my daughters when they were teenagers," Norma Parrott of Kansas City, Missouri, says. They prepared the dessert—butter brickle ice cream sandwiched between a buttered mixture of coconut, almonds, and rice cereal—for parties, showers, and get-togethers. But now Parrott says it's more important for her to eat healthfully since her daughters have children of their own. So we helped her out.

Instead of purchasing butter brickle ice cream, we made our own by adding crushed toffee bars to softened reduced-fat vanilla ice cream. This shaved about 40 calories and almost eight grams of fat per serving. And because the cereal, coconut, and almond mixture holds together when frozen with the ice cream, there is no need to use butter as a binder. We reduced it to two tablespoons for the whole recipe, which saved each portion another 55 calories and six grams of fat.

The last trouble spot was the toasted almonds and coconut. We reduced the amounts of both, and toasted both ingredients to intensify their flavors. We also decreased the amount of cereal and brown sugar, and added whole-grain cereal to boost the fiber.

Ice Cream Treasures

Use any combination of cereals you like. This frozen dessert would also be delicious with chocolate ice cream and chopped walnuts instead of almonds.

1½ cups (6 ounces) chocolate-covered English toffee candy bars (such as Heath), crushed
8 cups vanilla reduced-fat ice cream (such as Healthy Choice), softened
4 cups crispy rice cereal squares, crushed (such as Rice Chex)
2 cups whole-grain toasted oat cereal (such as Cheerios)
⅔ cup packed dark brown sugar
⅓ cup slivered almonds, toasted
⅓ cup flaked sweetened coconut, toasted
2 tablespoons butter, melted

1. Stir crushed candy into ice cream. Cover and freeze until ready to use.
2. Combine cereals and remaining 4 ingredients in a large bowl. Press half of cereal mixture in bottom of a 13 x 9–inch baking pan.
3. Let ice cream stand at room temperature 20 minutes or until softened. Spread ice cream mixture over cereal mixture; top evenly with remaining cereal mixture. Cover and freeze 8 hours or overnight. Yield: 16 servings (serving size: about ¾ cup).

CALORIES 265 (29% from fat); FAT 8.4g (sat 4.1g, mono 2.7g, poly 0.7g); PROTEIN 5.2g; CARB 41.7g; FIBER 1g; CHOL 25mg; IRON 3.6mg; SODIUM 194mg; CALC 156mg

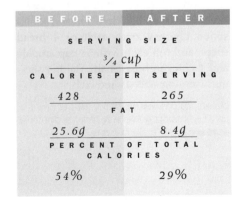

BEFORE	AFTER
SERVING SIZE	
¾ cup	
CALORIES PER SERVING	
428	265
FAT	
25.6g	8.4g
PERCENT OF TOTAL CALORIES	
54%	29%

reader recipes

Turkey Burgers with a Twist

A search for a leaner sandwich led this Tennessee reader to create a new take on a family favorite.

JoAnn Stanford of Lupton City, Tennessee, likes to experiment in the kitchen. So, when both she and her husband, Joey, decided they wanted to lose weight and focus on living a healthier lifestyle, she began experimenting with one of their all-time favorites: burgers. "I found that turkey, orange, and a little green onion go well together." Ground turkey can dry out easily, but the orange juice keeps the burgers moist and eliminates the need for a binder like egg.

Stanford tops her burgers with a slightly sweet and gingery "special sauce" that she created during her kitchen experiments. (She notes it's also delicious over salmon.) "We serve the burgers with plantains sautéed in a little bit of olive oil," Stanford says.

QUICK & EASY
Turkey Burgers with Special Sauce

Serve these great summertime burgers with table grapes for a refreshing and light meal.

¼ cup chopped green onions
2 tablespoons fresh orange juice
1 tablespoon low-sodium soy sauce
1 teaspoon finely chopped peeled fresh ginger
1 garlic clove, minced
1 pound ground turkey breast
Cooking spray
½ cup Special Sauce
4 (1½-ounce) whole wheat hamburger buns
4 curly leaf lettuce leaves

1. Prepare grill.
2. Combine first 6 ingredients in a large bowl. Divide turkey mixture into 4 equal

portions, shaping each into a ¾-inch-thick patty. Place patties on grill rack coated with cooking spray; grill 6 minutes on each side or until done.
3. Spread 2 tablespoons Special Sauce over top half of each bun. Place lettuce leaves on bottom halves of buns; top each with 1 patty and top half of bun. Cut each burger in half. Yield: 4 servings (serving size: 1 burger).

CALORIES 318 (21% from fat); FAT 7.3g (sat 1.6g, mono 1.8g, poly 3.3g); PROTEIN 32.5g; CARB 31.7g; FIBER 3.6g; CHOL 70mg; IRON 2.8mg; SODIUM 812mg; CALC 73mg

QUICK & EASY • MAKE AHEAD
SPECIAL SAUCE:

¾ cup reduced-fat mayonnaise
2 tablespoons Dijon mustard
1½ tablespoons finely chopped green onions
1 tablespoon honey
1 teaspoon fresh orange juice
1 teaspoon low-sodium soy sauce
½ teaspoon finely chopped peeled fresh ginger

1. Combine all ingredients in a medium bowl. Cover; refrigerate. Yield: ¾ cup (serving size: 2 tablespoons).

CALORIES 69 (58% from fat); FAT 4.5g (sat 1g, mono 1.1g, poly 2.2g); PROTEIN 0.4g; CARB 7.8g; FIBER 0.1g; CHOL 0mg; IRON 0.2mg; SODIUM 416mg; CALC 9mg

QUICK & EASY
Stacey's Broiled Salmon

"My boys like this with pasta and fresh steamed asparagus or broccoli."
—Stacey Keller, Federal Way, Washington

¼ cup water
Cooking spray
4 (6-ounce) salmon fillets (about 1 inch thick)
2 tablespoons brown sugar
2 tablespoons teriyaki sauce
2 teaspoons salt-free Creole seasoning
4 lemon wedges

1. Preheat broiler.
2. Pour ¼ cup water into a foil-lined
Continued

shallow roasting pan; place rack in pan. Lightly coat rack with cooking spray. Place fillets, skin side down, on rack. Pierce flesh liberally with a fork.

3. Combine sugar, teriyaki sauce, and seasoning in a small bowl; rub evenly over tops of fillets. Broil 13 minutes or until fish flakes easily when tested with a fork or until desired degree of doneness. Serve with lemon wedges. Yield: 4 servings (serving size: 1 salmon fillet and 1 lemon wedge).

CALORIES 298 (40% from fat); FAT 13.1g (sat 3.1g, mono 5.7g, poly 3.2g); PROTEIN 36.7g; CARB 6.4g; FIBER 0g; CHOL 87mg; IRON 0.8mg; SODIUM 427mg; CALC 27mg

---

Sweet Cabbage Salad

"I developed this recipe after my mom made a similar version. I changed a couple of her items and ended up with this sweet-tangy salad."

—Jenn Sitts, Oneonta, New York

  6 cups shredded cabbage (about ½ head)
  1 cup shredded carrot (about 1 medium)
  1 cup chopped green bell pepper (about 1 medium)
  ½ cup chopped red onion
  ½ cup sugar
  ½ cup white wine vinegar
  2 tablespoons olive oil
  1 teaspoon dry mustard
  ½ teaspoon celery seeds
  ½ teaspoon salt

1. Combine first 4 ingredients in a large bowl; toss well. Combine sugar and remaining 5 ingredients in a small bowl, stirring with a whisk. Pour vinegar mixture over cabbage mixture, tossing gently to combine. Cover; chill 1 hour. Yield: 6 servings (serving size: about ¾ cup).

CALORIES 147 (29% from fat); FAT 4.7g (sat 0.6g, mono 3.4g, poly 0.5g); PROTEIN 1.6g; CARB 25.3g; FIBER 3g; CHOL 0mg; IRON 0.8mg; SODIUM 225mg; CALC 54mg

---

Moroccan-Spiced Oranges

"Simple to prepare, this salad is a light and refreshing way to end a meal. The cinnamon-orange combination is a great one. You can also serve this over ice cream or frozen yogurt."

—Liz Brown, Portland, Oregon

2½ cups orange sections, cut into ½-inch pieces (about 6)
 ¼ cup slivered almonds
2½ tablespoons chopped pitted dates (about 4)
 1 tablespoon powdered sugar
 1 tablespoon fresh lemon juice
 ¼ teaspoon ground cinnamon
Ground cinnamon (optional)
Grated orange rind (optional)

1. Combine first 6 ingredients in a medium bowl, tossing to combine. Cover; chill 20 minutes. Garnish with cinnamon and rind, if desired. Yield: 4 servings (serving size: about ½ cup).

CALORIES 167 (19% from fat); FAT 3.6g (sat 0.3g, mono 2.2g, poly 0.9g); PROTEIN 3g; CARB 35g; FIBER 5.3g; CHOL 0mg; IRON 0.7mg; SODIUM 0mg; CALC 81mg

---

Fresh Fruit Salad with Honey Ginger Lime Dressing

"This dressing has the perfect balance of sweet and tangy, and it is especially delicious served with pork."

—Marie Meyer, Greensboro, North Carolina

1½ tablespoons honey
 1 tablespoon fresh lime juice
 ¼ teaspoon minced peeled fresh ginger
 2 cups sliced peeled peaches (about 2)
 1 cup blueberries
 1 cup seedless green grapes, halved

1. Combine first 3 ingredients in a small bowl; stir with a whisk.

2. Combine peaches, blueberries, and grapes in a bowl. Drizzle juice mixture over fruit mixture; toss gently to coat. Chill at least 1 hour. Yield: 8 servings (serving size: ½ cup).

CALORIES 53 (3% from fat); FAT 0.2g (sat 0g, mono 0g, poly 0.1g); PROTEIN 0.7g; CARB 13.8g; FIBER 1.3g; CHOL 0mg; IRON 0.3mg; SODIUM 1mg; CALC 6mg

---

Grilled Chicken Sandwiches with Arugula and Chutney

"The sweet chutney in this sandwich contrasts well with the peppery arugula."

—Lisa Richardson, Glendale, California

  4 (6-ounce) skinless, boneless chicken breast halves
  ½ teaspoon salt
  ½ teaspoon freshly ground black pepper
  2 tablespoons light mayonnaise
Cooking spray
  6 tablespoons mango chutney, divided
  4 (1-ounce) slices sourdough bread
  2 cups trimmed arugula

1. Prepare grill.

2. Sprinkle chicken with salt and pepper. Coat both sides of chicken breast halves with mayonnaise. Place chicken on a grill rack coated with cooking spray. Grill 3 minutes on each side or until done. Brush 1½ teaspoons chutney over each chicken breast half. Place bread slices on grill rack, and grill 1 minute on each side or until golden. Spread 1 tablespoon chutney onto each of 4 bread slices, and top each with ½ cup arugula and 1 chicken breast half. Yield: 4 servings (serving size: 1 sandwich).

CALORIES 323 (15% from fat); FAT 5.3g (sat 1.1g, mono 1.4g, poly 2.1g); PROTEIN 42.3g; CARB 25.2g; FIBER 1.7g; CHOL 101mg; IRON 2.9mg; SODIUM 622mg; CALC 70mg

QUICK & EASY • MAKE AHEAD
Golden Gazpacho

"This soup is light and perfect for summer."
—Linda Brodlieb, Sands Point, New York

3½ cups chopped seeded yellow tomato (about 1½ pounds)
2 cups chopped seeded peeled cucumber (about 1)
1 cup chopped yellow bell pepper (about 1 medium)
½ cup chopped red bell pepper
½ cup chopped green bell pepper
½ cup chopped red onion
2 garlic cloves, chopped
2 tablespoons white wine vinegar
1 tablespoon chopped fresh mint
1 tablespoon chopped fresh cilantro
1 tablespoon honey
2 teaspoons extravirgin olive oil
¾ teaspoon salt
¼ teaspoon ground cumin

1. Place first 7 ingredients in a blender; process until smooth. Add vinegar and remaining ingredients; pulse 5 times or until well combined. Cover and chill at least 1 hour or overnight. Yield: 6 servings (serving size: 1 cup).

CALORIES 77 (27% from fat); FAT 2.3g (sat 0.3g, mono 1.2g, poly 0.4g); PROTEIN 2.9g; CARB 13.9g; FIBER 2.7g; CHOL 0mg; IRON 1.4mg; SODIUM 342mg; CALC 37mg

inspired vegetarian

Time for Tempeh

Get all the goodness of soy—lean protein and fiber—from this flexible component in meatless meals.

Green Salad with Grilled Tempeh and Maple-Soy Vinaigrette

8 ounces organic tempeh, cut crosswise into ¼-inch slices
1 teaspoon butter, melted
¼ teaspoon salt
2½ tablespoons low-sodium soy sauce, divided
1½ tablespoons maple syrup, divided
4 cups trimmed arugula
4 cups baby spinach (about 3 ounces)
½ cup thinly sliced yellow bell pepper (about ½ medium)
¼ cup thinly sliced green onions (about 2)
2 tablespoons apple cider vinegar
1 teaspoon extravirgin olive oil
Dash ground red pepper
1 garlic clove, finely chopped

1. Lightly brush both sides of tempeh slices with butter; sprinkle with salt. Heat a grill pan over medium-high heat. Add tempeh slices in a single layer; cook 1 minute on each side or until tempeh begins to brown and grill marks appear. Remove from heat. Combine 1 tablespoon soy sauce and 1 tablespoon syrup; brush over both sides of tempeh while still warm. Cool tempeh completely; cut slices into bite-sized pieces.
2. Combine arugula, spinach, bell pepper, and onions in a large bowl. Combine 1½ tablespoons soy sauce, 1½ teaspoons syrup, vinegar, oil, red pepper, and garlic in a small bowl; stir well with a whisk. Drizzle soy mixture over greens mixture; toss to coat. Place 2 cups salad on each of 4 plates; top each serving with ½ cup tempeh. Serve immediately. Yield: 4 servings.

CALORIES 153 (31% from fat); FAT 5.3g (sat 1.8g, mono 1.9g, poly 1.3g); PROTEIN 14g; CARB 13.8g; FIBER 5g; CHOL 3mg; IRON 3.2mg; SODIUM 521mg; CALC 155mg

Tempeh Tasting

While three-grain, wild rice, and plain (soy) tempeh are generally interchangeable, here are basic flavor profiles of tempeh varieties available at large grocery stores and health-food stores.
Original: The crunchy and chewy bite and mild nutty flavor make for a great meat substitute in any recipe.
Flax: This has substantial bite but is a bit dry. It would be good in a breakfast casserole or marinated and simmered in a rich broth or tangy sauce.
Soy: A pleasing chewy texture gives way to the characteristic tang of the soy cake. This tempeh works best marinated or with a flavorful herb, spice, or nut sauce.
Garden vegetable: With carrots and bell peppers, this tempeh has bouillon undertones. Grate some to use as "croutons" on a salad, or use in a vegetable noodle soup.
Wild rice: This crunchy version imparts a black olive undertone. Use it crumbled in Italian red sauces, a roasted vegetable dish, or with sweet-and-sour Asian dishes.
Three-grain and five-grain: With a combination of millet, soybeans, brown rice, barley, or oats, these varieties have a mild taste that could pair well with any flavoring—barbecued, as a fajita filler, or even in a potpie.

Tempeh Tips

• Health- and natural-food stores generally carry larger selections of tempeh—and their inventories turn over quickly.
• Dark, black, or gray spots are a part of the culturing process and do not affect the texture, flavor, or shelf life.
• Refrigerate opened tempeh tightly wrapped for up to five days.
• Once opened, tempeh can be frozen up to one year from its sell-by date.

Tempeh Ratatouille

We swapped tempeh for traditional eggplant in this ratatouille. Use any fresh vegetable combination in this easy sauté.

- 1 teaspoon extravirgin olive oil
- 8 ounces organic tempeh, cut into ½-inch cubes
- Cooking spray
- 1 cup finely chopped onion (about 1 large)
- ¾ teaspoon kosher salt
- ¼ teaspoon crushed red pepper
- 2 garlic cloves, minced
- ½ cup organic vegetable broth (such as Swanson Certified Organic)
- 1 cup yellow squash, cut into 1-inch cubes (about ½ pound)
- 1 cup zucchini, cut into ½-inch cubes (about ½ pound)
- 1 (8-ounce) package mushrooms, halved
- 1 cup halved cherry tomatoes
- ½ cup ½-inch pieces red bell pepper (about ½ large pepper)
- 2 tablespoons chopped fresh basil
- 1 tablespoon chopped fresh flat-leaf parsley
- 1 teaspoon fresh lemon juice

1. Preheat oven to 500°.
2. Combine oil and tempeh in a baking pan coated with cooking spray, tossing to coat tempeh. Bake at 500° for 10 minutes or until tempeh is browned on the edges, stirring once.
3. Heat a large nonstick skillet over medium-high heat. Coat pan with cooking spray. Add onion; sauté 3 minutes or until browned. Stir in salt, crushed red pepper, and garlic; sauté 30 seconds. Add broth; bring to a boil. Stir in tempeh, squash, zucchini, and mushrooms; simmer 5 minutes. Stir in tomatoes and bell pepper; simmer 5 minutes. Remove from heat; stir in basil, parsley, and juice. Yield: 4 servings (serving size: 1 cup).

CALORIES 163 (26% from fat); FAT 4.7g (sat 1.3g, mono 1.8g, poly 1.4g); PROTEIN 16.3g; CARB 17.2g; FIBER 6.3g; CHOL 0mg; IRON 2.8mg; SODIUM 440mg; CALC 132mg

Tempeh-Mushroom Fricassee with Garlic Confit

To save time, use jarred peeled whole garlic found in the produce section of the grocery store. Serve stew over egg noodles.

- 1 tablespoon olive oil
- 16 garlic cloves, crushed
- Cooking spray
- 12 ounces organic tempeh, cut into ¼-inch cubes
- ¼ cup dry white wine
- 2 cups thinly sliced leek (about 2 medium)
- 1 pound mixed gourmet mushrooms (such as cremini, shiitake, or oyster), thickly sliced
- 3 cups organic vegetable broth (such as Swanson Certified Organic), divided
- 1 tablespoon all-purpose flour
- 2 teaspoons chopped fresh thyme
- ½ teaspoon salt
- ¼ teaspoon black pepper
- 1 tablespoon chopped fresh parsley

1. Combine oil and garlic in a large Dutch oven over low heat. Cook 10 minutes or until garlic is golden and fragrant, stirring frequently. Lightly coat Dutch oven and garlic mixture with cooking spray. Increase heat to medium-high; add tempeh, and sauté 8 minutes or until brown. Stir in wine; cook until liquid is almost evaporated (about 30 seconds). Transfer tempeh mixture to a bowl.
2. Return pan to medium-high heat. Recoat pan with cooking spray. Add leek and mushrooms; sauté until vegetables begin to brown and liquid is almost evaporated (about 10 minutes). Add 1 cup broth; cook 1 minute, scraping pan to loosen browned bits. Combine 2 cups broth and flour in a small bowl, stirring well with a whisk. Add broth mixture to pan. Reduce heat, and stir in tempeh mixture. Cover; simmer 30 minutes. Stir in thyme, salt, and pepper. Remove from heat; stir in parsley. Yield: 4 servings (serving size: 1½ cups).

CALORIES 297 (32% from fat); FAT 10.4g (sat 1.9g, mono 4.4g, poly 2.9g); PROTEIN 22.3g; CARB 31.1g; FIBER 8.9g; CHOL 0mg; IRON 4.6mg; SODIUM 751mg; CALC 85mg

Tempeh Coconut Curry

This is a traditional southeast Asian preparation for tempeh—highly flavored with warm and hot spices.

CURRY:
- 1 tablespoon canola oil
- 2 cups finely chopped onion
- 1 teaspoon salt, divided
- 2 teaspoons tamarind pulp
- 1 tablespoon finely chopped peeled fresh ginger
- 1 tablespoon finely chopped fresh garlic
- 1½ teaspoons ground coriander
- ½ teaspoon ground turmeric
- ½ teaspoon crushed red pepper
- 1 (3-inch) cinnamon stick
- 3 cups chopped peeled sweet potato (about 1 pound)
- 1 cup water
- 1 (13.5-ounce) can light coconut milk
- 8 ounces organic tempeh, cut into ¾-inch cubes
- 1 tablespoon fresh lime juice
- 2 teaspoons low-sodium soy sauce

RICE:
- 1½ cups uncooked basmati rice
- ⅓ cup chopped fresh cilantro
- ¼ teaspoon salt

1. To prepare curry, heat oil in a large nonstick skillet over medium-high heat. Add onion and ½ teaspoon salt. Cook 2 minutes or until onion is tender, stirring occasionally. Stir in tamarind; cook 2 minutes, stirring to break up tamarind. Add ginger and next 5 ingredients; cook 2 minutes, stirring frequently. Add ½ teaspoon salt, potato, 1 cup water, milk, and tempeh; bring to a boil. Cover, reduce heat, and simmer 15 minutes or until potato is tender. Uncover; stir in juice and soy sauce. Simmer 3 minutes or until slightly thick. Discard cinnamon stick.
2. To prepare rice, cook rice according to package directions, omitting salt and fat. Stir in cilantro and ¼ teaspoon salt. Serve with curry. Yield: 4 servings (serving size: 1 cup curry and about 1 cup rice).

CALORIES 381 (27% from fat); FAT 11.5g (sat 5.5g, mono 3.2g, poly 2.2g); PROTEIN 16.9g; CARB 53.7g; FIBER 6.3g; CHOL 0mg; IRON 2.9mg; SODIUM 870mg; CALC 112mg

Tempeh Sloppy Joes with Coleslaw

Topped with cool coleslaw, these saucy sandwiches are a great way to try tempeh for the first time. Substitute wild rice or three-grain tempeh, if available.

    1   tablespoon olive oil
    1   cup chopped onion (about
        1 medium)
    1   pound organic tempeh, crumbled
    3   tablespoons tomato paste
    2   tablespoons balsamic vinegar
    2   teaspoons brown sugar
    1   teaspoon Spanish smoked
        paprika
    ¾   teaspoon salt
    ¼   teaspoon freshly ground black
        pepper
    3   cups water
    2   tablespoons light mayonnaise
    2   teaspoons water
    ¼   teaspoon salt
    ¼   teaspoon freshly ground black
        pepper
    3   cups thinly shredded cabbage
    ½   cup shredded carrot (about
        1 medium)
    6   (1½-ounce) hamburger buns

1. Heat oil in a large nonstick skillet over medium-high heat. Add onion; sauté 2 minutes or until soft. Add tempeh; sauté 6 minutes or until tempeh begins to brown.
2. Combine tomato paste and next 5 ingredients in a small bowl. Add tomato mixture to tempeh; stir to combine. Stir in 3 cups water. Simmer until mixture is thick and liquid is almost evaporated (about 20 minutes), stirring frequently. Remove from heat; keep warm.
3. Combine mayonnaise and next 3 ingredients in a medium bowl. Add cabbage and carrot, tossing well to combine.
4. Top bottom half of each bun with about ¾ cup tempeh filling. Top each serving with about ⅓ cup cabbage mixture, and cover with top half of bun. Serve sloppy joes immediately. Yield: 6 servings (serving size: 1 sandwich).

CALORIES 319 (28% from fat); FAT 9.9g (sat 2.4g, mono 3.7g, poly 3.5g); PROTEIN 21.3g; CARB 37.6g; FIBER 7.4g; CHOL 2mg; IRON 4.2mg; SODIUM 727mg; CALC 203mg

dinner tonight

Down-Home Dinners

These classics require minimal effort for delicious down-home suppers.

Down-Home Menu 1
serves 4

Cornmeal-Crusted Catfish

Green beans with hot pepper vinegar

Creamy coleslaw with bacon*

*Combine ⅓ cup light mayonnaise, ⅓ cup reduced-fat sour cream, 1 tablespoon minced seeded jalapeño pepper, 1 tablespoon white wine vinegar, 2 teaspoons sugar, ½ teaspoon salt, and 3 cooked and crumbled bacon slices. Add 1 (16-ounce) package coleslaw, tossing well to coat. Cover and chill.

Game Plan

1. While bacon cooks:
  • Assemble ingredients for coleslaw
2. While catfish cooks:
  • Steam green beans

QUICK & EASY
Cornmeal-Crusted Catfish
(pictured on page 239)

The bacon drippings used to cook the catfish lend this southern family favorite authentic flavor. Use the bacon in the coleslaw, or reserve for another use.
TOTAL TIME: 32 MINUTES

    3   slices bacon
    ⅓   cup yellow cornmeal
    2   teaspoons salt-free Cajun
        seasoning
    ½   teaspoon salt
    4   (6-ounce) catfish fillets

1. Cook bacon in a large nonstick skillet over medium heat until crisp. Remove bacon from pan; reserve 2 teaspoons drippings in pan. Crumble bacon; reserve for another use.
2. Combine cornmeal, seasoning, and salt in a shallow dish. Dredge fillets in cornmeal mixture, shaking off excess.
3. Heat reserved drippings in pan over medium-high heat. Add fillets; cook 5 minutes on each side or until fish flakes easily when tested with a fork or until desired degree of doneness. Yield: 4 servings (serving size: 1 fillet).

CALORIES 277 (45% from fat); FAT 13.7g (sat 3.4g, mono 6.9g, poly 2.3g); PROTEIN 27.5g; CARB 8.9g; FIBER 0.9g; CHOL 93mg; IRON 1.6mg; SODIUM 412mg; CALC 13mg

QUICK & EASY
Sloppy Joes with Corn

If you need less than six servings for dinner, leftovers are great for lunch the next day. The meat mixture will keep in the refrigerator a few days stored in an airtight container. Reheat in a saucepan, adding water to thin as necessary. See Down-Home Menu 2 on page 196 for serving suggestions.
TOTAL TIME: 45 MINUTES

    1   teaspoon canola oil
    1   cup finely chopped onion
    1   cup finely chopped green bell
        pepper
    2   garlic cloves, minced
    1½ pounds lean ground beef
    1   (6-ounce) can no-salt-added
        tomato paste
    2   teaspoons chili powder
    1   teaspoon ground cumin
    ½   teaspoon salt
    1   (14-ounce) can fat-free,
        less-sodium chicken broth
    1   (15-ounce) can no-salt-added
        corn, rinsed and drained
    6   (1½-ounce) whole wheat
        hamburger buns, toasted

1. Heat oil in a large nonstick skillet over medium-high heat. Add onion, bell pepper, and garlic; sauté 3 minutes. Add meat to pan; cook 5 minutes or until browned, stirring to crumble. Stir in tomato paste; cook 2 minutes. Add chili
Continued

powder, cumin, salt, and broth. Reduce heat, and simmer 12 minutes or until thick, stirring occasionally. Stir in corn; cook 2 minutes or until thoroughly heated.

2. Spoon about 1 cup meat mixture on bottom half of each bun; cover with top half of each bun. Yield: 6 servings (serving size: 1 sandwich).

CALORIES 338 (20% from fat); FAT 7.5g (sat 2g, mono 2.5g, poly 1.7g); PROTEIN 31.7g; CARB 40g; FIBER 6.2g; CHOL 61mg; IRON 4.1mg; SODIUM 638mg; CALC 72mg

Down-Home Menu 2
serves 6

Sloppy Joes with Corn
(recipe on page 195)

Sliced tomatoes with crumbled blue cheese

Oven fries*

*Cut 3 medium baking potatoes into 24 wedges (about 1 inch thick); toss with 1 tablespoon canola oil. Arrange in a single layer on a baking sheet coated with cooking spray. Bake at 450° for 30 minutes or until browned, turning once. Sprinkle with ¼ teaspoon salt.

Game Plan

1. While oven fries bake:
  • Chop onion and bell pepper
  • Prepare meat mixture
2. While meat mixture simmers:
  • Slice tomatoes, and top with blue cheese
  • Toast buns
3. Assemble sandwiches.

Down-Home Menu 3
serves 4

Pork Chops with Country Gravy

Mashed potatoes

Succotash*

*Bring ⅔ cup water to a boil in a medium saucepan. Add 1 (10-ounce) package frozen lima beans and 1 (10-ounce) package frozen whole-kernel corn. Cover, reduce heat, and cook 8 minutes or until tender. Drain, stir in ¼ cup chopped green onions, 1 tablespoon butter, ¼ teaspoon salt, and ¼ teaspoon black pepper.

Game Plan

1. While potatoes cook:
  • Dredge pork in flour mixture
  • Cook pork chops
  • Prepare gravy
2. While lima beans and corn cook:
  • Chop green onions for succotash

QUICK & EASY
Pork Chops with Country Gravy

This recipe makes enough gravy to smother the pork chops, or you can spoon half over the chops and half over the mashed potatoes. Substitute dried basil if you don't have marjoram.

TOTAL TIME: 40 MINUTES

¼ cup all-purpose flour (about 1 ounce)
¾ teaspoon salt
¼ teaspoon dried marjoram
¼ teaspoon dried thyme
¼ teaspoon dried rubbed sage
4 (4-ounce) boneless center-cut loin pork chops (about ¾ inch thick)
1 tablespoon butter
Cooking spray
1½ cups 1% low-fat milk

1. Lightly spoon flour into a dry measuring cup; level with a knife. Place flour, salt, and next 3 ingredients in a shallow dish. Dredge pork in flour mixture, turning to coat; shake off excess. Reserve remaining flour mixture.

2. Melt butter in a large nonstick skillet coated with cooking spray over medium-high heat. Add pork to pan; cook 2 minutes on each side or until browned. Reduce heat, and cook 10 minutes or until done, turning pork once. Remove pork from pan; keep warm.

3. Combine reserved flour mixture and milk in a small bowl, stirring with a whisk until blended. Add milk mixture to pan; place over medium-high heat. Bring to a boil, scraping pan to loosen browned bits. Reduce heat, and simmer 2 minutes or until slightly thick, stirring constantly. Serve with chops. Yield: 4 servings (serving size: 1 chop and ½ cup gravy).

CALORIES 252 (34% from fat); FAT 9.6g (sat 4.4g, mono 3.6g, poly 0.8g); PROTEIN 28.9g; CARB 10.6g; FIBER 0.3g; CHOL 83mg; IRON 1.5mg; SODIUM 584mg; CALC 142mg

Down-Home Menu 4
serves 6

Creamy Stove-Top Macaroni and Cheese

Seven-layer salad*

Low-fat chocolate chip ice cream

*Layer 6 cups torn iceberg lettuce, 1 (15-ounce) can rinsed and drained kidney beans, 2 cups diced tomatoes, 1 cup diced cucumbers, and 1 cup julienne-cut carrot in a large bowl. Combine ½ cup fat-free sour cream and ½ cup light ranch dressing; spread sour cream mixture over carrot. Top with ½ cup (2 ounces) preshredded reduced-fat sharp Cheddar cheese; cover and chill.

Game Plan

1. While water for pasta comes to a boil:
  • Assemble salad
2. While pasta cooks:
  • Prepare cheese sauce

Creamy Stove-Top Macaroni and Cheese

Try this dish with any short pasta, such as fusilli, farfalle, or cavatappi. You can also vary the type of cheese; a combination of provolone and Asiago gives it an Italian flair.

TOTAL TIME: 40 MINUTES

    4   cups uncooked medium elbow
        macaroni
    3   tablespoons all-purpose flour
    1   teaspoon salt
    ¼   teaspoon black pepper
    2¼ cups fat-free milk
    ¼   cup (2 ounces) ⅓-less-fat cream
        cheese, softened
    2   teaspoons Dijon mustard
    2   teaspoons Worcestershire sauce
    ½   teaspoon bottled minced garlic
    1¼ cups (5 ounces) shredded
        reduced-fat Cheddar cheese

1. Cook pasta according to package directions, omitting salt and fat. Drain and set aside.
2. While pasta cooks, place flour, salt, and pepper in a large saucepan. Add milk, stirring with a whisk until well blended. Drop cream cheese by teaspoonfuls into milk mixture; bring to a boil over medium-high heat, stirring constantly. Reduce heat; simmer 2 minutes or until thick and cream cheese melts, stirring occasionally. Stir in mustard, Worcestershire, and garlic; simmer 1 minute. Remove from heat. Add Cheddar cheese, stirring until cheese melts. Combine pasta and cheese sauce in a large bowl; toss well. Yield: 6 servings (serving size: 1½ cups).

CALORIES 252 (29% from fat); FAT 8.2g (sat 5.1g, mono 0.1g, poly 0.3g); PROTEIN 14.5g; CARB 30.9g; FIBER 1.1g; CHOL 27mg; IRON 1.4mg; SODIUM 536mg; CALC 312mg

Young Chefs At Play

Spend quality time with your children, and have fun cooking these easy recipes.

Blueberry and Maple-Pecan Granola Parfaits

Kids will love to assemble their own parfaits.

    2   cups vanilla fat-free yogurt
    2   cups blueberries
    1   cup Maple-Pecan Granola

1. Spoon ¼ cup yogurt into each of 4 parfait glasses; top each serving with ¼ cup blueberries. Top each serving with ¼ cup Maple-Pecan Granola, ¼ cup yogurt, and ¼ cup blueberries. Yield: 4 servings (serving size: 1 parfait).

(Totals include ¼ cup Maple-Pecan Granola per serving) CALORIES 283 (18% from fat); FAT 5.6g (sat 0.8g, mono 2.8g, poly 1.8g); PROTEIN 8.8g; CARB 50.9g; FIBER 3.7g; CHOL 2mg; IRON 1.1mg; SODIUM 106mg; CALC 242mg

MAKE AHEAD

MAPLE-PECAN GRANOLA:

    2   cups regular oats
    ½   cup pecan pieces
    ½   cup maple syrup
    ¼   cup packed brown sugar
    2   tablespoons canola oil
    ⅛   teaspoon salt
    Cooking spray

1. Preheat oven to 300°.
2. Combine first 6 ingredients; spread on a large jelly-roll pan coated with cooking spray. Bake at 300° for 1 hour, stirring every 15 minutes. Cool completely. Yield: 4 cups (serving size: ¼ cup).
NOTE: Store in an airtight container up to one week.

CALORIES 129 (36% from fat); FAT 5.2g (sat 0.6g, mono 2.7g, poly 1.7g); PROTEIN 2.2g; CARB 19.3g; FIBER 1.9g; CHOL 0mg; IRON 0.8mg; SODIUM 21mg; CALC 20mg

Canadian Bacon and Pineapple Mini Pizzas

With preshredded cheese, pineapple tidbits, and prepared pizza sauce, the only thing adults need to be responsible for is chopping the bacon. For a pepperoni pizza variation that requires no chopping, use eight ounces pepperoni in place of the Canadian bacon and pineapple.

    6   English muffins, split
    1   (14-ounce) jar pizza sauce
    1   (8-ounce) can pineapple tidbits in
        juice, drained
    1   (6-ounce) package Canadian
        bacon, diced
    1½ cups (6 ounces) preshredded
        part-skim mozzarella cheese

1. Preheat oven to 425°.
2. Spread each muffin half with about 2 tablespoons sauce. Sprinkle pineapple and Canadian bacon evenly over sauce. Sprinkle evenly with cheese. Place on a baking sheet.
3. Bake at 425° for 12 minutes or until cheese is lightly browned. Yield: 6 servings (serving size: 2 mini pizzas).

CALORIES 273 (23% from fat); FAT 7g (sat 3.5g, mono 2.2g, poly 0.8g); PROTEIN 17.3g; CARB 34.9g; FIBER 2.9g; CHOL 30mg; IRON 2.7mg; SODIUM 867mg; CALC 289mg

Veggie Piglets in Blankets with Dipping Sauce

Expose your children to vegetarian sausage with this fun finger food that's good for breakfast or lunch. There's no need to thaw the sausage. Kids can help by cutting the dough with safety scissors. They can also roll dough around the sausages and make the dipping sauce.

    1   (8-ounce) package reduced-fat
        crescent roll dough
    16 meatless breakfast links (such as
        Boca)
    ¾   cup honey
    ¼   cup Dijon mustard

Continued

1. Preheat oven to 375°.

2. Unroll dough; divide along perforations into triangles. Cut each dough triangle in half to form 2 triangles. Wrap one dough triangle around center of each breakfast link, starting at wide end of triangle. Arrange wrapped breakfast links on a baking sheet. Bake at 375° for 15 minutes or until browned.

3. Combine honey and mustard; serve with piglets. Yield: 8 servings (serving size: 2 piglets and 2 tablespoons sauce).

CALORIES 277 (27% from fat); FAT 8.2g (sat 1.6g, mono 1.8g, poly 3.6g); PROTEIN 10.6g; CARB 44.2g; FIBER 2.2g; CHOL 0mg; IRON 9.1mg; SODIUM 754mg; CALC 15mg

Peanut Butter Jammies

Be ready for hand washing afterward: With peanut butter as the main ingredient, this dough is oily. Parents can beat the cookie dough ingredients and leave the shaping to the kids. Use a baby-food or demitasse spoon to spoon jam into the thumbprints.

⅓ cup all-purpose flour (about 1½ ounces)
¾ cup creamy peanut butter
¾ cup sugar
1 egg, lightly beaten
Cooking spray
6 tablespoons strawberry jam

1. Lightly spoon flour into a dry measuring cup; level with a knife. Place peanut butter, sugar, and egg in a medium bowl; beat with a mixer at medium speed until smooth. Add flour; stir well. Shape dough into 36 (1-inch) balls; place 1-inch apart on baking sheets coated with cooking spray. Press thumb into center of each cookie, leaving an indentation. Cover and chill 3 hours.

2. Preheat oven to 375°.

3. Bake cookies at 375° for 12 minutes or until golden. Remove from pans; cool on wire racks. Spoon ½ teaspoon jam into center of each cookie. Yield: 3 dozen (serving size: 1 cookie).

CALORIES 62 (42% from fat); FAT 2.9g (sat 0.6g, mono 1.4g, poly 0.8g); PROTEIN 1.6g; CARB 8.3g; FIBER 0.4g; CHOL 6mg; IRON 0.2mg; SODIUM 27mg; CALC 3mg

Spaghetti and Meatballs with a Surprise

Adults should cube the cheese and do all the cooking. Kids can shape the meatballs, which contain a surprise—melted cheese in the center.

¼ cup grated onion
1 teaspoon dried Italian seasoning
½ teaspoon salt
1½ pounds ground round
1 garlic clove, minced
3 ounces part-skim mozzarella cheese, cut into 16 cubes
1 (26-ounce) bottle fat-free pasta sauce
5½ cups hot cooked spaghetti (about 12 ounces uncooked pasta)

1. Combine first 5 ingredients in a bowl; shape into 16 (1-inch) meatballs. Working with 1 meatball at a time, flatten meatball, and place 1 cheese cube in center of meatball. Gather meatball around cheese cube, sealing well.

2. Heat a large nonstick skillet over medium-high heat. Add meatballs; cook 6 minutes, browning on all sides. Drain well. Wipe pan with a paper towel.

3. Return meatballs to pan. Add pasta sauce; bring to a simmer over medium heat. Cover and cook 10 minutes. Serve over pasta. Yield: 8 servings (serving size: about ⅔ cup pasta, about ⅓ cup sauce, and 2 meatballs).

CALORIES 397 (29% from fat); FAT 12.9g (sat 5.3g, mono 5.2g, poly 0.7g); PROTEIN 25.6g; CARB 42.9g; FIBER 2.7g; CHOL 58mg; IRON 3.3mg; SODIUM 478mg; CALC 86mg

QUICK & EASY
Cinnamon Buttons

Give children clean, kid-safe scissors for cutting the dough into pieces. Sprinkle any remaining cinnamon-sugar over top of dough before baking.

Cooking spray
2 tablespoons butter, melted
¼ cup sugar
½ teaspoon ground cinnamon
1 (11-ounce) can refrigerated soft breadstick dough

1. Preheat oven to 375°.

2. Lightly coat 6 muffin cups with cooking spray.

3. Pour melted butter into a shallow dish. Combine sugar and cinnamon in another shallow dish.

4. Unroll dough; separate into breadsticks. Cut each breadstick into 3 equal portions; shape each portion into a ball. Working with 1 ball at a time, dip into melted butter; gently roll in sugar mixture. Place 6 balls in each muffin cup.

5. Bake at 375° for 15 minutes. Remove rolls from pan. Serve warm. Yield: 6 servings (serving size: 1 roll).

CALORIES 213 (27% from fat); FAT 6.5g (sat 2.4g, mono 1.9g, poly 1.2g); PROTEIN 4.1g; CARB 33.8g; FIBER 0.8g; CHOL 10mg; IRON 1.5mg; SODIUM 413mg; CALC 4mg

QUICK & EASY
Chicken and Corn Quesadillas

Cooking the quesadillas together on a baking sheet is much quicker than cooking them separately in a skillet.

6 (8-inch) fat-free flour tortillas
Cooking spray
2 cups chopped roasted skinless, boneless chicken breast
1½ cups frozen whole-kernel corn, thawed and drained
2 cups (8 ounces) shredded reduced-fat Cheddar cheese
¾ cup bottled salsa
6 tablespoons reduced-fat sour cream

1. Preheat oven to 400°.

2. Coat one side of tortillas with cooking spray; place, coated side down, on a large baking sheet. Place ⅓ cup chicken over half of each tortilla; top each with ¼ cup corn and ⅓ cup cheese. Fold tortillas in half over filling, pressing firmly.

3. Bake at 400° for 10 minutes or until tortillas are crisp and cheese is melted. Cut each tortilla into quarters. Serve with salsa and sour cream. Yield: 6 servings (serving size: 4 quesadilla quarters, 2 tablespoons salsa, and 1 tablespoon sour cream).

CALORIES 359 (30% from fat); FAT 11.9g (sat 7g, mono 3.6g, poly 1g); PROTEIN 28.9g; CARB 36.5g; FIBER 2.5g; CHOL 72mg; IRON 1mg; SODIUM 446mg; CALC 301mg

Fresh Lime Chiffon Cake

Hollywood caterer Harry Baker invented the chiffon cake in the 1920s. He used vegetable oil and beaten egg whites to achieve the lightness of angel food cake and a tender, moist crumb.

Our updated three-layer version of this 1950s and 60s must-bake cake combines dazzling style with the refreshing crispness of fresh lime juice. Its good looks and great taste earned our Test Kitchens highest rating.

STAFF FAVORITE • MAKE AHEAD
Fresh Lime Chiffon Cake

FILLING:
- 1 teaspoon finely grated lime rind
- ¼ cup fresh lime juice (about 2 limes)
- 1 (14-ounce) can sweetened condensed milk

CAKE:
- Cooking spray
- 1 tablespoon cake flour
- 2 cups sifted cake flour (7½ ounces)
- 1¼ cups sugar, divided
- 2½ teaspoons baking powder
- ½ teaspoon salt
- 7 tablespoons canola oil
- 1 teaspoon finely grated lime rind
- ⅓ cup fresh lime juice (about 3 limes)
- 3 tablespoons water
- 1 teaspoon pure lemon extract
- 3 egg yolks
- 8 egg whites
- 1 teaspoon cream of tartar

FROSTING:
- 3 tablespoons sugar
- 2 tablespoons lime juice (about 1 lime)
- 2½ cups fat-free whipped topping, thawed
- Mint sprigs (optional)
- Fresh blueberries (optional)
- Lime wedges (optional)

1. To prepare lime filling, combine first 3 ingredients in a small bowl, stirring until blended. Cover and chill 3 hours.

2. Preheat oven to 325°.

3. To prepare cake, coat bottoms of 3 (8-inch) round cake pans with cooking spray (do not coat sides of pans); line bottoms with wax paper. Coat wax paper with cooking spray; dust with 1 tablespoon flour.

4. Combine 2 cups cake flour, 1 cup sugar, baking powder, and salt in a large bowl, stirring with a whisk until well combined.

5. Combine oil and next 5 ingredients in a medium bowl, stirring with a whisk. Add oil mixture to flour mixture; beat with a mixer at medium speed until smooth.

6. Place egg whites in a large bowl; beat with a mixer at high speed until foamy. Add cream of tartar; beat until soft peaks form. Gradually add ¼ cup sugar, 1 tablespoon at a time, beating until stiff peaks form. Gently stir one-fourth of egg white mixture into flour mixture; gently fold in remaining egg white mixture.

7. Divide cake batter equally among prepared pans, spreading evenly. Break air pockets by cutting through batter with a knife. Bake at 325° for 20 minutes or until cake springs back when lightly touched. Cool in pans 10 minutes on a wire rack; remove from pans. Remove wax paper from cake layers. Cool completely on wire rack.

8. To prepare frosting, combine 3 tablespoons sugar and 2 tablespoons lime juice in a small microwave-safe glass bowl. Microwave at HIGH 30 seconds or until sugar dissolves. Cool completely. Fold into whipped topping.

9. To assemble cake, place 1 cake layer on a plate; spread half of filling over cake layer. Top with second layer, remaining half of filling, and third layer. Spread frosting over top and sides of cake. Garnish with mint, blueberries, and lime wedges, if desired. Store cake loosely covered in refrigerator up to 3 days. Slice cake into wedges. Yield: 16 servings (serving size: 1 slice).

CALORIES 290 (29% from fat); FAT 9.3g (sat 2.1g, mono 4.6g, poly 2.1g); PROTEIN 5.3g; CARB 44.9g; FIBER 0.3g; CHOL 47mg; IRON 1.1mg; SODIUM 218mg; CALC 122mg

Chicken Rolls

Use this cooking method to prepare restaurant-quality fare at home.

If you feel like you've cooked chicken every conceivable way, stuffed poached chicken may be your chance to try something new. Although the result looks like fine-dining fare, the method is simple.

Julienne Vegetable-Stuffed Chicken with Ginger-Hoisin Sauce

Serve this dish with sesame noodles, if desired.

CHICKEN:
- 1½ teaspoons dark sesame oil
- 1 tablespoon minced peeled fresh ginger
- 3 garlic cloves, minced
- 2 cups matchstick-cut carrot
- 2 cups matchstick-cut zucchini
- 1 cup red bell pepper, cut into ¼-inch strips
- 1 tablespoon low-sodium soy sauce
- 2 teaspoons hoisin sauce
- ¼ cup panko (Japanese breadcrumbs)
- 4 (6-ounce) skinless, boneless chicken breast halves
- 3 quarts water

SAUCE:
- 5 teaspoons hoisin sauce
- 1 tablespoon finely chopped green onions
- 1 tablespoon seasoned rice vinegar
- 1 tablespoon low-sodium soy sauce
- 2 teaspoons minced peeled fresh ginger
- 2 teaspoons honey

1. To prepare chicken, heat oil in a large nonstick skillet over medium-high heat. Add ginger and garlic; sauté 15 seconds. Add carrot, zucchini, and bell pepper;
Continued

sauté 3 minutes or until crisp-tender. Add soy sauce and hoisin sauce; sauté 30 seconds. Place carrot mixture in a bowl; cool 5 minutes. Stir in panko.

2. Slice each breast half lengthwise, cutting to, but not through, other side. Open halves, laying breast flat. Place each breast half between 2 sheets of heavy-duty plastic wrap; pound to ¼-inch thickness using a meat mallet or small heavy skillet.

3. Divide carrot mixture into 4 equal portions; spoon 1 portion down center of each breast half, leaving a ½-inch border at each end. Fold breast sides over filling.

4. Place a 2-foot-long sheet of heavy-duty plastic wrap on a work surface with 1 long side hanging over counter's edge 2 inches. Place a stuffed breast half, seam side down, on edge farthest from you; tightly roll chicken toward you, jelly-roll fashion. Twist ends in opposite directions to form a cylinder. Tie plastic wrap in tight knots against chicken on each end. Trim off excess wrap close to knot. Place a second 2-foot-long sheet of heavy-duty plastic wrap on work surface; place rolled chicken on wrap, and repeat procedure. Repeat with remaining chicken breast halves.

5. Bring 3 quarts water to a boil in a large stockpot; add chicken. Simmer 15 minutes (do not boil), turning occasionally. Remove from water, and let stand 10 minutes before unwrapping and cutting into ½-inch-thick slices.

6. To prepare sauce, combine 5 teaspoons hoisin sauce and remaining 5 ingredients in a small bowl. Serve with chicken. Yield: 4 servings (serving size: 1 stuffed breast half and about 1½ tablespoons sauce).

CALORIES 289 (14% from fat); FAT 4.5g (sat 0.9g, mono 1.3g, poly 1.4g); PROTEIN 42g; CARB 18.7g; FIBER 2.4g; CHOL 99mg; IRON 1.8mg; SODIUM 638mg; CALC 46mg

Chorizo and Plantain-Stuffed Chicken

We enjoyed the Caribbean flair of this dish. Sweet plantain balances the mild spiciness of the chorizo and poblano pepper. Be sure plantains are very ripe. Serve with yellow rice.

  1 teaspoon extravirgin olive oil
  ½ cup finely chopped onion
  1 soft black plantain (about ½ pound), cut into ½-inch-thick slices
  ¾ cup (about 3 ounces) finely chopped chorizo (such as Goya brand)
  ½ cup finely chopped poblano chile
  ¾ teaspoon ground cumin
  ½ teaspoon salt, divided
  ¼ teaspoon freshly ground black pepper, divided
  4 (6-ounce) skinless, boneless chicken breast halves
  3 quarts water
  ½ cup green salsa
  2 tablespoons chopped fresh cilantro
Cilantro sprigs (optional)

1. Heat oil in a large nonstick skillet over medium-high heat. Add onion and plantain; cook 3 minutes or until lightly browned. Add chorizo, poblano, cumin, ¼ teaspoon salt, and ⅛ teaspoon pepper; cook 4 minutes or until plantain is very soft. Place plantain mixture in a bowl; mash with a fork. Cool 10 minutes.

2. Slice each breast half lengthwise, cutting to, but not through, other side. Open halves, laying breast flat. Place each breast half between 2 sheets of heavy-duty plastic wrap; pound to ¼-inch thickness using a meat mallet or small heavy skillet. Sprinkle chicken with ¼ teaspoon salt and ⅛ teaspoon pepper.

3. Divide plantain mixture into 4 equal portions; spoon 1 portion down center of each breast half, leaving a ½-inch border at each end. Fold sides over filling.

4. Place a 2-foot-long sheet of heavy-duty plastic wrap on a work surface with 1 long side hanging over counter's edge 2 inches. Place a stuffed breast half, seam side down, on edge farthest from you,

and tightly roll breast toward you, jelly-roll fashion. Twist ends in opposite directions to form a cylinder. Tie plastic wrap in tight knots against breast half on each end. Trim off excess wrap close to knot. Place a second 2-foot-long sheet of heavy-duty plastic wrap on work surface; place rolled chicken on wrap, and repeat procedure. Repeat with remaining chicken breast halves.

5. Bring 3 quarts of water to a boil in a large stockpot; add chicken. Simmer 15 minutes (do not boil), turning occasionally. Remove from water, and let stand 10 minutes before unwrapping and cutting into ½-inch-thick slices. Serve with salsa; sprinkle with chopped cilantro. Garnish with cilantro sprigs, if desired. Yield: 4 servings (serving size: 1 stuffed breast half, 2 tablespoons salsa, and 1½ teaspoons cilantro).

CALORIES 389 (27% from fat); FAT 11.8g (sat 3.9g, mono 5.4g, poly 1.4g); PROTEIN 45.6g; CARB 23.8g; FIBER 1.9g; CHOL 117mg; IRON 2.2mg; SODIUM 768mg; CALC 32mg

Chicken Stuffed with Leeks, Shiitakes, and Mozzarella

Shiitakes provide a mildly meaty flavor for this dish, though you can substitute cremini mushrooms, if you prefer.

  1 teaspoon extravirgin olive oil
  ½ cup finely chopped shallots
  4 garlic cloves, minced
 2½ cups thinly sliced shiitake mushrooms (about 6 ounces)
  1 cup thinly sliced leek (about 1 large)
  ½ teaspoon salt, divided
  ¼ teaspoon dried thyme
  ¼ teaspoon freshly ground black pepper, divided
  ¼ cup Madeira wine or dry sherry
  ½ cup (2 ounces) shredded sharp provolone
  ½ cup (2 ounces) shredded part-skim mozzarella cheese
  ¼ cup chopped fresh flat-leaf parsley
  4 (6-ounce) skinless, boneless chicken breast halves
  3 quarts water

1. Heat oil in a large nonstick skillet over medium-high heat. Add shallots and garlic; cook 1 minute, stirring occasionally. Add mushrooms, leek, ¼ teaspoon salt, thyme, and ⅛ teaspoon pepper; cook 4 minutes or until mushrooms are tender. Add Madeira; cook 1 minute or until liquid evaporates. Transfer mushroom mixture to a bowl; cool 5 minutes. Stir in cheeses and parsley.

2. Slice each breast half lengthwise, cutting to, but not through, other side. Open halves, laying breast flat. Place each breast half between 2 sheets of heavy-duty plastic wrap; pound to ¼-inch thickness using a meat mallet or small heavy skillet. Sprinkle chicken with ¼ teaspoon salt and ⅛ teaspoon pepper.

3. Divide mushroom mixture into 4 portions; spoon 1 portion down center of each breast half; leave a ½-inch border at each end. Fold sides over filling.

4. Place a 2-foot-long sheet of heavy-duty plastic wrap on a work surface with 1 long side hanging over counter's edge 2 inches. Place a stuffed breast half, seam side down, on edge farthest from you; tightly roll breast toward you, jelly-roll fashion. Twist ends in opposite directions to form a cylinder. Tie plastic wrap in tight knots against breast half on each end. Trim off excess wrap close to knot. Place a second 2-foot-long sheet of heavy-duty plastic wrap on work surface; place rolled breast on wrap, and repeat procedure. Repeat with remaining breast halves.

5. Bring 3 quarts water to a boil in a large stockpot; add chicken. Simmer 15 minutes (do not boil), turning occasionally. Remove from water, and let stand 10 minutes before unwrapping and cutting into ½-inch-thick slices. Yield: 4 servings (serving size: 1 stuffed breast half).

CALORIES 365 (25% from fat); FAT 10g (sat 5g, mono 3.3g, poly 0.8g); PROTEIN 48.7g; CARB 13.1g; FIBER 1.3g; CHOL 116mg; IRON 3.1mg; SODIUM 625mg; CALC 263mg

How to Make Chicken Rolls

Begin by butterflying and pounding breast halves to an even ¼-inch thickness; pounding promotes even cooking. Spoon the filling down the center of each breast half, leaving room at the ends.

1. *Fold sides over the filling. Breast halves vary in size; if you can't fit the filling neatly inside the chicken, remove filling a teaspoon at a time until the breast can envelop the filling. Place a two-foot-long sheet of heavy-duty plastic wrap on a work surface with a long side hanging over the counter's edge by an inch or two, which allows the plastic to grip the counter as you roll the chicken.*

2. *Place a stuffed breast half, seam side down, on the edge of the plastic farthest from you, and tightly roll the breast toward you, jelly-roll fashion. Twist the ends of the plastic wrap in opposite directions to form a cylinder. Knot the plastic wrap tightly against the chicken.*

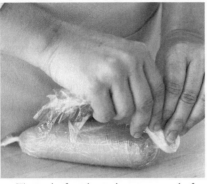

3. *To tie the first knot, brace one end of the twisted plastic between the edge of the work surface and your hip to keep the package from unraveling. Tie a tight knot against the chicken on the opposite end. Trim off excess wrap close to the knots. Place a second two-foot-long sheet of heavy-duty plastic wrap on the work surface.*

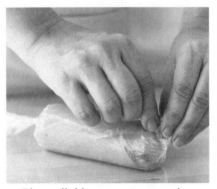

4. *Place rolled breast on wrap, and repeat procedure. (Double-wrapping ensures a tight seal.) Add the chicken to boiling water in a large stockpot. Place a metal colander on top of the pot to help keep the chicken submerged. If a colander isn't available, turn the chicken occasionally with tongs so it cooks on all sides. The chicken will bring the temperature of the water down immediately, but do not let the water boil; a gentle simmer will keep the chicken tender.*

Curried Couscous-Stuffed Chicken

If you can't fit the six stuffed breasts into the pot at once, cook in two batches for 15 minutes each.

    1   tablespoon olive oil
   ½   cup chopped onion
    2   teaspoons grated peeled fresh ginger
    3   garlic cloves, minced
    3   tablespoons golden raisins
    3   tablespoons sliced almonds
   ¼   cup water
   ¼   cup orange juice
 1½   tablespoons mango chutney
   ¾   teaspoon ground cumin
   ¾   teaspoon curry powder
   ¼   teaspoon salt
   ⅛   teaspoon ground red pepper
   ⅛   teaspoon ground cinnamon
   ⅓   cup uncooked couscous
    2   tablespoons minced fresh cilantro
    6   (6-ounce) skinless, boneless chicken breast halves
   ¾   teaspoon salt
   ¼   teaspoon black pepper
    3   quarts water
    6   tablespoons mango chutney (optional)

1. Heat oil in a small saucepan over medium-high heat. Add onion, ginger, and garlic; sauté 2 minutes or until onion is tender. Stir in raisins and almonds; sauté 1 minute. Stir in ¼ cup water and next 7 ingredients. Bring to a boil; gradually stir in couscous. Remove from heat; cover and let stand 5 minutes. Fluff with a fork.

Transfer couscous mixture to a bowl; cool 5 minutes. Stir in cilantro; set aside.

2. Slice each breast half lengthwise, cutting to, but not through, other side. Open halves, laying breast flat. Place each breast half between 2 sheets of heavy-duty plastic wrap; pound to ¼-inch thickness using a meat mallet or small heavy skillet.

3. Sprinkle chicken with ¾ teaspoon salt and black pepper. Divide couscous mixture into 6 equal portions; spoon 1 portion down center of each breast half, leaving a ½-inch border at each end. Fold sides over filling.

4. Place a 2-foot-long sheet of heavy-duty plastic wrap on a work surface with 1 of the long sides hanging over counter's edge 2 inches. Place a stuffed breast half, seam side down, on edge farthest from you, and tightly roll breast toward you, jelly-roll fashion. Twist ends in opposite directions to form a cylinder. Tie plastic wrap in tight knots against breast half on each end. Trim off excess wrap close to knot. Place a second 2-foot-long sheet of heavy-duty plastic wrap on work surface; place rolled breast on wrap, and repeat procedure. Repeat with remaining chicken breast halves.

5. Bring 3 quarts water to a boil in a large stockpot; add chicken. Simmer 20 minutes (do not boil), turning occasionally. Remove from water, and let stand 10 minutes before unwrapping and cutting into ½-inch-thick slices. Top each serving with 1 tablespoon mango chutney, if desired. Yield: 6 servings (serving size: 1 stuffed breast half).

CALORIES 301 (18% from fat); FAT 6.1g (sat 1g, mono 3.2g, poly 1.1g); PROTEIN 41.7g; CARB 17.7g; FIBER 1.5g; CHOL 99mg; IRON 1.7mg; SODIUM 570mg; CALC 43mg

Artichoke and Goat Cheese–Stuffed Chicken

   ½   cup Italian-seasoned breadcrumbs
   ½   cup (2 ounces) crumbled goat cheese
   ¼   cup chopped fresh basil
    6   canned artichoke hearts, rinsed, drained, and chopped
    1   bottled roasted red bell pepper, rinsed, drained, and chopped
    4   (6-ounce) skinless, boneless chicken breast halves
   ¼   teaspoon freshly ground black pepper, divided
   ⅛   teaspoon salt
    3   quarts water
    6   cups mixed baby greens
 1½   tablespoons fresh lemon juice
 1½   teaspoons extravirgin olive oil

1. Combine first 5 ingredients in a medium bowl; stir until well blended.

2. Slice each breast half lengthwise, cutting to, but not through, other side. Open halves, laying breast flat. Place each breast half between 2 sheets of heavy-duty plastic wrap; pound to ¼-inch thickness using a meat mallet or small heavy skillet. Sprinkle chicken with ⅛ teaspoon pepper and salt.

3. Divide artichoke mixture into 4 equal portions; spoon 1 portion down center of each breast half, leaving a ½-inch border at each end. Fold sides over filling.

4. Place a 2-foot-long sheet of heavy-duty plastic wrap on a work surface with 1 long side hanging over counter's edge 2 inches. Place a stuffed breast half, seam side down, on edge farthest from you; tightly roll chicken toward you, jelly-roll fashion. Twist ends in opposite directions to form a cylinder. Tie plastic wrap in tight knots against chicken on each end. Trim off excess wrap close to knots. Place a second 2-foot-long sheet of heavy-duty plastic wrap on work surface; place rolled chicken on wrap, and repeat procedure. Repeat with remaining breast halves.

5. Bring 3 quarts water to a boil in a large stockpot; add chicken. Simmer 15 minutes (do not boil), turning occasionally. Remove from water, and let stand 10 minutes before unwrapping and cutting into ½-inch-thick slices.

6. Combine greens, juice, oil, and ⅛ teaspoon pepper in a large bowl; toss well. Place about 1 cup greens mixture on each of 4 plates. Top each serving with 1 chicken breast half. Yield: 4 servings.

CALORIES 348 (20% from fat); FAT 7.7g (sat 2.9g, mono 2.5g, poly 0.8g); PROTEIN 47.2g; CARB 21.2g; FIBER 3.1g; CHOL 105mg; IRON 4.3mg; SODIUM 882mg; CALC 97mg

Stuffed chicken works well for a dinner party, since you can wrap the rolls the day before.

Ricotta, Spinach, and Sun-Dried Tomato–Stuffed Chicken

Serve this dish with your favorite marinara.

    2   cups boiling water
   10   sun-dried tomatoes, packed
        without oil
  1½   teaspoons extravirgin olive
        oil
    ½   cup finely chopped
        onion
  1½   teaspoons dried oregano
    4   garlic cloves, minced
    1   (10-ounce) package frozen
        chopped spinach, thawed,
        drained, and squeezed dry
    ¾   cup (3 ounces) shredded part-
        skim mozzarella cheese
    ⅔   cup fat-free ricotta cheese
    ¼   cup (1 ounce) grated Parmesan
        cheese
    ½   teaspoon salt, divided
    ¼   teaspoon black pepper,
        divided
    4   (6-ounce) skinless, boneless
        chicken breast halves
    3   quarts water

1. Combine 2 cups boiling water and sun-dried tomatoes in a bowl; let stand 30 minutes or until soft. Drain and chop.
2. Heat oil in a large nonstick skillet over medium-high heat. Add onion, oregano, and garlic; cook 3 minutes or until onion is tender, stirring occasionally. Add spinach; cook 3 minutes or until liquid almost evaporates. Add tomatoes; cook 1 minute. Place spinach mixture in a bowl, and cool 5 minutes. Stir in cheeses, ¼ teaspoon salt, and ⅛ teaspoon pepper.
3. Slice each breast half lengthwise, cutting to, but not through, other side. Open halves, laying breast flat. Place each breast half between 2 sheets of heavy-duty plastic wrap; pound to ¼-inch thickness using a meat mallet or small heavy skillet. Sprinkle chicken with ¼ teaspoon salt and ⅛ teaspoon pepper.
4. Divide spinach mixture into 4 equal portions, and spoon 1 portion down center of each breast half, leaving a ½-inch border at each end. Fold sides over filling.
5. Place a 2-foot-long sheet of heavy-duty plastic wrap on a work surface with 1 long side hanging over counter's edge 2 inches. Place a stuffed breast half, seam side down, on edge farthest from you, and tightly roll chicken toward you, jelly-roll fashion. Twist ends in opposite directions to form a cylinder. Tie plastic wrap in tight knots against chicken on each end. Trim off excess wrap close to knots. Place a second 2-foot-long sheet of heavy-duty plastic wrap on work surface; place rolled chicken on wrap, and repeat procedure. Repeat with remaining breast halves.
6. Bring 3 quarts water to a boil in a large stockpot; add chicken breasts. Simmer 15 minutes (do not boil), turning occasionally. Remove from water, and let stand 10 minutes before unwrapping and cutting into ½-inch-thick slices. Yield: 4 servings (serving size: 1 stuffed breast half).

CALORIES 377 (26% from fat); FAT 10.8g (sat 4.7g, mono 3.1g, poly 0.9g); PROTEIN 54.8g; CARB 12.6g; FIBER 3.2g; CHOL 122mg; IRON 3.4mg; SODIUM 814mg; CALC 473mg

WINE NOTE: In matching this dish with wine, the tomatoes, spinach, garlic, and cheeses are more important factors than the mild-flavored chicken. A terrific match for this savory lineup is the famous Italian light red wine Chianti Classico, especially *riservas*. Great producers include Querciabella, Ruffino, and Antinori.

Community Table

Weekly family-style dinners at The Kitchen in Boulder, Colorado, make strangers into friends.

Every Monday evening, a special dining experience takes shape at The Kitchen, a bustling restaurant in downtown Boulder, Colorado. It's Community Night, when chefs and co-owners Hugo Matheson and Kimbal Musk host a family-style meal for an adventurous group of up to 24 people.

The Kitchen's typical offerings employ seasonal ingredients and change daily. And although their regular dishes are worth eating any day of the week, for Monday's Community Night, Matheson and Musk let loose, improvising and spinning out giant bowls and platters of food that diners pass around a big table as they enjoy a multicourse supper for $35 per person. It's all part of the duo's wish to create community over a good meal—perhaps the oldest form of fellowship in the world. Here is a sampling of recipes you'll find at The Kitchen.

QUICK & EASY
Fresh English Pea Salad with Mint and Pecorino

You can substitute crumbled feta cheese for the pecorino. If you can't find fresh peas, use frozen thawed petite green peas.

    2   cups water
    1   cup shelled green peas (about
        1 pound unshelled)
    6   cups trimmed arugula
    ¼   cup chopped fresh mint
  1½   tablespoons fresh lemon juice
    1   tablespoon extravirgin olive oil
    ½   teaspoon salt
    ¼   teaspoon freshly ground black
        pepper
    ½   cup (2 ounces) shaved fresh
        pecorino Romano cheese

Continued

1. Bring 2 cups water to a boil in a medium saucepan. Add peas; cook 1 minute. Drain; plunge peas into ice water; drain.

2. Combine peas, arugula, and mint in a large bowl. Add lemon juice, olive oil, salt, and pepper; toss well. Sprinkle with cheese. Serve immediately. Yield: 8 servings (serving size: about 1 cup salad and 1 tablespoon cheese).

CALORIES 90 (40% from fat); FAT 4g (sat 1.3g, mono 1.4g, poly 0.2g); PROTEIN 5.6g; CARB 9.1g; FIBER 3.3g; CHOL 6mg; IRON 1.1mg; SODIUM 342mg; CALC 107mg

Grilled Tuna Niçoise Salad

The Kitchen's simple version of this classic dish is a great outdoor meal accompanied by a glass of dry white wine. You also can cook the tuna in a grill pan.

DRESSING:

  2   tablespoons red wine vinegar
  1   tablespoon extravirgin olive oil
  ½   teaspoon chopped fresh tarragon
  ½   teaspoon Dijon mustard
  ¼   teaspoon salt
  ¼   teaspoon freshly ground black pepper

SALAD:

  4   cups water
  ½   pound green beans, trimmed
  ½   pound quartered Yukon gold potatoes
  6   (6-ounce) Yellowfin tuna steaks
  ¼   teaspoon salt
  ¼   teaspoon freshly ground black pepper
      Cooking spray
  4   cups mixed salad greens (about 2 ounces)
  ¼   cup niçoise olives
  3   hard-cooked large eggs, halved

1. To prepare dressing, combine first 6 ingredients in a small bowl, stirring well with a whisk. Set dressing aside.

2. To prepare salad, bring 4 cups water to a boil in a large saucepan. Add beans; cook 2 minutes. Remove with a slotted spoon; plunge beans into ice water. Drain and set aside. Add potatoes to pan; cook 10 minutes or until tender. Drain potatoes, and set aside.

3. Prepare grill.

4. Sprinkle fish with ¼ teaspoon salt and ¼ teaspoon pepper. Place fish on a grill rack coated with cooking spray, and grill 3 minutes on each side or until desired degree of doneness.

5. Combine beans, potatoes, salad greens, olives, and dressing in a large bowl; toss well. Place salad mixture on a large platter. Arrange steaks and egg halves over salad mixture. Yield: 6 servings (serving size: 1 cup salad mixture, 1 steak, and 1 egg half).

CALORIES 295 (23% from fat); FAT 7.5g (sat 1.7g, mono 3.6g, poly 1.1g); PROTEIN 44.5g; CARB 10.1g; FIBER 2.3g; CHOL 183mg; IRON 2.4mg; SODIUM 362mg; CALC 70mg

Grilled Lamb with Anchoïade Dressing

"Whenever we put this on the menu, we need to make sure we have enough in the house to last the night, or there's an uproar if we sell out," says Kimbal Musk. "It's such a simple dish, but when the lamb combines with the salty anchovy and tart lemon, fireworks go off in your mouth." Serve it with roasted potato wedges and green beans.

LAMB:

  ⅓   cup extravirgin olive oil
  1½ tablespoons fresh lemon juice
  1   tablespoon chopped fresh rosemary
  2   garlic cloves, thinly sliced
  1   (3-pound) rolled boneless leg of lamb, trimmed
  ¼   teaspoon salt
  ¼   teaspoon freshly ground black pepper
      Cooking spray

DRESSING:

  1   tablespoon finely chopped fresh rosemary
  1½ tablespoons fresh lemon juice
  1   tablespoon extravirgin olive oil
  2   canned anchovy fillets, finely chopped

1. To prepare lamb, combine first 4 ingredients in a large zip-top plastic bag. Add lamb to bag; seal. Marinate in refrigerator 12 hours, turning bag occasionally.

2. Prepare grill.

3. Remove lamb from bag; discard marinade. Sprinkle lamb with salt and pepper. Place on a grill rack coated with cooking spray; grill 30 minutes, turning to cook all sides, or until a thermometer registers 145° (medium rare). Remove from grill, and let stand 20 minutes before slicing.

4. To prepare dressing, combine 1 tablespoon rosemary, 1½ tablespoons juice, 1 tablespoon oil, and anchovies in a small bowl, stirring well with a whisk. Serve with lamb. Yield: 10 servings (serving size: about 3 ounces lamb and about 1 teaspoon dressing).

CALORIES 185 (44% from fat); FAT 9.1g (sat 2.5g, mono 4.9g, poly 0.8g); PROTEIN 23.6g; CARB 0.6g; FIBER 0.1g; CHOL 76mg; IRON 2.1mg; SODIUM 161mg; CALC 11mg

make ahead

The Beauty of Barbecue Sauce

Prepare this simple condiment to flavor your next backyard feast.

Barbecue sauce can be made in advance, and in large batches (these recipes can be doubled or tripled). Once prepared, place the sauce in a glass jar or heat-proof plastic container; cover and refrigerate for up to a month. Or freeze in small batches for up to a year, defrosting as needed in the microwave or in a saucepan on the stovetop. In addition to offering make-ahead convenience, preparing your own sauce allows you to customize the flavor. Also, homemade sauces tend to be much lower in sodium than commercial ones.

Four-Alarm Barbecue Sauce

This sticky sauce is better for dipping than basting, since its sugars will cause food to stick to the grill. Try it with shrimp.

  2 teaspoons canola oil
  1 cup finely chopped onion
  2 garlic cloves, minced
  ¾ cup water
  ½ cup bottled chili sauce
  2 tablespoons red wine vinegar
  1 teaspoon chipotle chile powder
  1 teaspoon ground ancho chile pepper
  1 (12-ounce) can cola
  1 jalapeño pepper, chopped

1. Heat oil in a medium saucepan over medium-high heat. Add onion and garlic; cook 2 minutes or until onion is tender. Add ¾ cup water and remaining ingredients. Bring to a boil; reduce heat and simmer until reduced to 1½ cups (about 12 minutes).
2. Place half of chili sauce mixture in a blender. Remove center piece of blender lid (to allow steam to escape); secure blender lid on blender. Place a clean towel over opening in blender lid (to avoid spills). Blend until smooth. Pour into a large bowl. Repeat procedure with remaining chili sauce mixture. Yield: 1½ cups (serving size: 1½ tablespoons).

CALORIES 33 (19% from fat); FAT 0.7g (sat 0g, mono 0.4g, poly 0.2g); PROTEIN 0.2g; CARB 6.6g; FIBER 0.3g; CHOL 0mg; IRON 0.1mg; SODIUM 256mg; CALC 7mg

Chinese Barbecue Sauce

  ½ cup dry sherry
  ½ cup hoisin sauce
  ½ cup ketchup
  2 tablespoons minced peeled fresh ginger
  2 tablespoons rice vinegar
  1 tablespoon honey
  2 teaspoons Sriracha (hot chile sauce, such as Huy Fong)
  ¼ teaspoon five-spice powder
  1 garlic clove, minced

1. Combine all ingredients in a small saucepan over medium heat; bring to a simmer. Cook 5 minutes, stirring frequently. Yield: 1½ cups (serving size: 2 tablespoons).

CALORIES 47 (11% from fat); FAT 0.6g (sat 0g, mono 0.2g, poly 0.3g); PROTEIN 0.6g; CARB 9.2g; FIBER 0.2g; CHOL 0mg; IRON 0.2mg; SODIUM 314mg; CALC 4mg

Maple-Chipotle Barbecue Sauce

Serve this aromatic sauce with strong-flavored meats like lamb, game, or beef.

  1 small garlic head
1½ cups tomato sauce
  1 cup finely chopped onion (about 1 small)
  ½ cup maple syrup
  ¼ cup rice vinegar
  2 tablespoons Worcestershire sauce
  ½ teaspoon ground coriander
  ¼ teaspoon ground allspice
  ¼ teaspoon ground cloves
  ¼ teaspoon vanilla extract
  2 chipotle chiles, canned in adobo sauce, seeded and minced

1. Preheat oven to 350°.
2. Remove white papery skin from garlic head (do not peel or separate cloves). Wrap garlic head in foil. Bake at 350° for 1 hour; cool 10 minutes. Separate cloves, and squeeze to extract garlic pulp. Discard skins.
3. Combine garlic, tomato sauce, and remaining ingredients in a medium saucepan over medium heat; bring to a simmer. Cook 20 minutes, stirring frequently. Strain mixture through a sieve into a bowl, and discard solids. Yield: 1 cup (serving size: 2 tablespoons).

CALORIES 85 (3% from fat); FAT 0.3g (sat 0g, mono 0g, poly 0.1g); PROTEIN 1g; CARB 21.2g; FIBER 1.4g; CHOL 0mg; IRON 1.1mg; SODIUM 327mg; CALC 35mg

Asian-Inspired Barbecue Sauce

Beyond the grill, you can toss this sauce with udon or soba noodles, too.

  ⅔ cup low-sodium soy sauce
  ½ cup unsalted creamy peanut butter
  ¼ cup packed light brown sugar
  ¼ cup honey
2½ tablespoons fresh lemon juice
  2 tablespoons minced peeled fresh ginger
  1 tablespoon sesame seeds, toasted
  1 tablespoon dark sesame oil
1½ teaspoons freshly ground black pepper
  1 teaspoon onion powder
  1 garlic clove, minced

1. Combine all ingredients in a large bowl; stir well with a whisk. Yield: 1⅔ cups (serving size: about 2 tablespoons).

CALORIES 109 (50% from fat); FAT 6g (sat 1.2g, mono 2.7g, poly 1.9g); PROTEIN 3.2g; CARB 12.5g; FIBER 0.8g; CHOL 0mg; IRON 0.7mg; SODIUM 410mg; CALC 13mg

Peachy Barbecue Sauce

Fruit sauces are subtle, delicate additions to the grilling repertoire. This one is good with ham, pork, and chicken.

  1 cup organic vegetable broth (such as Swanson Certified Organic)
  1 cup peach preserves
  ¼ cup bottled chili sauce
  3 tablespoons finely chopped shallots
  2 tablespoons cider vinegar
  1 tablespoon minced peeled fresh ginger
  1 tablespoon low-sodium soy sauce
  2 teaspoons Dijon mustard
1½ teaspoons freshly ground black pepper
  ⅛ teaspoon ground cloves

Continued

1. Combine all ingredients in a medium saucepan; bring to a boil. Reduce heat, and simmer 20 minutes, stirring occasionally. Yield: 1⅓ cups (serving size: about 2 tablespoons).

CALORIES 94 (0% from fat); FAT 0g; PROTEIN 0.2g; CARB 24.2g; FIBER 0.1g; CHOL 0mg; IRON 0.2mg; SODIUM 316mg; CALC 3mg

QUICK & EASY • MAKE AHEAD
FREEZABLE
Brown Sugar Barbecue Sauce

This thick, classic-style sauce is particularly good on grilled chicken breasts with coleslaw and baked beans on the side, and it's much lower in sodium than commercial sauces. For a version with extra smoky flavor, use Spanish smoked paprika.

1½ cups no-salt-added tomato sauce
⅔ cup packed dark brown sugar
3 tablespoons cider vinegar
1½ tablespoons molasses
1 tablespoon Worcestershire sauce
2 teaspoons dry mustard
2 teaspoons chili powder
2 teaspoons paprika
2 teaspoons barbecue smoked seasoning (such as Hickory Liquid Smoke)
1 teaspoon salt
1 teaspoon onion powder
½ teaspoon garlic powder
¼ teaspoon celery seeds
¼ teaspoon ground cloves
¼ teaspoon ground red pepper
1 (6-ounce) can tomato paste

1. Combine all ingredients in a large saucepan over medium-high heat; bring to a simmer. Cook 15 minutes, stirring frequently. Yield: 2 cups (serving size: 2 tablespoons).

CALORIES 63 (4% from fat); FAT 0.3g (sat 0g, mono 0g, poly 0.1g); PROTEIN 0.7g; CARB 14.9g; FIBER 0.9g; CHOL 0mg; IRON 1mg; SODIUM 261mg; CALC 21mg

---

Beyond the Grill

A good barbecue sauce can serve a host of functions in the kitchen.
- Pour over scrambled eggs for a morning pick-me-up.
- Thin with vegetable broth, and use as a salad dressing.
- Use as a dip for crudités.
- Spread like mayonnaise in a wrap or on a sandwich.
- Ladle on a bare pizza crust.
- Toss with hot noodles and sliced vegetables for a twist on pasta salad.
- Use in a stir-fry as part of the sauce.
- Brush on oven roasts during the last 20 minutes of cooking.

---

superfast

...And Ready in Just About 20 Minutes

More than a week's worth of quick entrées to get dinner on the table in a flash

QUICK & EASY
Thai Beef Rolls

These wrap sandwiches take just a few minutes to assemble and make a quick lunch or supper. Serve with rice crackers and sautéed zucchini.

1½ tablespoons fresh lime juice
1 tablespoon dark sesame oil
1 tablespoon bottled ground fresh ginger (such as Spice World)
1 tablespoon bottled minced garlic
2 teaspoons fish sauce
¾ teaspoon sugar
4 (8-inch) flour tortillas
2 cups torn Boston lettuce
12 ounces thinly sliced deli roast beef
½ cup matchstick-cut carrots
¼ cup chopped fresh mint

1. Combine first 6 ingredients in a small bowl, stirring well with a whisk. Place tortillas on a work surface; brush lightly with 2 teaspoons juice mixture. Arrange ½ cup lettuce on each tortilla; top each with 3 ounces beef. Combine carrots and mint; arrange about 3 tablespoons carrot mixture over each serving. Drizzle each serving with about 1 tablespoon of remaining juice mixture; roll up. Yield: 4 wraps (serving size: 1 wrap).

CALORIES 294 (29% from fat); FAT 9.5g (sat 1.8g, mono 2.8g, poly 2g); PROTEIN 22.5g; CARB 30.3g; FIBER 1.1g; CHOL 47mg; IRON 3.8mg; SODIUM 967mg; CALC 127mg

QUICK & EASY
Lamb Rib Chops with Raisin-Almond Couscous

1½ cups water
⅓ cup golden raisins
1 teaspoon kosher salt, divided
¾ cup couscous
¼ teaspoon ground cumin
¼ teaspoon ground coriander
¼ teaspoon black pepper
8 (3-ounce) lamb rib chops, trimmed
¼ cup sliced almonds
¼ cup chopped fresh flat-leaf parsley

1. Preheat broiler.
2. Combine 1½ cups water, raisins, and ½ teaspoon salt in a medium saucepan; bring to a boil. Add couscous to pan. Remove from heat; cover and let stand 5 minutes. Fluff with a fork.
3. Combine ½ teaspoon salt, cumin, coriander, and pepper. Rub spice mixture evenly over lamb. Place lamb on a jelly-roll pan lined with aluminum foil. Broil lamb 10 minutes or until desired degree of doneness, turning once.
4. Heat a small skillet over medium heat. Add almonds to pan; cook 3 minutes or until lightly toasted, stirring constantly. Stir almonds and parsley into couscous mixture. Serve with lamb. Yield: 4 servings (serving size: 2 lamb chops and ¾ cup couscous).

CALORIES 328 (30% from fat); FAT 10.9g (sat 3g, mono 5.2g, poly 1.3g); PROTEIN 20.8g; CARB 36.3g; FIBER 3g; CHOL 50mg; IRON 1.9mg; SODIUM 523mg; CALC 50mg

Chicken Lettuce Wraps with Sweet and Spicy Sauce

You can serve these casual wraps buffet style. Arrange the lettuce leaves on a large platter, spoon the chicken salad in a bowl, and place the sauce in a small bowl on the side. Let people assemble their own wraps—it's one less step for the cook.

    3 tablespoons unsalted, dry-roasted
       peanuts
    3 tablespoons hoisin sauce
    2 tablespoons cider vinegar
    2 teaspoons low-sodium soy sauce
    1 teaspoon bottled ground fresh
       ginger (such as Spice World)
    1 teaspoon dark sesame oil
  ½ teaspoon crushed red pepper
  ½ teaspoon bottled minced garlic
    2 cups packaged cabbage-and-carrot
       coleslaw
    1 cup canned sliced water chestnuts,
       drained
    8 ounces grilled chicken breast
       strips (such as Louis Rich)
  12 Bibb lettuce leaves

1. Place peanuts in a small nonstick skillet over medium-high heat; cook 3 minutes or until lightly browned, shaking pan frequently. Remove pan from heat; set aside.
2. Combine hoisin and next 6 ingredients in a small bowl, stirring well with a whisk.
3. Combine peanuts, coleslaw, water chestnuts, and chicken in a medium bowl; toss well.
4. Spoon about ⅓ cup chicken salad in center of each lettuce leaf; top each with 2 teaspoons sauce. Roll up; secure with a wooden pick. Yield: 4 servings (serving size: 3 wraps).

CALORIES 197 (34% from fat); FAT 7.4g (sat 1.4g, mono 2.9g, poly 2.1g); PROTEIN 16.5g; CARB 18.2g; FIBER 3.4g; CHOL 37mg; IRON 1.9mg; SODIUM 825mg; CALC 40mg

Pork Medallions with Nectarine-Cranberry Chutney

CHUTNEY:

    1 tablespoon butter, divided
  ⅓ cup finely chopped onion
    2 cups chopped nectarine (about
       3 nectarines)
  ⅓ cup sweetened dried cranberries
    1 tablespoon balsamic vinegar
  ¼ teaspoon salt
  ¼ teaspoon ground cinnamon
  ⅛ teaspoon ground cloves

PORK:

    1 pound pork tenderloin, trimmed
  ½ teaspoon salt
  ¼ teaspoon freshly ground black
       pepper
       Cooking spray

1. To prepare chutney, melt 1 teaspoon butter in a medium saucepan over medium heat. Add onion; cook 4 minutes or until tender. Add nectarine, cranberries, and vinegar; cook 3 minutes or until nectarine is tender. Remove from heat; stir in ¼ teaspoon salt, cinnamon, cloves, and 2 teaspoons butter.
2. To prepare pork, cut pork crosswise into 8 (1-inch-thick) slices. Place each slice between 2 sheets of heavy-duty plastic wrap; pound to ½-inch thickness using a meat mallet or small heavy skillet. Sprinkle pork evenly with ½ teaspoon salt and pepper. Heat a large nonstick skillet over medium-high heat. Coat pan with cooking spray. Add pork; cook 3 minutes on each side or until desired degree of doneness. Serve pork with chutney. Yield: 4 servings (serving size: 2 pork slices and about ⅓ cup chutney).

CALORIES 233 (29% from fat); FAT 7.6g (sat 3.4g, mono 2.8g, poly 0.7g); PROTEIN 18.4g; CARB 23.1g; FIBER 1.6g; CHOL 64mg; IRON 1.4mg; SODIUM 507mg; CALC 12mg

Seared Chicken with Tomatillo-Avocado Salsa

Fix the salsa first so the flavors have time to develop. Serve with baked tortilla chips, reduced-fat sour cream, and frozen margaritas for a quick, festive dinner.

    4 ounces tomatillos (3 tomatillos)
  ¾ cup peeled chopped avocado
  ⅓ cup sliced radish
  ¼ cup chopped fresh cilantro
    2 tablespoons fresh lime
       juice
  ½ teaspoon salt
  ¼ teaspoon crushed red pepper
       Cooking spray
    4 (6-ounce) skinless, boneless
       chicken breast halves
  1½ teaspoons poultry seasoning

1. Discard husks and stems from tomatillos; finely chop. Combine tomatillos, avocado, and next 5 ingredients in a medium bowl.
2. Heat a large nonstick skillet over medium-high heat. Coat pan with cooking spray. Sprinkle chicken evenly with seasoning. Add chicken to pan; cook 3 minutes. Turn chicken over. Reduce heat, and cook 5 minutes or until done. Serve chicken with tomatillo mixture. Yield: 4 servings (serving size: 1 chicken breast half and ½ cup tomatillo mixture).

CALORIES 199 (28% from fat); FAT 6.2g (sat 1.2g, mono 3.1g, poly 1g); PROTEIN 30.5g; CARB 4.9g; FIBER 2.2g; CHOL 74mg; IRON 1.5mg; SODIUM 529mg; CALC 25mg

Quick Bouillabaisse Pasta

Toss together a salad, and serve with slices of crusty bread.

1 (9-ounce) package refrigerated fettuccine
1 tablespoon olive oil
1 teaspoon bottled minced garlic
2 teaspoons all-purpose flour
½ teaspoon herbes de Provence
¼ teaspoon ground turmeric
1 (14.5-ounce) can diced tomatoes, undrained
1 (8-ounce) bottle clam juice
12 medium mussels, cleaned and debearded
8 ounces medium shrimp, peeled and deveined
1 (8-ounce) halibut fillet, cut into 1-inch pieces
Chopped fresh basil (optional)

1. Cook fettuccine according to package directions, omitting salt and fat. Drain, and keep warm.
2. Heat oil in large nonstick skillet over medium-high heat. Add garlic to pan; cook 1 minute. Add flour to pan; cook 30 seconds, stirring constantly with a whisk. Stir in herbes de Provence, turmeric, tomatoes, and clam juice; bring to a boil. Stir in mussels, shrimp, and fish. Cover, reduce heat, and simmer 5 minutes or until mussels open. Discard any unopened shells.
3. Place 1 cup pasta in each of 4 bowls; top each serving with about ⅓ cup fish mixture and 3 mussels. Garnish with basil, if desired. Yield: 4 servings.

CALORIES 407 (18% from fat); FAT 8.3g (sat 1.2g, mono 3.5g, poly 2g); PROTEIN 37.5g; CARB 41.5g; FIBER 3.6g; CHOL 119mg; IRON 4.4mg; SODIUM 632mg; CALC 96mg

Summer Black Bean and Pasta Salad

Drain the pasta, and rinse it immediately with cold water to cool it quickly. If you can't find ditalini pasta, substitute tubetti or small elbow macaroni.

¾ cup uncooked ditalini (very short tube-shaped macaroni, 3 ounces)
1½ cups halved grape tomatoes
¾ cup diced peeled avocado
½ cup chopped seeded poblano chile (about 1)
½ cup chopped cucumber
⅓ cup chopped red onion
2 tablespoons chopped fresh cilantro
1 (15-ounce) can black beans, rinsed and drained
2 teaspoons grated lime rind
2 tablespoons fresh lime juice
1 tablespoon cider vinegar
2 teaspoons extravirgin olive oil
¾ teaspoon bottled minced garlic
¾ teaspoon salt
⅛ teaspoon ground red pepper
1 lime, cut in 4 wedges

1. Cook pasta according to package directions, omitting salt and fat. Drain, and cool completely.
2. Combine tomatoes and next 6 ingredients in a medium bowl, stirring well. Combine rind and next 6 ingredients in a small bowl, stirring well with a whisk. Add pasta and lime mixture to bean mixture; toss to combine. Serve with lime wedges. Yield: 4 servings (serving size: 1½ cups pasta mixture and 1 lime wedge).

CALORIES 214 (30% from fat); FAT 7.1g (sat 1.1g, mono 4.4g, poly 0.9g); PROTEIN 7.3g; CARB 35.5g; FIBER 7.2g; CHOL 0mg; IRON 2.4mg; SODIUM 656mg; CALC 47mg

Sesame Noodles with Chicken

Look for bottled toasted sesame seeds for a quick garnish.

8 ounces uncooked linguine
1 cup matchstick-cut carrots
⅔ cup organic vegetable broth (such as Swanson Certified Organic)
½ cup reduced-fat peanut butter
2 tablespoons rice vinegar
2 tablespoons low-sodium soy sauce
1 tablespoon bottled ground fresh ginger (such as Spice World)
2 teaspoons Sriracha (hot chile sauce, such as Huy Fong)
2 cups chopped cooked chicken breast
1 cup thinly sliced green onions
2 tablespoons sesame seeds, toasted

1. Cook pasta according to package directions, omitting salt and fat. Add carrots to pasta during the last 3 minutes of cooking. Drain well.
2. Place broth and next 5 ingredients in a food processor; process until smooth. Combine pasta mixture, chicken, and onions in a large bowl. Drizzle broth mixture over pasta mixture; toss well. Sprinkle with sesame seeds. Yield: 5 servings (serving size: 1 cup).

CALORIES 456 (27% from fat); FAT 13.9g (sat 3g, mono 6.1g, poly 4.1g); PROTEIN 31.1g; CARB 52.8g; FIBER 5.2g; CHOL 48mg; IRON 3.2mg; SODIUM 645mg; CALC 47mg

Salmon School

A chef, lodge owner, and cooking instructor shares her love of wild Alaskan fish.

Each year, Kirsten Dixon waits with pleasurable anticipation for that first excited phone call relating the news that will resonate throughout the valley. Someone has caught a king salmon, one of the five Pacific salmon species to arrive home from the ocean to spawn. Thus begins the daily arrival of fresh salmon to her kitchen door at Winterlake Lodge, almost 200 miles northwest of Anchorage, Alaska.

Guests visit Winterlake and Dixon's other property, Redoubt Bay Lodge, to fish for and dine on wild salmon, which are prized for their rich texture and succulent flavor.

QUICK & EASY
Salmon Burgers

Dress the burgers with lettuce, tomato, and your favorite condiments. Serve on toasted focaccia or hamburger buns with a simple fruit salad.

   1   cup finely chopped red onion
   ¼   cup thinly sliced fresh basil
   ¼   teaspoon salt
   ¼   teaspoon freshly ground black
         pepper
   1   (1-pound) salmon fillet, skinned
         and chopped
   1   tablespoon hot pepper sauce
   1   large egg white, lightly beaten
Cooking spray
   8   (¾-ounce) slices focaccia, toasted

1. Combine first 5 ingredients in a large bowl. Combine pepper sauce and egg white in a small bowl; add egg white mixture to salmon mixture, stirring well.
2. Divide mixture into 4 equal portions, shaping each into a ½-inch-thick patty. Heat a large nonstick skillet over medium-high heat. Coat pan with cooking spray. Add patties, and cook 3 minutes on each side or until desired degree of doneness. Serve patties on focaccia. Yield: 4 servings (serving size: 1 burger).

CALORIES 190 (42% from fat); FAT 8.8g (sat 2.1g, mono 3.8g, poly 2.1g); PROTEIN 25.2g; CARB 1.1g; FIBER 0.3g; CHOL 58mg; IRON 0.6mg; SODIUM 236mg; CALC 21mg

Broiled Salmon with Roasted Tomato Sauce

Roasting the tomatoes imbues them with flavor that's a delicious match for the rich fish. Garnish with a sprig of oregano.

   1   pound plum tomatoes, quartered
   ½   small onion, peeled and quartered
   2   garlic cloves
Cooking spray
   ¼   teaspoon salt
   ¼   teaspoon freshly ground black
         pepper
   2   tablespoons tomato paste
   1   cup organic vegetable broth (such
         as Swanson Certified Organic)
   2   tablespoons water
   1   teaspoon cornstarch
   4   (6-ounce) salmon fillets, skinned
   ⅛   teaspoon salt
   ¼   cup thinly sliced fresh basil
Coarsely ground black pepper
         (optional)

1. Preheat broiler.
2. Arrange tomatoes, onion, and garlic in an even layer on a jelly-roll pan coated with cooking spray. Sprinkle with ¼ teaspoon salt and ¼ teaspoon pepper. Broil 8 minutes; stir gently. Broil 5 minutes or until vegetables begin to blacken at edges.
3. Place tomato mixture and tomato paste in a blender or food processor; process until smooth. Place tomato mixture in a saucepan over medium heat. Stir in broth; bring to a simmer. Cook 10 minutes, stirring frequently. Strain mixture through a sieve into a large bowl; discard solids. Return tomato mixture to saucepan over medium heat.
4. Combine 2 tablespoons water and cornstarch in a small bowl. Stir cornstarch mixture into tomato mixture. Increase heat to medium-high; bring mixture to a boil. Cook 1 minute, stirring constantly. Remove from heat.
5. Place fish on a broiler pan lightly coated with cooking spray. Sprinkle evenly with ⅛ teaspoon salt. Broil 6 minutes or until fish flakes easily when tested with a fork or until desired degree of doneness.
6. Place about ¼ cup tomato mixture on each of 4 deep plates; top each with 1 salmon fillet. Sprinkle each with 1 tablespoon basil. Garnish with coarsely ground black pepper, if desired. Yield: 4 servings.

CALORIES 324 (38% from fat); FAT 13.5g (sat 3.2g, mono 5.7g, poly 3.4g); PROTEIN 37.9g; CARB 11.7g; FIBER 2.2g; CHOL 87mg; IRON 1.5mg; SODIUM 520mg; CALC 43mg

MAKE AHEAD
Hot-Smoked Salmon

   ¼   cup granulated sugar
   ¼   cup packed dark brown
         sugar
   2   tablespoons kosher salt
   1   tablespoon crushed black
         peppercorns
   1   teaspoon ground cardamom
   1   (1-pound) salmon fillet, pin bones
         removed
   2   cups wood chips
   2   cups water
Cooking spray

1. Combine first 5 ingredients in a small bowl. Rub sugar mixture into salmon flesh, and pack remaining rub around salmon. Wrap salmon tightly in plastic wrap and then in aluminum foil. Refrigerate 12 to 24 hours. Unwrap salmon, and rinse with cold water. Pat salmon dry.

Continued

2. Soak wood chips in water 30 minutes; drain well.

3. Prepare grill for indirect grilling, heating one side to high and leaving one side with low heat.

4. Place wood chips on hot coals. Place a disposable aluminum foil pan on unheated side of grill. Pour 2 cups water in pan. Coat grill rack with cooking spray; place on grill. Place salmon on grill rack over foil pan. Close lid; cook 15 minutes or until fish flakes easily when tested with a fork or until desired degree of doneness. Center of fish should be opaque and warm. Yield: 4 servings (serving size: 3 ounces salmon).

CALORIES 173 (38% from fat); FAT 7.3g (sat 1.1g, mono 2.4g, poly 2.9g); PROTEIN 22.5g; CARB 2.7g; FIBER 0g; CHOL 62mg; IRON 1mg; SODIUM 333mg; CALC 15mg

QUICK & EASY • MAKE AHEAD
Smoked Salmon-Cardamom Spread

This easy, no-cook spread has been a favorite in Kirsten's family for almost 20 years. It's terrific with any kind of cracker or crisp bread. Prepare it up to a day ahead, and refrigerate.

- ¾ cup reduced-fat sour cream
- 1 teaspoon finely grated lemon rind
- 1 tablespoon fresh lemon juice
- ¼ teaspoon ground cardamom
- ¼ teaspoon freshly ground black pepper
- 1 pound hot-smoked (kippered) boneless salmon fillet, divided
- ¼ cup chopped fresh chives
- Chopped fresh chives (optional)

1. Place first 5 ingredients and half of salmon in a food processor. Process until smooth. Transfer salmon mixture to a bowl.
2. Coarsely chop remaining salmon, and fold into salmon mixture. Gently fold in ¼ cup chives. Cover and chill. Garnish with additional chopped chives, if desired. Yield: 20 servings (serving size: 2 tablespoons).

CALORIES 39 (48% from fat); FAT 2.1g (sat 0.9g, mono 0.8g, poly 0.3g); PROTEIN 4.4g; CARB 0.5g; FIBER 0g; CHOL 9mg; IRON 0.2mg; SODIUM 182mg; CALC 13mg

Smoked Salmon Puffs

Bread flour lends these savory pastries height and structure.

- 1 cup bread flour (about 4¾ ounces)
- ½ teaspoon salt
- ¼ teaspoon freshly ground black pepper
- 1 cup water
- 2 tablespoons butter
- 2 large eggs, lightly beaten
- 4 large egg whites, lightly beaten
- ¼ cup chopped green onions
- 2 ounces hot-smoked (kippered) salmon, chopped
- Cooking spray

1. Preheat oven to 425°.
2. Lightly spoon flour into a dry measuring cup; level with a knife. Combine flour, salt, and pepper in a large bowl.
3. Combine 1 cup water and butter in a medium saucepan; bring to a boil over medium-high heat. Add flour mixture, and stir constantly with a wooden spoon until mixture forms a ball and pulls away from sides of pan (about 30 seconds). Cook 1 minute, stirring constantly. Remove from heat. Transfer flour mixture to a large bowl.
4. Add eggs, 1 at a time, beating well with a mixer after each addition. Add egg whites, 1 at a time, beating well after each addition. Stir in onions and salmon.
5. Spoon salmon mixture by rounded teaspoonfuls 1 inch apart on a baking sheet coated with cooking spray. Bake at 425° for 10 minutes.
6. Reduce oven temperature to 350° (do not remove puffs from oven). Bake an additional 20 minutes or until puffs have risen, are lightly browned, and feel dry on top and bottom. Remove from pan; cool completely on wire racks. Yield: 24 puffs (serving size: 2 puffs).

CALORIES 75 (35% from fat); FAT 2.9g (sat 1.3g, mono 1.2g, poly 0.2g); PROTEIN 4.5g; CARB 7.7g; FIBER 0.3g; CHOL 41mg; IRON 0.7mg; SODIUM 180mg; CALC 7mg

QUICK & EASY
Grilled Salmon Caesar Salad

- ½ cup plain fat-free yogurt
- ½ cup (2 ounces) freshly grated Parmesan cheese
- 2 tablespoons Dijon mustard
- 2 tablespoons fresh lemon juice
- ½ teaspoon Worcestershire sauce
- ½ teaspoon freshly ground black pepper
- ¼ teaspoon salt
- 2 garlic cloves, minced
- 1 (1-pound) salmon fillet
- ¼ teaspoon salt
- ¼ teaspoon freshly ground black pepper
- Cooking spray
- 8 cups torn romaine lettuce

1. Spoon yogurt onto several layers of heavy-duty paper towels; spread to ½-inch thickness. Cover with additional paper towels; let stand 5 minutes. Scrape into a food processor or blender using a rubber spatula. Add cheese and next 6 ingredients; process until smooth. Transfer yogurt mixture to a bowl; cover and chill 30 minutes.
2. Prepare grill.
3. Sprinkle skin side of salmon with ¼ teaspoon salt and ¼ teaspoon pepper. Place fish, skin side down, on a grill rack coated with cooking spray. Grill 8 minutes or until fish flakes easily when tested with a fork or until desired degree of doneness. Remove and discard skin. Break fish into large flakes with a fork.
4. Place lettuce in a large bowl. Drizzle with yogurt mixture, tossing to coat. Place 2 cups lettuce mixture on each of 4 large plates; top each serving with 3 ounces salmon. Yield: 4 servings.

CALORIES 271 (42% from fat); FAT 12.6g (sat 3.9g, mono 4.9g, poly 2.6g); PROTEIN 31.3g; CARB 8.9g; FIBER 2.6g; CHOL 67mg; IRON 1.9mg; SODIUM 724mg; CALC 215mg

WINE NOTE: The perfect wine for this dish must be clean, crisp, and bracing with enough body to balance a "meaty" fish like salmon. One to try: a California pinot gris like J Pinot Gris from the Russian River Valley, about $15.

Wild by Law

In Alaska, all salmon are wild. There are no farm-raised fish in Alaskan waters. In fact, it's illegal to farm-raise finfish. The thinking is that this will help preserve the pristine nature of Alaska's waters and the hearty genetic stock of our wild fish.

Wild salmon tend to be slightly lower in calories, fat, and sodium than their farmed cousins, and depending on the variety, they can have a bit more protein. Because salmon stop feeding once they re-enter the river, they're particularly high in heart-healthy omega-3 fatty acids and protein to fuel their long journey through icy-cold waters.

Alaskan salmon are either commercially caught in the ocean or sport-caught in freshwater streams. Guests who stay at Dixon's lodges often take some salmon home as an edible souvenir of their trip.

Cooking with Different Types

There are three species of Pacific salmon generally found as fresh fish in the market: king, coho, and sockeye. You can use any type of salmon in the recipes here, but keep in mind that each species cooks a little differently because of its fat content and average size. The idea is to avoid drying out or overcooking the fish. A general rule is to cook it about eight to 10 minutes per inch thickness of fish, however you're preparing it.

King are the favorite of professional chefs, in part because the high fat content of the fish keeps them moist as they cook. Try searing king salmon, then finish it in the oven and serve with a sauce.

Coho are best grilled, hot-smoked, pan-seared, or baked. During the summer, use fresh herbs and vegetables to create main-course salads topped with grilled salmon. If you grill salmon, select fish with the skin intact; it helps hold the fish together on the grill. Although you should usually remove skin after grilling, many people enjoy the taste of crispy, crunchy salmon skin.

Sockeye have become more popular over the past few years. On the day that fishermen can begin catching sockeye in Alaska's Copper River, restaurants across the country begin featuring them on menus. Sockeye have a deep red color that looks beautiful simply steamed and served with colorful vegetables.

What to Look For

When shopping for Alaskan salmon, usually you'll find fillets or steaks nicely portioned and packaged. You can ensure your fish is of good quality by looking for:
- Firm, resilient flesh
- Shiny skin, if it's still intact
- Pleasant sea smell—no ammonia
- No weeping fluids or dried-out flesh

Don't be afraid to buy fresh-frozen fish, also known as "fish frozen at sea" (FAS). It's often vacuum packed and frozen as soon as it's caught to preserve texture and flavor. It's a good alternative when fresh wild salmon isn't available.

Read the Label

Current labeling laws that require identification of origin make it easier to spot wild salmon. But there can still be some confusion. Keep in mind:
- All commercially available Atlantic salmon are farm-raised. Atlantic salmon typically are marketed alongside Pacific salmon, but they're a different genus and species of fish.
- Just because salmon is labeled "Pacific" doesn't mean it's wild. There are some farm-raised Pacific salmon imported from Canada and Chile.
- Look for salmon labeled "wild."

Internet Catch

Although you can find wild salmon in local stores, you may not have a choice of varieties. These Internet retailers ship several types of salmon (king, coho, sockeye, and keta), as well as smoked and canned fish. Most sell fish that has been fresh-frozen at sea, so it's available year-round.

Ed's Kasilof Seafoods
www.kasilofseafoods.com
800-982-2377
Wild Pacific Salmon
www.wildpacificsalmon.com
503-435-8003
SeaBear Wild Salmon
www.seabear.com
800-645-3474
ChefShop.com
(ships never-frozen wild salmon when it's in season)
www.chefshop.com
800-596-0885

How to Hot-Smoke a Salmon

Besides fresh fish at the seafood counter, keep an eye out for smoked salmon, either hot-smoked (kippered) or cold-smoked (lox). We recommend using hot-smoked salmon in the winter for pizzas and other savory dishes. Lox is more delicate and doesn't hold up to cooking, but we serve it with breakfast toast and with appetizers in the afternoon.

Although commercially smoked fish is readily available, you can also prepare your own on the grill with wood chips available in small bags from most markets. Use alder wood if it's available. Try smoked salmon in the recipes here, or add it to pasta, pizza, or a main-course salad.

Salmon Curry

    2 teaspoons ground turmeric
    2 teaspoons cider vinegar
    ¾ teaspoon salt
    ½ teaspoon ground cumin
    ½ teaspoon chili powder
    ½ teaspoon brown sugar
    1 (1-pound) skinless salmon fillet
    1 teaspoon olive oil
    1 cup thinly sliced onion (about 1
       small onion)
    2 garlic cloves, thinly sliced
    6 cups finely chopped tomato
  Cooking spray
    3 cups cooked basmati rice
  Chopped fresh cilantro (optional)

1. Combine first 6 ingredients in a small bowl, stirring to form a paste. Rub both sides of salmon with ½ teaspoon spice mixture; cover and chill. Set remaining spice mixture aside.
2. Heat oil in a large saucepan over medium-high heat. Add onion; sauté 5 minutes or until tender and just beginning to brown. Add garlic; sauté 1 minute or until garlic begins to brown. Stir in reserved spice mixture and tomato. Reduce heat, and simmer 15 minutes or until thickened, stirring frequently. Remove from heat; keep warm.
3. Preheat oven to 450°.
4. Place fish on a broiler pan coated with cooking spray. Bake at 450° for 10 minutes or until fish flakes easily when tested with a fork or until desired degree of doneness. Remove from oven; cool slightly. Break fish into chunks.
5. Place ¾ cup rice on each of 4 large plates. Top each serving with about ¾ cup tomato mixture and 3 ounces salmon. Sprinkle with cilantro, if desired. Yield: 4 servings.

CALORIES 416 (24% from fat); FAT 11g (sat 2.5g, mono 4.9g, poly 2.7g); PROTEIN 30.2g; CARB 48.8g; FIBER 4.6g; CHOL 58mg; IRON 3.2mg; SODIUM 516mg; CALC 70mg

Sweet Salmon with a Kick

    ¼ cup rice vinegar
    2 tablespoons honey
    1 tablespoon low-sodium soy
       sauce
    1 teaspoon ground red pepper
    ½ teaspoon kosher salt
    ½ teaspoon five-spice powder
    4 (6-ounce) salmon fillets
  Cooking spray
    ¼ cup sliced green onions

1. Preheat broiler.
2. Combine first 3 ingredients in a small bowl; stir with a whisk. Reserve ¼ cup vinegar mixture.
3. Combine red pepper, salt, and five-spice powder; rub evenly over skin side of salmon.
4. Place salmon, skin sides down, on a broiler pan coated with cooking spray. Broil 16 minutes or until fish flakes easily when tested with a fork or until desired degree of doneness, brushing frequently with vinegar mixture.
5. Place reserved ¼ cup vinegar mixture in a small microwave-safe glass bowl. Microwave at HIGH 20 seconds or until bubbly. Drizzle over fish; sprinkle with onions. Yield: 4 servings (serving size: 1 fillet, 1 tablespoon sauce, and 1 tablespoon onions).

CALORIES 281 (35% from fat); FAT 10.9g (sat 1.7g, mono 3.6g, poly 4.4g); PROTEIN 34.1g; CARB 10g; FIBER 0.4g; CHOL 94mg; IRON 1.7mg; SODIUM 446mg; CALC 25mg

lighten up

Better Broccoli Casserole

A favorite vegetable and cheese combo from childhood is renovated for a growing Ohio family.

Trisha Prenger of Columbus, Ohio, has enjoyed this cheesy, simple casserole since childhood. Now she can enjoy it in the future with our changes.

Zesty Broccoli Casserole

    3 (10-ounce) packages frozen
       broccoli florets, thawed
  Cooking spray
  1½ cups fat-free milk
  2½ tablespoons all-purpose flour
    ½ teaspoon salt
    ¼ teaspoon freshly ground black pepper
    ¾ cup (3 ounces) shredded sharp
       Cheddar cheese
    ½ cup (4 ounces) fat-free cream
       cheese, softened
    1 cup fat-free mayonnaise
    ¾ cup chopped onion
    1 (8-ounce) can water chestnuts,
       rinsed, drained, and sliced
    ¾ cup panko (Japanese breadcrumbs)
    2 teaspoons butter, melted

1. Preheat oven to 375°.
2. Arrange broccoli in an even layer in an 11 x 7–inch baking dish coated with cooking spray; set aside.
3. Combine milk, flour, salt, and pepper in a large saucepan over medium-high heat; bring to a boil. Cook 1 minute or until thick; stir constantly. Remove from heat. Add Cheddar and cream cheeses; stir until smooth. Stir in mayonnaise, onion, and water chestnuts. Spoon cheese mixture evenly over broccoli.
4. Place panko in a small bowl. Drizzle with butter, and toss. Sprinkle breadcrumb mixture evenly over cheese mixture. Lightly spray breadcrumb layer with cooking spray. Bake at 375° for 25 minutes or until mixture begins to bubble and breadcrumbs brown. Yield: 10 servings (serving size: about ¾ cup).

CALORIES 141 (31% from fat); FAT 4.9g (sat 2.6g, mono 1.3g, poly 0.7g); PROTEIN 8.6g; CARB 17.9g; FIBER 4.1g; CHOL 15mg; IRON 1mg; SODIUM 484mg; CALC 173mg

BEFORE	AFTER
SERVING SIZE	
¾ cup	
CALORIES PER SERVING	
351	141
FAT	
30.9g	4.9g
PERCENT OF TOTAL CALORIES	
79%	31%

Smooth As Velvet

A Wisconsin artist's smooth and delicious pudding appeases any sweet tooth.

Self-professed chocoholic Shelly Platten of Amherst, Wisconsin, loves to prepare desserts but is always looking for ways to reduce calories and make the sweet goodies she creates for her family more healthful. "I try to cut down the fat but keep the good taste," says Platten. Her smooth-textured and rich Velvety Fudge Pudding is comforting.

MAKE AHEAD
Velvety Fudge Pudding

(pictured on page 240)

This makes a thick, heavy pudding. Use less cornstarch if you prefer a lighter consistency.

- 1 cup 1% low-fat milk, divided
- 1 cup fat-free half-and-half
- ⅓ cup sugar
- ⅔ cup semisweet chocolate chips
- 3 tablespoons cornstarch
- 1 large egg, lightly beaten
- 1 large egg white, lightly beaten
- 1½ teaspoons vanilla extract
- Chocolate shavings

1. Combine ½ cup milk, half-and-half, and sugar in a medium saucepan over medium heat. Cook, stirring constantly, 2 minutes or just until mixture begins to simmer. Remove from heat, and add chocolate chips. Let stand 5 minutes; stir until smooth.

2. Place chocolate mixture over low heat; return to a simmer, stirring frequently. Combine ½ cup milk, cornstarch, egg, and egg white in a medium bowl; stir with a whisk. Gradually add 1 cup hot chocolate mixture to cornstarch mixture, stirring constantly with a whisk. Return mixture to pan. Cook, stirring constantly, over low heat 4 minutes or until thickened. Stir in vanilla. Serve warm, or cover and chill. Garnish with chocolate shavings. Yield: 4 servings (serving size: ½ cup).

CALORIES 314 (30% from fat); FAT 10.3g (sat 5.8g, mono 3.5g, poly 0.5g); PROTEIN 5.7g; CARB 49.1g; FIBER 1.7g; CHOL 55mg; IRON 1.2mg; SODIUM 126mg; CALC 132mg

MAKE AHEAD
Grilled Chicken and Lemon Salad

"When it's in season, I sometimes substitute thin, blanched, fresh asparagus for the sugar snap peas. Freshly squeezed lemon juice is essential to the flavor of this salad."

—Michael Ruggeberg, Aspen, Colorado

CHICKEN:
- ¾ cup fresh lemon juice
- ¼ cup olive oil
- 1 tablespoon fresh thyme leaves
- 1 teaspoon salt
- 4 (6-ounce) skinless, boneless chicken breast halves
- Cooking spray

SALAD:
- 1 cup sugar snap peas, trimmed
- ½ cup red bell pepper strips
- ½ cup yellow bell pepper strips
- ½ cup (¼-inch-thick) slices zucchini
- 2 tablespoons chopped fresh cilantro
- 1 tablespoon extravirgin olive oil
- ¼ teaspoon salt
- ¼ teaspoon freshly ground black pepper
- 4 lemon wedges (optional)

1. To prepare chicken, combine first 4 ingredients in a large zip-top plastic bag. Add chicken to bag, and seal. Marinate chicken in refrigerator 1 hour, turning occasionally.

2. Prepare grill.

3. Remove chicken from bag; discard marinade. Place chicken on a grill rack coated with cooking spray; grill 6 minutes on each side or until done. Cool completely; cut into ¼-inch-thick slices.

4. To prepare salad, cook peas in boiling water 30 seconds. Drain and rinse with cold water. Drain. Combine peas and next 7 ingredients in a large bowl; add chicken, tossing to combine. Place 1¾ cups chicken salad on each of 4 plates. Serve with lemon wedges, if desired. Yield: 4 servings.

CALORIES 259 (25% from fat); FAT 7.1g (sat 1.2g, mono 4g, poly 1g); PROTEIN 40.5g; CARB 5.3g; FIBER 0.8g; CHOL 99mg; IRON 1.5mg; SODIUM 332mg; CALC 35mg

Chipotle Tandoori Shrimp Wraps

"Chipotle chiles, not normally found in tandoori, add a wonderful smoky flavor to the marinade. Grilled shrimp, sweet mango, red onion, and fragrant cilantro all make for a striking combination of flavors."

—Edwina Gadsby, Great Falls, Montana

- 1½ cups plain low-fat yogurt, divided
- 2 tablespoons minced peeled fresh ginger
- 2 tablespoons minced garlic
- 2 tablespoons fresh lemon juice
- 1 tablespoon fresh lime juice
- ½ teaspoon salt
- ½ teaspoon ground turmeric
- ½ teaspoon ground cumin
- 1 teaspoon adobo sauce
- 2 chipotle chiles, canned in adobo sauce, seeded and minced
- 1½ pounds medium shrimp, peeled and deveined
- Cooking spray
- 8 (7-inch) flatbreads (such as Flatout)
- 1 cup diced peeled mango
- ½ cup thinly sliced red onion
- ¼ cup chopped fresh cilantro
- 2 thinly sliced jalapeño peppers
- 8 lime wedges

1. Combine 1 cup yogurt, ginger, and next 9 ingredients in a large zip-top plastic bag; seal bag. Toss well to coat. Marinate in refrigerator 1 hour, turning bag occasionally.

2. Prepare grill.

3. Remove shrimp from bag; discard marinade. Thread shrimp evenly onto 8 (10-inch) skewers. Place skewers on a grill rack coated with cooking spray, and grill 2 minutes on each side or until done. Let shrimp stand 5 minutes.

Continued

Remove shrimp from skewers. Divide shrimp evenly among 8 flatbreads. Top each serving with 2 tablespoons mango, 1 tablespoon onion, 1½ teaspoons cilantro, and 1 tablespoon yogurt. Divide jalapeño evenly among flatbreads; roll up. Serve with lime wedges. Yield: 8 servings (serving size: 1 topped flatbread and 1 lime wedge).

CALORIES 400 (25% from fat); FAT 11.1g (sat 2g, mono 4.3g, poly 4.1g); PROTEIN 28.8g; CARB 45.2g; FIBER 1.7g; CHOL 131mg; IRON 4.5mg; SODIUM 562mg; CALC 188mg

QUICK & EASY • MAKE AHEAD
Bulldog Salad

"I developed this lightened version of Waldorf salad for a teacher's luncheon at my children's school. When I served the leftovers to my family, 'Waldorf' somehow turned into 'Bulldog,' so that's what we call the dish."

—Becky Fulcher, Monument, Colorado

  3 cups diced Fuji or Gala apple
     (about 2 large)
2½ cups diced Granny Smith apple
     (about 1 large)
  1 cup seedless green grapes, halved
  1 cup seedless red grapes, halved
  1 cup finely chopped celery
  1 cup miniature marshmallows
 ⅓ cup golden raisins
 ¼ cup chopped pecans, toasted
 ¼ cup reduced-fat mayonnaise
 ¼ cup fat-free vanilla yogurt
  2 tablespoons reduced-fat sour cream

1. Combine all ingredients in a large bowl; stir well. Chill. Yield: 10 servings (serving size: 1 cup).

CALORIES 129 (32% from fat); FAT 4.6g (sat 0.7g, mono 1.8g, poly 1.8g); PROTEIN 1.4g; CARB 22.8g; FIBER 2.5g; CHOL 1mg; IRON 0.4mg; SODIUM 64mg; CALC 29mg

Dinner on the Deck Menu
serves 8

Prepare the salad and marinate the pork up to a day ahead to keep last-minute preparations to a minimum.

Balsamic Carrot Salad

Grilled pork tenderloin*

Smashed red potatoes

*Combine 2 tablespoons chopped fresh parsley, 2 tablespoons chopped fresh rosemary, 1 tablespoon chopped fresh thyme, 1 tablespoon olive oil, and 3 minced garlic cloves. Sprinkle 2 (1-pound) pork tenderloins with 1 teaspoon salt and ½ teaspoon black pepper; coat with herb mixture. Grill 20 minutes or until a thermometer registers 160° (slightly pink), turning to brown on all sides. Let pork stand 10 minutes. Cut crosswise into ½-inch-thick slices.

MAKE AHEAD
Balsamic Carrot Salad

"This is a unique vegetable salad that is great served hot or cold and for picnics or casual summer dinners."

—Silvina Bates, Orange, California

  4 cups (¼-inch-thick) slices carrot (about 2 pounds)
 ¼ cup minced fresh cilantro
  2 tablespoons white balsamic vinegar
  1 tablespoon extravirgin olive oil
  2 teaspoons minced fresh oregano
 ¼ teaspoon salt
 ¼ teaspoon black pepper
  2 garlic cloves, minced

1. Combine all ingredients in a large bowl, tossing to coat carrots. Cover and chill at least 1 hour or overnight to enhance flavors. Yield: 8 servings (serving size: ½ cup).

CALORIES 59 (29% from fat); FAT 1.9g (sat 0.3g, mono 1.3g, poly 0.2g); PROTEIN 0.8g; CARB 10.3g; FIBER 2.1g; CHOL 0mg; IRON 1.1mg; SODIUM 164mg; CALC 42mg

MAKE AHEAD
Annie's Salad

"Annie was a coworker who brought in this dish she had created. I liked the salad so much that I experimented with various ingredients to find what worked for me. This is a wonderful summer dish that I have served often and everyone loves."

—Stacy Wallace, Chatham, New York

  1 cup dried lentils
  1 (14-ounce) can fat-free, less-sodium chicken broth
  1 cup uncooked pearl barley
2¾ cups water
 ¾ cup diced red onion
 ½ cup chopped fresh parsley
 ½ cup fresh lemon juice
 ¼ cup olive oil
 ½ teaspoon salt
  2 garlic cloves, minced
Parsley sprigs (optional)

1. Combine lentils and broth in a large saucepan over medium-high heat; bring to a boil. Reduce heat, and simmer 10 minutes or just until liquid is absorbed, stirring occasionally. Stir in barley and 2¾ cups water; bring to a simmer. Cook 18 minutes or until liquid is absorbed, stirring occasionally. Transfer lentil mixture to a large bowl. Add onion and next 5 ingredients, stirring well. Cool to room temperature. Cover and chill at least 1 hour. Garnish with parsley sprigs, if desired. Yield: 6 servings (serving size: ¾ cup).

CALORIES 248 (26% from fat); FAT 7.1g (sat 1g, mono 5.1g, poly 0.8g); PROTEIN 10.5g; CARB 38.1g; FIBER 7.6g; CHOL 0mg; IRON 3.2mg; SODIUM 231mg; CALC 19mg

Bella Brunches

Unwind and entertain this weekend—
Mediterranean style.

A Taste of Capri Menu
serves 6

Classic Bruschetta

Tomato, Fresh Mozzarella, and Basil Salad

Caramelized Onion Frittata

Summer Berry Medley with Limoncello and Mint

Chilled greco di Tufo (or other light Italian white wine)

Game Plan

Up to a day in advance:
- Cook potato and onions.

Up to 30 minutes before serving:
- Prepare bruschetta.
- Assemble salad.
- Prepare berry medley.
- Prepare frittata.

QUICK & EASY
Classic Bruschetta

Toast the bread under the broiler if you don't have a grill pan.

- 6 ounces Italian bread, diagonally cut into 6 slices
- 3 garlic cloves, halved
- 1 tablespoon extravirgin olive oil
- ½ teaspoon dried oregano
- ¼ teaspoon salt

1. Heat a grill pan over medium-high heat. Place bread slices in pan; cook 2 minutes on each side or until lightly browned. Rub 1 side of each toast slice with cut sides of garlic cloves. Discard garlic. Drizzle bread with oil, and sprinkle with oregano and salt. Yield: 6 servings (serving size: 1 bruschetta).

CALORIES 89 (31% from fat); FAT 3.1g (sat 0.3g, mono 1.8g, poly 0.2g); PROTEIN 2.3g; CARB 14.3g; FIBER 1.5g; CHOL 0mg; IRON 0.6mg; SODIUM 240mg; CALC 17mg

QUICK & EASY
Tomato, Fresh Mozzarella, and Basil Salad

In Italy, this is known as *insalata caprese* (Capri-style salad). It's best in summer, when tomatoes are at their peak.

- 4 tomatoes, each cut into 6 slices (about 1½ pounds)
- ½ pound fresh mozzarella cheese, cut into 12 slices
- ¼ teaspoon kosher salt
- ¼ teaspoon freshly ground black pepper
- 1 tablespoon extravirgin olive oil
- ½ cup fresh basil leaves

1. Arrange 4 tomato slices and 2 mozzarella slices on each of 6 salad plates. Sprinkle evenly with salt and pepper; drizzle evenly with oil. Top evenly with basil. Yield: 6 servings.

CALORIES 150 (64% from fat); FAT 10.7g (sat 5.8g, mono 1.9g, poly 0.4g); PROTEIN 7.8g; CARB 5.4g; FIBER 1.5g; CHOL 30mg; IRON 0.6mg; SODIUM 138mg; CALC 231mg

Caramelized Onion Frittata

- 1 cup diced baking potato
- 3 tablespoons water
- Cooking spray
- 4 cups sliced onion (about 1 pound)
- ⅓ cup water
- 1 tablespoon chopped fresh sage
- ½ teaspoon salt
- ¼ teaspoon freshly ground black pepper
- ¼ cup (1 ounce) grated Parmigiano-Reggiano cheese, divided
- 2 tablespoons fat-free milk
- 6 large egg whites, lightly beaten
- 4 large eggs, lightly beaten

1. Place potato and 3 tablespoons water in a small microwave-safe bowl. Cover with plastic wrap, and vent. Microwave at HIGH 4 minutes or until tender, stirring once. Set aside.
2. Heat a 10-inch nonstick skillet over medium-high heat. Coat pan with cooking spray. Add onion. Cover and cook 10 minutes or until lightly browned, stirring occasionally. Uncover and cook 10 minutes or until golden brown, stirring frequently. While onion cooks, add ⅓ cup water, 1 tablespoon at a time, to prevent onion from sticking to pan. Stir in potato, sage, salt, and pepper. Spoon into a medium bowl; cool slightly.
3. Combine 3 tablespoons cheese, milk, egg whites, and eggs in a small bowl; stir with a whisk. Add egg mixture to potato mixture; stir well.
4. Preheat broiler.
5. Wipe pan with a paper towel; recoat pan with cooking spray. Pour potato mixture into pan. Cook over medium heat 7 minutes or until bottom of frittata is browned and top is almost set.
6. Wrap handle of pan with foil. Sprinkle 1 tablespoon cheese over frittata. Broil 5 minutes or until cheese melts and top is set. Cut into wedges. Yield: 6 servings (serving size: 1 wedge).

CALORIES 135 (29% from fat); FAT 4.4g (sat 1.6g, mono 1.6g, poly 0.5g); PROTEIN 10.5g; CARB 13.1g; FIBER 1.5g; CHOL 144mg; IRON 1mg; SODIUM 356mg; CALC 84mg

STAFF FAVORITE • QUICK & EASY
Summer Berry Medley with Limoncello and Mint

Limoncello (lee-mon-CHAY-low) is a lemon-flavored liqueur from Italy's Amalfi coast. It's often savored after a meal. Store it in the freezer, and serve over ice. If you have trouble finding it, substitute an orange-flavored liqueur such as Grand Marnier. This recipe earned our Test Kitchens' highest rating.

- 2 cups fresh blackberries
- 2 cups hulled fresh strawberries, quartered
- 2 cups fresh blueberries
- 1 cup fresh raspberries
- ¼ cup sugar
- 1 tablespoon grated lemon rind
- 2 tablespoons fresh lemon juice
- 2 tablespoons limoncello (lemon-flavored liqueur)
- ½ cup torn mint leaves

Continued

1. Combine first 8 ingredients in a bowl; let stand 20 minutes. Gently stir in mint using a rubber spatula. Yield: 6 servings (serving size: about 1 cup).

CALORIES 136 (5% from fat); FAT 0.8g (sat 0g, mono 0.1g, poly 0.4g); PROTEIN 1.9g; CARB 31.3g; FIBER 7.4g; CHOL 0mg; IRON 1mg; SODIUM 2mg; CALC 38mg

Summer in Piedmont Menu

serves 6

Marinated Heirloom Tomatoes with Mustard and Dill

Open-Faced Panini with Goat Cheese, Roasted Peppers, and Spicy Olive Topping

Pan-Roasted Asparagus with Lemon Rind

Mushroom Salad with Truffle Oil and Parmigiano-Reggiano

Broiled Peaches and Hazelnuts with Vanilla Ice Cream

Chilled barbera d'Asti (or other light Italian red wine)

Game Plan

Up to a day in advance:
• Roast peppers for panini, and prepare olive topping for panini.
• Cook asparagus.
• Roast hazelnuts, broil peaches, and grate chocolate for dessert.

Up to 30 minutes before serving:
• Marinate tomatoes.
• Prepare mushrooms.
• Prepare panini.
• Bring broiled peaches and hazelnuts to room temperature.

Marinated Heirloom Tomatoes with Mustard and Dill

Use different varieties of tomato for more color. Prepare just before serving so the tomatoes will hold their shape.

  2 tablespoons Dijon mustard
  1 tablespoon chopped fresh dill
  2 teaspoons grated lemon rind
  1 teaspoon fresh lemon juice
  ¼ teaspoon salt
  ⅛ teaspoon freshly ground black pepper
  2 pounds large heirloom tomatoes, cut into ¼-inch-thick slices

1. Combine first 6 ingredients in a large bowl. Add tomato slices, tossing gently to coat. Let stand 15 minutes. Yield: 6 servings (serving size: about 5 ounces tomato).

CALORIES 39 (23% from fat); FAT 1g (sat 0.1g, mono 0.2g, poly 0.3g); PROTEIN 1.6g; CARB 7.7g; FIBER 1.8g; CHOL 0mg; IRON 0.8mg; SODIUM 238mg; CALC 16mg

Open-Faced Panini with Goat Cheese, Roasted Peppers, and Spicy Olive Topping

(pictured on page 240)

For the best flavor, look for high-quality imported olives, available at gourmet markets or large supermarkets.

  2 red bell peppers
  ⅛ teaspoon salt
  6 (1-inch) slices Italian bread
  ¼ cup minced pitted ripe olives (about 6)
  2 tablespoons minced pitted green olives (about 8)
  1 tablespoon minced fresh basil
  2 teaspoons grated lemon rind
  2 teaspoons fresh lemon juice
  ⅛ teaspoon ground red pepper
  1 small garlic clove, minced
  3 tablespoons crumbled goat cheese

1. Prepare broiler.
2. Cut bell peppers in half lengthwise; discard seeds and membranes. Place pepper halves, skin sides up, on a foil-lined baking sheet; flatten with hand. Broil 15 minutes or until blackened. Place in a zip-top plastic bag; seal. Let stand 10 minutes. Peel and cut into strips. Combine peppers and salt in a medium bowl; set aside.
3. Place bread on a baking sheet; broil 1 minute on each side or until toasted.
4. Combine ripe olives and next 6 ingredients in a small bowl. Spoon about 1 tablespoon olive mixture onto each toast slice; top evenly with pepper strips, and sprinkle each serving with 1½ teaspoons crumbled goat cheese. Cut each panino in half. Serve immediately. Yield: 6 servings (serving size: 2 panini).

CALORIES 126 (31% from fat); FAT 4.4g (sat 1.1g, mono 1.5g, poly 0.8g); PROTEIN 4g; CARB 18.1g; FIBER 1.8g; CHOL 4mg; IRON 1.1mg; SODIUM 420mg; CALC 60mg

Pan-Roasted Asparagus with Lemon Rind

Add a few fresh sage leaves along with the garlic, rosemary, and lemon zest for more herbal flavor. You can serve this at room temperature or chilled. Haricots verts (delicate, thin green beans) work well as a substitute for asparagus.

  1 pound asparagus
  1 teaspoon olive oil
Cooking spray
  2 (2-inch) lemon rind strips
  2 garlic cloves, chopped
  1 (1-inch) rosemary sprig
  ½ cup water
  ½ teaspoon salt
  ¼ teaspoon freshly ground black pepper

1. Snap off tough ends of asparagus.
2. Heat oil in a large nonstick skillet coated with cooking spray over medium-high heat. Add asparagus, rind, garlic, and rosemary; sauté 3 minutes or until asparagus is lightly browned.
3. Add ½ cup water to pan; cook 5 minutes or until asparagus is crisp-tender

and liquid almost evaporates. Discard rind and rosemary. Sprinkle asparagus with salt and pepper; toss well. Yield: 6 servings (serving size: about 6 spears).

CALORIES 30 (24% from fat); FAT 0.8g (sat 0.1g, mono 0.6g, poly 0.1g); PROTEIN 1.7g; CARB 3.8g; FIBER 1.8g; CHOL 0mg; IRON 0.3mg; SODIUM 197mg; CALC 20mg

QUICK & EASY

Mushroom Salad with Truffle Oil and Parmigiano-Reggiano

(pictured on page 240)

The success of this dish depends on slicing or shaving the mushrooms, celery, and cheese as thinly as possible so that each bite will provide some flavor from all the ingredients.

 1 teaspoon truffle oil or extravirgin olive oil
 ½ teaspoon grated lemon rind
 2 tablespoons fresh lemon juice
 ¼ teaspoon salt
 ¼ teaspoon freshly ground black pepper
 5 cups thinly sliced large button mushrooms (about ¾ pound)
 1¼ cups thinly sliced celery (about 4 stalks)
 1 ounce fresh Parmigiano-Reggiano cheese, shaved

1. Combine first 5 ingredients in a bowl.
2. Combine mushrooms and celery in a large bowl. Drizzle with oil mixture; toss gently to coat.
3. Arrange 1 cup mushroom mixture on each of 6 plates; top each serving with about 2 teaspoons shaved cheese. Yield: 6 servings.

CALORIES 51 (53% from fat); FAT 3g (sat 1g, mono 1.6g, poly 0.3g); PROTEIN 3.8g; CARB 3.3g; FIBER 1.1g; CHOL 3mg; IRON 0.4mg; SODIUM 195mg; CALC 68mg

MAKE AHEAD

Broiled Peaches and Hazelnuts with Vanilla Ice Cream

You can also shave the chocolate with a vegetable peeler, if you wish.

 ¼ cup hazelnuts
 4 cups peeled sliced peaches (about 1 pound)
 ¼ cup sugar
 Cooking spray
 2 cups vanilla fat-free ice cream (such as Edy's or Dreyer's)
 1 ounce bittersweet chocolate, grated

1. Preheat oven to 350°.
2. Place hazelnuts on a baking sheet. Bake at 350° for 15 minutes, stirring once. Turn nuts out onto a towel. Roll up towel; rub off skins. Chop nuts.
3. Preheat broiler.
4. Combine hazelnuts, peaches, and sugar in a large bowl, tossing to coat. Arrange peach mixture in a single layer on a broiler pan coated with cooking spray; broil 5 minutes or until lightly browned. Cool.
5. Spoon ⅓ cup ice cream into each of 6 bowls; top each serving with 1 cup peach mixture and 2 teaspoons grated chocolate. Yield: 6 servings.

CALORIES 187 (27% from fat); FAT 5.7g (sat 1.3g, mono 2.8g, poly 0.5g); PROTEIN 3.9g; CARB 33.7g; FIBER 2.2g; CHOL 0mg; IRON 0.4mg; SODIUM 30mg; CALC 61mg

enlightened cook

Something For Everyone

In the heart of California's vineyards, Chef John Littlewood caters to diverse groups with eclectic cuisine.

The ultimate compliment for a chef is repeat business. Guests returning to Chef John Littlewood's tables collectively log thousands of miles each year to enjoy what's new in his repertoire of recipes.

Roasted Halibut with Romesco Sauce and Olive Relish

Make the romesco sauce and relish a day ahead; refrigerate separately in airtight containers. Serve with sautéed spinach or chard and roasted new potatoes or jasmine rice. The sauce is also good with grilled chicken, and you can serve the relish on toasted baguette slices as an appetizer.

ROMESCO SAUCE:
 1 red bell pepper
 2 plum tomatoes, halved and seeded
 1½ tablespoons sliced almonds, toasted
 3 tablespoons water
 1 tablespoon sherry vinegar
 1½ teaspoons low-sodium soy sauce
 ¼ teaspoon sugar
 ¼ teaspoon freshly ground black pepper
 ⅛ teaspoon ground red pepper
 2 garlic cloves, chopped

OLIVE RELISH:
 ½ cup chopped pitted kalamata olives
 3 tablespoons chopped fresh flat-leaf parsley
 1½ tablespoons capers
 1 tablespoon balsamic vinegar
 1 teaspoon chopped fresh oregano
 ¼ teaspoon freshly ground black pepper
 2 garlic cloves, minced

HALIBUT:
 ¼ cup dry white wine
 2 tablespoons finely chopped shallots
 1 tablespoon grated lemon rind
 2 tablespoons fresh lemon juice
 ½ teaspoon crushed red pepper
 ½ teaspoon freshly ground black pepper
 2 garlic cloves, minced
 4 (6-ounce) halibut fillets
 Cooking spray
 ½ teaspoon kosher salt
 Oregano sprigs (optional)

Continued

1. Preheat broiler.

2. To prepare sauce, cut bell pepper in half lengthwise; discard seeds and membranes. Place bell pepper and tomato halves, skin sides up, on a foil-lined baking sheet; flatten peppers with hand. Broil 12 minutes or until peppers blacken. Place peppers and tomatoes in a zip-top plastic bag; seal. Let stand 15 minutes. Peel peppers and tomatoes. Place peppers, tomatoes, almonds, and next 7 ingredients in a food processor, and process until smooth.

3. Reduce oven temperature to 400°.

4. To prepare relish, combine olives and next 6 ingredients in a small bowl.

5. To prepare fish, combine wine and next 6 ingredients in a large zip-top plastic bag. Add fillets to bag; seal and marinate in refrigerator 30 minutes, turning bag occasionally.

6. Remove fillets from bag; discard marinade. Place fillets on a jelly-roll pan coated with cooking spray. Sprinkle fillets with ½ teaspoon salt. Bake at 400° for 15 minutes or until fish flakes easily when tested with a fork or until desired degree of doneness. Serve with romesco sauce and olive relish. Garnish with oregano sprigs, if desired. Yield: 4 servings (serving size: 1 fillet, ¼ cup sauce, and 3 tablespoons relish).

CALORIES 289 (29% from fat); FAT 9.3g (sat 1.2g, mono 4.9g, poly 2.1g); PROTEIN 37.5g; CARB 10.6g; FIBER 1.5g; CHOL 54mg; IRON 2.5mg; SODIUM 738mg; CALC 119mg

---

MAKE AHEAD • FREEZABLE
Lemon Buttermilk Sherbet with Orange-Scented Berries

If you prepare and freeze this sherbet ahead, let it sit at room temperature for 20 minutes to soften a bit before serving. Find more recipes for homemade ice cream beginning on page 261.

SHERBET:
- ½ cup sugar
- 1 cup water
- 2 cups low-fat buttermilk
- 1 cup vanilla low-fat yogurt
- 1 tablespoon grated lemon rind
- 2 tablespoons lemon juice

REMAINING INGREDIENTS:
- 3 tablespoons orange-flavored liqueur (such as Triple Sec)
- 1 teaspoon grated orange rind
- 1½ cups mixed berries (such as raspberries, blueberries, and blackberries)
- 6 mint sprigs

1. To prepare sherbet, combine sugar and 1 cup water in a small saucepan; bring to a boil over medium-high heat. Cook until sugar dissolves, stirring frequently. Transfer syrup to a large bowl; cool. Add buttermilk, yogurt, lemon rind, and juice, stirring with a whisk. Pour mixture into freezer can of an ice-cream freezer; freeze according to manufacturer's instructions. Spoon sherbet into a freezer-safe container; cover and freeze 30 minutes or until firm.

2. Combine liqueur and orange rind in a small bowl; let stand 20 minutes. Serve with sherbet and berries. Garnish with mint. Yield: 6 servings (serving size: ⅔ cup sherbet, ¼ cup berries, 1 teaspoon liqueur mixture, and 1 mint sprig).

CALORIES 182 (7% from fat); FAT 1.4g (sat 0.7g, mono 0.2g, poly 0.2g); PROTEIN 4.8g; CARB 35.8g; FIBER 2.2g; CHOL 6mg; IRON 0.3mg; SODIUM 112mg; CALC 147mg

---

Pineapple-Jalapeño Coleslaw

For milder heat, seed the jalapeño pepper before chopping it.

- ¼ cup pineapple juice
- ¼ cup seasoned rice vinegar
- 3 tablespoons chopped jalapeño pepper
- 1½ tablespoons canola oil
- 1 tablespoon sugar
- 1 teaspoon grated lime rind
- ½ teaspoon kosher salt
- 6 cups thinly sliced napa (Chinese) cabbage
- 2 cups grated peeled jícama
- 1 cup grated peeled carrot
- ¾ cup thinly sliced green onions
- ¼ cup chopped fresh cilantro
- ¼ cup chopped fresh mint

1. Combine first 7 ingredients in a small bowl, stirring with a whisk.

2. Combine cabbage and remaining 5 ingredients in a large bowl. Pour dressing over cabbage mixture; toss gently to coat. Serve immediately. Yield: 8 servings (serving size: 1 cup).

CALORIES 72 (34% from fat); FAT 2.7g (sat 0.2g, mono 1.6g, poly 0.8g); PROTEIN 1.2g; CARB 11.2g; FIBER 3.3g; CHOL 0mg; IRON 0.4mg; SODIUM 139mg; CALC 58mg

---

MAKE AHEAD
Soybean Hummus

In this recipe, Littlewood uses frozen shelled edamame in place of chickpeas to prepare hummus. It's also good as a spread on flatbread for a wrap sandwich or as a dip with cut-up raw vegetables. Add extra flavor to the pita chips by lightly toasting them, then rubbing them with the cut side of a halved raw garlic clove.

- 1 cup frozen, shelled edamame (green soybeans)
- ¼ cup water
- 3 tablespoons olive oil
- 2 tablespoons fresh lemon juice
- 1 teaspoon kosher salt
- ½ teaspoon minced garlic
- ⅛ teaspoon hot pepper sauce
- 2 tablespoons chopped fresh flat-leaf parsley
- 6 (6-inch) pitas, each cut into 8 wedges

1. Combine soybeans and ¼ cup water in a small saucepan; bring to a boil. Reduce heat, and simmer 10 minutes. Drain soybeans.

2. Place soybeans, oil, juice, salt, garlic, and pepper sauce in a food processor; process until smooth. Add parsley, and process until blended. Serve with pita wedges. Yield: 12 servings (serving size: about 1½ tablespoons hummus and 4 pita wedges).

CALORIES 130 (29% from fat); FAT 4.2g (sat 0.5g, mono 2.5g, poly 0.5g); PROTEIN 4.1g; CARB 18.6g; FIBER 1.4g; CHOL 0mg; IRON 1.1mg; SODIUM 324mg; CALC 36mg

Fit Food on the Go

Try these tactics and recipes to pack good nutrition and exercise into a busy schedule.

Chances are you're not training for the Olympics, but if you exercise regularly, take a cue from elite and professional athletes regarding how to eat to gain the most from every workout. Sports nutritionists encourage the strategies on page 220 for eating before and after exercise depending on when—morning, noon, or after work—you exercise. Here are some recipes to get you started.

STAFF FAVORITE • QUICK & EASY
Fajita Turkey Burgers

Put together these turkey burgers for a speedy supper after a late-afternoon or early-evening workout. Use prechopped onion and bell pepper, if you prefer, so the burgers come together even more quickly. Garnish with fresh lettuce, tomato, and red onion, if desired.

¼   cup bottled tomatillo salsa
2   tablespoons chopped avocado
1   tablespoon chopped fresh cilantro
2   (1-ounce) slices white bread
Cooking spray
½   cup finely chopped onion
½   cup finely chopped red bell pepper
½   cup finely chopped green bell pepper
2   teaspoons fajita seasoning, divided
¼   teaspoon salt, divided
1   tablespoon tomato paste
1   pound ground turkey
1   egg white, lightly beaten
4   (1½-ounce) whole wheat hamburger buns, toasted

1. Combine first 3 ingredients; set aside.
2. Place bread in a food processor; pulse 10 times or until crumbs measure 1 cup.
3. Heat a large nonstick skillet over medium-high heat. Coat pan with cooking spray. Add onion and bell peppers; sauté 5 minutes or until tender. Stir in ½ teaspoon fajita seasoning and ⅛ teaspoon salt. Cool.

4. Combine breadcrumbs, onion mixture, 1½ teaspoons fajita seasoning, ⅛ teaspoon salt, tomato paste, turkey, and egg white in a large bowl. Using damp hands, divide turkey mixture into 4 equal portions, shaping each into a ¾-inch-thick patty. Heat pan over medium heat. Recoat pan with cooking spray. Add patties; cook 4 minutes on each side or until done. Place 1 patty on bottom half of each bun. Top each serving with 1½ tablespoons salsa mixture; top with remaining halves of buns. Yield: 4 servings (serving size: 1 burger).

CALORIES 349 (30% from fat); FAT 11.5g (sat 3.1g, mono 7g, poly 1.1g); PROTEIN 30.4g; CARB 34.5g; FIBER 4.6g; CHOL 71mg; IRON 2.7mg; SODIUM 876mg; CALC 110mg

QUICK & EASY • MAKE AHEAD
Fruit and Yogurt Shake

Sip this thick drink before or immediately after a morning workout.

1   cup frozen sweet cherries
1   cup plain yogurt
1   cup pomegranate cherry juice (such as POM)
1   (8-ounce) can crushed pineapple in juice, drained
1   banana, peeled and sliced crosswise

1. Place all ingredients in a blender; puree until smooth. Yield: 4 servings (serving size: about 1 cup).

CALORIES 142 (13% from fat); FAT 2.1g (sat 1.3g, mono 0.6g, poly 0.1g); PROTEIN 3g; CARB 28g; FIBER 2g; CHOL 8mg; IRON 0.3mg; SODIUM 38mg; CALC 95mg

MAKE AHEAD
Cheddar-Parmesan Biscotti

Keep a stash of these savory biscotti in your desk drawer for a quick snack. They'd also be good with soup or chili. They'll keep up to a week stored in an airtight container.

2¾   cups flour (about 12⅓ ounces)
½   cup (2 ounces) extrasharp reduced-fat shredded Cheddar cheese
⅓   cup (about 1½ ounces) freshly grated Parmesan cheese
¼   cup sun-dried tomato pieces
3   tablespoons yellow cornmeal
3   tablespoons pine nuts, toasted
2   teaspoons baking powder
¾   teaspoon salt
½   teaspoon dried basil
⅓   cup fat-free milk
1   tablespoon olive oil
2   large eggs, lightly beaten
1   large egg white, lightly beaten
Cooking spray

1. Preheat oven to 350°.
2. Lightly spoon flour into dry measuring cups; level with a knife. Combine flour, cheese, and next 7 ingredients in a bowl.
3. Combine milk, oil, eggs, and egg white; stir with a whisk. Add milk mixture to flour mixture, stirring until well blended. (Dough will be crumbly and slightly dry.)
4. Turn dough out onto a lightly floured surface; knead 7 times. Divide dough in half. Shape each portion into an 8-inch-long roll. Place rolls, 6 inches apart, on a baking sheet coated with cooking spray; flatten to 1-inch thickness. Bake at 350° for 25 minutes. Remove from baking sheet; cool 10 minutes on a wire rack.
5. Reduce oven temperature to 325°.
6. Cut each roll diagonally into 12 (½-inch) slices; stand slices upright on baking sheet. Bake at 325° for 25 minutes (cookies will be slightly soft in center but will harden as they cool). Remove from baking sheet; cool completely on wire rack. Yield: 24 servings (serving size: 1 biscotto).

CALORIES 91 (27% from fat); FAT 2.7g (sat 0.8g, mono 0.9g, poly 0.6g); PROTEIN 3.6g; CARB 12.8g; FIBER 0.5g; CHOL 20mg; IRON 1mg; SODIUM 173mg; CALC 62mg

Morning Wake-Up

Challenge: Fit in exercise and breakfast before work.

Strategy: No matter what time of day you exercise, your muscles need carbohydrates as fuel, says University of Pittsburgh sports nutritionist Leslie Bonci, R.D., the dietitian Pittsburgh Steelers football players seek for advice. And because you've had nothing to eat all night, your body needs fuel before exercising in the morning. Make it something "that's fairly easily digested" so that it doesn't feel heavy in the stomach, says Bonci. She suggests eating a small carbohydrate-rich snack about an hour before you work out.

If you're up too early for that, Seattle sports nutritionist and author Susan Kleiner, Ph.D., suggests drinking a glass of hot cocoa at bedtime the night before. That way, your muscles will have stored a little extra fuel for the morning.

Best food choices: "I'd advise you to divide your breakfast calorie allotment so you have something light, primarily a carbohydrate that will fuel your body for exercise first, and then have a more substantial breakfast after exercise," says Bonci. All you need before exercise is 100 to 200 calories, mostly carbohydrates with a little protein and fat, such as our Fruit and Yogurt Shake (recipe on page 219). That's enough to see you through a workout that lasts up to an hour. After exercising, have a Breakfast Fig and Nut "Cookie" (recipe on page 221) or a couple of Warmed Stuffed Peaches (recipe on page 221) with a glass of fat-free milk. If your morning workout is vigorous, you may also want something right after exercising. "There is a lot of research suggesting that after exercise simple carbs facilitate the body's ability to recover more effectively," Bonci explains. Have a handful of whole-grain toasted oat cereal (such as Cheerios), a sports drink, or a glass of orange juice. Once you are back at home or the office, sit down to a small, satisfying breakfast.

Lunchtime Workout

Challenge: Have enough energy to exercise before you eat lunch and not become ravenous afterward.

Strategy: You've eaten breakfast a few hours earlier, and the body has those nutrients digested, absorbed, and ready to be used, says Kleiner, though you could have a light snack with protein and carbohydrates before you work out. And you should plan to eat something immediately after. "Don't blow 45 minutes showering and changing before eating," says Kleiner, or you're more likely to overeat at lunch. "You need to have something in your gym bag to eat right away. Eating immediately after working out helps maximize your exercise by increasing calorie burn and building more muscle." Follow that with a meal that's a good balance of carbs and protein.

Best food choices: Chocolate milk is great post-workout fuel. "One study compared chocolate milk with a high-end recovery sports drink, and they were both equally effective," says Kleiner. A carton of yogurt works, too. Or have some crackers with that and a piece of fruit, she adds. "This is also the time to indulge a sweet tooth," Kleiner says, because the sugar will help muscles to recover. So stop by the coffeehouse for a skim-milk latte with a shot of flavored syrup. Once you're back at work, dig into a healthful lunch with complex carbs, protein, and healthy fats, like our Blue Cheese and Beef Roll-Ups (recipe on page 222).

After-Work Workout

Challenge: Exercising when you're beginning to get hungry for dinner.

Strategy: Since lunch was four or five hours ago, "eating something in the afternoon is critical," says Bonci. "Otherwise, you may overshoot your calorie allotment at dinner."

Best food choices: String cheese with whole wheat crackers or half a Peanut Butter–Plus Sandwich (recipe on page 222) are good afternoon snacks, says Bonci. Or try our Cheddar-Parmesan Biscotti (recipe on page 219) with a milk chaser. If you don't have time for a snack before exercising, Kleiner suggests nibbling a little something afterward while preparing dinner. A handful of nuts, for example, will quell your hunger enough that you won't overeat at supper. For dinner, prepare dishes with lean protein and complex carbs, like our Fajita Turkey Burgers (recipe on page 219) or grilled fish with rice and a tossed green salad.

Smart Snacks

Stock up on foods that boast high-quality protein and complex carbohydrates and are low in fat. If you keep the following items in the cupboard and refrigerator, it will be easier to eat well before and after exercise:

- Peanut butter
- Hard-cooked eggs
- String cheese
- Bananas
- Frozen whole-grain waffles
- Low-fat chocolate milk
- Whole-grain cereal
- Whole wheat crackers
- Graham crackers
- Fat-free or 1% low-fat milk
- Low-fat yogurt
- Dried fruit
- Fig cookies
- Sports bars
- Almonds and other nuts

Breakfast Fig and Nut "Cookies"

These oversized cookies are more like muffin tops, but calling them cookies makes them seem a bit more indulgent. Chock-full of exercise-friendly ingredients like dried fruit and nuts, they're ideal with a glass of fat-free milk for breakfast after a morning workout.

- ¾ cup packed brown sugar
- ¼ cup butter, melted
- 2 large eggs, lightly beaten
- ¼ cup finely chopped dried figs
- ¼ cup sweetened dried cranberries
- 1 teaspoon vanilla extract
- 1 cup all-purpose flour (about 4½ ounces)
- ½ cup whole wheat flour (about 2⅓ ounces)
- ½ cup unprocessed bran (about 1 ounce)
- ½ teaspoon baking soda
- ¼ teaspoon ground cinnamon
- ¼ teaspoon ground allspice
- ¼ cup sliced almonds
- 2 teaspoons granulated sugar

1. Preheat oven to 350°.
2. Combine first 3 ingredients in a large bowl. Stir in figs, cranberries, and vanilla.
3. Lightly spoon flours into dry measuring cups; level with a knife. Combine flours, bran, and next 3 ingredients, stirring with a whisk. Add flour mixture to egg mixture, stirring just until moist. Gently fold in almonds.
4. Drop by level ¼ cup measures 4 inches apart on 2 baking sheets lined with parchment paper. Sprinkle evenly with granulated sugar. Bake at 350° for 12 minutes or until almost set. Cool 2 minutes on pans. Remove from pans; cool completely on wire racks. Yield: 10 servings (serving size: 1 "cookie").

CALORIES 211 (31% from fat); FAT 7.1g (sat 3.3g, mono 2.4g, poly 0.8g); PROTEIN 4.5g; CARB 33.2g; FIBER 3.4g; CHOL 54mg; IRON 1.8mg; SODIUM 115mg; CALC 37mg

Orange Quinoa Salad

With protein-rich quinoa, dried fruit, and almonds, this salad is a good snack before or after exercise and a nice side dish with grilled pork. Or increase the serving size to ¾ cup and add feta cheese or shredded rotisserie chicken to make it a main dish.

DRESSING:
- ¼ cup fresh orange juice
- 2 tablespoons extravirgin olive oil
- 1½ tablespoons low-fat buttermilk
- 2 teaspoons honey
- ½ teaspoon salt
- ⅛ teaspoon freshly ground black pepper

SALAD:
- 1⅓ cups uncooked quinoa
- 2¾ cups water
- ½ teaspoon salt
- 1 cup thinly sliced green onions
- 1 cup sweetened dried cranberries
- ⅓ cup chopped fresh parsley
- 3 tablespoons sliced almonds, toasted

1. To prepare dressing, combine first 6 ingredients in a small bowl; stir with a whisk until well blended.
2. To prepare salad, place quinoa in a large nonstick skillet; cook 4 minutes over medium heat, stirring frequently. Place quinoa in a fine sieve; place sieve in a large bowl. Cover quinoa with water. Using your hands, rub grains together 30 seconds; rinse and drain. Repeat procedure twice. Drain well.
3. Combine quinoa, 2¾ cups water, and ½ teaspoon salt in a large saucepan; bring to a boil. Cover and reduce heat; simmer 20 minutes or until liquid is absorbed. Remove from heat, and cool to room temperature. Stir in dressing, onions, and remaining ingredients. Cover and chill. Yield: 10 servings (serving size: about ½ cup).

CALORIES 170 (28% from fat); FAT 5.2g (sat 0.6g, mono 3.1g, poly 1.1g); PROTEIN 3.5g; CARB 28.8g; FIBER 2.7g; CHOL 0mg; IRON 2.4mg; SODIUM 245mg; CALC 34mg

Sunday Breakfast Menu
serves 8

Brown the ham, make the quick glaze, and pop the bread in the toaster while the peaches bake.

Warmed Stuffed Peaches

Glazed ham*

Whole wheat toast

*Heat a large skillet over medium-high heat. Coat pan with cooking spray. Add 2 (4-ounce) slices 33%-less-sodium ham to pan; cook 3 minutes on each side or until browned. Repeat procedure in batches to yield 8 slices. Combine ¼ cup apricot jam, ¼ cup fat-free, less-sodium chicken broth, and 2 teaspoons Dijon mustard, stirring well with a whisk. Add jam mixture to pan. Cook 2 minutes or until slightly thick. Dredge ham slices in glaze.

Warmed Stuffed Peaches

You can prepare and refrigerate the stuffing before you go to bed, then assemble and bake the peaches in the morning. Enjoy one peach half as a pre- or post-workout snack. Or have two stuffed peach halves with an eight-ounce glass of skim milk or one ounce of string cheese for breakfast. The peach halves also are a nice addition to a brunch buffet.

- 4 peaches, halved and pitted
- ½ cup dried tropical mixed fruit (such as Sunkist brand)
- ¼ cup slivered almonds, toasted
- 2 tablespoons graham cracker crumbs
- 2 tablespoons brown sugar
- ¼ teaspoon ground allspice
- 1 (12-ounce) can peach nectar
- ½ cup vanilla yogurt

1. Preheat oven to 350°.
2. Scoop out peach pulp to form a 2-inch circle in center of each half. Finely chop pulp. Combine pulp, dried fruit, and next 4 ingredients. Divide pulp mixture evenly among peach halves. Place stuffed peach halves in an 11 x 7–inch
Continued

baking dish. Add nectar to dish. Bake at 350° for 40 minutes or until peaches are tender. Drizzle peach halves evenly with liquid from dish. Top evenly with yogurt. Yield: 8 servings (serving size: 1 peach half and 1 tablespoon yogurt).

CALORIES 134 (17% from fat); FAT 2.5g (sat 0.7g, mono 1.3g, poly 0.5g); PROTEIN 2.2g; CARB 27g; FIBER 2.1g; CHOL 2mg; IRON 0.5mg; SODIUM 30mg; CALC 39mg

QUICK & EASY • MAKE AHEAD

Peanut Butter–Plus Sandwiches

Half a sandwich makes a great post-exercise snack. Or enjoy a whole sandwich for lunch.

    3 tablespoons creamy peanut butter
    2 tablespoons honey
    1 cup mashed banana (about 1 large)
    3 tablespoons golden raisins
    1 tablespoon roasted salted sunflower seed kernels
    8 (1-ounce) slices whole wheat bread

1. Combine peanut butter and honey in a small microwave-safe bowl. Microwave at HIGH 20 seconds. Stir in banana, raisins, and sunflower seeds. Spread about ¼ cup peanut butter mixture on each of 4 bread slices. Top with remaining bread slices. Yield: 8 servings (serving size: ½ sandwich).

CALORIES 152 (29% from fat); FAT 4.9g (sat 1g, mono 2g, poly 1.5g); PROTEIN 4.8g; CARB 25.3g; FIBER 3g; CHOL 0mg; IRON 1.2mg; SODIUM 181mg; CALC 26mg

Drink Up

The American College of Sports Medicine recommends consuming 16 ounces of fluid two hours before exercise and an additional 8 ounces 20 minutes before working out. For vigorous workouts, sip 4 to 8 ounces every 20 minutes during exercise. And drink 18 to 24 ounces of fluid within 30 minutes after your workout.

QUICK & EASY • MAKE AHEAD

Blue Cheese and Beef Roll-Ups

Precut beef stir-fry strips used for the filling in this wrap add a dose of post-workout iron without the salt of deli roast beef. Combine the mayonnaise mixture and cook the beef the night before; refrigerate each separately and assemble the sandwich in the morning for a satisfying lunch after a midday workout.

    ⅓ cup fat-free mayonnaise
    2 tablespoons crumbled blue cheese
    ½ teaspoon prepared horseradish
    ¼ teaspoon freshly ground black pepper, divided
       Cooking spray
    ½ pound round tip steak strips
    ⅛ teaspoon salt
    4 cups finely chopped romaine lettuce
    1 cup halved grape tomatoes
    ¼ cup thinly sliced red onion
    4 (10-inch) reduced-fat flour tortillas

1. Combine mayonnaise, blue cheese, horseradish, and ⅛ teaspoon black pepper in a small bowl; cover and refrigerate 30 minutes.
2. Heat a large nonstick skillet over medium-high heat. Coat pan with cooking spray. Sprinkle steak with salt and ⅛ teaspoon pepper. Add steak to pan; sauté 4 minutes or until desired degree of doneness. Let stand 5 minutes; cut into 1-inch pieces.
3. Combine lettuce, tomatoes, and onion in a bowl. Spread about 2 tablespoons mayonnaise mixture evenly over each tortilla. Divide steak and lettuce mixture evenly among tortillas; roll up. Yield: 4 servings (serving size: 1 wrap).

CALORIES 281 (16% from fat); FAT 5.1g (sat 1.8g, mono 1.8g, poly 0.8g); PROTEIN 20.4g; CARB 37.9g; FIBER 5.3g; CHOL 36mg; IRON 2.1mg; SODIUM 763mg; CALC 69mg

Bastille Day Déjeuner

On July 14, savor Gallic flavors at lunch and celebrate France's Fête Nationale.

Family-Style Lunch Menu
serves 6

Sparkling Cassis Aperitif

French-Style Shrimp Salad

French bread

Vanilla Crème with Fresh Berry Jam

QUICK & EASY

Sparkling Cassis Aperitif

Crème de cassis (krehm deuh kah-SEES) is a liqueur made with black currant syrup.

    4 cups currant juice
    ¾ cup crème de cassis (black currant–flavored liqueur)
    2 tablespoons fresh lemon juice
    2 cups chilled sparkling water
    1 (750-milliliter) bottle chilled Champagne
    1 cup fresh blackberries

1. Combine first 3 ingredients in a large pitcher. Chill until ready to serve.
2. Before serving, add sparkling water and Champagne to currant mixture; stir well. Divide blackberries evenly among 9 glasses. Top each serving with about 1 cup Champagne mixture. Serve immediately. Yield: 9 servings.

CALORIES 199 (0% from fat); FAT 0.1g (sat 0g, mono 0g, poly 0g); PROTEIN 0.7g; CARB 24.5g; FIBER 0.8g; CHOL 0mg; IRON 0.4mg; SODIUM 6mg; CALC 29mg

French-Style Shrimp Salad

(pictured on page 241)

Assemble this salad in individual servings, or arrange it on a platter and serve family style. Niçoise olives are a small purplish-black variety; you can substitute kalamata. Serve with crusty French bread. This dish is a twist on the classic salade niçoise with tuna.

VINAIGRETTE:

- 6 garlic cloves, halved
- ⅔ cup fat-free, less-sodium chicken broth
- ¼ cup chopped fresh basil
- ¼ cup chopped fresh parsley
- 2 tablespoons fresh lemon juice
- 2 tablespoons tarragon vinegar
- 2 tablespoons extravirgin olive oil
- 2 teaspoons Dijon mustard
- ½ teaspoon freshly ground black pepper

SALAD:

- 2 pounds peeled and deveined large shrimp
- 12 small red potatoes (about ¾ pound)
- ½ pound haricots verts
- Cooking spray
- 5 cups gourmet salad greens
- 4 cups torn romaine lettuce
- 1 cup (¼-inch-thick) slices red bell pepper (about 1 medium)
- 3 tomatoes, each cut into 6 wedges
- 1 (14-ounce) can quartered artichoke hearts, drained
- 3 hard-cooked large eggs, each sliced into quarters
- ½ cup niçoise olives
- 2 tablespoons capers

1. To prepare vinaigrette, drop garlic through food chute with food processor on; process until minced. Add broth and next 7 ingredients; process until well blended.

2. To prepare salad, combine 2 table-spoons vinaigrette and shrimp in a large zip-top plastic bag; seal. Marinate in refrigerator 20 minutes, turning bag occasionally.

3. Place potatoes in a large saucepan; cover with water. Bring to a boil; cook

8 minutes. Add haricots verts to pan; cook 2 minutes or until haricots verts are crisp-tender and potatoes are tender. Drain and rinse with cold water; drain. Cut potatoes into ¼-inch-thick slices. Set aside.

4. Heat a large grill pan over medium-high heat. Coat pan with cooking spray. Remove shrimp from bag, and discard marinade. Add shrimp to pan. Cook 3 minutes on each side or until shrimp are done.

5. Combine potatoes, haricots verts, greens, and next 4 ingredients in a large bowl. Add remaining vinaigrette, tossing gently to coat. Place lettuce mixture on a serving platter. Arrange shrimp and eggs over lettuce mixture; sprinkle with olives and capers. Serve immediately. Yield: 6 servings (serving size: about 2½ cups salad mixture, 5 ounces shrimp, 2 pieces egg, 4 teaspoons olives, and 1 teaspoon capers).

CALORIES 366 (30% from fat); FAT 12g (sat 2.2g, mono 6g, poly 2.2g); PROTEIN 39.3g; CARB 26.1g; FIBER 6.4g; CHOL 336mg; IRON 6.7mg; SODIUM 798mg; CALC 179mg

Vanilla Crème with Fresh Berry Jam

Prepare the jam and custard up to a day ahead, and refrigerate separately. Assemble the desserts before serving. The jam is also good with toast, pancakes, or pound cake.

JAM:

- ⅓ cup water
- 3 tablespoons sugar
- 2 cups coarsely chopped strawberries, divided

CRÈME:

- 2 teaspoons unflavored gelatin
- 1¼ cups whole milk
- 1 (6-inch) piece vanilla bean, split lengthwise
- 6 tablespoons sugar
- 2 cups buttermilk
- Mint sprigs (optional)

1. To prepare jam, combine ⅓ cup water and 3 tablespoons sugar in a small saucepan over medium heat. Cook 3

minutes or until sugar dissolves. Add 1 cup chopped strawberries, and bring to a boil. Reduce heat, and simmer 10 minutes or until mixture is syrupy, mashing strawberries with a fork. Remove from heat, and stir in 1 cup chopped strawberries. Pour into a bowl, and cool completely. Cover and chill.

2. To prepare crème, sprinkle gelatin over whole milk in a small saucepan; let stand 10 minutes. Scrape seeds from vanilla bean, and add seeds and bean to milk mixture. Cook milk mixture over medium-low heat 10 minutes or until gelatin dissolves, stirring constantly with a whisk. Increase heat to medium, and add 6 tablespoons sugar, stirring until sugar dissolves. Remove from heat. Stir in buttermilk. Remove and discard vanilla bean. Spoon about ½ cup buttermilk mixture into each of 6 small glasses. Cover and chill 6 hours or until set. Top each serving with 3 tablespoons berry jam. Garnish with mint sprigs, if desired. Yield: 6 servings.

CALORIES 178 (23% from fat); FAT 4.6g (sat 2.6g, mono 0.4g, poly 0.3g); PROTEIN 5.5g; CARB 30g; FIBER 2.7g; CHOL 17mg; IRON 0.3mg; SODIUM 119mg; CALC 69mg

---

Lunch in Provence Menu
(recipes on page 224)
serves 6

Oven-Poached Halibut Provençale

Herbed Potato Salad

Haricots Verts with Warm Shallot Vinaigrette

Vanilla Crème with Fresh Berry Jam (recipe at left)

WINE NOTE: In Coastal Provence, seafood dishes like this halibut are invariably spiked with a generous amount of garlic, herbes de Provence, and olive oil, then accompanied by all sorts of vegetables. Such vivid flavors would significantly diminish a delicate white wine. That's why Provençal cooks often serve lunches like this with a snappy, bold, fruity, chilled dry rosé. A terrific bone-dry French rosé: Red Bicyclette ($8).

Oven-Poached Halibut Provençale

Herbes de Provence (EHRB duh proh-VAWNS) is a fragrant blend of dried herbs (basil, lavender, marjoram, rosemary, sage, thyme, summer savory, and fennel seed) commonly used in southern French cooking. The mixture is also good on lamb, beef, and poultry.

1 tablespoon olive oil
3 garlic cloves, minced
2 cups chopped fennel bulb
1½ cups chopped onion
1 teaspoon salt, divided
4 cups diced tomato
⅓ cup chopped fresh basil
⅓ cup chopped fresh flat-leaf parsley
6 (6-ounce) halibut fillets
1 cup dry white wine
⅓ cup dry breadcrumbs
2 tablespoons chopped pitted kalamata olives
1 teaspoon dried herbes de Provence
1 teaspoon olive oil
½ teaspoon coarsely ground black pepper
Flat-leaf parsley sprigs (optional)

1. Preheat oven to 450°.
2. Heat 1 tablespoon oil in a large non-stick skillet over medium-high heat. Add garlic; sauté 30 seconds. Add fennel, onion, and ½ teaspoon salt; sauté 8 minutes or until lightly browned. Stir in tomato; cook 2 minutes. Remove from heat; stir in basil and chopped parsley.
3. Spoon half of tomato mixture into a 13 x 9–inch baking dish. Place fillets over tomato mixture. Pour wine into dish; sprinkle fillets with ¼ teaspoon salt. Spoon remaining tomato mixture over fillets. Bake at 450° for 15 minutes or until fish flakes easily when tested with a fork or until desired degree of doneness.
4. Preheat broiler.
5. Combine breadcrumbs, next 4 ingredients, and ¼ teaspoon salt in a small bowl. Sprinkle breadcrumb mixture over fillets. Broil 5 minutes or until lightly browned. Serve immediately. Garnish with parsley sprigs, if desired. Yield: 6 servings (serving size: 1 fillet and about ½ cup tomato mixture).

CALORIES 315 (26% from fat); FAT 9g (sat 1.3g, mono 4.6g, poly 2g); PROTEIN 38.8g; CARB 19.3g; FIBER 4.4g; CHOL 54mg; IRON 3.1mg; SODIUM 653mg; CALC 158mg

Herbed Potato Salad

White wine, tarragon, and whole-grain mustard lend this potato salad traditional French flavor. Prepare it up to a day ahead.

3 pounds Yukon gold potatoes
1 cup dry white wine
3 tablespoons white wine vinegar
2 tablespoons extravirgin olive oil
1 tablespoon whole-grain Dijon mustard
¾ teaspoon salt
¾ teaspoon freshly ground black pepper
2 garlic cloves, minced
½ cup thinly sliced chives
2 tablespoons chopped fresh parsley
1 teaspoon chopped fresh tarragon

1. Place potatoes in a large saucepan; cover with water. Bring to a boil. Reduce heat, and simmer 20 minutes or until tender. Drain and cool 10 minutes. Cut each potato in half lengthwise. Cut each half crosswise into ½-inch-thick slices. Place potato slices in a large bowl.
2. Place wine in a small saucepan over medium-high heat; bring to a boil. Cook until reduced to ½ cup (about 6 minutes). Transfer wine to a bowl. Add vinegar and next 5 ingredients; stir with a whisk until well combined. Drizzle wine mixture over potatoes; sprinkle with chives, parsley, and tarragon. Toss gently to combine. Serve salad warm or chilled. Yield: 6 servings (serving size: about 1 cup).

CALORIES 239 (18% from fat); FAT 4.7g (sat 0.7g, mono 3.6g, poly 0.4g); PROTEIN 6.2g; CARB 42.3g; FIBER 3g; CHOL 0mg; IRON 2.3mg; SODIUM 374mg; CALC 14mg

Haricots Verts with Warm Shallot Vinaigrette

Haricots verts (ah-ree-koh VEHR) is French for "green beans." These beans are small, slender, and vivid green. If you can't find haricots verts, substitute regular green beans and increase the cooking time to five minutes.

1½ pounds haricots verts
1 tablespoon olive oil
½ cup chopped shallots (about 2 large)
½ cup red wine vinegar
½ teaspoon black pepper
¼ teaspoon salt

1. Place haricots verts in a large saucepan of boiling water; cook 3 minutes or until crisp-tender. Drain and plunge beans into ice water; drain.
2. Heat oil in a large nonstick skillet over medium-high heat. Add shallots; sauté 4 minutes or until golden. Stir in vinegar; cook 5 minutes or until mixture thickens slightly. Add haricots verts, pepper, and salt to pan; sauté 2 minutes or until beans are thoroughly heated. Serve warm or at room temperature. Yield: 6 servings (serving size: about 1⅓ cups).

CALORIES 65 (33% from fat); FAT 2.4g (sat 0.3g, mono 0.4g, poly 1.7g); PROTEIN 2.4g; CARB 10.5g; FIBER 4g; CHOL 0mg; IRON 1.4mg; SODIUM 107mg; CALC 48mg

Mexican Black Bean Sausage Chili,
page 45

Asian Coleslaw,
page 43

Café au Lait Chiffon Pie, page 21

Crunchy Shrimp with Toasted Couscous and Ginger-Orange Sauce, page 41

Pesto Chicken Salad Sandwiches,
page 60

Lentil and Spinach Soup with Roasted
Red Pepper and Pomegranate Molasses,
page 82

Three-Cheese Chicken Penne Florentine,
page 76

Classic Meat Loaf, page 92

Colorful Quick Quinoa Grecian Salad,
page 111

Spanish-Style Shrimp with Garlic,
page 65

Cheesecake with Fresh Strawberry Sauce,
page 112

Garlic Pork with Tomato and Basil, page 114

Marinated Vegetable Salad with Queso Fresco, page 99

Pineapple Teriyaki Salmon, page 151

Edamame Dip, page 151

Linguine with Asparagus,
Parmesan, and Bacon, page 158

Citrus Waffles with Marmalade
Compote, page 150

Spiced Chicken Skewers, page 176

Pulled Chicken Sandwiches,
page 172

238

Sweet Corn and Parmesan Flans, page 177

Cornmeal-Crusted Catfish, page 195

Velvety Fudge Pudding, page 213

Open-Faced Panini with Goat Cheese, Roasted Peppers, and Spicy Olive Topping, page 216 and Mushroom Salad with Truffle Oil and Parmigiano-Reggiano, page 217

French-Style Shrimp Salad, page 223

Flank Steak with Grilled Mango and
Watermelon Chutney, page 260

Jasmine Rice-Stuffed Peppers,
page 299

Chipotle Chicken Taco Salad,
page 279

Basic Grilled Steak, page 287

244

Sweet Pea Risotto with Corn Broth,
page 295

245

Chicken Poblano Casserole,
page 317

Poppy Seed Fruited Slaw, page 337

246

Pepperoni Pizza, page 336

Beef Carnitas Tacos,
page 325

Caramel Apple Upside-Down Cake,
page 315

Classic Scones,
page 351

Grilled Quail with White
Polenta, page 374

Bloody Mary,
page 342

Classic Beef Pot Roast,
page 363

Marsala-Glazed Ham,
page 387

Whole Wheat Bread with Caraway and
Anise, page 396

Harvest Pie, page 398

Fontina and Mascarpone Baked
Pasta, page 388

Roasted Beet, Fennel, and Walnut
Salad, page 427

Garlicky Roasted Potatoes with
Herbs, page 433

Barbecue-Rubbed Pork Loin
with Raisin-Mustard Chutney,
page 428

Orange Mini Bundt Cakes,
page 455

All-American Accompaniments

Traditional or modern, these dishes will be the main attractions at your next picnic, barbecue, or get-together.

When it comes to a summer gathering, certain dishes are standbys. Baked beans and a variety of salads (macaroni, three-bean, potato, and fruit) are longtime favorites because of their predictable broad appeal and ease of preparation. They're also best made ahead so the flavors can develop, and they hold well.

Here, we offer traditional and updated versions of each of these dishes. All are examples of culinary Americana—a bonus if you're preparing them to accompany burgers or steaks for a Fourth of July celebration.

Amber Ale Baked Beans

Just a little bacon gives a lot of flavor to this classic barbecue side, especially when you add it to sweet caramelized onions and a bottle of slightly fruity and malty ale.

- 2 cups water
- 4 (16-ounce) cans low-sodium pinto beans, rinsed and drained
- 1 (14-ounce) can fat-free, less-sodium chicken broth
- 2 bay leaves
- 1 yellow onion, peeled and quartered
- 2 bacon slices (uncooked), chopped
- 2 cups chopped yellow onion (about 2 medium)
- 1 tablespoon minced garlic
- 2 teaspoons chili powder
- ¾ cup no salt–added ketchup
- ⅓ cup packed brown sugar
- 3 tablespoons Dijon mustard
- 2 tablespoons Worcestershire sauce
- ¼ teaspoon freshly ground black pepper
- 1 (12-ounce) bottle amber ale (such as Redhook)

Cooking spray

1. Combine first 5 ingredients in a Dutch oven; bring to a boil. Reduce heat, and simmer 15 minutes. Drain in a colander over a large bowl, reserving ½ cup cooking liquid. Discard onion and bay leaves.

2. Preheat oven to 300°.

3. Cook bacon in a large nonstick skillet over medium heat until crisp. Remove bacon from pan, reserving 1 tablespoon drippings in pan; set bacon aside. Add chopped onion to drippings in pan; cook 10 minutes or until golden brown and caramelized, stirring frequently. Add garlic and chili powder to pan; cook 1 minute, stirring frequently. Add ½ cup reserved cooking liquid, ketchup, and next 5 ingredients to pan; bring to a boil. Add beans and bacon. Reduce heat, and simmer 10 minutes or until slightly thick. Transfer to a 13 x 9–inch baking dish coated with cooking spray. Bake at 300° for 45 minutes or until thick. Yield: 9 servings (serving size: ⅔ cup).

CALORIES 276 (14% from fat); FAT 4.3g (sat 1.3g, mono 1.7g, poly 0.6g); PROTEIN 11.5g; CARB 46.1g; FIBER 10.4g; CHOL 7mg; IRON 3.3mg; SODIUM 558mg; CALC 90mg

Honey-Chipotle Baked Beans

Dress up canned baked beans with flavor and richness—and minimal added fat—with this modern quick and simple dish. Since the sodium is high, use organic canned beans to keep sodium levels in check.

Cooking spray
- ½ cup minced shallots (about 5 ounces)
- 1 tablespoon ground cumin
- 1 tablespoon minced garlic
- ½ cup tomato puree
- 1 tablespoon canola oil
- ¼ cup honey
- ¼ cup cider vinegar
- 2 tablespoons molasses
- 1 tablespoon Worcestershire sauce
- ¼ teaspoon salt
- 2 chipotle chiles, canned in adobo sauce, seeded and chopped
- 2 (28-ounce) cans baked beans

1. Preheat oven to 300°.

2. Heat a large nonstick skillet over medium-high heat. Coat pan with cooking spray. Add shallots; sauté 4 minutes or until golden. Add cumin and garlic; sauté 1 minute. Add tomato puree and oil, and cook 2 minutes or until thick, stirring constantly. Add honey and next 5 ingredients. Reduce heat; simmer 10 minutes, stirring occasionally.

3. Combine beans and shallot mixture in a 2-quart baking dish. Bake at 300° for 1 hour or until thick and bubbly. Yield: 8 servings (serving size: ¾ cup).

CALORIES 286 (7% from fat); FAT 2.2g (sat 0.1g, mono 1.2g, poly 0.6g); PROTEIN 8.3g; CARB 54g; FIBER 9.9g; CHOL 0mg; IRON 2mg; SODIUM 709mg; CALC 88mg

All-American Potato Salad

Dressing the hot potatoes with a splash of vinegar ensures this traditional salad has flavor throughout. Sweet red bell peppers and sugar snap peas lend color and improve the nutritional profile. This dish can be made eight hours ahead and chilled.

- 3 pounds red potatoes (or baking potatoes), cut into ¾-inch pieces
- 8 teaspoons white wine vinegar, divided
- 3 hard-cooked large eggs
- ¼ cup reduced-fat mayonnaise
- ¼ cup reduced-fat sour cream
- ¼ cup buttermilk
- 3 tablespoons prepared mustard
- 1 teaspoon freshly ground black pepper
- ½ teaspoon kosher salt
- ⅔ cup chopped red onion
- ⅔ cup chopped red bell pepper
- ⅔ cup chopped sweet pickles
- ½ cup thinly sliced green onions (about 2 bunches)
- 6 ounces sugar snap peas, trimmed, blanched, and cut into ¾-inch pieces (about 2 cups)

1. Place potatoes in a large saucepan; cover with water. Bring to a boil. Reduce heat, and simmer 12 minutes or until tender; drain. Place potatoes in a large bowl. Add 2 tablespoons vinegar, and toss gently. Cool completely.

2. Chop egg whites (reserve yolks for another use); set aside.

3. Combine 2 teaspoons vinegar, mayonnaise, and next 5 ingredients in a small bowl; stir with a whisk. Add vinegar mixture, egg whites, onion, and remaining ingredients to potato mixture, stirring gently to coat. Yield: 10 servings (serving size: 1 cup).

CALORIES 169 (11% from fat); FAT 2.1g (sat 0.8g, mono 0.6g, poly 0.6g); PROTEIN 5.2g; CARB 33.1g; FIBER 3.4g; CHOL 3mg; IRON 1.5mg; SODIUM 334mg; CALC 43mg

Roasted Potato Salad with Mustard Dressing

This tangy side dish with sweet onions and honey pairs beautifully with burgers or steak. It's best chilled, but can stay at room temperature for up to two hours. You can also use sweet-hot mustard in place of the Dijon and honey for a zesty flavor.

- 3 pounds small red potatoes, cut into 1-inch pieces
- 1 tablespoon olive oil
- 2 teaspoons freshly ground black pepper
- ½ teaspoon kosher salt
- 2 bacon slices (uncooked), chopped
- 2 cups diced Vidalia or other sweet onion (about 2 medium)
- 2 garlic cloves, minced
- 3 tablespoons Dijon mustard
- 2 tablespoons reduced-fat mayonnaise
- 1½ tablespoons honey
- 1½ tablespoons sherry vinegar
- ¼ cup chopped fresh parsley

1. Preheat oven to 400°.

2. Combine first 4 ingredients in a large bowl; toss to coat. Arrange potatoes in a single layer on a jelly-roll pan. Bake at 400° for 40 minutes or until potatoes are tender, stirring once. Transfer potatoes to a large bowl.

3. Cook bacon in a large nonstick skillet over medium heat until crisp. Remove bacon from pan, reserving 1 tablespoon drippings in pan; set bacon aside. Add onion to drippings in pan; cook 15 minutes or until golden brown and caramelized, stirring frequently. Add garlic to pan; cook 30 seconds. Add onion mixture and bacon to potatoes; toss gently. Let stand 15 minutes.

4. Combine mustard, mayonnaise, honey, and vinegar in a small bowl; stir with a whisk. Add mustard mixture and parsley to potato mixture; toss gently. Yield: 8 servings (serving size: 1 cup).

CALORIES 224 (27% from fat); FAT 6.7g (sat 1.8g, mono 3.4g, poly 1.1g); PROTEIN 6g; CARB 36.3g; FIBER 3.7g; CHOL 7mg; IRON 1.8mg; SODIUM 427mg; CALC 41mg

Three-Bean Salad

This traditional salad features fresh green beans, canned Great Northerns, and kidney beans tossed in a vinegar dressing.

- ¼ cup cider vinegar
- 3 tablespoons grated onion
- 3 tablespoons extravirgin olive oil
- 2 tablespoons Dijon mustard
- 1 tablespoon sugar
- 1 teaspoon minced garlic
- ½ teaspoon dry mustard
- ½ teaspoon freshly ground black pepper
- ¼ teaspoon kosher salt
- 1 pound green beans, trimmed
- ½ cup minced red onion (about 1 small)
- ½ cup chopped fresh flat-leaf parsley
- ⅓ cup sliced green onions
- 1 (15.8-ounce) can Great Northern beans, rinsed and drained
- 1 (15-ounce) can kidney beans, rinsed and drained

1. Combine first 9 ingredients in a small bowl, and stir with a whisk.

2. Steam green beans, covered, 5 minutes or until crisp-tender. Drain and rinse with cold water; drain. Cut beans into 1-inch pieces; transfer to a large bowl. Add red onion and remaining 4 ingredients to bowl. Add vinegar mixture to bean mixture, tossing well to coat. Cover and chill 4 hours. Yield: 7 servings (serving size: about 1 cup).

CALORIES 207 (30% from fat); FAT 7g (sat 1g, mono 4.8g, poly 0.9g); PROTEIN 8.5g; CARB 29.7g; FIBER 9.2g; CHOL 0mg; IRON 2.4mg; SODIUM 368mg; CALC 95mg

Dijon Mustard

Dijon is often used to add bite to savory main dishes like lamb chops or pork tenderloin, but it can also be used to make zesty homemade vinaigrettes, or as a simple dip for pretzels. In fact, Dijon is so versatile you'll find lots of ways to season with it as we did in several of these recipes.

MODERN
Zesty Three-Bean and Roasted Corn Salad

This modern southwestern-accented recipe combines canned beans with sweet summer corn and red bell peppers for a colorful side dish.

Cooking spray
2½ cups (1-inch) cut green beans (about 1 pound)
¾ cup fresh corn kernels (about 2 medium ears)
¾ cup diced red bell pepper
½ cup minced red onion
¼ cup chopped fresh cilantro
1 tablespoon minced seeded jalapeño
1 (16-ounce) can cannellini beans or other white beans, rinsed and drained
1 (15-ounce) can black beans, rinsed and drained
¼ cup fresh lime juice
¼ cup red wine vinegar
1 tablespoon minced garlic
1 tablespoon olive oil
2 teaspoons ground cumin
1 teaspoon chili powder
½ teaspoon salt
¼ teaspoon red chile sauce (such as Cholula)
Dash of ground red pepper
1 cup diced seeded tomato (about 2 medium)
1 cup diced avocado

1. Heat a large nonstick skillet over medium-high heat. Coat pan with cooking spray. Add green beans and corn to pan; sauté 3 minutes or until lightly browned. Transfer green bean mixture to a large bowl. Add bell pepper and next 5 ingredients to bowl; toss well. Combine juice and next 8 ingredients in a small bowl; stir with a whisk. Add juice mixture to bean mixture; toss well. Cover and chill 30 minutes. Gently stir in tomato and avocado. Serve immediately. Yield: 10 servings (serving size: about 1 cup).

CALORIES 146 (33% from fat); FAT 5.3g (sat 0.6g, mono 3g, poly 0.7g); PROTEIN 6.6g; CARB 23.1g; FIBER 6.9g; CHOL 0mg; IRON 1.7mg; SODIUM 233mg; CALC 64mg

TRADITIONAL
Macaroni Salad with Bacon, Peas, and Creamy Dijon Dressing

The tangy traditional dressing contrasts well with the smoky bacon, sweet bell pepper, and red onion.

DRESSING:
½ cup (4 ounces) ⅓-less-fat cream cheese
¼ cup chopped shallots
¼ cup reduced-fat mayonnaise
2 tablespoons fat-free sour cream
2 tablespoons Dijon mustard
2 tablespoons lemon juice
1 tablespoon white wine vinegar
¾ teaspoon black pepper
½ teaspoon kosher salt

SALAD:
8 ounces uncooked large elbow macaroni
⅔ cup fresh green peas
⅔ cup finely diced red bell pepper
⅔ cup finely diced red onion
½ cup thinly sliced green onions
¼ cup chopped fresh flat-leaf parsley
½ teaspoon grated lemon rind
3 lower-sodium bacon slices, cooked and crumbled

1. To prepare dressing, place first 9 ingredients in a food processor, and process until smooth. Cover and chill.
2. To prepare salad, cook pasta according to package directions, omitting salt and fat; add peas during last 3 minutes of cooking time. Drain; rinse with cold water. Drain. Combine pasta mixture, bell pepper, and next 4 ingredients in a large bowl. Toss pasta mixture with half of dressing. Cover and chill until ready to serve. Toss salad with remaining dressing, and sprinkle with crumbled bacon; serve immediately. Yield: 8 servings (serving size: 1 cup salad and about 1 teaspoon bacon).

CALORIES 208 (30% from fat); FAT 7g (sat 3.2g, mono 2.2g, poly 1.4g); PROTEIN 8.6g; CARB 29.1g; FIBER 2.3g; CHOL 16mg; IRON 1.5mg; SODIUM 454mg; CALC 44mg

MODERN • MAKE AHEAD
Rotini Salad with Kalamata Olive Dressing

This recipe easily doubles to feed a crowd.

1 red bell pepper
½ yellow bell pepper
6 ounces uncooked rotini (corkscrew pasta)
¼ pound haricots verts, trimmed and cut into 1-inch pieces
1½ cups quartered cherry tomatoes
½ cup sliced fresh basil
1½ ounces diced fresh mozzarella
1 ounce prosciutto, chopped
4 pitted kalamata olives, sliced
Cooking spray
3 garlic cloves, peeled and sliced
1 large shallot, peeled and cut into ½-inch pieces
2½ tablespoons white balsamic vinegar
1 tablespoon water
1 teaspoon Dijon mustard
¼ teaspoon kosher salt
¼ teaspoon freshly ground black pepper

1. Preheat broiler.
2. Cut bell peppers in half lengthwise; discard seeds and membranes. Place red and yellow pepper halves, skin sides up, on a foil-lined baking sheet; flatten with hand. Broil 15 minutes or until blackened. Place in a zip-top plastic bag; seal. Let stand 10 minutes. Peel and dice; place in a large bowl.
3. Cook pasta according to package directions, omitting salt and fat. Add haricots verts to pasta during last 3 minutes of cooking time. Drain. Add pasta mixture, tomatoes, and next 4 ingredients to peppers; toss well.
4. Heat a small saucepan over medium-low heat. Coat pan with cooking spray. Add garlic and shallot to pan. Cook 15 minutes or until soft, stirring occasionally. Place garlic mixture, vinegar, and remaining 4 ingredients in a blender; process until smooth. Pour dressing over pasta mixture; toss well. Yield: 7 servings (serving size: about 1 cup).

CALORIES 147 (18% from fat); FAT 3g (sat 1.3g, mono 1.1g, poly 0.3g); PROTEIN 6.6g; CARB 23.9g; FIBER 2.2g; CHOL 8mg; IRON 1.3mg; SODIUM 205mg; CALC 59mg

Summertime Fruit Salad with Cream

The whipped cream topping can be made four hours ahead if kept chilled and covered. If you don't have Chambord, use Grand Marnier, crème de cassis (black currant–flavored liqueur), or two teaspoons raspberry extract for the sugar syrup.

⅓ cup water
5 tablespoons sugar
¼ cup Chambord (raspberry-flavored liqueur)
2 tablespoons fresh lemon juice
2 cups diced nectarines
1 cup pitted and halved sweet cherries
1 cup sliced strawberries
1 cup fresh raspberries
1 cup fresh blueberries
⅓ cup whipping cream
2 teaspoons sugar
1 teaspoon Chambord (raspberry-flavored liqueur)
3 tablespoons slivered almonds, toasted

1. Combine first 4 ingredients in a small saucepan over medium-low heat; bring to a boil. Simmer 8 minutes or until sugar dissolves, stirring frequently. Remove from heat, and cool.
2. Combine nectarines and next 4 ingredients in a large bowl. Add sugar mixture, and toss gently to coat.
3. Place whipping cream and 2 teaspoons sugar in a medium bowl, and beat with a mixer at high speed until stiff peaks form. Fold in 1 teaspoon Chambord. Serve whipped cream over fruit, and sprinkle with almonds. Yield: 8 servings (serving size: ½ cup fruit salad, 1½ tablespoons whipped cream, and about 1 teaspoon almonds).

CALORIES 163 (29% from fat); FAT 5.3g (sat 2.4g, mono 2g, poly 0.6g); PROTEIN 1.8g; CARB 24.6g; FIBER 3.1g; CHOL 14mg; IRON 0.5mg; SODIUM 5mg; CALC 27mg

Peaches and Mixed Greens Salad

2 cups raspberries, divided
3 tablespoons crème de cassis (black currant–flavored liqueur)
1 tablespoon sugar
2 tablespoons minced shallots
2 tablespoons crème fraîche
2 tablespoons Champagne vinegar
2 tablespoons honey
1 teaspoon Dijon mustard
½ teaspoon freshly ground black pepper
¼ teaspoon salt
6 cups mixed salad greens (about 8 ounces)
2 cups thinly sliced peeled peaches (about 2 large)
½ cup thinly sliced green onions (about 2 bunches)
⅓ cup chopped hazelnuts, toasted

1. Combine ½ cup raspberries, crème de cassis, and sugar in a small saucepan over medium heat; bring to a simmer. Cook 5 minutes or until raspberries are very tender; cool to room temperature. Press raspberry mixture through a fine sieve into a bowl, reserving liquid; discard solids. Combine raspberry liquid, shallots, and next 6 ingredients in a medium bowl, stirring with a whisk.
2. Combine 1½ cups raspberries, salad greens, and remaining 3 ingredients in a large bowl; add shallot mixture, tossing gently to coat greens. Serve immediately. Yield: 6 servings (serving size: 1 cup).

CALORIES 164 (30% from fat); FAT 5.5g (sat 1g, mono 3.3g, poly 0.8g); PROTEIN 3.3g; CARB 24.5g; FIBER 5.1g; CHOL 2mg; IRON 1.7mg; SODIUM 138mg; CALC 66mg

new american classics

Flank Steak with Grilled Mango and Watermelon Chutney

Flank Steak with Grilled Mango and Watermelon Chutney

(pictured on page 242)

STEAK:
1 tablespoon brown sugar
1 teaspoon salt
¾ teaspoon ground cumin
3 garlic cloves, minced
1 (1½-pound) flank steak, trimmed
Cooking spray

WATERMELON CHUTNEY:
2 peeled ripe mangoes, each cut into quarters (about 1 pound)
1 teaspoon olive oil
1 cup thinly vertically sliced onion
1 tablespoon minced peeled fresh ginger
⅓ cup cider vinegar
2 tablespoons brown sugar
2 tablespoons fresh lime juice
¼ teaspoon salt
¼ teaspoon ground red pepper
2 cups finely diced seedless watermelon (about ¾ pound)
1½ tablespoons chopped fresh cilantro
1½ tablespoons chopped fresh mint
Mint sprigs (optional)
Lime wedges (optional)

1. Prepare grill.
2. To prepare steak, combine first 4 ingredients. Sprinkle steak evenly with sugar mixture. Place steak on grill rack coated with cooking spray; grill 8 minutes on each side or until desired degree of doneness. Let stand 10 minutes. Cut steak diagonally across grain into thin slices.
3. To prepare chutney, place mango on grill rack coated with cooking spray; grill 4 minutes on each side. Cool; chop. Set aside.
4. Heat oil in a saucepan over medium-high heat. Add onion; sauté 4 minutes. Add ginger; sauté 1 minute. Add vinegar and next 4 ingredients; cook 5 minutes or until liquid almost evaporates. Stir in mango; cook 1 minute. Remove from heat. Stir in watermelon, cilantro, and chopped mint. Garnish with mint and lime, if desired. Yield: 6 servings (serving size: 3 ounces beef and ½ cup chutney).

CALORIES 274 (24% from fat); FAT 7.4g (sat 2.5g, mono 2.9g, poly 0.4g); PROTEIN 25.7g; CARB 26.8g; FIBER 2.3g; CHOL 37mg; IRON 2.3mg; SODIUM 553mg; CALC 57mg

Homemade Ice Cream

Straight from the churn, ice cream is one of summer's greatest pleasures. Learn how simple it is to master.

It's easy to make ice cream at home. Start by selecting the machine that best suits your needs. Prepare the ice-cream base (or mix), cool it, crank it, and put it in the freezer to "ripen" (firm) for about an hour. With just a bit of practice, you can churn out fabulous ice cream.

STAFF FAVORITE • MAKE AHEAD
FREEZABLE
Chocolate Fudge Brownie Ice Cream

Place the ice-cream freezer can and your freezer-safe dish for ripening the ice cream in the freezer while you make the custard. This helps the ice cream ripen quickly. We awarded this rich-tasting ice cream our Test Kitchens' highest rating.

BROWNIES:

½ ounce bittersweet chocolate, chopped
½ cup sugar
2 tablespoons butter, softened
½ teaspoon vanilla extract
1 large egg, lightly beaten
½ cup all-purpose flour (about 2¼ ounces)
⅓ cup unsweetened cocoa
¼ teaspoon baking powder
⅛ teaspoon salt
Cooking spray

ICE CREAM:

1⅓ cups sugar
⅓ cup unsweetened cocoa
3½ cups 2% reduced-fat milk, divided
3 large egg yolks, lightly beaten
½ cup half-and-half
2½ ounces bittersweet chocolate, chopped

1. Preheat oven to 350°.
2. To prepare brownies, place ½ ounce chocolate in a microwave-safe dish, and microwave at HIGH 30 seconds or until almost melted, stirring once. Combine chocolate, ½ cup sugar, and butter in a medium bowl; beat with a mixer at high speed until well blended. Add extract and egg; beat until combined. Lightly spoon flour into a dry measuring cup; level with a knife. Combine flour, ⅓ cup cocoa, baking powder, and salt. Add flour mixture to sugar mixture; beat just until blended. Spoon batter into a 9 x 5–inch loaf pan coated with cooking spray. Bake at 350° for 20 minutes or until a wooden pick inserted in center comes out clean. Cool brownies in pan on a wire rack.
3. To prepare ice cream, combine 1⅓ cups sugar and ⅓ cup cocoa in a medium, heavy saucepan over medium-low heat, stirring well with a whisk. Stir in ½ cup milk and egg yolks. Stir in 3 cups milk. Cook 12 minutes or until a thermometer registers 160°, stirring constantly. Remove from heat.
4. Place half-and-half in a medium microwave-safe bowl; microwave at HIGH 1½ minutes or until half-and-half boils. Add 2½ ounces chocolate; stir until smooth. Stir half-and-half mixture into milk mixture. Place pan in a large ice-filled bowl. Cool completely, stirring occasionally.
5. Pour mixture into freezer can of an ice-cream freezer; freeze according to manufacturer's instructions. Spoon ice cream into a freezer-safe container. Cut brownies into small squares; stir into ice cream. Cover and freeze 1 hour or until firm. Yield: 11 servings (serving size: about ⅔ cup).

CALORIES 297 (29% from fat); FAT 9.6g (sat 5.1g, mono 3.1g, poly 0.5g); PROTEIN 6.6g; CARB 49.2g; FIBER 2g; CHOL 90mg; IRON 1.4mg; SODIUM 105mg; CALC 37mg

MAKE AHEAD • FREEZABLE
Vanilla Bean Ice Cream

Substitute two teaspoons pure vanilla extract if you don't have a vanilla bean.

3⅓ cups 2% reduced-fat milk
1 cup half-and-half
1 (6-inch) vanilla bean, split lengthwise
1 cup sugar
3 large egg yolks

1. Combine milk and half-and-half in a medium, heavy saucepan. Scrape seeds from vanilla bean; add seeds and bean to pan. Bring milk mixture to a boil. Remove from heat. Remove bean; discard.
2. Combine sugar and egg yolks; beat with a mixer at high speed until thick and pale. Gradually add half of hot milk mixture to sugar mixture, stirring constantly with a whisk. Return milk mixture to pan. Cook over medium-low heat 2 minutes or until thermometer registers 160°; stir constantly.
3. Place pan in an ice-filled bowl. Cool, stirring occasionally. Pour mixture into freezer can of an ice-cream freezer; freeze according to manufacturer's instructions. Spoon ice cream into a freezer-safe container; cover and freeze 1 hour or until firm. Yield: 8 servings (serving size: ¾ cup).

CALORIES 213 (30% from fat); FAT 7.1g (sat 4g, mono 2.3g, poly 0.5g); PROTEIN 5.9g; CARB 32.1g; FIBER 0g; CHOL 96mg; IRON 0.3mg; SODIUM 76mg; CALC 186mg

1. *The most important piece of equipment is an ice-cream maker. You've got a couple of options: an old-fashioned bucket churn or a countertop freezer.*

2. *Traditional bucket-style freezers require rock salt and ice, but tabletop models rely strictly on a freezer bowl filled with a coolant.*

3. *Heat the milk, and combine the egg yolks and sugar separately. Gradually add half the hot milk to yolk mixture to slowly heat the yolk mixture.*

4. *It's important to completely cool the ice-cream mix before freezing it. Accomplish this quickly by placing the pan in a large ice-filled metal bowl.*

5. *Use coarse rock salt because it will not slip easily between the ice or drain through the cracks of the bucket.*

6. *Ripen the ice cream by transferring it to a freezer-safe container. Let it stand in the freezer at least one hour or until firm.*

7. *Let the ice cream stand at room temperature for about five minutes. If it's still frozen, heat the scoop under hot running water, pat it dry, and scoop.*

Straight from the churn, ice cream is one of summer's greatest pleasures. Learn how simple it is to master.

Pecan Pie Ice Cream

Stove-top custard reminiscent of pecan pie filling is swirled in after churning to create an ice cream that tastes like pecan pie à la mode. Because this is a large-yield recipe, you'll need to use an old-fashioned ice-cream churn. Or cut the recipe in half to use a countertop freezer. If you can't find brown sugar corn syrup, use dark corn syrup.

ICE CREAM:

    4 cups 2% reduced-fat milk
    1 cup half-and-half
 1¼ cups granulated sugar
    4 large egg yolks

FILLING:

 ¾ cup brown sugar corn syrup
 ½ cup packed brown sugar
    3 tablespoons cornstarch
 ⅛ teaspoon salt
    1 cup half-and-half
 ½ cup 2% reduced-fat milk
    2 large egg yolks, lightly beaten
    3 tablespoons chopped pecans, toasted
    2 tablespoons butter, softened
    1 teaspoon vanilla extract

GARNISH:

 ½ (15-ounce) package refrigerated pie dough (optional)
Cooking spray (optional)

1. To prepare ice cream, combine 4 cups milk and 1 cup half-and-half in a large, heavy saucepan; bring to a boil.
2. Combine granulated sugar and 4 egg yolks; beat with a mixer at high speed until thick and pale. Gradually add half of hot milk mixture to yolk mixture, stirring constantly. Return milk mixture to pan. Cook over medium-low heat 2 minutes or until a thermometer registers 160°, stirring constantly with a whisk. Remove from heat. Place pan in a large ice-filled bowl. Cool completely, stirring occasionally. Pour mixture into freezer can of an ice-cream freezer, and freeze according to manufacturer's instructions.
3. To prepare filling, combine corn syrup, brown sugar, cornstarch, and salt in a medium, heavy saucepan, stirring well with a whisk.
4. Combine 1 cup half-and-half, ½ cup milk, and 2 egg yolks, stirring well. Add milk mixture to sugar mixture; stir well with a whisk. Place pan over low heat; cook 12 minutes or until thick and bubbly, stirring constantly. Remove from heat; stir in pecans, butter, and vanilla. Transfer filling to a bowl. Place plastic wrap directly over filling; chill.
5. Spoon ice cream into a freezer-safe container; gently fold filling into ice cream. Cover and freeze 1 hour or until ice cream is firm.
6. Preheat oven to 350°.
7. To prepare garnish, place dough on a large cutting board or work surface. Cut 14 stars with a 1-inch star-shaped cookie cutter. Place stars on a baking sheet coated with cooking spray. Bake at 350° for 12 minutes or until browned. Serve with ice cream, if desired. Yield: 14 servings (serving size: about ¾ cup).

CALORIES 285 (30% from fat); FAT 9.4g (sat 4.7g, mono 3g, poly 0.9g); PROTEIN 5.2g; CARB 46.9g; FIBER 0.2g; CHOL 110mg; IRON 0.5mg; SODIUM 122mg; CALC 66mg

Blueberry Cheesecake Ice Cream

This recipe yields two quarts of ice cream, so if you make the entire recipe, use a traditional bucket-style freezer. Halve the recipe if you use a countertop model; they typically have a smaller capacity.

    2 cups granulated sugar
 ¾ cup (6 ounces) ⅓-less-fat cream cheese, softened
    4 large egg yolks
    3 cups 2% reduced-fat milk
    1 cup half-and-half
    3 cups fresh blueberries, coarsely chopped
 ¼ cup powdered sugar
 ¼ cup water

1. Combine first 3 ingredients in a large bowl; beat with a mixer at high speed until smooth. Combine milk and half-and-half in a medium, heavy saucepan; bring to a boil. Remove from heat. Gradually add half of hot milk mixture to cheese mixture, stirring constantly with a whisk. Return milk mixture to pan. Cook over medium-low heat 5 minutes or until a thermometer registers 160°, stirring constantly. Place pan in an ice-filled bowl. Cool completely, stirring occasionally.
2. Combine blueberries, powdered sugar, and ¼ cup water in a small saucepan; bring to a boil. Reduce heat, and simmer 10 minutes or until mixture thickens slightly, stirring frequently. Remove from heat, and cool completely.
3. Stir blueberry mixture into milk mixture. Pour mixture into freezer can of an ice-cream freezer; freeze according to manufacturer's instructions. Spoon ice cream into a freezer-safe container; cover and freeze 1 hour or until firm. Yield: 12 servings (serving size: about ⅔ cup).

CALORIES 268 (26% from fat); FAT 7.8g (sat 4.4g, mono 2.3g, poly 0.5g); PROTEIN 5.4g; CARB 45.8g; FIBER 0.9g; CHOL 90mg; IRON 0.3mg; SODIUM 100mg; CALC 49mg

Peanut Butter, Banana, and Honey Ice Cream

Mashed bananas and peanut butter add body to this no-cook ice cream.

 ¾ cup half-and-half
 ½ cup honey
 ½ cup sugar
 ⅓ cup chunky peanut butter
    1 teaspoon vanilla extract
 ⅛ teaspoon salt
    2 ripe bananas, mashed
 2½ cups 2% reduced-fat milk

1. Combine first 3 ingredients in a large bowl, stirring until sugar dissolves. Stir in peanut butter and next 3 ingredients. Stir in milk.
2. Pour mixture into the freezer can of an ice-cream freezer; freeze according to manufacturer's instructions. Spoon ice cream into a freezer-safe container; cover and freeze 1 hour or until firm. Yield: 8 servings (serving size: about ⅔ cup).

CALORIES 266 (29% from fat); FAT 8.7g (sat 3g, mono 3.4g, poly 1.7g); PROTEIN 6.4g; CARB 44.1g; FIBER 1.7g; CHOL 13mg; IRON 0.4mg; SODIUM 139mg; CALC 41mg

Make the Mix

Ice cream is a frozen custard (or milk mixture) with air whipped into it. The custard or mix, is a delicate balance of dairy products, sweetener, flavorings, and sometimes eggs. Each plays an important role in the overall outcome.

A substantial amount of half-and-half combined with two percent reduced-fat milk produces delicious lower-fat ice cream with velvety smooth texture and rich flavor. Most of our recipes begin by heating the milk mixture, then stirring a little of the hot mixture into the egg yolk and sugar mixture, a process known as *tempering,* to prevent the eggs from coagulating. The custard goes back over a low flame until the eggs reach a safe temperature (160°). It's only necessary to cook the custard if using eggs (or egg yolks), but bear in mind that heat dissolves the sugar as well, helping to avoid a gritty-textured ice cream.

If the heat is too high or the custard stays on the flame too long, the eggs may coagulate, leaving lumps. To ensure a smooth texture, strain the mix through a fine-mesh sieve over a bowl before cooling.

For no-cook ice cream, minimize the amount of granulated sugar, and opt for liquid sweeteners, such as maple syrup, honey, or sweetened condensed milk.

Egg yolks are a natural emulsifier. They also add fat, and therefore body, to the texture of the frozen ice cream.

Flavorings offer variety. The most popular flavors include fresh fruit, chocolate, caramel, toasted chopped nuts, candies, and cookies. When using fruit, it's best to pick soft, ripe fruit, and consider soaking it in sugar syrup or cooking it briefly. These tricks will prevent the fruit from freezing into large chunks that are difficult to eat. It's often best to add the fruit before freezing the ice cream because the dasher helps break it into smaller pieces.

Chill Out

It's important to completely cool the ice-cream mix before freezing it. The best way to accomplish this quickly is to nest the pan directly inside a large ice-filled bowl—preferably a metal bowl, which will conduct cold better than glass or plastic. Or simply make the mix in advance and refrigerate, a process known among professionals as *aging.* Aging involves chilling the mix for four to 24 hours, allowing the proteins to swell and bind with the water molecules, which makes for a creamier product. This makes homemade ice cream even easier and more convenient because not only can you prepare the mix ahead and pop it in the ice-cream maker the next day, but it also enhances the end result.

Freeze

It's important to follow the ice-cream maker manufacturer's instructions very carefully because each type of machine works differently. If you're using a bucket freezer, make sure to use plenty of salt. If not specified by the manufacturer, use about one cup of rock salt to every eight to 10 cups of ice. Use coarse rock salt since it will not easily slip between the ice or drain through the cracks of the bucket; this keeps a consistent temperature throughout the entire bucket.

Use crushed ice if it is available. Crushed ice puts more of the surface area of the ice in contact with the brine, and this maintains lower temperatures in the freezer.

Ripen

The ice cream will be a soft-serve consistency straight from the maker. To freeze (or *ripen*) the ice cream to a firmer texture, scrape it out of the canister or freezer bowl into a freezer-safe container. (To ensure the ice cream ripens quickly, place the container in the freezer while making the ice cream.)

This is the time to fold in cookies, candies, or sauces, such as caramel. Work quickly so the ice cream doesn't begin to thaw. And remember, less stirring is better. If you stir too long, the sauce will not ribbon or swirl through the ice cream.

Then ripen, or freeze, it for at least an hour or until it's firm. The ice cream will keep, frozen, up to a month.

If using a bucket-style maker, you can also remove the dasher, cork the top of the canister, and repack it in the bucket with fresh ice and salt so the ice cream ripens in the bucket. This way you can serve homemade ice cream out of the churn.

Serve

Let ice cream stand at room temperature for five to 10 minutes after it has ripened. This allows it to soften, so it will scoop more easily. Another trick is to heat the scoop under hot running water, pat it dry, and then use it.

Store-Bought vs. Homemade: What's the Difference?

Grocery stores stock a dizzying array of ice cream. But most are high in fat. Federal standards require any product labeled "ice cream" to contain at least 10 percent milk fat (or about 7 grams of fat per ½ cup serving—this doesn't account for additional fat from eggs and other flavorings). Most premium brands have much higher percentages. Guidelines also specify a maximum allowable amount of emulsifiers, stabilizers, and minimum weight for a gallon of ice cream.

Light ice cream versions offer lower-fat options. However, they're often made with added ingredients, such as milk powder, gelatin, or other emulsifiers. These ingredients boost the percentage of total milk solids and attempt to mimic the texture of fat, but they also add a noticeably different flavor and consistency.

Overrun is a term used to define the amount of air whipped into the mix. Producers are required by law not to exceed 100 percent overrun. Many premium ice creams have overrun well under 100 percent. Sometimes commercial manufacturers pump compressed air into the mix after it's frozen, and low-fat ice cream will accept more air than full fat. This is a technique used to increase the yield, and it also, in essence, reduces the amount of fat and calories per serving.

Homemade ice cream allows you to control the quality of the ingredients and texture of the final product. Our recipes strike a balance between flavor, texture, and nutrition.

Strawberry Mint Ice Cream

A simple syrup infused with the flavor of fresh mint sweetens this strawberry ice cream. Macerate the strawberries in the syrup before adding them to the ice cream to prevent the berries from freezing too hard. Refrigerate the mix just long enough to chill it thoroughly, or you can make it up to a day before you plan to freeze it.

  2   cups half-and-half
  1¼   cups 2% reduced-fat milk
  1½   cups sugar, divided
  3   large egg yolks
  ½   cup water
  1   (1-ounce) package fresh mint
  2   cups fresh strawberries,
       chopped

1. Combine half-and-half and milk in a heavy saucepan; bring to a boil.
2. Combine ½ cup sugar and egg yolks; beat with a mixer at high speed until thick and pale. Gradually add half of hot milk mixture to yolk mixture, stirring constantly with a whisk. Return milk mixture to pan. Reduce heat to medium-low, and cook 2 minutes or until a thermometer registers 160°, stirring constantly. Remove from heat. Place pan in a large ice-filled bowl. Cool milk mixture completely, stirring occasionally.
3. Combine 1 cup sugar and ½ cup water in a microwave-safe dish; microwave at HIGH 2½ minutes or until sugar dissolves. Add mint to hot syrup; steep 5 minutes. Remove mint; discard. Pour syrup over berries; let stand 20 minutes. Add berries and syrup to milk mixture; stir well. Cover and chill, stirring occasionally.
4. Pour mixture into freezer can of an ice-cream freezer, and freeze according to manufacturer's instructions. Spoon ice cream into a freezer-safe container; cover and freeze 1 hour or until firm. Yield: about 8 servings (serving size: ¾ cup).

CALORIES 274 (30% from fat); FAT 9.1g (sat 5.1g, mono 2.7g, poly 0.6g); PROTEIN 4.5g; CARB 45.6g; FIBER 0.9g; CHOL 101mg; IRON 0.4mg; SODIUM 48mg; CALC 84mg

Maple Walnut Buttercrunch Ice Cream

If you have a candy thermometer, use it while making the buttercrunch; cook the sugar mixture to 250°. If not, just cook the sugar until it's golden, as the recipe directs. Chop the buttercrunch into coarse pieces with the food processor, or place it in a zip-top plastic bag and break it with a rolling pin. This recipe earned our Test Kitchens' highest rating.

ICE CREAM:
  3½   cups 2% reduced-fat milk
  ⅔   cup half-and-half
  1¼   cups maple syrup
  3   large egg yolks, lightly beaten

BUTTERCRUNCH:
  Cooking spray
  ⅓   cup sugar
  2   tablespoons light corn
       syrup
  1   tablespoon water
  ¼   cup chopped walnuts
  2   tablespoons butter
  ⅛   teaspoon salt

1. To prepare ice cream, combine milk and half-and-half in a medium, heavy saucepan, and bring to a boil. Remove from heat.
2. Combine maple syrup and egg yolks, stirring well with a whisk. Gradually add half of hot milk mixture to yolk mixture, stirring constantly with a whisk. Return milk mixture to pan. Cook over medium-low heat 2 minutes or until a thermometer registers 160°, stirring constantly. Place pan in a large ice-filled bowl. Cool completely, stirring occasionally. Pour mixture into freezer can of an ice-cream freezer; freeze according to manufacturer's instructions.
3. To prepare buttercrunch, line a baking sheet with foil; coat foil with cooking spray. Combine sugar, corn syrup, and 1 tablespoon water in a small saucepan over medium-high heat; bring to a boil, stirring occasionally until sugar dissolves. Cook about 8 minutes or until golden (do not stir). Remove from heat.

Stir in walnuts, butter, and salt. Quickly spread buttercrunch in a thin layer on prepared baking sheet. Cool completely. Break buttercrunch into pieces. Place buttercrunch pieces in a food processor; pulse 4 times or until coarsely ground. Spoon ice cream into a freezer-safe container; stir in buttercrunch. Cover and freeze 1 hour or until firm. Yield: 10 servings (serving size: about ⅔ cup).

CALORIES 256 (29% from fat); FAT 8.2g (sat 3.7g, mono 2.1g, poly 1.6g); PROTEIN 5.2g; CARB 42.5g; FIBER 0.2g; CHOL 79mg; IRON 0.7mg; SODIUM 109mg; CALC 63mg

Double Chocolate Ice Cream

Enjoy this delicious ice cream plain, or stir in ingredients such as pitted chopped fresh cherries, chocolate chips, or marshmallows.

  1⅓   cups sugar
  ⅓   cup unsweetened cocoa
  2½   cups 2% reduced-fat milk, divided
  3   large egg yolks, lightly beaten
  ½   cup half-and-half
  2½   ounces bittersweet chocolate,
       chopped

1. Combine sugar and cocoa in a medium, heavy saucepan over medium-low heat. Stir in ½ cup milk and egg yolks. Stir in 2 cups milk. Cook 12 minutes or until a thermometer registers 160°, stirring constantly. Remove from heat.
2. Place half-and-half in a microwave-safe dish; microwave at HIGH 1½ minutes or until half-and-half boils. Add chocolate to half-and-half; stir until smooth. Add half-and-half mixture to pan; stir until smooth. Place pan in an ice-filled bowl. Cool completely, stirring occasionally.
3. Pour mixture into freezer can of an ice-cream freezer; freeze according to manufacturer's instructions. Spoon ice cream into a freezer-safe container; cover and freeze 1 hour or until firm. Yield: 8 servings (serving size: about ⅔ cup).

CALORIES 255 (30% from fat); FAT 8.4g (sat 4.3g, mono 1.4g, poly 0.3g); PROTEIN 5.6g; CARB 44.5g; FIBER 1.8g; CHOL 87mg; IRON 0.9mg; SODIUM 51mg; CALC 38mg

Bourbon Pecan Ice Cream

Bourbon lowers the freezing point of this ice cream, so it will probably be a soft-serve consistency even after ripening.

3½ cups 2% reduced-fat milk
1 cup half-and-half
2 teaspoons vanilla extract
1 (14-ounce) can fat-free sweetened condensed milk
½ cup chopped pecans, toasted
3½ tablespoons bourbon

1. Combine first 4 ingredients, stirring well with a whisk. Pour mixture into freezer can of an ice-cream freezer, and freeze according to manufacturer's instructions. Stir in pecans and bourbon. Spoon ice cream into a freezer-safe container; cover and freeze 4 hours or until almost firm. Yield: 10 servings (serving size: about ¾ cup).

CALORIES 238 (30% from fat); FAT 8g (sat 2.6g, mono 3.2g, poly 1.4g); PROTEIN 7.9g; CARB 30.5g; FIBER 0.6g; CHOL 16.7mg; IRON 0.2mg; SODIUM 97mg; CALC 151mg

Coconut Cream Pie Ice Cream

Crushed vanilla wafer cookies, stirred in after the ice cream freezes, add the flavor of a crumb crust.

1¾ cups 2% reduced-fat milk
1¼ cups light coconut milk
1 cup half-and-half
1½ cups sugar
3 large egg yolks
6 tablespoons sweetened flaked coconut, toasted
10 vanilla wafers, crushed

1. Combine first 3 ingredients in a medium, heavy saucepan, and bring to a boil. Remove milk mixture from heat.
2. Combine sugar and egg yolks; beat with a mixer at high speed until thick and pale. Gradually add half of hot milk mixture to sugar mixture, stirring constantly with a whisk. Return milk mixture to pan. Cook over medium-low heat 2 minutes or until a thermometer registers 160°, stirring constantly. Place pan in a large ice-filled bowl. Cool completely, stirring occasionally.
3. Pour mixture into freezer can of an ice-cream freezer; freeze according to manufacturer's instructions. Stir in coconut and cookies. Spoon ice cream into a freezer-safe container; cover and freeze 1 hour or until firm. Yield: 8 servings (serving size: ¾ cup).

CALORIES 288 (29% from fat); FAT 9.4g (sat 6g, mono 2g, poly 0.4g); PROTEIN 4.6g; CARB 48.7g; FIBER 0.3g; CHOL 92mg; IRON 0.6mg; SODIUM 78mg; CALC 50mg

Ice-Cream Makers

Bucket freezers and countertop ice-cream makers function according to the same principles: A metal canister is exposed to freezing temperature. The canister (or freezer bowl) is filled with cooled custard and fitted with a dasher. The canister rotates while the dasher scrapes frozen cream from the sides, incorporating air into the mixture as it freezes to create the characteristic silky smooth, creamy texture.

Type	Bucket	Countertop
How it works	A frozen metal canister is nestled in a brine of ice and rock salt inside a bucket. A powerful motor rotates the canister (and in some cases the dasher, as well) to incorporate air into the ice cream for a rich-tasting product. Premium models have a canister and dasher that rotate in opposite directions.	The machine comes with a freezer bowl filled (internally) with gel or liquid coolant. Place the bowl in the freezer for several hours (according to manufacturer's instructions). Then put the bowl in its base, fill it with the cooled ice-cream mix, close the machine, plug it in, and turn it on.
Pros	Best results because salt lowers temperature to freeze the ice cream below 22° (soft-serve consistency) so ice cream is firm, even straight from the churn. Especially good for light ice creams, which tend to have a lower freezing point because of their higher sugar content. Bucket freezers also have a large capacity, usually 4 to 6 quarts.	Convenient (requires no salt or ice); good for small batches (countertop models have a 1- to 1½-quart capacity). If you have space, keep the freezer bowl stashed in the freezer so you can make ice cream any time.
Cons	Cumbersome, loud, requires close supervision so the ice doesn't clump and stick, and you have to listen for the motor to slow or stop (as a sign the ice cream has frozen). Manual models require plenty of muscle power.	The freezer bowl will only get as cold as your freezer, so the best result, especially with light ice cream, is soft-serve consistency. Ice cream definitely needs time to ripen in the freezer. (If you have trouble getting ice cream to freeze in the countertop maker, lower the temperature of your freezer to about 10°.)
Cost	$30 to $200	$25 to $80

Peach Ice Cream

If your peaches are not ripe and soft, pulse them in the food processor.

> 2 cups 2% reduced-fat milk
> 1 cup half-and-half
> 1 cup sugar
> 1/8 teaspoon salt
> 4 large egg yolks
> 2 cups chopped peeled peaches

1. Combine milk and half-and-half in a medium, heavy saucepan, and bring to a boil. Remove from heat.

2. Combine sugar, salt, and egg yolks in a medium bowl; beat with a mixer at high speed until thick and pale. Gradually add half of hot milk mixture to yolk mixture, stirring well with a whisk. Return milk mixture to pan. Cook over medium-low heat 2 minutes or until a thermometer registers 160°, stirring constantly. Place pan in a large ice-filled bowl. Cool completely, stirring occasionally.

3. Pour mixture into freezer can of an ice-cream freezer, and add peaches. Freeze according to manufacturer's instructions. Spoon ice cream into a freezer-safe container; cover and freeze 1 hour or until firm. Yield: 8 servings (serving size: 1 cup).

CALORIES 210 (28% from fat); FAT 6.6g (sat 3.3g, mono 2g, poly 0.5g); PROTEIN 6.5g; CARB 32.1g; FIBER 0.4g; CHOL 121mg; IRON 0.5mg; SODIUM 117mg; CALC 54mg

superfast

. . . And Ready in Just About 20 Minutes

More than a week's worth of quick entrées to get dinner on the table in a flash

Fish Tacos with Cabbage Slaw

The sturdy texture of corn tortillas works best for these tacos, but you can use flour tortillas. Since the recipe makes more slaw than necessary for the tacos, serve the extra on the side.

> 4 cups very thinly presliced green cabbage
> 1 cup chopped plum tomatoes
> 1/3 cup thinly sliced green onions
> 1/4 cup chopped fresh cilantro
> 2 tablespoons fresh lime juice
> 5 teaspoons extravirgin olive oil, divided
> 1/2 teaspoon salt, divided
> 1 pound tilapia fillets
> 1 teaspoon chili powder
> 8 (6-inch) corn tortillas

1. Combine first 4 ingredients in a large bowl. Add juice, 1 tablespoon oil, and 1/4 teaspoon salt; toss well.

2. Heat 2 teaspoons oil in a large nonstick skillet over medium-high heat. Sprinkle fish evenly with chili powder and 1/4 teaspoon salt. Add fish to pan; cook 3 minutes on each side or until fish flakes easily when tested with a fork or until desired degree of doneness. Remove from heat, and cut fish into bite-sized pieces.

3. Warm tortillas according to package directions. Spoon about 1/4 cup cabbage mixture down center of each tortilla. Divide fish evenly among tortillas; fold in half. Serve tacos with remaining cabbage mixture. Yield: 4 servings (serving size: 2 tacos and about 1 cup cabbage mixture).

CALORIES 305 (29% from fat); FAT 9.8g (sat 2g, mono 4.9g, poly 1.2g); PROTEIN 26.5g; CARB 30.1g; FIBER 4.4g; CHOL 75mg; IRON 1.4mg; SODIUM 445mg; CALC 162mg

Shrimp Skewers with Mango Dipping Sauce

Set the finished skewers atop hot cooked rice tossed with chopped fresh cilantro. If using wooden skewers, soak them in water while you prepare the ingredients.

> 1 1/2 cups cherry tomatoes (about 12 ounces)
> 1 pound peeled and deveined large shrimp
> 1 red onion, cut into 1 1/2-inch pieces (about 1 cup)
> 1 green pepper, cut into 1 1/2-inch pieces (about 1 cup)
> Cooking spray
> 1/4 cup fresh lime juice, divided
> 1/4 teaspoon black pepper
> 1/8 teaspoon salt
> 1/2 cup mango chutney
> 1/4 cup chopped green onions
> 2 tablespoons low-sodium soy sauce
> 1/2 teaspoon bottled minced garlic

1. Preheat broiler.

2. Thread tomatoes, shrimp, red onion, and green pepper alternately onto 8 skewers. Place skewers on a wire rack coated with cooking spray; place rack on a roasting pan. Drizzle with 2 tablespoons juice; sprinkle with black pepper and salt. Broil 4 minutes or until shrimp are done, turning once.

3. Combine 2 tablespoons juice, chutney, and remaining 3 ingredients in a small bowl, stirring well. Serve sauce with skewers. Yield: 4 servings (serving size: 2 skewers and about 1/4 cup sauce).

CALORIES 217 (10% from fat); FAT 2.4g (sat 0.5g, mono 0.4g, poly 1g); PROTEIN 25.4g; CARB 24.8g; FIBER 3g; CHOL 172mg; IRON 3.8mg; SODIUM 522mg; CALC 98mg

Chicken Corn Chowder

> 1 tablespoon butter
> 6 green onions
> 2 tablespoons all-purpose flour
> 2 cups chopped cooked chicken breast
> 1/4 teaspoon salt
> 1/4 teaspoon freshly ground black pepper
> 2 (10-ounce) packages frozen corn kernels, thawed and divided
> 1 (14-ounce) can fat-free, less-sodium chicken broth
> 2 cups fat-free milk
> 1/2 cup (2 ounces) preshredded Cheddar cheese

Continued

1. Melt butter in a Dutch oven over medium-high heat. Remove green tops from onions. Chop green tops; set aside. Thinly slice white portion of onions. Add sliced onions to pan; sauté 2 minutes. Add flour; cook 1 minute, stirring constantly with a whisk. Stir in chicken, salt, pepper, 1 package of corn, and broth; bring to a boil. Reduce heat, and simmer 5 minutes.

2. While mixture simmers, place remaining corn and milk in a blender; process until smooth. Add milk mixture to pan; simmer 2 minutes or until thoroughly heated. Ladle 2 cups chowder into each of 4 soup bowls; sprinkle evenly with green onion tops. Top each serving with 2 tablespoons cheese. Yield: 4 servings.

CALORIES 394 (26% from fat); FAT 11.5g (sat 5.8g, mono 3.4g, poly 1.4g); PROTEIN 35.5g; CARB 40.7g; FIBER 4.5g; CHOL 84mg; IRON 2.2mg; SODIUM 534mg; CALC 293mg

Shrimp for Supper Menu
serves 4

A fresh green salad rounds out this weeknight meal. Follow our recipe for a quick homemade vinaigrette, or use a light bottled dressing in a pinch.

Chipotle-Spiced Shrimp

Green salad*

Angel food cake with fresh strawberries

*Combine 6 cups mixed salad greens, 2 cups halved cherry tomatoes, 1 cup thinly sliced radish, and ½ cup thinly sliced red onion. Combine 2 tablespoons sherry vinegar, 1 tablespoon extravirgin olive oil, 1 teaspoon Dijon mustard, ½ teaspoon salt, and ¼ teaspoon freshly ground black pepper, stirring well with a whisk. Drizzle dressing over salad mixture.

QUICK & EASY
Chipotle-Spiced Shrimp

Chipotle chile powder adds smoky, slightly sweet spiciness to the dish. Hot paprika makes a good substitute, or use sweet paprika for a milder heat.

 1   (3½-ounce) bag boil-in-bag long-grain rice
2½   tablespoons butter, divided
 1   teaspoon bottled minced garlic
 ¼   teaspoon salt
 ¼   teaspoon chipotle chile powder
36   large shrimp, peeled and deveined (about 1 pound)
 2   tablespoons dry vermouth
 1   tablespoon fresh lime juice
 ¼   teaspoon sugar
 2   tablespoons chopped fresh cilantro

1. Cook rice according to package directions, omitting salt and fat.
2. Melt 1½ tablespoons butter in a large nonstick skillet over medium-high heat. Add garlic to pan; sauté 30 seconds. Add salt, chile powder, and shrimp to pan; sauté 2 minutes. Stir in vermouth, juice, and sugar; cook 2 minutes or until shrimp are done. Remove from heat; stir in 1 tablespoon butter and cilantro. Serve over rice. Yield: 4 servings (serving size: 9 shrimp and about ½ cup rice).

CALORIES 290 (29% from fat); FAT 9.3g (sat 4.9g, mono 2.2g, poly 1.1g); PROTEIN 25.4g; CARB 24.3g; FIBER 0.4g; CHOL 191mg; IRON 3.8mg; SODIUM 317mg; CALC 73mg

QUICK & EASY
Seared Snapper Provençal

Most types of flaky white fish will work in this recipe. Serve with orzo pasta tossed with a bit of extravirgin olive oil, grated Parmesan cheese, and chopped fresh basil.

 2   cups grape tomatoes, halved
 ½   cup chopped bottled roasted red bell peppers
 ¼   cup kalamata olives, pitted and coarsely chopped
 3   tablespoons chopped fresh basil
 2   tablespoons chopped shallots

 1   tablespoon balsamic vinegar
 2   teaspoons extravirgin olive oil
 ¼   teaspoon salt, divided
Cooking spray
 4   (6-ounce) red snapper fillets
 ¼   teaspoon black pepper

1. Combine first 7 ingredients in a bowl; sprinkle with ⅛ teaspoon salt. Toss well.
2. Heat a large nonstick skillet over medium-high heat. Coat pan with cooking spray. Sprinkle fish with ⅛ teaspoon salt and pepper. Add fish to pan; cook 4 minutes on each side or until fish flakes easily when tested with a fork or until desired degree of doneness. Serve with tomato mixture. Yield: 4 servings (serving size: 1 fillet and about ¾ cup tomato mixture).

CALORIES 260 (30% from fat); FAT 8.6g (sat 1.3g, mono 5g, poly 1.6g); PROTEIN 36.4g; CARB 7.4g; FIBER 1.4g; CHOL 63mg; IRON 1mg; SODIUM 743mg; CALC 77mg

QUICK & EASY
Quick Romaine Salad with Pan-Grilled Chicken

With a quick, fresh Caesar dressing, this salad is a snap to prepare. Substitute shrimp for the chicken, if you prefer. Garlic breadsticks are good on the side.

 1   pound chicken breast tenders
 ½   teaspoon kosher salt
 ¼   teaspoon black pepper, divided
Cooking spray
 3   tablespoons reduced-fat mayonnaise
 2   tablespoons fresh lemon juice
 1   tablespoon water
 2   teaspoons extravirgin olive oil
 1   teaspoon capers
 1   teaspoon bottled minced garlic
 1   teaspoon anchovy paste
 1   teaspoon Dijon mustard
 2   (10-ounce) packages chopped romaine lettuce

1. Heat a grill pan over medium-high heat. Sprinkle chicken with salt and ⅛ teaspoon pepper. Coat pan with cooking spray. Add chicken to pan; cook 3 minutes on each side or until done. Remove chicken from pan.

2. While chicken cooks, place ⅛ teaspoon pepper, mayonnaise, and next 7 ingredients in a blender; process until smooth.

3. Cut chicken into ½-inch pieces. Combine chicken and lettuce in a large bowl; drizzle with mayonnaise mixture. Toss to coat. Serve immediately. Yield: 4 servings (serving size: about 2½ cups salad and 3 ounces chicken).

CALORIES 203 (28% from fat); FAT 6.4g (sat 1.1g, mono 3g, poly 1.6g); PROTEIN 28.2g; CARB 7.8g; FIBER 1.8g; CHOL 67mg; IRON 2.8mg; SODIUM 650mg; CALC 90mg

QUICK & EASY
Orange Pork with Scallions

1 pound pork tenderloin
2 tablespoons cornstarch, divided
⅓ cup fat-free, less-sodium chicken broth
¼ cup orange juice
2 tablespoons low-sodium soy sauce
1 teaspoon chili garlic sauce
¼ teaspoon salt
Cooking spray
1½ teaspoons canola oil
2 cups matchstick-cut carrots
¼ cup water
2 teaspoons bottled ground fresh ginger (such as Spice World)
2 teaspoons bottled minced garlic
⅓ cup diagonally cut green onions
Sliced green onions (optional)

1. Cut pork into 2 x ¼-inch strips. Combine pork and 1 tablespoon cornstarch in a bowl; toss well. Combine 1 tablespoon cornstarch, broth, and next 4 ingredients.

2. Heat a large nonstick skillet over medium-high heat. Coat pan with cooking spray. Add pork to pan; sauté 3 minutes or until desired degree of doneness; stir frequently. Remove pork from pan.

3. Heat oil in pan. Add carrots, ¼ cup water, ginger, and garlic to pan; cook 1½ minutes, scraping pan to loosen browned bits. Return pork to pan. Stir in broth mixture; bring to a boil. Cook 30 seconds. Stir in ⅓ cup onions. Serve immediately. Garnish with sliced onions, if desired. Yield: 4 servings (serving size: about 1 cup pork mixture).

CALORIES 214 (29% from fat); FAT 6.9g (sat 1.9g, mono 3.1g, poly 1g); PROTEIN 24.1g; CARB 12.7g; FIBER 2.2g; CHOL 65mg; IRON 1.7mg; SODIUM 586mg; CALC 37mg

dinner tonight
Weeknight Alternatives

Ground chicken provides new alternatives for weeknight suppers.

Weeknight Menu 1
serves 4

Spicy Chicken Cakes with Horseradish Aïoli

Steamed asparagus

Mashed sweet potatoes*

*Peel and dice 1½ pounds sweet potatoes. Cook in boiling water 10 minutes or until tender. Drain well, and place in a large bowl. Add ¼ cup fat-free milk and ¼ teaspoon salt. Mash with a potato masher to desired consistency.

Game Plan

1. While water boils for potatoes:
 • Peel and dice potatoes
2. While potatoes cook:
 • Prepare chicken cakes
3. While chicken cakes cook:
 • Steam asparagus
 • Prepare aïoli

STAFF FAVORITE • QUICK & EASY
Spicy Chicken Cakes with Horseradish Aïoli

Aïoli (ay-OH-lee) is a garlic mayonnaise from the Provence region in France and a popular condiment there for meat and vegetables. It can be made in advance and refrigerated.

TOTAL TIME: 45 MINUTES
QUICK TIP: With day-old bread, make breadcrumbs for future use. Freeze the breadcrumbs in a zip-top plastic bag up to six months.

CAKES:
2 (1½-ounce) slices whole wheat bread
1 pound skinless, boneless chicken breast
¼ cup chopped fresh chives
3 tablespoons low-fat mayonnaise
1 teaspoon Cajun seasoning
¼ teaspoon salt
2 large egg whites
2 teaspoons canola oil

AÏOLI:
2 tablespoons low-fat mayonnaise
2 teaspoons prepared horseradish
1 teaspoon bottled minced garlic
⅛ teaspoon salt

1. To prepare cakes, place bread in a food processor; pulse 10 times or until coarse crumbs measure 1 cup (discard remaining breadcrumbs). Set breadcrumbs aside.

2. Place chicken in food processor; pulse until ground. Combine breadcrumbs, chicken, chives, and next 4 ingredients in a medium bowl; mix well (mixture will be wet). Divide mixture into 8 equal portions, shaping each into a ½-inch-thick patty.

3. Heat oil in a large nonstick skillet over medium heat. Add patties; cook 7 minutes on each side or until done.

4. To prepare aïoli, combine 2 tablespoons mayonnaise and remaining 3 ingredients in a small bowl. Serve with cakes. Yield: 4 servings (serving size: 2 chicken cakes and about 1½ teaspoons aïoli).

CALORIES 242 (26% from fat); FAT 7.1g (sat 1.3g, mono 1.8g, poly 1.3g); PROTEIN 29.5g; CARB 12.5g; FIBER 0.5g; CHOL 66mg; IRON 1.6mg; SODIUM 749mg; CALC 44mg

Weeknight Menu 2

serves 4

Swedish Meatballs

Green peas

Buttered poppy seed noodles*

*Cook 8 ounces wide egg noodles according to package directions, omitting salt and fat; drain. Place noodles in a large bowl. Add 2 tablespoons chopped fresh parsley, 1½ tablespoons butter, 1 teaspoon poppy seeds, ¼ teaspoon salt, and ¼ teaspoon pepper; toss to combine.

Game Plan

1. While water for noodles comes to a boil:
- Prepare meatballs

2. While noodles cook:
- Cook meatballs

3. While meatballs simmer in sauce:
- Prepare peas
- Chop parsley for noodles

QUICK & EASY
Swedish Meatballs

Substitute white or whole wheat bread for the rye to bind the meatballs.

TOTAL TIME: 37 MINUTES

PREP TIP: Lightly coat your hands with cooking spray to shape the meatballs since the mixture is very moist.

2 (1-ounce) slices rye bread
1 pound skinless, boneless chicken breast
¾ teaspoon salt, divided
¼ teaspoon ground nutmeg
¼ teaspoon freshly ground black pepper
1 large egg white, lightly beaten
1 tablespoon canola oil
1 cup fat-free, less-sodium chicken broth
1 tablespoon all-purpose flour
1 (8-ounce) carton fat-free sour cream
2 tablespoons chopped fresh parsley

1. Place bread in a food processor; pulse 10 times or until coarse crumbs measure 1 cup. Place breadcrumbs in a medium bowl; set aside.

2. Place chicken in food processor, and pulse until ground. Add chicken, ½ teaspoon salt, nutmeg, pepper, and egg white to breadcrumbs in bowl; stir well. Shape mixture into 16 (1½-inch) meatballs.

3. Heat oil in a large nonstick skillet over medium-high heat. Add meatballs; cook 6 minutes, browning on all sides. Remove meatballs from pan. Add ¼ teaspoon salt, broth, and flour to pan, stirring with a whisk. Bring to a boil, and cook 1 minute or until slightly thickened, stirring constantly. Stir in sour cream, and return meatballs to pan. Reduce heat to medium-low; cook 10 minutes or until meatballs are done and sauce is thick. Sprinkle with parsley. Yield: 4 servings (serving size: 4 meatballs and ⅓ cup sauce).

CALORIES 269 (21% from fat); FAT 6.3g (sat 1.2g, mono 2.6g, poly 1.5g); PROTEIN 32.3g; CARB 18.6g; FIBER 1g; CHOL 72mg; IRON 1.5mg; SODIUM 783mg; CALC 117mg

Weeknight Menu 3

serves 4

Chicken Picadillo

Black beans and rice*

Flour tortillas

*Bring 1¼ cups fat-free, less-sodium chicken broth to a boil in a medium saucepan. Add ¾ cup long-grain rice. Cover, reduce heat, and simmer 18 minutes or until liquid is absorbed. Stir in 1 cup rinsed and drained canned black beans and ¼ cup chopped fresh cilantro; cook until thoroughly heated. Stir in ¼ teaspoon salt.

Game Plan

1. While water comes to a boil for rice:
- Assemble ingredients for picadillo

2. While rice cooks:
- Prepare picadillo
- Warm tortillas

QUICK & EASY
Chicken Picadillo

Any leftover chicken mixture can be reheated and served on hot tortillas; top with shredded lettuce, chopped tomatoes, and light sour cream.

TOTAL TIME: 30 MINUTES

QUICK TIP: To toast nuts quickly, place them on a paper plate, and microwave at HIGH 1 to 2 minutes or until nuts smell toasted.

1 pound skinless, boneless chicken breast
2 teaspoons olive oil
1 cup chopped onion
1½ teaspoons ground cumin
½ teaspoon salt
¼ teaspoon ground cinnamon
3 garlic cloves, minced
1 cup bottled salsa
⅓ cup golden raisins
¼ cup slivered almonds, toasted
¼ cup chopped fresh cilantro
Cilantro sprigs (optional)

1. Place chicken in a food processor; pulse until ground.

2. Heat oil in a large nonstick skillet over medium-high heat. Add onion, and cook 3 minutes, stirring occasionally. Add chicken, cumin, salt, cinnamon, and garlic, and cook 3 minutes or until chicken is done, stirring frequently. Stir in salsa and raisins. Cover, reduce heat, and simmer 5 minutes or until thoroughly heated. Stir in almonds and chopped cilantro. Garnish with cilantro sprigs, if desired. Yield: 4 servings (serving size: about 1 cup).

CALORIES 257 (26% from fat); FAT 7.5g (sat 1g, mono 4.2g, poly 1.5g); PROTEIN 29.6g; CARB 19g; FIBER 3.2g; CHOL 66mg; IRON 2.2mg; SODIUM 762mg; CALC 74mg

Make-Ahead Summer Buffet

Dine outdoors, Italian-style, with this collection of simple recipes.

This casual gathering is a snap to pull off when you plan—and prepare—ahead. Italian food lends itself well to this kind of dinner; the flavors meld and improve when the dishes are prepared in advance, and many of them taste best when served at room temperature. The recipes here also lend themselves to a potluck because they're easy for your guests to make ahead and tote to your house.

Make-Ahead Menu
serves 8

Mix and match recipes as you wish. Choose an entrée and several colorful sides and salads.

Entrées

Seafood Salad

Orecchiette with Shrimp, Arugula, and Cherry Tomatoes

Spicy Grilled Chicken over Sweet Peppers

Salads and Sides

Summer Rice Salad with Tuna

Steamed Asparagus with Lemon-Garlic Gremolata

Figs and Prosciutto with Mint and Shaved Parmigiano-Reggiano

Roasted Beets with Pine Nuts, Dill, and Red Onion

Marinated Heirloom Tomatoes with Tarragon

Dessert

Tuscan Almond Biscotti

Tuscan white wine

MAKE AHEAD
Seafood Salad

Cook and refrigerate the seafood up to one day in advance. Prepare the dressing, slice the fennel, tear the lettuce, and refrigerate separately. Assemble just before serving.

- ½ cup dry white wine
- 2 pounds mussels, scrubbed and debearded
- 1 pound medium shrimp, peeled and deveined
- 1 pound cleaned skinless squid, cut into 1-inch rings
- ⅓ cup fresh lemon juice, divided
- 2 tablespoons finely chopped fresh flat-leaf parsley
- 2 tablespoons extravirgin olive oil
- 1 tablespoon Dijon mustard
- ¾ teaspoon salt
- ¼ teaspoon freshly ground black pepper
- 1 garlic clove, minced
- 6 cups torn Bibb lettuce
- 4 cups thinly sliced fennel (about 1 medium bulb)

1. Combine wine and mussels in a Dutch oven over medium-high heat. Cover and cook 5 minutes or until mussels open; discard any unopened shells. Remove mussels from pan with a slotted spoon, reserving liquid. Remove meat from mussels, and discard shells. Place mussels in a large bowl. Line a sieve with dampened cheesecloth, allowing cheesecloth to extend over edge of sieve. Strain cooking liquid through sieve into a bowl, reserving liquid; discard cheesecloth.

2. Return liquid to pan; bring to a boil. Add shrimp and squid to pan; cook 4 minutes or until done, stirring occasionally. Remove shrimp and squid with a slotted spoon; discard liquid. Add shrimp and squid to mussels.

3. Combine ¼ cup lemon juice and next 6 ingredients in a bowl, stirring well with a whisk. Drizzle lemon juice mixture over shrimp mixture, tossing to coat.

4. Combine lettuce and fennel in a large bowl. Add 4 teaspoons lemon juice to fennel mixture; toss to coat. Arrange fennel mixture on a platter; top with shrimp mixture. Yield: 8 servings (serving size: 1½ cups salad).

CALORIES 249 (27% from fat); FAT 7.4g (sat 1.3g, mono 3.4g, poly 1.5g); PROTEIN 32.6g; CARB 10.4g; FIBER 1.3g; CHOL 248mg; IRON 6.9mg; SODIUM 730mg; CALC 93mg

MAKE AHEAD
Orecchiette with Shrimp, Arugula, and Cherry Tomatoes

If you want to cook the pasta ahead, toss it with the olive oil, and refrigerate for up to two days.

- ¾ teaspoon salt, divided
- 1 pound medium shrimp, peeled
- Cooking spray
- 1½ cups quartered cherry tomatoes
- 2 tablespoons fresh lemon juice
- 1½ tablespoons chopped pitted niçoise olives
- ½ teaspoon crushed red pepper
- ¼ teaspoon freshly ground black pepper
- 2 garlic cloves, minced
- 8 ounces uncooked orecchiette pasta ("little ears" pasta)
- 6 cups trimmed arugula
- 1½ tablespoons extravirgin olive oil
- ½ cup (2 ounces) grated fresh Parmigiano-Reggiano cheese

Continued

1. Prepare grill.
2. Sprinkle ¼ teaspoon salt over shrimp. Place shrimp in a wire grilling basket coated with cooking spray; place basket on grill rack. Grill 2 minutes on each side or until done. Cool completely. Combine shrimp, ½ teaspoon salt, tomatoes, and next 5 ingredients in a large bowl.
3. Cook pasta according to package directions, omitting salt and fat. Drain well; cool. Add pasta, arugula, and oil to shrimp mixture; toss gently. Sprinkle with cheese. Yield: 8 servings (serving size: 1 cup).

CALORIES 226 (28% from fat); FAT 7.1g (sat 2.1g, mono 3.9g, poly 0.7g); PROTEIN 16.4g; CARB 24.2g; FIBER 1.6g; CHOL 89mg; IRON 2.7mg; SODIUM 537mg; CALC 142mg

WINE NOTE: The arugula's light peppery bite, the tomatoes' acidity, and the brininess of the olives all call for a simple, crisp, bone-dry white wine that will act as a between-bite refresher. Italy is full of such wines. For one that's packed with personality, you can try Terruzi e Puthod's Terre di Tufo 2005, a vernaccia-chardonnay blend from Tuscany (about $24).

MAKE AHEAD
Spicy Grilled Chicken over Sweet Peppers

Prepare the peppers, omitting the basil so it doesn't darken and wilt, up to two days in advance. Add basil right before serving.

CHICKEN:
- 2 teaspoons chopped fresh thyme
- 2 teaspoons chopped fresh rosemary
- 2 teaspoons chopped fresh sage
- 1 teaspoon fennel seeds, coarsely crushed
- 1 teaspoon extravirgin olive oil
- ½ teaspoon crushed red pepper
- 4 garlic cloves, minced
- 6 (6-ounce) skinless, boneless chicken breast halves
- 3 tablespoons fresh lemon juice
- 1 teaspoon salt
- ½ teaspoon freshly ground black pepper
- Cooking spray

PEPPERS:
- 2 red bell peppers
- 2 yellow bell peppers
- 2 orange bell peppers
- 1 tablespoon chopped fresh basil
- 3 tablespoons fresh lemon juice
- 1 tablespoon extravirgin olive oil
- 1 tablespoon balsamic vinegar
- ½ teaspoon salt
- ¼ teaspoon freshly ground black pepper
- 1 garlic clove, thinly sliced

1. To prepare chicken, combine first 7 ingredients in a large zip-top plastic bag. Add chicken; seal. Marinate in refrigerator 8 hours or overnight, turning bag occasionally. Add 3 tablespoons lemon juice to chicken mixture; shake well. Marinate in refrigerator 20 minutes.
2. Prepare grill.
3. Remove chicken from bag; discard marinade. Sprinkle chicken evenly with 1 teaspoon salt and ½ teaspoon black pepper. Place chicken on grill rack coated with cooking spray; grill 6 minutes on each side or until done. Cool slightly; cut chicken crosswise into thin slices. Set aside.
4. To prepare peppers, cut bell peppers in half lengthwise; discard seeds and membranes. Place pepper halves, skin sides up, on a work surface; flatten with hand. Grill, skin sides down, 15 minutes or until blackened. Place in a zip-top plastic bag; seal. Let stand 10 minutes. Peel and cut into strips. Combine peppers, basil, and remaining 6 ingredients in a bowl. Arrange pepper mixture on a platter; top with chicken. Yield: 8 servings (serving size: about 3 ounces chicken and about ⅓ cup peppers).

CALORIES 155 (22% from fat); FAT 3.8g (sat 0.7g, mono 2.1g, poly 0.6g); PROTEIN 23.1g; CARB 6.8g; FIBER 1.8g; CHOL 56mg; IRON 1.2mg; SODIUM 508mg; CALC 28mg

MAKE AHEAD
Summer Rice Salad with Tuna

Use high-quality tuna, such as Bonito del Norte from Spain. Look for it in specialty or gourmet food markets.

- 1 red bell pepper
- 1 yellow bell pepper
- Cooking spray
- 1 eggplant, peeled and cut lengthwise into ½-inch-thick slices (about 1 medium)
- 3 cups hot cooked long-grain rice
- 1 cup frozen peas, thawed
- ¼ cup chopped kosher dill pickles
- 1 tablespoon extravirgin olive oil
- 1 tablespoon red wine vinegar
- 1 teaspoon salt
- ½ teaspoon hot pepper sauce (such as Tabasco)
- ¼ teaspoon freshly ground black pepper
- 6 ounces oil-packed white albacore tuna, rinsed and drained

1. Prepare grill.
2. Cut bell peppers in half lengthwise; discard seeds and membranes. Place halves, skin sides up, on a work surface; flatten with hand. Place skin sides down, on grill rack coated with cooking spray; grill 10 minutes or until blackened. Place in a zip-top plastic bag; seal. Let stand 10 minutes. Peel and coarsely chop.
3. Place eggplant on grill rack coated with cooking spray; grill 3 minutes on each side or until lightly browned. Cool slightly, and coarsely chop eggplant.
4. Combine peppers, eggplant, rice, and remaining ingredients, stirring to flake tuna with a fork. Yield: 8 servings (serving size: about ¾ cup salad).

CALORIES 177 (20% from fat); FAT 3.9g (sat 0.7g, mono 1.9g, poly 1g); PROTEIN 9.1g; CARB 26.5g; FIBER 3.6g; CHOL 7mg; IRON 1.7mg; SODIUM 388mg; CALC 19mg

Local markets are full of fresh fare, making it easy to create a colorful menu.

Steamed Asparagus with Lemon-Garlic Gremolata

Green beans work just as well as asparagus if the latter is no longer in season. Steam and refrigerate the asparagus a day ahead; arrange on a platter with the other ingredients a couple of hours before dinner.

 2 pounds fresh asparagus
 ½ teaspoon salt
 ¼ teaspoon freshly ground black pepper
1½ tablespoons extravirgin olive oil
 3 tablespoons minced fresh flat-leaf parsley
 ¾ teaspoon grated lemon rind
 1 garlic clove, minced

1. Snap off tough ends of asparagus. Steam asparagus, covered, 4 minutes or until crisp-tender. Plunge asparagus into ice water; drain. Place asparagus on a large platter. Sprinkle with salt and pepper. Drizzle with oil.
2. Combine parsley, rind, and garlic. Sprinkle over asparagus, tossing gently. Yield: 8 servings (serving size: about 3 ounces asparagus).

CALORIES 48 (53% from fat); FAT 2.8g (sat 0.4g, mono 2g, poly 0.3g); PROTEIN 2.6g; CARB 4.7g; FIBER 2.4g; CHOL 0mg; IRON 2.5mg; SODIUM 151mg; CALC 30mg

Figs and Prosciutto with Mint and Shaved Parmigiano-Reggiano

Ripe figs are the secret to this simple yet refined salad. It's best made just before serving.

 8 fresh figs, quartered
 2 teaspoons extravirgin olive oil
 ¼ teaspoon cracked black pepper
 1 ounce Parmigiano-Reggiano cheese, thinly shaved
12 mint leaves, thinly sliced
 4 ounces thinly sliced prosciutto

1. Place figs in a bowl; drizzle with oil. Sprinkle figs with pepper; toss gently. Place fig mixture in the center of a platter; top with cheese and mint. Top with prosciutto. Yield: 8 servings (serving size: 4 fig quarters, about ½ ounce prosciutto, and ⅛ ounce cheese).

CALORIES 90 (34% from fat); FAT 3.4g (sat 1.2g, mono 1.8g, poly 0.3g); PROTEIN 4.8g; CARB 9.5g; FIBER 1.4g; CHOL 11mg; IRON 0.3mg; SODIUM 270mg; CALC 64mg

Roasted Beets with Pine Nuts, Dill, and Red Onion

Golden or ruby beets work well in this summer salad. Roast the beets up to four days before serving, and combine with the other ingredients up to two hours before it goes to the table.

 2 pounds golden beets
 ½ cup water
 1 cup thinly vertically sliced red onion (about 1 small)
 2 tablespoons pine nuts, toasted
 2 tablespoons red wine vinegar
 1 tablespoon chopped fresh dill
 2 teaspoons extravirgin olive oil
 ½ teaspoon salt
 ¼ teaspoon freshly ground black pepper

1. Preheat oven to 450°.
2. Leave root and 1 inch of stem on beets; scrub with a brush. Place beets in a 13 x 9–inch baking dish; add ½ cup water to dish. Cover and bake at 450° for 40 minutes or until tender. Drain and rinse with cold water. Drain; cool. Trim off beet roots; rub off skins. Slice each beet into 8 wedges.
3. Combine beets, onion, and remaining ingredients in a bowl, stirring gently. Yield: 8 servings (serving size: about ⅔ cup).

CALORIES 79 (32% from fat); FAT 2.8g (sat 0.3g, mono 1.3g, poly 0.9g); PROTEIN 2.2g; CARB 12.6g; FIBER 3.4g; CHOL 0mg; IRON 1.1mg; SODIUM 236mg; CALC 21mg

Marinated Heirloom Tomatoes with Tarragon

A simple marinade of shallots, balsamic vinegar, and fresh tarragon makes the most of summer tomatoes. Try a variety of heirloom tomatoes in this dish for their different colors and flavors. Prepare this one hour before you eat, and serve it at room temperature.

 ¼ cup finely chopped shallots
 2 tablespoons balsamic vinegar
 4 teaspoons extravirgin olive oil
 1 tablespoon chopped fresh tarragon
 2 pounds (about 6 medium) heirloom tomatoes, cut into ¼-inch-thick slices
 ¼ teaspoon salt
 ¼ teaspoon freshly ground black pepper

1. Combine first 4 ingredients in a bowl, stirring well. Arrange tomatoes on a platter. Sprinkle tomatoes evenly with salt and pepper; drizzle with shallot mixture. Yield: 8 servings (serving size: about 3 tomato slices).

CALORIES 57 (43% from fat); FAT 2.7g (sat 0.3g, mono 1.8g, poly 0.2g); PROTEIN 0.9g; CARB 7.6g; FIBER 0.8g; CHOL 0mg; IRON 0.4mg; SODIUM 79mg; CALC 19mg

Tuscan Almond Biscotti

These crunchy, light cookies are a specialty of Prato, a city in Tuscany, where they are called *cantucci*. They're typically served with a glass of *vin santo*, a sweet dessert wine, at meal's end. The biscotti keep in airtight tins for up to a week.

1¾ cups all-purpose flour (about 7¾ ounces)
 1 cup sugar
 1 teaspoon baking powder
 ¼ teaspoon salt
 1 cup whole almonds, toasted
 2 large eggs, lightly beaten
 ½ teaspoon almond extract
Cooking spray

Continued

1. Preheat oven to 375°.

2. Lightly spoon flour into dry measuring cups; level with a knife. Combine flour, sugar, baking powder, and salt in a large bowl. Place almonds in a food processor; pulse 10 times. Stir nuts into flour mixture.

3. Combine eggs and extract, stirring well with a whisk. Add egg mixture to flour mixture, stirring just until blended (dough will be crumbly). Turn dough out onto a lightly floured surface; knead lightly 7 or 8 times. Divide dough into 2 equal portions. Shape each portion into a 6-inch-long roll. Place rolls 6 inches apart on a baking sheet coated with cooking spray, and pat to 1-inch thickness. Bake at 375° for 25 minutes or until lightly browned. Cool 5 minutes on a wire rack.

4. Cut each roll crosswise into 12 (½-inch) slices. Stand slices upright on baking sheet. Bake at 375° for 14 minutes (cookies will be slightly soft in center but will harden as they cool). Remove from baking sheet, and cool completely on a wire rack. Yield: 2 dozen (serving size: 1 biscotto).

CALORIES 102 (30% from fat); FAT 3.4g (sat 0.4g, mono 2.1g, poly 0.8g); PROTEIN 2.7g; CARB 15.7g; FIBER 0.9g; CHOL 18mg; IRON 0.8mg; SODIUM 51mg; CALC 28mg

lighten up

A More Fabulous Fettuccine

A decadent bacon, spinach, and cheese sauce receives a healthful makeover for a California reader.

Kathy Gordon of Mission Viejo, California, inherited a recipe for Spinach Fettuccine from her mom about 15 years ago. But she stopped making the dish about 10 years ago, when she and her husband, Mike, started eating more healthfully.

We modified several high-fat components yet still created a rich, creamy, and bacon-crisped result.

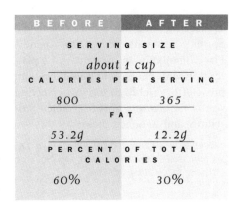

BEFORE	AFTER
SERVING SIZE	
about 1 cup	
CALORIES PER SERVING	
800	365
FAT	
53.2g	12.2g
PERCENT OF TOTAL CALORIES	
60%	30%

Spinach Fettuccine

You can use Asiago cheese for a slightly sweeter flavor, or Parmigiano-Reggiano for a sharper flavor than the pecorino Romano.

1   pound uncooked fettuccine
1   tablespoon butter
1   garlic clove, minced
¼   cup (2 ounces) ⅓-less-fat cream cheese
¾   cup fat-free, less-sodium chicken broth
3   tablespoons all-purpose flour
¾   cup (3 ounces) grated fresh pecorino Romano cheese
¾   cup half-and-half
1   teaspoon salt
½   teaspoon freshly ground black pepper
1   (10-ounce) package frozen chopped spinach, thawed, drained, and squeezed dry
10   center-cut bacon slices, cooked and crumbled (about 1¼ cups)
Parsley sprigs (optional)

1. Cook pasta according to package directions, omitting salt and fat. Drain pasta, reserving ½ cup pasta water.

2. Melt butter in a large nonstick skillet over medium-high heat. Add garlic; sauté 30 seconds. Add reserved pasta water and cream cheese, stirring with a whisk until smooth.

3. Combine broth and flour in a small bowl, stirring with a whisk until smooth. Add flour mixture to pan, stirring with a whisk to combine; bring to a boil. Cook 2 minutes or until mixture thickens, stirring constantly. Remove from heat; add pecorino Romano, stirring until smooth. Add half-and-half, salt, and pepper. Stir in spinach. Combine cheese mixture and pasta in a large bowl, tossing to coat. Place about 1 cup pasta mixture in each of 8 bowls; top each serving with 2½ tablespoons bacon. Garnish with parsley, if desired. Yield: 8 servings.

CALORIES 365 (30% from fat); FAT 12.2g (sat 6.3g, mono 3.3g, poly 0.6g); PROTEIN 15.9g; CARB 46.6g; FIBER 2.3g; CHOL 34mg; IRON 1.8mg; SODIUM 681mg; CALC 188mg

reader recipes

Stellar Baked Shells

A Maine reader puts heart-healthy ingredients to work to revamp a pasta favorite.

Toni Seger, a 57-year-old writer from Lovell, Maine, has always loved cooking and eating rich, flavorful foods such as creamy pasta dishes and vegetables covered with hollandaise sauce. But when her husband, Timothy, suffered a sudden heart attack several years ago, the couple sought healthier choices. "We had to change our lifestyle," says Seger. She started revising old recipe favorites to create a new lower-fat and -cholesterol diet.

Baked Stuffed Shells was one favorite Seger felt needed some heart-healthy tweaking. She substituted lean turkey sausage for full-fat sausage and swapped a 14-ounce package of light firm tofu for full-fat ricotta cheese. Tofu's creamy consistency maintains the stuffing's rich texture and absorbs the other flavors of the stuffing without the cholesterol and saturated fat of full-fat ricotta. She also used lower-fat cheeses (part-skim mozzarella and Parmesan).

Baked Stuffed Shells

SHELLS:

¼ cup boiling water
6 sun-dried tomatoes
1 cup (4 ounces) shredded part-skim mozzarella cheese
¼ cup (1 ounce) grated fresh Parmesan cheese
1 tablespoon chopped fresh parsley
¼ teaspoon freshly ground black pepper
⅛ teaspoon salt
1 (14-ounce) package reduced-fat firm tofu
1 egg, lightly beaten
18 cooked jumbo pasta shells

SAUCE:

1 tablespoon olive oil
1¾ cups chopped onion (about 1 large)
1 cup chopped green bell pepper (about 1 medium)
1 cup chopped red bell pepper (about 1 medium)
3 garlic cloves, minced
Cooking spray
¾ pound low-fat turkey breakfast sausage, casings removed
¼ cup red wine
2 tablespoons no-salt-added tomato paste
1 teaspoon dried oregano
1 teaspoon dried basil
½ teaspoon freshly ground black pepper
⅛ teaspoon salt
1 (28-ounce) can organic crushed tomatoes
2 tablespoons grated fresh Parmesan cheese

1. To prepare stuffing, combine ¼ cup boiling water and sun-dried tomatoes in a small bowl; let stand 20 minutes or until tomatoes soften. Drain and finely chop. Place chopped tomatoes, mozzarella, and next 6 ingredients in a food processor; process until smooth. Spoon 2 tablespoons stuffing into each shell. Set stuffed shells aside.

2. To prepare sauce, heat oil in a large skillet over medium-high heat. Add onion, bell peppers, and garlic; sauté

6 minutes or until tender. Place onion mixture in a bowl.

3. Coat pan with cooking spray; return pan to heat. Add sausage, and cook 6 minutes or until browned, stirring to crumble. Add wine; cook until wine is reduced to 2 tablespoons (about 3 minutes). Stir in onion mixture, tomato paste, and next 5 ingredients; bring to a simmer. Cook 25 minutes or until slightly thick.

4. Preheat oven to 350°.

5. Spread 2 cups sauce in an 11 x 7–inch baking dish coated with cooking spray. Arrange stuffed shells in a single layer in pan; top with remaining sauce. Sprinkle 2 tablespoons Parmesan over sauce. Bake at 350° for 40 minutes or until bubbly. Yield: 6 servings (serving size: 3 stuffed shells and about 1 cup sauce).

CALORIES 391 (32% from fat); FAT 13.8g (sat 4.8g, mono 5.2g, poly 2.3g); PROTEIN 27g; CARB 37.1g; FIBER 4.7g; CHOL 84mg; IRON 4mg; SODIUM 892mg; CALC 238mg

---

Breakfast Coffee Cake

"I like to have this on hand for snacking or taking to friends. It freezes nicely without the icing. I created this recipe when my son married a nutritionist."

—Kathy Frederickson,
Leominster, Massachusetts

½ cup granulated sugar
½ cup nutlike cereal nuggets (such as Grape-Nuts)
2 teaspoons instant espresso granules
1 teaspoon ground cinnamon
1¾ cups all-purpose flour (about 7¾ ounces)
1 cup granulated sugar
1 teaspoon baking soda
½ teaspoon baking powder
½ teaspoon salt
1 cup vanilla fat-free yogurt (about 8 ounces)
½ cup butter, softened
½ cup egg substitute
Cooking spray
1½ cups powdered sugar, sifted
2 tablespoons cooled brewed coffee

1. Preheat oven to 350°.

2. Combine first 4 ingredients in a small bowl; stir with a whisk. Set aside.

3. Lightly spoon flour into dry measuring cups; level with a knife. Combine flour, sugar, and next 3 ingredients in a large bowl. Add yogurt, butter, and egg substitute; beat with an electric mixer at low speed 1 minute or until combined. Spread half of batter in an 8-inch square baking dish coated with cooking spray. Sprinkle with cereal mixture; top with remaining batter. Bake at 350° for 45 minutes or until a wooden pick inserted in center comes out clean; cool in dish.

4. Combine powdered sugar and coffee in a small bowl; spread glaze evenly over top of cake. Cut into 12 pieces. Yield: 12 servings (serving size: 1 piece).

CALORIES 321 (22% from fat); FAT 7.9g (sat 4.9g, mono 2g, poly 0.4g); PROTEIN 4.6g; CARB 59.4g; FIBER 1g; CHOL 20mg; IRON 2.5mg; SODIUM 342mg; CALC 61mg

---

Corn and Black Bean Salad

"I wanted a side dish that had a little spicy heat to serve with my pan-fried tilapia. I came up with this Mexican-inspired salad."

—Peggy Kistler, Salem, Oregon

2 cups fresh corn kernels (about 4 ears)
1 cup diced red bell pepper (about 1 large)
½ cup thinly sliced green onions
½ cup chopped fresh cilantro
1 (15-ounce) can black beans, rinsed and drained
¼ cup red wine vinegar
2 teaspoons canola oil
1 teaspoon sugar
½ teaspoon garlic powder
½ teaspoon ground cumin
½ teaspoon chili powder
½ teaspoon freshly ground black pepper
Dash of salt

1. Combine first 5 ingredients in a medium bowl.

2. Combine vinegar and remaining
Continued

7 ingredients in a small bowl. Drizzle vinegar mixture over corn mixture; toss well. Cover and chill 30 minutes. Yield: 10 servings (serving size: ½ cup).

CALORIES 74 (28% from fat); FAT 2.3g (sat 0.1g, mono 0.6g, poly 0.3g); PROTEIN 3.4g; CARB 14.4g; FIBER 3.4g; CHOL 0mg; IRON 0.8mg; SODIUM 208mg; CALC 19mg

---

QUICK & EASY • MAKE AHEAD
Broccoli Salad

"Most broccoli salads have a creamy dressing, but I came up with this recipe using oil and vinegar instead."

—Paulette Kwiatkowski, Maumee, Ohio

4 cups broccoli florets (about 1 head)
¼ cup thinly vertically sliced red onion
¼ cup (1-inch-thick) slices red bell pepper
¼ cup raisins
2½ tablespoons sliced almonds, toasted
⅛ teaspoon salt
⅛ teaspoon freshly ground black pepper
1 center-cut bacon slice, cooked and crumbled (drained)
2 tablespoons white wine vinegar
2 tablespoons sugar
1½ teaspoons olive oil

1. Combine first 8 ingredients in a large bowl. Combine vinegar, sugar, and oil in a small bowl, stirring with a whisk to combine. Pour vinegar mixture over broccoli mixture; toss gently to coat. Yield: 6 servings (serving size: about ¾ cup).

CALORIES 84 (32% from fat); FAT 3g (sat 0.4g, mono 1.9g, poly 0.6g); PROTEIN 2.6g; CARB 13.5g; FIBER 2.1g; CHOL 1mg; IRON 0.6mg; SODIUM 84mg; CALC 35mg

---

MAKE AHEAD
Cacik

"I've also tried this cold Turkish soup as a dip with carrots, celery sticks, and pita triangles, so this recipe can certainly perform double duty."

—Peggy McGee, Green Valley, Arizona

1 garlic clove, crushed
2 cups plain low-fat yogurt
1½ cups grated cucumber (about 1 large seedless)
1 tablespoon white vinegar
2 teaspoons extravirgin olive oil
1½ teaspoons chopped fresh dill
1½ teaspoons chopped fresh mint
2 tablespoons water
Mint sprigs (optional)

1. Rub a large bowl with garlic; discard garlic. Combine yogurt and next 5 ingredients in bowl. Cover and chill 2 hours. Stir in 2 tablespoons water, and serve. Garnish with mint sprigs, if desired. Yield: 10 servings (serving size: ¼ cup).

CALORIES 48 (32% from fat); FAT 1.7g (sat 0.6g, mono 0.9g, poly 0.1g); PROTEIN 2.8g; CARB 5.4g; FIBER 0.2g; CHOL 3mg; IRON 0.2mg; SODIUM 36mg; CALC 95mg

---

inspired vegetarian

Veggie Burgers

Beans, tofu, and meaty mushrooms offer fresh options.

Open-Faced Falafel Burgers

This Middle Eastern vegetarian sandwich is typically stuffed in a pita, but our version offers a more eye-catching presentation. Garnish with parsley.

SAUCE:
1 cup hot water
¼ cup tahini (sesame-seed paste)
3 tablespoons fresh lemon juice
⅛ teaspoon salt
2 garlic cloves, minced

PATTIES:
1 cup chopped red onion
½ cup chopped fresh parsley
2 tablespoons fresh lemon juice
1 teaspoon ground cumin
1 teaspoon ground coriander
½ teaspoon salt
2 (15½-ounce) cans chickpeas (garbanzo beans), rinsed and drained
4 garlic cloves, minced
½ cup dry breadcrumbs, divided
4 teaspoons olive oil, divided

REMAINING INGREDIENTS:
6 mini pitas (about 5 inches wide)
3 cups chopped romaine lettuce
2 cups chopped tomato
2 cups sliced peeled cucumber
½ cup finely chopped red onion

1. To prepare sauce, place first 5 ingredients in a blender; process until smooth.
2. To prepare patties, place 1 cup onion and next 7 ingredients in a food processor, and process until smooth, scraping sides of bowl occasionally. Place bean mixture in a large bowl; stir in ¼ cup breadcrumbs. Divide bean mixture into 6 equal portions, shaping each into a ½-inch-thick patty. Place ¼ cup breadcrumbs in a shallow dish. Dredge patties in breadcrumbs.
3. Heat 2 teaspoons oil in a large non-stick skillet over medium-high heat. Add 3 patties to pan; cook 3 minutes on each side or until browned. Repeat procedure with 2 teaspoons oil and remaining patties.
4. Warm mini pitas according to package directions. Place 1 pita on each of 6 plates. Top each pita with ½ cup lettuce, ⅓ cup tomato, ⅓ cup cucumber, and 4 teaspoons onion. Drizzle each serving with about 3 tablespoons sauce; top each serving with 1 patty. Yield: 6 servings (serving size: 1 burger).

CALORIES 437 (24% from fat); FAT 11.6g (sat 1.7g, mono 4.1g, poly 4.6g); PROTEIN 14.8g; CARB 70.8g; FIBER 9.1g; CHOL 0mg; IRON 4.7mg; SODIUM 903mg; CALC 159mg

WINE NOTE: Light in body and tannin, pinot noir is the perfect red wine for robust vegetarian dishes. These burgers include spices like coriander and cumin, which are echoed in Kim Crawford Marlborough Pinot Noir ($15), with its savory nuances and aromas of smoke and dried herbs. Bright fruit and ample acidity help to cut the burgers' rich tahini sauce.

Hominy-Pinto Burgers with Roasted Poblano Chiles

For an easy side, combine fresh corn, chopped avocado, red onion, cilantro, and fresh lime juice. If you can't find masa harina, substitute dry polenta or cornmeal.

2 poblano chiles
Cooking spray
1 cup chopped onion
2 garlic cloves, minced
¼ teaspoon salt
1 (15.5-ounce) can pinto beans, rinsed and drained
1 (15-ounce) can hominy, rinsed and drained
¾ cup masa harina, divided
1 tablespoon canola oil
¾ cup (3 ounces) shredded Monterey Jack cheese with jalapeño peppers
2 tablespoons reduced-fat sour cream
2 tablespoons low-sodium salsa
4 (1½-ounce) whole wheat hamburger buns, toasted

1. Preheat broiler.
2. Place chiles on a foil-lined baking sheet; broil 3 inches from heat 8 minutes or until blackened and charred, turning after 6 minutes. Place in a heavy-duty plastic bag; seal. Let stand 15 minutes. Peel and discard skins. Cut each chile lengthwise into 4 strips; discard seeds.
3. Heat a large nonstick skillet over medium-high heat. Coat pan with cooking spray. Add onion and garlic; sauté 5 minutes. Place onion mixture, salt, beans, and hominy in a food processor; pulse until coarsely ground. Combine bean mixture and ½ cup masa in a medium bowl. Divide bean mixture into

4 equal portions, shaping each into a ½-inch-thick patty. Place ¼ cup masa in a shallow dish; dredge patties in masa.
4. Heat oil in skillet over medium heat. Add patties to pan; cook 4 minutes. Turn patties over. Top each patty with 3 tablespoons cheese; cook 4 minutes.
5. Combine sour cream and salsa in a small bowl. Spread 1 tablespoon sour cream mixture on top half of each bun. Place patties on bottom halves of buns; top each serving with 2 pepper strips. Cover with tops of buns. Yield: 4 servings (serving size: 1 burger).

CALORIES 475 (27% from fat); FAT 14.4g (sat 4.8g, mono 4.9g, poly 2.5g); PROTEIN 18.8g; CARB 71.5g; FIBER 11g; CHOL 25mg; IRON 4.9mg; SODIUM 864mg; CALC 234mg

Grilled Lemon-Basil Tofu Burgers

Marinated tofu slices acquire a golden crust when grilled; the olive-garlic mayonnaise on the sandwich adds a Mediterranean flavor. Serve with grilled asparagus.

⅓ cup finely chopped fresh basil
2 teaspoons grated lemon rind
¼ cup fresh lemon juice
2 tablespoons Dijon mustard
2 tablespoons honey
1 tablespoon extravirgin olive oil
½ teaspoon salt
¼ teaspoon freshly ground black pepper
4 garlic cloves, minced and divided
1 pound firm or extrafirm tofu, drained
Cooking spray
⅓ cup finely chopped pitted kalamata olives
3 tablespoons reduced-fat sour cream
3 tablespoons light mayonnaise
6 (1½-ounce) hamburger buns
6 (¼-inch-thick) slices tomato
1 cup trimmed watercress

1. Combine first 8 ingredients and 3 garlic cloves in a small bowl. Cut tofu crosswise into 6 slices. Pat each square dry with paper towels. Place tofu slices on a jelly-roll pan. Brush both sides of

tofu slices with lemon juice mixture; reserve remaining juice mixture. Let tofu stand 1 hour.
2. Prepare grill.
3. Place tofu slices on grill rack coated with cooking spray; grill 3 minutes on each side. Brush tofu with reserved juice mixture.
4. Combine 1 minced garlic clove, olives, sour cream, and mayonnaise in a small bowl; stir well. Spread about 1½ tablespoons mayonnaise mixture over bottom half of each bun; top each with 1 tofu slice, 1 tomato slice, about 2 tablespoons watercress, and top half of bun. Yield: 6 servings (serving size: 1 burger).

CALORIES 276 (37% from fat); FAT 11.3g (sat 1.9g, mono 5.7g, poly 2.2g); PROTEIN 10.5g; CARB 34.5g; FIBER 1.5g; CHOL 5mg; IRON 2.4mg; SODIUM 743mg; CALC 101mg

QUICK & EASY
Grilled Portobello Burgers

Portobello mushrooms' large size and substantial texture make them a natural choice for a vegetarian "burger." These are quick and supereasy to prepare.

2 tablespoons Worcestershire sauce
2 teaspoons honey mustard
¼ teaspoon black pepper
2 garlic cloves, minced
4 large portobello mushroom caps
1 red bell pepper, cut into 4 wedges
Cooking spray
4 (½-inch-thick) slices onion
8 (½-ounce) slices reduced-fat sharp Cheddar cheese
¼ cup ketchup
2 tablespoons prepared mustard
4 (1½-ounce) hamburger buns
4 Bibb lettuce leaves
8 sandwich-cut bread-and-butter pickles

1. Prepare grill.
2. Combine first 4 ingredients in a small bowl; brush both sides of mushroom caps with sauce mixture.
3. Place bell pepper on grill rack coated with cooking spray; grill 10 minutes or until blackened. Place in a zip-top plastic
Continued

bag; seal. Let stand 10 minutes. Peel. Place mushroom caps, top sides down, and onion on grill rack coated with cooking spray; grill 4 minutes on each side or until tender. Place 2 cheese slices on top of each mushroom cap; cover and grill 1 minute or until cheese melts.

4. Spread 1 tablespoon ketchup and 1½ teaspoons mustard over top half of each bun. Place mushroom caps on bottom halves of buns. Separate onion into rings; arrange onion evenly over mushrooms. Top each serving with 1 lettuce leaf, 2 pickles, and top half of bun. Yield: 4 servings (serving size: 1 burger).

CALORIES 283 (27% from fat); FAT 8.4g (sat 4.6g, mono 2.1g, poly 1.3g); PROTEIN 14.4g; CARB 37.7g; FIBER 3.2g; CHOL 20mg; IRON 2.9mg; SODIUM 995mg; CALC 299mg

Jamaican Black Bean Burgers

Plantains pair well with this Caribbean-inspired burger.

    4   teaspoons canola oil, divided
    2   cups chopped onion
    1   cup chopped red bell pepper
    2   teaspoons grated peeled fresh
        ginger
    3   garlic cloves, minced
    ¾   teaspoon ground allspice
    ½   teaspoon ground coriander
    ¼   teaspoon salt
    ¼   teaspoon ground red pepper
    1   cup cooked rice
    ⅔   cup dry breadcrumbs, divided
    1   (15-ounce) can black beans,
        rinsed and drained
    ¼   cup light mayonnaise
    4   (1½-ounce) whole wheat
        hamburger buns, toasted
    4   Boston lettuce leaves
    4   (⅛-inch-thick) slices red
        onion

1. Heat 1 teaspoon oil in a large nonstick skillet over medium heat until hot. Add chopped onion, bell pepper, ginger, and garlic; cook 7 minutes or until tender, stirring occasionally. Add allspice, coriander, salt, and red pepper; cook 1 minute, stirring constantly.

2. Place onion mixture, rice, ⅓ cup breadcrumbs, and black beans in a food processor; pulse 15 times or until finely chopped. Divide bean mixture into 4 equal portions, shaping each portion into a 1-inch-thick patty. Place ⅓ cup breadcrumbs in a shallow dish, and dredge patties in breadcrumbs. Heat 1 tablespoon oil in a large nonstick skillet over medium heat. Add patties to pan, and cook 3 minutes on each side or until browned and crisp.

3. Spread 1 tablespoon mayonnaise on top half of each bun. Place patties on bottom halves of buns; top each serving with 1 lettuce leaf, 1 onion slice, and top half of bun. Yield: 4 servings (serving size: 1 burger).

CALORIES 420 (28% from fat); FAT 13g (sat 2g, mono 6.9g, poly 3.5g); PROTEIN 11.5g; CARB 69.5g; FIBER 10.7g; CHOL 5mg; IRON 4mg; SODIUM 828mg; CALC 131mg

dinner tonight

No-Cook Meals

Beat the heat with three quick meals.

No-Cook Menu 1
serves 4

Lump Crab Salad

Marinated cucumbers*

Sesame crackers

*Combine 2 cups thinly sliced English cucumber, 3 tablespoons rice vinegar, 1½ teaspoons sugar, ½ teaspoon dark sesame oil, ¼ teaspoon salt, and ¼ teaspoon crushed red pepper. Cover and chill.

Game Plan

1. Prepare and refrigerate cucumbers.
2. Prepare crab salad.
3. Spoon salad into lettuce leaves just before serving.

QUICK & EASY
Lump Crab Salad

Though it can be expensive, crabmeat is great for quick and delicious dinners. Substitute canned lump crabmeat for fresh, if you prefer, but avoid using regular canned crabmeat; the meat is too flaky for this dish. Rinse canned crabmeat for the best flavor.

TOTAL TIME: 24 MINUTES
FLAVOR TIP: To get more juice from a lime, microwave it at HIGH 10 seconds before cutting it open.

DRESSING:

    ½   teaspoon grated lime rind
    3   tablespoons fresh lime juice
    1½ tablespoons extravirgin olive oil
    1   teaspoon sugar
    1   teaspoon Thai fish sauce (such as
        Three Crabs)
    ¼   teaspoon salt
    ⅛   teaspoon ground red pepper

SALAD:

    ¾   cup finely chopped celery
    ⅔   cup finely chopped red bell
        pepper
    ⅓   cup thinly sliced green
        onions
    3   tablespoons chopped fresh mint
    1   pound lump crabmeat, shell pieces
        removed
    4   Boston lettuce leaves

1. To prepare dressing, combine first 7 ingredients, stirring with a whisk.
2. To prepare salad, place celery and next 4 ingredients in a medium bowl; toss gently. Drizzle dressing over salad; toss gently to coat. Place 1 lettuce leaf on each of 4 plates; spoon 1 cup salad into each leaf. Yield: 4 servings.

CALORIES 202 (29% from fat); FAT 6.6g (sat 0.7g, mono 3.7g, poly 0.6g); PROTEIN 27.8g; CARB 5.3g; FIBER 1.3g; CHOL 128mg; IRON 1.5mg; SODIUM 730mg; CALC 160mg

No-Cook Menu 2

serves 4

Chipotle Chicken Taco Salad

Watermelon-mango salad*

Baked tortilla chips

*Combine 2 cups cubed seeded watermelon and 1 cup sliced peeled mango in a medium bowl. Combine 1½ tablespoons fresh lime juice, 2 teaspoons honey, and ⅛ teaspoon salt, stirring with a whisk. Drizzle juice mixture over fruit; toss gently to coat. Sprinkle with 1 teaspoon chopped fresh mint.

Game Plan

1. Prepare fruit salad; cover and chill.
2. While fruit salad refrigerates:
• Prepare taco salad dressing
• Combine taco salad ingredients
3. Toss taco salad with dressing just before serving.

QUICK & EASY

Chipotle Chicken Taco Salad

(pictured on page 243)

The dressing mellows the heat from the chiles.

TOTAL TIME: 34 MINUTES

DRESSING:

⅔ cup light sour cream
⅓ cup chopped fresh cilantro
4 teaspoons fresh lime juice
1 tablespoon minced chipotle chile, canned in adobo sauce
1 teaspoon ground cumin
1 teaspoon chili powder
¼ teaspoon salt

SALAD:

4 cups shredded romaine lettuce
2 cups chopped roasted skinless, boneless chicken breast (about 2 breast halves)
1 cup cherry tomatoes, halved
½ cup diced peeled avocado
⅓ cup thinly vertically sliced red onion
1 (15-ounce) can black beans, rinsed and drained
1 (8¾-ounce) can no-salt-added whole-kernel corn, rinsed and drained

1. To prepare dressing, combine first 7 ingredients, stirring well.
2. To prepare salad, combine lettuce and remaining 6 ingredients in a large bowl. Drizzle dressing over salad; toss gently to coat. Serve immediately. Yield: 4 servings (serving size: 2½ cups).

CALORIES 249 (30% from fat); FAT 8.2g (sat 2.8g, mono 2.9g, poly 0.7g); PROTEIN 23.3g; CARB 25.1g; FIBER 7g; CHOL 50mg; IRON 2.2mg; SODIUM 650mg; CALC 106mg

No-Cook Menu 3

serves 4

Shrimp and White Bean Salad with Creamy Lemon-Dill Dressing

Tomato wedges with spiced salt*

Pumpernickel bread

*Combine ¼ teaspoon kosher salt, ⅛ teaspoon chili powder, ⅛ teaspoon ground cumin, and ⅛ teaspoon ground red pepper. Cut each of 4 large plum tomatoes into 4 wedges, and lightly sprinkle with salt mixture.

Game Plan

1. Prepare shrimp mixture, and refrigerate.
2. While shrimp mixture chills:
• Prepare watercress mixture
• Prepare spiced salt
• Cut tomatoes
3. Just before serving:
• Spoon shrimp mixture onto watercress
• Sprinkle spiced salt on tomato wedges

STAFF FAVORITE • QUICK & EASY

Shrimp and White Bean Salad with Creamy Lemon-Dill Dressing

For a flavor variation, try arugula and basil in place of watercress and dill. You can also substitute chopped rotisserie chicken for shrimp.

TOTAL TIME: 32 MINUTES

QUICK TIP: Look for precooked peeled and deveined shrimp at the seafood counter, or purchase it frozen to keep on hand for quick toss-together meals.

3 tablespoons reduced-fat mayonnaise
2 tablespoons plain fat-free yogurt
1 tablespoon fresh lemon juice, divided
1½ teaspoons chopped fresh dill
¼ teaspoon salt, divided
¼ teaspoon freshly ground black pepper
¾ cup chopped fennel bulb
⅓ cup julienne-cut carrot
¼ cup thinly vertically sliced red onion
1¼ pounds cooked peeled and deveined large shrimp
1 (15.5-ounce) can Great Northern beans, rinsed and drained
1 teaspoon extravirgin olive oil
4 ounces trimmed watercress (about 1 bunch)

1. Combine mayonnaise, yogurt, 1½ teaspoons lemon juice, dill, ⅛ teaspoon salt, and pepper in a large bowl, stirring well with a whisk. Add fennel and next 4 ingredients; toss well.
2. Combine oil, watercress, 1½ teaspoons lemon juice, and ⅛ teaspoon salt in a large bowl; toss gently to coat. Divide watercress mixture evenly among 4 plates; top each serving with 1½ cups shrimp mixture. Yield: 4 servings.

CALORIES 252 (16% from fat); FAT 4.5g (sat 1g, mono 1.4g, poly 1.7g); PROTEIN 35.3g; CARB 16.8g; FIBER 3.9g; CHOL 277mg; IRON 5.7mg; SODIUM 761mg; CALC 144mg

A Little
DASH Will Do

Reap the benefits of a diet proven to reduce blood pressure by eating more food—especially fruits, vegetables, and low-fat dairy.

Many diets these days work on the premise of eliminating foods or including specialty products to promote some health benefit. Here's a refreshing twist: a meal plan that's been around for years, doesn't deprive you of tasty foods, and has been proven to work.

The Dietary Approaches to Stop Hypertension (DASH) diet doesn't lower blood pressure by cutting out certain foods. In fact, you can reap its benefits simply by adding more fruits and vegetables to your diet.

Instead of dishing out advice to quit eating this or cut out that, nutritionists now talk in terms of consuming more DASH plan foods, especially those rich in calcium, magnesium, and potassium, for better cardiovascular health.

QUICK & EASY
Banana Cream Pie Smoothie

A higher-fiber alternative to plain milk, this smoothie doubles as a smart breakfast or a milk shake–like treat. One serving of the smoothie contains 315 milligrams of calcium, roughly the same amount as a glass of milk. Freeze and store extra bananas in zip-top plastic bags so you can whip up this smoothie in a flash.

  1 cup sliced ripe banana (about 1 large)
  1 cup vanilla low-fat yogurt
  ½ cup 1% low-fat milk
  2 tablespoons whole wheat graham cracker crumbs (about ½ cookie sheet)
  1 tablespoon nonfat dry milk
  ½ teaspoon vanilla extract
  3 ice cubes (about ¼ cup)
Graham cracker crumbs

1. Arrange banana slices in a single layer on a baking sheet, and freeze until firm (about 1 hour).

2. Place frozen banana, yogurt, and next 5 ingredients in a blender. Process until smooth. Sprinkle each serving with graham cracker crumbs. Serve immediately. Yield: 2 servings (serving size: 1 cup).

CALORIES 216 (12% from fat); FAT 2.8g (sat 1.5g, mono 0.8g, poly 0.3g); PROTEIN 9.8g; CARB 39.3g; FIBER 1.9g; CHOL 9mg; IRON 0.4mg; SODIUM 145mg; CALC 315mg

Sesame Red Lentils

Lentils and sesame seeds combine in this savory, nutty side dish to provide about 10 percent of daily magnesium needs.

  2 teaspoons peanut oil
  1 teaspoon dark sesame oil
  ½ cup finely chopped shallots (about 4 medium)
  2 cups dried small red lentils
  1½ cups water
  2 tablespoons low-sodium soy sauce
  ¼ teaspoon salt
  1 (14-ounce) can fat-free, less-sodium chicken broth
  1 cup thinly sliced green onions
  1 tablespoon sesame seeds, toasted

1. Heat oils in a medium saucepan over medium heat. Add shallots; cook 3 minutes or until tender. Add lentils and next 4 ingredients; bring to a boil. Cover, reduce heat, and simmer 20 minutes or until lentils are tender, stirring occasionally. Stir in green onions. Sprinkle with sesame seeds. Yield: 8 servings (serving size: ½ cup).

CALORIES 210 (14% from fat); FAT 3.3g (sat 0.4g, mono 1g, poly 0.9g); PROTEIN 14.3g; CARB 31.5g; FIBER 7.7g; CHOL 0mg; IRON 3.1mg; SODIUM 310mg; CALC 45mg

Broccoli and Parmesan Casserole

Broccoli is one of the best vegetable sources of calcium. Here it's paired with a béchamel sauce thickened with cheese, which boosts the calcium even more.

  8 cups coarsely chopped broccoli florets (about 2 pounds)
  ⅓ cup all-purpose flour (about 1½ ounces)
  ¼ teaspoon salt
  ¼ teaspoon dry mustard
  1½ cups fat-free milk
  1 cup fat-free, less-sodium chicken broth
  1 cup (4 ounces) reduced-fat shredded extrasharp Cheddar cheese
  ½ cup (2 ounces) grated Parmesan cheese, divided
  2 tablespoons diced pimientos, drained
  ¼ teaspoon freshly ground black pepper
Cooking spray
  12 garlic melba toast rounds

1. Preheat oven to 400°.
2. Cook broccoli in boiling water 3 minutes or until crisp-tender; drain.
3. Lightly spoon flour into a dry measuring cup, and level with a knife. Place flour, salt, and mustard in a large, heavy saucepan over medium heat; gradually add milk and broth, stirring with a whisk until blended. Cook 8 minutes or until thick, stirring constantly. Remove from heat, and add Cheddar cheese and 6

tablespoons Parmesan cheese, stirring until melted. Stir in pimientos and pepper. Add broccoli, tossing to coat.

4. Spoon broccoli mixture into a 13 x 9–inch baking dish coated with cooking spray.

5. Place toast rounds in a food processor; pulse 10 times or until coarse crumbs measure 1 cup. Combine crumbs and 2 tablespoons Parmesan cheese, and sprinkle evenly over broccoli mixture. Spray top of casserole lightly with cooking spray. Bake at 400° for 15 minutes or until bubbly. Let stand 5 minutes before serving. Yield: 8 servings (serving size: about 1 cup).

CALORIES 154 (30% from fat); FAT 5.1g (sat 3g, mono 0.5g, poly 0.3g); PROTEIN 11.9g; CARB 16.6g; FIBER 3.7g; CHOL 15mg; IRON 1.5mg; SODIUM 415mg; CALC 274mg

---

MAKE AHEAD
Lima Bean Salad

Beans, legumes, and nuts are all rich in magnesium. We combine three magnesium-rich beans—lima, kidney, and garbanzo—in an easy-to-make side salad. You can substitute Great Northern beans, pinto beans, or navy beans.

    3 tablespoons fresh lemon juice
    ¼ teaspoon salt
    ¼ teaspoon pepper
    ¼ teaspoon Dijon mustard
    2 tablespoons olive oil
    1 cup cooked bulgur
    1 cup frozen lima beans, cooked
    1 cup chopped yellow bell pepper
    ¼ cup finely chopped red onion
    ¼ cup chopped fresh chives
    ¼ cup chopped fresh parsley
    1 tablespoon chopped fresh thyme
    1 (15½-ounce) can chickpeas
       (garbanzo beans), rinsed and drained
    1 (15-ounce) can kidney beans,
       rinsed and drained

1. Combine first 4 ingredients in a large bowl; add oil, stirring with a whisk. Add bulgur and remaining ingredients; toss well. Cover and chill. Yield: 6 servings (serving size: 1 cup).

CALORIES 182 (28% from fat); FAT 5.6g (sat 0.7g, mono 3.4g, poly 0.7g); PROTEIN 8g; CARB 26.8g; FIBER 7.5g; CHOL 0mg; IRON 2.4mg; SODIUM 347mg; CALC 51mg

---

Farmers' Market Fare Menu
serves 6

Celebrate a morning of smart shopping with this fresh-flavored meal.

Potato, Corn, and Leek Chowder

Tossed green salad*
Garlic breadsticks

*Combine 4 cups arugula and 4 cups baby spinach in a large bowl. Cut 2 large tomatoes into 6 wedges each. Add tomato wedges, 1 cup julienne-cut yellow bell pepper, and 1 cup thinly sliced English cucumber to bowl. Combine 1½ tablespoons lemon juice, 1 tablespoon extravirgin olive oil, 1 tablespoon chopped fresh basil, ¼ teaspoon salt, and ¼ teaspoon freshly ground black pepper; stir well with a whisk. Drizzle over salad; toss well.

QUICK & EASY
Potato, Corn, and Leek Chowder

This soup ends up being a good source of three blood pressure-lowering minerals since the milk adds calcium and the potatoes deliver a dose of potassium, as well as magnesium. Serve with hot sauce.

    2   tablespoons butter
    1   tablespoon olive oil
    1½   cups coarsely chopped leek (about
         1 large)
    ½   cup finely chopped celery
    ½   cup finely chopped red bell pepper
    2   cups whole milk
    3   tablespoons all-purpose flour
    3   cups fat-free, less-sodium chicken
         broth
    2   cups fresh corn kernels (about 4
         ears)
    2   pounds cubed peeled Yukon gold
         or red potatoes
    1   teaspoon salt
    ¼   teaspoon freshly ground black
         pepper
    ¼   cup finely chopped fresh parsley
    3   tablespoons chopped fresh chives

1. Heat butter and oil in a large Dutch oven over medium heat. Add leek, celery, and bell pepper; cook 4 minutes or until vegetables are tender, stirring frequently. Combine milk and flour in a small bowl, stirring with a whisk. Slowly add milk mixture to pan, stirring constantly. Stir in broth and next 4 ingredients; bring to a boil. Reduce heat, and simmer 20 minutes or until potato is tender. Stir in parsley and chives. Yield: 6 servings (serving size: 1⅓ cups).

CALORIES 331 (26% from fat); FAT 9.5g (sat 4.4g, mono 3.4g, poly 0.9g); PROTEIN 9.8g; CARB 54.9g; FIBER 5.3g; CHOL 18mg; IRON 1.8mg; SODIUM 701mg; CALC 127mg

---

QUICK & EASY
Spinach with Pine Nuts and Golden Raisins

This Spanish-inspired side dish is a sweet-savory combination of garlicky wilted spinach, buttery pine nuts, and golden raisins. One serving is a tasty way to pack in 114 milligrams of magnesium—about 25 percent of your daily needs.

    ½   cup boiling water
    ⅓   cup golden raisins
    2   (9-ounce) bags baby
         spinach
    2   tablespoons water
    1   teaspoon olive oil
    2   garlic cloves, minced
    ¼   teaspoon salt
    ¼   teaspoon freshly ground black
         pepper
    4   teaspoons pine nuts, toasted

1. Combine ½ cup boiling water and raisins; let stand 15 minutes or until raisins are plump. Drain.

2. Combine spinach and 2 tablespoons water in a large Dutch oven over medium-high heat. Cook 3 minutes or until spinach wilts, stirring frequently. Remove from pan. Wipe pan with a paper towel.

3. Heat oil in pan over medium heat. Add garlic; cook 30 seconds, stirring frequently. Add spinach, raisins, salt, and pepper; cook 1 minute or until thoroughly heated. Stir in pine nuts. Yield: 4 servings (serving size: ½ cup).

CALORIES 121 (23% from fat); FAT 3.1g (sat 0.3g, mono 1.4g, poly 1.1g); PROTEIN 3.9g; CARB 24.1g; FIBER 6.7g; CHOL 0mg; IRON 4.5mg; SODIUM 352mg; CALC 100mg

Easy Does It

Many foods supply several of the DASH nutrients. For example, trail mix with dried fruit and nuts offers potassium and magnesium; milk offers a healthy dose of both calcium and potassium.

According to the DASH diet, one fruit serving equals 6 ounces of juice or one piece of fruit, while a vegetable serving equals 1 cup raw leafy vegetables or ½ cup cooked vegetables. One 8-ounce glass of milk or 1½ ounces of low-fat cheese counts as one dairy serving. Whole grains and grain product servings add up with one slice of bread or ½ cup cooked grains as one serving. Receive a serving of seeds or nuts with 1 tablespoon of seeds or ⅓ cup nuts.

Our recipes offer a good boost of calcium, magnesium, and potassium toward your daily goal, but you'll need to add other foods, too. Here are daily intake goals (based on the DASH study) for each of the three minerals, along with good sources of each.

	Calcium 1,240 milligrams	Potassium 4,700 milligrams	Magnesium 500 milligrams
8 ounces fat-free milk	301mg	407mg	27mg
⅓ cup mixed nuts	30mg	254mg	96mg
¼ cup raisins	19mg	271mg	13mg
1 medium peach	5mg	193mg	7mg
1 carrot	19mg	233mg	11mg
1½ ounces low-fat cheese	177mg	29mg	8mg
2 tablespoons sunflower seeds	21mg	124mg	64mg

MAKE AHEAD

Mashed Potatoes with Cumin-Lime Butter

- 3 tablespoons finely chopped fresh cilantro
- 2 tablespoons finely chopped shallots
- 2 tablespoons butter, softened
- 4 teaspoons fresh lime juice
- 1½ teaspoons cumin seeds, toasted
- ½ teaspoon ground cumin
- 2½ pounds Yukon gold potatoes, peeled and quartered
- ¾ cup low-fat buttermilk
- ¾ teaspoon salt
- ¼ teaspoon freshly ground black pepper

1. Combine first 6 ingredients in a small bowl. Mash with a fork until blended. Cover and refrigerate.

2. Place potatoes in a large saucepan; cover with water. Bring to a boil. Reduce heat, and simmer 20 minutes or until tender; drain. Return potatoes to pan. Add buttermilk, salt, and pepper; beat with a mixer at medium speed until smooth. Serve with butter mixture. Yield: 6 servings (serving size: ¾ cup potatoes and 1 teaspoon butter mixture).

CALORIES 216 (19% from fat); FAT 4.5g (sat 2.6g, mono 1.1g, poly 0.2g); PROTEIN 4.6g; CARB 40.7g; FIBER 3.6g; CHOL 12mg; IRON 1.1mg; SODIUM 367mg; CALC 56mg

---

Peanut-Crusted Tofu Triangles

Tofu and peanuts contribute magnesium.

- 1 (14-ounce) package firm tofu, drained
- 1½ cups uncooked instant rice
- 1½ cups rice milk
- ½ cup thinly sliced green onions
- ⅓ cup chopped fresh cilantro
- 3 tablespoons finely chopped red bell pepper
- 1 teaspoon salt, divided
- 1 teaspoon water
- 1 large egg white, lightly beaten
- ⅓ cup dry-roasted peanuts
- ½ teaspoon garlic powder
- ½ teaspoon ground ginger
- ½ teaspoon crushed red pepper
- 2 teaspoons peanut oil, divided
- Cooking spray

1. Cut tofu crosswise into 8 equal pieces. Cut each piece into two triangles. Arrange tofu in a single layer on several layers of heavy-duty paper towels. Cover tofu with additional paper towels. Place a cutting board on top of tofu. Place a heavy pan on cutting board. Let stand 20 minutes. Pat tofu dry with paper towels.

2. Combine rice and milk in a medium saucepan; bring to a boil. Cover, reduce heat, and simmer 5 minutes. Stir in onions, cilantro, bell pepper, and ½ teaspoon salt. Cover and keep warm.

3. Combine 1 teaspoon water and egg white in a shallow dish. Place peanuts in a food processor; process until finely ground. Combine ground peanuts, garlic powder, ginger, red pepper, and ½ teaspoon salt in a shallow dish. Dip one side of each tofu triangle in egg mixture. Dredge same side in peanut mixture. Heat 1 teaspoon oil in a large nonstick skillet coated with cooking spray over medium heat. Add half of tofu; cook 2 minutes on each side or until browned. (Watch closely to prevent burning.) Repeat procedure with 1 teaspoon oil and remaining tofu. Serve tofu with rice. Yield: 4 servings (serving size: ¾ cup rice and 4 tofu triangles).

CALORIES 391 (35% from fat); FAT 15.1g (sat 2.5g, mono 5.5g, poly 6.6g); PROTEIN 17.6g; CARB 46.7g; FIBER 2.6g; CHOL 0mg; IRON 3.1mg; SODIUM 748mg; CALC 101mg

Indian-Spiced Chicken with Tomato Chutney

A serving of this dish provides about one-tenth of your daily potassium needs. Serve with broccoli and whole wheat pitas.

CHUTNEY:

1½ teaspoons olive oil
¼ cup chopped shallots
1 teaspoon minced seeded serrano chile
¼ teaspoon minced peeled fresh ginger
1 garlic clove, minced
1 cup coarsely chopped seeded tomato
2 tablespoons red wine vinegar
1 tablespoon sugar
1 teaspoon mustard seeds
½ teaspoon salt

CHICKEN:

2 teaspoons olive oil
½ teaspoon ground coriander
½ teaspoon curry powder
¼ teaspoon ground cumin
¼ teaspoon black pepper
4 (6-ounce) skinless, boneless chicken breast halves
½ teaspoon salt
Cooking spray

1. To prepare chutney, heat 1½ teaspoons oil in a small saucepan over medium heat. Add shallots and serrano; cook 2 minutes, stirring frequently. Add ginger and garlic; cook 30 seconds, stirring frequently. Add tomato and next 4 ingredients; bring to a boil. Cover, reduce heat, and simmer 10 minutes. Uncover and simmer 5 minutes or until mixture is thick. Set aside, and keep warm.
2. Prepare grill.
3. To prepare chicken, heat 2 teaspoons oil in a small saucepan over medium heat. Add coriander, curry, cumin, and black pepper; cook 1 minute, stirring frequently. Brush mixture evenly on both sides of chicken; sprinkle evenly with ½ teaspoon salt.
4. Place chicken on grill rack coated with cooking spray; grill 4 minutes on each side or until chicken is done. Serve chutney over chicken. Yield: 4 servings (serving size: 1 chicken breast half and about 2½ tablespoons chutney).

CALORIES 268 (30% from fat); FAT 8.9g (sat 1.9g, mono 4.7g, poly 1.5g); PROTEIN 40.6g; CARB 4.3g; FIBER 0.9g; CHOL 108mg; IRON 1.8mg; SODIUM 687mg; CALC 36mg

Fig, Date, and Walnut Quick Bread

Dried fruits like figs and dates are good sources of potassium and fiber. Here they're paired with heart-healthy walnuts and a mixture of whole wheat and white flours. One slice of this sweet, rich bread adds a generous 227 milligrams of potassium to your daily tally.

¾ cup low-fat buttermilk
½ teaspoon finely grated lemon rind
¼ teaspoon ground nutmeg
⅛ teaspoon ground cloves
⅔ cup chopped dried figs
⅓ cup chopped pitted dates
½ cup packed brown sugar
2 tablespoons canola oil
2 large eggs, lightly beaten
¾ cup whole wheat flour (about 3½ ounces)
¾ cup all-purpose flour (about 3⅓ ounces)
1½ teaspoons baking soda
⅛ teaspoon salt
Cooking spray
⅓ cup chopped walnuts

1. Preheat oven to 350°.
2. Heat first 4 ingredients in a small, heavy saucepan over medium heat just until bubbles begin to form around edge (do not boil). Remove from heat; stir in figs and dates. Let stand 20 minutes or until fruit softens.
3. Combine sugar, oil, and eggs in a large bowl; stir with a whisk until well blended. Stir in cooled buttermilk mixture.
4. Lightly spoon flours into dry measuring cups; level with a knife. Combine flours, baking soda, and salt in a large bowl; make a well in center of mixture. Add buttermilk mixture to flour mixture, stirring just until moist. Spoon batter into an 8 x 4–inch loaf pan coated with cooking spray. Sprinkle walnuts evenly over batter. Bake at 350° for 40 minutes or until a wooden pick inserted in center comes out clean. Cool 10 minutes in pan on wire rack; remove from pan. Cool completely on wire rack. Yield: 12 servings (serving size: 1 slice).

CALORIES 192 (27% from fat); FAT 5.8g (sat 0.8g, mono 2g, poly 2.5g); PROTEIN 4.4g; CARB 32.5g; FIBER 2.9g; CHOL 36mg; IRON 1.4mg; SODIUM 216mg; CALC 55mg

Label Lingo

Here are some points to keep in mind when you're reading a Nutrition Facts label to determine how a food fits into your daily meal plan. You can also visit the Food and Drug Administration's Web site to learn more: www.cfsan.fda.gov.

Serving Size: typically uses common kitchen measurements to identify the unit the nutrition information is based on. Serving size is especially important since some foods' nutrition information—like a canned drink or a purchased muffin—are often based on two servings.

Amount Per Serving: the number of grams or calories a serving contains

Percent Daily Value: percentage of a nutrient provided by one serving of that food based on Reference Daily Intakes and Dietary Reference Values. Even though not every nutrient has a Percent Daily Value (like trans fats, for example), many major nutrients do. As a general rule, foods low in a nutrient contribute five Percent Daily Value or less while foods supplying 20 Percent Daily Value or more would be considered a high amount of a nutrient.

Buy Local

In a growing trend, home cooks and chefs are discovering the great taste of foods made close to home—and helping reshape how we eat in America.

WINE NOTE: Green, vegetal flavors, like those found in this soup, call for sauvignon blanc's distinctive, herbaceous character. The wine's grassy, citrus qualities bring out the soup's fresh, crisp flavors. A good value from California is Dry Creek Vineyard Fumé Blanc ($13.50).

Dan Barber, the chef of Blue Hill at Stone Barns, is on the edge of a trend sweeping restaurants and home kitchens as more people embrace the benefits of cooking with ingredients that are grown, raised, or produced near the tables where they will be served. Home cooks have come to appreciate the vivid taste of fresh, in-season fruits and vegetables that are grown nearby and prepared soon after harvest. Chefs at white-tablecloth and casual restaurants highlight local and regional produce, heritage meats, artisanal cheeses, and other foods on their menus. Of course, the flavor of local goods is the greatest benefit, but there are other advantages, too, including supporting small-scale regional farmers.

Blue Hill at Stone Barns is located on the 80-acre Stone Barns Center for Food and Agriculture, which opened in May 2004 to educate the public about the entire farm-to-table process.

"We bring all the elements together," says Stone Barns Executive Director James Ford. "The point is to reconnect people to their food and where it comes from."

Cucumber Soup

Chef Dan Barber of Blue Hill at Stone Barns uses the farm's cucumber crop to prepare this fresh-tasting soup. Avocado lends the soup a creamy touch. It's a terrific way to start a summertime dinner party.

- 11 large cucumbers (about 8 pounds), divided
- ¼ cup honey, divided
- ¼ cup rice wine vinegar
- 1 ripe avocado, peeled and seeded
- 2 teaspoons chopped fresh dill
- ¼ teaspoon salt
- ¼ teaspoon freshly ground black pepper
- Cracked black pepper (optional)
- Dill sprigs (optional)

1. Cut 5 cucumbers into 3-inch chunks. Place half of cucumber chunks and 2 tablespoons honey in a blender or food processor; process until smooth. Pour pureed cucumber mixture into a cheesecloth-lined sieve over a bowl. Repeat procedure with remaining chunks. Cover and chill 8 hours or overnight.

2. Peel, seed, and thinly slice 6 cucumbers; place slices in a bowl. Add vinegar and 2 tablespoons honey; toss well to coat. Cover and chill 8 hours or overnight.

3. Working with cucumber mixture in sieve, press lightly with a wooden spoon or rubber spatula to squeeze out juice; discard solids. Set aside cucumber juice.

4. Place half of marinated cucumber slices, avocado, and 1¾ cups cucumber juice in a blender or food processor; process until smooth. Pour mixture into a bowl. Repeat with remaining cucumber slices and an additional 1¾ cups cucumber juice. Stir in chopped dill, salt, and ground pepper. Divide among each of 6 bowls. Garnish with cracked black pepper and dill sprigs, if desired. Yield: 9 cups (serving size: 1½ cups).

CALORIES 167 (32% from fat); FAT 6g (sat 0.9g, mono 3.2g, poly 0.7g); PROTEIN 3.8g; CARB 27.3g; FIBER 5.3g; CHOL 0mg; IRON 1.6mg; SODIUM 312mg; CALC 79mg

Chicken and Goat Cheese Quesadilla

Wanda Barras created this layered, baked quesadilla to showcase Belle Écorce's goat cheese. Serve with your favorite jarred salsa and a tossed green salad.

- ½ cup fat-free, less-sodium chicken broth
- 2 tablespoons chopped cilantro
- 2 tablespoons fresh lime juice
- 2 tablespoons extravirgin olive oil
- 2 jalapeño peppers, sliced
- 1 (6-ounce) skinless, boneless chicken breast half
- ½ teaspoon salt
- ¼ teaspoon freshly ground black pepper
- 1 onion, cut into ¼-inch slices
- Cooking spray
- 3 (8-inch) fat-free flour tortillas
- 6 tablespoons (3 ounces) crumbled soft goat cheese
- 1 tablespoon chopped fresh cilantro
- 4 teaspoons fat-free sour cream
- Cilantro sprigs (optional)
- Lime wedges (optional)

1. Place first 5 ingredients in a blender or food processor; process until smooth. Place chicken in a zip-top plastic bag. Add broth mixture. Seal and marinate in refrigerator 2 hours, turning bag occasionally.

2. Prepare grill.

3. Remove chicken from bag; discard marinade. Sprinkle chicken with salt and pepper. Place chicken and onion on grill rack coated with cooking spray. Grill onion 3 minutes on each side or until onion is browned. Grill chicken 6 minutes on each side or until done. Cool 5 minutes. Cut chicken into very thin slices.

4. Preheat oven to 400°.

5. Place 1 tortilla on a baking sheet coated with cooking spray. Sprinkle with 3 tablespoons cheese, half of chicken, half of onion, and 1½ teaspoons chopped cilantro. Top with 1 tortilla. Sprinkle with 3 tablespoons cheese, remaining chicken, remaining onion, and 1½ teaspoons chopped cilantro. Top with remaining tortilla. Coat tortilla with cooking spray. Bake at 400° for 15 minutes or until lightly browned. Let stand 5 minutes. Cut into 4 wedges. Top each wedge with 1 teaspoon sour cream. Garnish with cilantro sprigs, and serve with lime wedges, if desired. Yield: 4 servings (serving size: 1 wedge).

CALORIES 248 (33% from fat); FAT 9.2g (sat 4.1g, mono 3.3g, poly 0.8g); PROTEIN 17.4g; CARB 22.9g; FIBER 2.4g; CHOL 37mg; IRON 0.9mg; SODIUM 666mg; CALC 54mg

QUICK & EASY
Pork Chops with Cherry Preserves Sauce

Becky Courchesne of Frog Hollow Farm uses her preserves as a basis for a simple pan sauce. You can slice a one-pound pork tenderloin into four medallions to use in place of the pork chops, or try the sauce over duck breast. Either way, this classic flavor combination makes good use of high-quality cherry preserves. Serve over egg noodles.

Cooking spray
4 (4-ounce) boneless loin pork chops
½ teaspoon salt, divided
¼ teaspoon freshly ground black pepper, divided
1 cup cherry preserves
1 teaspoon balsamic vinegar
Chopped chives (optional)

1. Heat a large nonstick skillet over medium-high heat. Coat pan with cooking spray. Sprinkle pork with ¼ teaspoon salt and ⅛ teaspoon pepper. Add pork to pan; cook 4 minutes on each side

or until browned. Remove pork from pan, and keep warm.

2. Add preserves, vinegar, ¼ teaspoon salt, and ⅛ teaspoon pepper to pan. Cook 30 seconds, scraping pan to loosen browned bits. Serve with pork. Garnish with chopped chives, if desired. Yield: 4 servings (serving size: 1 pork chop and about ¼ cup sauce).

CALORIES 370 (17% from fat); FAT 6.8g (sat 2.4g, mono 3.1g, poly 0.7g); PROTEIN 25.1g; CARB 52.3g; FIBER 0g; CHOL 62mg; IRON 0.9mg; SODIUM 342mg; CALC 25mg

Local Heroes

Small producers are turning out all manner of foods, from honey and artisanal cheese to heritage meat to jams, salsas, and preserves. These food producers are representative of products found across the country.

Burgundy Pasture Beef (www.burgundy-pasturebeef.com or 817-866-2247). Self-described "beef artisans" Jon and Wendy Taggart of Grandview, Texas, raise, package, and home-deliver pasture-fed Angus beef, chicken, and lamb in Dallas. They say their dry-aged product has hearty flavor not found in commercial beef.

Broadwing Farm (www.broadwingfarm-cabins.com or 828-622-3647). Pete and Mary Dixon started their organic farm in Hot Springs, North Carolina, 12 years ago so their kids could have a traditional upbringing. They sell peppers, heirloom tomatoes, and other produce year-round at two farmers' markets in Asheville, but they're best known for plump, sweet Triple Crown blackberries. They also sell pesto made from homegrown herbs.

Blue Schoolhouse Farm (309-467-9228). Being laid off from an Illinois job worked out for Bill Davison, who moved his family to a century-old one-room schoolhouse on a farm in Congerville and began raising pasture-fed laying hens with complex flavor and tender texture. He sells out fast in Bloomington, Illinois, at the farmers' market, local grocery stores, and restaurants.

Belle Ècorce Farm (337-394-6683). Wanda Barras of St. Martinville, Louisiana, raises Adele, Fuzzy Wuzzy, and 30 or so other dairy goats in her five-acre backyard. Dining on wild berry bushes, the pets produce mild milk for a bright-white cheese called Très Belle Chévre, sold at Joey's Fine Foods in nearby Lafayette. She also sells spreads combining cheese with home-dried figs or dried tomatoes and herbs at the Saturday River Ranch Green Market in Lafayette and the once-a-month St. Martinville Creole Farmers' Market.

Frog Hollow Farm (www.froghollow.com or 888-779-4511). The renowned Northern California–based company began by selling organic cherries, peaches, apricots, and nectarines, and then branched out with gourmet pastries, preserves, and chutneys.

Summertime Gourmet Products (www.summertimeproducts.com or 865-947-8087). Gerald Hawkins founded G and H Foods Inc., parent company of Summertime Gourmet, in 2002 to employ residents of Hancock County, Tennessee, to grow, produce, and package the company's salsas, jams, marinades, and barbecue sauces. Today, Summertime Gourmet's products are sold at select Wal-Mart stores and at Fresh Market stores throughout the Southeast. The salsa, which is based on a 100-year-old family recipe from Hawkins's Latino son-in-law, is their big seller.

You'll probably have leftover bean dip. Try using it as filling for a burrito or quesadilla with shredded rotisserie chicken.

Tilapia Tacos with Peach Relish

Chipotle bean dip with chips*

Mexican beer

*Drain 1 (16-ounce) can pinto beans in a colander over a bowl. Place beans and 2 tablespoons drained liquid in a medium bowl; mash until smooth or desired consistency. Stir in ¼ cup finely chopped red bell pepper and 1 teaspoon chopped chipotle chile, canned in adobo sauce. Sprinkle with ¼ cup finely chopped green onions. Serve with baked tortilla chips.

QUICK & EASY

Tilapia Tacos with Peach Relish

Gotreaux Family Farms in Louisiana produces farm-raised tilapia. Locally raised or caught seafood is available at grocers and farmers' markets. You can substitute other seafood, such as salmon or shrimp.

SALSA:

2 cups finely chopped peeled peach (about 2 medium)
½ cup finely chopped red onion
2 tablespoons chopped cilantro
1 tablespoon fresh lime juice
½ teaspoon kosher salt
⅛ teaspoon ground red pepper
1 jalapeño pepper, seeded and finely chopped
1 garlic clove, minced

REMAINING INGREDIENTS:

½ cup panko (Japanese breadcrumbs)
½ teaspoon kosher salt
¼ teaspoon ground red pepper
1 pound tilapia, cut into 2-inch strips
Cooking spray
8 (6-inch) corn tortillas

1. To prepare salsa, combine first 8 ingredients in a medium bowl. Let stand 30 minutes at room temperature.

2. Preheat oven to 375°.

3. Combine panko, ½ teaspoon salt, and ¼ teaspoon pepper in a medium bowl. Add fish to bowl, tossing to coat. Place fish in a single layer on a baking sheet coated with cooking spray. Bake at 375° for 10 minutes or until desired degree of doneness, turning once.

4. Heat tortillas according to package directions. Divide fish and salsa evenly among tortillas. Yield: 4 servings (serving size: 2 tacos).

CALORIES 250 (15% from fat); FAT 4.1g (sat 1g, mono 0.5g, poly 0.9g); PROTEIN 25.8g; CARB 30.6g; FIBER 3.5g; CHOL 75mg; IRON 0.6mg; SODIUM 533mg; CALC 30mg

---

Indian-Style Marinated Chicken

Becky Courchesne of Frog Hollow Farms uses peach preserves as the basis of a spicy-sweet marinade for chicken. You can use any locally made peach preserves.

½ cup peach preserves
¼ cup lemon juice
1 tablespoon olive oil
½ teaspoon ground red pepper
¼ teaspoon cumin
¼ teaspoon ground coriander
¼ teaspoon garam masala
2 canned whole tomatoes, drained
2 garlic cloves
1 (½-inch) piece ginger, peeled and chopped
4 (6-ounce) skinless, boneless chicken breast halves
1 teaspoon salt
Cooking spray
1 cup water
3 cups hot cooked basmati rice

1. Place first 10 ingredients in a food processor; process until smooth. Combine preserves mixture and chicken in a zip-top plastic bag. Seal and marinate in refrigerator 2 hours, turning bag occasionally.

2. Prepare grill.

3. Remove chicken from bag; reserve marinade. Sprinkle chicken evenly with salt; place chicken on grill rack coated with cooking spray. Grill 6 minutes on each side or until chicken is done.

4. Combine reserved marinade and 1 cup water in a medium saucepan over medium-high heat; bring to a boil. Reduce heat, and simmer until reduced to ¾ cup (about 8 minutes). Serve sauce over chicken and rice. Yield: 4 servings (serving size: 1 chicken breast half, ¾ cup rice, and 3 tablespoons sauce).

CALORIES 327 (30% from fat); FAT 11g (sat 2.5g, mono 5.5g, poly 1.9g); PROTEIN 27.9g; CARB 29.4g; FIBER 0.6g; CHOL 77mg; IRON 1.2mg; SODIUM 649mg; CALC 22mg

---

QUICK & EASY

Summertime Gourmet Salsa Pizza

Look for locally made salsas at farmers' markets and groceries. They tend to be much lower in sodium than most commercial salsas.

6 (6-inch) pitas
1 (16-ounce) can fat-free spicy refried beans
¾ cup salsa
¾ cup (3 ounces) preshredded four-cheese Mexican blend cheese
1½ cups thinly sliced iceberg lettuce
6 tablespoons reduced-fat sour cream

1. Preheat oven to 400°.

2. Place pitas on a large baking sheet. Bake at 400° for 8 minutes, turning once. Cool slightly on a wire rack.

3. Spread about ¼ cup beans over each pita. Top each pita with 2 tablespoons salsa and 2 tablespoons cheese. Place pizzas on a large baking sheet. Bake at 400° for 8 minutes or until cheese melts. Remove from oven. Top each pizza with ¼ cup lettuce and 1 tablespoon sour cream. Yield: 6 servings (serving size: 1 pizza).

CALORIES 319 (20% from fat); FAT 7.1g (sat 4.3g, mono 1.5g, poly 0.3g); PROTEIN 13.1g; CARB 48.7g; FIBER 5.3g; CHOL 20mg; IRON 3.4mg; SODIUM 957mg; CALC 202mg

Wildflower Honey Mustard Sauce

This sauce is a tasty condiment for sandwiches and burgers.

¼ cup whole-grain Dijon mustard
¼ cup wildflower honey
2 tablespoons low-fat mayonnaise
1½ tablespoons sherry vinegar
1 tablespoon minced shallots
⅛ teaspoon kosher salt

1. Combine all ingredients in a small bowl; stir with a whisk until well blended. Yield: 8 servings (serving size: 1½ tablespoons).

CALORIES 57 (28% from fat); FAT 1.8g (sat 0.2g, mono 0.3g, poly 0.9g); PROTEIN 0.5g; CARB 10.7g; FIBER 0.3g; CHOL 1mg; IRON 0.3mg; SODIUM 214mg; CALC 7mg

Grilled Shrimp and Spinach Salad with Honey Vinaigrette

Chef Thomas Hogan of the Penthouse Grille in San Francisco developed this recipe using Marshall's Farm's honey.

1 teaspoon grated lemon rind
3 tablespoons fresh lemon juice
1 tablespoon extravirgin olive oil
1 teaspoon kosher salt
1 teaspoon honey
¼ teaspoon freshly ground black pepper
24 large shrimp, peeled and deveined (about 1 pound)
¼ cup chopped shallots
3 tablespoons Champagne vinegar
3 tablespoons honey
1 tablespoon extravirgin olive oil
⅛ teaspoon sea salt
⅛ teaspoon freshly ground black pepper
Cooking spray
1 (16-ounce) bag prewashed baby spinach
1 large head Belgian endive (about 4 ounces)
½ cup (2 ounces) crumbled blue cheese

1. Place first 6 ingredients in a blender or food processor; process until smooth. Combine juice mixture and shrimp in a plastic zip-top bag; seal. Marinate in refrigerator 20 minutes, turning bag occasionally.
2. Prepare grill.
3. Place shallots and next 5 ingredients in a blender or food processor; process 5 minutes or until smooth.
4. Remove shrimp from bag; discard marinade. Place shrimp on grill rack coated with cooking spray. Cook 2 minutes on each side or until done.
5. Combine spinach and endive in a large bowl. Add shallot mixture, tossing to coat. Place 2½ cups spinach mixture on each of 4 plates. Top each serving with 6 shrimp and 2 tablespoons cheese. Yield: 4 servings.

CALORIES 306 (29% from fat); FAT 9.8g (sat 3.7g, mono 4.3g, poly 0.5g); PROTEIN 28.9g; CARB 28g; FIBER 5g; CHOL 13mg; IRON 5.3mg; SODIUM 479mg; CALC 243mg

---

Where to Find Locally Made Goods

The Internet is a good place to search for local ingredients. Regional sites like BuyAppalachian.com and the national LocalHarvest.org have directories of producers. The sites can also help you find CSAs and farmers' markets. And the USDA's Agriculture Marketing Service maintains a state-by-state directory of some 3,600 farmers' markets at www.ams.usda.gov/farmersmarkets, and on its Farmers Market Hotline at 800-384-8704.

Many producers say customers often find them through word of mouth. Neighbors tell neighbors. Chefs at quality restaurants are usually willing to share information about their sources with customers.

---

technique

Grilled to Perfection

A sizzling steak right off the grill is something few can resist.

Basic Grilled Steak
(pictured on page 244)

Turn the steaks only once as you cook them. The more time they are in direct contact with the grill, the better. Serve with corn and Smoked Tomatoes (recipe on page 290).

4 (8-ounce) ribeye steaks, trimmed (about ¾ inch thick)
1 teaspoon salt
¾ teaspoon freshly ground black pepper
Cooking spray

1. Sprinkle both sides of steaks with salt and pepper. Let steaks stand at room temperature 20 minutes.
2. Prepare grill.
3. Pat steaks dry with a paper towel. Place steaks on grill rack coated with cooking spray; grill 2 minutes on each side or until desired degree of doneness. Remove from grill. Cover steaks loosely with foil; let stand 5 minutes. Yield: 4 servings (serving size: 1 steak).

CALORIES 350 (39% from fat); FAT 15.3g (sat 6.1g, mono 6.6g, poly 0.6g); PROTEIN 49.2g; CARB 0.3g; FIBER 0.1g; CHOL 155mg; IRON 3.4mg; SODIUM 683mg; CALC 29mg

Five Tips to a Great Steak

1. Choose a Cut. We work with ribeye, tenderloin, and flank steaks. We use ribeye for the Basic Grilled Steak (recipe on page 287) and the Grilled Herb Steak (recipe on page 289), since it's a tender, flavorful cut and needs little adornment. Tenderloin steaks offer exceptionally supple meat, but because of their lack of fat, they benefit from added flavorings, as in the Grilled Steak with Teriyaki Glaze (recipe on page 290). Flank steak lends itself nicely to salads when sliced very thin, as in Summer Steak Salad (recipe on page 288). Lean flank steak can be tough, which is why it requires thin slicing. When you take the flank off the grill, transfer it to a cutting board with a moat in order to capture juices as you slice.

2. Salt the Meat. Salt sprinkled on a raw steak draws out the juices and makes the surface of the meat moist, which in turn makes it difficult to brown. To avoid this, salt the meat when you start to bring it to room temperature, and pat it dry with a paper towel just before you put it on the grill. This allows the salt to seep into the steak and eliminates water drawn out by the salt.

3. Fire Up the Grill. Charcoal and gas fires each have advantages. A charcoal grill cooks hotter than gas, but it requires building a fire with briquettes. Gas grills are convenient because they need no fire building and it's easy to control the heat.

The best grills for individual steaks are those that allow you to adjust the distance of the rack from the coals. Set the distance between the coals and the steak according to the thickness of the meat—three inches or less for a steak thinner than an inch, three to six inches for thicker steaks. Thinner steaks require intense heat to form a desirable crust before the heat has a chance to penetrate and overcook the meat, whereas thicker cuts need less heat and longer time to allow the middle to cook without burning the exterior.

While the grill is preheating, let the steak come to room temperature; this helps ensure the meat cooks evenly.

4. Don't Overcook. There are four basic ways to determine doneness. The first two are best for novice cooks, while the last two are good for pros:

1. Cut into the steak in an unobtrusive place, and examine the interior to check the doneness.

2. Slide an instant-read thermometer through the side of the steak into the center to check the temperature. Keep in mind that the temperature of meat will increase five to 10 degrees after resting.

3. Use the touch test. A rare steak will feel fleshy, like an unflexed muscle; a rare to medium-rare steak will just begin to bounce back to the touch; a medium-rare to medium steak will feel firmer still.

4. Look for juices on the steak's surface. A rare steak doesn't release any juices. As the steak approaches medium rare, you'll begin to see red juices forming on the surface (you might also hear them sizzle as they drip over the coals). As the steak approaches medium, it releases more juices. As it approaches medium well and well, the juices will turn brown.

Remember, you can always put a steak back on the grill if it's too rare, but you can't uncook a well-done steak.

5. Let the Meat Rest. "Resting," or standing, after cooking allows the meat to reabsorb its flavorful juices. If you serve the steak right away, those tasty juices will spill out onto the plate as soon as you cut into the meat.

After the steak is done, transfer it from the grill to a platter, and loosely cover with foil. (Don't cover tightly or stack steaks, or they'll overcook.) Let rest for five minutes per inch of thickness. Residual heat will cook steaks five to 10 degrees more during resting.

Summer Steak Salad

Flank steak, sliced thin, lends itself nicely to salads.

  1 (1-pound) flank steak, trimmed
  ½ teaspoon salt
  ¼ teaspoon freshly ground black
       pepper
  ½ pound haricots verts, trimmed
       Cooking spray
  8 (½-ounce) slices French bread
  2 tablespoons white wine
       vinegar
  1 tablespoon water
  2 teaspoons extravirgin olive oil
  ¼ teaspoon salt
  ¼ teaspoon freshly ground black
       pepper
  ⅛ teaspoon sugar
  6 cups trimmed arugula
  1 cup torn fresh basil
  4 tomatoes, each cut into
       6 wedges
  2 hard-cooked large eggs, each cut
       into 4 wedges

1. Sprinkle both sides of steak with ½ teaspoon salt and ¼ teaspoon pepper. Let stand at room temperature 20 minutes.
2. Cook haricots verts in boiling water 2 minutes or until crisp-tender. Drain; rinse with cold water. Drain.
3. Prepare grill.
4. Pat steak dry with a paper towel. Place steak on grill rack coated with cooking spray; grill 5 minutes on each side or until desired degree of doneness. Add bread to grill rack; grill 2 minutes on each side or until lightly browned. Remove steak and bread from grill. Lightly cover steak with foil; let stand 10 minutes. Cut steak diagonally across grain into thin slices.
5. Combine vinegar and next 5 ingredients in a medium bowl; stir with a whisk. Add haricots verts, arugula, and basil to vinegar mixture; toss well. Place about 1½ cups arugula mixture on each of 4 plates. Top each serving with 3 ounces steak, 6 tomato wedges, 2 egg wedges, and 2 slices grilled bread. Yield: 4 servings.

CALORIES 353 (31% from fat); FAT 12.2g (sat 3.7g, mono 5.6g, poly 1.2g); PROTEIN 32.5g; CARB 27.9g; FIBER 4.7g; CHOL 143mg; IRON 4.2mg; SODIUM 707mg; CALC 157mg

WINE NOTE: With grilled steak, you should usually opt for a full throttle cabernet sauvignon. But this is a salad, and the peppery character of the arugula, the greenness of the basil and beans, and the acidity of the tomatoes are more important than the meat itself. So serve this with a bone-dry rosé, which combines the crispness of a white wine with the fruit and body of a red. A fabulous choice is the powerhouse Tablas Creek Rosé 2005 from California's Paso Robles region ($26).

STAFF FAVORITE

Tenderloin Sandwich

Cook the lean tenderloin to medium-rare so the meat stays moist.

- 4 (4-ounce) beef tenderloin steaks, trimmed (1 inch thick)
- ½ teaspoon salt
- ½ teaspoon freshly ground black pepper
- Cooking spray
- 4 (1½-ounce) hamburger buns, split
- ¼ cup Dijon mustard
- 4 romaine lettuce leaves
- 4 tomato slices
- 4 red onion slices

1. Sprinkle both sides of steaks with salt and pepper. Let stand at room temperature 20 minutes.
2. Prepare grill.
3. Pat steaks dry with a paper towel. Place steaks on grill rack coated with cooking spray; grill 3 minutes on each side or until desired degree of doneness. Grill buns, cut sides down, 2 minutes or until lightly browned. Remove steak and bread from grill. Cover steak loosely with foil; let stand 5 minutes. Spread mustard evenly over cut sides of buns. Place steaks on bottom halves of buns. Top each serving with 1 lettuce leaf, 1 tomato slice, 1 onion slice, and top half of bun. Yield: 4 servings (serving size: 1 sandwich).

CALORIES 294 (26% from fat); FAT 8.6g (sat 3.3g, mono 3.4g, poly 0.4g); PROTEIN 28.6g; CARB 23.1g; FIBER 1.3g; CHOL 67mg; IRON 3mg; SODIUM 741mg; CALC 81mg

Marks Matter

For an attractive presentation, grill crosshatches on the steak.

1. *Set steak on grill.*

2. *After about a minute—or halfway through the cooking time for the first side of the steak—rotate the meat a quarter-turn (45 degrees for diamond-shaped crosshatches, 90 degrees for square-shaped marks).*

3. *Flip steak over, and complete cooking. Only one side of the steak will show on the plate, so both sides don't require crosshatches. Do not flip steak back onto marked side while grilling.*

Grilled Herb Steak

Five different herbs lend the steak fresh flavor. Experiment with your own blends. For lighter flavor, refrigerate the herb-rubbed steaks for only two hours before cooking.

- 2 tablespoons fresh thyme leaves, minced
- 1 tablespoon fresh oregano leaves, minced
- 1 teaspoon fresh rosemary leaves, minced
- 1 teaspoon dried marjoram
- 1 teaspoon dried lavender buds
- 1 large garlic clove, minced
- 4 (8-ounce) ribeye steaks
- 1 teaspoon salt
- ½ teaspoon freshly ground black pepper
- Cooking spray

1. Combine first 6 ingredients in a small bowl. Rub both sides of steaks with herb mixture. Place steaks in a shallow dish; cover and refrigerate 4 hours.
2. Remove steaks from refrigerator. Sprinkle both sides of steaks with salt and pepper; let stand at room temperature 20 minutes.
3. Prepare grill.
4. Place steaks on grill rack coated with cooking spray; grill 2 minutes on each side or until desired degree of doneness. Remove from grill. Cover steaks loosely with foil; let stand 5 minutes. Yield: 4 servings (serving size: 1 steak).

CALORIES 354 (39% from fat); FAT 15.4g (sat 6.2g, mono 6.6g, poly 0.6g); PROTEIN 49g; CARB 1g; FIBER 0.3g; CHOL 155mg; IRON 3.8mg; SODIUM 684mg; CALC 43mg

Degrees of Doneness

While doneness standards can vary somewhat (one person's rare may be another's medium rare), we follow U.S. Department of Agriculture guidelines for steak temperatures. The USDA does not recommend serving rare steak.

Spicy Chile Paste

Use one tablespoon per eight ounces of raw steak. Store unused paste covered in the refrigerator up to two weeks.

  6 ancho chiles (about 3 ounces)
  2 tablespoons balsamic
     vinegar
  1 teaspoon ground cumin
  ½ teaspoon freshly ground black
     pepper
  ¼ teaspoon ground cinnamon

1. Heat a large skillet over medium-high heat. Add chiles; cook 4 minutes or until fragrant, turning frequently. Place chiles in a large bowl; cover with hot water. Let stand 30 minutes or until soft. Drain well, reserving 1 tablespoon of soaking liquid. Discard stems and seeds from chiles.
2. Place chiles, 1 tablespoon reserved liquid, and remaining ingredients in a blender or food processor, and process until well blended, scraping sides of container occasionally. Yield: 12 servings (serving size: 1 tablespoon).

CALORIES 23 (24% from fat); FAT 0.6g (sat 0.1g, mono 0g, poly 0.3g); PROTEIN 0.9g; CARB 4.1g; FIBER 1.6g; CHOL 0mg; IRON 0.9mg; SODIUM 4mg; CALC 7mg

Smoked Tomatoes

Use ripe tomatoes that are still slightly firm. Very ripe tomatoes will overcook and become mushy.

  2 cups wood chips, divided
Cooking spray
  3 ripe, firm tomatoes, cut in half
     crosswise and seeded (about
     1½ pounds)
  2 teaspoons extravirgin olive oil
  3 tablespoons finely chopped fresh
     parsley
  2 tablespoons grated fresh Parmesan
     cheese
  ½ teaspoon freshly ground black
     pepper
  ¼ teaspoon salt
  1 garlic clove, minced

1. Soak wood chips in water 30 minutes; drain well.
2. Prepare grill for indirect grilling, heating one side to high and leaving one side with no heat. Place 1 cup wood chips on hot coals. When chips begin to smoke, coat grill rack with cooking spray, and place on grill. Place tomato halves, cut sides down, on unheated side of grill. Cover and cook 18 minutes or just until tomatoes are tender. Add additional chips halfway through cooking time, if necessary.
3. Place tomatoes, cut sides up, on a serving platter; drizzle with oil. Combine parsley and remaining 4 ingredients; sprinkle over tomatoes. Serve warm. Yield: 6 servings (serving size: 1 tomato half).

CALORIES 47 (46% from fat); FAT 2.4g (sat 0.6g, mono 1.4g, poly 0.3g); PROTEIN 1.7g; CARB 5.7g; FIBER 1.4g; CHOL 1mg; IRON 0.7mg; SODIUM 134mg; CALC 28mg

Grilled Steak with Teriyaki Glaze

  ¾ cup mirin (sweet rice wine)
  ¾ cup low-sodium soy sauce
  2 teaspoons dark sesame oil
  8 (4-ounce) beef tenderloin steaks,
     trimmed (about ¾ inch thick)
Cooking spray

1. Combine mirin and soy sauce in a medium saucepan; bring to a boil over medium-high heat. Cook until reduced to ¾ cup (about 12 minutes). Pour into a bowl; cool completely. Stir in oil. (Mixture will thicken as it cools.)
2. Combine half of soy mixture and steaks in a shallow dish, turning to coat. Cover and marinate in refrigerator 2 hours, turning occasionally. Reserve remaining soy mixture.
3. Remove steaks from marinade; discard marinade. Let steaks stand at room temperature 20 minutes.
4. Prepare grill.
5. Pat steaks lightly with a paper towel. Place steaks on grill rack coated with cooking spray; grill 3 minutes. Turn steaks over; spoon reserved soy mixture over tops of steaks. Grill 3 minutes or until desired degree of doneness. Remove from grill. Let stand 5 minutes before serving. Yield: 8 servings (serving size: 1 steak).

CALORIES 238 (30% from fat); FAT 7.9g (sat 2.7g, mono 3.1g, poly 0.7g); PROTEIN 25.6g; CARB 9.1g; FIBER 0.2g; CHOL 67mg; IRON 2mg; SODIUM 850mg; CALC 21mg

---

Helpful Utensils

Tongs: A pair of spring-loaded kitchen tongs ($10 to $16) will help you turn steaks and other items on a hot grill while protecting your hands from the heat. Some cooks find that 16-inch tongs are ideal, while others prefer shorter tongs because they're easier to manipulate. Tongs longer than 16 inches may prove unwieldy.

Instant-read thermometer: Until you've mastered the touch test or can size up the doneness of your steak by sight, a digital instant-read thermometer ($8 to $19) is a smart tool.

Basting brush: Handy tools for spreading marinade or barbecue sauce as the meat cooks on the grill, basting brushes commonly feature heat-resistant silicone bristles and cost between $8 and $18. "They're easy to clean, and they don't soak up all your basting liquid," says *Cooking Light* Test Kitchens professional Mike Wilson. Some culinary professionals use high-quality paintbrushes.

Grill brush: Before grilling, scrub the grill wire with a metal brush or grill scrub pad ($6 to $17) to clean off carbon buildup and residue, which can occur even when the grill is coated with cooking spray. Heat the grill first, and the debris will simply blow away with little effort. Even better, clean your grill after cooking and before the grill has cooled, so it's ready to use next time.

Pudding, Please

Homemade pudding is an easy treat. Learn to prepare creamy custards in a delicious array of flavors.

All About Custards

Stove-Top Custards

The first step when preparing most stove-top custards is to heat the milk. The technique involves combining sugar, starch, and additional flavorings. Separately combine eggs or yolks with a bit of milk or cream, and stir the egg mixture into the sugar mixture. Then add half of the hot milk to the egg mixture. "Tempering" refers to a procedure for combining a hot liquid with a cool one, where the aim is to slowly bring the temperature of the cool mixture up to that of the hot one. This technique ensures the eggs reach the desired temperature gradually, and it protects them from coagulating immediately upon contact with the boiling liquid.

Eggs serve a dual purpose in the custard. They bind or thicken the liquid, but they also enrich the pudding, as well. For the most part, we use yolks, which have fat to lend the pudding a rich, smooth texture.

In most of our stove-top recipes, we use cornstarch in combination with the eggs. Cornstarch adds a silky sheen in addition to thickening the mixture. (See "Pudding Primer," on page 293.) Flour also works, but it clouds the appearance of the cooked pudding.

Once tempered, the mixture goes back into the pan and over a medium flame. Puddings thickened with cornstarch need to come to a boil and cook for 1 minute. This activates the thickening power of the cornstarch and cooks off its raw taste. Be sure to stir the pudding constantly with a whisk as it cooks so it will not clump or stick and burn to the bottom of the pan.

Butter is an additional ingredient used to enrich the flavor and texture of the custard. It's best to stir in cold butter just after the custard comes off the stove. This is also the time to stir in other flavorings that might be compromised by exposure to heat, such as vanilla extract.

Unless you're planning to serve the pudding warm, chill it as quickly as possible. Do this by spooning the pudding into a bowl and nesting the bowl in another ice-filled bowl, stirring occasionally until the pudding cools. Finally, cover the surface of the pudding directly with plastic wrap, and chill. The plastic must come in contact with the pudding, or a rubbery skin will form on the top. Store the covered pudding in the refrigerator until you're ready to serve—it will keep up to three days.

Baked Puddings

Baked custards contain many of the same ingredients as stove-top varieties and rely on the same principles. Delicate baked custards such as crème brûlée and flan account for one variety. But here we focus on the more forgiving baked puddings, such as bread pudding and Indian pudding. Instead of cornstarch, these recipes include bread cubes or other starchy ingredients to soak up the custard and help stabilize the egg-based mixture as it bakes.

Our custard recipes instruct you to bake the custard at a low temperature. The combination of the low temperature and the starchy ingredients insulates the custard and allows you to skip the step of tempering the eggs.

Jasmine Chai Rice Pudding

Although it keeps several days in the fridge, this pudding is at its best warm. Add a touch of extra milk to reheat, and top with whipped topping, nuts, and rind just before serving.

     2 cups 1% low-fat milk, divided
 1½ cups water
     2 teaspoons loose chai tea (about 4 tea bags)
 ⅛ teaspoon salt
     1 cup uncooked jasmine rice
 ¾ cup sweetened condensed milk
 ¼ cup diced dried mixed fruit
     2 large egg yolks, lightly beaten
     1 tablespoon butter
     6 tablespoons frozen fat-free whipped topping, thawed
     2 tablespoons chopped pistachios
 ½ teaspoon grated orange rind

1. Combine 1 cup milk, 1½ cups water, tea, and salt in a large saucepan; bring to a boil. Remove from heat; steep 1 minute. Strain milk mixture through a fine sieve into a bowl; discard solids. Return milk mixture to pan; place pan over medium heat. Stir in rice. Cover and simmer 10 minutes. Combine 1 cup milk, condensed milk, fruit, and egg yolks, stirring well with a whisk. Gradually add half of hot milk mixture to egg yolk mixture, stirring constantly with a whisk. Return milk mixture to pan; cook 10 minutes or until mixture is thick and rice is tender, stirring constantly. Remove from heat; stir in butter.

2. Place ⅔ cup rice pudding in each of 6 bowls. Top each serving with 1 tablespoon fat-free whipped topping. Combine nuts and rind. Sprinkle about 1 teaspoon nut mixture over each serving. Yield: 6 servings.

CALORIES 287 (28% from fat); FAT 8.8g (sat 4.5g, mono 3g, poly 0.8g); PROTEIN 8.3g; CARB 44g; FIBER 1.1g; CHOL 90mg; IRON 0.6mg; SODIUM 169mg; CALC 223mg

5 Steps to Great Stove-Top Pudding

1. *Stove-top pudding requires little more than a heavy saucepan, a whisk, a rubber spatula, and a little plastic wrap to prepare.*

2. *Most stove-top custard recipes combine dry ingredients, such as sugar and starch. This prevents the starch from clumping when it's added to the hot milk. Separately combine eggs with a bit of milk or cream.*

3. *Tempering is a process that combines a hot liquid with a cool one, protecting the delicate eggs from coagulating too quickly.*

4. *The pudding is thick enough if it coats the back of a spoon.*

5. *Place plastic wrap directly on the surface of the pudding to avoid a rubbery skin on top.*

Old-Fashioned Tapioca Pudding

Look for tapioca with pasta and grains in the supermarket. Small pearl tapioca is different from instant and takes longer to cook.

¾ cup water
⅓ cup uncooked small pearl tapioca
2¼ cups 2% reduced-fat milk
¼ teaspoon salt
⅓ cup sugar
2 large eggs, lightly beaten
½ teaspoon vanilla extract
Grated whole nutmeg (optional)

1. Combine ¾ cup water and tapioca in a medium saucepan; let stand 30 minutes.
2. Add milk and salt to tapioca mixture; bring to a boil. Reduce heat, and simmer 30 minutes or until mixture thickens, stirring frequently. Combine sugar and eggs, stirring well with a whisk. Gradually stir about ½ cup hot tapioca mixture into egg mixture. Return tapioca mixture to pan. Cook 4 minutes or until thickened, stirring constantly.
3. Remove from heat; stir in vanilla. Spoon pudding into a bowl. Place bowl in a large ice-filled bowl; let stand 15 minutes or until pudding is cool, stirring occasionally. Cover surface of pudding with plastic wrap. Chill. Garnish with grated nutmeg, if desired. Yield: 4 servings (serving size: ½ cup).

CALORIES 221 (22% from fat); FAT 5.3g (sat 2.5g, mono 1.8g, poly 0.5g); PROTEIN 7.7g; CARB 35.5g; FIBER 0.1g; CHOL 109mg; IRON 0.7mg; SODIUM 252mg; CALC 169mg

Mocha Pudding

1¾ cups fat-free milk
½ cup packed brown sugar
1 tablespoon cornstarch
1 tablespoon instant coffee granules
¼ teaspoon salt
¼ cup half-and-half
2 large egg yolks, lightly beaten
1 tablespoon butter
1 tablespoon Kahlúa (coffee-flavored liqueur)
2 tablespoons dark chocolate shavings

1. Place milk in a medium, heavy saucepan; bring to a boil. Combine sugar, cornstarch, coffee, and salt in a large bowl, stirring well. Combine half-and-half and egg yolks. Stir egg yolk mixture into sugar mixture. Gradually add half of hot milk to sugar mixture, stirring constantly with a whisk. Return hot milk mixture to pan; bring to a boil. Reduce heat, and simmer 1 minute or until thick, stirring constantly. Remove from heat. Stir in butter and liqueur.

2. Spoon pudding into a bowl. Place bowl in a large ice-filled bowl 15 minutes or until pudding is cool, stirring occasionally.

3. Cover surface of pudding with plastic wrap; chill. Sprinkle each serving with chocolate shavings. Yield: 6 servings (serving size: ½ cup pudding and 1 teaspoon shavings).

CALORIES 173 (29% from fat); FAT 5.6g (sat 3g, mono 1.5g, poly 0.4g); PROTEIN 3.8g; CARB 26.9g; FIBER 0.2g; CHOL 78mg; IRON 0.6mg; SODIUM 155mg; CALC 124mg

STAFF FAVORITE • MAKE AHEAD
Vanilla Bean Pudding

Vanilla beans can be expensive, but their superior flavor is worth the investment. Substitute vanilla paste or one teaspoon real vanilla extract if necessary. Stir extract in with the butter.

2½   cups 2% reduced-fat milk
  1   vanilla bean, split lengthwise
  ¾   cup sugar
  3   tablespoons cornstarch
  ⅛   teaspoon salt
  ¼   cup half-and-half
  2   large egg yolks, lightly beaten
  4   teaspoons butter

1. Place milk in a medium, heavy saucepan. Scrape seeds from vanilla bean; add seeds and bean to milk. Bring to a boil.

2. Combine sugar, cornstarch, and salt in a large bowl, stirring well. Combine half-and-half and egg yolks, stirring well. Stir egg yolk mixture into sugar mixture. Gradually add half of hot milk to sugar mixture, stirring constantly with a whisk. Return hot milk mixture to pan;

bring to a boil. Cook 1 minute, stirring constantly with a whisk. Remove from heat. Add butter, stirring until melted. Remove vanilla bean; discard.

3. Spoon pudding into a bowl. Place bowl in a large ice-filled bowl 15 minutes or until pudding cools, stirring occasionally. Cover surface of pudding with plastic wrap; chill. Yield: 6 servings (serving size: ½ cup).

CALORIES 216 (30% from fat); FAT 7.1g (sat 4.1g, mono 2.2g, poly 0.4g); PROTEIN 4.6g; CARB 34.2g; FIBER 0g; CHOL 86mg; IRON 0.2mg; SODIUM 125mg; CALC 142mg

PEANUT BUTTER PUDDING VARIATION: Omit vanilla bean, salt, and butter; stir in ¼ cup reduced-fat creamy peanut butter after custard is cooked. Yield: 6 servings (serving size: about ½ cup).

CALORIES 257 (30% from fat); FAT 8.6g (sat 3.3g, mono 3.6g, poly 1.6g); PROTEIN 6.9g; CARB 39.2g; FIBER 0.7g; CHOL 80mg; IRON 0.5mg; SODIUM 170mg; CALC 142mg

COCONUT PUDDING VARIATION: Omit vanilla bean. Omit ¾ cup milk, and replace it with ¾ cup light unsweetened coconut milk. Omit butter; stir in ½ cup toasted sweetened flaked coconut after pudding is cooked. Yield: 6 servings (serving size: about ½ cup).

CALORIES 224 (30% from fat); FAT 7.5g (sat 5.3g, mono 1.5g, poly 0.4g); PROTEIN 4.1g; CARB 36.8g; FIBER 0.3g; CHOL 77mg; IRON 0.5mg; SODIUM 115mg; CALC 105mg

STAFF FAVORITE • MAKE AHEAD
Chocolate Pudding

2½   cups fat-free milk, divided
  ⅓   cup sugar
  3   tablespoons cornstarch
  ¼   teaspoon salt
  2   large egg yolks, lightly beaten
  2   teaspoons butter
  1   teaspoon vanilla extract
  5   ounces semisweet chocolate, chopped

1. Place 2 cups milk in a medium, heavy saucepan; bring to a boil. Combine sugar, cornstarch, and salt in a large bowl, stirring well with a whisk. Combine ½ cup milk and egg yolks, stirring well with a whisk. Add egg yolk mixture to sugar mixture, stirring well.

Gradually add half of hot milk to egg yolk mixture, stirring constantly with a whisk. Return milk mixture to pan; bring to a boil. Reduce heat, and simmer 1 minute or until thick, stirring constantly. Remove from heat. Add butter, vanilla, and chocolate, stirring until melted.

2. Spoon pudding into a bowl. Place bowl in a large ice-filled bowl 15 minutes or until pudding is cool, stirring occasionally. Cover surface of pudding with plastic wrap; chill. Yield: 6 servings (serving size: about ½ cup).

CALORIES 246 (35% from fat); FAT 9.6g (sat 5.6g, mono 3.5g, poly 0.5g); PROTEIN 6.4g; CARB 35.8g; FIBER 0g; CHOL 74mg; IRON 0.8mg; SODIUM 157mg; CALC 150mg

Pudding Primer

Eggs work in tandem with cornstarch to thicken puddings. Custard recipes often call for egg yolks because they possess thickening qualities and add rich flavor to the final dish. Since yolks add fat, they're a secondary thickener in our recipes.

Rice releases starch into the liquid as it cooks. Stirring the rice releases more starch and disperses it throughout the pudding.

Cornmeal thickens the Indian Pudding (recipe on page 294) by slowly absorbing the liquid.

Cornstarch creates velvety-smooth puddings. In order to avoid lumps in the pudding, stir the cornstarch into the recipe's sugar. Although cornstarch begins to thicken the pudding just below the boiling point, be sure to cook another minute to eliminate any raw taste.

Tapioca comes from the cassava (or yuca) plant. These starchy pearls thicken puddings when cooked and stirred.

Bread soaks up the custard, thickening (along with the eggs) a bread pudding as it cooks.

Step-by-Step to Great Baked Pudding

1. *Baked puddings don't require specialty equipment. You'll need a mixing bowl, wooden spoon, and baking dish in an appropriate size.*

2. *With these baked puddings, you simply mix all the ingredients together, stir, and bake at a low temperature.*

MAKE AHEAD
Indian Pudding

This New England classic is thickened with cornmeal. When chilled, this pudding firms to the consistency of polenta.

　¼　cup butter
　4　cups fat-free milk
　¾　cup yellow cornmeal
　⅓　cup sugar
　⅓　cup molasses
　1　teaspoon pumpkin pie spice
　½　teaspoon salt
　2　large egg yolks, lightly beaten
　　Cooking spray
　9　tablespoons frozen fat-free whipped topping, thawed

1. Preheat oven to 275°.
2. Melt butter in a large, heavy saucepan over medium-high heat; cook 2 minutes or until browned. Add milk to pan; bring to a boil. Gradually add cornmeal, stirring constantly with a whisk. Cook 5 minutes or until mixture thickens, stirring constantly. Combine sugar and next 4 ingredients, stirring well with a whisk. Gradually add half of hot milk mixture to sugar mixture, stirring constantly. Return milk mixture to pan; cook 2 minutes or until sugar dissolves.
3. Pour cornmeal mixture into a 9-inch square baking pan coated with cooking spray. Bake at 275° for 1 hour and 15 minutes or until pudding barely moves when pan is touched. Cool to room temperature on a wire rack. Cover and chill 2 hours. Cut into 9 squares. Serve with whipped topping. Yield: 9 servings (serving size: 1 pudding square and 1 tablespoon whipped topping).

CALORIES 216 (28% from fat); FAT 6.8g (sat 3.7g, mono 1.8g, poly 0.4g); PROTEIN 5.3g; CARB 34.2g; FIBER 0.9g; CHOL 61mg; IRON 1.2mg; SODIUM 231mg; CALC 167mg

---

MAKE AHEAD
Cinnamon Apple Raisin Bread Pudding

For an alcohol-free version, substitute apple cider or apple juice for the brandy. Golden raisins, sweetened dried cranberries, or dried cherries can stand in for the raisins.

　½　cup raisins
　½　cup chopped dried apple
　2　tablespoons Calvados (apple brandy)
　3½　cups 2% reduced-fat milk
　¾　cup sugar
　1　tablespoon grated lemon rind
　1　tablespoon butter, melted
　½　teaspoon salt
　½　teaspoon ground cinnamon
　⅛　teaspoon grated whole nutmeg
　4　large eggs, lightly beaten
　5　cups (1½-inch) cubed cinnamon bread (about 12 ounces)
　　Cooking spray

1. Preheat oven to 325°.
2. Combine first 3 ingredients in a microwave-safe bowl. Microwave at HIGH 1 minute; cool. Combine milk and next 7 ingredients in a large bowl, stirring well with a whisk. Stir in bread cubes and raisin mixture. Let stand at room temperature 15 minutes.
3. Pour bread mixture into an 8-inch square baking pan coated with cooking spray. Bake at 325° for 50 minutes or until set. Serve warm. Yield: 10 servings.

CALORIES 285 (25% from fat); FAT 8g (sat 3g, mono 1.8g, poly 1.6g); PROTEIN 9.3g; CARB 45g; FIBER 3.4g; CHOL 94mg; IRON 1.6mg; SODIUM 341mg; CALC 120mg

---

enlightened cook

Sense of Place

Southern Chef Chris Hastings champions local fare to keep regional flavors and traditions alive.

Chef Chris Hastings's restaurant, the Hot and Hot Fish Club in Birmingham, Alabama, is brimming with local flavor. Farmstead cheeses, locally grown organic herbs and lettuces, and seafood from the nearby Gulf of Mexico are all given their proper appellation.

What you taste at Hot and Hot is fresh and new, yet pays homage to the past. (The recipes here are adaptations for home cooks of dishes Hastings serves at Hot and Hot.)

MAKE AHEAD
Preserved Lemon Vinaigrette

　2　tablespoons finely chopped preserved lemon, pith removed
　2　tablespoons fresh lemon juice
　1½　tablespoons extravirgin olive oil
　1　teaspoon minced shallots

1. Combine all ingredients in a small bowl, stirring until blended. Yield: ⅓ cup (serving size: about 1 tablespoon).

CALORIES 26 (89% from fat); FAT 2.6g (sat 0.4g, mono 2g, poly 0.2g); PROTEIN 0g; CARB 0.7g; FIBER 0.1g; CHOL 0mg; IRON 0mg; SODIUM 353mg; CALC 2mg

Grilled Wild Salmon and Vegetables

Hastings likes to use specialty onions, including red torpedo, bianco de maijio, and gold coin. Here, we call for more readily available varieties. Use a grill basket to cook the fish and vegetables.

      8 fingerling potatoes (about 8 ounces)
      4 small red onions, cut into 1-inch slices (about 1 pound)
      4 Vidalia spring onions, quartered (about 8 ounces)
      4 cipollini onions (about 4 ounces)
      2 cups sliced fennel (about 7 ounces)
      1 tablespoon extravirgin olive oil
         Cooking spray
    ½ teaspoon salt, divided
    ½ teaspoon freshly ground black pepper, divided
      1 tablespoon chopped fennel fronds
      1 tablespoon chopped fresh parsley
      4 (6-ounce) salmon fillets
      2 cups pea tendrils or baby spinach
    ¼ cup Preserved Lemon Vinaigrette (recipe on page 294)

1. Prepare grill.
2. Place potatoes in a large pan of boiling water; cook 8 minutes or until tender. Add onions and sliced fennel; cook 3 minutes or until onions are tender. Drain and plunge into ice water; drain.
3. Toss vegetables with oil. Place vegetables on grill rack coated with cooking spray; grill 4 minutes on each side or until tender and lightly browned. Sprinkle with ¼ teaspoon salt, ¼ teaspoon pepper, fennel fronds, and parsley.
4. Sprinkle salmon with ¼ teaspoon salt and ¼ teaspoon pepper. Place salmon on grill rack coated with cooking spray, and grill 5 minutes on each side or until fish flakes easily when tested with a fork or until desired degree of doneness. Place 1 salmon fillet onto each of 4 plates. Toss pea tendrils with Preserved Lemon Vinaigrette. Place about ½ cup pea tendril mixture over salmon on each plate. Add 1½ cups grilled vegetables to each serving, and serve immediately. Yield: 4 servings.

CALORIES 307 (47% from fat); FAT 16.2g (sat 4.1g, mono 8.1g, poly 3.6g); PROTEIN 24.3g; CARB 15.7g; FIBER 2.8g; CHOL 57mg; IRON 1.3mg; SODIUM 515mg; CALC 65mg

Sweet Pea Risotto with Corn Broth

(pictured on page 245)

CORN BROTH:

    2½ cups water
      2 cups fresh corn kernels
    ¼ teaspoon salt

RISOTTO:

      3 cups organic vegetable broth (such as Swanson Certified Organic)
      2 tablespoons butter
      1 cup uncooked arborio rice
    ½ cup diced onion
      3 tablespoons minced carrot
      3 tablespoons minced celery
      2 cups fresh green peas
      1 cup fresh corn kernels
    ½ cup diced fresh fennel
      2 tablespoons grated Parmesan cheese
      2 teaspoons chopped fresh thyme

REMAINING INGREDIENTS:

      1 tablespoon sherry vinegar
      1 tablespoon olive oil
      1 teaspoon sugar
    ¼ teaspoon salt
      1 garlic clove, minced
      2 tablespoons grated Parmesan cheese
      1 tablespoon chopped fresh parsley
      1 tablespoon chopped fresh chives

1. To prepare corn broth, combine 2½ cups water and 2 cups corn kernels in a small saucepan; bring to a boil. Reduce heat, and simmer 5 minutes or until corn is tender. Stir in ¼ teaspoon salt. Place corn mixture in blender; process until smooth. Strain corn mixture through a sieve into a bowl; discard solids. Set aside; keep warm.
2. To prepare risotto, bring broth to a simmer in a medium saucepan (do not boil); keep warm over low heat. Heat butter in a large saucepan over medium-high heat. Add rice; cook 1 minute, stirring constantly. Add onion, carrot, and celery; cook 3 minutes, stirring constantly. Add warm broth, ½ cup at a time, stirring constantly until each portion of broth is absorbed before adding next (about 20 minutes). Add peas and next 4 ingredients, stirring until blended and hot. Keep warm.

3. Combine vinegar and next 4 ingredients in a small bowl, stirring with a whisk until blended. Place about ⅓ cup corn broth in each of 6 bowls. Top each serving with about 1½ cups risotto; drizzle each with 1 teaspoon vinaigrette. Sprinkle each serving with 1 teaspoon cheese, ½ teaspoon parsley, and ½ teaspoon chives. Serve immediately. Yield: 6 servings.

CALORIES 250 (29% from fat); FAT 8.2g (sat 3g, mono 3.9g, poly 0.9g); PROTEIN 7.8g; CARB 38.9g; FIBER 5.3g; CHOL 13mg; IRON 1.5mg; SODIUM 582mg; CALC 65mg

Steamed Asparagus with Crawfish and Preserved Lemon Vinaigrette

Mâche is delicious but can be expensive and hard to find. You can substitute gourmet greens or arugula.

    12 asparagus spears
    12 white asparagus spears
    ¼ teaspoon ground black pepper
    ¼ cup Preserved Lemon Vinaigrette (recipe on page 294), divided
    1⅓ cups cooked peeled and deveined crawfish tail meat
      1 cup mâche
      1 tablespoon chopped fresh flat-leaf parsley

1. Snap tough ends off asparagus. Steam asparagus, covered, 2 minutes or until crisp-tender. Sprinkle with pepper. Toss with 2 tablespoons Preserved Lemon Vinaigrette; chill until ready to serve.
2. Combine crawfish, mâche, parsley, and 2 tablespoons Preserved Lemon Vinaigrette, tossing to coat. Arrange 3 green and 3 white asparagus spears on each of 4 plates; top each with about ½ cup salad mixture. Serve immediately. Yield: 4 servings.

CALORIES 83 (35% from fat); FAT 3.3g (sat 0.5g, mono 2.1g, poly 0.5g); PROTEIN 9.5g; CARB 5.3g; FIBER 0.5g; CHOL 57mg; IRON 2.6mg; SODIUM 401mg; CALC 52mg

superfast

. . . And Ready in Just About 20 Minutes

More than a week's worth of quick entrées to get dinner on the table in a flash.

QUICK & EASY
Spicy Tomato and White Bean Soup

Pair this soup with a simple grilled cheese sandwich for a quick and satisfying meal.

    1   (14-ounce) can fat-free, less-
        sodium chicken broth, divided
    2   teaspoons chili powder
    1   teaspoon ground cumin
    1   (16-ounce) can navy beans, rinsed
        and drained
    1   poblano chile, halved and
        seeded
  ½   onion, cut into ½-inch-thick
        wedges
    1   pint grape tomatoes
  ¼   cup chopped fresh cilantro
    2   tablespoons fresh lime juice
    1   tablespoon extravirgin
        olive oil
  ½   teaspoon salt
        Cilantro sprigs (optional)

1. Combine 1 cup broth, chili powder, cumin, and beans in a Dutch oven over medium-high heat. Place remaining broth, poblano, and onion in a food processor; pulse until vegetables are chopped. Add onion mixture to pan.
2. Place tomatoes and chopped cilantro in food processor, and process until coarsely chopped. Add tomato mixture to pan; bring to a boil. Cover, reduce heat, and simmer 5 minutes or until vegetables are tender. Remove from heat; stir in juice, oil, and salt. Garnish with cilantro sprigs, if desired. Yield: 4 servings (serving size: 1 cup).

CALORIES 157 (25% from fat); FAT 4.3g (sat 0.6g, mono 2.6g, poly 0.6g); PROTEIN 8.1g; CARB 23.1g; FIBER 6g; CHOL 0mg; IRON 2.4mg; SODIUM 828mg; CALC 65mg

QUICK & EASY
Middle Eastern Chicken Salad Wraps

Purchased salad dressing and roasted garlic hummus combine with lettuce and chicken breast for a no-cook sandwich.

    6   cups chopped romaine lettuce
  1½   cups chopped cooked chicken
        breast
  ½   cup chopped bottled roasted red
        bell peppers
  ¼   cup light Caesar dressing (such as
        Ken's)
  ½   cup hummus with roasted garlic
    4   (10-inch) whole wheat flatbread
        wraps (such as Toufayan)

1. Combine first 4 ingredients. Spread 2 tablespoons hummus over each wrap; top each wrap with about 2 cups lettuce mixture; roll up. Cut each wrap in half crosswise. Yield: 4 servings (serving size: 2 halves).

CALORIES 336 (22% from fat); FAT 8.1g (sat 1.1g, mono 2.6g, poly 3.4g); PROTEIN 25.8g; CARB 41.2g; FIBER 10.8g; CHOL 50mg; IRON 3.2mg; SODIUM 591mg; CALC 76mg

QUICK & EASY
Chicken and Summer Vegetable Tostadas

The tostadas can easily become soft tacos if you skip broiling the tortillas. Serve with black beans.

    1   teaspoon ground cumin
  ¼   teaspoon salt
  ¼   teaspoon black pepper
    2   teaspoons canola oil
  12   ounces chicken breast tenders
    1   cup chopped red onion (about 1)
    1   cup fresh corn kernels (about
        2 ears)
    1   cup chopped zucchini (about
        4 ounces)
  ½   cup green salsa
    3   tablespoons chopped fresh
        cilantro, divided
    4   (8-inch) fat-free flour tortillas
        Cooking spray
    1   cup (4 ounces) shredded
        Monterey Jack cheese

1. Preheat broiler.
2. Combine first 3 ingredients, stirring well. Heat oil in a large nonstick skillet over medium-high heat. Sprinkle spice mixture evenly over chicken. Add chicken to pan; sauté 3 minutes. Add onion, corn, and zucchini to pan; sauté 2 minutes or until chicken is done. Stir in salsa and 2 tablespoons cilantro. Cook 2 minutes or until liquid almost evaporates, stirring frequently.
3. Arrange 2 tortillas in a single layer on a baking sheet; lightly coat tortillas with cooking spray. Broil 3 minutes or until lightly browned. Spoon about ¾ cup chicken mixture in center of each tortilla; sprinkle each with ¼ cup cheese. Broil 2 minutes or until cheese melts. Repeat procedure with remaining tortillas, chicken mixture, and cheese. Sprinkle each serving with about ¾ teaspoon cilantro. Serve immediately. Yield: 4 servings.

CALORIES 398 (30% from fat); FAT 13.1g (sat 5.9g, mono 4.1g, poly 1.2g); PROTEIN 32.5g; CARB 36.7g; FIBER 3.1g; CHOL 75mg; IRON 1.4mg; SODIUM 799mg; CALC 236mg

QUICK & EASY
Seared Tofu with Gingered Vegetables

Drain the tofu while you cook the rice and prep the vegetables. This step ensures the tofu will brown nicely when it cooks. Radish sprouts add a fresh, peppery crunch. You can substitute broccoli sprouts or omit them altogether.

    1   pound reduced-fat extrafirm tofu
    1   (3½-ounce) bag boil-in-bag
        long-grain rice
  ¾   teaspoon salt, divided
    1   tablespoon dark sesame oil, divided
    1   tablespoon bottled minced garlic
    1   tablespoon bottled ground fresh
        ginger (such as Spice World)
    1   large red bell pepper, thinly sliced
    1   cup sliced green onions, divided
    2   tablespoons rice vinegar
    1   tablespoon low-sodium soy sauce
        Cooking spray
  ¼   teaspoon freshly ground black pepper
    1   tablespoon sesame seeds, toasted
    1   cup radish sprouts

1. Place tofu on several layers of paper towels; let stand 10 minutes. Cut tofu into 1-inch cubes.

2. Prepare rice according to package directions, omitting salt and fat. Add ¼ teaspoon salt to rice; fluff with a fork.

3. Heat 2 teaspoons oil in a large nonstick skillet over medium-high heat. Add garlic, ginger, and bell pepper to pan; sauté 3 minutes. Stir in ¾ cup onions, vinegar, and soy sauce; cook 30 seconds. Remove from pan. Wipe skillet with paper towels; coat pan with cooking spray.

4. Place pan over medium-high heat. Sprinkle tofu with ½ teaspoon salt and black pepper. Add tofu to pan; cook 8 minutes or until golden, turning to brown on all sides. Return bell pepper mixture to pan, and cook 1 minute or until thoroughly heated. Drizzle tofu mixture with 1 teaspoon oil; top with sesame seeds. Serve tofu mixture with rice; top with sprouts and ¼ cup onions. Yield: 4 servings (serving size: about ¼ cup rice, 1 cup tofu mixture, ¼ cup sprouts, and 1 tablespoon onions).

CALORIES 325 (28% from fat); FAT 10.2g (sat 2.6g, mono 2.7g, poly 4.6g); PROTEIN 28.2g; CARB 41.6g; FIBER 6.2g; CHOL 0mg; IRON 7.6mg; SODIUM 603mg; CALC 96mg

QUICK & EASY
Mozzarella, Ham, and Basil Panini

Serve these simple pressed sandwiches with a pickle and some vegetable chips.

  1 (16-ounce) loaf ciabatta, cut in half horizontally
  4 teaspoons Dijon mustard
  4 teaspoons balsamic vinegar
 1⅓ cups (8 ounces) thinly sliced fresh mozzarella cheese
 12 basil leaves
  8 ounces sliced 33%-less-sodium cooked deli ham (such as Healthy Choice)
  2 sweetened hot cherry peppers, sliced
  1 large plum tomato, thinly sliced
     Cooking spray

1. Brush cut side of bottom bread half with mustard; brush cut side of top half

with vinegar. Top bottom half with mozzarella, basil, ham, peppers, and tomato. Top with remaining bread half.

2. Heat a large nonstick skillet over medium heat. Coat pan with cooking spray. Add sandwich to pan; top with a heavy skillet. Cook 3 minutes on each side or until golden. Cut sandwich into 6 wedges. Yield: 6 servings (serving size: 1 wedge).

CALORIES 371 (30% from fat); FAT 12.5g (sat 6.1g, mono 5g, poly 0.6g); PROTEIN 20.2g; CARB 44.9g; FIBER 1.8g; CHOL 46mg; IRON 3mg; SODIUM 976mg; CALC 220mg

QUICK & EASY
Shrimp Fried Rice

Sauté snow peas for a side dish.

  3 (3½-ounce) bags boil-in-bag long-grain rice
  1 (10-ounce) package frozen green peas
     Cooking spray
  2 large eggs, lightly beaten
  1 tablespoon canola oil
  1 cup chopped green onions
  1 tablespoon bottled ground fresh ginger (such as Spice World)
 12 ounces medium shrimp, peeled and deveined
  2 tablespoons rice vinegar
  2 tablespoons low-sodium soy sauce
  1 teaspoon dark sesame oil
  ¼ teaspoon salt
     Dash of crushed red pepper

1. Cook rice according to package directions, omitting salt and fat. Drain. Remove rice from bags, and return to pan. Add peas to pan, stirring well. Cover and keep warm.

2. Heat a nonstick skillet over medium-high heat. Coat pan with cooking spray. Add eggs to pan; cook 1 minute or until set. Remove eggs from pan; coarsely chop. Return pan to heat; add canola oil to pan. Add onions and ginger to pan; sauté 1 minute. Add shrimp to pan; sauté 2 minutes or until shrimp are done.

3. Add shrimp mixture and eggs to rice mixture; stir well. Combine vinegar and remaining 4 ingredients, stirring well.

Drizzle vinegar mixture over rice mixture; stir well. Yield: 6 servings (serving size: about 1½ cups).

CALORIES 392 (15% from fat); FAT 6.7g (sat 1.1g, mono 2.8g, poly 1.9g); PROTEIN 19.3g; CARB 61.9g; FIBER 3.2g; CHOL 155mg; IRON 4.9mg; SODIUM 478mg; CALC 67mg

QUICK & EASY
Sautéed Tilapia with Honey-Scallion Dressing

Serve with fast-cooking rice noodles.

DRESSING:
 2½ tablespoons fresh lemon juice
  2 tablespoons chopped green onions
  1 tablespoon honey
  1 tablespoon low-sodium soy sauce
  1 teaspoon bottled ground fresh ginger (such as Spice World)
  ¼ teaspoon dark sesame oil

FISH:
  1 tablespoon canola oil
  4 (6-ounce) tilapia fillets
  ½ teaspoon salt
  ⅛ teaspoon black pepper
  4 cups gourmet salad greens

1. To prepare dressing, combine first 6 ingredients in a bowl, stirring well with a whisk.

2. To prepare fish, heat canola oil in a large nonstick skillet over medium-high heat. Sprinkle fish evenly with salt and pepper. Add fish to pan; cook 3 minutes on each side or until fish flakes easily when tested with a fork or until desired degree of doneness. Arrange 1 cup greens on each of 4 plates. Top each serving with 1 fish fillet; drizzle each with 2 tablespoons dressing. Yield: 4 servings.

CALORIES 230 (30% from fat); FAT 7.7g (sat 1.8g, mono 3.9g, poly 1.4g); PROTEIN 34.2g; CARB 7.5g; FIBER 1.4g; CHOL 113mg; IRON 1.4mg; SODIUM 485mg; CALC 35mg

QUICK & EASY
Lemon-Splashed Shrimp Salad

Purchase peeled and deveined shrimp to save prep time. Chop, measure, and prepare remaining ingredients while the pasta water comes to a boil. Chock-full of colorful ingredients, this makes a summery one-dish meal.

      8   cups water
      ⅔   cup uncooked rotini (corkscrew pasta)
    1½   pounds large shrimp, peeled and deveined
      1   cup halved cherry tomatoes
      ¾   cup sliced celery
      ½   cup chopped avocado
      ½   cup chopped seeded poblano chile
      2   teaspoons grated lemon rind
      3   tablespoons fresh lemon juice
      2   tablespoons chopped fresh cilantro
      2   teaspoons extravirgin olive oil
      ¾   teaspoon kosher salt

1. Bring 8 cups water to a boil in a large saucepan. Add pasta to pan; cook 5 minutes or until almost tender. Add shrimp to pan; cook 3 minutes or until done. Drain. Rinse with cold water; drain well.

Combine pasta mixture, tomatoes, and remaining ingredients in a bowl; toss well. Yield: 4 servings (serving size: about 1¾ cups).

CALORIES 250 (25% from fat); FAT 6.9g (sat 1.2g, mono 3.8g, poly 1.2g); PROTEIN 30.3g; CARB 17g; FIBER 2.6g; CHOL 252mg; IRON 5.1mg; SODIUM 667mg; CALC 74mg

WINE NOTE: The dominant green flavors here (avocado, celery), along with a nice hint of heat (poblanos) and citrus (lemon), all point to a perfect wine partner: sauvignon blanc. Sassy and herbal, sauvignon blanc itself is splashed with lemon flavors, making it a great mirror for the flavors of this salad. Try Girard Sauvignon Blanc 2005 from the Napa Valley ($15).

in season

Bell Weather

Enjoy creative ways to serve bell peppers— a sweet gift from the late-summer garden.

MAKE AHEAD
Roasted Red Pepper Soup

Adjust the amount of hot pepper sauce to suit your taste. Serve with crusty bread.

      8   red bell peppers (about 2¾ pounds)
      5   black peppercorns
      3   thyme sprigs
      1   bay leaf
      2   teaspoons olive oil
      2   cups diced onion (about 1 large)
      1   tablespoon minced fresh garlic
      4   cups fat-free, less-sodium chicken broth
      3   tablespoons white wine vinegar
      ¼   teaspoon hot pepper sauce (such as Tabasco)
      ½   teaspoon salt
      ¼   teaspoon freshly ground black pepper
      2   tablespoons chopped fresh chives

1. Preheat broiler.

2. Cut bell peppers in half lengthwise; discard seeds and membranes. Place pepper halves, skin sides up, on a foil-lined baking sheet; flatten with hand. Broil 15 minutes or until blackened. Place in a zip-top plastic bag; seal. Let stand 15 minutes. Peel and chop.

3. Place peppercorns, thyme, and bay leaf on a double layer of cheesecloth. Gather edges of cheesecloth together; tie securely.

4. Heat oil in a large Dutch oven over medium heat. Add onion and garlic; cook 15 minutes or until onion is lightly browned, stirring occasionally. Add bell peppers, cheesecloth bag, broth, vinegar, and hot pepper sauce to pan. Increase heat to medium-high, and bring to a boil. Cover, reduce heat, and simmer 20 minutes. Remove and discard cheesecloth bag; stir in salt and black pepper. Place half of bell pepper mixture in a blender. Remove center piece of blender lid (to allow steam to escape); secure blender lid on blender. Place a clean towel over opening in blender lid (to prevent splatters). Blend until smooth. Pour pureed mixture into a large bowl; repeat procedure with remaining soup. Sprinkle with chives. Yield: 6 cups (serving size: 1 cup soup and 1 teaspoon chives).

CALORIES 99 (22% from fat); FAT 2.4g (sat 0.4g, mono 1.2g, poly 0.5g); PROTEIN 3.7g; CARB 16.7g; FIBER 1.4g; CHOL 0mg; IRON 1.1mg; SODIUM 465mg; CALC 34mg

MAKE AHEAD
Bell Pepper Focaccia

This delicious flatbread makes a fine accompaniment for beef tenderloin, roast chicken, or grilled fish. Refrigerate for up to three days, and reheat servings in the oven.

DOUGH:

      1   package dry yeast (about 2¼ teaspoons)
      1   cup warm water (100° to 110°)
    1½   tablespoons extravirgin olive oil
      1   tablespoon honey
      ½   teaspoon salt
    2¾   cups all-purpose flour, divided (about 12⅓ ounces)
          Cooking spray

1 tablespoon olive oil,
divided
1 cup thinly sliced red onion
2 teaspoons chopped fresh
oregano
½ teaspoon salt, divided
1 red bell pepper, sliced into thin
rings
1 yellow bell pepper, sliced into
thin rings

1. To prepare dough, dissolve yeast in 1 cup warm water in a large bowl; let stand 5 minutes. Stir in 1½ tablespoons oil, honey, and ½ teaspoon salt, stirring until well blended. Lightly spoon flour into dry measuring cups; level with a knife. Stir 2½ cups flour into yeast mixture to form a dough. Turn dough out onto a floured surface. Knead until smooth and elastic (about 10 minutes); add enough of remaining ¼ cup flour, 1 tablespoon at a time, to prevent dough from sticking to hands (dough will feel sticky).

2. Place dough in a large bowl coated with cooking spray, turning to coat top. Cover and let rise in a warm place (85°), free from drafts, 45 minutes or until doubled in size. (Gently press two fingers into dough. If indentation remains, dough has risen enough.) Punch dough down, and turn out onto a jelly-roll pan coated with cooking spray; press into a 10 x 8–inch rectangle. Cover and let rise 30 minutes or until doubled in size.

3. Preheat oven to 400°.

4. To prepare topping, heat 2 teaspoons oil in a large nonstick skillet over medium heat. Add onion, oregano, ¼ teaspoon salt, and peppers to pan; cook 20 minutes or until peppers are tender.

5. Uncover dough. Make indentations in top of dough using handle of a wooden spoon or your fingertips. Gently brush dough with 1 teaspoon oil. Arrange pepper mixture evenly over dough; sprinkle with ¼ teaspoon salt. Bake at 400° for 28 minutes or until loaf is golden brown around edges and sounds hollow when tapped. Yield: 10 servings.

CALORIES 170 (24% from fat); FAT 4.6g (sat 0.5g, mono 3g, poly 0.7g); PROTEIN 4.1g; CARB 28.4g; FIBER 1.2g; CHOL 0mg; IRON 1.9mg; SODIUM 235mg; CALC 7mg

MAKE AHEAD
Pork and Bell Pepper Stew

1½ pounds boneless pork loin, cut
into ½-inch cubes
¾ teaspoon salt, divided
¾ teaspoon freshly ground black
pepper, divided
1 tablespoon olive oil, divided
Cooking spray
1 cup diced red onion
1 red bell pepper, cut into ½-inch
pieces
1 yellow bell pepper, cut into
½-inch pieces
1 orange bell pepper, cut into
½-inch pieces
¾ cup dry white wine
1 cup fat-free, less-sodium chicken
broth
1 teaspoon chopped fresh thyme
2 peeled baking potatoes, cut into
½-inch cubes (about 1 pound)
1 (14.5-ounce) can diced tomatoes,
undrained
1 bay leaf
2 teaspoons chopped fresh flat-leaf
parsley

1. Sprinkle pork with ¼ teaspoon salt and ¼ teaspoon black pepper. Heat 1½ teaspoons oil in a large Dutch oven over medium-high heat. Add half of pork to pan; cook 3 minutes or until lightly browned. Remove from pan with a slotted spoon. Add 1½ teaspoons oil to pan. Add remaining pork to pan; cook 3 minutes or until lightly browned. Remove from pan with a slotted spoon; keep warm.

2. Coat pan with cooking spray; add onion and bell peppers. Add wine, scraping pan to loosen browned bits. Return pork to pan. Add broth and next 4 ingredients. Bring to a boil; cover, reduce heat, and simmer 1½ hours or until pork is tender. Uncover and simmer 30 minutes or until sauce thickens. Discard bay leaf. Stir in ½ teaspoon salt and ½ teaspoon pepper. Sprinkle with parsley. Yield: 6 servings (serving size: 1⅓ cups).

CALORIES 284 (27% from fat); FAT 8.6g (sat 2.5g, mono 4.5g, poly 1g); PROTEIN 27.4g; CARB 19.2g; FIBER 2.4g; CHOL 62mg; IRON 1.8mg; SODIUM 499mg; CALC 52mg

Jasmine Rice–Stuffed Peppers
(pictured on page 243)

This recipe calls for green bell peppers, but feel free to use any color you like. Jasmine rice adds fragrance to this dish, but you can substitute basmati or another long-grain rice. Remove the seeds from the jalapeño if you prefer milder flavor. Serve with salad.

4 large green bell peppers
Cooking spray
½ cup chopped onion
2 garlic cloves, minced
1 jalapeño pepper, minced
½ cup uncooked jasmine rice
1 cup fat-free, less-sodium chicken
broth
2 cups tomato sauce, divided
½ cup (2 ounces) grated fresh
Parmesan cheese, divided
¼ teaspoon freshly ground black pepper
1 large egg, lightly beaten
⅔ pound ground sirloin, extra lean
⅓ pound ground turkey breast

1. Preheat oven to 400°.

2. Cut bell peppers in half lengthwise; discard seeds and membranes, leaving stems intact. Place on a foil-lined jelly-roll pan, cut sides up.

3. Heat a large nonstick skillet over medium-high heat. Coat pan with cooking spray. Add onion, garlic, and jalapeño to pan; sauté 5 minutes or until onion is lightly browned. Add rice, and cook 2 minutes, stirring frequently. Add broth; bring to a boil. Cover, reduce heat, and simmer 10 minutes. Remove from heat; cool completely.

4. Combine rice mixture, 1 cup tomato sauce, ¼ cup cheese, and remaining 4 ingredients in a large bowl, stirring until blended. Spoon about ½ cup meat mixture into each pepper half. Spoon 1 cup tomato sauce evenly over peppers. Cover and bake at 400° for 45 minutes. Uncover and sprinkle with ¼ cup cheese; bake 3 minutes or until cheese melts. Yield: 4 servings (serving size: 2 pepper halves).

CALORIES 312 (25% from fat); FAT 8.6g (sat 3.6g, mono 2.8g, poly 0.9g); PROTEIN 33.8g; CARB 28.6g; FIBER 2.6g; CHOL 115mg; IRON 4.1mg; SODIUM 994mg; CALC 168mg

Grilled Shellfish with Romesco Sauce

This thick, robust sauce hails from Spain and keeps for about a week refrigerated.

SAUCE:

- 2 (1½-ounce) slices white bread, crusts removed
- 1 red bell pepper
- 2 teaspoons extravirgin olive oil, divided
- 3 garlic cloves, minced
- 1 teaspoon Hungarian sweet paprika
- 3 plum tomatoes, peeled, seeded, and chopped (about ½ pound)
- 1 jalapeño pepper, seeded and minced
- 2 tablespoons dry sherry
- 3 tablespoons water
- 2 tablespoons white wine vinegar
- 2 tablespoons fresh lemon juice
- 2 tablespoons blanched almonds, toasted
- ½ teaspoon salt

SHELLFISH:

- 1 tablespoon chopped fresh flat-leaf parsley
- 1 teaspoon extravirgin olive oil
- 24 jumbo shrimp, peeled and deveined (about 1½ pounds)
- 1 garlic clove, minced
- Cooking spray
- 24 littleneck clams, scrubbed (about 2 pounds)
- 24 mussels, scrubbed and debearded (about 2 pounds)

1. Preheat broiler.

2. To prepare sauce, place bread directly onto oven rack. Broil 2 minutes on one side or until toasted; remove from oven and cut into cubes. Cut bell pepper in half lengthwise; discard seeds and membranes. Place pepper halves, skin sides up, on a foil-lined baking sheet; flatten with hand. Broil 15 minutes or until blackened. Place in a zip-top plastic bag; seal. Let stand 15 minutes. Peel and chop.

3. Heat 1 teaspoon oil in a large nonstick skillet over medium heat. Add 3 garlic cloves; cook 2 minutes, stirring occasionally. Add paprika, tomatoes, and jalapeño; cook 2 minutes, stirring occasionally. Add sherry; cover, reduce heat, and simmer 10 minutes. Remove from heat; stir in bread.

4. Place bread mixture, bell pepper, 1 teaspoon oil, 3 tablespoons water, and next 4 ingredients in a food processor; process until smooth.

5. To prepare shellfish, combine parsley and next 3 ingredients in a large zip-top plastic bag. Seal and refrigerate 30 minutes.

6. Prepare grill.

7. Remove shrimp from bag. Thread 4 shrimp on each of 6 (8-inch) skewers. Place skewers on grill rack coated with cooking spray; grill 4 minutes on each side or until done. Remove from grill. Place clams and mussels directly on grill rack; grill 10 minutes or until shells open. Discard any unopened shells. Serve shellfish with sauce. Yield: 6 servings (serving size: 4 shrimp, 4 clams, 4 mussels, and ¼ cup sauce).

CALORIES 227 (27% from fat); FAT 6.7g (sat 0.8g, mono 3.1g, poly 1.4g); PROTEIN 24.2g; CARB 15.4g; FIBER 1.5g; CHOL 86mg; IRON 14.5mg; SODIUM 537mg; CALC 83mg

new american classic

Peach Soufflés

Our Peach Soufflés make a light, airy finale for a summer supper.

Peach Soufflés

- Cooking spray
- 2 tablespoons granulated sugar
- 2 cups chopped peeled peaches (about 3 medium)
- ⅔ cup granulated sugar, divided
- 2 tablespoons cornstarch
- 2 tablespoons fresh lemon juice
- ⅛ teaspoon salt
- 2 large egg yolks, lightly beaten
- 2 tablespoons butter
- 1 teaspoon cream of tartar
- 5 large egg whites
- 1 teaspoon powdered sugar

1. Position oven rack to lowest level, and remove middle rack. Preheat oven to 425°.

2. Lightly coat 6 (8-ounce) soufflé dishes with cooking spray. Sprinkle evenly with 2 tablespoons granulated sugar. Set aside.

3. Place peaches and ⅓ cup granulated sugar in a food processor; process until smooth. Combine peach mixture, cornstarch, juice, salt, and egg yolks in a medium saucepan, stirring well with a whisk; bring to a boil. Cook 1 minute, stirring constantly with a whisk. Remove from heat; stir in butter. Cool 10 minutes.

4. Place cream of tartar and egg whites in a large mixing bowl, and beat with a mixer at high speed until soft peaks form. Add ⅓ cup granulated sugar, 2 tablespoons at a time, beating until stiff peaks form (do not overbeat). Gently stir ¼ of egg white mixture into peach mixture, and gently fold in remaining egg white mixture. Gently spoon mixture into prepared dishes. Sharply tap dishes 2 or 3 times on counter to level. Place dishes on a baking sheet, and place baking sheet on bottom rack of 425° oven. Immediately reduce oven temperature to 350° (do not remove soufflés from oven). Bake 28 minutes at 350° or until a wooden pick inserted in side of soufflé comes out clean. Sprinkle evenly with powdered sugar. Serve immediately. Yield: 6 servings (serving size: 1 soufflé).

CALORIES 147 (25% from fat); FAT 4.1g (sat 2.2g, mono 1.2g, poly 0.3g); PROTEIN 3.2g; CARB 24.8g; FIBER 0.4g; CHOL 59mg; IRON 0.2mg; SODIUM 94mg; CALC 9mg

Entertaining

Whether you're hosting a few friends for an evening or a group for the weekend, A Carolina Classic (page 301), Fall Foliage Retreat (page 304) and Common Cause (page 308) offer no-fuss menus and terrific recipes for memorable gatherings, large and small.

A Carolina Classic

Roll up your sleeves and gather your friends for a Lowcountry shrimp supper using our casual menu with make-ahead options.

Lowcountry Shrimp Boil Menu

serves 8

Have plenty of ice and paper towels on hand.

Appetizers

Grilled Herb Grit Cakes

Grilled Okra and Tomato Skewers

Main Dish

Frogmore Stew with Jalapeño Tartar Sauce and Zesty Chili Sauce

Sides

Broccoli and Apple Salad

Cheddar–Green Onion Muffins

Dessert

Benne Candy
or
Shortcakes with Fresh Berries

Beverages

Lemon and Mint Iced Tea

Beer

MAKE AHEAD
Grilled Herb Grit Cakes

Prepare the grits one day ahead; cover and refrigerate. Cut and grill the squares right before the party.

2¼ cups water
1 tablespoon butter
½ teaspoon kosher salt
2 garlic cloves, minced
¾ cup uncooked coarse-ground yellow grits
1 teaspoon chopped fresh basil
1 teaspoon chopped fresh thyme
1 teaspoon chopped fresh parsley
Cooking spray
8 teaspoons grated fresh Parmesan cheese

1. Combine first 4 ingredients in a medium saucepan; bring to a boil. Gradually add grits, stirring constantly with a whisk. Reduce heat, and simmer 10 minutes or until thick, stirring occasionally. Stir in basil, thyme, and parsley. Pour grits into an 8-inch square baking dish coated with cooking spray. Press plastic wrap onto surface of grits, and chill 2 hours or until firm.
2. Prepare grill.
3. Cut grits into 8 (2 x 4–inch) portions. Grill grit cakes 6 minutes. Carefully turn grit cakes over, and sprinkle each cake with 1 teaspoon cheese. Grill 6 minutes or until lightly browned and heated through. Yield: 8 servings (serving size: 1 grit cake).

CALORIES 75 (25% from fat); FAT 2.1g (sat 1.2g, mono 0.6g, poly 0.2g); PROTEIN 2g; CARB 12g; FIBER 0.3g; CHOL 5mg; IRON 0.6mg; SODIUM 155mg; CALC 22mg

---

QUICK & EASY • MAKE AHEAD
Grilled Okra and Tomato Skewers

Grill these appetizers when you cook Grilled Herb Grit Cakes (recipe at left). Assemble the skewers the night before; brush them with the oil mixture before grilling. Flavor the oil mixture with dried ground herbs to suit your taste. Look for okra pods of similar size to assure even grilling.

2 small onions, each cut into 8 wedges
24 okra pods (about ¾ pound), trimmed
16 cherry tomatoes (about ½ pound)
4 teaspoons olive oil
1 teaspoon kosher salt
1 teaspoon freshly ground black pepper
1 teaspoon water
½ teaspoon ground red pepper
⅛ teaspoon sugar
2 garlic cloves, minced
Cooking spray

1. Prepare grill.
2. Divide each onion wedge into 2 equal pieces. Thread 3 okra pods, 2 tomatoes, and 2 onion pieces alternately onto each of 8 (12-inch) skewers. Combine oil and next 6 ingredients in a small bowl, stirring with a whisk. Brush oil mixture over skewers. Place skewers on a grill rack coated with cooking spray, and grill 3 minutes on each side or until tender. Yield: 8 servings (serving size: 1 skewer).

CALORIES 44 (49% from fat); FAT 2.4g (sat 0.3g, mono 1.7g, poly 0.3g); PROTEIN 1.3g; CARB 5.5g; FIBER 1.9g; CHOL 0mg; IRON 0.5mg; SODIUM 241mg; CALC 42mg

Frogmore Stew

If you use frozen shrimp, be sure to thaw them before adding them to the other ingredients in the stockpot.

- 3 quarts water
- 1 tablespoon kosher salt
- 1 tablespoon crushed red pepper
- 1 tablespoon ground cumin
- 2 teaspoons dried thyme
- 2 teaspoons coarsely ground black pepper
- 8 garlic cloves, peeled and mashed
- 4 bay leaves
- 2 (12-ounce) cans beer
- 1 onion, cut into 8 wedges
- 2 pounds small red potatoes, quartered
- 1 pound low-fat smoked sausage or low-fat kielbasa (such as Hillshire Farms), cut into ½-inch-thick slices
- 4 ears shucked corn, halved crosswise
- 2 pounds large shrimp, unpeeled

1. Bring first 10 ingredients to a boil in an 8-quart stockpot. Add potatoes and sausage; cook 12 minutes. Add corn, and cook 4 minutes. Add shrimp, and cook 2 minutes or until shrimp are done. Drain and discard bay leaves. Yield: 8 servings (serving size: about 2¾ cups).

CALORIES 315 (11% from fat); FAT 4g (sat 1g, mono 1g, poly 1.2g); PROTEIN 31.5g; CARB 38.2g; FIBER 3.6g; CHOL 184mg; IRON 5.2mg; SODIUM 709mg; CALC 91mg

Corn, sausage, and shrimp spilled onto the table make an easy trip to your plate.

Jalapeño Tartar Sauce

This tangy, hot sauce doubles easily and can be made up to two days ahead. Leftovers would be great as a spread on a grilled fish sandwich. Use more pickled jalapeño if you like a spicy sauce.

- ½ cup reduced-fat mayonnaise
- ½ cup fat-free mayonnaise
- 2 tablespoons fresh lime juice
- 1 to 2 tablespoons finely chopped pickled jalapeño pepper
- ½ teaspoon grated lime rind
- ¼ teaspoon ground cumin
- Dash of kosher salt

1. Combine all ingredients in a small bowl. Cover and chill until ready to serve. Yield: 1¼ cups (serving size: 2 tablespoons).

CALORIES 32 (56% from fat); FAT 2g (sat 0.5g, mono 0.5g, poly 0.8g); PROTEIN 0.1g; CARB 3.9g; FIBER 0.3g; CHOL 1mg; IRON 0mg; SODIUM 220mg; CALC 2mg

Zesty Chili Sauce

The same amount of fresh horseradish can be substituted for prepared. More pungent and fiery than a freshly cut onion, fresh horseradish may irritate your eyes and nose when you grate it. We prefer to place a two-inch piece of horseradish root in the food processor and process until minced. Measure out two tablespoons for this recipe; reserve any extra for another use.

- 1 cup no-salt-added ketchup
- 3 tablespoons fresh lemon juice
- 2 tablespoons prepared horseradish
- 2 teaspoons hot sauce
- 1 teaspoon Worcestershire sauce
- ½ teaspoon minced garlic

1. Combine all ingredients in a small bowl, stirring with a whisk. Cover and chill. Yield: 1¼ cups (serving size: 2 tablespoons).

CALORIES 29 (3% from fat); FAT 0.1g (sat 0g, mono 0g, poly 0.1g); PROTEIN 0.5g; CARB 7.6g; FIBER 0.2g; CHOL 0mg; IRON 0.2mg; SODIUM 26mg; CALC 7mg

Broccoli and Apple Salad

Sweet, crunchy apple and broccoli create a refreshing, light side dish. Prepare this salad up to eight hours in advance.

- 6 tablespoons apple cider vinegar
- 2½ tablespoons sugar
- 2 tablespoons Dijon mustard
- 1 tablespoon canola oil
- ½ teaspoon freshly ground black pepper
- ¼ teaspoon salt
- 1 (1¼-pound) head of broccoli
- 1¼ cups chopped Braeburn or Fuji apple (about ½ pound)
- ¼ cup minced Walla Walla or other sweet onion

1. Combine first 6 ingredients in a large bowl, stirring well with a whisk.
2. Coarsely chop broccoli into 1½-inch pieces, and add to vinegar mixture. Add apple and onion, tossing to coat. Yield: 8 servings (serving size: about ¾ cup).

CALORIES 72 (30% from fat); FAT 2.4g (sat 0.2g, mono 1.2g, poly 0.6g); PROTEIN 2.8g; CARB 11.6g; FIBER 3g; CHOL 0mg; IRON 0.7mg; SODIUM 196mg; CALC 38mg

Cheddar-Green Onion Muffins

These muffins are delicious warm but can be made up to a month in advance and frozen.

- 1¾ cups all-purpose flour (about 7¾ ounces)
- ¼ cup yellow cornmeal
- 1 teaspoon baking powder
- ½ teaspoon salt
- ¼ teaspoon baking soda
- ¼ teaspoon freshly ground black pepper
- ½ cup (2 ounces) reduced-fat shredded extrasharp Cheddar cheese, divided
- 3 tablespoons chilled butter, cut into pieces
- 1¼ cups fat-free buttermilk
- 2 tablespoons chopped green onions
- 1 teaspoon minced garlic
- 1 large egg, lightly beaten
- Cooking spray

1. Preheat oven to 375°.

2. Lightly spoon flour into dry measuring cups; level with a knife. Place flour, cornmeal, and next 4 ingredients in a food processor; pulse 3 times to combine. Add 5 tablespoons cheese and butter; pulse 5 times or until mixture resembles coarse crumbs. Spoon mixture into a medium bowl. Combine buttermilk, onions, garlic, and egg; stir with a whisk. Add to flour mixture, stirring just until moist. Spoon into 12 muffin cups coated with cooking spray. Sprinkle evenly with 3 tablespoons cheese. Bake at 375° for 18 minutes or until a wooden pick inserted in center comes out clean. Cool 5 minutes in pan on a wire rack; remove from pan. Cool completely on a wire rack. Yield: 12 muffins (serving size: 1 muffin).

CALORIES 135 (30% from fat); FAT 4.5g (sat 2.7g, mono 0.9g, poly 0.2g); PROTEIN 4.9g; CARB 18.6g; FIBER 0.6g; CHOL 29mg; IRON 1.1mg; SODIUM 217mg; CALC 97mg

---

QUICK & EASY
Benne Candy

Carolinians adopted the West African ingredient *benne* (pronounced "benny")—or sesame seed—for this rich, brittle candy.

Cooking spray
2 cups sugar
½ cup water
2 teaspoons butter
1 teaspoon vanilla extract
¾ cup sesame seeds
1 teaspoon baking soda
½ teaspoon grated orange rind
⅛ teaspoon salt
⅛ teaspoon ground cardamom

1. Line a jelly-roll pan with foil. Coat foil with cooking spray.

2. Place sugar and ½ cup water in a medium, heavy saucepan over medium-high heat; bring to a boil (do not stir). Cook 10 minutes or just until sugar is golden. Remove from heat; add butter and vanilla, carefully stirring until butter melts (mixture will bubble vigorously). Stir in sesame seeds and remaining ingredients, stirring constantly, and return mixture to heat. Cook 30 seconds or until well combined. Rapidly spread mixture onto prepared pan. Cool completely, and break into small pieces. Yield: about 18 ounces (serving size: about 1 ounce).

CALORIES 125 (24% from fat); FAT 3.4g (sat 0.7g, mono 1.2g, poly 1.3g); PROTEIN 1.1g; CARB 23.7g; FIBER 0.7g; CHOL 1mg; IRON 0.9mg; SODIUM 90mg; CALC 59mg

---

MAKE AHEAD
Shortcakes with Fresh Berries

Make the shortcakes up to two days ahead, and store in an airtight container. Use a serrated knife to cut in half before serving. Prepare the berry filling up to 12 hours ahead, and refrigerate until serving. Use any combination of fresh berries available.

2 cups all-purpose flour (about 9 ounces)
3 tablespoons granulated sugar, divided
2 teaspoons baking powder
¼ teaspoon salt
3 tablespoons chilled butter, cut into small pieces
⅔ cup reduced-fat buttermilk
1 tablespoon canola oil
1 teaspoon vanilla extract
1 large egg, lightly beaten
Cooking spray
3½ teaspoons turbinado sugar, divided
½ cup apple jelly
3 tablespoons fresh lemon juice
3 cups strawberries, quartered (about 12 ounces)
2½ cups blackberries (about 12 ounces)
1 cup fat-free whipped topping

1. Preheat oven to 425°.

2. Lightly spoon flour into dry measuring cups; level with a knife. Combine flour, 2 tablespoons granulated sugar, baking powder, and salt in a large bowl, stirring with a whisk. Cut in butter with a pastry blender or two knives until mixture resembles coarse meal.

3. Combine buttermilk, oil, vanilla, and egg in a small bowl, stirring with a whisk. Add to flour mixture, stirring just until moist (dough will be sticky).

4. Turn dough out onto a baking sheet coated with cooking spray. Pat dough into an 8-inch circle. Cut dough into 8 wedges, cutting into, but not through, dough. Sprinkle 1½ teaspoons turbinado sugar over dough. Bake at 425° for 15 minutes or until golden. Cool 15 minutes.

5. Combine jelly, juice, and 1 tablespoon granulated sugar in a microwave-safe bowl; microwave at HIGH 1 minute. Stir mixture with a whisk until smooth. Combine jelly mixture, strawberries, and blackberries in a large bowl; toss to coat berries. Cover and chill.

6. Cut shortcake into 8 wedges. Cut each wedge in half horizontally; spoon ½ cup berry mixture over bottom half of each shortcake. Replace top half of shortcake. Top each serving with 2 tablespoons whipped topping; sprinkle evenly with 2 teaspoons turbinado sugar. Yield: 8 servings (serving size: 1 shortcake).

CALORIES 306 (22% from fat); FAT 7.5g (sat 3.2g, mono 2.4g, poly 1.1g); PROTEIN 5.7g; CARB 53.5g; FIBER 3.9g; CHOL 39mg; IRON 2.1mg; SODIUM 264mg; CALC 117mg

---

MAKE AHEAD
Lemon and Mint Iced Tea

This twist on sweet Southern iced tea is refreshingly tart. Serve well chilled.

8 cups water, divided
3 family-sized tea bags
1 sprig fresh mint (about ¼ cup leaves)
¾ cup sugar
¼ cup fresh lemon juice
8 lemon slices (optional)
8 mint sprigs (optional)

1. Bring 4 cups water to a boil in a medium saucepan. Add tea bags and 1 mint sprig to pan; steep 10 minutes. Remove and discard tea bags and mint.

2. Combine sugar and juice in a glass measuring cup. Add ½ cup hot tea mixture; stir until sugar dissolves. Pour sugar mixture into a 2-quart pitcher. Pour remaining hot tea mixture into pitcher. Add 4 cups cold water; stir. Serve over ice. Garnish with lemon slices and mint sprigs, if desired. Yield: 8 servings (serving size: 1 cup).

CALORIES 75 (0% from fat); FAT 0g; PROTEIN 0g; CARB 19.4g; FIBER 0g; CHOL 0mg; IRON 0mg; SODIUM 5mg; CALC 5mg

Fall Foliage Retreat

Every autumn, a group of Pennsylvania women convene to mountain bike, hike, unwind, and cook together. We provide the menu for their weekend getaway.

Friday-Night Welcome Menu
serves 10

Eggplant and Fig Caponata

Wild Mushroom and Goat Cheese Spread

Assorted cheeses

Wine

Saturday Breakfast Menu
serves 10

Chicken and Basil Sausage Patties

Scrambled eggs

Sliced melon

Toast

Coffee

Saturday Bikers' Lunch Menu
serves 10

Prosciutto and Smoked Gouda Panini

Tossed green salad

Fig and Almond Squares

Beer

Sparkling water

Eggplant and Fig Caponata

This satisfying spread is good to have on hand when guests arrive on Friday evening. Serve at room temperature with crackers and bread.

    1   (1-pound) eggplant
    Cooking spray
    2   tablespoons chopped shallots
    3   garlic cloves, minced
    ½   cup dried Calimyrna figs, finely
        chopped (about 5 whole figs)
    ½   cup water
    2   tablespoons white wine
        vinegar
    1   tablespoon fresh lemon juice
    1   tablespoon brown sugar
    ½   teaspoon kosher salt
    ¼   teaspoon crushed red pepper
    ¼   cup toasted pine nuts
    1   tablespoon chopped parsley
    1   teaspoon fresh lemon juice

1. Preheat oven to 450°.
2. Split eggplant in half lengthwise. Place eggplant, cut sides down, on a baking sheet coated with cooking spray. Bake at 450° for 20 minutes or until eggplant is tender and cut sides are browned. Remove from oven; cool completely. Using a fork, carefully remove flesh of eggplant from skin. Discard skin; finely chop flesh, and place in a bowl.
3. Heat a large nonstick skillet over medium-high heat. Coat pan with cooking spray. Add shallots and garlic to pan; sauté 2 minutes or until tender. Stir in figs and next 6 ingredients. Simmer 5 minutes or until liquid almost evaporates. Remove from heat. Stir in eggplant, pine nuts, parsley, and 1 teaspoon juice. Yield: 10 servings (serving size: about 3 tablespoons).

CALORIES 68 (33% from fat); FAT 2.5g (sat 0.2g, mono 0.7g, poly 1.2g); PROTEIN 1.4g; CARB 11.8g; FIBER 2.7g; CHOL 0mg; IRON 0.6mg; SODIUM 97mg; CALC 25mg

WINE NOTE: Oak-aged Chardonnay is tricky to pair with food, but the Eggplant and Fig Caponata is perfect with the wine's rich flavors. The toasted nuts and figs in the dish are echoed in many barrel-aged Chardonnays, like the toasty, spicy Voyager Estate Chardonnay 2004 ($22) from West Australia. This cool-climate wine also offers plenty of citrus and melon, along with bright acidity.

Make-Ahead Timeline

Even though part of the fun of a getaway with friends is cooking together, it's a good idea to do some of the work ahead.

Two days ahead:
• Combine ingredients for Cajun Spice Mix (recipe on page 306); store in a zip-top plastic bag.
• Prepare Homemade Granola (recipe on page 307); store in an airtight container.
• Bake Fig and Almond Squares (recipe on page 305); cool completely and store in an airtight container.

One day ahead:
• Prepare and chill Eggplant and Fig Caponata (recipe above) (bring to room temperature before serving).
• Assemble and chill Wild Mushroom and Goat Cheese Spread (recipe on page 305) (broil immediately before serving).
• Shred celeriac and fennel for Celery Root and Fennel Rémoulade (recipe on page 306).
• Combine ingredients for Chicken and Basil Sausage Patties (recipe on page 305); refrigerate in an airtight container.
• Chop onion and zucchini for Chicken, Chickpea, and Zucchini Stew (recipe on page 307); store separately in zip-top plastic bags.

Wild Mushroom and Goat Cheese Spread

Prepare the spread ahead of time, and chill; broil just before serving.

¼ cup boiling water
½ ounce dried porcini
    mushrooms
1 teaspoon butter
1 teaspoon extravirgin olive
    oil
1 tablespoon minced shallots
1 tablespoon finely chopped fresh
    thyme
1 tablespoon finely chopped fresh
    rosemary
½ teaspoon salt
¼ teaspoon freshly ground black
    pepper
2 garlic cloves, minced
8 ounces wild mushrooms, finely
    chopped
8 ounces cremini mushrooms, finely
    chopped
5 tablespoons sherry
6 tablespoons (3 ounces) goat
    cheese, divided
Cooking spray
1 tablespoon chopped fresh
    parsley

1. Combine ¼ cup boiling water and porcini mushrooms in a bowl; let stand 10 minutes. Strain porcini mushrooms through a sieve over a bowl, reserving liquid. Chop mushrooms; set aside.
2. Heat butter and oil in a large nonstick skillet over medium heat. Add shallots and next 5 ingredients; sauté 2 minutes. Stir in reserved porcini mushrooms, wild mushrooms, and cremini mushrooms. Cook 10 minutes or until liquid almost evaporates, stirring frequently. Stir in sherry and reserved mushroom liquid, scraping pan to loosen browned bits. Cook 5 minutes or until liquid almost evaporates. Remove from heat.
3. Preheat broiler.
4. Place mushroom mixture and 3 tablespoons cheese in a food processor; process until smooth. Scrape mushroom mixture into an 8-inch square baking dish coated with cooking spray. Sprinkle evenly with 3 tablespoons cheese. Broil 7 minutes or until edges of cheese begin to brown. Remove from heat, and sprinkle with parsley. Yield: 10 servings (serving size: about 3 tablespoons).

CALORIES 54 (47% from fat); FAT 2.8g (sat 1.6g, mono 0.9g, poly 0.1g); PROTEIN 3.3g; CARB 3.2g; FIBER 0.6g; CHOL 5mg; IRON 0.8mg; SODIUM 156mg; CALC 24mg

Chicken and Basil Sausage Patties

Chicken thighs make for moist, flavorful sausage; grind skinless, boneless thighs in a food processor. Combine the ingredients with your hands.

¼ cup chopped fresh basil
¼ cup (1 ounce) grated fresh
    Parmesan cheese
3 tablespoons dry white wine
1 teaspoon salt
1 teaspoon dried rubbed sage
½ teaspoon ground cumin
½ teaspoon ground coriander
½ teaspoon freshly ground black
    pepper
2 pounds ground chicken
2 garlic cloves, minced

1. Combine all ingredients in a large bowl. Divide chicken mixture into 12 equal portions, shaping each into a ½-inch-thick patty.
2. Heat a large nonstick skillet over medium heat. Add patties; cook 7 minutes on each side or until done. Yield: 12 servings (serving size: 1 patty).

CALORIES 104 (31% from fat); FAT 3.6g (sat 1.1g, mono 1.1g, poly 0.7g); PROTEIN 15.8g; CARB 0.5g; FIBER 0.2g; CHOL 64mg; IRON 0.9mg; SODIUM 300mg; CALC 41mg

Prosciutto and Smoked Gouda Panini

You'll need to cook the panini in batches; keep cooked panini warm in a 250° oven. The sandwiches make hearty lunch fare on their own, or serve them with a tossed green salad or Chicken, Chickpea, and Zucchini Stew (recipe on page 307).

20 (1-ounce) slices Italian bread
Cooking spray
6 ounces smoked Gouda cheese,
    thinly sliced
6 ounces thinly sliced prosciutto

1. Coat 1 side of each bread slice with cooking spray. Place 10 bread slices, coated sides down, on a work surface. Divide cheese and prosciutto evenly among 10 bread slices. Top with remaining bread slices, coated sides up.
2. Heat a large nonstick skillet over medium heat. Cook panini 5 minutes on each side or until lightly browned and cheese melts, pressing with a spatula to flatten. Yield: 10 servings (serving size: 1 panino).

CALORIES 265 (33% from fat); FAT 9.7g (sat 5g, mono 3g, poly 1.2g); PROTEIN 14.5g; CARB 28.9g; FIBER 1.5g; CHOL 36mg; IRON 1.9mg; SODIUM 772mg; CALC 204mg

Fig and Almond Squares

Prepare a double batch of these chewy, blondie-like treats so you can enjoy them with lunch on Saturday and take some on the road for the drive home on Sunday. Bake up to two days ahead, and store in an airtight container.

Cooking spray
¾ cup all-purpose flour (about
    3⅓ ounces)
½ teaspoon baking powder
⅛ teaspoon salt
¾ cup packed brown sugar
¼ cup butter, melted
1 tablespoon amaretto (almond-
    flavored liqueur)
1 teaspoon vanilla extract
1 large egg white, lightly beaten
1 large egg, lightly beaten
½ cup chopped dried figs
¼ cup flaked sweetened coconut
2 tablespoons sliced almonds,
    toasted
½ cup powdered sugar
2½ teaspoons hot water
¼ teaspoon amaretto (almond-
    flavored liqueur)

Continued

1. Preheat oven to 350°.

2. Coat bottom of an 8-inch square baking pan with cooking spray (do not coat sides of pan); set aside.

3. Lightly spoon flour into dry measuring cups; level with a knife. Combine flour, baking powder, and salt in a large bowl, stirring well with a whisk. Combine brown sugar and next 5 ingredients in a medium bowl, stirring with a whisk until well blended. Add brown sugar mixture, figs, coconut, and almonds to flour mixture; stir until blended. Spoon batter into prepared pan. Bake at 350° for 25 minutes or until a wooden pick inserted in center comes out clean. Cool in pan on a wire rack. Cut into 16 squares.

4. Combine powdered sugar, 2½ teaspoons hot water, and ¼ teaspoon amaretto in a small bowl, stirring with a whisk until smooth. Drizzle over squares. Yield: 16 servings (serving size: 1 square).

CALORIES 138 (27% from fat); FAT 4.2g (sat 2.4g, mono 1.3g, poly 0.3g); PROTEIN 1.6g; CARB 23.7g; FIBER 1g; CHOL 21mg; IRON 0.7mg; SODIUM 79mg; CALC 32mg

---

QUICK & EASY • MAKE AHEAD
Cajun Spice Mix

This spice mix is used in Blackened Grouper (recipe at right), Maque Choux (page 307), and Dirty Rice (page 307).

  3 tablespoons paprika
  2 tablespoons ground red pepper
  2 tablespoons dried thyme
  2 tablespoons dried oregano
  2 tablespoons onion powder
  2 tablespoons garlic powder
  1 tablespoon kosher salt
  1 tablespoon black pepper
  1 tablespoon sugar

1. Combine all ingredients in a small bowl. Yield: 1 cup (serving size: 1 tablespoon).

CALORIES 20 (13% from fat); FAT 0.3g (sat 0.1g, mono 0g, poly 0.2g); PROTEIN 0.7g; CARB 4.2g; FIBER 1.4g; CHOL 0mg; IRON 1.1mg; SODIUM 355mg; CALC 23mg

---

Saturday Cajun Dinner Menu
serves 10

Celery Root and Fennel Rémoulade

Blackened Grouper

Maque Choux

Dirty Rice

Low-fat almond-praline ice cream

Beer

Coffee

Easy Sunday Breakfast Menu
serves 10

Homemade Granola

Low-fat yogurt

Assorted fruit

Orange juice

Coffee

Farewell Sunday Lunch Menu
serves 10

Chicken, Chickpea, and Zucchini Stew

Tossed green salad

French bread

Sparkling water

Fig and Almond Squares (page 305)

QUICK & EASY
Celery Root and Fennel Rémoulade

Use the grater attachment of the food processor to quickly shred celeriac and fennel for this slawlike side.

  4 cups shredded peeled celeriac (celery root)
  2 cups shredded fennel bulb
  2 tablespoons fresh lemon juice
  ½ cup reduced-fat sour cream
  2 tablespoons Creole mustard
  2 teaspoons canola oil
  ½ teaspoon salt
  ½ teaspoon freshly ground black pepper
  ½ cup chopped green onions
  ¼ cup chopped fresh parsley

1. Combine first 3 ingredients in a large bowl. Combine sour cream and next 4 ingredients, stirring with a whisk. Add sour cream mixture, onions, and parsley to celeriac mixture; toss well. Cover and chill at least 30 minutes. Yield: 10 servings (serving size: about ⅔ cup).

CALORIES 66 (37% from fat); FAT 2.7g (sat 1.1g, mono 0.6g, poly 0.4g); PROTEIN 1.8g; CARB 9.5g; FIBER 2g; CHOL 6mg; IRON 0.7mg; SODIUM 217mg; CALC 58mg

---

QUICK & EASY
Blackened Grouper

Be careful when adding the fish to the pan, as the butter and oil may splatter.

 10 (6-ounce) grouper fillets
  ¼ cup Cajun Spice Mix (recipe at left)
  5 teaspoons canola oil, divided
  5 teaspoons butter, divided
 10 lemon wedges

1. Rub each side of fillets with Cajun Spice Mix. Heat 2½ teaspoons oil and 2½ teaspoons butter in a large nonstick skillet over medium-high heat. Add 5 fillets; cook 4 minutes on each side or until fish flakes easily when tested with a fork or until desired degree of doneness. Repeat procedure with 2½ teaspoons oil, 2½ teaspoons butter, and remaining fillets. Serve with lemon wedges. Yield: 10 servings (serving size: 1 fillet and 1 lemon wedge).

CALORIES 204 (27% from fat); FAT 6.1g (sat 1.8g, mono 2.2g, poly 1.4g); PROTEIN 33.3g; CARB 2.3g; FIBER 0.8g; CHOL 68mg; IRON 2mg; SODIUM 246mg; CALC 58mg

Maque Choux

There are several theories about the name of this side dish (pronounced "mock shoe"). Some say it's derived from the Native American name for corn.

    1   tablespoon butter
    5   cups fresh corn kernels (about
        8 ears)
    1   cup chopped onion
    ½   cup chopped poblano pepper
    1   (14.5-ounce) can diced tomatoes,
        undrained
    ½   cup fat-free, less-sodium chicken
        broth
    1   tablespoon Cajun Spice Mix
        (recipe on page 306)
    ½   teaspoon salt

1. Melt butter in a large skillet over medium-high heat. Add corn, onion, and pepper; sauté 10 minutes or until corn begins to brown. Add tomatoes and remaining ingredients; cook 20 minutes or until liquid almost evaporates, stirring occasionally. Yield: 10 servings (serving size: ½ cup).

CALORIES 104 (19% from fat); FAT 2.2g (sat 0.9g, mono 0.6g, poly 0.6g); PROTEIN 3.7g; CARB 20.3g; FIBER 3.5g; CHOL 3mg; IRON 1.2mg; SODIUM 258mg; CALC 23mg

Dirty Rice

Add more Cajun Spice Mix, a teaspoon at a time, if you enjoy spicy rice.

    4   cups fat-free, less-sodium chicken
        broth
    2   bay leaves
    2   cups long-grain rice
        Cooking spray
    2   cups chopped onion
    1   cup chopped celery
    1   cup chopped green bell
        pepper
    2   tablespoons Cajun Spice Mix
        (recipe on page 306)
    12 ounces chicken and apple sausage,
        chopped
    3   garlic cloves, minced
    ½   cup chopped fresh parsley

1. Bring broth and bay leaves to a boil in a medium saucepan; add rice. Cover, reduce heat, and simmer 20 minutes or until liquid is absorbed. Discard bay leaves. Place rice in a large bowl.
2. Heat a large nonstick skillet over medium-high heat. Coat pan with cooking spray. Add onion and next 5 ingredients; sauté 7 minutes. Add sausage mixture and parsley to rice, tossing to combine. Yield: 10 servings (serving size: 1 cup).

CALORIES 216 (15% from fat); FAT 3.7g (sat 1g, mono 1.6g, poly 0.8g); PROTEIN 8.5g; CARB 37.4g; FIBER 3.1g; CHOL 25mg; IRON 1.4mg; SODIUM 408mg; CALC 40mg

Homemade Granola

Prepare the granola up to two days ahead, and store in an airtight container. Serve for breakfast with low-fat yogurt and fruit.

    6   cups rolled oats
    ¼   cup chopped almonds
    ¼   cup chopped pecans
    2   tablespoons brown sugar
    ¼   teaspoon kosher salt
    ⅓   cup maple syrup
    ¼   cup honey
    ¼   cup pineapple juice
    ½   teaspoon almond extract
        Cooking spray
    ¼   cup dried cranberries
    ¼   cup chopped dried apricots

1. Preheat oven to 300°.
2. Combine first 5 ingredients in a large bowl. Add syrup, honey, juice, and almond extract; toss well. Spread mixture evenly onto a jelly-roll pan coated with cooking spray. Bake at 300° for 45 minutes, stirring every 15 minutes. Stir in cranberries and apricots. Cool completely. Store in a zip-top plastic bag. Yield: 10 servings (serving size: ½ cup).

CALORIES 384 (20% from fat); FAT 8.4g (sat 1.1g, mono 3.7g, poly 2.5g); PROTEIN 9.8g; CARB 68.1g; FIBER 7.8g; CHOL 0mg; IRON 3.4mg; SODIUM 52mg; CALC 57mg

Chicken, Chickpea, and Zucchini Stew

This stew is nice for lunch before or after a hike. To speed preparation, chop the onion and zucchini the night before.

    1   teaspoon olive oil
    1   cup chopped onion
    1½ teaspoons minced fresh
        rosemary
    2   garlic cloves, minced
    3   cups chopped zucchini
    ¼   teaspoon freshly ground black
        pepper
    ⅛   teaspoon salt
    ½   pound ground chicken
    4   cups fat-free, less-sodium chicken
        broth
    ¼   cup dry white wine
    3   tablespoons tomato paste
    ½   teaspoon crushed red pepper
    2   (15½-ounce) cans chickpeas
        (garbanzo beans), rinsed and
        drained
    2   (14.5-ounce) cans diced tomatoes
    1   bay leaf
    ¾   cup (3 ounces) grated Parmesan
        cheese

1. Heat oil in a large Dutch oven over medium heat. Add onion, rosemary, and garlic; sauté 2 minutes. Add zucchini, black pepper, salt, and chicken; cook 5 minutes or until chicken is browned, stirring to crumble.
2. Add broth and next 6 ingredients; bring to a boil. Reduce heat, and simmer 30 minutes. Discard bay leaf. Sprinkle with cheese. Yield: 10 servings (serving size: 1 cup stew and about 1 tablespoon cheese).

CALORIES 173 (25% from fat); FAT 4.8g (sat 1.7g, mono 1.1g, poly 0.5g); PROTEIN 11.4g; CARB 21g; FIBER 4.7g; CHOL 19mg; IRON 2mg; SODIUM 592mg; CALC 130mg

Common Cause

Drawn by a shared interest in good food, Cooking Light *Supper Clubs celebrate a camaraderie that spans generations.*

For all the *Cooking Light* supper clubs, we've developed a themed menu, which offers traditional yet lightened Cuban fare. Try these dishes with your group, and savor their flavorful Caribbean accents.

Cuban-Inspired Menu
serves 12

Prepare each of these dishes and allow your group to sample as they please, or prepare only one from each course.

Appetizers

Grilled Pineapple and Avocado Salad

Sofrito Fish Cakes with Creamy Chipotle Tartar Sauce

Havana Sandwich Bites

Entrées

Pork Tenderloin with Spicy Guava Glaze

Grilled Shrimp with Mango and Red Onion Relish

Cilantro Citrus Chicken

Sides

Sautéed Sweet Plantains

Cuban-Style Black Beans and Rice

Desserts

Guava and Cheese Empanadas

Tres Leches Cakes

Beverages

Rum Punch

WINE NOTE: The flavors in this menu are sweet, citrusy, fruity, earthy, and savory, with just a touch of spice and chiles. Pairing all these is a tall order for a single wine, but a good, rich zinfandel can do the trick. Zinfandel's plush fruitiness will both cushion and stand up to the flavors. Try the Folie à Deux 2003 zinfandel from Amador County, California ($16).

Grilled Pineapple and Avocado Salad

2 small pineapples, peeled, cored, and sliced
1 tablespoon sugar
¼ teaspoon ground red pepper
Cooking spray
8 cups torn Boston lettuce
1¾ cups chopped seeded cucumber
1 cup chopped red onion
¼ cup chopped fresh cilantro
3 tablespoons fresh lemon juice
1½ teaspoons salt
1 teaspoon extravirgin olive oil
¼ teaspoon freshly ground black pepper
1 diced peeled avocado

1. Prepare grill.
2. Pat pineapple dry with paper towels. Combine sugar and red pepper in a small bowl; sprinkle pineapple evenly with sugar mixture. Place pineapple on grill rack coated with cooking spray; grill 4 minutes on each side or until golden. Cool completely; chop.
3. Place pineapple in a large bowl. Add lettuce and remaining ingredients; toss well. Serve immediately. Yield: 12 servings (serving size: about 1 cup).

CALORIES 78 (36% from fat); FAT 3.1g (sat 0.3g, mono 1.9g, poly 0.4g); PROTEIN 1.5g; CARB 14.5g; FIBER 2.2g; CHOL 0mg; IRON 0.7mg; SODIUM 298mg; CALC 26mg

Sofrito Fish Cakes with Creamy Chipotle Tartar Sauce

SAUCE:
⅓ cup fat-free sour cream
⅓ cup reduced-fat mayonnaise
1 tablespoon sweet pickle relish
2 teaspoons drained capers, chopped
1 to 1½ teaspoons finely chopped chipotle chile, canned in adobo sauce

CAKES:
2 cups coarsely chopped green bell pepper
1¾ cups coarsely chopped red bell pepper
⅓ cup chopped fresh cilantro
3 garlic cloves, chopped
1 onion, quartered
Cooking spray
3 (1-ounce) slices white bread
1½ pounds cleaned red snapper, divided
1¾ teaspoons salt
½ teaspoon freshly ground black pepper
½ teaspoon grated orange rind
2 egg whites, lightly beaten
4 teaspoons olive oil, divided

1. To prepare sauce, combine first 5 ingredients in a small bowl. Set aside.
2. Preheat oven to 400°.
3. To prepare cakes, place green bell pepper and next 4 ingredients in a food processor; pulse until minced. Heat a large nonstick skillet over medium-high heat. Coat pan with cooking spray. Add bell pepper mixture; sauté 5 minutes or until vegetables are tender. Remove from heat; cool completely. Wipe pan clean with a paper towel.
4. Place bread in food processor; process until coarse crumbs measure 1 cup. Chop 1 pound of fish into ¼-inch pieces; place in a large bowl. Chop ½ pound fish; place in food processor. Pulse until finely minced; add to chopped fish. Add bell pepper mixture, breadcrumbs, salt, black pepper, orange rind, and egg whites to fish mixture; stir until well blended.
5. Divide fish mixture into 24 equal portions, shaping each into a ½-inch-thick patty. Heat 1 teaspoon oil in pan over medium-high heat. Add 6 patties; cook 2½ minutes on each side or until browned. Transfer patties to a baking sheet coated with cooking spray. Repeat process 3 times with remaining oil and patties. Bake at 400° for 10 minutes or until done. Serve with sauce. Yield: 12 servings (serving size: 2 patties and 1 tablespoon sauce).

CALORIES 126 (25% from fat); FAT 3.5g (sat 0.7g, mono 1.3g, poly 0.6g); PROTEIN 13.6g; CARB 9.8g; FIBER 1.3g; CHOL 22mg; IRON 0.6mg; SODIUM 543mg; CALC 46mg

QUICK & EASY
Havana Sandwich Bites

3 tablespoons Dijon mustard
4 (3-ounce) Portuguese- or Cuban-style rolls, split horizontally
8 (¾-ounce) slices reduced-fat Swiss cheese
6 ounces thinly sliced 96%-fat-free, less-sodium ham (such as Kraft)
2 tablespoons dill pickle relish
6 ounces thinly sliced, skinless 47%-lower-sodium turkey breast (such as Boar's Head)
Cooking spray

1. Spread mustard evenly over cut sides of rolls. Arrange 1 slice cheese, 1½ ounces ham, 1½ teaspoons relish, and 1½ ounces turkey over 4 roll halves. Top each serving with 1 slice cheese. Cover with top halves of rolls.
2. Heat a nonstick skillet over medium heat. Coat pan with cooking spray. Add sandwiches. Place a heavy cast-iron skillet on top of sandwiches; cook 6 minutes on each side or until golden brown. Cut each sandwich into 6 wedges. Yield: 12 servings (serving size: 2 wedges).

CALORIES 153 (22% from fat); FAT 3.7g (sat 2g, mono 0.4g, poly 0.4g); PROTEIN 13.5g; CARB 16.5g; FIBER 1.3g; CHOL 19mg; IRON 1mg; SODIUM 422mg; CALC 170mg

Pork Tenderloin with Spicy Guava Glaze

2 tablespoons garlic powder
1 tablespoon chili powder
1 tablespoon paprika
2 teaspoons ground coriander
¾ teaspoon ground cinnamon
½ teaspoon ground ginger
3 (1-pound) pork tenderloins, trimmed
2 teaspoons salt
½ cup finely chopped onion
½ cup orange juice
⅓ cup water
1 tablespoon cider vinegar
6 ounces commercial guava paste
2 garlic cloves, minced
1 jalapeño pepper, minced
Cooking spray

1. Prepare grill.
2. Combine first 6 ingredients in a small bowl. Sprinkle pork with salt, and rub pork with garlic powder mixture.
3. Combine onion and next 6 ingredients in a small saucepan over medium heat; bring to a boil. Cook 4 minutes or until guava paste dissolves, stirring constantly. Reduce heat, and simmer 4 minutes or until thickened, stirring occasionally. Remove from heat.
4. Place pork on a grill rack coated with cooking spray; grill 20 minutes or until a thermometer registers 160° (slightly pink), turning pork occasionally. Brush guava mixture over pork. Let stand 10 minutes before cutting into ½-inch-thick slices. Yield: 12 servings (serving size: 3 ounces pork).

CALORIES 195 (19% from fat); FAT 4.1g (sat 1.4g, mono 1.8g, poly 0.4g); PROTEIN 24.4g; CARB 14.2g; FIBER 0.8g; CHOL 74mg; IRON 1.7mg; SODIUM 467mg; CALC 17mg

Grilled Shrimp with Mango and Red Onion Relish

Serve this festive dish along with Cuban-Style Black Beans and Rice (recipe on page 310).

1 red onion, cut into ¼-inch-thick slices
Cooking spray
3 cups diced peeled mango
2 cups chopped seeded tomato
⅓ cup chopped fresh cilantro
2 tablespoons cider vinegar
2 teaspoons sugar
1 teaspoon salt
1 teaspoon grated lime rind
2 minced serrano chiles
1¼ teaspoons salt
1 teaspoon dried oregano
¼ teaspoon freshly ground black pepper
4 pounds jumbo shrimp, peeled and deveined
3 garlic cloves, minced

1. Prepare grill.

Continued

2. Lightly coat onion slices with cooking spray. Place onion on a grill rack coated with cooking spray; grill 4 minutes on each side. Cool and chop. Combine onion, mango, and next 7 ingredients in a large bowl.

3. Combine 1¼ teaspoons salt and remaining 4 ingredients in a large bowl, and toss well. Thread shrimp onto skewers. Place skewers on grill rack coated with cooking spray; grill for 2 minutes on each side or until done. Serve with relish. Yield: 12 servings (serving size: 4 ounces shrimp and ½ cup relish).

CALORIES 210 (12% from fat); FAT 2.8g (sat 0.6g, mono 0.5g, poly 1.1g); PROTEIN 31.5g; CARB 13.7g; FIBER 1.6g; CHOL 230mg; IRON 3.9mg; SODIUM 670mg; CALC 95mg

Cilantro Citrus Chicken

Chicken stays juicier and more flavorful when it cooks on the bone. You can cut up the leftover chicken and toss it with mixed greens and chopped vegetables for a healthful lunch salad.

     ½   cup chopped onion
     ⅓   cup fresh cilantro leaves
     ¼   cup fresh parsley leaves
     ¼   cup fresh orange juice
     ¼   cup fresh lime juice
     2   tablespoons olive oil
     6   garlic cloves
    12   (8-ounce) skinless, bone-in
         chicken breast halves
     2   teaspoons salt
     1   teaspoon ground cumin
     ½   teaspoon freshly ground black
         pepper
         Cooking spray

1. Place first 7 ingredients in a food processor; process until smooth. Place 6 chicken breast halves and half of herb mixture in a large zip-top plastic bag. Place remaining breast halves and remaining herb mixture in a second large zip-top plastic bag. Seal and marinate in refrigerator 1 hour, turning bags occasionally.

2. Prepare grill.

3. Remove chicken from bags; discard marinade. Let chicken stand 15 minutes.

Sprinkle chicken evenly with salt, cumin, and pepper. Place chicken, breast side down, on a grill rack coated with cooking spray. Grill 12 minutes on each side or until a thermometer registers 165°, turning once. Yield: 12 servings (serving size: 1 chicken breast half).

CALORIES 227 (26% from fat); FAT 6.6g (sat 1.5g, mono 3.1g, poly 1.2g); PROTEIN 37.3g; CARB 2.4g; FIBER 0.3g; CHOL 102mg; IRON 1.5mg; SODIUM 484mg; CALC 27mg

Sautéed Sweet Plantains
Maduros

Use plantains with completely black skins, which indicate that they're fully ripe.

     4   cups (½-inch-thick) slices soft
         black plantains (about 6)
     3   tablespoons sugar
     ¼   teaspoon salt
    1½   tablespoons butter

1. Combine first 3 ingredients in a large bowl; toss well.

2. Melt butter in a large nonstick skillet over medium-high heat. Add plantains; sauté 5 minutes or until browned and tender. Yield: 12 servings (serving size: about ⅓ cup).

CALORIES 134 (12% from fat); FAT 1.8g (sat 1g, mono 0.4g, poly 0.1g); PROTEIN 1.2g; CARB 31.7g; FIBER 2.1g; CHOL 4mg; IRON 0.5mg; SODIUM 62mg; CALC 3mg

Spread the Word

Simplify supper plans by using an online invitation service such as Evite (www.evite.com). These services are free and allow you to efficiently manage the guest list. Moreover, members can use the invitation response to announce what dishes they plan to bring, which guards against overlap and omitted courses.

Cuban-Style Black Beans and Rice
Moros y Cristianos

In Cuba, the name of this dish refers to the mix of African and Spanish cultures. Vegetarians can make an entrée of this soul-satisfying side.

     2   cups uncooked long-grain rice
     2   tablespoons olive oil
     2   cups chopped onion
     2   cups chopped green bell pepper
     6   garlic cloves, minced
     1   cup chopped seeded tomato
     2   tablespoons sherry vinegar
     2   teaspoons ground cumin
    1½   teaspoons dried oregano
     1   teaspoon ground coriander
     1   teaspoon fennel seeds, crushed
     ½   teaspoon salt
     ¼   teaspoon ground red pepper
     ¼   cup water
     3   (15-ounce) cans 50%-less-sodium
         black beans, rinsed and drained
     6   dashes hot pepper sauce (such as
         Tabasco)

1. Cook rice according to package directions, omitting salt and fat.

2. Heat oil in a large saucepan over medium-high heat. Add onion, bell pepper, and garlic to pan; cook 10 minutes or until tender, stirring occasionally. Add tomato; cook 2 minutes. Add vinegar and next 6 ingredients; cook 2 minutes. Stir in ¼ cup water, beans, and pepper sauce; bring to a boil. Reduce heat, and simmer 10 minutes or until thoroughly heated, stirring occasionally. Serve with rice. Yield: 12 servings (serving size: about ½ cup beans and ½ cup rice).

CALORIES 261 (9% from fat); FAT 2.7g (sat 0.4g, mono 1.7g, poly 0.4g); PROTEIN 10.5g; CARB 55.5g; FIBER 10.7g; CHOL 0mg; IRON 4.4mg; SODIUM 492mg; CALC 88mg

Guava and Cheese Empanadas

Guava paste with cream cheese or farmer's cheese is a classic Cuban combination. Cut guava paste cleanly by dipping your knife into a cup of hot water between slices. When cutting the dough, roll the scraps again if needed to make 24 circles.

DOUGH:

2¼ cups all-purpose flour (about 10 ounces)
⅓ cup sugar
¼ teaspoon baking powder
¼ teaspoon salt
5 tablespoons butter, cut into small pieces
6 ounces block-style fat-free cream cheese, cut into small pieces
3 tablespoons fat-free milk

FILLING:

¼ cup sugar
6 ounces Kraft farmer's cheese, cut into small pieces
1 tablespoon fat-free milk
1 large egg white, lightly beaten
6 ounces commercial guava paste, cut into 48 pieces
Cooking spray

TOPPING:

3 tablespoons sugar
½ teaspoon ground cinnamon

1. To prepare dough, lightly spoon flour into dry measuring cups; level with a knife. Place flour, ⅓ cup sugar, baking powder, and salt in a food processor; pulse to combine. Add butter and cream cheese; pulse 4 times or until mixture resembles coarse meal. With processor on, add 3 tablespoons milk through food chute, processing just until dough forms a ball. Press mixture gently into a 4-inch circle on plastic wrap; cover. Chill dough 1 hour.

2. To prepare filling, wipe food processor clean with a paper towel. Place ¼ cup sugar and farmer's cheese in processor; process 1 minute or until well blended. Cover and chill. Combine 1 tablespoon milk and egg white in a small bowl; set aside.

3. Preheat oven to 425°.

4. Roll dough to a ⅛-inch thickness on a heavily floured surface; cut with a 3-inch biscuit cutter into 24 circles. Discard any remaining dough scraps. Spoon about 2 teaspoons cheese mixture onto half of each circle; top each with 2 pieces guava paste, leaving ½-inch borders. Brush egg mixture around edge of each circle. Fold dough over filling; press edges together with a fork or fingers to seal. Place empanadas on 2 baking sheets coated with cooking spray; brush tops of empanadas with remaining egg mixture.

5. To prepare topping, combine 3 tablespoons sugar and cinnamon in a small bowl; sprinkle sugar mixture evenly over empanadas. Bake at 425° for 10 minutes or until golden. Remove from oven; cool completely on a wire rack. Yield: 12 servings (serving size: 2 empanadas).

CALORIES 285 (29% from fat); FAT 9.2g (sat 6.2g, mono 1.3g, poly 0.3g); PROTEIN 8g; CARB 42.5g; FIBER 0.8g; CHOL 26mg; IRON 1.2mg; SODIUM 284mg; CALC 152mg

---

STAFF FAVORITE
Tres Leche Cake

The name of the cake refers to the three types of milk used in the recipe.

CAKE:

Cooking spray
1 tablespoon all-purpose flour
6 large egg yolks
⅔ cup sugar
2 teaspoons vanilla extract
2 cups all-purpose flour (about 9 ounces)
2½ teaspoons baking powder
¼ teaspoon salt
½ cup fat-free milk
6 large egg whites
3 tablespoons sugar

MILK SAUCE:

1 (14-ounce) can fat-free sweetened condensed milk
1 (12-ounce) can evaporated fat-free milk
½ cup fat-free milk
2 tablespoons light rum

MERINGUE:

4 large egg whites
¼ teaspoon cream of tartar
⅛ teaspoon salt
1 cup sugar
½ cup water
1 teaspoon vanilla extract
Fresh grated whole nutmeg (optional)

1. Preheat oven to 375°.

2. To prepare cake, coat a 13 x 9–inch baking pan with cooking spray; dust with 1 tablespoon flour. Set aside.

3. Place egg yolks, ⅔ cup sugar, and 2 teaspoons vanilla in a large bowl; beat with a mixer at high speed until mixture is thick and pale, about 2 minutes.

4. Lightly spoon 2 cups flour into dry measuring cups; level with a knife. Combine flour, baking powder, and ¼ teaspoon salt; stir well with a whisk. Add flour mixture and ½ cup fat-free milk alternately to egg yolk mixture, beginning and ending with flour mixture.

5. Beat 6 egg whites in a large bowl with a mixer at high speed until foamy using clean, dry beaters. Add 3 tablespoons sugar, 1 tablespoon at a time, beating until stiff peaks form (about 2 minutes). Gently fold egg white mixture into flour mixture. Spoon batter into prepared baking pan. Bake at 375° for 20 minutes or until a wooden pick inserted in center comes out clean. Cool in pan 10 minutes on a wire rack. Turn cake out onto a platter with sides. Pierce entire top of cake with a fork.

6. To prepare sauce, combine condensed milk and next 3 ingredients; stir with a whisk. Slowly pour milk mixture evenly over cake. Cover with plastic wrap, and refrigerate at least 3 hours or overnight.

7. To prepare meringue, beat 4 egg whites, cream of tartar, and ⅛ teaspoon salt in a large bowl with a mixer at high speed until foamy using clean, dry beaters. Combine 1 cup sugar and ½ cup water in a saucepan; bring to a boil. Cook, without stirring, until candy thermometer registers 250°. Pour hot sugar syrup in a thin stream over egg whites, beating at high speed until stiff peaks

Continued

form (about 3 minutes). Stir in 1 teaspoon vanilla. Spread meringue evenly over top and sides of cake. Garnish with nutmeg, if desired. Yield: 16 servings.

CALORIES 277 (7% from fat); FAT 2.1g (sat 0.6g, mono 0.8g, poly 0.7g); PROTEIN 9g; CARB 54.5g; FIBER 0.4g; CHOL 84mg; IRON 1.3mg; SODIUM 228mg; CALC 200mg

MAKE AHEAD
Rum Punch

Substitute an additional cup of seltzer for the rum if you prefer to turn this summer cocktail into a refreshing tropical fruit punch.

- ½ cup sugar
- ½ cup water
- 4 cups mango juice, chilled (such as Looza brand)
- 3 cups pineapple juice, chilled
- 1½ cups dark rum
- ⅓ cup fresh lime juice (about 3 limes)
- ¼ cup grenadine
- 3 cups club soda, chilled

1. Combine sugar and ½ cup water in a small saucepan over high heat; bring to a boil. Cook until sugar dissolves, stirring occasionally. Remove from heat; transfer sugar mixture to a small bowl. Chill.
2. Combine sugar mixture, mango juice, and next 4 ingredients in a large bowl; mix well. Stir in soda. Serve over ice. Yield: 12 servings (serving size: about 1 cup).

CALORIES 191 (0% from fat); FAT 0.1g (sat 0g, mono 0g, poly 0g); PROTEIN 0.3g; CARB 31.1g; FIBER 0.2g; CHOL 0mg; IRON 0.2mg; SODIUM 19mg; CALC 13mg

lighten up

Quick Veggie Quiche

We lightened a California mom's crustless custard to fit her healthful goals.

Julie Schreader of San Rafael, California, doesn't make Garden Vegetable Crustless Quiche often because of the fat, so she's asked us to lighten it.

The main contributors to the fat count—eggs, butter, and Jack cheese—also added cholesterol. We used a combination of fat-free egg substitute, which is also cholesterol-free, and three eggs, which provide some fat to carry flavor and maintain richness. Rather than use ½ cup melted butter as the liquid, we substituted an equal amount of one percent milk, and sautéed the vegetables in cooking spray instead of a tablespoon of butter. Adjusting the eggs and swapping milk for butter shaved eight grams of fat (four of which were saturated) and 175 milligrams of cholesterol per serving.

Next, we focused on the cheeses. We used a combination of reduced-fat Monterey Jack and reduced-fat extrasharp Cheddar cheese. The Jack cheese has good melting properties for a creamy texture, and the reduced-fat extrasharp Cheddar cheese exerts a stronger flavor—so we were able to use less of it. We also swapped fat-free cottage cheese for the full-fat, which still provided ample body and creaminess in the quiche. These changes alone cut almost 11 grams of fat per serving (about half of which were saturated).

BEFORE	AFTER
SERVING SIZE	
1 piece	
CALORIES PER SERVING	
428	230
FAT	
31.7g	7.7g
PERCENT OF TOTAL CALORIES	
67%	30%

Garden Vegetable Crustless Quiche

Substitute corn or spinach for some of the vegetables, if you wish.

- 1½ cups egg substitute
- 3 large eggs
- 1½ cups (6 ounces) shredded reduced-fat extrasharp Cheddar cheese, divided
- 1½ cups (6 ounces) shredded reduced-fat Monterey Jack cheese, divided
- ½ cup 1% low-fat milk
- ½ cup all-purpose flour (about 2¼ ounces)
- 1 teaspoon baking powder
- ½ teaspoon salt
- 1 (16-ounce) carton fat-free cottage cheese
- Cooking spray
- 4 cups sliced zucchini (about 4)
- 2 cups diced potato with onion (such as Simply Potatoes)
- 1 cup finely chopped green bell pepper (about 1)
- 1 (8-ounce) package presliced mushrooms
- ½ cup chopped fresh parsley
- 2 tomatoes, thinly sliced

1. Preheat oven to 400°.
2. Beat egg substitute and eggs in a large bowl until fluffy. Add ¾ cup Cheddar cheese, ¾ cup Jack cheese, milk, and next 4 ingredients.
3. Heat a large nonstick skillet over medium-high heat. Coat pan with cooking spray. Add zucchini and next 3 ingredients; sauté 5 minutes or until tender. Add zucchini mixture and parsley to egg mixture. Pour mixture into a 3-quart casserole dish coated with cooking spray. Top with ¾ cup Cheddar cheese and ¾ cup Jack cheese. Arrange tomato slices over cheese. Bake at 400° for 15 minutes. Reduce oven temperature to 350° (do not remove dish from oven), and bake 35 minutes or until lightly browned and set. Yield: 10 servings.

CALORIES 230 (30% from fat); FAT 7.7g (sat 4.6g, mono 1.3g, poly 0.3g); PROTEIN 23g; CARB 18.1g; FIBER 1.9g; CHOL 84mg; IRON 2.1mg; SODIUM 716mg; CALC 382mg

WINE NOTE: Because of its eggy, custardy character, quiche is excellent with chardonnay. But this version goes in a "greener" direction, incorporating lots of zucchini, bell pepper, and parsley. So serve it with sauvignon blanc, a wine that has a touch of green flavor. Try the Honig Sauvignon Blanc 2005 from Napa Valley, California ($15).

reader recipes

Charming Chowder

A New England teacher perfects a unique clam chowder with a flavorful twist.

Living close to the New England coast in West Newbury, Massachusetts, has its advantages for Patti Marsh. The clams for her Plum Island Sound Clam Chowder are plentiful, and she and her husband, Larry, boat to the clam flats to dig for the mollusks whenever they have time. But even when fresh clams aren't available (usually June through September), she uses canned to fulfill the many requests for her chowder.

MAKE AHEAD
Plum Island Sound Clam Chowder

4   (6½-ounce) cans chopped clams
2   (8-ounce) bottles clam juice
5   slices center-cut bacon, cut into ½-inch pieces
¾   cup chopped onion
½   cup chopped celery
1½   teaspoons butter
2   cups cubed red potato
1   tablespoon fresh thyme leaves
½   teaspoon salt
¼   teaspoon freshly ground black pepper
1   bay leaf
2¼   cups evaporated fat-free milk
1½   cups 1% low-fat milk
1½   tablespoons dry sherry
1   tablespoon chopped fresh parsley

1. Drain clams in a colander over a bowl, reserving juice. Add bottled clam juice to reserved juice to equal 3½ cups. Set aside clams and juice.
2. Cook bacon in a Dutch oven over medium heat until crisp, stirring occasionally. Remove bacon from pan with a slotted spoon, reserving 2 teaspoons drippings in pan. Return bacon to pan; increase heat to medium-high. Add onion, celery, and butter; sauté 6 minutes or until vegetables are tender.
3. Add clam juice mixture, potato, and next 4 ingredients; bring to a boil. Cover, reduce heat, and simmer 15 minutes or until potato is tender. Stir in clams, evaporated milk, 1% milk, and sherry. Cook 5 minutes or until thoroughly heated, stirring occasionally. Discard bay leaf. Sprinkle with parsley. Yield: 10 servings (serving size: 1 cup).

CALORIES 145 (21% from fat); FAT 3.7g (sat 1.5g, mono 1.3g, poly 0.4g); PROTEIN 12.1g; CARB 16.2g; FIBER 0.8g; CHOL 23mg; IRON 5.6mg; SODIUM 476mg; CALC 248mg

Chicken for Dinner Menu
serves 4

Israeli couscous is pearl-sized pasta. If you can't find it, use regular couscous for the pilaf—the cook time will vary, so follow the package directions.

Orange Chicken
Couscous pilaf*
Sautéed Broccolini

*Bring 1½ cups fat-free, less-sodium chicken broth to a boil in a medium saucepan. Stir in 1 cup Israeli couscous. Cover, reduce heat, and simmer 10 minutes or until al dente. Fluff with a fork. Stir in ¼ cup chopped fresh flat-leaf parsley, ¼ cup finely chopped red onion, ¼ cup toasted pine nuts, ¼ teaspoon salt, and ⅛ teaspoon freshly ground black pepper.

Orange Chicken

"I love the simple flavor of this dish that my dad created. Sugar snap peas make a great side dish."

—Deborah Eckroat,
Pittsburgh, Pennsylvania

4   (6-ounce) skinless, boneless chicken breast halves
¼   teaspoon salt
¼   teaspoon freshly ground black pepper
⅓   cup all-purpose flour (about 1½ ounces)
2   teaspoons olive oil
2   teaspoons butter
½   cup white wine
½   cup fresh orange juice (about 2 oranges)

1. Place each chicken breast half between 2 sheets of heavy-duty plastic wrap; pound each piece to ½-inch thickness using a meat mallet or small heavy skillet. Sprinkle both sides of chicken evenly with salt and pepper; dredge chicken in flour.
2. Heat oil and butter in a large nonstick skillet over medium-high heat; cook 1 minute or until lightly browned, stirring occasionally. Add chicken to pan; cook 4 minutes on each side or until done. Remove chicken; cut into thin slices, and keep warm. Add wine and juice to pan; cook until reduced to ½ cup (about 4 minutes). Serve sauce over chicken. Yield: 4 servings (serving size: 1 chicken breast half and 2 tablespoons sauce).

CALORIES 261 (22% from fat); FAT 6.4g (sat 2.1g, mono 2.7g, poly 0.8g); PROTEIN 40.2g; CARB 8.2g; FIBER 0.3g; CHOL 104mg; IRON 1.7mg; SODIUM 274mg; CALC 26mg

Grilled Rosemary Steak

"A steak I had at a restaurant was so delicious, I came up with this version. I like to make this on special occasions for my family."

—Eileen Subiel,
Philadelphia, Pennsylvania

  1 tablespoon finely chopped fresh rosemary
  1 teaspoon grated lemon rind
  1 teaspoon freshly ground black pepper
  1 teaspoon extravirgin olive oil
  ¼ teaspoon kosher salt
  2 garlic cloves, minced
  4 (4-ounce) beef tenderloin steaks, trimmed (1 inch thick)
    Cooking spray

1. Combine first 6 ingredients in a small bowl. Rub rosemary mixture evenly over steaks; cover. Refrigerate 1 hour.
2. Prepare grill.
3. Place steaks on a grill rack coated with cooking spray; grill 5 minutes on each side or until desired degree of doneness. Yield: 4 servings (serving size: 1 steak).

CALORIES 179 (40% from fat); FAT 7.9g (sat 2.7g, mono 3.5g, poly 0.4g); PROTEIN 24.4g; CARB 1g; FIBER 0.3g; CHOL 67mg; IRON 1.6mg; SODIUM 168mg; CALC 22mg

---

MAKE AHEAD
Edamame and Barley Salad

"My boyfriend and I wanted to incorporate more soy into our diets, and my sister introduced us to edamame. This is an easy way to use the frozen, shelled beans. The recipe takes a little time to assemble, but if you chop the vegetables while the barley cooks, it's ready in 25 minutes."

—Maggie Knapp, Fort Worth, Texas

DRESSING:
  5 teaspoons olive oil
  1 tablespoon grated lemon rind
  2 tablespoons fresh lemon juice
  1 tablespoon whole-grain Dijon mustard
  ½ teaspoon freshly ground black pepper

SALAD:
  1 cup uncooked pearl barley
  1 cup coarsely chopped red bell pepper
  ¾ cup chopped red onion
  ¼ cup chopped fresh cilantro
  ¼ cup chopped fresh mint
  1¼ teaspoons salt
  1 (16-ounce) bag frozen shelled edamame (green soybeans), thawed

1. To prepare dressing, combine first 5 ingredients in a medium bowl, stirring with a whisk until blended; set aside.
2. To prepare salad, cook barley according to package directions, omitting salt and fat. Combine cooked barley, bell pepper, and remaining 5 ingredients in a large bowl, tossing well. Add dressing, and toss gently to coat evenly. Let stand 15 minutes. Yield: 8 servings (serving size: about 1 cup).

CALORIES 213 (30% from fat); FAT 7.2g (sat 0.9g, mono 2.9g, poly 2.3g); PROTEIN 10.4g; CARB 29.3g; FIBER 7g; CHOL 0mg; IRON 3.2mg; SODIUM 417mg; CALC 133mg

---

Potato Leek Soup

"I developed this soup for a hiking retreat with vegetarians. The pureed potatoes lend a creamy texture without adding extra fat."
—Lisa Gilbert, Steamboat Springs, Colorado

  1 tablespoon olive oil
  2½ cups thinly sliced leek (about 2 large)
  5 cups cubed peeled Yukon gold or red potato (about 2½ pounds)
  5 cups organic vegetable broth (such as Swanson Certified Organic)
  2 cups thinly sliced arugula
  ¼ teaspoon salt
  ¼ teaspoon freshly ground black pepper

1. Heat oil in a large saucepan over medium-high heat. Add leek; sauté 5 minutes or until tender. Add potato and broth; bring to a boil. Reduce heat, and simmer 25 minutes or until potato is tender. Place 3 cups potato mixture in a blender. Remove center piece of blender lid (to allow steam to escape); secure blender lid on blender. Place a clean towel over opening in blender lid (to avoid splatters). Blend until smooth. Return pureed mixture to pan; bring to a simmer. Stir in arugula, salt, and pepper; cook 2 minutes or until arugula wilts. Yield: 8 servings (serving size: 1 cup).

CALORIES 127 (13% from fat); FAT 1.9g (sat 0.3g, mono 1.2g, poly 0.3g); PROTEIN 2.2g; CARB 25.6g; FIBER 2.4g; CHOL 0mg; IRON 1mg; SODIUM 442mg; CALC 32mg

---

Mocha Fudge Bread Pudding

"This bread pudding is best served warm. I put it in the oven just as we are sitting down to dinner so it's done when we're ready for dessert."

—Kristin Fontaine, Burlington, Vermont

  1⅓ cups 1% low-fat milk
  1 cup hot strong brewed coffee
  ¼ cup packed dark brown sugar
  ½ cup egg substitute
  1 teaspoon vanilla extract
    Dash of salt
  2 large egg whites, lightly beaten
  8 cups (1-inch) cubed white bread (about 10 ounces)
    Cooking spray
  1¼ cups semisweet chocolate chips

1. Combine first 3 ingredients in a medium saucepan over medium-high heat; bring to a simmer, stirring until sugar dissolves. Remove from heat, and cool to room temperature. Add egg substitute, vanilla, salt, and egg whites, stirring with a whisk. Combine egg mixture and bread in a large bowl, tossing gently to coat. Let stand 30 minutes.
2. Preheat oven to 350°.
3. Spoon half of bread mixture into an 8-inch square baking dish coated with cooking spray, and sprinkle evenly with chocolate chips. Top chocolate chips with remaining bread mixture. Bake at 350° for 45 minutes or until center is set. Let stand 10 minutes before serving. Yield: 9 servings (serving size: ⅔ cup).

CALORIES 282 (28% from fat); FAT 8.7g (sat 4.6g, mono 2.7g, poly 0.7g); PROTEIN 8.1g; CARB 45.6g; FIBER 2.1g; CHOL 2mg; IRON 2.5mg; SODIUM 75mg; CALC 72mg

Food for Thought

Just as certain foods are beneficial for the heart and bones, nutrition can help improve brain function as well.

Multigrain Pilaf with Sunflower Seeds

Sunflower seeds and brown rice pack a double nutrition punch, enhancing this side dish with both vitamin E and niacin. This recipe calls for long-cooking barley and brown rice, but if you're in a hurry, substitute instant brown rice and quick-cooking barley. Just be sure to adjust cooking times according to package directions.

    4   teaspoons canola oil, divided
    ⅓   cup sunflower seed kernels
    ½   teaspoon salt, divided
    2   teaspoons butter
    1   cup thinly sliced leek (about 1
        large)
    2½ cups water
    1½ cups fat-free, less-sodium chicken
        broth
    ½   cup uncooked pearl barley
    ½   cup brown rice blend (such as
        Lundberg) or brown rice
    ½   cup dried currants
    ¼   cup uncooked bulgur
    ¼   cup chopped fresh parsley
    ¼   teaspoon freshly ground black
        pepper

1. Heat a Dutch oven over medium-high heat. Add 2 teaspoons oil, sunflower seeds, and ¼ teaspoon salt; sauté 2 minutes or until lightly browned. Remove from pan; set aside.
2. Heat pan over medium heat; add 2 teaspoons oil and butter. Add leek; cook 4 minutes or until tender, stirring frequently. Add 2½ cups water and next 3 ingredients; bring to a boil. Cover, reduce heat, and simmer 35 minutes. Stir in currants and bulgur; cover and simmer 10 minutes or until grains are tender. Remove from heat; stir in ¼ teaspoon

salt, sunflower seeds, parsley, and pepper. Serve immediately. Yield: 8 servings (serving size: ½ cup).

CALORIES 198 (30% from fat); FAT 6.6g (sat 1.1g, mono 2.2g, poly 2.6g); PROTEIN 5g; CARB 32.7g; FIBER 4.9g; CHOL 3mg; IRON 1.5mg; SODIUM 266mg; CALC 26mg

Caramel Apple Upside-Down Cake

(pictured on page 248)

Wheat germ and canola oil boost the nutrition profile of this simple dessert by adding vitamin E. Granny Smith apples remain firm and pleasantly tart when cooked. For a sweeter apple that also holds up well when cooked, try Braeburn.

        Cooking spray
    ⅓   cup fat-free caramel topping
    2   cups thinly sliced peeled
        Granny Smith apple (about 10
        ounces)
    1¼ cups all-purpose flour (about 5½
        ounces)
    ⅔   cup packed brown sugar
    ¼   cup toasted wheat germ
    ½   teaspoon ground cinnamon
    ¼   teaspoon salt
    ½   cup low-fat buttermilk
    ½   teaspoon baking soda
    ½   cup applesauce
    5   tablespoons canola oil
    1   teaspoon vanilla extract
    2   large egg whites, lightly
        beaten
    1   large egg, lightly beaten

1. Preheat oven to 350°.
2. Coat an 8-inch square baking pan with cooking spray. Drizzle caramel over bottom of pan. (Caramel will not completely

cover bottom of pan.) Arrange apple slices over caramel, overlapping slices slightly.
3. Lightly spoon flour into dry measuring cups; level with a knife. Combine flour, sugar, wheat germ, cinnamon, and salt in a large bowl, stirring with a whisk. Combine buttermilk and baking soda in a medium bowl, stirring with a whisk. Stir in applesauce and remaining 4 ingredients. Add buttermilk mixture to flour mixture; stir just until blended. Pour batter over apple slices in prepared pan. Bake at 350° for 35 minutes or until a wooden pick inserted in center comes out clean. Cool 10 minutes in pan on a wire rack. Place a plate upside down on top of cake; invert onto plate. Serve warm. Yield: 9 servings (serving size: 1 piece).

CALORIES 280 (29% from fat); FAT 9g (sat 0.9g, mono 4.9g, poly 2.6g); PROTEIN 4.7g; CARB 45.3g; FIBER 1.4g; CHOL 24mg; IRON 1.7mg; SODIUM 208mg; CALC 40mg

Almond-Chive Salmon

In this simple entrée, almonds supply vitamin E, while salmon delivers a good amount of niacin. Vary the herbs according to your preference; try dill, thyme, or basil.

    ¼   cup sliced almonds
    2   tablespoons chopped fresh
        chives
    1   tablespoon chopped fresh
        parsley
    ½   teaspoon grated lemon rind
    2   (1-ounce) slices white bread,
        torn
    ½   teaspoon salt, divided
    4   (6-ounce) salmon fillets (about
        1 inch thick)
    ¼   teaspoon freshly ground black
        pepper
        Cooking spray
    4   lemon wedges

1. Preheat oven to 400°.
2. Place first 5 ingredients in a food processor; add ¼ teaspoon salt. Process until finely chopped.
3. Sprinkle salmon with ¼ teaspoon salt
Continued

and pepper. Top fillets evenly with breadcrumb mixture; press gently to adhere. Place fillets on a baking sheet coated with cooking spray.

4. Bake at 400° for 10 minutes or until fish flakes easily when tested with a fork or until desired degree of doneness. Serve with lemon wedges. Yield: 4 servings (serving size: 1 fillet and 1 lemon wedge).

CALORIES 302 (42% from fat); FAT 14g (sat 2.8g, mono 6.6g, poly 3.4g); PROTEIN 33.5g; CARB 9.1g; FIBER 1.2g; CHOL 80mg; IRON 1.4mg; SODIUM 454mg; CALC 56mg

Roasted Green Beans with Mushrooms

Cremini mushrooms are a surprisingly good source of niacin. Roasting is a great way to cook green beans, giving them crisp browned edges and intensifying their flavor.

     6 cups quartered cremini mushrooms (about 1 pound)
     1 cup thinly sliced shallots
     5 garlic cloves, chopped
  1½ pounds green beans, trimmed
        Cooking spray
  1½ tablespoons canola oil
     1 tablespoon chopped fresh thyme
     ½ teaspoon freshly ground black pepper
     ¾ teaspoon salt

1. Preheat oven to 450°.
2. Combine first 4 ingredients on a jelly-roll pan coated with cooking spray. Drizzle with oil; sprinkle with thyme and pepper. Toss well to coat. Bake at 450° for 30 minutes or until beans are lightly browned. Sprinkle with salt; toss to combine. Yield: 6 servings (serving size: about 1⅓ cups).

CALORIES 107 (32% from fat); FAT 3.8g (sat 0.3g, mono 2.1g, poly 1.2g); PROTEIN 4.8g; CARB 16.7g; FIBER 4.6g; CHOL 0mg; IRON 1.9mg; SODIUM 310mg; CALC 75mg

Nepalese Red Lentil Soup

Turmeric gives this creamy soup a deep golden color, and the red lentils lend it a slightly sweeter flavor than brown or green lentils would. The lentils also provide niacin and plenty of folate, a B vitamin that may help delay cognitive decline.

     1 tablespoon canola oil
     1 tablespoon butter
     2 cups chopped red onion
     1 tablespoon minced peeled fresh ginger
     1 tablespoon finely chopped seeded jalapeño pepper
     6 cups water
     2 cups dried small red lentils
  1½ teaspoons salt
     ½ teaspoon ground turmeric
     ¼ teaspoon five-spice powder
     ⅓ cup chopped fresh cilantro
     2 tablespoons fresh lemon juice

1. Heat oil and butter in a Dutch oven over medium-high heat. Add onion, ginger, and jalapeño; sauté 4 minutes or until tender. Stir in 6 cups water and next 4 ingredients; bring to a boil. Cover, reduce heat, and simmer 15 minutes or until lentils are tender, stirring occasionally.
2. Place one-third of lentil mixture in a blender. Remove center piece of blender lid (to allow steam to escape); secure blender lid on blender. Place a clean towel over opening in blender lid (to avoid splatters). Blend until smooth. Pour pureed lentil mixture into a large bowl. Repeat procedure twice with remaining lentil mixture. Stir in cilantro and juice. Serve immediately. Yield: 8 servings (serving size: about 1 cup).

CALORIES 217 (17% from fat); FAT 4.2g (sat 1g, mono 1.6g, poly 1.1g); PROTEIN 13.5g; CARB 32.7g; FIBER 7.7g; CHOL 4mg; IRON 2.9mg; SODIUM 453mg; CALC 31mg

Smart Snacks

Foods rich in niacin and vitamin E don't corner the market on boosting brainpower. These between-meal choices may also sharpen cognitive function.

• **Apples.** Research at Cornell University in New York suggests that quercetin, an antioxidant that's abundant in fresh apples, may protect brain cells from the type of damage associated with Alzheimer's disease. Quercetin is concentrated in the skin, more so in red apples than green or yellow.

• **Avocados.** According to James Joseph, Ph.D., director of the Neuroscience Lab at the U.S. Department of Agriculture Human Nutrition Research Center on Aging at Tufts University in Boston, when avocado extract was put on distressed cells that provide protection to neurons—as those affected by Parkinson's disease or Alzheimer's—the result was less inflammation. "The flavonoids—which act as antioxidants—in avocados, blueberries, strawberries, concord grape juice, and cranberries inhibit enzymes and other factors involved in inflammation," says Joseph. The anti-inflammatory effects may help protect against cognitive decline.

• **Blueberries.** Try a handful of blueberries—dried or fresh—when you feel an afternoon slump coming on. Blueberries activate the signals that help brain neurons talk to one another. "At first we thought that because of blueberries' antioxidant and anti-inflammatory effects, the cells just worked better," explains Joseph. "But now we know the improvement is in addition to those effects."

• **Curried nuts.** Recharge with a handful of nuts toasted with a sprinkling of turmeric, an Indian spice often used in curries. A 2004 study at the University of California at Los Angeles (UCLA) suggests that the antioxidant and anti-inflammatory effects of the spice help protect against memory loss and dwindling brainpower.

Warm Sesame Spinach

Fresh spinach is an excellent source of folate and a fair source of niacin and vitamin E. You can serve this side dish warm or at room temperature.

 2 tablespoons low-sodium soy sauce
 1 tablespoon rice vinegar
 1 tablespoon sesame seeds, toasted
 2 teaspoons sugar
 2 teaspoons dark sesame oil
 3 garlic cloves, minced
 2 (10-ounce) packages fresh spinach
 (about 5 cups)

1. Combine first 4 ingredients in a small bowl, stirring with a whisk.
2. Heat oil in a large Dutch oven over medium heat. Add garlic, and cook 1 minute, stirring frequently. Gradually add spinach; cook 2 minutes or until spinach wilts, stirring constantly. Place spinach in a colander, pressing until barely moist. Place spinach in a medium bowl; drizzle with soy sauce mixture. Toss well to coat. Yield: 4 servings (serving size: about ⅓ cup).

CALORIES 84 (42% from fat); FAT 3.9g (sat 0.7g, mono 1.4g, poly 1.6g); PROTEIN 5g; CARB 9.2g; FIBER 3.2g; CHOL 0mg; IRON 7.3mg; SODIUM 379mg; CALC 146mg

Easy Entertaining Menu
serves 4

Get a head start on this quick menu by preparing the aïoli a day ahead. While the potatoes cook, the rest of the meal comes together in minutes.

Tuna with Avocado Green Goddess Aïoli

Garlic-roasted red potatoes*

Green beans

*Preheat oven to 425°. Combine 2 tablespoons olive oil, 1 tablespoon minced fresh garlic, ¾ teaspoon salt, ½ teaspoon freshly ground black pepper, and 1 (24-ounce) package refrigerated red potato wedges (such as Simply Potatoes) on a jelly-roll pan; toss well. Bake at 425° for 20 minutes or until golden.

Tuna with Avocado Green Goddess Aïoli

The aïoli features heart-healthy avocado, which contributes vitamin E to this dish. But the real nutritional standout is the tuna, which is rich in niacin.

AÏOLI:

 6 tablespoons chopped ripe peeled avocado
 ¼ cup fat-free sour cream
 2 tablespoons fat-free mayonnaise
 2 tablespoons chopped fresh cilantro
 1 tablespoon chopped fresh basil leaves
 1 tablespoon chopped fresh flat-leaf parsley
 1 teaspoon fresh lemon juice
 ¼ teaspoon salt
 1 garlic clove, chopped

TUNA:

 ¾ teaspoon ground coriander
 ½ teaspoon salt
 ½ teaspoon ground cumin
 ½ teaspoon garlic powder
 ¼ teaspoon chili powder
 ⅛ teaspoon freshly ground black pepper
 4 (6-ounce) tuna steaks (about 1 inch thick)
 Cooking spray

1. To prepare aïoli, place first 9 ingredients in a blender; process until smooth.
2. To prepare tuna, combine coriander and next 5 ingredients in a small bowl; sprinkle spice mixture evenly over tuna.
3. Heat a grill pan over medium-high heat. Coat pan with cooking spray. Add tuna; cook 2 minutes on each side or until medium-rare or desired degree of doneness. Serve with aïoli. Yield: 4 servings (serving size: 1 tuna steak and about 2½ tablespoons aïoli).

CALORIES 234 (24% from fat); FAT 6.1g (sat 1.8g, mono 2.6g, poly 1.2g); PROTEIN 39g; CARB 6.1g; FIBER 1.3g; CHOL 82mg; IRON 2.4mg; SODIUM 581mg; CALC 82mg

WINE NOTE: Tuna, like salmon, is a fish capable of handling lighter red wines, especially when it's grilled. A to Z Wineworks Willamette Valley Pinot Noir 2004 ($16) from Oregon is a great value. Along with red raspberry and strawberry fruit, this supple wine offers peppery spice that marries well with the chili powder, cumin, and coriander coating the tuna steak.

Chicken Poblano Casserole
(pictured on page 246)

Not only is this casserole a good source of niacin (mainly from the chicken), but one serving also supplies about 60 percent of your daily calcium needs. Fresh corn and corn tortillas offer an ample amount of folate, too.

 3 poblano chiles (about 12 ounces)
 1 large red bell pepper (about 8 ounces)
 3 ears shucked corn
 ⅓ cup all-purpose flour (about 1½ ounces)
 1 teaspoon salt, divided
 ¼ teaspoon freshly ground black pepper
 3½ cups 1% low-fat milk
 3 cups (12 ounces) preshredded reduced-fat 4-cheese Mexican blend cheese, divided
 ⅓ cup chopped red onion
 ⅓ cup chopped fresh cilantro
 2 large eggs, lightly beaten
 1 (15-ounce) carton part-skim ricotta cheese
 Cooking spray
 18 (6-inch) white corn tortillas
 3¾ cups chopped cooked chicken breast
 1 cup thinly sliced green onions

1. Preheat broiler.
2. Cut poblanos and bell pepper in half lengthwise; discard seeds and membranes. Place, skin sides up, on a foil-lined baking sheet; flatten with hand. Place corn on baking sheet. Broil 10 minutes or until poblanos and bell pepper are blackened and corn is lightly browned.

Continued

Place poblanos and bell pepper in a zip-top plastic bag; seal. Let stand 10 minutes. Peel and coarsely chop; set poblanos and bell pepper aside separately. Remove corn kernels from cobs.

3. Lightly spoon flour into a dry measuring cup; level with a knife. Place flour, ½ teaspoon salt, and black pepper in a large saucepan. Gradually add milk, stirring with a whisk. Cook over medium heat until slightly thick (about 12 minutes), stirring constantly. Remove from heat. Place 1 cup milk mixture and poblanos in a blender; process until smooth. Stir pureed poblano mixture into remaining milk mixture.

4. Preheat oven to 350°.

5. Combine bell pepper, corn, ½ teaspoon salt, 1 cup Mexican cheese, red onion, cilantro, eggs, and ricotta.

6. Coat bottom of a 13 x 9–inch baking dish with cooking spray. Spread ½ cup sauce in bottom of dish. Arrange 6 tor-

tillas over sauce, overlapping slightly. Spread half of ricotta mixture over tortillas; top with half of chicken. Sprinkle with ⅓ cup green onions and ⅔ cup Mexican cheese. Pour about 1 cup sauce over cheese. Repeat layers with 6 tortillas, remaining ricotta mixture, remaining chicken, ⅓ cup green onions, ⅔ cup Mexican cheese, 1 cup sauce, and 6 tortillas. Pour remaining sauce over tortillas. Coat 1 side of foil with cooking spray. Place foil, coated side down, over casserole. Bake at 350° for 30 minutes or until bubbly.

7. Uncover; sprinkle with ⅔ cup Mexican cheese and ⅓ cup green onions. Bake, uncovered, 15 minutes or until cheese melts. Let stand 15 minutes. Yield: 12 servings.

CALORIES 369 (29% from fat); FAT 11.9g (sat 6.1g, mono 2.9g, poly 1.2g); PROTEIN 33.1g; CARB 33.8g; FIBER 3.6g; CHOL 98mg; IRON 1.8mg; SODIUM 594mg; CALC 536mg

Cellophane Noodle Salad with Peanut Dressing

Canola oil and peanuts provide vitamin E and niacin in this make-ahead side salad. For a main dish with even more niacin, add shredded rotisserie chicken. Serve with hot sauce, such as Sriracha, for an extra kick.

DRESSING:
- ¼ cup water
- ¼ cup low-sodium soy sauce
- 2 tablespoons brown sugar
- 2 tablespoons rice vinegar
- 1 tablespoon grated peeled fresh ginger
- 1 tablespoon canola oil
- ¼ teaspoon crushed red pepper
- ¼ teaspoon five-spice powder
- 2 garlic cloves, minced

At-a-Glance: Niacin and Vitamin E

Here's a quick reference of common food sources of these two nutrients. Women need 14 milligrams of niacin per day; men should consume 16 milligrams. Both need 15 milligrams of vitamin E daily.

NIACIN			VITAMIN E		
FOOD	**AMOUNT**	**NIACIN**	**FOOD**	**AMOUNT**	**VITAMIN E**
Cooked Yellowfin tuna	4.5 ounces	15.2mg	Sunflower seed kernels	1 ounce	9.8mg
Cooked swordfish	4.5 ounces	15mg	Almonds	1 ounce	7.3mg
Roasted skinless, boneless chicken breast	3 ounces	11.7mg	Safflower oil	1 tablespoon	4.6mg
Cooked coho salmon	4.5 ounces	9.4mg	Toasted wheat germ	¼ cup	4.5mg
Roasted skinless, boneless turkey breast	3 ounces	6.4mg	Cooked spinach	1 cup	3.7mg
Roasted pork tenderloin	3 ounces	4.4mg	Cooked Swiss chard	1 cup	3.3mg
Dry-roasted peanuts	1 ounce	3.8mg	Cooked turnip greens	1 cup	2.7mg
Cooked enriched long-grain white rice	1 cup	2.3mg	Canola oil	1 tablespoon	2.4mg
Cooked green soybeans (edamame)	1 cup	2.3mg	Dry-roasted peanuts	1 ounce	2.2mg
Cremini mushrooms	2 ounces	2.2mg	Mashed avocado	⅓ cup	1.5mg
Cooked lentils	1 cup	2.1mg			

SALAD:

1½ cups matchstick-cut carrots (about 4 ounces)
4 ounces uncooked bean threads (cellophane noodles)
1 cup shredded bok choy
¾ cup thinly sliced green onions
½ cup snow peas, trimmed and cut into ½-inch pieces (about 2 ounces)
½ cup julienne-cut red bell pepper
3 tablespoons chopped fresh cilantro
2 tablespoons chopped fresh mint
3 tablespoons chopped dry-roasted peanuts, divided
6 Boston lettuce leaves

1. To prepare dressing, combine first 9 ingredients, stirring with a whisk, and set aside.
2. To prepare salad, cook carrots and noodles in boiling water 1 minute; drain. Place noodle mixture in a large bowl. Add bok choy and next 5 ingredients; toss gently to combine. Pour dressing over noodle mixture; sprinkle with 2 tablespoons peanuts. Toss gently to combine. Place 1 lettuce leaf on each of 6 plates. Top each leaf with 1 cup salad; sprinkle each serving with ½ teaspoon peanuts. Yield: 6 servings.

CALORIES 163 (29% from fat); FAT 5.2g (sat 0.5g, mono 2.7g, poly 1.7g); PROTEIN 2.7g; CARB 26g; FIBER 2.3g; CHOL 0mg; IRON 1mg; SODIUM 415mg; CALC 48mg

dinner tonight

Satisfying Suppers

Satisfying Suppers Menu 1
serves 4

Mustard and Tarragon Braised Lamb

Spinach salad with heirloom tomatoes and basil vinaigrette*

Mashed potatoes

*Combine 4 cups baby spinach and ½ cup sliced mushrooms in a large bowl. Cut 2 large heirloom tomatoes into 8 wedges each, and add to spinach mixture. Combine 1 tablespoon balsamic vinegar, 2 teaspoons thinly sliced fresh basil, 2 teaspoons extravirgin olive oil, ½ teaspoon salt, and ¼ teaspoon black pepper, stirring well with a whisk. Drizzle vinaigrette over spinach mixture, tossing to coat.

Game Plan

1. Trim and cube lamb.
2. Trim carrots.
3. While lamb mixture simmers:
 • Prepare salad
 • Heat mashed potatoes

QUICK & EASY
Mustard and Tarragon Braised Lamb

TOTAL TIME: 30 MINUTES

1 tablespoon all-purpose flour
½ teaspoon dry mustard
½ teaspoon black pepper
1 pound boneless leg of lamb, trimmed and cubed
1 tablespoon olive oil
2 cups frozen pearl onions, thawed
2 cups baby carrots with tops (about ¾ pound), trimmed
1⅓ cups less-sodium beef broth
⅔ cup white wine
2 tablespoons Dijon mustard
1 tablespoon minced fresh tarragon

1. Combine first 3 ingredients in a medium bowl; add lamb, tossing to coat.
2. Heat oil in a large nonstick skillet over medium-high heat. Add lamb mixture, and sauté 4 minutes or until browned. Add onions and carrots; sauté 4 minutes. Stir in broth and wine. Cover, reduce heat, and simmer 7 minutes or until carrots are crisp-tender. Stir in Dijon and tarragon. Increase heat to medium-high; cook, uncovered, 2 minutes or until slightly thickened. Yield: 4 servings (serving size: 1 cup).

CALORIES 332 (27% from fat); FAT 10g (sat 2.7g, mono 5g, poly 1.1g); PROTEIN 28.7g; CARB 25.3g; FIBER 1.9g; CHOL 75mg; IRON 3mg; SODIUM 341mg; CALC 67mg

Satisfying Suppers Menu 2
serves 4

Roasted Chicken with Dried Plums and Shallots (recipe on page 320)

Brussels sprouts with garlic and honey*

Israeli couscous

*Melt 1 tablespoon butter in a large nonstick skillet over medium-high heat. Add 1 pound quartered trimmed Brussels sprouts, ¼ teaspoon salt, and ¼ teaspoon black pepper; sauté 3 minutes. Add 3 thinly sliced garlic cloves; sauté 2 minutes or until lightly browned. Add 3 tablespoons water; cover and cook 3 minutes or until Brussels sprouts are tender. Drizzle with 1 tablespoon honey; toss well to coat.

Game Plan

1. Prepare garlic, shallots, and fennel for chicken.
2. While chicken roasts:
 • Combine flour and broth
 • Chop thyme
 • Cook couscous
 • Prepare Brussels sprouts

Roasted Chicken with Dried Plums and Shallots

Bone-in, unskinned chicken breast halves work well for roasting because the meat stays moist in the oven's high heat. Substitute dried apricot halves for dried plums, if you prefer.

TOTAL TIME: 50 MINUTES

QUICK TIP: Look for jars of peeled whole garlic cloves in your supermarket's produce section.

    2   teaspoons olive oil
    4   bone-in chicken breast halves
        (about 2 pounds)
    ¾   teaspoon salt, divided
    ½   teaspoon black pepper,
        divided
    8   garlic cloves, peeled
    4   large shallots, peeled and halved
        (about 8 ounces)
    2   thyme sprigs
    1   large fennel bulb, cut into 8
        wedges
   16   pitted dried plums
    ¾   cup fat-free, less-sodium chicken
        broth, divided
    ¼   cup dry white wine
    1   tablespoon all-purpose flour
    2   teaspoons chopped fresh
        thyme

1. Preheat oven to 450°.
2. Drizzle oil in a small roasting pan or bottom of a broiler pan. Place pan in oven 5 minutes or until oil is hot. Sprinkle chicken with ¼ teaspoon salt and ¼ teaspoon pepper. Place chicken, skin sides down, in pan. Arrange garlic, shallots, thyme sprigs, and fennel around chicken; sprinkle vegetables with ¼ teaspoon salt and ⅛ teaspoon pepper. Bake at 450° for 20 minutes. Remove pan from oven. Turn chicken over; stir vegetables. Add plums to pan. Bake an additional 15 minutes or until chicken is done. Remove chicken and vegetable mixture from pan; discard thyme sprigs. Discard skin. Loosely cover chicken and vegetable mixture; keep warm.
3. Place pan over medium-high heat. Add ½ cup broth and wine, stirring to loosen browned bits. Combine flour and ¼ cup broth, stirring with a whisk until smooth. Add flour mixture to pan; stir until well blended. Bring to a boil; cook 1 minute or until slightly thick. Stir in chopped thyme, ¼ teaspoon salt, and ⅛ teaspoon pepper. Serve sauce with chicken and vegetable mixture. Yield: 4 servings (serving size: 1 chicken breast half, about ⅓ cup vegetable mixture, and 3 tablespoons sauce).

CALORIES 384 (30% from fat); FAT 13g (sat 3.3g, mono 5.8g, poly 2.4g); PROTEIN 36.6g; CARB 31g; FIBER 5.1g; CHOL 96mg; IRON 3.1mg; SODIUM 632mg; CALC 95mg

---

Satisfying Suppers Menu 3
serves 4

Flank Steak with Shiitake Mushroom Sauce

Ginger-scallion rice*

Steamed baby bok choy

*Heat 1 tablespoon canola oil in a medium saucepan over medium-high heat. Add ½ cup chopped green onion bottoms, 2 teaspoons minced peeled fresh ginger, and 2 minced garlic cloves; sauté 2 minutes. Stir in 1 cup uncooked long-grain rice; sauté 1 minute. Stir in 2 cups fat-free, less-sodium chicken broth and ¼ teaspoon salt; bring to a boil. Cover, reduce heat, and simmer 15 minutes or until liquid is absorbed. Stir in ¼ cup chopped green onion tops.

Game Plan

1. While rice cooks and broiler preheats:
  • Trim steak
  • Slice mushrooms and mince green onions
2. While steak broils:
  • Prepare mushroom sauce
  • Steam bok choy

Flank Steak with Shiitake Mushroom Sauce

Allow the meat to rest for a few minutes after it cooks so the juices have time to redistribute. If you slice the steak immediately after removing it from the oven, all the tasty juices will run out. Balsamic vinegar lends slight tang to the sauce.

TOTAL TIME: 30 MINUTES

STEAK:

    ½   teaspoon salt
    ¼   teaspoon black pepper
    1   (1-pound) flank steak, trimmed
        Cooking spray

SAUCE:

    ½   cup chopped onion
    1   garlic clove, minced
    2   cups thinly sliced shiitake
        mushroom caps (about ½ pound
        mushrooms)
    1   cup less-sodium beef broth
    ⅓   cup dry white wine
    1   tablespoon balsamic vinegar
    ½   cup minced green onions

1. Preheat broiler.
2. To prepare steak, sprinkle salt and pepper evenly over both sides of steak. Place steak on a broiler pan coated with cooking spray; broil 5 minutes on each side or until desired degree of doneness. Remove steak from oven; loosely cover with foil.
3. To prepare sauce, heat a large non-stick skillet over medium-high heat. Coat pan with cooking spray. Add ½ cup onion and garlic; sauté 2 minutes. Add mushrooms; sauté 4 minutes. Add broth, wine, and vinegar. Bring to a boil; reduce heat to medium, and cook until reduced to 1¼ cups (about 6 minutes). Add green onions, and cook 1 minute.
4. Cut steak diagonally across grain into ¼-inch-thick slices. Serve steak with mushroom sauce. Yield: 4 servings (serving size: 3 ounces steak and about ⅓ cup sauce).

CALORIES 203 (35% from fat); FAT 8g (sat 3.3g, mono 3.2g, poly 0.4g); PROTEIN 25.4g; CARB 6.1g; FIBER 1.2g; CHOL 43mg; IRON 1.9mg; SODIUM 462mg; CALC 35mg

enlightened cook

Women Helping Women

An innovative culinary arts program in Denver helps low-income women gain financial independence.

Social worker Toni Schmid and chef Jane Berryman designed a culinary arts program called Work Options for Women (WOW) that provides women on welfare a place to learn skills in the food services industry. (Funding comes from private individuals, foundations, and corporations like womenswear retailer J. Jill; cafeteria sales provide 50 percent of the budget.)

WOW's 16-week hands-on course covers everything from knife skills, food preparation, and restaurant service to punching a time clock and kitchen sanitation. After completing the curriculum, women are placed in jobs that provide benefits, including child-care-friendly hours, medical coverage, and a living wage. Some 95 percent of WOW graduates have stayed off welfare by retaining their jobs for more than a year. WOW now trains 14 students at a time, with a waiting list of 25. Here are some of WOW's favorite recipes.

QUICK & EASY
Soft Chicken Tacos

Forty percent of WOW's cafeteria sales come from its healthful Mexican station, where tacos and burritos are assembled to order. Learning to prepare this recipe teaches students grilling techniques, as well as knowledge about Mexican spices and basic salsas. Thigh meat makes these tacos especially moist, but you can use breast meat instead. Serve with Pico de Gallo (recipe at right) or Tomatillo Salsa (recipe on page 322).

1 teaspoon chili powder
½ teaspoon salt
½ teaspoon ground cumin
½ teaspoon freshly ground black pepper
1 pound skinless, boneless chicken thighs
Cooking spray
12 (6-inch) white corn tortillas
1½ cups thinly sliced green cabbage
¼ cup (1 ounce) shredded reduced-fat Monterey Jack cheese (such as Tillamook)
Low-fat sour cream (optional)

1. Prepare grill.
2. Combine first 4 ingredients in a small bowl; rub spice mixture over chicken.
3. Place chicken on grill rack coated with cooking spray; grill 10 minutes on each side or until done. Let stand 5 minutes; chop.
4. Heat tortillas according to package directions. Divide chicken evenly among tortillas; top each tortilla with 2 tablespoons cabbage and 1 teaspoon cheese. Serve with sour cream, if desired. Yield: 4 servings (serving size: 3 tacos).

CALORIES 329 (34% from fat); FAT 12.5g (sat 3.5g, mono 3.5g, poly 2.9g); PROTEIN 27.4g; CARB 29.4g; FIBER 3.9g; CHOL 86mg; IRON 1.5mg; SODIUM 466mg; CALC 109mg

QUICK & EASY • MAKE AHEAD
Pico de Gallo

This is the most-requested salsa at the cafeteria's Mexican station. It uses all fresh ingredients, teaching students proper vegetable washing and knife skills. Remove the seeds from the jalapeño for milder flavor.

2½ cups chopped seeded plum tomato (about 6 medium)
⅔ cup finely chopped onion
2 tablespoons chopped fresh cilantro
2 tablespoons finely chopped jalapeño pepper (1 large)
2 tablespoons fresh lime juice
½ teaspoon salt
½ teaspoon garlic powder

1. Combine all ingredients in a serving bowl; toss well. Let stand 30 minutes before serving. Yield: 3½ cups (serving size: ¼ cup).

CALORIES 8 (11% from fat); FAT 0.1g (sat 0g, mono 0g, poly 0g); PROTEIN 0.3g; CARB 1.8g; FIBER 0.4g; CHOL 0mg; IRON 0.1mg; SODIUM 86mg; CALC 4mg

QUICK & EASY
Chicken Piccata with Capers

During preparation, WOW's trainees learn sautéing techniques, the proper temperature for serving the food, and tips to make the dish visually appealing. Garnish with lemon slices.

4 (6-ounce) skinless, boneless chicken breast halves
¼ cup all-purpose flour (about 1 ounce)
1 tablespoon butter
1 tablespoon olive oil
½ cup white wine
¼ cup fresh lemon juice
2 tablespoons capers
2 teaspoons minced fresh garlic
¼ teaspoon salt
¼ teaspoon freshly ground black pepper
4 cups hot cooked spaghetti (about 8 ounces uncooked)
2 tablespoons chopped fresh flat-leaf parsley
Lemon slices

1. Place each breast half between 2 sheets of heavy-duty plastic wrap; pound to ½-inch thickness using a meat mallet or small heavy skillet. Place flour in a shallow dish; dredge chicken in flour.
2. Heat butter and oil in a large skillet over medium-high heat. Add chicken, and cook 3 minutes on each side or until browned. Remove chicken from pan; keep warm. Add wine, lemon juice, capers, and garlic to pan; scrape pan to loosen browned bits. Cook 2 minutes or until slightly thick. Sprinkle with salt and pepper. Serve chicken over pasta. Top with sauce; sprinkle with parsley. Garnish with lemon slices. Yield: 4 servings
Continued

(serving size: 1 breast half, 1 cup spaghetti, 2 tablespoons sauce, and 1½ teaspoons parsley).

CALORIES 519 (21% from fat); FAT 12g (sat 3.7g, mono 4.9g, poly 1.8g); PROTEIN 48.1g; CARB 51g; FIBER 2.3g; CHOL 116mg; IRON 4mg; SODIUM 396mg; CALC 40mg

WINE NOTE: When a recipe calls for wine as an ingredient, it's nice to find a bottle that is delicious enough to drink but affordable enough to toss a little in the skillet. Mani Masianco 2005 ($15), an Italian blend of pinot grigio and verduzzo, fills the bill. It's aromatic, with apple, lemon, and floral notes. It also has the necessary acidity to greet the potent acid of the capers.

MAKE AHEAD
Tomatillo Salsa

With this salsa, students learn how to use fresh chiles to achieve different levels of heat. With the jalapeño seeds left in, this salsa is fiery. To tame the heat, remove the seeds.

    12 fresh tomatillos (about 1½
        pounds)
    1½ cups water
    ½   teaspoon salt
    4   seeded and chopped jalapeño
        peppers
    ½   cup chopped fresh cilantro

1. Discard husks and stems from tomatillos; cut into quarters. Place tomatillos, 1½ cups water, salt, and peppers in a large saucepan; bring to a boil. Cover, reduce heat, and simmer 15 minutes, stirring occasionally. Cool.
2. Place tomatillo mixture in a food processor, and process until smooth. Add cilantro, and pulse 5 times or until blended. Yield: 4 cups (serving size: ¼ cup).

CALORIES 18 (25% from fat); FAT 0.5g (sat 0.1g, mono 0.1g, poly 0.2g); PROTEIN 0.6g; CARB 3.2g; FIBER 1.1g; CHOL 0mg; IRON 0.4mg; SODIUM 85mg; CALC 4mg

technique
Creative Ways with Carnitas

The easy Mexican way of slow-cooking beef and pork yields tasty—and versatile—results.

Anyone who has traveled in Mexico has likely encountered carnitas. These slow-cooked chunks of meat (carnitas means "little meats" in Spanish) are sold by vendors on street corners and are on taqueria menus throughout the country.

And they've become increasingly popular here in the States. Basically, carnitas are a Mexican version of barbecue, only meat is slowly simmered in water or broth until deliciously tender, then browned in a skillet for a crisp exterior. This taco filling is often made from braised pork, but beef is common, too.

Beef Carnitas Empanada

Empanadas are Mexican-style pastries filled with meat, vegetables, or even dessert. This family-sized version is known as an empanada *gallega*.

FILLING:
    Cooking spray
    2 cups vertically sliced onion
    1 cup sliced green bell pepper
    1 cup chopped seeded tomato
    ¼ teaspoon crushed red pepper
    ¼ teaspoon salt
    3 cups Beef Carnitas (recipe on
       page 324)

DOUGH:
    9 tablespoons hot water
    ¼ teaspoon saffron threads, crushed
    1 teaspoon cider vinegar
    2 cups all-purpose flour (about 9
       ounces)
    1 teaspoon baking powder
    ½ teaspoon sugar
    ½ teaspoon salt
    2 tablespoons chilled butter, cut
       into small pieces

1. To prepare filling, heat a large nonstick skillet over medium-high heat. Coat pan with cooking spray. Add onion and bell pepper; sauté 5 minutes or until onion begins to brown. Stir in tomato, red pepper, and ¼ teaspoon salt, and sauté 2 minutes. Stir in Beef Carnitas, and cook 2 minutes, stirring frequently. Remove from heat; cool to room temperature.
2. Preheat oven to 400°.
3. To prepare dough, combine 9 tablespoons water and saffron; cool to room temperature. Stir in vinegar. Lightly spoon flour into dry measuring cups; level with a knife. Place flour, baking powder, sugar, and ½ teaspoon salt in a food processor; pulse 2 times to combine. Add butter; process until mixture resembles coarse meal. With processor on, slowly pour saffron mixture through food chute; process just until dough begins to form a ball (dough will be crumbly).
4. Divide dough into 2 equal portions. Press each portion into a 4-inch circle on heavy-duty plastic wrap. Cover with additional plastic wrap. Place dough in freezer 5 minutes or until plastic wrap can be easily removed.
5. Slightly overlap 2 sheets of plastic wrap on a slightly damp surface. Unwrap 1 dough portion; place on plastic wrap. Cover dough with 2 additional sheets of overlapping plastic wrap. Roll dough, still covered, into an 11-inch circle. Repeat procedure with remaining dough. Place both portions in freezer 5 minutes or until plastic wrap can be easily removed.
6. Remove plastic wrap from top of 1 dough portion; place dough, plastic wrap side up, on a large baking sheet coated with cooking spray. Remove top sheets of plastic wrap. Spoon filling onto dough, leaving a 1-inch border. Remove top sheets of plastic wrap from remaining dough. Place dough, plastic wrap side up, over filling. Remove top sheets of plastic wrap. Pinch edges together to seal. Cut several slits in top of dough to allow steam to escape. Bake at 400° for 30 minutes or until crust is crisp and beginning to brown. Cut into 8 wedges. Yield: 8 servings (serving size: 1 wedge).

CALORIES 251 (27% from fat); FAT 7.4g (sat 3g, mono 2.9g, poly 0.4g); PROTEIN 15.1g; CARB 30.4g; FIBER 1.9g; CHOL 43mg; IRON 3mg; SODIUM 470mg; CALC 57mg

Pork Carnitas Gorditas

Gordita is a term of endearment meaning "little fat one" in Spanish. It also refers to a thick, fried tortilla. Here, we use masa harina (available in the Latin foods aisle at large supermarkets) to make fresh gorditas. In a pinch, you can use store-bought corn tortillas as a base for this delicious dish.

1½ cups masa harina
¾ cup all-purpose flour (about 3⅓ ounces)
1 teaspoon baking powder
½ teaspoon salt
3 tablespoons chilled butter, cut into small pieces
1 cup fat-free, less-sodium chicken broth
Cooking spray
1 (15-ounce) can pinto beans, rinsed and drained
½ cup salsa verde (green salsa)
¼ cup diced peeled avocado
1 teaspoon fresh lime juice
1 cup Pork Carnitas (recipe at right)
2 tablespoons finely chopped red onion
2 tablespoons chopped fresh cilantro
Cilantro sprigs (optional)

1. Lightly spoon masa harina and flour into dry measuring cups; level with a knife. Combine masa harina, flour, baking powder, and salt in a medium bowl; cut in butter with a pastry blender or 2 knives until mixture resembles coarse meal. Add broth; stir just until moist. Turn dough out onto a lightly floured surface; knead lightly 5 or 6 times.
2. Divide dough into 6 equal portions. Shape each portion into a ball. Working with 1 portion at a time, press each ball into a 6-inch circle on a lightly floured surface (cover remaining balls to prevent drying). Heat a large nonstick skillet over medium-high heat. Coat pan with cooking spray. Place 1 gordita in pan; cook 2 minutes on each side or until lightly browned. Remove gordita from pan; cover and keep warm. Repeat procedure with cooking spray and remaining gorditas.
3. Place beans in a bowl; mash with a fork to desired consistency. Heat a large nonstick skillet over medium-high heat. Coat pan with cooking spray. Add beans; cook 2 minutes, stirring frequently. Stir in salsa verde; cook 2 minutes or until liquid almost evaporates, stirring frequently.
4. Combine avocado and lime juice; toss gently to coat. Spread about ¼ cup bean mixture on each gordita; top each with about 2½ tablespoons Pork Carnitas and 2 teaspoons avocado mixture. Sprinkle 1 teaspoon onion and 1 teaspoon chopped cilantro over each serving. Garnish with cilantro sprigs, if desired. Yield: 6 servings (serving size: 1 gordita).

CALORIES 359 (31% from fat); FAT 12.6g (sat 4.9g, mono 5.2g, poly 1.6g); PROTEIN 15.3g; CARB 46.6g; FIBER 6.3g; CHOL 41mg; IRON 3.1mg; SODIUM 782mg; CALC 109mg

MAKE AHEAD
Pork Carnitas

Trim the pork well to remove excess fat. Refrigerating the cooked pork overnight allows the solidified fat to rise to the top, so it's easy to remove.

2 tablespoons tomato paste
1 teaspoon salt
1 teaspoon freshly ground black pepper
10 garlic cloves, peeled
2¼ pounds boneless Boston butt pork roast, trimmed and cut into ½-inch pieces
1 cup fat-free, less-sodium chicken broth
1 tablespoon fresh lime juice

1. Preheat oven to 350°.
2. Combine first 5 ingredients in a large Dutch oven; pour broth over pork mixture. Cover and bake at 350° for 1½ hours or until pork is very tender.
3. Transfer pork mixture to a 13 x 9–inch baking dish, and cool to room temperature. Cover and chill 8 hours or overnight.
4. Skim solidified fat from surface; discard fat. Let pork stand at room temperature 30 minutes to soften. Heat a large nonstick skillet over medium-high heat. Add pork; cook 8 minutes or until liquid almost evaporates. Remove from heat; stir in juice. Yield: 3½ cups (serving size: about ⅓ cup).

CALORIES 154 (52% from fat); FAT 8.9g (sat 3.2g, mono 3.9g, poly 0.8g); PROTEIN 15.5g; CARB 2.3g; FIBER 0.5g; CHOL 52mg; IRON 1.2mg; SODIUM 363mg; CALC 25mg

How to Make Pork Carnitas

1. *Trim the pork well to remove excess fat.*

2. *Combine first 5 ingredients in a large Dutch oven; pour broth over pork mixture. Cover and bake at 350° for 1½ hours or until pork is very tender.*

3. *Skim the solidified fat from surface.*

Beef Carnitas

This simple recipe, which uses inexpensive beef stew meat, garnered our highest rating for great flavor and versatility. To freeze the carnitas, wrap them tightly in heavy-duty plastic wrap or foil, and place in a zip-top plastic freezer bag; they will keep in the freezer up to three months.

Cooking spray
1 cup chopped onion
3 garlic cloves, crushed
2 pounds beef stew meat, trimmed and cut into 1-inch pieces
1 cup less-sodium beef broth
1 teaspoon sugar
¾ teaspoon salt
½ teaspoon crushed red pepper
1 large unpeeled orange wedge

1. Heat a large Dutch oven over medium-high heat. Coat pan with cooking spray. Add onion; sauté 4 minutes or until tender. Add garlic; sauté 1 minute. Add beef; sauté 5 minutes or until beef is browned on all sides. Stir in broth, sugar, salt, and pepper; nestle orange wedge into beef mixture. Bring to a boil. Cover, reduce heat, and simmer 1½ hours or until beef is tender. Remove and discard orange. Continue simmering, uncovered, 8 minutes or until liquid almost evaporates, stirring frequently. Yield: 4 cups (serving size: ½ cup).

CALORIES 180 (40% from fat); FAT 8g (sat 3g, mono 3.4g, poly 0.3g); PROTEIN 22.2g; CARB 3.5g; FIBER 0.4g; CHOL 71mg; IRON 2.5mg; SODIUM 320mg; CALC 16mg

Traditional Toppings

Carnitas are about the meat, first and foremost, but the toppings deserve some consideration, too. Purists insist on fresh lime juice, chopped white onion, and fresh cilantro. For more embellishment, try a dollop of guacamole, crumbled queso fresco, and pico de gallo (see our recipe on page 321). Finish with chipotle salsa (with beef) or salsa verde (with pork), and wrap in a warm tortilla.

Pork Stew with Chickpeas and Sweet Potatoes

Serve over couscous or hot cooked rice.

1 teaspoon olive oil
Cooking spray
2 cups chopped onion
2 tablespoons grated peeled fresh ginger
½ teaspoon ground red pepper
¼ teaspoon ground cumin
¼ teaspoon ground allspice
¼ teaspoon ground nutmeg
¼ teaspoon ground cinnamon
⅛ teaspoon salt
4 garlic cloves, minced
½ cup water
2¼ cups (1-inch) cubed peeled sweet potato
1 cup fat-free, less-sodium chicken broth
1 (28-ounce) can whole peeled tomatoes, drained and coarsely chopped
1 (15½-ounce) can chickpeas (garbanzo beans), rinsed and drained
2 cups Pork Carnitas (recipe on page 323)
¼ cup golden raisins
1 tablespoon almond butter or peanut butter

1. Heat oil in a large Dutch oven lightly coated with cooking spray over medium-high heat. Add onion and next 8 ingredients; sauté 5 minutes or until onion is tender. Stir in ½ cup water, scraping pan to loosen browned bits. Add potato; sauté 5 minutes. Stir in broth, tomatoes, and chickpeas; bring to a boil. Cover, reduce heat, and simmer 20 minutes or until potato is tender, stirring occasionally.
2. Stir in Pork Carnitas and raisins; simmer, uncovered, 10 minutes or until mixture thickens slightly. Remove from heat; stir in almond butter. Yield: 6 servings (serving size: about 1⅓ cups).

CALORIES 340 (33% from fat); FAT 12.5g (sat 3.5g, mono 6g, poly 1.9g); PROTEIN 21g; CARB 36.4g; FIBER 6.5g; CHOL 52mg; IRON 3.4mg; SODIUM 781mg; CALC 105mg

Enchilada Casserole with Quick Mole Sauce

Tender carnitas meat is layered with corn tortillas and an easy Mexican mole sauce. This version of the sauce combines sweet plantains and dried cherries with spicy ancho chiles and savory pumpkinseed kernels; a touch of Mexican chocolate adds depth. Substitute Pork Carnitas (recipe on page 323) for the beef, if you prefer.

MOLE:
2 dried ancho chiles
1 cup boiling water
1 teaspoon olive oil
1 cup (½-inch-thick) slices soft black plantains (about 4 ounces)
½ cup chopped onion
¾ teaspoon salt
¼ teaspoon ground cumin
⅛ teaspoon ground cinnamon
2 garlic cloves, minced
1 cup less-sodium beef broth
2 tablespoons dried sweet cherries
2 tablespoons salted pumpkinseed kernels
½ ounce Mexican chocolate, chopped (such as Abuelita)
1 cup water

REMAINING INGREDIENTS:
Cooking spray
12 (6-inch) corn tortillas
1½ cups chopped Beef Carnitas (recipe at left)
⅓ cup (about 1¼ ounces) queso fresco

1. To prepare mole, heat a large skillet over medium-high heat. Add chiles, and cook 2 minutes on each side or until fragrant. Combine chiles and 1 cup boiling water in a small bowl; cover and let stand 10 minutes. Remove chiles from liquid, reserving liquid. Remove and discard stems and seeds from chiles. Set chiles and soaking liquid aside.
2. Heat oil in pan over medium-high heat. Add plantains; sauté 2 minutes. Add onion and next 4 ingredients; sauté 5 minutes. Stir in chiles, soaking liquid, broth, cherries, and pumpkinseed kernels; bring to a boil. Reduce heat, and simmer 10 minutes, stirring occasionally.

Remove from heat. Add chocolate, stirring until chocolate melts. Place mixture in a blender, and add 1 cup water. Process until smooth.

3. Preheat oven to 350°.

4. Spread 1 cup mole in bottom of a 13 x 9–inch baking dish lightly coated with cooking spray. Arrange 6 tortillas over mole; top with Beef Carnitas. Arrange remaining tortillas over Beef Carnitas. Spread remaining mole over tortillas; sprinkle with queso fresco. Bake at 350° for 30 minutes or until cheese begins to melt and casserole is thoroughly heated. Yield: 6 servings.

CALORIES 259 (29% from fat); FAT 8.6g (sat 2.8g, mono 3g, poly 1.2g); PROTEIN 11.6g; CARB 37.5g; FIBER 4.6g; CHOL 25mg; IRON 1.7mg; SODIUM 501mg; CALC 81mg

Spicy Beef Salad

Latin dishes are a natural with carnitas, but the tender meat is at home in Asian recipes, too. Sambal oelek (ground fresh chile paste) adds a fiery flavor to this tasty salad. To tame the heat, you can try just ½ teaspoon in the vinaigrette, or you can leave it out altogether.

VINAIGRETTE:
    3 tablespoons rice vinegar
    1 tablespoon fresh lime juice
    1 tablespoon brown sugar
    1 tablespoon chopped peeled fresh
        lemongrass
    1 tablespoon finely chopped
        shallot
    1 teaspoon dark sesame oil
    1 teaspoon Thai fish sauce
    1 teaspoon sambal oelek (ground
        fresh chile paste)
    ⅛ teaspoon salt
    1 garlic clove, minced

SALAD:
    2 cups Beef Carnitas (recipe on
        page 324)
    2 large tomatoes, each cut into
        8 wedges
    1 (10-ounce) package romaine salad
    ½ English cucumber, halved
        lengthwise and thinly sliced
        (about 1 cup)

1. To prepare vinaigrette, combine first 10 ingredients in a small bowl, stirring well with a whisk.

2. To prepare salad, combine Beef Carnitas and remaining 3 ingredients in a large bowl. Drizzle vinaigrette over salad, and toss gently to coat. Serve immediately. Yield: 4 servings (serving size: about 3 cups).

CALORIES 184 (33% from fat); FAT 6.8g (sat 2.2g, mono 2.8g, poly 0.8g); PROTEIN 17g; CARB 15.1g; FIBER 2.5g; CHOL 48mg; IRON 2.9mg; SODIUM 446mg; CALC 63mg

Beef Carnitas Tacos
(pictured on page 248)

These simple tacos are an ideal showcase for tender Beef Carnitas (recipe on page 324) or Pork Carnitas (recipe on page 323). Serve with a black bean salad and frozen margaritas or ice-cold beer. You can warm the tortillas in a nonstick skillet just until lightly browned.

    2 cups chopped plum tomato
        (about 2 medium)
    ⅓ cup chopped onion
    ¼ cup diced peeled avocado
    2 tablespoons minced fresh
        cilantro
    1 tablespoon fresh lime
        juice
    ⅛ teaspoon salt
    ⅛ teaspoon freshly ground black
        pepper
    8 (6-inch) corn tortillas
    2 cups Beef Carnitas (recipe on
        page 324)
    1 lime, cut into 8 wedges

1. Combine first 7 ingredients in a medium bowl; toss well. Warm tortillas according to package directions. Spoon ¼ cup Beef Carnitas onto each tortilla; top each with about 3 tablespoons avocado mixture. Fold in half; serve with lime wedges. Yield: 4 servings (serving size: 2 tacos and 2 lime wedges).

CALORIES 235 (30% from fat); FAT 7.9g (sat 2.2g, mono 3.2g, poly 0.9g); PROTEIN 17.6g; CARB 26g; FIBER 3.8g; CHOL 48mg; IRON 2mg; SODIUM 303mg; CALC 37mg

on hand

The Omnipotent Oat

This heart-healthy grain is good for more than just breakfast—sow it in desserts, entrées, soups, and breads.

MAKE AHEAD
Blackberry Crumb Cake

Finely ground oats give this cake a tender, moist texture. Stir frozen blackberries into the batter; the juices from thawed berries will turn the batter blue.

BATTER:
    2 cups regular oats
    ½ cup all-purpose flour (about
        2¼ ounces)
    ½ cup packed brown sugar
    2 teaspoons baking powder
    ½ teaspoon salt
    2½ tablespoons chilled butter, cut
        into small pieces
    1 cup 1% low-fat milk
    ½ cup egg substitute
    2 teaspoons vanilla extract
    1 (10-ounce) package frozen
        blackberries, unthawed
    Cooking spray

TOPPING:
    ½ cup regular oats
    ¼ cup packed brown sugar
    1 tablespoon chilled butter,
        softened
    ¼ cup chopped pecans, toasted

1. Preheat oven to 350°.

2. To prepare batter, place 2 cups oats in a food processor; process until finely ground (about 1 minute). Lightly spoon flour into a dry measuring cup; level with a knife. Add flour, ½ cup sugar, baking powder, and salt to food processor; process until well blended. Add butter; pulse 5 times or until combined. Spoon mixture into a large bowl. Combine milk, egg substitute, and vanilla, stirring

Continued

just until blended. Add to oat mixture, stirring to combine. Gently stir in blackberries. Pour mixture into a 9-inch square baking pan coated with cooking spray (batter will be thin).

3. To prepare topping, place ½ cup oats and remaining 3 ingredients in a food processor; process until finely chopped. Sprinkle evenly over batter. Bake at 350° for 45 minutes or until lightly browned and a wooden pick inserted in center comes out clean. Cool completely on a wire rack. Yield: 8 servings.

CALORIES 315 (29% from fat); FAT 10g (sat 3.3g, mono 4.2g, poly 1.5g); PROTEIN 7.9g; CARB 51g; FIBER 4.7g; CHOL 14mg; IRON 2.7mg; SODIUM 361mg; CALC 157mg

MAKE AHEAD
Simple Chicken and Oat Groat Soup

Once cooked, oat groats possess a resilient bite similar to that of wheat berries. They add a delightful textural contrast to the other elements of this satisfying soup.

2½ cups water
1 cup uncooked oat groats
1 tablespoon olive oil
1½ cups chopped onion
1 cup chopped celery
¾ cup chopped carrot
1 cup diced zucchini
2 garlic cloves, minced
4 cups fat-free, less-sodium chicken broth
2 cups chopped skinless, boneless rotisserie chicken breast
1 cup (1-inch) cut green beans
2 teaspoons chopped fresh thyme
½ teaspoon salt
1 (14.5-ounce) can diced tomatoes, undrained
1 cup frozen green peas, thawed
⅓ cup chopped fresh basil

1. Combine 2½ cups water and groats in a large saucepan; bring to a boil. Reduce heat, and simmer 45 minutes or until tender (do not overcook). Drain; wipe pan with a paper towel.
2. Heat oil in pan over medium-high heat. Add onion, celery, and carrot; sauté

8 minutes or until tender. Add zucchini and garlic; sauté 2 minutes. Add cooked groats, broth, and next 5 ingredients; bring to a boil. Reduce heat, and simmer 10 minutes. Stir in peas and basil. Yield: 6 servings (serving size: about 1⅔ cups).

CALORIES 285 (20% from fat); FAT 6.4g (sat 1.2g, mono 2.9g, poly 1.3g); PROTEIN 23.3g; CARB 35.2g; FIBER 7.4g; CHOL 40mg; IRON 3.1mg; SODIUM 635mg; CALC 87mg

Cheese-Onion Bannocks

Bannocks are Scottish oatcakes, similar to scones. Coarsely ground oats provide a hearty, slightly chewy texture to this savory version that's excellent as a snack or alongside a bowl of soup.

Cooking spray
¾ cup finely chopped onion
⅓ cup all-purpose flour (about 1½ ounces)
2 cups regular oats
1 teaspoon baking powder
½ teaspoon salt
⅛ teaspoon ground red pepper
2 tablespoons chilled butter, cut into small pieces
½ cup (2 ounces) grated fresh Parmesan cheese
¼ cup water
¼ cup egg substitute

1. Preheat oven to 400°.
2. Heat a small skillet over medium-high heat. Coat pan with cooking spray. Add onion; sauté 8 minutes or until tender. Remove from heat; cool.
3. Lightly spoon flour into a dry measuring cup; level with a knife. Place flour, oats, baking powder, salt, and pepper in a food processor; process until oats are coarsely ground (about 10 seconds). Add butter; pulse 3 times or until combined. Add onion and cheese; pulse 3 times or until blended. Place mixture in a medium bowl. Add ¼ cup water and egg substitute, stirring until moist. Let mixture stand 1 minute.
4. Place mixture onto a lightly floured surface; knead lightly 3 times (dough will be sticky). Divide dough in half; press each half into a 5-inch circle. Cut

each circle into 8 wedges. Place wedges on a baking sheet coated with cooking spray. Bake at 400° for 15 minutes or until lightly browned. Serve warm. Yield: 16 servings (serving size: 1 wedge).

CALORIES 75 (35% from fat); FAT 2.9g (sat 1.3g, mono 1g, poly 0.3g); PROTEIN 3.2g; CARB 9.7g; FIBER 1.1g; CHOL 6mg; IRON 0.7mg; SODIUM 161mg; CALC 54mg

Steel-Cut Oat Risotto with Butternut Squash and Mushrooms

Look for steel-cut oats, often labeled "steel-cut Irish oatmeal," on the cereal aisle in your supermarket. If the risotto becomes too thick after cooking, simply stir in hot water, one tablespoon at a time, until it reaches the desired consistency.

SQUASH:
2 cups diced peeled butternut squash (about ½ small squash)
1 tablespoon olive oil
½ teaspoon chopped fresh sage
¼ teaspoon salt
Dash of freshly ground black pepper

RISOTTO:
1½ cups water
2 (14-ounce) cans fat-free, less-sodium chicken broth
Cooking spray
¾ cup diced onion
2 garlic cloves, minced
2 cups steel-cut oats
1 cup dry white wine
¾ cup (3 ounces) grated fresh Parmigiano-Reggiano cheese, divided
2 teaspoons chopped fresh sage
¼ teaspoon freshly ground black pepper
1½ teaspoons butter
4 cups sliced cremini mushrooms (about 1 pound)
½ teaspoon salt
Coarsely ground black pepper (optional)

1. Preheat oven to 400°.

2. To prepare squash, combine first 5 ingredients in a jelly-roll pan; toss well to coat. Bake at 400° for 20 minutes or until tender and beginning to brown, stirring every 7 minutes. Set aside, and keep warm.

3. To prepare risotto, bring 1½ cups water and broth to a simmer in a medium saucepan (do not boil). Keep warm.

4. Heat a medium sauté pan over medium-high heat. Coat pan with cooking spray. Add onion and garlic; sauté 3 minutes or until golden. Add oats; cook 3 minutes or until oats become fragrant and begin to brown, stirring constantly. Add wine; cook 1 minute or until liquid is nearly absorbed, stirring constantly. Stir in 1 cup broth mixture; cook 4 minutes or until liquid is nearly absorbed, stirring constantly. Add remaining broth mixture,

½ cup at a time, stirring constantly until each portion of broth is absorbed before adding next (about 25 minutes). Remove risotto from heat; stir in ½ cup cheese, 2 teaspoons sage, and ¼ teaspoon pepper.

5. Melt butter in a large nonstick skillet over medium-high heat. Add mushrooms and ½ teaspoon salt; sauté 3 minutes or until tender and beginning to brown. Stir in squash; cook 1 minute or until thoroughly heated.

6. Spoon about ⅔ cup risotto into each of 6 bowls; top each serving with ½ cup mushroom mixture, 2 teaspoons cheese, and coarsely ground pepper, if desired. Yield: 6 servings.

CALORIES 356 (29% from fat); FAT 11.3g (sat 3.9g, mono 4.4g, poly 1.7g); PROTEIN 16.7g; CARB 51.4g; FIBER 8g; CHOL 15mg; IRON 3.9mg; SODIUM 738mg; CALC 242mg

Oatmeal-Crusted Chicken Tenders

Oatmeal in the breading adds crunch to these chicken tenders, which are sure to be a hit with adults and children alike. Serve with commercial honey mustard or light ranch dressing for dipping.

1   cup regular oats
¾   cup (3 ounces) grated fresh
    Parmesan cheese
1   teaspoon chopped fresh thyme
½   teaspoon salt
¼   teaspoon freshly ground black
    pepper
1   pound chicken breast tenders
Cooking spray

Continued

Meet the Oat Family

Type	Characteristics	Best Uses	Cooking Tip
Oat groats	Chewy, nutty-tasting grains similar to wheat berries	As a substitute for rice in a side dish or in soups and stews	Boil in a large pot of water 45 minutes or until tender; drain and combine with seasonings, or stir into soup.
Steel-cut oats (Irish Oatmeal)	Mild flavor similar to groats (steel-cut oats are whole groats cut into 2 to 3 pieces); starchy texture	Substituted for rice in a pilaf or risotto; cooked, chilled, and tossed with vinaigrette for a salad	Toast before cooking to enhance nutty flavor; steel-cut oats cook in about 15 to 20 minutes.
Regular or rolled oats (commonly called oatmeal)	Nutty flavor similar to groats (oatmeal is made from steamed groats that have been flattened by large rollers)	Added to meat loaf as a binder; combined with vegetables for stuffing; coarsely ground to bread chicken, fish, or pork	Toast oats in a dry skillet to maintain their shape and chewy texture in the final product.
Oat flour	Delicate texture that produces moist, tender baked goods	Baked in muffins, cakes, batter breads, and cookies; also nice in pancakes and waffles	Substitute one-third of regular flour with oat flour in baked goods.

1. Preheat oven to 450°.

2. Place oats in a food processor, and process 20 seconds or until coarsely ground. Add cheese, thyme, salt, and pepper. Pulse to combine, and place in a shallow bowl.

3. Place each chicken breast tender between 2 sheets of heavy-duty plastic wrap; pound to ¼-inch thickness using a meat mallet or small heavy skillet. Coat both sides of tenders with cooking spray; dredge tenders in oat mixture. Place tenders on a baking sheet coated with cooking spray. Bake at 450° for 15 minutes or until browned. Yield: 4 servings (serving size: about 4 ounces).

CALORIES 283 (26% from fat); FAT 8.3g (sat 4.1g, mono 2.4g, poly 0.8g); PROTEIN 36.9g; CARB 14.2g; FIBER 1.9g; CHOL 80mg; IRON 2mg; SODIUM 710mg; CALC 278mg

Roast Chicken with Fennel and Oat Stuffing

Based on the Scottish dish *skirlie*, the oatmeal stuffing is a great accompaniment to roasted poultry or meat. To ensure that everything is ready at the same time, place the stuffing in the oven for the last 20 minutes of the chicken's baking time.

CHICKEN:

  1 (4½-pound) roasting chicken
  Cooking spray

STUFFING:

  1½ cups regular oats
  2 tablespoons butter
  2 cups sliced leek (about 2 medium)
  2 cups chopped fennel bulb (about 1 large)
  1¼ cups fat-free, less-sodium chicken broth
  1 teaspoon salt
  1 teaspoon finely chopped fresh rosemary
  1 teaspoon grated orange rind
  1 egg white, lightly beaten

1. Preheat oven to 375°.

2. To prepare chicken, remove and dis-

card giblets and neck from chicken. Rinse chicken with cold water; pat dry. Trim excess fat. Place chicken, breast side up, on a broiler pan coated with cooking spray. Bake at 375° for 1 hour and 20 minutes or until a thermometer inserted into meaty part of thigh registers 175°. Let chicken stand 10 minutes. Remove and discard skin.

3. To prepare stuffing, cook oats in a large nonstick skillet over medium-high heat 10 minutes or until lightly toasted and fragrant, stirring frequently. Spoon into a medium bowl.

4. Melt butter in pan over medium-high heat. Add leek and fennel; sauté 8 minutes or until tender. Add leek mixture, broth, and remaining 4 ingredients to toasted oats, and stir well to combine. Spoon mixture into a 1-quart casserole dish coated with cooking spray. Bake at 375° for 20 minutes or until thoroughly heated. Serve with chicken. Yield: 6 servings (serving size: about 4 ounces meat and about ½ cup stuffing).

CALORIES 334 (27% from fat); FAT 10.1g (sat 3.3g, mono 3.5g, poly 1.7g); PROTEIN 40.3g; CARB 20.1g; FIBER 3.5g; CHOL 123mg; IRON 3.7mg; SODIUM 662mg; CALC 66mg

superfast

. . . And Ready in Just About 20 Minutes

More than a week's worth of quick entrées to get dinner on the table in a flash

QUICK & EASY
Balsamic and Black Pepper Filet Mignon

Add extra flavor to the steaks by drizzling them with any pan juices after they're cooked. Serve the steak with fast-cooking long-grain and wild rice pilaf tossed with dried fruit.

  2 tablespoons molasses
  2 teaspoons balsamic vinegar
  4 (4-ounce) beef tenderloin steaks, trimmed (1 inch thick)
  Cooking spray
  ¾ teaspoon salt
  ¾ teaspoon black pepper

1. Preheat broiler.

2. Combine molasses and vinegar in a medium bowl, stirring with a whisk. Add steaks, turning to coat. Place steaks on a baking sheet coated with cooking spray. Sprinkle steaks with salt and pepper.

3. Broil 6 minutes; turn steaks over. Broil 5 minutes or until desired degree of doneness. Serve immediately. Yield: 4 servings (serving size: 1 steak).

CALORIES 215 (37% from fat); FAT 8.9g (sat 3g, mono 3.5g, poly 0.7g); PROTEIN 24.7g; CARB 8.3g; FIBER 0.1g; CHOL 72mg; IRON 2.3mg; SODIUM 491mg; CALC 37mg

QUICK & EASY
Creamy Cajun Shrimp Linguine

Shrimp and pasta combine with a creamy sauce for a quick and delicious dish. Round out the meal with a Caesar salad.

  1 cup water
  1 (14-ounce) can fat-free, less-sodium chicken broth
  6 ounces uncooked linguine
  1 pound medium shrimp, peeled and deveined
  1½ tablespoons butter
  1 (8-ounce) package presliced mushrooms
  1 large red bell pepper, cut into ¼-inch-thick slices
  2 teaspoons all-purpose flour
  1 teaspoon Cajun seasoning
  ¼ teaspoon salt
  ⅔ cup half-and-half
  ¼ cup chopped fresh flat-leaf parsley

1. Combine 1 cup water and broth in a Dutch oven; bring to a boil. Break pasta in half; add to pan. Bring to a boil. Cover, reduce heat, and simmer 8 minutes. Add shrimp to pan. Cover and simmer 3 minutes or until shrimp are done; drain shrimp.

2. Melt butter in a large skillet over medium-high heat. Add mushrooms and pepper to pan; sauté 4 minutes or until moisture evaporates. Add flour, seasoning, and salt to pan; sauté 30 seconds. Stir in half-and-half; cook 1 minute or until thick, stirring constantly. Remove from heat. Add pasta mixture and parsley to pan; toss. Yield: 4 servings (serving size: 1½ cups).

CALORIES 365 (27% from fat); FAT 10.9g (sat 5.9g, mono 2.7g, poly 0.8g); PROTEIN 27.4g; CARB 38.1g; FIBER 2.2g; CHOL 194mg; IRON 4.1mg; SODIUM 685mg; CALC 101mg

---

QUICK & EASY

Sesame Tuna with Spicy Slaw

Sriracha chile sauce can be found in the ethnic foods aisle in large supermarkets or in Asian groceries. If you can't find Sriracha, substitute half the amount of Tabasco or other hot sauce. There isn't a good substitute for the one-of-a-kind flavor of fish sauce, though many cooks will use soy sauce in a pinch. Pair this dish with rice noodles.

    1   tablespoon dark sesame oil
    4   (6-ounce) tuna steaks
    2   tablespoons low-sodium soy sauce
    2   teaspoons coarsely ground black pepper
    1   teaspoon sesame seeds
    2   tablespoons water
    2   teaspoons sugar
    1   teaspoon Sriracha (hot chile sauce, such as Huy Fong)
    ¾   teaspoon fish sauce
    ½   teaspoon rice vinegar
    ½   teaspoon bottled ground fresh ginger (such as Spice World)
    4   cups packaged angel hair slaw
    2   tablespoons thinly sliced green onions

1. Heat oil in a large nonstick skillet over medium-high heat. Brush fish with soy sauce. Combine pepper and sesame seeds; sprinkle evenly over fish. Add fish to pan, and cook 2 minutes on each side or until fish flakes easily when tested with a fork or until desired degree of doneness.

2. Combine 2 tablespoons water and next 5 ingredients in a small bowl. Combine slaw and onions in a large bowl. Drizzle sugar mixture over slaw mixture; toss to coat. Serve with fish. Yield: 4 servings (serving size: 1 tuna steak and about ¾ cup slaw).

CALORIES 247 (20% from fat); FAT 5.5g (sat 1g, mono 1.8g, poly 2.1g); PROTEIN 40.1g; CARB 7.9g; FIBER 2.1g; CHOL 74mg; IRON 2mg; SODIUM 427mg; CALC 75mg

---

Spanish Supper Menu
serves 4

Dulce de leche is caramelized sweetened condensed milk, and it's available on the ethnic aisle in most supermarkets.

Shrimp and Sausage Paella

Tossed green salad

Dulce de leche parfait*

*Place ¼ cup fat-free vanilla ice cream in each of 4 footed glasses. Combine 6 tablespoons dulce de leche and 2 tablespoons hot water, stirring well; top each serving with 1 tablespoon dulce de leche mixture and 2 teaspoons chopped toasted almonds. Repeat layers.

QUICK & EASY

Shrimp and Sausage Paella

Saffron is expensive; fortunately, a pinch goes a long way.

    2   links Spanish chorizo sausage (about 6½ ounces) or turkey kielbasa, cut into ½-inch-thick slices
    1   cup chopped onion
    1   cup chopped green bell pepper (about 1 medium)
    2   teaspoons bottled minced garlic
    ¼   teaspoon black pepper
    ¼   teaspoon crushed saffron threads
    1½ cups instant rice
    ¾   cup water
    ½   teaspoon dried marjoram
    1   (14½-ounce) can no-salt-added diced tomatoes, undrained
    1   (8-ounce) bottle clam juice
    8   ounces medium shrimp, peeled and deveined

1. Heat a large nonstick skillet over medium-high heat. Add sausage to pan; sauté 1 minute. Add onion and bell pepper to pan; sauté 4 minutes. Stir in garlic, black pepper, and saffron; sauté 1 minute. Stir in rice and next 4 ingredients; bring to a boil. Cover, reduce heat, and simmer 4 minutes or until rice is almost tender. Stir in shrimp. Cover and simmer 3 minutes or until shrimp are done. Yield: 4 servings (serving size: about 1½ cups).

CALORIES 390 (30% from fat); FAT 13.2g (sat 4.6g, mono 5.8g, poly 1.5g); PROTEIN 23.3g; CARB 41.8g; FIBER 2.7g; CHOL 114mg; IRON 5.1mg; SODIUM 626mg; CALC 66mg

---

QUICK & EASY

Duck with Port and Cranberry-Cherry Sauce

This rich sauce pairs well with duck breast, chicken, or pork.

    1½ tablespoons butter, divided
    3   tablespoons chopped shallots
    ½   cup port
    ¼   cup red currant jelly
    1   tablespoon red wine vinegar
    1   teaspoon sugar
    ¼   cup sweetened dried cranberries
    3   tablespoons dried tart cherries
    ¾   teaspoon salt, divided
    ¼   teaspoon black pepper, divided
    2   teaspoons olive oil
    4   (6-ounce) boneless duck breast halves, skinned

1. Melt 1½ teaspoons butter over medium-high heat in a medium saucepan. Add shallots; sauté 1 minute. Add port, jelly, vinegar, and sugar; cook 2 minutes or until sugar dissolves. Stir in cranberries and cherries; cook 2 minutes or until slightly thick. Remove from heat. Stir in 1 tablespoon butter, ¼ teaspoon salt, and ⅛ teaspoon pepper.

2. While sauce cooks, heat oil in a medium nonstick skillet over medium-high heat. Sprinkle duck with ½ teaspoon salt and ⅛ teaspoon pepper. Add duck to

Continued

pan; cook 4 minutes on each side or until desired degree of doneness. Serve with sauce. Yield: 4 servings (serving size: 1 duck breast half and about 3 tablespoons sauce).

CALORIES 371 (24% from fat); FAT 9.8g (sat 3.8g, mono 3.9g, poly 0.9g); PROTEIN 35.7g; CARB 30.1g; FIBER 1.5g; CHOL 194mg; IRON 6.2mg; SODIUM 610mg; CALC 27mg

Pizza, Perfected

To make a pizzeria-quality pie at home with no special equipment, start with the crust.

QUICK & EASY
Fattoush

Fattoush (fah-TOOSH) is the Middle Eastern version of bread salad, made with torn bits of pita and lots of late-summer vegetables. This version is a main dish, thanks to the addition of chicken and kidney beans.

- ¼ cup fresh lemon juice
- 2 tablespoons extravirgin olive oil
- 1 teaspoon Dijon mustard
- ¼ teaspoon salt
- ¼ teaspoon black pepper
- 8 cups chopped romaine lettuce
- 2 cups shredded cooked chicken breast
- 1½ cups chopped peeled cucumber
- 1 cup thinly sliced fennel bulb
- ⅓ cup thinly sliced green onions
- ¼ cup chopped fresh mint
- ¼ cup chopped fresh flat-leaf parsley
- 2 (6-inch) pitas, torn into bite-sized pieces
- 1 (15-ounce) can kidney beans, rinsed and drained
- 1 pint cherry tomatoes, halved

1. Combine first 5 ingredients in a bowl, stirring with a whisk.
2. Combine lettuce and remaining 9 ingredients in a large bowl; toss gently. Drizzle juice mixture over chicken mixture; toss to coat. Serve immediately. Yield: 4 servings (serving size: 2 cups).

CALORIES 400 (30% from fat); FAT 13.4g (sat 2.6g, mono 7.1g, poly 2.2g); PROTEIN 30.3g; CARB 40.9g; FIBER 9.4g; CHOL 59mg; IRON 4.1mg; SODIUM 566mg; CALC 163mg

Pizza is comfort food for the ages: Flatbread made of flour, water, and (maybe) a little olive oil has existed in the Mediterranean region for millennia. But residents of the Italian peninsula embraced the simple dish and, ultimately, made it their own. Tomatoes weren't added until the 16th century, when explorers ferried the fruit back from the New World.

Italian immigrants brought pizza to our shores in the 19th century. New Yorkers favored a thin crust, while deep-dish pizza became a Chicago icon. Pizza became a nationwide favorite in the 1950s, when GIs returning from World War II brought foods from around the globe to small-town U.S.A.

Homemade pizza is a special treat because you control the ingredients, from what goes into the dough to the cheese sprinkled atop, and your pizza will be lower in fat and sodium than store-bought or pizzeria pies, yet every bit as delicious. With just a little practice, you can master preparing the dough and toppings.

MAKE AHEAD • FREEZABLE
Basic Pizza Dough

Mix up a batch of this dough whenever you're in the mood for homemade pizza. Use it in the recipes here, create your own versions, or add mix-ins to customize the crust. Don't worry about rolling the dough into a perfect circle.

- 2 teaspoons honey
- 1 package active dry yeast (about 2¼ teaspoons)
- ¾ cup warm water (100° to 110°)
- 2¼ cups all-purpose flour (about 10 ounces), divided
- ½ teaspoon salt
- Cooking spray
- 2 tablespoons stone-ground yellow cornmeal

1. Dissolve honey and yeast in ¾ cup warm water in a large bowl. Let stand 5 minutes or until bubbly. Lightly spoon flour into dry measuring cups; level with a knife. Add 2 cups flour and salt to yeast mixture; stir until a soft dough forms.

Turn dough out onto a lightly floured surface. Knead until smooth and elastic (about 6 minutes); add enough of remaining flour, 1 tablespoon at a time, to prevent dough from sticking to hands (dough will feel slightly sticky).
2. Place dough in a large bowl coated with cooking spray, turning to coat top. Cover and let rise in a warm place (85°), free from drafts, 30 minutes or until doubled in size. (Gently press two fingers into dough. If indentation remains, dough has risen enough.)
3. Roll dough into a 12-inch circle (about ¼ inch thick) on a lightly floured surface. Place dough on a rimless baking sheet sprinkled with cornmeal. Crimp edges of dough with fingers to form a rim. Lightly spray surface of dough with cooking spray, and cover with plastic wrap. Place dough in refrigerator up to 30 minutes. Bake according to recipe directions. Yield: 1 (12-inch) crust.

(Totals are for 1 [12-inch] pizza crust) CALORIES 1,155 (3% from fat); FAT 3.4g (sat 0.6g, mono 0.5g, poly 1.3g); PROTEIN 33.8g; CARB 242.5g; FIBER 10.8g; CHOL 0mg; IRON 14.3mg; SODIUM 1,195mg; CALC 49mg

Gather the Equipment

You'll need two rimless baking sheets, a rolling pin, and a spatula. If you don't have two rimless baking sheets, roll out the dough, and place it on the backside of a jelly-roll pan. Then, use a rimless baking sheet or a pizza stone (see "Pizza Extras" on page 336) to cook the pizza. Insulated baking sheets are less-efficient heat conductors, so bake the pizza about four minutes longer for a crisp crust if your baking sheet is insulated.

Use the rolling pin to punch down, roll out, and shape the dough. The rolling pin also doubles as a handy tool to transfer the dough from your work surface. Use the spatula to guide the dough onto the preheated baking sheet.

Prepare the Dough

Pizza dough is a bread dough, so it requires the use of yeast. Yeast is a living entity, which you'll observe when you combine it with warm water and honey. As the mixture stands, you'll be able to see tiny bubbles form on the surface as the yeast blooms. Then, stir in flour and a touch of salt to form a soft dough, which you turn out onto a lightly floured surface to knead.

Kneading is a process that develops the dough's gluten—long strands of protein that make the dough pliable and act as balloons to trap gas emitted by the yeast, which helps the dough rise. When kneading the dough, be sure to follow the visual and tactile clues ("soft and elastic") to know when it's ready. Avoid overkneading the dough, or you'll end up with a tough crust (dough is overkneaded when it becomes rough and breaks into pieces rather than feeling smooth and

stretchy). Then, put it in a bowl, and let it rise in a warm place for 30 minutes or until it doubles in size.

Shape the Dough

After the dough rises, use a rolling pin to roll it out on a lightly floured surface to *about* a 12-inch diameter. The objective is to roll the dough to about ¼-inch thickness so the crust cooks evenly. You may end up with a 12-inch circle, a 12-inch square, or some amorphous shape in between—it doesn't matter as long as it's an even thickness. (Another option: Shape smaller pizzas to serve as appetizers or individual portions.) Then, gently drape the dough over a rolling pin to transfer it to a baking sheet sprinkled with a little cornmeal, cover, and pop it into the refrigerator while the oven preheats. Refrigerating slows the growth of the yeast so the dough doesn't continue to rise.

Make the Sauce

You can use a commercial pizza sauce, as we do with our Cheese Pizza (recipe on page 336), or prepare sauce from scratch. You can cook the sauce ahead of time and refrigerate or freeze, or simply prepare it while the dough rises. Another option is to doctor a bottled sauce by adding sautéed fresh vegetables and meats, a strategy we use for our Sausage and Vegetable Deep-Dish Pizza (recipe on page 335). Or you can forgo sauce altogether.

Preheat the Baking Sheet

Place your second baking sheet on the lowest rack in the oven while the oven preheats. This is similar to using a pizza stone, which is preheated so the raw dough hits a hot surface and becomes

crisp and sturdy to support the toppings. If you don't preheat the baking sheet, that's OK. Just know that you will end up with a slightly softer crust.

Prebake the Crust

Before adding any toppings, bake the crust for a few minutes on the lowest rack in the oven. Use the cornmeal-coated baking sheet as an impromptu pizza peel to transfer the dough onto the preheated baking sheet. The layer of cornmeal under the dough helps it to slide more easily. Then, prebake the dough as directed.

Add the Topping

If you're preparing a sauce from scratch or want to cook vegetables or meats before adding them to the pizza, be sure to do so during the dough's first rise. The idea is to have all the toppings ready to go before the pizza goes into the oven so they're ready to add after the crust prebakes but while it's still hot. Add hearty toppings, such as sauce, cooked veggies, cheese, or meat to the prebaked crust.

Finish Baking and Serve

Once the toppings you select are on the crust, put the pizza back in the oven on the middle rack, and bake just until the cheese melts and the top and bottom crust are golden brown. Moving the pizza to the middle rack after toppings are added ensures the bottom of the crust doesn't overcook. Add fragile toppings like herbs or salad greens after removing the pizza from the oven and just before serving so they don't wilt. Then, slice the pizza with a pizza wheel, a large knife, or kitchen shears, and dig in.

1. All you'll need are two rimless baking sheets (use one as an improvised peel and the other to bake the pizza), a rolling pin to shape the dough, a spatula to guide the dough onto the preheated baking sheet, and a pizza wheel, large knife, or kitchen shears to cut the pizza.

2. Knead the dough on a lightly floured surface until it's smooth and elastic.

3. Roll the dough into a 12-inch circle. Don't worry about making it a perfect circle so much as ensuring it's an even thickness. That way it will cook evenly.

4. Drape the dough over the rolling pin to transfer it to a baking sheet sprinkled with cornmeal.

5. Crimp the edges of the dough to form a rim to corral the toppings on the surface of the pizza.

6. Holding the baking sheet at about a 45-degree angle and using a spatula to guide it, slide the dough onto the preheated sheet. Place the dough on the lowest oven rack to prebake.

7. Remove the prebaked crust from the oven. Add toppings, and return the pizza to the middle oven rack to bake until the crust is brown and the cheese melts.

Basic Pizza Sauce

This makes a chunky sauce; if you prefer a smoother consistency, you can puree the sauce in a food processor with one tablespoon water.

MAKE-AHEAD TIP: Prepare the sauce a day or two ahead and refrigerate it, or make a double batch and freeze the extra for up to one month.

Cooking spray
¼ cup finely chopped onion
1 garlic clove, minced
¼ cup white wine
2 tablespoons tomato paste
1 teaspoon dried oregano
⅛ teaspoon freshly ground black pepper
1 (14.5-ounce) can crushed tomatoes, undrained
1 tablespoon chopped fresh basil
½ teaspoon balsamic vinegar

1. Heat a large saucepan over medium-high heat. Coat pan with cooking spray. Add onion to pan; sauté 3 minutes or until tender. Add garlic to pan; sauté 30 seconds. Stir in wine; cook 30 seconds. Add tomato paste, oregano, pepper, and tomatoes. Reduce heat, and simmer 20 minutes or until thick. Remove from heat; stir in basil and vinegar. Cool. Yield: 1⅓ cups.

(Totals are for 1⅓ cups Basic Pizza Sauce) CALORIES 203 (1% from fat); FAT 0.3g (sat 0.1g, mono 0.1g, poly 0.1g); PROTEIN 9.6g; CARB 42.2g; FIBER 10.1g; CHOL 0mg; IRON 7.3mg; SODIUM 953mg; CALC 201mg

SPICY PIZZA SAUCE VARIATION:
Add ½ teaspoon crushed red pepper with oregano and black pepper; omit basil. Yield: 1⅓ cups.

(Totals are for 1⅓ cups Spicy Pizza Sauce) CALORIES 206 (2% from fat); FAT 0.4g (sat 0.1g, mono 0.1g, poly 0.2g); PROTEIN 9.6g; CARB 42.6g; FIBER 10.3g; CHOL 0mg; IRON 7.3mg; SODIUM 953mg; CALC 199mg

Grilled Shrimp Pizza

Green salsa (also known as "salsa verde") is available in most grocery stores either near Hispanic foods or stored with other bottled salsas. Queso fresco is a salty, crumbly Mexican cheese you'll find in most major supermarkets or at Latin markets.

DOUGH:
2 teaspoons honey
1 package active dry yeast (about 2¼ teaspoons)
1 cup warm water (100° to 110°)
2¼ cups all-purpose flour (about 10 ounces), divided
6 tablespoons stone-ground yellow cornmeal, divided
½ teaspoon salt
Cooking spray
2 teaspoons olive oil

REMAINING INGREDIENTS:
36 large shrimp, peeled and deveined (about 1 pound)
⅛ teaspoon salt
2 cups (8 ounces) shredded part-skim mozzarella cheese
2 cups (8 ounces) queso fresco, crumbled
6 tablespoons green salsa, divided
½ cup fresh cilantro leaves

1. To prepare dough, dissolve honey and yeast in 1 cup warm water in a large bowl; let stand 5 minutes. Lightly spoon flour into dry measuring cups; level with a knife. Add 2 cups flour, 2 tablespoons cornmeal, and ½ teaspoon salt to yeast mixture; stir until a soft dough forms. Turn dough out onto a floured surface. Knead until smooth and elastic (about 6 minutes); add enough of remaining flour, 1 tablespoon at a time, to prevent dough from sticking to hands (dough will feel slightly sticky).
2. Place dough in a large bowl coated with cooking spray, turning to coat top. Cover and let rise in a warm place (85°), free from drafts, 45 minutes or until doubled in size. (Gently press two fingers into dough. If indentation remains, dough has risen enough.)
3. Divide dough into 2 equal portions. Working with one portion at a time

(cover remaining dough), roll each into a 10-inch circle on a floured surface. Place dough on 2 rimless baking sheets, each sprinkled with 2 tablespoons cornmeal. Brush each portion with 1 teaspoon oil; coat lightly with cooking spray. Cover with plastic wrap; chill.
4. Prepare grill.
5. Thread 6 shrimp onto each of 6 (12-inch) wooden skewers. Sprinkle shrimp with ⅛ teaspoon salt. Place skewers on grill rack coated with cooking spray, and grill 2 minutes on each side or until shrimp are done. Cool slightly, and coarsely chop. Combine cheeses.
6. Remove plastic wrap from 1 dough portion; discard plastic. Slide dough onto grill rack coated with cooking spray, using a spatula as a guide. Grill 3 minutes or until lightly browned; turn. Spread 3 tablespoons salsa over crust, leaving a ¼-inch border. Top with half of shrimp and 2 cups cheese mixture. Grill 3 minutes or until crust is golden brown and cheese melts. Remove and keep warm. Repeat procedure with remaining dough, salsa, shrimp, and cheese mixture. Sprinkle each pizza with ¼ cup cilantro. Cut each pizza into 6 wedges. Yield: 6 servings (serving size: 2 wedges).

CALORIES 458 (25% from fat); FAT 12.8g (sat 6.4g, mono 4.1g, poly 1.3g); PROTEIN 35g; CARB 48.8g; FIBER 2.1g; CHOL 149mg; IRON 4.7mg; SODIUM 636mg; CALC 401mg

---

Freezing Extra Dough

You can prepare an extra batch of the dough to freeze and make pizza another time. Just follow the recipe through the first rise, and then punch the dough down to expel gas and redistribute the yeast. Form the dough into a ball, lightly dust it with flour, and seal it in a heavy-duty zip-top plastic bag. Freeze for up to two weeks. To use, thaw the dough overnight in the refrigerator; remove it from the fridge, and allow it to come to room temperature (about 30 minutes) before rolling it out and proceeding with the recipe as directed.

Fontina, Olive, and Tomato Pizza with Basil Whole Wheat Crust

This is a sauceless pizza. The whole wheat flour and fresh basil base is an earthy foil for the creamy cheese, tangy olives, and tomatoes.

DOUGH:

1 tablespoon honey
1 package active dry yeast (about 2¼ teaspoons)
1 cup warm water (100° to 110°)
1½ cups all-purpose flour (about 6¾ ounces), divided
1 cup whole wheat flour (about 4¾ ounces)
½ teaspoon salt
⅛ teaspoon freshly ground black pepper
¼ cup chopped fresh basil
Cooking spray
2 tablespoons stone-ground yellow cornmeal

REMAINING INGREDIENTS:

2 plum tomatoes, thinly sliced (about ½ pound)
1 cup (4 ounces) shredded fontina cheese
3 tablespoons chopped pitted kalamata olives
½ cup (2 ounces) shredded part-skim mozzarella cheese
1 tablespoon pine nuts, coarsely chopped
Cracked black pepper (optional)

1. To prepare dough, dissolve honey and yeast in 1 cup warm water in a large bowl; let stand 5 minutes. Lightly spoon flours into dry measuring cups; level with a knife. Add 1¼ cups all-purpose flour, whole wheat flour, salt, and ⅛ teaspoon pepper to yeast mixture; stir until a soft dough forms.
2. Turn dough out onto a lightly floured surface. Knead until soft and elastic (about 6 minutes); add enough of remaining all-purpose flour, 1 tablespoon at a time, to keep dough from sticking to hands (dough will feel slightly sticky). Knead in basil just until incorporated. Place dough in a large bowl

coated with cooking spray, turning to coat top. Cover and let rise in a warm place (85°), free from drafts, 40 minutes or until doubled in size. (Gently press two fingers into dough. If indentation remains, dough has risen enough.)
3. Roll dough into a 12-inch circle (about ¼ inch thick) on a lightly floured surface. Place dough on a rimless baking sheet sprinkled with cornmeal. Crimp edges of dough with fingers to form a rim. Lightly spray surface of dough with cooking spray; cover with plastic wrap. Place dough in refrigerator.
4. Position one oven rack in middle setting. Position another rack in lowest setting, and place a rimless baking sheet on bottom rack. Preheat oven to 500°.
5. Remove plastic wrap from dough; discard. Remove preheated baking sheet from oven; close oven door. Slide dough onto preheated baking sheet, using a spatula as a guide. Bake on lowest oven rack at 500° for 8 minutes.
6. Arrange tomato slices on paper towels. Cover with additional paper towels; let stand 5 minutes.
7. Sprinkle fontina over crust, leaving a ¼-inch border. Arrange tomato slices and olives over fontina; sprinkle with mozzarella. Top with pine nuts. Bake on middle rack an additional 8 minutes or until crust is golden brown and cheese melts. Garnish with cracked pepper, if desired. Cut into 12 wedges. Yield: 6 servings (serving size: 2 wedges).

CALORIES 341 (29% from fat); FAT 10.9g (sat 5g, mono 3.7g, poly 1.4g); PROTEIN 14.6g; CARB 47.3g; FIBER 4.5g; CHOL 27mg; IRON 2.9mg; SODIUM 502mg; CALC 186mg

Basil and Three-Cheese Thin-Crust Pizza

Inspired by the original Margherita pizza from Naples, this version features a spicy red sauce, ricotta and mozzarella cheeses, and a sprinkling of fresh basil. Use a gentle hand while rolling this thin crust. If the dough tears, just gather it into a ball, cover with plastic wrap, and let it rest for 10 minutes before re-rolling. Place the dough in the refrigerator for its first rise to ensure the crust stays thin.

DOUGH:

1 teaspoon honey
1½ teaspoons active dry yeast
½ cup warm water (100° to 110°)
1¼ cups all-purpose flour (about 5½ ounces), divided
¼ teaspoon salt
Cooking spray
2 tablespoons stone-ground yellow cornmeal
1½ teaspoons olive oil

REMAINING INGREDIENTS:

Spicy Pizza Sauce (recipe on page 333)
¾ cup (3 ounces) shredded part-skim mozzarella cheese
½ cup part-skim ricotta
2 tablespoons finely grated fresh Parmesan cheese
3 tablespoons thinly sliced fresh basil

1. To prepare dough, dissolve honey and yeast in ½ cup warm water in a large bowl; let stand 5 minutes. Lightly spoon flour into dry measuring cups; level with a knife. Add 1 cup flour and salt to yeast mixture; stir until a soft dough forms. Turn dough out onto a lightly floured surface. Knead until smooth and elastic (about 6 minutes); add enough of remaining flour, 1 tablespoon at a time, to prevent dough from sticking to hands (dough will feel slightly sticky). Place dough in a large bowl coated with cooking spray, turning to coat top. Cover and chill 1 hour.
2. Position one oven rack in middle setting. Position another rack in lowest setting, and place a rimless baking sheet on bottom rack. Preheat oven to 500°.
3. Roll dough into a 13-inch circle (about ¼ inch thick) on a lightly floured surface. Place dough on a rimless baking sheet sprinkled with cornmeal. Crimp edges of dough with fingers to form a rim. Brush oil over dough. Remove preheated baking sheet from oven; close oven door. Slide dough onto preheated baking sheet, using a spatula as a guide. Bake on lowest oven rack at 500° for 5 minutes. Remove from oven.
4. Spread Spicy Pizza Sauce in an even layer over crust, leaving a ¼-inch border.

Combine mozzarella and ricotta; sprinkle evenly over sauce. Top with Parmesan. Bake on middle rack an additional 10 minutes or until crust is golden brown and cheese melts. Sprinkle with basil. Cut into 8 wedges. Yield: 4 servings (serving size: 2 wedges).

CALORIES 328 (24% from fat); FAT 8.7g (sat 4.3g, mono 3.2g, poly 0.6g); PROTEIN 15.7g; CARB 45.7g; FIBER 4.2g; CHOL 23mg; IRON 3.2mg; SODIUM 520mg; CALC 283mg

Sausage and Vegetable Deep-Dish Pizza

Unlike our other pizzas, the crust for this pizza is intended to be thick. Use a spatula to serve its substantial squares straight from the pan.

DOUGH:

2 teaspoons honey
1 package active dry yeast (about 2¼ teaspoons)
1 cup warm water (100° to 110°)
2½ cups all-purpose flour (about 11¼ ounces), divided
1 tablespoon yellow cornmeal
½ teaspoon salt
Cooking spray

SAUCE:

2 cups chopped zucchini
¼ cup chopped onion
1 (8-ounce) package mushrooms, sliced
¼ cup white wine
⅛ teaspoon black pepper
2 cups fat-free garlic-and-onion pasta sauce (such as Muir Glen Organic)
8 ounces hot turkey Italian sausage

REMAINING INGREDIENTS:

2 teaspoons olive oil
1½ cups (6 ounces) shredded part-skim mozzarella cheese
½ cup (2 ounces) grated Parmesan cheese

1. To prepare dough, dissolve honey and yeast in 1 cup warm water in a large bowl; let stand 5 minutes. Lightly spoon flour into dry measuring cups; level with a knife. Add 2¼ cups flour, cornmeal, and salt to yeast mixture; stir until a soft dough forms. Turn dough out onto a lightly floured surface. Knead until smooth and elastic (about 6 minutes); add enough of remaining flour, 1 tablespoon at a time, to prevent dough from sticking to hands (dough will feel sticky). Place dough in a large bowl coated with cooking spray, turning to coat top. Cover and let rise in a warm place (85°), free from drafts, 45 minutes or until doubled in size. (Gently press two fingers into dough. If indentation remains, dough has risen enough.)

2. To prepare sauce, while dough rises, heat a large saucepan over medium-high heat. Coat pan with cooking spray. Add zucchini, onion, and mushrooms to pan; sauté 7 minutes or until vegetables are lightly browned. Add wine and pepper; cook 1 minute or until liquid almost evaporates. Stir in sauce. Remove from heat; cool.

3. Remove casings from sausage. Cook sausage in a large nonstick skillet over medium-high heat until browned, stirring to crumble. Drain; add to sauce.

4. Position one oven rack in middle setting. Position another rack in lowest setting. Preheat oven to 475°.

5. Brush a 13 x 9–inch baking pan with oil. Turn dough into pan. Gently press dough in bottom and up sides of pan. Lightly spray surface of dough with cooking spray. Cover with plastic wrap; let stand 5 minutes. Remove plastic wrap; discard. Spoon sauce mixture into crust. Bake on bottom rack at 475° for 20 minutes. Remove from oven.

6. Combine cheeses; sprinkle evenly over sauce. Bake on middle rack an additional 15 minutes or until crust is golden brown and cheese melts. Cool 10 minutes on a wire rack. Cut into 6 squares. Yield: 6 servings (serving size: 1 square).

CALORIES 434 (27% from fat); FAT 12.8g (sat 5.9g, mono 4.1g, poly 1.4g); PROTEIN 24.6g; CARB 54.2g; FIBER 3.9g; CHOL 45mg; IRON 3.8mg; SODIUM 682mg; CALC 336mg

Easy Crust Additions

Our Basic Pizza Dough (recipe on page 330) yields a delicious crust. And you can customize the flavor and texture by adding ingredients during the last minute or so of kneading to enhance the flavor of the crust without overwhelming the toppings.

Wheat Germ Dough: Replace ¼ cup all-purpose flour with ¼ cup toasted wheat germ.

Asian Dough: Add 2 teaspoons raw sesame seeds.

Herb Dough: Add 2 tablespoons chopped fresh herbs (use a mix of herbs or just one, such as basil or oregano).

Nutty Dough: Add 2 tablespoons finely chopped walnuts or pecans.

Cheese Dough: Add 2 tablespoons finely grated Parmesan, fontina, or other cheese.

Pepper Dough: Add 1 teaspoon coarsely ground black pepper.

STAFF FAVORITE
Wild Mushroom Pizza

Monterey Jack cheese pairs nicely with mushrooms and salty prosciutto. You can easily substitute your favorite mild white cheese, if you prefer.

1 teaspoon butter
2 teaspoons olive oil, divided
1½ pounds mixed wild mushrooms, sliced ¼ inch thick
¼ teaspoon salt
⅛ teaspoon freshly ground black pepper
Basic Pizza Dough (recipe on page 330)
1 cup (4 ounces) shredded Monterey Jack cheese
2 ounces thinly sliced prosciutto
1 tablespoon chopped fresh flat-leaf parsley

1. Position one oven rack in middle setting. Position another rack in the lowest
Continued

setting, and place a rimless baking sheet on bottom rack. Preheat oven to 500°.

2. Melt butter in a large nonstick skillet over medium-high heat; add 1 teaspoon oil to pan. Add mushrooms; sauté 10 minutes or until moisture evaporates. Sprinkle with salt and pepper; stir to combine.

3. Remove plastic wrap from Basic Pizza Dough; discard. Brush 1 teaspoon oil evenly over dough. Remove preheated baking sheet from oven; close oven door. Slide dough onto preheated baking sheet, using a spatula as a guide. Bake on lowest oven rack at 500° for 8 minutes. Remove from oven.

4. Spread mushroom mixture in an even layer over crust, leaving a ¼-inch border. Top with cheese. Slice prosciutto crosswise into thin strips; sprinkle over pizza. Bake on middle rack an additional 10 minutes or until crust is golden brown and cheese melts. Sprinkle with parsley. Cut into 12 wedges. Yield: 6 servings (serving size: 2 wedges).

CALORIES 324 (26% from fat); FAT 9.4g (sat 4.6g, mono 3.4g, poly 0.8g); PROTEIN 15.3g; CARB 45.3g; FIBER 2.5g; CHOL 24mg; IRON 3.1mg; SODIUM 552mg; CALC 172mg

---

Pizza Extras

Although our recipes don't require specialty equipment, consider these affordable items to make the task easier.

Pizza stone ($25): A round terra-cotta slab is the best tool for home cooks to mimic the conditions of a pizzeria oven. The stone absorbs excess moisture from the dough to create a crisp crust. Preheat the stone while the oven preheats, following the manufacturer's specifications for oven temperature.

Pizza peel ($15): This large, flat, usually wooden paddle is used to slide pizza dough onto a preheated baking sheet or pizza stone.

Pizza wheel ($10): A round blade attached to a handle, use this tool to slice pizza.

Look for pizza equipment at discount stores, houseware emporiums, kitchen shops, or online (www.amazon.com).

Pepperoni Pizza

(pictured on page 247)

Sautéed mushrooms add earthy flavor to this familiar favorite, but they're optional. Substitute white button mushrooms, if desired. Omit both if you prefer classic pepperoni pizza.

Cooking spray
2 cups thinly sliced cremini mushrooms (about 4 ounces)
Basic Pizza Dough (recipe on page 330)
2 teaspoons olive oil
Basic Pizza Sauce (recipe on page 333)
1½ cups (6 ounces) shredded part-skim mozzarella cheese
2 tablespoons grated fresh Parmesan cheese
2 ounces sliced turkey pepperoni (such as Hormel)

1. Position one oven rack in middle setting. Position another rack in lowest setting, and place a rimless baking sheet on bottom rack. Preheat oven to 500°.

2. Heat a large nonstick skillet over medium-high heat. Coat pan with cooking spray. Add sliced mushrooms to pan, and sauté 5 minutes or until moisture evaporates.

3. Remove plastic wrap from Basic Pizza Dough; discard. Brush oil over dough. Remove preheated baking sheet from oven; close oven door. Slide dough onto preheated baking sheet, using a spatula as a guide. Bake on lowest oven rack at 500° for 8 minutes. Remove from oven.

4. Spread Basic Pizza Sauce in an even layer over crust, leaving a ¼-inch border. Top sauce with mushrooms. Sprinkle mushrooms evenly with mozzarella and Parmesan. Arrange pepperoni in an even layer on top of cheese. Bake on middle rack an additional 10 minutes or until crust is golden brown and cheese melts. Cut into 12 wedges. Yield: 6 servings (serving size: 2 wedges).

CALORIES 346 (21% from fat); FAT 8.2g (sat 3.8g, mono 3g, poly 0.8g); PROTEIN 18.1g; CARB 49.5g; FIBER 3.6g; CHOL 29mg; IRON 4mg; SODIUM 692mg; CALC 249mg

---

WINE NOTE: A crisp, acidic Italian red like Chianti is absolutely the best choice for this pizza or for any pizzas that have many toppings.

Cheese Pizza

Since this recipe calls for commercial pizza sauce, all you need to prepare is the dough. If you prefer homemade sauce, ladle on our Basic Pizza Sauce (recipe on page 333) and substitute your favorite cheese instead.

Basic Pizza Dough (recipe on page 330)
2 teaspoons olive oil
1 cup fat-free bottled pizza sauce
2 cups (8 ounces) shredded part-skim mozzarella cheese
½ cup (2 ounces) grated fresh Parmesan cheese

1. Position one oven rack in middle setting. Position another rack in lowest setting, and place a rimless baking sheet on bottom rack. Preheat oven to 500°.

2. Remove plastic wrap from Basic Pizza Dough; discard plastic. Brush oil over dough. Remove preheated baking sheet from oven, and close oven door. Slide dough onto preheated baking sheet, using a spatula as a guide. Bake on lowest oven rack at 500° for 8 minutes. Remove from oven.

3. Spread sauce in an even layer over crust, leaving a ¼-inch border. Top with mozzarella and Parmesan cheeses. Bake on middle rack an additional 10 minutes or until crust is golden brown and cheese melts. Cut into 12 wedges. Yield: 6 servings (serving size: 2 wedges).

CALORIES 356 (27% from fat); FAT 10.8g (sat 5.8g, mono 3.7g, poly 0.7g); PROTEIN 19.1g; CARB 44.5g; FIBER 2.5g; CHOL 30mg; IRON 3mg; SODIUM 633mg; CALC 357mg

---

WINE NOTE: For a simple pizza such as this, a crisp white like a pinot grigio fills the bill. Pinot grigio is inexpensive and easy to find.

sidetracked

In the Bag

Prepackaged coleslaw mixes yield simple yet flavorful side dishes.

Although the weather is still pleasant enough for outdoor grilling, we find ourselves craving fresh side dishes at this point in the season. We want something with a little more crunch and more assertive flavor.

A crisp slaw can fill the bill. Fortunately, it's now easy to create your own fresh-tasting salad with the convenient preshredded bagged coleslaw mixes found in the supermarket produce section. They come in several sizes (eight-, 10-, 12-, and 16-ounce packages) and varieties.

Create your own simple dressing, add one or two more embellishments (diced fresh pineapple, raisins, pumpkinseed and sunflower seed kernels, walnuts, almonds, or pecans, to name a few), and you'll have a side dish that rounds out a late-summer dinner.

QUICK & EASY • MAKE AHEAD
Poppy Seed Fruited Slaw
(pictured on page 246)

COLESLAW:
- ½ cup orange sections
- 1 cup halved seedless red grapes
- 1 (16-ounce) package cabbage-and-carrot coleslaw

DRESSING:
- ¼ cup sugar
- 3 tablespoons cider vinegar
- 4 teaspoons canola oil
- 1 tablespoon minced fresh onion
- 1 teaspoon poppy seeds
- ½ teaspoon dry mustard
- ¼ teaspoon salt

1. To prepare coleslaw, chop orange sections. Combine oranges, grapes, and coleslaw in a large bowl.
2. To prepare dressing, combine sugar and remaining 6 ingredients, stirring with a whisk until sugar dissolves. Add dressing mixture to cabbage mixture, and toss well. Cover and chill for 30 minutes before serving. Yield: 6 servings (serving size: 1 cup).

CALORIES 114 (28% from fat); FAT 3.6g (sat 0.3g, mono 1.9g, poly 1.1g); PROTEIN 1.6g; CARB 21.3g; FIBER 1g; CHOL 0mg; IRON 0.7mg; SODIUM 114mg; CALC 56mg

QUICK & EASY • MAKE AHEAD
Superspeedy Broccoli Slaw

Look for bottled dressing in the refrigerated part of the produce section.

- 1 cup chopped fresh pineapple
- ¼ cup bottled light coleslaw dressing (such as Marzetti)
- 3 tablespoons toasted sunflower seed kernels
- 1 (12-ounce) package broccoli coleslaw

1. Combine all ingredients in a large bowl; toss well. Cover and chill. Yield: 6 servings (serving size: about 1 cup).

CALORIES 90 (43% from fat); FAT 4.4g (sat 0.5g, mono 0.4g, poly 1.3g); PROTEIN 2.5g; CARB 10.8g; FIBER 2.5g; CHOL 8mg; IRON 0.7mg; SODIUM 147mg; CALC 20mg

QUICK & EASY
Smoky Cabbage Slaw

- ½ cup chopped Oso Sweet or other sweet onion
- ½ cup diced red bell pepper
- 1 (16-ounce) package cabbage-and-carrot coleslaw
- 1 slice bacon, cooked and crumbled (drained)
- ½ cup seasoned rice wine vinegar
- ¼ cup sugar
- 1 tablespoon canola oil
- 2½ teaspoons dry mustard
- 1 teaspoon celery seeds

1. Combine first 4 ingredients in a large bowl.
2. Combine vinegar and remaining 4 ingredients in a small saucepan. Bring to a boil; cook 1 minute, stirring frequently.

Pour over cabbage mixture; toss gently. Serve immediately. Yield: 6 servings (serving size: 1 cup).

CALORIES 112 (28% from fat); FAT 3.6g (sat 0.4g, mono 1.6g, poly 0.8g); PROTEIN 2.3g; CARB 19.4g; FIBER 0.6g; CHOL 1mg; IRON 0.8mg; SODIUM 446mg; CALC 47mg

QUICK & EASY • MAKE AHEAD
Tart and Tangy Chopped Cabbage Slaw

- 1 (16-ounce) package cabbage-and-carrot coleslaw
- 2 tablespoons minced red onion
- ¼ cup low-fat mayonnaise
- 2 tablespoons sugar
- 1 tablespoon 2% reduced-fat milk
- 1 tablespoon low-fat buttermilk
- 1 tablespoon fresh lemon juice
- 1½ teaspoons prepared horseradish
- 1½ teaspoons white vinegar
- ¼ teaspoon salt
- ⅛ teaspoon black pepper

1. Place half of coleslaw in food processor; pulse 6 times. Place in a large bowl. Repeat with remaining coleslaw. Add onion to coleslaw.
2. Combine mayonnaise and remaining 8 ingredients, stirring with a whisk. Add to slaw mixture; toss well. Cover and chill. Yield: 6 servings (serving size: ⅔ cup).

CALORIES 57 (14% from fat); FAT 0.9g (sat 0.1g, mono 0.4g, poly 0.3g); PROTEIN 1.3g; CARB 12.2g; FIBER 0.3g; CHOL 0mg; IRON 0.5mg; SODIUM 214mg; CALC 43mg

QUICK & EASY • MAKE AHEAD
Spicy Asian Slaw

- 1 cup matchstick-cut carrots
- ½ cup thinly sliced green onions
- 1 (16-ounce) package cabbage-and-carrot coleslaw
- 3 tablespoons seasoned rice vinegar
- 2 tablespoons low-sodium soy sauce
- 1 tablespoon creamy peanut butter
- 1 tablespoon fresh lime juice
- 1 tablespoon canola oil
- 2 teaspoons chile paste with garlic (such as sambal oelek)
- 2 tablespoons chopped dry-roasted peanuts

Continued

1. Combine first 3 ingredients in a large bowl. Combine vinegar and next 5 ingredients, stirring well with a whisk. Add vinegar mixture and peanuts to cabbage mixture; toss well. Yield: 6 servings (serving size: 1 cup).

CALORIES 105 (49% from fat); FAT 5.7g (sat 0.9g, mono 2g, poly 1.2g); PROTEIN 3.3g; CARB 12.2g; FIBER 3g; CHOL 0mg; IRON 1.1mg; SODIUM 439mg; CALC 54mg

---

QUICK & EASY • MAKE AHEAD
Waldorf Slaw

Inspired by the original Waldorf salad, this slaw is good with grilled chicken or pork. Although we call for Braeburn, use your favorite crisp apple in this recipe.

  2 cups chopped Braeburn apple
     (about 1 large apple)
  1 cup chopped peeled Bartlett pear
     (about 1 pear)
  ½ cup raisins
  3 tablespoons chopped walnuts
  1 (16-ounce) package cabbage-and-
     carrot coleslaw
  ½ cup low-fat mayonnaise
  ½ cup low-fat buttermilk
  1 teaspoon grated lemon rind
  2 tablespoons fresh lemon juice
  ¼ teaspoon salt
  ⅛ teaspoon freshly ground black
     pepper

1. Combine first 5 ingredients in a large bowl.
2. Combine mayonnaise and remaining 5 ingredients, stirring well with a whisk. Drizzle mayonnaise mixture over cabbage mixture, and toss to coat. Cover and refrigerate 30 minutes. Yield: 10 cups (serving size: 1 cup).

CALORIES 89 (33% from fat); FAT 3.3g (sat 0.6g, mono 0.3g, poly 1.1g); PROTEIN 1.7g; CARB 15.4g; FIBER 1.2g; CHOL 0mg; IRON 0.5mg; SODIUM 187mg; CALC 44mg

---

new american classic
Spaghetti and Meatballs

Spaghetti and meatballs is an American specialty.

In Italy, pasta and meat are traditionally served separately. But immigrants who opened restaurants in this country discovered that American diners didn't have patience for a leisurely repast, so chefs created meatball red sauce. It's become a beloved addition to the American recipe box ever since. Our version takes some liberties with tradition. The meatballs are made with ground sirloin and turkey Italian sausage. Fresh herbs brighten the flavor. But we bow to tradition with a shower of Parmigiano-Reggiano added before serving for a classically delicious finish.

STAFF FAVORITE
Spaghetti and Meatballs

SAUCE:
   Cooking spray
  1 cup finely chopped onion
  3 garlic cloves, minced
  2 tablespoons tomato paste
  ¼ teaspoon salt
  1 (14-ounce) can less-sodium beef
     broth
  2 (28-ounce) cans whole peeled
     tomatoes, undrained and
     chopped

MEATBALLS:
  1 (1-ounce) slice white bread
  2 (4-ounce) links sweet turkey
     Italian sausage, casings removed
  ½ cup finely chopped onion
  ⅓ cup chopped fresh basil
  ¼ cup chopped fresh parsley
  2 tablespoons egg substitute
  ½ teaspoon freshly ground black
     pepper
  ¼ teaspoon salt
  2 garlic cloves, minced
  1 large egg, lightly beaten
  1 pound ground sirloin

REMAINING INGREDIENTS:
  ½ cup chopped fresh parsley
  ⅓ cup chopped fresh basil
  1 pound hot cooked spaghetti
  ½ cup (2 ounces) grated fresh
     Parmigiano-Reggiano
     Parsley sprigs (optional)

1. To prepare sauce, heat a large nonstick skillet over medium-high heat. Coat pan with cooking spray. Add 1 cup onion; sauté 3 minutes. Add 3 garlic cloves, and sauté 1 minute. Add tomato paste; cook 1 minute. Stir in ¼ teaspoon salt and broth. Cook 4 minutes. Stir in tomatoes. Reduce heat, and simmer 45 minutes, stirring occasionally.
2. Preheat broiler.
3. To prepare meatballs, place bread in a food processor; process until fine crumbs measure ½ cup. Combine crumbs, sausage, and next 9 ingredients in a bowl. With wet hands, shape sirloin mixture into 32 meatballs. Place meatballs on a broiler pan. Broil 15 minutes or until done. Add meatballs to sauce; simmer 15 minutes. Sprinkle with ½ cup parsley and ⅓ cup basil. Serve over spaghetti. Sprinkle with cheese; garnish with parsley sprigs, if desired. Yield: 8 servings (serving size: 1 cup spaghetti, about ½ cup sauce, 4 meatballs, and 1 tablespoon cheese).

CALORIES 291 (25% from fat); FAT 8g (sat 3.2g, mono 2.5g, poly 1.3g); PROTEIN 24.3g; CARB 32.2g; FIBER 4.1g; CHOL 76mg; IRON 7.4mg; SODIUM 873mg; CALC 163mg

WINE NOTE: Spaghetti and Meatballs is terrific with red or white wine as long as the wine has good acidity to mirror that of the tomatoes and act as a counterpoint to the meatballs. Because our recipe has fresh herbs, we prefer white wine with the dish—in particular, an herbal dry white from southern Italy such as Feudi di San Gregorio Greco di Tufo 2004 ($22).

Superfood in a Can

The antioxidant lycopene confers a host of health perks. And an excellent source is probably already in your pantry.

Scientists are finding evidence that the red-pigmented antioxidant lycopene, found in many fruits and vegetables—especially tomatoes—may play an important role in reducing risks of many diseases, including cancer. While acquiring lycopene can be as simple as smearing ketchup on a sandwich bun or sipping a cup of tomato juice, there are many ways to boost the antioxidant in your diet (see "Easy Ways to Add Lycopene" on page 342). The recipes here offer tasty options. Some, like Hearty Beef and Tomato Stew (recipe below) and Romesco Sauce (recipe on page 341), use several tomato products. Plus, you'll enjoy flavorful, satisfying new ways to reap the health benefits of lycopene.

MAKE AHEAD • FREEZABLE
Hearty Beef and Tomato Stew

Serve with crusty slices of a baguette. A double-dose of lycopene comes with tomato paste and canned tomatoes.
LYCOPENE COUNT: 11 milligrams per serving

- 2 teaspoons olive oil
- 2 pounds sirloin steak, trimmed and cut into ½-inch cubes
- 1 cup finely chopped onion (about 1 medium)
- 3 garlic cloves, minced
- 1 tablespoon tomato paste
- 1½ cups fat-free, less-sodium beef broth
- 4 cups cubed red potato (1½ pounds)
- 2 cups sliced carrot
- ¾ cup pinot noir or other spicy dry red wine
- 2 teaspoons chopped fresh thyme
- 1 (16-ounce) package frozen pearl onions
- 1 (28-ounce) can crushed tomatoes, undrained
- 1 rosemary sprig
- 1 bay leaf
- 1 teaspoon salt
- ¾ teaspoon freshly ground black pepper
- ½ cup chopped fresh parsley

1. Heat oil in a large Dutch oven over medium-high heat. Add beef; cook 5 minutes or until browned, stirring frequently. Remove beef from pan, reserving 1 tablespoon drippings in pan. Add onion and garlic to pan; sauté 2 minutes or until onion begins to brown. Add tomato paste; cook 1 minute, stirring frequently. Add broth; bring to a boil. Return meat to pan. Add potato and next 7 ingredients; bring to a simmer. Cover and cook 1 hour and 15 minutes or until vegetables are tender, stirring occasionally. Discard rosemary and bay leaf. Stir in salt and pepper. Top with parsley. Yield: 8 servings (serving size: 1½ cups stew and 1 tablespoon parsley).

CALORIES 329 (21% from fat); FAT 7.5g (sat 2.6g, mono 3.3g, poly 0.4g); PROTEIN 31.1g; CARB 33.3g; FIBER 4.1g; CHOL 51mg; IRON 4.3mg; SODIUM 630mg; CALC 93mg

More Than Lycopene

You can get lycopene in a supplement, but consuming foods like canned tomatoes or guava bestows benefits beyond lycopene, including vitamins A, C, and E; folate; potassium; and fiber. And these nutrients may work with lycopene to offer health benefits.

African Chicken in Spicy Red Sauce

This flavorful Ethiopian-inspired chicken stew uses Berbere, an Ethiopian spice blend. Store extra spice mix covered in a cool, dark place for up to two weeks. Use leftovers on salmon, flank steak, or chicken for fiery flavor. Serve with basmati rice.
LYCOPENE COUNT: 12 milligrams per serving

CHICKEN:

- 2 chicken breast halves, skinned (about ½ pound)
- 2 chicken drumsticks, skinned (about ½ pound)
- 2 chicken thighs, skinned (about ¾ pound)
- 3 tablespoons fresh lemon juice (1 lemon)
- ¾ teaspoon salt, divided
- Cooking spray
- 1½ cups chopped onion (2 medium)
- 1 tablespoon minced garlic
- 2 teaspoons Berbere (recipe on page 340)
- 1 tablespoon butter
- 1 tablespoon minced peeled fresh ginger
- ½ teaspoon ground nutmeg
- ½ teaspoon ground cardamom
- ½ cup dry red wine
- 1 (14-ounce) can fat-free, less-sodium chicken broth
- 1 (6-ounce) can no-salt-added tomato paste
- 2 tablespoons chopped fresh cilantro
- 4 lemon wedges

1. Place chicken in a shallow dish; drizzle with juice, and sprinkle with ½ teaspoon salt. Cover and marinate in refrigerator 30 minutes.
2. Heat a Dutch oven over medium heat. Coat pan with cooking spray. Add onion and garlic; cook 5 minutes (do not brown), stirring frequently. Add ¼ teaspoon salt, Berbere, and next 4 ingredients; cook 1 minute. Add wine, broth, and tomato paste; stir until well blended. Add chicken mixture; bring to a boil. Cover, reduce heat, and simmer 50 minutes or
Continued

until chicken is tender, turning chicken occasionally. Stir in cilantro. Serve with lemon wedges. Yield: 4 servings (serving size: 3 ounces chicken, about 1 cup sauce, and 1 lemon wedge).

(Totals include Berbere) CALORIES 373 (24% from fat); FAT 9.8g (sat 3.6g, mono 2.7g, poly 1.8g); PROTEIN 53.2g; CARB 17.3g; FIBER 3.6g; CHOL 175mg; IRON 4mg; SODIUM 848mg; CALC 72mg

QUICK & EASY • MAKE AHEAD
BERBERE:

- 2 tablespoons ground red pepper
- 1 tablespoon freshly ground black pepper
- 1 teaspoon ground ginger
- 1 teaspoon ground cinnamon
- ¼ teaspoon ground cloves

1. Combine all ingredients in a small bowl. Yield: ¼ cup (serving size: 1 teaspoon).

CALORIES 6 (30% from fat); FAT 0.2g (sat 0g, mono 0g, poly 0.1g); PROTEIN 0.2g; CARB 1.1g; FIBER 0.5g; CHOL 0mg; IRON 0.2mg; SODIUM 1mg; CALC 6mg

QUICK & EASY • MAKE AHEAD
FREEZABLE
Southwestern Chicken Chili

This meal comes together in a snap. Serve with baked tortilla chips and margaritas.
LYCOPENE COUNT: 20 milligrams per serving

- Cooking spray
- 1 cup chopped onion (1 medium)
- 1 cup diced green bell pepper (about 1)
- 2 garlic cloves, minced
- 1 pound skinless, boneless chicken breast, cut into ½-inch cubes
- ¼ cup chopped fresh cilantro
- ¼ cup strong brewed coffee
- 1 tablespoon chili powder
- 1 teaspoon brown sugar
- ½ teaspoon ground red pepper
- 2 (15-ounce) cans kidney beans, rinsed and drained
- 1 (28-ounce) can diced tomatoes, undrained
- 3 tablespoons water
- 1 tablespoon masa harina or finely ground cornmeal
- Chopped fresh cilantro (optional)

1. Heat a Dutch oven over medium heat. Coat pan with cooking spray. Add onion, bell pepper, and garlic; cook 5 minutes or until onion is translucent, stirring frequently. Add chicken; cook 5 minutes, stirring frequently. Stir in ¼ cup cilantro and next 6 ingredients; bring to a boil. Cover, reduce heat, and simmer 10 minutes.
2. Combine 3 tablespoons water and masa harina in a small bowl. Add to chicken mixture, stirring well. Simmer, uncovered, 10 minutes. Garnish with cilantro, if desired. Yield: 4 servings (serving size: about 1½ cups).

CALORIES 311 (10% from fat); FAT 3.5g (sat 0.8g, mono 1g, poly 0.9g); PROTEIN 33.6g; CARB 36.7g; FIBER 10.5g; CHOL 65mg; IRON 3.4mg; SODIUM 749mg; CALC 98mg

MAKE AHEAD
Tomato Chickpea Curry

Serve over steamed brown rice as a side with grilled chicken or pork. Look for garam masala in the spice section of the supermarket or Asian grocery store. Substitute yellow mustard seeds for the brown, or stir in 1½ teaspoons dry mustard or 1½ tablespoons prepared mustard with the chickpeas if you don't have mustard seeds.
LYCOPENE COUNT: 19 milligrams per serving

- 1 tablespoon canola oil
- 1 cup chopped onion (1 small)
- 1 tablespoon minced peeled fresh ginger
- 1 garlic clove, minced
- 2 teaspoons garam masala
- 1½ teaspoons brown mustard seeds
- ¼ to ½ teaspoon ground red pepper
- ½ cup light coconut milk
- 1 tablespoon chopped seeded jalapeño pepper
- 1 teaspoon sugar
- ½ teaspoon ground turmeric
- 2 (15½-ounce) cans chickpeas (garbanzo beans), rinsed and drained
- 1 (28-ounce) can diced tomatoes, undrained
- 1 (8-ounce) can no-salt-added tomato sauce
- 3 tablespoons chopped fresh cilantro

1. Heat oil in a large nonstick skillet over medium heat. Add onion, ginger, and garlic; cook 5 minutes. Stir in garam masala, mustard seeds, and red pepper; cook 2 minutes, stirring frequently. Stir in coconut milk and next 6 ingredients; bring to a boil.
2. Reduce heat, and simmer 35 minutes, stirring occasionally. Remove from heat; stir in cilantro. Yield: 6 servings (serving size: 1 cup).

CALORIES 213 (26% from fat); FAT 6.2g (sat 1.2g, mono 2.4g, poly 2.3g); PROTEIN 7.4g; CARB 34.3g; FIBER 8.6g; CHOL 0mg; IRON 3mg; SODIUM 459mg; CALC 81mg

Fettuccine with Clams and Tomato Sauce

Each serving provides what research indicates is a beneficial daily amount of lycopene.
LYCOPENE COUNT: 31 milligrams per serving

- 2 tablespoons olive oil
- 1 cup chopped onion (1 small)
- 3 garlic cloves, minced
- 2 cups low-sodium tomato juice
- ½ cup dry white wine
- ¼ teaspoon salt
- ¼ teaspoon crushed red pepper
- 48 littleneck clams in shells, scrubbed (about 2¾ pounds)
- 1 (28-ounce) can diced tomatoes, undrained
- ¼ cup chopped fresh parsley
- 4 cups hot cooked fettuccine (about 8 ounces uncooked pasta)

1. Heat oil in a large Dutch oven over medium heat. Add onion and garlic; cook 4 minutes or until onion is tender, stirring occasionally. Add juice and next 5 ingredients; bring to a boil. Cover, reduce heat, and simmer 8 minutes or until shells open. Remove clams from pan. Discard any unopened shells. Add parsley to pan; cook until liquid is reduced to 4 cups (about 15 minutes). Serve clams and sauce over pasta. Yield: 4 servings (servings size: 1 cup pasta, 1 cup sauce, and 12 clams).

CALORIES 475 (18% from fat); FAT 9.4g (sat 1.4g, mono 5.1g, poly 1.3g); PROTEIN 32.7g; CARB 65g; FIBER 6.4g; CHOL 59mg; IRON 27.7mg; SODIUM 590mg; CALC 151mg

Oven-Dried Tomato on Toast Rounds

These roasted tomatoes are a great alternative to common sun-dried tomatoes. If you like, serve the roasted tomatoes over polenta, pork, chicken, or duck.

LYCOPENE COUNT: 21 milligrams per serving

12 plum tomatoes, peeled, seeded, and cut in half lengthwise
3 tablespoons olive oil
2 tablespoons chopped fresh herbs (rosemary, thyme, oregano)
6 garlic cloves, thinly sliced
1 teaspoon freshly ground black pepper
½ teaspoon salt
24 (½-inch-thick) slices French bread baguette, toasted
24 fresh basil leaves

1. Preheat oven to 250°.
2. Arrange tomato halves in a single layer in a 13 x 9–inch baking dish. Drizzle with oil; sprinkle with herbs, garlic, pepper, and salt. Bake at 250° for 4 hours. Place one dried tomato half on each toast round. Garnish each with 1 basil leaf. Yield: 12 servings (serving size: 2 toast rounds).

CALORIES 114 (30% from fat); FAT 3.8g (sat 0.5g, mono 2.5g, poly 0.4g); PROTEIN 3.2g; CARB 17.1g; FIBER 1.4g; CHOL 0mg; IRON 1.2mg; SODIUM 266mg; CALC 14mg

Sweet and Spicy Menu
serves 6

The sweetness of pineapple balances the spiciness of the pork.

Indian-Spiced Pork in Tomato Sauce

Pineapple salad*

Basmati rice

*Combine 4 cups cubed fresh pineapple, ½ cup very thinly vertically sliced red onion, 1 tablespoon thinly sliced fresh mint, 1 tablespoon fresh lime juice, 1 tablespoon honey, and ⅛ teaspoon salt.

Indian-Spiced Pork in Tomato Sauce

Pita bread or basmati rice would be good with this saucy dish. Toasting the whole spices before adding them to the other ingredients intensifies their flavors.

LYCOPENE COUNT: 13 milligrams per serving

1 teaspoon ground red pepper
1 teaspoon cumin seeds
1 teaspoon mustard seeds
½ teaspoon ground coriander
½ teaspoon ground cardamom
½ teaspoon ground cinnamon
¼ teaspoon black peppercorns
2 cups chopped onion (1 medium)
3 tablespoons white vinegar
1 tablespoon finely chopped fresh ginger
2 teaspoons sugar
6 garlic cloves, crushed
2 pounds boneless pork loin, trimmed and cut into ½-inch cubes
Cooking spray
1 cup fat-free, less-sodium chicken broth
4 cups (1½ pounds) baking potato, cut into ½-inch cubes
¾ teaspoon salt
1 (28-ounce) can diced tomatoes, undrained
Chopped fresh cilantro (optional)

1. Heat first 7 ingredients in a dry skillet over medium heat about 3 minutes or until fragrant, stirring frequently. Place in a blender or food processor. Add onion and next 4 ingredients; process 2 minutes or until well blended.
2. Combine pork and spice mixture in a glass bowl, tossing to coat. Cover and chill 30 minutes.
3. Heat a Dutch oven over medium heat. Coat pan with cooking spray. Add half of pork mixture; cook 5 minutes or until pork begins to brown, stirring frequently. Transfer to a bowl. Repeat procedure with cooking spray and remaining pork. Add broth to pan, scraping pan to loosen browned bits. Add pork mixture to pan. Stir in potato, salt, and tomatoes; bring to a boil. Cover, reduce heat, and simmer 1 hour or until potato is cooked and pork is tender, stirring occasionally. Garnish with cilantro, if desired. Yield: 6 servings (serving size: about 1½ cups).

CALORIES 383 (26% from fat); FAT 10.7g (sat 3.9g, mono 4.6g, poly 0.9g); PROTEIN 36.1g; CARB 35.8g; FIBER 5g; CHOL 90mg; IRON 3.2mg; SODIUM 611mg; CALC 93mg

Romesco Sauce

Serve this robust and smoky sauce over firm white fish or pork.

LYCOPENE COUNT: 7 milligrams per serving

2 red bell peppers
1 (28-ounce) can whole plum tomatoes, undrained
2 garlic cloves, peeled
Cooking spray
½ cup dry breadcrumbs
3 tablespoons organic vegetable broth (such as Swanson Certified Organic)
2 tablespoons white vinegar
2 tablespoons slivered almonds, toasted
2 tablespoons chopped fresh parsley
1 teaspoon crushed red pepper
1 tablespoon olive oil
¾ teaspoon Spanish smoked paprika
½ teaspoon salt

1. Preheat broiler.
2. Cut bell pepper in half lengthwise; discard seeds and membranes. Place pepper halves, skin sides up, on a foil-lined baking sheet; flatten with hand. Broil 10 minutes or until blackened. Place in a zip-top plastic bag; seal. Let stand 5 minutes. Peel and coarsely chop. Set aside.
3. Preheat oven to 275°.
4. Combine tomatoes and garlic in a 13 x 9–inch baking dish coated with cooking spray. Bake at 275° for 2½ hours or until most of liquid has evaporated.
5. Place bell peppers, tomato mixture, breadcrumbs, and remaining ingredients in a food processor; process until smooth. Yield: 12 servings (serving size: about ¼ cup).

CALORIES 56 (37% from fat); FAT 2.3g (sat 0.2g, mono 1.3g, poly 0.4g); PROTEIN 1.8g; CARB 7.6g; FIBER 1.4g; CHOL 0mg; IRON 1.1mg; SODIUM 228mg; CALC 35mg

Bloody Mary

(pictured on page 250)

You can use rum or tequila instead of vodka. Tomato juice is a concentrated source of lycopene; a ½ cup serving supplies one-third of a daily lycopene dose.

LYCOPENE COUNT: 8 milligrams per serving

    4   cups tomato juice
    1   cup vodka
    2   tablespoons fresh lemon juice
    1   to 1½ tablespoons prepared
        horseradish
    2   teaspoons hot sauce
    2   teaspoons Worcestershire sauce
    ½   teaspoon brown sugar
    ¼   teaspoon freshly ground black
        pepper
    ¼   teaspoon ground celery seeds
    Fresh lemon slices and celery sticks

1. Combine first 9 ingredients in a pitcher, stirring well. Serve over ice. Garnish with lemon slices and celery sticks. Yield: 10 servings (serving size: ½ cup).

CALORIES 76 (1% from fat); FAT 0.1g (sat 0g, mono 0g, poly 0g); PROTEIN 0.8g; CARB 5g; FIBER 0.5g; CHOL 0mg; IRON 0.5mg; SODIUM 284mg; CALC 13mg

---

Easy Ways to Add Lycopene

Current research suggests 30 milligrams daily is enough to offer lycopene's health benefits. Cooked tomatoes or processed tomato products, which are available year-round, have a greater concentration of lycopene than raw tomatoes. Besides tomatoes, other pink- and red-hued fruits contain lycopene. These are the lycopene amounts for some often-used products:

• 1 tablespoon tomato ketchup:
  2.5 milligrams

• 1 tablespoon chili sauce: 2.2 milligrams

• ¼ cup cocktail sauce: 7.3 milligrams

• ¼ cup tomato sauce: 9.3 milligrams

• ½ cup spaghetti sauce: 20 milligrams

These are some non-tomato sources:

• ½ pound watermelon: 10.3 milligrams

• 1 whole pink grapefruit: 2.9 milligrams

• 1 papaya: 3 milligrams

---

lighten up

All-Star Apple-Date Bars

A Georgia reader's tempting treat receives a timely makeover.

Jenny Rhodes of Perry, Georgia, received this recipe for Apple-Date Bars more than 30 years ago from a friend who brought them to a church potluck. "Now I only make this dessert for special occasions," Rhodes says since she now aims for a more balanced diet. Our goal was to lower the fat, cholesterol, and calories without compromising the delicate, buttery topping. We used seven tablespoons of butter—less than 1½ teaspoons per serving—to preserve the rich, smooth flavor of the bars, as well as maintain the lovely crust. But instead of using two whole eggs, we used one, plus two egg whites and ¼ cup of fat-free applesauce to help keep the batter moist while shaving almost five grams of total fat and nearly halving the saturated fat and cholesterol counts per serving. Even though the original version's one cup of pecans added heart-healthy fats, they also supplied surplus calories. We reduced it to ⅔ cup, which is plenty to maintain the recipe's signature crunch. We also sprinkled the apples with some fresh lemon juice to perk up their flavor and tossed the chopped dates with a spoonful of flour in order to maintain their firmness.

BEFORE	AFTER
SERVING SIZE	
1 bar	
CALORIES PER SERVING	
324	279
FAT	
13.9g	*9g*
PERCENT OF TOTAL CALORIES	
39%	*29%*
SODIUM	
211mg	*193mg*

Apple-Date Bars

You can use walnuts instead of pecans, or substitute raisins for the dates.

    2   cups all-purpose flour (about
        9 ounces)
    1   teaspoon baking soda
    1   teaspoon baking powder
    ½   teaspoon ground cinnamon
    ¼   teaspoon salt
    2   cups sugar
    7   tablespoons butter, softened
    1   large egg
    2   large egg whites
    ¼   cup applesauce
    1   teaspoon vanilla extract
    1   cup chopped pitted dates
    1   teaspoon all-purpose flour
    1½ cups chopped peeled Granny
        Smith apple (about 1 large)
    1½ cups chopped peeled Red
        Delicious apple (about 1
        large)
    ½   teaspoon fresh lemon juice
    ⅔   cup chopped pecans
    Cooking spray

1. Preheat oven to 325°.
2. Lightly spoon 2 cups flour into dry measuring cups; level with a knife. Combine 2 cups flour, soda, and next 3 ingredients in a large bowl; stir with a whisk. Set aside.
3. Place sugar and butter in a large bowl, and beat with a mixer at high speed 2 minutes or until light and fluffy. Add egg and egg whites, beating well after each addition. Stir in applesauce and vanilla. Gradually add flour mixture to sugar mixture; stir just until combined to form a stiff batter. Toss dates with 1 teaspoon flour. Toss apples with juice. Add dates, apples, and nuts to flour mixture, stirring just until combined. Pour batter into a 13 x 9–inch baking dish coated with cooking spray. Bake at 325° for 1 hour and 5 minutes or until a wooden pick inserted in center comes out clean. Cool completely on a wire rack. Yield: 16 servings (serving size: 1 bar).

CALORIES 279 (29% from fat); FAT 9g (sat 3.6g, mono 3.4g, poly 1.4g); PROTEIN 3.3g; CARB 48.5g; FIBER 2g; CHOL 26mg; IRON 1.1mg; SODIUM 193mg; CALC 33mg

---

Taking Mom's Advice

A Philadelphia student dresses up salmon with the traditional Moroccan flavors of her childhood.

Moroccan Salmon

Sweet peppers, tangy lemon slices, and heady spices come together in this simple dish that yields tender fish and vegetables in a flavorful sauce. Serve in bowls over couscous or basmati rice to soak up the tasty juices.

½ cup chopped fresh parsley
2 teaspoons olive oil
1 teaspoon fresh lemon juice
½ teaspoon salt
¼ teaspoon ground ginger
¼ teaspoon garlic powder
¼ teaspoon ground red pepper
¼ teaspoon ground cumin
¼ teaspoon freshly ground black pepper
2 garlic cloves, minced
4 (6-ounce) salmon fillets (about 1 inch thick)
Cooking spray
1 lemon
1½ cups thinly sliced red bell pepper (about 1 medium)
1½ cups thinly sliced green bell pepper (about 1 medium)
2 tablespoons water
1 large plum tomato, cut crosswise into ¼-inch-thick slices

1. Preheat oven to 400°.
2. Combine first 10 ingredients in a large bowl. Add salmon, turning to coat. Cover and let stand 15 minutes. Remove salmon from bowl, reserving marinade. Place salmon, skin side down, in a 13 x 9–inch baking dish coated with cooking spray.
3. Cut lemon in half lengthwise; cut 1 lemon half crosswise into ⅛-inch-thick

slices. Reserve remaining lemon half for another use. Add lemon slices, red and green bell pepper, water, and tomato to marinade; stir gently to coat. Arrange lemon mixture in an even layer over salmon; cover with foil. Bake at 400° for 20 minutes or until fish flakes easily when tested with a fork or until desired degree of doneness.
4. Place 1 fillet on each of 4 plates. Top each serving with about ½ cup lemon mixture, and drizzle each serving with about 2½ tablespoons pan juices. Yield: 4 servings.

CALORIES 319 (44% from fat); FAT 15.6g (sat 3.5g, mono 7.4g, poly 3.5g); PROTEIN 37.5g; CARB 6.7g; FIBER 2.3g; CHOL 87mg; IRON 1.5mg; SODIUM 383mg; CALC 50mg

MAKE AHEAD
Butternut Squash–Leek Soup

"I love my local organic farmers' market and like to cook with seasonal fare. I'm a professional organizer and include seasonal recipes in my newsletters for my clients. This was last winter's recipe." It's great as a side or a light main dish with a salad.

—Shannon Simmons, Redding, California

1 whole garlic head
4 teaspoons olive oil
6 cups thinly sliced leek (about 4 large)
4 cups (¾-inch) cubed peeled butternut squash (about 1 medium)
2 cups water
2 cups fat-free, less-sodium chicken broth
½ teaspoon salt
½ teaspoon freshly ground black pepper

1. Preheat oven to 350°.
2. Remove white papery skin from garlic head (do not peel or separate cloves). Wrap head in foil. Bake at 350° for 1 hour; cool 10 minutes. Separate cloves, and squeeze to extract garlic pulp. Discard skins.
3. Heat oil in a large saucepan over medium-high heat. Add leek; sauté 5

minutes or until tender. Stir in garlic, squash, and remaining ingredients; bring to a boil. Reduce heat, and simmer 10 minutes or until squash is tender. Place half of squash mixture in a blender. Remove center piece of blender lid (to allow steam to escape); secure lid on blender. Place a clean towel over opening in lid (to avoid splatters). Blend until smooth. Pour pureed soup into a bowl. Repeat procedure with remaining squash mixture. Yield: 6 servings (serving size: about 1 cup).

CALORIES 167 (19% from fat); FAT 3.5g (sat 0.5g, mono 2.2g, poly 0.6g); PROTEIN 4.1g; CARB 33.5g; FIBER 5.3g; CHOL 0mg; IRON 3.3mg; SODIUM 351mg; CALC 144mg

WINE NOTE: The creamy texture of the pureed soup matches well with a plump but crisp Chardonnay like J.J. Vincent Bourgogne Blanc ($15). It's suitably rich, round, and fruity, with gently buttery flavors and good acidity to balance the natural sweetness of the squash.

QUICK & EASY
Chicken Saltimbocca

"My husband first had this dish at a restaurant and loved the overall flavor but found it a bit too salty. We experimented at home to create our own recipe, which isn't as salty and still has all of the original taste."

—Amy Miller, Colgate, Wisconsin

4 (6-ounce) skinless, boneless chicken breast halves
1 teaspoon salt-free chicken seasoning (such as McCormick Grill Mates)
¼ teaspoon salt
¼ teaspoon freshly ground black pepper
4 fresh sage leaves, finely chopped
4 very thin slices prosciutto
½ cup all-purpose flour (about 2¼ ounces)
2 tablespoons olive oil
½ cup Marsala wine
½ cup fat-free, less-sodium chicken broth

Continued

1. Place each chicken breast half between 2 sheets of heavy-duty plastic wrap; pound to ¼-inch thickness using a meat mallet or small heavy skillet. Combine chicken seasoning, salt, and pepper; sprinkle over both sides of chicken. Sprinkle sage evenly onto undersides of breast halves; top each with 1 prosciutto slice. Place flour in a shallow dish; carefully dredge chicken in flour.

2. Heat oil in a large nonstick skillet over medium-high heat. Arrange chicken, prosciutto side up, in pan; cook 3 minutes. Carefully turn over; cook 3 minutes or until done. Add wine and broth to pan; simmer 5 minutes or until reduced to about ¼ cup. Serve sauce over chicken. Yield: 4 servings (serving size: 1 chicken breast half and 1 tablespoon sauce).

CALORIES 333 (28% from fat); FAT 10.5g (sat 2g, mono 6.2g, poly 1.4g); PROTEIN 44.5g; CARB 8.9g; FIBER 0.4g; CHOL 110mg; IRON 1.9mg; SODIUM 683mg; CALC 29mg

Spiced Caramel-Apple Soufflés

"What goes better with apple than caramel? The spiced apple offers a crisp bite and caramel syrup adds just enough contrast to the light soufflé to tantalize."

—Helen Fields, Springtown, Texas

1 tablespoon butter, softened and divided
1 tablespoon granulated sugar
1 tablespoon all-purpose flour
1 tablespoon brown sugar
2 large egg yolks, lightly beaten
1 (6-ounce) carton caramel fat-free yogurt
¼ teaspoon cream of tartar
4 large egg whites
¼ cup chopped bottled spiced apple rings (such as Lucky Leaf)
2 tablespoons fat-free caramel sundae syrup

1. Preheat oven to 425°.
2. Spread ½ teaspoon butter in each of 4 (8-ounce) ramekins; sprinkle evenly with granulated sugar.

3. Combine 1 teaspoon butter, flour, and next 3 ingredients in a medium bowl, stirring well with a whisk.
4. Place cream of tartar and egg whites in a large bowl; beat with a mixer at high speed until stiff peaks form. Gently fold one-fourth of egg white mixture into yogurt mixture; gently fold in remaining egg white mixture. Divide mixture evenly among prepared ramekins.
5. Place ramekins on a baking sheet. Bake at 425° for 10 minutes or until puffy and set.
6. Combine apple and caramel syrup; spoon 1 tablespoon apple mixture into center of each hot soufflé. Serve immediately. Yield: 4 servings (serving size: 1 soufflé).

CALORIES 160 (29% from fat); FAT 5.1g (sat 2.2g, mono 2.1g, poly 0.5g); PROTEIN 6.7g; CARB 21.9g; FIBER 0.2g; CHOL 111mg; IRON 0.6mg; SODIUM 138mg; CALC 90mg

Sunday Supper Menu
serves 8

Truffle oil and Parmesan cheese dress up ordinary mashed potatoes, but the potatoes remain comforting as ever in this meal fit for a family gathering.

Truffle-Parmesan Mashed Potatoes

Lemon-herb roasted chicken*

Steamed haricots verts

*Preheat oven to 400°. Combine 2 teaspoons chopped fresh rosemary, 2 teaspoons chopped fresh thyme, 2 teaspoons grated lemon rind, 1 teaspoon salt, ¾ teaspoon black pepper, and 3 minced garlic cloves; rub under skin of a 7-pound whole roasting chicken. Place chicken on a broiler pan coated with cooking spray. Bake at 400° for 1 hour and 10 minutes or until thermometer registers 165°. Let stand at least 15 minutes; discard skin.

Truffle-Parmesan Mashed Potatoes

"I try to experiment with making everyday foods (like mashed potatoes) healthier by cutting the fat and increasing the flavor. You only need a small amount of truffle oil and cheese to produce big flavor."

—LeeAnn Camut, Warrington, Pennsylvania

6 cups (1-inch) cubed peeled baking potato (about 2½ pounds)
½ cup (2 ounces) grated Parmigiano-Reggiano cheese
½ cup 2% reduced-fat milk
¼ cup fat-free, less-sodium chicken broth
2 tablespoons reduced-fat sour cream
1 tablespoon butter
1 teaspoon white truffle oil
½ teaspoon salt
¼ teaspoon freshly ground black pepper

1. Place potato in a medium saucepan; cover with water. Bring to a boil. Reduce heat, and simmer 20 minutes or until tender. Drain. Return potato to pan; add cheese and remaining ingredients. Beat with a mixer at medium speed until smooth, or mash with a potato masher until desired consistency. Yield: 8 servings (serving size: ⅔ cup).

CALORIES 185 (24% from fat); FAT 4.9g (sat 2.7g, mono 1.6g, poly 0.3g); PROTEIN 6.1g; CARB 29.8g; FIBER 2.6g; CHOL 13mg; IRON 0.5mg; SODIUM 295mg; CALC 109mg

Lovely Little Pies

These handmade pastries are a perfect marriage of light crust and delightful fillings.

Take your pick, and make a batch of sweet or savory dough to use with the fillings listed here. Or try stuffing our dough with the filling from your favorite pie recipe. One of the best features of these single-serving sides, entrées, and desserts is that they can be made ahead of time and refrigerated or frozen, so you can bake only what you need at the moment (see "Getting Ahead" on page 348).

Keep in mind that most pies, particularly fruit-filled ones, are best eaten the same day they're baked. For savory meat- and vegetable-filled turnovers or empanadas, leftovers will stay fresh for one to two days in the refrigerator. To reheat, place them on a baking sheet in a 300° oven for 10 to 15 minutes. The filling will be warm, and the crust—just the way you like it.

MAKE AHEAD • FREEZABLE
Brandied Apricot-Peach Pies

The honey-citrus notes of dried apricots enhance the frozen peaches in this baked version of the classic fried pie.

PIES:
- ½ cup diced dried apricots
- ¼ cup granulated sugar
- 1 tablespoon fresh lemon juice
- ½ teaspoon ground cinnamon
- ⅛ teaspoon ground nutmeg
- 1 (16-ounce) bag frozen sliced peaches, thawed, chopped, and drained
- 1½ tablespoons butter
- 1 tablespoon brandy
- 2½ teaspoons cornstarch
- 12 Sweet Cream Cheese Dough circles (recipe on page 348)

GLAZE:
- 1 cup sifted powdered sugar
- 2 tablespoons 2% reduced-fat milk
- ½ teaspoon vanilla extract

1. To prepare pies, combine first 6 ingredients in a medium saucepan; cook over medium heat 8 minutes or until liquid almost evaporates. Remove from heat. Add butter, stirring until butter melts. Stir in brandy and cornstarch. Cool slightly.

2. Working with 1 Sweet Cream Cheese Dough circle at a time, remove plastic wrap from dough. Place dough on a lightly floured surface. Spoon about 2 tablespoons peach mixture into center of circle. Fold dough over filling; press edges together with a fork or fingers to seal. Place pie on a large baking sheet covered with parchment paper. Repeat procedure with remaining Sweet Cream Cheese Dough circles and remaining peach mixture. Freeze 30 minutes.

3. Preheat oven to 425°.

4. Remove pies from freezer. Pierce top of each pie once with a fork. Place baking sheet on bottom rack in oven. Bake at 425° for 18 minutes or until edges are lightly browned and filling is bubbly. Cool completely on a wire rack.

5. To prepare glaze, combine powdered sugar, milk, and vanilla, stirring well. Drizzle evenly over pies. Yield: 12 pies (serving size: 1 pie).

CALORIES 235 (26% from fat); FAT 6.7g (sat 3.4g, mono 2.5g, poly 0.3g); PROTEIN 3.2g; CARB 40.9g; FIBER 1g; CHOL 18mg; IRON 1.3mg; SODIUM 96mg; CALC 26mg

MAKE AHEAD • FREEZABLE
Bacon, Potato, and Leek Turnovers

With a filling of mashed potatoes, bacon, chives, and cheese, these pies taste like a stuffed baked potato. They make a great accompaniment to steak and broccoli rabe.

- 3 cups (½-inch) cubed red or Yukon gold potato
- 2 cups chopped leek
- ¾ cup water
- 2 tablespoons chopped fresh chives
- 2 tablespoons grated fresh Parmesan cheese
- 2 tablespoons low-fat buttermilk
- ¾ teaspoon salt
- ¼ teaspoon freshly ground black pepper
- 2 bacon slices, cooked and crumbled
- 12 Savory Cornmeal–Whole Wheat Dough circles (recipe on page 348)

1. Combine first 3 ingredients in a microwave-safe pie plate or bowl; lightly cover with wax paper. Microwave at HIGH 8 minutes or until tender, stirring every 3 minutes. Coarsely mash mixture with a fork. Stir in chives and next 5 ingredients. Cool slightly.

2. Preheat oven to 425°.

3. Place Savory Cornmeal–Whole Wheat Dough circles on a lightly floured surface. Spoon ¼ cup potato mixture into center of each dough circle. Fold dough over filling; press edges together with a fork or fingers to seal. Place turnovers on a large baking sheet lined with parchment paper. Pierce top of each turnover once with a fork. Bake at 425° for 17 minutes or until lightly browned. Serve warm. Yield: 12 servings (serving size: 1 turnover).

CALORIES 202 (28% from fat); FAT 6.2g (sat 3.5g, mono 1.7g, poly 0.4g); PROTEIN 5.1g; CARB 31.5g; FIBER 2.1g; CHOL 32mg; IRON 1.8mg; SODIUM 307mg; CALC 58mg

How to Make Pies

1. *Fold dough over filling; press edges together with a fork or fingers to seal.*

2. *Pierce top of each pie once with a fork.*

MAKE AHEAD • FREEZABLE
Double-Cherry Pies

The white, creamy chocolate topping drizzles the pies with sweetness.

  1 cup dried sweet cherries
  ¼ cup sugar
  1 tablespoon fresh lemon juice
  ½ teaspoon ground cinnamon
  1 (16-ounce) bag frozen sour cherries, thawed and drained
  1 tablespoon butter
  2½ teaspoons cornstarch
  ½ teaspoon vanilla extract
  12 Sweet Cream Cheese Dough circles (recipe on page 348)
  ¼ cup white chocolate baking chips

1. Combine first 5 ingredients in a medium saucepan; cook over medium heat 7 minutes or until liquid almost evaporates. Remove from heat. Add butter, stirring until butter melts. Stir in cornstarch and vanilla. Cool slightly.
2. Working with 1 Sweet Cream Cheese

Dough circle at a time, remove plastic wrap from dough. Place dough on a lightly floured surface. Spoon about 2 tablespoons cherry mixture into center of circle. Fold dough over filling; press edges together with a fork or fingers to seal. Place pie on a large baking sheet covered with parchment paper. Repeat procedure with remaining Sweet Cream Cheese Dough circles and remaining cherry mixture. Freeze 30 minutes.
3. Preheat oven to 425°.
4. Remove pies from freezer. Pierce top of each pie once with a fork. Place baking sheet on bottom rack in oven. Bake at 425° for 19 minutes or until edges are lightly browned and filling is bubbly. Cool completely on a wire rack.
5. Place chocolate chips in a heavy-duty zip-top plastic bag; microwave at HIGH 1 minute or until chips are soft. Knead bag until smooth. Snip a tiny hole in corner of bag; drizzle chocolate over cooled pies. Yield: 12 servings (serving size: 1 pie).

CALORIES 244 (27% from fat); FAT 7.4g (sat 3.8g, mono 2.7g, poly 0.4g); PROTEIN 3.9g; CARB 40.5g; FIBER 2.2g; CHOL 16mg; IRON 1.4mg; SODIUM 93mg; CALC 34mg

MAKE AHEAD • FREEZABLE
Creamy Apple-Raisin Turnovers

You can substitute other kinds of dried fruits, such as cranberries, currants, or cherries, for the raisins.

PIES:
  1½ tablespoons butter
  2 cups coarsely chopped peeled Granny Smith apple (about 2 apples)
  2 cups coarsely chopped peeled Rome apple (about 2 apples)
  ¼ cup packed brown sugar
  ¼ cup raisins
  ¼ teaspoon ground cinnamon
  ⅛ teaspoon ground nutmeg
  2 tablespoons ⅓-less-fat cream cheese, softened
  1 tablespoon reduced-fat sour cream
  1 teaspoon all-purpose flour
  ½ teaspoon vanilla extract
  1 large egg white, lightly beaten
  12 Sweet Cream Cheese Dough circles (recipe on page 348)

GLAZE:
  ½ cup powdered sugar
  1 tablespoon 1% low-fat milk
  1 tablespoon reduced-fat sour cream
  ¼ teaspoon vanilla extract

1. To prepare pies, melt butter in a large nonstick skillet over medium heat. Add apples; cook 15 minutes or until tender and lightly browned, stirring occasionally. Stir in brown sugar, raisins, cinnamon, and nutmeg; cook 1 minute or until sugar melts. Remove from heat; cool slightly.
2. Combine cream cheese and next 4 ingredients, stirring with a whisk until well blended. Gently fold into apple mixture.
3. Working with 1 Sweet Cream Cheese Dough circle at a time, remove plastic wrap from dough. Place dough on a lightly floured surface. Spoon about 3 tablespoons apple mixture into center of circle. Fold dough over filling, and press edges together with a fork or fingers to seal. Place turnover on a large baking sheet covered with parchment paper. Repeat procedure with remaining Sweet Cream Cheese Dough circles and remaining apple mixture. Freeze 30 minutes.
4. Preheat oven to 425°.
5. Remove turnovers from freezer. Pierce top of each turnover once with a fork. Place baking sheet on bottom rack in oven. Bake at 425° for 19 minutes or until edges are lightly browned and filling is bubbly. Cool completely on a wire rack.
6. To prepare glaze, combine powdered sugar and remaining 3 ingredients, stirring with a whisk until well blended. Drizzle glaze over turnovers. Yield: 12 turnovers (serving size: 1 turnover).

CALORIES 228 (30% from fat); FAT 7.5g (sat 3.9g, mono 2.7g, poly 0.4g); PROTEIN 3.7g; CARB 37.4g; FIBER 1.2g; CHOL 20mg; IRON 1.2mg; SODIUM 110mg; CALC 29mg

Turnovers offer a delicious proportion of pastry to filling.

Chocolate, Fig, and Marsala Pastries

Marsala's deep, smoky flavor enhances the sweetness of dried figs. For a nonalcoholic version, substitute apple cider.

    ⅔ cup water
    ⅔ cup Marsala wine
    ½ cup packed brown sugar
    1 (8-ounce) bag dried Calimyrna figs, stems removed and chopped
    1 teaspoon vanilla extract
    ¼ teaspoon ground nutmeg
    ⅓ cup semisweet chocolate chips
    1 large egg yolk, lightly beaten
   12 Sweet Cream Cheese Dough circles (recipe on page 348)
    1 tablespoon powdered sugar

1. Combine first 4 ingredients in a medium saucepan; bring to a boil. Reduce heat, and simmer 25 minutes or until figs are tender and liquid almost evaporates. Remove from heat. Stir in vanilla and nutmeg. Cover and chill 1 hour. Stir in chocolate and egg yolk.
2. Working with 1 Sweet Cream Cheese Dough circle at a time, remove plastic wrap from dough. Place dough on a lightly floured surface. Spoon about 2 tablespoons fig mixture into center of circle. Fold dough over filling; press edges together with a fork or fingers to seal. Place pie on a large baking sheet covered with parchment paper. Repeat procedure with remaining Sweet Cream Cheese Dough circles and remaining fig mixture. Freeze 30 minutes.
3. Preheat oven to 425°.
4. Remove pies from freezer. Pierce top of each pie once with a fork. Place baking sheet on bottom rack in oven. Bake at 425° for 19 minutes or until edges are lightly browned and filling is bubbly. Cool completely on a wire rack. Sprinkle with powdered sugar. Yield: 12 pies (serving size: 1 pie).

CALORIES 270 (25% from fat); FAT 7.4g (sat 3.9g, mono 2.1g, poly 0.4g); PROTEIN 4g; CARB 47g; FIBER 2.9g; CHOL 31mg; IRON 1.6mg; SODIUM 88mg; CALC 54mg

Pork Picadillo Empanadas

These Latin-spiced turnovers are filling enough to be a main dish. Serve with a tossed salad of lettuce, avocado slices, and orange wedges.

    2 teaspoons canola oil
    1 cup chopped onion
    1 tablespoon minced seeded jalapeño pepper
    1 tablespoon chili powder
    1 teaspoon dried oregano
    1 teaspoon ground cumin
    ½ teaspoon ground cinnamon
   Dash of cloves
    ¾ pound pork tenderloin, trimmed and cut into ½-inch pieces
    ⅓ cup raisins
    2 tablespoons tomato paste
    ½ teaspoon salt
    1 (14.5-ounce) can petite diced tomatoes, undrained
   12 Savory Cornmeal–Whole Wheat Dough circles (recipe on page 348)

1. Heat oil in a large nonstick skillet over medium-high heat. Add onion and jalapeño; sauté 4 minutes or until tender. Stir in chili powder and next 4 ingredients; cook 1 minute. Add pork; sauté 5 minutes or until pork is browned on all sides. Stir in raisins, tomato paste, salt, and tomatoes. Reduce heat, and simmer 10 minutes or until most of liquid evaporates. Cool slightly.
2. Preheat oven to 425°.
3. Place Savory Cornmeal–Whole Wheat Dough circles on a lightly floured surface. Spoon ¼ cup pork mixture into center of each circle. Fold dough over filling; press edges together with a fork or fingers to seal. Place empanadas on a large baking sheet lined with parchment paper. Pierce top of each once with a fork. Bake at 425° for 18 minutes or until lightly browned. Serve warm. Yield: 12 servings (serving size: 1 empanada).

CALORIES 223 (29% from fat); FAT 7.3g (sat 3.6g, mono 2.3g, poly 0.7g); PROTEIN 9.9g; CARB 29.7g; FIBER 2.8g; CHOL 49mg; IRON 2mg; SODIUM 275mg; CALC 46mg

Sweet Potato Samosas

Stirring frozen peas into hot mashed sweet potatoes means there's no need for thawing. Serve with lamb.

    3 cups (½-inch) cubed peeled sweet potato (about 1 pound)
    ½ cup water
   1½ cups frozen petite green peas
    2 teaspoons olive oil
    ½ cup chopped onion
    4 garlic cloves, minced
   1½ teaspoons mustard seeds
   1½ teaspoons curry powder
    ½ teaspoon salt
    ⅛ to ¼ teaspoon ground red pepper
   12 Savory Cornmeal–Whole Wheat Dough circles (recipe on page 348)

1. Combine sweet potato and ½ cup water in a microwave-safe pie plate or bowl; lightly cover with wax paper. Microwave at HIGH 8 minutes or until tender, stirring every 3 minutes. Drain; coarsely mash sweet potato. Stir in peas.
2. Heat oil in a medium nonstick skillet over medium-high heat. Add onion and garlic; sauté 4 minutes. Add mustard seeds and curry powder; sauté 2 minutes. Add onion mixture, salt, and pepper to potato mixture; stir well. Cool slightly.
3. Preheat oven to 425°.
4. Place Savory Cornmeal–Whole Wheat Dough circles on a lightly floured surface. Spoon ¼ cup potato mixture into center of each dough circle. Fold dough over filling; press edges together with a fork or fingers to seal. Place samosas on a large baking sheet lined with parchment paper. Pierce top of each samosa once with a fork. Bake at 425° for 19 minutes or until lightly browned. Serve warm. Yield: 12 servings (serving size: 1 samosa).

CALORIES 205 (28% from fat); FAT 6.3g (sat 3.3g, mono 2.1g, poly 0.5g); PROTEIN 5g; CARB 32g; FIBER 3.3g; CHOL 30mg; IRON 1.8mg; SODIUM 231mg; CALC 50mg

MAKE AHEAD • FREEZABLE

Sweet Cream Cheese Dough

Packing the dough into a measuring cup helps the dough come together without overworking. Because this dough is significantly lower in fat than most sweet pastry doughs, ensure even browning by freezing the assembled pies for a half-hour before baking. Be sure to bake the pies on the bottom rack of the oven.

- 2 cups all-purpose flour (about 9 ounces)
- ¼ cup sugar
- ¼ teaspoon baking powder
- ⅛ teaspoon salt
- ¼ cup chilled butter, cut into small pieces
- ¼ cup (2 ounces) chilled ⅓-less-fat cream cheese, cut into small pieces
- 1 tablespoon cider vinegar
- 4 to 5 tablespoons ice water

1. Lightly spoon flour into dry measuring cups; level with a knife. Place flour, sugar, baking powder, and salt in a food processor; pulse 3 times or until combined. Add butter, cream cheese, and vinegar; pulse 4 times. Add ice water

through food chute, 1 tablespoon at a time, pulsing just until combined (do not form a ball). (Mixture may appear crumbly but will stick together when pressed between fingers.)

2. Place half of dough into a 1-cup measuring cup, pressing to compact dough. Remove dough from cup, and form into a ball. Divide ball into 6 equal portions. Repeat procedure with remaining dough. Cover and chill 15 minutes.

3. Place each dough portion between 2 sheets of plastic wrap. Roll each dough portion, still covered, into a 5-inch circle; chill until ready to use. Yield: 12 servings (serving size: 1 dough circle).

CALORIES 138 (33% from fat); FAT 5.1g (sat 2.6g, mono 1.9g, poly 0.3g); PROTEIN 2.7g; CARB 20.3g; FIBER 0.6g; CHOL 14mg; IRON 1mg; SODIUM 81mg; CALC 14mg

MAKE AHEAD • FREEZABLE

Savory Cornmeal–Whole Wheat Dough

- 1 cup all-purpose flour (about 4½ ounces)
- ½ cup whole wheat flour (about 2¼ ounces)
- 1 cup yellow cornmeal
- 1 teaspoon baking powder
- ¾ teaspoon garlic salt
- ½ cup water
- 5 tablespoons chilled butter, cut into small pieces
- 1 large egg, lightly beaten

1. Lightly spoon flours into dry measuring cups; level with a knife. Place flours, cornmeal, baking powder, and garlic salt in a food processor; pulse 3 times or until combined. Add water, butter, and egg; pulse 3 times or just until combined (do not form a ball). Place dough on a lightly floured surface; knead gently 4 or 5 times. Divide dough into 12 equal portions. Roll each portion into a 5½-inch circle on a lightly floured surface. Stack dough circles between layers of wax paper or plastic wrap to prevent sticking; chill dough until ready to use. Yield: 12 servings (serving size: 1 dough circle).

CALORIES 152 (31% from fat); FAT 5.3g (sat 3.2g, mono 1.4g, poly 0.3g); PROTEIN 3.2g; CARB 22.4g; FIBER 1.2g; CHOL 30mg; IRON 1.1mg; SODIUM 108mg; CALC 29mg

How to Make Dough

1. *Mixture may appear crumbly, but will stick together when pressed between fingers.*

2. *Place half of dough into a 1-cup measuring cup, pressing to compact dough. Remove dough from cup, and form into a ball. Divide ball into 6 equal portions. Repeat procedure with remaining dough.*

3. *Place each dough portion between 2 sheets of plastic wrap. Roll each dough portion, still covered, into a 5-inch circle; chill until ready to use.*

Potpie Tonight

These potpies have speedy, crusty toppings that make them simple to prepare.

Potpie Menu 1

serves 4

Shrimp Potpies with Oyster Cracker Topping

Fruit salad with lemon-ginger dressing*

Garlic bread

*Combine 2 cups halved strawberries, 1 cup cubed cantaloupe, and 1 cup cubed pineapple. Combine 1½ tablespoons honey, 1 tablespoon fresh lemon juice, 1 teaspoon olive oil, and ¼ teaspoon minced peeled fresh ginger; stir with a whisk. Drizzle over fruit; toss to coat.

Game Plan

1. While oven preheats:
   • Prepare potpies
2. While potpies bake:
   • Prepare fruit salad
   • Prepare garlic bread

QUICK & EASY
Shrimp Potpies with Oyster Cracker Topping

These individual servings make a special entrée, whether you're serving them as a weeknight dinner for your family or entertaining a small group.

TOTAL TIME: 40 MINUTES

  1 tablespoon butter
  1 cup chopped onion
  ½ cup chopped celery
  ½ cup chopped carrot
  2 garlic cloves, minced
  2 tablespoons brandy
  ½ cup half-and-half
  3 tablespoons tomato paste
  2 (8-ounce) bottles clam juice
1½ tablespoons cornstarch
  1 tablespoon water
  2 tablespoons chopped fresh parsley

  ¼ teaspoon salt
  ¼ teaspoon freshly ground black pepper
  ¾ pound cooked shrimp, chopped (about 1½ cups)
Cooking spray
  1 cup oyster crackers, coarsely crushed

1. Preheat oven to 400°.
2. Melt butter in a large nonstick skillet over medium-high heat. Add onion, celery, carrot, and garlic; sauté 5 minutes or until tender. Add brandy; cook 30 seconds. Stir in half-and-half, tomato paste, and clam juice; bring to a boil. Cook 4 minutes, stirring occasionally. Combine cornstarch and 1 tablespoon water. Add cornstarch mixture, parsley, salt, pepper, and shrimp to pan; cook 1 minute, stirring constantly.
3. Divide shrimp mixture evenly among 4 (10-ounce) ramekins coated with cooking spray. Top each serving with ¼ cup cracker crumbs. Arrange ramekins on a baking sheet. Bake at 400° for 10 minutes or until bubbly and lightly browned. Yield: 4 servings (serving size: 1 potpie).

CALORIES 267 (30% from fat); FAT 8.8g (sat 4.4g, mono 2.8g, poly 0.8g); PROTEIN 21.5g; CARB 19.9g; FIBER 1.8g; CHOL 188mg; IRON 4.5mg; SODIUM 875mg; CALC 111mg

---

Potpie Menu 2

serves 6

Beef and Vegetable Potpie

Mixed green salad

Gingersnap ice cream sandwiches*

*Place 12 gingersnap cookies, bottom sides up, on a work surface. Top each with 1 tablespoon low-fat vanilla ice cream; top each with another cookie. Arrange sandwiches on a baking sheet; freeze.

Game Plan

1. While oven preheats:
   • Prepare potpie
2. While potpie bakes:
   • Prepare ice cream sandwiches
   • Prepare salad

QUICK & EASY
Beef and Vegetable Potpie

The beef filling is first cooked in a large skillet on the stove top, then spooned into a baking dish. Finish the casserole in the oven to brown the breadstick dough topping.

TOTAL TIME: 42 MINUTES

QUICK TIP: Remove the can of breadsticks from the refrigerator before you prepare the filling. The dough will be more pliable and easy to handle.

  1 tablespoon olive oil, divided
  1 pound ground sirloin
  2 cups chopped zucchini
  1 cup prechopped onion
  1 cup chopped carrot
  1 teaspoon dried basil
  ½ teaspoon dried thyme
  1 (8-ounce) package presliced mushrooms
  3 garlic cloves, minced
  ½ cup dry red wine
  ¼ cup tomato paste
1½ teaspoons Worcestershire sauce
  ½ teaspoon freshly ground black pepper
  1 (14-ounce) can fat-free, less-sodium beef broth
  2 tablespoons cornstarch
  2 tablespoons water
Cooking spray
  1 (11-ounce) can refrigerated soft breadstick dough

1. Preheat oven to 400°.
2. Heat 1½ teaspoons oil in a large nonstick skillet over medium-high heat. Add beef; cook 3 minutes or until browned, stirring to crumble. Drain. Wipe drippings from pan with a paper towel. Heat 1½ teaspoons oil in pan. Add zucchini and next 6 ingredients; sauté 7 minutes or until vegetables are tender. Return beef to pan. Stir in wine and next 4 ingredients. Bring to a boil; cook 3 minutes. Combine cornstarch and 2 tablespoons water in a small bowl; stir with a whisk. Add cornstarch mixture to pan; cook 1 minute, stirring constantly.

Continued

3. Spoon beef mixture into an 11 x 7–inch baking dish coated with cooking spray. Separate breadstick dough into strips. Arrange strips in a lattice fashion over beef mixture. Bake at 400° for 12 minutes or until browned. Yield: 6 servings (serving size: 1⅓ cups).

CALORIES 313 (24% from fat); FAT 8.5g (sat 1.7g, mono 3g, poly 0.7g); PROTEIN 22g; CARB 37.6g; FIBER 2.7g; CHOL 40mg; IRON 3.9mg; SODIUM 679mg; CALC 41mg

---

Potpie Menu 3
serves 6

Biscuit-Topped Chicken Potpie

Sautéed baby spinach*

Mixed berries dolloped with vanilla yogurt

*Heat 1 tablespoon olive oil in a Dutch oven; add 1 (10-ounce) bag baby spinach; sauté 1 minute or until wilted. Place cooked spinach in a medium bowl. Add 1 (10-ounce) bag baby spinach to Dutch oven; sauté 1 minute or until wilted. Add to spinach in bowl; sprinkle with ¼ teaspoon salt and ¼ teaspoon freshly ground black pepper. Serve with lemon wedges.

Game Plan

1. While oven preheats:
  • Prepare chicken filling
  • Prepare biscuit topping
2. While potpie bakes:
  • Sauté spinach
  • Wash berries

QUICK & EASY
Biscuit-Topped Chicken Potpie

This tastes like Mom's potpie, but we've taken some shortcuts to slash the cooking time.

TOTAL TIME: 45 MINUTES

QUICK TIP: To clean leek, chop and place in a strainer; rinse under running water.

  1 tablespoon butter
  2 cups chopped leek
  ¼ cup chopped shallot
  ¾ teaspoon chopped fresh or ¼ teaspoon dried thyme
  1½ cups refrigerated diced potatoes with onions (such as Simply Potatoes)
  ⅓ cup dry white wine
  1 teaspoon Dijon mustard
  1 (14-ounce) can fat-free, less-sodium chicken broth
  2 cups chopped roasted chicken breast
  1½ cups frozen mixed vegetables
  ¼ teaspoon salt
  ¼ teaspoon freshly ground black pepper
  2 tablespoons water
  1½ tablespoons cornstarch
  ⅔ cup half-and-half
  Cooking spray
  1¼ cups low-fat baking mix (such as Bisquick Heart Smart)
  ½ cup fat-free milk
  1 large egg white, lightly beaten

1. Preheat oven to 425°.
2. Melt butter in a large nonstick skillet over medium-high heat. Add leek, shallot, and thyme; sauté 2 minutes. Add potatoes; sauté 2 minutes. Add wine; cook 1 minute or until liquid evaporates. Stir in mustard and broth; bring to a boil. Cook 4 minutes, stirring occasionally. Stir in chicken, mixed vegetables, salt, and pepper; cook 1 minute. Combine 2 tablespoons water and cornstarch in a small bowl, stirring with a whisk. Add cornstarch mixture and half-and-half to pan. Reduce heat, and simmer 2 minutes, stirring constantly. Spoon mixture into a 13 x 9–inch baking dish coated with cooking spray.

3. Lightly spoon baking mix into dry measuring cups; level with a knife. Combine baking mix, milk, and egg white in a medium bowl, stirring with a whisk. Spoon batter evenly over chicken mixture. Bake at 425° for 20 minutes or until topping is golden and filling is bubbly. Let stand 10 minutes. Yield: 6 servings (serving size: 1½ cups).

CALORIES 348 (24% from fat); FAT 9.2g (sat 4.1g, mono 2.2g, poly 0.9g); PROTEIN 23.5g; CARB 43.3g; FIBER 4.4g; CHOL 55mg; IRON 3.1mg; SODIUM 634mg; CALC 131mg

---

Potpie Menu 4
serves 6

Turkey Tamale Potpie

Tossed salad with poppy seed dressing and orange sections

Warm spiced apples with vanilla frozen yogurt*

*Toss 3 cups sliced peeled apple with 2 teaspoons lemon juice. Melt 2 teaspoons butter in a large nonstick skillet over medium-high heat. Add apple; sauté 6 minutes or until tender. Stir in 1 tablespoon maple syrup, ¼ teaspoon ground cinnamon, and ⅛ teaspoon ground nutmeg; cook 1 minute. Scoop ½ cup vanilla frozen yogurt into each of 6 bowls; top evenly with spiced apples.

Game Plan

1. While oven preheats:
  • Make potpie filling
  • Prepare corn bread topping
  • Scoop yogurt into dessert dishes; place in freezer
2. While potpie bakes:
  • Toss salad
  • Sauté apple for dessert; keep warm

Turkey Tamale Potpie

This dish has the ingredients of tamales, but the meat filling is topped with a cornmeal batter and baked instead of being wrapped in a corn husk.

TOTAL TIME: 38 MINUTES

FLAVOR TIP: Substitute lean ground beef and black beans for turkey and kidney beans, if desired.

FILLING:

Cooking spray
1 cup chopped onion
¾ cup chopped red bell pepper
4 garlic cloves, minced
1 pound ground turkey breast
1 tablespoon chili powder
1 teaspoon dried oregano
½ teaspoon salt
1 (14.5-ounce) can no-salt-added diced tomatoes, undrained
1 (15-ounce) can kidney beans, rinsed and drained

TOPPING:

1 cup all-purpose flour (about 4½ ounces)
¾ cup yellow cornmeal
1 teaspoon sugar
1 teaspoon baking powder
½ teaspoon salt
¼ teaspoon baking soda
1 cup low-fat buttermilk
1 large egg, lightly beaten

1. Preheat oven to 425°.
2. To prepare filling, heat a large nonstick skillet over medium-high heat. Coat pan with cooking spray. Add onion, bell pepper, garlic, and turkey; cook 5 minutes or until turkey loses its pink color. Add chili powder and next 4 ingredients; cook 3 minutes. Spoon turkey mixture into an 11 x 7–inch baking dish coated with cooking spray.
3. To prepare topping, lightly spoon flour into a dry measuring cup; level with a knife. Combine flour, cornmeal, and next 4 ingredients in a bowl. Combine buttermilk and egg; add to dry ingredients, stirring just until moist. Spread cornmeal mixture evenly over turkey mixture. Bake at 425° for 18 minutes or

until topping is golden. Yield: 6 servings (serving size: 1¾ cups).

CALORIES 329 (8% from fat); FAT 3g (sat 0.9g, mono 0.5g, poly 0.4g); PROTEIN 27.6g; CARB 47.6g; FIBER 6.8g; CHOL 67mg; IRON 2.4mg; SODIUM 705mg; CALC 120mg

enlightened cook

Taste of Home

This college women's dormitory welcomes its international residents with foods from their homelands.

Twice a day the residents at Bayridge Residence in Boston gather to share meals that often reflect their varied cultures. The residence, a private, nonprofit entity, is home to female students attending more than a dozen Boston-area colleges.

Kelly O'Leary, 42, a dynamo in chef's whites, is the guiding spirit behind those meals. Her philosophy is simple: "It's really home-style cooking. It's just the students all come from different homes."

José's Chicken

Sous-chef Roxana Pareja and her husband, José, created this guest-worthy roast chicken.

1 (4-pound) whole chicken
1 tablespoon chopped fresh oregano
1 tablespoon chopped fresh parsley
1 tablespoon chopped fresh cilantro
2 teaspoons butter, softened
1 teaspoon kosher salt
1 teaspoon ground cumin
¾ teaspoon freshly ground black pepper
½ teaspoon paprika
2 garlic cloves, crushed
1 small orange, quartered
1 small onion, quartered
Cooking spray

1. Preheat oven to 375°.
2. Remove and discard giblets and neck from chicken; trim excess fat. Starting at neck cavity, loosen skin from breasts and

drumsticks by inserting fingers, gently pushing between skin and meat.
3. Combine oregano and next 7 ingredients. Rub oregano mixture under loosened skin and over breasts and drumsticks. Place garlic in body cavity; arrange orange and onion in cavity. Tie ends of legs together with twine. Lift wing tips up and over back; tuck under chicken. Place chicken, breast side up, on a roasting pan coated with cooking spray. Bake at 375° for 1 hour and 20 minutes or until thermometer registers 165°. Let stand 10 minutes. Discard skin. Remove orange quarters; squeeze juice over chicken. Discard oranges, garlic cloves, and onions. Yield: 4 servings (serving size: about 4 ounces chicken).

CALORIES 279 (27% from fat); FAT 8.3g (sat 2.8g, mono 2.4g, poly 1.6g); PROTEIN 47.3g; CARB 0.8g; FIBER 0.4g; CHOL 155mg; IRON 2.7mg; SODIUM 659mg; CALC 36mg

Classic Scones
(pictured on page 249)

These barely sweet scones are delicious with strawberry jam. Try substituting other dried fruits, such as cranberries or blueberries, for the currants.

2 cups all-purpose flour (about 9 ounces)
3 tablespoons granulated sugar
1½ teaspoons baking powder
½ teaspoon salt
5 tablespoons chilled butter, cut into small pieces
½ cup fat-free milk
¼ teaspoon vanilla extract
1 large egg white, lightly beaten
⅓ cup dried currants
2 teaspoons fat-free milk
2 teaspoons turbinado or granulated sugar

1. Preheat oven to 425°.
2. Lightly spoon flour into dry measuring cups; level with a knife. Combine flour, sugar, baking powder, and salt in a bowl; stir with a whisk. Cut in butter with a pastry blender or 2 knives until mixture resembles coarse meal.

Continued

3. Combine ½ cup milk, vanilla, and egg white in a bowl. Add milk mixture to flour mixture, stirring just until moist (dough will be soft). Turn dough out onto a lightly floured surface. Sprinkle dough with currants. With floured hands, knead 4 times or just until currants are incorporated.

4. Pat dough into an 8-inch circle on a baking sheet lined with parchment paper. Cut dough into 12 wedges, cutting into, but not through, dough. Brush 2 teaspoons milk over dough; sprinkle with turbinado sugar. Bake at 425° for 17 minutes or until golden. Serve warm, or cool on a wire rack. Yield: 12 servings (serving size: 1 scone).

CALORIES 149 (30% from fat); FAT 5g (sat 3g, mono 1.3g, poly 0.3g); PROTEIN 3g; CARB 23.4g; FIBER 0.8g; CHOL 13mg; IRON 1.2mg; SODIUM 203mg; CALC 56mg

Thai Rice

    1   tablespoon olive oil
    2   cups chopped onion (1 medium)
    1   tablespoon finely chopped peeled
        fresh lemongrass
    1   teaspoon finely chopped peeled
        fresh ginger
    ¼   teaspoon ground coriander
    ¼   teaspoon ground cumin
    1   cup brown basmati rice
    2¾ cups fat-free, less-sodium chicken
        broth
    1   teaspoon grated lime rind
    ¼   teaspoon salt
    ¼   cup finely chopped fresh cilantro
    6   lime wedges

1. Heat oil in a large nonstick skillet over medium-high heat. Add onion and next 4 ingredients; sauté 3 minutes or until onion is tender. Add rice; sauté 1 minute. Stir in broth, rind, and salt; bring to a boil. Cover, reduce heat, and simmer 45 minutes or until rice is tender. Remove from heat. Let stand, covered, 10 minutes. Stir in cilantro. Serve with lime wedges. Yield: 6 servings (serving size: ⅔ cup rice and 1 lime wedge).

CALORIES 168 (20% from fat); FAT 3.7g (sat 0.7g, mono 2.2g, poly 0.7g); PROTEIN 4.2g; CARB 31.6g; FIBER 2.9g; CHOL 0mg; IRON 0.8mg; SODIUM 280mg; CALC 24mg

Good Things Come in Pears

Sweet and succulent, this fruit serves a feast for the senses.

With their appearance, scent, taste, and texture, pears are one of the most sensuous fruits. In a bowl, they inspire still-life paintings. In hand, they offer sweet, subtle fragrance and flavor. Pears just seem to make you look more closely, inhale more deeply, and chew more thoughtfully.

MAKE AHEAD
Pear Upside-Down Spice Cake

This attractive cake is a good choice to round out a fall menu. Use Bartlett or Anjou pears, if you prefer.

CAKE:

    3   cups sliced peeled Bosc pears
        (about 3 pears)
        Cooking spray
    2   cups all-purpose flour (about 9
        ounces)
    ½   teaspoon salt
    ½   teaspoon baking powder
    ½   teaspoon instant coffee
        granules
    ½   teaspoon ground nutmeg
    ¼   teaspoon ground ginger
    ¼   teaspoon ground allspice
    ¼   teaspoon ground cinnamon
    1   cup granulated sugar
    5   tablespoons butter,
        softened
    1   teaspoon vanilla extract
    1   large egg, lightly beaten
    ¾   cup buttermilk

GLAZE:

    2   tablespoons butter
    1   tablespoon water
    ½   teaspoon fresh lemon juice
    ¾   cup packed dark brown sugar
    1½ tablespoons buttermilk

1. Preheat oven to 350°.

2. To prepare cake, arrange pear slices spokelike in bottom of a 9-inch cake pan coated with cooking spray, working from center of pan to edge.

3. Lightly spoon flour into dry measuring cups; level with a knife. Combine flour, salt, and next 6 ingredients in a large bowl.

4. Combine granulated sugar and 5 tablespoons butter in a large bowl; beat with a mixer at medium speed until light and fluffy. Add vanilla and egg; beat well. Add flour mixture and ¾ cup buttermilk alternately to sugar mixture, beginning and ending with flour mixture. Spoon batter over pears; spread evenly.

5. Bake at 350° for 1 hour or until a wooden pick inserted in center comes out clean. Cool completely on a wire rack. Loosen cake from sides of pan using a narrow metal spatula; invert cake onto plate. Let rest 2 minutes, and remove pan.

6. To prepare glaze, combine 2 tablespoons butter, 1 tablespoon water, and juice in a medium saucepan over medium-high heat, stirring until butter melts. Stir in brown sugar; bring to a boil. Remove from heat; stir in 1½ tablespoons buttermilk. Let stand 2 minutes; pour glaze evenly over cake. Yield: 12 servings (serving size: 1 wedge).

CALORIES 295 (25% from fat); FAT 8.1g (sat 4.7g, mono 1.9g, poly 0.4g); PROTEIN 3.6g; CARB 53.4g; FIBER 1.6g; CHOL 38mg; IRON 1.4mg; SODIUM 198mg; CALC 37mg

Know Your Pears

One of the world's oldest crops, pears were domesticated in China and Europe about 3,000 years ago. The western United States—chiefly California, Washington, and Oregon—provide some of America's best pears. Of the roughly 5,000 varieties grown throughout the world, here are a few of the most familiar:

Comice

The sweetest and juiciest of all widely available pears, green and amber Comice pears have rotund bottoms and narrow shoulders. Often smaller than other varieties, they're best enjoyed raw.

Anjou

With a yellowish-green skin that can blush slightly amber when ripe, Anjou pears are juicy and appropriate for cooking or eating out of hand. Originally from France, these pears have a slightly tannic flavor.

Bosc

Russet-toned with an elegant, almost teardrop shape, Bosc pears boast dense, buttery flesh. This pear has slightly rough skin and a long, curving stem often left intact to make poached or baked pears more attractive. Because it's less juicy than some other varieties, the Bosc is a good pear for cooking.

Seckel

Most often used for cooking and baking rather than eating out of hand, Seckel pears are one of the crisper varieties. They're among the smallest pears and are green with a deep red blush.

Asian

Unlike other pears, ripe Asian pears are crisp and firm textured, and often called pear-apples for this reason. They're large and globe shaped, with a delicate skin that bruises easily.

Bartlett

Bell-shaped with a yellow-green skin, Bartletts are an early-season pear that can be cooked or eaten raw. This variety is known to be aromatic and sweet, and is often considered the "classic" pear variety.

Homestead Pear Crisp

A delicious way to use the bounty from a you-pick orchard, this dessert serves a crowd. Served with hot coffee or chai tea, it warms up a brisk fall evening.

CRISP:
- ⅓ cup packed brown sugar
- 2 tablespoons cornstarch
- 2 tablespoons fresh lemon juice
- 2 teaspoons ground cinnamon
- ¼ teaspoon salt
- 12 peeled Bartlett pears, cored and cut into ½-inch pieces (about 5 pounds)
- Cooking spray

TOPPING:
- ½ cup all-purpose flour (about 2¼ ounces)
- 1 cup regular oats
- ⅓ cup packed brown sugar
- ½ teaspoon ground cinnamon
- 6 tablespoons chilled butter, cut into small pieces

1. Preheat oven to 350°.
2. To prepare crisp, combine first 6 ingredients in a large bowl; toss well. Spoon into a 13 x 9–inch baking dish coated with cooking spray.
3. To prepare topping, lightly spoon flour into a dry measuring cup; level with a knife. Combine flour, oats, ⅓ cup sugar, and ½ teaspoon cinnamon in a large bowl. Cut in butter with a pastry blender or 2 knives until mixture resembles coarse meal. Sprinkle flour mixture over pear mixture. Bake at 350° for 1 hour or until topping is golden and fruit is tender. Serve warm. Yield: 12 servings (serving size: about 1 cup).

CALORIES 251 (23% from fat); FAT 6.5g (sat 3.7g, mono 1.7g, poly 0.5g); PROTEIN 2.3g; CARB 49.2g; FIBER 6.7g; CHOL 15mg; IRON 1.4mg; SODIUM 96mg; CALC 43mg

MAKE AHEAD
Free-Form Pear Pie

Top this easy pie with crumbled blue cheese. Substitute ¼ cup granulated sugar for turbinado in the filling, or use Bosc or Anjou pears instead of Bartletts, if desired.

- ½ (15-ounce) package refrigerated pie dough (such as Pillsbury)
- 5 cups coarsely chopped peeled Bartlett pear (about 5 medium)
- ¼ cup turbinado sugar
- 1 tablespoon cornstarch
- 1 tablespoon lemon juice
- ½ teaspoon ground ginger
- ½ teaspoon ground cinnamon
- ⅛ teaspoon salt
- Cooking spray
- 1 tablespoon turbinado sugar or granulated sugar

1. Preheat oven to 425°.
2. Roll dough into a 14-inch circle on a lightly floured surface. Place dough circle on a baking sheet lined with parchment paper.
3. Combine pear and next 6 ingredients; toss well. Arrange pear mixture in center of dough, leaving a 3-inch border. Fold edges of dough toward center, pressing gently to seal (dough will only partially cover pear mixture). Lightly coat with cooking spray, and sprinkle evenly with 1 tablespoon sugar.
4. Bake at 425° for 20 minutes on lowest oven rack. Reduce oven temperature to 350° (do not remove from oven); bake an additional 15 minutes or until fruit is tender and crust is golden brown. Cool on a wire rack. Cut into wedges. Yield: 8 servings (serving size: 1 wedge).

CALORIES 211 (30% from fat); FAT 7g (sat 2.5g, mono 3.1g, poly 1.2g); PROTEIN 0.9g; CARB 37.4g; FIBER 3.3g; CHOL 3mg; IRON 0.3mg; SODIUM 146mg; CALC 11mg

Crepes with Sautéed Pears in Wine Sauce

Make the crepes in advance, and store in the refrigerator until needed. If the first crepe doesn't turn out, keep in mind that subsequent crepes usually turn out perfectly once the pan is seasoned.

CREPES:
- ¾ cup all-purpose flour (about 3⅓ ounces)
- ½ cup 2% reduced-fat milk
- ½ cup water
- ½ cup egg substitute
- 2 tablespoons lemon juice
- 1 teaspoon sugar
- Dash of salt
- 2 tablespoons melted butter

FILLING:
- 5 Bosc pears (about 2½ pounds)
- 1 teaspoon butter
- ½ cup light brown sugar, divided

REMAINING INGREDIENTS:
- ½ cup pear nectar
- ½ cup riesling or other dry white wine
- 1 tablespoon cornstarch
- Powdered sugar (optional)
- 9 mint sprigs (optional)

1. To prepare crepes, lightly spoon flour into a dry measuring cup; level with a knife. Place flour, milk, and next 5 ingredients in a blender; process until smooth, scraping sides. Let stand 30 minutes.

2. Heat an 8-inch crepe pan or nonstick skillet over medium heat. Brush pan lightly with melted butter. Pour a scant ¼ cup batter into pan; quickly tilt pan in all directions so batter covers pan with a thin film. Cook about 2 minutes. Carefully lift edge of crepe with a spatula to test for doneness. The crepe is ready to turn when it can be shaken loose from pan and underside is lightly browned. Turn crepe over, and cook 30 seconds or until center is set.

3. Place crepe on a towel; cool completely. Repeat procedure with remaining batter, stirring batter between crepes. Stack crepes between single layers of wax paper to prevent sticking.

4. To prepare filling, peel pears, reserving peels; thinly slice pears. Melt 1 teaspoon butter in a large nonstick skillet over medium-high heat. Add pear slices in a single layer to pan; sauté 1 minute on each side or until slightly softened. Add 1 tablespoon brown sugar to pan; sauté 6 minutes or until golden. Remove pears from pan.

5. Add peels and 7 tablespoons brown sugar to pan; cook 1 minute or until sugar dissolves, stirring constantly. Combine pear nectar, wine, and cornstarch in a small bowl; stir well with a whisk. Add nectar mixture to pan; bring to a boil. Reduce heat, and simmer 2 minutes or until thickened, stirring constantly. Strain sauce through a fine sieve into a bowl, pressing to extract all of liquid. Discard solids.

6. Spoon about ⅓ cup pear mixture in center of each crepe; fold sides and ends over. Place, seam side down, on a plate. Drizzle each serving with about 5 teaspoons sauce. Garnish with powdered sugar and mint, if desired. Yield: 9 servings (serving size: 1 crepe).

CALORIES 212 (15% from fat); FAT 3.5g (sat 2.1g, mono 0.9g, poly 0.2g); PROTEIN 3.4g; CARB 44.2g; FIBER 4.3g; CHOL 9mg; IRON 1.3mg; SODIUM 80mg; CALC 47mg

Chai-Spiced Bosc Pears with Pound Cake

You can substitute any slightly sweet white wine for late-harvest riesling. Heat the pound cake on a grill pan before serving to create attractive grill marks.

- 2 cups late-harvest riesling
- 2 cups water
- 1 cup pear nectar
- 25 cardamom pods, crushed
- 12 whole cloves
- 3 (3-inch) cinnamon sticks, broken
- 2 tablespoons black tea leaves (such as Darjeeling or Assam)
- 4 peeled Bosc pears, cored and halved
- ¼ cup mascarpone cheese
- 1 tablespoon butter
- 1 (10.75-ounce) loaf frozen low-fat pound cake (such as Sara Lee), thawed and cut into 8 slices

1. Combine first 6 ingredients in a large saucepan; bring to a boil. Cover, reduce heat, and simmer 15 minutes. Stir in tea leaves; simmer 2 minutes. Strain mixture through a fine sieve into a bowl; discard solids.

2. Return wine mixture to pan; add pear halves, cut sides down. Cover; simmer 15 minutes or until tender. Remove pears with a slotted spoon; place in a shallow dish. Set pears aside; keep warm.

3. Bring wine mixture to a boil over medium-high heat; cook until reduced to 1 cup (about 10 minutes). Add mascarpone, stirring with a whisk until well blended. Remove from heat; add butter, stirring until butter melts.

4. Place 1 pound cake slice on each of 8 plates, and top each slice with 1 pear half. Spoon about 2 tablespoons sauce over each serving. Serve warm. Yield: 8 servings.

CALORIES 258 (24% from fat); FAT 6.8g (sat 3.5g, mono 1.2g, poly 0.3g); PROTEIN 2.9g; CARB 38.8g; FIBER 3.1g; CHOL 42mg; IRON 0.9mg; SODIUM 165mg; CALC 65mg

Stilton-Stuffed Baked Pears

Stilton, an English blue cheese, is a classic accompaniment for pears. Use ripe but firm pears that will hold their shape once cooked. You can substitute toasted walnuts for pecans.

- ½ cup packed brown sugar
- 2 tablespoons butter, softened
- ½ cup (2 ounces) crumbled Stilton cheese
- ¼ cup dried cranberries
- ¼ cup chopped pecans, toasted
- 8 peeled Bartlett pears (about 3¾ pounds)
- ¼ cup apple juice
- 1 tablespoon port

1. Preheat oven to 375°.

2. Combine sugar and butter in a small bowl, and stir until well blended. Add cheese, cranberries, and pecans; stir well.

3. Cut 1 inch off stem end of each pear; reserve top. Remove core from stem end, and scoop out about 2 tablespoons pulp from each pear half to form a cup, using a melon baller or spoon. If necessary, cut about ¼ inch from base of pears so they will sit flat. Place pears in a 13 x 9–inch baking dish. Fill each pear with about 2 tablespoons sugar mixture, and replace top on each.

4. Combine juice and port in a small bowl; pour into baking dish. Bake pears at 375° for 30 minutes or until tender. Serve warm. Yield: 8 servings (serving size: 1 pear).

CALORIES 246 (30% from fat); FAT 8.2g (sat 3.6g, mono 3g, poly 1g); PROTEIN 2.8g; CARB 43.8g; FIBER 5.7g; CHOL 14mg; IRON 0.7mg; SODIUM 145mg; CALC 75mg

Chicken with Pear-Sage Skillet Chutney

Keeping the skin on the pears boosts fiber content and helps the ripe fruit hold its shape even after cooking.

- 2   teaspoons canola oil, divided
- 6   (6-ounce) skinless, boneless chicken breast halves
- ¾   teaspoon salt, divided
- ¾   teaspoon freshly ground black pepper, divided
- ⅓   cup finely chopped red onion
- ⅓   cup finely chopped red bell pepper
- 2   tablespoons brown sugar
- 3   tablespoons cider vinegar
- 1½ teaspoons chopped fresh sage
- ½   teaspoon mustard seeds
- 2   cups cored, finely chopped Bartlett pear (about 2 pears)

1. Preheat oven to 375°.
2. Heat 1 teaspoon oil in a large non-stick skillet over medium-high heat. Sprinkle chicken evenly with ½ teaspoon salt and ½ teaspoon black pepper. Add chicken to pan; cook 2 minutes on each side or until browned. Remove from pan.
3. Reduce heat to medium; add 1 teaspoon oil. Add onion and bell pepper to pan. Cook 3 minutes, stirring frequently. Add ¼ teaspoon salt, ¼ teaspoon black pepper, sugar, and next 3 ingredients to pan; bring to a boil. Reduce heat; simmer

5 minutes. Add pear. Increase heat to medium; cook 10 minutes or until pear is tender, stirring frequently.

4. Place chicken in pan on top of chutney. Cover pan loosely with foil; bake at 375° for 15 minutes or until chicken is done. Yield: 6 servings (serving size: 1 chicken breast half and about 2 tablespoons chutney).

CALORIES 282 (20% from fat); FAT 6.3g (sat 1.4g, mono 2.6g, poly 1.5g); PROTEIN 40g; CARB 14.6g; FIBER 2g; CHOL 108mg; IRON 1.6mg; SODIUM 388mg; CALC 34mg

WINE NOTE: Pinot gris, the same grape as pinot grigio, is known for producing fuller-bodied whites brimming with fruit flavors like apple and pear when grown in the cool climate of Oregon's Willamette Valley. Ponzi Vineyards Pinot Gris 2005 ($17), with its clove and almond notes, echoes the concentrated pear and herbal flavors that are found in the chutney.

MAKE AHEAD
Amaretto-Pear Streusel Cake

Warm slices in the microwave, if desired.

TOPPING:
- ½   cup packed brown sugar
- 2   tablespoons regular oats
- 2   tablespoons all-purpose flour
- 1   tablespoon butter, softened
- 1   teaspoon ground cinnamon
- ⅓   cup slivered almonds

CAKE:
- 2   cups all-purpose flour (about 9 ounces)
- 1   teaspoon baking soda
- 1   teaspoon baking powder
- ½   teaspoon salt
- 1   cup granulated sugar
- ⅓   cup butter, softened
- 3   large eggs
- ¾   cup reduced-fat sour cream
- ¼   cup amaretto (almond-flavored liqueur)
- 1½ cups peeled Bosc pear, cored and finely chopped (about 2)
- Cooking spray

1. Preheat oven to 350°.
2. To prepare topping, combine first 5 ingredients in a small bowl. Stir in almonds; set aside.
3. To prepare cake, lightly spoon 2 cups flour into dry measuring cups; level with a knife. Combine flour, baking soda, baking powder, and salt.
4. Place granulated sugar and ⅓ cup butter in a large bowl; beat with a mixer at high speed 5 minutes or until well blended. Reduce mixer speed to medium; add eggs, 1 at a time, beating well after each addition. Add flour mixture and sour cream alternately to sugar mixture, beginning and ending with flour mixture. Stir in amaretto and pear.
5. Spoon batter into a 13 x 9–inch baking pan coated with cooking spray; sprinkle topping evenly over batter. Bake at 350° for 30 minutes or until a wooden pick inserted in center comes out clean. Cool in pan on a wire rack. Yield: 15 servings (serving size: 1 piece).

CALORIES 264 (29% from fat); FAT 8.5g (sat 4.1g, mono 2.6g, poly 0.7g); PROTEIN 4.4g; CARB 42.1g; FIBER 1.5g; CHOL 59mg; IRON 1.4mg; SODIUM 259mg; CALC 57mg

MAKE AHEAD • FREEZABLE
Pear-Vanilla Freezer Jam

Enjoy the taste of ripe, in-season pears all year long with this simple jam. Spread on toast or English muffins, or try on gingerbread, bran muffins, and hot cross buns. The jam also makes a tasty glaze for pork tenderloin.

- 4   cups coarsely chopped peeled Bartlett pear (about 5 large)
- 1   teaspoon grated lemon rind
- 6   tablespoons fresh lemon juice
- 1   vanilla bean, split lengthwise
- 1   (1.75-ounce) package pectin crystals
- 4   cups sugar

1. Place pear in a food processor; pulse until finely chopped. Place pear, rind, juice, and vanilla bean in a large saucepan. Stir in pectin. Place pan over high heat; bring to a boil. Stir in sugar; cook 5 minutes or until sugar dissolves.
Continued

Bring to a boil; cook 1 minute, stirring constantly.

2. Remove from heat. Skim foam from surface; discard. Remove vanilla bean. Scrape seeds into pear mixture; discard bean. Stir 5 minutes to ensure fruit is suspended in jam. Cover and chill overnight. Yield: 44 servings (serving size: 2 tablespoons).

NOTE: Refrigerate Pear-Vanilla Freezer Jam in airtight containers up to three weeks, or freeze up to six months.

CALORIES 93 (2% from fat); FAT 0.2g (sat 0g, mono 0g, poly 0g); PROTEIN 0.2g; CARB 23.9g; FIBER 0.8g; CHOL 0mg; IRON 0mg; SODIUM 2mg; CALC 4mg

Pear and Cranberry Stuffed Pork Roast

If your butcher can't butterfly the roast for you and time is short, buy a tied loin roast. Separate it into two pieces, spread the filling between the halves, and truss tightly.

Cooking spray
¼ cup sliced onion
½ teaspoon dried thyme
½ teaspoon dried rubbed sage
2 garlic cloves, minced
½ cup fat-free, less-sodium chicken broth
1½ cups chopped peeled pear (about 2)
¼ cup dried cranberries
¼ cup apple juice
1 (2-pound) boneless pork loin roast, trimmed and butterflied
1 teaspoon salt
1 teaspoon freshly ground black pepper

1. Heat a large nonstick skillet over medium-high heat. Coat pan with cooking spray. Add onion, thyme, sage, and garlic. Sauté 3 minutes or until onion is tender. Stir in broth, scraping pan to loosen browned bits. Cook 5 minutes or until liquid is almost evaporated. Add pear; cook 5 minutes or until pear is lightly browned, stirring frequently. Add cranberries and apple juice; cook 5 minutes or until liquid is evaporated. Remove from heat; cool to room temperature.

2. Preheat oven to 400°.

3. Unroll roast; sprinkle both sides with salt and pepper. Spread pear mixture over roast, leaving a 2-inch margin around edges. Roll up roast, jelly-roll fashion, starting with short side. Secure at 1-inch intervals with twine. Place roast on rack of a broiler pan or roasting pan coated with cooking spray.

4. Bake at 400° for 15 minutes. Reduce heat to 325° (do not remove from oven); cook 1 hour and 10 minutes or until a thermometer registers 160° (slightly pink). Let stand 10 minutes before cutting into 1-inch-thick slices. Yield: 10 servings (serving size: 1 slice).

CALORIES 171 (34% from fat); FAT 6.4g (sat 2.3g, mono 2.7g, poly 0.5g); PROTEIN 19.2g; CARB 8.9g; FIBER 1.1g; CHOL 54mg; IRON 0.8mg; SODIUM 301mg; CALC 25mg

menu of the month

Oktoberfest

Germany's celebration of beer and the fall harvest prompt this festive meal.

Oktoberfest Supper Menu
serves 8

Herring and Apple Salad

Pork Loin Braised with Cabbage
or
Turkey Bratwurst Patties

Warm Potato Salad with Beer and Mustard Dressing

Brown Beer Rye Bread

Ginger Cake

Beer

BEER NOTE: The robust foods of this Oktoberfest menu call for an authentic beer like Paulaner Oktoberfest-Märzen ($8 for a six-pack). This German beer uses a small proportion of hops, allowing the chewy malt to shine through with flavors of toffee, caramel, and nuts. The beer is clean, slightly sweet, and full-bodied, which makes it a perfect choice with the bread and the tang of the potato salad.

MAKE AHEAD
Brown Beer Rye Bread

Hearty breads like rye and pumpernickel are German culinary standards. This version uses stone-ground rye flour and caraway seeds, a favorite spice in German cooking. Serve with Herring and Apple Salad (recipe on page 357), or use it to make sandwiches with Pork Loin Braised with Cabbage (recipe on page 357) or Turkey Bratwurst Patties (recipe on page 358).

1 tablespoon olive oil
½ cup chopped onion
1⅛ teaspoons sugar, divided
2 packages dry yeast (about 4½ teaspoons)
¾ cup warm brown beer (100° to 110°)
½ cup plain low-fat yogurt
1 tablespoon white vinegar
1 tablespoon caraway seeds
1½ teaspoons salt
1 large egg, lightly beaten
2¾ cups all-purpose flour, divided (about 12⅓ ounces)
1 cup stone-ground rye flour (about 4½ ounces) (such as Bob's Red Mill)
Cooking spray
1 teaspoon water
1 large egg white, lightly beaten

1. Heat oil in a large skillet over medium-high heat. Add onion; sauté 4 minutes or until golden brown. Cool.

2. Dissolve ⅛ teaspoon sugar and yeast in warm beer; let stand 5 minutes. Stir in yogurt and next 3 ingredients. Add 1 teaspoon sugar and egg; stir with a whisk until combined.

3. Lightly spoon flours into dry measuring cups; level with a knife. Add 2½ cups all-purpose flour and rye flour to yeast mixture; stir until a soft dough forms. Stir in onion mixture. Turn dough out onto a floured surface. Knead until smooth and elastic (about 8 minutes); add enough of remaining flour, 1 tablespoon at a time, to prevent dough from sticking to hands (dough will feel tacky).

4. Place dough in a large bowl coated with cooking spray, turning to coat top.

Cover and let rise in a warm place (85°), free from drafts, 45 minutes or until doubled in size. (Press two fingers into dough. If indentation remains, dough has risen enough.) Punch dough down; cover and let rest 5 minutes.

5. Shape dough into a 12-inch oval loaf on a lightly floured surface. Place on a baking sheet lined with parchment paper. Lightly coat loaf with cooking spray. Cover with plastic wrap; let rise 30 minutes or until doubled in size.

6. Preheat oven to 400°.

7. Combine 1 teaspoon water and egg white in a small bowl. Gently brush egg white mixture over surface of loaf. Bake at 400° for 28 minutes or until loaf is golden brown and sounds hollow when tapped; let cool on a wire rack. Yield: 1 loaf; 20 servings (serving size: 1 slice).

CALORIES 101 (12% from fat); FAT 1.4g (sat 0.3g, mono 0.7g, poly 0.2g); PROTEIN 3.5g; CARB 18.7g; FIBER 1.5g; CHOL 11mg; IRON 1.1mg; SODIUM 189mg; CALC 20mg

MAKE AHEAD
Herring and Apple Salad

This is a version of *Heringsalat* (herring salad), which is traditionally prepared with herring, apples, and raw onions. You can substitute smoked trout for herring. Serve with a well-chilled lager and Brown Beer Rye Bread (recipe on page 356). Garnish with dill sprigs.

 2 cups finely diced Granny Smith apple (about 1 medium)
 ½ cup chopped Rio or other sweet onion
 ¼ cup chopped green onions
 1 teaspoon chopped fresh dill
 ½ teaspoon sugar
 Dash of freshly ground black pepper
 2 hard-cooked large eggs, finely chopped
 1 (12-ounce) jar kippered herring in wine sauce, drained and cut into ¼-inch pieces
 1 cup thinly sliced English cucumber

1. Combine first 8 ingredients in a bowl. Cover and chill 4 hours. Arrange cucumber slices on a serving platter; top with

herring salad. Yield: 8 servings (serving size: ½ cup).

CALORIES 106 (38% from fat); FAT 4.5g (sat 1.2g, mono 1.8g, poly 1g); PROTEIN 5.8g; CARB 9.6g; FIBER 0.7g; CHOL 73mg; IRON 0.3mg; SODIUM 348mg; CALC 14mg

MAKE AHEAD
Ginger Cake

To prepare this cake a day ahead, cool completely, wrap it with plastic wrap, and store at room temperature. Frost the cake with whipped topping just before serving.

 Cooking spray
 1¼ cups all-purpose flour (about 5½ ounces)
 ½ teaspoon ground ginger
 ½ teaspoon ground cinnamon
 1 teaspoon baking soda
 ¼ teaspoon salt
 ½ cup packed dark brown sugar
 4½ tablespoons butter, softened
 1 large egg
 ⅓ cup applesauce
 ¼ cup molasses
 ⅓ cup flat Guinness stout
 ¾ cup frozen reduced-calorie whipped topping (such as Cool Whip Lite), thawed

1. Preheat oven to 350°.

2. Coat a 9-inch round cake pan with cooking spray; line bottom of pan with wax paper. Coat wax paper with cooking spray; set aside.

3. Lightly spoon flour into dry measuring cups; level with a knife. Combine flour, ginger, and next 3 ingredients in a bowl, stirring with a whisk.

4. Place sugar and butter in a large bowl; beat with a mixer at medium-high speed until well blended (about 3 minutes). Add egg; beat well. Beat in applesauce and molasses (batter may look slightly curdled). Reduce mixing speed to low. Add one-third of flour mixture, and beat just until blended. Repeat procedure twice with remaining flour mixture. Add stout, and beat just until combined.

5. Scrape batter into prepared pan. Bake at 350° for 30 minutes or until a wooden pick inserted in center comes out clean. Cool in pan on a wire rack 10 minutes;

remove from pan. Cool completely. Spread cake with whipped topping. Cut into 8 wedges. Yield: 8 servings (serving size: 1 wedge).

CALORIES 244 (30% from fat); FAT 8g (sat 5g, mono 1.9g, poly 0.4g); PROTEIN 3g; CARB 40.1g; FIBER 0.8g; CHOL 43mg; IRON 2mg; SODIUM 295mg; CALC 43mg

MAKE AHEAD
Pork Loin Braised with Cabbage

Pork is typically served with cabbage at the German table. Use red cabbage, if you like, for slightly sweeter flavor. You can prepare the dish a day ahead, and chill it overnight. Cut the roast into ¼-inch slices. Gently reheat the meat with the cabbage mixture in a Dutch oven over medium-low heat.

 2 teaspoons Hungarian sweet paprika
 1 teaspoon chopped fresh thyme
 1 teaspoon kosher salt
 1 teaspoon freshly ground black pepper
 1 teaspoon chopped fresh sage
 1 (2-pound) boneless pork loin, trimmed
 Cooking spray
 ¾ cup diced Canadian bacon (about 4 ounces)
 14 cups thinly sliced cabbage (about 2 pounds)
 2½ cups thinly sliced onion (about 2 medium)
 ¾ cup thinly sliced carrot (about 1)
 1 tablespoon tomato paste
 2 teaspoons Hungarian sweet paprika
 1 teaspoon chopped fresh thyme
 ½ teaspoon freshly ground black pepper
 ½ teaspoon caraway seeds
 1 (12-ounce) bottle dark lager
 ½ teaspoon kosher salt

1. Preheat oven to 350°.

2. Combine first 5 ingredients; rub over pork. Heat a large ovenproof Dutch oven over medium-high heat. Coat pan with cooking spray. Add pork to pan;
Continued

cook 5 minutes, browning on all sides. Remove pork from pan.

3. Add bacon to pan; cook 3 minutes. Add cabbage, onion, and carrot. Cover, reduce heat to medium, and cook 15 minutes or until cabbage begins to wilt, stirring occasionally. Stir in tomato paste and next 5 ingredients. Return pork to pan. Cover and bake at 350° for 2 hours or until tender. Sprinkle with ½ teaspoon salt. Yield: 8 servings (serving size: 3 ounces pork and ¾ cup cabbage mixture).

CALORIES 255 (32% from fat); FAT 9g (sat 3.3g, mono 4g, poly 0.8g); PROTEIN 28.7g; CARB 11.9g; FIBER 3.7g; CHOL 76mg; IRON 1.7mg; SODIUM 596mg; CALC 84mg

---

QUICK & EASY
Warm Potato Salad with Beer and Mustard Dressing

Known as *Kartoffelsalat,* this side dish is popular throughout Germany. Use pale lager when preparing the salad, as a darker beer will discolor the potatoes. We enjoyed the variety of flavors from the different types of onions, but you can use all yellow onions, if you prefer. Garnish with chopped parsley, if desired.

SALAD:
- 3 pounds red potatoes
- ½ cup finely chopped red onion
- ¼ cup thinly sliced green onions
- ¼ cup finely chopped celery
- ¼ cup chopped fresh parsley
- ¼ cup finely chopped sweet pickles
- 2 tablespoons beer
- 2 tablespoons cider vinegar

DRESSING:
- ¼ cup olive oil, divided
- ¾ cup finely chopped yellow onion
- ¾ cup beer
- ¼ cup cider vinegar
- 1 teaspoon sugar
- ¾ teaspoon salt
- ⅛ teaspoon freshly ground black pepper
- 2 tablespoons Dijon mustard

1. To prepare salad, place potatoes in a large saucepan; cover with water. Bring to a boil. Reduce heat, and simmer 25 minutes or until tender. Drain; cool. Cut potatoes into ¼-inch slices. Combine potatoes, red onion, and next 6 ingredients; toss gently.

2. To prepare dressing, heat 2 tablespoons oil in a small skillet over medium-high heat. Add yellow onion to pan; sauté 3 minutes or until tender. Add ¾ cup beer and next 4 ingredients; bring to a boil. Cook until reduced to ½ cup (about 6 minutes). Place mixture in a food processor. Add mustard; process until smooth. With processor on, slowly pour 2 tablespoons oil through food chute, processing until smooth. Pour dressing over potato mixture; toss gently. Serve immediately. Yield: 8 servings (serving size: 1¼ cups).

CALORIES 223 (31% from fat); FAT 7.6g (sat 1.1g, mono 5.2g, poly 1.1g); PROTEIN 3.8g; CARB 33.6g; FIBER 3.5g; CHOL 0mg; IRON 1.6mg; SODIUM 247mg; CALC 32mg

---

QUICK & EASY
Turkey Bratwurst Patties

Germans are master sausage makers, producing an estimated 1,500 varieties. This recipe includes typical bratwurst spices like ginger and nutmeg; lean ground turkey is a lower-fat alternative to traditional pork and veal. Serve these patties with Brown Beer Rye Bread (recipe on page 356) and mustard for a hearty sandwich.

- 1 teaspoon kosher salt
- 1 teaspoon freshly ground black pepper
- ½ teaspoon sugar
- ½ teaspoon ground coriander
- ½ teaspoon dried rubbed sage
- ¼ teaspoon ground nutmeg
- ¼ teaspoon ground ginger
- 1 tablespoon fat-free milk
- 2 pounds lean ground turkey
Cooking spray

1. Combine all ingredients except cooking spray, and mix well. Divide mixture into 8 equal portions, shaping each into a ½-inch-thick patty. Heat a large non-stick skillet over medium-high heat. Coat pan with cooking spray. Add 4 patties; cook 4 minutes on each side or until done. Repeat procedure with cooking spray and remaining patties. Yield: 8 servings (serving size: 1 patty).

CALORIES 172 (49% from fat); FAT 9.4g (sat 2.6g, mono 3.5g, poly 2.3g); PROTEIN 19.9g; CARB 0.6g; FIBER 0.1g; CHOL 90mg; IRON 1.5mg; SODIUM 343mg; CALC 19mg

---

on hand

Cider Rules

A seasonal favorite, this fresh beverage delivers deep apple essence in cakes, roasts, salads, and other dishes.

Duck Breasts with Cider-Farro Risotto

Farro is also known as spelt; look for it alongside other specialty grains.

RISOTTO:
- 2 cups farro
- 3 cups fat-free, less-sodium chicken broth
- 3 cups apple cider
- 2 tablespoons butter
- 4 cups chopped fennel bulb (about 2)
- 1½ cups dry white wine
- 1 cup water (optional)
- 1½ teaspoons grated lemon rind
- 1 teaspoon salt
- 1 teaspoon freshly ground black pepper
- ½ teaspoon ground cinnamon

DUCK:
- 8 (6-ounce) boneless duck breast halves, thawed and skinned
- ½ teaspoon salt
- ½ teaspoon chopped fresh thyme
- ¼ teaspoon freshly ground black pepper
- 2 garlic cloves, minced
- 2 tablespoons olive oil, divided

1. To prepare risotto, place farro in a large bowl; cover with water to 1 inch above farro. Let stand 30 minutes; drain.
2. Combine broth and cider in a large

saucepan; bring to a simmer (do not boil). Keep warm over low heat.

3. Melt butter in a large saucepan over medium-high heat. Add fennel, and sauté 5 minutes or until lightly browned and tender. Remove fennel from pan. Add farro, and cook 3 minutes over medium heat, stirring constantly. Add wine, and cook 5 minutes or until liquid is nearly absorbed, stirring constantly. Add broth mixture, 1 cup at a time, stirring constantly until each portion is absorbed before adding next (about 35 minutes total). Add up to 1 cup water as needed until farro is al dente. Stir in fennel, lemon rind, and next 3 ingredients. Remove from heat. Cover and keep warm.

4. To prepare duck, sprinkle duck with ½ teaspoon salt, thyme, and ¼ teaspoon pepper; rub with garlic. Heat 1 tablespoon oil in a large nonstick skillet over medium-high heat. Add 4 breast halves, and cook 2½ minutes or until browned. Turn breasts over; cook over medium-low heat 5½ minutes or until desired degree of doneness. Repeat procedure with 1 tablespoon oil and remaining breast halves. Serve duck with farro risotto. Yield: 8 servings (serving size: 1 breast half and about ½ cup farro risotto).

CALORIES 459 (22% from fat); FAT 11.2g (sat 3.2g, mono 4.6g, poly 1.1g); PROTEIN 42.9g; CARB 50.5g; FIBER 2.1g; CHOL 190mg; IRON 8.4mg; SODIUM 659mg; CALC 63mg

Hard Facts

Hard cider dates back thousands of years and is historically more prevalent than sweet cider, in part because hard cider didn't require refrigeration. Ancient Celts made a simple alcoholic brew from small, hard, wild apples. Romans arrived in England in 55 B.C. to find the natives enjoying their own version of cider.

Hard cider is so named not because of its alcohol content but for the small, rock-hard cider apples from which the juice is extracted. American hard cider ranges from four to eight percent alcohol content, and can be still or sparkling. Use hard cider in cooking just as you would beer or wine.

Poached Shrimp Salad with Cider Dressing

Cider's bright, fresh-pressed flavor comes through in both the shrimp and dressing for this dish. For more tartness, you can substitute Granny Smith apples for Fujis.

SHRIMP:

    4 cups apple cider
    ¼ cup thinly sliced peeled fresh ginger
    3 tablespoons fresh lemon juice (about 1 lemon)
    4 teaspoons Worcestershire sauce
   10 black peppercorns
    2 (3-inch) cinnamon sticks
    2 star anise
   1½ pounds large shrimp, peeled and deveined

DRESSING:

    ½ cup apple cider
    2 tablespoons cider vinegar
    1 tablespoon plain low-fat yogurt
   1½ teaspoons extravirgin olive oil
    ½ teaspoon prepared horseradish

SALAD:

    5 cups torn Boston lettuce (about 2 small heads)
    4 cups trimmed watercress (about 2 bunches)
    2 Fuji apples, cored and cut into ¼-inch-thick wedges
    ½ thinly sliced peeled avocado

1. To prepare shrimp, combine first 7 ingredients in a large saucepan; bring to a boil. Reduce heat, and simmer 10 minutes. Strain cider mixture through a sieve into a large bowl; discard solids. Return cider mixture to pan; bring to a boil. Stir in shrimp; reduce heat, and simmer 5 minutes. Remove pan from heat. Let stand 30 minutes. Remove shrimp from cider mixture, and discard cider mixture. Chop shrimp; chill.

2. To prepare dressing, combine ½ cup cider and next 4 ingredients in a medium bowl, stirring with a whisk.

3. To prepare salad, place lettuce and remaining 3 ingredients in a large bowl. Drizzle ½ cup dressing over lettuce mixture; toss gently to coat. Add shrimp to remaining dressing; toss to coat. Arrange shrimp on top of salad. Yield: 4 servings (serving size: about 2 cups).

CALORIES 308 (26% from fat); FAT 8.7g (sat 1.2g, mono 1.8g, poly 1.4g); PROTEIN 37.6g; CARB 22g; FIBER 3g; CHOL 259mg; IRON 5.4mg; SODIUM 279mg; CALC 163mg

Pork Tenderloin with Shallot-Cider Sauce

While five-spice powder is a mainstay of the Chinese kitchen, it contains standard American companions for pork and apples, including cinnamon, cloves, and fennel seed. You'll find the spice mix at Asian markets and the spice section of grocery stores.

PORK:

    1 (1-pound) pork tenderloin, trimmed
    1 tablespoon olive oil
    1 garlic clove, minced
    ½ teaspoon salt
    ¼ teaspoon freshly ground black pepper
       Cooking spray

SAUCE:

    ⅓ cup finely chopped shallots
   1½ cups apple cider
    ½ cup less-sodium beef broth
    ½ cup applesauce
    ½ teaspoon salt
    ¼ teaspoon five-spice powder
    ¼ teaspoon freshly ground black pepper
    3 tablespoons fresh lemon juice (about 1 lemon)

1. Preheat oven to 400°.

2. To prepare pork, rub pork with oil and garlic; sprinkle with ½ teaspoon salt and ¼ teaspoon pepper. Place pork on grill rack or broiler pan coated with cooking spray. Bake at 400° for 30 minutes or until a thermometer registers 160° (barely pink). Let stand 5 minutes before slicing.

3. To prepare sauce, heat a medium saucepan over medium heat. Coat pan with cooking spray. Add shallots, and

Continued

cook 1½ minutes or until tender, stirring occasionally. Stir in cider and next 5 ingredients; bring to a boil. Cook until reduced to 1 cup (about 10 minutes); stir in lemon juice. Serve sauce with pork. Yield: 4 servings (serving size: 3 ounces pork and about ¼ cup sauce).

CALORIES 262 (26% from fat); FAT 7.6g (sat 1.9g, mono 4.1g, poly 0.7g); PROTEIN 25.1g; CARB 23.2g; FIBER 0.6g; CHOL 67mg; IRON 1.7mg; SODIUM 703mg; CALC 16mg

MAKE AHEAD
Hot Mulled Cider

A steaming fragrant mug of this cider is a welcome treat on a brisk fall afternoon. Garnish with a cinnamon stick or lemon slice, if desired.

    4   cups apple cider
    ¼   cup fresh orange juice
   10   black peppercorns
    6   whole cloves
    5   whole white cardamom pods, crushed
    4   star anise
    3   (¼-inch-thick) slices lemon
    3   cinnamon sticks
    1   (½-inch) piece peeled fresh ginger, thinly sliced

1. Combine all ingredients in a medium saucepan over medium heat; bring to a simmer. Cook 30 minutes. Strain cider mixture through a fine sieve into a bowl, and discard solids. Serve cider hot. Yield: 4 servings (serving size: about ¾ cup).

CALORIES 127 (0% from fat); FAT 0g; PROTEIN 0.1g; CARB 11.2g; FIBER 0g; CHOL 0mg; IRON 0mg; SODIUM 0mg; CALC 2mg

MAKE AHEAD
Spice Cake with Cider Glaze

The glaze boosts the apple essence of this cake without making it overly sweet.

CAKE:
   3½   cups all-purpose flour (about 15¾ ounces)
    2   teaspoons baking soda
    2   teaspoons apple-pie spice
    1   teaspoon baking powder
    ½   teaspoon ground cardamom
    ¼   teaspoon salt
    1   cup sugar
    ¼   cup butter, softened
    2   tablespoons walnut oil or canola oil
    4   large eggs
    1   cup reduced-fat buttermilk
    1   cup apple cider
    ½   teaspoon vanilla extract
        Cooking spray

GLAZE:
    1   cup apple cider
    1   teaspoon sugar

1. Preheat oven to 350°.
2. To prepare cake, lightly spoon flour into dry measuring cups; level with a knife. Combine flour, baking soda, and next 4 ingredients in a large bowl; stir with a whisk.
3. Combine 1 cup sugar, butter, and oil in a large bowl; beat with a mixer at medium speed until light and fluffy (about 5 minutes). Add eggs, 1 at a time, beating well after each addition. Combine buttermilk and 1 cup cider in a small bowl. Add flour mixture and cider mixture alternately to sugar mixture, beginning and ending with flour mixture. Stir in vanilla. Pour into a Bundt pan coated with cooking spray. Bake at 350° for 45 minutes or until a wooden pick inserted in center comes out clean. Cool in pan 10 minutes on a wire rack; remove from pan. Cool completely on wire rack.
4. To prepare glaze, combine 1 cup cider and 1 teaspoon sugar in a small saucepan over medium-low heat; bring to a simmer. Cook until reduced to ¼ cup (about 15 minutes). Drizzle glaze over each serving of cake. Yield: 16 servings (serving size: 1 slice and ¾ teaspoon glaze).

CALORIES 235 (25% from fat); FAT 6.4g (sat 2.6g, mono 1.7g, poly 1.5g); PROTEIN 5.2g; CARB 39.2g; FIBER 0.9g; CHOL 62mg; IRON 1.6mg; SODIUM 276mg; CALC 53mg

Chicken with Cider and Dried Plums

This dish is inspired by the simple country braises served in the Dordogne region of southwest France. Serve with rice or over egg noodles.

    2   tablespoons olive oil
    6   (6-ounce) skinless, boneless chicken breast halves
    2   cups chopped onion (about 1 large)
    ¾   cup finely chopped shallots (about 4)
    2   cups apple cider
    ½   cup golden raisins
    2   tablespoons fresh lemon juice
   1½   teaspoons curry powder
    1   teaspoon salt
    1   teaspoon freshly ground black pepper
    1   cup pitted dried plums, halved

1. Heat oil in a large Dutch oven over medium-high heat. Add chicken; cook 3 minutes on each side or until browned. Remove chicken from pan. Add onion and shallots to pan; sauté 3 minutes or until lightly browned, stirring occasionally. Stir in cider and next 5 ingredients. Add chicken; bring to a boil. Cover, reduce heat, and simmer 5 minutes. Uncover and cook 25 minutes, turning chicken occasionally. Stir in plums; cook 5 minutes. Yield: 6 servings (serving size: 1 chicken breast half and about ⅓ cup sauce).

CALORIES 427 (19% from fat); FAT 9.2g (sat 1.9g, mono 4.9g, poly 1.5g); PROTEIN 41.9g; CARB 43.8g; FIBER 3.3g; CHOL 108mg; IRON 2.4mg; SODIUM 498mg; CALC 59mg

Pot Roast Primer

Learn to master this satisfying and wonderfully rich classic.

To most people, "pot roast" means slow-cooked beef with carrots, potatoes, or other vegetables added partway through cooking. The term actually refers either to the cooking method or the dish. Many of these recipes can be made ahead, and some freeze well. A single roast easily feeds six to eight and often offers the promise of future meals made from leftovers.

MAKE AHEAD • FREEZABLE
Pork Roast with White Beans and Cranberries

This rich dish balances sweet and tart flavors from the cranberries with savory notes from the pork and sage.

  1 pound dried navy beans (about 2 cups)
  1 (5-pound) pork shoulder blade roast, trimmed
1½ teaspoons kosher salt, divided
 ¼ teaspoon freshly ground black pepper
  2 tablespoons minced fresh sage, divided
    Cooking spray
1½ cups sliced shallots (about 8 medium)
  5 cups water
  3 fresh sage sprigs
 ½ cup dried cranberries

1. Sort and wash beans; place in a large Dutch oven. Cover with water to 2 inches above beans; cover and let stand 8 hours. Drain.
2. Preheat oven to 350°.
3. Sprinkle pork roast with 1 teaspoon salt and pepper. Rub surface of roast with 4 teaspoons minced sage. Heat a Dutch oven over medium-high heat. Coat pan with cooking spray. Add roast to pan; cook 15 minutes, turning to brown on all sides. Remove roast from pan. Add shallots to pan; sauté 3 minutes or until tender. Return roast to pan. Add ½ teaspoon salt,

beans, 5 cups water, and sage sprigs to pan; bring to a simmer. Cover and bake at 350° for 2 hours. Add cranberries to pan; bake an additional 30 minutes or until roast is tender. Remove sage sprigs; discard. Remove roast from pan; shred pork with 2 forks. Sprinkle with 2 teaspoons minced sage. Serve roast with bean mixture. Yield: 13 servings (serving size: about 3 ounces roast and ½ cup beans).

CALORIES 407 (32% from fat); FAT 14.4g (sat 5g, mono 6.3g, poly 1.5g); PROTEIN 36.1g; CARB 34g; FIBER 8.7g; CHOL 103mg; IRON 4.4mg; SODIUM 284mg; CALC 83mg

MAKE AHEAD
Pot-Roasted Rosemary Lamb with Fingerling Potatoes

This dish works well for entertaining a crowd. Small red potatoes stand in nicely for fingerlings, if necessary. Garnish each serving with a rosemary sprig, if desired.

  2 tablespoons fresh rosemary leaves
20 garlic cloves, peeled
  1 (4-pound) boneless leg of lamb, trimmed
  1 teaspoon kosher salt
  1 teaspoon freshly ground black pepper
  2 teaspoons olive oil
  2 cups fat-free, less-sodium beef broth
  1 cup sweet vermouth
  2 pounds fingerling potatoes
  1 tablespoon cornstarch

1. Preheat oven to 300°.
2. Place rosemary and garlic in a food processor; process until finely chopped. Sprinkle lamb evenly with salt and pepper; rub surface of roast with garlic mixture. Heat oil in a large Dutch oven over medium-high heat. Add lamb to pan; cook 7 minutes, turning to brown on all sides. Stir in broth and vermouth; bring to a simmer. Cover and bake at 300° for 2½ hours.
3. Add potatoes to pan. Cover and bake an additional 30 minutes or until potatoes are tender. Remove lamb from pan. Cover and keep warm. Drain potato mixture through a sieve over a bowl. Reserve potatoes, and keep warm. Return cooking liquid to pan; bring to a boil over medium-high heat. Cook 10 minutes or until reduced to 3 cups. Add cornstarch to pan, stirring with a whisk; bring to a boil. Cook 1 minute, stirring constantly.
4. Shred lamb with 2 forks. Serve with potatoes and sauce. Yield: 13 servings (serving size: about 3 ounces meat, ¼ cup potatoes, and about ¼ cup sauce).

CALORIES 337 (40% from fat); FAT 14.9g (sat 6g, mono 6.5g, poly 1.1g); PROTEIN 31.7g; CARB 14.5g; FIBER 1.4g; CHOL 111mg; IRON 2.9mg; SODIUM 294mg; CALC 39mg

---

Recycling Leftovers

• Make hash using leftover meat and potatoes. You can also peel and chop potatoes to pan-fry with the meat.

• Shred leftover beef, lamb, or pork, and add it along with more broth, if necessary, to pasta dishes.

• Shred or chop leftover beef or pork, and combine it with chopped canned green chiles, chopped white onion, and chopped fresh cilantro to use as a filling for burritos or tacos.

• Add chopped leftover meat to vegetable or bean soups.

• Use leftover meat for sandwiches.

Pot Roast 101

Choose the Pot

In keeping with pot roast's down-home roots, the dish requires little in the way of specialty equipment. A pot with a tight-fitting lid is crucial. Many cooks prefer a heavy cast-iron pot, often called a Dutch oven. Enameled cast iron (a French oven) is another good option. Although this kind of pot is a bit pricier, enameled cast iron cooks beautifully on the stove and in the oven, and cleanup is straight-forward.

A heavy pot is important so you don't burn or scorch the meat and aromatics when browning, and it conducts heat evenly to insulate the contents during roasting. A heavy cast-iron pot delivers more intense flavor because it cooks hot and browns evenly. Of course, any large, heavy, stainless steel, aluminum, or other nonreactive pan with a tight-fitting lid will work as long as the pan is large enough to accommodate the roast.

You'll need a pair of sturdy tongs to transfer the roast in and out of the pot. If you have two pairs of tongs, use both of them—one to handle the uncooked roast and the second to move the cooked meat. Otherwise, be sure to wash the tongs after handling raw or partially cooked meat. A wooden spoon is also handy to stir aromatics as they brown or to mix vegetables into the pot partway through cooking.

Select the Right Cut of Meat

Pot roasting is a great technique for less expensive, tough cuts of meat, such as those from the shoulder and neck, arm, or hip and leg. These sections are typi-cally fattier and therefore more flavorful, but they're also tough because they con-tain more connective tissue than more expensive cuts. Cooking tough cuts slowly in a flavorful liquid melts the fat away and breaks down the tough connec-tive tissue, resulting in fork-tender meat.

Beef pot roasts generally come from the chuck (cut from entire shoulder section, between the neck and arm). Brisket, rump roast, and top and bottom round are a bit leaner than chuck and suitable for pot-roasting as well. Leg of lamb and pork shoulder roasts will also work.

Whichever meat or cut you choose, look for a roast that's well marbled. The smaller marbling creates smaller pockets of fat, contributing to a moist and compact roast. Avoid roasts with large ribbons of fat, as they will yield a greasy, misshapen, and fatty pot roast.

Brown the Meat

Season the meat before you cook it. Salt and freshly ground black pepper are the basics, but you can make spice pastes or rubs with fresh garlic, chopped fresh herbs, and ground spices to rub on the meat. Then heat a Dutch oven, and brown the meat on all sides. Since the meat will simmer in liquid, this step is critical to de-velop color and flavor. The natural sugars in the paste or rub have a chance to caramelize, while the browned exterior makes the finished dish look attractive and appetizing.

Cook It

Pot roast is braised, which means the meat cooks in a few inches of liquid. You can cook it on the stove top or in the oven. When roasted in the oven, the temperature range is usually between 300° and 350°. Any higher and the meat will likely be dry and tough. Atop the stove, maintain the liquid at a slow simmer (about 180°) over medium-low heat.

Add the Vegetables

You should be able to cut the cooked pot roast on your plate with a fork. To ensure that both the meat and the vegetables will be cooked perfectly, it's usually best to cook the meat until it is almost done before adding most vegetables. Test for doneness by inserting a long, thin skewer or long fork tines into the meat. If there is little or no resistance, the meat is properly cooked. Add vegetables, such as carrots or potatoes, at this point, and continue cooking until the vegetables are tender.

Use the Pan Juices

While some pot roasts cook with a gener-ous amount of liquid, others have just enough wine or broth to yield a moist roast and provide flavorful pan juices to drizzle over the meat. If the cooking liquid is too thick or thin, you can always adjust it to suit your tastes. To thicken pan juices, cook them over medium-high heat to re-duce the liquid, or stir in a little cornstarch. If pan juices are too thick, add a bit of wine, broth, or water and simmer briefly to achieve your desired consistency.

Serve It

Simply remove the meat from the pan, shred with two forks or slice it thinly, and serve with the vegetables and pan juices or gravy. Chopped fresh herbs, herb sprigs, or grated fresh citrus rind are fitting gar-nishes for these hearty, earthy dishes.

Freeze It

Make sure the cooked, cooled meat is completely covered with liquid before you freeze it. You can accomplish this by cut-ting the meat into smaller pieces and im-mersing them in pan juices. Or add a bit of broth to the gravy or pan juices until it cov-ers the roast. If you add broth, boil the liq-uid mixture after you thaw to thicken its consistency and concentrate the flavor. You may prefer not to freeze most vegeta-bles, as they tend to deteriorate when frozen. You can roast fresh potatoes, car-rots, or other vegetables and add them to the thawed roast and pan juices.

Chinese-Style Stove-Top Pot Roast with Noodles

Ginger, soy sauce, star anise, and Chinese five-spice powder infuse this dish with Asian flavor.

    4   teaspoons peanut oil, divided
    1   (2½-pound) sirloin tip roast,
        trimmed
    1   teaspoon Chinese five-spice
        powder
    ¼   teaspoon kosher salt
    5   cups fat-free, less-sodium beef
        broth
    ½   cup dry sherry
    ¼   cup thinly sliced peeled fresh
        ginger
    3   tablespoons low-sodium soy
        sauce
    ¼   teaspoon crushed red pepper
    4   garlic cloves, crushed
    3   star anise
    2   cups sliced shiitake mushroom
        caps
    2   cups (2-inch) julienne-cut carrot
        (about 2 large)
    4   baby bok choy, halved lengthwise
        (about 1¾ pounds)
    12 ounces fresh uncooked Chinese
        egg noodles
    ¼   cup thinly sliced green onions

1. Heat 2 teaspoons oil in a large Dutch oven over medium-high heat. Sprinkle roast evenly with five-spice powder and salt. Add meat to pan; cook 5 minutes, turning to brown on all sides. Add broth and next 6 ingredients to pan; bring to a simmer. Cover, reduced heat, and simmer 3½ hours or until meat is tender. Remove meat from pan. Cover; keep warm.
2. Strain cooking liquid through a sieve into a bowl; discard solids. Heat 2 teaspoons oil in pan over medium-high heat. Add mushrooms and carrot; sauté 5 minutes. Add bok choy and 4 cups reserved cooking liquid. Cover and cook 5 minutes or until bok choy is tender.
3. Cook noodles according to package directions, omitting salt and fat. Drain. Divide noodles evenly among 8 bowls. Shred meat with 2 forks; arrange 3 ounces meat over each serving. Top each serving with 2 tablespoons vegetable mixture and ½ cup broth. Place 1 bok choy half on each serving; sprinkle each serving with 1½ teaspoons green onions. Yield: 8 servings.

CALORIES 414 (31% from fat); FAT 14.2g (sat 4.6g, mono 6.5g, poly 1.4g); PROTEIN 40.1g; CARB 29.8g; FIBER 3.1g; CHOL 82mg; IRON 4.2mg; SODIUM 846mg; CALC 207mg

Classic Beef Pot Roast

(pictured on page 250)

Cuts of beef that perform well for pot roasting go by many different names: Blade roast, cross-rib roast (or shoulder clod), seven-bone pot roast, arm pot roast, and boneless chuck roast are all acceptable cuts for this traditional recipe.

    1   teaspoon olive oil
    1   (3-pound) boneless chuck roast,
        trimmed
    1   teaspoon kosher salt
    ¼   teaspoon freshly ground black
        pepper
    2   cups coarsely chopped onion
    1   cup dry red wine
    4   thyme sprigs
    3   garlic cloves, chopped
    1   (14-ounce) can fat-free,
        less-sodium beef broth
    1   bay leaf
    4   large carrots, peeled and cut
        diagonally into 1-inch pieces
    2   pounds Yukon gold potatoes,
        peeled and cut into 2-inch pieces
    Thyme leaves (optional)

1. Preheat oven to 350°.
2. Heat oil in a large Dutch oven over medium-high heat. Sprinkle roast with salt and pepper. Add roast to pan; cook 5 minutes, turning to brown on all sides. Remove roast from pan. Add onion to pan; sauté 8 minutes or until tender.
3. Return roast to pan. Add wine and next 4 ingredients; bring to a simmer. Cover and bake at 350° for 1½ hours or until roast is almost tender.
4. Add carrots and potatoes to pan. Cover and bake an additional 1 hour or until vegetables are tender. Remove thyme sprigs and bay leaf; discard. Shred meat with 2 forks. Serve roast with vegetable mixture and cooking liquid. Garnish with thyme leaves, if desired. Yield: 10 servings (serving size: 3 ounces roast, about ¾ cup vegetables, and about 3 tablespoons cooking liquid).

CALORIES 307 (31% from fat); FAT 10.4g (sat 3.5g, mono 4.8g, poly 0.5g); PROTEIN 28.6g; CARB 23.7g; FIBER 2.8g; CHOL 85mg; IRON 3.9mg; SODIUM 340mg; CALC 34mg

Argentinean-Style Pot Roast

This is a simplified version of *matambre*, a stuffed, rolled pot roast from Argentina.

    1   (2-pound) flank steak, trimmed
    1½ teaspoons salt
    ½   teaspoon freshly ground black
        pepper
    ¼   teaspoon Spanish smoked paprika
    Cooking spray
    1½ cups chopped onion (about
        1 medium)
    1   cup chopped red bell pepper
        (about 1 small)
    5   garlic cloves, minced
    2   cups loosely packed baby spinach
        leaves
    1   cup Argentinean malbec or other
        dry red wine
    1   (14-ounce) can fat-free,
        less-sodium beef broth
    1   teaspoon chopped fresh oregano

1. Preheat oven to 350°.
2. Cut horizontally through center of steak, cutting to, but not through, other side using a sharp knife; open flat as you would a book. Combine salt, black pepper, and paprika, stirring well; rub both sides of steak with salt mixture.
3. Heat a large Dutch oven over medium-high heat. Coat pan with cooking spray. Add onion and bell pepper; sauté 5 minutes or until tender. Add garlic; sauté 1 minute. Add spinach; sauté 30 seconds or until wilted.
4. Spread onion mixture over steak, leaving a ½-inch margin around edges; fold top over onion mixture, and secure with wooden picks.

Continued

5. Wipe pan with paper towels; place over medium-high heat. Recoat pan with cooking spray. Add steak to pan; cook 5 minutes. Add wine and broth to pan; bring to a simmer. Cover and bake at 350° for 45 minutes or until steak is tender. Remove steak from pan. Cover and keep warm.

6. Place pan over medium-high heat; bring broth mixture to a boil. Cook until liquid is reduced to 1 cup (about 10 minutes). Cut steak into thin slices; serve with sauce. Sprinkle with oregano. Yield: 8 servings (serving size: 3 ounces steak and 2 tablespoons sauce).

CALORIES 188 (43% from fat); FAT 8.9g (sat 3.8g, mono 3.7g, poly 0.3g); PROTEIN 20.2g; CARB 6g; FIBER 1.2g; CHOL 48mg; IRON 2.9mg; SODIUM 596mg; CALC 23mg

---

MAKE AHEAD • FREEZABLE

Slow Cooker Beef Pot Roast with Gremolata

To produce a successful slow cooker pot roast, the classic recipe needs a flavor boost (here, from sun-dried tomatoes) and less liquid than oven or stove-top versions. A mixture of garlic, herbs, and lemon rind, gremolata is traditionally served in Italy with veal shanks.

POT ROAST:

  1 (2½-pound) boneless cross-rib chuck roast, trimmed
1½ teaspoons salt
  1 teaspoon freshly ground black pepper
  1 teaspoon olive oil
Cooking spray
  2 cups chopped onion (about 1 large)
  1 cup fat-free, less-sodium beef broth
  ¾ cup dry red wine
  ¼ cup chopped drained oil-packed sun-dried tomato halves
  ¼ teaspoon crushed red pepper
  4 thyme sprigs
  4 garlic cloves, crushed
  2 bay leaves
  3 large carrots, peeled and cut into 1-inch pieces
  2 pounds baking potatoes, peeled and cut into 1-inch pieces

GREMOLATA:

  2 tablespoons chopped fresh flat-leaf parsley
  1 teaspoon chopped fresh thyme
  ½ teaspoon grated lemon rind
  1 garlic clove, minced

1. To prepare pot roast, sprinkle roast evenly with salt and black pepper. Heat oil in a large nonstick skillet over medium-high heat. Coat pan with cooking spray. Add roast to pan; cook 5 minutes, turning to brown on all sides. Transfer roast to an electric slow cooker. Recoat pan with cooking spray. Add onion to pan; sauté 8 minutes or until tender. Add broth and next 6 ingredients to pan; bring to a simmer. Add broth mixture to slow cooker. Arrange carrots and potatoes around roast in slow cooker. Cover and cook on high 2 hours. Reduce heat to low; cook 4 hours. Remove bay leaves and thyme sprigs from slow cooker; discard. Remove roast from slow cooker; shred with 2 forks.

2. To prepare gremolata, combine parsley and remaining 3 ingredients in a small bowl, stirring well. Serve with roast and vegetable mixture. Yield: 10 servings (serving size: 3 ounces meat, about ¾ cup vegetable mixture, and about 1 teaspoon gremolata).

CALORIES 309 (31% from fat); FAT 10.8g (sat 3.6g, mono 5.1g, poly 0.6g); PROTEIN 29.1g; CARB 23.3g; FIBER 2.5g; CHOL 84mg; IRON 4.5mg; SODIUM 480mg; CALC 41mg

WINE NOTE: Slow-cooked pot roast has a tender meatiness that's simple but luscious, especially when the roast's flavors are entwined with the earthiness of long-simmered root vegetables. Wines that work well with a dish like this are also soft, earthy, and (usually) red. Supple zinfandel such as Bogle's Old Vine Zinfandel from California ($11) is a good choice.

MAKE AHEAD • FREEZABLE

Brisket Pot Roast with Butternut Squash, Sweet Potatoes, and Apricots

Brisket, a big flat roast, requires a large Dutch oven. A roasting pan with a tight-fitting lid will work as well for this recipe.

  2 teaspoons olive oil
  1 (3-pound) beef brisket, trimmed
1½ teaspoons kosher salt
  ½ teaspoon freshly ground black pepper
  2 cups chopped onion
  1 cup Madeira
  1 (14-ounce) can fat-free, less-sodium beef broth
  4 garlic cloves, chopped
  1 bay leaf
  4 cups (1-inch) cubed peeled butternut squash (about 1¼ pounds)
  4 cups (1-inch) cubed peeled sweet potato (about 2 medium)
  1 cup dried apricots, chopped
  3 tablespoons chopped fresh flat-leaf parsley

1. Preheat oven to 350°.

2. Heat oil in a large Dutch oven over medium-high heat. Sprinkle brisket with salt and pepper. Add brisket to pan; cook 5 minutes, turning to brown on all sides. Remove from pan. Add onion to pan; sauté 8 minutes or until browned. Return beef to pan. Add Madeira, broth, garlic, and bay leaf to pan; bring to a simmer. Cover and bake at 350° for 1½ hours.

3. Add squash, potato, and apricots to pan. Cover and bake an additional 1 hour or until vegetables are tender. Remove bay leaf from pan, and discard. Remove brisket from pan; cut diagonally across grain into thin slices. Sprinkle with parsley. Serve with vegetables and cooking liquid. Yield: 11 servings (serving size: 3 ounces meat, ½ cup vegetables, and about 2 tablespoons cooking liquid).

CALORIES 329 (25% from fat); FAT 9.3g (sat 3.4g, mono 4.2g, poly 0.4g); PROTEIN 31.3g; CARB 25.9g; FIBER 3g; CHOL 42mg; IRON 3.7mg; SODIUM 383mg; CALC 62mg

Seven Steps to Great Pot Roast

1. *Gather the right equipment. All you need to prepare pot roast are a heavy, nonreactive pot with a tight-fitting lid, such as a Dutch oven; at least one pair of sturdy tongs; and a wooden spoon.*

2. *Select the proper cuts of meat to ensure success. Pot roasting works well to tenderize tougher cuts of meat from the shoulder, arm, or leg sections.*

3. *Season the meat before you cook it. Salt and pepper are essential, and some recipes include spice blends or chopped fresh herbs.*

4. *Brown the meat before you braise it. This builds flavor and gives the cooked roast an appealing golden-brown appearance.*

5. *A flavorful broth mixture yields tasty results. The cooking liquid usually consists of broth, wine, and seasonings, such as garlic, fresh herbs, bay leaves, or other aromatic ingredients.*

6. *Most vegetables cook more quickly than the large cuts of meat used for pot roast. In order to cook both to perfection, add the vegetables to the pan partway through cooking.*

7. *Use two forks to shred the tender meat before serving.*

Newcastle Pot Roast

England's famous dark beer has an affinity for beef and caramelized onions. Serve over egg noodles, if you prefer.

POT ROAST:

- 2 tablespoons butter
- 12 cups sliced onion (about 1½ pounds)
- Cooking spray
- 1 (4-pound) beef rump roast, trimmed
- 1½ teaspoons kosher salt
- ½ teaspoon freshly ground black pepper
- 1 cup fat-free, less-sodium beef broth
- 1 tablespoon fresh thyme leaves
- 1 (12-ounce) bottle dark beer (such as Newcastle)
- 3 tablespoons cornstarch

POTATOES:

- 4 cups fat-free milk
- 4 pounds baking potatoes, peeled and cubed
- 1 teaspoon poppy seeds
- ¾ teaspoon kosher salt
- ½ teaspoon freshly ground black pepper

1. Preheat oven to 300°.
2. To prepare pot roast, melt butter in a large Dutch oven over medium-high heat. Add onion to pan; sauté 12 minutes or until almost tender. Reduce heat to medium-low; cook 40 minutes or until onions are caramelized, stirring frequently. Transfer onions to a bowl.
3. Place pan over medium-high heat. Coat pan with cooking spray. Sprinkle roast evenly with 1½ teaspoons salt and ½ teaspoon pepper. Add roast to pan; cook 5 minutes, turning to brown on all sides. Add onion mixture, broth, thyme, and beer to pan; bring to a simmer. Cover and bake at 300° for 2 hours or until tender, turning roast over after 1 hour.
4. Remove roast from pan. Cover and keep warm. Place pan over medium-high heat. Add cornstarch to pan, stirring with a whisk; bring to a boil. Cook 1 minute, stirring constantly.
5. To prepare potatoes, place milk and potatoes in a large saucepan; bring to a boil. Reduce heat, and simmer 15 minutes or until tender. Mash potatoes; stir in poppy seeds, ¾ teaspoon salt, and ½ teaspoon pepper.
6. Serve roast with potatoes and sauce. Yield: 10 servings (serving size: about 3 ounces roast, about ¾ cup potatoes, and ⅔ cup sauce).

CALORIES 445 (26% from fat); FAT 13g (sat 5.3g, mono 5g, poly 0.6g); PROTEIN 48g; CARB 31.1g; FIBER 7g; CHOL 122mg; IRON 5.3mg; SODIUM 610mg; CALC 212mg

---

Seasoning Cast Iron

A well-seasoned cast-iron pot helps avoid chemical reactions caused by acidic ingredients, such as vinegar, wine, or tomatoes, that can affect the flavor of the dish and/or discolor the pan. Preseasoned cast iron is now available, though it's easy enough to season a pan yourself. Most unseasoned cast-iron skillets or pots come with seasoning instructions, which typically direct you to scrub and clean the pan. Then you dry it, oil it, and bake it at 350° for 1½ to 2 hours. Next, cool the pan and repeat the oiling and baking process a second time, cool it, and wipe away any residual oil with paper towels. This process seals the pores of the iron to prevent rust and any possible reactions.

Cast iron can rust if handled or stored improperly. Follow a few basic maintenance and storage tips to preserve and extend the life of your pot:

- Never wash cast iron in the dishwasher.
- Make sure to dry it thoroughly and rub on a little oil before storing it.
- If exposed to acidic foods, cast iron may corrode. To restore a pot, scrub the rust away with steel wool and reseason it.

Stuffed Spuds

Delicious fillings turn baked potatoes into crowd-pleasing sides.

While most people at your table would be perfectly content with a bit of butter or sour cream on top of a potato, why stop there? A baked potato practically begs to be dressed. Explore the possibilities with these recipes.

Yukon Gold Potatoes with Gorgonzola and Pancetta

First developed in Canada in the early 1980s, Yukon gold potatoes are a cross between a North American white-fleshed potato and a yellow-fleshed South American potato. Their smooth texture and buttery flavor are well suited to the rich Gorgonzola filling.

- 6 large Yukon gold potatoes (about 3 pounds)
- ½ cup fat-free sour cream
- ¼ cup (1 ounce) crumbled Gorgonzola cheese
- 3 ounces pancetta, finely diced
- 2 garlic cloves, minced
- 3 tablespoons finely chopped chives

1. Preheat oven to 375°.
2. Pierce potatoes with a fork, and bake at 375° for 1 hour or until tender. Cool potatoes slightly.
3. Combine sour cream and cheese in a small bowl; partially mash with a fork.
4. Heat a small nonstick skillet over medium heat. Add pancetta; cook 2 minutes. Add garlic; cook 1 minute.
5. Split potatoes lengthwise, cutting to, but not through, other side. Spoon 2 tablespoons cheese mixture into each potato. Top each serving with 4 teaspoons pancetta mixture and 1½ teaspoons chives. Yield: 6 servings (serving size: 1 stuffed potato).

CALORIES 269 (20% from fat); FAT 5.9g (sat 3g, mono 2.4g, poly 0.5g); PROTEIN 9.1g; CARB 42.6g; FIBER 2.9g; CHOL 14mg; IRON 2mg; SODIUM 336mg; CALC 55mg

Baked Potatoes with Corn and Crema Mexicana

6 baking potatoes (about 3 pounds)
1 teaspoon cumin seeds
¼ cup finely chopped jalapeño pepper
2 tablespoons finely chopped fresh cilantro
2 tablespoons fresh lime juice
¼ teaspoon salt
1 (15.25-ounce) can whole-kernel corn, drained
1 garlic clove, minced
6 tablespoons crema Mexicana

1. Preheat oven to 375°.
2. Pierce potatoes with a fork, and bake at 375° for 1 hour or until tender. Cool potatoes slightly.
3. Cook cumin seeds in a small skillet over medium heat 1 minute or until toasted. Combine cumin seeds and next 6 ingredients in a medium bowl; stir well.
4. Split potatoes lengthwise, cutting to, but not through, other side. Spoon ¼ cup corn mixture into each potato. Top each serving with 1 tablespoon crema Mexicana. Yield: 6 servings (serving size: 1 stuffed potato).

CALORIES 240 (14% from fat); FAT 3.8g (sat 2g, mono 1.1g, poly 0.4g); PROTEIN 6.4g; CARB 47.1g; FIBER 5.1g; CHOL 6mg; IRON 2.5mg; SODIUM 267mg; CALC 56mg

---

Microwaved "Baked" Potatoes

If time is an issue, remember that microwave ovens cook potatoes much faster than conventional ovens. But the results differ. A microwaved potato is more steamed than baked, so the skin is softer than an oven-baked spud, and the flesh may be less fluffy.

Pierce washed potatoes several times with a fork. Microwave the potatoes at HIGH for 5 to 10 minutes or more until tender. Microwave cooking times vary depending on the microwave. If your oven doesn't feature a carousel tray, turn the potatoes halfway through cooking.

Baked Sweet Potatoes with West African–Style Peanut Sauce

Peanuts are integral to West African cooking. The nutty, spicy flavors in the filling complement the sweet potato.

6 sweet potatoes (about 3 pounds)
1 teaspoon canola oil
⅓ cup finely chopped onion
1 tablespoon grated peeled fresh ginger
2 garlic cloves, minced
1½ teaspoons ground cumin
1½ teaspoons ground coriander
⅛ teaspoon ground red pepper
¾ cup water
¾ cup tomato sauce
¼ cup peanut butter
1 teaspoon sugar
¼ teaspoon salt
2 tablespoons chopped fresh cilantro

1. Preheat oven to 375°.
2. Pierce potatoes with a fork, and bake at 375° for 1 hour or until tender. Cool potatoes slightly.
3. Heat oil in a medium skillet over medium-low heat. Add onion, ginger, and garlic; cook 3 minutes. Add cumin, coriander, and pepper; cook 1 minute. Add ¾ cup water and next 4 ingredients, stirring until smooth; bring to a simmer. Cook 2 minutes or until thick.
4. Split potatoes lengthwise, cutting to, but not through, other side. Spoon about ¼ cup sauce into each potato. Top each serving with 1 teaspoon cilantro. Yield: 6 servings (serving size: 1 stuffed potato).

CALORIES 231 (25% from fat); FAT 6.4g (sat 1.2g, mono 3.1g, poly 1.7g); PROTEIN 5.4g; CARB 38.7g; FIBER 5.5g; CHOL 0mg; IRON 1.5mg; SODIUM 355mg; CALC 37mg

---

Rosemary-Scented Potatoes Topped with Caramelized Onions and Gruyère

Cooking onions without salt helps them caramelize better. Add ¼ teaspoon salt to the onion mixture once it has browned, if desired.

6 baking potatoes (about 3 pounds)
1 tablespoon butter
7 cups thinly sliced onion (about 4)
4 garlic cloves, minced
2 teaspoons finely chopped fresh rosemary
½ teaspoon freshly ground black pepper
¾ cup (3 ounces) shredded Gruyère cheese

1. Preheat oven to 375°.
2. Pierce potatoes with a fork, and bake at 375° for 1 hour or until tender. Cool potatoes slightly.
3. Melt butter in a large nonstick skillet over medium heat. Add onion and garlic; cook 20 minutes or until browned. Stir in rosemary and pepper.
4. Preheat broiler.
5. Split potatoes lengthwise, cutting to, but not through, other side. Spoon about ⅓ cup onion mixture into each potato. Sprinkle each serving with 2 tablespoons cheese. Broil 3 minutes or until cheese is lightly browned. Yield: 6 servings (serving size: 1 stuffed potato).

CALORIES 264 (23% from fat); FAT 6.6g (sat 3.8g, mono 1.9g, poly 0.4g); PROTEIN 9.2g; CARB 42.7g; FIBER 4.8g; CHOL 20mg; IRON 2mg; SODIUM 74mg; CALC 183mg

---

Roasted Russets with Wild Mushrooms, Leeks, and Goat Cheese

6 baking potatoes (about 3 pounds)
Cooking spray
2 cups thinly sliced leek (about 2 large)
3 (4-ounce) packages exotic mushroom blend (such as shiitake, cremini, and oyster), chopped
½ cup fat-free sour cream
½ cup fat-free, less-sodium chicken broth
⅓ cup (3 ounces) goat cheese
½ teaspoon salt
⅛ teaspoon freshly ground black pepper
1 tablespoon finely chopped fresh tarragon

Continued

1. Preheat oven to 375°.
2. Pierce potatoes with a fork, and bake at 375° for 1 hour or until tender. Cool potatoes slightly.
3. Heat a large nonstick skillet over medium heat. Coat pan with cooking spray. Add leek; cook 5 minutes or until tender, stirring frequently. Add mushrooms; cook 5 minutes or until tender, stirring occasionally. Stir in sour cream, broth, cheese, salt, and pepper. Reduce heat, and cook 2 minutes, stirring constantly (do not boil). Stir in tarragon.
4. Split potatoes lengthwise, cutting to, but not through, other side. Spoon ¾ cup mushroom mixture into each potato. Yield: 6 servings (serving size: 1 stuffed potato).

CALORIES 253 (12% from fat); FAT 3.3g (sat 2.1g, mono 0.7g, poly 0.2g); PROTEIN 9.9g; CARB 46.3g; FIBER 5.3g; CHOL 7mg; IRON 3.5mg; SODIUM 328mg; CALC 98mg

---

Tater Tips

Follow a few preliminary steps to guarantee success with baked potatoes. First, wash the potato thoroughly, paying particular attention to indentations, eyes, and anywhere else dirt might collect. Pierce the skin a few times with a fork to keep the potato from bursting as it bakes. And unless you like potato skin soft, don't wrap it in foil before baking. A foil wrapper will cause the potato to steam, rather than bake, and prevent the skin from becoming crisp.

Stuffed Potatoes with Tomato-Olive Salad

Expand the Mediterranean-flavored filling by adding diced red onion, pepperoncini, roasted red bell peppers, artichoke hearts, or anchovies. Serve with seared tuna or flank steak.

    6   baking potatoes (about 3 pounds)
    1   cup finely chopped seeded peeled tomato (about 1 large)
    ½   cup finely chopped pitted kalamata olives
    2   tablespoons capers
    1   tablespoon extravirgin olive oil
    ¼   teaspoon freshly ground black pepper
    ⅛   teaspoon salt
    2   garlic cloves, minced
    ½   cup fat-free sour cream
    ¼   cup chopped fresh basil

1. Preheat oven to 375°.
2. Pierce potatoes with a fork, and bake at 375° for 1 hour or until tender. Cool potatoes slightly.
3. Combine tomato and next 7 ingredients in a small bowl; toss well.
4. Split potatoes lengthwise, cutting to, but not through, other side. Spoon about ¼ cup tomato mixture into each potato. Top each serving with 2 teaspoons basil. Yield: 6 servings (serving size: 1 stuffed potato).

CALORIES 263 (26% from fat); FAT 7.6g (sat 1g, mono 5.5g, poly 0.9g); PROTEIN 6g; CARB 42.7g; FIBER 4.7g; CHOL 0mg; IRON 2.2mg; SODIUM 484mg; CALC 34mg

---

. . . And Ready in Just About 20 Minutes

More than a week's worth of quick entrées to get dinner on the table in a flash

QUICK & EASY
Thai Green Curry Mussels

Green curry paste can be spicy; use less for milder flavor. Available in the ethnic foods aisle at the supermarket, the paste keeps several months in the refrigerator. Substitute shrimp for mussels, if you like.

    1   (3½-ounce) bag boil-in-bag long-grain white rice
    1   cup water
    1   teaspoon grated lime rind
    2   tablespoons fresh lime juice
    1½   teaspoons green curry paste
    1   teaspoon sugar
    1   teaspoon fish sauce
    1   (13.5-ounce) can light coconut milk
    1   (8-ounce) bottle clam juice
    80   mussels (about 2 pounds), scrubbed and debearded
    ⅓   cup chopped fresh cilantro
         Lime wedges (optional)

1. Cook rice according to package directions, omitting salt and fat.
2. Combine 1 cup water and next 7 ingredients in a large Dutch oven over medium-high heat. Add mussels to pan; bring to a boil. Cover and steam 5 minutes or until mussels open; discard any unopened shells. Stir in cilantro. Place about ½ cup rice in each of 4 bowls; ladle about 20 mussels and 1 cup coconut mixture over rice. Garnish with lime wedges, if desired. Yield: 4 servings.

CALORIES 349 (25% from fat); FAT 9.6g (sat 5.2g, mono 1.2g, poly 1.4g); PROTEIN 30.5g; CARB 34.8g; FIBER 0.1g; CHOL 65mg; IRON 10.3mg; SODIUM 954mg; CALC 70mg

---

Potato Potential

Mix and match to create delicious combinations with these stuffing suggestions:

Vegetable		Sauce | Seasoning	
• Artichoke hearts	• Sautéed spinach	• Fontina	• Curry powder
• Asparagus	• Wilted mustard greens	• Light cream cheese	• Hot sauce
• Bell peppers	**Cheese**	• Stilton	• Pesto
• Broccoli	• Brie	**Sauce | Seasoning**	• Spanish smoked paprika
• Butternut squash	• Cheddar	• Barbecue sauce	
• Pumpkin	• Cottage cheese	• Chili powder	
	• Feta	• Chipotle chiles	

To turn a stuffed potato into a main course, simply add meat or other proteins:

• Diced, cooked chicken	• Diced ham	• Sautéed lean ground beef	• Seared tofu
	• Pulled pork		

Veggie Burger and Fries Menu
serves 4

Meaty mushrooms and garlicky aïoli sauce update traditional diner fare.

Portobello Cheeseburgers

Oven fries with aïoli*

Vanilla low-fat ice cream with hot fudge sauce

*Preheat oven to 400°. Cut 2 pounds peeled baking potatoes into ¼-inch-thick strips. Place potatoes on a jelly-roll pan. Drizzle with 1 tablespoon canola oil and sprinkle with ½ teaspoon salt; toss to coat. Bake at 400° for 20 minutes or until tender and golden. Toss with 1½ tablespoons melted butter and 1½ tablespoons chopped fresh parsley. Combine ¼ cup reduced-fat mayonnaise, 2 teaspoons fresh lemon juice, ⅛ teaspoon ground red pepper, and 1 minced garlic clove. Serve with fries.

QUICK & EASY
Portobello Cheeseburgers

Portobello mushrooms are well-paired with pungent Gorgonzola cheese. Use crumbled blue cheese to save even more time.

- 2 teaspoons olive oil
- 4 (4-inch) portobello caps
- ¼ teaspoon salt
- ¼ teaspoon black pepper
- 1 tablespoon bottled minced garlic
- ¼ cup (1 ounce) crumbled Gorgonzola cheese
- 3 tablespoons reduced-fat mayonnaise
- 4 (2-ounce) sandwich rolls
- 2 cups trimmed arugula
- ½ cup sliced bottled roasted red bell peppers

1. Heat oil in a large nonstick skillet over medium-high heat. Sprinkle mushrooms with salt and black pepper. Add mushrooms to pan; sauté 4 minutes or until tender, turning once. Add garlic to pan; sauté 30 seconds. Remove mushroom mixture from heat.

2. Combine cheese and mayonnaise, stirring well. Spread about 2 tablespoons mayonnaise mixture over bottom half of each roll; top each serving with ½ cup arugula and 2 tablespoons bell peppers. Place 1 mushroom on each serving, and top with top halves of rolls. Yield: 4 servings (serving size: 1 burger).

CALORIES 278 (32% from fat); FAT 9.9g (sat 3g, mono 1.7g, poly 0.4g); PROTEIN 9.3g; CARB 33.7g; FIBER 2.4g; CHOL 6mg; IRON 1.7mg; SODIUM 726mg; CALC 129mg

QUICK & EASY
Turkey Cutlets with Prosciutto

Pair this dish with garlic mashed potatoes. Garnish with sage sprigs, if desired.

- 4 (4-ounce) turkey breast cutlets
- ⅛ teaspoon salt
- ⅛ teaspoon black pepper
- 1½ ounces prosciutto, julienned
- 2 teaspoons finely chopped fresh sage
- 1 tablespoon olive oil
- 3 tablespoons finely chopped shallots
- ⅓ cup dry white wine

1. Place each cutlet between 2 sheets of heavy-duty plastic wrap; pound to ¼-inch thickness using a meat mallet or small heavy skillet. Sprinkle both sides of cutlets with salt and pepper. Divide prosciutto into 4 equal portions; place 1 portion in center of each cutlet. Sprinkle each portion with ½ teaspoon sage. Roll up cutlets, jelly-roll fashion, starting with narrow end.

2. Heat oil in a large nonstick skillet over medium-high heat. Add cutlets to pan; cook 6 minutes or until thoroughly cooked, turning to brown on all sides. Remove cutlets from pan; cover and keep warm. Reduce heat to medium-low. Add shallots to pan; cook 2 minutes, stirring occasionally. Add wine; bring to a simmer. Cook 30 seconds. Serve with cutlets. Yield: 4 servings (serving size: 1 cutlet and 1 tablespoon sauce).

CALORIES 180 (26% from fat); FAT 5.2g (sat 1.1g, mono 2.5g, poly 0.5g); PROTEIN 31.1g; CARB 1.6g; FIBER 0.1g; CHOL 54mg; IRON 1.8mg; SODIUM 380mg; CALC 7mg

QUICK & EASY
Southwestern Couscous Salad

You can use boneless, skinless chicken breast halves instead of turkey.

- Cooking spray
- 1 (1-pound) turkey tenderloin, cut into 1-inch pieces
- ½ teaspoon salt, divided
- ¼ teaspoon black pepper, divided
- 2 cups fat-free, less-sodium chicken broth
- 2 cups frozen corn kernels
- 1½ cups uncooked couscous
- 1 cup diced plum tomato (about 2 medium)
- ½ cup prechopped green bell pepper
- ¼ cup chopped fresh cilantro
- ¼ cup fresh lime juice
- 2 tablespoons canola oil
- 1 teaspoon ground cumin
- 1 teaspoon hot pepper sauce (such as Tabasco)

1. Heat a large nonstick skillet over medium-high heat. Coat pan with cooking spray. Sprinkle turkey with ¼ teaspoon salt and ⅛ teaspoon black pepper. Add turkey to pan; sauté 6 minutes.

2. Place broth in a medium saucepan; bring to a boil. Add corn; cook 3 minutes. Add couscous. Remove from heat; cover and let stand 5 minutes. Fluff with a fork.

3. Combine ¼ teaspoon salt, ⅛ teaspoon black pepper, tomato, and remaining 6 ingredients in a large bowl. Add turkey and couscous mixture to bowl, and toss well. Yield: 6 servings (serving size: 1⅔ cups).

CALORIES 353 (16% from fat); FAT 6.1g (sat 0.7g, mono 3.1g, poly 1.9g); PROTEIN 27g; CARB 47.7g; FIBER 4.5g; CHOL 47mg; IRON 2mg; SODIUM 377mg; CALC 34mg

Swordfish Siciliana

Cooking spray
- 4 (6-ounce) swordfish steaks
- ½ teaspoon salt
- ½ teaspoon freshly ground black pepper
- 1 tablespoon sliced almonds
- 2 teaspoons bottled minced garlic
- 2 tablespoons raisins
- 2 tablespoons fresh orange juice
- 1½ tablespoons chopped pitted kalamata olives
- 1½ tablespoons chopped bottled roasted red bell peppers

1. Heat a large nonstick skillet over medium-high heat. Coat pan with cooking spray. Sprinkle fish evenly with salt and black pepper. Add fish to pan; sauté 5 minutes on each side or until fish flakes easily when tested with a fork or until desired degree of doneness. Remove fish from pan; cover and keep warm.

2. Recoat pan with cooking spray; add nuts and garlic to pan. Sauté 30 seconds. Add raisins, juice, olives, and bell pepper to pan; cook 1 minute or until liquid evaporates. Serve with fish. Yield: 4 servings (serving size: 1 fish steak and 2 tablespoons olive mixture).

CALORIES 246 (30% from fat); FAT 8.3g (sat 2g, mono 3.6g, poly 1.9g); PROTEIN 34.6g; CARB 6.5g; FIBER 0.7g; CHOL 66mg; IRON 1.8mg; SODIUM 503mg; CALC 23mg

Turkey Reuben Sandwiches

- 2 tablespoons Dijon mustard
- 8 slices rye bread
- 4 (1-ounce) slices reduced-fat, reduced-sodium Swiss cheese (such as Alpine Lace)
- 8 ounces smoked turkey, thinly sliced
- ⅔ cup sauerkraut, rinsed and drained
- ¼ cup fat-free Thousand Island dressing
- 1 tablespoon canola oil, divided

1. Spread about ¾ teaspoon mustard over each bread slice. Place 1 cheese slice on each of 4 bread slices. Divide turkey evenly over cheese. Top each serving with 2½ tablespoons sauerkraut and 1 tablespoon dressing. Top each serving with 1 bread slice, mustard side down.

2. Heat 1½ teaspoons oil in a large non-stick skillet over medium-high heat. Add 2 sandwiches to pan; top with another heavy skillet. Cook 3 minutes on each side or until golden; remove sandwiches from pan, and keep warm. Repeat procedure with 1½ teaspoons oil and remaining sandwiches. Yield: 4 servings (serving size: 1 sandwich).

CALORIES 255 (38% from fat); FAT 10.7g (sat 4.8g, mono 3.9g, poly 1.5g); PROTEIN 19.6g; CARB 18.9g; FIBER 3.4g; CHOL 44mg; IRON 0.7mg; SODIUM 865mg; CALC 311mg

Hot and Sour Soup with Shrimp

- 3 cups fat-free, less-sodium chicken broth
- ½ cup presliced mushrooms
- 1 tablespoon low-sodium soy sauce
- 1 (8-ounce) can sliced bamboo shoots, drained
- 2½ tablespoons fresh lemon juice
- 1 teaspoon white pepper
- 1½ pounds medium shrimp, peeled and deveined
- 8 ounces reduced-fat firm tofu, drained and cut into 1-inch cubes
- 2 tablespoons water
- 1 tablespoon cornstarch
- 1 large egg white, beaten
- ¼ teaspoon chili oil
- 2 tablespoons chopped green onions

1. Combine first 4 ingredients in a large saucepan; bring to a boil. Reduce heat, and simmer 5 minutes. Add juice, pepper, shrimp, and tofu to pan; bring to a boil. Cook 2 minutes or until shrimp are almost done. Combine water and cornstarch in a small bowl, stirring until smooth. Add cornstarch mixture to pan; cook 1 minute, stirring constantly with a whisk. Slowly drizzle egg white into pan, stirring constantly. Remove from heat; stir in chili oil and onions. Yield: 4 servings (serving size: 1¾ cups).

CALORIES 233 (18% from fat); FAT 4.7g (sat 1g, mono 0.8g, poly 1.3g); PROTEIN 38g; CARB 9.4g; FIBER 2.3g; CHOL 252mg; IRON 5.7mg; SODIUM 736mg; CALC 98mg

Citrus Chicken

The spicy sauce works equally well with fish or pork.

- ¼ cup orange juice
- ½ teaspoon grated lime rind
- 2 tablespoons fresh lime juice
- 2 tablespoons chopped fresh thyme
- 2 teaspoons bottled minced garlic
- 1 teaspoon grated orange rind
- ¼ teaspoon salt
- ⅛ teaspoon ground red pepper
- 1 pound skinless, boneless chicken breast cutlets
- 1 tablespoon olive oil
Cooking spray
- 6 cups bagged prewashed baby spinach

1. Combine first 8 ingredients in a small bowl, stirring well with a whisk. Pour ¼ cup juice mixture into a large zip-top plastic bag. Add chicken to bag. Seal; let stand 5 minutes. Add oil to remaining juice mixture; stir well with a whisk.

2. Heat a large nonstick skillet over medium-high heat. Coat pan with cooking spray. Remove chicken from bag; discard marinade. Add chicken to pan; cook 4 minutes on each side or until done. Place 1½ cups spinach on each of 4 plates. Divide chicken evenly among servings; top each serving with 1 tablespoon juice mixture. Yield: 4 servings.

CALORIES 183 (24% from fat); FAT 4.9g (sat 0.9g, mono 2.8g, poly 0.7g); PROTEIN 27.4g; CARB 7.1g; FIBER 2.1g; CHOL 66mg; IRON 2.3mg; SODIUM 278mg; CALC 50mg

Szechuan Shrimp with Spinach

Serve this tasty dish with hot cooked rice to soak up the garlicky sauce.

- 2 tablespoons bottled minced garlic
- 2 tablespoons dry sherry
- 1½ tablespoons bottled ground fresh ginger (such as Spice World)
- 1½ tablespoons low-sodium soy sauce
- 1 tablespoon chili garlic sauce (such as Lee Kum Kee)
- 1 teaspoon sugar
- 24 large shrimp, peeled and deveined (about 1 pound)
- ½ cup fat-free, less-sodium chicken broth
- 2 teaspoons cornstarch
- 1 tablespoon canola oil
- 2 (6-ounce) packages fresh baby spinach

1. Combine first 6 ingredients in a bowl, stirring well. Add shrimp to bowl; toss to coat. Let stand 5 minutes. Remove shrimp with a slotted spoon, and reserve marinade. Combine broth and cornstarch in a small bowl, stirring with a whisk.

2. Heat oil in a large nonstick skillet over medium-high heat. Add shrimp to pan; sauté 3 minutes or until done. Remove shrimp from pan. Add reserved marinade to pan; cook 1 minute or until slightly thick. Add broth mixture to pan; bring to a boil. Add spinach to pan; cook 1 minute or until spinach wilts. Serve with shrimp. Yield: 4 servings (serving size: about 6 shrimp and ½ cup spinach).

CALORIES 216 (23% from fat); FAT 5.5g (sat 0.6g, mono 2.4g, poly 1.8g); PROTEIN 26g; CARB 15.2g; FIBER 4.4g; CHOL 172mg; IRON 5.9mg; SODIUM 712mg; CALC 131mg

Haunted House Welcome

Answer the knock on the door with a special dinner for trick-or-treaters (and their parents).

Welcome folks to your Halloween open house party with this simple, mostly make-ahead menu that's appropriate for kids and grown-ups alike. There are plenty of savory dishes to offset all the candy the little ones are sure to amass over the evening. The recipes are scaled to feed a big crowd but can easily be halved for a smaller gathering.

Halloween Open House Menu
serves 16

Spiced Apple-Pomegranate Cider

Avocado-Yogurt Dip with Cumin

Cinnamon-Sugar Popcorn

Maple-Chile Popcorn

Spinach-Pear Salad with Honey-Bacon Vinaigrette

Pepita Corn Bread

Three-Bean Chili with Vegetables

Chocolate Cupcakes with Vanilla Cream Cheese Frosting

Spiced Apple-Pomegranate Cider

Keep this crimson-hued beverage warm in a slow cooker on the kitchen counter, and set out a stack of paper cups and a ladle for guests to help themselves. Substitute cranberry juice for pomegranate juice, if you prefer.

- 1 gallon apple cider
- 6 whole cloves
- 5 star anise
- 3 (2-inch-long) strips lemon rind
- 2 cinnamon sticks
- ½ vanilla bean
- 2 cups pomegranate juice

1. Combine first 5 ingredients in a large stockpot over medium-high heat; bring to a boil. Reduce heat to low. Add vanilla bean; cover and simmer 15 minutes. Remove from heat; let stand at room temperature 1 hour or up to 4 hours. Discard solids. Stir in pomegranate juice. Reheat over medium heat until warm. Yield: 16 servings (serving size: about 1 cup).

CALORIES 158 (0% from fat); FAT 0g; PROTEIN 1.1g; CARB 39.4g; FIBER 0g; CHOL 0mg; IRON 0mg; SODIUM 4mg; CALC 5mg

Avocado-Yogurt Dip with Cumin

Scoop this creamy dip with pita chips and carrot, celery, red bell pepper, and jícama sticks. Prepare up to eight hours in advance, and refrigerate in an airtight container.

- ¾ cup plain fat-free yogurt
- ½ cup finely chopped red onion
- 3 tablespoons chopped fresh cilantro
- 2 tablespoons fresh lime juice
- 1 tablespoon finely chopped seeded jalapeño pepper
- 1 tablespoon ground cumin
- ½ teaspoon salt
- 3 ripe peeled avocados, seeded and coarsely chopped
- 1 garlic clove, minced

Continued

1. Place all ingredients in a food processor or blender, and process until smooth. Yield: 16 servings (serving size: 2 tablespoons).

CALORIES 70 (76% from fat); FAT 5.9g (sat 0.9g, mono 3.6g, poly 0.7g); PROTEIN 1.3g; CARB 4.6g; FIBER 2g; CHOL 0mg; IRON 0.4mg; SODIUM 83mg; CALC 21mg

MAKE AHEAD
Cinnamon-Sugar Popcorn

Prepare this simple snack a couple of hours before the party. Store in an airtight container to keep it fresh.

8 cups popcorn (popped without salt or fat)
Cooking spray
2 tablespoons sugar
1 teaspoon ground cinnamon
½ teaspoon salt
1½ tablespoons butter, melted

1. Place popcorn in a large bowl. Lightly coat popcorn with cooking spray; toss well. Repeat procedure.
2. Combine sugar, cinnamon, and salt in a small bowl. Drizzle popcorn with melted butter; toss well. Sprinkle with sugar mixture; toss well to coat. Yield: 16 servings (serving size: ½ cup).

CALORIES 31 (38% from fat); FAT 1.3g (sat 0.7g, mono 0.3g, poly 0.1g); PROTEIN 0.5g; CARB 4.8g; FIBER 0.7g; CHOL 3mg; IRON 0.2mg; SODIUM 81mg; CALC 2mg

MAKE AHEAD
Maple-Chile Popcorn

A heatproof spatula works best to combine and spread the ingredients into the pan. Kids may prefer this without the red pepper.

Cooking spray
8 cups popcorn (popped without salt or fat)
½ cup maple syrup
1 tablespoon butter
½ teaspoon salt
½ teaspoon ground red pepper

1. Preheat oven to 300°.
2. Coat a 15 x 10–inch jelly-roll pan or other large rimmed baking pan with cooking spray. Place popcorn in a large metal or glass bowl lightly coated with cooking spray.
3. Combine syrup, butter, salt, and pepper in a saucepan over medium heat. Bring to a boil, stirring just until combined. Cook, without stirring, 2 minutes. Pour syrup mixture over popcorn in a steady stream, stirring to coat.
4. Spread popcorn mixture in an even layer into prepared pan. Bake at 300° for 15 minutes. Remove from oven, and cool completely in pan. Yield: 16 servings (serving size: ½ cup).

CALORIES 48 (17% from fat); FAT 0.9g (sat 0.5g, mono 0.2g, poly 0.1g); PROTEIN 0.5g; CARB 9.9g; FIBER 0.6g; CHOL 2mg; IRON 0.2mg; SODIUM 79mg; CALC 7mg

MAKE AHEAD
Spinach-Pear Salad with Honey-Bacon Vinaigrette

Although this pleasantly wilted salad is best made shortly before serving, you can prepare and chill the vinaigrette up to a day in advance; microwave at HIGH for 30 seconds, and stir well before tossing with the salad ingredients.

VINAIGRETTE:
4 bacon slices
¼ cup cider vinegar
¼ cup rice vinegar
2 tablespoons honey
2 teaspoons Dijon mustard
¼ teaspoon salt
⅛ teaspoon freshly ground black pepper

SALAD:
⅓ cup thinly vertically sliced red onion
2 large ripe Bartlett pears, cored and cut lengthwise into ¼-inch-thick slices (about 3 cups)
1 (10-ounce) package fresh spinach

1. To prepare vinaigrette, cook bacon in a medium nonstick skillet over medium heat until crisp. Remove bacon from pan, reserving 1 teaspoon drippings in pan. Crumble bacon; set aside. Add vinegars, honey, mustard, salt, and pepper to drippings in pan, stirring with a whisk; bring to a boil. Remove from heat.
2. To prepare salad, combine onion, pears, spinach, and bacon in a large bowl. Drizzle with vinaigrette, and toss gently to coat. Yield: 16 servings (serving size: about 1⅓ cups).

CALORIES 41 (22% from fat); FAT 1g (sat 0.3g, mono 0.4g, poly 0.1g); PROTEIN 1.2g; CARB 7.2g; FIBER 1.3g; CHOL 2mg; IRON 0.7mg; SODIUM 103mg; CALC 21mg

Pepita Corn Bread

Hulled pumpkinseeds are often labeled pepitas. They're common to many Mexican recipes and can be found on the nut aisle or in the Latin foods section of many supermarkets. This bread is best served the day it's made—easy, since it comes together in a snap.

1½ cups all-purpose flour (6¾ ounces)
1½ cups cornmeal
1 teaspoon baking soda
1 teaspoon salt
1¼ cups low-fat buttermilk
2 tablespoons olive oil
2 tablespoons honey
3 large eggs, lightly beaten
Cooking spray
⅓ cup pumpkinseed kernels

1. Preheat oven to 350°.
2. Lightly spoon flour and cornmeal into dry measuring cups; level with a knife. Combine flour, cornmeal, baking soda, and salt in a large bowl. Combine buttermilk, oil, honey, and eggs. Add buttermilk mixture to cornmeal mixture; stir just until moist (batter will look slightly lumpy). Spoon batter into an 11 x 7–inch baking dish coated with cooking spray.
3. Sprinkle batter evenly with pumpkinseeds. Bake at 350° for 20 minutes or until a wooden pick inserted in center comes out clean. Cool in pan 10 minutes. Serve warm. Yield: 16 servings (serving size: 1 piece).

CALORIES 150 (27% from fat); FAT 4.5g (sat 0.9g, mono 2g, poly 1.1g); PROTEIN 4.8g; CARB 22.7g; FIBER 1.4g; CHOL 40mg; IRON 1.7mg; SODIUM 259mg; CALC 31mg

Three-Bean Chili with Vegetables

Chipotle chiles add a smokiness and a touch of spicy heat. Cook this hearty, kid-friendly dish up to two days ahead. Thin it with a little water when reheating, if necessary.

  1½ tablespoons canola oil
  2 cups chopped onion
  ⅔ cup chopped carrot
  4 garlic cloves, minced
  4 cups water
  2 cups frozen whole-kernel corn
  1 cup chopped red bell pepper (about 1 large)
  1 cup chopped zucchini
  2 tablespoons chili powder
  2 teaspoons dried oregano
  2 teaspoons ground cumin
  ¾ teaspoon salt
  2 (28-ounce) cans crushed tomatoes
  2 (16-ounce) cans pinto beans, rinsed and drained
  2 (16-ounce) cans kidney beans, rinsed and drained
  2 (15-ounce) cans black beans, rinsed and drained
  1 (6-ounce) can no-salt-added tomato paste
  1½ tablespoons rice vinegar
  1½ teaspoons to 1 tablespoon finely chopped chipotle chile, canned in adobo sauce
  1 cup chopped fresh cilantro
  1 cup (4 ounces) shredded reduced-fat Cheddar cheese
  1 cup reduced-fat sour cream

1. Heat oil in a large stockpot over medium-high heat. Add onion, carrot, and garlic; sauté 5 minutes. Stir in 4 cups water and next 12 ingredients; bring to a boil. Cover, reduce heat, and simmer 25 minutes or until carrot is tender, stirring occasionally. Stir in vinegar and chipotle. Top with cilantro, cheese, and sour cream. Yield: 16 servings (serving size: 1¼ cups chili, 1 tablespoon cilantro, 1 tablespoon cheese, and 1 tablespoon sour cream).

CALORIES 211 (26% from fat); FAT 6.1g (sat 2.4g, mono 1.5g, poly 0.9g); PROTEIN 10.3g; CARB 34.6g; FIBER 8.8g; CHOL 11mg; IRON 3.5mg; SODIUM 708mg; CALC 159mg

Chocolate Cupcakes with Vanilla Cream Cheese Frosting

To repeat the Halloween theme, decorate them with plastic cake toppers, licorice, jelly beans, or candy sprinkles.

CUPCAKES:
  1 cup granulated sugar
  ½ cup egg substitute
  ¼ cup canola oil
  ½ teaspoon vanilla extract
  1½ cups all-purpose flour (about 6¾ ounces)
  ½ cup unsweetened cocoa
  1 teaspoon baking soda
  1 teaspoon instant coffee granules
  ½ teaspoon baking powder
  ¼ teaspoon salt
  1 cup fat-free buttermilk

FROSTING:
  1 cup powdered sugar
  ½ teaspoon vanilla extract
  Dash of salt
  1 (8-ounce) block ⅓-less-fat cream cheese, softened

1. Preheat oven to 350°.
2. To prepare cupcakes, place first 4 ingredients in a large bowl; beat with a mixer at medium speed until well blended (about 2 minutes).
3. Lightly spoon flour into dry measuring cups; level with a knife. Combine flour, cocoa, and next 4 ingredients, stirring well with a whisk. Stir flour mixture into sugar mixture alternately with buttermilk, beginning and ending with flour mixture; mix after each addition just until blended.
4. Place 16 paper muffin cup liners in muffin cups; spoon about 2½ tablespoons batter into each cup. Bake at 350° for 18 minutes or until a wooden pick inserted in center of a cupcake comes out with moist crumbs attached (do not overbake). Remove cupcakes from pans; cool on a wire rack.
5. To prepare frosting, combine powdered sugar and remaining 3 ingredients in a medium bowl. Beat with a mixer at medium speed until combined. Increase speed to medium-high, and beat until smooth. Spread about 1 tablespoon frosting on top of each cupcake. Yield: 16 servings (serving size: 1 cupcake).

CALORIES 203 (30% from fat); FAT 6.8g (sat 2.1g, mono 3g, poly 1.3g); PROTEIN 4.8g; CARB 32.4g; FIBER 1.2g; CHOL 8mg; IRON 1.3mg; SODIUM 211mg; CALC 53mg

classics

Wild About Game

Even if you don't hunt, or know a hunter, you can enjoy the taste and nutritional benefits of free-range meat and fowl.

Easy Elk Chili

Substitute ground venison, buffalo, or lean beef for the elk. Freeze leftovers in individual freezer-safe zip-top plastic bags for up to two months.

  1 pound ground elk
  2 cups chopped yellow onion
  1 cup dry red wine
  1½ cups water
  1 tablespoon chipotle chile powder
  2 teaspoons ground cumin
  2 teaspoons dried oregano
  ½ teaspoon salt
  2 (14.5-ounce) can diced tomatoes, undrained
  2 (14-ounce) cans less-sodium beef broth
  1 (15-ounce) can red kidney beans, rinsed and drained
  ¼ cup reduced-fat sour cream
  ¼ cup (1 ounce) reduced-fat shredded Cheddar cheese
  2 tablespoons chopped green onions

1. Combine elk and yellow onion in a Dutch oven; cook over medium-high heat until lightly browned, stirring to crumble. Add wine; bring to a boil. Cook 3 minutes. Stir in 1½ cups water and next
Continued

7 ingredients; bring to a boil. Partially cover, reduce heat, and simmer 2 hours (add more water if mixture becomes too thick). Ladle about 1 cup chili into each of 6 bowls; spoon 2 teaspoons sour cream over each. Sprinkle each with 2 teaspoons cheese and 1 teaspoon green onions. Yield: 6 servings.

CALORIES 282 (25% from fat); FAT 7.8g (sat 3.8g, mono 2.1g, poly 0.5g); PROTEIN 23g; CARB 24.3g; FIBER 7.9g; CHOL 51mg; IRON 3.3mg; SODIUM 685mg; CALC 106mg

QUICK & EASY

Jerk-Seasoned Buffalo Hamburger Steak with Mango-Pineapple Salsa

Naturally lean and rich-tasting buffalo is now widely available in grocery stores. Its flavor is milder than other wild red meats. You also can use ground elk, deer, or lean beef for the patties. Cook the patties on a grill pan if it's too chilly to grill outdoors. Serve with baked tortilla chips.

    1   cup chopped peeled mango
    ¾   cup chopped pineapple
    ½   cup finely chopped red onion
    ¼   cup chopped fresh cilantro
    1   tablespoon fresh lime juice
    ½   teaspoon salt
    1   small jalapeño pepper, seeded and finely chopped
    1   pound ground buffalo
    2   teaspoons salt-free Jamaican jerk seasoning
    ½   teaspoon salt
    Cooking spray

1. Prepare grill.
2. Combine first 7 ingredients in a medium bowl. Set aside.
3. Divide buffalo into 4 equal portions, shaping each into a ½-inch-thick patty. Sprinkle patties with jerk seasoning and ½ teaspoon salt. Place patties on grill rack coated with cooking spray; grill 5 minutes on each side or until done. Serve with salsa. Yield: 4 servings (serving size: 1 patty and ½ cup salsa).

CALORIES 195 (20% from fat); FAT 4.3g (sat 1.6g, mono 1.4g, poly 0.9g); PROTEIN 24.8g; CARB 14.1g; FIBER 2g; CHOL 55mg; IRON 3.1mg; SODIUM 629mg; CALC 20mg

Roast Canada Goose with Mushroom-Port Gravy

Goose sizes vary widely, so adjust the cooking time accordingly. Plan on cooking 12 minutes per pound or until a thermometer registers 165°.

    1   (7- to 8-pound) whole dressed Canada goose, skin on
    ¾   teaspoon salt, divided
    ½   teaspoon freshly ground black pepper, divided
    1   yellow onion, quartered
    1   small red bell pepper, seeded and quartered
    2   (3-inch) fresh parsley sprigs
    ¼   cup finely chopped shallots
    1   (8-ounce) package sliced mixed wild mushrooms
    ½   cup fat-free, less-sodium chicken broth
    ½   cup port
    1   tablespoon all-purpose flour
    1   (12-ounce) can fat-free evaporated milk

1. Preheat oven to 325°.
2. Sprinkle cavity of goose with ½ teaspoon salt and ¼ teaspoon black pepper. Stuff cavity loosely with onion, bell pepper, and parsley sprigs. Tie legs together with string. Place goose, breast side up, on rack of a roasting pan. Bake at 325° for 1 hour and 15 minutes or until a thermometer registers 165°. Let stand 10 minutes. Discard skin, onion, bell pepper, and parsley sprigs. Reserve 1 tablespoon goose fat from roasting pan.
3. Heat reserved goose fat in a large nonstick skillet over medium-high heat. Add shallots and mushrooms; sauté 5 minutes. Add broth and port; cook 6 minutes or until liquid almost evaporates.
4. Combine flour, milk, ¼ teaspoon salt, and ¼ teaspoon black pepper in a small bowl, stirring well with a whisk. Reduce heat to medium-low. Add milk mixture to pan; cook 2 minutes or until thick. Serve gravy with goose. Yield: 6 servings (serving size: 3 ounces goose and ⅓ cup gravy).

CALORIES 175 (21% from fat); FAT 4.1g (sat 1.5g, mono 1.4g, poly 0.5g); PROTEIN 15.2g; CARB 13.9g; FIBER 0.5g; CHOL 32mg; IRON 1.7mg; SODIUM 424mg; CALC 198mg

Grilled Quail with White Polenta

(pictured on page 249)

The most delicately flavored of all game birds, quail needs very little embellishment. You can use game hens in place of the quail, if you prefer. This company-worthy recipe is inspired by Chef Mark Monette of The Flagstaff House in Boulder, Colorado, who regularly features game on his menu.

    ¾   cup 2% reduced-fat milk
    ½   cup fat-free half-and-half
    ¼   cup white cornmeal
    1½   teaspoons butter
    ½   teaspoon salt, divided
    ½   teaspoon freshly ground black pepper, divided
    ⅛   teaspoon ground nutmeg
    4   (4-ounce) semiboneless quail
    1½   teaspoons minced fresh parsley
    Cooking spray
    4   lemon wedges
    Parsley sprigs (optional)

1. Prepare grill.
2. Bring milk and half-and-half to a simmer over medium-high heat in a small, heavy saucepan. Gradually add cornmeal, stirring with a whisk. Reduce heat to low, and cook 5 minutes or until polenta is thick and creamy, stirring occasionally. Stir in butter, ¼ teaspoon salt, ¼ teaspoon pepper, and nutmeg. Keep warm.
3. Place quail, breast sides down, on a cutting surface. Cut quail in half lengthwise along backbone, cutting to, but not through, other side. Sprinkle with ¼ teaspoon salt, ¼ teaspoon pepper, and minced parsley. Place quail on grill rack coated with cooking spray, and grill 6 minutes on each side or until done. Discard skin. Serve quail with polenta and lemon wedges. Garnish with parsley sprigs, if desired. Yield: 4 servings (serving size: 1 quail, about ⅓ cup polenta, and 1 lemon wedge).

CALORIES 213 (26% from fat); FAT 6.2g (sat 2.6g, mono 1.7g, poly 1.1g); PROTEIN 21.4g; CARB 14.7g; FIBER 1.1g; CHOL 68mg; IRON 4.2mg; SODIUM 388mg; CALC 90mg

Grilled Venison with Fennel Rub

Serve alongside roasted carrots, onions, red peppers, and potatoes.

  2 teaspoons fennel seeds
  1 teaspoon black peppercorns
  ½ teaspoon salt
  ½ teaspoon garlic powder
  1 (1-pound) venison tenderloin
     Cooking spray

1. Prepare grill.
2. Grind fennel and peppercorns with a mortar and pestle. Stir in salt and garlic powder. Rub fennel mixture over venison.
3. Place venison on grill rack coated with cooking spray; grill 12 minutes or until desired degree of doneness, turning occasionally. Let stand 10 minutes. Cut venison diagonally across grain into thin slices. Yield: 4 servings (serving size: 3 ounces).

CALORIES 141 (19% from fat); FAT 2.9g (sat 1.1g, mono 0.9g, poly 0.6g); PROTEIN 26.3g; CARB 0.9g; FIBER 0.5g; CHOL 96mg; IRON 4.1mg; SODIUM 362mg; CALC 19mg

---

Where to Find Farm-Raised Game Meats

Ranch- or farm-raised game tastes somewhat milder than its wild counterpart but still retains a unique, rich flavor. Another farm-raised advantage is consistent quality. If you can't find farm-raised game meats at local specialty stores or supermarkets, check out these mail-order sources.
Arrowhead Game Meats: 816-370-6328 or www.gamemeat.com
The Fort Trading Company: 877-229-2844 or www.forttradingco.com
House of Smoke: 800-738-2750 or www.houseofwildgame.com
Seattle's Finest Exotic Meats: 800-680-4375 or www.exoticmeats.com
Shaffer Venison Farms Inc.: 800-446-3745 or www.shafferfarms.com
Venison America: 800-310-2360 or www.venisonamerica.com

Slow Cooker Venison Stew

Substitute elk or beef stew meat, if you prefer. This stew can be frozen in an airtight container for up to three months; add a little more water or beer when reheating.

  2 cups (1-inch) cubed peeled Yukon gold or red potato
  2 cups cremini mushrooms, quartered
  1 cup (1-inch) cubed onion
  1 cup (1-inch-thick) slices celery
  1 cup (1-inch-thick) slices carrot
  ⅓ cup tomato paste
  2 teaspoons chopped fresh oregano
1½ teaspoons sugar
1½ teaspoons chopped fresh thyme
  1 teaspoon chopped fresh rosemary
  ¾ teaspoon freshly ground black pepper
  ½ teaspoon salt
  2 large garlic cloves, minced
  1 bay leaf
  ¼ cup all-purpose flour (about 1 ounce)
  ⅛ teaspoon salt
  ⅛ teaspoon black pepper
  1 pound venison tenderloin, cut into 1½-inch pieces
  1 tablespoon canola oil
  1 cup brown ale (such as Newcastle)
  1 (14-ounce) can less-sodium beef broth

1. Layer first 14 ingredients in an electric slow cooker.
2. Combine flour, ⅛ teaspoon salt, and ⅛ teaspoon pepper in a shallow dish; dredge venison in flour mixture. Heat oil in a large nonstick skillet over medium-high heat; add venison. Cook 4 minutes or until browned on all sides, turning frequently. Add venison to slow cooker. Pour ale and broth over venison. Cover and cook on low 7½ hours or until meat is tender. Discard bay leaf. Yield: 6 servings (serving size: about 1¼ cups).

CALORIES 232 (17% from fat); FAT 4.4g (sat 0.9g, mono 1.9g, poly 1.2g); PROTEIN 21.7g; CARB 26.3g; FIBER 2.8g; CHOL 64mg; IRON 3.6mg; SODIUM 445mg; CALC 39mg

---

Braised Pheasant in Mixed Peppercorn Sauce

This is an easy and tasty stove-top dinner. Adjust the amount of peppercorns according to your taste. Serve with sautéed broccoli rabe and mashed potatoes.

  1 (3¼-pound) pheasant, skinned and quartered
  ¼ teaspoon salt
  ¼ teaspoon freshly ground black pepper
  2 teaspoons butter
  2 teaspoons olive oil
  ½ cup fat-free, less-sodium chicken broth
  ½ cup dry white wine
  1 cup evaporated fat-free milk
  1 teaspoon cornstarch
  3 tablespoons minced yellow onion
  2 teaspoons mixed green, red, and white peppercorns, crushed

1. Sprinkle pheasant with salt and pepper. Melt butter and oil in large skillet over medium heat. Add pheasant; cook 2 minutes on each side or until browned. Add broth and wine; bring to a boil. Cover, reduce heat, and simmer 35 minutes. Remove pheasant from pan, and keep warm.
2. Combine milk and cornstarch in a small bowl.
3. Increase heat to medium-high. Bring broth mixture to a boil; cook until reduced to ½ cup (about 6 minutes). Add onion; cook 3 minutes. Add milk mixture and peppercorns. Simmer 2 minutes or until sauce thickens, stirring frequently. Serve with pheasant. Yield: 4 servings (serving size: 1 piece of pheasant and ¼ cup sauce).

CALORIES 362 (29% from fat); FAT 11.6g (sat 3.8g, mono 4.8g, poly 1.5g); PROTEIN 52.1g; CARB 9.5g; FIBER 0.4g; CHOL 139mg; IRON 2.7mg; SODIUM 368mg; CALC 220mg

Prosciutto-Wrapped Duck Appetizers

Duck is available at most supermarkets. Don't overmarinate the duck, or it will become tough. You can use dove or goose instead of duck, and substitute turkey bacon for the prosciutto.

½ cup dry red wine
¼ cup fresh lemon juice
3 tablespoons olive oil
2 teaspoons bottled minced garlic
½ teaspoon dry mustard
½ teaspoon freshly ground black pepper
1 bay leaf
1 (12-ounce) package boneless whole duck breast, thawed, skinned, and cut into 12 (1-inch) pieces
6 slices prosciutto, cut in half lengthwise
Cooking spray

1. Combine first 7 ingredients in a large zip-top plastic bag. Add duck to bag, and seal. Marinate in refrigerator 30 minutes. Remove duck from bag, and discard marinade.
2. Prepare grill.
3. Wrap each piece of duck with 1 strip prosciutto. Thread 2 pieces duck onto each of 6 (6-inch) skewers. Place skewers on a grill rack coated with cooking spray, and grill 5 minutes on each side or until desired degree of doneness. Yield: 6 servings (serving size: 1 skewer).

CALORIES 42 (35% from fat); FAT 1.7g (sat 0.3g, mono 0.6g, poly 0.1g); PROTEIN 4.7g; CARB 0.4g; FIBER 0g; CHOL 22mg; IRON 0.1mg; SODIUM 85mg; CALC 1mg

Grilled Pheasant with Dijon-Tarragon Sauce

Because wild pheasant is lean, baste it frequently during cooking, and avoid overcooking. If you substitute skinless, boneless chicken, cook until the meat is no longer pink in the middle.

2 tablespoons extravirgin olive oil
2 tablespoons fresh lemon juice
¼ teaspoon freshly ground black pepper
1 (3¼-pound) pheasant, skinned and quartered
¼ cup Champagne vinegar
¼ cup dry white wine
2 tablespoons white balsamic vinegar
1 tablespoon chopped fresh tarragon
½ teaspoon dried chervil
¼ cup Dijon mustard
1 tablespoon butter, cut into small pieces
Cooking spray

1. Combine first 3 ingredients in a large zip-top plastic bag. Add pheasant; seal and marinate in refrigerator 1 hour, turning bag occasionally.
2. Prepare grill.
3. Combine Champagne vinegar and next 4 ingredients in a small saucepan; bring to a boil. Cook until reduced to ¼ cup (about 4 minutes). Remove from heat. Add mustard and butter, stirring with a whisk.
4. Remove pheasant from bag, and discard marinade. Place pheasant on grill rack coated with cooking spray; grill 2½ minutes on each side or until done, basting frequently with vinegar mixture. Yield: 4 servings (serving size: 1 piece pheasant).

CALORIES 356 (34% from fat); FAT 13.6g (sat 4.7g, mono 5.6g, poly 1.7g); PROTEIN 50.2g; CARB 5.7g; FIBER 0.1g; CHOL 139mg; IRON 2.9mg; SODIUM 438mg; CALC 47mg

Soft Tacos with Spicy Marinated Goose

Prepared this way, wild goose tastes like the finest marinated steak. If you don't have wild goose, substitute a lean cut of beef, such as flank steak.

⅓ cup low-sodium soy sauce
¼ cup extravirgin olive oil
2 tablespoons minced yellow onion
1 tablespoon bottled minced garlic
1½ teaspoons sugar
1 teaspoon chili powder
½ teaspoon black pepper
½ teaspoon dried oregano
1 (1½-pound) boneless goose breast, skinned
1 cup chopped tomato
½ cup chopped green onions
¼ cup chopped fresh cilantro
1 tablespoon minced jalapeño pepper
1 teaspoon lemon juice
½ teaspoon salt
Cooking spray
8 (6-inch) white corn tortillas
½ cup (4 ounces) crumbled feta cheese
1½ cups finely shredded green cabbage

1. Prepare grill.
2. Combine first 9 ingredients in a large zip-top plastic bag; seal and marinate in refrigerator overnight, turning bag occasionally. Remove goose from bag, reserving marinade.
3. Combine tomato and next 5 ingredients in a medium bowl.
4. Place goose on grill rack coated with cooking spray; grill 10 minutes or until a thermometer registers 165°, turning and basting frequently with marinade. Let stand 10 minutes. Cut goose diagonally across grain into thin slices. Keep warm.
5. Warm tortillas according to package directions. Place 3 ounces goose in each tortilla. Top each with 2 tablespoons tomato mixture, 1 tablespoon cheese, and 3 tablespoons cabbage. Yield: 8 servings (serving size: 1 taco).

CALORIES 268 (42% from fat); FAT 12.4g (sat 4.4g, mono 5.4g, poly 1.5g); PROTEIN 22.8g; CARB 15.8g; FIBER 2.3g; CHOL 80mg; IRON 2.9mg; SODIUM 550mg; CALC 113mg

Go Global

Enjoy main dishes inspired by world fare—and made with supermarket ingredients.

Preparing tasty vegetarian dishes from around the globe needn't involve a trip to a specialty market. With fresh produce, spices, flavorful cheeses, and other supermarket ingredients, you can enjoy meals with European, Asian, or Latin flair.

QUICK & EASY
Vegetarian Chipotle Nachos

Cooking spray
1 cup chopped green bell pepper (about 1 medium)
1 cup chopped onion (about 1 medium)
1 (12-ounce) package meatless fat-free crumbles (such as Lightlife Smart Ground)
1 (7-ounce) can chipotle chiles in adobo sauce
1 (15-ounce) can pinto beans, rinsed and drained
1 (14.5-ounce) can diced tomatoes with basil, garlic, and oregano, undrained
¼ cup chopped fresh cilantro
8 cups baked corn tortilla chips (6 ounces)
2 cups shredded romaine lettuce
1 cup diced peeled avocado (about 1 medium)
¾ cup vertically sliced red onion
¾ cup (3 ounces) shredded sharp Cheddar cheese
6 tablespoons fat-free sour cream

1. Heat a large nonstick skillet over medium heat. Coat pan with cooking spray. Add bell pepper, chopped onion, and crumbles; cook 5 minutes, stirring occasionally. Remove 1 chile and 1 tablespoon sauce from can; reserve remaining chiles and sauce for another use. Chop chile; add chile, sauce, beans, and tomatoes to pan. Cover, reduce heat, and simmer 5 minutes. Remove from heat; stir in

cilantro. Arrange 1⅓ cups chips on each of 6 plates. Top each serving with 1 cup bean mixture, ⅓ cup lettuce, about 2½ tablespoons avocado, 2 tablespoons onion, 2 tablespoons cheese, and 1 tablespoon sour cream. Yield: 6 servings.

CALORIES 408 (26% from fat); FAT 11.8g (sat 4g, mono 4.2g, poly 2.5g); PROTEIN 23.8g; CARB 53.7g; FIBER 11g; CHOL 16mg; IRON 3.6mg; SODIUM 906mg; CALC 316mg

Triple-Mushroom Stir-Fry with Tofu

SAUCE:
1¼ cups organic vegetable broth (such as Swanson Certified Organic)
¼ cup low-sodium soy sauce
2 tablespoons water
2 tablespoons hoisin sauce
1½ tablespoons cornstarch
1½ teaspoons sugar
1 teaspoon grated peeled fresh ginger
½ teaspoon crushed red pepper
½ teaspoon dark sesame oil
3 garlic cloves, minced

STIR-FRY:
1½ tablespoons canola oil, divided
½ pound extrafirm tofu, drained and cut into 1-inch cubes
2 cups presliced button mushrooms
2 cups sliced shiitake mushroom caps (about 3 ounces)
1 cup snow peas, trimmed
½ cup red bell pepper strips
1 (8-ounce) can sliced water chestnuts, drained
2 cups sliced oyster mushroom caps (about 4 ounces)
¾ cup (1-inch) slices green onions

REMAINING INGREDIENT:
5 cups hot cooked long-grain rice

1. To prepare sauce, combine first 10 ingredients, stirring well with a whisk.
2. To prepare stir-fry, heat 1 tablespoon canola oil in a large nonstick skillet over medium-high heat. Add tofu; cook 8 minutes or until lightly browned, turning occasionally. Remove from pan. Add 1½ teaspoons oil and button and shiitake mushrooms to pan; sauté 3 minutes or

until almost tender. Add peas, bell pepper, and water chestnuts; sauté 1 minute. Stir in broth mixture, tofu, oyster mushrooms, and onions; cook 2 minutes or until slightly thick. Serve over rice. Yield: 5 servings (serving size: 1 cup mushroom mixture and 1 cup rice).

CALORIES 385 (20% from fat); FAT 8.5g (sat 1.1g, mono 3.3g, poly 3.2g); PROTEIN 14.5g; CARB 63.6g; FIBER 5.1g; CHOL 0mg; IRON 4.6mg; SODIUM 692mg; CALC 104mg

Black Soybean Risotto with Spinach

5 cups organic vegetable broth (such as Swanson Certified Organic)
2 teaspoons olive oil
1 cup finely chopped onion
2 teaspoons finely chopped fresh rosemary
2 teaspoons finely chopped peeled fresh ginger
2 garlic cloves, minced
1 cup uncooked Arborio rice
¼ teaspoon salt
⅛ teaspoon crushed red pepper
½ cup (2 ounces) grated fresh Parmesan cheese
1 (15-ounce) can black soybeans, rinsed and drained (such as Eden Organic)
2 (6-ounce) packages fresh baby spinach
1 tablespoon butter

1. Bring broth to a simmer in a medium saucepan (do not boil). Keep warm over low heat.
2. Heat oil in a large saucepan or Dutch oven over medium heat. Add onion; cook 5 minutes or until tender, stirring occasionally. Add rosemary, ginger, and garlic; cook 2 minutes, stirring frequently. Add rice; cook 3 minutes, stirring constantly. Stir in ½ cup broth, salt, and pepper; cook 1 minute or until liquid is nearly absorbed, stirring constantly. Add remaining broth, ½ cup at a time, stirring constantly until each portion of broth is absorbed before adding the next (about 20 minutes total). Stir in
Continued

Parmesan cheese and beans. Add spinach in batches, stirring constantly until spinach wilts. Stir in butter. Yield: 6 servings (serving size: 1⅓ cups).

CALORIES 260 (29% from fat); FAT 8.5g (sat 3.4g, mono 2.8g, poly 1.6g); PROTEIN 11.7g; CARB 36.1g; FIBER 5.4g; CHOL 11mg; IRON 2.7mg; SODIUM 794mg; CALC 202mg

Ratatouille Bread Pudding

 2 teaspoons olive oil
 2 cups chopped onion (about
    2 medium)
 2 cups (1-inch) cubed peeled
    eggplant (about 6 ounces)
1½ cups chopped zucchini (about
    12 ounces)
 1 cup chopped red bell pepper
    (about 1 medium)
 ¼ cup chopped fresh basil
 ½ teaspoon salt
 ¼ teaspoon black pepper
 2 garlic cloves, minced
 1 (28-ounce) can diced tomatoes,
    undrained
 1 cup 1% low-fat milk
 ¾ cup (3 ounces) grated fresh
    Parmesan cheese, divided
 3 large eggs, lightly beaten
 2 large egg whites, lightly beaten
 8 ounces (1-inch) cubed day-old
    Italian bread (about 9 cups)
 Cooking spray

1. Preheat oven to 350°.
2. Heat oil in a large Dutch oven over medium-high heat. Add onion; reduce heat to medium-low. Cover and cook 10 minutes or until golden brown, stirring occasionally. Add eggplant and next 6 ingredients; cover and cook 10 minutes or until tender, stirring occasionally. Increase heat to medium-high. Add tomatoes; cook, uncovered, 15 minutes or until liquid almost evaporates, stirring occasionally. Remove from heat; cool slightly.
3. Combine milk, ¼ cup cheese, eggs, and egg whites in a large bowl, stirring with a whisk. Stir in eggplant mixture. Add bread; stir gently to combine. Let stand 10 minutes. Spoon mixture into a 2-quart baking dish coated with cooking spray. Sprinkle with ½ cup cheese. Bake

at 350° for 45 minutes or until pudding is set and lightly browned. Yield: 6 servings (serving size: 1 piece).

CALORIES 299 (29% from fat); FAT 9.7g (sat 3.9g, mono 3.6g, poly 1.2g); PROTEIN 16.7g; CARB 37.6g; FIBER 5.9g; CHOL 118mg; IRON 2.5mg; SODIUM 886mg; CALC 307mg

Pumpkin and Red Lentil Curry

 1 tablespoon extravirgin olive oil
 2 cups chopped onion (about
    2 medium)
 5 cups (½-inch) cubed peeled fresh
    pumpkin (about 1¾ pounds)
 1 teaspoon ground ginger
 1 teaspoon ground cumin
 1 teaspoon ground coriander
 ¾ teaspoon ground turmeric
 ¼ teaspoon ground red pepper
 3 garlic cloves, minced
 1 small jalapeño pepper, seeded and
    finely chopped
 4 cups organic vegetable broth
    (such as Swanson Certified
    Organic)
 1 (14.5-ounce) can diced tomatoes,
    undrained
 1 cup dried small red lentils
 ¼ teaspoon salt
 ¼ teaspoon freshly ground black
    pepper
 ¼ cup chopped fresh cilantro
 6 lime wedges

1. Heat oil in a large saucepan over medium heat. Add onion; cook 5 minutes, stirring occasionally. Stir in pumpkin and next 7 ingredients; cook 30 seconds, stirring constantly. Add broth and tomatoes; bring to a boil. Cover, reduce heat, and simmer 10 minutes or until pumpkin is just tender. Stir in lentils; cook 10 minutes or until lentils are tender. Stir in salt and black pepper. Ladle stew into individual bowls; sprinkle with cilantro. Serve with lime wedges. Yield: 6 servings (serving size: about 1⅓ cups stew, 2 teaspoons cilantro, and 1 lime wedge).

CALORIES 222 (11% from fat); FAT 2.8g (sat 0.4g, mono 1.8g, poly 0.4g); PROTEIN 10.3g; CARB 41.9g; FIBER 8.7g; CHOL 0mg; IRON 4mg; SODIUM 657mg; CALC 123mg

STAFF FAVORITE
Cheese Pie with Peppers

 Cooking spray
1½ cups chopped green bell pepper
 1 tablespoon finely chopped
    seeded jalapeño pepper (about
    1 medium)
 ½ cup semolina or pasta flour (about
    2¼ ounces)
1½ cups fat-free milk, divided
 1 cup plain fat-free yogurt
 1 cup (4 ounces) crumbled feta
    cheese
 1 cup (4 ounces) shredded
    reduced-fat extrasharp Cheddar
    cheese
 ¼ cup (1 ounce) crumbled blue
    cheese
 ½ teaspoon salt
 ¼ teaspoon freshly ground black
    pepper
 2 large egg whites
 8 (18 x 14–inch) sheets frozen
    phyllo dough, thawed

1. Preheat oven to 400°.
2. Heat a large nonstick skillet over medium-high heat. Coat pan with cooking spray. Add bell pepper and jalapeño; sauté 5 minutes. Lightly spoon flour into a measuring cup; level with a knife. Stir in flour; remove from heat. Set aside 2 tablespoons milk. Gradually add remaining milk to pan, stirring well with a whisk. Stir in yogurt; bring to a boil. Remove from heat; stir 2 minutes or until thick. Cool 5 minutes. Stir in cheeses, salt, black pepper, and egg whites.
3. Working with 1 phyllo sheet at a time (cover remaining dough to keep from drying), place 2 phyllo sheets in a 13 x 9–inch baking pan coated with cooking spray; gently press sheets onto bottom and sides of pan, allowing ends to extend over edges of pan. Coat top sheet with cooking spray. Fold 1 phyllo sheet in half crosswise; place on sheets in bottom of pan, and coat with cooking spray. Top with 1 phyllo sheet, gently pressing sheet onto bottom and sides of pan; coat with cooking spray. Spread cheese mixture evenly over phyllo. Fold 1 phyllo sheet in half crosswise; gently press on cheese mixture in pan, and coat with

cooking spray. Top with 3 phyllo sheets, coating each sheet with cooking spray. Cut ends of sheets extending over pan. Fold edges of phyllo to form a rim; flatten rim with a fork. Cut 4 slits with a sharp knife in top of phyllo; brush with reserved 2 tablespoons milk. Bake at 400° for 22 minutes. Reduce oven temperature to 375° (do not remove pie from oven); bake 20 minutes or until browned. Remove from oven; let stand 15 minutes. Yield: 8 servings (serving size: 1 piece).

CALORIES 243 (32% from fat); FAT 8.7g (sat 5.2g, mono 1.7g, poly 0.4g); PROTEIN 13.3g; CARB 27.6g; FIBER 1.4g; CHOL 27mg; IRON 1.5mg; SODIUM 641mg; CALC 292mg

How to Line Pan with Phyllo

1. *The phyllo that hangs over the rim tends to dry out, so trim it off.*

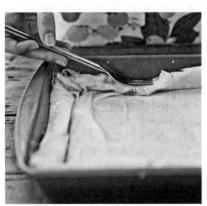

2. *Fold the phyllo to form a rim, and press with a fork to help the dough adhere.*

happy endings

Here's to Good Taste

Sweetly heady liqueurs spike these grown-up desserts.

STAFF FAVORITE • MAKE AHEAD
Irish Cream Brownies

Be sure to cook the brownies until a wooden pick inserted in the center comes out *almost* clean. If you wait until the pick is clean, the brownies will be overcooked.

    1   cup all-purpose flour (about
        4½ ounces)
    ½   cup unsweetened cocoa
    ¼   teaspoon baking soda
    ¼   teaspoon salt
    ⅓   cup semisweet chocolate chips
    ¼   cup butter
    1   cup sugar
    ½   cup egg substitute
    ¼   cup Baileys Irish Cream
    1   teaspoon vanilla extract
        Cooking spray

1. Preheat oven to 350°.
2. Lightly spoon flour into a dry measuring cup; level with a knife. Combine flour, cocoa, baking soda, and salt in a small bowl, stirring with a whisk.
3. Place chocolate chips and butter in a large microwave-safe bowl. Microwave at HIGH 1½ minutes or until chocolate chips and butter melt, stirring every 30 seconds. Cool slightly. Add sugar and next 3 ingredients, stirring well with a whisk. Microwave at HIGH 1 minute or until sugar dissolves, stirring every 30 seconds. Fold in flour mixture, stirring just until moist. Spread batter in a 9-inch square baking pan coated with cooking spray. Bake at 350° for 20 minutes or until a wooden pick inserted in center comes out almost clean. Cool on a wire rack. Yield: 16 servings (serving size: 1 brownie).

CALORIES 145 (30% from fat); FAT 4.9g (sat 3g, mono 0.9g, poly 0.2g); PROTEIN 2.5g; CARB 23.8g; FIBER 1.1g; CHOL 8mg; IRON 0.9mg; SODIUM 93mg; CALC 8mg

MAKE AHEAD
Hazelnut Cheesecake

Frangelico gives the cheesecake a delicate hazelnut taste, while chopped hazelnuts in the crust add crunch and more nutty flavor. You can use Amaretto (almond-flavored liqueur) and almonds instead.

CRUST:

    1   cup reduced-fat vanilla wafer
        crumbs (about 30 cookies)
    3   tablespoons sugar
    3   tablespoons finely chopped
        hazelnuts, toasted
    1   tablespoon butter, melted
        Cooking spray

FILLING:

    2   (8-ounce) blocks ⅓-less-fat cream
        cheese, softened
    1   (8-ounce) block fat-free cream
        cheese, softened
    1   cup fat-free sour cream
    1⅓ cups sugar
    2   tablespoons all-purpose
        flour
    ¼   teaspoon salt
    4   large egg whites
    1   large egg
    ¼   cup Frangelico (hazelnut-flavored
        liqueur)
    2   teaspoons vanilla extract

1. Preheat oven to 400°.
2. To prepare crust, combine first 3 ingredients in a medium bowl. Drizzle with butter; toss with a fork until moist. Press mixture into bottom of a 9-inch springform pan coated with cooking spray. Bake at 400° for 7 minutes or until lightly browned. Cool on a wire rack.
3. Reduce oven temperature to 325°.
4. To prepare filling, place cheeses in a large bowl; beat with a mixer at medium speed until smooth. Add sour cream; beat until combined. Combine 1⅓ cups sugar, flour, and salt, stirring with a whisk. Beating at low speed, gradually add sugar mixture to cheese mixture. Add egg whites and egg, 1 at a time, beating well after each addition. Beat in liqueur and vanilla. Pour mixture into
Continued

prepared pan. Bake at 325° for 1 hour or until cheesecake center barely moves when pan is touched. Remove cheesecake from oven; run a knife around outside edge. Cool to room temperature. Cover and chill at least 8 hours. Yield: 16 servings (serving size: 1 wedge).

CALORIES 238 (33% from fat); FAT 8.6g (sat 4.6g, mono 2.9g, poly 0.4g); PROTEIN 7.4g; CARB 31.3g; FIBER 0.2g; CHOL 38mg; IRON 0.4mg; SODIUM 184mg; CALC 69mg

MAKE AHEAD
Orange Liqueur Rice Pudding

Arborio rice, the traditional rice for risotto, releases starch as it cooks, yielding a creamy, orange-scented rice pudding. Serve warm or chilled. If you don't have Grand Marnier, substitute Cointreau.

3½   cups 2% reduced-fat milk
½   cup uncooked Arborio rice
6   tablespoons sugar
¼   teaspoon salt
1   large egg, lightly beaten
2   tablespoons Grand Marnier
      (orange-flavored liqueur)
1   tablespoon butter
1   teaspoon vanilla extract
1½   tablespoons slivered almonds,
      toasted
1½   tablespoons chopped dry-roasted
      pistachios

1. Combine first 4 ingredients in a medium saucepan; bring to a boil, stirring frequently. Reduce heat; simmer, uncovered, 20 minutes, stirring occasionally.
2. Place egg in a medium bowl. Gradually stir about one-fourth of hot rice mixture into egg; return egg mixture to pan, stirring constantly. Simmer, uncovered, 20 minutes or until mixture is thick and rice is tender, stirring occasionally. Remove from heat; add liqueur, butter, and vanilla, stirring until butter melts. Combine nuts in a small bowl; sprinkle nuts evenly over pudding. Yield: 6 servings (serving size: about ½ cup pudding and about 1½ teaspoons nuts).

CALORIES 215 (30% from fat); FAT 7.2g (sat 3.3g, mono 2.6g, poly 0.8g); PROTEIN 7.1g; CARB 28.4g; FIBER 0.5g; CHOL 51mg; IRON 0.5mg; SODIUM 203mg; CALC 185mg

Bread Pudding with Irish Cream Sauce

Just a splash of intensely flavored Baileys Irish Cream is all you need in the sauce. Cooking the pudding in a water bath ensures creamy results. We call for chopped dates and golden raisins in this recipe, but you may substitute any dried fruit you like.

PUDDING:
⅔   cup packed brown sugar
5   large eggs, lightly beaten
2⅔   cups 2% reduced-fat milk
2   teaspoons vanilla extract
½   teaspoon ground cinnamon
9   cups (½-inch) cubed French
      bread, crusts removed (about
      12 ounces)
¼   cup chopped pitted dates
¼   cup golden raisins
Cooking spray

SAUCE:
2   tablespoons brown sugar
2   egg yolks
½   cup 2% reduced-fat milk
1   tablespoon Baileys Irish Cream

1. To prepare pudding, combine ⅔ cup sugar and eggs in a large bowl, stirring with a whisk. Heat 2⅔ cups milk, vanilla, and cinnamon in a medium, heavy saucepan over medium heat to 180° or until tiny bubbles form around edge (do not boil). Gradually add hot milk mixture to egg mixture, stirring constantly with a whisk. Return milk mixture to pan; cook over low heat 6 minutes or until mixture coats the back of a spoon, stirring constantly with a whisk. Remove from heat. Combine bread, dates, and raisins in a large bowl. Pour milk mixture over bread mixture; toss well to coat. Spoon bread mixture into an 8-inch square baking dish coated with cooking spray. Cover and refrigerate 4 hours or up to overnight.
2. Preheat oven to 350°.
3. Place baking dish in a 13 x 9–inch baking pan; add hot water to pan to a depth of 1 inch. Bake, covered, at 350° for 20 minutes. Uncover and bake an additional 40 minutes or until a knife inserted in center comes out clean.

4. To prepare sauce, combine 2 tablespoons sugar and egg yolks in a medium bowl, stirring with a whisk. Heat ½ cup milk in a small, heavy saucepan over medium heat to 180° or until tiny bubbles form around edge (do not boil). Gradually add hot milk to egg yolk mixture, stirring constantly with a whisk. Place milk mixture in pan; cook over low heat 6 minutes or until mixture coats back of a spoon, stirring constantly with a whisk. Remove from heat; stir in liqueur. Place pan in a large ice-filled bowl 5 minutes or until sauce cools to room temperature, stirring constantly. Serve sauce over warm pudding. Yield: 9 servings (serving size: 1 bread pudding piece and about 1½ tablespoons sauce).

CALORIES 306 (20% from fat); FAT 6.8g (sat 2.6g, mono 2.4g, poly 0.9g); PROTEIN 10.6g; CARB 50.4g; FIBER 1.8g; CHOL 169mg; IRON 2.2mg; SODIUM 322mg; CALC 175mg

MAKE AHEAD
Individual Amaretto Flans

These make-ahead custards take on a lot of amaretto flavor. Resist the urge to stir the sugar-water mixture, as doing so can cause it to crystallize.

½   cup sugar
2   tablespoons water
Cooking spray
⅔   cup sugar
⅛   teaspoon salt
3   large eggs, lightly beaten
2   large egg yolks, lightly beaten
2   cups whole milk
¼   cup amaretto (almond-flavored
      liqueur)

1. Preheat oven to 325°.
2. Combine ½ cup sugar and 2 tablespoons water in a small, heavy saucepan. Cook over medium-high heat until sugar dissolves, and continue cooking 5 minutes or until golden brown (do not stir). Immediately pour into 6 (6-ounce) custard cups or ramekins coated with cooking spray, tipping quickly until caramelized sugar coats bottoms of cups.
3. Combine ⅔ cup sugar, salt, eggs, and egg yolks in a medium bowl, stirring well with a whisk.

4. Heat milk over medium-high heat in a small, heavy saucepan to 180° or until tiny bubbles form around edge (do not boil). Gradually add hot milk to egg mixture, stirring with a whisk. Stir in liqueur. Strain mixture through a sieve into a bowl, and discard solids. Divide mixture evenly among prepared custard cups. Place cups in bottom of a broiler pan; add hot water to pan to a depth of 1 inch. Bake at 325° for 40 minutes or until flan centers barely move when custard cups are touched. Remove cups from pan; cool completely on a wire rack. Cover and chill at least 8 hours.

5. Loosen edges of flans with a knife. Place a dessert plate, upside down, on top of each cup, and invert onto plates. Yield: 6 servings (serving size: 1 flan).

CALORIES 271 (22% from fat); FAT 6.6g (sat 2.8g, mono 2.3g, poly 0.7g); PROTEIN 6.6g; CARB 45g; FIBER 0g; CHOL 182mg; IRON 0.6mg; SODIUM 122mg; CALC 103mg

---

MAKE AHEAD
Banana Cupcakes with Amaretto Buttercream

A hint of almond liqueur in the frosting makes these a special treat for grown-ups.

CUPCAKES:
Cooking spray
1 cup granulated sugar
¼ cup butter, softened
2 large eggs
1½ cups all-purpose flour (about 6¾ ounces)
½ teaspoon baking soda
¼ teaspoon salt
⅔ cup mashed ripe banana (about 1 large)
⅓ cup plain fat-free yogurt
1¼ teaspoons vanilla extract

FROSTING:
⅓ cup butter, softened
2½ tablespoons amaretto (almond-flavored liqueur)
¼ teaspoon vanilla extract
2 cups powdered sugar
⅛ teaspoon salt
2 tablespoons chopped almonds, toasted

1. Preheat oven to 350°.

2. To prepare cupcakes, place 12 muffin cup liners in muffin cups; coat liners with cooking spray. Set aside.

3. Place granulated sugar and ¼ cup butter in a large bowl; beat with a mixer at medium speed until well blended (about 4 minutes). Add eggs, 1 at a time, beating well after each addition.

4. Lightly spoon flour into dry measuring cups; level with a knife. Combine flour, baking soda, and ¼ teaspoon salt, stirring with a whisk. Combine banana, yogurt, and 1¼ teaspoons vanilla, stirring well. Beating at low speed, add flour mixture and banana mixture alternately to sugar mixture, beginning and ending with flour mixture. Spoon batter into prepared muffin cups (cups will be full). Bake at 350° for 20 minutes or until a wooden pick inserted into center of 1 cupcake comes out clean. Remove cupcakes from pan; cool completely on a wire rack.

5. To prepare frosting, place ⅓ cup butter, liqueur, and ¼ teaspoon vanilla in a large bowl; beat with a mixer at medium speed until smooth. Gradually add powdered sugar and ⅛ teaspoon salt, beating just until smooth. Spread frosting evenly over cupcakes; sprinkle evenly with almonds. Yield: 12 servings (serving size: 1 cupcake).

CALORIES 325 (29% from fat); FAT 10.6g (sat 6g, mono 3.1g, poly 0.7g); PROTEIN 3.5g; CARB 53.8g; FIBER 0.9g; CHOL 59mg; IRON 1mg; SODIUM 205mg; CALC 22mg

---

Luscious Liqueurs

The flavors of specialty liqueurs are distinct. Here are some classic combinations to help you create your own desserts.

Liqueur	Origin	Flavor	Best with
Amaretto (am-ah-REHT-toh)	Saronno, Italy, in 1525	Though it tastes like almonds, amaretto traditionally is made from apricot pits steeped in brandy.	Apricots, almonds, and peaches; also good with chocolate, bananas, and pumpkin
Baileys Irish Cream	Ireland, in 1974	Irish whiskey and cream, with a touch of cocoa	Chocolate
Frangelico (fran-JELL-ih-koh)	Italy's Piedmont region, in the 17th century	Hazelnut, cocoa, vanilla	Chocolate, coffee; also nice with peaches
Grand Marnier (GRAN-mahr-NYAY)	France, in 1880	Cognac flavored with bitter Haitian oranges, vanilla, and spices	Chocolate; excellent drizzled over vanilla ice cream
Chambord (sham-BORD)	France, in 1685	Cognac, raspberries, vanilla, honey, herbs	Vanilla and chocolate (dark and white), almonds, lemon, raspberries

Lemon Pound Cake with Chambord Glaze

CAKE:

Cooking spray
2 tablespoons granulated sugar
2½ cups all-purpose flour (about 11¼ ounces)
½ teaspoon baking powder
½ teaspoon baking soda
¼ teaspoon salt
2 cups granulated sugar
¾ cup butter, softened
3 large eggs
1½ tablespoons grated lemon rind
¼ cup fresh lemon juice
1½ teaspoons vanilla extract
¾ cup fat-free buttermilk
2 tablespoons Chambord (raspberry-flavored liqueur)

GLAZE:

¾ cup powdered sugar
2½ tablespoons Chambord (raspberry-flavored liqueur)
1 tablespoon fresh lemon juice
1 tablespoon butter, melted

1. Preheat oven to 350°.
2. To prepare cake, coat a 12-cup Bundt pan with cooking spray; dust with 2 tablespoons granulated sugar. Set aside.
3. Lightly spoon flour into dry measuring cups; level with a knife. Combine flour, baking powder, baking soda, and salt, stirring well with a whisk.
4. Place 2 cups granulated sugar and ¾ cup butter in a large bowl; beat with a mixer at medium speed until light and fluffy (about 4 minutes). Add eggs, 1 at a time, beating well after each addition. Add rind, ¼ cup juice, and vanilla; beat until combined. Beating at low speed, add flour mixture and buttermilk alternately to sugar mixture, beginning and ending with flour mixture; beat just until combined (batter will be thick).
5. Spoon batter into prepared pan. Bake at 350° for 1 hour or until a wooden pick inserted in center comes out clean. Cool in pan 10 minutes on a wire rack. Loosen cake from sides of pan using a narrow metal spatula. Place a plate upside down on top of cake; invert onto plate. Pierce cake liberally with a wooden pick. Brush 2 tablespoons liqueur over warm cake.
6. To prepare glaze, combine powdered sugar, 2½ tablespoons liqueur, 1 tablespoon juice, and melted butter, stirring with a whisk until smooth. Drizzle slowly over warm cake. Cool completely. Yield: 16 servings (serving size: 1 slice).

CALORIES 314 (30% from fat); FAT 10.4g (sat 6.2g, mono 2.8g, poly 0.6g); PROTEIN 3.7g; CARB 50.4g; FIBER 0.6g; CHOL 64mg; IRON 1.1mg; SODIUM 182mg; CALC 35mg

Chocolate-Hazelnut Mousse

¼ cup sugar
¼ cup unsweetened cocoa
2½ tablespoons cornstarch
¼ teaspoon salt
2 large eggs, lightly beaten
2 cups 2% reduced-fat milk
¼ cup Frangelico (hazelnut-flavored liqueur)
½ teaspoon vanilla extract
3 ounces bittersweet chocolate, chopped
2 cups frozen fat-free whipped topping, thawed
2 tablespoons chopped hazelnuts, toasted

1. Combine first 5 ingredients in a medium bowl, stirring well with a whisk.
2. Heat milk over medium-high heat in a small, heavy saucepan to 180° or until tiny bubbles form around edge (do not boil). Gradually add hot milk to sugar mixture, stirring constantly with a whisk. Place milk mixture in pan, and cook over medium heat until very thick and bubbly (about 5 minutes), stirring constantly. Spoon mixture into a medium bowl, and add liqueur, vanilla, and chocolate, stirring until chocolate melts. Place bowl in a large ice-filled bowl 15 minutes or until mixture is cool, stirring occasionally.
3. Remove bowl from ice. Gently fold in one-third of whipped topping. Fold in remaining topping. Cover and chill at least 3 hours. Sprinkle with hazelnuts. Yield: 6 servings (serving size: about ⅔ cup mousse and 1 teaspoon hazelnuts).

CALORIES 278 (30% from fat); FAT 9.2g (sat 4.4g, mono 3.5g, poly 0.5g); PROTEIN 6.9g; CARB 39g; FIBER 2.2g; CHOL 77mg; IRON 1mg; SODIUM 177mg; CALC 115mg

new american classic

Oven-Fried Chicken

This all-American favorite will become a mainstay at your family's Sunday dinners and holiday picnics.

Oven-Fried Chicken

1 cup low-fat buttermilk
2 large egg whites, beaten
1 cup all-purpose flour (about 4½ ounces)
⅓ cup cornmeal
1 teaspoon salt, divided
¾ teaspoon freshly ground black pepper
¼ teaspoon ground red pepper
2 chicken breast halves, skinned (about 1 pound)
2 chicken thighs, skinned (about ½ pound)
2 chicken drumsticks, skinned (about ½ pound)
2 tablespoons canola oil
Cooking spray

1. Preheat oven to 425°.
2. Cover a large baking sheet with parchment paper. Combine buttermilk and egg whites in a shallow dish; stir well with a whisk. Combine flour, cornmeal, ½ teaspoon salt, black pepper, and red pepper in a separate shallow dish; stir well. Sprinkle chicken evenly with ½ teaspoon salt. Dip chicken in buttermilk mixture; dredge in flour mixture.
3. Heat oil in a large nonstick skillet over medium-high heat. Add chicken to pan; cook 4 minutes on each side or until lightly browned. Place chicken on prepared baking sheet; lightly coat chicken with cooking spray. Bake at 425° for 30 minutes or until chicken is done. Yield: 4 servings (serving size: 1 chicken breast half or 1 drumstick and 1 thigh).

CALORIES 450 (28% from fat); FAT 13.8g (sat 2.5g, mono 6.1g, poly 3.6g); PROTEIN 43.5g; CARB 35.3g; FIBER 1.7g; CHOL 109mg; IRON 3.2mg; SODIUM 803mg; CALC 88mg

The *Cooking Light*® Holiday Cookbook

Our very best dishes, from festive appetizers to make-ahead gifts; plus, tips and techniques to pull them off with panache

---

Starters

For casual or formal get-togethers, kick off the festivities with these appetizers.

QUICK & EASY
Apple Martinis

Combine the ingredients for the martini mix before the party so it's ready to go into the shaker as soon as guests arrive.

    1   cup water
    ¼   cup sugar
    ¾   cup vodka
    1   cup apple juice
    1   cup apple liqueur (such as Sour Apple Pucker)
    Crushed ice

1. Combine water and sugar in a glass measuring cup. Microwave at HIGH 2 minutes or until sugar dissolves, stirring once; cool. Combine sugar mixture, vodka, juice, and liqueur in a pitcher.
2. Place ice in a martini shaker. Add vodka mixture to martini shaker in batches; shake well to chill. Strain about ½ cup vodka mixture in shaker into each of 10 glasses; repeat procedure with remaining vodka mixture, refilling ice as necessary. Serve immediately. Yield: 10 martinis (serving size: about ½ cup).

CALORIES 160 (0% from fat); FAT 0g; PROTEIN 0.1g; CARB 16.2g; FIBER 0g; CHOL 0mg; IRON 0mg; SODIUM 0mg; CALC 0mg

STAFF FAVORITE
Spicy Shrimp Cakes with Corn and Avocado Salsa

CAKES:

    1   pound medium shrimp, peeled and deveined
    Cooking spray
    1   cup finely chopped red bell pepper
    1   garlic clove, minced
    ¼   cup thinly sliced green onions
    3   tablespoons reduced-fat mayonnaise
    1   tablespoon fresh lime juice
    1½ teaspoons hot sauce
    ½   teaspoon sugar
    ¼   teaspoon salt
    1   large egg, lightly beaten
    ¼   cup finely chopped fresh cilantro
    ¾   cup panko (Japanese breadcrumbs), divided

SALSA:

    1   cup frozen white corn, thawed
    ¾   cup diced peeled avocado
    ¼   cup chopped fresh cilantro
    3   tablespoons finely chopped red onion
    2   tablespoons finely chopped seeded poblano pepper
    1   tablespoon fresh lime juice
    ¼   teaspoon salt

1. To prepare cakes, place shrimp in a food processor; pulse 10 times or until finely chopped. Set aside.
2. Heat a large nonstick skillet over medium heat. Coat pan with cooking spray. Add bell pepper to pan, and sauté 3 minutes. Add garlic to pan; sauté 1 minute. Remove from heat. Place bell pepper mixture in a large bowl. Add shrimp, green onions, and next 6 ingredients, stirring well. Stir in cilantro and ¼ cup panko.
3. Divide shrimp mixture into 10 equal portions, shaping each portion into a ½-inch-thick patty. Dredge both sides of patties in ½ cup panko. Chill at least one hour.
4. Heat pan over medium-high heat. Coat pan with cooking spray. Add 5 cakes to pan; cook 4 minutes on each side or until browned. Remove from pan; cover and keep warm. Repeat procedure with remaining cakes.
5. To prepare salsa, combine corn and remaining 6 ingredients; stir gently. Serve immediately with shrimp cakes. Yield: 10 servings (serving size: 1 shrimp cake and about 3 tablespoons salsa).

CALORIES 121 (29% from fat); FAT 3.9g (sat 0.8g, mono 1.4g, poly 0.7g); PROTEIN 11.5g; CARB 10.6g; FIBER 1.6g; CHOL 90mg; IRON 1.5mg; SODIUM 252mg; CALC 34mg

Pumpkin and Yellow Pepper Soup with Smoked Paprika

Pumpkinseed kernels are also known as *pepitas*. Garnish soup with parsley sprigs.

- 1 tablespoon olive oil
- 3½ cups chopped yellow bell pepper (about 2 large)
- 1½ cups chopped carrot (about 2 medium)
- 1 cup chopped onion (about 1 medium)
- ½ teaspoon Spanish smoked paprika
- 2 garlic cloves, chopped
- 5 cups fat-free, less-sodium chicken broth, divided
- ¼ teaspoon freshly ground black pepper
- 1 (15-ounce) can salt-free pumpkin puree
- 2 tablespoons fresh lemon juice
- 2 tablespoons unsalted pumpkinseed kernels, toasted
- 1 tablespoon chopped fresh parsley

1. Heat oil in a Dutch oven over medium-high heat. Add bell pepper, carrot, and onion; cook 10 minutes or until tender, stirring occasionally. Add paprika and garlic; sauté 1 minute. Add 3 cups broth and black pepper; bring to a boil. Cover, reduce heat, and simmer 20 minutes or until vegetables are tender.

2. Place one-third of vegetable mixture in a blender. Remove center piece of blender lid (to allow steam to escape); secure blender lid on blender. Place a clean towel over opening in blender lid (to avoid spills). Blend until smooth. Pour into a large bowl. Repeat procedure with remaining vegetable mixture.

3. Return pureed vegetable mixture to Dutch oven; stir in 2 cups broth and pumpkin. Cook over low heat 10 minutes or until thoroughly heated, stirring frequently. Remove from heat; stir in juice. Ladle 1 cup soup into each of 7 bowls; top each serving with about 1 teaspoon pumpkinseed kernels and about ½ teaspoon parsley. Serve immediately. Yield: 7 servings.

CALORIES 88 (28% from fat); FAT 2.7g (sat 0.5g, mono 1.6g, poly 0.5g); PROTEIN 3.6g; CARB 14g; FIBER 4.4g; CHOL 0mg; IRON 1.6mg; SODIUM 296mg; CALC 45mg

---

QUICK & EASY
Mini Smoked Salmon Pizzas

If you can't find gyoza skins, substitute round wonton wrappers.

- 24 gyoza skins
- Cooking spray
- 4 (1-ounce) slices cold-smoked salmon
- ½ cup (4 ounces) ⅓-less-fat cream cheese
- 2 tablespoons finely chopped red onion
- 1 tablespoon capers
- 1 teaspoon chopped fresh dill
- ½ teaspoon grated lemon rind
- 48 (½-inch) chive pieces

1. Preheat oven to 400°.
2. Arrange wrappers in a single layer on 2 baking sheets. Lightly coat wrappers with cooking spray. Bake at 400° for 6 minutes or until crisp; cool.
3. Cut each salmon slice into 6 equal portions. Combine cheese and next 4 ingredients, stirring well. Spread 1 teaspoon cheese mixture on each wrapper; top each with 1 salmon piece. Garnish each with 2 chive pieces. Yield: 12 servings (serving size: 2 pizzas).

CALORIES 84 (31% from fat); FAT 2.9g (sat 1.5g, mono 0.9g, poly 0.3g); PROTEIN 4.4g; CARB 9.8g; FIBER 0.4g; CHOL 11mg; IRON 0.7mg; SODIUM 230mg; CALC 18mg

---

Mushroom Pizza

Serve with a tossed green salad. Prepare the topping while the dough rises.

DOUGH:
- 1 package dry yeast (about 2¼ teaspoons)
- 1 teaspoon sugar
- 1 cup warm water (100° to 110°)
- 2¼ cups all-purpose flour (about 10 ounces), divided
- ¼ cup whole wheat flour (about 1 ounce)
- ¼ cup yellow cornmeal
- 1 teaspoon salt
- 1 teaspoon olive oil
- Cooking spray

MUSHROOM TOPPING:
- 2 teaspoons olive oil
- 6 cups sliced cremini mushrooms (about 1 pound)
- 2 cups thinly sliced onion (about 1 large)
- 1 garlic clove, minced
- 1 tablespoon chopped fresh thyme
- ½ teaspoon salt

REMAINING INGREDIENTS:
- 1 tablespoon yellow cornmeal
- ½ cup (2 ounces) shredded fontina cheese
- 3 tablespoons chopped fresh parsley

1. To prepare dough, dissolve yeast and sugar in 1 cup warm water in a large bowl; let stand 5 minutes. Lightly spoon flours into dry measuring cups; level with a knife. Add 2 cups all-purpose flour, whole wheat flour, and next 3 ingredients to yeast mixture; stir until a soft dough forms. Turn dough out onto a floured surface. Knead until smooth and elastic (about 8 minutes); add enough of remaining flour, 1 tablespoon at a time, to prevent dough from sticking to hands. Place dough in a large bowl coated with cooking spray, turning to coat top. Cover and let rise in a warm place (85°), free from drafts, 1 hour or until doubled in size. (Gently press two fingers into dough. If indentation remains, dough has risen enough.)

2. To prepare topping, heat 2 teaspoons oil in a large nonstick skillet over medium-high heat. Add mushrooms, onion, and garlic; sauté 8 minutes or until mushrooms are tender and liquid almost evaporates. Remove from heat; stir in thyme and ½ teaspoon salt.

3. Preheat oven to 475°.
4. Punch dough down; cover and let rest 5 minutes. Roll dough into a 13-inch round on a lightly floured surface. Lightly coat a large baking sheet with cooking spray, and sprinkle with 1 tablespoon cornmeal. Place dough on baking sheet. Spread mushroom mixture over dough, leaving a 1-inch border; sprinkle with cheese. Bake at 475° on bottom rack of oven 13 minutes or until crust is

lightly brown and cheese melts. Sprinkle with parsley. Cut into 12 wedges. Serve warm or cold. Yield: 12 servings (serving size: 1 wedge).

CALORIES 149 (18% from fat); FAT 3g (sat 1.1g, mono 1.3g, poly 0.3g); PROTEIN 5.6g; CARB 25.5g; FIBER 1.8g; CHOL 5mg; IRON 1.7mg; SODIUM 337mg; CALC 42mg

Baked Eggplant Dip

For a traditional and beautiful seasonal garnish, sprinkle this classic Middle Eastern appetizer with pomegranate seeds. You can also try the dip as a sandwich spread.

    2   eggplants (about 3 pounds)
   1/3 cup tahini (sesame-seed
         paste)
   1/4 cup fresh lemon juice
    1   tablespoon grated onion
    1   tablespoon minced garlic (about
         3 cloves)
   3/4 teaspoon salt
   1/4 teaspoon ground cumin
    1   tablespoon chopped fresh
         parsley
    6   (6-inch) pitas, each cut into
         6 wedges

1. Preheat oven to 450°.
2. Pierce eggplants several times with a fork; place on a jelly-roll pan. Bake at 450° for 1 hour or until tender. Remove from baking sheet. Cool slightly; peel. Drain pulp in a colander 30 minutes.
3. Place drained pulp, tahini, and next 5 ingredients in a food processor; process until smooth. Place dip in a serving bowl; sprinkle with parsley. Serve with pita wedges. Yield: 12 servings (serving size: 1/4 cup dip and 3 pita wedges).

CALORIES 148 (27% from fat); FAT 4.5g (sat 0.6g, mono 1.5g, poly 2g); PROTEIN 5.1g; CARB 23.8g; FIBER 1.4g; CHOL 0mg; IRON 1.2mg; SODIUM 312mg; CALC 44mg

Roasted Oysters with Prosciutto and Spinach

    1   (6-ounce) package fresh baby
         spinach
    1   ounce finely chopped prosciutto
   1/4 teaspoon freshly ground black
         pepper
   18   shucked oysters
    2   tablespoons pine nuts, toasted

1. Preheat oven to 450°.
2. Heat a large nonstick skillet over medium heat. Add spinach to pan; cook 3 minutes or until spinach is wilted, stirring occasionally. Add prosciutto; sauté 1 minute or until crisp. Stir in pepper. Remove from heat; cool.
3. Arrange oysters in a single layer in a broiler pan; spoon about 1 tablespoon spinach mixture onto each oyster. Sprinkle oysters evenly with pine nuts. Bake at 450° for 5 minutes or until oysters are opaque. Serve immediately. Yield: 6 servings (serving size: 3 oysters).

CALORIES 59 (47% from fat); FAT 3.1g (sat 0.5g, mono 0.8g, poly 1.3g); PROTEIN 4.5g; CARB 3.8g; FIBER 0.8g; CHOL 13mg; IRON 3.4mg; SODIUM 168mg; CALC 48mg

Hot Crab Dip

Serve warm with melba toast or pita chips.

    1   cup fat-free cottage cheese
   1/2 teaspoon grated lemon rind
    2   tablespoons lemon juice
    1   tablespoon Dijon mustard
  1 1/2 teaspoons Worcestershire sauce
    1   teaspoon hot sauce
   1/2 teaspoon salt
   1/8 teaspoon freshly ground black
         pepper
    1   garlic clove, minced
    1   (8-ounce) block 1/3-less-fat cream
         cheese, softened
    2   tablespoons chopped green onions
    1   pound lump crabmeat, shell pieces
         removed
         Cooking spray
    2   tablespoons grated fresh Parmesan
         cheese
   1/4 cup dry breadcrumbs

1. Preheat oven to 375°.
2. Place first 9 ingredients in a food processor; process until smooth.
3. Combine cottage cheese mixture, cream cheese, and onions in a large bowl; gently fold in crab. Place crab mixture in an 11 x 7–inch baking dish coated with cooking spray. Bake at 375° for 30 minutes. Sprinkle with Parmesan and breadcrumbs. Bake at 375° for 15 minutes or until lightly golden. Yield: 20 servings (serving size: about 3 tablespoons).

CALORIES 63 (53% from fat); FAT 3.1g (sat 1.8g, mono 0.1g, poly 0g); PROTEIN 6.8g; CARB 1.9g; FIBER 0.1g; CHOL 30mg; IRON 0.3mg; SODIUM 264mg; CALC 29mg

Phyllo Triangles with Onion Jam

JAM:

    2   teaspoons butter
    4   cups vertically sliced onion
    1   cup thinly sliced shallots
    1   tablespoon sugar
    4   garlic cloves, minced
   1/4 cup dry white wine
   1/4 cup fat-free, less-sodium chicken
         broth
   1/3 cup (1 1/2 ounces) blue cheese
         (such as Maytag)
    3   tablespoons finely chopped fresh
         chives
  1 1/2 tablespoons chopped fresh thyme
         leaves
         Dash of salt

REMAINING INGREDIENTS:

    6   (18 x 14–inch) sheets frozen
         phyllo dough, thawed
         Cooking spray
    4   teaspoons butter, melted

1. To prepare jam, heat 2 teaspoons butter in a large nonstick skillet over medium-high heat. Add onion, shallots, and sugar; sauté 8 minutes or until onion is lightly browned. Add garlic, and sauté 1 minute. Stir in wine and broth; cook 5 minutes or until liquid evaporates. Remove from heat, and stir in cheese, chives, thyme, and salt.
2. Preheat oven to 400°.

Continued

3. Place 1 phyllo sheet on a large cutting board or work surface (cover remaining phyllo to prevent drying). Cut sheet in quarters lengthwise; lightly coat with cooking spray. Spoon 1 level tablespoon onion mixture onto 1 short end of each strip, leaving a 1-inch border. Fold 1 corner of edge with 1-inch border over mixture, forming a triangle; continue folding back and forth into a triangle to end of strip. Repeat procedure with remaining phyllo, cooking spray, and onion mixture. Place triangles, seam sides down, on a baking sheet coated with cooking spray. Brush tops of triangles evenly with 4 teaspoons melted butter. Lightly coat tops with cooking spray. Bake at 400° for 11 minutes or until golden. Yield: 24 triangles (serving size: 2 triangles).

CALORIES 98 (34% from fat); FAT 3.7g (sat 2g, mono 0.9g, poly 0.2g); PROTEIN 2.5g; CARB 14.1g; FIBER 1g; CHOL 8mg; IRON 0.7mg; SODIUM 144mg; CALC 39mg

Wild Rice and Leek Soup

4½ cups water, divided
½ teaspoon salt, divided
2 bay leaves
½ cup uncooked wild rice
Cooking spray
4 cups thinly sliced leek (about 3 large)
2 teaspoons minced fresh thyme
4 cups fat-free, less-sodium chicken broth
1 cup chopped peeled red potato
⅛ teaspoon freshly ground black pepper
¼ cup whipping cream

1. Bring 3½ cups water, ¼ teaspoon salt, and bay leaves to a boil in a large saucepan. Stir in rice. Reduce heat, and simmer 50 minutes or until rice is tender. Remove rice from pan, draining if necessary. Discard bay leaves.
2. Heat pan over medium-high heat. Coat pan with cooking spray. Add leek and thyme; sauté 5 minutes. Stir in 1 cup water, ¼ teaspoon salt, cooked rice, broth, potato, and pepper; bring to a boil. Reduce heat, and simmer 30 minutes or until potato is tender.

3. Place 2 cups rice mixture in a blender. Remove center piece of blender lid (to allow steam to escape); secure blender lid on blender. Place a clean towel over opening in blender lid (to avoid spills). Blend until smooth. Return pureed mixture to pan. Stir in cream. Cook over medium heat just until heated. Yield: 6 servings (serving size: 1 cup).

CALORIES 153 (25% from fat); FAT 4.3g (sat 2.3g, mono 1.4g, poly 0.5g); PROTEIN 6.7g; CARB 23.6g; FIBER 2g; CHOL 11mg; IRON 1.8mg; SODIUM 263mg; CALC 47mg

---

QUICK & EASY
Endive Salad with Pomegranate Seeds, Persimmon, and Pecan Vinaigrette

Look for plump, soft persimmons with bright orange-red skin. You can use the common Hachiya (also called Japanese persimmon and kaki) or Fuyu.

CHOICE INGREDIENT: To seed a pomegranate, cut off the fruit's puckered crown and score the rind from top to bottom. Submerge fruit in a large bowl filled with water; pull apart each section. The seeds will sink to the bottom. Strain the seeds and use them to add crunch and flavor to this salad.

8 cups torn green leaf lettuce
4 cups (1-inch) sliced Belgian endive
1 cup pomegranate seeds
½ cup thinly sliced shallots
¼ cup finely chopped pecans, toasted
2 ripe persimmons, peeled and cut into thin wedges
3 tablespoons sherry vinegar
2 tablespoons honey
1 tablespoon Dijon mustard
2 teaspoons extravirgin olive oil
½ teaspoon salt

1. Combine first 6 ingredients in a large bowl. Combine vinegar and remaining 4 ingredients in a small bowl, stirring with a whisk. Drizzle vinegar mixture over lettuce mixture; toss gently to coat. Serve immediately. Yield: 8 servings (serving size: about 1½ cups).

CALORIES 91 (42% from fat); FAT 4.2g (sat 0.4g, mono 2.4g, poly 1g); PROTEIN 1.7g; CARB 13.8g; FIBER 2.6g; CHOL 0mg; IRON 1.1mg; SODIUM 181mg; CALC 39mg

---

The Ever-Ready Host

With a few ingredients on hand during the holidays, you can serve guests at a moment's notice.
• Keep a batch of vodka mixture for the Apple Martinis (recipe on page 383) in a pitcher in the refrigerator so you can shake these cocktails anytime.
• Stock up on prosciutto and smoked salmon to use in the recipes here, or simply lay slices out on a plate with crackers. Pair prosciutto with melon; top cream cheese-smeared crackers with pieces of smoked salmon.
• Use gyoza or wonton wrappers to prepare Mini Smoked Salmon Pizzas (recipe on page 384), or coat them with cooking spray, sprinkle with sugar and cinnamon, and bake at 400° for 6 minutes or until crisp.

QUICK & EASY
Pumpkin Mixed Greens Salad with Maple Vinaigrette

Small pumpkins, which have succulent, tender flesh, are best for cooking. They may be labeled as "sweet" or "pie" pumpkins. When chopping the pumpkin, be sure to save the seeds for the salad.

2 tablespoons raw green pumpkinseed kernels
Cooking spray
1 cup (½-inch) cubed peeled pumpkin (about 8 ounces)
½ teaspoon fresh minced thyme
3 tablespoons red wine vinegar
1 tablespoon extravirgin olive oil
2 teaspoons maple syrup
¼ teaspoon salt
⅛ teaspoon freshly ground black pepper
8 cups mixed salad greens

1. Preheat oven to 400°.
2. Place pumpkinseeds in a medium nonstick skillet over medium heat. Cook 5 minutes or until toasted, stirring frequently. Remove from pan.

3. Coat pan with cooking spray. Add pumpkin, and cook 8 minutes or until browned and tender. Remove from pan. Add thyme to pumpkin, tossing to combine. Cool.

4. Combine vinegar, oil, syrup, salt, and pepper, stirring with a whisk. Drizzle over salad greens; toss well to coat. Add pumpkin and pumpkinseeds; toss. Yield: 6 servings (serving size: 1½ cups salad).

CALORIES 51 (64% from fat); FAT 3.6g (sat 0.6g, mono 2.1g, poly 0.8g); PROTEIN 8.2g; CARB 18.7g; FIBER 7.4g; CHOL 0mg; IRON 0.8mg; SODIUM 398mg; CALC 11mg

Warm Garlic Spread

Serve this creamy spread with crisp crackers or flatbread.

    4 whole garlic heads
    1 cup evaporated fat-free milk
    ½ teaspoon salt
    ⅛ teaspoon black pepper
    2 large egg yolks
    1 large egg
    Cooking spray

1. Preheat oven to 350°.

2. Remove white papery skin from garlic heads (do not peel or separate cloves). Wrap each head separately in foil. Bake at 350° for 1 hour; cool 10 minutes. Separate cloves; squeeze to extract garlic pulp. Discard skins.

3. Place garlic pulp, milk, and next 4 ingredients in a blender or food processor; process until smooth. Pour garlic mixture into a shallow 1½-quart baking dish or gratin coated with cooking spray. Place dish in a large baking pan; add hot water to pan to a depth of 1 inch. Bake at 350° for 30 minutes or just until set in center. Remove from pan; cool briefly on a rack. Serve warm or at room temperature. Yield: 20 servings (serving size: 2 tablespoons spread).

CALORIES 24 (26% from fat); FAT 0.7g (sat 0.2g, mono 0.3g, poly 0.1g); PROTEIN 1.6g; CARB 2.8g; FIBER 0.1g; CHOL 32mg; IRON 0.2mg; SODIUM 80mg; CALC 42mg

Main Dishes

Entrées to suit every occasion throughout this merry season

MAKE AHEAD
Roasted Garlic and Butternut Squash Cassoulet

To get a head start, roast the garlic, caramelize the onions, and even assemble this robust casserole the day before you plan to serve it. Use leftover roasted garlic to flavor soups, or combine with olive oil as a spread for toasted baguette slices. Pancetta is Italian unsmoked bacon. You can substitute regular smoked bacon, but use less, as the smoky flavor is more assertive.

    1   whole garlic head
    4   ounces pancetta, chopped
    2   cups vertically sliced onion
    1   tablespoon olive oil
    1   tablespoon white wine vinegar
    4½ cups (½-inch) cubed peeled
        butternut squash (about 2 pounds)
    ½   cup organic vegetable broth (such
        as Swanson Certified Organic)
    ½   teaspoon dried thyme
    ¼   teaspoon salt
    ⅛   teaspoon freshly ground black
        pepper
    4   (16-ounce) cans cannellini or
        other white beans, rinsed and
        drained
    1   bay leaf
    2   (1-ounce) slices white bread
    2   tablespoons grated fresh Parmesan
        cheese
    ½   teaspoon olive oil
    1   tablespoon chopped fresh
        parsley

1. Preheat oven to 350°.

2. Remove white papery skin from garlic head (do not peel or separate cloves). Wrap garlic head in foil. Bake at 350° for 1 hour; cool 10 minutes. Separate cloves; squeeze to extract garlic pulp. Set half of garlic pulp aside; reserve remaining garlic pulp for another use. Discard skins.

3. Heat a large Dutch oven over medium-high heat. Add pancetta; sauté 5 minutes or until crisp. Remove pancetta from pan, reserving drippings in pan. Add onion and 1 tablespoon oil to drippings in pan; sauté 5 minutes. Reduce heat to medium-low; cook 25 minutes or until onion is very tender and browned, stirring frequently. Stir in vinegar.

4. Preheat oven to 375°.

5. Add garlic pulp, pancetta, squash, and next 6 ingredients to onion mixture, stirring well. Place bread in a food processor, and pulse 10 times or until coarse crumbs measure about 1 cup. Combine breadcrumbs, cheese, and ½ teaspoon oil; sprinkle evenly over squash mixture. Cover and bake at 375° for 50 minutes or until squash is tender. Uncover and bake an additional 15 minutes or until topping is browned. Discard bay leaf. Sprinkle with parsley. Yield: 8 servings (serving size: 1¾ cups).

CALORIES 259 (27% from fat); FAT 7.7g (sat 2.6g, mono 3.6g, poly 1.4g); PROTEIN 9.5g; CARB 38.8g; FIBER 8g; CHOL 11mg; IRON 3mg; SODIUM 679mg; CALC 131mg

MAKE AHEAD
Marsala-Glazed Ham

Gorgeously roasted and nicely spiced, this ham is a fitting centerpiece for a large gathering. It feeds a crowd but still leaves plenty of leftovers for sandwiches. Garnish the serving platter with orange wedges and fresh herbs.

    1¼ cups sweet Marsala or Madeira
    ½   cup packed brown sugar
    1   tablespoon ground coriander
    ½   teaspoon ground allspice
    1   (10-pound) bone-in 33%-less-
        sodium smoked, fully cooked ham
        half
    20 whole cloves
    Cooking spray

1. Preheat oven to 350°.

2. Combine first 4 ingredients in a small saucepan; bring to a boil. Reduce heat, and simmer until mixture is reduced to ⅔ cup (about 8 minutes). Remove mixture from heat.

Continued

3. Trim fat and rind from ham. Score outside of ham in a diamond pattern; stud with cloves. Place ham on a broiler pan coated with cooking spray. Brush ham with ¼ cup Marsala mixture. Bake at 350° for 1 hour. Baste with ¼ cup Marsala mixture; bake an additional 1½ hours or until thermometer registers 140°. Baste with remaining Marsala mixture, and bake an additional 10 minutes. Remove from oven; let stand 15 minutes before slicing. Yield: 42 servings (serving size: about 3 ounces).

CALORIES 172 (49% from fat); FAT 9.4g (sat 3.5g, mono 4.4g, poly 1.2g); PROTEIN 12.4g; CARB 6.6g; FIBER 0.3g; CHOL 46mg; IRON 0.1mg; SODIUM 913mg; CALC 8mg

How to Prepare Ham

1. *Trim fat and rind from ham.*

2. *Score outside of ham in a diamond pattern; stud with cloves.*

Fontina and Mascarpone Baked Pasta

The nutty flavor of fontina and creaminess of mascarpone create a delicious updated version of mac and cheese. If your supermarket doesn't stock mascarpone cheese, substitute full-fat cream cheese. For a dinner party, bake the pasta in individual gratin dishes for 15 minutes.

　1　pound uncooked penne
　¼　cup all-purpose flour (about 1 ounce)
　3　cups fat-free milk
　2　cups (8 ounces) shredded fontina cheese
　¼　cup (2 ounces) mascarpone cheese
　¾　teaspoon salt
　¼　teaspoon freshly ground black pepper
　　　Cooking spray
　3　(1-ounce) slices white bread
　1　tablespoon butter
　1　small garlic clove, minced
1½　tablespoons chopped fresh parsley

1. Cook pasta according to package directions, omitting salt and fat. Drain; keep warm.
2. Preheat oven to 350°.
3. Lightly spoon flour into a dry measuring cup; level with a knife. Combine flour and milk in a large saucepan over medium heat, stirring with a whisk. Cook 10 minutes or until thick, stirring constantly. Remove from heat; add cheeses, stirring with a whisk until smooth. Stir in salt and pepper. Add cooked pasta, stirring to coat. Spoon pasta mixture into a 13 x 9–inch baking dish coated with cooking spray.
4. Tear bread into several pieces. Place bread in a food processor; process until fine crumbs measure 1½ cups.
5. Melt butter in a skillet over medium heat. Add garlic; cook 30 seconds. Remove from heat. Stir in breadcrumbs. Sprinkle breadcrumb mixture evenly over pasta. Bake at 350° for 25 minutes or until bubbly. Sprinkle with parsley. Yield: 8 servings (serving size: 1¼ cups).

CALORIES 423 (30% from fat); FAT 14.3g (sat 8.2g, mono 3.7g, poly 0.7g); PROTEIN 19.3g; CARB 54.6g; FIBER 2.1g; CHOL 46mg; IRON 2.4mg; SODIUM 550mg; CALC 298mg

Fettuccine with Butternut and Gorgonzola Sauce

This rich dish works well for a dinner party—simply add a tossed salad, bread, and wine. To help cut prep time, look for prechopped butternut squash, which some large supermarkets stock in the produce section.

　1　tablespoon butter
　3　cups vertically sliced onion
　3　cups (1-inch) cubed peeled butternut squash (about 1 pound)
1¼　teaspoons salt, divided
　½　teaspoon freshly ground black pepper
　2　garlic cloves, minced
　3　cups 1% low-fat milk, divided
　3　tablespoons all-purpose flour
1½　cups (6 ounces) crumbled Gorgonzola cheese, divided
　8　cups hot cooked fettuccine (about 1 pound uncooked pasta)
　¼　cup chopped fresh parsley
　¼　cup coarsely chopped walnuts, toasted
　1　teaspoon grated lemon rind

1. Melt butter in a large nonstick skillet over medium-high heat. Add onion, squash, ¼ teaspoon salt, and pepper; sauté 6 minutes or until squash is almost tender. Add garlic; sauté 1 minute. Cover and set aside.
2. Bring 2 cups milk to a boil in a saucepan. Combine 1 cup milk and flour, stirring well with a whisk; gradually add to boiling milk, stirring constantly. Reduce heat to medium, and cook 5 minutes or until slightly thick, stirring constantly. Remove from heat. Add 1 cup cheese, and stir until smooth.
3. Combine squash mixture, pasta, and cheese mixture in a large bowl. Sprinkle with 1 teaspoon salt; toss well to combine. Sprinkle with parsley, walnuts, lemon rind, and ½ cup cheese. Serve immediately. Yield: 8 servings (serving size: 1¼ cups).

CALORIES 429 (25% from fat); FAT 11.9g (sat 6.6g, mono 2.2g, poly 2g); PROTEIN 17.6g; CARB 65.5g; FIBER 5.4g; CHOL 26mg; IRON 3mg; SODIUM 723mg; CALC 299mg

Gnocchi Gratin

1 (22-ounce) package gnocchi
1 tablespoon butter
⅓ cup all-purpose flour (about
    1½ ounces)
¼ teaspoon salt
¼ teaspoon freshly ground black
    pepper
2 cups fat-free milk
½ cup fat-free, less-sodium chicken
    broth
¾ cup (3 ounces) shredded Gruyère
    cheese
⅓ cup chopped fresh chives
2 bacon slices, cooked and
    crumbled
Cooking spray
¼ cup (1 ounce) grated fresh
    Parmesan cheese

1. Preheat oven to 400°.
2. Cook gnocchi according to package directions, omitting salt and fat. Drain.
3. Melt butter in a large saucepan over medium heat. Lightly spoon flour into a dry measuring cup; level with a knife. Add flour, salt, and pepper to pan; cook 1 minute, stirring constantly. Gradually add milk and broth, stirring with a whisk until blended. Bring to a boil; cook until thick, stirring constantly. Remove from heat. Add Gruyère, chives, and bacon; stir until smooth. Add gnocchi; toss well.
4. Spoon mixture into an 11 x 7–inch baking dish coated with cooking spray; sprinkle with Parmesan. Bake at 400° for 20 minutes or until lightly browned. Serve immediately. Yield: 6 servings (serving size: about ¾ cup).

CALORIES 328 (25% from fat); FAT 9.2g (sat 5.1g, mono 2.7g, poly 0.5g); PROTEIN 14.1g; CARB 47.7g; FIBER 1.7g; CHOL 29mg; IRON 1.3mg; SODIUM 726mg; CALC 304mg

WINE NOTE: With creamy dishes like this, the texture of the dish is as important as the flavors. A suitably rich and full-bodied white, like chardonnay, is a good match for the richness of Gruyère and bacon. Try Mezzacorona Chardonnay Vigneti delle Dolomiti 2005 ($8), from the north of Italy. It offers bright, fresh fruit and a touch of buttery flavor to complement the cheese.

Leg of Lamb with Roasted Pear and Pine Nut Relish

You can also serve the relish with roast beef, pork, or chicken.

RELISH:

6 firm ripe Anjou pears, peeled,
    cored, and quartered
1 Rio or other sweet onion, cut into
    ¼-inch-thick slices
Cooking spray
2 teaspoons grated lemon rind
1 tablespoon fresh lemon juice
1 tablespoon honey
2 teaspoons olive oil
¼ teaspoon salt
¼ teaspoon ground cumin
¼ teaspoon ground coriander
¼ teaspoon black pepper
¼ cup pine nuts, toasted

LAMB:

1 tablespoon grated lemon rind
¼ cup fresh lemon juice
1 tablespoon olive oil
2 teaspoons ground cumin
2 teaspoons ground coriander
½ teaspoon salt
½ teaspoon paprika
½ teaspoon freshly ground black
    pepper
¼ teaspoon ground red pepper
4 garlic cloves
1 small onion, cut into 8 wedges
1 (5-pound) boneless leg of lamb,
    trimmed

1. Preheat oven to 400°.
2. To prepare relish, arrange pears in a single layer in a 13 x 9–inch baking dish. Arrange onion slices in a single layer in another 13 x 9–inch baking dish; lightly coat onion slices with cooking spray. Bake pears and onion slices at 400° for 40 minutes or until tender; turn once. Cool; chop.
3. Combine 2 teaspoons rind and next 7 ingredients in a large bowl; add chopped onion and pears, tossing gently to combine. Stir in nuts just before serving.
4. To prepare lamb, place 1 tablespoon lemon rind and next 10 ingredients in a food processor; process until finely chopped. Roll roast, and secure at 3-inch

intervals with twine. Spread garlic mixture over lamb; cover and refrigerate 8 hours or overnight.
5. Preheat oven to 450°.
6. Place lamb on rack of a broiler pan coated with cooking spray; place rack in pan. Bake at 450° for 20 minutes. Decrease oven temperature to 300° (do not remove lamb from oven); bake an additional 1 hour or until thermometer registers 145° (medium-rare) to 160° (medium). Let stand 10 minutes before slicing. Serve relish with lamb. Yield: 18 servings (serving size: about 3 ounces lamb and about 3 tablespoons relish).

CALORIES 246 (37% from fat); FAT 10g (sat 3.2g, mono 4.3g, poly 1.2g); PROTEIN 25.3g; CARB 13.7g; FIBER 2.6g; CHOL 80mg; IRON 2.3mg; SODIUM 165mg; CALC 21mg

White Bean–Chard Soup with Rosemary Croutons

Enjoy half of this soup now, and freeze the other half for later. For best results, prepare the croutons shortly before serving.

SOUP:

1 pound dried Great Northern beans
2 tablespoons olive oil
2 cups chopped onion
¾ cup chopped carrot (about
    2 medium)
6 garlic cloves, thinly sliced
1 cup dry white wine
½ teaspoon salt
½ teaspoon crushed red pepper
1 rosemary sprig
6 cups water
4 (14-ounce) cans fat-free,
    less-sodium chicken broth
6 cups coarsely chopped Swiss
    chard (about 2 bunches)

CROUTONS:

2 tablespoons olive oil
4 ounces sourdough bread, cut into
    1-inch cubes
1 tablespoon chopped fresh rosemary

REMAINING INGREDIENT:

½ cup (2 ounces) grated fresh
    Parmesan cheese

Continued

1. To prepare soup, sort and wash beans; place in a large Dutch oven. Cover with water to 2 inches above beans; cover and let stand 8 hours or overnight. Drain beans; set aside.

2. Heat 2 tablespoons oil in Dutch oven over medium heat. Add onion and carrot; cook 8 minutes, stirring frequently. Add garlic; cook 1 minute, stirring frequently. Increase heat to medium-high. Add wine; cook until liquid is reduced to ½ cup (about 5 minutes). Add salt, pepper, and rosemary sprig; cook 30 seconds, stirring constantly. Stir in beans, 6 cups water, and broth; bring to a boil. Reduce heat; simmer 1½ hours or until beans are tender, stirring occasionally. Add chard; cook 15 minutes or until chard is tender. Discard rosemary sprig.

3. Preheat oven to 400°.

4. To prepare croutons, combine 2 tablespoons oil and bread; toss to coat. Add chopped rosemary; toss to combine. Arrange bread in a single layer on a baking sheet. Bake at 400° for 10 minutes or until golden, turning once. Ladle about 1½ cups soup into each of 8 bowls; divide croutons evenly among bowls. Sprinkle each serving with 1 tablespoon cheese. Yield: 8 servings.

CALORIES 339 (27% from fat); FAT 10g (sat 2.5g, mono 5.7g, poly 1.3g); PROTEIN 19g; CARB 45.8g; FIBER 12.7g; CHOL 5mg; IRON 4.9mg; SODIUM 741mg; CALC 250mg

---

Ready-to-Go Ingredients

Holiday recipes are meant to be special, so some require a bit more chopping and prepping than usual. But many chopped, sliced, and even cooked ingredients are available at the supermarket, including these:

- Chopped and sliced onion
- Chopped bell pepper and celery
- Matchstick-cut carrots
- Grated fresh Parmesan cheese
- Cooked and crumbled bacon

Pork Tenderloin with Pomegranate Glaze

For safety reasons, a portion of the glaze is kept separate to baste the pork while raw and during cooking; the remainder is served with the cooked roast. The glaze will thicken significantly if made ahead; microwave at HIGH for a few seconds at a time, stirring after each heating, until the glaze is thinned.

2 cups pomegranate juice
¼ cup sugar
2 (¾-pound) pork tenderloins, trimmed
½ teaspoon salt
¼ teaspoon freshly ground black pepper
Cooking spray

1. Preheat oven to 450°.

2. Combine juice and sugar in a medium saucepan over medium heat, and bring to a boil. Cook until reduced to ½ cup (about 8 minutes). Pour half of glaze into a small bowl; set aside.

3. Sprinkle pork evenly with salt and pepper. Place pork on rack of a broiler pan coated with cooking spray; place rack in pan. Brush pork with half of glaze in saucepan. Bake at 450° for 15 minutes or until a thermometer registers 145°. Baste pork with remaining glaze in saucepan; bake an additional 5 minutes or until thermometer registers 155°.

4. Remove pork from oven; baste with half of glaze in bowl. Let pork stand 10 minutes. Cut pork across grain into thin slices. Serve pork with remaining glaze mixture. Yield: 6 servings (serving size: 3 ounces pork and 2 teaspoons glaze mixture).

CALORIES 215 (16% from fat); FAT 3.9g (sat 1.3g, mono 1.8g, poly 0.4g); PROTEIN 24.2g; CARB 20.1g; FIBER 0g; CHOL 74mg; IRON 1.5mg; SODIUM 263mg; CALC 19mg

---

Turkey-Tortilla Soup

This flavorful favorite is a quick fix when made with leftover Thanksgiving turkey. If you love the flavor but simply want to turn up the heat, add a touch of ground red (cayenne) pepper. Prepare the soup and tortilla strips ahead, and store them separately.

4 (6-inch) corn tortillas
Cooking spray
2¼ teaspoons salt-free chili powder, divided
1½ teaspoons olive oil
1 cup finely chopped onion
2 garlic cloves, minced
4 cups fat-free, less-sodium chicken broth
½ teaspoon ground cumin
1 (14.5-ounce) can Mexican-style stewed tomatoes with jalapeño peppers and spices, undrained
2 cups shredded cooked turkey breast (about 12 ounces)
3 tablespoons fresh lime juice
3 tablespoons chopped fresh cilantro
¼ cup (1 ounce) crumbled queso fresco

1. Preheat oven to 375°.

2. Stack tortillas on a cutting board, and cut into ¼-inch strips. Place strips in a bowl; lightly coat with cooking spray, tossing to coat. Sprinkle ¼ teaspoon chili powder over strips, tossing to coat. Arrange strips in an even layer on a baking sheet. Bake at 375° for 10 minutes; stir. Bake an additional 5 minutes or until lightly browned and crisp. Cool on pan.

3. Heat oil in a Dutch oven over medium-high heat. Add onion; sauté 4 minutes or until tender. Add garlic; sauté 1 minute. Stir in broth, 2 teaspoons chili powder, cumin, and tomatoes; bring to a boil. Cover, reduce heat, and simmer 10 minutes. Stir in turkey; cover and simmer 5 minutes. Remove from heat; stir in juice and cilantro. Ladle 1½ cups soup into each of 4 bowls. Top each serving with 1 tablespoon cheese and about ¾ cup tortilla strips. Serve immediately. Yield: 4 servings.

CALORIES 271 (13% from fat); FAT 3.9g (sat 1g, mono 1.8g, poly 0.7g); PROTEIN 31.7g; CARB 26.5g; FIBER 4.7g; CHOL 73mg; IRON 2.7mg; SODIUM 877mg; CALC 123mg

Beef Stew with Poblanos, Tomatillos, and Potatoes

Tomatillos lend this Latin-inspired stew tangy taste, while roasted poblano chiles offer modest heat. Look for canned tomatillos with the Latin/Mexican foods in your grocery store.

    2 poblano chiles
    1 tablespoon olive oil, divided
    2 cups chopped onion
    ⅓ cup all-purpose flour (about
       1½ ounces)
    2 pounds lean beef stew meat, cut
       into bite-sized pieces
    1 teaspoon salt, divided
    1 (12-ounce) bottle pale Mexican
       beer (such as Corona)
    2 cups water
    1 cup chopped green bell pepper
       (about 1 medium)
    1 tablespoon chopped fresh
       oregano
  1½ teaspoons ground cumin
    6 garlic cloves, minced
    1 (28-ounce) can tomatillos, drained
       and crushed
    1 (14-ounce) can less-sodium beef
       broth
    6 cups (1-inch) cubed peeled white
       potato (about 2 pounds)
    ½ teaspoon freshly ground black
       pepper
    ¾ cup (3 ounces) crumbled queso
       fresco
       Chopped fresh cilantro (optional)

1. Preheat broiler.

2. Place chiles on a foil-lined baking sheet; broil 10 minutes or until blackened and charred, turning chiles occasionally. Place in a heavy-duty zip-top plastic bag; seal. Let stand 15 minutes. Peel chiles; cut in half lengthwise. Discard seeds and membranes. Chop chiles; set aside.

3. Heat 1 teaspoon oil in a large Dutch oven over medium-high heat. Add onion; sauté 10 minutes or until onion is tender and golden brown. Spoon onion into a large bowl.

4. Place flour in a shallow bowl or pie plate. Dredge beef in flour, shaking off excess. Heat 2 teaspoons oil in pan over medium-high heat. Add half of beef mixture; sprinkle with ¼ teaspoon salt. Cook 6 minutes, browning on all sides. Add browned beef to onion. Repeat procedure with remaining beef mixture and ¼ teaspoon salt.

5. Add beer to pan, scraping pan to loosen browned bits. Add chopped chiles, 2 cups water and next 6 ingredients; bring to a simmer. Stir in beef mixture. Cover, reduce heat to medium-low, and simmer 1 hour or until beef is just tender.

6. Stir in potato. Simmer, uncovered, 50 minutes or until beef and potato are very tender and sauce is thick, stirring occasionally. Stir in ½ teaspoon salt and black pepper. Ladle 1⅓ cups stew into each of 8 bowls, and sprinkle each serving with 1½ tablespoons cheese. Garnish with cilantro, if desired. Yield: 8 servings.

CALORIES 385 (29% from fat); FAT 12.2g (sat 3.8g, mono 5.8g, poly 0.6g); PROTEIN 27.9g; CARB 38.7g; FIBER 6.2g; CHOL 74mg; IRON 4.5mg; SODIUM 597mg; CALC 84mg

Rosemary Salt–Crusted Venison with Cherry-Cabernet Sauce

This recipe also works well with rich meats such as pork tenderloin and duck breast.

    8 large shallots, peeled and quartered
       (about ½ pound)
    4 teaspoons olive oil, divided
    2 venison tenderloins, trimmed
       (about 9 ounces each)
    1 teaspoon Rosemary Salt, divided
    ½ teaspoon coarsely ground black
       pepper
    1 cup cabernet sauvignon or other
       dry red wine
    ¾ cup dried cherries
  1½ cups less-sodium beef broth
    1 tablespoon water
    1 tablespoon cornstarch
  1½ tablespoons chilled butter, cut
       into small pieces
    1 tablespoon fresh lemon juice
       Rosemary sprigs (optional)

1. Preheat oven to 400°.

2. Combine shallots and 2 teaspoons oil; toss well. Arrange shallots in a single layer in a shallow roasting pan.

3. Rub venison evenly with ½ teaspoon Rosemary Salt and pepper. Heat 2 teaspoons oil in a large nonstick skillet over medium-high heat. Add venison; cook 6 minutes, browning on all sides. Remove venison from pan; arrange on top of shallots in roasting pan. Bake at 400° for 17 minutes or until a thermometer registers 145° (medium-rare). Remove venison and shallots from pan. Keep venison warm. Chop shallots.

4. Heat skillet over medium-high heat. Add shallots, wine, and cherries; cook until liquid is reduced to ½ cup (about 3 minutes), scraping pan to loosen browned bits. Add broth and ½ teaspoon Rosemary Salt; bring to a boil. Reduce heat, and simmer until reduced to 2 cups (about 5 minutes). Combine 1 tablespoon water and cornstarch in a small bowl. Add cornstarch mixture to pan; bring to a boil. Cook 1 minute, stirring constantly. Remove from heat; stir in butter and juice. Cut venison across grain into thin slices; serve venison with sauce. Garnish with rosemary sprigs, if desired. Yield: 4 servings (serving size: about 3 ounces venison and about ½ cup sauce).

(Totals include Rosemary Salt) CALORIES 362 (29% from fat); FAT 11.7g (sat 4.4g, mono 5.2g, poly 1.2g); PROTEIN 28.8g; CARB 31.8g; FIBER 3.8g; CHOL 108mg; IRON 5.1mg; SODIUM 589mg; CALC 57mg

ROSEMARY SALT:

    ¼ cup chopped fresh rosemary
    3 tablespoons kosher salt
    3 juniper berries, crushed

1. Place all ingredients in a mini food processor; process until finely chopped. Yield: ¼ cup (serving size: ¼ teaspoon).

CALORIES 0 (0% from fat); FAT 0g; PROTEIN 0g; CARB 0.1g; FIBER 0g; CHOL 0mg; IRON 0mg; SODIUM 353mg; CALC 1mg

Seafood Lasagna

This shrimp- and scallop-filled lasagna is refined enough for a dinner party.

⅓ cup all-purpose flour (about 1½ ounces)
3 cups 2% reduced-fat milk
1 tablespoon butter
1 tablespoon chopped fresh thyme
¼ teaspoon salt
¼ teaspoon freshly ground black pepper
2 cups (8 ounces) grated Parmigiano-Reggiano cheese, divided
⅛ teaspoon grated whole nutmeg
Cooking spray
2 cups thinly sliced onion
6 garlic cloves, minced
⅓ cup (3 ounces) block-style ⅓-less-fat cream cheese, softened
½ cup half-and-half
½ cup chopped fresh parsley, divided
¾ pound medium shrimp, peeled, deveined, and coarsely chopped
¾ pound scallops, coarsely chopped
3 large eggs
1 (15-ounce) carton fat-free ricotta cheese
12 no-cook lasagna noodles

1. Preheat oven to 350°.
2. Lightly spoon flour into a dry measuring cup; level with a knife. Place a large saucepan over medium heat; add flour to pan. Gradually add milk to pan, stirring constantly with a whisk until smooth; cook 1 minute. Stir in butter, thyme, salt, and pepper; bring to a boil. Cook 5 minutes or until thick, stirring constantly. Remove pan from heat; stir in 1¼ cups Parmigiano and nutmeg. Set cheese sauce aside.
3. Heat a large nonstick skillet over medium-high heat. Coat pan with cooking spray. Add onion; sauté 4 minutes. Add garlic; sauté 1 minute. Remove from heat. Add cream cheese; stir until cheese melts. Stir in half-and-half, ¼ cup parsley, shrimp, and scallops. Place eggs and ricotta in a food processor; process until smooth. Stir ricotta mixture into seafood mixture.
4. Spoon 1 cup cheese sauce into bottom

of a 13 x 9–inch baking dish coated with cooking spray. Arrange 4 noodles over sauce; top with half of ricotta mixture. Repeat layers with 4 noodles, remaining ricotta mixture, and 4 noodles. Pour remaining cheese sauce over noodles; sprinkle with ¾ cup Parmigiano. Bake at 350° for 45 minutes or until lightly browned. Sprinkle lasagna with ¼ cup parsley. Let stand 10 minutes before serving. Yield: 12 servings (serving size: 1 piece).

CALORIES 383 (30% from fat); FAT 12.9g (sat 7g, mono 3.6g, poly 0.9g); PROTEIN 31.5g; CARB 33.1g; FIBER 1.4g; CHOL 150mg; IRON 3.3mg; SODIUM 583mg; CALC 428mg

WINE NOTE: The rich, mellow flavor and creamy texture of this Seafood Lasagna demands a white wine that's soft and full on the palate. Chardonnay is a great answer–especially a luscious, full-bodied Italian version like Antinori's Cervaro della Sala 2003 from Umbria ($45).

On the Side

These stellar accompaniments complete any meal with panache.

Brussels Sprouts with Honey-Glazed Pearl Onions and Capocollo

Capocollo is a delicious, tangy Italian-style cured ham. Look for it sliced in the supermarket deli section. If you can't find capocollo, substitute prosciutto.

3 quarts water
3 cups pearl onions
5 cups trimmed and quartered Brussels sprouts (about 1¾ pounds)
Cooking spray
½ cup (2 ounces) chopped capocollo ham
¼ cup water
½ teaspoon freshly ground black pepper
¼ teaspoon kosher salt
3 tablespoons honey

1. Bring 3 quarts water to a boil in a Dutch oven. Add onions; cook 1 minute. Remove onions with a slotted spoon. Drain and rinse with cold running water; drain. Set aside. Add Brussels sprouts to boiling water; boil 2 minutes or until crisp-tender. Drain. Pinch stem end of each onion; discard peels.
2. Heat a large nonstick skillet over medium-high heat. Coat pan with cooking spray. Add ham; sauté 5 minutes or until lightly browned. Remove from pan. Wipe pan with a paper towel; recoat pan with cooking spray. Add peeled onions; cook over medium heat 5 minutes. Add Brussels sprouts and ¼ cup water; cover and cook 8 minutes or tender, stirring occasionally. Sprinkle with pepper and salt. Drizzle with honey; stir gently. Top with ham. Yield: 10 servings (serving size: ½ cup).

CALORIES 100 (18% from fat); FAT 2g (sat 0.9g, mono 0g, poly 0.1g); PROTEIN 3.5g; CARB 19g; FIBER 2.2g; CHOL 4mg; IRON 1mg; SODIUM 171mg; CALC 45mg

Green Beans with Toasted Hazelnut–Lemon Butter

Prepare the butter up to a week ahead and refrigerate, or up to three weeks in advance and freeze.

1½ tablespoons butter, softened
3 tablespoons finely chopped hazelnuts, toasted
1½ teaspoons grated lemon rind
½ teaspoon salt
8 cups water
1¾ teaspoons salt
1½ pounds green beans, trimmed

1. Combine first 4 ingredients in a small bowl; stir with a fork until well blended.
2. Bring 8 cups water and 1¾ teaspoons salt to a boil in a large saucepan. Add beans; cook 3 minutes. Drain. Return pan to medium heat. Add beans and butter mixture, and cook 3 minutes or until butter mixture melts. Toss gently to coat. Yield: 6 servings (serving size: 1⅓ cups).

CALORIES 54 (52% from fat); FAT 3.1g (sat 0.8g, mono 1.9g, poly 0.3g); PROTEIN 1.7g; CARB 6.4g; FIBER 3.8g; CHOL 3mg; IRON 0.6mg; SODIUM 400mg; CALC 51mg

Oyster Dressing

Oysters are a traditional highlight in dressings along the southern coastal states.

    3   slices center-cut bacon, diced
        (uncooked)
    1   cup diced onion (about 1
        medium)
    ½   cup diced celery (about 1 stalk)
    ¼   cup diced green onions
    1   teaspoon minced garlic
    ½   teaspoon minced fresh thyme
    ¼   teaspoon salt
    ¼   teaspoon ground red pepper
    6   cups (1-inch) cubed, toasted
        Italian bread (about 8 ounces)
    ½   cup fat-free, less-sodium chicken
        broth
    ¼   cup water
    2   large egg whites, lightly beaten
    1   cup shucked oysters, rinsed
        (about 16)
        Cooking spray
    ¼   cup (1 ounce) shredded Parmesan
        cheese

1. Preheat oven to 350°.
2. Cook bacon in a large skillet over medium-high heat until crisp. Remove bacon from pan, reserving 2 teaspoons drippings in pan; set bacon aside. Add 1 cup onion and celery; sauté 5 minutes or until tender. Add green onions and next 4 ingredients; sauté 1 minute. Remove from heat.
3. Combine bread, onion mixture, and bacon in a large bowl. Add broth, water, and egg whites, stirring gently. Gently fold in oysters. Spoon mixture into an 11 x 7–inch baking dish coated with cooking spray. Cover and bake at 350° for 30 minutes. Uncover; sprinkle with cheese. Bake an additional 30 minutes or until golden brown. Let stand 5 minutes before serving. Yield: 8 servings (serving size: about 1 cup).

CALORIES 145 (27% from fat); FAT 4.4g (sat 1.6g, mono 1.5g, poly 0.9g); PROTEIN 7.6g; CARB 18.2g; FIBER 1.3g; CHOL 20mg; IRON 2.7mg; SODIUM 431mg; CALC 74mg

Mashed Potato Gratin

Although Yukon gold potatoes give this cheesy gratin extra buttery flavor and color, russets also will work.

    4   pounds Yukon gold potatoes,
        peeled and cut into 2-inch chunks
    1   cup (4 ounces) fontina cheese,
        shredded and divided
    ¾   cup (3 ounces) Gruyère cheese,
        shredded and divided
    1½ tablespoons butter
    1   teaspoon salt
    ¼   teaspoon freshly ground black
        pepper
    1   cup warm 1% low-fat milk (100°
        to 110°)
        Cooking spray

1. Preheat oven to 400°.
2. Place potatoes in a large Dutch oven. Cover with water; bring to a boil. Reduce heat, and simmer 15 minutes or until tender; drain. Return potatoes to pan. Add ¾ cup fontina cheese, ½ cup Gruyère cheese, butter, salt, and pepper to pan; mash with a fork or potato masher until well combined. Add warm milk to pan; continue mashing potato mixture until desired consistency. Spoon into a 13 x 9–inch baking dish coated with cooking spray; sprinkle evenly with ¼ cup fontina cheese and ¼ cup Gruyère cheese. Cover with aluminum foil lightly sprayed with cooking spray. Bake at 400° for 20 minutes. Remove from oven; uncover.
3. Preheat broiler.
4. Broil gratin 5 minutes or until cheese is brown and bubbly. Yield: 14 servings (serving size: ½ cup).

CALORIES 188 (29% from fat); FAT 6g (sat 3.6g, mono 1.7g, poly 0.4g); PROTEIN 6.9g; CARB 27.1g; FIBER 2.3g; CHOL 20mg; IRON 0.4mg; SODIUM 276mg; CALC 134mg

QUICK & EASY
Maple-Sage Glazed Turnips

    1   pound small turnips, trimmed and
        peeled
    ¼   cup water
    3   tablespoons maple syrup
    2   teaspoons chopped fresh sage
    ¼   teaspoon salt
    ¼   teaspoon freshly ground black
        pepper

1. Cut turnips in half lengthwise and into ½-inch wedges. Combine ¼ cup water and remaining 4 ingredients in a large nonstick skillet over medium-high heat. Add turnips, turning to coat; bring to a boil. Cover, reduce heat, and simmer 15 minutes or until tender. Uncover and cook 7 minutes or until turnips are glazed. Yield: 4 servings (serving size: ½ cup).

CALORIES 65 (0% from fat); FAT 0.1g (sat 0g, mono 0g, poly 0.1g); PROTEIN 0.8g; CARB 15.9g; FIBER 2.3g; CHOL 0mg; IRON 0.4mg; SODIUM 167mg; CALC 50mg

---

The American Larder

Maple syrup: Colonists learned how to tap maple trees for sap from the American Indians, who boiled it to an elixir they called "sweetwater."

Pecans: These native American nuts are a fall favorite. They also have a high fat content (more than 70 percent), which means they can go rancid quickly. Once the pecans are shelled, you can refrigerate them in an airtight container for up to three months, or freeze them up to six months.

Quinoa: This high-protein grain was a staple among the ancient Incas.

Wheat Berry–Cranberry Salad

Serve this salad at room temperature or chilled. Find more dried and fresh cranberry recipes starting on page 412.

    1½ cups uncooked wheat berries
         (hard winter wheat)
    1   teaspoon salt, divided
    1   cup fresh cranberries
    ¼   cup maple syrup
    ¼   cup cranberry juice
    2   tablespoons olive oil
    1   tablespoon white wine vinegar
    2   teaspoons Dijon mustard
    ¼   teaspoon freshly ground black
         pepper
    ½   cup diced celery
    ⅓   cup thinly sliced green onions
    ⅓   cup chopped fresh flat-leaf parsley
    ⅓   cup chopped pecans, toasted

1. Place wheat berries in a medium bowl, and cover with water to 2 inches above wheat berries. Cover and let stand 8 hours. Drain.
2. Place wheat berries and ½ teaspoon salt in a medium saucepan. Cover with water to 2 inches above wheat berries; bring to a boil. Cover, reduce heat, and cook 1 hour or until tender. Drain; cool to room temperature.
3. Combine cranberries and syrup in a small saucepan over medium heat; bring to a boil. Cook 4 minutes or until cranberries pop, stirring frequently. Transfer to a large bowl; cool 10 minutes.
4. Add ½ teaspoon salt, juice, and next 4 ingredients to cranberry mixture; stir well to combine. Add wheat berries, celery, onions, parsley, and pecans; stir well. Serve at room temperature, or cover and chill. Yield: 8 servings (serving size: about ½ cup).

CALORIES 223 (31% from fat); FAT 7.6g (sat 0.9g, mono 4.6g, poly 1.7g); PROTEIN 5.3g; CARB 36.9g; FIBER 5.8g; CHOL 0mg; IRON 0.6mg; SODIUM 248mg; CALC 23mg

Sausage, Apple, and Fennel Corn Bread Dressing

Prepare the corn bread up to two days ahead.

CORN BREAD:

    1   cup all-purpose flour (about 4½
         ounces)
    ¾   cup yellow cornmeal
    1   teaspoon baking powder
    ½   teaspoon salt
    1   cup fat-free milk
    2   tablespoons canola oil
    1   large egg, lightly beaten
    Cooking spray

DRESSING:

    2   teaspoons olive oil
    6   ounces lean, low-sodium smoked
         turkey sausage, finely chopped
         (about 1 cup)
    2   cups finely chopped onion
    1   bay leaf
    1½ cups diced Granny Smith apple
         (about 1 large)
    ½   cup diced celery
    ½   cup diced fennel bulb
    1   teaspoon minced garlic
    ¼   teaspoon dried rubbed sage
    ¼   teaspoon poultry seasoning
    ¼   teaspoon salt
    ⅛   teaspoon ground red pepper
    ⅛   teaspoon freshly ground black
         pepper
    1½ cups fat-free, less-sodium chicken
         broth
    2   large eggs, lightly beaten

1. Preheat oven to 425°.
2. To prepare corn bread, lightly spoon flour into a dry measuring cup; level with a knife. Combine flour and next 3 ingredients in a large bowl; make a well in center of mixture. Combine milk, canola oil, and 1 egg in a small bowl. Add to flour mixture, stirring just until moist. Spoon batter into an 8-inch square baking pan coated with cooking spray. Bake at 425° for 16 minutes or until a wooden pick inserted in center comes out clean. Cool 5 minutes in pan on a wire rack. Remove from pan; cool completely.

3. Reduce oven temperature to 375°.
4. To prepare dressing, heat olive oil in a large nonstick skillet over medium-high heat. Add sausage; cook 5 minutes or until browned, stirring occasionally. Add onion and bay leaf; cook 8 minutes or until onion starts to brown, stirring occasionally. Add apple, celery, and fennel; cook 5 minutes. Add garlic and next 5 ingredients; cook 1 minute. Remove from heat; discard bay leaf. Cool to room temperature.
5. Crumble corn bread into a large bowl. Add sausage mixture to bowl; toss to combine. Add broth and 2 eggs, and toss to combine. Spoon into a 13 x 9–inch baking dish coated with cooking spray. Bake at 375° for 50 minutes or until top is crisp and golden brown. Yield: 10 servings (serving size: about ¾ cup).

CALORIES 212 (31% from fat); FAT 7.2g (sat 1.3g, mono 3.5g, poly 1.7g); PROTEIN 9.2g; CARB 26.9g; FIBER 1.7g; CHOL 79mg; IRON 1.8mg; SODIUM 458mg; CALC 83mg

Quinoa Stuffing with Leeks, Walnuts, and Cherries

Use sweet or tart dried cherries, or you can substitute dried cranberries.

    2   cups fat-free, less-sodium chicken
         broth
    ½   teaspoon kosher salt, divided
    1   cup uncooked quinoa
    1   tablespoon butter
    Cooking spray
    2   cups thinly sliced leek (about
         ¾ pound)
    ½   cup chopped celery
    ½   teaspoon freshly ground black
         pepper
    ½   teaspoon dried rubbed sage
    4   garlic cloves, minced
    ¾   cup dried cherries, coarsely
         chopped
    ¼   cup chopped walnuts, toasted

1. Bring broth and ¼ teaspoon salt to a boil in a medium saucepan. Add quinoa. Cover, reduce heat, and simmer 20 minutes or until liquid is absorbed. Let stand 5 minutes; fluff with a fork.

2. Melt butter in a large nonstick skillet coated with cooking spray over medium heat. Add leek, celery, ¼ teaspoon salt, pepper, and sage; cook 10 minutes or until tender, stirring occasionally. Add garlic; cook 1 minute. Stir in cooked quinoa, cherries, and walnuts; cook until thoroughly heated. Yield: 8 servings (serving size: about ½ cup).

CALORIES 202 (22% from fat); FAT 4.9g (sat 1.1g, mono 1.4g, poly 2.1g); PROTEIN 5.3g; CARB 33.2g; FIBER 4.4g; CHOL 4mg; IRON 2.8mg; SODIUM 245mg; CALC 63mg

---

QUICK & EASY

Roast Lemon and Pepper Brussels Sprouts with Parmesan

Use good-quality Parmesan for the most robust flavor.

 1 tablespoon sugar
 2 teaspoons olive oil
 ½ teaspoon salt
 2 pounds Brussels sprouts, trimmed and quartered
 Cooking spray
 ¼ cup chopped fresh parsley
 2 teaspoons butter, softened
 1 teaspoon freshly ground black pepper
 ¾ teaspoon grated lemon rind
 ½ ounce shaved Parmesan cheese

1. Preheat oven to 400°.
2. Combine first 4 ingredients in a large bowl; toss well. Place Brussels sprouts mixture in a single layer on a jelly-roll pan coated with cooking spray. Bake at 400° for 20 minutes or until edges of Brussels sprouts are lightly browned.
3. Combine parsley, butter, pepper, and rind, stirring well. Add butter mixture to Brussels sprouts mixture, and toss well. Sprinkle with cheese. Yield: 8 servings (serving size: ½ cup).

CALORIES 81 (32% from fat); FAT 2.9g (sat 1.1g, mono 1.1g, poly 0.3g); PROTEIN 4.6g; CARB 12.1g; FIBER 4.5g; CHOL 4mg; IRON 1.7mg; SODIUM 200mg; CALC 73mg

---

Roquefort, Polenta, and Prosciutto Spoon Bread

These individual spoon breads are an elegant accompaniment to roast beef or pork. Or serve them with a tossed salad, such as Endive Salad with Pomegranate Seeds, Persimmon, and Pecan Vinaigrette (recipe on page 386), as a light supper.

 Cooking spray
 ¼ cup dry breadcrumbs
 2 cups fat-free milk
 ½ cup dry polenta
 ½ cup (2 ounces) crumbled Roquefort blue cheese
 ⅓ cup finely chopped prosciutto (about 1½ ounces)
 5 large egg whites

1. Preheat oven to 425°.
2. Lightly coat 6 (8-ounce) soufflé dishes with cooking spray; sprinkle evenly with breadcrumbs. Set aside.
3. Combine milk and polenta in a medium saucepan, stirring with a whisk. Bring to a boil, stirring constantly. Reduce heat; simmer 4 minutes or until thick. Remove from heat. Add cheese and prosciutto, stirring until cheese melts.
4. Beat egg whites with a mixer at high speed until stiff peaks form (do not overbeat). Gently stir one-fourth of egg whites into polenta mixture; gently fold in remaining egg whites. Gently spoon mixture into prepared dishes; arrange dishes on a baking sheet. Place spoon breads in 425° oven. Immediately reduce oven temperature to 350°. Bake at 350° for 25 minutes or until spoon breads are set. Serve immediately. Yield: 6 servings (serving size: 1 spoon bread).

CALORIES 186 (27% from fat); FAT 5.5g (sat 2.6g, mono 0.9g, poly 0.3g); PROTEIN 12.7g; CARB 21.1g; FIBER 1.3g; CHOL 18mg; IRON 1.8mg; SODIUM 576mg; CALC 205mg

---

Extras

Round out the menu with this variety of must-make breads and condiments.

MAKE AHEAD

Jezebel Sauce

Serve with roast chicken, pork, or lamb, or pair it with goat cheese and crackers.

 ½ cup boiling water
 ¼ cup dried apricots
 ⅔ cup pineapple preserves
 ⅓ cup red pepper jelly
 1 tablespoon Dijon mustard
 ½ teaspoon prepared horseradish
 Dash of freshly ground black pepper

1. Combine ½ cup boiling water and apricots in a bowl; let stand 10 minutes. Drain. Finely chop apricots.
2. Combine apricots, preserves, and remaining ingredients in a bowl. Cover and chill. Yield: 9 servings (serving size: about 2 tablespoons).

CALORIES 95 (0% from fat); FAT 0g; PROTEIN 0.2g; CARB 24.2g; FIBER 0.3g; CHOL 0mg; IRON 0.2mg; SODIUM 38mg; CALC 2mg

---

MAKE AHEAD

Easy Baked Applesauce

The sauce is delicious with roast turkey or pork; prepare it up to three days ahead.

 5 tablespoons water
 ¼ cup packed brown sugar
 2 tablespoons fresh lemon juice
 1 teaspoon ground cinnamon
 4 pounds apples, peeled, cored, and halved

1. Preheat oven to 375°.
2. Combine all ingredients in a large Dutch oven; toss to coat. Cover and bake at 375° for 1 hour and 15 minutes or until apples are tender, stirring once after 45 minutes. Yield: 8 servings (serving size: ½ cup).

CALORIES 137 (2% from fat); FAT 0.3g (sat 0.1g, mono 0g, poly 0.1g); PROTEIN 0.6g; CARB 36.2g; FIBER 3.1g; CHOL 0mg; IRON 0.4mg; SODIUM 3mg; CALC 21mg

Pumpkin Muffins

Prepare these golden muffins up to two days ahead.

2¼ cups all-purpose flour (about 10 ounces)
2 teaspoons pumpkin pie spice
1½ teaspoons baking soda
1 teaspoon ground ginger
¼ teaspoon salt
1 cup golden raisins
1 cup packed brown sugar
1 cup canned pumpkin
⅓ cup buttermilk
⅓ cup canola oil
¼ cup molasses
1 teaspoon vanilla extract
2 large eggs, lightly beaten
Cooking spray
2 tablespoons granulated sugar

1. Preheat oven to 400°.
2. Lightly spoon flour into dry measuring cups; level with a knife. Combine flour and next 4 ingredients in a medium bowl, stirring well with a whisk. Stir in raisins; make a well in center of mixture. Combine brown sugar and next 6 ingredients, stirring well with a whisk. Add sugar mixture to flour mixture; stir just until moist.
3. Spoon batter into 18 muffin cups coated with cooking spray. Sprinkle with granulated sugar. Bake at 400° for 15 minutes or until a wooden pick inserted in center comes out clean. Remove muffins from pans immediately; cool on a wire rack. Yield: 18 servings (serving size: 1 muffin).

CALORIES 202 (23% from fat); FAT 5.1g (sat 0.8g, mono 2g, poly 1.9g); PROTEIN 2.9g; CARB 37.5g; FIBER 1.2g; CHOL 24mg; IRON 1.7mg; SODIUM 159mg; CALC 35mg

Chipotle-Cranberry Compote

Be sure you grate the rind before juicing the oranges.

1¼ cups sugar
¼ cup fresh orange juice
2 (12-ounce) packages fresh cranberries
1 tablespoon chipotle chile, canned in adobo sauce
1½ teaspoons grated orange rind
½ teaspoon ground cinnamon
¼ teaspoon ground coriander
¼ teaspoon salt

1. Combine first 3 ingredients in a large saucepan; bring to a boil. Cook 7 minutes or until cranberries begin to pop, stirring occasionally. Stir in chipotle and remaining ingredients. Reduce heat, and cook 20 minutes or until mixture is thick, stirring occasionally. Chill. Yield: 14 servings (serving size: about ¼ cup).

CALORIES 95 (1% from fat); FAT 0.1g (sat 0g, mono 0g, poly 0.1g); PROTEIN 0.2g; CARB 24.5g; FIBER 2.4g; CHOL 0mg; IRON 0.2mg; SODIUM 55mg; CALC 6mg

Sweet Potato Latkes

Like traditional latkes, these are good with sour cream and applesauce.

4 cups shredded peeled sweet potato (about 1 pound)
2½ cups shredded peeled baking potato (about 12 ounces)
¼ cup grated shallots (about 2 medium)
1 (1-ounce) slice white bread
½ cup all-purpose flour (about 2¼ ounces)
1 tablespoon brown sugar
1 teaspoon salt
¼ teaspoon black pepper
1 large egg, lightly beaten
1 tablespoon butter, divided
1 tablespoon olive oil, divided

1. Line colander with paper towels. Place potatoes and shallots in colander, and let stand 15 minutes. Squeeze out excess moisture.

2. Place bread in a food processor; pulse 10 times or until coarse crumbs measure ¼ cup. Lightly spoon flour into a dry measuring cup; level with a knife. Combine potato mixture, breadcrumbs, flour, sugar, salt, pepper, and egg in a bowl. Divide mixture into 8 equal portions, shaping each portion into a ¼-inch-thick patty.
3. Melt 1½ teaspoons butter in a large nonstick skillet over medium-high heat. Add 1½ teaspoons oil to pan. Add 4 patties to pan; cook 3 minutes on each side or until golden brown. Repeat procedure with remaining butter, oil, and patties. Yield: 8 servings (serving size: 1 patty).

CALORIES 166 (22% from fat); FAT 4.1g (sat 1.4g, mono 1.9g, poly 0.4g); PROTEIN 3.7g; CARB 29g; FIBER 2.6g; CHOL 30mg; IRON 1.2mg; SODIUM 354mg; CALC 31mg

Whole Wheat Bread with Caraway and Anise

Aniseed and caraway seeds give this braided bread a licorice flavor. Leave either or both of them out, if you prefer.

2 tablespoons honey
1 package dry yeast (about 2¼ teaspoons)
1 cup warm water (100° to 110°)
1 teaspoon water
1 large egg
2⅓ cups all-purpose flour, divided (about 10½ ounces)
1 cup whole wheat flour (about 4¾ ounces)
1½ teaspoons kosher salt
1 teaspoon caraway seeds, divided
½ teaspoon aniseed
Cooking spray

1. Dissolve honey and yeast in 1 cup warm water in a large bowl; let stand 5 minutes. Combine 1 teaspoon water and egg, stirring well with a whisk. Place 1 tablespoon egg mixture in a small bowl. Cover and chill. Add remaining egg mixture to yeast mixture.
2. Lightly spoon flours into dry measuring cups; level with a knife. Add 2 cups all-purpose flour, whole wheat flour, salt, ½ teaspoon caraway seeds, and aniseed

to yeast mixture; stir to form a soft dough. Turn dough out onto a floured surface. Knead until smooth and elastic (about 10 minutes); add enough of remaining all-purpose flour, 1 tablespoon at a time, to prevent dough from sticking to hands (dough will feel sticky).

3. Place dough in a large bowl coated with cooking spray, turning to coat top. Cover and let rise in a warm place (85°), free from drafts, 45 minutes or until doubled in size. (Gently press two fingers into dough. If indentation remains, dough has risen enough.) Punch dough down; cover and let rest 5 minutes. Divide dough in half. Working with one portion at a time, roll each portion into a 12-inch rope on a lightly floured surface. Twist ropes together, and pinch ends to seal. Place dough in an 8-inch loaf pan coated with cooking spray. Cover and let rise 30 minutes or until doubled in size.

4. Preheat oven to 375°.

5. Uncover dough. Brush reserved egg mixture over loaf, and sprinkle with ½ teaspoon caraway seeds. Bake at 375° for 30 minutes or until loaf is browned on bottom and sounds hollow when tapped. Remove from pan; cool on a wire rack. Yield: 12 servings (serving size: 1 slice).

CALORIES 142 (6% from fat); FAT 0.9g (sat 0.2g, mono 0.2g, poly 0.2g); PROTEIN 2.8g; CARB 29.1g; FIBER 2.1g; CHOL 18mg; IRON 1.8mg; SODIUM 243mg; CALC 12mg

How to Shape Loaf

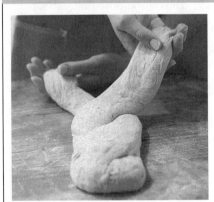

1. *Working with one portion at a time, roll each portion into a 12-inch rope on a lightly floured surface. Twist ropes together, and pinch ends to seal.*

MAKE AHEAD • FREEZABLE
Multigrain Rolls

Whole wheat, rye, bran, and cornmeal combine with all-purpose flour for the heartiness of whole-grain bread with the lightness of a dinner roll. Loaves of this bread were popular in mid-19th-century America.

- ¼ cup cornmeal
- ¼ cup wheat bran cereal (such as All-Bran)
- ¼ cup golden raisins
- ¾ cup boiling water
- ¼ cup packed brown sugar, divided
- 1 tablespoon molasses
- 1 package dry yeast (about 2¼ teaspoons)
- ¼ cup warm water (100° to 110°)
- 2 tablespoons butter, melted
- ¾ teaspoon salt
- 2 cups all-purpose flour, divided (about 9 ounces)
- ¼ cup whole wheat flour (about 1 ounce)
- ¼ cup rye flour (about 1 ounce)
- Cooking spray

1. Combine first 3 ingredients in a bowl. Stir in ¾ cup boiling water. Let stand 15 minutes.

2. Dissolve 1 tablespoon sugar, molasses, and yeast in ¼ cup warm water in a large bowl; let stand 5 minutes. Stir in cornmeal mixture, 3 tablespoons sugar, butter, and salt.

3. Lightly spoon flours into dry measuring cups; level with a knife. Add 1¾ cups all-purpose flour, whole wheat flour, and rye flour to yeast mixture; stir until a soft dough forms. Turn dough out onto a lightly floured surface. Knead until smooth and elastic (about 8 minutes); add enough of remaining all-purpose flour, 1 tablespoon at a time, to prevent dough from sticking to hands (dough will feel tacky).

4. Place dough in a large bowl coated with cooking spray, turning to coat top. Cover and let rise in a warm place (85°), free from drafts, 1½ hours or until doubled in size. (Gently press two fingers into dough. If indentation remains, dough has risen enough.)

5. Punch dough down; cover and let rest 5 minutes. Divide dough into 16 equal portions. Working with one portion at a time (cover remaining dough to prevent drying), roll dough into a ball. Place rolls 1 inch apart on a baking sheet coated with cooking spray. Cover and let rise in a warm place (85°), free from drafts, 45 minutes or until doubled in size.

6. Preheat oven to 400°.

7. Bake rolls at 400° for 15 minutes or until golden brown. Cool on wire racks. Yield: 16 servings (serving size: 1 roll).

CALORIES 119 (13% from fat); FAT 1.7g (sat 0.9g, mono 0.4g, poly 0.1g); PROTEIN 2.6g; CARB 23.7g; FIBER 1.1g; CHOL 4mg; IRON 1.3mg; SODIUM 128mg; CALC 11mg

MAKE AHEAD
Northwest Waldorf Salad

A salad with origins in New York City takes on Northwest flair with juicy pears, hazelnuts, and dried cherries.

- ¾ cup finely chopped celery
- ½ cup chopped dried cherries
- ¼ cup chopped hazelnuts, toasted
- ⅓ cup plain fat-free yogurt
- 3 tablespoons reduced-fat sour cream
- 1 tablespoon fresh lemon juice
- ¼ teaspoon salt
- 2 Bartlett pears (about 1 pound)

1. Combine first 3 ingredients in a large bowl. Combine yogurt, sour cream, juice, and salt in a bowl, stirring well with a whisk. Drizzle yogurt mixture over celery mixture; toss gently.

2. Peel, core, and chop pears. Add pears to salad, and toss gently. Cover and chill 1 hour. Yield: 6 servings (serving size: about ⅔ cup).

CALORIES 132 (29% from fat); FAT 4.2g (sat 0.8g, mono 2.2g, poly 0.4g); PROTEIN 2.6g; CARB 21.7g; FIBER 3.4g; CHOL 4mg; IRON 0.5mg; SODIUM 127mg; CALC 71mg

Desserts

Create a winning finale from our tasty line-up of recipes with lots of make-ahead tips.

STAFF FAVORITE • MAKE AHEAD
Harvest Pie

Butternut squash stands in for pumpkin in this pie, which received our Test Kitchens' highest rating.

  1 large butternut squash, halved and seeded (about 2¼ pounds)
     Cooking spray
  ½ cup fat-free evaporated milk
  ¾ cup granulated sugar
  ½ cup egg substitute
  1 teaspoon vanilla extract
  ½ teaspoon ground cinnamon
  ⅛ teaspoon ground allspice
  ⅛ teaspoon ground cloves
  ¼ cup all-purpose flour (about 1 ounce)
  ¼ cup packed dark brown sugar
  2 tablespoons chilled butter, cut into small pieces
  3 tablespoons chopped pecans
  ½ (15-ounce) package refrigerated pie dough (such as Pillsbury)
 10 tablespoons fat-free whipped topping (optional)

1. Position oven rack to lowest setting. Preheat oven to 400°.
2. Place squash, cut sides down, on a foil-lined baking sheet coated with cooking spray. Bake at 400° 30 minutes or until squash is tender. Cool slightly, and peel. Mash pulp to measure 2½ cups. Place pulp and milk in a food processor; process until smooth. Add granulated sugar and next 5 ingredients; process until smooth.
3. Increase oven temperature to 425°.
4. Lightly spoon flour into a dry measuring cup; level with a knife. Combine flour and brown sugar in a medium bowl; cut in butter using two knives or a pastry blender. Add pecans; toss to combine.
5. Roll dough into a 13-inch circle; fit into a 9-inch deep-dish pie plate coated with cooking spray. Fold edges under; flute. Pour squash mixture into prepared

crust. Place pie plate on bottom rack; bake at 425° for 15 minutes. Remove pie from oven.
6. Reduce oven temperature to 350°.
7. Sprinkle flour mixture evenly over filling; shield edges of piecrust with foil. Return pie plate to bottom rack; bake at 350° for an additional 40 minutes or until center is set. Cool on a wire rack. Garnish each serving with 1 tablespoon whipped topping, if desired. Yield: 10 servings (serving size: 1 wedge).

CALORIES 294 (34% from fat); FAT 11g (sat 3.9g, mono 4.9g, poly 1.5g); PROTEIN 4.6g; CARB 46.2g; FIBER 3.5g; CHOL 7mg; IRON 1.7mg; SODIUM 200mg; CALC 97mg

MAKE AHEAD
Cranberry-Orange Trifle

The cranberries and pastry cream can be made up to three days ahead. Then, simply assemble and refrigerate the trifle up to 24 hours before you plan to serve it.

CRANBERRIES:

  ¾ cup sugar
  ¾ cup fresh orange juice
  ¼ cup Grand Marnier (or other orange liqueur)
  1 (12-ounce) package fresh cranberries

PASTRY CREAM:

  ½ cup sugar
  5 tablespoons cornstarch
 2½ cups 2% reduced-fat milk
  2 large eggs, lightly beaten
  2 teaspoons vanilla extract
  ⅛ teaspoon salt

REMAINING INGREDIENTS:

  1 (10.75-ounce) loaf pound cake (such as Sara Lee), cut into ½-inch cubes
  1 teaspoon orange rind

1. To prepare cranberries, combine first 3 ingredients in a medium saucepan over medium-high heat; cook 3 minutes until sugar dissolves, stirring occasionally. Add cranberries; bring to a boil. Reduce heat; simmer 8 minutes or until cranberries pop. Spoon mixture into a bowl; cover and chill.

2. To prepare pastry cream, combine ½ cup sugar and cornstarch in a medium, heavy saucepan over medium heat. Gradually add milk, stirring with a whisk until blended; bring to a boil. Cook 1 minute, stirring constantly. Remove from heat. Gradually add half of hot milk mixture to eggs, stirring constantly with a whisk. Return milk mixture to pan; cook over medium heat 1 minute or until thick, stirring constantly. Remove from heat. Stir in vanilla and salt. Place pan in a large ice-filled bowl until custard cools to room temperature (about 25 minutes), stirring occasionally.
3. Arrange half of cake cubes in bottom of a 2-quart trifle dish. Spoon 1½ cups cranberry mixture over cake; top with 1½ cups pastry cream. Repeat layers. Garnish with rind. Cover loosely with plastic wrap, and chill at least 4 hours. Yield: 12 servings (serving size: about ¾ cup).

CALORIES 265 (21% from fat); FAT 6.2g (sat 3.2g, mono 1.9g, poly 0.4g); PROTEIN 4.6g; CARB 46.5g; FIBER 1.7g; CHOL 75mg; IRON 0.5mg; SODIUM 155mg; CALC 84mg

MAKE AHEAD
Chocolate Chip Blondies with Caramel-Bourbon Drizzle

Use an extra teaspoon of bourbon for heightened flavor, or omit it, if you prefer.

BLONDIES:

 1½ cups all-purpose flour (about 6¾ ounces)
  ½ cup quick-cooking oats
  1 teaspoon baking powder
  ¼ teaspoon salt
  1 cup packed brown sugar
  ⅓ cup butter, softened
  ½ cup egg substitute
  1 large egg, lightly beaten
  ⅓ cup semisweet mini chocolate chips
  1 teaspoon vanilla extract
     Cooking spray

DRIZZLE:

  ½ cup packed brown sugar
  1 tablespoon butter
  1 tablespoon whipping cream
  1 teaspoon bourbon

1. Preheat oven to 350°.

2. To prepare blondies, lightly spoon flour into dry measuring cups, and level with a knife. Combine flour and next 3 ingredients, stirring well with a whisk.

3. Place 1 cup sugar and ⅓ cup butter in a large bowl; beat with a mixer at medium speed until well blended. Add egg substitute and egg to sugar mixture; beat well. Add flour mixture; beat just until combined. Stir in chocolate chips and vanilla.

4. Spoon batter into a 9-inch square baking pan coated with cooking spray. Bake at 350° for 25 minutes or until a wooden pick inserted into center comes out clean. Cool on a wire rack.

5. To prepare drizzle, combine ½ cup sugar, 1 tablespoon butter, whipping cream, and bourbon in a medium saucepan over medium heat; bring to a boil. Cook 1 minute, stirring constantly with a whisk. Pour mixture into a bowl; chill 1 hour. Drizzle bourbon mixture over blondies; cut into 24 bars. Yield: 24 servings (serving size: 1 bar).

CALORIES 141 (29% from fat); FAT 4.5g (sat 2.7g, mono 1g, poly 0.2g); PROTEIN 2.1g; CARB 23.2g; FIBER 0.4g; CHOL 18mg; IRON 0.9mg; SODIUM 85mg; CALC 29mg

Lemon Polenta Cake with Winter Fruit Compote

This rustic cake has a slight crunch from cornmeal, and a mixture of winter fruits balances the tangy lemon flavor. The compote is best served at room temperature or slightly warm.

CAKE:
Cooking spray
1¼ cups all-purpose flour (about 5½ ounces)
1 cup sugar
½ cup yellow cornmeal
½ teaspoon baking soda
¼ teaspoon salt
⅔ cup reduced-fat buttermilk
¼ cup extravirgin olive oil
2 large eggs, lightly beaten
2 teaspoons grated lemon rind

COMPOTE:
1 cup unsweetened apple juice
½ cup golden raisins
½ cup fresh cranberries
1¾ cups finely chopped, peeled pear (about 2)
2 teaspoons fresh lemon juice

1. Preheat oven to 350°.

2. To prepare cake, coat an 8-inch round cake pan with cooking spray; line bottom of pan with parchment paper. Coat paper with cooking spray. Set aside.

3. Lightly spoon flour into dry measuring cups; level with a knife. Combine flour and next 4 ingredients in a large bowl, stirring well with a whisk. Make a well in center of mixture. Combine buttermilk, oil, eggs, and rind, stirring well with a whisk. Add buttermilk mixture to flour mixture, stirring until moist. Pour batter into prepared pan. Bake at 350° for 40 minutes or until a wooden pick inserted in center comes out clean. Cool in pan 10 minutes on a wire rack; remove from pan. Cool completely on wire rack.

4. To prepare compote, combine apple juice and raisins in a small saucepan over medium-high heat; bring to a boil. Reduce heat, and cook until reduced to ⅔ cup (about 4 minutes). Add cranberries to pan; cook 3 minutes or until cranberries pop. Add pear to pan; cook 2 minutes or until pears are tender. Remove from heat; stir in lemon juice. Serve with cake. Yield: 12 servings (serving size: 1 cake wedge and about 2½ tablespoons compote).

CALORIES 243 (22% from fat); FAT 6g (sat 1.1g, mono 3.7g, poly 0.7g); PROTEIN 3.8g; CARB 44.7g; FIBER 1.7g; CHOL 36mg; IRON 1.2mg; SODIUM 127mg; CALC 35mg

WINE NOTE: With a modestly sweet dessert like this, try a classic Madeira like Blandy's 5-Year-Old Verdelho ($21), which echoes the dried fruit with raisin and apricot flavors while adding its own touch of caramel sweetness. Serve it slightly chilled to contrast the warm cake. And don't worry about finishing the bottle; Madeira lasts almost indefinitely, even after it's been opened.

Oatmeal Pecan Pie

Rolled oats add heartiness to the filling of this classic Thanksgiving dessert. Make the pie up to a day ahead, but store it in the refrigerator if you do.

½ (15-ounce) package refrigerated pie dough (such as Pillsbury)
Cooking spray
1 cup packed dark brown sugar
1 cup light corn syrup
⅔ cup regular oats
½ cup chopped pecans
2 tablespoons butter, melted
1 teaspoon vanilla extract
¼ teaspoon salt
2 large eggs, lightly beaten
2 large egg whites, lightly beaten

1. Preheat oven to 325°.

2. Roll dough into an 11-inch circle. Fit into a 9-inch pie plate coated with cooking spray. Fold edges under; flute.

3. Combine sugar and remaining 8 ingredients, stirring well with a whisk. Pour into prepared crust. Bake at 325° for 50 minutes or until center is set. Cool completely on a wire rack. Yield: 12 servings (serving size: 1 wedge).

CALORIES 311 (33% from fat); FAT 11.3g (sat 3.5g, mono 5g, poly 2.6g); PROTEIN 3.2g; CARB 51.4g; FIBER 1g; CHOL 42mg; IRON 0.8mg; SODIUM 181mg; CALC 30mg

Homemade Pie Crust

1 cup all-purpose flour (about 4½ ounces)
¼ teaspoon salt
2 tablespoons chilled butter, cut into small pieces
1½ tablespoons vegetable shortening
3 tablespoons ice water
1 teaspoon fresh lemon juice
Cooking spray

1. Lightly spoon flour into a dry measuring cup; level with knife. Combine flour and salt in a medium bowl. Cut in butter and shortening with a pastry blender or two knives until mixture resembles
Continued

coarse meal. Combine 3 tablespoons water and juice. Sprinkle surface of flour mixture with water mixture, 1 tablespoon at a time; toss with a fork until moist. Gently press mixture into a 4-inch circle on plastic wrap; cover. Chill 30 minutes.

2. Preheat oven to 325°.

3. Unwrap and place chilled dough on a lightly floured surface. Roll dough to an 11-inch circle. Fit dough into a 9-inch pie plate coated with cooking spray. Fold edges under; flute. Fill crust, and bake as pie recipe directs.

CALORIES 822 (46% from fat); FAT 41.9g (sat 21.3g, mono 11.2g, poly 6.6g); PROTEIN 13.2g; CARB 95.8g; FIBER 3.4g; CHOL 60mg; IRON 5.8mg; SODIUM 754mg; CALC 26mg

---

Start with the Crust

Both the Harvest Pie (recipe on page 398) and Oatmeal Pecan Pie (recipe on page 399) rely on the convenience of a refrigerated pastry dough. You can usually substitute store-bought dough for homemade crust and vice versa. Store-bought pastry saves time, but there is a nutrition price.

We did a comparison of our Homemade Pie Crust (page 399) and an average (9-inch) store-bought pastry dough. Here are the results:

	HOMEMADE	STORE-BOUGHT
CALORIES	822 (46% from fat)	960 (53% from fat)
FAT	41.9g sat 21.3g mono 11.2g poly 6.6g	56g sat 20g mono 24.6g poly 14.6g
PROTEIN	13.2g	4g
CARB	95.8g	104g
FIBER	3.4g	0g
CHOL	60mg	24mg
IRON	5.8mg	0mg
SODIUM	754mg	880mg
CALC	26mg	0mg
		(Totals are for 1 [9-inch] pastry crust.)

Stout Gingerbread with Citrus Sauce

Make the sauce just before serving.

GINGERBREAD:
Cooking spray
2 cups all-purpose flour (about 9 ounces)
2 teaspoons ground ginger
1½ teaspoons ground cinnamon
1 teaspoon baking soda
¼ teaspoon salt
¼ teaspoon ground nutmeg
¼ teaspoon ground cloves
¾ cup sugar
½ cup butter, softened
1 large egg
¼ cup molasses
1 tablespoon grated fresh ginger
1 cup stout beer (such as Guinness)

SAUCE:
½ cup sugar
½ cup water
1 tablespoon cornstarch
1 tablespoon butter
1 tablespoon grated lemon rind
⅓ cup fresh lemon juice
¼ teaspoon vanilla extract

1. Preheat oven to 350°.

2. To prepare gingerbread, coat a 9-inch round cake pan with cooking spray; line bottom of pan with parchment paper. Coat paper with cooking spray, and set aside.

3. Lightly spoon flour into dry measuring cups; level with a knife. Combine flour and next 6 ingredients in a bowl, stirring with a whisk. Combine ¾ cup sugar and ½ cup butter in a large bowl; beat with a mixer at medium speed until light and fluffy. Add egg; beat until blended. Beat in molasses and fresh ginger. Add flour mixture and beer alternately to sugar mixture, beginning and ending with flour mixture. Pour batter into prepared pan. Bake at 350° for 40 minutes or until a wooden pick inserted in center comes out clean. Cool in pan 10 minutes on a wire rack; remove from pan. Cool completely on wire rack.

4. To prepare sauce, combine ½ cup sugar, ½ cup water, and cornstarch in a medium saucepan; bring to a boil. Cook 1 minute, stirring constantly. Remove from heat. Add 1 tablespoon butter, stirring until smooth. Stir in rind, juice, and vanilla. Cool to room temperature. Serve with gingerbread. Yield: 12 servings (serving size: 1 gingerbread slice and about 1 tablespoon sauce).

CALORIES 274 (30% from fat); FAT 9.2g (sat 5.6g, mono 2.4g, poly 0.5g); PROTEIN 3g; CARB 44.5g; FIBER 0.9g; CHOL 40mg; IRON 1.5mg; SODIUM 224mg; CALC 28mg

---

Caramelized Pears with Blue Cheese and Ginger Gastrique

A gastrique is a reduction sauce made with vinegar and sugar.

½ cup plus 2 tablespoons granulated sugar
½ cup water
¼ cup champagne vinegar
1 tablespoon minced fresh ginger
2 tablespoons brown sugar
1 tablespoon butter
½ teaspoon chopped fresh thyme
½ teaspoon fresh lemon juice
¼ teaspoon salt
2 peeled Bosc pears, cored and each cut into 4 wedges
½ cup (2 ounces) blue cheese, crumbled
Dash of cracked black pepper
Thyme sprigs (optional)

1. Combine first 4 ingredients in a small saucepan over high heat; bring to a boil. Reduce heat; cook until reduced to ½ cup (about 8 minutes), stirring occasionally until sugar dissolves. Strain mixture through a fine sieve into a bowl, reserving liquid; discard solids. Cool.

2. Melt brown sugar and butter in a large nonstick skillet over medium-high heat. Cook 2 minutes. Stir in chopped thyme, juice, and salt. Add pears, cut-sides down, to pan. Reduce heat to low; cook 2 minutes or until tender, turning once.

3. Arrange 2 pear wedges on each of 4 plates; drizzle pears evenly with pan juices. Sprinkle 2 tablespoons cheese over each serving; top each serving with 2 tablespoons reserved cooking liquid. Sprinkle with cracked black pepper. Garnish with thyme sprigs, if desired. Yield: 4 servings.

CALORIES 289 (22% from fat); FAT 7g (sat 4.3g, mono 1.8g, poly 0.2g); PROTEIN 3.5g; CARB 56.3g; FIBER 3.3g; CHOL 20mg; IRON 0.5mg; SODIUM 367mg; CALC 93mg

MAKE AHEAD
Individual Apple Tarts

Prepare the tarts up to a day ahead, and glaze just before serving.

TARTS:
Cooking spray
1 tablespoon canola oil
1 tablespoon butter, melted
10 (14 x 9–inch) sheets frozen phyllo dough, thawed
2 large apples, peeled, cored, and thinly sliced
2 teaspoons sugar
½ teaspoon ground cinnamon

GLAZE:
1 cup sugar
¼ cup water

1. Preheat oven to 400°.
2. To prepare tarts, line a baking sheet with parchment paper; coat paper with cooking spray. Combine oil and butter in a small bowl, stirring well. Place 1 phyllo sheet on a large cutting board or work surface (cover remaining sheets to prevent drying); lightly brush with oil mixture. Repeat layers with remaining phyllo sheets and oil mixture. Gently press phyllo layers together. Cut through phyllo layers crosswise with a sharp knife to form 2 (14 x 4½–inch) strips; cut each strip into 4 (4½ x 3½–inch) rectangles to form 8 rectangles. Carefully place rectangles on prepared baking sheet.
3. Arrange apple slices evenly on rectangles. Combine 2 teaspoons sugar and cinnamon; sprinkle over apples. Bake at 400° for 30 minutes or until browned. Cool slightly on a wire rack.
4. To prepare glaze, combine 1 cup

sugar and ¼ cup water in a heavy saucepan over medium-low heat; cook 13 minutes, stirring just until sugar dissolves. Cover, increase heat to medium, and boil 1 minute. (This will dissolve any sugar crystals clinging to sides of pan.) Uncover and boil 10 additional minutes or until golden. (Do not stir.) Remove from heat; let stand 1 minute. Working quickly, gently brush glaze over apples. Serve immediately. Yield: 8 servings (serving size: 1 tart).

CALORIES 228 (19% from fat); FAT 4.7g (sat 1.4g, mono 2.2g, poly 0.8g); PROTEIN 1.8g; CARB 46g; FIBER 1.8g; CHOL 3.8mg; IRON 0.9mg; SODIUM 126mg; CALC 8.3mg

MAKE AHEAD
Citrus Pound Cake with Blood Orange Sauce

Use regular oranges if you can't find blood oranges. Prepare the cake up to two days in advance.

CAKE:
Cooking spray
1 tablespoon all-purpose flour
2¼ cups all-purpose flour (about 10 ounces)
1 teaspoon baking powder
¼ teaspoon salt
1¾ cups sugar, divided
10 tablespoons butter, softened
½ cup (4 ounces) ⅓-less-fat cream cheese, softened
1 teaspoon grated lemon rind
1 teaspoon grated orange rind
3 large eggs
½ cup low-fat buttermilk
¼ cup fresh orange juice
2 tablespoons fresh lemon juice
3 large egg whites

SAUCE:
2 cups fresh blood orange juice (about 12 oranges)
⅔ cup sugar

1. Preheat oven to 325°.
2. To prepare cake, coat a 10-inch tube pan with cooking spray; dust with 1 tablespoon flour. Set aside. Lightly spoon 2¼ cups flour into dry measuring cups; level

with a knife. Combine flour, baking powder, and salt; stir well with a whisk.
3. Combine 1½ cups sugar, butter, and cheese in a large bowl; beat with a mixer at medium speed until well blended (about 7 minutes). Add rinds; beat well. Add 3 eggs, 1 at a time, beating well after each addition. Combine buttermilk, ¼ cup orange juice, and lemon juice. Add flour mixture and buttermilk mixture alternately to sugar mixture, beginning and ending with flour mixture.
4. Place egg whites in a medium bowl. Beat with a mixer at high speed until soft peaks form, using clean, dry beaters. Add ¼ cup sugar, 1 tablespoon at a time, beating until stiff peaks form. Gently fold one-third of egg white mixture into batter, and fold in remaining egg white mixture. Spoon batter into prepared pan.
5. Bake at 325° for 1 hour and 10 minutes or until a wooden pick inserted in center comes out clean. Cool in pan on a wire rack 10 minutes. Remove cake from pan; cool completely on wire rack.
6. To prepare sauce, combine blood orange juice and ⅔ cup sugar in a large, heavy saucepan; bring to a boil, stirring until sugar dissolves. Reduce heat, and simmer until reduced to 1 cup (about 30 minutes). Serve sauce with cake. Yield: 16 servings (serving size: 1 cake slice and 1 tablespoon sauce).

CALORIES 316 (29% from fat); FAT 10.1g (sat 5.9g, mono 2.7g, poly 0.5g); PROTEIN 5.3g; CARB 52.1g; FIBER 0.7g; CHOL 64mg; IRON 1.2mg; SODIUM 178mg; CALC 50mg

Chocolate Orange Sauce Sundaes

Prepare the sauce several days ahead, chill it, and reheat just before serving. You can also use this sauce for fondue.

1½   cups 2% reduced-fat milk
¼   cup half-and-half
1   tablespoon butter
8   ounces bittersweet chocolate, chopped
2   teaspoons grated orange rind
1½   tablespoons fresh orange juice
1   teaspoon Grand Marnier (orange-flavored liqueur)
12   cups vanilla fat-free frozen yogurt

1. Heat milk and half-and-half in a heavy saucepan over medium-high heat to 180° or until tiny bubbles form around edge (do not boil). Remove from heat; add butter and chocolate, stirring until smooth. Stir in rind, juice, and liqueur. Serve sauce with frozen yogurt. Yield: 16 servings (serving size: ¾ cup frozen yogurt and 2½ tablespoons sauce).

CALORIES 245 (28% from fat); FAT 7.7g (sat 4g, mono 2.5g, poly 0.2g); PROTEIN 7.9g; CARB 40.2g; FIBER 1g; CHOL 5mg; IRON 1.1mg; SODIUM 138mg; CALC 183mg

Upside-Down Cardamom-Pear Cake

An ideal spice for sweet, juicy pears, cardamom has a pronounced, slightly spicy flavor similar to ginger. This cake is best served warm.

PEARS:
2   tablespoons butter
¼   cup packed brown sugar
¼   teaspoon ground cardamom
Cooking spray
2   peeled Bartlett or Anjou pears, cored and each cut into 12 wedges

CAKE:
1½   cups all-purpose flour (about 6¾ ounces)
2   teaspoons baking powder
¼   teaspoon ground cardamom
⅛   teaspoon salt
¾   cup granulated sugar
¼   cup butter, softened
2   large eggs
¾   cup 2% reduced-fat milk
1   teaspoon vanilla extract

1. Preheat oven to 350°.
2. To prepare pears, melt 2 tablespoons butter in a small nonstick skillet over medium heat. Add brown sugar and ¼ teaspoon cardamom; cook 3 minutes or until sugar dissolves, stirring constantly. Pour sugar mixture into a 9-inch round cake pan coated with cooking spray. Arrange pears in an overlapping circle over sugar mixture; set aside.
3. To prepare cake, lightly spoon flour into dry measuring cups; level with a knife. Sift together flour, baking powder, ¼ teaspoon cardamom, and salt in a large bowl, stirring well. Place granulated sugar and ¼ cup butter in a large bowl; beat with a mixer at medium speed until well blended. Add eggs; beat until blended. Add flour mixture to egg mixture alternately with milk, beginning and ending with flour mixture. Stir in vanilla. Spoon batter into center of prepared pan; gently spread batter to cover fruit.
4. Bake at 350° for 50 minutes or until a wooden pick inserted in center comes out clean. Cool in pan 10 minutes on a wire rack; run a knife around outside edge. Place a plate upside down on top of pan; invert onto plate. Let cake stand 2 minutes before removing pan. Cut into wedges. Yield: 8 servings (serving size: 1 wedge).

CALORIES 316 (30% from fat); FAT 10.7g (sat 6.1g, mono 2.8g, poly 0.6g); PROTEIN 5.1g; CARB 51.3g; FIBER 1.7g; CHOL 77mg; IRON 1.6mg; SODIUM 251mg; CALC 120mg

Gifts

Surprise those on your list with thoughtful homemade treats.

Gingerbread People

For a whimsical presentation, arrange these cookies in a lunch box lined with colorful packing paper. Use a variety of cookie cutter sizes to create "families." If you don't want to cut the dough into shapes, roll it into two logs, cover, chill, and slice into ⅛-inch rounds. Refrigerate the dough up to three days, or freeze up to one month.

COOKIES:
2¼   cups all-purpose flour (about 10 ounces)
1½   teaspoons ground ginger
1   teaspoon ground cinnamon
½   teaspoon baking powder
¼   teaspoon baking soda
¼   teaspoon salt
¼   teaspoon ground nutmeg
¼   teaspoon ground cloves
¾   cup granulated sugar
¼   cup butter, softened
½   cup molasses
1   large egg

DECORATIONS:
1¼   cups powdered sugar
2   tablespoons 2% milk
¼   cup colored sugar sprinkles

1. To prepare cookies, lightly spoon flour into dry measuring cups; level with a knife. Combine flour, ginger, and next 6 ingredients in a large bowl, stirring with a whisk.
2. Place granulated sugar and butter in a large bowl; beat with a mixer at medium speed until smooth and well blended. Add molasses and egg; beat until well blended. Stir flour mixture into sugar mixture until well blended. Divide dough in half; shape each portion into a flat disk. Wrap separately in plastic wrap; chill 1 hour or until firm.

3. Preheat oven to 350°.

4. Remove one dough portion from refrigerator; remove plastic wrap. Roll dough to a ⅛-inch thickness on a floured surface. Cut with a 3-inch boy or girl cookie cutter. Place cookies ½ inch apart on parchment paper–lined baking sheets. Repeat procedure with remaining dough portion. Bake at 350° for 11 minutes or until edges of cookies are lightly browned. Remove from pans; cool completely on wire racks.

5. To prepare decorations, combine powdered sugar and milk, stirring until smooth. Spoon mixture into a heavy-duty zip-top plastic bag. Snip a tiny hole in 1 corner of bag. Pipe onto cookies. Decorate as desired with sugar sprinkles. Yield: about 5 dozen cookies (serving size: 1 cookie).

CALORIES 56 (14% from fat); FAT 0.9g (sat 0.5g, mono 0.2g, poly 0.1g); PROTEIN 0.6g; CARB 11.5g; FIBER 0.2g; CHOL 6mg; IRON 0.4mg; SODIUM 27mg; CALC 10mg

---

MAKE AHEAD
Amaretti

Package these crunchy cookies in a gift box with a pound of your favorite coffee beans. Look for almond paste on your supermarket's baking aisle, and for best results, don't substitute marzipan, which is sweeter and more finely textured, in place of the paste.

  1 cup granulated sugar
  1 (7-ounce) package almond
     paste
  1 teaspoon amaretto (almond-
     flavored liqueur)
  2 large egg whites
  ¼ cup turbinado sugar

1. Preheat oven to 350°.
2. Place granulated sugar and almond paste in a large bowl; beat with a mixer at medium speed until almond paste is broken into small pieces. Add amaretto and egg whites; beat mixture at high speed 4 minutes or until smooth. Chill batter 20 minutes.
3. Drop batter by teaspoonfuls 1 inch apart on parchment paper–lined baking sheets. Sprinkle evenly with turbinado

sugar. Bake at 350° for 10 minutes or until edges of cookies are golden brown. Cool completely on pans; carefully remove cookies from parchment. Cool on wire racks. Yield: 40 cookies (serving size: 1 cookie).

CALORIES 48 (26% from fat); FAT 1.4g (sat 0.1g, mono 0.9g, poly 0.3g); PROTEIN 0.6g; CARB 8.6g; FIBER 0.2g; CHOL 0mg; IRON 0.1mg; SODIUM 3mg; CALC 9mg

---

MAKE AHEAD
Sun-Dried Tomato Jam

Spoon this sweet-savory jam into a pretty glass jar, and tie with a ribbon. You can also attach a rosemary sprig and a card with serving suggestions—as an appetizer spread on baguette slices with goat cheese; as a chutney over chicken, beef, or pork; or as the sauce for a pizza with shredded chicken, goat cheese, and chives.

  3 cups vertically sliced onion
  3 tablespoons sugar
  3 garlic cloves, minced
  3 (7-ounce) jars oil-packed sun-
     dried tomatoes, drained and
     coarsely chopped
  ½ cup red wine vinegar
  ¼ cup red wine
  1 cup water
  ½ cup fat-free, less-sodium chicken
     broth
  1 tablespoon finely chopped fresh
     rosemary
  ¾ teaspoon salt

1. Heat a medium saucepan over medium-high heat. Add first 4 ingredients; cook 8 minutes or until tomatoes are soft, stirring occasionally. Add vinegar and wine; cook 3 minutes or until liquid evaporates. Add 1 cup water and broth; bring to boil. Reduce heat; simmer 45 minutes or until liquid evaporates, stirring occasionally. Stir in rosemary and salt. Yield: 4 cups (serving size: ¼ cup).

CALORIES 77 (44% from fat); FAT 3.8g (sat 0.5g, mono 2.3g, poly 0.6g); PROTEIN 1.7g; CARB 11g; FIBER 1.9g; CHOL 0mg; IRON 0.8mg; SODIUM 195mg; CALC 20mg

---

MAKE AHEAD
Candied Orange Slices with Ganache Dipping Sauce

Because the orange slices are sticky, layer them between sheets of wax paper or parchment paper, and arrange in a small box or glassine bag. Spoon the sauce into a ramekin, and secure with plastic wrap and a ribbon. Include a note to microwave the sauce for 15 seconds and stir before serving.

ORANGES:
  8 (¼-inch-thick) unpeeled orange
     slices (about 2 oranges)
2½ cups granulated sugar
  2 cups turbinado sugar
1½ cups water
  1 tablespoon Grand Marnier
     (orange-flavored liqueur)
Dash of salt

GANACHE:
  2 tablespoons 2% milk
  ½ cup semisweet chocolate chips

1. To prepare oranges, place orange slices in a medium saucepan; cover with water. Bring to a boil; drain orange slices on paper towels.
2. Combine sugars, 1½ cups water, liqueur, and salt in a medium saucepan. Bring to a boil (do not stir); reduce heat and simmer, without stirring, until a candy thermometer registers 220° (about 8 minutes). Add orange slices; simmer, without stirring, 45 minutes or until peel becomes translucent. Remove orange slices from syrup with a slotted spoon; drain on parchment paper 5 minutes or until cool enough to handle. Place on a wire rack, and cool completely. Cut orange slices into quarters.
3. To prepare ganache, place milk in a small microwave-safe bowl. Microwave at HIGH 1 minute. Add chocolate chips; let stand 5 minutes, stirring occasionally until chocolate melts. Serve orange wedges with ganache. Yield: 8 servings (serving size: 4 orange wedges and 1 tablespoon ganache).

CALORIES 99 (30% from fat); FAT 3.3g (sat 1.9g, mono 1.1g, poly 0.1g); PROTEIN 0.9g; CARB 18.5g; FIBER 1.4g; CHOL 0mg; IRON 0.4mg; SODIUM 23mg; CALC 26mg

Golden Pumpkin-Walnut Loaf

Seal this quick bread in plastic, wrap it with a pretty kitchen towel, and tie it up with a ribbon. Add a card that suggests toasting slices of this moist bread for breakfast and spreading with light cream cheese for a special treat. You can even include a small crock of cream cheese in a basket with the bread for a hand-delivered gift.

1¼ cups all-purpose flour (about 5½ ounces)
½ cup yellow cornmeal
1½ teaspoons baking powder
1 teaspoon ground ginger
½ teaspoon salt
¼ teaspoon baking soda
¼ teaspoon ground cardamom
¼ teaspoon ground mace
¾ cup packed dark brown sugar
½ cup granulated sugar
2 large eggs, lightly beaten
1 cup canned pumpkin
3 tablespoons canola oil
1½ teaspoons vanilla extract
1 cup golden raisins
½ cup chopped walnuts
Cooking spray

1. Preheat oven to 350°.
2. Lightly spoon flour into dry measuring cups; level with a knife. Combine flour, cornmeal, and next 6 ingredients in a large bowl; make a well in center of mixture.
3. Combine sugars and eggs in a medium bowl, stirring with a whisk. Add pumpkin, oil, and vanilla; stir well. Stir in raisins and nuts; add to flour mixture, stirring just until moist. Spoon batter into a 9 x 5–inch loaf pan coated with cooking spray. Bake at 350° for 50 minutes or until a wooden pick inserted in center comes out clean. Cool 10 minutes in pan on a wire rack, and remove from pan. Cool completely on wire rack. Yield: 16 servings (serving size: 1 slice).

CALORIES 209 (25% from fat); FAT 5.9g (sat 0.7g, mono 2.1g, poly 2.7g); PROTEIN 3.2g; CARB 37g; FIBER 1.5g; CHOL 26mg; IRON 1.5mg; SODIUM 190mg; CALC 52mg

Glazed Honey Nuts

Serve these nuts as a snack, or toss them in your favorite salad. Spreading the nuts on a baking sheet before they're completely cooled prevents them from clumping.

1 teaspoon salt
¼ teaspoon curry powder
¼ teaspoon ground red pepper
Cooking spray
1 cup unsalted pecan halves
1 cup unsalted walnut halves
2 tablespoons honey

1. Combine first 3 ingredients.
2. Heat a large nonstick skillet over medium-high heat. Coat pan with cooking spray. Add pecans, walnuts, and honey. Cook 4 minutes or until nuts are toasted, stirring constantly. Sprinkle nuts evenly with spice mixture, tossing well to coat.
3. Spread nut mixture on a baking sheet coated with cooking spray. Cool completely. Store in an airtight container. Yield: 16 servings (serving size: 2 tablespoons).

CALORIES 96 (83% from fat); FAT 8.9g (sat 0.8g, mono 3.3g, poly 4.4g); PROTEIN 1.6g; CARB 4g; FIBER 1.1g; CHOL 0mg; IRON 0.4mg; SODIUM 146mg; CALC 11mg

Pack the Glazed Honey Nuts in a glass apothecary jar or other attractive airtight container.

Mailing Food Gifts

Some items are better candidates for sending through the mail than others. In general, safe bets are baked goods such as cookies, bar cookies, quick breads, and unfrosted cakes (like pound cake); candies; and other items that can be stored at room temperature. Follow these tips to ensure your goodies arrive intact:

• **Cool off.** Allow any baked goods to cool completely before packaging to prevent moisture from condensing inside the package.

• **Wrap for freshness.** Wrap quick breads or cakes in plastic wrap and then aluminum foil, and seal inside a zip-top plastic bag. Keep quick breads, brownies, or bar cookies in the pan they baked in, and wrap with plastic wrap and foil; if you can, seal the pan inside a zip-top plastic bag. Place cookies or spiced nuts directly into a zip-top plastic bag.

• **Cushion the food.** Place food into one container (a zip-top plastic bag or metal tin lined with tissue paper, for example), and place inside a larger box lined on all sides with crumpled tissue paper, bubble wrap, or other packaging material.

• **Give delicates extra care.** If you've decorated cookies, ensure that they'll arrive in good shape. Align two cookies back-to-back, and wrap in tissue paper. Nestle pairs of wrapped cookies into a tissue paper– or bubble wrap–lined tin.

• **Bank on one week.** Most homemade baked goods have a shelf life of about a week, so take this into consideration when deciding how quickly to have the gift delivered.

• **Alert the recipient.** Let the person to whom you're mailing the gift know when to expect the package.

Six Holiday Menus

To make planning meals easier, we composed six all-occasion menus with recipes from our November issue of Cooking Light *magazine.*

Cocktail Party Menu
serves 10

Apple Martinis
(recipe on page 383)

Mini Smoked Salmon Pizzas
(recipe on page 384)

Phyllo Triangles with Onion Jam
(recipe on page 385)

Glazed Honey Nuts
(recipe on page 404)

Cheese and fruit platter

Feed a Crowd Menu
serves 12

Assemble the lasagna up to a day ahead, then bake just before serving. The refrigerated dish may require an extra five to 10 minutes in the oven.

Seafood Lasagna
(recipe on page 392)

Garlic breadsticks*

Tossed salad

*Unroll 1 (11-ounce) can refrigerated breadstick dough; separate it into 12 pieces. Combine 3 tablespoons grated Parmesan cheese and 1½ teaspoons minced garlic. Brush 1 tablespoon butter evenly over dough pieces. Sprinkle cheese mixture evenly over dough pieces; press lightly. Twist each piece several times, forming spirals. Bake at 375° for 13 minutes or until lightly browned.

Holiday Menu
serves 4

Sautéed pork chops

Jezebel Sauce

Long-grain and wild rice

Sautéed broccoli

Chocolate Chip Blondies with Caramel-Bourbon Drizzle
(recipe on page 398)

Holiday Dinner Menu
serves 8

Endive Salad with Pomegranate Seeds, Persimmon, and Pecan Vinaigrette
(recipe on page 386)

Marsala-Glazed Ham
(recipe on page 387)

Sweet Potato Casserole
(recipe on page 426)

Sautéed broccoli rabe

Dinner rolls

Oatmeal Pecan Pie
(recipe on page 399)

Iced tea

Dinner Party Menu
serves 8

Leg of Lamb with Roasted Pear and Pine Nut Relish
(recipe on page 389)

Mashed Potato Gratin
(recipe on page 393)

Roast Lemon and Pepper Brussels Sprouts with Parmesan
(recipe on page 395)

Caramelized Pears with Blue Cheese and Ginger Gastrique
(recipe on page 400)

Tawny port

Casual Entertaining Menu
serves 6

Pork Tenderloin with Pomegranate Glaze
(recipe on page 390)

Wild rice pilaf*

Green beans

*Melt 1 tablespoon butter in a large saucepan over medium-high heat. Add ¼ cup diced shallots; sauté 2 minutes. Stir in 1 cup long-grain and wild rice blend; sauté 1 minute. Stir in 2 cups fat-free, less-sodium chicken broth; 1 cup water; ¼ teaspoon salt; and ¼ teaspoon freshly ground black pepper. Bring to a boil. Cover, reduce heat, and simmer 30 minutes. Stir in ½ cup dried cherries; cover and cook 10 minutes or until liquid is absorbed. Remove from heat; stir in ⅓ cup chopped fresh parsley and ⅓ cup toasted chopped pecans.

Fine Fruit Butter

Seattle schoolteacher Patricia St. John substitutes a different spice to create a fabulous fall preserve.

Spanish Salad of Oranges, Fennel, Red Onion, and Mint with Dressing

—Lillian Julow, Gainesville, Florida

2 cups thinly sliced red onion (about 1 large)
3 large navel oranges (about 5 pounds)
3 cups thinly sliced fennel bulb (about 1 pound)
¼ cup loosely packed fresh mint leaves
3 tablespoons plain fat-free yogurt
2 tablespoons frozen orange juice concentrate, thawed
2 tablespoons red wine vinegar
4 teaspoons extravirgin olive oil
1 teaspoon coriander seeds, toasted and crushed
½ teaspoon sea salt
¼ teaspoon freshly ground black pepper

1. Place onion in a medium bowl; cover with ice water, and soak 15 minutes. Drain well.
2. Carefully remove rind and white pithy part of rind from oranges; discard rind and pith. Cut each orange in half vertically; remove white pithy core portion, and discard. Cut oranges crosswise into ¼-inch-thick slices, reserving about ⅓ cup juice for dressing.
3. Layer onion, fennel, and orange evenly in a bowl or on a platter, and sprinkle with mint. Combine reserved juice, yogurt, and remaining 6 ingredients in a small bowl, and stir with a whisk. Drizzle evenly over salad; serve immediately. Yield: 6 servings (serving size: about 1 cup).

CALORIES 163 (19% from fat); FAT 3.5g (sat 0.5g, mono 2.3g, poly 0.4g); PROTEIN 3.4g; CARB 32.8g; FIBER 7g; CHOL 0mg; IRON 1.3mg; SODIUM 241mg; CALC 134mg

MAKE AHEAD
Ginger Cardamom Pear Butter

—Patricia St. John, Seattle, Washington

4 cups coarsely chopped peeled Bartlett pear (about 2½ pounds)
1 cup sugar
2 teaspoons minced peeled fresh ginger
2 teaspoons fresh lemon juice
1 teaspoon ground cardamom
¼ teaspoon salt

1. Place pears in a blender or food processor; process until smooth. Combine pear puree, sugar, and remaining ingredients in a medium sauté pan over medium heat; bring to a simmer, stirring occasionally. Cook 3 hours or until mixture is thick. Yield: 1¼ cups (serving size: 1 tablespoon).

CALORIES 72 (1% from fat); FAT 0.1g (sat 0g, mono 0g, poly 0g); PROTEIN 0.2g; CARB 18.9g; FIBER 1.8g; CHOL 0mg; IRON 0.1mg; SODIUM 30mg; CALC 6mg

MAKE AHEAD
Whole Wheat Apple Scones

"These scones are great in the morning with coffee or as an afternoon pick-me-up."
—Sarah Green, Ilwaco, Washington

1 cup plus 2 tablespoons all-purpose flour (about 5 ounces)
1 cup whole wheat flour (about 4¾ ounces)
¼ cup sugar
2 teaspoons baking powder
1 teaspoon ground cinnamon
½ teaspoon baking soda
½ teaspoon salt
Dash of ground nutmeg
¼ cup chilled butter, cut into small pieces
1 cup shredded peeled Granny Smith apple (about ½ pound)
½ cup 1% low-fat milk
1 teaspoon vanilla extract
Cooking spray
2 tablespoons 1% low-fat milk
2 teaspoons sugar

1. Preheat oven to 425°.
2. Lightly spoon flours into dry measuring cups and tablespoons; level with a knife. Combine flours, sugar, and next 5 ingredients in a large bowl; stir with a whisk. Cut in butter with a pastry blender or 2 knives until mixture resembles coarse meal. Add apple, ½ cup milk, and vanilla, stirring just until moist (dough will be sticky).
3. Turn dough out onto a lightly floured surface, and knead lightly 4 times with floured hands. Divide dough in half; pat each portion into a 6-inch circle on a baking sheet coated with cooking spray. Cut each circle into 5 wedges, cutting into, but not through, dough. Brush tops of wedges with 2 tablespoons milk, and sprinkle evenly with 2 teaspoons sugar. Bake at 425° for 15 minutes or until golden. Serve warm. Yield: 10 servings (serving size: 1 wedge).

CALORIES 170 (27% from fat); FAT 5.1g (sat 3g, mono 1.3g, poly 0.3g); PROTEIN 3.7g; CARB 28.1g; FIBER 2.1g; CHOL 13mg; IRON 1.3mg; SODIUM 319mg; CALC 84mg

One-Dish Barley, Wild Rice, and Chicken Pilaf

"This recipe has some of the creamy texture of a risotto but requires far less stirring."
—Diana Hubbell, Sudbury, Massachusetts

½ cup hot water
¼ cup dried porcini mushrooms, chopped
1 tablespoon olive oil
1 cup finely chopped onion (about 1 medium)
3 garlic cloves, minced
¾ cup uncooked pearl barley
¼ cup wild rice
2 teaspoons chopped fresh thyme
1 (14-ounce) can fat-free, less-sodium chicken broth
2 cups chopped cooked chicken breast
½ cup (2 ounces) grated fresh Parmesan cheese
¼ cup chopped fresh parsley
¼ teaspoon salt
¼ teaspoon ground black pepper

1. Combine ½ cup hot water and mushrooms; let stand 10 minutes or until mushrooms are tender. Set aside.

2. Heat oil in a large nonstick skillet over medium heat. Add onion; cook 1 minute, stirring frequently. Add garlic; cook 30 seconds, stirring frequently. Add barley, rice, and thyme; cook 5 minutes or until lightly browned, stirring frequently. Stir in mushroom mixture and broth. Cover, reduce heat, and simmer 40 minutes or until barley is tender. Stir in chicken and cheese; cook 5 minutes or until thoroughly heated. Stir in parsley, salt, and pepper. Yield: 4 servings (serving size: 1 cup).

CALORIES 409 (27% from fat); FAT 12.4g (sat 3.9g, mono 5.6g, poly 2g); PROTEIN 31.6g; CARB 42.8g; FIBER 7.7g; CHOL 68mg; IRON 2.7mg; SODIUM 515mg; CALC 160mg

Classic Chicken Parmesan

—Jocelyn Pickford, Arlington, Virginia

  4 (6-ounce) skinless, boneless chicken breast halves
  2 cups (3½ ounces) low-fat whole wheat crackers (such as Breton)
  2 teaspoons dried oregano, divided
  1 teaspoon garlic powder
Cooking spray
  1 cup finely chopped onion (about 1 medium)
  3 garlic cloves, minced
  ¼ cup dry red wine
  1 (28-ounce) can crushed tomatoes, undrained
  ¼ teaspoon salt
  ¼ teaspoon freshly ground black pepper
  ⅓ cup (about 1½ ounces) grated fresh Parmesan cheese
  4 cups hot cooked linguine (about 8 ounces uncooked pasta)
Flat-leaf parsley sprigs (optional)

1. Preheat oven to 350°.

2. Place each chicken breast half between 2 sheets of heavy-duty plastic wrap, and pound to ½-inch thickness using a meat mallet or small heavy skillet.

3. Place crackers, 1 teaspoon oregano, and garlic powder in a food processor; pulse 5 times or until coarse crumbs measure 1¼ cups. Place cracker mixture in a shallow bowl, and dredge chicken in cracker mixture. Place chicken in a 13 x 9–inch baking dish coated with cooking spray. Bake at 350° for 25 minutes or until chicken is done.

4. Heat a large nonstick skillet over medium-high heat. Coat pan with cooking spray. Add onion; sauté 2 minutes. Add garlic; sauté 1 minute or until mixture begins to brown. Add wine; cook 1 minute or until most of liquid evaporates. Stir in tomatoes, 1 teaspoon oregano, salt, and pepper. Reduce heat to low, and simmer 5 minutes or until thoroughly heated.

5. Spoon 2 cups tomato mixture over cooked chicken; sprinkle evenly with cheese. Bake at 350° for 5 minutes or until cheese melts and sauce is bubbly. Remove from oven; let stand 5 minutes. Pour remaining tomato mixture over pasta, and toss. Serve pasta with chicken. Garnish with parsley sprigs, if desired. Yield: 4 servings (serving size: 1 cup pasta and 1 topped chicken breast half).

CALORIES 577 (10% from fat); FAT 6.7g (sat 1.8g, mono 1.5g, poly 1.2g); PROTEIN 54.9g; CARB 71.9g; FIBER 6.7g; CHOL 105mg; IRON 5.4mg; SODIUM 774mg; CALC 203mg

MAKE AHEAD

Healthy Banana Bread

—Helen Oetjen, Burlington, Vermont

  ½ cup sugar
  5 tablespoons butter, softened
  2 large eggs
1½ cups all-purpose flour (about 6¾ ounces)
  1 teaspoon baking soda
  1 teaspoon salt
  ½ teaspoon ground cinnamon
  ¼ teaspoon ground nutmeg
  ⅛ teaspoon ground cloves
  1 (6-ounce) carton vanilla low-fat yogurt
  ¾ cup ripe mashed bananas (about 1½ bananas)
  ¼ teaspoon vanilla extract
Cooking spray

1. Preheat oven to 350°.

2. Place sugar and butter in a large bowl; beat with a mixer at medium speed until well blended (about 5 minutes). Add eggs, 1 at a time, beating well after each addition.

3. Lightly spoon flour into dry measuring cups; level with a knife. Sift together flour, baking soda, and next 4 ingredients. Add flour mixture and yogurt alternately to sugar mixture, beginning and ending with flour mixture. Fold in bananas and vanilla. Pour into an 8 x 4–inch loaf pan coated with cooking spray. Bake at 350° for 1 hour or until a wooden pick inserted in center comes out clean. Cool 10 minutes in pan on a wire rack; remove from pan. Cool completely on wire rack. Yield: 10 servings (serving size: 1 slice).

CALORIES 204 (31% from fat); FAT 7.1g (sat 4.1g, mono 1.9g, poly 0.4g); PROTEIN 4.3g; CARB 31g; FIBER 1.2g; CHOL 58mg; IRON 1.2mg; SODIUM 428mg; CALC 41mg

simple suppers

Leftover Bounty

Make over your Thanksgiving feast into more delicious dishes.

Toasted Turkey and Brie Sandwiches

You may need a knife and fork to eat this sandwich. Serve with a side of cranberry sauce and sweet potato chips.

  4 sourdough English muffins, split and toasted
  4 teaspoons honey mustard
  2 cups shredded cooked turkey breast (about ½ pound)
  ¼ cup thinly sliced red onion
  5 ounces Brie, sliced
  ¼ teaspoon salt
  ¼ teaspoon ground black pepper
  ½ cup trimmed arugula

1. Preheat broiler.

Continued

2. Arrange muffin halves, cut sides up, on a baking sheet. Spread 1 teaspoon mustard over each of 4 halves; top each with ½ cup turkey and one-fourth of onion. Divide cheese evenly among remaining 4 halves. Broil 2 minutes or until cheese melts and turkey is warm. Top turkey halves evenly with salt, pepper, and arugula. Top each turkey half with 1 cheese muffin half. Yield: 4 servings (serving size: 1 sandwich).

CALORIES 340 (31% from fat); FAT 11.6g (sat 6.8g, mono 3.1g, poly 0.7g); PROTEIN 29.8g; CARB 28.8g; FIBER 2.3g; CHOL 83mg; IRON 3.5mg; SODIUM 686mg; CALC 174mg

MAKE AHEAD • FREEZABLE
White Bean and Turkey Chili

Using canned beans and chicken broth makes this crowd-pleasing chili convenient.

 1 tablespoon canola oil
 2 cups diced yellow onion (about 2 medium)
1½ tablespoons chili powder
 1 tablespoon minced garlic
1½ teaspoons ground cumin
 1 teaspoon dried oregano
 3 (15.8-ounce) cans Great Northern beans, rinsed and drained
 4 cups fat-free, less-sodium chicken broth
 3 cups chopped cooked turkey
 ½ cup diced seeded plum tomato (about 1)
 ⅓ cup chopped fresh cilantro
 2 tablespoons fresh lime juice
 ½ teaspoon salt
 ½ teaspoon freshly ground black pepper
 8 lime wedges (optional)

1. Heat oil in a large Dutch oven over medium-high heat. Add onion; sauté 10 minutes or until tender and golden. Add chili powder, garlic, and cumin; sauté 2 minutes. Add oregano and beans; cook 30 seconds. Add broth; bring to a simmer. Cook 20 minutes.
2. Place 2 cups of bean mixture in a blender or food processor, and process until smooth. Return pureed mixture to pan. Add turkey, and cook 5 minutes or

until thoroughly heated. Remove from heat. Add tomato and next 4 ingredients, stirring well. Garnish with lime wedges, if desired. Yield: 8 servings (serving size: about 1 cup).

CALORIES 286 (19% from fat); FAT 6g (sat 1.2g, mono 2.1g, poly 1.6g); PROTEIN 32.4g; CARB 24.3g; FIBER 5.5g; CHOL 85mg; IRON 4.8mg; SODIUM 435mg; CALC 105mg

Turkey Pies with Mashed Potato-Asiago Topping

Chopped onions, fresh herbs, and mashed potatoes jazz up this twist on turkey potpie. Use your own leftover mashed potatoes in place of the prepared ones—you may need to cut the amount of pepper or cheese depending on how the potatoes are seasoned.

 2 teaspoons olive oil
 2 teaspoons butter
 ⅔ cup finely chopped yellow onion
 ⅓ cup minced shallots (about 3)
 ¾ cup frozen petite green peas
 2 tablespoons dry white wine
 3 cups diced cooked turkey
 1 tablespoon chopped fresh flat-leaf parsley
 1 tablespoon chopped fresh sage
1½ cups fat-free, less-sodium chicken broth
 2 tablespoons all-purpose flour
 ¾ teaspoon salt
 ¼ teaspoon freshly ground black pepper, divided
 3 cups refrigerated mashed potatoes (such as Simply Potatoes)
 ½ cup (2 ounces) finely grated Asiago cheese
Cooking spray

1. Preheat oven to 400°.
2. Heat oil and butter in a large nonstick skillet over medium heat. Add onion and shallots; cook 6 minutes or until tender, stirring frequently. Add peas and wine; cook 2 minutes. Add turkey, parsley, and sage. Combine broth and flour in a small bowl, and stir well with a whisk. Add broth mixture to pan; bring to a boil. Cook 1 minute, stirring constantly. Stir in salt and ⅛ teaspoon pepper.

3. Combine ⅛ teaspoon pepper, mashed potatoes, and cheese in a small bowl. Spoon turkey mixture evenly into each of 6 (8-ounce) ramekins coated with cooking spray. Top evenly with potato mixture. Place ramekins on a baking sheet. Bake at 400° for 20 minutes or until lightly browned and bubbly. Let stand 8 minutes before serving. Yield: 6 servings (serving size: 1 potpie).

CALORIES 283 (27% from fat); FAT 8.5g (sat 3.3g, mono 2.6g, poly 0.9g); PROTEIN 27g; CARB 23.6g; FIBER 3g; CHOL 81mg; IRON 2.3mg; SODIUM 794mg; CALC 139mg

Roast Turkey and Butternut Squash Risotto

Gently reheat the roasted turkey before adding it to the cooked risotto. That way you won't overcook the dish trying to warm the turkey thoroughly before serving.

3¾ cups fat-free, less-sodium chicken broth, divided
1½ cups water
 2 tablespoons olive oil, divided
 2 cups (½-inch) cubed peeled butternut squash (about 1¼ pounds)
 ¾ cup finely chopped shallots (about 5 medium)
 ½ cup dry white wine, divided
 1 tablespoon minced fresh sage
 ¼ teaspoon kosher salt
 ¼ teaspoon freshly ground black pepper
 1 cup dry Arborio rice
1½ cups reheated diced cooked turkey (about ¾ pound)
 ½ cup (2 ounces) crumbled goat cheese

1. Bring 3¼ cups chicken broth and 1½ cups water to a simmer in a large saucepan (do not boil). Keep mixture warm over low heat.
2. Heat 1 tablespoon oil in a Dutch oven over medium-high heat. Add squash and shallots; sauté 5 minutes or until lightly browned. Stir in ½ cup broth, ¼ cup wine, sage, salt, and pepper. Cover, reduce heat, and simmer 3 minutes or

until squash is tender. Remove squash mixture from pan, and keep warm.

3. Increase heat to medium-high; add 1 tablespoon oil and rice to pan. Sauté 2 minutes or until lightly browned. Stir in 1 cup broth mixture and ¼ cup wine; cook 5 minutes or until liquid is nearly absorbed, stirring constantly. Add remaining broth mixture, ½ cup at a time, stirring constantly until each portion of broth mixture is absorbed before adding next (about 35 minutes total). Gently stir in squash mixture and turkey. Top each serving with cheese. Yield: 4 servings (serving size: about 1¼ cups risotto and 2 tablespoons cheese).

CALORIES 456 (24% from fat); FAT 12g (sat 3.6g, mono 6g, poly 1.3g); PROTEIN 30g; CARB 58.8g; FIBER 5.7g; CHOL 69mg; IRON 3.5mg; SODIUM 595mg; CALC 121mg

Roast Turkey and Prosciutto Pizza

Top a store-bought pizza crust with balsamic-splashed turkey, peppery arugula, creamy fontina, and nutty Parmigiano-Reggiano for a quick one-dish dinner.

  1 (12-ounce) prebaked pizza crust (such as Mama Mary's)
  ¾ cup tomato and basil pasta sauce
  ½ cup (2 ounces) shredded fontina cheese
  1 cup shredded cooked turkey breast
  1 tablespoon balsamic vinegar
  ½ cup thinly sliced red onion
  ¼ cup (1 ounce) grated Parmigiano-Reggiano cheese
  ¼ teaspoon coarsely ground black pepper
  1 cup torn arugula leaves
  3 slices prosciutto, finely chopped (about 2 ounces)

1. Preheat oven to 425°.
2. Place crust on a baking sheet. Spread sauce over crust; sprinkle with fontina. Toss turkey with vinegar. Top pizza with turkey, onion, Parmigiano-Reggiano, and pepper.
3. Bake at 425° for 12 minutes or until crust is browned. Remove from oven.

Sprinkle with arugula and prosciutto. Yield: 4 servings (serving size: 1 wedge).

CALORIES 509 (29% from fat); FAT 16.4g (sat 5.5g, mono 4.3g, poly 5.6g); PROTEIN 42.4g; CARB 47.6g; FIBER 2.4g; CHOL 99mg; IRON 4.7mg; SODIUM 937mg; CALC 259mg

Gingered Noodles with Roast Turkey

  2 tablespoons dark sesame oil
  2 cups thinly sliced shiitake mushroom caps (about 3½ ounces mushrooms)
  1 cup chopped Rio or other sweet onion (about 1 large)
  1 cup chopped carrot
  1 tablespoon minced peeled fresh ginger
  2 tablespoons hoisin sauce
  2 tablespoons low-sodium soy sauce, divided
  3 cups fat-free, less-sodium chicken broth
  1 (8-ounce) package uncooked soba noodles (buckwheat noodles)
  4 cups thinly sliced napa (Chinese) cabbage (1 head)
  3 cups chopped cooked turkey breast
  ½ cup thinly sliced green onions

1. Heat oil in a large nonstick skillet over medium-high heat. Add mushroom, chopped onion, and carrot; sauté 3 minutes. Add ginger; sauté 1 minute. Stir in hoisin and 1 tablespoon soy sauce. Add broth and noodles; bring to a boil. Cover, reduce heat, and simmer 8 minutes or until noodles are done, stirring frequently. Place cabbage and turkey in a large bowl. Add noodle mixture to turkey mixture; toss gently to coat. Stir in 1 tablespoon soy sauce and green onions. Yield: 6 servings (serving size: 1⅓ cups).

CALORIES 358 (17% from fat); FAT 6.6g (sat 1g, mono 2.1g, poly 2.4g); PROTEIN 35.9g; CARB 38.6g; FIBER 2.5g; CHOL 70mg; IRON 2.9mg; SODIUM 647mg; CALC 89mg

Roast Turkey and Mushroom Pasta with White Wine Cheese Sauce

Use presliced mushrooms to shave prep time. Instead of using a high-sodium canned white sauce, our recipe employs a simple homemade, flour-thickened, creamy one.

  2 teaspoons olive oil
  5 cups sliced cremini mushrooms (about 1 pound)
  ½ cup finely chopped onion
  ½ cup finely chopped shallots (about 3 medium)
  ¾ cup dry white wine, divided
  2 teaspoons chopped fresh thyme
  1 teaspoon kosher salt, divided
  ½ teaspoon freshly ground black pepper, divided
  3 tablespoons butter
  5 tablespoons all-purpose flour
  2 cups fat-free, less-sodium chicken broth
  2 cups fat-free milk
  ¾ cup (3 ounces) grated fontina cheese
  ½ cup (2 ounces) grated fresh Parmigiano-Reggiano, divided
  6 cups hot cooked fusilli (short twisted spaghetti; about 12 ounces uncooked)
  2 cups chopped cooked turkey breast (about 1½ pounds)
Cooking spray

1. Preheat oven to 375°.
2. Heat oil in a large nonstick skillet over medium-high heat. Add mushrooms, onion, and shallots; sauté 5 minutes or until onion and shallots are lightly golden. Stir in ¼ cup wine, thyme, ½ teaspoon salt, and ¼ teaspoon pepper; cook 1 minute or until liquid evaporates, scraping pan to loosen browned bits. Set aside.
3. Melt butter in a large saucepan over medium-high heat. Add flour; cook 30 seconds, stirring constantly with a whisk. Add ½ cup wine, broth, and milk; bring to a boil, stirring constantly. Reduce heat, and cook 5 minutes or until slightly thick, stirring constantly. Remove pan from heat, and stir in
Continued

fontina, ¼ cup Parmigiano-Reggiano, ½ teaspoon salt, and ¼ teaspoon pepper. Add mushroom mixture, pasta, and turkey; toss gently to combine. Place in a 13 x 9–inch baking dish coated with cooking spray; sprinkle with ¼ cup Parmigiano-Reggiano. Bake at 375° for 12 minutes or until lightly browned. Let stand 10 minutes before serving. Yield: 8 servings (serving size: about 1½ cups).

CALORIES 458 (24% from fat); FAT 12.2g (sat 6.6g, mono 3.6g, poly 0.8g); PROTEIN 41.9g; CARB 44.7g; FIBER 2.4g; CHOL 102mg; IRON 3.6mg; SODIUM 634mg; CALC 257mg

entertaining

Freeze Now, Party Later

Appetizers you can prepare, freeze, then heat and serve as needed are a real gift this time of year.

MAKE AHEAD • FREEZABLE
Mini Turkey Burgers with Gorgonzola

½ teaspoon garlic powder
¼ teaspoon salt
¼ teaspoon freshly ground black pepper
1¼ pounds ground turkey breast
½ cup (2 ounces) crumbled Gorgonzola cheese
Cooking spray
¼ cup reduced-fat mayonnaise
2 tablespoons minced sweet gherkin pickle (about 2 small)
⅛ teaspoon freshly ground black pepper
12 (1-ounce) dinner rolls
6 curly leaf lettuce leaves, torn in half

1. Combine first 4 ingredients in a large bowl. Add cheese, stirring with a fork just until combined. Divide turkey mixture into 12 equal portions, shaping each into a ¼-inch-thick patty.
2. Heat a large nonstick skillet over medium-high heat. Coat pan with cooking

spray. Add 4 patties; cook 2 minutes. Carefully turn patties over; cook 2 minutes or until done. Place patties on a large baking sheet in a single layer. Repeat procedure twice with remaining patties. Cool patties to room temperature. Cover with plastic wrap; freeze until firm. Place in a single layer in zip-top plastic bags; freeze up to 3 months.
3. Thaw patties overnight in refrigerator.
4. Preheat oven to 400°.
5. Coat a large baking sheet with cooking spray. Place patties on baking sheet in a single layer; cover with foil. Bake at 400° for 10 minutes or until thoroughly heated. Keep warm.
6. Combine mayonnaise, pickle, and ⅛ teaspoon pepper in a small bowl. Cut rolls in half horizontally. Spread about 1 teaspoon mayonnaise mixture on bottom half of each roll; top each with 1 turkey patty and 1 piece lettuce. Cover with tops of rolls. Serve immediately. Yield: 12 servings (serving size: 1 burger).

CALORIES 169 (26% from fat); FAT 4.9g (sat 1.9g, mono 1.1g, poly 0.4g); PROTEIN 14.5g; CARB 17.1g; FIBER 0.9g; CHOL 23mg; IRON 1.3mg; SODIUM 374mg; CALC 62mg

MAKE AHEAD • FREEZABLE
Chicken and Black Bean Taquitos with Adobo Sour Cream

TAQUITOS:
1½ teaspoons olive oil
½ pound diced skinless, boneless chicken breast
1 cup (4 ounces) preshredded reduced-fat 4-cheese Mexican blend cheese
½ cup canned black beans, rinsed and drained
1 (4-ounce) can diced green chiles, undrained
10 (8-inch) flour tortillas
Cooking spray

ADOBO SOUR CREAM:
1 cup reduced-fat sour cream
2 tablespoons chopped fresh cilantro
2 to 3 teaspoons minced chipotle chile, canned in adobo sauce

1. To prepare taquitos, heat oil in a large nonstick skillet over medium heat. Add chicken, and sauté 5 minutes or until done. Place chicken in a food processor. Add cheese, beans, and green chiles; pulse 15 times or until beans are coarsely chopped.
2. Spoon about 3 tablespoons chicken mixture across lower third of each tortilla; roll up. Cut each tortilla in half; secure with wooden picks. Place taquitos in a large zip-top plastic bag; freeze up to 3 months.
3. Preheat oven to 400°.
4. Place frozen taquitos on a large baking sheet coated with cooking spray. Bake at 400° for 10 minutes; turn taquitos, and coat with cooking spray. Bake an additional 10 minutes or until golden.
5. To prepare adobo sour cream, combine sour cream, cilantro, and chipotle chile. Stir well. Serve with taquitos. Yield: 20 servings (serving size: 1 taquito and about 2½ teaspoons dip).

CALORIES 125 (30% from fat); FAT 4.1g (sat 1.8g, mono 1.2g, poly 0.5g); PROTEIN 6.9g; CARB 15.3g; FIBER 1.1g; CHOL 13mg; IRON 1.1mg; SODIUM 250mg; CALC 79mg

---

Cold Facts on Freezing

To ensure your food doesn't suffer during freezing and thawing, follow a few guidelines:

• Freezer temperature should be below 0° to freeze foods safely.

• The faster foods freeze, the less they will be affected by the process. Chill freshly prepared foods in the refrigerator. Then, before freezing, wrap or package them tightly—with freezer-safe plastic wrap, zip-top plastic bags, or airtight plastic containers—in small portions, which will freeze faster than larger helpings.

• Label each bag or container with the date and contents. Also, include instructions for reheating on the label, if desired, as a reminder for yourself and others.

• To avoid food safety problems, always thaw frozen appetizers in the refrigerator, not at room temperature.

Turkey Empanaditas

Chill the filling before forming the empanaditas to help the dough stay tender. Rotate the baking sheets halfway through baking to ensure even browning. Serve with salsa verde.

FILLING:

Cooking spray
12 ounces ground turkey breast
2 teaspoons chili powder
1 teaspoon ground cumin
½ teaspoon salt
¼ teaspoon freshly ground black pepper
½ cup water
1 (6-ounce) can no-salt-added tomato paste
1 cup reduced-fat shredded Cheddar cheese

DOUGH:

3 cups all-purpose flour (about 13½ ounces)
1½ teaspoons baking powder
1 teaspoon sugar
¼ teaspoon salt
¼ cup chilled butter, cut into small pieces
¾ cup ice water

1. To prepare filling, heat a large skillet over medium-high heat. Coat pan with cooking spray. Add turkey, and cook 5 minutes or until browned, stirring to crumble. Stir in chili powder and next 3 ingredients; cook 1 minute, stirring frequently. Stir in ½ cup water and tomato paste. Cook 2 minutes or until turkey mixture thickens. Remove from heat; stir in cheese. Place in a bowl, and cool to room temperature; cover and chill 30 minutes.

2. To prepare dough, lightly spoon flour into dry measuring cups; level with a knife. Place flour and next 3 ingredients in a food processor; pulse 2 times or until combined. Add butter; pulse 4 times or until mixture resembles coarse meal. With processor on, add ¾ cup ice water through food chute, processing just until combined (do not form a ball). Turn dough out onto a floured surface; knead lightly 4 times with floured hands.

3. Divide dough into 24 equal portions. Place 1 portion on a floured surface (cover remaining portions to keep dough from drying); roll into a 3½-inch circle. Spoon 1 rounded tablespoon turkey mixture onto half of circle. Fold dough over filling; press edges together to seal. Place on a large baking sheet. Repeat procedure with remaining dough and filling. Cover with plastic wrap; freeze until firm. Place in zip-top plastic bags; freeze up to 3 months.

4. Preheat oven to 400°.

5. Place frozen empanaditas on 2 baking sheets coated with cooking spray. Bake at 400° for 30 minutes or until bottoms are golden brown and tops begin to brown. Serve warm. Yield: 24 servings (serving size: 1 empanadita).

CALORIES 110 (28% from fat); FAT 3.4g (sat 2g, mono 0.5g, poly 0.2g); PROTEIN 6.5g; CARB 13.8g; FIBER 0.8g; CHOL 14mg; IRON 1.1mg; SODIUM 135mg; CALC 59mg

Crab Cakes with Chive Sauce

We brown the cakes before freezing them, so they go from the freezer to the table in less than 30 minutes.

CRAB CAKES:

½ cup reduced-fat mayonnaise
3 tablespoons quick-cooking oats
2 tablespoons dry breadcrumbs
2 teaspoons chopped fresh oregano
1 teaspoon Old Bay seasoning
1 teaspoon chopped fresh parsley
1 teaspoon Dijon mustard
¼ teaspoon freshly ground black pepper
2 pounds lump crabmeat, shell pieces removed
Cooking spray

SAUCE:

6 tablespoons plain fat-free yogurt
6 tablespoons reduced-fat mayonnaise
2 tablespoons chopped fresh chives
½ teaspoon fresh lemon juice
⅛ teaspoon ground red pepper

1. To prepare crab cakes, combine first 9 ingredients in a large bowl, stirring gently

just until mixture is combined and will hold a shape. Divide mixture into 30 equal portions (about 2 tablespoons each), shaping each into a 2-inch patty.

2. Heat a large nonstick skillet over medium-high heat. Coat pan with cooking spray. Add 8 patties; cook 2 minutes. Carefully turn patties over. Cook 2 minutes or until golden. Place patties on a large baking sheet in a single layer. Repeat procedure with cooking spray and remaining patties. Cover patties with plastic wrap, and freeze until firm. Place in zip-top plastic bags; freeze up to 3 months.

3. Thaw cakes overnight in refrigerator.

4. Preheat oven to 400°.

5. Coat a large baking sheet with cooking spray; place patties on baking sheet in a single layer. Bake at 400° for 20 minutes or until thoroughly heated.

6. To prepare sauce, combine yogurt and remaining 4 ingredients in a small bowl. Serve with crab cakes. Yield: 15 servings (serving size: 2 crab cakes and about 2½ teaspoons sauce).

CALORIES 96 (29% from fat); FAT 3.1g (sat 0.6g, mono 0.2g, poly 0.5g); PROTEIN 12.8g; CARB 3.8g; FIBER 0.2g; CHOL 61mg; IRON 0.7mg; SODIUM 351mg; CALC 74mg

Phyllo Knishes

Freeze in an airtight container instead of zip-top plastic bags because frozen phyllo can be fragile. Serve with bottled chutney.

1 pound Yukon gold potatoes, peeled and cut into 2-inch pieces
2 tablespoons reduced-fat sour cream
½ teaspoon salt-free garlic and herb seasoning
¼ teaspoon salt
⅛ teaspoon freshly ground black pepper
2 tablespoons chopped green onions
18 (14 x 9–inch) sheets frozen phyllo dough, thawed
Cooking spray

Continued

1. Place potatoes in a saucepan; cover with water. Bring to a boil. Reduce heat, and simmer 15 minutes or until tender; drain. Return potatoes to pan. Add sour cream and next 3 ingredients; mash with a fork or potato masher until smooth. Stir in onions. Cool to room temperature.

2. Place 1 phyllo sheet on a large cutting board or work surface; layer with 2 additional phyllo sheets (cover remaining dough to keep from drying). Cut phyllo stack in half crosswise. Top each half with about 2 tablespoons potato mixture, leaving ½-inch borders. Roll up jelly-roll fashion, starting with short side. Tuck ends under; place rolls, seam sides down, on a baking sheet coated with cooking spray. Repeat with remaining phyllo and potato mixture to total 12 knishes. Lightly coat knish tops with cooking spray. Place knishes in an airtight container; freeze up to 3 months.

3. Preheat oven to 400°.

4. Place frozen knishes on a baking sheet coated with cooking spray. Bake at 400° for 25 minutes or until browned and crisp. Serve immediately. Yield: 12 servings (serving size: 1 knish).

CALORIES 120 (15% from fat); FAT 2g (sat 0.6g, mono 1g, poly 0.3g); PROTEIN 3g; CARB 21.9g; FIBER 1g; CHOL 1mg; IRON 1.2mg; SODIUM 190mg; CALC 7mg

---

MAKE AHEAD • FREEZABLE
Pork Pot Stickers

Look for round gyoza skins or wonton wrappers in most supermarkets or in Asian groceries.

Cooking spray
8 ounces lean ground pork
⅓ cup chopped green onions (about 2)
1 tablespoon low-sodium soy sauce
1 teaspoon sesame oil
1½ cups packaged cabbage-and-carrot coleslaw
3 tablespoons water
½ teaspoon cornstarch
30 gyoza skins
1 tablespoon peanut oil
1 cup water

1. Heat a large nonstick skillet over medium-high heat. Coat pan with cooking spray. Add pork; cook 6 minutes or until done, stirring to crumble. Add onions, soy sauce, and sesame oil; cook 30 seconds. Stir in coleslaw, and cook 30 seconds or until cabbage wilts, stirring frequently.

2. Combine 3 tablespoons water and cornstarch in a small bowl. Add cornstarch mixture to pork mixture; cook 1 minute, stirring constantly. Remove from heat; cool to room temperature.

3. Working with 1 gyoza skin at a time (cover remaining skins to prevent drying), spoon 1 scant tablespoon pork mixture into center of each skin. Moisten edges of skin with water. Fold in half, pinching edges together to seal. Place on a baking sheet in a single layer (cover loosely with a towel to prevent drying). When all skins are filled, remove towel and cover with plastic wrap; freeze until firm. Place in zip-top plastic bags, and freeze up to 3 months.

4. Arrange frozen pot stickers in a single layer on a baking sheet; cover with plastic wrap, and thaw in refrigerator overnight.

5. Heat peanut oil in a large nonstick skillet over medium heat. Arrange pot stickers in pan in a single layer; cook 2 minutes or until browned on bottom. Add 1 cup water to pan; cover and cook 5 minutes. Uncover and cook until liquid evaporates, about 2 minutes. Serve immediately. Yield: 10 servings (serving size: 3 pot stickers).

CALORIES 118 (30% from fat); FAT 3.9g (sat 1.1g, mono 0.8g, poly 0.6g); PROTEIN 7g; CARB 14g; FIBER 1.1g; CHOL 17mg; IRON 0.7mg; SODIUM 190mg; CALC 8mg

---

in season

Cranberry Harvest

For Martha's Vineyard's Wampanoag people, these tart, nutritious berries have been a source of sustenance for centuries.

MAKE AHEAD
Cranberry-Orange Ginger Chutney

Try this tangy condiment with roast turkey, pork, or chicken, or on breakfast toast.

1 teaspoon olive oil
½ cup minced shallots
1 tablespoon finely chopped peeled fresh ginger
¼ cup fresh orange juice
2 cups fresh or frozen cranberries, thawed
½ cup sugar
2 tablespoons cider vinegar
¼ teaspoon kosher salt
¼ teaspoon ground allspice

1. Heat oil in a medium saucepan over medium heat. Add shallots and ginger; cook 5 minutes or until golden, stirring occasionally. Add juice, scraping pan to loosen browned bits. Add cranberries and remaining ingredients. Reduce heat; simmer 15 minutes or until slightly thickened. Cover and chill 2 hours. Yield: 6 servings (serving size: ¼ cup).

CALORIES 102 (7% from fat); FAT 0.8g (sat 0.1g, mono 0.6g, poly 0.1g); PROTEIN 0.6g; CARB 24.1g; FIBER 1.6g; CHOL 0mg; IRON 0.3mg; SODIUM 81mg; CALC 10mg

---

QUICK & EASY • MAKE AHEAD
Cranberry Syrup

Serve warm over pancakes, or use as a glaze for chicken or ham.

1 cup fresh or frozen cranberries, thawed
½ cup maple syrup
¼ cup sugar
¼ cup water
⅛ teaspoon salt
1 tablespoon lemon juice

1. Combine first 5 ingredients in a saucepan; bring to a boil. Reduce heat; simmer 8 minutes or until cranberries pop, stirring occasionally. Stir in juice. Yield: 10 servings (serving size: 2 tablespoons).

CALORIES 66 (0% from fat); FAT 0g; PROTEIN 0g; CARB 17g; FIBER 0.4g; CHOL 0mg; IRON 0.2mg; SODIUM 31mg; CALC 12mg

Stuffed Pork Loin with Caramelized Onion–Cranberry Sauce

For the deepest flavor, caramelize the onions in the same pan you use to brown the pork loin. Substitute apple for pear in the stuffing, if you prefer. Garnish with flat-leaf parsley.

    1   (2-pound) boneless pork loin
        roast, trimmed
    2   cups cranberry juice
    1   cup water
    ¼   cup kosher salt
    2   tablespoons sugar
    ¾   cup Bosc pear, diced (about 1 large)
    ¼   cup (1 ounce) crumbled blue
        cheese
    2   tablespoons dried cranberries,
        chopped
    ⅛   teaspoon salt
    ⅛   teaspoon freshly ground black
        pepper
    1   tablespoon olive oil
    Cooking spray
    1   cup minced onion
    1   cup fresh or frozen cranberries,
        thawed
    ½   cup cranberry juice
    3   tablespoons sugar

1. Cut horizontally through center of roast, cutting to, but not through, other side using a sharp knife; open flat as you would a book. Place roast between 2 sheets of plastic wrap; pound to a ¼-inch thickness using a meat mallet or small heavy skillet.

2. Combine 2 cups juice and next 3 ingredients in a large bowl; stir until sugar and salt dissolve. Pour juice mixture into a large zip-top plastic bag. Add roast to bag; seal. Marinate in refrigerator 4 hours, turning occasionally. Remove roast from bag, and pat dry; discard marinade.

3. Preheat oven to 350°.

4. Combine pear, cheese, and dried cranberries; sprinkle over roast, leaving a ½-inch margin around edges. Roll up roast, jelly-roll fashion, starting with long side. Secure at 2-inch intervals with twine. Sprinkle with ⅛ teaspoon salt and pepper.

5. Heat oil in a large nonstick skillet over medium-high heat. Add roast; cook 5 minutes, turning to brown on all sides. Place roast on a broiler pan coated with cooking spray. Bake at 350° for 40 minutes or until a thermometer registers 160° (slightly pink). Let stand 15 minutes before slicing; cut roast into ¼-inch-thick slices.

6. While roast bakes, add onion to skillet; sauté 8 minutes or until onion is browned, stirring frequently. Add fresh cranberries, ½ cup juice, and 3 tablespoons sugar to pan, scraping pan to loosen browned bits. Reduce heat; simmer 5 minutes or until cranberries pop and sauce thickens. Serve sauce with roast. Yield: 6 servings (serving size: 3 ounces roast and about ¼ cup sauce).

CALORIES 226 (26% from fat); FAT 6.4g (sat 2.2g, mono 3.1g, poly 0.8g); PROTEIN 26.5g; CARB 14.8g; FIBER 1.4g; CHOL 67mg; IRON 0.7mg; SODIUM 584mg; CALC 38mg

Cranberry-Cherry Crumble

Serve warm with low-fat vanilla ice cream or fat-free whipped topping.

    3   cups fresh or frozen cranberries,
        thawed
    3   cups frozen pitted dark sweet
        cherries, thawed
    ¾   cup granulated sugar
    ¼   cup dried cranberries,
        chopped
    ¼   cup dried cherries, chopped
    1   tablespoon all-purpose flour
    1½ teaspoons cornstarch
    Cooking spray
    ¼   cup slivered almonds, chopped
    ¼   cup regular oats
    ¼   cup whole wheat flour (about 1⅛
        ounces)
    ¼   cup packed brown sugar
    ¼   teaspoon salt
    ⅛   teaspoon ground nutmeg
    ⅛   teaspoon ground cinnamon
    ⅛   teaspoon almond extract
    2   tablespoons chilled butter, cut
        into small pieces

1. Preheat oven to 375°.

2. Combine first 7 ingredients in a large bowl, tossing gently to coat fruit. Spoon cranberry mixture into an 8-inch square baking dish coated with cooking spray.

3. Combine almonds and next 7 ingredients in a medium bowl; cut in butter with a pastry blender or 2 knives until mixture resembles coarse meal. Sprinkle oat mixture evenly over cranberry mixture. Bake at 375° for 45 minutes or until filling is bubbly and topping is golden. Yield: 8 servings.

CALORIES 265 (19% from fat); FAT 5.6g (sat 2.1g, mono 2g, poly 0.9g); PROTEIN 2.9g; CARB 53.6g; FIBER 4.5g; CHOL 8mg; IRON 1.1mg; SODIUM 99mg; CALC 37mg

Oatmeal-Cranberry Chocolate Chip Cookies

Dried cranberries add sweet-tart notes. These drop cookies would make a nice holiday gift.

    1   cup whole wheat flour (about
        4¾ ounces)
    ¼   cup all-purpose flour (about 1
        ounce)
    ¾   cup regular oats
    1   teaspoon baking soda
    ½   teaspoon salt
    1½ cups packed brown sugar
    ¼   cup butter, softened
    ¼   cup reduced-fat sour cream
    1   teaspoon vanilla extract
    2   large egg whites
    ¾   cup sweetened dried cranberries,
        coarsely chopped
    ½   cup semisweet chocolate chips

1. Preheat oven to 350°.

2. Lightly spoon flours into dry measuring cups; level with a knife. Combine flours, oats, baking soda, and salt in a medium bowl. Place sugar, butter, and sour cream in a large bowl; beat with a mixer at high speed until smooth. Add vanilla and egg whites; beat well. Gradually add flour mixture, stirring until blended. Fold in cranberries and chocolate chips.

3. Drop dough by rounded teaspoonfuls 2 inches apart onto 2 baking sheets lined

Continued

with parchment paper. Bake at 350° for 15 minutes or until edges of cookies are browned. Cool on pan 5 minutes. Remove cookies from pan; cool on wire racks. Yield: 27 servings (serving size: 2 cookies).

CALORIES 128 (23% from fat); FAT 3.3g (sat 1.8g, mono 0.8g, poly 0.3g); PROTEIN 1.8g; CARB 24.2g; FIBER 1g; CHOL 6mg; IRON 0.8mg; SODIUM 114mg; CALC 21mg

Crisp Cornish Game Hens with Spiced Cranberry-Honey Glaze

First coat the measuring cup with cooking spray; the honey will slip out easily.

HENS:
2 (1¼-pound) Cornish hens
1 teaspoon thyme, minced
½ teaspoon kosher salt
½ teaspoon freshly ground black pepper
2 garlic cloves, minced

GLAZE:
4 teaspoons olive oil, divided
1 garlic clove, minced
½ cup fresh or frozen cranberries, thawed
¼ cup cranberry juice
¼ cup honey
¼ teaspoon ground cinnamon
⅛ teaspoon ground red pepper
Cooking spray

1. Preheat oven to 425°.
2. To prepare hens, remove and discard giblets and necks from hens. Remove skin; trim excess fat. Split hens in half lengthwise. Combine thyme and next 3 ingredients. Rub hen halves with thyme mixture.
3. To prepare glaze, heat 1 teaspoon oil in a small saucepan over medium heat. Add 1 minced garlic clove; cook 1 minute. Add cranberries and next 4 ingredients, and bring to a simmer. Cook 5 minutes or until slightly syrupy.
4. Heat 1 tablespoon oil in a large nonstick skillet over medium-high heat. Add hens, breast side down; cook 3 minutes. Place hens, breast side up, on a broiler pan coated with cooking spray. Brush

hens with half of glaze. Bake at 425° for 25 minutes or until a thermometer registers 165°, brushing occasionally with remaining glaze. Yield: 4 servings (serving size: 1 hen half).

CALORIES 407 (28% from fat); FAT 12.8g (sat 2.7g, mono 5.9g, poly 2.5g); PROTEIN 49.9g; CARB 21.6g; FIBER 0.8g; CHOL 225mg; IRON 1.9mg; SODIUM 372mg; CALC 41mg

WINE NOTE: Both game birds and cranberry sauce are terrific partners for pinot noir. Because pinot noir has an earthy, sweet character, it perfectly highlights the meaty sweetness of a roasted bird. At the same time, pinot noir's good acidity is just the ticket as a complement to the cranberries. Try La Crema Pinot Noir 2004 from Russian River Valley, California ($29).

Warm Spinach Salad with Apples, Bacon, and Cranberries

To wilt the spinach, toss the salad while the dressing is still hot.

1 cup sliced Granny Smith apple (about 1 small)
¾ cup thinly sliced red onion
½ cup dried cranberries, chopped
1 (10-ounce) package fresh baby spinach
⅓ cup balsamic vinegar
2 tablespoons cranberry juice
1 tablespoon sugar
1 teaspoon Dijon mustard
¼ teaspoon salt
¼ teaspoon freshly ground black pepper
2 tablespoons reduced-fat sour cream
2 bacon slices, cooked and crumbled (drained)

1. Combine first 4 ingredients in a large bowl; toss well.
2. Combine vinegar and next 5 ingredients in a small saucepan. Bring to a boil over medium heat; cook 1 minute. Remove from heat, and stir in sour cream. Drizzle warm dressing over spinach mixture; toss well. Sprinkle

with bacon; serve immediately. Yield: 6 servings (serving size: about 2 cups).

CALORIES 117 (32% from fat); FAT 4.1g (sat 1.4g, mono 1.5g, poly 0.5g); PROTEIN 2.6g; CARB 18.5g; FIBER 2.2g; CHOL 7mg; IRON 1.5mg; SODIUM 220mg; CALC 59mg

Cranberry Vinaigrette

Serve with arugula and goat cheese for a tart, peppery salad.

1 cup cranberry juice
½ cup chopped fresh or frozen cranberries, thawed
1 tablespoon extravirgin olive oil
1 tablespoon red wine vinegar
1 tablespoon honey
2 teaspoons minced chives
⅛ teaspoon salt
⅛ teaspoon freshly ground black pepper

1. Place juice and cranberries in a small saucepan; bring to a boil. Cook until reduced to ¼ cup (about 5 minutes). Combine cranberry mixture, oil, and remaining ingredients in a small bowl; stir well with a whisk. Yield: 6 servings (serving size: 4 teaspoons).

CALORIES 53 (39% from fat); FAT 2.3g (sat 0.3g, mono 1.6g, poly 0.2g); PROTEIN 0.1g; CARB 8.4g; FIBER 0.5g; CHOL 0mg; IRON 0.1mg; SODIUM 52mg; CALC 8mg

---

Healthful Harvest

Food science has long touted the high levels of antioxidants in cranberries, and in recent clinical trials, researchers found them to contain anti-adhesion compounds that may ward off the bacteria that cause urinary tract infections and ulcers. Cranberries may also inhibit and even reverse the work of certain bacteria that cause plaque and gum disease. For more information, go to www.cranberryinstitute.org.

cooking class

Talking Turkey

With a few basic guidelines, you can choose from several cooking methods for a tender, juicy bird that will highlight your holiday meal.

Turkey, the main dish of most traditional Thanksgiving dinners, is something many of us cook only once a year. For this reason, a refresher is always useful. We consulted chef, cooking teacher, and turkey expert Rick Rodgers for pointers. Author of *Thanksgiving 101* and *The Turkey Cookbook*, among 25 other cookbooks, Rodgers has cooked more than 1,000 turkeys, by his own estimate.

Although it often causes stress for novice cooks, roasting a turkey is essentially the same process as roasting a chicken, only on a larger scale. Just follow a few guidelines, and the turkey will be the standout of your holiday meal, be it your first or your fiftieth.

High-Heat Roast Turkey

1 (12-pound) fresh turkey
2 cups chopped onion (about 1 medium)
½ cup chopped carrot (about 1 medium)
½ cup chopped celery (about 1 stalk)
2 teaspoons chopped fresh rosemary
2 teaspoons chopped fresh sage
2 teaspoons chopped fresh thyme
1 teaspoon salt, divided
1 teaspoon freshly ground black pepper, divided
2 cups water
3 cups Make-Ahead Gravy (recipe at right)

1. Preheat oven to 450°.
2. Remove and discard giblets and neck from turkey. Trim excess fat. Combine onion, next 5 ingredients, ½ teaspoon salt, and ½ teaspoon pepper in bowl. Stuff body cavity with onion mixture. Tie legs together with kitchen string. Lift wing tips up and over back; tuck under turkey. Sprinkle turkey with ½ teaspoon salt and ½ teaspoon pepper. Place turkey, breast side up, on a roasting rack in a roasting pan; pour 2 cups water into pan.
3. Bake at 450° for 1½ hours or until a thermometer inserted in meaty part of thigh registers 165°. Remove turkey from oven; let stand at least 30 minutes before carving. Discard onion mixture and skin.
4. Place a zip-top plastic bag inside a 2-cup glass measure. Pour drippings into bag; let stand 10 minutes (fat will rise to top). Seal bag; carefully snip off 1 bottom corner. Drain drippings into a bowl, stopping before fat layer reaches opening; discard fat.
5. Place roasting pan over two burners on medium heat. Add drippings and Make-Ahead Gravy, scraping pan to loosen browned bits. Reduce heat to medium-low; cook until gravy mixture is reduced to 3 cups, stirring occasionally (about 5 minutes). Serve gravy with turkey. Yield: 12 servings (serving size: 6 ounces turkey and ¼ cup gravy).

CALORIES 377 (20% from fat); FAT 8.4g (sat 3.2g, mono 2g, poly 2g); PROTEIN 67.6g; CARB 3.4g; FIBER 0.5g; CHOL 228mg; IRON 4.7mg; SODIUM 421mg; CALC 56mg

MAKE AHEAD
Make-Ahead Gravy

3 tablespoons all-purpose flour
2 tablespoons butter, softened
5 cups Roasted Turkey Stock (recipe on page 420), divided
2 teaspoons chopped fresh sage
¼ teaspoon salt
¼ teaspoon freshly ground black pepper

1. Combine flour and butter in a medium bowl.
2. Heat a large saucepan over high heat. Add 2 cups stock; bring to a boil. Cook until reduced to ½ cup (about 5 minutes). Add 3 cups stock; bring to a boil.
3. Add 1 cup stock to flour mixture, stirring with a whisk until smooth. Pour mixture into saucepan; reduce heat to medium-low, and cook until thickened, about 5 minutes. Stir in sage, salt, and pepper. Yield: 12 servings (serving size: ¼ cup).

CALORIES 29 (75% from fat); FAT 2.4g (sat 1.3g, mono 0.7g, poly 0.2g); PROTEIN 0.4g; CARB 1.6g; FIBER 0.1g; CHOL 6mg; IRON 0.1mg; SODIUM 63mg; CALC 2mg

---

Temperatures

Earlier in the year, the United States Department of Agriculture lowered its recommended safe minimum internal temperature for poultry from 180° to 165°. Also, the USDA advises keeping the bird in the oven until it has reached 165°, rather than pulling it from the heat five or 10 degrees earlier and letting the temperature rise as it rests. "That's because we're just not sure how much the temperature will rise," says USDA meat and poultry hotline manager Diane Van.

Still, Rick Rodgers recommends cooking the turkey to 180°; he feels dark meat might be tough if cooked only to 165°. We find cooking turkey to 165° yields juicier white meat than higher temperatures. "If consumers cook to higher temperatures for taste, that's their choice," Van says.

Buy the Right Bird

We favor fresh turkeys over frozen because we prefer their texture, flavor, and moistness. But there are other considerations. You can also choose among organic, heritage-breed, and free-range birds.

Heritage-breed turkeys, such as Bourbon Red and Narragansett, have stronger-flavored meat than their hybrid counterparts.

Fresh organic turkeys can be considerably more expensive than mainstream frozen ones, and heritage breeds are most expensive of all. (For a comparison of turkey types, see "Turkey Test," page 417.)

Gear Up

A fundamental piece of turkey-roasting equipment is a high-quality, thick-construction roasting pan with solid handles. Some models may cost $150 or more, but you can find a suitable roasting pan for about $40. (Measure the pan before purchasing to be sure it fits comfortably in your oven.)

Lesser vessels, particularly disposable aluminum pans, can't compare. Disposable roasting pans aren't sturdy enough to support a heavy bird.

Roasting pans with nonstick surfaces are superior for making gravy. Some might argue that nonstick surfaces don't properly develop browned bits while cooking on the stove top. However, when the dark-colored nonstick surface is surrounded by heat in the oven, it helps the roasting juices caramelize, leading to richer gravy. The roasting pan should also be equipped with a sturdy wire rack, which allows hot air to circulate beneath the bird and keeps it from sitting in its drippings.

A good meat thermometer is another essential tool. Use a digital probe thermometer with a readout that stands outside the oven, so you don't have to open the oven door to check the temperature (each time you open the oven door, the temperature drops 25° to 50°). Use pop-up thermometers as a backup only.

Use a bulb baster to moisten the turkey skin as it roasts. Because we call for discarding the skin before serving, basting merely serves to enhance the appearance of the turkey if you bring it to the table. While basting will help brown the skin, the liquid will not penetrate the skin into the meat.

Also important: an oven thermometer. Although your oven dial is set, the actual temperature may be significantly higher or lower because oven settings become uncalibrated over time.

Store and Handle Correctly

Buy a fresh turkey no more than two days before cooking. If you choose a frozen bird, allow 24 hours defrosting time for every five pounds. Defrost the turkey in the refrigerator, never at room temperature, which would allow harmful bacteria to grow. Be certain that the turkey has thawed completely before roasting, or the meat will cook unevenly. Whether fresh or frozen, keep the turkey in a shallow pan in the refrigerator to catch any drips.

The United States Department of Agriculture no longer calls for rinsing whole turkeys before roasting. Rinsing turkey in a sink can be an unwieldy process and is likely to splash water and spread bacteria.

To guard against cross contamination, wash knives or cutting boards that have come in contact with raw turkey before using them again. Similarly, be sure to wash your hands thoroughly after handling raw turkey so you don't potentially spread bacteria to other food.

Cook to Perfection

The basic challenge with turkey is that white meat cooks faster than dark. To mitigate this problem, cover the turkey breast with foil for most techniques (except for high-heat roasting). The foil deflects the heat and slows the cooking time for the breast.

Rest Before Carving

Let the turkey rest for at least 30 minutes before carving. If you carve too soon, juices will flood out, and you'll be left with dry meat. Resting allows the juices to settle, resulting in moister turkey. While half an hour may seem like a long time to let the turkey stand, it won't cool off.

When it comes time to carve, make sure that the carving knife is sharp. Inexperienced carvers may want to slice the bird in the kitchen to avoid the gaze of a tableside audience. First, remove and discard the skin. Remove the thigh quarters by cutting through the joint where the thigh attaches to the body. Then cut through the joint that attaches the leg to the thigh. Serve these pieces whole, or cut meat away from the bone, depending on demand for dark meat. Carve white meat by slicing parallel to the breast, or cut the breast off entirely and then slice it crosswise.

Bags and Brining

Two other turkey techniques: oven bags and brining. Oven bags produce tender meat, but the turkey steams, and it may taste more like stew than anything else.

Brining is a process that requires a method of holding the turkey in a chilled, salted marinade for 12 to 24 hours. Place the turkey in a double layer of oven bags, cover it in brine, then place the sealed bag in an ice chest and add ice packs. The procedure can be cumbersome and can change the flavor and texture of the meat. Nevertheless, we have had success with brined turkeys in the past.

Turkey Test

We conducted an in-house taste test of four basic types of turkey: frozen, fresh, organic, and heritage breed. Our Test Kitchens roasted each turkey the same way, following the High-Heat Roast Turkey recipe (page 415). Each had its strengths and weaknesses, and no clear winner emerged. Rather, we found that the bird that's best depends on your tastes, needs, and cooking methods.

Type	Pros	Cons	Cost	Our Findings
Frozen	Available at any supermarket; cheaper than other types	Needs considerable time to thaw; may be injected with saline solution	About $1.25 to $1.50 per pound	Moist and salty throughout (presumably because the turkey had been injected with a flavored saline solution to keep it moist). But the same solution seemed to make the meat taste like chicken broth rather than turkey.
Fresh	Doesn't need time to thaw; the texture of the meat hasn't been affected by freezing	Not as widely available as frozen turkey	About $1.40 to $2.30 per pound	Slightly stringy texture; tasters thought the bird might benefit from roasting at a much lower temperature or even brining.
Organic	Free of pesticides, antibiotics, and other foreign substances	More difficult to track down than frozen turkeys, though they're becoming more readily available	$5 to $7 per pound	Dense meat that some tasters considered full-flavored, others thought gamey. Low-temperature roasting would be the best approach.
Heritage	The oldest pure breeds of turkey, they're free range and don't contain antibiotics or additives.	Not widely available; will probably be shipped frozen to you	$7 or more per pound	Strong turkey taste, not particularly juicy, with much less white meat than a commercially bred bird. This turkey rendered more fat in the pan than other types.

Turkey with Sausage, Apricot, and Sage Stuffing

1 pound sweet turkey Italian sausage (about 4 links)
2 cups chopped onion (about 1 large)
1 cup chopped celery (about 4 stalks)
1¼ cups coarsely chopped dried apricots
¼ cup chopped fresh parsley
1 tablespoon chopped fresh sage
¼ teaspoon salt
¼ teaspoon freshly ground black pepper
1 (14-ounce) package country-style stuffing mix (such as Pepperidge Farm)
3¼ cups hot Roasted Turkey Stock (recipe on page 420)
1 (12-pound) fresh or frozen turkey, thawed
Cooking spray
1 tablespoon canola oil
½ teaspoon salt
½ teaspoon freshly ground black pepper
3 cups water, divided

1. Preheat oven to 325°.

2. Remove casings from sausage. Heat a large nonstick skillet over medium-high heat. Add sausage; cook 5 minutes or until browned, stirring to crumble. Add onion and celery. Cover, reduce heat, and cook 10 minutes or until tender, stirring occasionally.

3. Place sausage mixture in a large bowl. Add apricots and next 5 ingredients. Drizzle with hot Roasted Turkey Stock; toss well. Remove and discard giblets and neck from turkey. Trim excess fat. Do not trim excess skin around neck. Lift wing tips up and over back; tuck under turkey. Stuff 2 cups sausage mixture into neck cavity. Fold skin over sausage mixture, and loosely secure with several wooden picks. Stuff 3 cups sausage mixture into body cavity. Spoon remaining sausage mixture into an 11 x 7–inch baking dish coated with cooking spray. Cover dish with foil, and refrigerate until ready to bake. Tie legs together with kitchen string. Place turkey, breast side up, on a roasting rack in a roasting pan.

Brush turkey with oil; sprinkle with ½ teaspoon salt and ½ teaspoon pepper. Cover breast with foil. Pour 2 cups water into pan.

4. Bake at 325° for 2 hours; remove foil, and baste turkey with pan juices. Add 1 cup water to pan, if needed. Bake an additional 2 hours or until thermometer inserted in meaty part of thigh registers 165°, basting every 30 minutes. Remove turkey from oven; let stand at least 30 minutes before carving. Remove and discard wooden picks.

5. Increase oven temperature to 350°. Bake remaining stuffing, covered, 25 minutes or until thoroughly heated. Serve with turkey. Yield: 12 servings (serving size: 6 ounces turkey and about 1 cup stuffing).

CALORIES 506 (21% from fat); FAT 11.5g (sat 2.8g, mono 4g, poly 3.1g); PROTEIN 79.6g; CARB 38.1g; FIBER 3.2g; CHOL 251mg; IRON 7mg; SODIUM 872mg; CALC 74mg

Six Steps to Great Turkey

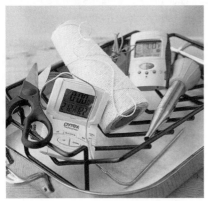

1. *Equipment: Roasting pan, roasting rack, remote-read digital thermometer, bulb baster, oven thermometer, kitchen twine, kitchen shears, and foil.*

2. *Trim excess fat.*

3. *Tie legs together with kitchen twine for an attractive presentation. Lift wing tips up and over back; tuck under turkey.*

4. *Cover breast with foil to keep the white meat from cooking too fast.*

5. *Check temperature in meaty part of thigh, making sure not to touch bone. The turkey is ready when the thermometer registers 165°.*

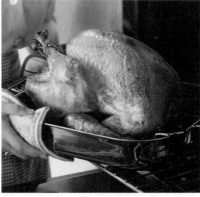

6. *Once you've presented the finished turkey to guests, remove and discard the skin to dramatically reduce fat intake.*

Turkey Techniques

We present five techniques for turkey. Our Classic Roast Turkey (recipe on page 419) is slow-roasted at 325° for about two and a half hours. (Because of such variables as actual oven temperature and how cold the turkey is when it goes in the oven, cooking times are approximate; rely more on your meat thermometer.) Fresh herbs in the body cavity help flavor the cooking juices, while Make-Ahead Gravy (recipe on page 415) provides the finishing touch. High-Heat Roast Turkey (recipe on page 415) cooks at 450° and takes about an hour and a half. A high-quality, heavy-duty roasting pan is imperative for this method in order to insulate the drippings and make them less likely to scorch. Clean the oven beforehand to prevent excessive smoking and, because turkey tends to splatter when cooked at high heat, do a follow-up cleaning afterward.

With the Turkey with Sausage, Apricot, and Sage Stuffing (recipe on page 417), you fill the cold bird with freshly made, warm stuffing and roast immediately. For food safety reasons, never use chilled stuffing or refrigerate a stuffed bird overnight. Don't overstuff the bird, because the stuffing will expand from the moisture, and the bird could split open from internal pressure. This dish should finish cooking in about four hours, longer than an unstuffed turkey.

Apple-Grilled Turkey (recipe on page 419) is a delicious option for people in warmer climates or die-hard grillers. Indirect grilling and applewood smoke give the turkey an attractive exterior and smoky flavor.

Provençal Turkey Breast (recipe on page 419) is ideal for a small gathering with a preference for white meat. This dish also saves time—it cooks in about an hour and 20 minutes.

Apple-Grilled Turkey with Cider Gravy

2 cups applewood chips, divided
1 (12-pound) fresh or frozen turkey, thawed
2 cups chopped onion (about 1 medium)
2 cups chopped Granny Smith apple (about 1)
1 tablespoon chopped fresh sage
1 teaspoon salt, divided
1 teaspoon freshly ground black pepper, divided
1 tablespoon canola oil
1 (12-ounce) bottle hard apple cider
3 cups Make-Ahead Gravy (recipe on page 415)

1. Soak wood chips in water 30 minutes. Drain well.

2. Remove and discard giblets and neck from turkey. Trim excess fat. Combine onion, apple, sage, ½ teaspoon salt, and ½ teaspoon pepper in a bowl. Stuff body cavity with onion mixture. Tie legs together with kitchen string. Lift wing tips up and over back; tuck under turkey. Brush turkey with oil; sprinkle with ½ teaspoon salt and ½ teaspoon pepper. Cover breast with foil. Place turkey in a disposable aluminum foil pan.

3. To prepare grill for indirect grilling, preheat grill, heating one side to medium and leaving one side with no heat. Maintain temperature at 350°.

4. Place 1 cup wood chips on hot coals. Place pan on unheated side of grill. Cover and cook 45 minutes. Place 1 cup wood chips on hot coals; cover and cook 45 minutes. Add coals as needed to maintain temperature at 350°. Remove foil from breast; cover and cook 35 minutes or until a thermometer inserted in meaty part of thigh registers 165°. Remove turkey from grill; let stand at least 30 minutes before carving. Discard onion mixture and skin.

5. Place a zip-top plastic bag inside a 2-cup glass measure. Pour drippings from pan into bag; let stand 10 minutes (fat will rise to top). Seal bag; carefully snip off 1 bottom corner. Drain drippings into a bowl, stopping before fat layer reaches opening; discard fat.

6. Place cider in a large saucepan; bring to a boil. Cook until reduced to ¾ cup (about 4 minutes). Add pan drippings and Make-Ahead Gravy; bring to a boil. Cook until reduced to 3 cups (about 5 minutes). Yield: 12 servings (serving size: 6 ounces turkey and ¼ cup gravy).

CALORIES 394 (22% from fat); FAT 9.5g (sat 3.3g, mono 2.7g, poly 2.3g); PROTEIN 67.4g; CARB 2.9g; FIBER 0.1g; CHOL 228mg; IRON 4.6mg; SODIUM 363mg; CALC 48mg

Provençal Turkey Breast with Jus

1 (5-pound) whole turkey breast
1 tablespoon dried herbes de Provence
¾ teaspoon salt
½ teaspoon freshly ground black pepper
2 garlic cloves, minced
1 tablespoon olive oil
12 garlic cloves, unpeeled
2 cups Roasted Turkey Stock (recipe on page 420)
¾ cup dry white wine
⅛ teaspoon salt
⅛ teaspoon freshly ground black pepper

1. Preheat oven to 400°.

2. Loosen skin from breast by inserting fingers, gently pushing between skin and meat. Combine herbes de Provence and next 3 ingredients in a small bowl. Rub seasoning mixture under loosened skin. Rub turkey with oil. Place 12 garlic cloves in a roasting pan; place turkey on cloves. Bake at 400° for 1 hour and 15 minutes or until a thermometer registers 165°. Let stand 15 minutes. Discard skin. Squeeze cloves to extract garlic pulp. Set aside. Discard skins.

3. Place a zip-top plastic bag inside a 2-cup glass measure. Pour drippings from pan into bag; let stand 10 minutes (fat will rise to top). Seal bag; carefully snip off 1 bottom corner. Drain drippings into a bowl, stopping before fat layer reaches opening; discard fat.

4. Place roasting pan over 2 burners on medium heat. Add pan drippings, Roasted Turkey Stock, white wine, and reserved garlic, scraping pan to loosen browned bits. Cook 10 minutes or until reduced to 1½ cups. Stir in ⅛ teaspoon salt and ⅛ teaspoon pepper. Serve with turkey. Yield: 8 servings (serving size: 4 ounces turkey and 3 tablespoons jus).

CALORIES 266 (11% from fat); FAT 3.3g (sat 0.7g, mono 1.6g, poly 0.6g); PROTEIN 53.7g; CARB 2.2g; FIBER 0.2g; CHOL 147mg; IRON 2.9mg; SODIUM 353mg; CALC 34mg

Classic Roast Turkey with Fresh Herbs and Make-Ahead Gravy

1 (12-pound) fresh or frozen turkey, thawed
2 cups chopped onion (about 1 medium)
½ teaspoon salt
½ teaspoon freshly ground black pepper
6 thyme sprigs, coarsely chopped
6 sage sprigs, coarsely chopped
6 marjoram sprigs, coarsely chopped
6 parsley sprigs, coarsely chopped
4 rosemary sprigs, coarsely chopped
1 tablespoon canola oil
½ teaspoon salt
½ teaspoon freshly ground black pepper
2 cups water
1 cup water (optional)
3 cups Make-Ahead Gravy (recipe on page 415)
2 teaspoons chopped fresh sage

1. Preheat oven to 325°.

2. Remove and discard giblets and neck from turkey. Trim excess fat. Combine onion and next 7 ingredients in a small bowl. Stuff body cavity with onion mixture. Tie legs together with kitchen string. Lift wing tips up and over back; tuck under turkey. Brush turkey with canola oil; sprinkle with ½ teaspoon salt and ½ teaspoon pepper. Cover breast with foil. Place turkey, breast side up, on a roasting rack in a roasting pan. Pour 2 cups water into pan.

3. Bake at 325° for 1½ hours; remove foil, and baste turkey with pan juices.
Continued

Add 1 cup water to pan, if needed. Bake an additional hour or until a thermometer inserted in meaty part of thigh registers 165°, basting every 30 minutes. Remove turkey from oven; let stand at least 30 minutes before carving. Discard onion mixture and skin.

4. Place a zip-top plastic bag inside a 2-cup glass measure. Pour drippings from pan into bag; let stand 10 minutes (fat will rise to top). Seal bag; carefully snip off 1 bottom corner. Drain drippings into a bowl, stopping before fat layer reaches opening; discard fat.

5. Place roasting pan over 2 burners on medium heat. Add turkey drippings, Make-Ahead Gravy, and 2 teaspoons chopped fresh sage, scraping pan to loosen browned bits. Reduce heat, and cook until gravy mixture is reduced to 3 cups, stirring occasionally (about 5 minutes). Serve with turkey. Yield: 12 servings (serving size: 6 ounces turkey and ¼ cup gravy).

CALORIES 380 (23% from fat); FAT 9.5g (sat 3.3g, mono 2.7g, poly 2.3g); PROTEIN 67.4g; CARB 1.7g; FIBER 0.1g; CHOL 228mg; IRON 4.6mg; SODIUM 363mg; CALC 49mg

MAKE AHEAD • FREEZABLE
Roasted Turkey Stock

3 pounds turkey wings
1 gallon water, divided
2 teaspoons canola oil
2 cups chopped onion (about 1 medium)
½ cup chopped carrot (about 1 medium)
½ cup chopped celery (about 1 stalk)
½ teaspoon black peppercorns
½ teaspoon dried thyme
4 parsley sprigs
1 bay leaf

1. Preheat oven to 450°.
2. Place wings in a single layer on a jelly-roll pan. Bake at 450° for 1 hour or until browned. Remove wings from pan. Place pan over medium-high heat; stir in 1 cup water, scraping pan to loosen browned bits. Remove from heat.
3. Heat oil in a large Dutch oven over medium-high heat. Add onion, carrot, and celery, and cook 5 minutes or until

tender. Add turkey, pan liquid, 15 cups water, peppercorns, thyme, parsley, and bay leaf. Bring to a simmer; cook 3 hours or until reduced to 12 cups. Strain through a sieve into a bowl; discard solids. Cover and chill overnight. Skim solidified fat from surface; discard. Yield: 12 cups (serving size: 2 cups).

CALORIES 24 (79% from fat); FAT 2.1g (sat 0.3g, mono 1.1g, poly 0.6g); PROTEIN 0.9g; CARB 0.4g; FIBER 0.1g; CHOL 3mg; IRON 0.2mg; SODIUM 4mg; CALC 4mg

dinner tonight

International Suppers

Take a break from the ordinary with these internationally inspired suppers.

International Menu 1
serves 4

Pork and Edamame Fried Rice
Egg rolls with dipping sauce*
Lemon sorbet

*Bake 4 frozen white-meat chicken egg rolls (such as Pagoda) according to package directions. While egg rolls bake, combine 1 tablespoon minced green onions, 2 tablespoons low-sodium soy sauce, 1 tablespoon rice vinegar, 2 tablespoons duck sauce, and 1 teaspoon Thai chili sauce (such as Sriracha). Serve sauce with egg rolls.

Game Plan

1. While water comes to a boil for the rice:
  • Preheat oven for egg rolls
  • Chop and measure ingredients for fried rice
2. While egg rolls bake:
  • Cook long-grain rice
  • Scoop sorbet into individual bowls; freeze
  • Prepare dipping sauce
3. Prepare fried rice.

QUICK & EASY
Pork and Edamame Fried Rice

The best fried rice starts with leftover cooked rice; the grains are less moist, which makes them better to "fry" than fresh-cooked rice.

TOTAL TIME: 40 MINUTES

1 (3½-ounce) bag boil-in-bag long-grain rice
3 tablespoons canola oil, divided
1 tablespoon chopped peeled fresh ginger
3 garlic cloves, minced
6 ounces pork tenderloin, trimmed and cut into thin strips
½ cup shelled edamame (green soybeans)
½ cup preshredded carrot
¾ cup diagonally cut green onions
½ cup (¼-inch-thick) slices red bell pepper, each cut in half
2 tablespoons low-sodium soy sauce
½ cup fat-free, less-sodium chicken broth
2 tablespoons chopped fresh cilantro
1½ tablespoons seasoned rice vinegar
1 tablespoon Thai chili sauce (such as Sriracha)
½ teaspoon salt
¼ teaspoon black pepper
2 tablespoons unsalted, dry-roasted peanuts

1. Cook rice according to package directions; set aside.
2. Heat ½ teaspoon oil in a wok or large nonstick skillet over medium-high heat. Add ginger and garlic; sauté 1 minute. Add pork; sauté 3 minutes or until pork loses its pink color. Place pork mixture in a large bowl; cover and keep warm.
3. Add 1 teaspoon oil to pan. Add edamame and carrot; sauté 2 minutes. Add onions and bell pepper; sauté 2 minutes. Add carrot mixture to pork mixture in bowl; keep warm.
4. Heat 2½ tablespoons oil in pan. Add cooked rice and soy sauce to pan; sauté 3 minutes. Return pork mixture to pan. Stir in broth and next 5 ingredients; cook 2 minutes or until thoroughly heated. Spoon 1½ cups fried rice onto each of

4 plates; top each serving with 1½ teaspoons peanuts. Yield: 4 servings.

CALORIES 473 (29% from fat); FAT 15.1g (sat 2.6g, mono 6.6g, poly 4.3g); PROTEIN 17.8g; CARB 64.8g; FIBER 5g; CHOL 28mg; IRON 4.2mg; SODIUM 810mg; CALC 32mg

---

International Menu 2
serves 4

Yucatán Shrimp Cocktail Salad

Jack cheese tortilla wedges*

Fresh pineapple chunks

*Sprinkle 4 (6-inch) corn tortillas with 1 teaspoon ground cumin and ¼ teaspoon crushed red pepper. Top each tortilla with 2 tablespoons shredded Monterey Jack cheese. Place tortillas on a baking sheet; broil until cheese melts. Cut each tortilla into 4 wedges.

Game Plan

1. Cook shrimp; cool.
2. While broiler heats for tortilla wedges:
   • Prepare salad ingredients
3. Broil tortilla wedges.
4. Combine salad ingredients; add shrimp.

QUICK & EASY
Yucatán Shrimp Cocktail Salad

TOTAL TIME: 30 MINUTES

Cooking spray
1½ pounds peeled and deveined medium shrimp
⅛ teaspoon ground red pepper
¼ cup fresh lime juice
2 tablespoons cider vinegar
1 tablespoon honey
½ teaspoon salt
1 cup chopped seeded peeled cucumber
1 cup halved cherry tomatoes
1 cup chopped seeded Anaheim chile
½ cup thinly sliced celery
½ cup sliced green onions
½ cup chopped fresh cilantro
½ cup diced peeled avocado

1. Heat a large nonstick skillet over medium-high heat. Coat pan with cooking spray. Add shrimp and red pepper; sauté 4 minutes. Remove from heat; set aside.
2. Combine juice, vinegar, honey, and salt in a large bowl, stirring well with a whisk. Add cucumber and remaining 6 ingredients; toss well. Add shrimp mixture; toss well. Yield: 4 servings (serving size: 1¾ cups).

CALORIES 271 (23% from fat); FAT 7g (sat 1.2g, mono 2.9g, poly 1.7g); PROTEIN 35.8g; CARB 12.8g; FIBER 2.7g; CHOL 259mg; IRON 4.7mg; SODIUM 569mg; CALC 117mg

---

QUICK & EASY
Mussels Ravigote

Mussels and fries are a classic pairing in Belgium and France. *Ravigote* is a traditional French vinegar-herb sauce that is often served with seafood.

TOTAL TIME: 25 MINUTES

¼ cup finely chopped red onion
3 tablespoons sliced cornichons
2 tablespoons chopped fresh parsley
1 tablespoon minced fresh tarragon
1 tablespoon white wine vinegar
2 teaspoons capers
1½ teaspoons extravirgin olive oil
1 teaspoon Dijon mustard
1 garlic clove, minced
1 cup dry white wine
1 (8-ounce) bottle clam juice
48 mussels (about 2 pounds), scrubbed and debearded

1. Combine first 9 ingredients in a small bowl; set aside.
2. Bring wine and clam juice to a boil in a Dutch oven. Add mussels; cover and cook 2 minutes or until shells open. Remove mussels from pan with a slotted spoon; discard any unopened shells. Keep warm.
3. Bring wine mixture to a boil over high heat; cook until reduced to ⅓ cup (about 15 minutes). Pour liquid over mussels. Add cornichon mixture; toss. Yield: 2 servings (serving size: 24 mussels and about 3 tablespoons wine mixture).

CALORIES 244 (30% from fat); FAT 8.1g (sat 1.3g, mono 3.6g, poly 1.6g); PROTEIN 24.4g; CARB 18.2g; FIBER 0.9g; CHOL 57mg; IRON 9mg; SODIUM 1,141mg; CALC 96mg

---

International Menu 3
serves 2

Mussels Ravigote

Parmesan-parsley fries*

Frozen yogurt with chopped bananas, chopped walnuts, and fat-free caramel sauce

*Cut 1 large baking potato into ¼-inch-thick strips. Combine potato strips, 2 teaspoons olive oil, and ⅛ teaspoon pepper on a baking sheet coated with cooking spray. Bake at 500° for 25 minutes or until golden, turning once after 10 minutes. Toss with 3 tablespoons grated fresh Parmesan, ¼ teaspoon salt, and 1 tablespoon chopped fresh parsley. Serve immediately.

Game Plan

1. While oven preheats:
   • Cut potato into strips
2. While fries bake:
   • Chop onion
   • Slice cornichons
   • Prepare herbs and garlic

QUICK & EASY
Black Bean and Chicken Chilaquiles

A traditional Mexican breakfast favorite, *chilaquiles* (chee-lah-KEE-lays) is a sauté of day-old tortilla strips, fresh tomato sauce, cream, and cheese. This hearty version is baked.

TOTAL TIME: 45 MINUTES

Cooking spray
1 cup thinly sliced onion
5 garlic cloves, minced
2 cups shredded cooked chicken breast
1 (15-ounce) can black beans, rinsed and drained
1 cup fat-free, less-sodium chicken broth
1 (7¾-ounce) can salsa de chile fresco (such as El Pato)
15 (6-inch) corn tortillas, cut into 1-inch strips
1 cup shredded queso blanco (about 4 ounces)

Continued

1. Preheat oven to 450°.

2. Heat a large nonstick skillet over medium-high heat. Coat pan with cooking spray. Add onion; sauté 5 minutes or until lightly browned. Add garlic; sauté 1 minute. Add chicken; cook 30 seconds. Transfer mixture to a medium bowl; stir in beans. Add broth and salsa to pan; bring to a boil. Reduce heat, and simmer 5 minutes, stirring occasionally. Set aside.

3. Place half of tortilla strips in bottom of an 11 x 7–inch baking dish coated with cooking spray. Layer half of chicken mixture over tortillas; top with remaining tortillas and chicken mixture. Pour broth mixture evenly over chicken mixture. Sprinkle with cheese. Bake at 450° for 10 minutes or until tortillas are lightly browned and cheese is melted. Yield: 6 servings.

CALORIES 293 (15% from fat); FAT 4.9g (sat 1.7g, mono 1.5g, poly 1.2g); PROTEIN 22.9g; CARB 40g; FIBER 5.9g; CHOL 46mg; IRON 2.3mg; SODIUM 602mg; CALC 200mg

---

International Menu 4

serves 6

Black Bean and Chicken Chilaquiles

Green salad*

Store-bought angel food cake with sliced strawberries and fat-free whipped topping

*Combine 11 cups torn red leaf lettuce, 2 cups plum tomato wedges, and ¾ cup thinly sliced green onions in a large bowl. Combine ¼ cup fresh lemon juice, 2 tablespoons sherry vinegar, 1 tablespoon extravirgin olive oil, 1 tablespoon Dijon mustard, and ½ teaspoon salt, stirring with a whisk. Drizzle over lettuce mixture, tossing to coat. Serve immediately.

Game Plan

1. While onion cooks:
   • Drain and rinse beans
   • Cut tortillas into strips
   • Shred cheese
2. While chilaquiles bake:
   • Prepare vinaigrette
   • Tear lettuce; slice tomatoes and onion
   • Assemble salad
3. Slice cake and strawberries.

---

superfast

. . . And Ready in Just About 20 Minutes

More than a week's worth of quick entrées to get dinner on the table in a flash

QUICK & EASY
Chicken and Mushrooms in Garlic White Wine Sauce

Substitute your favorite dried herb for the tarragon, if you prefer. Dried basil or parsley would both work in this dish.

    4   ounces uncooked medium egg
        noodles
    1   pound skinless, boneless chicken
        breast halves
    2   tablespoons all-purpose flour,
        divided
    ½   teaspoon salt, divided
    ¼   teaspoon black pepper, divided
    2   tablespoons olive oil, divided
    1   tablespoon bottled minced garlic
    ½   teaspoon dried tarragon
    1   (8-ounce) package presliced
        mushrooms
    ½   cup dry white wine
    ½   cup fat-free, less-sodium chicken
        broth
    ¼   cup grated Parmesan cheese

1. Cook noodles according to package directions, omitting salt and fat. Drain and keep warm.

2. Cut chicken into 1-inch pieces. Place in a shallow dish. Combine 1 tablespoon flour, ¼ teaspoon salt, and ⅛ teaspoon pepper, stirring well with a whisk. Sprinkle flour mixture over chicken; toss to coat.

3. Heat 1 tablespoon oil in a large nonstick skillet over medium-high heat. Add chicken to pan; sauté 4 minutes or until browned. Remove chicken from pan. Add 1 tablespoon oil to pan. Add garlic, tarragon, and mushrooms to pan; sauté

3 minutes or until liquid evaporates and mushrooms darken. Add wine to pan, and cook 1 minute. Stir in 1 tablespoon flour; cook 1 minute, stirring constantly. Stir in broth, ¼ teaspoon salt, and ⅛ teaspoon pepper; cook 1 minute or until slightly thick, stirring frequently.

4. Return chicken to pan. Cover and simmer 2 minutes. Uncover; cook 1 minute or until chicken is done. Stir in noodles; cook 1 minute or until thoroughly heated. Place about 1½ cups chicken mixture on each of 4 plates; top each serving with 1 tablespoon cheese. Yield: 4 servings.

CALORIES 350 (29% from fat); FAT 11.1g (sat 2.6g, mono 6.2g, poly 1.4g); PROTEIN 34.3g; CARB 26.5g; FIBER 1.2g; CHOL 99mg; IRON 2.5mg; SODIUM 502mg; CALC 91mg

---

QUICK & EASY
Hoisin Pork and Snow Pea Stir-Fry

The slightly sweet, soy-based hoisin sauce is to Chinese food what ketchup is to American food. Look for hoisin and rice noodles with other Asian foods in most supermarkets.

    4   ounces uncooked rice noodles or
        rice
    2   tablespoons low-sodium soy
        sauce, divided
    1   (1-pound) pork tenderloin,
        trimmed and thinly sliced
    ¾   cup fat-free, less-sodium chicken
        broth
    ¼   cup hoisin sauce
    1   tablespoon cornstarch
    1   tablespoon honey
    4   teaspoons dark sesame oil, divided
    3   cups snow peas, trimmed (about
        ½ pound)
    ½   cup sliced red bell pepper
    1   tablespoon bottled ground fresh
        ginger
    1   teaspoon bottled minced garlic
    ½   cup chopped green onions

1. Prepare noodles according to package directions, omitting salt and fat. Drain and keep warm.

2. Combine 1 tablespoon soy sauce and pork, tossing to coat. Set aside.

3. Combine 1 tablespoon soy sauce, broth, hoisin, cornstarch, and honey in a medium bowl, stirring with a whisk until smooth.

4. Heat 1 tablespoon oil in a large non-stick skillet over medium-high heat. Add pork mixture to pan; sauté 3 minutes or until browned. Remove pork from pan. Add 1 teaspoon oil to pan. Stir in peas, bell pepper, ginger, and garlic; sauté 30 seconds. Return pork mixture to pan; stir in broth mixture. Simmer 2 minutes or until thick, stirring occasionally. Remove from heat, and stir in onions. Serve over noodles. Yield: 4 servings (serving size: ¾ cup noodles and about 1 cup pork mixture).

CALORIES 395 (22% from fat); FAT 9.6g (sat 2.1g, mono 3.7g, poly 2.5g); PROTEIN 28.1g; CARB 43.7g; FIBER 2.4g; CHOL 74mg; IRON 2.5mg; SODIUM 690mg; CALC 53mg

Lowcountry Shrimp Pilaf

Serve this quick dish with a green salad and crusty bread.

1½   tablespoons canola oil
1½   cups prechopped green bell pepper
  1   cup prechopped onion
  1   tablespoon bottled minced garlic
  2   teaspoons Old Bay seasoning
  1   pound peeled and deveined large shrimp
  ½   cup dry white wine
  1   (8-ounce) bottle clam juice
1½   cups instant white rice
  2   tablespoons chopped fresh thyme, divided
  1   (14.5-ounce) can diced tomatoes with jalapeños, undrained

1. Heat oil in large nonstick skillet over medium-high heat. Add bell pepper and onion to pan; sauté 2 minutes. Add garlic and Old Bay seasoning; sauté 1 minute. Add shrimp, wine, and clam juice; bring to a boil. Stir in rice; cover and remove from heat. Let stand 5 minutes or until liquid is absorbed.

2. Place pan over medium-high heat. Stir in 1 tablespoon thyme and tomatoes; cook 2 minutes or until thoroughly heated, stirring occasionally. Sprinkle

with 1 tablespoon thyme. Yield: 4 servings (serving size: 1½ cups).

CALORIES 365 (20% from fat); FAT 8g (sat 0.8g, mono 3.5g, poly 2.4g); PROTEIN 27.8g; CARB 44.7g; FIBER 3.9g; CHOL 174mg; IRON 6mg; SODIUM 756mg; CALC 117mg

Speedy Soup and Salad Menu
serves 4

Jícama, a round root vegetable commonly found in supermarkets and Latin groceries, adds crunch to the salad. For a sweeter version, substitute apple.

Chipotle Chicken and Tomato Soup

Orange and jícama salad*

Baked tortilla chips

*Combine 2 cups orange sections, 1 cup julienne-cut jícama, and ½ cup vertically sliced red onion in a large bowl. Combine 2 tablespoons fresh lime juice, 1 tablespoon extravirgin olive oil, 1 tablespoon honey, and ¼ teaspoon salt, stirring well with a whisk. Drizzle over salad; toss gently to coat. Sprinkle 1 tablespoon chopped chives over salad.

Chipotle Chicken and Tomato Soup

A chipotle chile (canned smoked jalapeño pepper) adds smoky heat to this soup. If you want to tame the spice, substitute ½ teaspoon smoked paprika for the chile.

  ½   teaspoon ground cumin
  1   (15.5-ounce) can navy beans, rinsed and drained
  1   (14.5-ounce) can no-salt-added stewed tomatoes
  1   (14-ounce) can fat-free, less-sodium chicken broth
  1   chipotle chile, canned in adobo sauce, finely chopped
  2   cups chopped cooked chicken breast (about ½ pound)
  1   tablespoon extravirgin olive oil
  ½   cup reduced-fat sour cream
  ¼   cup chopped fresh cilantro

1. Combine first 5 ingredients in a large saucepan; bring to a boil. Cover, reduce heat, and simmer 10 minutes. Partially mash tomatoes and beans with a potato masher. Stir in chicken; cook 2 minutes or until thoroughly heated. Remove from heat; stir in oil. Place 1¼ cups soup in each of 4 bowls. Top each serving with 2 tablespoons sour cream and 1 tablespoon cilantro. Yield: 4 servings.

CALORIES 325 (28% from fat); FAT 10g (sat 3.6g, mono 4.4g, poly 1.1g); PROTEIN 28.9g; CARB 30.4g; FIBER 7.5g; CHOL 58mg; IRON 3.1mg; SODIUM 741mg; CALC 120mg

Ozark Catfish Sandwiches with Warm Pan Slaw

     Cooking spray
  3   tablespoons yellow cornmeal
  ¾   teaspoon chopped fresh thyme
  ½   teaspoon salt, divided
  ½   teaspoon black pepper, divided
  1   pound catfish fillets, cut into 4 pieces
  3   cups cabbage-and-carrot coleslaw
  1   tablespoon fresh lemon juice
  1   tablespoon fat-free mayonnaise
  4   crusty sandwich rolls, halved horizontally (about 2 ounces each)

1. Heat a large nonstick skillet over medium-high heat. Coat pan with cooking spray. Combine cornmeal, thyme, ¼ teaspoon salt, and ¼ teaspoon pepper in a shallow dish, stirring well with a fork. Dredge fish in cornmeal mixture. Add fish to pan; cook 4 minutes on each side or until fish flakes easily when tested with a fork. Transfer fish to a plate.

2. Add coleslaw to pan; cook 2½ minutes or until slightly wilted. Remove from heat. Add ¼ teaspoon salt, ¼ teaspoon pepper, juice, and mayonnaise; toss to coat. Place 1 fish piece on each of 4 bottom halves of rolls; top each sandwich with about ⅓ cup slaw mixture. Place top halves of rolls on sandwiches. Serve immediately. Yield: 4 servings (serving size: 1 sandwich).

CALORIES 356 (29% from fat); FAT 11.4g (sat 2g, mono 4.1g, poly 3.5g); PROTEIN 24.3g; CARB 40g; FIBER 3.6g; CHOL 54mg; IRON 3.1mg; SODIUM 655mg; CALC 78mg

Pan-Roasted Chicken Cutlets with Maple-Mustard Dill Sauce

Pounding chicken breast halves ensures they'll cook quickly and evenly. Serve with pasta to soak up all the flavorful sauce.

  4 (6-ounce) skinless, boneless chicken breast halves
¼ teaspoon salt
¼ teaspoon black pepper
Cooking spray
  2 tablespoons chopped red onion
  6 tablespoons maple syrup
¼ cup Dijon mustard
  1 tablespoon water
  1 teaspoon chopped fresh dill
  1 teaspoon grated orange rind

1. Place each chicken breast half between 2 sheets of heavy-duty plastic wrap; pound to ¼-inch thickness using a meat mallet or small heavy skillet. Sprinkle chicken evenly with salt and pepper. Heat a large nonstick skillet over medium-high heat. Coat pan with cooking spray. Add chicken to pan; cook 4 minutes or each side or until done. Remove chicken from pan.

2. Reduce heat to medium. Add onion to pan; cook 1 minute. Add syrup and remaining 4 ingredients; cook 1 minute or until thoroughly heated, stirring frequently. Serve sauce with chicken. Yield: 4 servings (serving size: 1 chicken breast half and about 2 tablespoons sauce).

CALORIES 287 (11% from fat); FAT 3.5g (sat 0.6g, mono 1g, poly 0.9g); PROTEIN 40.3g; CARB 22.5g; FIBER 0.3g; CHOL 99mg; IRON 2mg; SODIUM 640mg; CALC 63mg

Herbed Fish and Red Potato Chowder

If you can't find halibut, substitute cod or other flaky white fish. Serve with bread.

  2 bacon slices
  3 cups diced red potato (about 1 pound)
  1 cup chopped onion
  3 tablespoons all-purpose flour
  2 (8-ounce) bottles clam juice
  2 cups 2% reduced-fat milk
  1 tablespoon chopped fresh thyme
¼ teaspoon salt
¼ teaspoon black pepper
12 ounces skinless halibut fillets, cut into 1-inch pieces
  2 tablespoons chopped fresh flat-leaf parsley

1. Cook bacon in a Dutch oven over medium-high heat until crisp. Remove from pan. Reserve 1 tablespoon drippings in pan; discard remaining drippings. Cool bacon; crumble. Set aside. Add potato and onion to drippings in pan; sauté 3 minutes or until onion is tender. Add flour to pan; cook 1 minute, stirring constantly. Stir in clam juice; bring to a boil. Cover, reduce heat, and simmer 6 minutes or until potato is tender. Stir in milk; bring to a simmer over medium-high heat, stirring constantly (do not boil). Stir in thyme, salt, pepper, and fish; cook 3 minutes or until fish flakes easily when tested with a fork or until desired degree of doneness. Stir in parsley. Sprinkle with bacon. Yield: 4 servings (serving size: 2 cups).

CALORIES 307 (24% from fat); FAT 8.1g (sat 3.5g, mono 3g, poly 0.9g); PROTEIN 24.4g; CARB 33.9g; FIBER 2.5g; CHOL 57mg; IRON 2.2mg; SODIUM 611mg; CALC 198mg

inspired vegetarian

Breakfast Casseroles

These hearty dishes are easy to cook first thing in the morning.

Brie and Egg Strata

The night before, assemble and layer the casserole without the egg mixture (steps one and two); cover and refrigerate. Combine the egg mixture (step three), and refrigerate in a separate container. In the morning, pour the egg mixture over the bread mixture; allow the strata to stand for 30 minutes before baking. Substitute a French baguette or sourdough loaf for the flat Italian bread, ciabatta, if desired. Freeze the Brie for about 15 minutes to make chopping easier.

  2 teaspoons olive oil
  2 cups chopped onion
1½ cups diced unpeeled Yukon gold potato (1 large)
  1 cup chopped red bell pepper
  1 cup halved grape tomatoes
  1 teaspoon salt, divided
¾ pound ciabatta, cut into 1-inch cubes, toasted
Cooking spray
  4 ounces Brie cheese, rind removed and chopped
  1 cup egg substitute
  2 large eggs
  1 teaspoon herbes de Provence
¼ teaspoon freshly ground black pepper
  3 cups 1% low-fat milk
  2 tablespoons chopped fresh parsley

1. Heat oil in a large nonstick skillet over medium-high heat. Add onion, potato, and bell pepper; sauté 4 minutes or until tender. Stir in tomatoes; sauté 2 minutes. Stir in ½ teaspoon salt. Combine onion mixture and bread.

2. Place half of bread mixture into a 13 x 9–inch baking dish coated with cooking spray. Sprinkle with half of Brie. Top with remaining bread mixture and remaining Brie.

3. Place egg substitute and eggs in a medium bowl. Add ½ teaspoon salt, herbes de Provence, and pepper. Add milk, stirring with a whisk until well blended. Pour egg mixture over bread mixture. Let stand 30 minutes.

4. Preheat oven to 350°.

5. Bake at 350° for 50 minutes or until

set. Sprinkle with parsley. Serve immediately. Yield: 12 servings (serving size: 1 piece).

CALORIES 205 (30% from fat); FAT 6.9g (sat 2.7g, mono 3g, poly 0.8g); PROTEIN 10.8g; CARB 26.1g; FIBER 1.7g; CHOL 47mg; IRON 2mg; SODIUM 534mg; CALC 120mg

Marmalade French Toast Casserole

Grapefruit or mixed fruit marmalade will work just as well as the orange marmalade called for in the recipe. Serve the casserole with honey or pancake syrup warmed with orange rind and a splash of orange juice (add one teaspoon rind and two tablespoons juice per ½ cup syrup). This easy casserole can be assembled in less than 15 minutes and stored in the refrigerator overnight.

  3   tablespoons butter, softened
  1   (16-ounce) sourdough French bread loaf, cut into 24 (½-inch) slices
  Cooking spray
  1   (12-ounce) jar orange marmalade
  2¾ cups 1% low-fat milk
  ⅓   cup sugar
  1   teaspoon vanilla extract
  ¼   teaspoon ground nutmeg
  6   large eggs, lightly beaten
  ⅓   cup finely chopped walnuts

1. Spread butter on one side of each bread slice. Arrange 12 bread slices, buttered side down, slightly overlapping in a single layer in a 13 x 9–inch baking dish coated with cooking spray. Spread marmalade evenly over bread; top with remaining 12 bread slices, buttered side up.
2. Combine milk and next 4 ingredients, stirring with a whisk. Pour egg mixture over bread. Cover and refrigerate 8 hours or overnight.
3. Preheat oven to 350°.
4. Sprinkle casserole with walnuts. Bake at 350° for 45 minutes or until golden. Let stand 5 minutes before serving. Yield: 12 servings (serving size: 1 piece).

CALORIES 293 (28% from fat); FAT 9g (sat 3.2g, mono 2.2g, poly 2.3g); PROTEIN 9.1g; CARB 46.4g; FIBER 1.6g; CHOL 116mg; IRON 2.2mg; SODIUM 315mg; CALC 132mg

Broccoli and Three-Cheese Casserole

Broccoli remains crisp-tender in this recipe, though you can substitute any leftover cooked vegetables. Assemble the casserole the night before. Cover, refrigerate, and bake in the morning.

  2   cups cooked white rice
  6   tablespoons (1½ ounces) freshly grated Parmesan cheese, divided
  ¾   teaspoon salt, divided
  ½   teaspoon dried fines herbes
  3   egg whites, lightly beaten
  Cooking spray
  ½   cup (2 ounces) shredded fontina cheese
  4   cups coarsely chopped broccoli florets (about 1 bunch)
  1   cup finely chopped onion
  ¼   cup (1 ounce) reduced-fat shredded extrasharp Cheddar cheese
  ¾   cup egg substitute
  ¾   cup 1% low-fat milk
  ¼   teaspoon black pepper
  2   (1-ounce) slices firm white bread

1. Preheat oven to 400°.
2. Combine rice, ¼ cup Parmesan, ¼ teaspoon salt, fines herbes, and egg whites. Press mixture into an 11 x 7–inch baking dish coated with cooking spray. Sprinkle fontina evenly over rice mixture. Set aside
3. Cook broccoli in boiling water 4 minutes or until tender; drain well.
4. Heat a large nonstick skillet over medium heat. Coat pan with cooking spray. Add onion; cook 4 minutes or until tender, stirring occasionally. Stir in broccoli. Spoon broccoli mixture evenly over rice mixture. Top with Cheddar.
5. Combine egg substitute, milk, ½ teaspoon salt, and pepper in a small bowl; stir well with a whisk. Pour egg mixture over broccoli mixture.
6. Place bread in a food processor; pulse 10 times or until coarse crumbs measure 1¼ cups. Combine breadcrumbs and 2 tablespoons Parmesan. Sprinkle evenly over broccoli. Bake at 400° for 23 minutes

or until set. Yield: 6 servings (serving size: 1 piece).

CALORIES 242 (28% from fat); FAT 7.6g (sat 4g, mono 1.6g, poly 0.9g); PROTEIN 16.3g; CARB 27.8g; FIBER 2.5g; CHOL 20mg; IRON 2.2mg; SODIUM 613mg; CALC 259mg

Baked Grits Casserole

This casserole uses quick-cooking grits. If you have time, use longer cooking stone-ground grits, which yield even more flavor.
NOTE: The casserole falls slightly as it cools. Serve with fried eggs and vegetarian sausage or bacon.

  4   cups 1% low-fat milk
  2   cups water
  1   teaspoon salt, divided
  1¼ cups uncooked quick-cooking grits
  1   cup (4 ounces) shredded Parmesan cheese
  ½   teaspoon freshly ground black pepper
  5   large egg whites
  6   tablespoons finely chopped fresh chives
  Cooking spray
  2   teaspoons butter, melted

1. Preheat oven to 350°.
2. Combine milk, 2 cups water, and ½ teaspoon salt in a medium saucepan over medium-high heat; bring to a boil. Add grits, stirring with a whisk. Cover, reduce heat, and cook 8 minutes or until liquid is absorbed. Remove from heat; stir in ¼ teaspoon salt, cheese, and pepper. Cool 5 minutes.
3. Place ¼ teaspoon salt and egg whites in a large bowl. Beat with a mixer at high speed until stiff peaks form (do not overbeat). Gently fold grits mixture and chives into egg whites; spoon mixture into a 13 x 9–inch baking dish coated with cooking spray. Brush evenly with butter. Bake at 350° for 40 minutes or until browned. Let stand 10 minutes before serving. Yield: 8 servings (serving size: about 1 cup).

CALORIES 220 (27% from fat); FAT 6.7g (sat 3.9g, mono 1.8g, poly 0.3g); PROTEIN 13.7g; CARB 26.1g; FIBER 0.7g; CHOL 20mg; IRON 0.9mg; SODIUM 616mg; CALC 313mg

Sweet Potato Casserole

Our version of this classic side dish, which earned our Test Kitchens' highest rating, uses fresh sweet potatoes and half-and-half for a subtle, satisfying sweetness.

STAFF FAVORITE • MAKE AHEAD

Sweet Potato Casserole

POTATOES:

2¼ pounds sweet potatoes, peeled and chopped
1 cup half-and-half
¾ cup packed brown sugar
1 teaspoon salt
2 teaspoons vanilla extract
2 large eggs
Cooking spray

TOPPING:

1½ cups miniature marshmallows
½ cup all-purpose flour (about 2¼ ounces)
¼ cup packed brown sugar
¼ teaspoon salt
2 tablespoons chilled butter, cut into small pieces
½ cup chopped pecans, toasted

1. Preheat oven to 375°.
2. To prepare potatoes, place potatoes in a Dutch oven, and cover with water. Bring to a boil. Reduce heat, and simmer 20 minutes or until very tender. Drain; cool slightly.
3. Place potatoes in a large bowl. Add half-and-half, ¾ cup sugar, 1 teaspoon salt, and vanilla. Beat with a mixer at medium speed until smooth. Add eggs; beat well (mixture will be thin). Spoon mixture into a 13 x 9–inch baking dish coated with cooking spray.
4. To prepare topping, sprinkle miniature marshmallows over top of casserole. Lightly spoon flour into a dry measuring cup; level with a knife. Combine flour, ¼ cup sugar, and ¼ teaspoon salt in a medium bowl. Cut in butter with a pastry blender or 2 knives until mixture resembles coarse meal. Stir in pecans, and sprinkle over potato mixture and marshmallows. Bake at 375° for 30 minutes or until golden brown. Yield: 16 servings.

CALORIES 193 (29% from fat); FAT 6.3g (sat 2.4g, mono 2.6g, poly 1g); PROTEIN 2.9g; CARB 31.4g; FIBER 1.9g; CHOL 38mg; IRON 1.1mg; SODIUM 235mg; CALC 54mg

Family Favorite

A go-to soup recipe receives a healthful makeover and rave reviews.

Beer Cheese Soup became part of the Vujnov family Christmas Eve tradition 31 years ago, when they moved from Oregon back to California, and Linda Vujnov's mother-in-law prepared a spread of cold cuts, relishes, cheeses, breads, and this rich, savory soup.

By sautéing the aromatics in cooking spray instead of butter, we shaved 300 calories, 34 grams of fat (most of which was saturated), 242 milligrams of sodium, and most of the cholesterol from each serving. To achieve buttery flavor and a smooth texture without butter, we cooked rich Yukon gold potatoes in fat-free, less-sodium chicken broth, pureed the mixture, and added it back to the soup. Instead of using all fat-free cheeses, we opted for a mixture of sharp reduced-fat Cheddar and full-fat Cheddar.

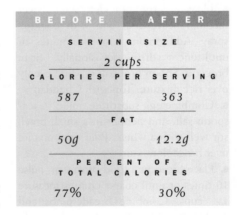

BEFORE	AFTER
SERVING SIZE	
2 cups	
CALORIES PER SERVING	
587	363
FAT	
50g	12.2g
PERCENT OF TOTAL CALORIES	
77%	30%

MAKE AHEAD

Beer Cheese Soup

4½ cups fat-free, less-sodium chicken broth, divided
1¼ cups cubed peeled Yukon gold potato (about 10 ounces)
Cooking spray
½ cup finely diced onion
½ cup finely diced celery
½ cup finely diced carrot
1 teaspoon minced garlic
½ cup all-purpose flour (about 2¼ ounces)
2½ cups 1% low-fat milk
¾ cup (3 ounces) shredded sharp Cheddar cheese
½ cup (2 ounces) shredded reduced-fat extrasharp Cheddar cheese
½ teaspoon dry mustard
½ teaspoon Worcestershire sauce
¼ teaspoon black pepper
⅛ teaspoon salt
1 (12-ounce) can beer

1. Simmer 2 cups broth and potato in a small saucepan. Cook 15 minutes or until potato is tender. Place potato mixture in a blender. Remove center piece of blender lid (to allow steam to escape); secure lid on blender. Place a clean towel over opening in lid (to avoid spills). Blend until smooth. Set aside.
2. Heat a large Dutch oven over medium heat. Coat pan with cooking spray. Add onion, celery, and carrot to pan; cook 5 minutes or until tender, stirring occasionally. Add garlic to pan; cook 30 seconds.
3. Lightly spoon flour into a dry measuring cup; level with a knife. Combine flour, 2½ cups broth, and milk in a medium bowl; stir with a whisk. Add flour mixture to pan; bring to a boil. Cook 1 minute or until slightly thick; stir constantly with a whisk. Add potato mixture, sharp Cheddar cheese, and next 5 ingredients to pan; cook 1 minute or until cheese melts, stirring constantly. Add beer to pan; bring to a simmer. Cook 15 minutes or until thoroughly heated. Yield: 4 servings (serving size: 2 cups).

CALORIES 363 (30% from fat); FAT 12.2g (sat 7.7g, mono 3.5g, poly 0.6g); PROTEIN 20.7g; CARB 41.8g; FIBER 3.4g; CHOL 39mg; IRON 2.1mg; SODIUM 884mg; CALC 480mg

Open House

Welcome one and all with a reception that can be casual or refined.

H osting a buffet-style open house is an easy way to entertain. Since most of the food is prepared in advance, you're free to mingle with guests. Partygoers come and go throughout the event, helping avoid bottlenecks at the buffet or bar. And while it's an inherently relaxed format, you can make it as formal as you like, depending on your guest list and menu choices.

Casual Buffet Dinner Menu
serves 12

Mini Bacon and Potato Frittatas

Roasted Beet, Fennel, and Walnut Salad

Barbecue-Rubbed Pork Loin with Raisin-Mustard Chutney

Garlic and Herb Roasted Turkey Breast with Tarragon Mayonnaise

Asiago and Balsamic Caramelized Onion Focaccia

Broccolini with lemon and shaved Parmesan

Citrus-Drizzled Cranberry-Oatmeal Cookies

Peppermint Stick Hot Chocolate

MAKE AHEAD • FREEZABLE
Mini Bacon and Potato Frittatas

The Italian version of omelets, frittatas make tasty appetizers. Prepare them a day ahead, chill, and reheat just before serving. You can also freeze them for up to a month. Run a sharp knife around the edges of the muffin cups to loosen them from the pans. If you don't have a mini-muffin pan, cook the frittata in a 13 x 9–inch pan at 375° for 15 minutes, and cut into 36 squares.

2 cups finely chopped peeled baking potato (about 12 ounces)
5 bacon slices (uncooked)
½ cup finely chopped sweet onion
1 teaspoon salt, divided
¼ teaspoon dried thyme
½ cup chopped fresh chives, divided
2 tablespoons grated fresh Parmesan cheese
¼ teaspoon freshly ground black pepper
7 large egg whites, lightly beaten
3 large eggs, lightly beaten
Cooking spray
6 tablespoons fat-free sour cream

1. Preheat oven to 375°.
2. Place potato in a medium saucepan; cover with water. Bring to a boil; cook 4 minutes or until almost tender. Drain.
3. Cook bacon in a large nonstick skillet over medium heat until crisp. Remove bacon from pan, reserving 2 teaspoons drippings in pan. Crumble bacon; set aside. Add potato, onion, ¼ teaspoon salt, and thyme to drippings in pan; cook 8 minutes over medium-high heat or until potato is lightly browned. Remove from heat; cool.
4. Combine potato mixture, bacon, remaining ¾ teaspoon salt, 2 tablespoons chives, cheese, pepper, egg whites, and eggs, stirring well with a whisk. Coat 36 mini-muffin cups with cooking spray. Spoon about 1 tablespoon egg mixture into each muffin cup. Bake at 375° for 16 minutes or until

lightly brown. Cool 5 minutes on a wire rack. Remove frittatas from muffin cups. Top each with ½ teaspoon sour cream and ½ teaspoon chives. Yield: 18 servings (serving size: 2 frittatas).

CALORIES 59 (35% from fat); FAT 2.3g (sat 0.8g, mono 0.9g, poly 0.3g); PROTEIN 4.1g; CARB 5.6g; FIBER 0.8g; CHOL 38mg; IRON 0.5mg; SODIUM 218mg; CALC 35mg

Roasted Beet, Fennel, and Walnut Salad
(pictured on page 254)

Roast the beets, toast the walnuts, and prepare the dressing three days in advance. Slice the fennel and endive, and toss the salad just before serving.

SALAD:
6 beets
1½ teaspoons canola oil
2 (1¼-pound) fennel bulbs with stalks
2 cups sliced Belgian endive (about 2 small heads)
⅓ cup coarsely chopped walnuts, toasted
1 (6-ounce) package fresh spinach (about 8 cups)
½ teaspoon kosher salt
¼ teaspoon freshly ground black pepper

DRESSING:
3 tablespoons red wine vinegar
3 tablespoons honey
1 teaspoon grated orange rind
2 tablespoons fresh orange juice
2 tablespoons chopped fresh basil
2 teaspoons extravirgin olive oil
2 teaspoons Dijon mustard
½ teaspoon kosher salt

1. Preheat oven to 400°.
2. To prepare salad, leave root and 1 inch of stem on beets; scrub with a vegetable brush. Place beets on a jelly-roll pan. Drizzle with canola oil; toss well to coat. Bake at 400° for 45 minutes or until beets are tender, stirring every 20 minutes. Peel and cut beets into ½-inch-thick wedges.
3. Trim tough outer leaves from fennel;
Continued

mince feathery fronds to measure 2 tablespoons. Remove and discard stalks. Cut fennel bulbs in half lengthwise; discard cores. Cut bulbs into ¼-inch slices. Combine fennel slices, endive, and next 4 ingredients in a large bowl; toss gently.

4. To prepare dressing, combine vinegar and remaining ingredients, stirring well with a whisk. Drizzle dressing mixture over fennel mixture. Add beets to bowl; toss to combine. Sprinkle with chopped fennel fronds. Serve immediately. Yield: 12 servings (serving size: about 1 cup).

CALORIES 87 (38% from fat); FAT 3.7g (sat 0.4g, mono 1.2g, poly 1.9g); PROTEIN 2.2g; CARB 13.1g; FIBER 3.4g; CHOL 0mg; IRON 1.2mg; SODIUM 232mg; CALC 48mg

---

Set up with Style

Use these tips for arranging a beautiful, inviting—and practical—open house buffet that guests will remember.

Spread it out. Put stations of your buffet in different rooms to promote mingling, prevent tie-ups at the buffet table, and help guests circulate through the house.

Set up a side table near the start of the buffet to hold plates, silverware, and napkins. Place glasses at the end of the buffet line so guests don't have to carry them while plating their food. Set up your table so guests can approach it from both sides to help lines move smoothly.

Consider the centerpiece. Flowers and plants are always good choices. For example, blooming amaryllis bulbs make a great winter centerpiece. Other flowers such as roses, hypericum, and tulips also add color to the table.

Light the night. Candles provide both decoration and warm light. Choose candles with at least a four-hour burn time.

Choose fresh accents. Use miniature fruits such as lady apples or Seckel pears as stoppers for wine decanters. Fresh seasonal fruits like kumquats, satsuma tangerines, cranberries, clementines, and pomegranates look pretty in bowls or arranged in wreaths. Put them to use in recipes for sauces, baked goods, and other edible gifts after the party.

Barbecue-Rubbed Pork Loin with Raisin-Mustard Chutney

(pictured on page 255)

Prepare the chutney a day or two in advance, but roast the pork just before serving. Serve with focaccia and roasted Broccolini.

CHUTNEY:

- 1 tablespoon olive oil
- 1 cup chopped onion
- 2 teaspoons grated peeled fresh ginger
- 2 garlic cloves, minced
- 1 cup apple juice
- 1 cup golden raisins
- 1 cup raisins
- 2 tablespoons white wine vinegar
- 2 teaspoons sugar
- 1 teaspoon curry powder
- ½ teaspoon ground cumin
- ⅓ cup apple jelly
- 1 tablespoon Dijon mustard
- ¼ teaspoon salt

PORK:

- 1 tablespoon sugar
- 2 teaspoons ground cumin
- 1½ teaspoons salt
- 1½ teaspoons paprika
- ¾ teaspoon curry powder
- ½ teaspoon ground allspice
- ½ teaspoon ground ginger
- ½ teaspoon garlic powder
- ¼ teaspoon ground red pepper
- 1 (3¾-pound) boneless pork loin, trimmed
- Cooking spray

1. To prepare chutney, heat oil in a large saucepan over medium-high heat. Add onion, 2 teaspoons fresh ginger, and garlic; sauté 4 minutes. Stir in juice and next 6 ingredients; bring to a boil. Reduce heat, and simmer 15 minutes or until liquid is almost absorbed. Remove from heat; let stand 10 minutes. Stir in jelly, mustard, and ¼ teaspoon salt. Spoon into a bowl; cover and chill.

2. Preheat oven to 350°.

3. To prepare pork, combine sugar and next 8 ingredients; rub over pork. Place pork on a rack coated with cooking spray; place rack in pan. Bake at 350° for 1 hour and 20 minutes or until a meat thermometer registers 160° (slightly pink). Let stand 20 minutes. Cut into thin slices. Serve with chutney. Yield: 12 servings (serving size: about 3 ounces pork and 3 tablespoons chutney).

CALORIES 391 (23% from fat); FAT 10g (sat 3.2g, mono 4.3g, poly 0.9g); PROTEIN 40.5g; CARB 33.2g; FIBER 2g; CHOL 112mg; IRON 3mg; SODIUM 446mg; CALC 32mg

---

Garlic and Herb Roasted Turkey Breast with Tarragon Mayonnaise

Prepare the mayonnaise a day ahead, and refrigerate.

TURKEY:

- 1 (6-pound) whole bone-in turkey breast
- 2 tablespoons chopped fresh tarragon
- 1 tablespoon chopped fresh sage
- 1 tablespoon extravirgin olive oil
- 2 teaspoons grated lemon rind
- 1 teaspoon salt
- ¼ teaspoon freshly ground black pepper
- 4 garlic cloves, minced
- Cooking spray
- 1½ cups water

MAYONNAISE:

- 1 cup light mayonnaise
- 2 tablespoons chopped fresh tarragon
- 1 tablespoon Dijon mustard
- ¾ teaspoon tarragon vinegar

1. Preheat oven to 350°.

2. To prepare turkey, trim excess fat. Starting at neck cavity, loosen skin from breast by inserting fingers, gently pushing between skin and meat.

3. Combine 2 tablespoons tarragon and next 6 ingredients, stirring well. Rub tarragon mixture under loosened skin and over breast meat. Place turkey, breast side up, on a wire rack coated with cooking spray. Place rack in a roasting pan. Pour 1½ cups water into pan. Bake at 350° for 1 hour. Baste turkey with pan juices. Bake an additional 30 minutes or until a thermometer registers 165°.

Remove turkey from oven. Loosely cover with foil; let stand 20 minutes. Remove skin; discard. Thinly slice.

4. To prepare mayonnaise, combine mayonnaise and remaining ingredients, stirring well. Serve with turkey. Yield: 12 servings (serving size: 4 ounces turkey and 1 tablespoon mayonnaise).

CALORIES 295 (27% from fat); FAT 8.9g (sat 1.5g, mono 2.6g, poly 4.3g); PROTEIN 48.2g; CARB 2.3g; FIBER 0.1g; CHOL 139mg; IRON 2.5mg; SODIUM 456mg; CALC 27mg

Asiago and Balsamic Caramelized Onion Focaccia

This bread complements poultry and pork.

  2 tablespoons plus 2 teaspoons extravirgin olive oil, divided
  1 cup chopped onion
  2 tablespoons honey, divided
  ¼ teaspoon dried thyme
  2 tablespoons balsamic vinegar
1½ teaspoons salt, divided
  1 package dry yeast (about 2¼ teaspoons)
1¼ cups warm water (100° to 110°)
3¾ cups all-purpose flour (about 17 ounces), divided
    Cooking spray
  ¾ cup (3 ounces) grated fresh Asiago cheese

1. Heat 2 teaspoons oil in a nonstick skillet over medium-high heat. Add onion, 1 tablespoon honey, and thyme; cook 5 minutes or until browned, stirring occasionally. Remove from heat; stir in vinegar and ¼ teaspoon salt. Cool completely.

2. Dissolve yeast and remaining 1 tablespoon honey in 1¼ cups warm water in a large bowl; let stand 5 minutes. Lightly spoon flour into dry measuring cups; level with a knife. Add onion mixture, remaining 2 tablespoons oil, remaining 1¼ teaspoons salt, and 3½ cups flour to yeast mixture; stir until a soft dough forms. Turn dough out onto a floured surface. Knead until smooth and elastic (about 8 minutes). Add enough of remaining flour, 1 tablespoon at a time, to prevent dough from sticking to hands.

3. Place dough in a large bowl coated with cooking spray, turning to coat top. Cover and let rise in a warm place (85°), free from drafts, 1 hour or until doubled in size. (Gently press two fingers into dough. If indentation remains, dough has risen enough.) Punch dough down; cover and let rest 5 minutes. Gently press dough into a 15 x 10–inch jelly-roll pan coated with cooking spray. Cover and let rise 25 minutes or until almost doubled in size.

4. Preheat oven to 400°.

5. Sprinkle dough with cheese. Bake at 400° for 18 minutes or until browned. Cool in pan on a wire rack 10 minutes. Remove from pan; cool completely on rack. Yield: 16 servings.

CALORIES 160 (23% from fat); FAT 4.1g (sat 1.3g, mono 1.7g, poly 0.4g); PROTEIN 4.6g; CARB 26g; FIBER 1g; CHOL 5mg; IRON 1.5mg; SODIUM 288mg; CALC 46mg

Citrus-Drizzled Cranberry-Oatmeal Cookies

Sweetened dried cranberries add color and sweet-tartness to these oatmeal cookies. Make them up to three days ahead, and store in an airtight container.

COOKIES:

  2 cups all-purpose flour (about 9 ounces)
  2 cups quick-cooking oats
  1 teaspoon baking powder
  1 teaspoon ground cinnamon
  ½ teaspoon baking soda
  ½ teaspoon salt
  ½ teaspoon ground nutmeg
  1 cup packed brown sugar
  ¾ cup granulated sugar
  ¾ cup butter, softened
1½ teaspoons vanilla extract
  2 large eggs
  1 cup sweetened dried cranberries
    Cooking spray

GLAZE:

1½ cups powdered sugar
  3 tablespoons fresh lemon juice
  2 teaspoons grated orange rind

1. Preheat oven to 350°.

2. To prepare cookies, lightly spoon flour into dry measuring cups; level with a knife. Combine flour, oats, and next 5 ingredients in a bowl. Combine brown sugar, granulated sugar, and butter in a large bowl; beat with a mixer at medium speed until well blended. Add vanilla and eggs; beat well. Gradually add flour mixture and cranberries; beat at low speed until combined. Shape dough into 55 (1-inch) balls. Place balls 2 inches apart on baking sheets coated with cooking spray. Bake at 350° for 15 minutes or until almost firm. Let stand on baking sheets 2 minutes. Remove cookies from baking sheets; cool completely on wire racks.

3. To prepare glaze, combine powdered sugar and remaining ingredients in a bowl, stirring with a whisk. Spoon mixture into a small zip-top plastic bag. Snip a small hole in 1 corner of bag; drizzle glaze over cooled cookies. Yield: 55 cookies (serving size: 1 cookie).

CALORIES 101 (27% from fat); FAT 3g (sat 1.7g, mono 0.8g, poly 0.2g); PROTEIN 1.2g; CARB 17.7g; FIBER 0.7g; CHOL 14mg; IRON 0.5mg; SODIUM 62mg; CALC 13mg

Peppermint Stick Hot Chocolate

For an adults-only party, consider spiking this drink with mint liqueur, such as peppermint schnapps or crème de menthe.

  8 cups 2% reduced-fat milk
  ¾ cup packed dark brown sugar
  ⅓ cup unsweetened cocoa
  1 teaspoon vanilla extract
  ⅛ teaspoon ground nutmeg
  3 ounces semisweet chocolate, finely chopped
 12 candy canes
  ¾ cup miniature marshmallows
    Whole grated nutmeg (optional)

1. Combine first 6 ingredients in a large saucepan over medium-low heat. Cook 25 minutes or until chocolate melts and mixture is smooth, stirring occasionally. Serve with candy canes and marshmallows.

Continued

Garnish with whole grated nutmeg, if desired. Yield: 12 servings (serving size: ¾ cup hot chocolate, 1 candy cane, and 1 tablespoon marshmallows).

CALORIES 194 (18% from fat); FAT 3.9g (sat 2.3g, mono 0g, poly 0g); PROTEIN 7g; CARB 34g; FIBER 0.8g; CHOL 10mg; IRON 0.6mg; SODIUM 96mg; CALC 32mg

Cocktail Dinner Menu
serves 12

Endive with Caramelized Pears and Blue Cheese

Mushroom-Stuffed Black Peppercorn Filet of Beef

Haricots Verts with Champagne-Shallot Vinaigrette

Oatmeal Dinner Rolls

Pecan–White Chocolate Oat Biscotti

WINE NOTE: This menu calls for a wine that is versatile but still robust enough for red meat. We chose Hogue Cellars Genesis Washington Merlot 2002 ($16), which shows some real muscle. The ripe black cherry and raspberry flavors complement the blue cheese. And aromas of smoke and savory dill make it a natural with earthy mushrooms, while firm tannins stand up nicely to steak.

QUICK & EASY
Endive with Caramelized Pears and Blue Cheese

The classic combination of pears, blue cheese, and walnuts yields a nice appetizer that comes together quickly.

Cooking spray
1½ cups chopped peeled Bosc pear (about 3 medium)
1 tablespoon sugar
⅔ cup (about 3 ounces) crumbled blue cheese
2 tablespoons chopped walnuts, toasted
⅛ teaspoon salt
24 small Belgian endive leaves (about 3 heads)
1 teaspoon chopped fresh parsley

1. Heat a large nonstick skillet over medium-high heat. Coat pan with cooking spray. Add pear and sugar to pan; sauté 2 minutes or until tender. Cool.
2. Place pear mixture, blue cheese, walnuts, and salt in a bowl; stir gently to combine. Spoon about 1½ tablespoons pear mixture into each endive leaf. Arrange leaves on a platter; sprinkle evenly with parsley. Yield: 12 servings (serving size: 2 filled endive leaves).

CALORIES 83 (34% from fat); FAT 3.1g (sat 1.4g, mono 0.7g, poly 0.7g); PROTEIN 3.6g; CARB 12.1g; FIBER 5.3g; CHOL 5mg; IRON 1.2mg; SODIUM 152mg; CALC 109mg

Mushroom-Stuffed Black Peppercorn Filet of Beef

To more easily serve this at a buffet, cut the uncooked, stuffed tenderloin in half crosswise. Cook half the tenderloin for about 30 minutes before the party; cook the other half midway through the party.

2 teaspoons butter
½ cup finely chopped shallots (2 medium)
½ cup finely chopped onion (1 small)
4 garlic cloves, minced
2 cups thinly sliced shiitake mushroom caps (about 6 ounces)
2 cups chopped oyster mushrooms (about 6 ounces)
2 teaspoons chopped fresh oregano
1 teaspoon chopped fresh thyme
1½ teaspoons salt, divided
⅓ cup dry sherry
1 (1½-ounce) slice white bread
1 (3-pound) beef tenderloin, trimmed
2 teaspoons coarsely ground black pepper
Cooking spray

1. Preheat oven to 450°.
2. Melt butter in a large nonstick skillet over medium-high heat. Add shallots, onion, and garlic to pan; sauté 3 minutes. Add mushrooms, oregano, thyme, and ½ teaspoon salt to pan; sauté 5 minutes or until liquid evaporates and mushrooms darken. Add sherry to pan; cook 2 minutes or until liquid evaporates.

Transfer mixture to a large bowl. Place bread in a food processor; pulse 10 times or until coarse crumbs measure 1 cup. Stir breadcrumbs into mushroom mixture. Cool.
3. Slice beef lengthwise, cutting to, but not through, other side. Open halves, laying beef flat. Slice each half lengthwise, cutting to, but not through, other side. Place heavy-duty plastic wrap over beef; pound to an even thickness using a meat mallet or small heavy skillet. Spread mushroom mixture down center of beef, leaving a ½-inch border. Roll up beef, jelly-roll fashion, starting with long side. Secure at 2-inch intervals with heavy string. Rub beef with remaining 1 teaspoon salt and pepper.
4. Place beef on a broiler pan coated with cooking spray. Bake at 450° for 40 minutes or until a thermometer registers 135° or until desired degree of doneness. Remove beef from oven; let stand 10 minutes. Slice. Yield: 12 servings (serving size: 3 ounces beef).

CALORIES 188 (34% from fat); FAT 7.1g (sat 2.8g, mono 2.7g, poly 0.3g); PROTEIN 23.2g; CARB 6g; FIBER 0.9g; CHOL 61mg; IRON 2mg; SODIUM 373mg; CALC 26mg

QUICK & EASY
Haricots Verts with Champagne-Shallot Vinaigrette

Haricots verts are slender French green beans.

1 gallon water
1½ teaspoons salt, divided
3 pounds haricots verts, trimmed
¼ cup champagne vinegar
¼ cup finely chopped shallots
2 tablespoons Dijon mustard
2 tablespoons honey
½ teaspoon freshly ground black pepper
2½ tablespoons extravirgin olive oil

1. Bring 1 gallon water and 1 teaspoon salt to a boil in a Dutch oven. Add beans to pan; cook 3 minutes or until crisp-tender. Drain and plunge beans into ice water; drain.
2. Combine remaining ½ teaspoon salt,

vinegar, and next 4 ingredients in a large bowl, stirring well with a whisk. Slowly drizzle oil into vinegar mixture; stir well with a whisk. Add beans to vinegar mixture; toss to coat. Yield: 12 cups (serving size: 1 cup).

CALORIES 67 (38% from fat); FAT 2.8g (sat 0.4g, mono 2.1g, poly 0.3g); PROTEIN 1.5g; CARB 10.9g; FIBER 4.2g; CHOL 0mg; IRON 0.6mg; SODIUM 151mg; CALC 57mg

---

Oatmeal Dinner Rolls

Store leftover rolls in an airtight container for up to three days, or freeze for up to a month.

    1   cup 2% reduced-fat milk
    ¾   cup water
    ¼   cup honey
    1   package dry yeast (about
        2¼ teaspoons)
    3   tablespoons butter, melted
    1   large egg, lightly beaten
    4¼ cups all-purpose flour (about
        19 ounces), divided
    1   cup regular oats
    1½ teaspoons salt
        Cooking spray

1. Combine milk, ¾ cup water, and honey in a small saucepan. Heat milk mixture over medium-high heat to 100° to 110°; remove from heat. Dissolve yeast in milk mixture; let stand 5 minutes. Stir in butter and egg.
2. Lightly spoon flour into dry measuring cups; level with a knife. Combine 4 cups flour, oats, and salt in a large bowl, stirring well. Add yeast mixture to flour mixture; stir until a soft dough forms. Turn dough out onto a lightly floured surface. Knead until smooth and elastic (about 8 minutes); add enough remaining flour, 1 tablespoon at a time, to prevent dough from sticking to hands.
3. Place dough in a large bowl coated with cooking spray; turn to coat top. Cover and let rise in a warm place (85°), free from drafts, 1 hour or until doubled in size.
4. Punch dough down, reshape into a ball, and return to bowl. Cover and let rise 1 hour or until doubled in size.
5. Punch dough down; turn out onto a

lightly floured surface. Knead dough 3 or 4 times; let rest 5 minutes. Divide mixture into 24 equal portions; shape each portion into a ball. Place balls 1 inch apart on a jelly-roll pan coated with cooking spray. Cover and let rise in a warm place (85°), free from drafts, 30 minutes or until doubled in size.
6. Preheat oven to 425°.
7. Bake rolls at 425° for 12 minutes or until browned. Remove rolls from pan; cool on a wire rack. Yield: 24 rolls (serving size: 1 roll).

CALORIES 131 (16% from fat); FAT 2.4g (sat 1.2g, mono 0.6g, poly 0.3g); PROTEIN 3.7g; CARB 23.6g; FIBER 1.2g; CHOL 13mg; IRON 1.3mg; SODIUM 167mg; CALC 22mg

---

Pecan–White Chocolate Oat Biscotti

These cookies will keep in an airtight container for up to one week.

    2   cups regular oats
    ¾   cup all-purpose flour (about
        3⅓ ounces)
    ¾   cup sugar
    2   teaspoons baking powder
    ½   teaspoon salt
    ½   teaspoon ground ginger
    2   tablespoons water
    2   large eggs, lightly beaten
    ⅓   cup chopped pecans
        Cooking spray
    ¼   cup white chocolate baking chips
    1   teaspoon canola oil

1. Preheat oven to 350°.
2. Place oats in a food processor; process until finely ground (about 1 minute). Place ground oats in a large bowl. Lightly spoon flour into dry measuring cups; level with a knife. Add flour, sugar, baking powder, salt, and ginger to oats; stir well with a whisk. Combine 2 tablespoons water and eggs; stir with a whisk. Add egg mixture to oat mixture, and stir until well combined. Stir in pecans.
3. Turn dough out onto a lightly floured surface; knead lightly 7 times. Shape dough into 2 (8-inch-long) rolls. Place rolls 3 inches apart on a baking sheet coated with cooking spray; pat to 1-inch

thickness. Bake at 350° for 30 minutes. Remove rolls from baking sheet; cool 10 minutes on a wire rack.
4. Reduce oven temperature to 325°.
5. Cut each roll diagonally into 10 slices. Place, cut sides down, on baking sheet. Bake at 325° for 10 minutes. Turn cookies over; bake an additional 10 minutes (cookies will harden as they cool). Remove from baking sheet; cool completely on wire rack.
6. Combine chips and oil in a small microwave-safe bowl. Microwave at HIGH 30 seconds or until chips melt; stir gently. Drizzle evenly over biscotti. Yield: 20 biscotti (serving size: 1 biscotto).

CALORIES 111 (29% from fat); FAT 3.5g (sat 0.8g, mono 1.5g, poly 0.7g); PROTEIN 2.6g; CARB 18.2g; FIBER 1.1g; CHOL 21mg; IRON 0.8mg; SODIUM 117mg; CALC 41mg

---

great starts

Pancakes for Breakfast

Four great flapjack recipes to mix and match with simple sauces

Leek and Cheddar Pancakes

Serve these savory pancakes with bottled salsa. They also would make a filling, yet light, supper with a tossed green salad on the side.

    1⅔ cups all-purpose flour (about
        7½ ounces)
    ½   cup (2 ounces) shredded sharp
        Cheddar cheese
    1   tablespoon sugar
    1   teaspoon baking powder
    1   teaspoon salt
    2   teaspoons olive oil
    ½   cup sliced leek
    1½ cups 2% reduced-fat milk
    1   tablespoon butter, melted
    1   large egg, lightly beaten

Continued

1. Lightly spoon flour into dry measuring cups; level with a knife. Combine flour, cheese, and next 3 ingredients in a large bowl, stirring with a whisk. Set aside.

2. Heat oil in a small skillet over medium-high heat. Add leek; sauté 3 minutes or until tender and lightly browned. Stir leek mixture into flour mixture. Combine milk, butter, and egg; add milk mixture to flour mixture, stirring until smooth.

3. Pour about ¼ cup batter per pancake onto a hot nonstick griddle or nonstick skillet. Cook 3 minutes or until tops are covered with bubbles and edges look cooked. Carefully turn pancakes over; cook 2 minutes or until bottoms are lightly browned. Yield: 4 servings (serving size: 3 pancakes).

CALORIES 374 (32% from fat); FAT 13.2g (sat 6.6g, mono 4.7g, poly 1g); PROTEIN 13.7g; CARB 49.1g; FIBER 1.6g; CHOL 82mg; IRON 3mg; SODIUM 629mg; CALC 234mg

---

QUICK & EASY • MAKE AHEAD

Cranberry Citrus Sauce

Serve this jewel-toned sauce with Buttermilk Pancakes (recipe at right) or Whole Wheat Pancakes (recipe at right). It's also good as a glaze over angel food cake.

    ⅔ cup sugar
    ¼ cup water
    ½ cup fresh cranberries
    2 tablespoons fresh orange
       juice
    2 teaspoons grated lime rind
    2 tablespoons fresh lime juice
    2 teaspoons butter

1. Combine sugar and ¼ cup water in a small saucepan over medium-high heat; cook 2 minutes or until sugar dissolves, stirring constantly. Reduce heat; stir in cranberries, orange juice, rind, and lime juice. Cook 5 minutes or until mixture foams and cranberries pop. Remove from heat; stir in butter. Yield: 1¼ cups (serving size: 2½ tablespoons).

CALORIES 78 (10% from fat); FAT 0.9g (sat 0.6g, mono 0g, poly 0g); PROTEIN 0.1g; CARB 18.2g; FIBER 0.3g; CHOL 3mg; IRON 0mg; SODIUM 9mg; CALC 2mg

---

QUICK & EASY

Buttermilk Pancakes

Classic and universally appealing, these pancakes pair well with all our sauces or just maple syrup.

    1½ cups all-purpose flour (about
         6¾ ounces)
     2 tablespoons sugar
     1 teaspoon baking powder
     ½ teaspoon salt
    1½ cups fat-free buttermilk
     1 tablespoon butter, melted
     1 large egg, lightly beaten

1. Lightly spoon flour into dry measuring cups; level with a knife. Combine flour, sugar, baking powder, and salt in a large bowl; stir with a whisk. Combine buttermilk, butter, and egg; add to flour mixture, stirring until smooth.

2. Pour about ¼ cup batter per pancake onto a hot nonstick griddle or nonstick skillet. Cook 2 minutes or until tops are covered with bubbles and edges look cooked. Carefully turn pancakes over; cook 2 minutes or until bottoms are lightly browned. Yield: 4 servings (serving size: 3 pancakes).

CALORIES 272 (15% from fat); FAT 4.5g (sat 2.2g, mono 1.3g, poly 0.5g); PROTEIN 9.8g; CARB 47.4g; FIBER 1.3g; CHOL 61mg; IRON 2.4mg; SODIUM 583mg; CALC 126mg

---

QUICK & EASY

Whole Wheat Pancakes

These flapjacks have a hearty texture that suits a chilly morning and makes them ideal for a chunky sauce.

    1 cup all-purpose flour (about
       4½ ounces)
    ⅔ cup whole wheat flour (about
       3 ounces)
    2 tablespoons brown sugar
    1½ teaspoons baking powder
    ¾ teaspoon salt
    1⅔ cups 2% reduced-fat milk
    1 tablespoon butter, melted
    1 large egg, lightly beaten

1. Lightly spoon flours into dry measuring cups; level with a knife. Combine

---

flours, sugar, baking powder, and salt in a large bowl. Combine milk, butter, and egg; add milk mixture to flour mixture, stirring until smooth.

2. Pour about ¼ cup batter per pancake onto a hot nonstick griddle or nonstick skillet. Cook 2 minutes or until tops are covered with bubbles and edges look cooked. Carefully turn pancakes over; cook 2 minutes or until bottoms are lightly browned. Yield: 4 servings (serving size: 3 pancakes).

CALORIES 293 (20% from fat); FAT 6.6g (sat 3.5g, mono 1.9g, poly 0.6g); PROTEIN 10.9g; CARB 47.8g; FIBER 3.3g; CHOL 68mg; IRON 2.6mg; SODIUM 691mg; CALC 146mg

---

QUICK & EASY

Double Coconut Pancakes

These pancakes cook to a light brown.

    1½ cups all-purpose flour (about
         6¾ ounces)
     2 tablespoons sugar
     2 tablespoons flaked sweetened
        coconut
     1 teaspoon baking powder
     ½ teaspoon salt
     1 (13.5-ounce) can light coconut
        milk
     1 tablespoon butter, melted
     1 large egg, lightly beaten

1. Lightly spoon flour into dry measuring cups; level with a knife. Combine flour, sugar, and next 3 ingredients in a large bowl. Combine coconut milk, butter, and egg; stir well. Add coconut milk mixture to flour mixture, stirring until smooth.

2. Pour about ¼ cup batter per pancake onto a hot nonstick griddle or nonstick skillet. Cook 3 minutes or until tops are covered with bubbles and edges look cooked. Carefully turn pancakes over; cook 2 minutes or until bottoms are lightly browned. Yield: 4 servings (serving size: 3 pancakes).

CALORIES 300 (29% from fat); FAT 9.7g (sat 7.1g, mono 1.3g, poly 0.5g); PROTEIN 7.6g; CARB 46.6g; FIBER 1.4g; CHOL 60mg; IRON 2.9mg; SODIUM 521mg; CALC 14mg

Vanilla Pear Sauce

Try this cardamom-spiced sauce over Double Coconut Pancakes (recipe on page 432).

    1   cup sugar
    ½   cup water
    2   teaspoons butter
    2   cups sliced peeled pear (about
        10 ounces)
    1   tablespoon fresh lemon juice
    1   teaspoon vanilla extract
    ¼   teaspoon ground cardamom
    Dash freshly ground black pepper

1. Combine sugar and ½ cup water in a small saucepan over medium-high heat. Cook 3 minutes or until sugar dissolves, stirring constantly. Transfer syrup to a small bowl; set aside.

2. Melt butter in pan over medium heat. Add pear to pan; cook 3 minutes or until soft, stirring frequently. Return syrup to pan; stir in juice and remaining ingredients. Cook 5 minutes or until sauce is slightly thickened. Yield: 2 cups (serving size: ¼ cup).

CALORIES 131 (7% from fat); FAT 1g (sat 0.6g, mono 0g, poly 0g); PROTEIN 0.2g; CARB 3.7g; FIBER 1.3g; CHOL 3mg; IRON 0.1mg; SODIUM 9mg; CALC 5mg

Bourbon Pecan Sauce

This rich-tasting sauce has grown-up appeal, thanks to the bourbon, and makes a delicious accompaniment with Whole Wheat Pancakes (recipe on page 432) or the Buttermilk Pancakes (recipe on page 432).

    1   cup sugar
    ⅓   cup water
    ⅓   cup chopped pecans, toasted
    2   tablespoons fat-free milk
    1½   tablespoons butter
    1   tablespoon bourbon
    2   teaspoons vanilla extract

1. Combine sugar and ⅓ cup water in a small saucepan over medium-high heat. Cook 5 minutes or until sugar dissolves, stirring constantly. Stir in pecans and remaining ingredients. Reduce heat, and

cook 3 minutes or until mixture is thick and bubbly. Yield: 1¼ cups (serving size: 2½ tablespoons).

CALORIES 158 (32% from fat); FAT 5.6g (sat 1.6g, mono 2g, poly 1.1g); PROTEIN 0.6g; CARB 26g; FIBER 0.5g; CHOL 6mg; IRON 0.1mg; SODIUM 20mg; CALC 9mg

reader recipes

Cookie Confidential

A Rochester, New York, reader and her friend do some sleuthing to create their own lighter version of a local favorite.

When Allyn Stelljes-Young and her friend, Joyce Steel, discovered delicious "no-guilt cookies" at a Rochester, New York, deli, they wanted the recipe. When the deli wouldn't share its secret recipe, she and her friend scoured cookbooks to create their own adaptation. Thanks to their culinary detective work, you can bake a batch for a holiday gathering.

Cranberry-Nut Chocolate Chip Cookies

This cookie dough needs to be chilled for several hours or overnight before baking.

    ¾   cup all-purpose flour (about 3⅓ ounces)
    ¾   cup whole wheat flour (about 3½ ounces)
    ¾   cup regular oats
    ½   teaspoon baking powder
    ¼   teaspoon baking soda
    ¼   teaspoon salt
    ¼   cup dried cranberries
    2½   tablespoons finely chopped walnuts
    2½   tablespoons semisweet chocolate minichips
    ¾   cup packed brown sugar
    5   tablespoons butter, softened
    2   tablespoons honey
    ¾   teaspoon vanilla extract
    1   large egg
    1   large egg white
    Cooking spray

1. Lightly spoon flours into dry measuring cups; level with a knife. Combine flours, oats, baking powder, and next 5 ingredients in a large bowl.

2. Place sugar and butter in a large bowl; beat with a mixer at medium speed until light and fluffy. Add honey, vanilla, egg, and egg white; beat well. Add flour mixture to sugar mixture; beat at low speed until well blended. Cover and refrigerate 8 hours or overnight.

3. Preheat oven to 350°.

4. Drop batter by tablespoonfuls onto a baking sheet coated with cooking spray. Bake at 350° for 10 minutes. Cool 2 minutes on pans. Remove from pans, and cool completely on wire racks. Yield: 36 cookies (serving size: 1 cookie).

CALORIES 75 (31% from fat); FAT 2.6g (sat 1.3g, mono 0.7g, poly 0.4g); PROTEIN 1.4g; CARB 12.1g; FIBER 0.8g; CHOL 10mg; IRON 0.5mg; SODIUM 49mg; CALC 12mg

Garlicky Roasted Potatoes with Herbs
(pictured on page 254)

"Always looking for ways to use fresh herbs, I came up with these parslied roasted potatoes. You can also use a mixture of herbs like basil and thyme."

—Marti LoSasso, Arvada, Colorado

    2   tablespoons chopped garlic
    1   tablespoon olive oil
    1½   pounds quartered Yukon gold or
         red potatoes (about 4 cups)
    Cooking spray
    ½   teaspoon sea salt
    ¼   teaspoon freshly ground black
         pepper
    ¼   cup chopped fresh flat-leaf parsley
    ½   teaspoon grated lemon rind

1. Preheat oven to 475°.

2. Combine garlic and oil in a small saucepan over medium heat. Cook 2 minutes or until golden, stirring frequently. Remove garlic with a slotted spoon; set aside. Drizzle remaining oil evenly over potatoes in a large bowl, tossing well to coat. Arrange potatoes in a single layer on a baking sheet coated

Continued

with cooking spray, and sprinkle with salt and pepper. Bake at 475° for 30 minutes or until potatoes are golden. Combine reserved garlic, parsley, and lemon rind in a small bowl; sprinkle garlic mixture evenly over potatoes. Yield: 4 servings (serving size: 1 cup).

CALORIES 195 (19% from fat); FAT 4.2g (sat 0.5g, mono 2.5g, poly 0.4g); PROTEIN 4.1g; CARB 32g; FIBER 2.2g; CHOL 0mg; IRON 1.6mg; SODIUM 299mg; CALC 7mg

Pork Medallions with Gingered Cranberry Sauce

"The sliced pork cooks faster than a whole tenderloin, and this gingered cranberry sauce not only has wonderful flavor, but it's also quick and easy."
—Linda Drinkard, Vero Beach, Florida

    2   teaspoons butter
    1   (1-pound) pork tenderloin, trimmed and cut into 1-inch-thick slices
    ¼   teaspoon salt
    ¼   teaspoon freshly ground black pepper
    1   tablespoon olive oil
    ½   teaspoon finely minced peeled fresh ginger
    1   garlic clove, minced
    ½   cup port or other sweet red wine
    1   cup canned whole-berry cranberry sauce
    ¼   cup fat-free, less-sodium chicken broth
    1½   teaspoons balsamic vinegar

1. Melt butter in a large nonstick skillet over medium-high heat. Sprinkle both sides of pork evenly with salt and pepper. Add pork to pan; cook 2 minutes on each side or until browned. Remove pork from pan; keep warm.
2. Add oil to pan. Add ginger and garlic; sauté 30 seconds. Add port, scraping pan to loosen browned bits; cook until reduced to ¼ cup (about 5 minutes). Add cranberry sauce and broth; cook 3 minutes or until slightly thick, stirring occasionally. Stir in vinegar; return pork to pan. Cook 1 minute, turning to coat

pork. Yield: 4 servings (serving size: 3 ounces pork and 3 tablespoons sauce).

CALORIES 310 (27% from fat); FAT 9.2g (sat 3g, mono 4.7g, poly 0.9g); PROTEIN 24.1g; CARB 28.7g; FIBER 1.1g; CHOL 79mg; IRON 1.5mg; SODIUM 259mg; CALC 10mg

Brown Sugar and Spice Cookies

"I developed these cookies from an old gingerbread recipe. Since a piece of gingerbread is sometimes overpowering to me, this cookie has all the good flavor in a smaller portion."
—Rae Castillo, Pittsburg, California

COOKIES:
    ⅓   cup granulated sugar
    ⅓   cup packed light brown sugar
    ⅓   cup butter, softened
    1   teaspoon vanilla extract
    1   large egg
    1¼   cups all-purpose flour (about 5½ ounces)
    ⅓   cup whole wheat flour (about 1½ ounces)
    ½   teaspoon baking powder
    ½   teaspoon ground cinnamon
    ¼   teaspoon salt
    ¼   teaspoon ground ginger
    ⅛   teaspoon ground nutmeg
         Cooking spray

TOPPING:
    1   tablespoon granulated sugar
    ¼   teaspoon ground cinnamon
         Dash of ground nutmeg
         Dash of ground allspice

1. Preheat oven to 350°.
2. To prepare cookies, combine ⅓ cup granulated sugar, brown sugar, and butter in a large bowl; beat with a mixer at medium speed until light and fluffy. Add vanilla and egg; beat well. Lightly spoon flours into dry measuring cups; level with a knife. Combine flours, baking powder, and next 4 ingredients in a medium bowl, stirring with a whisk. Add flour mixture to sugar mixture; beat at low speed until well blended.
3. Shape dough into 30 balls. Place 2 inches apart on baking sheets coated

with cooking spray; flatten cookies with bottom of a glass.
4. To prepare topping, combine 1 tablespoon granulated sugar, ¼ teaspoon cinnamon, dash of nutmeg, and allspice in a small bowl. Sprinkle evenly over cookies.
5. Bake at 350° for 9 minutes. Cool 10 minutes on pans. Remove from pans; cool completely on wire racks. Yield: 30 servings (serving size: 1 cookie).

CALORIES 64 (32% from fat); FAT 2.3g (sat 1.3g, mono 0.6g, poly 0.1g); PROTEIN 1g; CARB 10.1g; FIBER 0.3g; CHOL 12mg; IRON 0.4mg; SODIUM 46mg; CALC 10mg

Stuffed Mushrooms

"These are easy to make, and people have no idea that I've used lower fat ingredients."
—Tiffany Bryson, San Antonio, Texas

    24   large button mushrooms (about 1¾ pounds)
         Cooking spray
    3   tablespoons chopped green onions
    1   garlic clove, minced
    4   ounces 50%-less-fat pork sausage (such as Jimmy Dean 50% less fat)
    ½   teaspoon crushed red pepper
    ¼   teaspoon kosher salt
    ⅛   teaspoon black pepper
    ¼   cup (2 ounces) ⅓-less-fat cream cheese, softened
    ¼   cup dry breadcrumbs
    3   tablespoons grated fresh Parmesan cheese

1. Preheat oven to 400°.
2. Clean mushrooms, and remove stems; finely chop stems.
3. Heat a large nonstick skillet over medium-high heat. Coat pan with cooking spray. Add onions and garlic; sauté 1 minute. Add sausage; cook until browned, stirring to crumble. Add reserved mushroom stems, red pepper, salt, and black pepper; sauté 2 minutes or until stems are tender. Remove from heat; stir in cream cheese and breadcrumbs. Stuff 1 tablespoon sausage mixture into each mushroom cap. Arrange mushroom caps in a 13 x 9–inch baking dish coated with cooking spray; sprinkle evenly with Parmesan. Bake at 400° for

30 minutes or until lightly golden and thoroughly heated. Yield: 12 servings (serving size: 2 stuffed mushrooms).

CALORIES 64 (46% from fat); FAT 3.3g (sat 1.5g, mono 1.3g, poly 0.2g); PROTEIN 4g; CARB 4.5g; FIBER 0.2g; CHOL 11mg; IRON 0.5g; SODIUM 159mg; CALC 23mg

---

QUICK & EASY
Quick and Easy Turkey Vegetable Soup

"The mild cheese complements this slightly spicy soup."
—Tara Bennett, Raleigh, North Carolina

Cooking spray
1   cup finely chopped celery (about 2 stalks)
½   cup finely chopped onion
1½ teaspoons bottled minced garlic
1½ pounds ground turkey breast
3   cups water
1   cup sliced carrot (about 2 large)
½   cup frozen French-cut green beans
½   cup frozen whole-kernel corn
1½ teaspoons ground cumin
1   teaspoon chili powder
2   bay leaves
2   beef-flavored dry bouillon cubes, chopped
1   (15-ounce) can kidney beans, rinsed and drained
1   (14.5-ounce) can diced tomatoes and green chiles, undrained
6   tablespoons shredded Monterey Jack cheese

1. Heat a Dutch oven over medium-high heat. Coat pan with cooking spray. Add celery, onion, garlic, and turkey. Cook 5 minutes or until turkey is browned, stirring to crumble. Add 3 cups water and remaining ingredients except cheese; bring to a boil. Cover, reduce heat, and simmer 20 minutes or until vegetables are tender. Discard bay leaves. Ladle 1½ cups soup into each of 6 bowls; top each serving with 1 tablespoon cheese. Yield: 6 servings.

CALORIES 238 (16% from fat); FAT 4.3g (sat 2g, mono 0.7g, poly 0.2g); PROTEIN 31.9g; CARB 18.4g; FIBER 5.5g; CHOL 52mg; IRON 1.9mg; SODIUM 899mg; CALC 102mg

Hanukkah for Moderns

Two menus inspired by culinary customs from the Mediterranean, North Africa, and the Middle East suit today's worldly tastes.

When you think of Hanukkah, chances are you imagine potato pancakes with applesauce, brisket, kugel, and rugelach. That's traditional—if your roots trace back to Eastern Europe, as those of many American Jews do. But for Sephardic Jews, whose ancestors hailed from Spain or Portugal and later migrated throughout the Mediterranean region to North Africa, Turkey, Greece, and other destinations, culinary traditions are quite different. Here are two menus that spotlight Sephardic flavors: a company-worthy dinner to share with friends and a casual supper to enjoy with family.

Hanukkah-with-Friends Menu
serves 8

Leek and Potato Fritters with Lemon-Cumin Yogurt

Romaine Salad with Oranges and Pine Nuts

Roasted Chicken with Lemons and Thyme

Bulgur Salad with Lemon Vinaigrette

Pear-Walnut Cake with Honey-Orange Syrup

MAKE AHEAD
Leek and Potato Fritters with Lemon-Cumin Yogurt

This is based on *keftes de prasa*, a traditional Sephardic recipe for fritters. Leeks add an aromatic note to traditional Hanukkah latkes (potato pancakes). Fritters and latkes are typically fried with olive oil; here, we use canola oil, which has a mild flavor and high smoke point to brown the fritters. To prepare fritters ahead, place cooked fritters in a 250° oven to stay warm until you're ready to serve. Garnish with parsley sprigs.

YOGURT:
1½ cups plain nonfat yogurt
½   teaspoon minced garlic
½   teaspoon grated lemon rind
¼   teaspoon ground cumin
⅛   teaspoon salt
⅛   teaspoon freshly ground black pepper

FRITTERS:
Cooking spray
4   cups thinly sliced leek (about 1½ pounds)
6   tablespoons water, divided
1   teaspoon salt, divided
¾   teaspoon freshly ground black pepper, divided
1   (20-ounce) package refrigerated shredded hash brown potatoes (such as Simply Potatoes)
2   large eggs
2   large egg whites
8   teaspoons canola oil, divided

1. To prepare yogurt, spoon yogurt onto several layers of heavy-duty paper towels; spread to ½-inch thickness. Cover with additional paper towels; let stand 5 minutes. Scrape into a bowl using a rubber spatula. Combine yogurt and next 5 ingredients in a small bowl. Cover and chill.

Continued

2. To prepare fritters, heat a large non-stick skillet over medium-high heat. Coat pan with cooking spray. Add leek, 2 tablespoons water, ¼ teaspoon salt, and ¼ teaspoon pepper. Sauté 10 minutes or until golden, adding remaining ¼ cup water as necessary to prevent leeks from sticking to pan. Place leeks and potatoes in a large bowl. Combine ½ teaspoon salt, ¼ teaspoon pepper, eggs, and egg whites; stir well with a whisk. Add egg mixture to potato mixture.

3. Heat 4 teaspoons oil in a large non-stick skillet coated with cooking spray over medium-high heat. Spoon about 3 tablespoons potato mixture for each of 8 fritters into pan. Cook 3 minutes on each side or until browned. Remove from pan. Repeat procedure with remaining 4 teaspoons oil and potato mixture. Sprinkle fritters with remaining ¼ teaspoon salt and remaining ¼ teaspoon pepper. Serve with yogurt sauce. Yield: 8 servings (serving size: 2 fritters and 1½ table-spoons sauce).

CALORIES 200 (28% from fat); FAT 6.2g (sat 0.8g, mono 3.2g, poly 1.7g); PROTEIN 7.5g; CARB 30.6g; FIBER 2.5g; CHOL 54mg; IRON 2.1mg; SODIUM 446mg; CALC 116mg

QUICK & EASY
Romaine Salad with Oranges and Pine Nuts

Honey and fresh oranges lend a touch of Spanish flair to this winter salad.

- ½ cup thinly sliced red onion
- ¼ cup thinly sliced fresh basil
- 2 navel oranges, peeled, halved, and sliced
- 1 (10-ounce) package prewashed romaine lettuce, torn
- ½ English cucumber, peeled, halved lengthwise, and sliced (about 1 cup)
- 3 tablespoons red wine vinegar
- 1 tablespoon canola oil
- 1 tablespoon honey
- ¼ teaspoon kosher salt
- ¼ teaspoon freshly ground black pepper
- 1 small garlic clove, minced
- ¼ cup pine nuts, toasted

1. Place first 5 ingredients in a large bowl. Combine vinegar and next 5 ingredients in a small bowl, stirring with a whisk until blended. Drizzle over lettuce mixture; toss to coat. Sprinkle with pine nuts. Serve immediately. Yield: 8 servings (serving size: 1½ cups).

CALORIES 81 (54% from fat); FAT 4.9g (sat 0.4g, mono 1.9g, poly 2.1g); PROTEIN 1.6g; CARB 9.6g; FIBER 2g; CHOL 0mg; IRON 0.7mg; SODIUM 63mg; CALC 34mg

Roasted Chicken with Lemons and Thyme

- 1 (6-pound) roasting chicken
- 2 teaspoons Hungarian paprika
- 2 tablespoons chopped fresh thyme, divided
- 1 teaspoon salt, divided
- 1 teaspoon freshly ground black pepper, divided
- 2 lemons, divided
- Cooking spray
- 1 teaspoon olive oil
- 2 tablespoons all-purpose flour
- ½ cup dry white wine (such as sauvignon blanc)
- 1 cup fat-free, less-sodium chicken broth
- 1 tablespoon fresh lemon juice
- 2 teaspoons sugar
- Lemon slices (optional)
- Thyme sprigs (optional)

1. Preheat oven to 425°.

2. Remove and discard giblets and neck from chicken. Trim excess fat. Starting at neck cavity, loosen skin from breast and drumsticks by inserting fingers, gently pushing between skin and meat. Combine paprika, 1 tablespoon thyme, ½ teaspoon salt, and ¼ teaspoon pepper; rub under loosened skin. Thinly slice 1 lemon; arrange slices under loosened skin. Cut remaining lemon into quarters. Place lemon quarters inside chicken cavity. Add remaining 1 tablespoon thyme to chicken cavity.

3. Place chicken on rack of a broiler pan or roasting pan coated with cooking spray. Brush oil over skin. Cover chicken with aluminum foil. Bake at 425° for 30 minutes. Uncover, and bake 50 minutes or until an instant-read thermometer inserted into thigh registers 165°. Transfer chicken to a cutting board; cover with foil and let stand 15 minutes before carving.

4. Place a zip-top plastic bag in a 2-cup glass measure. Pour drippings into bag; let stand 10 minutes (fat will rise to top). Seal bag, and carefully snip off 1 bottom corner of bag. Drain drippings into measuring cup, stopping before fat layer reaches opening; discard fat. Place pan on stove top over medium heat. Sprinkle flour into pan. Add wine; bring to a boil, stirring constantly with a whisk. Add drippings, broth, juice, sugar, remaining ½ teaspoon salt, and remaining ¾ teaspoon pepper to pan, stirring constantly with a whisk until slightly thickened. Remove from heat.

5. Remove skin and lemon slices from chicken, and lemon wedges from cavity; discard. Carve chicken and arrange on a serving platter. Serve with gravy. Garnish with additional lemon slices and thyme sprigs, if desired. Yield: 8 servings (serving size: about 3 ounces meat and 3 tablespoons gravy).

CALORIES 174 (35% from fat); FAT 6.7g (sat 1.8g, mono 2.7g, poly 1.5g); PROTEIN 23.5g; CARB 3.2g; FIBER 0.1g; CHOL 69mg; IRON 1.3mg; SODIUM 417mg; CALC 21mg

MAKE AHEAD
Bulgur Salad with Lemon Vinaigrette

Sephardic Jews who migrated to Syria, Lebanon, and Turkey learned to use bulgur as an alternative to rice.

- 1¼ cups uncooked bulgur
- 1¼ cups boiling water
- 1 cup diced seedless cucumber
- 1 cup diced seeded plum tomato (about 2 tomatoes)
- ½ cup chopped fresh flat-leaf parsley
- ½ cup chopped radishes
- ¼ cup chopped green onions
- ½ teaspoon grated lemon rind
- ¼ cup fresh lemon juice
- 1½ tablespoons extravirgin olive oil
- ¾ teaspoon salt
- ½ teaspoon freshly ground black pepper

1. Combine bulgur and 1¼ cups boiling water in a large bowl. Cover and let stand 30 minutes or until bulgur is tender. Drain; return bulgur to bowl. Add cucumber and next 4 ingredients.
2. Combine rind and remaining ingredients in a small bowl, stirring with a whisk. Drizzle over bulgur mixture; toss well. Cover and chill at least 1 hour. Yield: 8 servings (serving size: ¾ cup).

CALORIES 107 (24% from fat); FAT 2.9g (sat 0.4g, mono 1.9g, poly 0.4g); PROTEIN 3.1g; CARB 19g; FIBER 4.6g; CHOL 0mg; IRON 1mg; SODIUM 228mg; CALC 20mg

MAKE AHEAD
Pear-Walnut Cake with Honey-Orange Syrup

This is similar to *pan d'Espanya* (Spanish bread), which is what Sephardic Jews call sponge cake. Brushing the honey-orange syrup over the warm cake infuses it with moisture and delicate aromas. For a second-day treat, try toasting a slice. Garnish with orange rind curls and star anise.

CAKE:
  Cooking spray
  2 tablespoons all-purpose flour
1¾ cups sugar
  4 large eggs
  3 cups all-purpose flour (about 13½ ounces)
  1 tablespoon baking powder
  1 teaspoon aniseed, crushed
  ½ teaspoon kosher salt
  ½ teaspoon ground cinnamon
  1 teaspoon finely grated orange rind
  ½ cup fresh orange juice
  ½ cup canola oil
  1 teaspoon vanilla extract
  2 cups chopped peeled pear (about 3)
  ¼ cup chopped walnuts, toasted

SYRUP:
  ⅓ cup honey
  2 tablespoons fresh orange juice

1. Preheat oven to 375°.
2. To prepare cake, coat a 10-inch tube pan with cooking spray; dust with 2 tablespoons flour. Set aside.

3. Place sugar and eggs in a large bowl; beat with a mixer at medium speed until thick and pale (about 3 minutes).
4. Lightly spoon 3 cups flour into dry measuring cups; level with a knife. Combine flour, baking powder, anise, salt, and cinnamon, stirring well with a whisk.
5. Combine rind, ½ cup juice, oil, and vanilla. Add flour mixture to egg mixture alternately with juice mixture, beginning and ending with flour mixture; blend after each addition just until combined. Stir in pear and walnuts. Pour batter into prepared pan. Bake at 375° for 55 minutes or until a wooden pick inserted in center comes out clean. Cool in pan on a wire rack 15 minutes; loosen cake from sides of pan using a narrow metal spatula or knife. Place a plate upside down on top of cake pan; carefully invert cake onto plate.
6. To prepare syrup, combine honey and 2 tablespoons juice in a small saucepan over medium heat. Cook 2 minutes, stirring constantly. Brush warm syrup over top and sides of cake. Cool completely. Yield: 18 servings (serving size: 1 slice).

CALORIES 271 (30% from fat); FAT 8.9g (sat 0.9g, mono 4.3g, poly 2.9g); PROTEIN 4.1g; CARB 45.4g; FIBER 1.4g; CHOL 47mg; IRON 1.4mg; SODIUM 176mg; CALC 15mg

---

Family Festival of Lights Supper Menu
serves 8

Roasted Garlic and Potato Spread

Leek and Potato Fritters with Lemon-Cumin Yogurt (recipe on page 435)

Braised Lamb with Butternut Squash and Dried Fruit

or

White Bean and Beef Soup with Tomatoes and Onions

Basmati Pilaf with Vermicelli and Onions

Pear-Walnut Cake with Honey-Orange Syrup (recipe at left)

MAKE AHEAD
Roasted Garlic and Potato Spread

Serve with bread or crudités.

  1 large whole garlic head, unpeeled
3½ cups cubed peeled baking potato (about 1½ pounds)
  ½ cup plain fat-free yogurt
  2 tablespoons extravirgin olive oil
  ½ teaspoon grated lemon rind
  1 tablespoon fresh lemon juice
  ¾ teaspoon kosher salt
  ¼ teaspoon freshly ground black pepper
  ⅛ teaspoon ground red pepper
  2 tablespoons chopped fresh parsley

1. Preheat oven to 400°.
2. Remove white papery skin from garlic head (do not peel or separate the cloves). Wrap head in foil. Bake at 400° for 30 minutes, remove from oven; cool 10 minutes.
3. Place potato in a medium saucepan, and cover with water; bring to a boil. Cook 19 minutes or until very tender. Drain, reserving ½ cup cooking liquid. Place potatoes in a large bowl.
4. Separate garlic cloves; squeeze to extract garlic pulp. Discard skins. Add pulp, yogurt, and next 6 ingredients to potatoes. Mash potato mixture with a potato masher. Stir in reserved cooking liquid, 2 tablespoons at a time, until mixture is almost smooth. Sprinkle with parsley. Yield: 8 servings (serving size: about ⅓ cup).

CALORIES 126 (25% from fat); FAT 3.5g (sat 0.5g, mono 2.5g, poly 0.4g); PROTEIN 3.2g; CARB 21.2g; FIBER 2.2g; CHOL 0mg; IRON 1.1mg; SODIUM 193mg; CALC 43mg

Braised Lamb with Butternut Squash and Dried Fruit

Filled with dried fruit and squash, this lamb stew boasts the flavors of Morocco and Algeria. Serve with Basmati Pilaf with Vermicelli and Onions (recipe at right) or couscous.

    2 pounds boneless leg of lamb,
       trimmed and cut into 1-inch
       pieces
    1 teaspoon kosher salt, divided
    1 teaspoon ground cinnamon,
       divided
    1 teaspoon freshly ground black
       pepper, divided
   ¼ teaspoon ground red pepper
   ⅛ teaspoon ground cloves
    1 teaspoon olive oil
  Cooking spray
    2 cups chopped onion (about 1
       large)
    4 garlic cloves, minced
    4 cups fat-free, less-sodium chicken
       broth
    4 cups (1-inch) cubed peeled
       butternut squash
   ½ cup dried plums
   ½ cup dried apples, coarsely
       chopped
   ½ cup dried apricots, coarsely
       chopped
    2 teaspoons grated orange rind
    1 (14.5-ounce) can diced tomatoes,
       undrained

1. Sprinkle lamb with ¼ teaspoon salt, ½ teaspoon cinnamon, ¼ teaspoon black pepper, red pepper, and cloves. Heat oil in a Dutch oven coated with cooking spray over medium-high heat. Add lamb; sauté 7 minutes or until browned. Remove from pan.
2. Add onion to pan; sauté 5 minutes or until tender. Add garlic; sauté 1 minute. Add broth, scraping pan to loosen browned bits. Return lamb to pan. Add remaining ¾ teaspoon salt, remaining ½ teaspoon cinnamon, and remaining ¾ teaspoon black pepper; bring to a boil. Cover, reduce heat, and simmer 1 hour, stirring occasionally.
3. Add squash and remaining ingredients; bring to a boil. Reduce heat; simmer, uncovered, 30 minutes or until lamb and squash are tender. Yield: 8 servings (serving size: 1¼ cups stew).

CALORIES 378 (27% from fat); FAT 11.3g (sat 4.6g, mono 4.6g, poly 0.6g); PROTEIN 31g; CARB 39g; FIBER 6g; CHOL 104mg; IRON 4mg; SODIUM 706mg; CALC 103mg

White Bean and Beef Soup with Tomatoes and Onions

White beans braised in a savory sauce are enjoyed year-round in Sephardic households.

    1 (16-ounce) package dried navy
       beans
    1 teaspoon kosher salt, divided
   ½ teaspoon freshly ground black
       pepper
   ¾ pound sirloin, cut into 1-inch
       cubes
  Cooking spray
  1½ cups chopped Rio or other sweet
       onion
  4½ cups Beef Stock
    2 cups water
    3 bay leaves
    2 (8-ounce) cans tomato sauce

1. Sort and wash beans; place in a large Dutch oven. Cover with water to 2 inches above beans; cover and let stand 8 hours. Drain beans.
2. Sprinkle ½ teaspoon salt and pepper evenly over beef. Heat a Dutch oven over medium-high heat. Coat pan with cooking spray. Add beef; sauté 7 minutes or until lightly browned. Remove beef from pan.
3. Add onion to pan; sauté 5 minutes or until tender. Return beef to pan. Add Beef Stock, 2 cups water, and bay leaves, scraping pan to loosen browned bits. Add beans; bring to a boil. Cover, reduce heat, and simmer 45 minutes, stirring occasionally.
4. Add tomato sauce and remaining ½ teaspoon salt to pan. Cook, uncovered, 45 minutes or until beans are tender, pressing some of beans against side of pan with a wooden spoon to thicken liquid. Discard bay leaves. Yield: 8 servings (serving size: about 1 cup).

(Totals include Beef Stock) CALORIES 282 (9% from fat); FAT 2.8g (sat 0.8g, mono 0.9g, poly 0.7g); PROTEIN 23.5g; CARB 42g; FIBER 15.2g; CHOL 19mg; IRON 4.5mg; SODIUM 602mg; CALC 113mg

MAKE AHEAD • FREEZABLE
BEEF STOCK:

    8 cups water
    1 teaspoon kosher salt
   ½ teaspoon freshly ground black
       pepper
   ½ pound beef bones and lean trimmings
    2 bay leaves
    1 large carrot, cut into 4 pieces
    1 large onion, quartered
    1 garlic bulb, crushed
    1 bunch fresh flat-leaf parsley

1. Place all ingredients in a Dutch oven or stockpot; bring to a boil. Cover, reduce heat, and simmer 1 hour. Strain broth through a sieve into a large bowl; discard solids. Cool stock to room temperature. Cover and chill stock 8 to 24 hours. Skim solidified fat from surface of broth; discard. Yield: 7 cups (serving size: about 1 cup).
NOTE: Refrigerate broth in an airtight container for up to one week or freeze for up to three months.

CALORIES 6 (15% from fat); FAT 0.1g (sat 0g, mono 0.1g, poly 0g); PROTEIN 0.8g; CARB 0.5g; FIBER 0.1g; CHOL 1mg; IRON 0.1mg; SODIUM 76mg; CALC 8mg

Basmati Pilaf with Vermicelli and Onions

    5 teaspoons olive oil
   ¾ cup chopped Rio or other sweet
       onion
    2 cups uncooked basmati rice
   ¾ cup (2 ounces) uncooked vermicelli,
       broken into 2-inch pieces
    3 cups fat-free, less-sodium chicken
       broth
   ½ teaspoon kosher salt
   ¼ teaspoon freshly ground black
       pepper
   ¼ cup chopped fresh flat-leaf parsley
   ¼ cup chopped green onions

1. Preheat oven to 350°.

2. Heat oil in a Dutch oven over medium heat. Add ¾ cup onion; cook 3 minutes or until tender, stirring frequently. Add rice and pasta; cook 2 minutes or until rice is opaque, stirring frequently. Stir in broth, salt, and pepper; bring to a boil. Cover and bake at 350° for 15 minutes. Remove from oven. Let stand 15 minutes. Uncover; stir in parsley and green onions. Yield: 8 servings (serving size: about 1 cup).

CALORIES 140 (19% from fat); FAT 3g (sat 0.4g, mono 2.1g, poly 0.3g); PROTEIN 3.1g; CARB 25.2g; FIBER 0.8g; CHOL 0mg; IRON 0.6mg; SODIUM 289mg; CALC 10mg

dinner tonight

Wrap and Roll

Wrap and roll your way to speedy, easy suppers.

Wrap and Roll Menu 1

serves 4

Fish Tacos with Lime-Cilantro Crema

Pinto salad*

Mango slices with slivered almonds

*Combine 1 cup diced plum tomatoes, ½ cup diced yellow bell pepper, ¼ cup minced fresh cilantro, 2 tablespoons lime juice, 2 teaspoons olive oil, ⅛ teaspoon freshly ground black pepper, and 1 (15-ounce) can drained and rinsed pinto beans; stir well.

Game Plan

1. While oven preheats:
- Prepare crema.
- Prepare salad.

2. While fish bakes:
- Shred cabbage.
- Heat tortillas.

QUICK & EASY
Fish Tacos with Lime-Cilantro Crema

You can use crisp lettuce such as romaine in place of cabbage. Peeled and deveined medium shrimp is an alternative for the snapper. Cook 2 minutes or just until shrimp are done.

TOTAL TIME: 40 MINUTES

FLAVOR TIP: Smoked paprika adds complex flavor to this versatile taco spice mixture, but you can substitute regular paprika.

CREMA:

- ¼ cup thinly sliced green onions
- ¼ cup chopped fresh cilantro
- 3 tablespoons fat-free mayonnaise
- 3 tablespoons reduced-fat sour cream
- 1 teaspoon grated lime rind
- 1½ teaspoons fresh lime juice
- ¼ teaspoon salt
- 1 garlic clove, minced

TACOS:

- 1 teaspoon ground cumin
- 1 teaspoon ground coriander
- ½ teaspoon smoked paprika
- ¼ teaspoon ground red pepper
- ⅛ teaspoon salt
- ⅛ teaspoon garlic powder
- 1½ pounds red snapper fillets
- Cooking spray
- 8 (6-inch) corn tortillas
- 2 cups shredded cabbage

1. Preheat oven to 425°.

2. To prepare crema, combine first 8 ingredients in a small bowl; set aside.

3. To prepare tacos, combine cumin and next 5 ingredients in a small bowl; sprinkle spice mixture evenly over both sides of fish. Place fish on a baking sheet coated with cooking spray. Bake at 425° for 9 minutes or until fish flakes easily when tested with a fork or until desired degree of doneness. Place fish in a bowl; break into pieces with a fork. Heat tortillas according to package directions. Divide fish evenly among tortillas; top each with ¼ cup cabbage and 1 tablespoon crema. Yield: 4 servings (serving size: 2 wraps).

CALORIES 394 (14% from fat); FAT 6.3g (sat 1.5g, mono 1.5g, poly 1.5g); PROTEIN 40.3g; CARB 40.1g; FIBER 5.5g; CHOL 70mg; IRON 3.5mg; SODIUM 857mg; CALC 233mg

---

Wrap and Roll Menu 2

serves 4

Curried Chicken Salad in Naan

Baked sweet potato chips

Cranberry spritzers*

*Combine 2 cups cranberry juice, 1 cup sparkling water, and 1 cup orange juice in a small pitcher; chill. Pour 1 cup cranberry mixture into each of 4 ice-filled glasses.

Game Plan

1. Prepare cranberry spritzers.

2. While spritzers chill:
- Prepare salad and sandwiches.

QUICK & EASY
Curried Chicken Salad in Naan

This fruited sandwich filling is a natural for breads such as naan (an Indian flatbread) or pita, but it's also tasty on pumpernickel or sourdough bread.

TOTAL TIME: 35 MINUTES

QUICK TIP: To chop dried apricots, coat the knife blade with cooking spray to keep the fruit from sticking to the blade. You can also use a sharp pair of kitchen shears.

- 6 tablespoons reduced-fat mayonnaise
- ½ teaspoon grated orange rind
- 1½ teaspoons orange juice
- 1 teaspoon curry powder
- ½ teaspoon grated peeled fresh ginger
- 2½ cups diced roasted boneless, skinless chicken breast (about ¾ pound)
- ¾ cup green seedless grapes, halved
- ¼ cup diced dried apricots
- ¼ cup thinly sliced green onions
- 2 tablespoons chopped, unsalted cashews
- 1 tablespoon chopped fresh parsley
- 4 (6-inch) naan breads
- 3 cups trimmed watercress

1. Combine first 5 ingredients in a large bowl; stir with a whisk. Add chicken and next 5 ingredients to mayonnaise mixture, tossing to coat.

Continued

2. Heat naan according to package directions, if desired.

3. Spoon about ¾ cup chicken mixture onto each naan. Top with ¾ cup watercress; fold over. Yield: 4 servings (serving size: 1 sandwich).

CALORIES 458 (24% from fat); FAT 12.2g (sat 3g, mono 4.1g, poly 3.8g); PROTEIN 35.5g; CARB 52.7g; FIBER 5.5g; CHOL 72mg; IRON 3.8mg; SODIUM 602mg; CALC 83mg

Wrap and Roll Menu 3

serves 4

Lamb Pitas with Lemon-Mint Sauce

Greek salad*

Vanilla frozen yogurt with honey

*Combine 4 cups fresh baby spinach, 1 cup peeled diced cucumber, ⅓ cup thinly sliced red onion, 2 tablespoons sliced ripe olives, 2 tablespoons crumbled feta cheese, and 4 plum tomatoes, cut into wedges. Combine 3 tablespoons lemon juice, 1 tablespoon olive oil, 2 teaspoons minced fresh oregano, ⅛ teaspoon salt, and ⅛ teaspoon black pepper in a small bowl, stirring with a whisk. Add to spinach mixture; toss well.

Game Plan

1. Prepare lemon-mint sauce.
2. Prepare ingredients for Greek salad.
3. Simmer meat mixture; toss salad.
4. Make sandwiches.

QUICK & EASY
Lamb Pitas with Lemon-Mint Sauce

A chilled yogurt sauce is a refreshing contrast to the zesty seasoned meat mixture.

TOTAL TIME: 41 MINUTES

TASTE TIP: Heat pitas 1 minute on each side in a small skillet before preparing the meat filling; wrap them in foil to keep warm.

SAUCE:
  ⅔ cup plain low-fat yogurt
  2 tablespoons chopped fresh mint
  2 teaspoons grated lemon rind
  ¼ teaspoon ground black pepper
  ⅛ teaspoon salt

SANDWICHES:
  6 ounces ground lamb
  6 ounces ground sirloin
  Cooking spray
  ½ cup finely chopped red onion
  1 teaspoon minced fresh thyme
  ¼ teaspoon ground cumin
  ¼ teaspoon salt
  ⅛ teaspoon crushed red pepper
  2 garlic cloves, minced
  ¼ cup minced fresh parsley
  4 (6-inch) pitas, cut in half
  1 cup peeled seeded thinly sliced cucumber
  2 bottled roasted red bell peppers, cut into ¼-inch strips (about ½ cup)

1. To prepare sauce, combine first 5 ingredients in a small bowl; cover and chill until ready to serve.

2. To prepare sandwiches, heat a large nonstick skillet over medium-high heat. Add lamb and beef to pan; cook 5 minutes or until browned; stirring to crumble. Drain well, and set aside. Wipe pan dry with a paper towel.

3. Lightly coat pan with cooking spray; return to heat. Add onion; sauté 3 minutes or until tender. Stir in meat mixture, thyme, cumin, ¼ teaspoon salt, crushed red pepper, and garlic. Reduce heat to low; cook 2 minutes, stirring occasionally. Remove from heat; stir in parsley. Fill each pita half with ¼ cup lamb mixture, 2 tablespoons cucumber, about 1 tablespoon roasted peppers, and about 1 tablespoon sauce. Yield: 4 servings (serving size: 2 stuffed pita halves).

CALORIES 381 (28% from fat); FAT 11.8g (sat 4.7g, mono 4.5g, poly 1.2g); PROTEIN 27.1g; CARB 40.9g; FIBER 2.4g; CHOL 66mg; IRON 3.8mg; SODIUM 680mg; CALC 163mg

Wrap and Roll Menu 4

serves 4

Chipotle Pork Tacos

Radish, celery, and fennel salad*

Fresh pineapple spears

*Combine 1 cup thinly sliced radishes, 1 cup thinly sliced fennel bulb, ½ cup thinly sliced celery, and 1 tablespoon finely chopped niçoise or kalamata olives in a large bowl. Combine 3 tablespoons fresh lemon juice, 2 tablespoons white wine vinegar, 2 teaspoons extravirgin olive oil, 1½ teaspoons honey, ¼ teaspoon salt, and ¼ teaspoon freshly ground black pepper in a small bowl; stirring with a whisk. Drizzle over salad; toss gently to coat.

Game Plan

1. Prepare salad and dressing.
2. Prepare taco filling.
3. While tortillas heat:
   • Toss salad.
4. Assemble tacos.

QUICK & EASY
Chipotle Pork Tacos

TOTAL TIME: 40 MINUTES

QUICK TIP: Pounding the tenderloin while it's still whole is quicker and takes less effort than pounding pieces of sliced pork.

  1 (1-pound) pork tenderloin, trimmed
  1½ teaspoons grated lime rind
  1 tablespoon fresh lime juice
  2 teaspoons minced fresh or ½ teaspoon dried oregano
  2 teaspoons chopped chipotle chile canned in adobo sauce
  2 teaspoons bottled minced garlic
  1 teaspoon brown sugar
  ¼ teaspoon salt
  Cooking spray
  1 cup thinly sliced shallots (about 3 large shallots)
  2 teaspoons olive oil
  8 (6-inch) corn tortillas
  ¼ cup reduced-fat sour cream
  Chopped fresh cilantro (optional)

1. Place tenderloin between 2 sheets of

heavy-duty plastic wrap, and pound to ¼-inch thickness using a meat mallet or small, heavy skillet. Cut meat crosswise into thin strips, and place in a medium bowl. Add rind and next 6 ingredients; stir well.

2. Heat a large nonstick skillet over medium-high heat. Coat pan with cooking spray. Add shallots; sauté 4 minutes or until lightly browned. Place shallots in a large bowl.

3. Heat oil in pan over medium-high heat. Add pork mixture; cook 3 minutes or until pork loses its pink color, stirring frequently. Add pork to shallots in bowl; stir well to combine.

4. Warm tortillas according to package directions. Spoon about ⅓ cup meat mixture onto each tortilla; top each tortilla with 1½ teaspoons sour cream. Garnish with chopped cilantro, if desired; fold in half. Yield: 4 servings (serving size: 2 tacos).

CALORIES 299 (28% from fat); FAT 9.3g (sat 2.8g, mono 3.9g, poly 1.2g); PROTEIN 27.3g; CARB 27.4g; FIBER 2.6g; CHOL 80mg; IRON 2mg; SODIUM 253mg; CALC 61mg

enlightened cook

Nice Guys, Nice Food

Three Portland, Oregon, chefs cook family-style meals for patrons in a unique community setting.

Simpatica Dining Hall is tucked into the basement of a funky yellow building in southeast Portland's warehouse district. This underground eatery operates only on weekend evenings, Sunday mornings, and special holidays.

But the moment the doors swing open, the simple cement-floored room turns into a cozy supper club. Although anyone who visits the simpaticacatering.com Web site can sign up for the mailing list to find out about the multicourse, prix-fixe dinners (which typically cost $30 to $40), once seated at Simpatica's dining tables, patrons feel like friends or family rather than strangers at an ordinary restaurant.

Beer-Braised Beef with Italian Salsa Verde

This meat dish is a specialty at Simpatica Dining Hall. You can prepare and refrigerate the salsa verde up to two weeks in advance. It's good with chicken or fish, too, or simply atop grilled bread as an appetizer. Serve the beef and salsa over mashed potatoes instead of toasted bread, if desired.

SALSA VERDE:

- 1 cup chopped fresh mint
- ⅔ cup chopped fresh dill
- ⅓ cup chopped fresh flat-leaf parsley
- ¼ cup finely chopped shallots
- 1 tablespoon chopped capers
- 3 tablespoons extravirgin olive oil
- ½ teaspoon sea salt
- ¼ teaspoon freshly ground black pepper

BEEF:

- 2 pounds boneless chuck roast, trimmed and cut into 3-inch cubes
- ½ teaspoon sea salt
- ¼ teaspoon freshly ground black pepper
- Cooking spray
- 1 teaspoon olive oil
- 3 cups vertically sliced onion (about 1 large)
- 1 cup fat-free, less-sodium beef broth
- 1 (12-ounce) can Guinness Stout

REMAINING INGREDIENT:

- 1 (16-ounce) loaf Italian bread, cut into 16 (1-ounce) slices, toasted

1. To prepare salsa, combine first 8 ingredients in a small bowl. Cover and chill until ready to serve.

2. To prepare beef, sprinkle beef with ½ teaspoon salt and ¼ teaspoon pepper. Heat a Dutch oven over medium-high heat. Coat pan with cooking spray. Add beef; cook 5 minutes or until browned. Remove from pan.

3. Add 1 teaspoon oil and onion to pan. Reduce heat, and cook 12 minutes or until golden brown, stirring occasionally.

4. Return beef to pan. Add broth and beer; bring to a boil. Cover, reduce heat, and simmer 1 hour and 30 minutes or until tender. Remove beef from pan; shred beef with 2 forks. Return beef to pan; stir. Spoon ¼ cup beef mixture over each bread slice; top each with 1½ tablespoons salsa. Yield: 8 servings (serving size: 2 topped slices).

CALORIES 387 (29% from fat); FAT 12.4g (sat 3g, mono 6.8g, poly 1.5g); PROTEIN 29.9g; CARB 34.7g; FIBER 2.1g; CHOL 47mg; IRON 4.3mg; SODIUM 788mg; CALC 78mg

Orange and Red Onion Salad with Red Pepper

This simple salad is a refreshing start to winter meals at Simpatica Dining Hall. Garnish with fresh mint or flat-leaf parsley, if desired.

- 18 (¼-inch-thick) orange slices (about 4 oranges)
- ½ cup vertically sliced red onion
- ½ teaspoon sea salt
- ¼ teaspoon freshly ground black pepper
- ¼ teaspoon ground red pepper
- 2 tablespoons extravirgin olive oil

1. Arrange orange slices in a single layer on a platter. Top evenly with onion. Sprinkle with salt, black pepper, and red pepper. Drizzle with oil. Serve immediately. Yield: 6 servings (serving size: 3 orange slices and about 5 onion pieces).

CALORIES 93 (54% from fat); FAT 4.9g (sat 0.7g, mono 3.6g, poly 0.5g); PROTEIN 0.8g; CARB 12.7g; FIBER 2.6g; CHOL 0mg; IRON 0.2mg; SODIUM 192mg; CALC 46mg

Olive Oil Cake

Olive oil is the star ingredient in this lightened version of Dining Hall's cake, so be sure to use a good-quality extravirgin oil.

Cooking spray
2 tablespoons all-purpose flour
2½ cups granulated sugar
1½ cups fat-free milk
¾ cup egg substitute
½ cup extravirgin olive oil
2 tablespoons lemon rind
3 tablespoons fresh lemon juice
2¼ cups all-purpose flour (about 10 ounces)
1 teaspoon baking powder
1 teaspoon salt
½ teaspoon baking soda
¼ cup orange marmalade
2 tablespoons powdered sugar

1. Preheat oven to 350°.
2. Coat a 12-cup Bundt pan with cooking spray; dust with 2 tablespoons flour.
3. Combine granulated sugar, milk, egg substitute, oil, rind, and juice in a large bowl; stir with a whisk until well combined.
4. Lightly spoon flour into dry measuring cups; level with a knife. Combine flour, baking powder, salt, and baking soda; stir well with a whisk. Add flour mixture to oil mixture, stirring with whisk until smooth.
5. Pour batter into prepared pan. Bake at 350° for 55 minutes or until golden brown and cake begins to pull away from sides of pan. Cool cake completely in pan on wire rack. Loosen edges of cake with a spatula. Place a plate upside down on top of cake; invert onto plate.
6. Place marmalade in a microwave-safe bowl. Microwave at HIGH 1 minute. Stir, and spoon hot marmalade evenly over cake. Cool completely. Sift powdered sugar over top of cake. Yield: 16 servings.

CALORIES 284 (24% from fat); FAT 7.6g (sat 1.1g, mono 5.5g, poly 0.9g); PROTEIN 4.2g; CARB 50.7g; FIBER 0.6g; CHOL 1mg; IRON 1.1mg; SODIUM 253mg; CALC 62mg

Feast of the Seven Fishes

Let this Italian Christmas Eve tradition draw your family together at the table.

Celebrate an ancient Italian Christmas Eve tradition—the Feast of the Seven Fishes or *La Vigilia di Natale* (The Vigil of the Birth).

Opinions differ on the origins of this predominantly Southern Italian, Roman Catholic tradition, but it's most commonly attributed to the seven days it took for the Virgin Mary to travel to Bethlehem, the seven sacraments, the seven days of the week, the seven days of creation, or the seven deadly sins. Prepare the whole meal, or those dishes that best suit your family's tastes.

Italian Christmas Eve Feast
serves 6

This menu feeds a small group, but you can easily double the recipes to accommodate a larger gathering. Prepare all the recipes for a true feast, or pick just a couple of entrées for a low-key evening.

White Bean Bruschetta

Mussels in Red Sauce

Mixed Seafood Salad

Crabmeat Ravioli with Clam Sauce

Southern Italian Fish Soup

Flounder Rolls with Cherry Tomatoes and Spinach

Tricolor Salad

Garlicky Broccoli Rabe

Poached Pears with Cardamom Cream

Grandma Babe's Lemon Knots

Hazelnut Dessert Coffee

White Bean Bruschetta

For the best flavor, use high-quality extravirgin olive oil. Prepare and chill the white bean spread up to two days in advance; bring to room temperature before serving. Toast the baguette slices up to a day ahead, and store in a zip-top plastic bag.

¼ cup chopped fresh flat-leaf parsley
1½ tablespoons fresh lemon juice
½ teaspoon salt
½ teaspoon freshly ground black pepper
1 large garlic clove
1 (19-ounce) can cannellini beans or other white beans, rinsed and drained
3 tablespoons extravirgin olive oil
2 teaspoons water
1 (10-ounce) French bread baguette, cut into 24 (½-inch-thick) slices

1. Preheat oven to 350°.
2. Place parsley, juice, salt, pepper, garlic, and beans in a food processor; process until smooth. With processor on, slowly add oil through food chute. Add water, 1 teaspoon at a time; process until creamy.
3. Place bread on a baking sheet. Bake at 350° for 5 minutes on each side or until

lightly browned. Serve with white bean spread. Yield: 12 servings (serving size: 2 baguette slices and about 2 tablespoons spread).

CALORIES 123 (26% from fat); FAT 3.5g (sat 0.5g, mono 2.5g, poly 0.5g); PROTEIN 3.6g; CARB 19.7g; FIBER 1.9g; CHOL 0mg; IRON 1.4mg; SODIUM 310mg; CALC 14mg

Mussels in Red Sauce

1½ teaspoons olive oil
¼ cup finely chopped
   onion
1 garlic clove, chopped
1 (28-ounce) can crushed tomatoes, undrained
2 tablespoons chopped fresh flat-leaf parsley
1½ tablespoons chopped fresh oregano
¼ to ½ teaspoon crushed red pepper
2 pounds mussels, scrubbed and debearded

1. Heat oil in a large Dutch oven over medium-high heat. Add onion; sauté 3 minutes or until tender. Add garlic; sauté 1 minute. Stir in tomatoes; partially cover, reduce heat, and simmer 30 minutes. Add parsley and remaining ingredients; cook 5 minutes or until shells open, stirring occasionally. Remove from heat; discard any unopened shells. Yield: 6 servings (serving size: about 1½ cups).

CALORIES 113 (24% from fat); FAT 3g (sat 0.5g, mono 1.2g, poly 0.7g); PROTEIN 10g; CARB 13.1g; FIBER 2.7g; CHOL 18mg; IRON 4.4mg; SODIUM 359mg; CALC 70mg

MAKE AHEAD
Mixed Seafood Salad

Brimming with a combination of six types of fresh seafood, this simply seasoned salad could be the star of your dinner. Use any combination you like. Flavorings are minimal to allow the seafood to shine. To ensure the octopus becomes tender, it needs lengthy cooking in barely simmering water. Cook the seafood a day ahead and refrigerate; toss with remaining ingredients a couple of hours before serving.

6 cups water
1 teaspoon salt
½ pound cleaned squid
½ pound medium shrimp, peeled and deveined
½ pound bay scallops
½ pound cleaned octopus
½ pound cooked lobster meat, cut into 1-inch pieces (about 3 tails)
½ pound lump crabmeat, drained and shell pieces removed
¼ cup fresh lemon juice
3 tablespoons chopped fresh flat-leaf parsley
3 tablespoons chopped fresh chives
2 tablespoons extravirgin olive oil
2 garlic cloves, minced
Lemon wedges (optional)
Parsley sprigs (optional)

1. Bring 6 cups water and salt to boil in a large saucepan over medium-high heat. Add squid; cook 3 minutes or until squid is just tender. Remove squid from pan with a slotted spoon. Plunge squid into ice water; drain. Cut squid into 1-inch pieces. Place squid in a large bowl.
2. Add shrimp to boiling water; cook 3 minutes or until done. Remove shrimp from pan with a slotted spoon. Plunge shrimp into ice water; drain. Add shrimp to bowl with squid.
3. Place a vegetable steamer in pan. Reduce heat to medium-low. Arrange scallops in steamer; cook over simmering water 6 minutes or until done. Plunge scallops into ice water; drain. Add scallops to bowl. Cover scallop mixture, and chill.
4. Remove steamer from pan. Add octopus to simmering water; cover and simmer 2 to 2½ hours or until fork-tender (add additional water, if necessary, to cover octopus.) Plunge octopus into ice water; drain. Rub off skin. Cut octopus into 1-inch pieces. Add octopus, lobster, and crabmeat to scallop mixture. Add juice and next 4 ingredients; toss gently to combine. Chill at least 2 hours. Garnish with lemon wedges and parsley sprigs, if desired. Yield: 6 servings (serving size: 1 cup).

CALORIES 247 (27% from fat); FAT 7.3g (sat 1g, mono 3.6g, poly 1.4g); PROTEIN 38.8g; CARB 5.1g; FIBER 0.2g; CHOL 237mg; IRON 3.9mg; SODIUM 608mg; CALC 108mg

MAKE AHEAD
Crabmeat Ravioli with Clam Sauce

Cook the sauce up to two days ahead, and reheat gently over medium-low heat before serving. Prepare a double batch of the sauce while you're at it, and freeze half to toss with pasta for a quick dinner later. You can prepare the ravioli filling up to a day in advance; fill and cook the ravioli just before serving. For a lovely garnish, tuck a fresh oregano sprig into each serving.

SAUCE:

1 tablespoon olive oil
⅓ cup finely chopped onion
2 garlic cloves, minced
1 (28-ounce) can crushed tomatoes, undrained
1 (14.5-ounce) can no-salt-added diced tomatoes
2 tablespoons chopped fresh flat-leaf parsley
1 tablespoon chopped fresh oregano
¼ teaspoon salt
¼ teaspoon crushed red pepper
¼ teaspoon freshly ground black pepper
1 (10-ounce) can whole clams, drained

RAVIOLI:

½ pound lump crabmeat, drained and shell pieces removed
½ cup finely chopped red bell pepper
2 tablespoons panko (Japanese breadcrumbs)
1 tablespoon chopped fresh chives
⅛ teaspoon salt
½ cup part-skim ricotta
24 round wonton wrappers or gyoza skins

1. To prepare sauce, heat oil in a Dutch oven over medium-high heat. Add onion; sauté 3 minutes or until tender. Add garlic; sauté 1 minute. Add tomatoes; bring to a boil. Reduce heat, and simmer 30 minutes. Add parsley and next 5 ingredients; simmer 10 minutes. Remove from heat; set aside.
2. To prepare ravioli, combine crab and
Continued

next 4 ingredients in a medium bowl. Add ricotta; stir gently to combine. Working with 1 wonton wrapper at a time (cover remaining wrappers with a damp towel to keep them from drying), spoon about 1 tablespoon crab mixture into center of wrapper. Moisten edges of wrapper with water. Fold in half, pinching edges together to seal and create a half-moon shape. Repeat procedure with remaining wonton wrappers and crab mixture.

3. Fill a large Dutch oven with water; bring water to a boil. Add half of ravioli; cook 4 minutes or until done. Remove ravioli from pan with a slotted spoon; keep warm. Repeat procedure with remaining ravioli. Serve ravioli immediately with sauce. Yield: 6 servings (serving size: 4 ravioli and about ⅔ cup sauce).

CALORIES 272 (18% from fat); FAT 5.3g (sat 1.4g, mono 2.2g, poly 0.6g); PROTEIN 22.7g; CARB 35.7g; FIBER 5.2g; CHOL 49mg; IRON 10mg; SODIUM 706mg; CALC 171mg

MAKE AHEAD
Southern Italian Fish Soup

If you have a great seafood market nearby, try adding other fish or seafood—clams or chopped scallops or cod, for example. You can make the broth for this fresh, fast soup the day before. Follow the recipe through step 1, cover, and chill. To finish, bring the broth to a simmer and proceed with step 2.

   Cooking spray
  2 teaspoons olive oil
2½ cups chopped leek (about 2 large)
  2 garlic cloves, minced
2½ cups water
  1 cup dry white wine
  1 (14.5-ounce) can diced tomatoes, undrained
  1 thyme sprig
 ½ teaspoon salt
 ¼ teaspoon freshly ground black pepper
  8 ounces medium shrimp, peeled, deveined, and coarsely chopped
  8 ounces grouper or other firm white fish fillets, cut into 2-inch pieces
 ⅓ cup chopped fresh flat-leaf parsley

1. Heat a Dutch oven over medium-high heat. Coat pan with cooking spray. Add oil to pan, swirling to coat. Add leek; sauté 8 minutes or until tender and lightly browned. Add garlic; sauté 1 minute. Stir in 2½ cups water, wine, tomatoes, and thyme; bring to a boil. Cover, reduce heat, and simmer 20 minutes. Discard thyme.

2. Stir in salt, pepper, shrimp, and grouper; simmer 6 minutes or until fish is done. Remove from heat; stir in parsley. Serve immediately. Yield: 6 servings (serving size: about 1 cup).

CALORIES 125 (19% from fat); FAT 2.7g (sat 0.4g, mono 1.3g, poly 0.6g); PROTEIN 16.2g; CARB 9g; FIBER 1.8g; CHOL 71mg; IRON 2.5mg; SODIUM 368mg; CALC 68mg

MAKE AHEAD
Flounder Rolls with Cherry Tomatoes and Spinach

Ask your fishmonger to remove the skin from the flounder fillets. Another time-saver: Stuff and roll the fillets a day in advance. Cover and refrigerate until you're ready to cook them.

1½ tablespoons olive oil, divided
  1 tablespoon chopped shallots
  1 teaspoon minced fresh garlic
  1 cup cherry tomatoes, quartered and divided
  2 tablespoons chopped fresh flat-leaf parsley
  2 tablespoons fresh lemon juice
 ½ teaspoon salt, divided
 ½ teaspoon freshly ground black pepper, divided
 ¼ teaspoon Old Bay seasoning
 ½ cup panko (Japanese breadcrumbs)
  6 (6-ounce) skinless flounder fillets
   Cooking spray
1½ cups dry white wine
  1 (10-ounce) package fresh spinach

1. Preheat oven to 400°.

2. Heat 1 teaspoon oil in a small skillet over medium-high heat. Add shallots; sauté 3 minutes or until tender and lightly browned. Add garlic; sauté 30 seconds. Spoon shallot mixture into a food processor. Add ½ cup tomatoes, parsley, juice, ¼ teaspoon salt, ¼ teaspoon pepper, and Old Bay; process just until combined. Spoon shallot mixture into a bowl; stir in panko.

3. Place each fillet between 2 sheets of heavy-duty plastic wrap; pound to ½-inch thickness using a meat mallet or small heavy skillet. Spoon about 1½ tablespoons shallot mixture on small end of each fillet. Beginning with small end, roll up jelly-roll fashion; secure with toothpicks. Arrange rolls on a jelly-roll pan coated with cooking spray. Drizzle with 2 teaspoons oil; sprinkle with ⅛ teaspoon salt and ⅛ teaspoon pepper. Add remaining ½ cup tomatoes and wine to pan. Bake at 400° for 25 minutes or until fish flakes easily when tested with a fork or until desired degree of doneness.

4. Heat remaining 1½ teaspoons oil in a large nonstick skillet over medium-high heat. Gradually add spinach; sauté 3 minutes or until spinach wilts. Remove from heat; sprinkle with remaining ⅛ teaspoon salt and remaining ⅛ teaspoon pepper. Remove fish and tomatoes from oven; discard wine. Serve fish and tomatoes over spinach. Yield: 6 servings (serving size: 1 fish roll, about ⅓ cup spinach, and about 2 tomato halves).

CALORIES 224 (23% from fat); FAT 5.8g (sat 1g, mono 2.9g, poly 1g); PROTEIN 34.5g; CARB 7.5g; FIBER 1.6g; CHOL 82mg; IRON 2.2mg; SODIUM 414mg; CALC 86mg

WINE NOTE: Flounder's delicate flavor gets a sophisticated boost from the herbal-tart character of the spinach and tomatoes. It's just the sort of dish Italians love to marry with a bone-dry Italian white wine like vermentino. With hints of wild herbs and a crisp minerally tang, vermentino is perfectly balanced for a seafood dish like this. Try Antinori Vermentino. The 2005 is about $21.

Tricolor Salad

Here's a great make-ahead trick: A couple of hours before dinner, pour the prepared dressing into the bottom of the serving bowl, and assemble the salad greens on top. When you bring the salad to the table, all you need to do is toss—and you won't have soggy greens.

    1   tablespoon minced shallots
    1   tablespoon balsamic vinegar
    1   tablespoon fresh lemon juice
    1   tablespoon water
    2   teaspoons extravirgin olive oil
    2   teaspoons Dijon mustard
    ¼   teaspoon sugar
    ⅛   teaspoon salt
    ⅛   teaspoon freshly ground black
        pepper
    2   cups torn Belgian endive (about 2
        heads)
    2   cups torn radicchio (about ½ head)
    1   (5-ounce) package fresh baby
        arugula (about 8 cups loosely
        packed)

1. Combine first 9 ingredients in a large bowl, stirring well with a whisk. Add endive, radicchio, and arugula; toss gently to coat. Serve immediately. Yield: 6 servings (serving size: about 1 cup).

CALORIES 34 (50% from fat); FAT 1.9g (sat 0.3g, mono 1.2g, poly 0.3g); PROTEIN 1.2g; CARB 3.9g; FIBER 1.5g; CHOL 0mg; IRON 0.6mg; SODIUM 102mg; CALC 49mg

Garlicky Broccoli Rabe

Boiling the broccoli rabe helps remove some bitterness before it's sautéed in the garlic-infused oil.

    2   pounds broccoli rabe (rapini),
        trimmed
    1   tablespoon olive oil
    2   large garlic cloves, thinly sliced
    ½   teaspoon salt
    ½   teaspoon freshly ground black
        pepper
    ¼   teaspoon crushed red pepper

1. Cook broccoli rabe in boiling water

6 minutes or until crisp-tender. Drain and plunge broccoli rabe into ice water; drain. Coarsely chop.

2. Heat oil in a large skillet over medium heat. Add garlic; cook 2 minutes, stirring constantly. Stir in broccoli rabe, salt, and peppers. Yield: 6 servings (serving size: ½ cup).

CALORIES 67 (31% from fat); FAT 2.3g (sat 0.3g, mono 1.6g, poly 0.3g); PROTEIN 5.4g; CARB 7.6g; FIBER 0.1g; CHOL 0mg; IRON 1.3mg; SODIUM 241mg; CALC 74mg

Poached Pears with Cardamom Cream

Make the components for this dessert a day ahead; assemble shortly before serving.

PEARS:

    6   peeled Bosc pears
    3   cups water
    2   cups orange juice
    ¼   cup sugar
    6   black peppercorns
    1   (2-inch) piece vanilla bean, split
        lengthwise
    1   (1.5-liter) bottle Asti Spumante or
        other sweet sparkling wine

CREAM:

    1½ cups vanilla ice cream
    2   cardamom pods, crushed
        Mint sprigs (optional)
        Ground cardamom (optional)

1. To prepare pears, working with 1 pear at a time, hold pear, stem side down, in 1 hand. Make 3 or 4 quick cuts into pear from bottom, using a melon baller (do not remove stem). If necessary, cut about ¼ inch from base of pears so they will sit flat when served.

2. Combine 3 cups water and next 5 ingredients in a large stockpot over medium heat; bring to a simmer. Cook 6 minutes or until sugar dissolves, stirring occasionally. Add pears; using tongs, place a small clean plate on top of pears to weigh them down. Return to a simmer; cook 15 minutes or until tender. Remove pot from heat; cool mixture to room temperature. Cover and chill 4 hours or up to overnight (do not remove plate).

3. To prepare cream, melt ice cream in a small heavy saucepan over medium-low heat. Remove from heat.

4. Heat a small skillet over medium-high heat. Add crushed cardamom; cook 2 minutes or until fragrant, shaking pan frequently. Stir cardamom into melted ice cream; cook over medium-low heat 5 minutes, stirring occasionally. Remove from heat. Strain mixture through a fine sieve over a bowl; discard solids. Cool cream to room temperature; cover and chill.

5. Remove plate from chilled pears. Remove pears from liquid with a slotted spoon; discard liquid. Spoon about 2½ tablespoons cream onto bottom of each of 6 small dessert plates or shallow bowls; top each serving with 1 pear. Garnish with mint sprigs and ground cardamom, if desired. Yield: 6 servings.

CALORIES 183 (30% from fat); FAT 6.2g (sat 3.7g, mono 1.8g, poly 0.3g); PROTEIN 2g; CARB 32.9g; FIBER 4.3g; CHOL 23mg; IRON 0.4mg; SODIUM 25mg; CALC 60mg

Grandma Babe's Lemon Knots

Store these tangy cookies in an airtight container at room temperature for up to one week.

COOKIES:

    ½   cup granulated sugar
    6   tablespoons butter, softened
    1   tablespoon finely grated lemon
        rind
    ¼   cup fresh lemon juice
    2   large eggs
    3   cups flour (about 13½ ounces)
    2   teaspoons baking powder
    ¼   teaspoon salt
        Cooking spray

GLAZE:

    2   cups powdered sugar
    3   tablespoons fresh lemon
        juice
    1   tablespoon low-fat buttermilk

1. Preheat oven to 375°.

2. To prepare cookies, place granulated sugar and butter in a large bowl; beat
Continued

with a mixer at medium speed 3 minutes or until light and fluffy. Beat in rind and ¼ cup juice. Add eggs, 1 at a time, beating well after each addition (mixture will look curdled).

3. Lightly spoon flour into dry measuring cups; level with a knife. Combine flour, baking powder, and salt, stirring well with a whisk. Add flour mixture to sugar mixture; stir with a wooden spoon to form a stiff dough. Turn dough out onto a floured surface; knead 10 to 15 times to form a smooth dough.

4. Divide dough into 8 equal portions. Working with 1 portion at a time (cover remaining dough to prevent drying), shape portion into a 30-inch-long rope; cut rope crosswise into 6 (5-inch) pieces. Tie each dough piece into a knot. Place knots on 2 baking sheets coated with cooking spray. Bake 1 sheet at a time at 375° for 8 minutes or until bottoms of cookies are lightly browned and tops are still pale. Remove cookies from pan; cool on wire racks.

5. To prepare glaze, combine powdered sugar, 3 tablespoons juice, and buttermilk; stir until smooth. Dip tops of cookies into glaze; dry on racks. Yield: 4 dozen cookies (serving size: 1 cookie).

CALORIES 72 (21% from fat); FAT 1.7g (sat 1g, mono 0.5g, poly 0.1g); PROTEIN 1.1g; CARB 13.3g; FIBER 0.2g; CHOL 13mg; IRON 0.4mg; SODIUM 34mg; CALC 15mg

---

QUICK & EASY
Hazelnut Dessert Coffee

Serve with Grandma Babe's Lemon Knots (recipe on page 445). Use any other liqueur that you prefer, such as Grand Marnier or Chambord.

 6 tablespoons Frangelico (hazelnut-flavored liqueur)
 3 cups hot strong brewed coffee
 2 tablespoons frozen reduced-calorie whipped topping, thawed
 Ground cinnamon (optional)

1. Place liqueur in a microwave-safe bowl; microwave at HIGH 10 seconds or until warm. Add warm liqueur to coffee. Pour about ½ cup coffee mixture into each of 6 cups; top each serving with

1 teaspoon whipped topping, and sprinkle with cinnamon, if desired. Yield: 6 servings.

CALORIES 131 (1% from fat); FAT 0.2g (sat 0.2g, mono 0g, poly 0g); PROTEIN 0.1g; CARB 23.9g; FIBER 0g; CHOL 0mg; IRON 0mg; SODIUM 2mg; CALC 2mg

---

superfast
. . . And Ready in Just About 20 Minutes

More than a week's worth of quick entrées to get dinner on the table in a flash

---

QUICK & EASY
Turkey and Blue Cheese Salad

Bottled ranch dressing gets customized with garlic and dill; try other combinations, such as shallots and oregano, if you'd like. Serve with breadsticks or rolls. Leftovers are great folded up in a flatbread or stuffed in a pita.

 ⅓ cup light ranch dressing
 1 tablespoon 1% low-fat milk
 1 teaspoon bottled minced garlic
 ½ teaspoon dried dill
 ¼ teaspoon salt
 1 cup chopped plum tomato
 ½ cup chopped celery
 ½ cup chopped green onions
 4 ounces roasted turkey, cut into thin strips
 2 ounces crumbled blue cheese
 1 (8-ounce) bag preshredded lettuce
 1 (15½-ounce) can chickpeas (garbanzo beans), rinsed and drained
 1 Anaheim chile, sliced into thin rounds

1. Combine first 5 ingredients in a small bowl; set aside.
2. Combine tomato, celery, and remaining ingredients in a large bowl; pour

dressing over salad. Toss gently to coat. Yield: 4 servings (serving size: about 2 cups).

CALORIES 232 (30% from fat); FAT 7.7g (sat 2.8g, mono 1.9g, poly 1.4g); PROTEIN 16.5g; CARB 24.2g; FIBER 5.5g; CHOL 34mg; IRON 2.3mg; SODIUM 774mg; CALC 136mg

---

QUICK & EASY
One-Dish Chicken and Kielbasa Rice

The turmeric, chicken broth, and sausage add layers of flavor to the rice. If you want to splurge, you can substitute a few crushed saffron threads for the turmeric.

 2 cups fat-free, less-sodium chicken broth
 ⅛ teaspoon ground turmeric
 8 ounces turkey kielbasa, cut into ½-inch pieces
 2 cups long-grain parboiled rice (such as Uncle Ben's)
 2 teaspoons olive oil
 8 ounces skinless, boneless chicken thighs, cut into bite-sized pieces
 1 cup prechopped onion
 1 cup prechopped green bell pepper
 ½ cup frozen green peas
 ¼ cup sliced pitted stuffed manzanilla (or green) olives
 1 tablespoon bottled minced garlic

1. Combine first 3 ingredients in a medium saucepan; bring to a boil. Stir in rice. Cover, reduce heat, and simmer 5 minutes. Remove from heat, and let stand 5 minutes.
2. Heat oil in a large skillet over high heat. Add chicken; cook 2 minutes or until browned, stirring occasionally. Add onion and bell pepper; sauté 4 minutes or until tender. Stir in peas, olives, and garlic; sauté 1 minute. Add rice mixture; cook 1 minute or until thoroughly heated, stirring constantly. Yield: 4 servings (serving size: 1½ cups).

CALORIES 428 (24% from fat); FAT 11.5g (sat 2.6g, mono 5.4g, poly 2.4g); PROTEIN 26.7g; CARB 53.1g; FIBER 4g; CHOL 84mg; IRON 5.2mg; SODIUM 891mg; CALC 60mg

Sausage, Escarole, and White Bean Ragoût

Italian turkey sausage and bold escarole are filling additions to this French-accented stew. Substitute mustard greens to mimic the bitter flavor of escarole, or use spinach for milder flavor. Serve with a crusty baguette or rolls.

12 ounces sweet turkey Italian sausage
Cooking spray
1 cup prechopped onion
1 cup cubed peeled red potatoes (about 6 ounces)
⅓ cup chardonnay or other dry white wine
1 tablespoon bottled minced garlic
1 (16-ounce) can cannellini beans or other white beans, rinsed and drained
1 (14-ounce) can fat-free, less-sodium chicken broth
4 cups sliced escarole (about 4 ounces)
1 teaspoon chopped fresh rosemary
2 tablespoons grated fresh Parmesan cheese

1. Remove casings from sausage.
2. Heat a large nonstick skillet over medium-high heat. Coat pan with cooking spray. Add Italian sausage and onion to pan, and cook 4 minutes or until sausage browns, stirring to crumble. Drain sausage mixture well; return to pan. Stir in potatoes, wine, garlic, beans, and chicken broth; bring to a simmer. Cover and cook 7 minutes. Stir in escarole and rosemary, and cook 4 minutes or until escarole wilts, stirring occasionally. Ladle 1¼ cups soup into each of 4 shallow bowls, and sprinkle each serving with 1½ teaspoons cheese. Yield: 4 servings.

CALORIES 254 (33% from fat); FAT 9.2g (sat 2.9g, mono 3.2g, poly 2.7g); PROTEIN 21g; CARB 21.2g; FIBER 4.9g; CHOL 74mg; IRON 2.6mg; SODIUM 929mg; CALC 86mg

WINE NOTE: The creaminess of the white beans, bitter herbalness of the escarole, and rich meatiness of the sausage are in perfect counterpoint in this dish. When bitter and fat flavors are involved, one of the best wines is often Italian red Chianti—even in a dish like this that calls for white wine. Try the Banfi Chianti Classico Riserva. The 2002 is $18.

Pan-Seared Chicken with Italian Salsa Verde

The fresh flavors of parsley and mint carry the piquant capers, garlic, and vinegar in this simple chicken recipe. It's especially good atop fettuccine.

1 tablespoon all-purpose flour
¼ teaspoon salt
¼ teaspoon freshly ground black pepper
4 (6-ounce) skinless, boneless chicken breast halves
5 teaspoons olive oil, divided
¾ cup fresh flat-leaf parsley leaves
2 tablespoons water
2 tablespoons red wine vinegar
1 teaspoon bottled minced garlic
1 teaspoon capers, rinsed and drained
4 (2-inch) fresh mint sprigs
1 (2-ounce) slice peasant bread, crust removed

1. Combine first 4 ingredients in a large zip-top plastic bag; seal and shake well to coat. Heat 1 tablespoon oil in a large nonstick skillet over medium-high heat. Add chicken to pan; cook 6 minutes on each side or until done.
2. Place remaining 2 teaspoons oil, parsley, and remaining ingredients, except bread, in a food processor; process 10 seconds or until finely chopped. Tear bread into pieces; add to processor, and process 4 seconds or until well blended. Thinly slice each chicken breast half; serve topped with salsa verde. Yield: 4 servings (serving size: 1 chicken breast half and 2 tablespoons salsa verde).

CALORIES 280 (27% from fat); FAT 8.3g (sat 1.5g, mono 4.7g, poly 1.3g); PROTEIN 40.9g; CARB 8.1g; FIBER 1g; CHOL 99mg; IRON 2.7mg; SODIUM 345mg; CALC 51mg

Ponzu-Glazed Flank Steak

Quick-cooking rice with green onions is an ideal side to soak up the pan sauce.

2 tablespoons fresh lemon juice
2 tablespoons fresh lime juice
2 tablespoons low-sodium soy sauce
1 tablespoon honey
2 teaspoons bottled ground fresh ginger (such as Spice World)
1 (1-pound) flank steak, trimmed

1. Preheat broiler.
2. Combine first 5 ingredients in a small saucepan over medium-high heat; bring to a boil. Cook 3 minutes, and remove from heat.
3. Place steak on a foil-lined broiler pan. Brush half of soy mixture over steak; broil 5 minutes or until browned. Turn steak over; brush with remaining soy mixture. Broil 5 minutes or until browned. Remove from oven; wrap foil around steak. Let stand 5 minutes before slicing. Serve steak with pan juices. Yield: 4 servings (serving size: 3 ounces steak and 1 tablespoon pan juices).

CALORIES 188 (30% from fat); FAT 6.2g (sat 2.3g, mono 2.2g, poly 0.2g); PROTEIN 25.1g; CARB 7.1g; FIBER 0.3g; CHOL 37mg; IRON 2.1mg; SODIUM 330mg; CALC 31mg

Chicken-Couscous Bibb Salad

Rinsing the couscous with cold water cools it quickly.

½ cup water
⅓ cup uncooked couscous
2 cups chopped cooked chicken breast
1 cup chopped cucumber
½ cup finely chopped red onion
½ cup chopped fresh mint
¼ cup chopped fresh parsley
2 tablespoons fresh lemon juice
2 teaspoons chopped fresh oregano
1 tablespoon extravirgin olive oil
½ teaspoon salt
12 Bibb lettuce leaves

Continued

1. Bring ½ cup water to a boil in a small saucepan; stir in couscous. Remove from heat; cover and let stand 5 minutes. Fluff with a fork. Place couscous in a fine-mesh strainer; rinse with cold water. Drain.

2. Combine couscous, chicken, and next 6 ingredients in a medium bowl. Stir in oil and salt. Place 3 lettuce leaves on each of 4 plates; spoon about ¼ cup chicken mixture in the center of each leaf. Yield: 4 servings (serving size: 3 lettuce cups).

CALORIES 225 (25% from fat); FAT 6.3g (sat 1.2g, mono 3.4g, poly 1g); PROTEIN 24.9g; CARB 16.6g; FIBER 2.4g; CHOL 60mg; IRON 2.3mg; SODIUM 355mg; CALC 64mg

---

QUICK & EASY
Shrimp Garam Masala

Find the peppery Indian spice blend garam masala in the spice aisle of large grocery stores. Try it on meat and poultry, or broccoli, cauliflower, or potatoes. If you can't find garam masala, substitute equal parts ground cumin, pepper, cloves, and nutmeg. Ladle this dish over basmati rice.

1½ pounds peeled and deveined large shrimp
1½ teaspoons garam masala
1½ tablespoons canola oil
1½ cups prechopped green bell pepper
 1 cup prechopped onion
 ⅓ cup dry white wine
 ¼ cup chopped cilantro, divided
 ¼ teaspoon salt
 ¼ teaspoon black pepper
 4 lime wedges

1. Sprinkle shrimp evenly with garam masala, and let stand 5 minutes.
2. Heat oil in a large nonstick skillet over medium-high heat. Add bell pepper and onion; sauté 5 minutes or until vegetables are crisp-tender. Add shrimp; sauté 3 minutes or until shrimp are done. Stir in wine, 3 tablespoons cilantro, salt, and black pepper. Cook 30 seconds. Sprinkle with remaining 1 tablespoon cilantro. Serve with lime wedges. Yield: 4 servings (serving size 1 cup shrimp mixture and 1 lime wedge).

CALORIES 260 (29% from fat); FAT 8.4g (sat 1g, mono 3.5g, poly 2.8g); PROTEIN 35.5g; CARB 9.6g; FIBER 2g; CHOL 259mg; IRON 4.5mg; SODIUM 405mg; CALC 112mg

---

QUICK & EASY • MAKE AHEAD
Smoky Chili Joes

Increase the ground chipotle powder if you prefer more heat. Serve with corn chips.

 Cooking spray
 ½ pound extralean ground beef
 ½ cup prechopped onion
 1 teaspoon bottled minced garlic
 1 teaspoon ground cumin
 ½ teaspoon chili powder
 ⅛ teaspoon chipotle chile powder
 ¼ cup ketchup
 1 (15-ounce) can red kidney beans, rinsed and drained
 1 (14.5-ounce) can diced tomatoes with green pepper and onions, undrained
 6 (1½-ounce) hamburger buns
 6 tablespoons shredded sharp Cheddar cheese
12 sandwich-cut bread-and-butter pickles

1. Heat a large nonstick skillet over medium-high heat. Coat pan with cooking spray. Add ground beef to pan; cook 4 minutes or until browned, stirring to crumble. Add onion and garlic to pan; cook 2 minutes, stirring frequently. Add cumin, chili powder, and chipotle chile powder; cook 30 seconds. Stir in ketchup, beans, and tomatoes; cook 6 minutes or until slightly thickened. Spoon about ⅔ cup beef mixture evenly over 6 bottom bun halves; top each with 1 tablespoon cheese and 2 pickles. Top with remaining bun halves. Yield: 6 servings (serving size: 1 sandwich).

CALORIES 334 (22% from fat); FAT 8.1g (sat 3.1g, mono 2g, poly 1g); PROTEIN 22.2g; CARB 49.6g; FIBER 8.1g; CHOL 21mg; IRON 2.7mg; SODIUM 866mg; CALC 132mg

---

lighten up

Landing Lobster Thermidor

We transform a French classic so a Chicago businesswoman can ring in a healthful New Year.

STAFF FAVORITE
Lobster Thermidor

To save time, buy fresh lobster tails and have them steamed at the store. If using whole lobster, reserve the shells to cook the meat in, and use the body and claw shells to simmer in the milk.

 3 cups water
 4 large lobster tails (about 28 ounces)
 2 cups fat-free milk
 1 teaspoon olive oil
 3 tablespoons chopped shallots (about 1 large)
 2 (8-ounce) packages presliced mushrooms
 3 tablespoons dry sherry
1½ tablespoons all-purpose flour
 ¼ teaspoon freshly ground black pepper
 Dash of white pepper
 1 tablespoon chopped fresh basil
 2 teaspoons chopped fresh tarragon
 3 tablespoons whipping cream
 ¼ teaspoon kosher salt
 Cooking spray
 ¾ cup (3 ounces) shredded reduced-fat, reduced-sodium Swiss cheese (such as Alpine Lace)
 ⅔ cup panko (Japanese breadcrumbs)
 2 teaspoons unsalted butter, melted

1. Bring 3 cups water to a boil in a stockpot. Place a vegetable steamer or rack in bottom of pan. Add lobster tails. Cover and steam 8 minutes or until done. Cool to room temperature. Remove meat from cooked lobster tails; chop meat into bite-sized pieces (you should have about 1¾ cups chopped meat). Cover and chill.

2. Place lobster shells in a large zip-top plastic bag. Coarsely crush shells using a meat mallet or rolling pin. Combine shells and milk in a small saucepan over medium heat. Bring to a simmer; cook 5 minutes (do not boil). Remove from heat; cover and let stand 30 minutes. Strain mixture through a fine mesh sieve into a bowl; discard solids. Set aside.

3. Preheat oven to 450°.

4. Heat oil in a large nonstick skillet over medium-high heat. Add shallots; sauté 2 minutes or until soft. Add mushrooms; sauté 4 minutes or until liquid begins to evaporate. Stir in sherry; cook 1 minute.

5. Combine reserved milk mixture, flour, black pepper, and white pepper in a small bowl; stir with a whisk until smooth. Add milk mixture to pan; bring to a boil. Cook 1 minute or until thickened, stirring constantly. Stir in basil and tarragon; cook 1 minute, stirring occasionally. Add reserved lobster meat, cream, and salt, stirring to combine. Divide mixture evenly among each of 4 (1½-cup) gratin dishes coated with cooking spray.

6. Combine cheese, panko, and melted butter in a small bowl; toss to combine. Sprinkle about ⅓ cup panko mixture over each gratin. Bake at 450° for 12 minutes or until topping is browned. Yield: 4 servings (serving size: 1 gratin).

CALORIES 419 (29% from fat); FAT 13.5g (sat 7.1g, mono 4.1g, poly 0.7g); PROTEIN 50.2g; CARB 23.3g; FIBER 1.7g; CHOL 159mg; IRON 1.7mg; SODIUM 883mg; CALC 480mg

new american classic

Herb-Crusted Standing Rib Roast

This roast features beef with a flavorful paste of Dijon mustard, shallots, garlic, and herbs.

Herb-Crusted Standing Rib Roast

1 (4½-pound) standing rib roast, trimmed
Cooking spray
1 tablespoon whole black peppercorns, cracked
2 teaspoons salt, divided
3 tablespoons Dijon mustard
½ cup sliced shallots (about 2 medium)
3 garlic cloves, crushed
3 tablespoons chopped fresh rosemary
2 tablespoons chopped fresh thyme
1½ cups fat-free, less-sodium beef broth
1 cup dry red wine
1 teaspoon butter

1. Preheat oven to 450°.

2. Place roast on a rack coated with cooking spray; place rack in a roasting pan. Sprinkle roast evenly with pepper and 1½ teaspoons salt; rub with mustard. Place shallots and garlic in a mini food processor; pulse to coarsely chop. Add rosemary and thyme; process until finely chopped. Rub shallot mixture evenly over roast. Bake at 450° for 25 minutes.

3. Reduce heat to 350° (do not remove roast from oven). Bake roast at 350° for 1 hour and 20 minutes or until a thermometer registers 145° (medium-rare) or until desired degree of doneness. Let stand 10 minutes before slicing.

4. Combine broth and wine in a small saucepan; bring to a boil. Cook until reduced to ⅔ cup (about 15 minutes). Remove from heat; stir in butter and remaining ½ teaspoon salt. Serve with roast. Yield: 12 servings (serving size: about 3 ounces beef and 1 tablespoon sauce).

CALORIES 143 (54% from fat); FAT 8.6g (sat 3.4g, mono 3.5g, poly 0.3g); PROTEIN 13.6g; CARB 1.8g; FIBER 0.4g; CHOL 63mg; IRON 1.2mg; SODIUM 528mg; CALC 19mg

inspired vegetarian

Pasta Pleasers

Warm up a winter night with a hearty, homey supper.

Baked Goat Cheese and Roasted Winter Squash over Garlicky Fettuccine

The goat cheese rounds are baked at a high temperature to crisp the breadcrumb coating and heat the cheese just enough to melt when you cut into one.

6 cups (1-inch) cubed peeled kabocha or butternut squash (about 2¼ pounds)
1 large red bell pepper, cut into 1-inch pieces
1½ tablespoons olive oil, divided
Cooking spray
1 teaspoon salt, divided
1 teaspoon chopped fresh or ¼ teaspoon dried rosemary
¼ teaspoon freshly ground black pepper
2 (4-ounce) packages goat cheese
½ cup dry breadcrumbs
1 pound uncooked fettuccine
¼ teaspoon crushed red pepper
2 garlic cloves, minced
Rosemary sprigs (optional)

1. Preheat oven to 425°.

2. Place squash and bell pepper in a large bowl. Add 1 tablespoon oil; toss well. Arrange vegetables in a single layer on a jelly-roll pan coated with cooking spray. Sprinkle with ½ teaspoon salt, rosemary, and black pepper. Bake at 425° for 40 minutes, stirring once.

3. Place goat cheese in freezer 10 minutes. Cut cheese crosswise into 8 equal rounds. Place breadcrumbs in a shallow bowl. Dredge each round in breadcrumbs; place on a baking sheet. Bake at 425° for 6 minutes.

4. Cook pasta according to package directions, omitting salt and fat. Drain,
Continued

reserving ½ cup pasta cooking water. Return pasta to pan; add reserved pasta cooking water, remaining 1½ teaspoons oil, remaining ½ teaspoon salt, red pepper, and garlic, tossing to coat. Place 1¼ cups pasta in each of 8 shallow bowls; top each with about ½ cup squash mixture and 1 cheese round. Garnish with rosemary, if desired. Yield: 8 servings.

CALORIES 423 (30% from fat); FAT 14.1g (sat 7.4g, mono 4.2g, poly 0.7g); PROTEIN 17.8g; CARB 54.7g; FIBER 2.7g; CHOL 30mg; IRON 2.1mg; SODIUM 439mg; CALC 290mg

Three-Cheese Baked Pasta

- 1 tablespoon olive oil
- 1¼ cups diced onion
- ⅓ cup diced carrot
- ¼ cup diced celery
- ¼ cup minced garlic (about 12 cloves)
- ¼ cup chopped sun-dried tomatoes (packed without oil)
- 1¼ teaspoons chopped fresh or ½ teaspoon dried thyme
- ½ teaspoon crushed red pepper
- 2 (28-ounce) cans diced tomatoes, undrained
- 1½ cups (6 ounces) grated fresh pecorino Romano cheese, divided
- 1 cup part-skim ricotta cheese
- 1 tablespoon chopped fresh parsley
- 1 large egg white, lightly beaten
- 1 pound uncooked penne rigate (tube-shaped pasta)
- 1 cup (4 ounces) diced provolone cheese
- Cooking spray

1. Preheat oven to 400°.
2. Heat oil in a large nonstick skillet over medium heat. Add onion, carrot, and celery; cook 10 minutes or until onion is tender, stirring frequently. Add garlic; cook 1 minute, stirring constantly. Add sun-dried tomatoes, thyme, pepper, and diced tomatoes; cook 25 minutes or until thickened, stirring occasionally.
3. Combine 1 cup Romano, ricotta, parsley, and egg white in a bowl.
4. Cook pasta according to package directions, omitting salt and fat. Drain; return pasta to pan. Add ricotta mixture to pan, stirring to coat. Add tomato mixture

and provolone, tossing just until combined (do not overstir). Spoon pasta mixture into a 13 x 9–inch baking dish coated with cooking spray. Sprinkle with remaining ½ cup Romano. Bake at 400° for 25 minutes or until bubbly and top is browned. Yield: 8 servings (serving size: about 1½ cups).

CALORIES 459 (28% from fat); FAT 14.1g (sat 8.4g, mono 4.8g, poly 0.9g); PROTEIN 23g; CARB 59.2g; FIBER 5.8g; CHOL 33mg; IRON 2.9mg; SODIUM 810mg; CALC 517mg

WINE NOTE: Cheese often works better with white wine than red. Try this cheesy baked pasta casserole with a crisp white such as pinot grigio. A favorite: Bollini Pinot Grigio from Italy. The 2004 is $10.

Spinach and Butternut Squash Lasagna

Prepare the white sauce, roast the squash, and sauté the spinach; refrigerate until you're ready to assemble the dish.

- 3 cups 2% reduced-fat milk
- ¼ cup all-purpose flour (about 1 ounce)
- 2 tablespoons butter
- ⅓ cup minced shallots
- 1¼ teaspoons salt, divided
- ½ teaspoon freshly ground black pepper, divided
- 8 cups (¾-inch) cubed peeled butternut squash (about 2¼ pounds)
- 1 tablespoon balsamic vinegar
- 4 teaspoons olive oil, divided
- Cooking spray
- 1 teaspoon chopped fresh or ¼ teaspoon dried thyme
- ¼ teaspoon crushed red pepper
- 4 garlic cloves, minced
- 3 (6-ounce) bags fresh baby spinach
- 9 cooked lasagna noodles (8 ounces uncooked noodles)
- 1 cup (4 ounces) shredded Asiago cheese
- 1 cup (4 ounces) grated fresh Parmigiano-Reggiano cheese

1. Cook milk in a small, heavy saucepan over medium-high heat to 180° or until tiny bubbles form around edge (do not boil). Remove from heat; keep warm.

2. Lightly spoon flour into a dry measuring cup; level with a knife. Melt butter in a medium nonstick saucepan over medium heat. Add shallots; cook 2 minutes or until tender. Reduce heat; add flour to pan, and cook 5 minutes or until smooth and golden, stirring constantly. Remove from heat; add about 2 tablespoons warm milk to flour mixture, stirring constantly with a whisk. Gradually add remaining warm milk, about ½ cup at a time, until mixture is smooth, stirring constantly with a whisk. Stir in ½ teaspoon salt and ¼ teaspoon black pepper. Bring to a boil; reduce heat, and cook until smooth and thickened. Remove from heat. Cover surface of milk mixture with plastic wrap; set aside.
3. Preheat oven to 425°.
4. Place squash in a large bowl. Add vinegar; toss to coat. Add 1 tablespoon oil; toss to coat. Arrange squash in a single layer on a jelly-roll pan coated with cooking spray. Sprinkle with ½ teaspoon salt, remaining ¼ teaspoon black pepper, and thyme. Bake at 425° for 30 minutes, stirring after 15 minutes.
5. Combine remaining 1 teaspoon oil, red pepper, and garlic in a Dutch oven over medium heat; cook 2 minutes, stirring constantly. Add spinach, 1 bag at a time; cook until wilted, stirring frequently. Add remaining ¼ teaspoon salt; cook until liquid evaporates, stirring frequently.
6. Reduce oven temperature to 350°.
7. Spoon ⅓ cup milk mixture in bottom of a 13 x 9–inch baking pan coated with cooking spray. Arrange 3 noodles over milk mixture; top with spinach mixture, ⅔ cup milk mixture, ½ cup Asiago, and ¼ cup Parmigiano-Reggiano. Arrange 3 noodles over cheese; top with squash mixture, ⅔ cup milk mixture, remaining ½ cup Asiago, and ¼ cup Parmigiano-Reggiano. Arrange remaining 3 noodles on cheese; spread remaining ½ cup milk mixture over noodles. Sprinkle with remaining ½ cup Parmigiano-Reggiano. Bake at 350° for 30 minutes or until bubbly. Let stand 15 minutes before serving. Yield: 8 servings (serving size: 1 piece).

CALORIES 445 (30% from fat); FAT 15g (sat 8.1g, mono 4.2g, poly 0.7g); PROTEIN 20.7g; CARB 61.5g; FIBER 7.3g; CHOL 36mg; IRON 4.8mg; SODIUM 758mg; CALC 599mg

Artichoke, Spinach, and Feta Stuffed Shells

To fill the shells, simply spoon the cheese mixture into a heavy-duty zip-top plastic bag; squeeze out the air. Snip a one-inch hole in one corner of the bag, and pipe the filling into the shells.

   1   teaspoon dried oregano
 ¼   cup chopped pepperoncini peppers
   1   (28-ounce) can fire-roasted crushed tomatoes with added puree (such as Progresso)
   1   (8-ounce) can no-salt-added tomato sauce
   1   cup (4 ounces) shredded provolone cheese, divided
   1   cup (4 ounces) crumbled feta cheese
 ½   cup (4 ounces) fat-free cream cheese, softened
 ¼   teaspoon freshly ground black pepper
   1   (9-ounce) package frozen artichoke hearts, thawed and chopped
 ½   (10-ounce) package frozen chopped spinach, thawed, drained, and squeezed dry
   2   garlic cloves, minced
 20   cooked jumbo shell pasta (about 8 ounces uncooked pasta)
Cooking spray

1. Preheat oven to 375°.
2. Combine first 4 ingredients in a medium saucepan. Place over medium heat; cook 12 minutes or until slightly thick, stirring occasionally. Remove from heat; set aside.
3. Combine ½ cup provolone, feta, and next 5 ingredients in a medium bowl. Spoon or pipe about 1½ tablespoons cheese mixture into each pasta shell; place stuffed shells in a 13 x 9–inch baking dish coated with cooking spray. Spoon tomato mixture over shells; sprinkle with remaining ½ cup provolone. Bake at 375° for 25 minutes or until thoroughly heated and cheese melts. Yield: 5 servings (serving size: 4 stuffed shells).

CALORIES 394 (28% from fat); FAT 12.4g (sat 7.7g, mono 2.9g, poly 0.7g); PROTEIN 21.3g; CARB 48.9g; FIBER 8.7g; CHOL 38mg; IRON 5mg; SODIUM 954mg; CALC 455mg

---

STAFF FAVORITE • QUICK & EASY
Farfalle with Creamy Wild Mushroom Sauce

This recipe scored high in our Test Kitchens for its rich flavor and ultracreamy texture. The presliced exotic mushroom blend is sold in eight-ounce packages. If unavailable, use all cremini mushrooms.

   1   pound uncooked farfalle (bow tie pasta)
   1   tablespoon butter
 12   ounces presliced exotic mushroom blend (such as shiitake, cremini, and oyster)
 ½   cup chopped onion
 ⅓   cup finely chopped shallots
   1   tablespoon minced garlic
 1½   teaspoons salt, divided
 ¼   teaspoon freshly ground black pepper
 ¼   cup dry white wine
 ⅔   cup whipping cream
 ½   cup (2 ounces) grated fresh Parmigiano-Reggiano cheese
   2   tablespoons chopped fresh parsley
Minced fresh parsley (optional)

1. Cook pasta according to package directions, omitting salt and fat; drain.
2. Melt butter in a large nonstick skillet over medium-high heat. Add mushrooms, onion, shallots, garlic, 1 teaspoon salt, and pepper; cook 12 minutes or until liquid evaporates and mushrooms are tender, stirring occasionally. Add wine; cook 2 minutes or until liquid evaporates, stirring occasionally. Remove from heat.
3. Add pasta, cream, cheese, and 2 tablespoons parsley, tossing gently to coat. Stir in remaining ½ teaspoon salt. Garnish with minced fresh parsley, if desired. Serve immediately. Yield: 8 servings (serving size: 1¼ cups).

CALORIES 336 (31% from fat); FAT 11.4g (sat 6.9g, mono 3.1g, poly 0.4g); PROTEIN 12.1g; CARB 47.5g; FIBER 2.3g; CHOL 36mg; IRON 2.3mg; SODIUM 577mg; CALC 124mg

---

QUICK & EASY
Gemelli with Roasted Fennel and Sun-Dried Tomatoes

Fusilli, cavatappi, or penne rigate can be substituted for the gemelli. Cook the pasta while the fennel bakes to save time.

   2   large fennel bulbs (about 2¼ pounds)
Cooking spray
   2   tablespoons olive oil, divided
   1   teaspoon salt, divided
 ½   teaspoon freshly ground black pepper, divided
 ¾   pound uncooked gemelli (short tube-shaped pasta)
 ¾   cup (3 ounces) crumbled feta cheese
 ½   cup drained oil-packed sun-dried tomatoes
 ¼   cup chopped fresh parsley
   3   tablespoons chopped fresh basil
   2   teaspoons grated fresh lemon rind

1. Preheat oven to 425°.
2. Trim tough outer leaves from fennel. Cut fennel bulbs in half crosswise; discard cores. Cut into ½-inch-thick pieces. Place fennel pieces in a large roasting pan. Coat fennel with cooking spray. Add 1 tablespoon oil, ½ teaspoon salt, and ¼ teaspoon pepper; toss to coat. Bake at 425° for 20 minutes. Stir fennel; bake an additional 10 minutes or until tender.
3. Cook pasta according to package directions, omitting salt and fat. Drain, reserving 2 tablespoons pasta cooking water. Return pasta to pan. Add reserved pasta cooking water, fennel, remaining 1 tablespoon oil, remaining ½ teaspoon salt, remaining ¼ teaspoon pepper, feta, and remaining ingredients; toss well. Yield: 4 servings (serving size: 2 cups).

CALORIES 494 (27% from fat); FAT 14.7g (sat 4.7g, mono 7.1g, poly 1.1g); PROTEIN 16.9g; CARB 76.6g; FIBER 7.5g; CHOL 19mg; IRON 4.5mg; SODIUM 923mg; CALC 195mg

Bake Me a Cake

Everyone appreciates a homemade cake. We show you how to bake a winner every time.

From birthdays to weddings and occasions in between, cakes often define life's great moments. We turned to Test Kitchens Professional Jan Moon to teach us a few tricks of the trade. Moon has been baking cakes professionally for 10 years, and she's turned out too many of them to count during her career. She shares all her secrets so you, too, can have sweet success.

STAFF FAVORITE • MAKE AHEAD

Cranberry Upside-Down Coffee Cake

Serve this buttery cake for a make-ahead brunch dish, or at the end of a casual meal.

CAKE:

Cooking spray
- 1 tablespoon all-purpose flour
- 1 cup fresh cranberries
- ½ cup coarsely chopped pitted dates
- 2 tablespoons chopped walnuts
- 1 teaspoon grated orange rind
- ½ cup butter, softened and divided
- ½ cup packed dark brown sugar
- 2 tablespoons fresh orange juice
- ¼ teaspoon ground cinnamon
- 1½ cups all-purpose flour (about 6¾ ounces)
- 1 teaspoon baking powder
- ½ teaspoon salt
- 1 cup granulated sugar
- 1 teaspoon vanilla
- 1 large egg
- ½ cup fat-free buttermilk

GLAZE:

- 1 cup powdered sugar
- 1 teaspoon butter, melted
- 2 tablespoons fresh orange juice

1. Preheat oven to 350°.

2. To prepare cake, coat a 9-inch square baking pan with cooking spray; dust with 1 tablespoon flour. Combine cranberries, dates, walnuts, and rind in a bowl. Melt 2 tablespoons butter in a small saucepan over medium heat. Stir in brown sugar, 2 tablespoons juice, and cinnamon; cook 3 minutes, stirring constantly. Pour brown sugar mixture into prepared pan. Sprinkle cranberry mixture evenly over brown sugar mixture.

3. Lightly spoon 1½ cups flour into dry measuring cups; level with a knife. Combine flour, baking powder, and salt in a bowl, stirring well with a whisk. Place granulated sugar and remaining 6 tablespoons butter in a large bowl; beat with a mixer at medium speed until well blended. Add vanilla and egg; beat well. Add flour mixture and buttermilk alternately to granulated sugar mixture, beginning and ending with flour mixture. Spoon batter over cranberry mixture.

4. Bake at 350° for 40 minutes or until a wooden pick inserted in center comes out clean. Cool in pan 5 minutes on a wire rack; run a knife around outside edges. Invert cake onto a plate; cool.

5. To prepare glaze, combine powdered sugar and remaining ingredients in a small bowl, stirring until smooth. Drizzle over cake. Cut cake into squares. Yield: 12 servings (serving size: 1 square).

CALORIES 312 (26% from fat); FAT 9.1g (sat 5.1g, mono 1g, poly 2.3g); PROTEIN 3g; CARB 55.7g; FIBER 1.4g; CHOL 39mg; IRON 1.2mg; SODIUM 236mg; CALC 32mg

MAKE AHEAD

Chocolate Cupcakes with Peppermint Frosting

CUPCAKES:

- 1 cup packed brown sugar
- 6 tablespoons butter, softened
- 2 large eggs
- 1¼ cups all-purpose flour (about 5½ ounces)
- ½ cup unsweetened cocoa
- 1 teaspoon baking powder
- ½ teaspoon baking soda
- ½ teaspoon salt
- ½ cup low-fat buttermilk
- 1 teaspoon vanilla extract

PEPPERMINT FROSTING:

- 2 cups powdered sugar
- ½ cup (4 ounces) tub-style light cream cheese
- ⅛ teaspoon peppermint extract
- 16 hard peppermint candies, finely crushed (about ⅓ cup)

1. Preheat oven to 350°.

2. To prepare cupcakes, place brown sugar and butter in a large bowl; beat with a mixer at medium speed 2 minutes or until well blended. Add eggs, 1 at a time, beating well after each addition. Lightly spoon flour into dry measuring cups; level with a knife. Combine flour, cocoa, baking powder, baking soda, and salt in a bowl, stirring well with a whisk. Add flour mixture to sugar mixture alternately with buttermilk, beginning and ending with flour mixture. Stir in vanilla extract.

3. Spoon batter into 18 muffin cups lined with paper liners. Bake at 350° for 12 minutes or until cupcakes spring back when touched lightly in the center. Cool in pan 10 minutes on a wire rack; remove from pan. Cool completely on wire rack.

4. To prepare frosting, combine powdered sugar, cream cheese, and peppermint extract in a bowl, stirring until smooth. Spread about 4 teaspoons frosting on each cupcake; sprinkle evenly with crushed candies. Yield: 18 cupcakes (serving size: 1 cupcake).

CALORIES 214 (26% from fat); FAT 6.2g (sat 3.7g, mono 1.3g, poly 0.3g); PROTEIN 3g; CARB 38.2g; FIBER 1g; CHOL 38mg; IRON 1.1mg; SODIUM 205mg; CALC 45mg

All About Baking Cakes

Start with the Right Equipment
Good-quality cake pans are important. Choose aluminum pans with a dull finish since this metal absorbs and conducts heat efficiently. Avoid shiny pans, which deflect heat, and dark metal pans, which cause the outer edges of the cake to cook more quickly than the center and overbrown, rendering the cake dry and tough. When preparing layer cakes, use a pan with tall, straight sides. According to Moon, three-inch sides are best since the depth allows the cake to rise to its maximum height.

A stand mixer is ideal for mixing most cakes since the powerful motor aerates the butter, sugar, and egg mixture, which in turn helps the cake rise nicely while it bakes. A handheld mixer works just fine, though you should mix the butter and sugar just a minute or two longer to incorporate as much air as the stand mixer does.

Your oven is another essential component in baking. It's important to know the oven's true temperature and know how it performs. Be aware of any hot or cold spots in the oven, and compensate by rotating the cake pans throughout baking, if necessary.

Preheat the Oven
Preheat the oven so you can put the cake batter in as soon as it's ready. If it stands long after it's mixed, the air in the batter (a result of beating the butter and sugar, as well as the leavening) may escape, causing the final result to be tough and dense.

Prepare the Pan(s)
Next, prepare the pans. Simply coat them with cooking spray, and dust with a bit of flour. As the cake bakes, the flour provides traction to help the cake rise to its full potential. It's often a good idea to line the bottom of the pan with wax paper as well, so the cake doesn't tear when removed from the pan. This is especially true if the recipe calls for cake flour, which is usually used in delicate cakes. Cakes baked in tube, Bundt, or other hard-to-line specialty pans are exceptions to this rule.

Mix the Batter
For best results, begin with ingredients at approximately room temperature (65° to 75°). Simply leave eggs, butter, milk, and any other refrigerated items out on the kitchen counter for about 20 minutes while you measure and gather all of the remaining ingredients and equipment. Softened butter accepts more air, which is desirable for a moist and light-textured cake. If you add cold ingredients, such as eggs or milk, later in the process, the butter can seize (clump), decreasing the volume of the batter and inhibiting the incorporation of the other ingredients. Place the softened butter and sugar in a large bowl, and beat with an electric mixer until thoroughly blended.

Measure flour carefully. This is especially important in low-fat baking because just a bit too much or too little flour can have a big impact on the cake's texture. If you don't have a kitchen scale, it's best to lightly spoon flour into dry measuring cups and level with a knife—never scoop flour directly from the canister with the measuring cup. This packs flour down and increases the amount in the cup.

Combine flour with all the dry ingredients in a bowl, and stir with a whisk to evenly disperse any salt or leavening agent. With an electric mixer speed on low, add the flour mixture to the batter alternately with milk, beginning and ending with the flour mixture. This procedure allows the flour to be incorporated into the batter thoroughly and completely. Mix just until the ingredients are combined. Once liquid is added to the mixture, the flour and liquid combine to form gluten. Overmixing increases the amount of gluten and causes the cake to be tough.

Bake the Cake
After it's mixed, place the batter in the oven as quickly as possible so the leavening will be fully active.

Avoid baking cakes on different levels in the oven, and place them at least two inches apart and two inches away from the oven walls to promote even baking. (If you have to bake the layers on different racks, rotate the pans halfway through baking.)

Once the cakes are in the oven, keep the oven door closed tightly because the temperature fluctuates each time the door opens. If the temperature drops, the cake will probably bake more slowly, and it may sink in the center. As the oven reheats to the desired temperature, the edges of the cake will be exposed to more extreme temperatures and could possibly result in a dry, tough cake.

The best way to determine doneness for most cakes is the wooden pick test. Insert a wooden pick in the center of the cake. If it comes out clean, the cake is done. If batter clings to the pick, the cake needs to bake one to three minutes longer. If you see the sides of the cake pulling away from the pan, this is another sign of doneness.

Let It Cool
Most cakes need to cool in the pan on a wire rack for a few minutes. If you try to remove a cake from the pan too soon, it may not hold together. This is especially true of cakes made with cake flour. Turn the cake out of the pan after five to 10 minutes, remove the wax paper, and cool completely on a wire rack before frosting, wrapping, or storing.

Bake Ahead, Save Time
Cakes are ideal make-ahead desserts for the holidays or any time of year. You can bake the layers up to a month ahead, cool them, wrap them tightly in two layers of plastic wrap, and freeze. Simply thaw frozen cakes at room temperature. Moon often frosts cakes while they're still partially frozen since this helps prevent stray crumbs from getting in the frosting, and she finds the cakes sturdier and easier to work with.

Pumpkin Pound Cake with Buttermilk Glaze

Drain the canned pumpkin before making the cake batter to keep the cake's texture light.

CAKE:

Cooking spray
1 tablespoon all-purpose flour
1 (15-ounce) can pumpkin
¾ cup granulated sugar
¾ cup packed dark brown sugar
½ cup butter, softened
4 large eggs
1 teaspoon vanilla extract
3 cups all-purpose flour (about 13½ ounces)
1½ teaspoons pumpkin pie spice
1 teaspoon baking powder
½ teaspoon baking soda
½ teaspoon salt
¾ cup fat-free buttermilk

GLAZE:

⅓ cup fat-free buttermilk
¼ cup granulated sugar
2 tablespoons butter
2 teaspoons cornstarch
⅛ teaspoon baking soda

1. Preheat oven to 350°.
2. To prepare cake, lightly coat a 10-inch tube pan with cooking spray; dust with 1 tablespoon flour. Spread pumpkin over 2 layers of paper towels; cover with 2 additional layers of paper towels. Let stand about 10 minutes. Scrape drained pumpkin into a bowl.
3. Place ¾ cup granulated sugar, brown sugar, and ½ cup butter in a large bowl; beat with a mixer at medium speed 3 minutes or until well blended. Add eggs, 1 at a time, beating well after each addition. Beat in pumpkin and vanilla. Lightly spoon 3 cups flour into dry measuring cups; level with a knife. Combine flour, pie spice, and next 3 ingredients in a bowl, stirring well with a whisk. Add flour mixture and ¾ cup buttermilk alternately to sugar mixture, beginning and ending with flour mixture.
4. Spoon batter into prepared pan. Bake at 350° for 55 minutes or until a wooden pick inserted in center comes out clean.

Cool in pan 10 minutes on a wire rack. Remove from pan; cool completely on wire rack.
5. To prepare glaze, combine ⅓ cup buttermilk and remaining ingredients in a small saucepan over medium heat; bring to a boil. Cook 1 minute or until thick, stirring constantly; remove from heat. Drizzle cake with glaze. Yield: 16 servings (serving size: 1 slice).

CALORIES 273 (29% from fat); FAT 8.7g (sat 5g, mono 2.4g, poly 0.5g); PROTEIN 5g; CARB 44.6g; FIBER 1.4g; CHOL 72mg; IRON 2mg; SODIUM 243mg; CALC 66mg

Coconut Cake with Buttercream Frosting

Garnish the cake plate with sugar-frosted cranberries and rosemary sprigs. (See page 457 for directions.)

CAKE:

Cooking spray
1 tablespoon cake flour
2½ cups cake flour (about 10 ounces)
2 teaspoons baking powder
½ teaspoon salt
2 cups sugar
6 tablespoons butter, softened
¼ cup egg substitute
2 large eggs
¾ cup light coconut milk
¼ teaspoon coconut extract

FROSTING:

1 cup sugar
¼ cup water
5 large egg whites
½ teaspoon cream of tartar
⅛ teaspoon salt
¼ cup butter, softened
¼ teaspoon coconut extract (optional)
3 tablespoons toasted flaked sweetened coconut

1. Preheat oven to 350°.
2. To prepare cake, coat 3 (8-inch) round cake pans with cooking spray; line bottoms of pans with wax paper. Lightly coat wax paper with cooking spray; dust pans with 1 tablespoon flour.

3. Lightly spoon 2½ cups flour into dry measuring cups; level with a knife. Combine flour, baking powder, and salt, stirring with a whisk. Place 2 cups sugar and 6 tablespoons butter in a large bowl; beat with a mixer at medium speed 2 minutes or until well blended. Add egg substitute and eggs to sugar mixture; beat well. Add flour mixture and coconut milk alternately to sugar mixture, beginning and ending with flour mixture. Stir in ¼ teaspoon extract.
4. Spoon batter into prepared pans. Sharply tap pans once on countertop to remove air bubbles. Bake at 350° for 25 minutes or until a wooden pick inserted in center comes out clean. Cool in pans 10 minutes on wire racks; remove from pans. Remove wax paper; discard. Cool cakes on wire racks.
5. To prepare frosting, combine 1 cup sugar and ¼ cup water in a saucepan; bring to a boil. Cook 3 minutes, without stirring, or until a candy thermometer registers 250°. Combine egg whites, cream of tartar, and ⅛ teaspoon salt in a large bowl; using clean, dry beaters, beat with a mixer at high speed until foamy. Pour hot sugar syrup in a thin stream over egg whites, beating at high speed until stiff peaks form, about 3 minutes. Reduce mixer speed to low; continue beating until egg white mixture cools (about 12 minutes).
6. Beat ¼ cup butter until light and fluffy; stir in ¼ teaspoon extract, if desired. Fold in 1 cup egg white mixture. Fold butter mixture into remaining egg white mixture, stirring until smooth.
7. Place 1 cake layer on a plate; spread with 1 cup frosting. Repeat twice with cake layers and 1 cup frosting, ending with cake layer; spread remaining frosting over top and sides of cake. Sprinkle with toasted coconut. Chill until set. Yield: 16 servings (serving size: 1 slice).

CALORIES 317 (25% from fat); FAT 8.8g (sat 5.5g, mono 0.3g, poly 0.2g); PROTEIN 4.4g; CARB 55.6g; FIBER 0.4g; CHOL 45mg; IRON 1.9mg; SODIUM 267mg; CALC 10mg

Six Steps to Great Cakes

1. *An electric mixer incorporates the most air into cake batter. You'll also need a spoon, dry measuring cups (or kitchen scale), quality cake pans, a rubber spatula, wax paper, and a cooling rack.*

2. *Coat pans with cooking spray, and dust them lightly with flour. For layer cakes, it's often a good idea to line the bottoms of pans with wax paper as well.*

3. *Be sure to measure carefully. Lightly spoon flour into dry measuring cups, and level with a knife. If you have a kitchen scale, use it for accurate measurements.*

4. *Whip the butter and sugar until fluffy and well blended to incorporate air into the mixture and improve the texture of the cake; continue beating until the eggs are thoroughly incorporated.*

5. *Add flour and milk (or buttermilk) alternately to the cake batter. Always begin and end with the flour mixture, and the ingredients will blend evenly and thoroughly.*

6. *Remove the wax paper as soon as you remove the cakes from pans, and always cool the cakes completely before frosting or freezing them.*

MAKE AHEAD
Orange Mini Bundt Cakes
(pictured on page 256)

Baked in mini Bundt pans (about $30 at most kitchen specialty stores and home stores), these cakes make delicious holiday gifts. The decorative Garland Bundtlette pan used to bake our cover cakes is available at Williams-Sonoma (www.williams-sonoma.com). You can bake the cake in a standard 12-cup Bundt pan for one hour or until a wooden pick inserted in the center comes out clean.

CAKE:

Cooking spray
1¾ cups granulated sugar
10 tablespoons butter, softened
1 teaspoon vanilla extract
½ cup egg substitute
2 large eggs
3 cups all-purpose flour (about 13½ ounces)
½ teaspoon baking soda
¼ teaspoon salt
1 cup chopped orange slice candy, (about 10 pieces)
1 cup pitted dates, diced
½ cup flaked sweetened coconut
¼ cup chopped pecans, toasted
1 cup fat-free buttermilk

GLAZE:

1 cup powdered sugar
2 tablespoons fresh orange juice

ADDITIONAL INGREDIENT:

1 tablespoon powdered sugar (optional)

1. Preheat oven to 350°.
2. To prepare cake, heavily coat mini Bundt pans with cooking spray; turn pan upside down to drain excess. Place granulated sugar, butter, and vanilla in a large bowl; beat with a heavy-duty mixer at medium speed 2 minutes or until well blended. Add egg substitute and eggs to sugar mixture; beat well. Lightly spoon flour into dry measuring cups; level with a knife. Combine flour, baking soda, and salt in a bowl, stirring well. Sprinkle candy, dates, coconut, and nuts over

Continued

flour; stir well to disperse and coat candies. Add flour mixture to sugar mixture alternately with buttermilk, beginning and ending with flour mixture.

3. To prepare glaze, combine 1 cup powdered sugar and juice in a bowl, stirring until smooth.

4. Spoon ⅓ cup batter into each mini Bundt cup. Bake at 350° for 16 minutes or until a wooden pick inserted in center of 1 cake comes out clean. Cool in pans 5 minutes. Remove cakes from pans; brush top of each warm cake with about 2 teaspoons glaze. Cool completely on a wire rack. Garnish cakes with 1 tablespoon powdered sugar, if desired. Yield: 18 cakes (serving size: 1 cake).

CALORIES 329 (25% from fat); FAT 9.2g (sat 4.9g, mono 2.6g, poly 0.9g); PROTEIN 4.7g; CARB 58.3g; FIBER 1.6g; CHOL 40mg; IRON 1.4mg; SODIUM 154mg; CALC 34mg

---

Degrees of Doneness

Different pieces of equipment may yield slightly different results. When preparing Orange Mini Bundt Cakes (recipe on page 455), keep these variables in mind:

- Ovens cook slightly differently. Use an oven thermometer to monitor the actual temperature.
- Darker nonstick-coated pans cook their contents more quickly. If your pan has a dark coating, check the cakes for doneness a few minutes before the recipes directs.
- Mini Bundt pan cups can vary in size. Depending on the volume of the pan you use, the size of the cakes and the cook time may vary slightly.
- Check the cakes with a wooden pick after 16 minutes as the recipes directs, even if the flat bottoms of the cakes don't appear done.

STAFF FAVORITE • MAKE AHEAD
Mississippi Mud Cake

CAKE:

¾ cup boiling water
½ cup unsweetened cocoa
¾ cup granulated sugar
½ cup butter, softened
1 teaspoon vanilla extract
½ cup egg substitute
1⅓ cups all-purpose flour (about 6 ounces)
1 teaspoon baking soda
¼ teaspoon salt
½ cup fat-free buttermilk
Cooking spray
3½ cups miniature marshmallows

FROSTING:

¼ cup unsweetened cocoa
¼ cup evaporated fat-free milk
3 tablespoons butter, melted
⅛ teaspoon salt
2 cups powdered sugar
1 teaspoon vanilla extract

1. Preheat oven to 350°.

2. To prepare cake, combine ¾ cup boiling water and ½ cup cocoa, stirring until blended. Cool. Place granulated sugar, ½ cup softened butter, and 1 teaspoon vanilla in a large bowl; beat with a mixer at medium speed until blended. Add cocoa mixture and egg substitute; beat well. Lightly spoon flour into dry measuring cups; level with a knife. Combine flour, baking soda, and ¼ teaspoon salt in a bowl, stirring well. Add flour mixture and buttermilk alternately to sugar mixture, beginning and ending with flour mixture. Spoon batter into a 13 x 9–inch baking pan coated with cooking spray. Bake at 350° for 20 minutes or until a wooden pick inserted in center comes out clean. Top with marshmallows. Bake an additional 2 minutes or until marshmallows are soft.

3. To prepare frosting, combine ¼ cup cocoa, evaporated milk, 3 tablespoons melted butter, and ⅛ teaspoon salt in a medium, heavy saucepan over medium heat. Cook 4 minutes, stirring frequently. Stir in powdered sugar and 1 teaspoon vanilla. Cook 2 minutes, stirring constantly. Drizzle frosting over cake. Cool.

Cut cake into squares. Yield: 15 servings. (serving size: 1 square).

CALORIES 278 (30% from fat); FAT 9.4g (sat 5.7g, mono 2.5g, poly 0.5g); PROTEIN 3.9g; CARB 47.5g; FIBER 1.8g; CHOL 22mg; IRON 1.4mg; SODIUM 240mg; CALC 37mg

---

MAKE AHEAD
Chocolate Peanut Butter Cake with Bittersweet Ganache

A light, sheer chocolate glaze similar to ganache provides the finishing touch to this decadent cake.

CAKE:

Cooking spray
1 tablespoon cake flour
½ cup unsweetened cocoa
½ cup boiling water
1 (1-ounce) square bittersweet chocolate
¾ cup granulated sugar
½ cup packed dark brown sugar
¼ cup butter, softened
½ cup egg substitute
2 cups cake flour (about 8 ounces)
1½ teaspoons baking soda
¼ teaspoon salt
1 cup fat-free buttermilk
⅓ cup fat-free sour cream
2 teaspoons vanilla extract

FILLING:

¾ cup peanut butter and milk chocolate chips
2 cups frozen reduced-calorie whipped topping, thawed

GANACHE:

⅔ cup granulated sugar
⅓ cup evaporated fat-free milk
1 tablespoon butter
⅛ teaspoon salt
2 (1-ounce) squares bittersweet chocolate, chopped
1 teaspoon vanilla extract

1. Preheat oven to 350°.

2. To prepare cake, coat 2 (9-inch) round cake pans with cooking spray; line bottoms of pans with wax paper. Lightly coat wax paper with cooking spray; dust pans with 1 tablespoon flour.

3. Combine cocoa, ½ cup boiling water, and 1 ounce bittersweet chocolate in a small bowl, stirring until smooth; cool. Place ¾ cup granulated sugar, ½ cup dark brown sugar, and ¼ cup butter in a large bowl; beat with a mixer at medium speed 2 minutes or until well blended. Add egg substitute; beat well.

4. Lightly spoon 2 cups flour into a dry measuring cups; level with a knife. Combine flour, baking soda, and salt, stirring well with a whisk. Combine buttermilk, sour cream, and 2 teaspoons extract, stirring well. Add flour mixture and buttermilk mixture alternately to sugar mixture, beginning and ending with flour mixture. Stir in cocoa mixture.

5. Spoon batter into prepared pans. Sharply tap pans once on counter to remove air bubbles. Bake at 350° for 25 minutes or until a wooden pick inserted in center comes out clean. Cool in pans 10 minutes; remove from pans. Remove wax paper; discard. Cool cakes completely on wire racks.

6. To prepare filling, place chips in a microwave-safe bowl; microwave at HIGH 1 minute, stirring every 15 seconds. Cool slightly. Fold ¼ cup whipped topping into melted chips. Repeat procedure 7 times with remaining whipped topping. Chill 1 hour.

7. To prepare ganache, combine ⅔ cup granulated sugar and next 4 ingredients in a medium saucepan over medium heat; bring to a boil. Cook 2 minutes or until sugar dissolves and chocolate melts, stirring constantly. Remove from heat. Stir in 1 teaspoon vanilla; cool completely. Chill mixture 30 minutes or until thick.

8. Place 1 cake layer on a plate; top with filling, spreading out to edges. Place remaining cake layer on filling. Spread ganache evenly over top of cake; let drip down sides. Chill 20 minutes or until set. Yield: 16 servings (serving size: 1 slice).

CALORIES 308 (30% from fat); FAT 10.3g (sat 6.9g, mono 1.1g, poly 0.3g); PROTEIN 4.6g; CARB 52.5g; FIBER 1.4g; CHOL 11mg; IRON 1.9mg; SODIUM 260mg; CALC 61mg

Flour Power

Some of our recipes call for cake flour, while others use all-purpose flour. Cake flour generally contains less protein than all-purpose. It yields cakes with a finer crumb and more delicate texture for layer cakes, such as Chocolate Peanut Butter Cake with Bittersweet Ganache (recipe on page 456). Substitute ¾ cup all-purpose flour plus 2 tablespoons cornstarch for 1 cup cake flour, if necessary. All-purpose flour is fine for homey sheet cakes like Mississippi Mud Cake (recipe on page 456).

Frostings or Glazes

Frostings and glazes make a cake special and add flavor. Test Kitchens Professional Jan Moon shares tips for finishing touches.

• Turn the bottom of each cake layer up to create a smooth surface when decorating.

• Trim bumps or bulges with a serrated knife.

• Brush layers lightly with a pastry brush before frosting. This will reduce the amount of crumbs that can become trapped in the frosting.

• Apply a thin layer of frosting (known as a crumb coat) to the cake. Then, let it stand until set. This is especially helpful with light-colored frostings used on a dark cake.

• Apply frosting with a metal offset spatula, which has a long, thin, flexible blade that's easy to maneuver around the cake (about $10 at housewares stores).

• Decorate with simple garnishes such as fresh herbs, edible flowers, fresh fruit, chocolate shavings, citrus rind curls, citrus slices, or frosting tinted with food coloring.

How to Sugar-Frost Garnishes

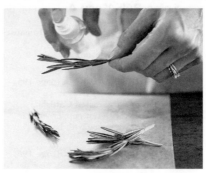

1. *Spray rosemary sprigs and cranberries with water.*

2. *Dip in granulated sugar.*

3. *Let dry on a wire rack.*

Menu Index

A topical guide to all the menus that appear in Cooking Light *Annual Recipes 2006.*
See page 479 for the General Recipe Index.

Dinner Tonight

Eggs Menu 1 (page 27)
serves 4
Cajun Quiche in a Rice Crust
Bibb-strawberry salad
Low-fat butter pecan ice cream with low-fat
caramel sauce

Eggs Menu 2 (page 28)
serves 4
Quick Avgolemono, Orzo, and Chicken Soup
Ricotta-garlic pita wedges
Tossed salad with bottled Greek dressing

Eggs Menu 3 (page 28)
serves 4
Shrimp and Egg Flower Soup
Snow pea and water chestnut salad
Store-bought almond cookies

Eggs Menu 4 (page 29)
serves 4
Sunny Frittata
Pineapple salad
Mango sorbet

Indonesian Dinner Menu 1 (page 74)
serves 4
Chicken Saté with Peanut Sauce
Assorted vegetable sauté
White rice with green onions

Indonesian Menu 2 (page 74)
serves 4
Fried Rice (Nasi Goreng)
Spinach soup
Fresh pineapple cubes

Indonesian Dinner Menu 3 (page 75)
serves 4
Steamed Clams with Thai Basil and Chiles
Rice noodles with cilantro
Cardamom-spiced iced coffee

Indonesian Dinner Menu 4 (page 75)
serves 4
Shrimp in Yellow Sauce
Coconut rice
Shrimp crackers

Chicken Supper Menu 1 (page 109)
serves 4
Chicken with Lime Sauce
Cumin roasted potatoes
Green beans

Chicken Supper Menu 2 (page 110)
serves 4
Chicken Enchiladas with Salsa Verde
Spanish rice
Black beans

Chicken Supper Menu 3 (page 110)
serves 4
Penne and Chicken Tenderloins with Spiced
Tomato Sauce
Romaine salad with anchovy and
fresh basil vinaigrette
Warm sourdough bread

Spice Rub Menu 1 (page 143)
serves 4
Pork Chops with Carolina Rub
Stove-top barbecue beans
Coleslaw

Spice Rub Menu 2 (page 143)
serves 4
Grilled Beef and Pepper Sandwich
Vegetable chips
Pineapple shake

Spice Rub Menu 3 (page 144)
serves 4
Roadhouse Steaks with Ancho Chile Rub
Mashed potatoes
Iceberg wedges with creamy blue cheese dressing

Spice Rub Menu 4 (page 144)
serves 4
Spice-Rubbed Pork Skewers with Tomatoes
Peanutty couscous
Limeade

Down-Home Menu 1 (page 195)
serves 4
Cornmeal-Crusted Catfish
Green beans with hot pepper vinegar
Creamy coleslaw with bacon

Down-Home Menu 2 (page 196)
serves 6
Sloppy Joes with Corn
Sliced tomatoes with crumbled blue cheese
Oven fries

Down-Home Menu 3 (page 196)
serves 4
Pork Chops with Country Gravy
Mashed potatoes
Succotash

Down-Home Menu 4 (page 196)
serves 6
Creamy Stove-Top Macaroni and Cheese
Seven-layer salad
Low-fat chocolate chip ice cream

Weeknight Menu 1 (page 269)
serves 4
Spicy Chicken Cakes with Horseradish Aïoli
Steamed asparagus
Mashed sweet potatoes

Weeknight Menu 2 (page 270)
serves 4
Swedish Meatballs
Green peas
Buttered poppy seed noodles

Weeknight Menu 3 (page 270)
serves 4
Chicken Picadillo
Black beans and rice
Flour tortillas

No-Cook Menu 1 (page 278)
serves 4
Lump Crab Salad
Marinated cucumbers
Sesame crackers

No-Cook Menu 2 (page 279)
serves 4
Chipotle Chicken Taco Salad
Watermelon-mango salad
Baked tortilla chips

No-Cook Menu 3 (page 279)
serves 4
Shrimp and White Bean Salad with Creamy
Lemon-Dill Dressing
Tomato wedges with spiced salt
Pumpernickel bread

Satisfying Suppers Menu 1 (page 319)
serves 4
Mustard and Tarragon Braised Lamb
Spinach salad with heirloom
tomatoes and basil vinaigrette
Mashed potatoes

Satisfying Suppers Menu 2 (page 319)
serves 4
Roasted Chicken with Dried Plums
and Shallots
Brussels sprouts with garlic and honey
Israeli couscous

Satisfying Suppers Menu 3 (page 320)
serves 4
Flank Steak with Shiitake
Mushroom Sauce
Ginger-scallion rice
Steamed baby bok choy

Spanish Supper Menu (page 329)
serves 4
Shrimp and Sausage Paella
Tossed green salad
Dulce de leche parfait

Simple Suppers

Breakfast, Brunch, and Lunch

Winter Breakfast Menu (page 44)
serves 6
Baked Pears with Streusel Filling
Smoked Salmon and Onion Frittata
Bagels
Fruit salad
Coffee

**Lunch on the Snowshoe
Trail Menu** (page 44)
serves 6
Lentil Soup with Balsamic-Roasted Winter
Vegetables
or
Mexican Black Bean Sausage Chili
Onion and Fontina Beer Batter Bread
Orange-Infused Cherry-Almond Biscotti
Hot chocolate

A Taste of Capri Menu (page 215)
serves 6
Classic Bruschetta
Tomato, Fresh Mozzarella, and Basil Salad
Caramelized Onion Frittata
Summer Berry Medley with
Limoncello and Mint
Chilled greco di Tufo
(or other light Italian white wine)

Summer in Piedmont Menu (page 216)
serves 6
Marinated Heirloom Tomatoes with Mustard and Dill
Open-Faced Panini with Goat Cheese, Roasted
Peppers, and Spicy Olive Topping
Pan-Roasted Asparagus with Lemon Rind
Mushroom Salad with Truffle Oil and
Parmigiano-Reggiano
Broiled Peaches and Hazelnuts with Vanilla Ice Cream
Chilled barbera d'Asti (or other light Italian red wine)

Sunday Breakfast Menu (page 221)
serves 8
Warmed Stuffed Peaches
Glazed ham
Whole wheat toast

Family-Style Lunch Menu (page 222)
serves 6
Sparkling Cassis Aperitif
French-Style Shrimp Salad
French bread
Vanilla Crème with Fresh Berry Jam

Lunch in Provence Menu (page 223)
serves 6
Oven-Poached Halibut Provençale
Herbed Potato Salad
Haricots Verts with Warm Shallot Vinaigrette
Vanilla Crème with Fresh Berry Jam

Saturday Breakfast Menu (page 304)
serves 10
Chicken and Basil Sausage Patties
Scrambled eggs
Sliced melon
Toast
Coffee

Saturday Bikers' Lunch Menu (page 304)
serves 10
Prosciutto and Smoked Gouda Panini
Tossed green salad
Fig and Almond Squares
Beer and Sparkling water

Easy Sunday Breakfast Menu (page 306)
serves 10
Homemade Granola
Low-fat yogurt
Assorted fruit
Orange juice and Coffee

Farewell Sunday Lunch Menu (page 306)
serves 10
Chicken, Chickpea, and Zucchini Stew
Tossed green salad
French bread
Sparkling water
Fig and Almond Squares

Casual Entertaining

Classic for Company Menu (page 22)
serves 4
Herb-crusted pork tenderloin
Wild Mushroom and Rice Timbales
Steamed green beans with minced shallots

Fresh Spring Fare Menu (page 128)
serves 4
Orecchiette with Fresh Fava Beans, Ricotta, and
Shredded Mint
Roasted asparagus with
lemon and Parmesan
Garlic bread

Garden Party Menu (page 136)
serves 6
Blackberry-Chambord Royale
Truffled Asparagus Crostini
Melon, Serrano Ham, and Arugula Salad
Curried Chicken Salad Sandwiches
Lemon Angel Food Cupcakes

Dinner on the Deck Menu (page 214)
serves 8
Balsamic Carrot Salad
Grilled pork tenderloin
Smashed red potatoes

Fast and Flavorful Menu (page 298)
serves 4
Lemon-Splashed Shrimp Salad
Spicy Broccolini
Angel food cake with berries

**Lowcountry Shrimp Boil
Menu** (page 301)
serves 8
<u>Appetizers</u>
Grilled Herb Grit Cakes
Grilled Okra and Tomato Skewers
<u>Main Dish</u>
Frogmore Stew with Jalapeño Tartar Sauce and
Zesty Chili Sauce
<u>Sides</u>
Broccoli and Apple Salad
Cheddar–Green Onion Muffins
<u>Dessert</u>
Benne Candy
or
Shortcakes with Fresh Berries
<u>Beverages</u>
Lemon and Mint Iced Tea
Beer

Friday-Night Welcome Menu (page 304)
serves 10
Eggplant and Fig Caponata
Wild Mushroom and Goat Cheese Spread
Assorted cheeses
Wine

**Saturday Cajun Dinner
Menu** (page 306)
serves 10
Celery Root and Fennel Rémoulade
Blackened Grouper
Maque Choux
Dirty Rice
Low-fat almond-praline ice cream
Beer
Coffee

Easy Entertaining Menu (page 317)
serves 4
Tuna with Avocado Green Goddess Aïoli
Garlic-roasted red potatoes
Green beans

Sunday Supper Menu (page 344)
serves 8
Truffle-Parmesan Mashed Potatoes
Lemon-herb roasted chicken
Steamed haricots verts
Feed a Crowd Menu (page 405)
serves 12
Seafood Lasagna
Garlic breadsticks
Tossed salad

Casual Entertaining Menu (page 405)
serves 6
Pork Tenderloin with Pomegranate Glaze
Wild rice pilaf
Green beans

Casual Buffet Dinner Menu (page 427)
serves 12
Mini Bacon and Potato Frittatas
Roasted Beet, Fennel, and Walnut Salad
Barbecue-Rubbed Pork Loin with Raisin-
Mustard Chutney
Garlic and Herb Roasted Turkey Breast with
Tarragon Mayonnaise
Asiago and Balsamic Caramelized
Onion Focaccia
Broccolini with lemon and shaved Parmesan
Citrus-Drizzled Cranberry-Oatmeal Cookies
Peppermint Stick Hot Chocolate

Special Occasions

Valentine's Day Menu (page 29)
serves 2
Wild Mushroom Soup
Toasted baguette slices
Rosemary Shrimp Scampi Skewers
Carrot Couscous with Fresh Chives
Steamed haricots verts
Bittersweet Chocolate Pudding with Raspberries
Chardonnay
Espresso

Easter/Passover Menu (page 117)
Appetizers
Smoked Trout Mousse
Asparagus Spears with Smoked Salmon Spirals
Entrées
Potato and Double-Horseradish Salmon or
Marinated Lamb with Orange Chimichurri or
Vanilla Balsamic Chicken
Sides
Roast Vegetable Medley
Date-Nut Haroset
Dessert
Fallen Chocolate Cake with Cherry Red Wine Sauce
Kosher pinot noir

Oktoberfest Supper Menu (page 356)
serves 8
Herring and Apple Salad
Pork Loin Braised with Cabbage
or
Turkey Bratwurst Patties
Warm Potato Salad with Beer and Mustard Dressing
Brown Beer Rye Bread
Ginger Cake
Beer

Halloween Open House Menu (page 371)
serves 16
Spiced Apple-Pomegranate Cider
Avocado-Yogurt Dip with Cumin
Cinnamon-Sugar Popcorn
Maple-Chile Popcorn
Spinach-Pear Salad with Honey-Bacon Vinaigrette
Pepita Corn Bread
Three-Bean Chili with Vegetables
Chocolate Cupcakes with
Vanilla Cream Cheese Frosting

Cocktail Party Menu (page 405)
serves 10
Apple Martinis
Mini Smoked Salmon Pizzas
Phyllo Triangles with Onion Jam
Glazed Honey Nuts
Cheese and fruit platter

Holiday Menu (page 405)
serves 4
Sautéed pork chops
Jezebel Sauce
Long-grain and wild rice
Sautéed broccoli
Chocolate Chip Blondies with
Caramel-Bourbon Drizzle

Holiday Dinner Menu (page 405)
serves 8
Endive Salad with Pomegranate Seeds,
Persimmon, and Pecan Vinaigrette
Marsala-Glazed Ham
Sweet Potato Casserole
Sautéed broccoli rabe
Dinner rolls
Oatmeal Pecan Pie
Iced tea

Dinner Party Menu (page 405)
serves 8
Leg of Lamb with Roasted Pear and
Pine Nut Relish
Mashed Potato Gratin
Roast Lemon and Pepper Brussels
Sprouts with Parmesan
Caramelized Pears with Blue Cheese and Ginger
Gastrique
Tawny port

Cocktail Dinner Menu (page 430)
serves 12
Endive with Caramelized Pears and Blue Cheese
Mushroom-Stuffed Black Peppercorn
Filet of Beef
Haricots Verts with
Champagne-Shallot Vinaigrette
Oatmeal Dinner Rolls
Pecan–White Chocolate Oat Biscotti

Hanukkah-with-Friends Menu (page 435)
serves 8
Leek and Potato Fritters with
Lemon-Cumin Yogurt
Romaine Salad with Oranges and Pine Nuts
Roasted Chicken with Lemons and Thyme
Bulgur Salad with Lemon Vinaigrette
Pear-Walnut Cake with
Honey-Orange Syrup

Family Festival of Lights Supper Menu (page 437)
serves 8
Roasted Garlic and Potato Spread
Leek and Potato Fritters with
Lemon-Cumin Yogurt
Braised Lamb with Butternut Squash and Dried
Fruit
or
White Bean and Beef Soup
with Tomatoes and Onions
Basmati Pilaf with Vermicelli and Onions
Pear-Walnut Cake with
Honey-Orange Syrup

Italian Christmas Eve Feast (page 442)
serves 6
White Bean Bruschetta
Mussels in Red Sauce
Mixed Seafood Salad
Crabmeat Ravioli with Clam Sauce
Southern Italian Fish Soup
Flounder Rolls with Cherry
Tomatoes and Spinach
Tricolor Salad
Garlicky Broccoli Rabe
Poached Pears with Cardamom Cream
Grandma Babe's Lemon Knots
Hazelnut Dessert Coffee

Global Kitchen

China Pattern Menu (page 43)
serves 4
Five-spice chicken
Asian Coleslaw
Steamed sugar snap peas

Creole Cookin' Menu (page 68)
serves 6
Chicken and Andouille Jambalaya
Spinach-orange salad
Mango sorbet

A Taste of Baja Menu (page 286)
serves 4
Tilapia Tacos with Peach Relish
Chipotle bean dip with chips
Mexican beer

Make-Ahead Menu (page 271)
serves 8
Entrées
Seafood Salad
Orecchiette with Shrimp, Arugula, and Cherry
Tomatoes
Spicy Grilled Chicken over
Sweet Peppers
Salads and Sides
Summer Rice Salad with Tuna
Steamed Asparagus with
Lemon-Garlic Gremolata
Figs and Prosciutto with Mint and
Shaved Parmigiano-Reggiano
Roasted Beets with Pine Nuts, Dill, and Red
Onion
Marinated Heirloom Tomatoes with Tarragon
Dessert
Tuscan Almond Biscotti
Tuscan white wine

Cuban-Inspired Menu (page 308)
serves 12
Appetizers
Grilled Pineapple and Avocado Salad
Sofrito Fish Cakes with Creamy Chipotle Tartar
Sauce
Havana Sandwich Bites
Entrées
Pork Tenderloin with Spicy Guava Glaze
Grilled Shrimp with Mango and Red Onion
Relish
Cilantro Citrus Chicken
Sides
Sautéed Sweet Plantains
Cuban-Style Black Beans and Rice
Desserts
Guava and Cheese Empanadas
Tres Leches Cakes
Beverages
Rum Punch

Recipe Title Index

An alphabetical listing of every recipe title that appeared
in the magazine in 2006. See page 479 for the General Recipe Index.

Month-by-Month Index

A month-by-month listing of every food story with recipe titles that appeared in the magazine in 2006. See page 479 for the General Recipe Index.

December

General Recipe Index

A listing by major ingredient and food category for every recipe that appeared in the magazine in 2006.

HOW TO USE IT AND WHY Glance at the end of any *Cooking Light* recipe, and you'll see how committed we are to helping you make the best of today's light cooking. With seven chefs, two registered dietitians, four home economists, and a computer system that analyzes every ingredient we use, *Cooking Light* gives you authoritative dietary detail like no other magazine. We go to such lengths so you can see how our recipes fit into your healthful eating plan. If you're trying to lose weight, the calorie and fat figures will probably help most. But if you're keeping a close eye on the sodium, cholesterol, and saturated fat in your diet, we provide those numbers, too. And because many women don't get enough iron or calcium, we can also help there, as well. Finally, there's a fiber analysis for those of us who don't get enough roughage.

Here's a helpful guide to put our nutrition analysis numbers into perspective. Remember, one size doesn't fit all, so take your lifestyle, age, and circumstances into consideration when determining your nutrition needs. For example, pregnant or breast-feeding women need more protein, calories, and calcium. And men older than 50 need 1,200mg of calcium daily, 200mg more than the amount recommended for younger men.

IN OUR NUTRITIONAL ANALYSIS, WE USE THESE ABBREVIATIONS:

sat	saturated fat	**CHOL**	cholesterol
mono	monounsaturated fat	**CALC**	calcium
poly	polyunsaturated fat	**g**	gram
CARB	carbohydrates	**mg**	milligram

Daily Nutrition Guide

	WOMEN AGES 25 TO 50	WOMEN OVER 50	MEN OVER 24
Calories	2,000	2,000 or less	2,700
Protein	50g	50g or less	63g
Fat	65g or less	65g or less	88g or less
Saturated Fat	20g or less	20g or less	27g or less
Carbohydrates	304g	304g	410g
Fiber	25g to 35g	25g to 35g	25g to 35g
Cholesterol	300mg or less	300mg or less	300mg or less
Iron	18mg	8mg	8mg
Sodium	2,300mg or less	1,500mg or less	2,300mg or less
Calcium	1,000mg	1,200mg	1,000mg

The nutritional values used in our calculations either come from The Food Processor, Version 7.5 (ESHA Research), or are provided by food manufacturers.

Credits

Contributing Recipe Developers:

Bruce Aidells
Melanie Barnard
Judith Barrett
Lidia Bastianich
Lisa Bell
Peter Berley
Mark Bittman
David Bonom
Elisa Bosley
Holly Rudin-Braschi
Frank Brigtsen
Barbara Seelig Brown
Jennifer Brulé
Maureen Callahan
Viviana Carballo
Claudia M. Caruana

Katie Chin
Leeann Chin
Katherine Cobbs
Martha Condra
Lorrie Hulston Corvin
Kirsten Dixon
Linda Eckhardt
Charity Ferreira
Allison Fishman
Brian Glover
Jaime Harder
Chris Hastings
Mary Lou Heiss
Lia Huber
Nancy Hughes
Dana Jacobi
Bill Jamison
Cheryl Jamison
Wendy Kalen

Elizabeth Karmel
Jeanne Thiel Kelley
Aglaia Kremezi
Jean Kressy
Barbara Lauterbach
Karen Levin
Alison Lewis
John Littlewood
Judy Lockhart
Donata Maggipinto
Domenica Marchetti
Jennifer Martinkus
Dana McCauley
Robin Miller
Jackie Mills
Paulette Mitchell
Krista Montgomery
Kitty Morse
Micol Negrin

Cynthia Nicholson
Cynthia Nims
Michel Nischan
Greg Patent
Marge Perry
James Peterson
Steve Petusevsky
Joanna Pruess
Rick Rodgers
Mark Scarbrough
Marie Simmons
Marcia Whyte Smart
Lisë Stern
Billy Strynkowski
Elizabeth Taliaferro
Kate Washington
Robyn Webb
Bruce Weinstein
Joanne Weir

Su-Mei Yu
Joy E. Zacharia,
R.D.Liz Zack
Laura Zapalowski

Wine Note Contributors:

Jeffery Lindenmuth
Karen MacNeil

Contributing Photo Stylists:

Melanie J. Clarke
Elizabeth Taliaferro
Ashley Johnson Wyatt

Contributing Photographers:

Colleen Duffley
Beau Gustafson
Lee Harrelson
Jeff Kauck
Becky Luigart-Stayner
Howard L. Puckett